Case Study

Video Cases

Marketing Miscues

Critical Thinking Cases

Marketing

fifth canadian edition

Marketing
fifth canadian edition

Charles W. Lamb, Jr.

M.J. Neeley Professor of Marketing
M.J. Neeley School of Business
Texas Christian University

Joseph F. Hair, Jr.

Alvin C. Copeland Endowed Chair
of Franchising and Director,
Entrepreneurship Institute
Louisiana State University

Carl McDaniel

Chair, Department of Marketing
College of Business Administration
University of Texas at Arlington

A.J. Faria

Chairman, Department of Marketing
Odette School of Business
University of Windsor

William J. Wellington

Associate Professor of Marketing
Odette School of Business
University of Windsor

NELSON / EDUCATION

NELSON EDUCATION

Marketing, Fifth Canadian Edition

by Charles W. Lamb, Jr., Joseph F. Hair, Jr., Carl McDaniel,
A.J. Faria, and William J. Wellington

**Vice President,
Editorial Director:**
Evelyn Veitch

**Editor-in-Chief,
Higher Education:**
Anne Williams

Acquisitions Editor:
Amie Plourde

Marketing Manager:
Kathaleen McCormick

Developmental Editor:
My Editor Inc.

Photo Researcher:
Julie Pratt

Permissions Coordinator:
Julie Pratt

Content Production Manager:
Claire Horsnell

Production Service:
MPS Limited, a Macmillan
Company

Copy Editor:
Wendy Thomas

Proofreader:
Jennifer A. McIntyre

Indexer:
Maura Brown

**Senior Manufacturing
Coordinator:**
Joanne McNeil

Design Director:
Ken Phipps

Managing Designer:
Franca Amore

Interior Design:
Peter Papayanakis

Cover Design:
Peter Papayanakis

Cover Image:
Debbie Yea/Nelson Education Ltd.

Map Design (cover):
Dave McKay

Compositor:
MPS Limited, a Macmillan
Company

Printer:
RR Donnelly

**Library and Archives Canada
Cataloguing in Publication Data**

Marketing / Charles W. Lamb, Jr . . .
[et al.]. — 5th Canadian ed.

First ed., published 1997, had ed.
statement: Canadian 3rd ed.;
2nd ed. published as: The subject
is marketing.

Includes bibliographical references
and index.
ISBN 978-0-17-650407-6

1. Marketing—Textbooks.
2. Marketing—Management—
Textbooks. I. Lamb, Charles W.

HF5415.M29325 2011   658.8
C2010-905660-4

Brief Contents

Contents

PART 2
Analyzing Marketing Opportunities 87

PART 3
Product Decisions   243

PART 4
Distribution Decisions   323

PART 5
Promotion Decisions   403

PART 6
Pricing Decisions 509

PART 7

Managing Marketing-Created Relationships 569

Preface

ABOUT THIS EDITION

Your students experience marketing through billboards, television commercials, and even in the aisles of super-markets and department stores. *Marketing*, Fifth Canadian Edition with its engaging presentation of concepts will give your students the ability to recognize how much marketing principles play a role in their day-to-day lives. With coverage of current marketing practices and exciting new features Lamb, Hair, McDaniel, Faria, and Wellington's *Marketing*, Fifth Canadian Edition will have your students saying, "Now that's marketing."

SO WHAT'S NEW?

If you're already familiar with *Marketing*, you may be asking, "So what's new?" The answer is quite a bit.

New Content

In addition to the dozens of new examples in each chapter, we have added new topical content and revised and updated existing material throughout the book. Each one of the chapter opening vignettes is updated or completely new in this edition. Further, we have added a section on marketing metrics and on sales forecasting to the text.

PART 1   We have retained the proven format of Chapter 1 (An Overview of Marketing) while stream-lining the chapter into fewer sections for easier reading and comprehension. Examples and cases are all updated and current. Chapter 2 (Strategic Planning for Competitive Advantage) has been expanded to provide more detail on the crucial aspects of developing mar-keting plans, the discussion on building the marketing mix through the use of the BCG portfolio has been revised, and the chapter now culminates in a detailed marketing plan outline. Added to Chapter 2 is a discussion of measuring marketing performance through clearly defined marketing performance metrics. A thoroughly revised Chapter 3 (Ethics and the Marketing Environment) tackles the issue of sustainability and offers new content on demographics, including new material on women as principal economic decision makers. We have completely revised the sections on tweens, teens, Generation Y, Generation X, baby boomers, and older consumers, and

on marketing to the growing ethnic and visible minority markets in Canada. The chapter contains new material on purchasing power and household income distribution while bringing discussion of the important issues of social, ethical, and environmental issues in marketing to the start of the chapter.

PART 2   Chapter 4 (Consumer Decision Making) has new material on how consumers use social media as part of their consumer information search. In addition, the theoretical discussion on alternative evaluation, purchase behaviour, and postpurchase behaviour has been consid-erably strengthened. Updated research on Canadian values is also presented in this chapter. The discussion of culture incorporates material on Canada's Aboriginal people as a subculture that marketers need to consider. The use of blogs as part of opinion leadership study is introduced in this edition. Chapter 5 (Business Marketing) has an updated and revised section on busi-ness marketing on the Internet. Chapter 6 (Segmenting and Targeting Markets) has been streamlined down to nine learning objectives from eleven. The sections on age and gender segmentation have been updated and the sections on one-to-one marketing have been reduced into one. Chapter 7 (Decision Support Systems and Marketing Research) introduces the topic of marketing research aggregator services and provides more coverage of observational research methods such as mystery shop-pers, ethnographic research, and virtual shopping. The use of the Internet for marketing research has been updated to include discussions on the use of Web com-munities, consumer-generated media, and behavioural targeting in relation to marketing research. Finally, Chapter 7 contains a new section on sales forecasting and sales forecasting methods.

PART 3   Chapter 8 (Product Concepts) has all-new discussions of the product mix, branding strategies, and trademark laws, and an expanded look at global product issues. Chapter 9 (Developing and Managing Products) has a completely updated section on the importance of innovation and revised material on the marketing implications of the diffusion process. Chapter 10 (Services and Nonprofit Organization Marketing) uses new exam-ples to illustrate the gap model and contains the latest projections on the fast-growing employment market within the services sector.

PART 4 Companies everywhere are working to squeeze inefficiencies out of their supply chain, so in Chapter 11 (Marketing Channels and Supply Chain Management) expanded coverage is given to channel structures, channel strategies, and supply chain integration while new materials on CRM, CSM, demand management, order fulfillment, manufacturing flow, supplier relationships, returns management and supply-chain performance measurement are added. Chapter 12 (Retailing) has been updated with the most recent statistics and reflects the most recent Canadian retailing trends; it discusses the impact of the do not call registry on telemarketing and the impact of technology on automatic vending, presents additional information sources on franchising, and includes a section on the retail phenomenon of pop-up shops.

PART 5 Promotion decisions are still presented in three chapters but redundant discussions between concepts introduced in Chapter 13 (Integrated Marketing Communications) and the later chapters have been reduced through a reorganization of Chapter 13. Chapter 13 now begins by discussing the role of promotion, followed by the process of communication, which includes a discussion of the impact of social media. These topics are followed by a discussion of the goals and tasks of promotion. It is after this that the elements of promotion are briefly introduced. Then the AIDA model is presented, followed by the concept of integrated marketing communication. The chapter now concludes with the factors affecting the promotional mix. Chapter 14 (Advertising and Public Relations) contains updated statistics and examples, but the section on alternative media adds discussions on video-game advertising, mobile phones, and stealth marketing. In addition, some new measures for the impact of public relations are presented. Chapter 15 (Sales Promotion and Personal Selling) is structured the same as in the fourth edition but includes new examples of unique sales promotion tools like "video couponing" using mobile phones. In addition, the chapter adds discussions on the use of social media as part of networking to generate sales leads.

PART 6 Chapter 16 (Pricing Concepts) includes a revised section on pricing power and new material on targeting technology and on guaranteed price matching. The chapter also includes a revised section on the impact of Internet auctions on pricing. New content on the impact of competition on pricing is included in Chapter 17 (Setting the Right Price), along with new discussions on markdown money and avoiding discounts.

PART 7 Chapter 18 (Customer Relationship Management) presents the same structure as the fourth edition but highlights some of the technological advances companies are employing to manage their databases to more effectively undertake CRM strategies. Chapter 19 (Marketing on the Web) presents this important topic in light of the major advent of the increasing use of smartphone technology to access the Web. All the material in this chapter was updated to represent the state of Web marketing and e-commerce at the writing of the text. Despite the best efforts of the authors, given the rapid state of change of smartphone applications and Web applications, it is likely that some material will still become dated. As was the case in the fourth edition, to reflect the dynamics of the World Wide Web, Chapter 19 is made available to students and instructors through the textbook website rather than in the printed text.

New Annotated Marketing Plan

Our new marketing plan, which can be used starting with Chapter 2, includes annotations that tie each part of the plan to the material throughout the book. Students will see the correlation between the chapters in the book and the elements of a professional marketing plan for a real company. The Marketing Plan is provided on the CourseMate website for *Marketing* accessible at www.nelsonbrain.com (also accessible from www.lamb5e.nelson.com).

New Marketing & You Surveys

Today's students demand that their courses be relevant, and to help make that connection, we have added a short survey to each chapter opener. Adapted from material in the *Marketing Scales Handbook*, these short polls are an engaging way to introduce students to a new concept. Even though this is their first marketing course, Marketing & You polls show them that they already have experience with marketing. Scoring instructions are given and general results provided. Marketing & You is not meant to be used in a scientific context; it is just an interesting and fun way to introduce the chapter material.

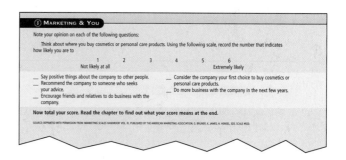

New Customer Experiences Boxes

At its very best, marketing is about creating an excellent experience for the consumer. Thus, we have added a new feature in this edition that showcases a very current example of the **Customer Experience** in action in light of the chapter's topic. For example, has the customer experience at WestJet—an integral part of that company's brand and a huge factor in customer loyalty—been watered down in recent years? What is Bass Pro Shops in Canada doing to create a unique customer experience at each of the outlets? Students will enjoy reading each of these customer experience examples.

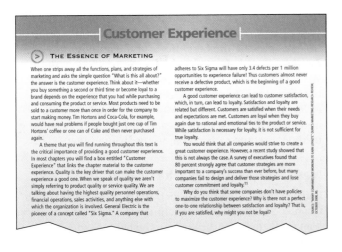

CLASSIC FEATURES HAVE BEEN UPDATED AND ENHANCED

Visual Learning Outcome Summaries

Through our years of teaching, we have found that not all students learn material in the same way. Some can read books and easily understand the concepts presented. Others need to rewrite the material in their own words. Still others learn best from diagrams and illustrations.

For this reason, every Learning Outcome topic in the fifth edition concludes with an updated graphic depiction of the material discussed. These **Review Learning Outcomes** are designed to give students a picture of the content that they can use to help them recall the material. For example, Learning Objective 2 in Chapter 6 discusses the importance of market segmentation. This discussion ends with the following simple diagram:

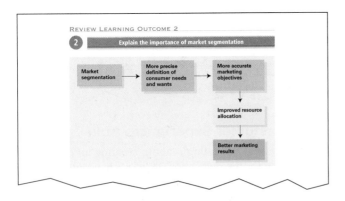

These reviews are meant to provide visual cues that prompt the student to recall the salient points in the chapter. The new visual reviews do not replace the end-of-chapter review and application summaries, as some students prefer the written summary to the visual summary. So we now offer a choice to meet the needs of different students.

Marketing Happens

Each chapter begins with a current, real-world story about a marketing decision or situation facing a company. These vignettes, called **Marketing Happens**, have been carefully prepared to stimulate student interest in the topics to come in the chapter and can be used to begin class discussions. The opening examples include well-known companies like Tim Hortons, Rona, Sobeys, Lululemon Athletica, Loblaw, Mastercard Canada, Nestlé Canada, Research in Motion, Rogers Communications, Pop Shoppe, and The Great Canadian Dollar Store; niche companies like James Ready Brewing Company and WestJet Vacations; new start-up Canadian companies like PlentyOfFish and organicKidz; medium-size industrial firms like Anchor-Danly; hoteliers like the Georgian Court Hotel in British Columbia; and finally, the Government of Canada!

Global Perspectives Boxes

Today most businesses compete not only locally and nationally, but globally as well. Companies that may have never given a thought to exporting now face competition abroad. Thinking globally should be part of every manager's tactical and strategic planning. Accordingly, global marketing is fully integrated throughout the book, cases, and videos. Our **Global Perspectives** boxes provide expanded global examples of the marketing issues facing companies around the world. Each box concludes with thought-provoking questions carefully prepared to stimulate class discussion. You'll read about leading Canadian companies and the problems, opportunities, and unusual situations they face in markets around the world.

Ethics in Marketing Boxes

In this edition of *Marketing* we continue our emphasis on ethics. The **Ethics in Marketing** boxes, complete with questions focusing on ethical decision making, have all been revised. This feature offers provocative examples of how ethics comes into play in many marketing decisions. Is it ethical to target young children and teens at school? Should pharmaceutical companies use customer information to develop target markets for their ads? Are organic claims about products misleading? Should companies use sex to sell their products? These and many other issues will be examined.

Review and Applications

To help students focus their study time, we continue to group end-of-chapter discussion and writing questions with their related learning outcome summary. Questions are numbered according to the learning outcome to which they correspond. For example, the summary point for Chapter 9 Learning Outcome 2 has four related questions. They are numbered 2.1, 2.2, 2.3, and 2.4. This organization helps students identify questions pertinent to the learning outcome they are studying.

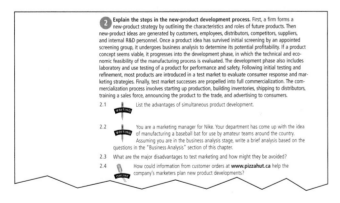

Application Exercises

Those familiar with *Marketing* know that we have always emphasized the application of marketing principles. **Application Exercises** at the end of each chapter give students the opportunity to work with marketing concepts in various real-world contexts. Each chapter

contains a new application exercise that gives students the opportunity to work with marketing concepts in a real-world context. We incorporate activities (rather than simple questions) to help students appreciate the width and depth of marketing.

The Application Exercises are designed to help students get into marketing by creating an ethnic dining guide, playing a world geography game, drafting a plan to revive the Hydrox cookie brand, collecting a list of 100 new products and graphing the distribution of new product types, comparing two retail stores according to their retailing mixes, researching the complete supply chain for a product of their choosing, creating an advertising campaign for a product, role-playing a televised interview after a marketing crisis, and much more.

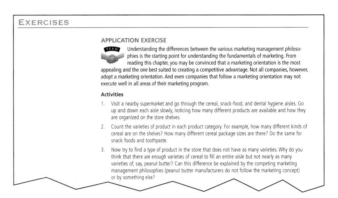

Ethics Exercises

To put more emphasis on the ethical issues facing marketing managers, in addition to the Ethics in Marketing Boxes and the ethics discussions found throughout the text, an **Ethics Exercise** is included at the end of each chapter. The Ethics Exercise provides a brief scenario that puts students in a situation where the right thing to do is not always clear. To help students make appropriate ethical decisions, we refer students to information sources that provide guidelines to follow. This gives students resource material for the exercise and helps to reinforce the ethical standards that marketers should uphold.

ETHICS EXERCISE
Cameron Stock, a purchasing manager for a sports equipment manufacturer, is responsible for buying $5 million of supplies every year. He has a preferred list of certified suppliers, many of which are awarded a large percentage of this business annually. Cameron has been offered an all-expense-paid weekend for two in Las Vegas as a Christmas present from a major supplier with whom he has done business for close to a decade and with whom he has built a very good relationship.

Questions
1. Would it be legal and ethical for Cameron Stock to accept this gift?
2. How is this situation addressed in the PMAC Code of Ethics? Go to the "Ethics in Marketing" box in the chapter and review the PMAC Code of Ethics. Also visit the CMA website at **www.the-cma.org** and read the CMA's Code of Ethics. Write a brief paragraph summarizing where PMAC and the CMA stand on the issue of supplier gifts.

Case Studies

One of the most powerful illustrations of how marketing concepts operate in the real world is the case study. All new **Case Studies** highlighting the challenges facing marketing managers in the 21st century are included at the end of each chapter. The cases focus on a wide range of companies and products including Harmonix's *Guitar Hero*, Disney, Burger King, men's clothing retailing, Mountain Equipment Co-op, HBO's show *True Blood*, and others. Your students will find these cases an exciting and challenging aspect of each chapter.

CASE STUDY

HARMONIX: EMBRACE YOUR INNER ROCK STAR

Just a few years ago, you had probably never heard of Harmonix. In 2005, the videogame design studio released Guitar Hero, which became the fastest video game in history to top $1 billion in sales. Guitar Hero focuses on a plastic guitar-shaped controller. Players press coloured buttons along the guitar neck to match a series of dots that scroll down the TV screen in time to music from famous rock tunes. Players score points based on their accuracy. In November 2007, Harmonix released Rock Band, adding drums, vocals, and bass guitar options to the game. Rock Band has sold over 5 million units at a price three to five times higher than the standard video game. In 2006, the founders of Harmonix sold the company to Viacom for $175 million, maintaining their operational autonomy while providing them greater budgets for product development and licensing music for their games.

The company, founded by Alex Rigopulos and Eran Egozy in 1995, focused on demo software they had created in grad school and a company vision of providing a way for people without much musical training or talent to experience the joy of playing and creating music. Their software, which was dubbed The Axe, provided basic music tutorials and allowed participants to use a joystick to improvise solos to popular music tracks. Alex and Eran attempted to market their creation through an interface with Japanese karaoke machines, a demo package deal with Intel, and an exhibition at Disney's Epcot. Although the software always proved technically impressive, people generally expressed little initial interest in trying it out.

In 2000, Rigopulos and Egozy hit on a concept that would engage consumers, and Harmonix became a video game company. The Axe software provided an improvisation program with no set goal, but most video games were designed with a purpose and offered competition among players,

---

Video Cases

Video is a valuable teaching tool, so this edition has retained its comprehensive video package. The videos are sourced from both the CBC and Canada's Business News Network (BNN), and they feature companies like Air Canada, CargoJet, Eureka! Inventing, easyhome rent-to-own outlets, Canadian Tire, and Amazon.ca. In addition, some of the videos focus on business situations such as the counterfeiting of brand-name merchandise, consumer buying behaviour, and the use of gift cards by Canadian merchants. A **Video Case** is built around each of these videos, putting the student into the role of a marketing manager having to respond to a real-world situation.

Marketing Miscues

Mistakes may have serious consequences but they also offer good learning opportunities. At the end of each text section you will find new cases that describe good and bad ideas that didn't make it in the marketplace. Often amusing and always interesting, these cases—showing how Unilever upset many of their customers with an ill-conceived promotional campaign, mistakes made by Apple Computer with a new product launch, pricing problems at Ryanair, Google Street View's infringements on consumer privacy, Dr. Pepper's mishandling of a co-promotion with rock band Guns N' Roses, and other missteps—will help your students avoid similar mistakes.

Critical Thinking Cases

We have developed an enormous capacity for generating data but our ability to use the data has lagged behind. To better prepare your students to analyze information and make better decisions, *Marketing*, Fifth Canadian Edition, includes a more challenging comprehensive case at the end of each text section—all of them new. The **Critical Thinking Cases** feature well-known companies and products like Tic Tac Breath Mints, Kindle e-reader, The Insurance Brokers Association of Canada, and the Coca-Cola Company.

OUR PEDAGOGY IS DESIGNED WITH YOUR STUDENTS IN MIND

All of our new and exciting content is anchored by the cornerstone of our text, our **Integrated Learning System (ILS)**. The text and all major supplements are organized around the learning outcomes that appear at the beginning of each chapter, so *Marketing* is both easy for instructors to teach from and for students to learn from. This organization is employed in the instructor ancillaries prepared for *Marketing*. In addition, we consider multiple learning styles in the organization of our text pedagogy.

Integrated Learning System Is More Important Than Ever

Since the Canadian first edition, the **Integrated Learning System** has been one of the hallmarks of *Marketing*. In the current edition, the ILS is more important than ever. Traditional pedagogical models assume that students have the ability to focus exclusively on studies and that professors have the ability to focus exclusively on class preparation, delivery, and evaluation. We propose an alternative model that meets the needs of today's students and professors without diminishing the importance of the material being studied.

The ILS breaks each chapter into cohesive blocks of content organized around the learning outcomes that are identified in the margin throughout each chapter. A visual learning summary concludes the presentation of each learning outcome. Students know exactly where a learning outcome begins and ends. At the end of each chapter, review questions are located after the appropriate summary point. Students are prompted to answer questions that relate to the material they have just read.

The same organization underpins the instructor materials that accompany *Marketing*. All 3500 items in the Test Bank are grouped by chapter and by learning outcome so professors can design tests that reflect the content covered in class. Each PowerPoint slide is identified by the corresponding learning outcome.

Changing Psychographics

In the past, students focused almost exclusively on their studies. Many of today's students, however, do not have this luxury. They work, commute, and volunteer, and may have families to raise. For students with active lifestyles, study time often comes in blocks of minutes rather than hours. This can make it hard to read a chapter in a single sitting. With ongoing starting and stopping of studying, it can be hard to retain chapter concepts.

Changing Demographics

Well over 80 percent of high school students entering college or university regularly use a computer. Most have a shorter attention span than previous cohorts of students. Today's students are used to receiving information in bullet points and other abbreviated formats. As an example, watch a music video. You will experience hundreds of images during a three- to four-minute song. Video directors piece together frames of imagery that often appear for only a few seconds and result in the inter-splicing of images to create virtually unconscious visual stimulation.

Real-World Application: The Marketing Plan

A series of Marketing Plan exercises and Marketing Plan worksheets on the Lamb CourseMate site are designed to encourage students to apply the marketing principles and strategies they've just learned. At the completion of each exercise, students are one step closer to building a complete strategic marketing plan for a company of their choosing.

Our Text Pedagogy Excites and Reinforces Learning

Pedagogical features are meant to reinforce learning. We have created teaching tools within the text that will excite student interest as well as teach. Not one of our features is casually included. Each has been designed to meet a specific learning need, level, or style.

- **Opening Vignettes:** Each chapter begins with a real-world story about a marketing decision or situation facing a well-known company. **Marketing Happens** helps illustrate how the chapter material relates to real-world marketing.
- **Marketing & You:** At the start of each chapter there is a short marketing survey on the topic area of the chapter. What your responses say about you, as a consumer, is summarized at the end of the chapter.
- **Terms:** Key terms appear in boldface in the text with definitions in the margins, making it easy for students to check their understanding of key definitions. A complete alphabetical list of key terms appears at the end of each chapter as a study checklist, with page citations for easy reference.
- **Review and Applications:** This is a detailed summary that distills the main points of each chapter. Chapter summaries are organized around the learning outcomes so that students can use them as a quick learning check. Discussion questions and activities are included under the learning outcomes.

- **Writing Questions:** To help students improve their writing skills, we have included writing exercises in the review section at the end of each chapter. These exercises are marked with the icon shown here. The writing questions are designed to be brief so that students can accomplish these assignments in a short time and instructor grading time is minimized.
- **Team Activities:** The ability to work collaboratively is a key to success in today's business world. End-of-chapter team activities, identified by the icon shown here, give students the opportunity to work together by engaging in consensus building and problem solving.
- **Online Activities:** Understanding how to use the Internet for professional (and academic) purposes is critical in today's business environment. End-of-chapter activities accompanied by the icon to the left give the students the opportunity to hone their skills in this area.
- **Application Exercise:** These exercises allow students to explore the principles of marketing in greater detail through engaging and enjoyable activities.
- **Video Case:** Each chapter includes a video around which a marketing strategy case is developed.
- **Ethics Exercise:** Short ethical dilemmas help students practise doing the right thing. Questions following each scenario prompt students to make an ethical decision and explain the rationale behind it.
- **Case Studies:** All chapters contain a case study with questions to help students work through problems facing real companies today.

INNOVATIVE AND VALUABLE INSTRUCTOR SUPPLEMENTS

All components of our comprehensive support package have been developed to help instructors prepare lectures and tests as quickly and easily as possible. We provide a wealth of information and activities beyond the text to supplement your lectures, as well as teaching aids in a variety of formats to fit your teaching style.

Introducing NETA

The **Nelson Education Teaching Advantage (NETA) program** delivers research-based resources that promote student engagement and higher-order thinking and enable the success of Canadian students and educators.

The primary NETA components are NETA Engagement (instructor's manuals and other teaching aids for instructors) and NETA Assessment (test banks and computerized test banks). Details about the NETA components specifically prepared for *Marketing* are included in the description of the Instructor's Resource CD that follows.

NETA Engagement's foundational principles are based on student-centred learning, deep learning, active learning, and creating positive classroom environments. Resources supporting NETA Engagement include enriched instructor manuals, classroom engagement activities, and the *Instructor's Guide to Classroom Engagement*, a manual that sets out the research underlying NETA Engagement and provides instructors with the framework to create engaging classrooms. The structure of the *Guide* was created by Dr. Roger Fisher and validated by an interdisciplinary board of scholars of teaching and learning.

NETA Assessment is a research-based program that was created in partnership with David DiBattista, a 3M National Teaching Fellow, professor of psychology at Brock University, and researcher in the area of multiple-choice testing. Working with Prof. DiBattista, Nelson Education has developed and enforced guidelines that improve the quality of our test banks by ensuring they measure not just recall (as is typical with test banks) but *higher-level thinking* skills as well. In addition, Prof. DiBattista's *Multiple-Choice Tests: Getting Beyond Remembering* established guidelines to help our test bank authors and copy editors recalibrate poorly worded questions that students might find confusing or ambiguous. Questions and answers developed under NETA test students' knowledge and understanding, not their skill at predicting answer outcomes based on unconscious clues in wording or playing the odds.

A Value-Added Instructor's Resource Like No Other

Managing your classroom resources is now easier than ever. The new **Instructor Resource CD-ROM** (ISBN 0-17-660834-6) contains all key instructor supplements: NETA Enriched Instructor's Manual, NETA Test Bank in printable and ExamView® computerized formats, and PowerPoint® slides.

Our Enriched Instructor's Manual is the core of our **Integrated Learning System**. Here is a list of the features that will reduce your class preparation time:

- NETA *Instructor's Guide to Classroom Engagement* provides instructors with an overview of the theory and models of active learning.
- Classroom Engagement Activities (suggested lesson plans for each chapter, including a lecture lesson plan, a small-group work lesson plan, and a video lesson plan).
- Suggested syllabi.
- A pedagogy grid for each chapter that sets out the chapter resources and the key points to feature from the chapter.
- Traditional instructor manual features like the detailed chapter outline, lists of support material,

additional class activities, solutions for all end-of-chapter materials, and teaching tips for all chapter materials.

The NETA Test Bank includes over 3500 questions in multiple choice, true-false, scenario, and essay formats. Test Bank files are provided in rich text format for easy editing and printing with all common word-processing formats. To complete the **Integrated Learning System**, our Computerized Test Bank runs on ExamView® software, which allows instructors to prepare tests that cover all learning outcomes, or emphasize those you feel are most important. This updated Computerized Test Bank is one of the most comprehensive on the market. The easy-to-use ExamView® platform is compatible with Microsoft Windows and Mac. Create tests by selecting questions from the question bank, modifying these questions as desired, and adding new questions you write yourself. You can administer quizzes online and export tests to WebCT, Blackboard, and other formats. The NETA Test Bank for *Marketing* is accompanied by *Multiple-Choice Tests: Getting Beyond Remembering*.

The Instructor's Resource CD also includes PowerPoint® lecture slides that present key concepts from *Marketing* with generous use of figures, photographs, and short tables from the text, as well as an Image Library. The Image Library allows instructors to customize their own PowerPoint presentations using figures, tables, illustrations, and photographs provided from the book in jpeg format.

Video Package (ISBN 0-17-660856-7)

The video package to accompany *Marketing* is quite comprehensive. These CBC and BNN videos showcase the nuts and bolts of marketing at existing companies. Also, Company Clips videos are found in CourseMate (accessible from www.nelsonbrain.com or www.lamb5e .nelson.com), along with the accompanying case studies, which will help to reinforce what your students have learned by showcasing people who are doing marketing every day.

Marketing CourseMate

Cengage Learning's **CourseMate** brings course concepts to life with interactive learning, study, and exam preparation tools that support the printed textbook. Watch student comprehension soar as your class works with the printed textbook and the textbook-specific website.

CourseMate includes an *integrated eBook*, *interactive teaching* and *learning tools* including quizzes, flashcards, videos, and more; downloadable instructor supplements; and *Engagement Tracker*, a first-of-its-kind tool that allows instructors to monitor student engagement in the course.

More information can be found at www.lamb5e .nelson.com. Please contact your Nelson representative to package Marketing CourseMate with your textbook.

Aplia aplia

Aplia is a dynamic homework system dedicated to improving students' learning by increasing their effort and engagement with your course. Founded by an instructor for other instructors, Aplia offers students premium, automatically graded assignments with detailed explanations that ensure they put forth effort on a regular basis.

Aplia saves instructors valuable time they'd otherwise spend on routine grading while giving students an easy way to stay on top of coursework with regularly scheduled assignments.

More information can be found at www.aplia.com. Please contact your Nelson representative to package Aplia with your textbook.

Music2Go Marketing: Principles of Marketing Simulation by Smartsims

Through the Smartsims easy-to-use interface, students will be taught the key principles of marketing and gain hands-on experience at the development and implementation of marketing strategy. The competitive nature of Music2Go encourages involvement and learning in a way that no other teaching methodology can, and your students will have fun in the process!

More information can be found at www.smartsims.com. Please contact your Nelson representative to package Music2Go Marketing with your textbook.

INNOVATIVE AND VALUABLE STUDENT SUPPLEMENTS

Marketing provides an excellent vehicle for learning the fundamentals. For students to gain a true understanding of marketing, however, it's best if they can apply the principles that they're learning. And it's best if they have the study aids that address their learning style. Our student supplements meet these needs.

Marketing CourseMate  CourseMate

CourseMate for *Marketing* includes an interactive eBook that allows students to take notes, highlight, bookmark, search the text, and use in-context glossary definitions. This online component also provides interactive learning tools including quizzes, flashcards, videos, and decision-making scenarios. Available at www.nelsonbrain.com; also accessible through www.lamb5e.nelson.com.

Aplia aplia

Aplia is a dynamic homework system that offers marketing students additional opportunities to review their text, stay engaged with class material, and master the basics of their course. Aplia includes the following features:

- An interactive textbook that contains all the content of the physical textbook, but takes advantage of the digital environment.
- Interactive questions to keep students engaged and prepare them for class discussion.
- Automatic grading of every question, with immediate explanations that link back to the online text so that students can review concepts.
- Automated recording of student grades are automatically in the instructor's Aplia gradebook.

Available at www.nelsonbrain.com.

Music2Go Marketing : Principles of Marketing Simulation by Smartsims

Music2Go is a Principles of Marketing Simulation enabling students to formulate and implement their own sales and marketing campaign for an MP3 player manufacturer, while competing online against other students within their course.

Students undertake market research and analyze market data to formulate their own strategic marketing plan, while keeping to a fixed marketing budget. They make key decisions involving price, forecasts, advertising, promotion activities, distribution, and R&D, just like sales and marketing executives in the real world.

More information can be found at www.smartsims.com.

MEET THE AUTHORS

Charles W. Lamb, Jr.
Texas Christian University

Charles W. Lamb, Jr., has a Ph.D. from Kent State University and is the M. J. Neeley Professor of Marketing, M. J. Neeley School of Business, Texas Christian University. He served as chair of the department of marketing from 1982 to 1988 and again from 1997 to 2003. He is currently chair of the Department of Information Systems and Supply Chain Management and is a former president of the Academy of Marketing Science and the Southwestern Marketing Association.

Lamb has authored or co-authored more than a dozen books and anthologies on marketing topics and over 150 articles that have appeared in academic journals and conference proceedings. In 1997, he was awarded the prestigious Chancellor's Award for Distinguished Research and Creative Activity at TCU. This is the highest honour that the university bestows on its faculty. Other key honours he has received include the M. J. Neeley School of Business Research Award, selection as a Distinguished Fellow of the Academy of Marketing Science, and a Fellow of the Southwestern Marketing Association.

Joseph F. Hair, Jr.
Louisiana State University

Joseph Hair is Professor of Marketing at Kennesaw State University. He previously held the Alvin C. Copeland

Endowed Chair of Franchising and was Director, Entrepreneurship Institute, Louisiana State University. Hair also held the Phil B. Hardin Chair of Marketing at the University of Mississippi. He has taught graduate and undergraduate marketing and marketing research courses.

A member of the American Marketing Association, Academy of Marketing Science, Southern Marketing Association, and Southwestern Marketing Association, Hair has authored 40 books, monographs, and cases and over 70 articles in scholarly journals. He serves on the editorial review boards of several journals and was the 2004 recipient of the Academy of Marketing Science Excellence in Teaching Award and the 2007 Innovative Marketer of the Year Award by the Marketing Management Association. Hair serves as a consultant to many businesses. Hair has a doctorate in marketing from the University of Florida.

Carl McDaniel
University of Texas, Arlington

Carl McDaniel is a professor of marketing at the University of Texas–Arlington, where he was chairman of the marketing department for 32 years. He has been an instructor for more than 40 years and is the recipient of several awards for outstanding teaching. McDaniel has also been a district sales manager for Southwestern Bell Telephone Company. Currently, he serves as a board member of the North Texas Higher Education Authority and is a member of the American Marketing Association, Academy of Marketing Science, Southern Marketing Association, Southwestern Marketing Association, and Western Marketing Association.

In addition to *Marketing*, McDaniel has authored or co-authored over 50 textbooks, and his research has appeared in such publications as the *Journal of Marketing, Journal of Business Research, Journal of the Academy of Marketing Science,* and the *California Management Review.* McDaniel is co-owner of a marketing research firm and has been a consultant to the International Trade Centre.

A.J. Faria
University of Windsor

A.J. Faria is a professor of marketing and chairman of the Department of Marketing in the Odette School of Business at the University of Windsor. He has taught for over 40 years at five different universities. He has also worked in industry in sales and marketing management positions and has served as a consultant to more than 50 corporations, industry trade associations, and government departments. Faria has run marketing strategy seminars across North America as well as in Russia, China, Estonia, France, the Netherlands, Singapore, and Hong Kong. Faria is also Co-Director of the Office of Automotive and Vehicle Research in the Odette School of Business and President of Marcon Marketing Consultants.

In addition to *Marketing*, Faria has authored seven other texts, 12 chapters for others' texts, and more than 180 refereed journal articles and conference papers. He has won 11 conference best-paper awards and is currently the business editor for *Simulation & Gaming*. Faria not only undertakes many consulting assignments in the automotive industry but does more than 200 media interviews each year on automotive industry topics. He was named a Fellow of the Association for Business Simulation and Experiential Learning in 1995 and received a Lifetime Achievement Award from the organization in 2006. Faria received the Senior Research Excellence Award from the Odette School of Business in 2005, the Distinguished Research Award from the University of Windsor in 2006, and the Kevin Doyle Award for Service to the Media in 2009. He has a doctorate in marketing from Michigan State University.

William J. Wellington
University of Windsor

William J. Wellington is an associate professor in the Department of Marketing in the Odette School of Business at the University of Windsor, where he has held an appointment since 1986. He also held an administrative appointment as Associate Dean of the Odette School of Business from 1999 through 2002. He has an Honours Bachelor of Science from the University of Western Ontario, an MBA from the University of Windsor, and a Ph.D. in Marketing and Transportation from Michigan State University. Wellington is both a Fellow and a Past President of the Association for Business Simulation and Experiential Learning. His teaching interests lie in the areas of introductory marketing, advertising and promotion, sales management, marketing management, and strategic marketing management.

Wellington's research interests lie in the areas of marketing education and strategic marketing management. In addition to *Marketing*, He has authored seven other books, two chapters for others' books, seven journal articles, and over 30 refereed conference proceedings. He has edited one book, published three abstracts, and delivered six papers as well as five invited addresses to professional associations.

Acknowledgments

There are many individuals to whom we owe gratitude for their help in making *Marketing*, Fifth Canadian Edition, a reality. In particular, we would like to thank the team at Nelson Education Limited: Evelyn Veitch, Amie Plourde, and Kathaleen McCormick. We are grateful for the expertise of the production team including Claire Horsnell, copy editor Wendy Thomas, and the tireless efforts of permissions editor, Julie Pratt. A special thanks goes to the development team of Katherine Goodes and Kim Watson at My Editor Inc. This project could not have been realized without their outstanding commitment and expertise.

We are especially indebted to the reviewers, past and present, who took the time to comment on the discipline's market analysis and Lamb contents pages of *Marketing*, Fifth Canadian Edition. We would like to extend our gratitude to the following:

Harish Kapoor, *Acadia University*

Jennifer Monk, *Algonquin College*

Jayne Van Dusen, *Algonquin College*

Anne-Marie Webb-Hughes, *British Columbia Institute of Technology*

David Butterton, *Canadian Tourism College*

Elaine MacNeil, *Cape Breton University*

Dwight Dyson, *Centennial College*

Bruce Bennett, *College of New Caledonia*

Janice Edwards, *College of the Rockies*

Mary Ann Cipriano, *Concordia University*

Christopher Ross, *Concordia University*

Robert Soroka, *Concordia University*

Allen Richert, *Confederation College*

Diana Serafini, *Dawson College*

Patrick Kidd, *Dawson College*

Henry Klaise, *Durham College*

Ted Seath, *Durham College*

Heather Stevens, *George Brown College*

Margery Taylor, *George Brown College*

Peter Burgess, *George Brown College*

Gary Dover, *Georgian College*

Bill Corcoran, *Grande Prairie Regional College*

Jeff Ryan, *Grant MacEwan College*

Edmund Baumann, *Humber College*

Pat Browne, *Kwantlen Polytechnic University*

Mehdi Zahaf, *Lakehead University*

Don Hill, *Langara College*

Kandey Larden, *Langara College*

Keith Murray, *Langara College*

Ann Pegoraro, *Laurentian University*

Ray Friedman, *Lethbridge Community College*

Alan Chapelle, *Vancouver Island University*

Vivian Vaupshas, *McGill University*

Janice Shearer, *Mohawk College*

Mark Valvasori, *Mohawk College*

Wes Zaboschuk, *Northern Alberta Institute of Technology*

Moira Hudson, *New Brunswick Community College*

Terri Champion, *Niagara College*

Brad MacDonald, *Nova Scotia Community College*

Wendy McGill, *Nova Scotia Community College*

Megan Mills, *Okanagan College*

Lawrence Ashworth, *Queen's University*

Craig Dyer, *Red River College*

Keith Penhall, *Red River College*

Maria Vincenten, *Red River College*

Steve Tissenbaum, *Ryerson University*

Denton Anthony, *Saint Francis Xavier University*

Gordon Fullerton, *Saint Mary's University*

Danny Wadden, *Saint Mary's University*

Miguel Morales, *Saint Mary's University*

Carlos E. Fernandez, *Seneca College*

Clayton Rolfe, *Seneca College*

Ingrid Mueller, *Seneca College*

Haizley Trevor-Smith, *Simon Fraser University*

David Nowell, *Sheridan College*

Susan Ronchka, *Sheridan College*

David Nowell, *Sheridan College*

Rae Varity, *Southern Alberta Institute of Technology*

Steve Janisse, *St. Clair College*

Paul Myers, *St. Clair College*

Dianne West, *Thompson Rivers University*

Paul Cubbon, *UBC, Sauder School of Business*

Ed Li, *University of the Fraser Valley*

Marc Boivin, *University of Calgary*

Lynne Ricker, *University of Calgary*

Scott Coldwell, *University of Guelph*

Roberto Bello, *University of Lethbridge*

Tanya Drollinger, *University of Lethbridge*

Sergio Carvalho, *University of Manitoba*

Rajesh V. Manchanda, *University of Manitoba*

Shelley Rinehart, *University of New Brunswick*

Richard Genest, *University of Saskatchewan*

Ian Skurnik, *University of Toronto*

Dilip Soman, *University of Toronto*

Mark Colgate, *University of Victoria*

Brent McKenzie, *University of Western Ontario*

Jacqueline Kappers, *University of Western Ontario*

Lou Gervino, *University of Winnipeg*

Rene Jamieson, *University of Winnipeg*

Jocelyn Starr, *Yellowquill College*

Ashwin Joshi, *York University*

PART

The World
of Marketing

1 An Overview of Marketing

SOURCE: KRISTIINA PAUL

LEARNING OUTCOMES

1 Define the term *marketing*

2 Describe four marketing management philosophies

3 Discuss the differences between sales and market orientations

4 Describe several reasons for studying marketing

(V) MARKETING & YOU

Note your opinion on each of the following questions:

Think about where you buy cosmetics or personal care products. Using the following scale, record the number that indicates how likely you are to

1	2	3	4	5	6
Not likely at all					Extremely likely

__ Say positive things about the company to other people.
__ Recommend the company to someone who seeks your advice.
__ Encourage friends and relatives to do business with the company.

__ Consider the company your first choice to buy cosmetics or personal care products.
__ Do more business with the company in the next few years.

Now total your score. Read the chapter to find out what your score means at the end.

SOURCE: REPRINTED WITH PERMISSION FROM *MARKETING SCALES HANDBOOK* VOL. III, PUBLISHED BY THE AMERICAN MARKETING ASSOCIATION, G. BRUNER, K. JAMES, H. HENSEL, EDS. SCALE #920.

With over 3,600 locations, Tim Hortons is the best-known and most successful coffee franchise in Canada. So popular is the company, that when it put only 15 percent of the firm up for sale in March 2006, the initial public stock offering fetched nearly $1 billion! This put the total value of the company at about $6.6 billion—making it more valuable than such corporate giants as Air Canada and Bombardier. So how did this company, founded by a legendary hockey player and a Hamilton, Ontario, police officer, manage to grow to a point where its sales exceed McDonald's in Canada?

Some marketing experts say that several strategies employed by Ron Joyce (the Hamilton police officer) have been instrumental in growing Tim Hortons from its first outlet (opened in Hamilton in May 1964) to the over 3,600 outlets that it has today, with sales volume growing past $2.3 billion.

Most important to its success, Tim Hortons has maintained its made-in-Canada appeal, even though there are nearly 600 Tim Hortons outlets outside of Canada today. "They still have the persona of small-town Canada," says Gordon Hendren, president of Charlton Strategic Research. The company markets its roots in advertisements that feature Canadian travellers in distant places yearning for a cup of Tim Hortons' coffee and through its sponsorship of youth hockey in almost every town across Canada. "Tim Bits, the community-based support program for young hockey players, is promoted at NHL venues across the country," noted Mr. Hendren.

Tim Hortons reaches out to Canadians in many other ways as well. For example, Canadian troops serving in Afghanistan get a taste of home through the Canadian Forces Personnel Support Agency (CFPSA), which brings Tim Hortons coffee and doughnuts to the troops. The commander of Canadian forces in Afghanistan, Major-General Doug Langton, told the soldiers,

"This is about serving you as you continue to do the outstanding job Canada asks of you. We hope this little piece of home makes your lives in Afghanistan just a little bit easier." Tim Hortons coffee and doughnuts are available to Canadian troops in Iraq as well.

The annual "Roll Up the Rim to Win" contest "has become a bit of a cultural touchstone," according to Gordon Hendren. "They have captured the element that everybody can win a prize. They have high participation in it and they have good prizes."

A second very important element in the success of Tim Hortons was the decision by Ron Joyce in the late 1980s to expand the Tim Hortons menu beyond coffee and doughnuts. The menu expansion started with chili, soup, and bagels. The big jump in revenue and profits, though, came with the addition of sandwiches in the 1990s. The soup and sandwiches additions expanded Tim Hortons sales dramatically beyond the normal morning coffee hours.

"Sandwiches were a risk for them, and you have to give them credit for working it out operationally so that it wouldn't be an issue with people waiting in line," said Ken Wong, a marketing professor at Queen's University's School of Business. Today, Tim Hortons is the largest seller of soup among food services firms in Canada and sells one out of every two bagels sold through restaurants in Canada.

To expand breakfast sales, Tim Hortons added a $2.49 breakfast sandwich. The success of the breakfast sandwich and fresh wraps has contributed to the nearly 7 percent increase in same-store year-over-year sales that Tim Hortons has been achieving. Most recently, Tim Hortons has added Cold Stone Creamery ice cream to a growing number of outlets in British Columbia, Alberta, Nova Scotia, New Brunswick, Ontario, and Quebec. Importantly, as with

their coffee and doughnuts, all new food items have to be of the same high Tim Hortons quality whether being sold in Vancouver, Toronto, Montreal, or Yellowknife. That type of consistency is important in a successful franchise, whether it is consistency in the food offering or in the wait times to be served.

Finally, realizing the importance of time and convenience, Tim Hortons led the movement to drive-through windows in Canada. Ten years ago, one in 10 quick-service meals were bought at a drive-through window; now it is one in four, largely due to the efforts of Tim Hortons. All together, these product and marketing strategies have resulted in many very loyal Tim Hortons' customers. Over 40 percent of customers visit a Tim Hortons' outlet four or more times each week!

Whether it's wide market coverage through nearly 3,600 outlets, consistent product quality and customer service, catering to its Canadian heritage, or successful promotional programs and an expanding product line-up, Tim Hortons' focus on always fresh quality products, good customer value, and community leadership has allowed it to grow into the largest quick-service restaurant chain in Canada.

Tim Hortons is now looking at major international growth. Although there currently are Tim Hortons kiosks serving troops in Afghanistan and Iraq and 290 self-serve Tim Hortons kiosks in Spar convenience stores in Ireland and England, Tim Hortons does not have the international presence of a competitor like Starbucks, which has outlets in 51 countries. This will soon change. "We are in the process right now of developing an international strategic plan, and we are going to present that to the board," said Don Schroeder, CEO of Tim Hortons at the 2010 annual general meeting. Soon, Canadians travelling outside of North America will still be able to get their favourite coffee.[1]

SOURCE: HOLLIE SHAW, "TIM HORTONS LOOKS TO GO GLOBAL," THE WINDSOR STAR, MAY 15, 2010, A16; HOLLIE SHAW, "STAYING FRESH WITH SMART MARKETING," FINANCIAL POST, MARCH 1, 2006, FP3; "BREAKFAST SANDWICH HEATS UP TIMS QUARTERLY SALES," GLOBE AND MAIL, JANUARY 6, 2007, B6; WWW.TIMHORTONS.COM.

Define the term *marketing*

What does the term *marketing* mean to you? Many people think it means the same thing as personal selling. Others think that marketing is the same as advertising and promotion. Still others believe that marketing has something to do with making products available in stores, arranging displays, and maintaining inventories of products for future sales. Actually, marketing includes all these activities and many more. Marketing is involved with developing and managing the company's products, services and ideas; promoting and pricing the company's offerings; and distributing the company's offerings. This combination of marketing activities is often referred to as the 4 P's of marketing.

Marketing has two facets. First, it is a philosophy, an attitude, or a business management orientation that stresses customer satisfaction. Second, marketing is a set of activities used to implement this philosophy. The definition of marketing adopted for this text encompasses both perspectives: "**Marketing** is an organizational function and a set of processes for creating, communicating, and delivering value to customers and for managing customer relationships in ways that benefit the organization and its stakeholders."[2]

marketing
An organizational function and a set of processes for creating, communicating, and delivering value to customers and for managing customer relationships in ways that benefit the organization and its stakeholders.

exchange
The idea that people give up something to receive something they would rather have.

THE CONCEPT OF EXCHANGE

Exchange is a key part of marketing. The concept of **exchange** is quite simple. It means that people give up something to receive something they would rather have. Normally, we think of money as the medium of exchange. We "give up" money to "get" the goods and services we want. Exchange does not require money, however. Two people may barter or trade such items as hockey cards, books, or cars.

Five conditions must normally exist for an exchange to take place:

1. There are at least two parties.

2. Each party has something that might be of value to the other party.

3. Each party is capable of communication and delivery.

4. Each party is free to accept or reject the exchange offer.

5. Each party believes it is appropriate or desirable to deal with the other party.[3]

Exchange will not necessarily take place even if all these conditions exist. These conditions are necessary, however, for exchange to be possible. For example, you may

REVIEW LEARNING OUTCOME 1

① **Define the term *marketing***

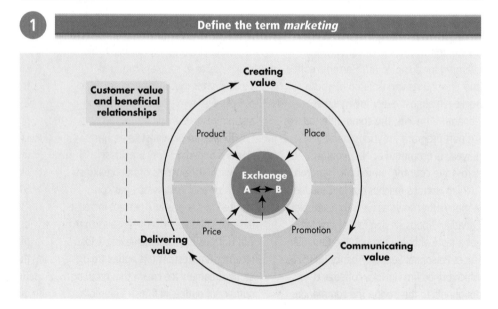

place an advertisement in your local newspaper stating that your used automobile is for sale at a certain price. Several people may call you to ask about the car, some may test-drive it, and one or more may even make an offer. All five conditions necessary for an exchange are present. But unless you reach an agreement with a buyer and actually sell the car, an exchange will not take place. Notice that marketing can occur even if an exchange does not occur. In the example just discussed, you would have engaged in marketing activities even if no one bought your used automobile.

2 MARKETING MANAGEMENT PHILOSOPHIES

Describe four management philosophies of business

Four competing philosophies strongly influence an organization's marketing activities. These philosophies are commonly referred to as the production, sales, market, and societal marketing orientations.

PRODUCTION ORIENTATION

production orientation
A philosophy that focuses on the internal capabilities of the firm rather than on the desires and needs of the marketplace.

A **production orientation** is a philosophy that focuses on the internal capabilities of the firm rather than on the desires and needs of the marketplace. A production orientation means that management assesses its resources and asks these questions: "What can we do best?" "What can our engineers design?" "What is easy to produce, given our equipment?" In the case of a service organization, managers ask, "What services are most convenient for the firm to offer?" and "Where do our talents lie?" Some have

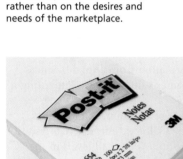

SOURCE: © ROSE ALCORN

referred to this orientation as a *Field of Dreams* orientation, referring to the movie line "If we build it, they will come." The furniture industry is infamous for its disregard of customers and for its slow cycle times. This has always been a production-oriented industry.

There is nothing wrong with assessing a firm's capabilities; in fact, such assessments are major considerations in strategic marketing planning (see Chapter 2). A production orientation falls short because it does not consider whether the goods and services the firm produces most efficiently meet the needs of the marketplace. Sometimes what a firm can best produce is exactly what the market wants. For example, the research and development department of 3M's commercial tape division developed and patented the adhesive component of Post-it Notes a year before a commercial application was identified. Clodhoppers candy, a huge success, was developed by a Winnipeg grandmother as a family treat and was also a product accepted by consumers when her grandson began marketing the product.[4] In yet other situations, as when competition is weak or demand exceeds supply, a production-oriented firm can survive and even prosper. More often, however, firms that succeed in competitive markets have a clear understanding that they must first determine what customers want and then produce it, rather than focus on what company management thinks should be produced.

SALES ORIENTATION

sales orientation
The idea that people will buy more goods and services if aggressive sales techniques are used and that high sales result in high profits.

A **sales orientation** is based on the ideas that people will buy more goods and services if aggressive sales techniques are used and that high sales result in high profits. Sales to the final buyer are emphasized, and intermediaries are encouraged to push manufacturers' products more aggressively. To sales-oriented firms, marketing means selling things and collecting money.

The fundamental problem with a sales orientation, as with a production orientation, is a lack of understanding of the needs and wants of the marketplace. Sales-oriented companies often find that, despite the quality of their sales personnel, they cannot convince people to buy goods or services that are neither wanted nor needed.

Many sales-oriented firms lack an understanding of what is important to their customers. Many so-called dot-com businesses that came into existence in the late 1990s are no longer around because they focused on the technology that they offered rather than on the customer.

MARKET ORIENTATION

marketing concept
The idea that the social and economic justification for an organization's existence is the satisfaction of customer wants and needs while meeting organizational objectives.

The **marketing concept** is a simple and intuitively appealing philosophy. It states that the social and economic justification for an organization's existence is the satisfaction of customer wants and needs while meeting organizational objectives. It is based on an understanding that a sale does not depend on an aggressive sales force, but rather on a customer's decision to purchase a product. What a business thinks it produces is not of primary importance to its success. Instead, what customers think they are buying—the perceived value—defines the business. The marketing concept includes the following:

1. Focusing on customer wants and needs so that the organization can distinguish its product(s) from competitors' offerings.

2. Integrating all the organization's activities, including production, to satisfy customer wants.

3. Achieving long-term goals for the organization by satisfying customer wants and needs legally and responsibly.

The recipe for success is to consistently deliver a unique experience that your competitors cannot match and that satisfies the intentions and preferences of your target buyers. This requires a thorough understanding of your customers and distinctive capabilities that enable your company to execute plans on the basis of this customer understanding, and delivering the desired experience using and integrating all the resources of the firm.[5]

market orientation
A philosophy that assumes that a sale does not depend on aggressive sales force efforts but rather on a customer's decision to purchase a product. A market orientation is synonymous with the marketing concept.

Firms that adopt and implement the marketing concept are said to be market oriented. Achieving a **market orientation** involves obtaining information about customers, competitors, and markets; examining the information from a total business perspective; determining how to deliver superior customer value; and implementing actions to provide value to customers.

Today, companies of all types are adopting a market orientation. Bill Marriott, Marriott International's CEO, logs an average of 250,000 kilometres every year visiting the company's hotels, inspecting them, and talking to employees at all levels in the organization. Burton Snowboards became the best-known brand in one of the world's fastest-growing sports by identifying its most important customers, figuring out the product that those customers wanted, and then designing it. Almost every day Burton staffers visit with some of the 300 professional riders worldwide who advise the company. These conversations take place on the slopes and on the phone. If one of the riders has a suggestion or a problem, a Burton employee calls back within 24 hours. Riders help develop virtually every Burton product.[6]

Understanding your competitive arena and competitors' strengths and weaknesses is a critical component of a market orientation. This includes assessing what existing or potential competitors might be intending to do tomorrow as well as what they are doing today. Western Union failed to define its competitive arena as telecommunications, concentrating instead on telegraph services, and was eventually outflanked by fax technology. Had Western Union been a market-oriented company, its management might

SOURCE: BILL GREENBLATT/UPI/LANDOV

Adopting a market orientation requires top-management leadership and involvement. Bill Marriott knows this, so each year he travels widely, visiting the company's hotels to ensure that every Marriott delivers superior customer value.

have better understood the changes taking place in the telecommunications market, seen the competitive threat, and developed strategies to counter the threat.

SOCIETAL MARKETING ORIENTATION

societal marketing orientation
The idea that an organization exists not only to satisfy customer wants and needs and to meet organizational objectives but also to preserve or enhance individuals' and society's long-term best interests.

One reason a market-oriented organization may choose not to deliver the benefits sought by customers is that these benefits may not be good for individuals or society. This philosophy, called a **societal marketing orientation,** states that an organization exists not only to satisfy customer wants and needs and to meet organizational objectives but also to preserve or enhance individuals' and society's long-term best interests. Marketing products and containers that are less toxic than normal, are more durable, contain reusable materials, or are made of recyclable materials is consistent with a societal marketing orientation. For example, Turtle Wax car wash products and detergents are biodegradable and can be "digested" by waste treatment plants. The company's plastic containers are made of recyclable plastic, and its spray products do not use propellants that damage the ozone layer in the earth's upper atmosphere.

Although the societal marketing concept has been discussed for over 30 years, it did not receive widespread support until the early 2000s. Concerns such as climate change, the depleting ozone layer, fuel shortages, pollution, and raised health concerns have caused consumers to be more aware of the need for companies and consumers to adopt measures that conserve resources and cause less damage to the environment.

Studies reporting consumers' attitudes toward, and intentions to buy, more environmentally friendly products show varying results. Many studies show that while consumers want to buy more environmentally friendly products, they are not willing to pay higher prices. Some believe that consumers want to "go green" but don't know where to start. Many marketers have made substantial commitments to either produce products using more environmentally friendly processes or make more environmentally friendly products. Coca-Cola has committed to spending $44 million to build the world's largest plastic-bottle-to-bottle recycling plant.[7] Adopting a societal marketing orientation and clearly communicating the decision and the actions that support it helps firms differentiate themselves from competitors and strengthens their positioning.

"Have we met before?" Recycling a single aluminum can saves enough energy to power a TV for three hours.

SOURCE: © AP IMAGES/PRNEWSFOTO/PEPSI-COLA COMPANY

REVIEW LEARNING OUTCOME 2

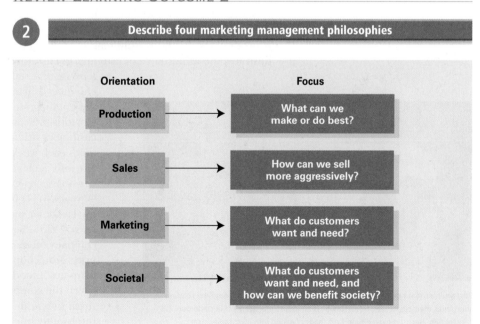

2 | Describe four marketing management philosophies

Orientation	Focus
Production	What can we make or do best?
Sales	How can we sell more aggressively?
Marketing	What do customers want and need?
Societal	What do customers want and need, and how can we benefit society?

Discuss the differences between
sales and market orientations

The differences between sales and market orientations are substantial. The two orientations can be compared using five characteristics: the organization's focus, the firm's business, those to whom the product is directed, the firm's primary goal, and the tools used to achieve those goals.

THE ORGANIZATION'S FOCUS

Personnel in sales-oriented firms tend to be "inward looking," focusing on selling what the organization makes rather than making what the market wants. Many of the historic sources of competitive advantage—technology, innovation, and economies of scale—allowed companies to focus their efforts internally and prosper. Today, many successful firms derive their competitive advantage from an external, market-oriented focus. A market orientation has helped companies such as Bombardier, Dell Computer, TD Canada Trust, and WestJet outperform their competitors. These companies put customers at the centre of their business.

A sales orientation has led to the demise of many firms, including Eaton's, Streamline.com, and the Digital Entertainment Network. Kmart Canada illustrates the problems companies face when they lose their customer focus. Kmart failed in Canada a number of years ago and exited the market. What was Kmart's biggest problem? Kmart focused on trying to match Zellers' products and prices rather than on determining what its customers wanted.

Customer Value

customer value
The relationship between
benefits and the sacrifice
necessary to obtain those
benefits.

Customer value is the relationship between benefits and the sacrifice necessary to obtain those benefits. Customer value is not simply a matter of high quality. A high-quality product that is available only at a high price will not be perceived as a good value, nor will bare-bones service or low-quality goods selling for a low price. Instead, customers value goods and services that are of the quality they expect and that are sold at prices they are willing to pay. Value can be used to sell a $209,000 Porsche 911 Turbo Cabriolet as well as a $4.99 package of President's Choice chocolate chip cookies.

Delivering customer value means elevating the customer experience, improving customer satisfaction, and paying close attention to customer feedback. The customer-oriented firm constantly changes itself in order to deliver more value to customers.

Marketers interested in customer value do the following:

- *Offer products that perform*: This is the bare minimum requirement. Consumers have lost patience with shoddy merchandise. Procter & Gamble, a company that alters its product formulations from market-to-market to suit customer preferences, illustrates the importance of listening to customers.

- *Earn trust*: A stable base of loyal customers enhances a firm's ability to grow and prosper. As the opening Marketing Happens example on Tim Hortons indicated, 40 percent of Tim Hortons customers visit a Tim Hortons outlet four or more times each week. That's over 200 visits to Tim Hortons each year—a very loyal customer base!

- *Give consumers more than they expect*: For more than 40 years, MTD Canada has been intent on raising the customer service bar. For many of its well-known Yard-Man and McCulloch products, the company offers lifetime parts warranties and 90-day price protection. The price protection and service plans are intended to demonstrate the extent to which the company stands behind all its products.

- *Avoid unrealistic pricing*: E-marketers are leveraging Internet technology to redefine how prices are set

SOURCE: ASSOCIATED PRESS

Customer-intimate companies achieve great success by building longtime relationships with their customers. Home Depot is an industry benchmark in customer satisfaction. Here, employee Juan Cruz loads plywood into a customer's car.

and negotiated. With lower costs, e-marketers can often offer lower prices than their bricks-and-mortar counterparts. The enormous popularity of auction sites such as eBay and Amazon.com and the customer-bid model used by Priceline illustrate that on-line customers are interested in bargain prices. Many are not willing to pay a premium for the convenience of examining the merchandise and taking it home with them.

- *Give the buyer facts*: Today's sophisticated consumer wants informative advertising and knowledgeable salespeople. It is becoming very difficult for business marketers to differentiate themselves from competitors. Rather than trying to sell products, salespeople need to find out what the customer needs. In other words, salespeople must start with the needs of the customer and work toward a solution.
- *Offer organization-wide commitment in service and after-sales support*: Organizations should incorporate customer service as a wide-ranging business strategy. People fly WestJet Airlines because the airline offers superior value. Passengers may not always get preassigned seats or meals, but its service is reliable and friendly and costs less. All WestJet employees are involved in the effort to satisfy customers. Pilots tend the boarding gate when their help is needed and ticket agents help move luggage.

Customer Satisfaction

customer satisfaction
Customers' evaluation of a good or service based on whether it has met their needs and expectations.

Customer satisfaction is the customers' evaluation of your goods and services based on whether they have met the customers' needs and expectations. Keeping current customers satisfied is just as important as attracting new ones and a lot less expensive. Firms that have a reputation for delivering high levels of customer satisfaction do things differently from their competitors. Top management is obsessed with customer satisfaction, and employees throughout the organization understand the link between

Global Perspectives

 MOLSON COORS TAPS INTO MAJOR GLOBAL MARKETS

When Molson and Coors merged in 2005, the fifth-largest brewing company in the world was formed. The combined Molson Coors could boast sales of nearly $9 billion and net income of over $700 million.

Molson Coors is the largest brewing company in Canada. However, with beer sales slowing in Canada, the company has been looking to growing markets around the world. In June 2010, Molson Coors Brewing Company announced that it had just launched Coors Light in Russia, the world's fourth-largest beer market. Coors Light would immediately be available in supermarkets, grocery stores, convenience stores, bars, and other neighbourhood stores across Moscow. As quickly as possible, distribution would be expanded throughout Russia.

Molson Coors will handle the marketing and advertising for the Coors Light brand in Russia, while the Moscow Brewing Company, Russia's leading importer of beer with brewery facilities in Moscow, will brew and distribute the brand. "We are very optimistic about the future success of Coors Light in Russia as we have put in place all the ingredients required to build a winning brand," said Mauricio Cardenas, Chief Officer, Latin America, Russia, India, and Africa at Molson Coors.

Kandy Anand, president of Molson Coors International, said, "As the fourth-largest beer market in the world, Russia has always been an attractive opportunity for us to expand our brand presence, particularly with Coors Light, which is quickly emerging as a global brand."

In September 2010, just three months after the announcement of the Coors Light's expansion into Russia, Molson Coors announced that it had purchased 51 percent of the Hebei Si'hai Beer Company of China. The newly formed Molson Coors Si'hai Brewing Company will brew and distribute Coors Light and Si'hai beers across China.

"As a leading global brewer, Molson Coors is proud to combine centuries of family brewing heritage and pioneering spirit with a trusted, local brewer such as Si'hai," said Kandy Anand. Mr. Wang Si'hai, president of Si'hai Brewing Company commented, "This is an exceptional partnership between our two companies, and I believe we have a very bright future ahead. Molson Coors global brand expertise and innovation combined with Si'hai's deep understanding of the local market will be a winning formula for beer drinkers across China."

In addition to the new partnerships in Russia and China, Molson Coors has also recently announced partnerships with Mahou San Miguel in Spain and with Viet Thai in Vietnam.[8]

Companies today must be prepared to compete in a global market. How might Molson Coors' marketing mix vary from one market to another? What do you think some of the most significant differences in the company's marketing mix might be among Canada, Russia, China, Spain, and Vietnam?

SOURCE: "MOLSON COORS ENTERS RUSSIA WITH COORS LIGHT," "MOLSON COORS-SI'HAI BEER COMPANY LAUNCHES IN CHINA," AND "MOLSON COORS ACQUIRES MAJORITY STAKE IN NEW JOINT VENTURE WITH SI'HAI BEER COMPANY OF CHINA," WWW.MOLSONCOORS.COM, ACCESSED OCTOBER 1, 2010.

their job and satisfied customers. The culture of the organization is to focus on delighting customers rather than on selling products.

Staples, the office supply retailer, offers great prices on its paper, pens, fax machines, and other office supplies, but its main strategy is to grow by providing customers with the best solutions to their problems. Its approach is to emulate customer-intimate companies like Home Depot and FedEx. These companies do not pursue one-time transactions. They cultivate relationships.

Building Relationships

Attracting new customers to a business is only the beginning. The best companies view new customer attraction as the launching point for developing and enhancing a long-term relationship. Companies can expand market share in three ways: by attracting new customers, by increasing business with existing customers, and by retaining current customers. Building relationships with existing customers directly addresses two of the three possibilities and indirectly addresses the other. The Customer Experience box provides more information about providing customers with rewarding experiences that lead to long-term relationships.

relationship marketing
A strategy that entails forging long-term partnerships with customers.

Relationship marketing is a strategy that entails forging long-term partnerships with customers. It begins with developing a clear understanding of who your customers are, what they value, what they want to buy, and how they prefer to interact with you and be served by you.[9] Companies then build relationships with customers by offering value and providing customer satisfaction. They are rewarded with repeat sales and referrals that lead to increases in sales, market share, and profits. Costs also fall because serving existing customers is less expensive than attracting new ones. Lee Iacocca, former president of both Ford and Chrysler, says that if you "take care of your customers, everything else will fall into place. You have to understand your customers, and you have to follow them. You have to change as your customers' lives change."[10]

Customer Experience

 ## THE ESSENCE OF MARKETING

When one strips away all the functions, plans, and strategies of marketing and asks the simple question "What is this all about?" the answer is the customer experience. Think about it—whether you buy something a second or third time or become loyal to a brand depends on the experience that you had while purchasing and consuming the product or service. Most products need to be sold to a customer more than once in order for the company to start making money. Tim Hortons and Coca-Cola, for example, would have real problems if people bought just one cup of Tim Hortons' coffee or one can of Coke and then never purchased again.

A theme that you will find running throughout this text is the critical importance of providing a good customer experience. In most chapters you will find a box entitled "Customer Experience" that links the chapter material to the customer experience. Quality is the key driver that can make the customer experience a good one. When we speak of quality we aren't simply referring to product quality or service quality. We are talking about having the highest quality personnel operations, financial operations, sales activities, and anything else with which the organization is involved. General Electric is the pioneer of a concept called "Six Sigma." A company that adheres to Six Sigma will have only 3.4 defects per 1 million opportunities to experience failure! Thus customers almost never receive a defective product, which is the beginning of a good customer experience.

A good customer experience can lead to customer satisfaction, which, in turn, can lead to loyalty. Satisfaction and loyalty are related but different. Customers are satisfied when their needs and expectations are met. Customers are loyal when they buy again due to rational and emotional ties to the product or service. While satisfaction is necessary for loyalty, it is not sufficient for true loyalty.

You would think that all companies would strive to create a great customer experience. However, a recent study showed that this is not always the case. A survey of executives found that 80 percent strongly agree that customer strategies are more important to a company's success than ever before, but many companies fail to design and deliver those strategies and lose customer commitment and loyalty.[11]

Why do you think that some companies don't have policies to maximize the customer experience? Why is there not a perfect one-to-one relationship between satisfaction and loyalty? That is, if you are satisfied, why might you not be loyal?

SOURCE: "MANY COMPANIES NOT WORKING TO EARN LOYALTY," QUIRK'S MARKETING RESEARCH REVIEW, OCTOBER 2008, 80.

Most successful relationship marketing strategies depend on customer-oriented personnel, effective training programs, employees with the authority to make decisions and solve problems, and teamwork.

Customer-Oriented Personnel

For an organization to be focused on building relationships with customers, employees' attitudes and actions must be customer oriented. An employee may be the only contact a particular customer has with the firm. In that customer's eyes, the employee *is* the firm. Any person, department, or division that is not customer oriented weakens the positive image of the entire organization. For example, a potential customer who is greeted discourteously may well assume that the employee's attitude represents that of the whole firm.

Isadore Sharp, founder and CEO of the Four Seasons hotel chain, says that "personal service is not something you can dictate as a policy. It comes from the culture. How you treat your employees is how you expect them to treat the customer."[12] Some companies have appointed chief customer officers (CCOs). These customer advocates provide an executive voice for customers and report directly to the company CEO. Their responsibilities include ensuring that the company maintains a customer-centric culture and that all employees remain focused on delivering customer value.

The Role of Training

Leading marketers recognize the role of employee training in customer service and relationship building. Edward Jones Company, ranked number one among *Fortune*'s "100 Best Companies to Work For" for two straight years, spends nearly 4 percent of its payroll on training and provides an average of 146 hours of training for each employee.[13] It is no coincidence that the companies on *Fortune*'s list, such as Cisco Systems, perform much better than other firms in their respective industries.

Empowerment

empowerment
Delegation of authority to solve customers' problems quickly—usually by the first person the customer notifies regarding the problem.

In addition to training, many marketing-oriented firms are giving employees more authority to solve customer problems on the spot. The term used to describe this delegation of authority is **empowerment**. Employees develop ownership attitudes when they are treated like part owners of the business and are expected to act the part. These employees manage themselves, are more likely to work hard, account for their own performance and the company's, and take prudent risks to build a stronger business and sustain the company's success. FedEx customer service representatives are trained and empowered to resolve customer problems. Although the average FedEx transaction is for less than $20, the customer service representatives are empowered to spend up to $100 to resolve a customer problem.

After Pierre Derome, general manager of Real's Truck Stop in Lancaster, Ontario, committed to empowering his employees, profit margins increased significantly. Real's Truck Stop, on Highway 401 just west of the Quebec border, includes gas and service facilities for cars and large trucks, a motel, a restaurant, and a convenience store. Giving employees more responsibility resulted in each taking a greater interest in his or her job and in the performance of the entire business. Truckers noticed the difference and have been giving additional business to Real's.

Empowerment gives customers the feeling that their concerns are being addressed and gives employees the feeling that their expertise matters. The result is greater satisfaction for both customers and employees.

Teamwork

teamwork
Collaborative efforts of people to accomplish common objectives.

Many organizations, such as WestJet Airlines and MTD Canada, which are frequently noted for delivering superior customer value and providing high levels of customer satisfaction, assign employees to teams and teach them team-building skills. **Teamwork** entails the collaborative efforts of people to accomplish common objectives. Job

SOURCE: COURTESY OF FEDERAL EXPRESS CANADA LTD.

Empowering employees not only boosts job satisfaction, but also boosts customer satisfaction. Each FedEx customer service representative has the authority to spend $100 to resolve a customer's complaint on the spot. FedEx customer service representatives are trained and empowered to resolve customer problems.

performance, company performance, product value, and customer satisfaction all improve when people in the same department or work group begin supporting and assisting each other and emphasize cooperation instead of competition. Performance is also enhanced when people in different areas of responsibility such as production and sales or sales and service practise teamwork, with the ultimate goal of delivering superior customer value and satisfaction.

THE FIRM'S BUSINESS

A sales-oriented firm defines its business (or mission) in terms of goods and services. A market-oriented firm defines its business in terms of the benefits its customers seek. People who spend their money, time, and energy expect to receive benefits, not just goods and services. This distinction has enormous implications.

Because of the limited way it defines its business, a sales-oriented firm often misses opportunities to serve customers whose wants can be met through a wide range of product offerings instead of specific products. For example, in 1989, 220-year-old Britannica had revenues of $650 million and a worldwide sales force of 7,500. Just five years later, after three consecutive years of losses, the sales force had collapsed to as few as 280 representatives. How did this respected company sink so low? Britannica managers saw that competitors were beginning to use CD-ROMs to store huge masses of information but chose to ignore the new computer technology, as well as an offer to team up with Microsoft.

It's not hard to see why parents would rather give their children an encyclopedia on a compact disk instead of a printed one. The CD-ROM versions were either given away or sold by other publishers for under $400. A full 32-volume set of *Encyclopedia Britannica* weighs about 55 kg, costs a minimum of $1,500, and takes up nearly a metre and a half of shelf space. If Britannica had defined its business as providing information instead of publishing books, it might not have suffered such a precipitous fall.

Adopting a "better late than never" philosophy, Britannica has made its complete 32-volume set available free on the Internet. The company no longer sells door-to-door and hopes to return to profitability by selling advertising on its website.

Answering the question "What is this firm's business?" thinking of the benefits customers seek, instead of thinking of goods and services, offers at least three important advantages:

- It ensures that the firm keeps focusing on customers and avoids becoming preoccupied with goods, services, or the organization's internal needs.
- It encourages innovation and creativity by reminding its people that there are many ways to satisfy customer wants.
- It stimulates an awareness of changes in customer desires and preferences so that product offerings are more likely to remain relevant.

Having a market orientation and focusing on customer wants does not mean that customers will always receive everything they want. It may not be possible, for example, to profitably manufacture and market automobile tires that will last for 200,000 kilometres and sell for $25. Furthermore, customers' preferences must be mediated by sound professional judgment as to how to deliver the benefits they seek. As Henry Ford once said, "If I had listened to the marketplace, I would have built a faster, cheaper horse."[14] Consumers have a limited set of experiences. They are unlikely to request anything beyond their experiences because they are not aware of the benefits they may gain from other potential offerings. For example, before the Internet, many people thought that shopping for some products was boring and time consuming, but could not express their need for electronic shopping.

THOSE TO WHOM THE PRODUCT IS DIRECTED

A sales-oriented organization targets its products at "everybody" or "the average customer." A market-oriented organization aims at specific groups of people. The fallacy

SOURCE: ASSOCIATED PRESS

A market-oriented organization recognizes that customer groups and their wants vary, so it creates products and services to address these differences. Grace magazine embodies the full-fashioned lifestyle with features and columns that highlight relevant fashion, beauty, and style tips for larger women. But while fashion features are definitely geared to the 30 percent of Canadian women size 14 and up, the rest of the magazine is of far more general interest.

of developing products directed at the average user is that relatively few average users actually exist. Typically, populations are characterized by diversity. An average is simply a midpoint in some set of characteristics. Because most potential customers are not "average," they are not likely to be attracted to an average product marketed to the average customer. Consider the market for shampoo as one example. There are shampoos for oily hair, dry hair, and dandruff. Some shampoos remove the grey or add colour to hair. Special shampoos are marketed for infants and elderly people. There is even shampoo for people with average or normal hair (whatever that is), but this is a fairly small portion of the total market for shampoo.

A market-oriented organization recognizes that different customer groups want different features or benefits. It may, therefore, need to develop different goods, services, and promotional appeals. A market-oriented firm carefully analyzes the market and divides it into groups of people who are fairly similar in selected characteristics. Then the firm develops marketing programs that will bring about mutually satisfying exchanges with one or more of those groups.

THE FIRM'S PRIMARY GOAL

A sales-oriented organization seeks to achieve profitability through sales volume and tries to convince potential customers to buy, even if the seller knows that the customer and product are mismatched. Sales-oriented organizations place a higher premium on making a sale than on developing a long-term relationship with a customer. In contrast, the ultimate goal of most market-oriented organizations is to make a profit by creating customer value, providing customer satisfaction, and building long-term relationships with customers.

TOOLS THE ORGANIZATION USES TO ACHIEVE ITS GOALS

Sales-oriented organizations seek to generate sales volume through intensive promotional activities, mainly personal selling and advertising. In contrast, market-oriented organizations recognize that promotion decisions are only one of four basic marketing mix decisions that have to be made: the total mix is made up of product, place (or distribution), promotion, and pricing decisions. A market-oriented organization recognizes each of these four components as important. Furthermore, a market-oriented organization recognizes that marketing is not just the responsibility of the marketing department—skills and resources throughout the organization are needed to deliver superior customer service and value.

REVIEW LEARNING OUTCOME 3

3	Discuss the differences between sales and market orientations				
	What is the organization's focus?	What business are you in?	To whom is the product directed?	What is your primary goal?	How do you seek to achieve your goal?
Sales Orientation	Inward, on the organization's needs	Selling goods and services	Everybody	Profit through maximum sales volume	Primarily through intensive promotion
Market Orientation	Outward, on the wants and preferences of customers	Satisfying customer wants and needs and delivering superior value	Specific groups of people	Profit through customer satisfaction	Through coordinated marketing and inter-functional activities.

WHY STUDY MARKETING?

Describe several reasons for studying marketing

Now that you understand the meaning of the term *marketing*, the importance of adopting a marketing orientation, how organizations implement this philosophy, and how relationship marketing is evolving, you may be asking, "What's in it for me?" or "Why should I study marketing?" There are several important reasons to study marketing, even if you are not majoring in marketing: marketing plays an important role in society, marketing is important to businesses, marketing offers outstanding career opportunities, and marketing affects your life every day.

SOURCE: COURTESY OF ROM

Businesses are not the only entities that conduct marketing activities. Not-for-profit organizations like the Royal Ontario Museum in Toronto, Ontario, provide career opportunities in marketing as well.

MARKETING PLAYS AN IMPORTANT ROLE IN SOCIETY

As you read this text, Canada's population will be moving toward 35 million people. Think about how many transactions are needed each day to feed, clothe, and shelter a population of this size. The number is huge. And yet it all works quite well, partly because the well-developed Canadian economic system efficiently distributes the output of farms and factories. A typical Canadian family, for example, consumes 2.5 tonnes of food a year. Marketing makes food available when we want it, in desired quantities, at accessible locations, and in sanitary and convenient packages and forms (such as instant and frozen foods).

MARKETING IS IMPORTANT TO BUSINESSES

The fundamental objectives of most businesses are survival, profits, and growth. Marketing contributes directly to achieving these objectives. Marketing includes the following activities, which are vital to business organizations: assessing the wants and satisfactions of current and potential customers, designing and managing product offerings, determining prices and pricing policies, developing distribution strategies, and communicating with current and potential customers.

All businesspeople, regardless of specialization or area of responsibility, need to be familiar with the terminology and fundamentals of accounting, finance, management, and marketing. People in all business areas need to be able to communicate with specialists in other areas. Furthermore, marketing is not just a job done by people in a marketing department. Marketing is a part of everyone's job in the organization. As David Packard of Hewlett-Packard put it: "Marketing is far too important to be left only to the marketing department." Marketing is not a department so much as a company-wide orientation. Therefore, a basic understanding of marketing is important to all businesspeople.

MARKETING OFFERS OUTSTANDING CAREER OPPORTUNITIES

Between one-quarter and one-third of the entire civilian workforce performs marketing activities. Marketing offers great career opportunities in such areas as professional selling, marketing research, advertising, retail and industrial buying, distribution management, product management, product development, and wholesaling. Marketing career opportunities also exist in a variety of nonbusiness organizations, including hospitals, museums, universities, the armed forces, sports organizations, and various government and social service agencies.

As the global marketplace becomes more challenging, companies all over the world and of all sizes are going to have to become better marketers. For a

4 **Describe several reasons for studying marketing**

Why Study Marketing?

Important to society

Important to business

Good career opportunities

+

Marketing affects you every day!

comprehensive look at career opportunities in marketing and a variety of other useful information about careers, visit our website at **www.lamb5e.nelson.com**.

MARKETING AFFECTS YOUR LIFE EVERY DAY

Marketing plays a major role in your everyday life. You participate in the marketing process as a consumer of goods and services. About half of every dollar you spend pays for marketing costs, such as marketing research, product development, packaging, transportation, storage, advertising, and sales expenses. By developing a better understanding of marketing, you will become a better-informed consumer. You will better understand the buying process and be able to negotiate more effectively with sellers. Moreover, you will be better prepared to demand satisfaction when the goods and services you buy do not meet the standards promised by the manufacturer or the marketer.

REVIEW AND APPLICATIONS

1 **Define the term *marketing*.** Marketing is an organizational function and a set of processes for creating, communicating, and delivering value to customers and for managing customer relationships in ways that benefit the organization and its stakeholders.

1.1 What is the American Marketing Association (AMA)? What does it do? How do its services benefit marketers across North America (see **www.marketingpower.com**)? Now check out the Canadian Marketing Association (CMA) (**www.the-cma.org**). How does the CMA differ from the AMA and what are the similarities?

2 **Describe four marketing management philosophies.** The role of marketing and the character of marketing activities within an organization are strongly influenced by management's philosophy and orientation. A production-oriented organization focuses on the internal capabilities of the firm rather than on the desires and needs of the marketplace. A sales orientation is based on the beliefs that people will buy more products if aggressive sales techniques are used and that high sales volumes produce high profits. A market-oriented organization focuses on satisfying customer wants and needs while meeting organizational objectives. A societal marketing orientation goes beyond a market orientation to include the preservation or enhancement of individuals' and society's long-term best interests.

2.1 Your company president has decided to restructure the firm to make it more market oriented. She is going to announce the changes at an upcoming meeting. She has asked you to prepare a short speech outlining the general reasons for the new company orientation.

2.2 Donald E. Petersen, former chairman of the board of Ford Motor Company, remarked, "If we aren't customer driven, our cars won't be either." Explain how this statement reflects the marketing concept.

2.3 Give an example of a company that might be successfully following a production orientation. Why might a firm in this industry be successful following such an orientation?

3 **Discuss the differences between sales and market orientations.** First, sales-oriented firms focus on their own needs; market-oriented firms focus on customers' needs and preferences. Second, sales-oriented companies consider themselves to be deliverers of goods and services, whereas market-oriented companies view themselves as satisfiers of customers. Third, sales-oriented firms direct their products to everyone; market-oriented firms aim at specific segments of the population. Fourth, although the primary goal of both types of firms is profit, sales-oriented businesses pursue maximum sales volume through intensive promotion, whereas market-oriented businesses pursue customer satisfaction through coordinated activities.

3.1 A friend of yours agrees with the adage "People don't know what they want—they only want what they know." Write your friend a letter expressing the extent to which you think marketers shape consumer wants.

3.2 Your local supermarket's slogan is "It's your store." However, when you asked one of the stock people to help you find a particular product, he told you it was not his job and that you should look a little harder. On your way out, you noticed a sign with an address for complaints. Draft a letter explaining why the supermarket's slogan will never be credible unless the employees carry it out.

3.3 How do tobacco companies handle the sensitive issues associated with marketing tobacco products? Go to the website of any tobacco company. What kind of information does the company's website provide about smoking and its negative effects on health? How does the company justify the sale of products that are hazardous to people's health? Examining the website in total, do you think that the company you selected is trustworthy?

 Describe several reasons for studying marketing. First, marketing affects the allocation of goods and services that influence a nation's economy and standard of living. Second, an understanding of marketing is crucial to understanding most businesses. Third, career opportunities in marketing are diverse, profitable, and expected to increase significantly during the coming decade. Fourth, understanding marketing makes consumers more informed.

4.1 Write a letter to a friend or family member explaining why you think a course in marketing will help you in your career in some field other than marketing.

TERMS

customer satisfaction 9
customer value 8
empowerment 11
exchange 4

market orientation 6
marketing 4
marketing concept 6
production orientation 5

relationship marketing 10
sales orientation 5
societal marketing orientation 7
teamwork 11

EXERCISES

APPLICATION EXERCISE

Understanding the differences between the various marketing management philosophies is the starting point for understanding the fundamentals of marketing. From reading this chapter, you may be convinced that a marketing orientation is the most appealing and the one best suited to creating a competitive advantage. Not all companies, however, adopt a marketing orientation. And even companies that follow a marketing orientation may not execute well in all areas of their marketing program.

Activities

1. Visit a nearby supermarket and go through the cereal, snack-food, and dental hygiene aisles. Go up and down each aisle slowly, noticing how many different products are available and how they are organized on the store shelves.

2. Count the varieties of product in each product category. For example, how many different kinds of cereal are on the shelves? How many different cereal package sizes are there? Do the same for snack foods and toothpaste.

3. Now try to find a type of product in the store that does not have as many varieties. Why do you think that there are enough varieties of cereal to fill an entire aisle but not nearly as many varieties of, say, peanut butter? Can this difference be explained by the competing marketing management philosophies (peanut butter manufacturers do not follow the marketing concept) or by something else?

4. Have you ever wanted to see a particular kind of cereal or snack food available for sale? Think of some product varieties (like strawberry-flavoured toothpaste or chocolate-covered popcorn) that you have never seen but would be interested in trying if someone sold it. Write a letter or send an e-mail to an appropriate company, suggesting that the company add your product idea to its current product line.

ETHICS EXERCISE

In today's business environment, ethics are extremely important. In recent years, there have been numerous scandals and trials that stem from a lack of ethical judgment. For this reason, we are including an ethical exercise at the end of each chapter. A brief scenario will present you with a situation in which the right thing to do may or may not be clear, and you will need to decide the ethical way out of the dilemma. To help you with these decisions, we will refer you to the CMA Code of Ethics at **www.the-cma.org** or the AMA's Code of Ethics, found on-line at **www.marketingpower.com**. These websites will give you a resource for the ethics exercises and will also help reinforce the ethical standards that marketers should uphold.

C. J. Sinnott Pharmaceuticals is the maker of several popular drugs used to treat high blood pressure and arthritis. Over time, the company has developed a good relationship with many of the patients who use its medications through a quarterly newsletter that offers all the latest news on new medical research findings as well as general health and fitness articles. Sinnott Pharmaceuticals has just been acquired by a group of investors who also own Soothing Waters Hot Tubs and Spas. The marketing director for Soothing Waters would like to use Sinnott's mailing list for a direct-mail promotion.

Questions

1. What should management of C. J. Sinnott Pharmaceuticals do?

2. Do you think it is ethical to use customer information across several divisions of the same company? Explain.

3. To which marketing management philosophy do you think the marketing director for Soothing Waters subscribes? Explain.

CASE STUDY

HARMONIX: EMBRACE YOUR INNER ROCK STAR

Just a few years ago, you had probably never heard of Harmonix. In 2005, the videogame design studio released Guitar Hero, which became the fastest video game in history to top $1 billion in sales. Guitar Hero focuses on a plastic guitar-shaped controller. Players press coloured buttons along the guitar neck to match a series of dots that scroll down the TV screen in time to music from famous rock tunes. Players score points based on their accuracy. In November 2007, Harmonix released Rock Band, adding drums, vocals, and bass guitar options to the game. Rock Band has sold over 5 million units at a price three to five times higher than the standard video game. In 2006, the founders of Harmonix sold the company to Viacom for $175 million, maintaining their operational autonomy while providing them greater budgets for product development and licensing music for their games.

The company, founded by Alex Rigopulos and Eran Egozy in 1995, focused on demo software they had created in grad school and a company vision of providing a way for people without much musical training or talent to experience the joy of playing and creating music. Their software, which was dubbed The Axe, provided basic music tutorials and allowed participants to use a joystick to improvise solos to popular music tracks. Alex and Eran attempted to market their creation through an interface with Japanese karaoke machines, a demo package deal with Intel, and an exhibition at Disney's Epcot. Although the software always proved technically impressive, people generally expressed little initial interest in trying it out.

In 2000, Rigopulos and Egozy hit on a concept that would engage consumers, and Harmonix became a video game company. The Axe software provided an improvisation program with no set goal, but most video games were designed with a purpose and offered competition among players, which helped engage, direct, and motivate the players. At the time, the market for music-based games, in which players would tap different combinations of buttons in time with a beat or a tune, was becoming increasingly popular. Harmonix created two games, Frequency and Amplitude, in which players hit buttons along with a beat, unlocking tracks for different layers of instruments in a song. Neither of the games proved especially successful, however, as both were very complex and the expense of generating initial interest proved too high for their publisher, Sony, to continue funding them.

Harmonix finally found some measure of success with its 2004 release of Karaoke Revolution, in which players would use a microphone or headset peripheral to score points singing along to pop songs. In a way, it allowed gamers to play a role and be a part of the music. In 2005, RedOctane, a company that had found success making peripheral video game controllers, contacted Harmonix about creating Guitar Hero.

Guitar Hero put players in the role of the lead guitarist in a rock band, climbing its way to stardom. The game soundtrack, filled with remixes of classic rock 'n' roll hits, found appeal among a broader musical audience, and the guitar controller put the iconic instrument of rock 'n' roll directly into the player's hands. Guitar Hero was released in November 2005, and when retailers set up in-store demo kiosks, game sales went through the roof.

After the initial success of Guitar Hero, even real rock stars began to pick it up, demonstrating its broad appeal. Music labels started to jump on the bandwagon, allowing the licensing of actual songs rather than just composition rights. Rock Band 2, which came out in September 2008, included songs by AC/DC and Bob Dylan. Gamers could also download additional songs, like The Who's greatest hits at $1.99 per song. Licences for Beatles songs were also secured. As the market for music video games has matured, sales of Harmonix products are expanding beyond the traditional gamers to first-time gamers and even families. The Rock Band franchise alone has sold over 7 million units since the first Rock Band release in 2007, and with the release of Rock Band 2 (2009), The Beatles: Rock Band (2009), and Green Day: Rock Band (2010), the hits just keep coming.[15]

Questions

1. What marketing management philosophy did Harmonix use at first and how did their philosophy change?

2. As a firm, how do you think Harmonix would describe its business?

3. To whom was Harmonix's original products directed and how did they create a product that would appeal to that audience?

VIDEO CASE

CBC

WORMBOY

Toronto native Tom Szaky went to university to study economics and ended up starting a company that makes worm poop. Tom, who graduated from Toronto's Upper Canada College in 2001, came across his business idea during his first year of university. While on a field trip to Montreal with some university classmates, he visited a friend who was using what is called a vermiculture composter in his kitchen to make homemade plant food from worm poop. Tom was so intrigued by the idea that he talked another friend into joining him to develop a business plan.

The result of the business plan was the formation of TerraCycle in a university dorm room. The basic concept for the company was to take waste, process it, and turn it into a useful product. The original business plan developed by Tom Szaky and his friend Jon Beyer (also from Toronto) was entered into a business plan contest. Tom and Jon's plan won and, with the first-prize money of $5,000, TerraCycle was started. From this modest starting point, TerraCycle grew into a company with 40 employees and 12 products that achieved $6 million in sales by 2007.

TerraCycle's products were made entirely from garbage and worm power. The company's products have been rated as the most eco-friendly in North America, and TerraCycle is the only consumer products company in North America to receive the Zerofootprint seal indicating that its products and manufacturing processes have virtually no negative environmental impact.

Almost all aspects of TerraCycle's business are as environmentally friendly as possible. The vermiculture composters that store the worms are made from vats retrieved from a landfill.

Organic waste that would otherwise go to landfills is used to feed the worms. The finished worm poop products are packaged in recycled plastic soft drink bottles. The finished product is packaged in recycled cardboard boxes. Even the desks, chairs, computers, telephones, cubicles, and other furnishings for the TerraCycle offices are all second-hand. Tom and Jon even turned down a much-needed $1 million in financing from an outside investor because the investor wanted the company to purchase new production materials and packaging rather than use recycled materials. You can read about TerraCycle's environmentally friendly production process, their "Bottle Brigade" program to retrieve used bottles, their intern program to hire university students and give them business experience, the company's aggressive program to obtain waste materials to recycle into finished products (and benefit charities at the same time), and their product line-up (which now includes a surprisingly large line of products—all made from waste materials) at the company website (**www.terracycle.net**). The TerraCycle products include fertilizers, a potting mix, flower pots, seed starters, animal repellents, school supplies, packaging materials, toys, and much more— all made from worm poop and other waste materials.

Being an environmentally conscious company does not guarantee business success, however. It is often more costly to produce eco-friendly products than synthetic products, and Tom and Jon want to sell their products at competitive prices to encourage consumers to use them. TerraCycle does not advertise but has benefited from considerable free publicity (which Tom and Jon work hard to get) due to the eco-friendly nature of the business (see their website for examples of the publicity the company has received). With a little luck and some on-going sales growth, Tom and Jon are hoping to show their first ever profit and prove that an entirely eco-friendly company can be a business success.

The company has no experienced sales people (student interns are trained to make sales calls), but TerraCycle products can now be found in Walmart Canada and Home Depot Canada. TerraCycle hopes to get its products in U.S. Walmart and Home Depot stores as well as in Target stores in the United States. As Tom and Jon attempt to keep their company as eco-friendly as possible, watch the problems that arise when you have an inexperienced all-student workforce, watch TerraCycle's first big sales breakthrough as it gets its products on The Shopping Channel, and watch the TerraCycle team in action on a sales "road show."[16]

Questions

1. Is TerraCycle a production, sales, marketing oriented, or societal marketing oriented firm? Why?

2. Has being so fully dedicated to ecology and the environment helped or hindered the growth of TerraCycle?

3. Do you feel that Tom and Jon are correct in their feeling that TerraCycle's products must be priced competitively? Why do you feel the way you do?

4. At this stage in its development, what must TerraCycle do to continue to grow?

5. Go to the TerraCycle website (**www.terracycle.net**) and take a look at the current line-up of company products and programs. What surprises you the most from its website?

MARKETING & YOU RESULTS

The higher your score, the more likely you are to do business with the company you thought of and recommend it to others. That is, you have a commitment to the organization and are likely a loyal customer. As you read in Chapter 1, building relationships is a central part of a market orientation.

for Competitive Advantage

SOURCE: DICK LOEK/GETSTOCK.COM

LEARNING OUTCOMES

1 Understand the importance of strategic marketing and know a basic outline for a marketing plan

2 Develop an appropriate business mission statement

3 Describe the components of a situation analysis

4 Explain the criteria for stating good marketing objectives

5 Identify sources of competitive advantage

6 Identify strategic alternatives

7 Discuss target market strategies

8 Describe the elements of the marketing mix

9 Explain why implementation, evaluation, and control of the marketing plan are necessary

10 Identify several techniques that help make strategic planning effective

MARKETING & YOU

What do you think about planning? Record your answers on the lines provided.

1	2	3	4	5	6	7
Not at all						All the time

__ I start my work without spending too much time on planning.*

__ I list the steps necessary for completing a task before starting it.

__ I think about strategies I will fall back on if problems arise.

__ Because so many aspects of my work are unpredictable, planning is not useful.*

__ I keep good records of the projects I'm working on.

__ I set personal goals for myself.

__ Each week I make a plan for what I need to do.

__ I do not waste time thinking about what I should do.*

__ I am careful to work on the highest priority tasks first.

__ Planning is a waste of time.*

__ Planning is an excuse for not working.

__ I don't need to develop a strategy for completing my assignments.*

Now total your score, reversing your score for items with asterisks—that is, if you entered a 2, score it as a 6, and vice versa. Read the chapter, and see what your score means at the end.

SOURCE: REPRINTED WITH PERMISSION FROM *MARKETING SCALES HANDBOOK* VOL. III, PUBLISHED BY THE AMERICAN MARKETING ASSOCIATION, G. BRUNER, K. JAMES, H. HENSEL, EDS. SCALE #646, P. 196.

Since its founding in 1939, Canada's leading home improvement retailer, Rona Inc., has been catering to tradespeople and those homeowners who are very handy with household repairs. Not everyone, however, is a do-it-yourselfer. And Rona is shifting its marketing strategy to capitalize on that.

Rona Inc. is Canada's largest home improvement retailer with sales of over $6 billion and a 17.5 percent share of the home improvement market. As successful as the company has been, Rona management is seeking further growth and is making a major adjustment in its marketing strategy to target the growing "do-it-for-me" market. This strategy shift will further intensify Rona's rivalry with Home Depot Canada, which is a close second in the Canadian home improvement market.

Rona's change in strategy represents a bold shift for the Boucherville, Quebec–headquartered retailer. The vast majority of Rona's customers—nearly 90 percent by company estimates—are do-it-yourself home renovators. However, Rona has recognized that there is a growing and very lucrative market among consumers who don't have the time or the ability to hang kitchen cabinets, lay tile or carpeting, install plumbing fixtures, or do the many other jobs necessary when undertaking home improvements.

As home construction across the country slowed in 2008 and 2009 and home renovations picked up, Rona wanted to make sure that it was getting its full share of this market by introducing installed services across the nearly 700 company-owned and franchised Rona outlets across the country. "Home Depot has really been pushing services in the past two years, and these two are competing head-to-head in all of the same markets, so it is a naturally competitive response," says Peter Norman, vice-president of Toronto-based Clayton Research. "This is also a natural extension of the products and services that Rona provides."

Rona, which first tested installation services at some of its outlets in Western Canada, has now extended the program to all but the smallest Rona outlets. According to company spokesman Sylvain Morisette, the new program will offer installed services for customers, including roofing, flooring, doors and windows, and kitchens and bathrooms. Previously, Rona handed out the cards of local contractors to customers who wanted installation services. Home Depot had moved into installation services a few years earlier than Rona when it recognized that there would eventually come a saturation point for its big-box outlets in Canada. Home Depot has also begun to open smaller stores in smaller markets in Canada, similar to the typical Rona small market outlets.

Installation services represented only about 6 percent of Home Depot's sales just a few years ago, but its installation services have been growing by about 30 percent per year and likely help the sale of other Home Depot products. This type of one-stop shopping should also help Rona sales to grow. Peter Norman estimates that installation services had accounted for less than 0.5 percent of Rona's sales in the past. "I suspect that the impact on Rona's bottom line will be relatively minor but they probably will find it easier to move product. If they are going to sell someone a hardwood floor, it makes it easier to close that sale if they can tell the customer it can be installed by the end of next week."

What else is Rona up to these days? It has been adding convenience stores and gas bars at the largest Rona outlets. Beyond this, Rona is looking into specialty stores that will cater to women and environmentally conscious consumers. Finally, Rona has explored the U.S. market and, while not moving into the United States yet, is still examining the possibility. The strategy planning room at Rona, it would seem, will be quite busy over the next few years.[1]

SOURCE: SCOTT ANDERSON, "RONA AIMS FOR 10–15% EPS GROWTH," FINANCIAL POST (HTTP://WWW.FINANCIALPOST.COM/MARKETS/NEWS-RELEASES/STORY.HTML?ID=2482458), JANUARY 25, 2010; ERIC LAM, "RONA IMPROVES Q1 SALES AND PROFITS," FINANCIAL POST, MAY 12, 2010, 23; HOLLIE SHAW, "RONA TARGETS "DO-IT-FOR-ME" CONSUMERS," FINANCIAL POST, FEBRUARY 21, 2006, FP1, FP3; MARINA STRAUSS, "RONA COULD ASK: DO YOU WANT GAS WITH THOSE NAILS?" GLOBE AND MAIL, AUGUST 10, 2006, B3; WWW.RONA.CA; WWW.HOMEDEPOT.CA.

THE NATURE OF STRATEGIC PLANNING

Understand the importance of
strategic marketing and know a
basic outline for a marketing plan

strategic planning
The managerial process of
creating and maintaining a fit
between the organization's
objectives and resources and
evolving market opportunities.

Strategic planning is the managerial process of creating and maintaining a fit between the organization's objectives and resources and the evolving market opportunities. The goal of strategic planning is long-run profitability and growth. Thus, strategic decisions require long-term commitments of resources.

A strategic error can threaten a firm's survival. On the other hand, a good strategic plan can help protect and grow the firm's resources. For instance, Metaldyne, an automotive parts maker with a number of plants in Ontario and sales of over $2 billion, was experiencing declining sales and profitability. Nearly 94 percent of Metaldyne's sales were to General Motors, Ford, and Chrysler, companies that have lost market share in North America over the past 20 years. To broaden its customer reach, Metaldyne merged with Asahi Tec Corp. of Japan. This merger opened up sales opportunities to Toyota, Honda, and Nissan for Metaldyne. Importantly, the market shares of Toyota, Honda, and Nissan have been growing in North America.

Strategic marketing management addresses two questions: What is the organization's main activity at a particular time? And how will it reach its goals? Here are some examples of strategic decisions:

- General Electric initiated an effort called "Ecomagination," which will ensure that the company becomes more environmentally conscious and one that is working to solve the planet's most critical environmental issues. This effort represents a major transformation in strategy for GE that is changing the way it develops products, sells to customers, and enters emerging markets.[2]
- Toys "R" Us has suffered as younger and younger children abandon traditional toys for electronic entertainment and because parents tend to buy toys during weekly trips to one-stop stores like Walmart. The company responded by expanding its infant line, Babies "R" Us, and is using it to lure parents of older children into their toy selections.[3]
- The Jean Coutu Group (PJC) Inc. spent $2.4 billion (U.S.) to acquire 1,539 Eckerd drugstores from J.C. Penney. This decision changed the Quebec-based drugstore chain from essentially an eastern Canadian regional operation into the fourth largest drugstore chain in North America with combined sales of over $15 billion.[4]
- Sobeys is converting its 87 Price Chopper stores to a new format, concentrating on fresh foods and is renaming the stores FreshCo. Sobeys is hoping to cater to a growing ethnic market that is more attracted to fresh products rather than just low prices.[5]

All these decisions have affected or will affect each organization's long-run direction, its allocation of resources, and ultimately its financial success. In contrast, an operating decision, such as changing the package design for Post's cornflakes or altering the sweetness of a Kraft salad dressing, probably won't have a big impact on the long-run profitability of each company.

How do companies go about strategic marketing planning? How do employees know how to implement the long-term strategies of the firm? The answer is the marketing plan.

WHAT IS A MARKETING PLAN?

planning
The process of anticipating future
events and determining the
strategies to achieve organizational objectives.

marketing planning
Designing activities relating to
marketing objectives and the
changing marketing
environment.

marketing plan
A written document that acts as a
guidebook of marketing activities
for the marketing manager.

Planning is the process of anticipating future events and determining the appropriate strategies to achieve organizational objectives. **Marketing planning** involves designing activities relating to marketing objectives and the changing marketing environment. Marketing planning is the basis for all marketing strategies and decisions. Issues such as product lines, distribution channels, marketing communications, and pricing are all outlined in the marketing plan. The **marketing plan** is a written document that acts as a guidebook of marketing activities for the marketing manager. In this chapter, you will learn the importance of writing a marketing plan and the types of information contained in a marketing plan.

Why Write a Marketing Plan?

By specifying objectives and defining the actions required to attain them, a marketing plan provides the basis by which actual and expected performance can be compared. Marketing can be one of the most expensive and complicated business activities, but it is also one of the most important. The written marketing plan provides clearly stated activities that help employees and managers understand and work toward common goals.

Writing a marketing plan allows you to examine the marketing environment in conjunction with the inner workings of the business. Once the marketing plan is written, it serves as a reference point for the success of future activities. The marketing plan allows the marketing manager to enter the marketplace with an awareness of possibilities and problems.

Marketing Plan Elements

Marketing plans can be presented in many different ways. Most businesses need a written marketing plan because the scope of a marketing plan is large and can be complex. Details about tasks and activity assignments may be lost if communicated orally. Regardless of the way a marketing plan is presented, some elements are common to all marketing plans. These include defining the business mission and objectives, performing a situation analysis, identifying a target market, and establishing components of the marketing mix. Exhibit 2.1 shows these elements, which will be described on the following pages. Other elements that may be included in the marketing plan are budgets, implementation timetables, required marketing research efforts, and elements of advanced strategic planning. A detailed marketing planning outline is provided in the appendix to this chapter.

Writing the Marketing Plan

The creation and implementation of a complete marketing plan will allow the organization to achieve its marketing objectives and succeed. However, the marketing plan is only as good as the information it contains and the effort, creativity, and thought that went into its creation. Having a good marketing information system and a wealth of competitive intelligence is critical to a thorough and accurate situation analysis. The role of managerial intuition is also important in the creation and selection of marketing strategies. Managers must weigh any information against its accuracy and their own judgment when making a marketing decision.

Note that the overall structure of the marketing plan (Exhibit 2.1) should not be viewed as a series of sequential steps. Many of the marketing plan elements are decided on in conjunction with one another. Further, every marketing plan has a different content, depending on the organization, its mission, objectives, targets, and marketing mix components. The marketing plan outline in the chapter appendix should not be regarded as the only correct format for a marketing plan. Many organizations have their own distinctive format or terminology for creating a marketing plan. Every marketing plan should be unique to the firm for which it was created. Remember that, although the format and order of presentation is flexible, the same types of questions and topic areas should be covered in any marketing plan. As you can see by the extent of the marketing plan outline in the chapter appendix, creating a complete marketing plan is not a simple effort.

EXHIBIT 2.1

Elements of a Marketing Plan

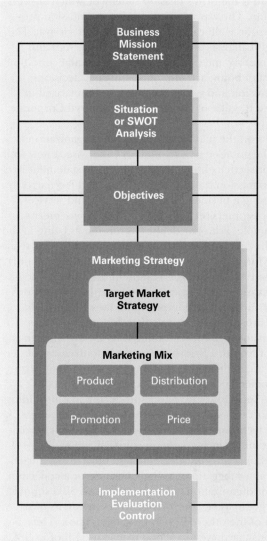

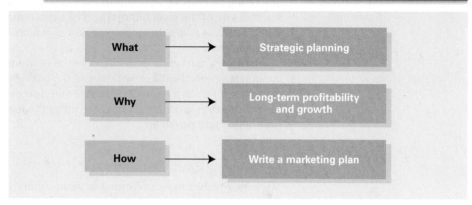

2 DEFINING THE BUSINESS MISSION

Develop an appropriate business mission statement

mission statement
A statement of the firm's business based on a careful analysis of benefits sought by present and potential customers and analysis of existing and anticipated environmental conditions.

marketing myopia
Defining a business in terms of goods and services rather than in terms of the benefits that customers seek.

EXHIBIT 2.2

WestJet's Mission

- To provide safe and affordable travel
- To become one of the most successful international airlines by 2016
- To be appreciative of customers by providing caring and friendly service

SOURCE: http://www.westjet.com/guest/en/aboutUs/corporateProfile/westJetCulture.shtml

strategic business unit (SBU)
A subgroup of a single business or collection of related businesses within the larger organization.

The foundation of any marketing plan is the firm's **mission statement**, which answers the question "What business are we in?" The way a business defines its mission profoundly affects the firm's long-run resource allocation, profitability, and survival. The mission statement is based on a careful analysis of benefits sought by present and potential customers and analysis of existing and anticipated environmental conditions. The firm's mission statement establishes boundaries for all subsequent decisions, objectives, and strategies. WestJet's mission and values statement is summarized in Exhibit 2.2. WestJet has been awarded the title of Canada's Most Admired Corporate Culture for three years in a row!

A mission statement should focus on the market or markets the organization is attempting to serve rather than on the good or service offered. Otherwise, a new technology may quickly make the good or service obsolete and the mission statement irrelevant to company functions. Business mission statements that are stated too narrowly suffer from **marketing myopia**—defining a business in terms of goods and services rather than in terms of the benefits customers seek. In this context, *myopia* means narrow, short-term thinking. For example, Frito-Lay defines its mission as being in the snack-food business rather than in the corn chip business. The mission of sports teams is not just to play games but to serve the interests of the fans. Telus does not sell only camera telephones or long-distance services; it markets communications technology.

Alternatively, business missions may be stated too broadly. "To provide products of superior quality and value that improve the lives of the world's consumers" is probably too broad a mission statement for any firm except Procter & Gamble. Care must be taken when stating what business a firm is in. The mission statement of Norco, a British Columbia manufacturer of performance bikes, states: "We are dedicated to building rewarding, long-term relationships with our Customers, our Employees, and our Suppliers. We are driven by our customers to supply innovative cycle products and outstanding service and marketing support that will promote their growth and success."[6] Once a firm correctly states its business mission in terms of the benefits that customers seek, the foundation for its marketing plan is set.

A large business may need to define a mission statement and objectives for each **strategic business unit (SBU)**, which is a subgroup of a single business or a collection of related businesses within the larger organization. A properly defined SBU should have a distinct mission, a specific target market, control over its resources, its own competitors, and plans independent of the other SBUs in the organization. Thus, a large firm such as Kraft General Foods may have marketing plans for each of its SBUs, which include breakfast foods, desserts, pet foods, and beverages.

Develop an appropriate business mission statement

Q: What business are we in?

A: Business mission statement
└─▶ Too narrow ─▶ marketing myopia
  Too broad ─▶ no direction
  Just right ─▶ focus on markets
    served and benefits
    customers seek

3 CONDUCTING A SITUATION ANALYSIS

Describe the components of a situation analysis

SWOT analysis
Identifying internal strengths (S) and weaknesses (W) and also examining external opportunities (O) and threats (T).

Marketers must understand the current and potential environment that their product or service will be marketed in. A situation analysis is sometimes referred to as a **SWOT analysis**; that is, the firm should identify its internal strengths (S) and weaknesses (W) and also examine external opportunities (O) and threats (T).

When examining internal strengths and weaknesses, the marketing manager should focus on organizational resources such as production costs, marketing skills, financial resources, company or brand image, employee capabilities, and available technology. For example, a potential weakness for Algoma Steel is that it is the smallest of Canada's major steel companies; this means that it may lack economies of scale in comparison with other steel makers. Other possible weaknesses include high labour rates and high management turnover. A potential strength is the low operating costs of its newest mill in Sault Ste. Marie, Ontario, which incorporates the latest technology in the industry. Another issue that might be covered in this section of the marketing plan is the historical background of the firm, including its sales and profit history.

environmental scanning
Collection and interpretation of information about forces, events, and relationships in the external environment that may affect the future of the organization or the implementation of the marketing plan.

When examining external opportunities and threats, marketing managers must analyze all important aspects of the marketing environment. This process is called **environmental scanning**—the collection and interpretation of information about forces, events, and relationships in the external environment that may affect the future of the organization or the implementation of the marketing plan. Environmental scanning helps identify market opportunities and threats and provides guidelines for the design of the marketing strategy. The six most often-studied macroenvironmental forces are social, demographic, economic, technological, political and legal, and competitive. These forces are examined in detail in the next chapter.

3 **Describe the components of a situation analysis**

SETTING MARKETING PLAN OBJECTIVES

Explain the criteria for stating good marketing objectives

marketing objective
A statement of what is to be accomplished through marketing activities.

Before the details of a marketing plan can be developed, goals and objectives for the plan must be stated. Without objectives, there is no basis for measuring the success of marketing plan activities. A **marketing objective** is a statement of what is to be accomplished through marketing activities. To be useful, stated objectives should meet several criteria:

- *Realistic*: Managers should develop objectives that have a chance of being met. For example, it may be unrealistic for a start-up firm or a new product to command a leading market share.
- *Measurable*: Managers need to be able to quantitatively measure whether an objective has been met. For example, it would be difficult to determine success for an objective that states "To improve performance." Does improving performance mean increasing sales, increasing profits, increasing customer satisfaction, or something else? Instead, a specific number should be set such as "To increase sales from $200 million to $240 million."
- *Time-specific*: By what time should the objective be met? "To increase sales from $200 million to $240 million by December 21, 2012," would be time-specific.
- *Compared to a benchmark*: If the objective is to increase sales by 20 percent, it is important to know the baseline against which the objective will be measured. Will it be current sales? Last year's sales? For example, "To increase 2012 sales by 20 percent over 2011 sales of $200 million."

Objectives must also be consistent with and indicate the priorities of the organization. Specifically, objectives flow from the business mission statement to the rest of the marketing plan. Exhibit 2.3 shows some well-stated and poorly stated objectives. Notice how well they do or do not meet the preceding criteria.

Carefully specified objectives serve several functions. First, they communicate the firm's marketing philosophies and provide direction for lower-level marketing managers so that marketing efforts are integrated and pointed in a consistent direction. Objectives also serve as motivators by creating something for employees to strive to reach. When objectives are attainable and challenging, they motivate those charged with achieving the objectives. Additionally, the process of writing specific objectives forces executives to clarify their thinking. Finally, objectives form a basis for control. The effectiveness of a plan can be gauged in light of the stated objectives.

REVIEW LEARNING OUTCOME 4

4 Explain the criteria for stating good marketing objectives

Realistic, measurable, and time-specific objectives consistent with the firm's objectives:

1. Communicate marketing management philosophy
2. Provide management direction
3. Motivate employees
4. Force executives to think clearly
5. Allow for better evaluation of results

EXHIBIT 2.3

Examples of Marketing Objectives

Poorly Stated Objectives	Well-Stated Objectives
Our objective is to be a leader in the industry in new-product development.	Our objective is to introduce five new products in each of 2012 and 2013 by spending 12 percent of sales revenue on R&D activities in each of 2012 and 2013.
Our objective is to maximize profits.	Our objective is to achieve a 10 percent return on investment during 2012, with a payback on new investments of no longer than four years.
Our objective is to better serve customers.	Our objective is to obtain customer satisfaction ratings of at least 90 percent on the 2012 annual customer satisfaction survey, and to retain at least 85 percent of our 2011 customers as repeat purchasers in 2012.
Our objective is to be the best that we can be.	Our objective is to increase market share from 30 percent in 2012 to 40 percent in 2013 by increasing promotional expenditures by 14 percent in 2013 over 2012.

COMPETITIVE ADVANTAGE

Identify sources of competitive advantage

competitive advantage
The set of unique features of a company and its products that are perceived by the target market as significant and superior to the competition.

Performing a SWOT analysis allows firms to identify their competitive advantage. A **competitive advantage** is a set of unique features of a company and its products that are perceived by the target market as significant and superior to the competition. A competitive advantage exists when a firm is able to deliver the same benefits as competitors but at a lower cost, or deliver benefits that exceed those of competing companies. A competitive advantage is what causes customers to patronize one firm over its competitors. There are three types of competitive advantages: cost, product/service differentiation, and niche/focus advantages.

COST COMPETITIVE ADVANTAGE

Cost leadership can result from obtaining inexpensive raw materials, creating an efficient scale of plant operations, designing products for ease of manufacture, controlling overhead costs, outsourcing and vertical integration, and avoiding marginal customers. DuPont, for example, has an exceptional cost competitive advantage in the production of titanium dioxide. Technicians created a production process using low-cost feedstock, giving DuPont a 20 percent cost advantage over its competitors. Having a **cost competitive advantage** means being the low-cost competitor in an industry while maintaining satisfactory profit margins.

cost competitive advantage
Being the low-cost competitor in an industry while maintaining satisfactory profit margins.

A cost competitive advantage enables a firm to deliver superior customer value. Walmart, the world's largest low-cost general merchandiser, offers good value to customers through focusing on providing a large selection of merchandise at low prices. Walmart is able to keep its prices down through strong buying power, closely monitoring all operating expenses, and a very efficient distribution network.

There are many sources of cost competitive advantage, including the following:

experience curves
Curves that show costs declining at a predictable rate as experience with a product increases.

- *Experience curves*: **Experience curves** tell us that costs decline at a predictable rate as experience with a product increases. The experience curve effect encompasses a broad range of manufacturing, marketing, and administrative costs. Experience curves reflect learning by doing, technological advances, and economies of scale. Firms like Bombardier and MTD Canada use historical experience curves as a basis for predicting and setting prices. Experience curves allow management to forecast costs and set prices based on anticipated costs as opposed to current costs.
- *Efficient labour*: Labour costs can be an important component of total costs in low-skill, labour-intensive industries such as product assembly and apparel manufacturing. Many manufacturers such as Nike, Levi Strauss, and Liz Claiborne have gone offshore to achieve lower manufacturing costs. Many automotive parts companies are also moving production to countries with lower labour costs, such as Argentina, China, India, and Thailand.
- *No-frills goods and services*: Marketers can lower costs by removing frills and options from a product or service. This is true of airlines (like WestJet), grocery stores (like No Frills), and retailers (like A Buck or Two).
- *Government subsidies*: Governments may provide grants and interest-free loans to targeted industries. Such government assistance enabled Japanese semiconductor manufacturers to become global leaders. Government subsidies are now assisting Chinese automotive assemblers and parts makers to expand into global markets.
- *Product design*: Cutting-edge design technology can help offset high labour costs. BMW is a world leader in designing cars for ease of manufacture and assembly. Reverse engineering—the process of disassembling a product piece by piece to learn its components and clues as to the manufacturing process—can also mean savings. Japanese engineers have reversed many products, such as computer chips, and have been able to build them at lower cost.
- *Re-engineering*: Re-engineering entails fundamental rethinking and redesign of business processes to achieve dramatic improvements in critical measures of performance. Chrysler Canada, for example, re-engineered its minivan assembly plant in

Nike shoes blends production innovation, efficient labour, and product design into a cost-competitive advantage that fully supports the build-to-order business model it follows. A strong, long-lasting product and service competitive advantage is the outcome that provides the company with superior performance results.

Windsor to make it more flexible (it can assemble five varieties of vehicles at the same time) and to accept larger modules (combinations of parts, such as entire front ends or interiors) onto the assembly line. The end result—more minivans can now be assembled with fewer workers and J. D. Power, a leading automotive consulting firm, has rated Windsor Assembly as the most efficient minivan plant in North America.

- *Production innovations*: Production innovations such as new technology and simplified production techniques help lower the average cost of production. Technologies such as computer-aided design and computer-aided manufacturing (CAD/CAM) and increasingly sophisticated robots help companies like Bombardier, Ford, and General Electric reduce their manufacturing costs.
- *New methods of service delivery*: Medical expenses have been substantially lowered by the use of outpatient surgery and walk-in clinics. Airlines are lowering reservation and ticketing costs by encouraging passengers to use the Internet to book flights, promoting "ticketless travel," and providing self-check-in kiosks at airports.

PRODUCT/SERVICE DIFFERENTIATION COMPETITIVE ADVANTAGE

product/service differentiation competitive advantage
The provision of something that is unique and valuable to buyers beyond simply offering a lower price than the competition.

Because cost competitive advantages are subject to continual erosion, product/service differentiation often provides a longer-lasting competitive advantage. The durability of this strategy tends to make it more attractive to many top managers. A **product/service differentiation competitive advantage** exists when a firm provides something unique that is valuable to buyers besides simply offering a low price. Examples include brand names (Lexus), a strong dealer network (Caterpillar Tractor for construction work), product reliability (Maytag appliances), image (Calvin Klein), or service (FedEx). A great example of a company that has a strong product/service competitive advantage is Nike. Nike's advantage is built around one idea—innovation. The company's goal is to think of something that nobody has thought of before or to improve something that already exists. Nike Air, ACG, Nike Swift, and Nike Shox are examples of innovative shoes introduced by Nike.[7] The value added by the uniqueness of the product may allow the firm to charge a premium price for it. The higher price should more than cover the extra costs that may be incurred in providing the differentiated product or service.

NICHE COMPETITIVE ADVANTAGE

niche competitive advantage
The advantage achieved when a firm seeks to target and effectively serve a small segment of the market.

A **niche competitive advantage**, sometimes referred to as a focus advantage or strategy, seeks to target and effectively serve a single segment of the market. For small companies with limited resources that potentially face giant competitors, niching may be the only viable option. A market segment that has good growth potential but is not crucial to the success of major competitors is a good candidate for developing a niche strategy.

Many companies using a niche strategy serve only a limited geographic market. TBQ is a very successful restaurant chain but is found only in the Windsor, Ontario, market. Migros is the dominant grocery chain in Switzerland but it has no stores outside that small country.

Block Drug Company uses niching by focusing its product line on tooth products. It markets Polident to clean false teeth, Poligrip to hold false teeth, and Sensodyne toothpaste for people with sensitive teeth. The Orvis Company, a very successful nicher, manufactures and sells everything that anyone might ever need for fly-fishing. Niche strategy firms often develop a high level of customer loyalty that keeps potential competitors out of the market.

BUILDING A SUSTAINABLE COMPETITIVE ADVANTAGE

sustainable competitive advantage
An advantage that cannot be readily copied by the competition.

The key to having a competitive advantage is the ability to sustain that advantage. A **sustainable competitive advantage** is one that cannot be easily copied by the competition. It is a competitive advantage that can be maintained over time. Nike, discussed earlier, is a good example of a company that has a sustainable competitive advantage. Others include Rolex (high-quality watches), Caterpillar Tractor (service), and Magna (patented hydroforming technology for shaping automotive parts). In contrast, when Datril was introduced into the pain-reliever market, it was touted as being exactly like Tylenol, only cheaper. Tylenol responded by lowering its price, thus destroying Datril's competitive advantage and ability to remain on the market. In this case, low price was not a sustainable competitive advantage. Without a competitive advantage, target customers don't have any reason to patronize an organization instead of its competitors.

The notion of competitive advantage means that a successful firm will stake out a position unique in some way from its rivals. Imitation of competitors indicates a lack of competitive advantage and almost ensures mediocre performance. Companies need to build their own competitive advantages rather than copy a competitor. The sources of tomorrow's competitive advantages are the skills and assets of the organization. Assets include patents, copyrights, locations, equipment and technology that are superior to those of the competition, and better people. Skills are functions such as customer service and promotion that the firm performs better than its competitors. Travelocity, for example, is known for the ease of its on-line travel reservations. Marketing managers should continually focus the firm's skills and assets on sustaining and creating competitive advantages.

Remember, a sustainable competitive advantage is a function of the speed with which competitors can imitate a leading company's strategy and plans. Imitation requires a competitor to identify the leader's competitive advantage, determine how it is achieved, and then learn how to duplicate it.

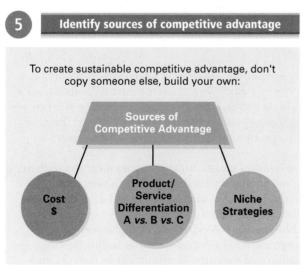

REVIEW LEARNING OUTCOME 5

5 Identify sources of competitive advantage

To create sustainable competitive advantage, don't copy someone else, build your own:

Sources of Competitive Advantage

Cost $

Product/ Service Differentiation A *vs.* B *vs.* C

Niche Strategies

Customer Experience

Bass Pro Shops (with outlets in Alberta and Ontario and expanding) has been named the "Outdoor Retailer of the Year" by *Sporting Goods Business* magazine. The award is due, in part, to the fact that the company understands how to offer the customer a quality and entertaining experience while they shop. This experiential aspect of Bass Pro Shops provides them with a strong competitive advantage.

Bass Pro Shop locations are designed to showcase the characteristics of the area where they are located. The stores bring in elements of a natural history museum, an art gallery, and an aquarium. Taxidermy mounts on the walls are animals native to the store's area and stores have an indoor water feature that contains indigenous fish species. One Bass Pro Shop store features the hull of a sunken ship while another has a 10-metre-long blue whale on display.

In some of the aquariums, professional fishermen and store staff hold demonstrations that show customers how to use artificial bait. Classes are offered at the stores, ranging from fly-casting, Dutch-oven cooking, archery hunting, and GPS navigation. Most stores also feature full-service restaurants. Bass Pro Shops is also the sponsor of the Lake Simcoe Open, Canada's premier bass fishing tournament.

The design details of the stores are a feature that enhances the customer experience. Bass Pro Shops has its own shop that builds the pine and cedar log buildings, and 55 artisans, including coppersmiths, blacksmiths, carvers, and painters who hand-make lighting fixtures, wood carvings, and iron work that is used throughout the store. Artists paint large murals on the walls and ceilings that incorporate mounted animals. Go to the website of any of the Bass Pro Shops in Canada for pictures of the stores.

Stores, such as the one in Vaughan, Ontario, receive over 3 million visitors a year. In fact, Bass Pro Shops have assumed the status of a tourist destination. Some people spend their vacations driving from store to store.[8]

How might the concept of retail entertainment be applied to other types of retail stores or shopping areas and malls? Either think of examples you have experienced, or create a new idea for using this concept.

SOURCE: STORE REVIEW, BASS PRO SHOPS, FLYFISHINGABOUT.COM, DECEMBER 1, 2008.

6 STRATEGIC DIRECTIONS

Identify strategic alternatives

The end result of a SWOT analysis and the identification of a competitive advantage is to determine the strategic direction of the firm, the next step in the strategic planning process.

STRATEGIC ALTERNATIVES

To discover a marketing opportunity, management must know how to identify possible alternatives. One method for developing alternatives is Ansoff's strategic opportunity matrix (see Exhibit 2.4), which matches products with markets. Firms can explore these four options:

market penetration
A marketing strategy that tries to increase market share among existing customers.

- *Market penetration*: A firm using the **market penetration** alternative would try to increase market share among existing customers. If Kraft General Foods started a major campaign for Maxwell House coffee, with aggressive advertising and cents-off coupons, it would be following a penetration strategy. McDonald's sold the most Happy Meals in its history with a promotion that included Ty's Teeny Beanie Babies.

market development
A marketing strategy that entails attracting new customers to existing products.

- *Market development*: **Market development** means attracting new customers to existing products. Ideally, new uses for old products stimulate additional sales among existing customers while also bringing in new buyers. McDonald's, for example, has opened restaurants in Russia, China, and Italy and is eagerly expanding into Eastern European countries. Bombardier has expanded its high-speed rail equipment sales into the Chinese market. In the nonprofit area, the growing emphasis on continuing education and executive development by colleges and universities is a market development strategy.

EXHIBIT 2.4

Ansoff's Strategic Opportunity Matrix

	Present Product	New Product
Present Market	**Market penetration:** McDonald's sells more Happy Meals with Disney movie promotions.	**Product development:** McDonald's introduces premium salads and McWater.
New Market	**Market development:** McDonald's opens restaurants in China.	**Diversification:** McDonald's introduces line of children's clothing

product development
A marketing strategy that entails the creation of new products for existing customers.

- *Product development*: A **product development** strategy entails the creation of new products for present markets. Nike, the famous maker of athletic shoes, has introduced sleek ergonomic running watches, a high-altitude wrist compass, and a portable heart-rate monitor. These new offerings are targeted at athletes who want to time their daily jog and monitor how fast their heart is beating. The company has formed a new division called Techlab to develop sports-technology products.[9] McDonald's introduced yogurt parfaits, entrée salads, and fruit to offer their current customers more healthy options. Tim Hortons is now introducing Cold Stone Creamery ice cream to many of its outlets. Managers following the product development strategy can rely on their extensive knowledge of their target audience. They usually have a good feel for what customers like and dislike about current products and what existing needs are not being met. In addition, managers can rely on established distribution channels.

diversification
A strategy of increasing sales by introducing new products into new markets.

- *Diversification*: **Diversification** is a strategy of increasing sales by introducing new products into new markets. For example, Magna, the largest automotive parts manufacturer in Canada, diversified into the entertainment business with its acquisition of racetracks and amusement parks. Sony practised a diversification strategy when it acquired Columbia Pictures; although motion pictures are not a new product in the marketplace, they were a new product for Sony. Coca-Cola manufactures and markets water-treatment and water-conditioning equipment, which has been a very challenging task for the traditional soft drink company. A diversification strategy can be risky when a firm is entering unfamiliar markets. On the other hand, it can be very profitable when a firm is entering markets with little or no competition.

SELECTING A STRATEGIC ALTERNATIVE

Selecting which strategic alternative to pursue depends on the overall company philosophy and the tool used to make the decision. Companies generally have one of two philosophies about when they expect profits. They either pursue profits right away or first seek to increase market share and then pursue profits. In the long run, market share and profitability are compatible goals. Michelin, the tire producer, consistently sacrifices short-term profits to achieve market share. On the other hand, IBM stresses profitability and stock valuation over market share. Over the past several years, General Motors has been content to give up market share in North America to concentrate on more profitable sales.

Portfolio Matrix

Recall that large organizations engaged in strategic planning may operate a number of strategic business units. Each SBU has its own rate of return on investment, growth potential, and risk. Management must find a balance among the SBUs that yields the overall organization's desired growth and profits with an acceptable level of risk. Some SBUs generate large amounts of cash while others need cash to foster growth. The challenge is to balance the organization's "portfolio" of SBUs for the best long-term firm performance. For a single SBU, the portfolio matrix may be used by positioning different products sold by the business unit on the matrix.

portfolio matrix
A tool for allocating resources among products or strategic business units on the basis of relative market share and market growth rate.

star
In the portfolio matrix, a business unit that is a fast-growing market leader.

cash cow
In the portfolio matrix, a business unit that generates more cash than it needs to maintain its market share.

To determine the future cash contributions and cash requirements expected for each SBU, or each product within an SBU, managers can use the Boston Consulting Group's portfolio matrix. This **portfolio matrix** classifies each SBU by its present or forecasted growth and market share. The underlying assumption is that market share and profitability are strongly linked. The measure of market share used in the portfolio approach is *relative market share,* the ratio between the company's share and the share of its largest competitor. For example, if firm A has a 50 percent share and its largest competitor has 5 percent, the ratio is 10 to 1 (or 10×). If firm A has a 10 percent market share and its largest competitor has 20 percent, the ratio is 0.5 to 1 (or 0.5×).

Exhibit 2.5 is a hypothetical portfolio matrix for a large computer manufacturer. The size of the circle in each cell of the matrix represents dollar sales of the SBU relative to dollar sales of the company's other SBUs. The following categories are used in the matrix:

- *Stars*: A **star** is a market leader in a fast-growing market. For example, computer manufacturers have identified subnotebook, handheld models, and tablet PCs as stars. Star SBUs usually have large profits but need a lot of cash to finance rapid growth. The best marketing tactic is to protect existing market share by reinvesting earnings in product improvement, better distribution, more promotion, and production efficiency. Management must strive to capture most of the new users as they enter the market.

- *Cash cows*: A **cash cow** is an SBU that generates more cash than it needs to maintain its market share. It is in a low-growth market, but the product has a dominant market share. Personal computers and laptops are categorized as cash cows in Exhibit 2.5. The basic strategy for a cash cow is to maintain market dominance and making technological improvements in the product. Managers should resist pressure to extend the basic line unless they can dramatically increase demand. Instead, they should allocate excess cash to the product categories where growth prospects are the greatest. For instance, the Clorox Company owns Kingsford charcoal, the Glad brand of products, Fresh Step, Scoop Away and other pet litters, Brita water filtration systems, and K.C. Masterpiece barbecue sauce, among others. Traditionally, the company's cash cow has been Clorox bleach, which owns the lion's share of a low-growth market. The Clorox Company has been highly successful in stretching the Clorox line to include scented chlorine bleach, as well as Clorox 2, a chlorine-free bleach for coloured clothing. For Heinz, with a large manufacturing plant in Leamington, Ontario, ketchup is a cash cow.

- *Problem children*: A **problem child**, also called a **question mark**, shows rapid growth but poor profit margins. It has a low market share in a high-growth industry. Problem children need a great deal of cash. Without cash support, they eventually become dogs. The strategy options are to invest heavily to gain better market

EXHIBIT 2.5

Portfolio Matrix for a Large Computer Manufacturer

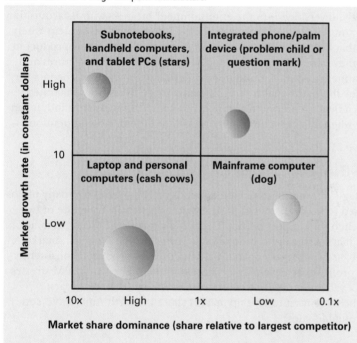

NOTE: The size of the circle represents the dollar-size sales relative to sales of other SBUs on the matrix.

problem child (question mark)
In the portfolio matrix, a business unit that shows rapid growth but poor profit margins.

dog
In the portfolio matrix, a business unit that has low growth potential and a small market share.

share, acquire competitors to get the necessary market share, or drop the SBU. Sometimes a firm, through a successful marketing strategy, can reposition the question-mark products of the SBU to move them into the star category.

- *Dogs*: A **dog** has low growth potential and a small market share. Most dogs eventually leave the marketplace. In the computer manufacturer example, the mainframe computer has become a dog. Two other examples of dogs are Warner-Lambert's Reef mouthwash and Campbell's Red Kettle soups. Frito-Lay has produced several dogs, including Stuffers cheese-filled snacks, Rumbles granola nuggets, and Toppels

SOURCE: © 2010 THE CLOROX COMPANY. CLOROX® IS A REGISTERED TRADEMARK OF THE CLOROX COMPANY. USED WITH PERMISSION.

SOURCE: © 2010 THE CLOROX COMPANY. CLOROX 2® IS A REGISTERED TRADEMARK OF THE CLOROX COMPANY. USED WITH PERMISSION.

Cash cows generate more cash than they need to maintain their market share. Clorox is a cash cow. It has a 60 percent market share and has successfully introduced numerous scents as well as a chlorine-free bleach for coloured clothes.

cheese-topped crackers—a trio irreverently known as Stumbles, Tumbles, and Twofers. The strategy options for dogs are to harvest or divest.

After classifying the company's SBUs or products on the Boston Consulting Group matrix, the next step is to allocate future resources for each. The four basic strategy options are to do one of the following:

- *Build*: If an organization has an SBU that it believes has the potential to be a star (probably a problem child at present), building would be an appropriate goal. The organization may decide to give up short-term profits and use its financial resources to achieve this goal. Procter & Gamble built Pringles from a money loser to a record profit maker.
- *Hold*: If an SBU is a very successful cash cow, a key goal would surely be to hold or preserve market share so that the organization can take advantage of the very positive cash flow. Bisquick has been a prosperous cash cow for General Mills for over two decades.
- *Harvest*: This strategy may be appropriate for all SBUs except those classified as stars. The basic goal is to increase the short-term cash return without too much concern for the long-run impact. It is especially worthwhile when more cash is needed from a cash cow with unfavourable long-run prospects due to a low market growth rate. For instance, Lever Brothers has been harvesting Lifebuoy soap for a number of years, giving the product little promotional backing.
- *Divest*: Getting rid of SBUs with low shares of low-growth markets is often appropriate. Problem children and dogs are most suitable for this strategy. Procter & Gamble dropped Cincaprin, a coated aspirin, because of its low growth potential.

REVIEW LEARNING OUTCOME 6

6 | **Identify strategic alternatives**

Market development	= ↑	customers
Market penetration	= ↑	share
Product development	= ↑	products
Diversification	= ↑	new products + ↑ new markets

Ethics in Marketing

 ## SURROGATE ADS

Indian law prohibits companies from advertising tobacco and liquor. However, companies that sell these products are among the largest advertisers in the country. They accomplish this by using what are known as "surrogate advertisements" that, instead of featuring cigarettes and alcoholic beverages, focus on unrelated, cheap-to-make products that they also produce. Surrogate products include CDs, playing cards, and bottled water that all have the same brand name as the companies' spirits and smokes. These ads have been blamed for luring India's young people (10 to 14 years old) to take up smoking. One study showed that current use of tobacco was five times lower among students who had not watched surrogate promotions. The companies say that they buy ads for the actual products advertised and deny that they use surrogate advertising.

India's health minister has asked the Information and Broadcasting Ministry to take action against the companies that are showing surrogate ads. The government has asked that broadcasters stop airing ads from tobacco and liquor companies for products with brand names that are the same as their tobacco and liquor brands, regardless of the product being advertised. If broadcasters comply, they could experience an estimated $50 million loss of advertising revenue and even more if the government extends the ban on surrogate ads to other forms of media.

Government actions against surrogate ads are causing the liquor and tobacco companies to use sponsorships of sporting events, concerts, and other entertainment venues as an alternative to promoting their products. For example, the chairman of the UB Group, which markets Kingfisher beer and Royal Challenge whisky, bought a professional cricket team. The team was named the "Royal Challengers" and the colours and logos of the team are the same as those of the whisky brand. Bacardi Martini India sells a line of music CDs with the brand name Bacardi Blast, which is also the branding used for high-profile events.[10] Is it ethical for India's tobacco and liquor companies to use surrogate advertising to get their brand names in front of customers? Take a stand and defend your answer.

SOURCE: NIRAJ SHERTH, "INDIA LIQUOR, TOBACCO FIRMS SHIFT TACK," THE WALL STREET JOURNAL, MAY 6, 2008, B8; KOUNTEYA SINHA, "SURROGATE ADS LURING KIDS TO SMOKING: STUDY," EPAPER.TIMESOFINDIA.COM, DECEMBER 1, 2008; "SURROGATE ADS WILL BE STOPPED, ASSURES I&B," TIMESOFINDIA.INDIATIMES.COM, DECEMBER 1, 2008.

 # DESCRIBING THE TARGET MARKET

Discuss target market strategies

A **marketing strategy** involves the activities of selecting and describing one or more target markets and developing and maintaining a marketing mix that will produce mutually satisfying exchanges with the selected target markets.

marketing strategy
The activities of selecting and describing one or more target markets and developing and maintaining a marketing mix that will produce mutually satisfying exchanges with the target markets.

TARGET MARKET STRATEGY

A market segment is a group of individuals or organizations that share one or more characteristics. They therefore may have relatively similar product needs. For example, parents of newborn babies need products such as formula, diapers, and special foods. A target market strategy identifies the market segment or segments on which the firm will focus. This process begins with a **market opportunity analysis (MOA)**—the description and estimation of the size and sales potential of market segments that are of interest to the firm and the assessment of key competitors in these market segments. After the firm describes the market segments, it may target one or more of them. There are three general strategies for selecting target markets. Target market(s) can be selected by appealing to the entire market with one marketing mix, concentrating on one segment, or appealing to multiple market segments using multiple marketing mixes.

market opportunity analysis (MOA)
The description and estimation of the size and sales potential of market segments that are of interest to the firm and the assessment of key competitors in these market segments.

Any market segment that is targeted must be fully described. Chapter 6 describes the process of segmenting and targeting markets. A target market may be described in terms of demographics, psychographics, and buyer behaviour. Buyer behaviour is covered in Chapters 4 and 5. If segments are differentiated by ethnicity, the multicultural aspects of the marketing mix must be examined. If the target market is international, it is especially important to describe differences in culture, economic and technological development, and the political structure that may affect the marketing plan.

7 | Discuss target market strategies

Target Market Options

| Entire Market | Multiple Markets | Single Market |

 THE MARKETING MIX

Describe the elements of the marketing mix

marketing mix
A unique blend of product, place, promotion, and pricing strategies designed to produce mutually satisfying exchanges with a target market.

four Ps
Product, place, promotion, and price, which together make up the marketing mix.

The term **marketing mix** refers to a unique blend of product, place (distribution), promotion, and pricing strategies designed to produce mutually satisfying exchanges with a target market. The marketing mix is often referred to as the **four Ps**. The marketing manager controls each component of the marketing mix, but the strategies for all four components must be blended to achieve optimal results. Any marketing mix is only as good as its weakest component. For example, the first pump toothpastes were distributed over cosmetic counters and failed. Not until pump toothpastes were distributed the same way as tube toothpastes did the products succeed. The best promotion and the lowest price cannot save a poor product. Similarly, excellent products with poor distribution, pricing, or promotion will likely fail.

Successful marketing mixes have been carefully designed to satisfy specific target markets. At first glance, McDonald's and Wendy's may appear to have roughly identical marketing mixes because they are both in the fast-food hamburger business. However, McDonald's has been most successful with targeting parents with young children for lunchtime meals, whereas Wendy's targets the adult crowd for lunches and dinner. McDonald's has playgrounds, Ronald McDonald the clown, and children's Happy Meals. Wendy's has salad bars, carpeted restaurants, and no playgrounds.

Variations in marketing mixes do not occur by chance. Astute marketing managers devise marketing strategies to gain advantages over competitors and best serve the needs and wants of a particular target market segment. By manipulating elements of the marketing mix, marketing managers can fine-tune the customer offering and achieve success.

SOURCE: COURTESY OF WENDY'S INTERNATIONAL, INC.

Although competing in the saturated fast-food industry, Wendy's does an excellent job of differentiating itself through its product mix. Rather than cater to families with young children, Wendy's tailors its offerings to meet the needs and wants of the adult lunch crowd. Its salad offerings are part of this strategy.

PRODUCT STRATEGIES

Typically, the marketing mix starts with the product "P." The heart of the marketing mix is the product offering and product strategy. It is hard to design a place strategy, decide on a promotion campaign, or set a price without knowing the product to be marketed.

The product includes the physical item along with its package, warranty, after-sale service, brand name, company image, value, and many other factors. A Godiva chocolate has many product elements: the chocolate itself, a fancy gold wrapper, a customer satisfaction guarantee, and the prestige of the Godiva brand name. We buy things not only for what they do (benefits) but also for what they mean to us (status, quality, or reputation). Products can be tangible goods such as computers, ideas like those offered by a consultant, or services such as medical care. Product decisions are covered in Chapters 8 and 9 while services marketing is detailed in Chapter 10.

PLACE (DISTRIBUTION) STRATEGIES

Place strategies are concerned with making products available when and where customers want them and providing the means for buyers to take ownership. Would you rather buy a kiwi fruit at the 24-hour grocery store within walking distance or fly to Australia to pick your own? A part of this place "P" is physical distribution, which involves all the business activities concerned with storing and transporting raw materials or finished products. The goal of distribution is to make sure products arrive in usable condition at designated places when needed. Distribution strategies are covered in Chapters 11 and 12.

PROMOTION STRATEGIES

Promotion includes personal selling, advertising, sales promotion, and public relations. Promotion's role in the marketing mix is to bring about mutually satisfying exchanges with target markets by informing, educating, persuading, and reminding your target customers of the benefits of your organization and products. A good promotion strategy, like using the Dilbert character in a national promotion strategy for Office Depot, can dramatically increase sales. Good promotion strategies do not guarantee success, however. Each element of the promotion "P" is coordinated and managed with the others to create a promotional blend or mix. These integrated marketing communications activities are described in Chapters 13, 14, and 15. Technology-driven aspects of promotional marketing are covered in Chapters 18 and 19.

Marketing Mix

Product · Place · Price · Promotion

PRICING STRATEGIES

Price is what a buyer must give up to obtain a product. It is often the most flexible of the four marketing mix elements—the quickest element to change. Marketers can raise or lower prices more frequently and easily than they can change other marketing mix variables. Price is an important competitive weapon and is very important to the organization because price multiplied by the number of units sold equals total revenue for the firm. Pricing decisions are covered in Chapters 16 and 17.

9 FOLLOWING UP ON THE MARKETING PLAN

Explain why implementation, evaluation, and control of the marketing plan are necessary

IMPLEMENTATION

Implementation is the process that turns marketing plans into action assignments and ensures that these assignments are executed in a way that accomplishes the plan's objectives. Implementation activities may involve detailed job assignments, activity

implementation
The process that turns marketing plans into action assignments and ensures that these assignments are executed in a way that accomplishes the plan's objectives.

evaluation
Gauging the extent to which the marketing objectives have been achieved during the specified time period.

control
Provides the mechanisms for evaluating marketing results in light of the plan's goals and for correcting actions that do not help the organization reach those objectives within budget guidelines.

marketing audit
A thorough, systematic, periodic evaluation of the objectives, strategies, structure, and performance of the marketing organization.

descriptions, timelines, budgets, and lots of communication. Although implementation is essentially "doing what you said you were going to do," many organizations repeatedly experience failures in strategy implementation. Brilliant marketing plans are doomed to fail if they are not properly communicated and implemented.

EVALUATION AND CONTROL

After a marketing plan is implemented, it should be evaluated. **Evaluation** entails gauging the extent to which marketing objectives have been achieved during the specified time period. Four common reasons for failing to achieve a marketing objective are unrealistic marketing objectives, inappropriate marketing strategies in the plan, poor implementation, and changes in the environment after the objective was specified and the strategy was implemented.

Once a plan is chosen and implemented, its effectiveness must be monitored. **Control** provides the mechanisms for evaluating marketing results in light of the plan's objectives and for correcting actions that do not help the organization reach those goals within budget guidelines. Firms need to establish formal and informal control programs to make the entire operation more efficient.

Perhaps the broadest control device available to marketing managers is the **marketing audit**—a thorough, systematic, periodic evaluation of the objectives, strategies, structure, and performance of the marketing organization. A marketing audit helps management allocate marketing resources efficiently. It has four characteristics:

- *Comprehensive*: The marketing audit covers all the major marketing issues facing an organization and not just trouble spots.
- *Systematic*: The marketing audit takes place in an orderly sequence and covers the organization's marketing environment, internal marketing system, and specific marketing activities. The diagnosis is followed by an action plan with both short-run and long-run proposals for improving overall marketing effectiveness.
- *Independent*: The marketing audit is normally conducted by an inside or outside party who is independent enough to have top management's confidence and to be objective.
- *Periodic*: The marketing audit should be carried out on a regular schedule, not just in crisis situations. Whether successful or in trouble, any organization can benefit greatly from such an audit.

A major part of the marketing audit is the establishment of marketing performance metrics. **Marketing performance metrics** tell us how well a business is performing in the market. Most businesses use financial performance metrics that report important ratios for profits, costs, and assets. Financial metrics, however, do not provide any insight into how the business is performing in the market. Further, while financial metrics are internal, marketing performance metrics are external—they serve as leading market indicators of what the future financial performance of the company

marketing performance metrics
Marketing performance metrics are measures that tell us how well a business is performing in the market.

will be. For example, if customers' intentions to repurchase are declining, sales and profitability can be expected to decline. Some examples of marketing and financial metrics are shown in Exhibit 2.6.

Marketing metrics are at the heart of an evaluation and control system as they tell management how the business is performing in the market. Marketing metrics are a barometer of future financial performance. Some marketing performance metrics examine current performance in the market (such as market share); some gauge the company's performance with their customers (such as customer satisfaction and retention); and some examine a company's performance relative to major competitors (such as relative product performance and service quality).

EXHIBIT 2.6

Sample Marketing and Financial Performance Metrics

Marketing Metrics	Financial Metrics
• Market Growth	• Return on Sales
• Company Sales Growth	• Return on Assets
• Market Share	• Return on Capital
• Customer Satisfaction	• Cost of Goods Sold
• Customer Retention	• Marketing Expenses
• Relative Product Performance	• Asset Turnover
• Relative Service Quality	• Accounts Receivable (days)
	• Inventory (days)

SOURCE: Adapted from Roger Best, MARKET-BASED MANAGEMENT, 5TH Ed. © 2009. Printed and Electronically reproduced by permission of Pearson Education, Inc., Upper Saddle River, New Jersey.

9 **Explain why implementation, evaluation, and control of the marketing plan are necessary**

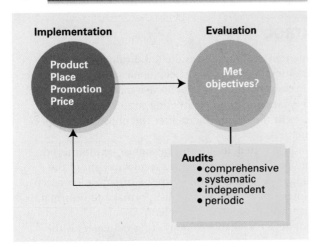

10 **Identify several techniques that help make strategic planning effective**

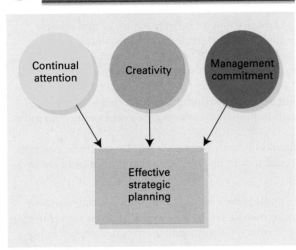

10 EFFECTIVE STRATEGIC PLANNING

Identify several techniques that help make strategic planning effective

Effective strategic planning requires constant attention, creativity, and management commitment as described within the following points:

- Strategic planning is not an annual exercise, in which managers go through the motions and then forget about strategic planning until the next year. It should be an ongoing process because the environment is constantly changing and the firm's resources and capabilities are constantly evolving.

- Sound strategic planning is based on creativity. Managers should challenge assumptions about the firm and its environment and establish new strategies. For example, major oil companies developed the concept of the gasoline service station in an age when cars needed frequent and rather elaborate servicing. They held on to the full-service approach, but independents were quick to respond to the new realities of the market and moved to lower-cost self-service and convenience store operations. The majors took several decades to catch up.

- Perhaps the most critical element in successful strategic planning is top management's support and participation. For example, Pete Mateja, while president of Home & Park Motorhomes, one of the largest manufacturers of customized travel and camper vans in Canada, always took direct leadership responsibility in the development of the short- and long-term marketing plans at Home & Park. Mateja worked directly with the heads of all departments in the company to ensure that input was received from everyone. All employees were assured that their concerns would be addressed so there would be complete company buy-in to the plan. Mateja then racked up hundreds of hours of travel time visiting Home & Park distributors to include them in the development of the plan and to make sure they would come on board.

REVIEW AND APPLICATIONS

1 **Understand the importance of strategic marketing and know a basic outline for a marketing plan.** Strategic marketing planning is the basis for all marketing strategies and decisions. The marketing plan is a written document that acts as a guidebook of marketing activities for the marketing manager. By specifying objectives and defining the actions required to attain them, a marketing plan provides the basis on which actual and expected performance can be compared.

Although there is no set formula for a marketing plan or a single correct outline, basic factors that should be covered include stating the business mission, performing a situation analysis of internal and external environmental forces, setting objectives, selecting target market(s), delineating a marketing mix (product, place, promotion, and price), and establishing ways to implement, evaluate, and control the plan.

1.1 Your cousin wants to start his own business and he is in a hurry. He has decided not to write a marketing plan because he thinks that preparing such a document would take too long. He says he doesn't need a formal proposal because he has already received funding from your uncle. Explain why it is important for him to write a plan anyway.

1.2 After graduation, you decide to take a position as the marketing manager for a small snack-food manufacturer. The company, Shur Snak, is growing and this is the first time that the company has ever employed a marketing manager. Consequently, there is no marketing plan in place for you to follow. Outline a basic marketing plan for your boss to give her an idea of the direction you want to take the company.

1.3 How are Coke and Pepsi using their websites, **www.coca-cola.com** and **www.pepsi.com**, to promote their newest product offerings? Do you see hints of any future strategies the companies might implement? Where?

2 **Develop an appropriate business mission statement.** The mission statement is based on a careful analysis of benefits sought by present and potential customers and an analysis of existing and anticipated environmental conditions. The firm's mission statement establishes boundaries for all subsequent decisions, objectives, and strategies. A mission statement should focus on the market or markets the organization is attempting to serve rather than on the good or service offered.

2.1 How can a new company best define its business mission statement? Can you find examples of good and bad mission statements on the Internet? How might you improve the bad ones?

2.2 Thinking back to question 1.2, write a business mission statement for Shur Snak. What elements should you include? Evaluate the mission statement you wrote against some of those you found on-line in question 2.1.

3 Describe the components of a situation analysis. In the situation (or SWOT) analysis, the firm should identify its internal strengths (S) and weaknesses (W) and also examine external opportunities (O) and threats (T). When examining external opportunities and threats, marketing managers must analyze aspects of the marketing environment through a process called environmental scanning. The six most often-studied macroenvironmental forces are social, demographic, economic, technological, political and legal, and competitive. During the situation analysis, it is crucial for the marketer to identify a competitive advantage and establish that it is a sustainable competitive advantage.

3.1 Competition in the private courier sector is fierce. UPS and FedEx dominate, but other companies, such as DHL, Emery, and even Canada Post, still have a decent chunk of the express package delivery market. Perform a mini-situation analysis on one of the companies listed below by stating one strength, one weakness, one opportunity, and one threat. You may want to consult the following websites as you build your grid:

United Parcel Service (UPS) **www.ups.com**

FedEx **www.fedex.com**

DHL **www.dhl-usa.com**

USPS **www.usps.com**

Canada Post **www.canadapost.ca**

4 **Explain the criteria for stating good marketing objectives.** Objectives should be realistic, measurable, and time specific. Objectives must also be consistent and indicate the priorities of the organization.

4.1 Building on your Shur Snak example, imagine that your boss has stated that the marketing objective of the company is to do the best job of satisfying the needs and wants of the customer. Explain that although this objective is admirable, it does not meet the criteria for good objectives. What are these criteria? What is a specific example of a better objective for Shur Snak?

5 **Identify sources of competitive advantage.** A competitive advantage is a set of unique features of a company and its products that are perceived by the target market as significant and superior to the competition. There are three types of competitive advantages including cost, product or service differentiation, and niche strategies. Sources of cost-competitive advantages include experience curves, efficient labour, no-frills goods and services, government subsidies, product design, re-engineering, product innovations, and new methods of service delivery. Product or service differentiation exists when a firm provides something unique that is valuable to buyers besides just low price. Niche competitive advantages come from targeting market segments with specific needs and wants and ignored by other firms. The goal of all these sources of competitive advantage is to be sustainable.

5.1   **TEAM**   Break into small groups and discuss examples (at least two per person) of the last few products you have purchased. What specific strategies are used by the makers of these products to achieve a competitive advantage? Is that advantage sustainable against competitors?

6 **Identify strategic alternatives.** The strategic opportunity matrix can be used to help management develop strategic alternatives. The four options are market penetration, product development, market development, and diversification. In selecting a strategic alternative, managers may use a portfolio matrix, which classifies strategic business units as stars, cash cows, problem children, or dogs, depending on their present or projected growth and market share.

6.1   Based on your SWOT analysis, decide what the strategic growth options are for the company you chose in question 3.1. Also, decide where your company's products fit in the Boston Consulting Group matrix (see Exhibit 2.5).

7 **Discuss target market strategies.** The target market strategy identifies which market segment or segments to focus on. This process begins with a market opportunity analysis (MOA), which describes and estimates the size and sales potential of market segments that are of interest to the firm. In addition, an assessment of key competitors in these market segments is performed. After the market segments are described, the firm may target one or more of them. The three strategies for selecting target markets are appealing to the entire market with one marketing mix, concentrating on one segment, or appealing to multiple market segments using multiple marketing mixes.

7.1   You are given the task of deciding the marketing strategy for a transportation company. How do the marketing mix elements change when the target market is (a) low-income workers without personal transportation, (b) corporate international business travellers, or (c) companies with urgent documents or perishable materials to get to customers?

8 **Describe the elements of the marketing mix.** The marketing mix (or four Ps) is a blend of product, place, promotion, and pricing strategies designed to produce mutually satisfying exchanges with a target market. The starting point of the marketing mix is the product offering. Products can be tangible goods, ideas, or services. Place strategies are concerned with making products available when and where customers want them and providing for the transfer of ownership. Promotion includes personal selling, advertising, sales promotion, and public relations. Price is what a buyer must give up to obtain a product and is often the easiest to change of the four marketing mix elements.

8.1   **TEAM**   Choose three or four other students and make up a team. Create a marketing plan to increase enrollment in your school. Describe the four marketing mix elements that make up the plan.

9 **Explain why implementation, evaluation, and control of the marketing plan are necessary.** Before a marketing plan can work, it must be implemented; that is, people must perform the actions in the plan. The plan should also be evaluated to see if it has achieved its objectives. Poor implementation can be a major factor in a plan's failure. Control provides the mechanisms for evaluating marketing results in light of the plan's goals and for correcting actions that do not help the organization reach those goals within budget guidelines. Marketing and financial performance metrics should be established as part of the control process.

9.1 Have your school enrollment marketing plan team (from question 8.1) develop a plan to implement, evaluate, and control the marketing strategy.

10 **Identify several techniques that help make strategic planning effective.** First, management must realize that strategic planning is an ongoing process and not a once-a-year exercise. Second, good strategic planning involves a high level of creativity. The last requirement is top management's support and cooperation.

10.1 What techniques can make your school enrollment marketing plan more effective?

TERMS

cash cow 32
competitive advantage 27
control 37
cost competitive advantage 27
diversification 31
dog 32
environmental scanning 25
evaluation 37
experience curves 27
four Ps 35
implementation 37
market development 30

market opportunity analysis (MOA) 34
market penetration 30
marketing audit 37
marketing mix 35
marketing myopia 24
marketing objective 26
marketing performance metrics 37
marketing plan 22
marketing planning 22
marketing strategy 34
mission statement 24

niche competitive advantage 29
planning 22
portfolio matrix 32
problem child (question mark) 32
product development 31
product/service differentiation 28
star 32
strategic business unit (SBU) 24
strategic planning 22
sustainable competitive advantage 29
SWOT analysis 25

EXERCISES

APPLICATION EXERCISE

As you know from reading this chapter, an important part of developing marketing strategies is scanning the environment for changes that will affect your marketing efforts. This exercise is designed to introduce you to the business press and to help you make the connection between the concepts you learn in the classroom and real-world marketing activities.

Activities

1. Find a current article of marketing substance in the business press (the Business Report section of *The Globe and Mail,* the *Financial Post, Canadian Business, Marketing, Fortune, Business Week,* or the business section of your local newspaper). Although this is only Chapter 2, you will be surprised by the amount of terminology you have already learned. If you are having trouble finding an article, read through the table of contents at the beginning of the book to familiarize yourself with the names of concepts that will be presented later in the course. Read your article carefully, making notes about relevant content.

2. **WRITING** Write a one-paragraph summary of the key points in your article; then write a list of the terms or concepts critical to understanding the article. Provide definitions for those terms. If you are unfamiliar with a term or concept in the article, do some research in this textbook or talk to your professor. Relate the key points in your article to concepts covered in this text.

3. What environmental issues, target markets, and/or marketing-mix issues are covered in the article? How has the article added to your understanding of these issues?

ETHICS EXERCISE

Abercrombie & Fitch, a $3-billion U.S. clothing chain with stores in Ontario and Alberta, launched a line of thong underwear for preteen girls. Words like "eye candy" and "wink wink" were printed on the front of the skimpy underwear that some argued would fit girls aged five to ten. Abercrombie is known for its provocative ads (you can see examples of its ads on its website) and sexually oriented catalogues. Supporters of the strategy claim that producing thong-style underwear for the age 10 to 16 crowd is a good move. Critics think that the line is tasteless and that marketing it to young girls is not appropriate.

Questions

1. Is marketing adult-styled undergarments to a younger audience unethical or in poor taste? Would Abercrombie have been in the spotlight had the sexy words been omitted from the product?

2. Take a look at the Abercrombie & Fitch website (**www.abercrombie.com**). What do you think of the young models displayed on the website? The website puts out a call for new young models (male and female). Would you consider applying?

CASE STUDY

DISNEY: THE HAPPIEST BRAND ON EARTH

In 2006, Disney's Pixar released the hit movie *Cars*, which grossed over $500 million worldwide. But movie box office sales were only the beginning. Since its release, *Cars* merchandise (including toys, games, books, recordings, clothing items, and more) has generated over $2 billion in sales each year! Pixar has since created a series of *Cars* shorts shown on the Disney Channel that have also been released on DVD. An on-line *Cars* virtual gaming world has been released, a *Cars* sequel is on its way to movie theatres, and a 12-acre *Cars* Land attraction will open at Disney California in 2012.

At Disney, the brand is the name of the game, and the cross-platform success of the *Cars* franchise is by no means the exception. Disney also has the Jonas Brothers, *Hanna Montana*, *Toy Story*, *High School Musical*, *Pirates of the Caribbean*, the Disney Princesses, and the list goes on. The man behind the magic is Disney's CEO, Bob Iger. When Iger took over as CEO in 2005, he shifted Disney's strategy to focus on its stable of "franchises." These franchises are distributed across Disney's multiple company platforms and divisions, such as Disney's various television broadcast platforms (the Disney Channel, Disney XD, Playhouse Disney, ABC, and ESPN), its consumer products business, theme parks, Disney's Hollywood Records music label, and Disney's publishing arm.

Iger's franchise strategy has been supported by the other major move he made upon first becoming CEO. On his first day on the job, Iger told the board that revitalizing Disney's animation business was a top priority, which would be improved through the purchase of Pixar. As part of Iger's franchise strategy, the deal made perfect sense, as many of Disney's latest TV shows, Disneyland rides, and merchandise were based on Pixar characters.

Finding a new market to push the Disney franchise became a priority as well. With the Disney brand growing flat, it was becoming evident that Disney had missed some opportunities for broader success due to a narrowing of its target market, which was largely younger children.

Iger's first move was to broaden Disney's viewership by moving the Disney Channel from premium to basic cable and launching local versions in key global markets. Then Disney began pushing franchises to capture the rapidly growing tween market. Putting its support behind the Disney Channel's *High School Musical* and *Hannah Montana* and the Jonas Brothers, who were emerging out of Disney's music label, Disney quickly generated a series of franchise juggernauts in the tween girl market.

Though Disney's focus has remained family-friendly fare, Iger has shown a new willingness to look to even broader markets if it fits with the Disney brand. Disney's *Pirates of the Caribbean*, the first Disney film with a PG-13 rating, played a major role in refocusing the brand, being based on the classic theme park ride, and it also helped expand the Disney appeal to older kids and even adults. The *Pirates of the Caribbean* and *Cars* franchises also provided preliminary steps for Disney's latest endeavours to crack the tween boy market, one traditionally difficult for media companies to capture. Its efforts focus on the new Disney XD channel, with a broad range of offerings, such as potential new franchises like the science fiction action-adventure show *Aaron Stone*. Disney will also be able to leverage ESPN to create original sports-based programming. The channel will be accompanied by a Disney HD website, which will promote the channel's programs, as well as offer games and original videos, social networking, and on-line community opportunities.

As it continues to expand and provide new franchise offerings, Disney looks to have relatively strong momentum, even in the midst of rising economic challenges.[11]

Questions

1. Do a brief market opportunity analysis for Disney, identifying the major markets that Disney has expanded into.

2. How does Disney's cross-platform franchising help create sustainable competitive advantage?

3. Describe the marketing mix for one of Disney's franchises.

4. Describe the major components of Bob Iger's strategic plan.

VIDEO CASE

CBC

TOWN DOCTOR: BIG-TIME MARKETING STRATEGY PLANNING COMES TO TOFINO, B.C.

Since founding Richard Saunders International in 1986, Doug Hall's client list has read like the *Fortune* 500. Companies that have paid $150,000 and more for three-day sessions at the Eureka! Ranch headquarters of Richard Saunders International include Coca-Cola, Procter & Gamble, Frito-Lay, PepsiCo, Disney, Labatt's, Compaq Computer, Nike, Ford, Chrysler, Johnson & Johnson, American Express, and NASCAR.

After graduating with a degree in chemical engineering, Doug Hall spent 10 years in marketing at Procter & Gamble. There, even among the vast marketing talent at this giant company, Doug stood out. In one year, Doug helped bring nine new products to market. With this valuable experience behind him, Doug decided to strike out on his own. Richard Saunders International was formed in Doug's basement in 1986 (Richard Saunders was the pen name used by Benjamin Franklin).

Richard Saunders International was to include both a new product idea division and a market research division. Doug, however, was more interested in new product work and soon sold the market research business. After considerable early success, Richard Saunders International moved from Doug's basement to an estate he named the Eureka Mansion. In 1997, Doug built a much larger complex alongside the Eureka Mansion and gave it the name Eureka! Ranch. The seminars and training programs conducted by Doug's company are held at the Eureka! Ranch while Doug and his family now live in the Eureka Mansion.

Doug's company, which is divided into three strategic business units (SBUs), undertakes a full range of marketing planning and marketing strategy activities for its clients. Sessions at Eureka! Ranch take place in large "play" rooms filled with video games, jukeboxes, and toys. It is not unusual for a Eureka! Ranch session to begin with a Nerf gunfight. Doug feels that fun leads to more creative output.

Eureka! Invention & Research is the largest of the three-company SBUs. Eureka! Invention sessions generally run for three days at the Eureka! Ranch and include the client's top marketing people and a team from Doug's company. The unorthodox and highly creative sessions might be geared toward generating new product ideas, new line extensions, new advertising campaigns, programs to reposition existing products, turnaround strategies for failing products, or entire marketing plans. Eureka! Winning Ways, a second SBU, is a training program that improves the ability of a company's personnel to invent more creative and effective ideas for growing the business. The final SBU is Merwyn Technology. Merwyn is a computer simulation test marketing and expert coaching software program. Merwyn assists clients in forecasting the probability for success of new product concepts and makes recommendations for improving the concepts' chances for success.

The success of Richard Saunders International has made Doug Hall rich and famous. He now commands over $25,000 for talks to business groups. Doug is still young (under 50) and is searching for more to do. Among other things, he has decided to provide the expertise of Eureka! Invention & Research to small businesses that would not otherwise be able to afford these services. As a start, Doug offered his services to four small businesses on Prince Edward Island back in 2001. Why there? Doug's mother is from New Brunswick and Doug has a vacation home on PEI.

A one-day creativity seminar was arranged for four small PEI businesses: Cavendish Figurines, Wooly Wares, Island Winds, and Mic Mac Productions. Cavendish Figurines creates and sells heirloom-quality figurines based on characters from great literary classics (*Anne of Green Gables* is a leading seller). The company has been in business since 1989 and has 13 employees. Wooly Wares is a retail store operated on John and Carol MacLeod's sheep farm. Wooly Wares sells handmade wool felt products. Island Winds is a one-man operation. Peter Baker makes and sells hand-tuned wind chimes. Mic Mac Productions sells handmade native crafts such as beadwork, carvings, drums, pipes, masks, pottery, rattles, headdresses, and moccasins.

After the one-day creativity seminar with the owners of each of the four PEI businesses, Doug arranged to meet with each owner for a two-hour session. Inside of two hours at Cavendish Figurines, Doug and his crew developed a new promotional brochure for the business, recommended a new display for the most popular figurines, developed a new promotional message, and recommended a new product assortment. Wooly Wares was persuaded to concentrate on several product offerings that were clearly superior to others, and Doug and his group came up with some catchy brand names for the products. Peter Baker at Island Winds was advised to stay with top-of-the-line chimes, where he had an advantage over the competition, and not get into low-priced products. As well, new product ideas were developed, along with new brand names and a new promotional campaign. Mic Mac Productions was advised to change its name to Mic Mac Legends, build a new promotional campaign around the legends associated with its products, expand its product lines, develop a new pricing strategy, and organize product combination packages.

Just this past year, Doug Hall agreed to visit the other end of Canada and look at three small businesses in Tofino, B.C. Could Doug Hall's magic be used to help the Whale Centre, Dust Bunnies Cleaning Services, and West Coast Market and Garden? Watch as Doug Hall meets with the owners of these small businesses and, with only 48 hours of time available, develops new business concepts for each of the business owners.[12]

Questions

1. What do you think Doug Hall's corporate mission statement might have been in 1986 when he founded Richard Saunders International, and what do you think it might be today?

2. What do you think is the major competitive advantage of Richard Saunders International?

3. Into which cell of the portfolio matrix do you feel that each SBU of Richard Saunders International would fall?

4. Can the marketing strategies used for the large clients of Doug Hall work for small businesses?

5. What is your assessment of the business concepts developed by Doug Hall for the three Tofino businesses? What other business ideas might you be able to offer to these business owners?

MARKETING & YOU RESULTS

The higher your score, the greater importance you place on planning. You also develop plans more often and devote more energy to the planning process. High scores also indicate a motivation to work "smart" and efficiently. If your score was low, you are less inclined to spend energy planning and, as a result, may have lower performance.

APPENDIX

MARKETING PLAN OUTLINE

I   BUSINESS MISSION

II SITUATION ANALYSIS
    (SWOT ANALYSIS)
    A. Internal Strengths and Weaknesses
    B. External Opportunities and Threats

III OBJECTIVES

IV MARKETING STRATEGY
    A. Target Market Strategy
    B. Marketing Mix
       1. Product
       2. Place/Distribution
       3. Promotion
       4. Price

V IMPLEMENTATION, EVALUATION, AND CONTROL

As you read in Chapter 2, there is more than one correct format for a marketing plan. Many organizations have their own distinctive format or terminology for creating a marketing plan, and every marketing plan should be unique to the firm for which it was created. The format and order of presentation, therefore, must be flexible. This appendix presents only one way to organize a marketing plan. The outline is meant to give you a more detailed look at what you need to include, topics you need to cover, and the types of questions you must answer in any marketing plan. But, depending on the product or service for which you are drafting a plan, this set of questions may only be the starting point for more industry-specific issues you need to address.

If you are assigned a marketing plan as a course requirement, this appendix can help you organize your work. In addition, worksheets that guide you through the process of marketing planning are available on your textbook's companion site. The worksheets can be completed electronically or printed out and filled in by hand.

I Business Mission

- What is the mission of the firm? What business is it in? How well is its mission understood throughout the organization? Five years from now, what business does it wish to be in?

- Does the firm define its business in terms of benefits its customers want rather than in terms of goods and services?

II Situation Analysis
(SWOT Analysis)

- Have one or more competitive advantages been identified in the SWOT analysis?

- Are these advantages sustainable against the competition?

A. Internal Strengths and Weaknesses

- What is the history of the firm, including sales, profits, and organizational philosophies?

- What is the nature of the firm and its current situation?

- What are the firm's resources (financial, human, time, experience, asset, skill)?

- What policies inhibit the achievement of the firm's objectives with respect to organization, resource allocation, operations, hiring, training, and so on?

B. External Opportunities and Threats

- *Social*: What major social and lifestyle trends will have an impact on the firm? What action has the firm been taking in response to these trends?

- *Demographics*: What impact will forecasted trends in the size, age, profile, and distribution of population have on the firm? How will the changing nature of the family, the increase in the proportion of women in the workforce, and changes in the ethnic composition of the population affect the firm? What action has the firm taken in response to these developments and trends? Has the firm re-evaluated its traditional products and expanded the range of specialized offerings to respond to these changes?

- *Economic*: What major trends in taxation and income sources will have an impact on the firm? What action has the firm taken in response to these trends?

- *Political, Legal, and Financial*: What laws are now being proposed at international, federal, provincial, and local levels that could affect marketing strategy and tactics? What recent changes in regulations and court decisions affect the firm? What political changes are taking place at each government level? What action has the firm taken in response to these legal and political changes?

- *Competition*: Which organizations are competing with the firm directly by offering a similar product? Which organizations are competing with the firm indirectly by securing its prime prospects' time, money, energy, or commitment? What new competitive trends seem likely to emerge? How effective is the competition? What benefits do competitors offer that the firm does not? Is it appropriate for the firm to compete?

- *Technological*: What major technological changes are occurring that affect the firm?

- *Ecological*: What is the outlook for the cost and availability of natural resources and energy needed by the firm? Are the firm's products, services, and operations environmentally friendly?

III Objectives

- Is the firm's mission statement able to be translated into operational terms regarding the firm's objectives?

- What are the stated objectives of the organization? Are they formally written down? Do they lead logically to clearly stated marketing objectives? Are objectives based on sales, profits, or customers?

- Are the organization's marketing objectives stated in hierarchical order? Are they specific so that progress toward achievement can be measured? Are the objectives reasonable in light of the organization's resources? Are the objectives ambiguous? Do the objectives specify a time frame?

- Is the firm's main objective to maximize customer satisfaction or to get as many customers as possible?

IV Marketing Strategy

A. Target Market Strategy

- Are the members of each market homogeneous or heterogeneous with respect to geographic, sociodemographic, and behavioural characteristics?

- What are the size, growth rate, and national and regional trends in each of the organization's market segments?

- Is the size of each market segment sufficiently large or important to warrant a unique marketing mix?

- Are market segments measurable and accessible to distribution and communication efforts?

- Which are the high- or low-opportunity segments?

- What are the evolving needs and satisfactions being sought by target markets?

- What benefits does the organization offer to each segment? How do these benefits compare with benefits offered by competitors?

- Is the firm positioning itself with a unique product? Is the product needed?

- How much of the firm's business is repeat versus new business? What percentage of the public can be classified as nonusers, light users, or heavy users?

- How do current target markets rate the firm and its competitors with respect to reputation, quality, and price? What is the firm's image with the specific market segments it seeks to serve? Does the firm try to direct its products only to specific groups of people or to everybody?

- Who buys the firm's products? How does a potential customer find out about the organization? When and how does a person become a customer?

- What are the major objections given by potential customers as to why they do not buy the firm's products?

- How do customers find out about and decide to purchase the product? When and where?

- Should the firm seek to expand, contract, or change the emphasis of its selected target markets? If so, in which target markets, and how vigorously?

- Could the firm more usefully withdraw from some areas where there are alternative suppliers and use its resources to serve new, unserved customer groups?
- What publics other than target markets (financial, media, government, citizen, local, general, and internal) represent opportunities or problems for the firm?

B. Marketing Mix
- Does the firm seek to achieve its objective chiefly through coordinated use of marketing activities (product, place, promotion, and pricing) or only through intensive promotion?
- Are the objectives and roles of each element of the marketing mix clearly specified?

1. Product
- What are the major product or service offerings of the firm? Do they complement each other, or is there unnecessary duplication?
- What are the features and benefits of each product offering?
- Where are the firm and each major product in the life cycle?
- What are the pressures among various target markets to increase or decrease the range and quality of products?
- What are the major weaknesses in each product area? What are the major complaints? What goes wrong most often?
- Is the product name easy to pronounce? Spell? Recall? Is it descriptive, and does it communicate the benefits the product offers? Does the name distinguish the firm or product from all others?
- What warranties are offered with the product? Are there other ways to guarantee customer satisfaction?
- Does the product offer good customer value?
- How is customer service handled? How is service quality assessed?

2. Place/Distribution
- Should the firm try to deliver its offerings directly to customers, or can it better deliver selected offerings by involving other organizations? What channel(s) should be used in distributing product offerings?
- What physical distribution facilities should be used? Where should they be located? What should be their major characteristics?
- Are members of the target market willing and able to travel some distance to buy the product?
- How good is access to facilities? Can access be improved? Which facilities need priority attention in these areas?
- How are facility locations chosen? Is the site accessible to the target markets? Is it visible to the target markets?
- What are the location and atmosphere of retail establishments? Do these retailers satisfy customers?
- When are products made available to users (season of year, day of week, time of day)? Are these times most appropriate?

3. Promotion
- How does a typical customer find out about the firm's products?
- Does the message the firm delivers gain the attention of the intended target audience? Does it address the wants and needs of the target market, and does it suggest benefits or a means for satisfying these wants? Is the message appropriately positioned?
- Does the promotion effort effectively inform, persuade, educate, and remind customers about the firm's products?
- Does the firm establish budgets and measure effectiveness of promotional efforts?

a. Advertising

- Which media are currently being used? Has the firm chosen the types of media that will best reach its target markets?
- Are the types of media used the most cost-effective, and do they contribute positively to the firm's image?
- Are the dates and times the ads will appear the most appropriate? Has the firm prepared several versions of its advertisements?
- Does the organization use an outside advertising agency? What functions does the ad agency perform for the organization?
- What system is used to handle consumer inquiries resulting from advertising and promotions? What follow-up is done?

b. Public Relations

- Is there a well-conceived public relations and publicity program? Does the program have the ability to respond to bad publicity?
- How is public relations normally handled by the firm? By whom? Have those responsible nurtured working relationships with media outlets?
- Is the firm using all available public relations avenues? Is an effort made to understand each of the publicity outlet's needs and to provide each with story types that will appeal to its audience in readily usable forms?
- What does the annual report say about the firm and its products? Who is being effectively reached by this vehicle? Does the benefit of the publication justify the cost?

c. Personal Selling

- How much of a typical salesperson's time is spent soliciting new customers as compared to serving existing customers?
- How does the sales force determine which prospect will be called on and by whom? How is the frequency of contacts determined?
- How is the sales force compensated? Are there incentives for encouraging more business?
- How is the sales force organized and managed?
- Has the sales force prepared an approach tailored to each prospect?
- Has the firm matched sales personnel with the target market characteristics?
- Is there appropriate follow-up to the initial personal selling effort? Are customers made to feel appreciated?
- Can database or direct marketing be used to replace or supplement the sales force?

d. Sales Promotion

- What is the specific purpose of each sales promotion activity? Why is it offered? What does it try to achieve?
- What categories of sales promotion are being used? Is sales promotion directed to the trade, the final consumer, or both?
- Is the effort directed at all the firm's key publics or restricted to only potential customers?

4. Price

- What levels of pricing and specific prices should be used?
- What mechanisms does the firm have to ensure that the prices charged are acceptable to customers?
- How price sensitive are customers?
- If a price change is put into effect, how will the number of customers change? Will total revenue increase or decrease?

- Which method is used for establishing a price: going rate, demand oriented, or cost based?
- What discounts are offered, and with what rationale?
- Has the firm considered the psychological dimensions of price?
- Have price increases kept pace with cost increases, inflation, or competitive levels?
- How are price promotions used?
- Do interested prospects have opportunities to sample products at an introductory price?
- What methods of payment are accepted? Is it in the firm's best interest to use these various payment methods?

V   Implementation, Evaluation, and Control

- Is the marketing organization structured appropriately to implement the marketing plan?
- What specific activities must take place? Who is responsible for these activities?
- What is the implementation timetable?
- What other marketing research is necessary?
- What will be the financial impact of this plan on a one-year projected income statement? How does projected income compare with expected revenue if the plan is not implemented?
- What are the performance standards?
- What monitoring procedures (audits) will take place and when?
- Does the firm seem to be trying to do too much or not enough?
- Are the core marketing strategies for achieving objectives sound? Are the objectives being met, and are the objectives appropriate?
- Are enough resources (or too many resources) budgeted to accomplish the marketing objectives?

3 Ethics and the Marketing Environment

Ready to serve.

SOURCE: KRISTIINA PAUL

LEARNING OUTCOMES

1 Discuss corporate social responsibility

2 Describe the role of ethics and ethical decisions in business

3 Discuss the external environment of marketing and explain how it affects a firm

4 Describe the social factors that affect marketing

5 Explain the importance to marketing managers of current demographic trends

6 Explain the importance to marketing managers of multiculturalism and growing ethnic markets

7 Identify consumer and marketer reactions to the state of the economy

8 Identify the impact of technology on a firm

9 Discuss the political and legal environment of marketing

10 Explain the basics of foreign and domestic competition

MARKETING & YOU

Using the following scale, enter the numbers that reflect your opinions.

1	2	3	4	5	6	7	8	9
Completely disagree								Completely agree

___ The ethics and social responsibility of a firm are essential to its long-term profitability.

___ Business ethics and social responsibility are critical to the survival of a business enterprise.

___ The overall effectiveness of a business can be determined to a great extent by the degree to which it is ethical and socially responsible.

___ Good ethics is often good business.

___ Business has a social responsibility beyond making a profit.

___ Corporate planning and goal-setting sessions should include discussions of ethics and social responsibility.

___ Social responsibility and profitability can be compatible.

Now total your score. Find out what it means after you read the chapter.

SOURCE: REPRINTED WITH PERMISSION FROM *MARKETING SCALES HANDBOOK* VOL. III, PUBLISHED BY THE AMERICAN MARKETING ASSOCIATION, G. BRUNER, K. JAMES, H. HENSEL, EDS. SCALE #646, P. 196.

The battle over okra and karela is really starting to heat up. Sobeys Inc., the second-largest supermarket chain in Canada, is working to earn a bigger share of the ethnic food market with a new store format focusing on fresh foods that appeal to the multicultural market. The new stores will be called FreshCo.

The Canadian marketing environment is in a constant state of change, and among the ongoing changes are the rapidly growing ethnic market segments in Canada. According to Gavin Barrett, one of the owners of Rao Barrett and Welsh, a Toronto advertising agency that specializes in multicultural marketing, visible minorities represent a market in excess of $80 billion in Canada. Visible minorities will make up one-third of the Canadian market by 2031. In a bid to cater to the food needs of ethnic market segments, grocery chains are stocking specialty products such as basmati rice and chocolate-covered pocky sticks and undertaking research that will help them customize their offerings to the local neighbourhoods that they are serving.

A Sobeys supermarket in Thornhill, Ontario, for example, employs two full-time rabbis who oversee a kosher section of the store, which covers about half of the total store area. In the northeastern section of Calgary, a Calgary Co-op supermarket offers a wide selection of East Indian foods. A Sobeys in Scarborough, Ontario, carries Oriental noodle dishes for its customers. "I feel like I'm back at home," says Ruth Yablonsky, who moved to Canada from Israel and shops at the Thornhill Sobeys store.

More and more supermarkets across the country are targeting their offerings to the specific characteristics of the neighbourhoods that they serve. "We're starting to see this institutionalized as a standard activity," says Sharon Skurnac, senior director of consumer marketing services at A. C. Nielsen in Toronto. A. C. Nielsen, as well, has recognized the changing demographic marketplace as a business opportunity for its research services. In the past year, A. C. Nielsen has started to track various communities' needs and has begun to provide grocers and their suppliers with localized demographic data to help them stock their shelves better.

At the Sobeys store in Thornhill, Rabbi Moshe Bensalmon mingles with the predominantly Jewish clientele, including a busload who came all the way from Rochester, New York, to stock up on Israeli tomatoes, tahini salad, and chocolate cakes. Rabbi Bensalmon ensures that meat preparation follows Jewish dietary rules and that bakery goods are milk-free. Over the years that Kevin Hopps has been the store manager at the Thornhill Sobeys, the kosher section of the store has been tripled in size. The store's productivity and profits are among Sobeys' highest.

Sobeys, of course, targets other neighbourhoods in other ways. A Sobeys in Brampton, Ontario, for instance, has a large East Indian food selection that includes basmati rice and curried sauces. A Sobeys in Malton, Ontario, carries halal meat for its Muslim customers.

Sobeys isn't alone in catering to growing ethnic markets across the country. Costco Wholesale carries chocolate-covered pocky biscuits for its Asian customers in Richmond and Grandview, B.C., and Mississauga, Ontario; big bags of arborio rice in Woodbridge, Ontario, and Ville d'Anjou, Quebec, for its Italian customers; and kosher foods in a number of outlets in Toronto and Montreal. Calgary Co-op, which operates 23 stores, conducts research in the neighbourhoods surrounding each of its stores to determine the right product offerings for each outlet. For example, some Calgary Co-op outlets will have larger Asian food sections while others will have larger Caribbean sections. Loblaw carries Passover goods at over 40 of its stores in Ontario and Quebec. In addition, some private-label President's Choice foods are certified kosher. Metro Inc., with its Food Basics stores, and Walmart Canada supercentres have also joined the battle for the ethnic shopper.

In addition to its many kosher selections, Loblaw reports that its East Indian food sales have been growing at "double-digit" rates. Loblaw has had great success with its President's Choice butter chicken frozen entrée and a new line of President's Choice East Indian sauces. In addition, Loblaw, the largest supermarket chain in Canada, recently acquired T&T Supermarket Inc., a specialist in Asian foods. Taking a big plunge and direct aim at Loblaw, Sobeys is converting its 87 Price Choppers stores to the FreshCo format.[1] Clearly, supermarkets in Canada are catering to the growing ethnic markets across the country.

SOURCE: MARINA STRAUSS, "LOW FRILLS, HIGH STAKES," GLOBE AND MAIL, MAY 12, 2010, B1, B5; MARINA STRAUSS, "GROCERS DEVELOPING APPETITE FOR ETHNIC MARKET," GLOBE AND MAIL, APRIL 5, 2004, B1, B6; APARITA BHANDARI, "ETHNIC MARKETING—IT'S MORE THAN SKIN DEEP," GLOBE AND MAIL, SEPTEMBER 7, 2005, B3; ANDY MUKHERJEE, "HALAL FINALLY SPOTTED ON THE RADAR SCREEN," GLOBE AND MAIL, AUGUST 11, 2006, B6.

CORPORATE SOCIAL RESPONSIBILITY

Discuss corporate social responsibility

corporate social responsibility
A business's concern for society's welfare.

sustainability
The idea that socially responsible companies will outperform their peers by focusing on the world's social problems, viewing them as opportunities to build profits and help the world at the same time.

Corporate social responsibility is a business's concern for society's welfare. This concern is demonstrated by managers who consider both the long-term best interests of the company and the company's relationship to the society within which it operates. The newest theory in social responsibility is called **sustainability**. This refers to the idea that socially responsible companies will outperform their peers by focusing on the world's social problems, viewing them as opportunities to build profits and helping the world at the same time. Starbucks, for example, has partnered with Conservation International, a nonprofit organization devoted to conserving the earth's natural heritage, to help coffee growers in developing countries produce shade-grown beans to increase the size of their crops and reduce the loss of rain forests. It is also the notion that companies cannot thrive for long (that is, they will lack sustainability) in a world where billions of people are suffering because they are desperately poor. Thus it is in business's interest to find ways to attack society's ills.

Some critics say that business should focus on making a profit and leave social and environmental problems to nonprofit organizations and the government. Economist Milton Friedman believed that the free market, and not businesses, should decide what is best for the world. Friedman argued that to the degree that business executives spend more money than they have to—to purchase vehicles with hybrid engines, or to pay higher wages in developing countries, or even to donate company money to charities—they are spending the shareholders' money to further their own interests. Friedman claims that it is better to pay higher dividends and let the shareholders give the money away as they see fit.[2] Another argument against corporate social responsibility is that businesses are created to produce goods and services and not to handle welfare activities. Finally, being socially aware increases the cost of doing business, which will lead to higher prices.

Supporters of corporate social responsibility say those are false arguments. Smart companies can prosper and build shareholder value by tackling global problems. The most basic argument for social responsibility is that it is simply the right thing to do. Another, more pragmatic, reason for being socially responsible is that if business isn't responsible, the government will step in and create new laws and regulations that will force business to follow government-created regulations. Finally, social responsibility can be a profitable undertaking. Walmart has reduced its electricity bill by 17 percent by using more efficient light bulbs and adding skylights for natural light in their stores. Walmart is also saving nearly $3 million each year by using less packaging on its house-brand toy products.[3] The social responsibility of business is growing around the world. A study of social responsibility in selected countries asked the following question, "Does your company consider social responsibility factors when making business decisions?" The percentage of firms that said yes were Brazil, 62 percent; Canada, 54 percent; Australia, 52 percent; United States, 47 percent; India, 38 percent; China, 35 percent; and Mexico, 26 percent.[4]

pyramid of corporate social responsibility
A model that suggests corporate social responsibility is composed of economic, legal, ethical, and philanthropic responsibilities and that the firm's economic performance supports the entire structure.

One theorist suggests that total corporate social responsibility has four components: economic, legal, ethical, and philanthropic.[5] The **pyramid of corporate social responsibility** portrays economic performance as the foundation for the other three responsibilities. At the same time that it pursues profits (economic responsibility), a business is expected to obey the law (legal responsibility); to do what is right, just, and fair (ethical responsibility); and to be a good corporate citizen (philanthropic responsibility). These four components are distinct but together constitute the whole. At the base, however, if the company doesn't make a profit, then the other three responsibilities cannot be fulfilled.

In many ways, companies are working to make the world a better place to live. LeBlanc Estate Winery in Harrow, Ontario, grows grapes organically, relying on natural pest control; Ben & Jerry's Ice Cream uses unbleached paper in its cartons and purchases only steroid-free milk; Abbot Laboratories funds free hearing examinations for the elderly in countries where they are not covered by government-funded health programs; Burger King has donated millions of dollars to assist the victims of natural disasters around the world; and H. J. Heinz has donated millions of nutritional supplement packets to children in Indonesia, Guyana, Mongolia, Pakistan, Haiti, and Ghana.

green marketing
The development and marketing of products designed to minimize negative effects on the physical environment or to improve the environment.

An outgrowth of the social responsibility movement is green marketing. **Green marketing** is the development and marketing of products designed to minimize negative effects on the physical environment or to improve the environment. One company that has done an excellent job of going green is Waste Management, which disposes waste for 22 million customers. The company produces more renewable energy each year than the entire North American solar industry; its Wheelabrator division creates electricity by combustion. Waste Management has also had 33 working landfills certified as wildlife habitat preserves. The firm hopes to have 100 certified by the Wildlife Habitat Council before 2020.[6]

Does being socially responsible create additional demand for a firm's products or services? The answer is not easy. In some cases it may be yes while in others it may be no. For example, one factor is the issue on which the company focuses, such as health, education, or charitable giving, and how the issue is perceived by the company's target market. Other factors are product or service quality and how the target market perceives the importance of social responsibility. The evidence that corporate social responsibility drives profit and growth is inconclusive. Socially responsible investment funds have only done about as well as the overall market. A recent study by Governance Metrics International, though, which rates companies on their governance policies, labour practices, environmental activities, and litigation history, found that the stocks of more socially responsible companies outperformed those of less responsible companies.[7]

Global Perspectives

 ## BOMBARDIER'S GLOBAL GROWTH LEADS TO PROBLEMS

Why would a $15-billion company sign a $78-million contract, on which it would likely lose money, when the contract had the potential to ignite protests around the world? "We don't think it's our responsibility to settle political differences between China and Tibet," explained Laurent Beaudoin, CEO of Bombardier Inc. Bombardier's contract with the Chinese Ministry of Railways called for Bombardier to build 361 specially developed pressurized rail-cars to travel the high-altitude railway that connects China's national railway system to Lhasa, the capital of Tibet.

As expected, there was immediate reaction to Bombardier's contract. A group called Students for a Free Tibet immediately called for global demonstrations to be held at Bombardier facilities and Chinese embassies (**www.studentsforafreetibet.org**). Tibetans and their supporters organized a mass demonstration at Bombardier's annual general meeting in Montreal. Canadian Jessica Spanton made the front pages of the *Montreal Gazette* when she disrupted a meeting between Bombardier officials and China's ambassador to Canada. A group called Save Tibet distributed a 70-page report on the China-Tibet railway that heavily criticized Bombardier's role (**www.savetibet.org**). An International Day of Action was called with protesters asked to call Bombardier offices around the world. A website was developed that asked people to submit their photo and a statement "giving Bombardier a piece of their mind" (**www.bombardieroutoftibet.org**).

What are the protests about? The protest groups claim that the Tibet railway is simply a means to accelerate the colonization of Tibet. China occupied Tibet in 1950 and has since repressed religious and cultural expression there. Chinese officials claim that the rail line will have economic benefits for Tibet. Tibetans counter with these points: (1) the railway makes it easier for Chinese settlers and military forces to enter Tibet; (2) the railway consolidates China's control over Tibet; (3) the railway facilitates the removal of natural resources that belong to Tibet; (4) the railway facilitates the rapid deployment of China's military forces and may lead to the stockpiling of nuclear weapons and missiles in Tibet; and (5) the railway is causing widespread erosion, damage to vegetation, disruption of migration patterns, and contamination of water bodies in Tibet.

Bombardier's management expected protests to take place. An internal company memo outlined the reasons for the protests, what to expect, how to react to the protesters, how to respond to the media, and what to say in Bombardier's defence.

So why did Bombardier sign a small and possibly money-losing contract when they expected problems? In the months after this contract, Bombardier signed additional contracts with the Chinese Ministry of Railways. The additional contracts were for $477 million to supply 40 high-speed trains, $326 million to supply 51 Movia metro trains, and $89 million to build an automated tram system at the Beijing International Airport. In addition, an exclusive 20-year contract to supply up to 400 additional high-speed trains, with potential revenue to Bombardier of $5 billion, was signed. "Bombardier sees China as an emerging market with good potential," says Bombardier spokeswoman Helene Gagnon.[8]

What is your view of Bombardier's business dealings in China? How does Bombardier management balance social or ethical responsibilities against their responsibilities to the shareholders of the company?

SOURCE: KONRAD YAKABUSKI, "BOMBARDIER'S NEW IMAGE PROBLEM," GLOBE AND MAIL, JUNE 29, 2005, B4; BERTRAND MAROTTE, "BOMBARDIER LANDS BIG ORDER IN CHINA," GLOBE AND MAIL, NOVEMBER 7, 2006; WWW.STUDENTSFORAFREETIBET.ORG; WWW.ACTIONNETWORK.ORG; WWW.SAVETIBET.ORG; WWW.BOMBARDIEROUTOFTIBET.ORG.

1   Discuss corporate social responsibility

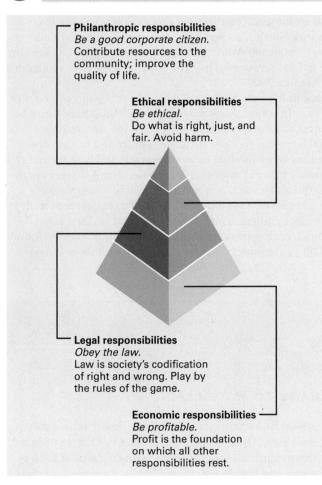

Philanthropic responsibilities
Be a good corporate citizen.
Contribute resources to the community; improve the quality of life.

Ethical responsibilities
Be ethical.
Do what is right, just, and fair. Avoid harm.

Legal responsibilities
Obey the law.
Law is society's codification of right and wrong. Play by the rules of the game.

Economic responsibilities
Be profitable.
Profit is the foundation on which all other responsibilities rest.

ethics
The moral principles or values that generally govern the conduct of an individual.

laws
The values and standards enforceable by the courts.

morals
The rules people develop as a result of cultural values and norms.

2 ETHICAL BEHAVIOUR IN BUSINESS

Describe the role of ethics and ethical decisions in business

Social responsibility and ethics are closely related. **Ethics** refers to the moral principles or values that generally govern the conduct of an individual. Ethics can also be viewed as the standard of behaviour by which conduct is judged. Standards that are legal may not always be ethical, and vice versa. **Laws** are the values and standards enforceable by the courts. Ethics consists of personal moral principles and values rather than societal prescriptions.

Defining the boundaries between what is ethical and what is legal can be difficult. Often judgment is needed to determine whether an action that may be legal is also ethical. For example, bogus surveys may be used as a way of finding prospects for the sale of products. This is legal, but is it ethical? As a marketing student, what is your view on this issue?

Morals are the rules people develop as a result of cultural values and norms. Culture is a socializing force that dictates what is right and wrong. Moral standards may also reflect the laws and regulations that affect social and economic behaviour. Thus morals can be considered a foundation of ethical behaviour.

Morals are usually characterized as good or bad. "Good" and "bad" have different connotations, including "effective" and "ineffective." A good salesperson makes or exceeds the assigned quota. If the salesperson sells a new stereo or television set to a disadvantaged consumer—knowing full well that the person can't keep up the monthly payments—is the salesperson still a good one? What if the sale enables the salesperson to exceed his or her quota? What would you do if you were the manager of this salesperson?

"Good" and "bad" can also refer to "conforming" and "deviant" behaviours. A lawyer who advertises that he or she will get drunk drivers their licences back may be engaged in legal behaviour but might not conform to the norms of the general public. "Bad" and "good" are also used to express the distinction between criminal and law-abiding behaviour. Different religions define "good" and "bad" in markedly different ways. A Muslim who eats pork would be considered bad, as would a fundamentalist Christian who drinks whisky.

MORALITY AND BUSINESS ETHICS

Business ethics are a subset of major life values that are learned from birth. The values businesspeople use to make decisions have been acquired through family as well as through educational and religious institutions.

While ethical values are often situation-specific and time-oriented, everyone must have an ethical base that applies to their conduct in the business world and in personal life. One approach to developing a personal set of ethics is to examine the consequences of a particular act. Who is helped or hurt? How long-lasting are the consequences? What actions produce the greatest good for the greatest number of people? A second approach stresses the importance of rules. Rules come in the form

Perhaps the most egregious example of unethical business practices in recent memory was the Enron scandal, which extended to the company's auditing firm, the venerable Arthur Andersen. Thousands of employees were negatively affected by the scandal.

of customs, laws, professional standards, and common sense. Consider these examples of rules:

- Always treat others as you would like to be treated.
- Copying copyrighted computer software is against the law.
- It is wrong to lie, bribe, or exploit.

Moral character and ethical development can be thought of as progressing, or growing, through three levels:

- *Preconventional morality*, the most basic level, is childlike. It is calculating, self-centred, and even selfish, and is based on what will be immediately punished or rewarded. Fortunately, most businesspeople have progressed beyond the self-centred and manipulative actions of preconventional morality.
- *Conventional morality* moves from an egocentric viewpoint toward the expectations of society. Loyalty and obedience to the organization (or society) become paramount. At the level of conventional morality, an ethical marketing decision would be concerned with whether it is legal and how others will view it. This type of morality could be likened to the adage "When in Rome, do as the Romans do."
- *Postconventional morality* represents the morality of the mature adult. At this level, people are less concerned about how others might see them and more concerned about how they see and judge themselves. A marketing decision maker who has attained a postconventional level of morality might ask, "Even though it is legal and will increase company profits, is it right in the long run? Might it do more harm than good in the end?"

SOURCE: BRIAN SNYDER/REUTERS/LANDOV

EXHIBIT 3.1

Unethical Practices Marketing Managers May Have to Deal With

- Entertainment and gift giving
- False or misleading advertising
- Misrepresentation of goods, services, and company capabilities
- Lying to customers in order to get the sale
- Manipulation of data (falsifying or misusing statistics or information)
- Misleading product or service warranties
- Unfair manipulation of customers
- Exploitation of children and/or disadvantaged groups
- Stereotypical portrayals of women, minority groups, or senior citizens
- Invasion of customer privacy
- Sexually oriented advertising appeals
- Product or service deception
- Unsafe products or services
- Price deception
- Price discrimination
- Unfair or inaccurate statements about competitors
- Smaller amounts of product in the same size packages

ETHICAL DECISION MAKING

How do businesspeople make ethical decisions? There is no easy answer to this. Some of the ethical issues that managers face are shown in Exhibit 3.1. Studies show that the following factors tend to influence ethical decision making and management judgments[9]:

- *Extent of ethical problems within the organization*: Marketing professionals who see fewer ethical problems in their organizations tend to disapprove more strongly of "unethical" or questionable practices than those who see more ethical problems. The healthier the ethical environment in the company, the greater is the likelihood that marketers will take a strong stand against questionable practices.
- *Top-management actions on ethics*: Top managers can influence the behaviour of marketing professionals by encouraging ethical behaviour. Research has shown that three ethics-related actions by managers have the greatest impact on employee ethics. These

are setting a good example, keeping promises and commitments, and supporting others in adhering to ethical standards.

- *Potential magnitude of the consequences*: The greater the harm done to victims, the more likely it is that marketing professionals will recognize the behaviour as unethical.
- *Social consensus*: The greater the degree of agreement among managerial peers that an action is harmful, the more likely it is that marketers will recognize the behaviour as unethical.
- *Probability of a harmful outcome*: The greater the likelihood that an action will result in a harmful outcome, the more likely it is that marketers will recognize the behaviour as unethical.

- *Length of time between the decision and the onset of consequences*: The shorter the length of time between the action and the onset of negative consequences, the more likely it is that marketers will perceive the behaviour as unethical.
- *Number of people to be affected*: The greater the number of people affected by a negative outcome, the more likely it is that marketers will recognize the behaviour as unethical.

ETHICAL GUIDELINES

Most businesses and marketing managers have become more interested in ethical issues. One sign of this interest is the increase in the number of large companies that appoint ethics officers—from virtually none five years ago to over 30 percent of large corporations now. Both Ontario Power Generation Inc. and Imperial Oil have appointed high-level ethics officers to champion ethics issues and to help resolve ethics problems and concerns among employees. In addition, many companies have developed a **code of ethics** as a guideline to help marketing managers and other employees make better decisions. A recent study found that 60 percent of the companies surveyed maintained a code of ethics, 33 percent offered ethics training, and 33 percent employed an ethics officer.[10]

Creating ethics guidelines offers several advantages for companies:

- The guidelines help employees identify what their firm recognizes as acceptable business practices.
- A code of ethics can be an effective internal control on behaviour, which is more desirable than external controls like government regulation.
- A written code helps employees avoid confusion when determining whether their decisions are ethical.
- The process of formulating the code of ethics facilitates discussion among employees about what is right and wrong and ultimately leads to better decisions.

Businesses must be careful not to make their code of ethics too vague. Codes that are too vague give little guidance to employees in their day-to-day activities. The checklist in Exhibit 3.2 is an example of a simple but helpful set of ethical guidelines. Following the checklist will not

EXHIBIT 3.2

Ethics Checklist

- Does the decision benefit one person or group but hurt or not benefit other individuals or groups? In other words, is my decision fair to all concerned?
- Would individuals or groups, particularly customers, be upset if they knew about my decision?
- Has important information been overlooked because my decision was made without input from other knowledgeable individuals or groups?
- Does my decision presume that my company is an exception to a common practice in this industry and that I, therefore, have the authority to break a rule?
- Would my decision offend or upset qualified job applicants?
- Will my decision create conflict between individuals or groups within the company?
- Will I have to pull rank or use coercion to implement my decision?
- Would I prefer to avoid the consequences of my decision?
- Did I avoid truthfully answering any of the above questions by telling myself that the risks of getting caught are low or that I could get away with the potentially unethical behaviour?

code of ethics
A guideline to help marketing managers and other employees make better decisions.

SOURCE: TERRI MILLER/E-VISUAL COMMUNICATIONS INC. © WORKING VALUES, LTD., DILBERT © UNITED FEATURE SYNDICATE, INC.

In an effort to ensure that employees know how to act in an ethical manner, many companies have a code of ethics or ethical guidelines. Some companies use games to practise ethical decision making. There is even a game based on the popular cartoon character, Dilbert.

guarantee the "rightness" of a decision, but it will improve the chances that the decision will be ethical.

Although many companies have issued policies on ethical behaviour, marketing managers must still put the policies into effect. They must address the classic "matter of degree" issue. For example, marketing researchers must sometimes resort to deception to obtain unbiased answers to their research questions. Asking for a few minutes of a respondent's time is dishonest if the researcher knows the interview will last 45 minutes. Not only must management post a code of ethics, but it must also give examples of what is ethical and unethical for each item in the code. Moreover, top management must stress to all employees the importance of adhering to the company's code of ethics. Without a detailed code of ethics and top management's support, creating ethical guidelines is an empty exercise. Ethics training is an excellent way to help employees put good ethics into practice. In the final analysis, you, the marketing manager, must be satisfied with the decisions you are making. At the end of each workday, are you okay with what you did that day?

REVIEW LEARNING OUTCOME 2

2 | Describe the role of ethics and ethical decisions in business

MORALITY		
Preconventional	**Conventional**	**Postconventional**
What's in it for me?	Everyone else is doing it!	Is this good in the long run?
Will I get caught?	When in Rome . . .	

ETHICAL CLIMATE

TOP-MANAGEMENT'S ETHICS

MAGNITUDE OF CONSEQUENCES

SOCIAL CONSENSUS

PROBABILITY OF HARM

LENGTH OF TIME BETWEEN
DECISION AND IMPACT

NUMBER OF PEOPLE AFFECTED

ETHICAL TRAINING

3 THE EXTERNAL MARKETING ENVIRONMENT

Discuss the external environment of marketing, and explain how it affects a firm

If there is one constant in the external environment of the firm, it is that things constantly change. If the organization doesn't understand or fails to react to the changing world around it, it will be a follower, not a leader. In the worst-case scenario, the firm will fail. Applebee's was once a hot, trendy restaurant chain. In recent years, the company has faced falling profits. What happened? Applebee's didn't adapt quickly enough to the changing environment. Newer competitors offered slick interiors in contrast with Applebee's busy walls full of photos and sports memorabilia. Menus at many newer restaurants stress the freshness or naturalness of the food. Applebee's continued to focus on fried and breaded items.

Perhaps the most important decisions a marketing manager must make relate to the creation of the marketing mix. Recall that a marketing mix is a firm's unique combination of product, place (distribution), promotion, and price strategies. The marketing mix is, of course, under the firm's control and is designed to appeal to a specific group of potential buyers. A **target market** is a defined group that managers feel is most likely to buy a firm's product.

target market
A defined group most likely to buy a firm's products.

As the Applebee's example shows, managers must alter the marketing mix because of changes in the environment in which consumers live, work, and make

Philips Electronics is a firm that tries to keep a step ahead of the latest environmental trends. The firm's new strategic plan focuses on "sense and sensibility."

purchasing decisions. Also, as markets mature, some new consumers become part of the target market; others drop out. Although managers can control the marketing mix, they cannot control the elements in the external environment that continually mould and reshape the target market. Review Learning Outcome 3 shows the controllable and uncontrollable variables that affect the target market. The uncontrollable elements surrounding the target market continually evolve and cause changes in the target market. In contrast, marketing managers shape and reshape the marketing mix, shown on the left side of the exhibit, to influence the target market. That is, marketing managers react to the changing external environment to create a more effective marketing program.

UNDERSTANDING THE EXTERNAL ENVIRONMENT

Unless marketing managers understand the external environment, the firm cannot intelligently plan for the future. Thus many organizations assemble teams of specialists to continually collect and evaluate environmental information, a process called *environmental scanning*. The goal in gathering environmental data is to identify future market opportunities and threats.

Philips Electronics, operating in Canada since 1934, is a firm that tries to keep a step ahead of the latest environmental trends. The firm's new strategic plan focuses on "sense and simplicity." The idea is to give consumers what they want in the way of electronic products in the health, lifestyle, and technology areas. Because Philips is dominated by engineers, it decided that if it was really going to create products that are simple to use and consumer-oriented, it needed help. The company created an advisory group of opinion leaders from around the globe. The group meets several days each month to help Philips understand how the environment of business is changing. Their goal is to help Philips create intuitive, easy-to-use products that meet specific needs. Andrea Ragnatti, chief marketing officer for Philips, notes, "In the past we just developed the technology and hoped someone would buy it. Now we are starting from the point of discovering what exactly consumers want a product to do."[11]

ENVIRONMENTAL MANAGEMENT

No one business is large or powerful enough to create major change in the external environment. Thus marketing managers are basically adapters rather than agents of change. For example, despite the huge size of General Motors and Ford, these companies are continually challenged by the Japanese auto companies to maintain their share of the Canadian automobile market. Competition is one of the uncontrollable elements in the external environment.

A firm is not always completely at the mercy of the external environment, however. Sometimes a firm can influence external events. For example, extensive lobbying by FedEx enabled it to acquire virtually all the Japanese routes it had been seeking. Japan had originally opposed new cargo routes for FedEx, but the company's lobbying efforts won out for it. When a company implements strategies that attempt to shape the external environment within which it operates, it is engaging in **environmental management**.

environmental management
When a company implements strategies that attempt to shape the external environment within which it operates.

The factors within the external environment that are important to marketing managers can be classified as social, demographic, economic, technological, political and legal, and competitive.

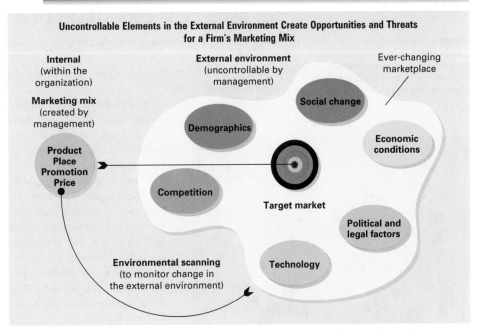

Uncontrollable Elements in the External Environment Create Opportunities and Threats for a Firm's Marketing Mix

 SOCIAL FACTORS

Describe the social factors that affect marketing

Social change is perhaps the most difficult external variable for marketing managers to forecast, influence, or integrate into marketing plans. Social factors include our attitudes, values, and lifestyles. Social factors influence the products people buy, the prices they pay for products, the effectiveness of specific promotions, and how, where, and when people expect to purchase products.

MARKETING-ORIENTED VALUES OF TODAY

A *value* is a strongly held and enduring belief. Four basic values have influenced Canadian consumers' attitudes and lifestyles:

- *Self-sufficiency*: Every person should have the opportunity to stand on his or her own two feet.
- *Upward mobility*: Success should come to everyone who gets an education, works hard, and plays by the rules.
- *Work ethic*: Hard work, dedication to family, and frugality are moral and right.
- *Conformity*: No one should expect to be treated differently from everybody else.

These core values still hold for a majority of Canadians today. A person's values are key determinants of what is important and not important, what actions to take or not to take, and how one behaves in social situations.

A person's values are typically formed through interaction with family, friends, and other influencers such as teachers, religious leaders, and politicians. The changing environment can also play a key role in shaping what one values. For example, people born during the 1980s and 1990s tend to be more comfortable with technology and its importance in the home than people born in the 1950s and 1960s and thus place a higher value on these changes.

Values also influence our buying habits. Today's consumers are demanding, inquisitive, and discriminating. No longer willing to tolerate products that break down, consumers are insisting on high-quality goods that save time, energy, and often calories. Shoppers are also concerned about nutrition and want to know what's in their food, and many consumers have environmental concerns.

THE GROWTH OF COMPONENT LIFESTYLES

component lifestyles
The practice of choosing goods and services that meet one's diverse needs and interests rather than conforming to a single, traditional lifestyle.

Many of today's consumers are piecing together **component lifestyles.** A lifestyle is a mode of living; it is the way people decide to live their lives. Consumers are choosing products and services that meet diverse needs and interests rather than conforming to traditional stereotypes.

In the past, a person's profession—for instance, banker—defined his or her lifestyle. Today, a person can be a banker and also a gourmet, fitness enthusiast, dedicated single parent, and Internet guru. Each of these lifestyles is associated with different goods and services and represents a target audience. For example, for the gourmet, marketers offer cooking utensils, wines, and exotic foods through magazines like *Bon Appetit.* The fitness enthusiast buys Adidas equipment and special jogging outfits and reads *Runner* magazine. Component lifestyles increase the complexity of consumers' buying habits. The banker may own a BMW but change the oil himself or herself. He or she may buy fast food for lunch but French wine for dinner, own sophisticated photographic equipment and a low-priced home stereo, and shop for socks at Zellers and suits or dresses at Harry Rosen or high-priced fashion boutiques.

A growing number of homeowners are single women. Rona and Home Depot have been finding that a growing number of shoppers in their stores are women. As a result, both companies are adapting their marketing strategies to better cater to women.

SOURCE: COURTESY OF RONA LTD.

THE CHANGING ROLE OF FAMILIES AND WORKING WOMEN

Component lifestyles have evolved because consumers can choose from a growing number of goods and services, and most have the money to exercise more options. The growth of dual-income families has resulted in increased purchasing power. Nearly two-thirds of all women between 18 and 65 are now in the workforce, and women's participation in the labour force will continue to grow. The phenomenon of working women has probably had a greater effect on marketing than has any other social change.

As women's earnings grow, so do their levels of expertise, experience, and authority. Working-age women are not the same group that businesses targeted 30 years ago. They expect different things in life—from their jobs, from their spouses, and from the products and services they buy. Home improvement centres like Rona and Home Depot know that women shoppers are vital to their success, accounting for half the sales in these traditional male outlets.[12] More women are involved in home repairs as evidenced by Mag Ruffman, the tool-savvy host of WTN's *A Repair to Remember* and books such as Aliza Sherman's *PowerTools for Women in Business.* Women are the principal buyers for over 40 percent of all cars and trucks sold and purchase over half of all electronics products. Both the Toronto Blue Jays and the Canadian Football League have developed advertising campaigns directed to women.

The growth in the number of working women has meant an increase in dual-career families. Although dual-career families typically have greater household incomes, they have less time for family activities. With the growth in the number of working women, Calgary-based Mark's Work Wearhouse, which traditionally carried only men's work and casual clothes, has launched an advertising campaign in national magazines including *Canadian Living* and *Chatelaine* to target female buyers. The sale of women's clothing now accounts for 15 percent of Mark's sales at its 280 stores across Canada.[13]

Customer Experience

 HARLEY-DAVIDSON NAVIGATES DOWN NEW ROADS

Harley-Davidson Inc. has operations in 77 countries including nearly 60 dealership outlets in Canada and is the leader in heavyweight motorcycle sales. The company, more than century old, has sales approaching $7 billion. A leather jacket, a weathered tan, and a rough smattering of whiskers have long been the hallmarks of a Harley-Davidson rider—but no longer. The company says the number of female Harley-Davidson owners has tripled in the past 20 years, and female buyers now account for 12 percent of new Harley-Davidson purchases, up from 4 percent in 1990. For years, Harley-Davidson primarily had tailored both its product design and its marketing to a target market of 35- to 55-year-old males. Now Harley-Davidson wants more women to move from the back of the bike onto the driver's seat. Says Leslie Prevish, Harley-Davidson's women's outreach manager: "We have marketed to women for decades and have an advertisement in our archives from 1920 that encourages women to ride, but we've boosted our efforts in the last five years as we've increased our overall marketing efforts to grow the sport."

The challenge for Harley-Davidson is to maintain its tough, road-tested brand identity while finding new ways to connect with female consumers—and to continue to play to its strengths rather than indulging in female stereotypes. "Women riders are diverse, so some like the black and chrome, while others prefer purples and pinks," Prevish says. "Our materials and initiatives appeal to a common personality trait of strong, independent women who enjoy taking on a challenge and feeling of adventure."

The company started by making its product more accessible to females, modifying motorcycles to fit women's smaller frames and offering an instructional manual and courses to teach women how to handle their bikes. Rider's Edge New Rider courses have become an important marketing vehicle with which Harley-Davidson can encourage women to enter the sport. "While there are some shifts in the emphasis of the brand as we continue to increase relevance for the women's market, we remain true to the brand," says Ken Ostermann, general manager of outreach marketing. A financial analyst for Harley-Davidson adds, "I don't think we're going to see any pink Harley-Davidsons on the road. . . . There is a market that they're going after that is 'I want to be free, I want to be independent, I want to be my own person,' and that person can be a guy or a girl," he says. "They don't have to add bigger mirrors so women can do their cosmetics. . . . They want to sell Harleys to women, and they want to sell them to women who want to ride a Harley."[14]

Do you think that targeting women will alienate Harley-Davidson's core male market? Why? Should Harley produce a motorcycle directed only to the female market?

SOURCE: ELISABETH A. SULLIVAN, "HOG-HARLEY-DAVIDSON SHOWS BRAND STRENGTH AS IT NAVIGATES DOWN NEW ROADS—AND PICKS UP MORE FEMALE RIDERS ALONG THE WAY," MARKETING NEWS, NOVEMBER 1, 2008, 8. REPRINTED WITH PERMISSION FROM THE AMERICAN MARKETING ASSOCIATION.

REVIEW LEARNING OUTCOME 4

4 | **Describe the social factors that affect marketing**

Component lifestyles

Values

Changing role of women

Social Factors

demography
The study of people's vital statistics, such as their age, race and ethnicity, and location.

Cost is a more important factor in decisions made by women, whereas quality is relatively more important to men. When it comes to big-ticket, long-term items, women are active in the decision-making process, although most say they are likely to make these decisions with a spouse. More working women means an ever-increasing demand for timesaving devices and products, particularly for the kitchen.

5 DEMOGRAPHIC FACTORS

Explain the importance to marketing managers of current demographic trends

Another uncontrollable variable in the external environment, and extremely important to marketing managers, is **demography**, the study of people's vital statistics, such as their age, race and ethnicity, and location. Demographics are significant because the basis for any market is people. Demographic characteristics are strongly related to consumers' buying behaviour in the marketplace. Some general demographic characteristics for Canada and the rest of the world are shown in Exhibit 3.3. This exhibit tells marketers many things. For example, Canada is growing much more slowly than the rest of the world. Faster growth, if it is coupled with rising incomes, means expanding markets. The longer life

EXHIBIT 3.3

The Demographic Facts of Life*

	Canada	Planet Earth
Population	33,930,830	6.9 billion
Area, in square kilometres	9,984,670	84,900,846
Births per 1,000 population	11.1	20.4
Deaths per 1,000 population	7.2	80.2
Doubling time in years at current rate	130	63
Projected population, 2050	41,900,000	9.4 billion
Infant deaths per 1,000 live births	5.1	46
Life expectancy	80.7	69
Percentage of population under age 15	16.6	27
Percentage of population over 65	13.9	8
Population per square kilometre	3.4	78
Percentage urban population	80.2	45
Percentage of labour force in agriculture	1.7	49
Percentage of labour force in industry	20.3	20
Percentage of labour force in services	78.0	31

*Data as of January 2010

SOURCE: Population Connection (http://www.populationconnection.org) and Statistics Canada (www.statcan.ca)

span of Canadians suggests a growing market for products and services targeted toward the elderly. Look through the table and see what other implications for marketers you can identify.

POPULATION

The most basic statistic of all is population because people are the basis of all markets. As of the beginning of 2010, the Canadian population was closing in on 34 million people. Canada's population grew a little more slowly in 2009 than in 2008 as both international migration into Canada and the number of births slowed. Population growth remains faster in Western Canada with British Columbia, Alberta, Saskatchewan, and Manitoba leading Canada's population growth. With only 3.3 people per square kilometre, Canada would seem to have plenty of room for population growth.

We now turn our attention to a closer look at age groups, their impact, and the opportunities they present for marketers. The cohorts have been given the names of tweens, teens, Generation Y, Generation X, baby boomers, and seniors. Each cohort group has its own needs, values, and consumption patterns.

TWEENS

They watch cable channels designed just for them, they cruise the Net with ease, they know what they want—and usually get it. They are Canada's **tweens** (pre- and early adolescents, ages 9 to 14), a group of just over 2.3 million. With attitudes, access to information, and sophistication well beyond their years, and purchasing power to match, these young consumers spend over $2 billion annually. If one adds in the amount parents spend on tweens, the total spending is estimated at over $30 billion.[15]

Tweens' styles don't reflect those of their parents. They want their own look, and parents spend over $250 per tween on back-to-school clothes to accommodate that. There are even special clothing lines for tweens, but clothing is not the only product area that has caught the eye of "tween marketers." Cellphone usage by tweens will be the industry's biggest growth area over the next few years.

tweens
Pre- and early adolescents, ages 9 to 14.

Tweens recognize television commercials for what they are—"just advertising." Most regard billboards and radio spots as paid advertising and recognize product placements on television shows. What is really important to tweens? Research shows that it is being happy, getting along with family, getting good grades, being healthy, the school he or she attends and being good with money. Tweens also enjoy being pampered at the Peaches & Cream Spa in Vancouver, where feet are buffed, nails meticulously polished, and shoulders massaged with hot stones.[16] Tweens shop at Claire's, Limited Too, The Gap, Walmart, and Old Navy.

Tweens
Ages 9–14
Pop. 2.3 million
Spend over $2 billion/year
Heavy buying influence on parents
Biggest growth area: cell phone usage

SOURCE: © RUBBERBALL/JUPITER IMAGES

teens
With some overlap, those between tweens and Generation Y, roughly 13 to 19 years of age.

TEENS

There are over 3 million teens in Canada, and they spend nearly $10 billion annually. They spend over 70 hours per week tuned in electronically. This includes TV, Internet, music, video games, cellphones, and text messages. Many teens participate in on-line social networks such as MySpace, and most have created profiles on MySpace, Zanga, or Facebook.[17]

While the average teen will spend over 10 hours a week on-line, they prefer reality over virtual reality. Teens would rather have real friends than on-line friends, date someone from school rather than someone met on the Internet, and shop in a store over shopping on-line (though most do shop on-line). Clothes and music are the most frequently purchased on-line items followed by books and electronics.

For teens, shopping has become a social sport on-line or at the mall. They patronize the big-box retailers like Best Buy and are attracted to luxury brands like Armani, Gucci, and Coach. Teens also like Taco Bell and drink Coke. Other interesting facts about teens are that they earn about $30 a week and spend over 40 percent of their earnings on fashion; music and entertainment are critical to their everyday life; over 90 percent of teens engage in on-demand entertainment; life often revolves around the mall, where over two-thirds go at least once a week to shop and socialize; and the average teen spends over 40 minutes per day reading books and magazines.[18]

Teens
Ages 13–19
Pop. 3 million
Spend $10 billion/year
Two-thirds go to a mall once a week.
90 percent engage in on-demand media/entertainment.

SOURCE: © RUBBERBALL/JUPITER IMAGES

Generation Y
People born between 1979 and 1994.

GENERATION Y

Those designated as **Generation Y** were born between 1979 and 1994. They are over 7 million strong in Canada, a little bigger than Generation X. Most Gen Yers are the children of baby boomers and are often referred to as "echo boomers" or the "millennial generation." The marketing impact of Generation Y has been immense. They spend about $20 billion annually. Many have already started their careers and are making major purchases such as cars and homes and are big purchasers of computers, MP3 players, cellphones, and sneakers.

Gen Yers tend to be a fickle group, demanding the latest trend in the shortest possible time. They are more likely to buy a product on the spur of the moment than their parents. They change brands very quickly as well. They are critical, though, and don't like the "hard sell." They are very brand and fashion conscious but, as one advertising manager learned, you have to get the "merchandise in front of them without being in their face."[19] A retail chain that has done this very successfully is West 49. While just over 10 years old, West 49 has grown to 90 stores and over $130 million in sales by catering to the sports-loving side of Gen Yers. West 49's media campaign has centred on the "brotherhood of the board" theme, and the stores are packed with skateboarding and snowboarding products and apparel. The result has been average store sales of $678 per square foot, about double that of comparable retail outlets.[20]

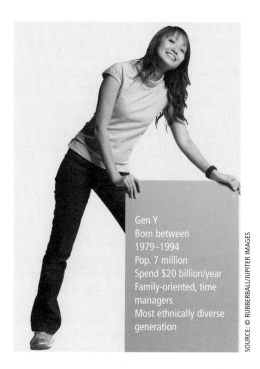

Gen Y
Born between
1979–1994
Pop. 7 million
Spend $20 billion/year
Family-oriented, time
managers
Most ethnically diverse
generation

SOURCE: © RUBBERBALL/JUPITER IMAGES

Researchers have found Gen Yers to be

- *Impatient*: Gen Y has grown up in a world that's always been automated. They've had access to computers, CD-ROMS, the Internet, DVD players, chat rooms, and instant messaging so it's no surprise that they expect things to be done now.
- *Family-oriented*: Unlike Gen X before them, Gen Yers had relatively stable childhoods. They grew up in a very family-focused time when even big companies strived to become more family and kid friendly.
- *Inquisitive*: Knowing more than their parents about computers and technology has always been a source of pride for the echo boomers. It's led to natural inquisitiveness that many of this group possesses. They want to know why things happen, how things work, and what they can do next.
- *Opinionated*: From the time they were children, Gen Yers have been encouraged by their parents, teachers, and other authority figures to share their opinions. That's translated to a group who feel that their opinions are always needed and welcomed.
- *Diverse*: This is an ethnically diverse generation and many don't identify themselves as being only one race. They are much more accepting of people who are different from themselves.
- *Time managers*: Their entire lives have been scheduled—from playgroups to soccer to hockey. So it's no surprise that they've picked up a knack for planning along the way.
- *"Street Smart"*: The term isn't used in a literal sense, but means that these young people have seen a lot. With the Internet and 24-hour cable TV news exposing them to recounts of violence, war, and sexuality at a young age, they're not easily shocked. They're very aware of the world around them.
- *Connected*: Most use social networking sites like MySpace or Facebook, and many have created profiles featuring photos, hobbies, and interests.[21]

Gen Yers care about the environment. They will often seek out "green" products. They also look to brands for information about the environment. Many Gen Yers applauded Honest Tea's switch to plastic when it was explained via the product's packaging that less fuel is used to ship plastic than heavier glass bottles.

GENERATION X

Generation X
People born between 1965 and 1978.

Generation X—people born between 1965 and 1978—consists of about 6.7 million consumers across Canada. It is the first generation of latchkey children—products of dual-career households or, in roughly half of the cases, of divorced or separated parents. Gen Xers have been bombarded by multiple media since their cradle days and are savvy and cynical consumers.

Gen Xers, now in their 30s and 40s, are reaching the age where they are sending their kids off to university. Gen Xers tend to be more protective and involved with their kids than were the baby boomer generation. They value the importance of education.

Gen Xers are buying homes and spending money to decorate and renovate them. They are also avid buyers of the latest clothes, technology, and recreational products. Now that they have advanced in the corporate world, they are demanding certain values from the retailers they patronize. Gen Xers want frankness, client service, reliability, and authenticity. Gen Xers are careful shoppers when it comes to home furnishings. They check an average of four stores before buying and do not exhibit much retail brand loyalty.

Researchers have found that a male Gen X traveller is more likely than a boomer to pick a hotel with a sports bar. But the pub must be genuine and the workout room cutting edge. So Holiday Inn Select is adding Sporting News Grill restaurants and Fitness by Nautilus workout centres to its offerings. In-room amenities include Wolfgang Puck coffee, Moen showerheads, and Garden Botanika bath products. A study of over 5,000 Gen Xers in 17 countries determined that their favourite brands were Google, Sony, Nokia, and BMW.[22]

baby boomers
People born between 1946 and 1964.

BABY BOOMERS: A MASS MARKET

When Vespa motor scooters came puttering back into Canada in 2001 after a 16-year absence, managers at the Italian company figured their biggest customers would be twentysomethings looking for a cheap way to get around, but executives at Piaggio, Vespa's parent company, noticed something odd. The most enthusiastic audience was often aging baby boomers who remembered the candy-coloured bikes from their youth. It turns out that boomers have lost none of their affection for Vespa. Better yet, they now can afford to buy top-of-the-line models with all the trimmings. Much to the company's surprise, consumers age 50 and older now buy a quarter of the scooters Vespa sells in its 30 dealerships across Canada.[23]

The nearly 9 million **baby boomers** in Canada, born between 1946 and 1964, represent over 26 percent of the total population, the largest population segment in the country. The oldest boomers are now over 60 and, with an ever-increasing life expectancy, view middle age as a new start on life. Many boomers expect to continue working past 65.

Many marketers believe that consumers' brand preferences are locked in by age 40. That might have been true for previous generations but not today's over-50 crowd who are just as likely as younger consumers to try new brands. In some categories such as cosmetics and electronics, older consumers are even more willing to brand-hop than younger consumers. Procter & Gamble's Cover Girl brand, which depends on women older than 55 for 20 percent of its sales, has just launched its first line of makeup aimed at older women. The name of the product, Advanced Radiance Age-Defying makeup, hints that advancing age can be pretty. And although ads still show a stunningly gorgeous face, that face belongs to an older woman—57-year-old supermodel Christie Brinkley.

A recent study divided the boomer market into four segments:

- *"Looking for balance" boomers*: About 27 percent of boomers fall into this active and busy segment. They represent an excellent market for companies that can offer them time-saving products and services. Though money is important, saving time is equally important to this segment. Companies engaged in travel-related businesses and food-service businesses will find key opportunities here.
- *"Confident and living-well" boomers*: Confident and living-well boomers represent 23 percent of all boomers. They have the highest incomes of all the segments and relish the chance to be the first to purchase a new product or service. They are technologically oriented and care about what is stylish and trendy. They are the most active boomers and travel is one of their favourite interests. Marketers offering luxury goods and services will find prime boomer prospects here.
- *"At-ease" boomers*: At-ease boomers represent 31 percent of all boomers. They are at peace with themselves and do not worry about the future, job security, or financial security. They express the least interest in luxury goods and services and don't travel much. They are the most home-centric and family-oriented segment of the boomers. Marketers of traditional household products and services will find this group of boomers most receptive to their offerings. New products and innovations are least likely to appeal to this group. Established and trusted brand names will resonate most strongly with this boomer segment.
- *"Overwhelmed" boomers*: As the smallest segment of the boomer population, overwhelmed boomers represent less than 20 percent of boomers. This group has the lowest income of all the segments. They worry about the future and their financial security. This segment is also the least active, and health is a big concern for them. They are also the least social boomers, spending little time with family and friends. These boomers are also far less accepting of technology and are well below average on using electronic, digital, and tech products.[24]

Baby boomers, because of the sheer size of the segment, account for a significant part of all shopping dollars spent on consumer packaged goods. Baby boomers frequently ask each other for advice on products and services and they trust the information received from friends. At every stage of their lives, boomers

have challenged the status quo. Brands that convey a totally new benefit will appeal to boomers' inherent desire to break from the norm. Boomers don't need to be reminded of how old they are. Rather than stress age, Centrum Silver uses advertising to reflect older consumers' passion to continue doing the things they love.

OLDER CONSUMERS: NOT JUST GRANDPARENTS

The generation preceding the baby boomers has crossed the 65-year threshold that many demographers use to define the "mature market." Today's mature consumers are wealthier, healthier, and better educated than those of earlier generations. Nearly 4.7 million Canadians are now 65 or older, making up nearly 14 percent of the population. Consumers in the mature market keep up with the times, are quite definite about their wants and needs, and exhibit a series of unique behaviour patterns. They vacation often, eat out often, and are light television viewers.

Mature consumers are often not happy with the way they are treated by marketers and advertisers. For the most part, they believe marketers and advertisers do not have their interests or needs in mind when developing products, designing packaging, and preparing advertising. More than half feel marketers do only a fair to poor job in considering their needs when they develop new products. Two out of five say marketers do a fair to poor job in considering their needs when they develop packaging. And almost half of all mature consumers feel that advertisers and their agencies ignore them in preparing their campaigns.[25]

Marketers who want to actively pursue the mature market must understand it. Aging consumers create some obvious opportunities. Easy Dressing brand clothes feature Velcro-fastened clothing for women with arthritis or other ailments, who may have difficulty with zippers or buttons.

SOURCE: YURI ARCURS/SHUTTERSTOCK

Windex comes in a bottle with an indented neck that is easier to grip. Cadaco offers a line of games with easy-to-read big print and larger game pieces. Trivia buffs more familiar with Mitch Miller than Guns 'n' Roses can play Parker Brothers' "The Vintage Years" edition of *Trivial Pursuit*. The game, aimed at the 65-plus crowd, poses questions covering the era from Arthur Conan Doyle to Rocket Richard. The mature market also likes to buy "made in Canada" products.

As important as the mature market is today, it will be even more important to businesses in the future. It is the fastest-growing age segment of the population. By 2031, Statistics Canada forecasts that the over 65-age group will grow to 9.4 million and will make up nearly 23 percent of the total population!

REVIEW LEARNING OUTCOME 5

5	Explain the importance to marketing managers of current demographic trends				
	Tweens	**Teens**	**Gen Y**	**Gen X**	**Baby Boomers**
Age	9 to 14 yrs	13 to 19 yrs	20 to 31 yrs	32 to 45 yrs	46 to 64 yrs
	2 million	3 million	7 million	6.7 million	9 million

⑥ GROWING ETHNIC MARKETS

Explain the importance to marketing managers of multiculturalism and growing ethnic markets

visible minority
Persons, other than Aboriginal peoples, who are non-Caucasian in race or non-white in colour.

The 2006 census reported Canada's "visible minority" population at approximately 5.3 million, about the size of Canada's total population in 1900. By 2031, Canada's "visible minority" population will reach 12.8 million, the size of Canada's total population in 1948. **Visible minorities**, according to the Employment Equity Act, are persons, other than Aboriginal peoples, who are non-Caucasian in race or non-white in colour.

Canada is becoming a truly multicultural society. Immigrants are Canada's main source of population growth, with nearly 250,000 newcomers arriving in the country each year. Over three-quarters of the immigrants to Canada are now classified as visible minorities and 16 percent of all Canadians are now visible minorities. By 2031, 31 percent of all Canadians will be visible minorities. As shown in Exhibit 3.4, the largest groups of visible minorities in Canada are South Asians, Chinese, Blacks, Filipinos, Latin Americans, Arabs, Southeast Asians, West Asians, Koreans, and Japanese. Furthermore, nearly 23 percent of all visible minorities in Canada are under 14 while less than 17 percent of non-visible minority Canadians are under 14 years of age.

EXHIBIT 3.4

Population of Visible Minorities in Canada for 2006 and Projected to 2031

	2006	2031
South Asian	1,320,000	3,640,000
Chinese	1,269,000	2,714,000
Black	815,000	1,809,000
Filipino	427,000	1,020,000
Latin American	317,000	733,000
Arab	276,000	930,000
Southeast Asian	250,000	449,000
West Asian	164,000	523,000
Korean	148,000	407,000
Japanese	85,000	142,000
Other	213,000	489,000

SOURCE: Adapted from Statistics Canada Projections of the Diversity of the Canadian Population 91-551-XWE 2010001 2006 to 2031 Released March 9, 2010.

Over the 2006 to 2031 period, the visible minority population of Canada is expected to grow by nearly 59 percent while the rest of the population will grow by less than 7 percent. The major reasons for the high growth rate of the visible minority population are higher immigration of visible minorities, higher fertility rates, and a younger population.

Nearly 50 percent of visible minorities in Canada in 2031 will be South Asian and Chinese. Also by 2031, Blacks and Filipinos will become the third and fourth visible minority groups to exceed 1 million in population. As is currently the case, over 70 percent of all visible minorities in Canada in 2031 will be living in Toronto, Vancouver, and Montreal. By 2031, visible minorities will represent about 60 percent of the populations of both Vancouver and Toronto—making them what's called majority-minority cities. In fact, Toronto's projected visible minority population of 5.6 million in 2031 would be the largest city in Canada today![26]

ETHNIC AND CULTURAL DIVERSITY

multiculturalism
When all major ethnic groups in an area—such as a city, county, or census metropolitan area—are roughly equally represented.

Multiculturalism occurs when all major ethnic groups in an area—such as a city, county, or census metropolitan area—are roughly equally represented. The trend in Canada is clearly toward greater multiculturalism.

The greatest degree of multiculturalism is found in the largest census metropolitan areas across the country, such as Toronto, Vancouver, Montreal, Calgary, Ottawa, and Edmonton. In the 2006 census, over 20 percent of the people in these cities listed neither English nor French as their first language. In recognition of this, a number of companies are now including visible minorities in their advertising. Air Canada, Nabisco, and TD Bank are among the companies advertising in languages other than English and French. Radio stations such as CHIN in Toronto and Ottawa broadcast in more than 30 languages. Over 60 percent of the television broadcasting of OMNI.1 (CFMT) is in languages other than English and French. People whose mother tongue is neither English nor French will make up over 30 percent of the population by 2031.

Across the provinces, visible minorities range from just over 1 percent of the population in Newfoundland and Prince Edward Island to 22.8 percent of the population in Ontario and 24.8 percent in British Columbia. Toronto, Montreal, and Vancouver

EXHIBIT 3.5

Visible Minority Population in Selected Major Canadian Cities

	2006	2017	2031
Vancouver	42.2%	51.0%	59.2%
Toronto	41.9	50.5	62.8
Ottawa	20.8	27.4	31.5
Calgary	19.5	23.6	37.7
Windsor	15.8	21.4	32.8
Montreal	15.4	19.4	31.1
Edmonton	15.3	17.5	28.6
Winnipeg	13.3	15.7	26.6
Kitchener	12.0	15.1	28.2
Hamilton	11.1	14.5	24.3

SOURCE: Statistics Canada, Demography Division, Population Projections of Visible Minority Groups, Canada, Provinces and Regions, Catalogue no. 91-541-XIE, July 2006; CANSIM table 91-551-X, Population by visible minority group and place of residence, Canada, 2031, May 5, 2010, www.statcan.ca.

account for 34.4 percent of Canada's total population but are home to 71.8 percent of Canada's visible minorities. Although Toronto, Vancouver, and Montreal have large visible minority populations, they are different. South Asians and Chinese are the two largest visible minority populations in Toronto and Vancouver, while Blacks and Arabs are the largest visible minority groups in Montreal. Exhibit 3.5 shows the visible minority populations in 10 CMAs across Canada with a projection to 2031. Look at the growth in visible minorities in all 10 CMAs.

MARKETING IMPLICATIONS OF MULTICULTURALISM

The marketer's task is more challenging in a diverse society because of the many differences across ethnic segments. What's more, ethnic markets are not homogeneous. There is not an Asian market or a Chinese market, any more than there is a single English or French market. Instead, there are many niches within ethnic markets that require micromarketing strategies. Among the Chinese population in Canada, some are from the People's Republic of China, some are from Hong Kong, and some are from Taiwan; some of the Chinese population report Cantonese as their mother tongue, some report that it's Mandarin, while others report many other dialects.

According to Manifold Data Mining, a Canadian research firm, ethnic spending in Canada exceeds $100 billion annually. In Toronto alone, both the South Asians and Chinese are spending over $13 billion each year.[27] "M&M Meat Shops has recognized the growing ethnic market in Canada and is investigating how to best service this potentially profitable group. Traditional methods do not necessarily apply when attracting this consumer and we need to find new and innovative ways to expose our brand to them," says Michelle Lewis of M&M Meat Shops, which operates over 400 stores across Canada.[28]

Providing service to customers who do not speak English or French could be a problem, but not for the Habib family, which owns Global Quality Market in Windsor, Ontario. Each staff member hired at Global Quality Market speaks at least two languages; these languages include Italian, Lebanese, Chinese, and Hindi. Why? "Because we are in the centre of a European, Middle East, Egyptian, and Pakistani population of over 20,000 people," says Sam Habib, one of the family members running the successful $3-million market.[29]

Some entrepreneurs are building large enclosed malls that cater to Asian consumers. At the Aberdeen Centre near Vancouver, nearly 80 percent of the merchants are Chinese Canadians, as are 80 percent of the customers. The mall offers fashions made in Hong Kong, a shop for traditional Chinese medicines, and a theatre showing Chinese movies. Kung fu martial-arts demonstrations and Chinese folk dances are held in the mall on weekends.

Sears Canada has increased its emphasis on the multicultural market. Sears has a number of stores located in urban areas with large Asian populations. Recently, the company recognized an opportunity to boost fall sales in those stores by forging a connection with the Asian Moon Festival.

If Sears, or any other company, is looking for a new place to advertise to the Asian community, *Jasmine* magazine, a glossy lifestyle magazine, hit the newsstands in Canada a few years ago. *Jasmine* is targeted to Asian-Canadian women aged 18 to 34. It is published four times a year and features many of the same sections as other women's magazines—health, beauty, travel, and careers—but with a distinct Asian focus. *Jasmine* addresses such topics as Asian-specific illnesses (like osteoporosis and lupus), interracial dating, and workplace barriers.[30]

Multicultural marketing has found great success on the Internet. Numerous sites provide information and services targeted toward a variety of minority groups. This site, from Citizenship and Immigration Canada (www.cic.gc.ca), provides links for immigrants and members of visible minorities.

THE INTERNET GOES MULTICULTURAL

Growth in Internet usage within many ethnic markets is outpacing growth among the general public, according to Forrester Research.[31] Eighty-eight percent of ethnic Canadians use the Internet, slightly above the usage for the general population. Ethnic Canadians also spend, on average, more time each day on the Internet. Chinese Canadians are particularly active Internet users, averaging 2.4 hours per day on the Internet as compared to 1.7 hours for the rest of the population.

The huge growth in the multicultural on-line market has resulted in a proliferation of websites targeted to specific ethnic groups. Examples include AsianAvenue.com, a site for the Asian market; StarMedia Network, which focuses on Latinos; and iMinorities.com, a job site for minorities. One of the more popular sites for the Black market is BlackPlanet.com, which averages 300 million views per month across Canada and the United States.[32]

REVIEW LEARNING OUTCOME 6

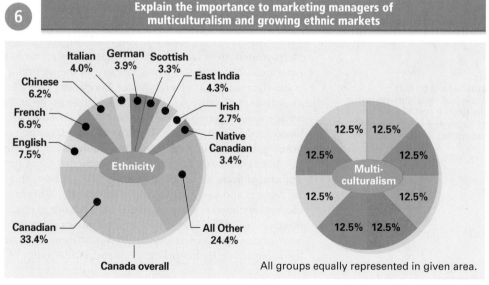

6 Explain the importance to marketing managers of multiculturalism and growing ethnic markets

Ethnicity — Canada overall:
- Italian 4.0%
- German 3.9%
- Scottish 3.3%
- East India 4.3%
- Chinese 6.2%
- Irish 2.7%
- French 6.9%
- Native Canadian 3.4%
- English 7.5%
- Canadian 33.4%
- All Other 24.4%

Multiculturalism: 12.5% 12.5% 12.5% 12.5% 12.5% 12.5% 12.5% 12.5%
All groups equally represented in given area.

Source: Statistics Canada, Population by Selected Ethnic Origins, July 5, 2010

7 ECONOMIC FACTORS

Identify consumer and marketer reactions to the state of the economy

In addition to social and demographic factors, marketing managers must understand and react to the economic environment. The economic areas of greatest concern to most marketers are consumers' incomes, purchasing power, inflation, and recession.

CONSUMERS' INCOMES

As disposable (or after-tax) incomes rise, more families and individuals can afford the "good life." Canadian incomes have continued to rise, although at a rather slow pace. After adjusting for inflation, average disposable incomes in Canada rose by less than 2 percent per year between 2004 and 2010.[33] The median household income in Canada today is $66,550.[34] This means that half of all Canadian households earn more than this amount and half earn less.

Today, just over 40 percent of all Canadian households earn a "middle-class" income. The rough boundaries for a middle-class income are $35,000 (above poverty) to $90,000 (short of wealth). More than 37 percent of households now earn above $90,000.[35] As a result, Canadians are buying more goods and services than ever before. For example, in raising a child to age 17, a family will spend over $190,000 in 2001 dollars. The new level of affluence in Canada is not limited to professionals or even individuals within specific age or education brackets. Rather, it cuts across all household types, well beyond what businesses traditionally consider to be markets for high-priced goods and services. This rising affluence stems primarily from the increasing number of dual-income families.

Income does vary across the country. By province, median family income is higher in Alberta ($82,030) and Ontario ($69,190) and lower in Newfoundland ($55,210) and New Brunswick ($56,930). Median family income for selected Canadian cities is shown in Exhibit 3.6. The average Canadian household has over $17,000 in discretionary income to spend each year. Education, of course, is the primary determinant of a person's earning potential. University-educated workers are thirteen times more likely to earn over $100,000 per year than those with only a high school education.[36] Some marketers are concentrating their efforts on higher-quality, higher-priced goods and services, such as the Lexus automobile, Breitling watches, and five-star resort hotels.

As can be seen in Exhibit 3.6, most of the cities shown have median family incomes higher than the Canada-wide median ($66,550). This would suggest, of course, that major Census Metropolitan Areas have higher average incomes than found in smaller markets and in rural areas. However, this is only one side of the spending equation for marketers. There is also the issue of purchasing power. **Purchasing power** is measured by comparing income to the relative cost of a set standard of goods and services in different geographic areas, usually referred to as the cost of living. Another way to think of purchasing power is income minus cost of living. The cost of living takes into consideration the cost of housing, food and groceries, transportation, utilities, clothing, and other expenses.

Just as median family incomes are higher in major market areas, so is the cost of living. The cost of living is much higher in Calgary, Oshawa, and Ottawa (where median incomes are higher) and lower in places like Yellowknife, Whitehorse, and St. John (where median incomes are lower). When income is high relative to cost of living, people have more *discretionary income*. This means that they have more money to spend on nonessential items. This is important information for marketers. Consumers with more discretionary income have the ability to buy higher priced items and a wider range of nonessential goods.

EXHIBIT 3.6

Median Family Income for Selected Canadian Cities (2007)

City	Median Family Income
Calgary (Alta.)	$87,970
Edmonton (Alta.)	83,460
Oshawa (Ont.)	81,570
Ottawa (Ont./Que.)	81,300
Regina (Sask.)	77,170
Kitchener (Ont.)	74,750
Victoria (B.C.)	74,730
Hamilton (Ont.)	74,480
Saskatoon (Sask.)	72,970
Kingston (Ont.)	71,980
Thunder Bay (Ont.)	71,480
Quebec (Que.)	70,920
Windsor (Ont.)	70,810
Halifax (N.S.)	70,610
Winnipeg (Man.)	67,900
St. John's (N.L.)	67,760
Toronto (Ont.)	66,560
Vancouver (B.C.)	66,330
Montreal (Que.)	63,790

SOURCE: Adapted from the Statistics Canada CANSIM database http://cansim2.statcan.gc.ca table number 111-0009, accessed March 29, 2010.

purchasing power
A comparison of income versus the relative cost of a set standard of goods and services in different geographic areas.

inflation
A measure of the decrease in the value of money, expressed as the percentage reduction in value since the previous year.

INFLATION

Inflation is a measure of the decrease in the value of money, generally expressed as the percentage reduction in value since the previous year, which is the rate of inflation.

In simple terms, an inflation rate of 5 percent means that you will need 5 percent more income than you would have needed last year to buy the same basket of products. Fortunately, Canada has had a low rate of inflation for well over a decade. The late 1990s and early 2000s have been marked by an inflation rate under 4 percent. By 2007, Statistics Canada reported that the inflation rate had dropped to 2.2 percent, and in 2009 and 2010 the inflation rate had dropped to under 2 percent. The low rate of inflation is due to the tremendous productivity of the high-tech sector of the economy and the stability of the price of services. Both education and health-care costs are rising more slowly than in the past. The current rate of inflation would have been even lower except for the fact that the cost of energy rose by nearly 10 percent in 2009 and 2010. These economic conditions benefit marketers, because real wages, and hence purchasing power, go up when inflation stays down. A significant increase in inflation almost always depresses real wages and the ability to buy more goods and services.

In times of low inflation, businesses seeking to increase their profit margins can do so only by increasing their efficiency. If they significantly increase prices, no one will purchase their goods or services.

In more inflationary times, marketers use a number of pricing strategies to cope. But in general, marketers must be aware that inflation causes consumers to either build up or diminish their brand loyalty. In one research session, a consumer panellist noted, "I used to use just Betty Crocker mixes, but now I think of either Betty Crocker or Duncan Hines, depending on which is on sale." Inflation pressures consumers to make more economical purchases. Nevertheless, most consumers try hard to maintain their standard of living.

In creating marketing strategies to cope with inflation, managers must realize that, despite what happens to the seller's cost, the buyer is not going to pay more for a product than the subjective value he or she places on it. No matter how compelling the justification might be for a 10 percent price increase, marketers must always examine its impact on demand. Many marketers try to hold prices level as long as is practical.

RECESSION

recession
A period of economic activity characterized by negative growth, which reduces demand for goods and services.

A **recession** is a period of economic activity characterized by negative growth, which reduces demand for goods and services. During recession, the growth rates of income, production, and employment all fall to below zero percent. In a true recession, you wouldn't receive a smaller raise than in previous years; you would receive no raise or a pay cut. The problems of inflation and recession go hand in hand, yet recession requires different marketing strategies.

During the economic downturn of 2008 and 2009, Procter & Gamble experienced a sales increase for their bargain-priced Gain detergent. Sales of McCormick spices increased as consumers were eating out less and cooking more at home. Snack foods, beer and wine, and movie sales remain solid in slower economic times, as well, as consumers find escapism for short periods of time from these products. Also, as people hang on to durable goods longer in recessionary periods there is an increased need for repair services, remodelling services, and do-it-yourself products. Retailers and manufacturers redouble their efforts to cut costs during a recession and they often try to lower prices to attract new customers and hold existing ones.

REVIEW LEARNING OUTCOME 7

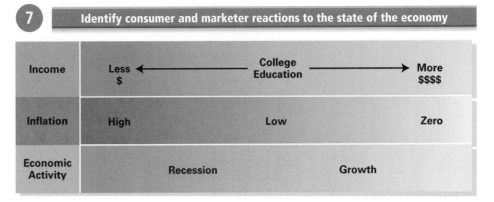

7	Identify consumer and marketer reactions to the state of the economy		
Income	Less $ ←	College Education	→ More $$$$
Inflation	High	Low	Zero
Economic Activity	Recession		Growth

Identify the impact of technology on a firm

basic research
Pure research that aims to confirm an existing theory or to learn more about a concept or phenomenon.

applied research
An attempt to develop new or improved products.

New technology is often an effective weapon against inflation and recession. New machines that reduce production costs can be one of a firm's most valuable assets. The power of a personal-computer microchip doubles about every 18 months. Our ability, as a country, to maintain and build wealth depends in large part on the speed and effectiveness with which we invent and adopt machines that lift productivity. For example, coal mining is typically thought of as unskilled, backbreaking labour. But visit a coal mine today and you will find workers with push-button controls who walk along massive machines that shear metre-long slices from the mine walls. Laptop computers help the miners track equipment breakdowns and water quality.

Canada excels at basic research and is improving at applied research. **Basic research** (or *pure research*) attempts to expand the frontiers of knowledge but is not aimed at a specific, pragmatic problem. Basic research aims to confirm an existing theory or to learn more about a concept or phenomenon. For example, basic research might focus on high-energy physics. **Applied research**, in contrast, attempts to develop new or improved products. Canada is improving its track record in applied research. Some Canadian companies spend heavily on R&D, as shown in Exhibit 3.7. According to Research Infosource Inc., R&D spending in Canada was flat in 2009 as compared to 2008 but had been growing at a pace of 3 percent per year previously. A total of 19 Canadian companies spent in excess of $100 million on R&D in 2009.[37]

As a group, the highest R&D spending, at nearly 19 percent of revenue, was among communications/telecommunications equipment companies. The top 100 R&D companies in Canada spent over $100 billion on research in 2009. Research intensity, or R&D spending as a share of revenue, was 2.7 percent among Canadian companies.

Information technology and the Internet have been the innovations driving increased productivity for the past decade. When Oracle wanted to boost operating margins, it automated such functions as office supply purchasing. That helped keep the company workforce stable even as sales soared. The company saved about $1 billion and margins jumped from 20 percent to 33 percent.[38] Dell uses WebMethods software to act as a type of translator enabling instant communication between Dell's order management system and customers' procurement systems. By making it easier for corporate customers to use the Internet to place orders, Dell has dramatically reduced procurement errors and shaved approximately $5 million a year off its costs. Dell also uses TradeMatrix software to run its plants. This system allows Dell to see

EXHIBIT 3.7

Canada's Top Corporate R&D Spenders for 2009

Company	R&D Spending	R&D as Percent of Revenue
Nortel Networks Corp.	$1,677,884,000	15.1%
BCE Inc.	985,500,000	5.6%
Magna International Inc.	692,900,000	2.7%
Pratt & Whitney Canada	442,000,000	12.3%
IBM Canada Ltd.	397,000,000	nd
Research In Motion Limited	383,577,000	6.0%
Atomic Energy of Canada Limited	329,406,000	56.6%
Alcatel-Lucent	237,000,000	nd
Apotex Inc.	218,944,000	16.2%
Sanofi-Aventis Group	211,542,000	37.5%

nd = not disclosed
SOURCE: Research Infosource Inc., http://www.researchinfosource.com

deep inside suppliers' business processes and vice versa. It tells suppliers which parts to get to which plant and when. TradeMatrix has saved Dell millions of dollars and has become a major competitive advantage. Dell's inventory averages one-tenth the average level of its rivals.[39]

Rather than innovation for the sake of innovation, many firms are turning to the marketing concept to guide their research. To give its scientists guidance, Dow first interviews customers to find out their wants and needs. A wish list of products and/or technical characteristics helps the scientists create innovations with market value. Dow recently created a fiber called XLA after learning that apparel makers wanted a "soft stretch" fibre with natural feel.

Businesses today must seek out new technology that will make them better competitors. New technology is making a significant impact on business. Canadian automotive assembly plants, for example, are able to produce 20 percent more cars with 8 percent fewer workers than just ten years ago. Companies not aware of technology changes can find their products rendered obsolete. Digital cameras significantly outsell traditional cameras that use film. You can imagine the impact of this on Kodak, which still generates 40 percent of its revenue from the sale of consumer film and photo-finishing services.

Innovation pays off big for creative organizations. One study found that the most innovative firms have an average profit margin growth of 3 percent higher than the typical firm.[40] Innovation starts with a country's educational system. In 2009, according to Research Infosource Inc., over $6 billion was spent on research at Canada's universities. Leading the way was the University of Toronto, where $845 million was spent on research. In all, 17 universities in Canada spent over $100 million on research in 2009.

REVIEW LEARNING OUTCOME 8

8 Identify the impact of technology on a firm

9 POLITICAL AND LEGAL FACTORS

Discuss the political and legal environment of marketing

Business needs government regulation to protect innovators of new technology, the interests of society in general, one business from another, and consumers. In turn, government needs business, because the marketplace generates taxes that support public efforts to build and maintain roads, educate our youth, protect health care, and so on. The private sector also serves as a counterweight to government. The decentralization of power inherent in a private-enterprise system such as ours places limits on the government that is essential for the survival of democracy.

Every aspect of a company's marketing mix is subject to laws and restrictions. It is the duty of marketing managers or their legal assistants to understand the laws and conform to them, because failure to comply with regulations can have major consequences for a firm. Sometimes just sensing trends and taking corrective action before a government agency acts can help avoid regulation. This didn't happen in the tobacco industry. As a result, it is facing tougher and tougher restrictions on its promotional activities. The legal environment is particularly challenging as laws are created at the federal, provincial, and municipal levels and often overlap. Moreover, laws are constantly changing.

The challenge is not simply to keep the marketing department out of trouble, but to help it implement creative new programs to accomplish marketing objectives. It is all too easy for a marketing manager or sometimes a lawyer to say no to a marketing innovation that actually entails little risk. For example, an overly cautious lawyer could hold up sales of a desirable new product by warning that the package design could prompt a copyright infringement suit. Thus it is important to have a thorough understanding of the laws established by the federal government, provincial governments, municipal governments, and regulatory agencies that control marketing-related issues.

FEDERAL LEGISLATION

The Combines Investigation Commission was established in 1888 to protect small businesses that were suffering as a result of collusive practices by larger businesses. In 1923, the Combines Investigation Act was passed to prevent anticompetitive conduct among businesses. Until 1975, this was the most important act affecting the legal environment of business.

Dissatisfaction with the Combines Investigation Act led to the passage in 1975 of Bill C-2, known as the Competition Act. At first, the Bureau of Competition Policy, which was part of Consumer and Corporate Affairs Canada, administered this act. Bill C-2 was updated in 1986 and is now administered by the Competition Bureau of Industry Canada. The Competition Bureau is an independent law-enforcement agency that contributes to the prosperity of Canadians by protecting and promoting competitive markets and enabling informed consumer choice.

Criminal offences under the Competition Act include the following: price fixing, bid rigging, false and misleading representations (e.g., saying that your product will do something that it won't), deceptive notice of winning a prize, abuse of a dominant position, price maintenance (i.e., manufacturers requiring retailers to charge a specific price), price discrimination, predatory pricing, misleading advertising, refusal to deal, and deceptive practices (such as bait-and-switch selling, certain forms of pyramid selling, and double-ticketing). Noncriminal matters dealt with by the act include mergers, exclusive dealing, consignment selling, and tied selling.

Competition Bureau
The federal department charged with administering most marketplace laws.

Headed by the Commissioner of Competition, the **Competition Bureau** is responsible for the administration and enforcement of the Competition Act, the Consumer Packaging and Labelling Act, the Textile Labelling Act, and the Precious Metals Marking Act. This bureau has several agencies (see Exhibit 3.8) and is responsible for enforcing the laws covering bankruptcy, trade practices, competition, credit, labelling and packaging, copyrights, hazardous products, patents, pensions, precious metals, and trademarks. The bureau's website, **www.competitionbureau.gc.ca**, lists the full range of responsibilities of the Competition Bureau and updates to the Competition Act and recent important Competition Bureau cases.

PROVINCIAL LAWS

For national companies, provincial legislation often poses difficulties because laws vary from province to province. Quebec's Bill 101 requires that French be the primary (and sometimes exclusive) language in all promotional and advertising activities in the province. Also, advertisers in Quebec are forbidden to target children directly. There are many provincial laws regulating pricing, business start-ups, door-to-door selling, Sunday business openings, and the sale of alcoholic beverages. As well, there are provincial laws that apply to certain types of businesses (e.g., travel agents, car dealers, realtors) and to certain types of business activities (e.g., billboards and direct mail advertising). Marketing managers must be aware of any legislation that directly affects their businesses. For example, Walmart (and other) stores in Ontario can sell wine, but the Liquor Control Board of Ontario sets the minimum price that these outlets can charge for each bottle of wine.

SELF-REGULATION

self-regulation
Programs voluntarily adopted by business groups to regulate the activities of their members.

Some business groups make efforts to police themselves. This is referred to as **self-regulation**. The Canadian Code of Advertising Standards, for example, was established by Canada's largest advertising agencies to monitor honesty and fairness in advertising. The Canadian Broadcasting Association, whose members include Canada's major television and radio stations, has developed its own code of ethics. The Canadian Marketing Association, whose members do over 80 percent of all telemarketing in Canada, has established guidelines for its members with regard to protecting consumers' privacy and right to not be contacted. Businesses that belong to the Better Business Bureau voluntarily agree to maintain fair business practices.

EXHIBIT 3.8

Organization of the Competition Bureau

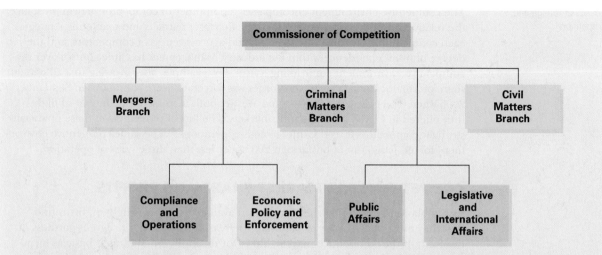

Commissioner of Competition: The current Commissioner of Competition is Melanie L. Aitken, appointed in August 2009.

Mergers Branch: Reviews merger transactions to assess whether a proposed merger is likely to prevent or substantially lessen competition.

Criminal Matters Branch: Enforces criminal matters such as conspiracies that lessen competition, price fixing, bid-rigging, price discrimination, predatory pricing, and restricting supply.

Civil Matters Branch: Reviews anticompetitive behaviour, such as abuse of a dominant position, restraints imposed by a supplier on a customer, refusal to supply, exclusive dealings, tied selling, price maintenance, etc.

Fair Business Practices Branch: Enforces provisions of the Competition Act dealing with false and misleading advertising, false representations, deceptive marketing practices, deceptive telemarketing, pyramid selling, misleading price claims, and ensuring that standards and regulations are met under the Consumer Packaging and Labelling Act, Precious Metals Marking Act and the Textile Labelling Act.

Compliance and Operations Branch: Responsible for ensuring that the various branches work within approved policies and procedures and have the resources they need to do their work.

Economic Policy and Enforcement Branch: Responsible for providing expertise on leading economic theory, advice on enforcement matters and policy/advocacy activities of the bureau, and for developing and disseminating economic knowledge.

Public Affairs Branch: Responsible for providing leadership, support, and advice in communicating to the public the bureau's contribution to competition. It is also the focal point for interactions between the bureau and Parliament, business, and consumer groups.

Legislative and International Affairs Branch: Responsible for input into legislative proposals relating to the Competition Act and other legislation administered and enforced by the bureau.

SOURCE: Competition Bureau of Canada, *What Is the Competition Bureau?* www.competitionbureau.gc.ca

REVIEW LEARNING OUTCOME 9

9   **Discuss the political and legal environment of marketing**

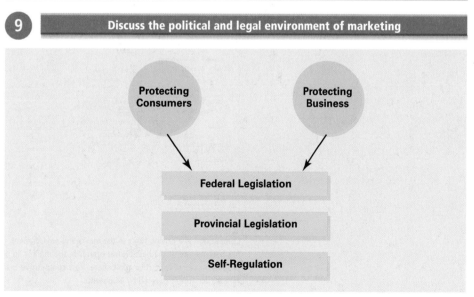

10 COMPETITIVE FACTORS

Explain the basics of foreign and domestic competition

The competitive environment encompasses the number of competitors a firm must face, the relative size of the competitors, the specific target markets and marketing strategies each competitor is pursuing, the strength and aggressiveness of competitors, and the degree of interdependence within the industry. Management has little control over the competitive environment confronting a firm. For example, after growing to a 20 percent share of Atlantic Canada air travel, CanJet was forced to cease operations in September 2006 when larger rivals Air Canada and WestJet both increased the number of flights they offered in CanJet's core Atlantic markets. The loss of passengers to these financially stronger competitors forced CanJet to cease operations.[41] The same competitive environment forced Jetsgo out of business in 2005 after less than three years of operation.

COMPETITION FOR MARKET SHARE AND PROFITS

As population growth slows, costs rise, and available resources tighten, firms find that they must work harder to maintain their profits and market share regardless of the form of the competitive market. Take, for example, something as basic as facial tissues. Kimberly-Clark and Procter & Gamble go head-to-head in this market. Kimberly-Clark is marketing its new three-ply tissue as the company's biggest innovation for Kleenex Facial Tissues in four decades. The new Kleenex Facial Tissue with Lotion is softer and 17 percent stronger than its predecessor, according to the company. P&G has added shea butter, a moisturizer, to its Puffs Plus line of lotion tissues as well as new box designs for three of its primary Puffs products. Lotion tissues make up 20 percent of the market and have been the fastest-growing segment. In the last few years, Kleenex, the market leader, has lost a few points of market share while Puffs

SOURCE: © THE PROCTER & GAMBLE COMPANY

Competition is a driving force in the marketing environment, including laundry detergent. Tide has become one of the best-known brands in the market, in part by continually improving its product and increasing its market share. How competitive is the world of detergents? The formula for Tide is covered by 44 patents.

has picked up a few points. The tissue battle is one of millions that goes on every day in the Canadian marketplace.[42]

In recent years, nobody has played the competition game better than P&G with its Tide brand. While the rest of the industry stagnated, Tide's sales climbed by over 40 percent to pass $2 billion. It now owns 40 percent of the laundry detergent market. What was the strategy used for Tide? First, P&G spends over $100 million a year promoting the Tide brand name through advertising on TV, billboards, subways, buses, magazines, and the Internet. Tide is the sponsor of a Nascar race car and youth soccer leagues. It holds publicity stunts, such as its U.S-wide Dirtiest Kid contest. Tide has made itself a brand icon—right up there with Coke and McDonald's.

But the real genius of Tide's strategy is its relentless stream of new and improved products. Each year, P&G spends heavily on R&D, a large portion of which goes toward developing new formulations of Tide. There's Tide With Bleach, Tide Free (which has no fragrance), Tide WearCare (which purports to keep fabrics vibrant longer), Tide Kick (whose package includes a nozzle to rub detergent directly into fabrics), and Tide HE (high-efficiency) for use in front-loading washers. In all, Tide has spawned more than 60 variations of itself. Has P&G's strategy been working? Procter & Gamble's sales have grown by over 30 percent from 2005 to 2009 and earnings over this time period have grown by 48.5 percent! P&G's sales are nearly $80 billion and earnings exceed $13 billion.[43]

REVIEW LEARNING OUTCOME 10

10 | **Explain the basics of foreign and domestic competition**

Highly Competitive Marketplace

Mature Industries

Slow growth/
No growth

Can only increase
market share by
taking it from a competitor.

GLOBAL COMPETITION

Walmart, Costco, Unilever, and Procter & Gamble are savvy international competitors conducting business throughout the world. Although these companies are not headquartered in Canada, they are leading sellers in many product categories in Canada. More and more foreign companies are looking at Canada as a ripe target market. Thus Canadian marketing managers can no longer worry about only domestic competitors. In automobiles, automotive parts, textiles, pharmaceuticals, retailing, steel, and many other areas, foreign competition has been strong and is getting stronger. In the past, many foreign firms penetrated Canadian markets by concentrating on price; today the emphasis has switched to product quality. Nestlé, Sony, Rolls-Royce, and premium imported wine and beer are noted for quality, not low prices. As Canadian companies formulate their marketing mixes, more and more it will be within an external environment consisting of a growing number of strong foreign competitors. Importantly, as has been witnessed over the past ten years in the Canadian automotive parts industry, as foreign competitors come into the market, it is not the weakest of the foreign firms that come here, it is the strongest.

REVIEW AND APPLICATIONS

1 **Discuss corporate social responsibility.** Responsibility in business refers to a firm's concern for the way its decisions affect society. Social responsibility has four components: economic, legal, ethical, and philanthropic. These are intertwined, yet the most fundamental is earning a profit. If a firm does not earn a profit, the other three responsibilities are moot. Most businesspeople believe they should do more than pursue profits. Although a company must consider its economic needs first, it must also operate within the law, do what is ethical and fair, and be a good corporate citizen. The concept of sustainability is that socially responsible companies will outperform their peers by focusing on the world's social problems and viewing them as an opportunity to earn profits and help the world at the same time.

1.1 Describe at least three situations in which you would not purchase the products of a firm even though that firm is very socially responsible.

1.2   A firm's only responsibility to society is to earn a fair profit. Comment.

1.3   Is sustainability a viable concept for Canadian businesses?

1.4   Illustrate how there can be conflicts between the needs and desires of various stakeholders.

2 **Describe the role of ethics and ethical decisions in business.** Business ethics may be viewed as a subset of the values of society as a whole. The ethical conduct of business-people is shaped by societal elements, including family, education, religion, and social movements. As members of society, businesspeople are morally obligated to consider the ethical implications of their decisions.

Ethical decision making is approached in three basic ways. The first approach examines the consequences of decisions. The second approach relies on rules and laws to guide decision making. The third approach is based on a theory of moral development that places individuals or groups in one of three developmental stages: preconventional morality, conventional morality, or postconventional morality.

Many companies develop a code of ethics to help their employees make ethical decisions. A code of ethics can help employees identify acceptable business practices, can be an effective internal control on behaviour, can help employees avoid confusion when determining whether decisions are ethical, and can facilitate discussion about what is right and wrong.

2.1   **WRITING** Write a paragraph discussing the ethical dilemma in the following situation and identify possible solutions: An insurance agent forgets to get the required signature from one of her clients who is buying an automobile insurance policy. The client acknowledges the purchase by giving the agent a signed personal cheque for the full amount. To avoid embarrassment and inconvenience, the agent forges the client's signature on the insurance application and sends it to the insurance company for processing.

2.2   Discuss the relationship between ethics and social responsibility.

3 **Discuss the external environment of marketing and explain how it affects a firm.** The external marketing environment consists of social, demographic, economic, technolog-ical, political and legal, and competitive variables. Marketers generally cannot control the elements of the external environment. Instead, they must understand how the external environment is changing and the impact of that change on the target market. Then marketing managers can create a marketing mix to effectively meet the needs of target customers.

3.1   What is the purpose of environmental scanning? Give an example.

3.2   **TEAM** Form six teams and make each one responsible for one of the uncontrollable elements in the marketing environment. Your boss, the company president, has asked each team to provide one-year and five-year forecasts of the major trends the firm will face. The firm is in the telecommunications equipment industry. It has no plans to become a telecommunications service provider like, for example, Verizon. Each team should use the library, the Internet, and other data sources to make its forecasts. Each team member should examine a minimum of one data source. The team should then pool its data and prepare its recommendation. A spokesperson for each team should present the findings to the class.

4 **Describe the social factors that affect marketing.** Within the external environment, social factors are perhaps the most difficult for marketers to anticipate. Several major social trends are currently shaping marketing strategies. First, people of all ages have a broader range of interests, defying traditional consumer profiles. Second, changing gender roles are bringing more women into the workforce and increasing the number of men who shop. Third, a greater number of dual-career families have created a demand for timesaving goods and services.

4.1   Every country has a set of core values and beliefs. These values may vary somewhat from region to region of the country. Identify five core values for your area of the country. Clip magazine advertisements that reflect these values and bring them to class.

4.2   Give an example of component lifestyles based on someone you know.

5 **Explain the importance to marketing managers of current demographic trends.** Today, several basic demographic patterns are influencing marketing mixes. Because the population is growing at a slower rate, marketers can no longer rely on profits from generally expanding markets. Marketers are also faced with increasingly experienced consumers among the younger generations such as tweens and teens. And because the population is also growing older, marketers are offering more products that appeal to middle-aged and older consumers.

5.1 Baby boomers in Canada are aging. Describe how this might affect the marketing mix for the following:

   a. Health clubs

   b. McDonald's

   c. Whirlpool Corporation

   d. Niagara Falls

   e. Zellers

5.2 **WRITING** You have been asked to address a local Chamber of Commerce on the subject of "Generation Y." Prepare an outline for your talk.

5.3 How should Ford Motor Company market differently to Generation Y, Generation X, and baby boomers?

6 **Explain the importance to marketing managers of multiculturalism and growing ethnic markets.** Multiculturalism occurs when all major ethnic groups in an area are roughly equally represented. Growing multiculturalism makes the marketer's task more challenging. Canada is not a melting pot but numerous mini-melting pots. Ethnic minorities are the fastest-growing segment of the population. Many companies are now creating departments and committees to effectively target multicultural market segments. Companies have found that ethnic markets are not homogeneous.

6.1 **WRITING** Go to the library and look up a minority market such as the Chinese or South Asian market. Write a memo to your boss that details the many submarkets within the minority segment.

6.2 **ONLINE** Use the Internet to find examples of large companies that direct marketing mixes to different ethnic groups.

7 **Identify consumer and marketer reactions to the state of the economy.** In recent years, incomes have risen at a slow pace. At the same time, the financial power of women has increased and they are making the purchasing decisions for many products in traditionally male-dominated areas. During a time of inflation, marketers generally attempt to maintain level pricing to avoid losing customer brand loyalty. During times of recession, many marketers maintain or reduce prices to counter the effects of decreased demand; they also concentrate on increasing production efficiency and improving customer service.

7.1 Explain how consumers' buying habits may change during a recessionary period.

7.2 **WRITING** Periods of inflation require firms to alter their marketing mix. Suppose a recent economic forecast predicts inflation to be almost 10 percent during the next 18 months. Your company manufactures hand tools for the home gardener. Write a memo to the company president explaining how the firm may have to alter its marketing mix.

8 **Identify the impact of technology on a firm.** Monitoring new technology is essential to keeping up with competitors in today's marketing environment. Information technology and the Internet have been driving increased productivity for the past decade. Without innovation, companies can't compete in global markets.

8.1 Give three examples of how technology has benefited marketers. Also, give several examples of how firms have been hurt by not keeping up with technological changes.

9 Discuss the political and legal environment of marketing. All marketing activities are subject to municipal, provincial, and federal laws and the rulings of regulatory agencies. Marketers are responsible for remaining aware of and abiding by such regulations.

9.1 Governments have been both praised and criticized for their regulation of marketing activities. To what degree do you think the government should regulate marketing? Explain your position.

9.2 Can you think of any areas where consumer protection laws are needed or need to be strengthened?

10 Explain the basics of foreign and domestic competition. The competitive environment encompasses the number of competitors a firm must face, the relative sizes of the competitors, how the companies compete, and the degree of interdependence within the industry. Declining population growth, rising costs, and shortages of resources have heightened domestic competition. Meanwhile, dwindling international barriers are bringing in more foreign competitors and offering expanding opportunities for Canadian companies abroad.

10.1 Explain how the nature of competition is changing in Canada.

10.2 Might there be times when a company becomes too competitive? If so, what could be the consequences?

TERMS

applied research 72
baby boomers 65
basic research 72
code of ethics 56
Competition Bureau 74
component lifestyles 60
corporate social responsibility 52
demography 61
environmental management 58

ethics 54
Generation X 64
Generation Y 63
green marketing 53
inflation 70
laws 54
morals 54
multiculturalism 67
purchasing power 70

pyramid of corporate social
  responsibility 52
recession 71
self-regulation 74
sustainability 52
target market 57
teens 63
tweens 62
visible minority 67

EXERCISES

APPLICATION EXERCISE

 Demographic factors play a big role in shaping the external marketing environment. One of those demographic factors is culture. The importance of cultural understanding cannot be overstated, especially in today's global marketplace and our own multicultural country. Many of us, though, are quick to prejudge other cultural norms as wrong, or unimportant, just because they are different.

One way to be exposed to another culture is by examining the foods typical of that culture. In this exercise, you will need to work in a team to create a guide to ethnic dining in your city or area. The finished guide will be descriptive in nature and it is not meant to be a rating guide.

Activities

1. Identify ethnic dining categories for inclusion in your guide. Once you have identified categories for your area, make a list of restaurants for each category.

2. You will need to create a data collection form so that the same information is collected from each restaurant. For example, you will want to include the name, address, and phone number for each restaurant. Think of other information that would be helpful.

3. Divide up the restaurant list your team generated in activity 1 so that each team member is responsible for collecting information from a certain number of restaurants. Consider dividing the

list geographically so that each team member can visit an assortment of ethnic restaurants. If possible, eat at a few of the restaurants in addition to collecting information. After you have all the information collected, meet to review and compare findings.

4. Was there a meal or type of food that you particularly liked? Disliked? Which type of ethnic restaurant seemed most foreign to you? Why was that?

ETHICS EXERCISE

Gary Caplan has developed a new "energy drink" designed to burn calories while sleeping, which he intends to market to overweight consumers. Data suggest that at least 20 percent of the population is obese. Gary's father, a doctor, argues that it's unethical to target the obese—that they are as vulnerable a target market as the elderly and children.

Questions

1. Is Gary targeting a "vulnerable" market?

2.  Does the CMA Code of Ethics address this issue? Go to **www.the-cma. org/consumer/ethics.cfm** and review the code. Then write a brief paragraph on what the CMA Code of Ethics contains that relates to Gary's marketing situation.

CASE STUDY

STARBUCKS: SELLING COFFEE IN THE LAND OF TEA

Starbucks, which has been operating in Canada since 1987 and now has over one thousand outlets across the country, has been doing business in China since 1999 when it opened its first outlet in Beijing. Today, hundreds of Starbucks stores sell coffee in the land of tea, including one at the Great Wall. Starbucks has become one of the most popular brands among the country's 20- to 40-year-old upwardly mobile Chinese, or "Chuppies," as they are called. So far, China accounts for about 10 percent of Starbucks' global sales. Chairman Howard Schultz believes that China will someday be the company's largest market outside North America. "The market response," he says, "has exceeded our expectations."

This may seem surprising when you consider the fact that the majority of China's 1.1 billion-plus population are tea drinkers who didn't know what coffee was until Nestlé introduced a powdered version to store shelves in the 1980s. But Starbucks is betting that it can win the new generation over by marketing its signature product as an emblem of modern China's new sophistication.

"Coffee represents the change," says Wang Jinlong, president of Starbucks Greater China. "The disposable income is concentrated on the young people, and this is the place they want to come." Success in China could depend on how well Starbucks markets itself to what Wang calls the "little emperors." China's one-child law has spawned a generation that isn't interested in collective goals, he says. Instead, they embrace the Western belief in individuality that Starbucks embodies.

After surveying Chinese consumers, Starbucks compiled a list of the top reasons they go to cafés. Surprisingly, the number one reason was "to gather with family and friends," while "to drink coffee" lagged behind at number six. Living spaces are generally small and cramped in China, making places to congregate important to the Chinese.

Da Wei Sun, manager of outlets in Beijing, believes that Starbucks found success in China because it took this idea of a place to gather and gave people in the cities a "third space" beyond work and home, making it cool to have a latte and hang out. Starbucks offers more food on the Chinese menu, including duck sandwiches, moon pies, and green-tea cheesecake, than in other countries—and more seating as well. Only 20 percent of Canadian customers eat and drink inside a Starbucks store after ordering, but the number is close to 90 percent in China.

China remains a communist country, so a change in its one-party dictatorship could potentially affect business overnight. Schultz says the key to establishing stores there is to first find local partners who understand the changing political and business landscapes. Starbucks initially entered China by authorizing local developers to use its brand and setting up joint ventures with partners.

Industry analyst Pei Liang advised that for long-term success in China, Starbucks would need to acquire controlling stakes in its joint ventures. This, Pei explained, would strengthen management's control and put them in a position to reap more of the profits as the market grew. "Licensing or holding a minority stake is an effective tool when first stepping into a new market because it involves a small investment," says Pei. "But Starbucks, the brand's owner, receives only royalty fees from the licensee."

In late 2006, Starbucks announced that it was buying out its partner in China and taking control of 60 stores. The market had changed after Beijing entered the World Trade Organization in 2001, making it easier for foreign companies to navigate alone. "Buying out one's partner is becoming more common," says industry consultant Kent D. Kedl. "Starbucks probably feels they know better how China works now so they can go it on their own."

Chairman Howard Schultz says that Starbucks will concentrate most of its future expansion efforts in China, and Kedl predicts it will see continued success there: "It's not just a drink in China. It's a destination. It's a place to be seen and a place to show how modern one is." And with China's economy continuing to grow in double digits, the number of Chuppies willing to pay $3.63 for a Mocha Frappuccino Grande is likely to grow too.[44]

Questions

1. Many of the same environmental factors, such as cultural factors, that operate in the domestic market also exist internationally. Discuss key cultural factors Starbucks had to consider as it expanded into China.

2. Discuss the key political and legal factors Starbucks had to consider in the Chinese marketplace. What are the risks of entering a country with these factors? What changes have occurred in China's political and legal structure to the advantage of foreign companies?

3. What demographic factors were important for Starbucks to understand in China? What were the demographics they decided to target?

4. What was the initial global-market strategy Starbucks employed to enter China? Discuss the advantages and disadvantages to this early strategy. How has its strategy changed since then and why?

VIDEO CASE

CBC

A LOOK AT THE EDUCATIONAL TOY MARKET

New parents, of course, try to bring up their child as best they can. Some may buy books to read with titles like *How to Raise a Brighter Child, How to Maximize Your Child's Learning Ability,* or *Your Child Can Think Like a Genius* to help their upbringing skills. There's also another option offered to parents: educational toys or "edu-toys" for short. Educational toys are now a billion-dollar-plus market in Canada. But do they work?

Visit any toy store and you'll find a large section of educational toys marketed to toddlers as young as three to six months of age. Some of the largest educational toy companies are Baby Einstein (now owned by Disney), Brainy Baby, and Baby Genius. Each of these companies has North America–wide total sales ranging from over $300 million to nearly $1 billion. Clearly parents are responding to the educational toy market. What parent wants their child to lag behind in learning? And the educational toy makers feed on this parental concern.

According to Dr. Hillel Goelman, a professor of early childhood development at the University of British Columbia, "There's no research that shows that kids who use educational toys learn faster, better, or learn more. There's no data right now that I've seen that shows these kids outperform any other kids who don't use these materials. What the research shows is that parents are buying them."

The toy companies don't directly promise to increase your baby's IQ. They use terms like "develop," "discover," "sensory stimulation," and "motor skills development" in their advertising and on their packaging. Dr. Goelman explains that "sensory development" means that the child can see and hold the toy. "Motor development" means that the child can use its fingers to make a noise come out of the toy. These kinds of claims make a toy sound more impressive and, as Dr. Goelman puts it, "make[s] the toy much more marketable." And parents are reacting to this marketing.

It seems the companies making these educational toy products do very little research into the learning benefits of their products. Their research shows only that the child plays with the products. In fact, the founders of Baby Einstein even claim that the name chosen for their company and line of products has nothing to do with the fact that Einstein was a genius, the name was chosen because Einstein was a great humanitarian!

A group called the Campaign for a Commercial-Free Childhood filed a complaint against the major makers of educational toys for toddlers for false and deceptive advertising (see the group's website **www.commercialfreechildhood.org** for details on the complaint). Let's take a look at the educational toy market and hear from some of the makers of these toys.[45]

Questions

1. What are your first impressions of educational toys? Are the companies marketing these toys being completely honest with parents?

2. Examine the websites of the major educational toy producers. What do they say about their products and how do they justify the claims that they make?

3. What do you see as the main ethical issues when selling infant products for which there is little research to support their benefits?

4. If you are not yet a parent, do you think that you will buy educational toys for your first child? Why or why not?

MARKETING & YOU RESULTS

The higher your score, the more important you think ethics and socially responsible behaviour are to achieving corporate objectives. A high score also suggests that you are an ethical idealist, or someone who sees right and wrong as absolute, rather than an ethical relativist, or someone who sees right and wrong as situation dependent.

MARKETING MISCUE

HAS UNILEVER BEGUN TO RETOUCH THE REAL?

In 2004, Unilever undertook a major appraisal of Dove, the top-selling cleansing soap brand in Canada. The appraisal found that only 2 percent of women worldwide (and only 1 percent in Canada) described themselves as beautiful. Nearly 80 percent of women in Canada thought that the media set unrealistic standards of beauty—standards that most women would never be able to achieve. These marketplace perceptions were coming at a time when women seemed prepared to spend money on themselves, and Dove brand managers wanted that money to be spent on its line of new and existing products.

Unilever launched the "Real Beauty" campaign, developed in part by the Toronto office of Ogilvy & Mather, for Dove shortly after the appraisal. This first campaign used women scouted off the streets, not models. Thus the ads featured "real women" with appearances that did not fit the common stereotype about advertising models. The advertising invited viewers to judge the women in the ads with respect to traditional norms about beauty—weight, skin, hair—and to cast their votes on the campaign's dedicated website, **www.campaignforrealbeauty.com.**

The second phase of the Real Beauty campaign featured six women, with emphasis on the women's real bodies and real curves. Dove's intention was to feature real women who were not the products of Botox procedures, silicone-based hair serums, dental bleaching, or the tanning salon.

In 2007, the third phase of the campaign celebrated women who were over 50 years of age. The campaign, photographed by world-renowned photographer Annie Leibovitz, brought the beauty of the 50-plus woman to life–wrinkles, age spots, and grey hair included!

The fourth phase of the ad campaign focused on younger females and how they were bombarded with unrealistic messages about beauty. Implementing this phase of the campaign, Dove engaged the forces of Hollywood—the place where young females see the more unrealistic body images via young movie stars in the print media and on the screen. Dove released on-line films about girls, self-esteem, and physical appearance. The short film, *Evolution,* showed the accelerated transformation of a girl going from frumpy (natural) to billboard ready. *Evolution* won Cyber and Film Grand Prix awards at the Cannes Lions International Advertising Festival.

But did Dove go too far in its efforts? In late 2007, a *Business Week* story questioned whether Dove was really building self-esteem among girls or if it was actually encouraging girls to pass

SOURCE: COURTESY OF UNILEVER CANADA INC.

SOURCE: COURTESY OF UNILEVER CANADA INC

judgment on other girls. Interviews with females in the target age group for the fourth phase of the ad campaign raised the following issues with respect to the on-line films:

- Dove depicted self-esteem as a "girl" issue—males have self-esteem problems too (was Dove essentially reinforcing the age-old bias that girls are weak?).

- Perfection and self-respect were not synonymous.

- Wanting to look good did not have to mean that a female was vain.

- Obsessive behaviours (eating disorders, compulsive plastic surgeries) were not necessarily the result of the beauty industry.

Then, in 2008, another magazine story suggested that the photos of the "real" women in Dove's ads had been retouched. Dove, the photographer, and the photo retoucher claimed that the photos were not digitally altered, except to remove dust and to do colour correction. They were adamant that the photos still portrayed "real" women but the brouhaha surrounding the story cast doubt on the images Dove used to portray women in their 50s, 60s, and 70s.[1]

Questions

1. Is it Unilever's job to promote self-esteem among women, or is it the company's role to get the Dove brand into the hands of consumers?

2. What are examples from other companies in which social issues are linked to the company or the company's brands?

CRITICAL THINKING CASE

CUTCO CORPORATION: GOING GREEN. GOING FORWARD

CUTCO Corporation, the largest marketer of high-quality kitchen cutlery and accessories in Canada, celebrated its 60th anniversary in 2009. Over 100 kitchen cutlery products are sold under the CUTCO name, as well as a variety of kitchen gadgets, utensils, and flatware. The company also carries a line of cookware, sporting and pocket knives, and garden tools.

Boasting millions of satisfied customers and annual sales in excess of $200 million, CUTCO's commitment to quality and innovation is evident throughout the manufacture and marketing of the company's products. CUTCO stands behind each and every product with a "Forever" satisfaction guarantee. The guarantee has four components:

1. "Forever" Performance Guarantee

2. "Forever" Sharpness Guarantee

3. "Forever" Replace Service Agreement for Misuse or Abuse

4. 15-day Unconditional Money Back Guarantee

The company's "Forever" guarantee ensures that CUTCO cutlery stays in the family for generations to come. Given this backdrop of the company's high-quality product offering in difficult economic times, the company initiated a "going green" effort in 2009.

Everyone, from individual consumers to corporate decision makers, is talking about sustainability, going green, and reducing the carbon footprint. However, some companies' efforts are more "greenwashing" than truly intended for the well-being of the environment. Greenwashing is what companies do (e.g., promotional efforts) to make themselves look more environmentally friendly than they really are.

For CUTCO Corporation, however, the plan is not for a "go-green project" or to engage in "greenwashing." Rather, the company is instilling "going green" initiatives that, like the product's "Forever" guarantee, stay with the company forever. CUTCO's marketing coordinator, Pam Bailey, was given the opportunity to create and coordinate a companywide "Going Green" effort. The focus initially was the "low-hanging fruit" (things that were easy to do). Within one year, Bailey, the Green Team, and CUTCO had accomplished the following:

- Implemented computer power management for estimated savings of $41,000 annually.

- Turned off centre row lighting on one floor of the administration building for estimated savings of $7,500 annually.

- Created a recycling program to collect plastic, glass, aluminum, and tin cans, as well as reuse or recycle CUTCO product components, all resulting in a 26 percent decrease in garbage from all CUTCO facilities.

- Set company printers to automatically duplex; departments switched to two-sided reports; paper use decreased 27 percent.

- Printed company newsletter on 50 percent recycled paper.

- Encouraged its employees to bring their own reusable plates, cups, and utensils to Christmas lunch, resulting in only two bags of garbage from the party.

CUTCO Corporation's "Going Green. Going Forward" effort is part and parcel of the company's internal processes, and the company plans to continually work toward going green. It is not holding itself up as a company that has "gone green," nor is it touting its initiatives externally. Rather, like the CUTCO product, the results will speak for themselves.[2]

Questions

1. Differentiate between "going green" and "greenwashing" within the context of a marketing philosophy.

2. Are there any particular market demographics that are more or less suitable to environmental sustainability initiatives?

PART

2

Analyzing
Marketing
Opportunities

4 ⟩ Consumer Decision Making

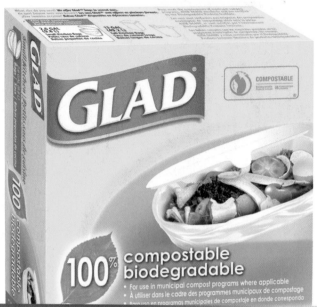

SOURCE: © 2010 THE GLAD PRODUCTS COMPANY. GLAD® IS A REGISTERED
TRADEMARK OF THE GLAD PRODUCTS COMPANY. USED WITH PERMISSION.

LEARNING OUTCOMES

1 Explain why marketing managers should understand consumer behaviour

2 Analyze the components of the consumer decision-making process

3 Explain the consumer's postpurchase evaluation process

4 Identify the types of consumer buying decisions and discuss the significance of consumer involvement

5 Identify and understand the cultural factors that affect consumer buying decisions

6 Identify and understand the social factors that affect consumer buying decisions

7 Identify and understand the individual factors that affect consumer buying decisions

8 Identify and understand the psychological factors that affect consumer buying decisions

(ⱽ) MARKETING & YOU

What is your buying behaviour?
  Using the scales below, enter your answers or record them on a separate page.

1	2	3	4	5
Very Often		Sometimes		Never

__ I feel others would be horrified if they knew of my spending habits.
__ I've bought things even though I knew I couldn't afford them.
__ I've written a cheque when I knew I didn't have enough money in the bank to cover it.

__ I've bought myself something in order to make myself feel better.
__ I've felt anxious or nervous on days I didn't go shopping.
__ I've made only the minimum payments on my credit cards.

1	2	3	4	5
Strongly agree				Strongly disagree

__ If I have any money left at the end of the pay period, I just have to spend it.
__ Having more money would solve my problems.
__ I have bought something, arrived home, and didn't know why I had bought it.

Now total your score. Read the chapter to find out what your score means at the end.

SOURCE: REPRINTED WITH PERMISSION FROM *MARKETING SCALES HANDBOOK* VOL. III, PUBLISHED BY THE AMERICAN MARKETING ASSOCIATION, G. BRUNER, K. JAMES, H. HENSEL, EDS. SCALE #98, P. 185.

Understanding how consumers shop, what they are looking for when they evaluate products, and why they purchase or not is extremely important to marketers. Astute marketers recognize the importance of coming up with unique ways to respond to particular concerns of consumers to achieve marketing success. Consider the grocery industry where marketers have learned that Canadian consumers are interested in environmentally friendly "green" products but this interest is tempered by "saving" money as well.

A survey of 25,000 Canadians by BrandSpark International reported the following factors as the key motivating forces behind new product purchases: "provide better value for money"—95 percent of respondents; "offers better quality"—94.5 percent of respondents; "offers a healthier option"—91 percent of respondents; "is longer lasting/more durable"—89 percent of respondents; "is better for the environment"—84.5 percent of respondents; and "is easier to use"—83 percent of respondents.

Although 84.5 percent of respondents reported that being better for the environment was an important consideration in selecting products, only 51 percent stated they were willing to pay more for such products.

The survey looked at which new grocery product brands that Canadian consumers felt were the best and the result was that GLAD® kitchen bags were rated as the best new product in Canada. Consumers commented that the GLAD® garbage bags were "an environmentally friendly product that works well." However, before marketers jump on to the green bandwagon with both feet, some other findings from this survey of consumers need to be taken into account. For example, 90 percent of consumers said that "manufacturers still have a long way to go to reduce packaging"; 83 percent said, "Some companies are exploiting environmentally friendly claims for marketing purposes," meaning that the claims were not seen as genuine; 66 percent said, "I am trying to buy less bottled water"; 63 percent said they were "trying to buy products that were as natural as possible"; while only 49 percent said they believed "organic products are healthier" and only 32 percent were "willing to pay more for products that are organic."

One of the key conclusions from BrandSpark's survey is that although consumers want environmentally friendly products, this desire does not come at the expense of buying good brands that are trusted. If you can combine all three characteristics as GLAD® compostable bags managed to do, then you have a winner![1]

Is the trend to environmentally friendly products really as strong as some marketers think? How can marketers "truly" tap into this trend without being perceived as exploiting the situation rather than demonstrating a "genuine" concern? What factors affect the buying decision for consumer products? Questions like these will be considered as you read this chapter on the consumer decision-making process and its influences.

SOURCE: REBECCA HARRIS, "BAGGING A WINNER," MARKETING MAGAZINE, MARCH 23, 2009, 34–35.

1 THE IMPORTANCE OF UNDERSTANDING CONSUMER BEHAVIOUR

Explain why marketing managers should understand consumer behaviour

consumer behaviour
Processes a consumer uses to make purchase decisions, as well as to use and dispose of purchased goods or services; also includes factors that influence purchase decisions and product use.

Consumers' product and service preferences are constantly changing. Marketing managers must understand these desires in order to create a proper marketing mix for a well-defined market. Therefore, it is critical for marketing managers to have a thorough knowledge of consumer behaviour. **Consumer behaviour** describes how consumers make purchase decisions and how they use and dispose of the purchased goods or services. The study of consumer behaviour also includes the factors that influence purchase decisions and product use.

Understanding how consumers make purchase decisions can help marketing managers in several ways. For example, if an automobile marketing manager knows through research that fuel economy is the most important attribute for new car selection in a certain target market, the manufacturer can redesign the product to meet that requirement. If the company cannot change the design in the short run, it can use promotion in an effort to change consumers' decision-making criteria—for example, by promoting style, durability, and cargo capacity.

REVIEW LEARNING OUTCOME 1

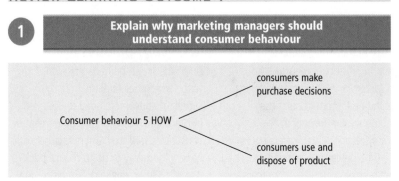

2 THE CONSUMER DECISION-MAKING PROCESS

Analyze the components of the consumer decision-making process

consumer decision-making process
A five-step process used by consumers when buying goods or services.

When buying products, consumers generally follow the **consumer decision-making process** shown in Exhibit 4.1: (1) need recognition, (2) information search, (3) evaluation of alternatives, (4) purchase, and (5) postpurchase behaviour. These five steps represent a basic process that can be used as a guide for studying how consumers make decisions. It is important to note, though, that consumers' decisions do not always proceed in order through all these steps. In fact, the consumer may end the process at any time and may not even make a purchase. The section on the types of consumer buying decisions later in the chapter discusses why a consumer's progression through these steps may vary. We begin, however, by examining the basic purchase process in greater detail.

NEED RECOGNITION

need recognition
Result of an imbalance between actual and desired states.

want
The way a consumer goes about addressing a need.

stimulus
Any unit of input affecting one or more of the five senses: sight, smell, taste, touch, hearing.

The first stage in the consumer decision-making process is need recognition. **Need recognition** occurs when consumers are faced with an imbalance between actual and desired states that arouses and activates the consumer decision-making process. A **want** is the way that a consumer goes about addressing a need. For example, have you ever got blisters from an old running shoe? Or maybe you have seen a TV commercial for a new electrically powered car and wanted to buy it. Need recognition is triggered when a consumer is exposed to either an internal or an external **stimulus**. *Internal stimuli* are things you feel or experience like thirst or hearing your stomach growl. *External stimuli* are influences on your thoughts and senses from an outside source like the smooth feel of the drive in your friend's new car, the flavour of the new gum sample you tried at the grocery store, the unique design of a package, a brand name

EXHIBIT 4.1

Consumer Decision-Making Process

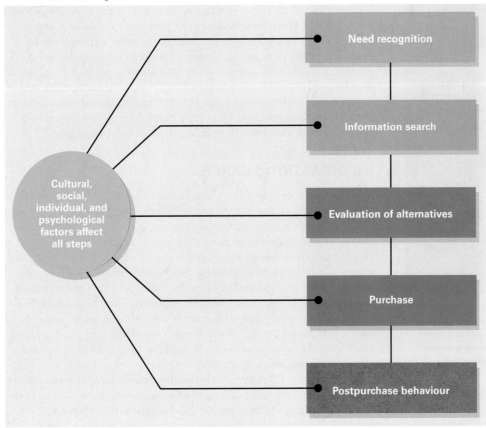

Need recognition

Information search

Cultural, social, individual, and psychological factors affect all steps

Evaluation of alternatives

Purchase

Postpurchase behaviour

mentioned by a friend, a product ad on a television show, and the smell of cologne worn by a stranger.

A marketing manager's objective is to get consumers to recognize an imbalance between their present status and their preferred state. Marketers most often use advertising and sales promotion to provide a need recognition stimulus. Surveying buyer preferences provides marketers with information about consumer wants and needs that can be used to tailor products and services. Marketing managers can influence the creation of wants on the part of the consumer. For example, when college and university students move into their own apartment or residence for the first time, they often need to furnish it, and they prefer new furniture rather than hand-me-downs from family and friends. A want can be for a specific product or it can be for a certain attribute or feature of a product. College and university students not only need home furnishings, but also want furnishings that reflect their personal sense of style. Similarly, consumers may want fast-food drive-throughs, on-demand cable movies, and Internet banking to fulfill their need for convenience.

Another way that marketers create new wants is by coupling them with existing wants. For example, Ikea, the home furnishings giant, watches home decor trends and then creates affordable, trendy furniture that they display in their stores. To create new wants, "in between display units, Ikea uses subtle push marketing to promote good-to-go products. These include picture frames, kitchen ware, trailing gangs, stationery, home tools and even candles that may or may not be part and parcel of the adjacent display units. This in itself instigates desire for a purchase, sometimes just to bring something home from the Ikea experience."[2]

Consumers recognize unfulfilled wants in various ways. The two most common occur when a current product isn't performing properly and when the consumer is about to run out of something that is generally kept on hand. Consumers may also recognize unfulfilled wants if they become aware of a product whose features make it seem superior to the one currently used. Such wants are usually created by advertising and other promotional activities. For example, going well beyond the difficult-to-access features in most "wireless" phones devices, Apple has been at the forefront of developing portable media and communication centres with its iPhone touch-screen device. When it was introduced, its competitors used primarily key-based phone interfaces whereas the Apple touch-screen interface allowed users to more easily make phone calls, send text messages, access e-mail, take photos, shoot movies, watch movies, watch televisions shows, listen to music, play video games, and browse the Internet on Wi-Fi or through a subscription provider; provided portable GPS navigation; and even had thousands of specific software applications. As the competitors scramble to catch up, Apple continues to innovate and introduced the iTablet in 2010.[3]

SOURCE: © PRNEWSFOTO/STONYFIELD FARM/AP IMAGES

Unlike nonmarketing-controlled information, which is neutral, marketing-controlled information is biased toward a specific product. This ad from Stonyfield Farm might be doing double duty—attempting to build bias for hormone-free Stonyfield products and against its possibly growth-hormone-using competitors' products.

internal information search
The process of recalling past information stored in the memory.

external information search
The process of seeking information in the outside environment.

nonmarketing-controlled information source
A product information source that is not associated with advertising or promotion.

Marketers selling their products in global markets must carefully observe the needs and wants of consumers in various regions. Unilever hit on an unrecognized need of European consumers when it introduced Persil tablets, a form of premeasured laundry detergent in tablet form. Though the tablets are more expensive than regular laundry detergents, Unilever found that European consumers considered laundry a chore and wanted the process to be as simple and uncomplicated as possible. Unilever launched the tablets as less messy and more convenient. The tablets proved so popular in the United Kingdom that Unilever's Persil brand edged ahead of rival Procter & Gamble's best-selling Ariel powder detergent.[4]

INFORMATION SEARCH

After recognizing a need or want, consumers search for information about the various alternatives available to satisfy it. For example, as gasoline prices increase, many people are searching for information on vehicles that use alternatives to gasoline, like Chevrolet's new electric car, the Volt. An information search can occur internally or externally, or both. In an **internal information search**, the person recalls information stored in his or her memory. This stored information stems largely from previous experience with a product. For example, while travelling with your family, you encounter a hotel where you stayed during winter break earlier that year. By searching your memory, you can probably remember whether the hotel had clean rooms and friendly service.

In contrast, an **external information search** seeks information in the outside environment. There are two basic types of external information sources: nonmarketing-controlled and marketing-controlled. A **nonmarketing-controlled information source** is not associated with marketers promoting a product. These information sources include personal experiences (trying or observing a new product); personal sources (family, friends, acquaintances, co-workers who may recommend a product or service); and public sources, such as the Canadian Standards Association (CSA), the Canadian Automobile Association (CAA), and other rating organizations that comment on products and services. If you are in the mood to go to the movies, you may search your memory for past experiences at various theatres when determining which one to go to (personal experience). To choose which movie you will see, you may rely on the recommendations of your friends and family members (personal sources). Alternatively, you may read the critical reviews in the local paper, go on-line, or watch the long-running television show *At the Movies* (public sources). Marketers gather information on how these information sources work and use this information to attract customers. For example, automobile manufacturers know that younger customers are likely to get information from friends and family, so they try to develop enthusiasm for their products via word of mouth.

In the digital age, consumers have access to many sources of nonmarketing-controlled information. On the Internet there are blogs, bulletin boards, activist websites, web forums, and specific opinion sites such as the Canadian Toy Testing Council (**www.toy-testing.org**) and the Automobile Protection Association (**www.apa.ca**) among many others. Aside from Internet, the use of social media such as Facebook, MySpace, and Twitter are also key sources of nonmarketing-controlled information for consumers. "Facebook is Canada's dominant social network and 87% of Canadians using social media have tried Facebook, compared with 33% for MySpace and 13% for Twitter."[5] It is important to note that marketers are also active participants in the nonmarketing-controlled information arena as they seek alternative ways to reach out to consumers.

According to statistics from the most recent report of the Canadian Internet Project (**www.ciponline.ca**), Canadian Internet users were on-line for over 17 hours per week, and the most recent estimate from **www.internetworldstats.com** reports that over 28 million Canadians are Internet users, meaning there is over 84 percent usage penetration in the Canadian population.[6]

The latest research has examined how consumers use information picked up on the Internet. For example, in Web forums, the information seeker has normally never met the information provider or interacted with the person before. Researchers found that an information provider's response speed, the extent to which the provider's previous responses within the forum had been positively evaluated by others, and the breadth of the provider's previous responses across different but related topics affected the information seeker's judgment about the value of the information. So, for example, if other information seekers had found the provider trustworthy, then the current seeker tended to believe the information.[7]

marketing-controlled information source
A product information source that originates with marketers promoting the product.

A **marketing-controlled information source** is biased toward a specific product because it originates with marketers promoting that product. Marketing-controlled information sources include mass-media advertising (radio, newspaper, television, and magazine advertising), sales promotion (contests, displays, premiums, and so forth), salespeople, product labels and packaging, and the Internet. One survey of Canadians reports that "today's advertising is a non-stop barrage . . . to 73 percent of Canadians. . . . But 56 percent of them are totally okay with that. . . . Only 31 percent . . . call the ceaseless bombardment of advertising unacceptable."[8] Many consumers, however, are wary about the information they receive from marketing-controlled sources, arguing that most marketing campaigns stress the product's positive attributes and ignore its faults. These sentiments tend to be stronger among better-educated and higher-income consumers. Commercially funded media like television networks, newspapers, radio stations, and magazines are normally strongly influenced by marketers who fund them through their advertising. However, they may become uncontrollable in the case of a crisis. For example, in 2010 the massive Toyota automotive faulty accelerator pedal recall of over 270,000 Canadian-sold cars was heavily reported on in the media. The media provided information that there had been similarly reported problems in some Toyota vehicles years before the company enacted their recall. Many consumers felt betrayed by Toyota, whose long-running advertisements had promised quality and reliability, attributes that were now highly questionable in the wake of the company's massive accelerator pedal recall.[9]

The extent to which an individual conducts an external search depends on his or her perceived risk, knowledge, prior experience, and level of interest in the good or service. Generally, as the perceived risk of the purchase increases, the consumer enlarges the search and considers more alternative brands. For instance, say you want to buy a large-screen high-definition television. The decision is a relatively risky one owing to the expense and the technical nature of the television's features, so you are motivated to search for information about models, options, and capabilities. You may decide to compare attributes of many different brands by visiting **www.cnet.com** and take a couple of hours to view all the written and video reviews on the televisions. You may believe that the value of the time expended in finding information will be less than the cost of buying the wrong television. In contrast, more than 60 percent of bar patrons don't know what they will drink until seconds before they place their order, challenging the marketers of alcoholic beverages to find ways of "educating" potential customers on the spot.[10]

A consumer's knowledge about the product or service will also affect the extent of an external information search. A consumer who is knowledgeable and well informed about a potential purchase is less likely to search for additional information. In addition, the more knowledgeable the consumers are, the more efficiently they will conduct the search process, thereby requiring less time to search. For example, many consumers know that on-line travel services like Expedia and Travelocity have great package prices so they don't bother visiting the websites of the airlines and hotels they might be interested in.

The extent of a consumer's external search is also affected by confidence in one's decision-making ability. A confident consumer not only has sufficient stored information about the product but also feels self-assured about making the right decision. People lacking this confidence will continue an information search even when they know a great deal about the product. Consumers with prior experience in buying a certain product will have less perceived risk than inexperienced consumers. Therefore, they will spend less time searching and limit the number of products they consider.

A third factor influencing the external information search is product experience. Consumers who have had a positive prior experience with a product are more likely to limit their search to only those items relating to the positive experience. For example, when flying, consumers are likely to choose airlines with which they have had positive experiences, such as consistent on-time arrivals. They will avoid airlines with which they have had a negative experience, such as lost luggage.

Finally, the extent of the search undertaken is positively related to the amount of interest a consumer has in a product. A consumer who is more interested in a product will spend more time searching for information and alternatives. Suppose you are a dedicated runner who reads jogging and fitness magazines and catalogues. In searching for a new pair of running shoes, you may enjoy reading about the new brands available and spend more time and effort than other buyers in deciding on the right shoe.

evoked set (consideration set)
Group of brands, resulting from an information search, from which a buyer can choose.

The consumer's information search should yield a group of brands, sometimes called the buyer's **evoked set** (or **consideration set**), which are the consumer's most preferred alternatives. From this set, the buyer will further evaluate the alternatives and make a choice. Consumers do not consider all the brands available in a product category, but they do seriously consider a much smaller set. For example, there are about 41 different automobile makes in Canada, each with many different available models, yet most consumers seriously contemplate only five when faced with a purchase decision.[11] Having too many choices can, in fact, confuse consumers and cause them to delay the decision to buy or, in some instances, cause them to decide not to buy at all.

EVALUATION OF ALTERNATIVES AND PURCHASE

After getting information and constructing an evoked set of alternative products, the consumer is ready to make a decision. A consumer will use the information stored in memory and obtained from outside sources to develop a set of criteria. Recent research has shown that exposure to certain cues in your everyday environment can affect decision criteria and purchase. For example, when the Pathfinder spacecraft landed on Mars, the event drew worldwide media coverage. The candy maker of the Mars chocolate bar noted an unusual increase in sales at this time. Although the Mars Bar takes its name from the company's founder and not the planet, consumers apparently responded to news about the plant Mars by purchasing more Mars Bars! In a recent lab experiment, participants who used an orange pen chose more orange products while those who used a green pen chose more green products. The researchers concluded that conceptual cues or primers (the pen colours) influenced product evaluations and purchase likelihood.[12]

The environment, internal information, and external information help consumers evaluate and compare alternatives. One way to begin narrowing the number of choices in the evoked set is to pick a product attribute and then exclude all products in the set that don't have that attribute. Assume that Pam and Chris are second-year university students who have decided to room off campus together. They want a two-bedroom apartment, reasonably priced and located near campus. They want the apartment to have a swimming pool, washer and dryer, and covered parking. Pam and Chris begin their search with all apartments in the area and systematically eliminate possibilities that lack the features they want. Hence, if there are 50 alternatives in the area, they may reduce their list to just 10 apartments that possess all the desired attributes.

Another way to narrow the number of choices is to use cutoffs. Cutoffs are either minimum or maximum levels of an attribute that an alternative must pass to be considered. Suppose that Pam and Chris set a maximum of $1,000 per month to spend on combined rent and utilities. Then all apartments with rent and utilities higher than $1,000 per month will be eliminated, further reducing the list of apartments from ten to seven. A final way to narrow the choices is to rank the attributes under consideration in order of importance and evaluate the apartments based on how well they perform on the most important attributes. To reach a final decision on one of the seven remaining apartments, Pam and Chris may decide that being close to campus is the most important attribute. Therefore they would rent the apartment that is closest to campus.

If new brands are added to an evoked set, the consumer's evaluation of the existing brands in that set will change. Suppose Pam and Chris find two apartments that are equally close to campus. One has a rent of $800 per month and the other is $750. Faced with this choice, they may decide that the $800 apartment is too expensive, given that a comparable apartment is cheaper. If they add a $900 per month apartment to the list because it is an easier walk, they may perceive the $800 apartment as being more reasonably priced and decide to rent it.

The purchase decision process described above is a piecemeal process. That is, the evaluation is made by examining alternative advantages and disadvantages along important product attributes. A different way consumers can evaluate a product is according to a categorization process. The evaluation of an alternative depends on the particular category to which it is assigned. Categories can be very general (e.g., motorized forms of transportation), or they can be very specific (a Chevrolet Volt). Typically, these categories are associated with some degree of liking or disliking. To the extent that the product can be assigned membership to a particular category, it will receive an evaluation similar to that of the category to which it is attached. For example, if you go to the grocery store and see a new organic food on the shelf, you will evaluate it in accordance with your opinions of whether you like organic foods or not.

So when consumers rely on a categorization process, a product's evaluation depends more on the particular category to which it is perceived to belong to. Given this, marketers need to understand whether consumers are using categories that evoke the desired evaluations. Indeed, how a product is categorized can strongly influence consumer demand. For example, what products come to mind when you think about the category of "morning beverage"? Soft drink makers have to live with the disappointment of knowing that few consumers put pop into this category. So far, all attempts by soft drink makers to get consumers to include pop in the breakfast meal have failed!

Brand extensions, in which a well-known and respected brand name from one product category is extended into other product categories, is one way companies employ categorization to their advantage. Brand extensions are a common business practice. For example, Nielsen-Cadbury has extended its brand-name chocolate bars into the ice cream market with Crispy Crunch Ice Cream and Caramilk Ice Cream Bars. Disney has extended in brand beyond cartoons and amusement parks to include cruise lines. However, the company that is the "master" of brand extensions has got to be the Virgin Group, which operates many different business ventures under the Virgin name, including Virgin-Atlantic Airlines (an airline), Virgin Drinks (a beverage company), Virgin Health Bank (stores stem cells from newborn babies), Virgin Megastore (a record and video store), Virgin Radio (a radio station), Virgin Money U.S. (a bank), and Virgin Mobile Canada (a wireless phone provider).[13]

brand extension
A well-known and respected brand name from one product category is extended into other product categories

To Buy or Not to Buy

Ultimately the consumer has to decide whether to buy. Specifically, consumers must decide

1. Whether to buy

2. When to buy

3. What to buy (product type and brand)

4. Where to buy (type of retailer, specific retailer, on-line or in-store)

5. How to pay

When a person is buying an expensive or complex item, it often a *fully planned purchase* based on a lot of information. It would be unthinkable for a person to buy a new home simply on impulse. Often consumers will make a *partially planned purchase* where they know the product category they want to buy (shirts, pants, reading lamp, car floor mats) but wait until they get to the store to choose a specific style or brand. Finally, there is the unplanned purchase where people buy on impulse. Research has found that up to 68 percent of the items bought during major shopping trips and 54 percent on smaller shopping trips are unplanned![14]

REVIEW LEARNING OUTCOME 2

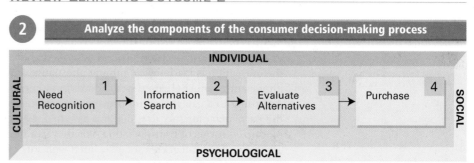

② Analyze the components of the consumer decision-making process

INDIVIDUAL

CULTURAL

| Need Recognition 1 | → | Information Search 2 | → | Evaluate Alternatives 3 | → | Purchase 4 |

SOCIAL

PSYCHOLOGICAL

③ POSTPURCHASE BEHAVIOUR

Explain the consumer's postpurchase evaluation process

When buying products, consumers expect certain outcomes from the purchase. How well these expectations are met determines whether the consumer is satisfied or dissatisfied with the purchase. For example, if a person bids on a used video-game console from eBay and wins, the person may have fairly low expectations regarding performance. If the video-game system turns out to perform with high quality, then the person's satisfaction will be high because their expectations were exceeded. Conversely, if the person bid on the newest PlayStation system expecting high quality and excellent performance, but the system broke down in the first month, the person would be very dissatisfied because expectations were not met. Price often influences the level of expectations for a product or service.

Marketers usually measure customer satisfaction directly by asking consumers to complete postpurchase surveys that are included in the product packaging or are combined with the warranty registration process. The majority of these surveys request that customers go on-line and evaluate their purchasing experience and provide a product evaluation. Alternatively, marketers might rely on third-party research firms to assist them in evaluating customer satisfaction. For example, automotive purchasers often look at *Consumer Reports* to get detailed information on customer satisfaction for automobile purchases. Another routine source of customer satisfaction measurement is the American Customer Satisfaction Index undertaken by the University of Michigan's School of Business. For example, in 2009 the survey found that North American auto makers had improved their satisfaction ratings despite having gone through a very tough economic cycle that saw General Motors and Chrysler seek Canadian and U.S. government bailouts to prevent bankruptcy. "GM's Cadillac and Toyota's Lexus brands tied for first place in the survey with scores of 89 out of 100. That marked a 4 point increase for Cadillac from its 2008 results and a 2 point improvement for Lexus, which also ranked first in last year's survey. GM's Buick brand, Honda and Ford's Lincoln Mercury vehicles all received an 88. The Lincoln Mercury score marked a 5 point increase over its results for the previous year, while Buick's score rose by 3 points."[15]

For the marketer, an important element of any postpurchase evaluation is reducing any lingering doubts that the decision was sound. This is particularly important because 75 percent of all consumers say they had a bad experience in the previous year with a product or service they purchased.[16] When people recognize inconsistency between their values or opinions and their behaviour, they tend to feel an inner tension called **cognitive dissonance**. Suppose Megan is interested in tanning

cognitive dissonance
Inner tension that a consumer experiences after recognizing an inconsistency between behaviour and values or opinions.

her skin and that she normally tans in a tanning bed. She decides to try a new "airbrush" tanning method, called a "Hollywood" or "mystic" tan. Mystic tanning costs $30 to $50, significantly more than "fake tanner" products or a tanning bed. Megan may feel inner tension or anxiety prior to spending more on the tan, which is a feeling of dissonance. The feeling occurs because she knows the product has some disadvantages, such as being expensive, and some advantages, such as being free of harmful ultraviolet rays. In this case, the disadvantage of higher cost battles the advantage of avoiding harmful UV rays.[17]

Consumers try to reduce dissonance by justifying their decision. They may seek new information that reinforces positive ideas about the purchase, avoid information that contradicts their decision, or revoke the original decision by returning the product. Consumers like Megan who are using the "mystic tanning" method mentioned above may ask several friends about their experiences, do on-line research, and talk with the tanning booth representative to obtain additional information about the procedure, thereby reducing dissonance while also increasing satisfaction. Sometimes, people deliberately seek contrary information in order to refute it and reduce dissonance. Dissatisfied customers sometimes rely on word of mouth to reduce cognitive dissonance, by letting friends and family know they are displeased.

Marketing managers can help reduce dissonance through effective communication with purchasers. A customer service manager may slip a note inside the package

Customer Experience

 ## AT ZAPPOS.COM, SERVICE IS ALWAYS ON

Zappos.com is an on-line retailer known originally for footwear, but also offering clothing, handbags, and accessories. Founded in 1999 and renowned for its unparalleled customer service, Zappos offers 500 brand names and 90,000 styles and stocks over 2 million pairs of shoes![18]

While Zappos is familiar to shoppers because of its wide selection of brands, styles, and sizes, the company is focused on positioning itself as the absolute on-line service leader. The company's website states, "We are a service company that happens to sell _____." Shoppers love the company for its free shipping and returns, 365-day return policy, and 24/7 customer service. But that's just the beginning of Zappos' corporate culture of service. The company and its employees embrace ten core concepts, the first of which is to "deliver WOW through service." Other concepts include being open and honest, driving change, and having fun. "Customer service is everything to us, and the reason we can stay focused and successful is that it's ingrained into our culture," says Aaron Magness, who works in business development for Zappos.

Zappos' service-oriented culture starts in the hiring process. According to Magness, half of the initial interview is dedicated to finding out if potential hires have the right technical skills for the job, and the other half is about making sure they're a good cultural fit. "Getting customers excited about the service they had at Zappos has to come naturally," he says. "You can't teach it; you have to hire for it."

Once hired, all new employees, regardless of position, are required to complete a four-week customer loyalty training program in the call centre to learn the history of the company, get immersed in its culture, and make sure they're a good fit. To ensure that's the case, CEO Tony Hsieh steps in during the second week of training and offers $2,000 to anyone who wants to quit. Magness says that only about 1 percent of the trainees actually take the offer.

Once Zappos wins over shoppers (roughly 75 percent of its orders are placed by repeat customers), the company works to keep them engaged through various on-line and social media outlets, including inviting customers to submit on-line reviews. It also maintains an active presence on Facebook and Twitter. "We want to let our customers speak for themselves on our site. If someone wants to say 'I really don't like this shirt,' we want other customers to know. We're not afraid to hear good reviews and bad reviews," Magness says.

On Twitter, Hsieh has about 12,000 followers who read his posts on topics associated with Zappos business and then give him feedback. According to Magness, not only does this ability to relate to the company help create a stronger relationship with shoppers, but it also provides the company with valuable consumer insight.[19]

How does Zappos' great customer service help reduce cognitive dissonance? Can a company put too much emphasis on customer service? Have you ever had poor customer service from an on-line vendor? If so, what did it do to your level of dissonance?

3 | **Explain the consumer's postpurchase evaluation process**

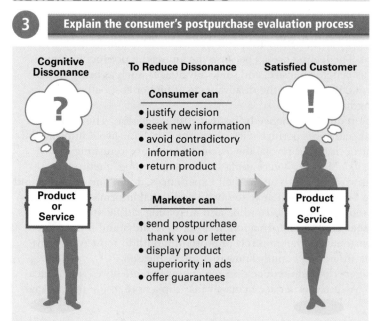

congratulating the buyer on making a wise decision. Postpurchase letters sent by manufacturers and dissonance-reducing statements in instruction booklets may help customers feel at ease with their purchase. Advertising that displays the product's superiority over competing brands or guarantees can also help relieve the possible dissonance of someone who has already bought the product. Hyundai Auto Canada promotes the quality of its automobile brands through its website, on which it lists a number of quality awards their brands have won. Examples: "2009 Hyundai Genesis—'Canadian Car of the Year'—AJAC (Automobile Journalists Association of Canada)"; "2009 Hyundai Sonata—'Winner of the AutoPacific Vehicle Satisfaction Award'"; and "2009 Elantra—'Highest Ranked Compact Car in Initial Quality in the U.S.'" in J. D. Power and Associates—2009 Initial Quality Study.[20] The Customer Experience Box illustrates how Zappos.com reduces cognitive dissonance for its patrons.

4 TYPES OF CONSUMER BUYING DECISIONS AND CONSUMER INVOLVEMENT

Identify the types of consumer buying decisions and discuss the significance of consumer involvement

involvement
The amount of time and effort a buyer invests in the search, evaluation, and decision processes of consumer behaviour.

routine response behaviour
The type of decision making exhibited by consumers buying frequently purchased, low-cost goods and services; requires little search and decision time.

limited decision making
The type of decision making that requires a moderate amount of time for gathering information and deliberating about an unfamiliar brand in a familiar product category.

All consumer buying decisions generally fall along a continuum of three broad categories: routine response behaviour, limited decision making, and extensive decision making (see Exhibit 4.2). Goods and services in these three categories can best be described in terms of five factors: level of consumer involvement, length of time to make a decision, cost of the good or service, degree of information search, and number of alternatives considered. The level of consumer involvement is perhaps the most significant determinant in classifying buying decisions. **Involvement** is the amount of time and effort a buyer invests in the search, evaluation, and decision processes of consumer behaviour.

Frequently purchased, low-cost goods and services are generally associated with **routine response behaviour**. These goods and services can also be called low-involvement products because consumers spend little time on search and decision before making the purchase. Usually, buyers are familiar with several different brands in the product category but stick with one brand and even one version of the brand. For example, a person may routinely buy Pulp-free Tropicana Orange Juice with Calcium and Vitamin D. Consumers engaged in routine response behaviour normally don't experience need recognition until they are exposed to advertising or see the product displayed on a store shelf. Consumers buy first and evaluate later, whereas the reverse is true for extensive decision making. A consumer who has previously purchased a whitening toothpaste and was satisfied with it will probably walk to the toothpaste aisle and select the same brand without spending 20 minutes examining all other alternatives. Interestingly, when marketers change or update packaging to attract new customers they risk alienating their highly loyal customers who are used to recognizing the product in its old packaging but now have to learn to recognize their familiar product in a new package!

Limited decision making typically occurs when a consumer has previous product experience but is unfamiliar with the current brands available. Limited decision making is also associated with lower levels of

EXHIBIT 4.2

Continuum of Consumer Buying Decisions

	Routine	Limited	Extensive
Involvement	Low	Low to moderate	High
Time	Short	Short to moderate	Long
Cost	Low	Low to moderate	High
Information search	Internal only	Mostly internal	Internal and external
Number of alternatives	One	Few	Many

involvement (although higher than routine decisions) because consumers do expend moderate effort in searching for information or in considering various alternatives. But what happens if the consumer's usual brand of whitening toothpaste is not readily apparent because it has been sold out or, as mentioned earlier, the packaging has changed so the consumer can't readily find it? Assuming that toothpaste is an immediate need, the consumer will look to choose another brand. Before making a final decision, the consumer will likely evaluate several other brands based on their active ingredients, their promotional claims, and the consumer's prior experiences. If the consumer discovers their usual brand choice in its new package as a result of this examination, they will likely buy it. However, the marketer who has changed packages risks putting their loyal customers into limited decision-making mode and it is possible that they will choose another brand, which now might become their "preferred" choice.

The type of decision making that consumers use to purchase a product does not necessarily remain constant. For instance, if a routinely purchased product no longer satisfies, consumers may practise limited or **extensive decision making** to switch to another brand. As mentioned before, a marketer's customers may move from routine response behaviour into limited problem-solving behaviour in response to product stock-outs or package changes. And people who first use extensive decision making may then use limited or routine decision making for future purchases. A new mother may first extensively evaluate several brands of disposable diapers before selecting one. Subsequent purchases of diapers will then become routine.

FACTORS DETERMINING THE LEVEL OF CONSUMER INVOLVEMENT

The level of involvement in the purchase depends on five factors: previous experience, interest, perceived risk, situation, and social visibility.

- *Previous experience.* When consumers have had previous experience with a good or service, the level of involvement typically decreases. After repeated product trials, consumers learn to make quick choices. Because consumers are familiar with the product and know whether it will satisfy their needs, they become less involved in the purchase. For example, a consumer purchasing cereal has many brands to choose from—picture any grocery store cereal aisle. If the consumer always buys the same brand because it satisfies their taste, they would have a low level of involvement. When a consumer purchases cereal for the first time, however, it will likely be a much more involving purchase.
- *Interest.* Involvement is directly related to consumer interests, as in cars, music, movies, bicycling, and electronics. Naturally, these areas of interest vary from one individual to another. People who are highly involved in bike racing will be very interested in the type of bike they own and will spend quite a bit of time evaluating different bikes and shop in specialty bike shops. People who simply want a bike for recreation will be far less involved in the purchase and will likely search for a bike from the most convenient retail location.
- *Perceived risk of negative consequences.* As the perceived risk in purchasing a product increases, so does a consumer's level of involvement. The types of risks that concern consumers include financial risk, social risk, and psychological risk. First, *financial risk* is exposure to loss of wealth or purchasing power. Because high risk is associated with high-priced purchases, consumers tend to become extremely involved. Therefore, price and involvement are usually directly related: as price increases, so does the level of involvement. Someone who is thinking of buying a home (high perceived risk) will normally spend much time and effort to find the right one. Second, consumers take *social* risks when they buy products that can affect people's social opinion of them (e.g., driving an old, beat-up car or wearing unstylish clothes). Finally, buyers undergo *psychological* risk if they feel that making the wrong decision might cause some concern or anxiety. For example, many Canadian consumers have been feeling guilty about buying highly visible foreign-made automobiles when their friends and neighbours work for domestic manufacturers who have been struggling for sales.

extensive decision making
The most complex type of consumer decision making, used when buying an unfamiliar, expensive product or an infrequently bought item; requires use of several criteria for evaluating options and much time for seeking information.

- *Situation.* The circumstances of a purchase may temporarily transform a low-involvement decision into a high-involvement one. High involvement comes into play when the consumer perceives risk in a specific situation. For example, an individual might routinely stay at limited-service low-budget hotels when travelling alone. When travelling with a partner, the same consumer might make a high-involvement decision and stay at up-market hotels with far more services.
- *Social visibility.* Involvement also increases as the social visibility of a product increases. Products often on social display include clothing (especially designer labels), jewellery, cars, and furniture. All these items make a statement about the purchaser and, therefore, carry a social risk.

MARKETING IMPLICATIONS OF INVOLVEMENT

Marketing strategy varies according to the level of involvement associated with the product. For high-involvement product purchases, marketing managers have several responsibilities. First, promotion to the target market should be extensive and informative. A good advertisement gives consumers the information they need for making the purchase decision as well as specifying the benefits and unique advantages of owning the product. Manufacturers of high-tech computers and peripheral equipment such as scanners, printers, and modems run lengthy ads that detail technical information about such attributes as performance, resolution, and speed. To make the purchase decision easier, major auto makers now enable their customers to go on-line and build and price their ideal vehicle before going to a local dealer. They can see what their "new" car will look like and cost as they review different combinations of chassis designs, major options, colours, fabrics, and so forth. Some websites, like **www.driving.ca**, will even take you on a test drive conducted by an expert driver. The illustrated Anatomy of Buying Decision: Car provides a full picture of this high-involvement decision.

For low-involvement product purchases, consumers may not recognize their wants until they are in the store. Therefore, in-store promotion is an important tool when promoting low-involvement products. Here, marketing managers must focus on package design so that the product will be eye-catching and be easily recognized on the shelf. Products that take this approach include Campbell's soups, Tide detergent, Velveeta cheese, and Heinz ketchup. In-store displays also stimulate sales of low-involvement products. A good display can explain the product's purpose and prompt recognition of a want. Displays of health and beauty-aid items in supermarkets have been known to increase sales many times above normal. Coupons, cents-off

ANATOMY OF a Buying Decision: Car

For a high-involvement purchase, such as buying a car, a consumer typically practices extensive decision making. Several factors ultimately affect her buying decision.

SOCIAL FACTORS

Before deciding to buy a car, this woman may seek out others' opinions or observe what others purchase.

ADVICE FROM HER REFERENCE GROUP

EXAMPLE OF OPINION LEADER

INDIVIDUAL FACTORS:

LIFESTYLE

SELF-CONCEPT

Her buying decision will be influenced by her personality, self-concept, and lifestyle.

PSYCHOLOGICAL FACTORS:

The consumer's perception, motivation, learning, values, beliefs, and attitudes will influence her decision on which car to buy, too.

ATTITUDE

"Should I try a new brand, or stick with the familiar one?"

?

EXHIBIT 4.3

Factors That Affect the Consumer Decision-Making Process

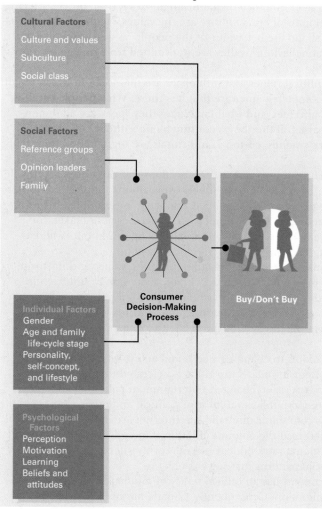

4 **Identify the types of consumer buying decisions and discuss the significance of consumer involvement**

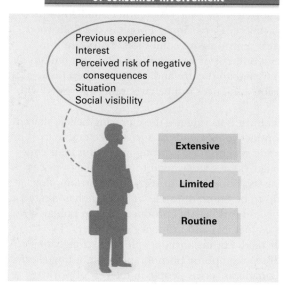

Previous experience
Interest
Perceived risk of negative
    consequences
Situation
Social visibility

Extensive

Limited

Routine

deals, and two-for-one offers also promote low-involvement items effectively.

Another tactic that marketing managers can use to increase the sales of a low-involvement product is to link the product to a higher-involvement issue. Many food products are no longer just nutritious but also low in fat or cholesterol. Packaged food is normally a low-involvement product; however, reference to health issues raises the involvement level. To take advantage of aging baby boomers' interest in healthier foods, a recent ad from H.J. Heinz Company linked its ketchup with a growing body of research that suggests that lycopene, an antioxidant found in tomatoes, can reduce the risk of prostate and cervical cancers.[21] Similarly, food products, such as SoyaWorld's So Good Omega soy milk, tout their health benefits in reducing the risk of coronary heart disease, preventing certain cancers, and reducing the symptoms of menopause. Manufacturers of soy-based products, which have long been shunned in Canada for their strong taste, are planning to tap into strong consumer interest in nutritional eating as a result of these health claims.[22]

FACTORS INFLUENCING CONSUMER BUYING DECISIONS

The consumer decision-making process does not occur in a vacuum. On the contrary, underlying cultural, social, individual, and psychological factors strongly influence the decision process. They have an effect from the time a consumer perceives a stimulus through postpurchase behaviour. Cultural factors, which include culture and values, subculture, and social class, exert a broad influence over consumer decision making. *Social* factors sum up the social interactions between a consumer and influential groups of people, such as reference groups, opinion leaders, and family members. *Individual* factors, which include gender, age, family life-cycle stage, personality, self-concept, and lifestyle, are unique to each individual and play a major role in the types of products and services consumers want. *Psychological* factors determine how consumers perceive and interact with their environments and influence the ultimate decisions consumers make. They include perception, motivation, learning, beliefs, and attitudes. Exhibit 4.3 summarizes these influences.

5 CULTURAL INFLUENCES ON CONSUMER BUYING DECISIONS

Identify and understand the cultural factors that affect consumer buying decisions

Of all the factors that affect consumer decision making, cultural factors exert the broadest and deepest influence. Marketers must understand the way people's culture and its accompanying values, as well as their subculture and social class, influence buying behaviour.

CULTURE AND VALUES

culture
The set of values, norms, attitudes, and other meaningful symbols that shape human behaviour and the artifacts, or products, of that behaviour as they are transmitted from one generation to the next.

Culture is the essential character of a society that distinguishes it from other societal groups. The underlying elements of every culture are the values, language, myths, customs, rituals, and laws that shape the behaviour of the people, as well as the material artifacts, or products, of that behaviour as they are transmitted from one generation to the next.

Culture is pervasive. Cultural values and influences are the ocean in which we all swim, yet most people are completely unaware that it is there. What people eat, how they dress, what they think and feel, and what languages they speak are all dimensions of culture. It encompasses all the things consumers do without conscious choice because their culture's values, customs, and rituals are ingrained in their daily habits.

Culture is functional. Human interaction creates values and prescribes acceptable behaviour for each culture. By establishing common expectations, culture gives order to society. Sometimes these expectations are coded into laws; for example, drivers in our culture must stop at a red light. Other times these expectations are taken for granted; for example, convenience stores and hospitals are open 24 hours whereas banks are open only during bankers' hours.

Culture is learned. Consumers are not born knowing the values and norms of their society. Instead, they must *learn* what is acceptable from family and friends. Children learn the values that will govern their behaviour from parents, teachers, and peers. As members of our society, they learn to shake hands when they greet someone, to drive on the right-hand side of the road, and to eat pizza and drink coffee.

Culture is dynamic. It adapts to changing needs and an evolving environment. The rapid growth of technology in today's world has accelerated the rate of cultural change. In the 20th century, television changed entertainment patterns and family communication and heightened public awareness of political and other news events. In the 21st century, wireless communication and the Internet are influencing a global culture. Automation has increased the amount of leisure time we have and, in some ways, has changed the traditional work ethic. Cultural norms will continue to evolve because of our need for social patterns that solve problems.

Canada's federal government has an official policy of multiculturalism and encourages large-scale immigration. Consequently, Canada has been undergoing rapid changes in diversity, causing major shifts in culture. For example, the 2006 census of Canada reported more than 200 different ethnic origins in Canada, and many of them are visible minorities. In 1991, approximately 10 percent of Canadians were classified as visible minorities; by 2006, the figure was 16.2 percent, and it is projected that by 2017, approximately 20 percent of Canadians will be classified as visible minorities.[23] The rapid growth of these ethnic groups will have a dramatic impact on the food, music, clothing, and entertainment industries in Canada. Telus sought to target the South Asian community, reported to be over 1.3 million Canadians, with a significant product placement of a Blackberry Curve Smart Phone in the Bollywood movie *Jag Jeondeyan De Mele*. The movie's central figure comes to Canada and purchases this device from Telus and uses a number of its features, including a built-in GPS. Telus hopes the movie's current Canadian theatre audiences and then the follow-up video purchasers and television audiences will be favourably impressed with the role of its products in the film.[24]

value
The enduring belief that a specific mode of conduct is personally or socially preferable to another mode of conduct.

The most defining element of a culture is its **values**—the enduring beliefs shared by a society that a specific mode of conduct is personally or socially preferable to another mode of conduct. People's value systems have a strong impact on their consumer behaviour. Consumers with similar value systems tend to react alike to prices and other marketing-related inducements. Values also correspond to consumption patterns. For example, Canadians tend to be brand disloyal.[25] This value has created highly competitive markets for generic and private-label products such as Loblaw's No Name and President's Choice brands. Values can also influence consumers' TV viewing habits and the magazines they read. For instance, people who strongly object to violence avoid crime shows, and those who oppose pornography do not buy *Hustler*. A recent joint study of the values of Canadians versus people in the rest of world

EXHIBIT 4.4

Canadian Values

Moral Issues and the Role of Religion	Canadians are fairly religious with 89% believing in God, but despite this, 67% believe that religious leaders should not have an influence on government decisions. Interestingly, 30% of Canadians support conservative thinking on the role of women and same-sex marriages but only 20% believe government should be involved in setting moral standards.
Welfare and Self-Reliance	Canadians support the concept of social safety nets but 60% of Canadians feel that a person should blame themselves, not the system, for not getting ahead. Only a slim majority (51% of Canadians) believed children should be taught the concept of hard work, compared to 61% of Americans.
Economic	Canadians accept the concept of free enterprise but total devotion to the profit motive is viewed with skepticism. A slim majority of Canadians (53%) believed the government should regulate businesses to keep them from becoming too powerful, while 38% of Canadians felt government regulation caused more harm than good. Interestingly, 68% of Canadians felt that competition in business was a good thing and, although the majority believed in government regulation, 60% favoured private ownership of business over government ownership.
Environment	A majority of Canadians (57%) felt that protecting the environment was very important, even more important than protecting jobs!

SOURCE: Adapted from The Canadian Values Study: A Joint Project of Innovative Research Group, the Dominion Institute (now The Historica-Dominion Institute) and the National Post, "Canadians Values Similar to Other Advanced Democracies," Toronto—September 28, 2005 www.innovativeresearch.ca/ Canadian%20Values%20Study_Factum%20280905.pdf

undertaken by the *National Post*, the Dominion Institute, and Innovative Research Group concluded that "Canadians hold very similar views to people from other advanced industrial democracies."[26] A summary of a number of the findings of this survey on the values of Canadians is presented in Exhibit 4.4.

Values represent what is most important in people's lives. It follows that marketers must understand consumers' values. The values that Citizenship and Immigration Canada seeks to imprint on immigrants are stated as follows: " [Canadian citizenship] involves pride. A belief in equality and diversity. Respect for others. It means accepting the shared values that make Canadians who they are, and respecting both the rights and the privileges of being Canadian."[27] Canadian values that marketers and social commentators have identified in the past include the following: support for collective responsibility; confidence in social institutions (e.g., education, health care, and the police); tolerance for diversity and differences; freedom of choice; democracy; and fiscal responsibility. Also, Canadians tend to be brand disloyal, pessimistic and skeptical, health conscious, and frugal.[28]

Recently, Canadian advertising agency Bensimon Byrne undertook consumer research that looked at Canadian values according to whether people lived in urban or less populated areas. The researchers termed this the "density divide" and examined three levels of population: under 100,000; 100,000 to 1 million; and over 1 million. They reported the following findings: 36 percent of Canadians live in towns of under 100,000 and have different values from those living in the larger urban centres of more than 100,000. For example, small-town Canadians believe more strongly in "hard work, saving, community involvement, having a family, tradition, order and security, cooperation and charitable giving." The people in small towns "are more satisfied with the crime rate . . . the quality of the local environment and its suitability to raise children. . . . They are much less satisfied with arts and culture options and job opportunities. They are more focused on both getting a good deal and getting the lowest price. They also place a much higher value on buying Canadian, and on corporate community support."[29]

UNDERSTANDING CULTURE DIFFERENCES

As more companies expand their operations globally, the need to understand the cultures of foreign countries is becoming more important. A firm has little chance of selling products in a culture it does not understand. Like people, products have cultural values and rules that influence their perception and use. Culture, therefore, must be understood before the behaviour of individuals within the cultural context

PepsiCo vies with Coca-Cola Co. in the world's fastest-growing soft-drinks arena—China. China's exanding market is the biggest after the United States and Mexico for the competing drinks giants. Which marketing elements do you think will give Pepsi an advantage over Coca-Cola or vice versa?

SOURCE: © CLARO CORTES IV/REUTERS/LANDOV

subculture
A homogeneous group of people who share elements of the overall culture as well as unique elements of their own group.

can be understood. Colours, for example, may have different meanings in global markets than they do at home. In China, brides wear red, and white is the colour to wear when mourning someone who has died. In Canada, brides wear white and people wear black when mourning.

Language is another important aspect of culture that global marketers must deal with. When translating product names, slogans, and promotional messages into foreign languages, the translation must not convey the wrong message. General Motors discovered too late that Nova (the name of an economical car) literally means "doesn't go" in Spanish; Coors encouraged its English-speaking customers to "turn it loose," but the phrase in Spanish means "suffer from diarrhea"; and when Frank Perdue, CEO of one of the largest chicken producers in the United States, said, "It takes a tough man to make a tender chicken," the translation into Spanish came out "It takes a sexually stimulated man to make a chicken affectionate."

Though marketers expanding into global markets generally adapt their products and business formats to the local culture, some fear that increasing globalization, as well as the proliferation of the Internet, will result in a homogeneous world culture in the future. Canadians have long worried about being submerged by American culture and American companies, but it's not just Canada that is being Americanized. U.S. companies are Americanizing most of the world by exporting bastions of American culture, such as McDonald's restaurants, Starbucks cafés, Microsoft software, and American movies and entertainment.

SUBCULTURE

A culture can be divided into subcultures on the basis of demographic characteristics, geographic regions, national and ethnic background, political beliefs, and religious beliefs. A **subculture** is a homogeneous group of people who share elements of the overall culture as well as cultural elements unique to their own group. Within subcultures, people's attitudes, values, and purchase decisions are even more similar than they are within the broader culture. Subcultural differences may result in considerable variation within a culture regarding what, how, when, and where people buy goods and services.

Canada is a multicultural society, with French Canadian being the dominant subculture in the country as 6.9 million Canadians identified themselves as francophones—having a mother-tongue language of French in the 2006 census. Most French Canadians live in Quebec, but Canada being a bilingual nation, French-Canadian culture is found on a national scale as well. Language is a critical factor for marketers when they are designing campaigns for French Canadians; however, language is not the only distinguishing feature of Canada's largest subculture. Compared to other North Americans, French Canadians are "more concerned about living in the moment than planning for the future." A Quebecer's sense of humour is stimulated by "over-the-top absurdity and slapstick" versus the "dry, observational sarcasm favoured by the rest of the continent. Quebecers are less likely to read detailed labels and are more likely to make purchases based on emotion and impulse."[30]

Canada's Aboriginal people represent another Canadian subculture with nearly 560,000 people registered as status Indians under Canada's Indian Act in 2006 and nearly 1.2 million people in total identifying themselves as Aboriginal in the 2006 Census of Canada. Status Indians are entitled to live on Indian reserves, which are located throughout Canada, although the largest land portions are in the northern regions. According to a TD Canada Economic Report, Aboriginal people operate an estimated 27,000 businesses both, on and off reserves. Many of the businesses are linked to Canada's resource sectors but Aboriginal entrepreneurs are also operating small airlines and mining supply and business service enterprises. As Aboriginal enterprises enter the mainstream economy, the report says, they do so with two main core values: "the protection of land and the environment. For example, in recent years, Aboriginal entrepreneurs are beginning to make a real mark in establishing environmentally-focused ventures in areas such as renewable and alternative energy development, which offer substantial opportunities for growth over the longer run. Within the energy sector, emerging technologies—such as run-of-the-river used for hydro development—are helping to reduce environmental impacts and, thus, foster Aboriginal involvement."[31]

According to the most recent information from the Census of Canada, besides French Canadians, there are more than 200 different ethnic groups in Canada. However, nearly one-third of the population (10.1 million people) reported themselves as "Canadian," making them the largest group. "After Canadian, the ethnic origins that people most frequently reported were English, Irish, French, Scottish, German, Italian, Chinese, North American Indian, Ukrainian and Dutch."[32]

In the past, most of Canada's immigrants were from Europe, but according to the 2006 Census of Canada, in the period from January 1, 2001, to May 16, 2006, 1.1 million immigrants entered Canada. Statistics Canada tells us, "Canada's largest group of recent immigrants were from Asia (including the Middle East), accounting for 58% of immigrants in 2006. Europe, in second place, accounted for 16%, compared with 61% in the 1971 Census. Central and South America and the Caribbean accounted for 11%, while 11% came from Africa." In 2006, nearly 20 percent of the Canadian population reported they were born outside of Canada and the majority of those that reported this had settled in one of the three major urban areas of Canada. For example, in "Toronto, one in two residents was born outside Canada. In the city of Montréal, one in three was foreign-born. In Richmond, British Columbia, it was three out of five residents."[33]

Other subcultures are geographically dispersed. For example, farmers, people who are hearing or visually impaired, Harley-Davidson bikers, university professors, and people who are gay or lesbian are found throughout the country. Yet they have identifiable attitudes, values, and needs that distinguish them from the broader culture.

If marketers can identify subcultures, they can design special marketing programs to serve their needs. One problem for Canadian companies is that the cost of research is extremely high and many of the subcultures are relatively small. In addition, many people are highly sensitive to questions about their ethnicity. Ford of Canada ran into this issue when it asked about ethnicity in a survey of customers. Several customers complained about the question, the media got wind of the complaints, and Ford of Canada received negative publicity. It responded by pulling the question from all its surveys. Clearly, research on ethnicity can be difficult to conduct. At the same time, though, Canadian marketers enjoy a wide choice of media vehicles for reaching out to both ethnic subcultures and other subcultures. For example, to reach ethnic groups, marketers can access a range of media: 10 analog and 79 digital stations represent 40 languages; 67 radio stations broadcast in a total of 69 languages; and 230 different publications are designed for 42 different ethnic language groups.[34] To reach other subcultures, there are specialty media vehicles such as *Ontario Farmer Magazine*, which targets farmers; *Inside Motorcycles Magazine*, which might appeal to Harley-Davidson riders; *University Affairs*, which would appeal to university professors; and digital television channel Out TV and *Xtra Magazine*, which target gay and lesbian lifestyles.[35]

SOCIAL CLASS

social class
A group of people in a society who are considered nearly equal in status or community esteem, who regularly socialize among themselves both formally and informally, and who share behavioural norms.

Like other societies, Canada has a class system. A **social class** is a group of people who are considered nearly equal in status or community esteem, who regularly socialize among themselves both formally and informally, and who share behavioural norms.

A number of techniques have been used to measure social class, and a number of criteria have been used to define it. One view of the Canadian status structure is shown in Exhibit 4.5. As you can see from that exhibit, the capitalist/executive class is made up of a small segment of affluent and wealthy Canadians. The capitalist/

EXHIBIT 4.5

Canadian Social Classes by Sex (%)

	Men	Women	Population total
Capitalist/executive	8.8	2.7	6.2
New middle class	25.3	24.4	24.9
Old middle class	15.7	5.1	11.3
Working class	50.3	67.9	57.6
Total	100.0	100.0	100.0

SOURCE: Adapted from Simon Langlois, "Empirical Studies on Social Stratification in Quebec and Canada," in Yannick Lemel and Heinz-Herbert Noll, eds., *Changing structures of inequality: a comparative perspective*, Montreal: McGill-Queen's Universtity Press, © 2002, p. 83. Reprinted with permission.

executive class is more likely than other classes to contribute something to society—for example, by volunteer work or through active participation in civic affairs. With regard to consumer buying patterns, the affluent are more likely to own their own home and purchase new cars and trucks and are less likely to smoke. The very rich flex their financial muscle by spending more on owned vacation homes, vacations and cruises, and housekeeping and gardening services. The most affluent consumers are more likely to attend art auctions and galleries, dance performances, opera, the theatre, museums, concerts, and sporting events.[36] Marketers often pay attention to the superwealthy. For example, the Mercedes-Benz SLR McLaren Roadster is a luxury convertible aimed at this group. Priced at $495,000, it is listed as having the fastest automatic transmission in the world and is able to reach 100 km/hour in 3.8 seconds; the driver can further accelerate to the vehicle's top speed of 330 km/hour. Add to this the joint effort of Mont Blanc and Van Cleef and Arpels to produce the Limited Edition Mystery Masterpiece Pen, which is priced at an astounding $730,000. The pen has 840 diamonds and 20 carats of gemstones. Owners of the McLaren Roadster will want this pen to sign the many traffic tickets they will earn if they decide to test out the top speed rating of their car![37]

The majority of Canadians today define themselves as middle class, regardless of their actual income or educational attainment. This phenomenon is most likely due to the fact that working-class Canadians tend to aspire to the middle-class lifestyle while some of those who do achieve affluence may downwardly aspire to respectable middle-class status as a matter of principle.[38] Attaining goals and achieving status and prestige are important to middle-class consumers. People falling into the middle class live in the gap between the haves and the have-nots. They aspire to the lifestyle of the more affluent but are constrained by the economic realities and cautious attitudes they share with the working class.

The working class perceives itself as middle class. Interest in organized labour is one of the attributes most common among the working class. This group is more likely to rate job security as the most important reason for taking a job.[39] The working-class person depends heavily on relatives and the community for economic and emotional support. The emphasis on family ties is one sign of the group's intensely local view of the world. They like the local news far more than do middle-class audiences, who favour national and world coverage. They are also more likely to vacation closer to home.

Social class is typically measured as a combination of occupation, income, education, wealth, and other variables. For instance, affluent capitalist/executive consumers are more likely to be salaried executives or self-employed professionals with at least an undergraduate degree. New middle-class consumers are also likely to have an undergraduate degree or college diploma and to work in salaried and professional occupations. Older middle-class and working-class consumers are more likely to be hourly service workers or blue-collar employees with only a high school education. Educational attainment, however, seems to be the most reliable indicator of a person's social and economic status. Those with university or graduate degrees are more likely to fall into the capitalist/executive or new middle class, while those with some university experience but no degree fall closest to the old middle class.

Marketers are interested in social class for two main reasons. First, social class often indicates which medium to use for advertising. If an insurance company is seeking to sell its policies to middle-class families, it might advertise during the local evening news because middle-class families tend to watch more TV than other classes do. If the company wants to sell more policies to upscale individuals, it might place a print ad in a business publication such as the *Financial Post*. The Internet, long the domain of more educated and affluent families, is becoming an important advertising

5 Identify and understand the cultural factors that affect consumer buying decisions

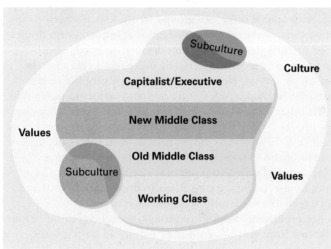

outlet for advertisers hoping to reach blue-collar workers and homemakers. As the middle class rapidly adopts the medium, marketers are having to do more research to find out which websites will reach their audience.[40]

Second, knowing which products appeal to which social classes can help marketers determine where to distribute their products. Tourism BC has targeted the Mexican upper middle class to come and ski during Mexican Whistler Ski Week, which is held at the end of January. Eleven weekly flights are scheduled between Vancouver and Mexico City, and Mexican citizens do not need a visa to visit Canada whereas they do need one to visit the United States. Since the timing of the ski season is generally between the usual Christmas and Easter vacation periods for families, Tourism BC is hoping that upper middle class travellers will be interested because they generally can afford to undertake "getaways" during nontraditional holiday seasons.[41]

6 SOCIAL INFLUENCES ON CONSUMER BUYING DECISIONS

Identify and understand the social factors that affect consumer buying decisions

reference group
A group in society that influences an individual's purchasing behaviour.

Many consumers seek out the opinions of others to reduce their search and evaluation effort or uncertainty, especially as the perceived risk of the decision increases. Consumers may also seek out others' opinions for guidance on new products or services, on products with image-related attributes, or on products for which attribute information is lacking or uninformative. Specifically, consumers interact socially with reference groups, opinion leaders, and family members to obtain product information and decision approval.

EXHIBIT 4.6

Types of Reference Groups

Reference groups

- **Direct** Face-to-face membership
  - **Primary** Small, informal group
  - **Secondary** Large, formal group
- **Indirect** Nonmembership
  - **Aspirational** Group that someone would like to join
  - **Nonaspirational** Group that someone wants to avoid being identified with

REFERENCE GROUPS

All the formal and informal groups that influence the buying behaviour of an individual are that person's **reference groups**. Consumers may use products or brands to identify with or become a member of a group. They learn from observing how members of their reference groups consume, and they use the same criteria to make their own consumer decisions.

Reference groups can be categorized very broadly as direct or indirect (see Exhibit 4.6). *Direct* reference groups are face-to-face membership groups that touch people's lives directly. They can be either primary or secondary. **Primary membership groups** include all

primary membership group
A reference group with which people interact regularly in an informal, face-to-face manner, such as family, friends, and fellow employees.

secondary membership group
A reference group with which people associate less consistently and more formally than a primary membership group, such as a club, professional group, or religious group.

aspirational reference group
A group that someone would like to join.

norm
A value or attitude deemed acceptable by a group.

nonaspirational reference group
A group with which an individual does not want to associate.

groups with which people interact regularly in an informal, face-to-face manner, such as family, friends, and co-workers. In contrast, people associate with **secondary membership groups** less consistently and more formally. Some examples of secondary membership groups are clubs, professional groups, and religious groups.

Consumers also are influenced by many indirect, nonmembership reference groups to which they do not belong. **Aspirational reference groups** are those that a person would like to join. To join an aspirational group, a person must at least conform to the norms of that group. (**Norms** are the values and attitudes deemed acceptable by the group.) Thus, a person who wants to be elected to a public office may begin to dress more conservatively, as other politicians do. He or she may go to many of the restaurants and social engagements that city and business leaders attend and try to play a role that is acceptable to voters and other influential people. Similarly, teenagers today may dye their hair or experiment with body piercing and tattoos. Athletes are an aspirational group for several market segments. To appeal to the younger market, Coca-Cola signed basketball star Le Bron James to be the spokesperson for its Sprite and Powerade brands, and Nike signed a sneaker deal with him reportedly worth $90 million. Coca-Cola and Nike assumed James would encourage consumers to drink Coke brands and buy Nike shoes because they would like to identify with him.

Nonaspirational reference groups, or dissociative groups, influence our behaviour when we try to maintain distance from them. A consumer may avoid buying some types of clothing or certain brands of automobiles, not patronize certain restaurants or stores, and will even refuse to consider a home purchase in particular neighbourhoods in order to avoid being associated with an undesirable reference group.

The activities, values, and goals of reference groups directly influence consumer behaviour. For marketers, reference groups have three important implications: (1) they serve as information sources and influence perceptions; (2) they affect an individual's aspiration levels; and (3) their norms either constrain or stimulate consumer behaviour.

Understanding the effect of reference groups on a product is important for marketers as they track the life cycles of their products. Youthography, a Toronto-based research company helps businesses understand the youth market. Youthography regularly surveys about 1,800 Canadians ages 9 through 34, asking them questions about their behaviours, attitudes, and social values. Using this information, the company publishes a quarterly report titled *Ping*, which has information marketers can use to get a handle on the activities and values of young people. For example, a recent *Ping* survey revealed that only 7.1 percent of 9- to 13-year-old Canadians answered, "I do not play video games." When the survey data for this age group were broken out by gender, only 1.2 percent of males answered "I do not play video games" as did 12.9 percent of females. The conclusion drawn by Youthography strategic manager Mike Farrell was that "videogaming is . . . about as bonafide a mainstream diversion as can be found in contemporary society. . . . The demographics and psychographics gaming now represents are just about as diverse as the population itself."[42]

OPINION LEADERS

opinion leader
An individual who influences the opinions of others.

Reference groups frequently include individuals known as group leaders, or **opinion leaders**—those who influence others. Obviously, it is important for marketing managers to persuade such people to purchase their goods or services. Many products and services that are integral parts of Canadians' lives today got their initial boost from opinion leaders. For example, opinion leaders embraced DVD players and sport utility vehicles well ahead of the general public.

Opinion leaders are often the first to try new products and services out of pure curiosity. They are typically self-indulgent, which makes them more likely to explore unproven but intriguing products and services.[43] Technology companies have found that teenagers, because of their willingness to experiment, are key opinion leaders for the success of new technologies. For example, text messaging, which first appealed to teenagers, has gained widespread popularity. Many technology companies see creating a buzz among teens as a critical part of their marketing programs.[44]

Opinion leadership is a casual, face-to-face phenomenon and usually inconspicuous, so locating opinion leaders can be a challenge. Marketers often try to *create*

Yes. She checks herself out in the mirror.

1 in 5 Americans will develop skin cancer in their lifetime. That's why Jennifer Garner made a promise to herself to examine her skin every month and see her dermatologist for a screening every year.

The Neutrogena Partnership for Skin Health, working with the American Academy of Dermatology (AAD), invites you to join them in their mission to stop skin cancer before it strikes. Empower their cause by wearing broad-spectrum sun protection, covering up and seeking shade between 10:00 am and 4:00 pm. Perform self-examinations regularly and report any changes in existing moles or birthmarks to your doctor. Because with early detection, skin cancer is 98% curable. And that's a statistic we love to share.

Protect yourself starting today.
The AAD and the Neutrogena Partnership for Skin Health encourage you to get a free skin cancer screening in May, June or July. Find one in your area by visiting aad.org or neutrogenaskinhealth.com. Mark the date of your screening on this slip as a healthy reminder.

Neutrogena®
PARTNERSHIP FOR
SKIN HEALTH

The activities, values, and goals of reference groups directly influence consumer behaviour. Consumers may use the Neutrogena brand—and participate in skin cancer prevention behaviour as she does—because they aspire to be like actress Jennifer Garner.

opinion leaders. They may use high school cheerleaders to model new fall fashions or civic leaders to promote insurance, new cars, and other merchandise. On a national level, companies sometimes use movie stars, sports figures, and other celebrities to promote products, hoping they are appropriate opinion leaders. The effectiveness of celebrity endorsements depends largely on how credible and attractive the spokesperson is and how familiar people are with him or her. Endorsements are most likely to succeed if an association between the spokesperson and the product can be reasonably established.

Celebrities and sports figures aren't the only people marketers consider opinion leaders. Managers at BMW are rethinking who opinion leaders are for their brand. Historically, the auto maker targeted car enthusiasts. Today, the company is looking at the "idea class," a group composed of architects, professionals, innovators, and entrepreneurs who are more interested in design, authenticity, and independent thinking.[45]

Respected organizations such as the Heart and Stroke Foundation may also serve as opinion leaders. Both Maple Leaf's Simply Savour Chicken Breast Strips and So Good's Soy Milk have the seal of approval of the Canadian Heart and Stroke Association. Marketers also seek endorsements from schools, churches, cities, and fraternal organizations as a form of group opinion leadership. Salespeople often ask to use opinion leaders' names as a means of achieving greater personal influence in a sales presentation.

How Blogs Are Defining Today's Opinion Leaders

Increasingly marketers are looking to Web logs (or blogs, as they're commonly called) to find opinion leaders. A new blog is created every second of every day according to Technorati, a blog-monitoring site, so it's getting harder to separate the true opinion leaders from intermediate Web users who are just looking to share random thoughts or vacation photos with family and friends. Technorati.com indexes millions of blog posts in real time and surfaces them in seconds.[46] McDonald's Restaurants of Canada decided to use blogging to develop some grassroots opinion leaders. They developed an initiative they called the "Moms' Quality Correspondents program" and provided a website entitled mcdonaldsmoms.ca. The company chose five women from among more than 300 applicants to take part in "behind-the-scenes field trips." McDonald's did not pay the women a salary but the company did cover the cost of the trips and provided the participants with laptops to blog on. The mothers made reports on the website, saying things such as "McDonald's hamburgers are made from 100 percent Canadian beef. No fillers, no additives. No preservatives. Beef. That's it. I promise. And I can make this promise to you . . . because I was there to see it"; "My mind is a little more at ease now, knowing what extent they do go to accommodate the best interest of the cattle and the people handling them. They do handle things as humanely as possible."[47]

One way marketers are identifying true opinion leaders is by looking to teen blogs to identify the social trends that are shaping consumer behaviour. During the research phase of development for its teen-targeted RED Blogs service, AOL discovered that over 50 percent of teens do not mind sharing their feelings in public forums. This is especially evident at social networking sites like Facebook, MySpace, and Xanga, where teens and twenty somethings post extensive personal profiles, photo collections, links to user groups they belong to, and detailed descriptions of their social events.

Raised with Much Music, 500-channel cable service, broadband Internet service, and multifunction wireless telephones, teens have unprecedented access to the world around them. Furthermore, they are no longer passive observers of the culture their parents have created. They can follow their favourite bands, performers, or athletes via their websites and blogs and even interact with their idols instead of simply admiring them from afar. With their ability to network and communicate with each other, young people rely on each other's opinions far more than marketing communications when they make their purchase decisions. And blogs are becoming a key way in which

EXHIBIT 4.7

Tweens and Teens Weigh in on Advertising Tactics

Ad Tactic	Like		Dislike	
	8–12 yrs	13–18 yrs	8–12 yrs	13–18 yrs
Famous person uses product	39%	21%	12%	22%
Person in a movie uses product	33%	20%	12%	19%
Cartoon or TV show about product	31%	13%	25%	34%
Popular kids give free product	24%	12%	43%	44%
Product advertised on cellphones	5%	4%	41%	55%
Product mentioned in on-line chats	5%	4%	37%	45%
Product written about on a blog site	14%	10%	24%	32%

SOURCE: Based on "Today's Youth Look to Advertising as Much as Their Friends When Making Purchase Decisions", 'PR Newswire', August 21, 2006.

socialization process
How cultural values and norms are passed down to children.

teens communicate their opinions (see Exhibit 4.7). Consequently, today's marketers are reading teen blogs, developing products that meet the very specific needs that teens express there, and learning unique and creative ways to put key influencers in charge of marketing their brands for them.

FAMILY

The family is the most important social institution for many consumers, strongly influencing values, attitudes, self-concept—and buying behaviour. For example, a family that strongly values good health will have a grocery list distinctly different from that of a family that views every dinner as a gourmet event. Moreover, the family is responsible for the **socialization process**—that is, the passing down of cultural values and norms to children. Children learn by observing their parents' consumption patterns and tend to shop in similar patterns.

Decision-making roles among family members tend to vary significantly, depending on the type of item purchased. Family members assume a variety of roles in the purchase process. *Initiators* suggest, initiate, or plant the seed for the purchase process. The initiator can be any member of the family. For example, Sister might initiate the product search by asking for a new bicycle as a birthday present. *Influencers* are those members of the family whose opinions are valued. In our example, Mom might function as a price-range watchdog, an influencer whose main role is to veto or approve price ranges. Brother may give his opinion on certain makes of bicycles. The *decision maker* is the member of the family who actually makes the decision to buy or not to buy. For example, Mom or Dad is likely to choose the final brand and model of bicycle to buy after seeking further information from Sister about cosmetic features such as colour and then imposing additional criteria of their own, such as durability and safety. The *purchaser* (probably Dad or Mom) is the one who actually exchanges money for the product. Finally, the *consumer* is the actual user—Sister, in the case of the bicycle.

Marketers should consider family purchase situations along with the distribution of consumer and decision-maker roles among family members. Ordinary marketing views the individual as both decision maker and consumer. Family marketing adds several other possibilities: sometimes more than one family member or all family members are involved in the decision; sometimes only children are involved in the decision; sometimes more than one consumer is involved; and sometimes the decision maker and the consumer are different people. Exhibit 4.8 represents the patterns of family purchasing relationships that are possible.

In most households when parental joint decisions are being made, spouses consider their partner's needs and perceptions to maintain decision fairness and harmony.[48] This tends to minimize family conflict. Research also shows that in harmonious households the spouse that has "won" a previous decision is less likely to use strong influence in a subsequent decision.[49] This balancing factor is key in maintaining long-term family harmony.

EXHIBIT 4.8

Relationships among Purchasers and Consumers in the Family

		Purchase Decision Maker		
		Parent(s) Only	Child/Children Only	Some or All Family Members
Consumer	Parent(s)	• golf clubs • cosmetics • wine	• Mother's Day card	• Christmas • gifts • minivan
	Child/Children	• diapers • breakfast cereal	• candy • small toys	• bicycle
	Some Family Members	• videos • long-distance phone service	• children's movies	• computers • sports events
	All Family Members	• clothing • life insurance	• fast-food restaurant	• swim club • membership • vacations

SOURCE: Reprinted with permission from "Pulling the Family's Strings" by Robert Boutillier in the August 1993 issue of 'American Demographics'. Copyright © 2004 Crain Communications, Inc.; permission conveyed through Copyright Clearance Center, Inc.

SOURCE: ASSOCIATED PRESS

As the proportion of children in the Canadian population swells, this market segment is becoming increasingly important to marketers wanting to influence the kids that influence their parents' purchasing habits. Heinz's coloured ketchups in the E-Z Squirt bottles are designed to do just that.

Children can have great influence over the purchase decisions of their parents. In many families, with both parents working and short on time, children are encouraged to participate. In addition, children in single-parent households become more involved in family decisions at an earlier age. Children are especially influential in decisions about food and eating out. Exactly how much of an influence kids have varies depending on factors such as age, race, socioeconomic status, and region. For example, a recent study reported that children age 5 or younger frequently influence restaurant visits, while children ages 6 to 18 have only occasional influence.[50] Children influence purchase decisions for many more products and services than food. Even though they are usually not the actual purchasers of such items, they often participate in decisions about toys, clothes, vacations, recreation, automobiles, and many other products.

Traditionally, children learn about consumption from their parents. In today's technologically overloaded world, this trend is reversing as parents are now learning about consumption from their children. Teenagers and adult children often contribute information and influence the purchase of parents' technology products.[51] Often they even help with installation and show the parents how to use the product!

REVIEW LEARNING OUTCOME 6

6 Identify and understand the social factors that affect consumer buying decisions

Reference Groups	Direct		Indirect	
	Primary	Secondary	Aspirational	Non-Aspirational

Opinion Leaders	People you know	Celebrities

Family	Socialization Process		
	Initiators	Decision Makers	Consumers
	Influencers		Purchasers

7 INDIVIDUAL INFLUENCES ON CONSUMER BUYING DECISIONS

Identify and understand the individual factors that affect consumer buying decisions

A person's buying decisions are also influenced by personal characteristics that are unique to each individual, such as gender; age, life-cycle stage; personality, self-concept, and lifestyle. Individual characteristics are generally stable over the course of one's life. For instance, most people do not change their gender, and the act of changing personality or lifestyle requires a complete reorientation of one's life. In the case of age and life-cycle stage, these changes occur gradually over time.

GENDER

Physiological differences between men and women result in different needs such as health and beauty products. Just as important are the distinct cultural, social, and economic roles played by men and women and the effects these have on their decision-making processes. For example, in Canada English-language television networks such as Slice, Viva, W Network, Cosmopolitan TV, and Showcase Diva, have programming targeted to women, while the programming on Men TV and Spike TV is specifically designed for men. Despite their targeting intentions, the network ratings of Canadian English-language networks indicate that both females and males are watching! For example, women 18 and over report watching the W Network for an average of 1.9 hours per week and Men TV for an average of .5 hours per week. In contrast, men 18 and over report watching the W Network for an average of 0.9 hours per week and Men TV for an average of 0.5 hours per week. What network do women 18 and over spend the most time watching? It is Playhouse Disney at 4.5 hours per week! What do the men spend the most time watching? You probably guessed it—TSN at 2.5 hours per week.[52]

Men and women also shop differently. Studies show that men and women share similar motivations about where to shop—that is, everyone seeks reasonable prices, merchandise quality, and a friendly, low-pressure environment. However, men and women don't necessarily feel the same about shopping in general. Most women enjoy shopping; most men claim that they dislike the experience and they shop only out of necessity. Furthermore, men desire convenience, simple shopping experiences, and stores with less variety. Stores that are easy to shop in, are near home or office, or have knowledgeable personnel appeal more to men than to women.[53] The Internet appeals to men who find that it's an easier and more enjoyable way to shop for clothing and gifts. Many Internet retailers are designing their sites to attract male gift buyers. FindGift.com's website is designed to take the worry out of gift buying. The site has a gift registry so that you can choose a gift from your special person's wish list. If you find the perfect gift idea while browsing the website, but the occasion is still months away, you can bookmark the gift and return at a later date to purchase it. Finally, the site provides an e-mail service that will remind you about upcoming special occasions.[54]

Trends in gender marketing are influenced by the changing roles of men and women in society. For instance, as women around the world are working and earning more, many industries are trying to attract new customers by marketing to women. Consulting firm Omnicomm created a special group they called G23 to consult on marketing to women around the world. G23 undertook a survey of 8,000 women living in 16 countries to try to understand their buying behaviour. The survey results were very revealing, to say the least. For example, G3 discovered that "women now make roughly 80% of the spending decisions." The research also found that "in purchasing a computer for the household, 89% of women have equal or more say in the decision; 39% have primary or sole control over the purchase." G3 also learned that "attitudes among 30-something women in China are consistent with those of 50-something women in the United States. They share the same attitudes about how they shop. They're conservative shoppers. They're thoroughly technologically savvy. They research everything that they shop for."[55]

The changing roles of men and women are also forcing companies that have traditionally targeted women to develop new strategies. For example, Dove, traditionally viewed as a female brand, launched a new line of Dove Men+Care products using advertising on the 2010 Super Bowl. Unilever, the company that makes Dove, decided to target "real men" as opposed to the typical post-adolescent males usually targeted for male personal-care products as exemplified by their Axe Body Spray brand. Canadian Dove brand manager Sharon MacLeod comments: "It's a celebration of men who feel comfortable in their own skin. It's an acknowledgement and celebration of these guys. That's the premise of Dove's philosophy when it comes to men's care. My hope is people will start talking about what it means to be a man today." The product launch was supported by in-store displays and a new website, **Dovemencare.com**, featuring a video for the new line of products.[56] It is often difficult for marketers to know how to respond as gender roles evolve and change.

AGE AND FAMILY LIFE-CYCLE STAGE

The age and family life-cycle stage of a consumer can have a significant impact on consumer behaviour. A consumer's age generally indicates what products he or she may be interested in purchasing. Consumer tastes in food, clothing, cars, furniture, and recreation are often age related; therefore, Toronto magazine publisher Bayard Canada targets children ages 3 to 6 with *Chirp*, ages 6 to 9 with *Chickadee*, and ages 9 to 13 with *Owl*. But as these children become teenagers, their tastes in magazines diverge in favour of sports titles for boys and fashion and lifestyle titles for girls.[57]

Related to a person's age is his or her place in the family life cycle. As Chapter 6 explains in more detail, the *family life cycle* is an orderly series of stages through which consumers' attitudes and behavioural tendencies evolve as a consequence of maturity, experience, and changing income and status. Marketers often define their target markets by family life cycle—"young singles," "young married with children," "middle-aged married without children," and so on. For instance, young singles spend more than average on alcoholic beverages, education, and entertainment. New parents typically increase their spending on health care, clothing, housing, and food and decrease their spending on alcohol, education, and transportation. Households with older children spend more on food, entertainment, personal-care products, and education, as well as on cars and gasoline. After their children leave home, spending by older couples on vehicles, women's clothing, health care, and long-distance calls typically increases. For instance, the presence of children in the home is the most significant determinant of the type of vehicle that's driven off the new car lot. Parents are the ultimate need-driven car consumers, requiring larger cars and trucks to haul their children and all their belongings. It comes as no surprise, then, that for all households with children, sport utility vehicles rank either first or second among new vehicle purchases, followed by minivans.

Marketers should also be aware of the many nontraditional life-cycle paths that are common today—paths that provide insights into the needs and wants of such consumers as divorced parents, lifelong singles, and childless couples. Four decades ago the majority of Canadian families were traditional families: married couples with children under 18. The average family size back in 1971 was 3.7 people and only 10 percent of families were single-parent families. Yet by 2006, the Canadian census was reporting an average family size of less than 3.0 people. In 2006, there were 8.9 million Canadian families; 68.6 percent were married families, 15.5 percent were common-law families, and 15.9 percent were lone-parent families, the majority of which were headed by a female (80.1 percent of all lone-parent families). Single-parent households headed by women represent over 20 percent of all households with children and are part of a broader societal change that has put more women on the career track. In addition, the sanctioning of gay marriages by Canadian courts in 2003 has changed the definition of family for marketers, with the 2006 census reporting same-sex couples as representing 0.6 percent of all couples in Canada. Although many marketers continue to be wary of targeting nontraditional families, Bank of Montreal Financial Group targeted single fathers in a print advertising campaign designed around the idea of letting people know they would be treated as individuals. The print ads featured a split-screen shot of two men, each walking and talking on a wireless phone. One of the men was middle-aged and carrying a set of golf clubs on his back; the second man was younger and walking with a baby strapped to his back in a carryall. The tag line was "For the world you live in."[58]

SOURCE: COURTESY OF BMO

Bank of Montreal Financial Group recognizes the many different lifestyles that people have today with its "For the world you live in" campaign.

Life Events

Another way to look at the life cycle is to look at major events in one's life over time. Life-changing events such as moving to a different place, marriage, birth or adoption of a child, getting fired, divorce, retirement, and death of a spouse are common in most people's lives and the specific timing is unpredictable. Typically, such events are quite stressful and consumers often take steps to minimize that stress. Many times such life-changing events will mean new consumption patterns.[59] A person moving to a different city (e.g., students who travel away from home to study) will need to find a new grocery store, a new auto service centre, a new hair salon, a new dentist, and a new doctor and these represent just a few of the needs that the person will have to find new providers for. Marketers have long understood that life events involve an opportunity to acquire new customers. The Welcome Wagon has operated in Canada since 1930, and although its original purpose was founded on helping area newcomers get settled with free gifts and information, the firm's mission has evolved. Its website states the following: "We greet people who are undergoing lifestyle changes with a friendly visit including moving to a new neighbourhood, planning a wedding, expecting a baby, a new executive, manager or professional, or new grandparents."[60]

PERSONALITY, SELF-CONCEPT, AND LIFESTYLE

Each consumer has a unique personality. **Personality** is a broad concept that can be thought of as a way of organizing and grouping how an individual typically reacts to situations. Thus personality combines psychological makeup and environmental forces. It includes people's underlying dispositions, especially their most dominant characteristics. Although personality is one of the least useful concepts in the study of consumer behaviour, some marketers believe that personality influences the types and brands of products purchased. For instance, the type of car, clothes, or jewellery a consumer buys may reflect one or more personality traits. Personality traits such as those listed in Exhibit 4.9 can be used to describe a consumer's personality.

Self-concept, or self-perception, is how consumers perceive themselves. Self-concept includes attitudes, perceptions, beliefs, and self-evaluations. Although self-concept may change, the change is often gradual. Through self-concept, people define their identity, which in turn provides for consistent and coherent behaviour.

Self-concept combines the **ideal self-image** (the way an individual would like to be) with the **real self-image** (how an individual actually perceives himself or herself). Generally, we try to raise our real self-image toward our ideal (or at least narrow the gap). Consumers seldom buy products that jeopardize their self-image. For example, someone who sees herself as a trendsetter wouldn't buy clothing that doesn't project a contemporary image.

Human behaviour depends largely on self-concept. Because consumers want to protect their identity as individuals, the products they buy, the stores they patronize, and the credit cards they carry support their self-image. No other product quite reflects a person's self-image as much as the car he or she drives. For example, many young consumers do not like family sedans such as the Honda Accord and the Toyota Camry and say they would buy one for their mother but not for themselves. Likewise, Mitsubishi found that car buyers did not want to sacrifice their youthful self-image just because they have new responsibilities in life. Thus advertising for their line of cars uses the positioning statement "Drive@Earth and encourages would-be car buyers to experience the exhilaration of driving stylish, exciting cars.[61] Positioning is discussed in more detail in Chapter 6.

By influencing the degree to which consumers perceive a good or service to be self-relevant, marketers can affect consumers' motivation to learn about, shop for, and buy a certain brand. Marketers also consider self-concept important because it helps explain the relationship between individuals' perceptions of themselves and their consumer behaviour.

An important component of self-concept is *body image*, the perception of the attractiveness of one's own physical features. Individuals who have cosmetic surgery often experience significant improvement in their overall body image and

---

personality
A way of organizing and grouping the consistencies of an individual's reactions to situations.

self-concept
How consumers perceive themselves in terms of attitudes, perceptions, beliefs, and self-evaluations.

ideal self-image
The way an individual would like to be.

real self-image
The way an individual actually perceives himself or herself.

EXHIBIT 4.9

Some Common Personality Traits
- Adaptability
- Need for affiliation
- Aggressiveness
- Need for achievement
- Ascendancy
- Autonomy
- Dominance
- Deference
- Defensiveness
- Emotionalism
- Orderliness
- Sociability
- Stability
- Self-confidence

SOURCE: ATANAS BOZHIKOV-ATANAS.DK/SHUTTERSTOCK

Although fitness is categorized most closely as a physiological need, it can also be considered a self-esteem need, especially regarding the prestigious health club memberships it often entails. Even during a recession, members will not sacrifice expensive memberships; to do so would be a subtle admission of financial difficulties.

lifestyle
A mode of living as identified by a person's activities, interests, and opinions.

self-concept. Moreover, a person's perception of body image can be a stronger reason for weight loss than either good health or other social factors.[62] With the median age of Canadians rising, many companies are introducing products and services aimed at aging baby boomers who are concerned about their age and physical appearance. Sales of hair-colouring products for men, for instance, have more than doubled over the past decade, and television and print ads aimed at getting men to dye the grey out of their hair have tripled. Similarly, many companies, including PepsiCo with its Tropicana juices and Pfizer with Viagra, are repositioning their products to focus on lifestyle.[63]

Personality and self-concept are reflected in **lifestyle**. A lifestyle is a mode of living, as identified by a person's activities, interests, and opinions. *Psychographics* is the analytical technique used to examine consumer lifestyles and to categorize consumers. Unlike personality characteristics, which are hard to describe and measure, lifestyle characteristics are useful in segmenting and targeting consumers. Lifestyle and psychographic analysis explicitly addresses how consumers outwardly express their inner selves in their social and cultural environment.

Many companies now use psychographics to better understand their market segments. For many years, marketers selling products to mothers conveniently assumed that all moms were fairly homogeneous and concerned about the same things—the health and well-being of their children—and that they could all be reached with a similar message. But recent lifestyle research has shown that there are traditional, blended, and non-traditional mothers, and companies like Procter & Gamble and Pillsbury are using strategies to reach these different types of mothers. Psychographics is also effective with other market segments. Ford of Canada targeted women car buyers in Toronto with a special promotion combined with L'Oreal to raise funds for the Canadian Breast Cancer Foundation. Ford donated a Ford Fusion to be auctioned off, with the proceeds going to the foundation, and it knew that many of the bidders would be women. Ford arranged for Andy Thê-Anh, a well known Montreal-based women's fashion designer, to customize the interior of the donated car so it would have a distinctive look that would appeal specifically to women bidders. Ford's research indicated that women represent 50 percent of actual car buyers in Canada. The research also showed that women approach car buying differently from men. Ford public affairs manager Christine Hollander commented: "Women look for companies that are good corporate citizens. They want to buy from companies that have a corporate soul. Men are impulse buyers. They see a car and boom, they buy it. Women do the research . . . they want to understand what's going on."[64] Psychographics and lifestyle segmentation are discussed in more detail in Chapter 6.

REVIEW LEARNING OUTCOME 7

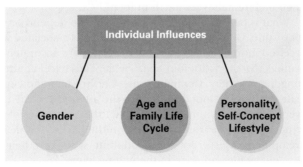

7 **Identify and understand the individual factors that affect consumer buying decisions**

Individual Influences

Gender | **Age and Family Life Cycle** | **Personality, Self-Concept Lifestyle**

PSYCHOLOGICAL INFLUENCES ON CONSUMER BUYING DECISIONS

(8)

Identify and understand the psychological factors that affect consumer buying decisions

An individual's buying decisions are further influenced by psychological factors: perception, motivation, learning, and beliefs and attitudes. These factors are what consumers use to interact with their world. They are the tools consumers use to recognize their feelings, gather and analyze information, formulate thoughts and opinions, and take action. Unlike the other three influences on consumer behaviour, psychological influences can be affected by a person's environment because they are applied on specific occasions. For example, you will perceive different stimuli and process these stimuli in different ways depending on whether you are sitting in class concentrating on the instructor, sitting outside class talking to friends, or sitting in your residence room watching television.

PERCEPTION

perception
The process by which people select, organize, and interpret stimuli into a meaningful and coherent picture.

selective exposure
The process by which a consumer notices certain stimuli and ignores others.

The world is full of stimuli. A stimulus is any unit of input affecting one or more of the five senses: sight, smell, taste, touch, and hearing. The process by which we select, organize, and interpret these stimuli to form a meaningful and coherent picture is called **perception**. In essence, perception is how we see the world around us and how we recognize that we need some help in making a purchasing decision.

People cannot perceive every stimulus in their environment. Therefore they use **selective exposure** to decide which stimuli to notice and which to ignore. A typical consumer is exposed to more than 2,500 advertising messages a day but notices only between 11 and 20 of them.

The familiarity of an object, contrast, movement, intensity (such as increased volume), and smell are cues that influence perception. Consumers use these cues to identify and define products and brands. The shape of a product's packaging—Coca-Cola's signature contour bottle, for instance—can influence perception. Colour is another cue, and it plays a key role in consumers' perceptions. Packaged food manufacturers use colour to trigger unconscious associations for grocery shoppers, who typically make their shopping decisions in the blink of an eye. When Pepsi departed from its usual blue can for a red can in a marketing campaign for the 2008 Summer Olympics in Beijing, China, they risked brand confusion with Coca-Cola. One Pepsi drinker in China said, "This is so weird. I usually go for the blue can; it's so easy to spot . . . the red can just doesn't look right." Pepsi officials say they coordinated the can with the colour of China's flag to highlight their sponsorship of Team China. Pepsi had used national colours on promotional packages before, such as yellow and green cans when they sponsored Brazilian teams.[65]

Fashion Trend (**www.fashiontrendsetter.com**) reports on global cultural trends to make forecasts of what colours will be popular. For example, in forecasting for the summer of 2010 this e-Zine reported the following: "Wide-ranging agreement at the latest biannual colour meeting organized by Eurovet: stylists and industrialists agreed that the market demands colour. Stars of the season: the greens. Guests of honour: nuances of red and soft and refined pinks, mauves and neutrals in full evolution. And essential are bright—almost neon—accents targeted at beachwear which is ever more influenced by the street and clubbing. Last but not least, white (colour 26!) and indigo blue remain very much in focus."[66]

What is perceived by consumers may also depend on the stimulus's vividness or shock value. Graphic warnings of the hazards associated with a product's use are perceived more readily and remembered more accurately than less vivid warnings or warnings that are written in text. "Sexier" ads excel at attracting the attention of younger consumers. Companies like Calvin Klein and Guess use sensuous ads to create a fantasy or mood to capture the attention of the target audience. Fragrance advertisements often make promises of the "outcome" of wearing their product, often the promise of role transformation on the part of the wearer. David Rubin, brand development director for Axe deodorant, says Axe's theme from the very start has been "giving guys an edge in the mating game."[67]

selective distortion
A process whereby a consumer changes or distorts information that conflicts with his or her feelings or beliefs.

Two other concepts closely related to selective exposure are selective distortion and selective retention. **Selective distortion** occurs when consumers change or distort information that conflicts with their feelings or beliefs. For example, people who smoke and have no plans to quit may distort information from medical reports about the links between smoking and cancer and ignore the strong Health Canada warnings such as "Smoking Can Kill You" that are prominently displayed on cigarette packages. Conversely, marketers who are aware of selective distortion use this tactic to get our attention. Mailings that look like cheques are quickly opened by consumers to reveal a direct marketing solicitation. Sometimes companies send us an actual cheque that obligates us to a contract if we cash it. Some people don't understand the implication; they just think they are cashing a cheque. The Ethics in Marketing Box illustrates a case in point.

Ethics in Marketing

 ## Did You Read That Cheque before you cashed it?

As we have discussed in this chapter, marketers study the psychology of consumers to identify unmet needs, develop products and services to meet those needs, and find a way to sell the products to those consumers. However, sometimes they use their knowledge and create promotional schemes that can mislead consumers.

Consider the case of energy deregulation in Ontario. Designed to promote free market competition and give consumers access to lower prices, it has spawned a number of competing energy companies that have been aggressively trying to sign up customers. They have been accused by a number of customers of stepping beyond the bounds of what one might call "ethical" business practices. Aggressive independent salespeople representing these companies were discovered to be using a number of unscrupulous and even illegal tactics. For example, the representatives would knock on doors and not clearly identify themselves, letting homeowners assume they were working for the homeowners' current utility company. The sales agents would claim to be doing an energy audit and ask to see the homeowner's energy bill. Compliant homeowners would show them the bill and then the salesperson would get their account numbers. Shortly after, the homeowner would find their energy accounts had been switched to a new supplier at a higher fixed price. These were the illegal tactics as a signature was required to make these switches and some of the sales agents were "forging" signatures on contracts. Of course, the companies they represented claimed they didn't know about the tactics and were merely executing their normal business activities. Homeowners caught up in this situation often had to resort to arbitration through the Better Business Bureau and utility regulators to get their contracts cancelled.

In other instances, when homeowners agreed to the audits, the salespeople would simply misrepresent what they were offering. Homeowners would be told that they needed to sign on for a new energy protection plan (actually switching energy suppliers) so they would sign contracts thinking they were dealing with their original supplier. Homeowners weren't told about their rights to get out of these contracts if they cancelled within 10 days. Many consumers found they were locked into long-term deals at fixed prices that were higher than the energy rates they had been paying and there was nothing they could do. They had unwisely signed a legal contract that they had not read.

Moving to a different approach, one that was less reliant on salespeople who might operate on the edge, Universal Energy, a gas and electricity marketer, designed a unique promotion to encourage Ontario consumers to sign up for its electrical energy distribution service.

Universal Energy distributed a direct mailing package with a cover letter, described by a marketing journalist as "explaining the electricity supply offer, a brochure containing the associated terms and conditions of the contract, and a perforated page containing a $50 cheque on the back of which was a signature line and a notation confirming that the recipient would, by cashing the cheque, become enrolled in a five-year electricity supply program with Universal Energy."

Some recipients of the offer displayed selective distortion in that they cashed the cheque thinking it was a rebate from their regular energy supplier only to discover they had actually changed their energy provider. When they sought recourse, they were shocked to discover that they had signed a legal contract to switch their energy suppliers and that the $50 cheque was a small recompense for the price increase they were charged by their new supplier, Universal Energy. For its part, Universal Energy states that it disclosed everything to the consumer in its offer. It is not the company's responsibility if consumers don't read the details (even the ones on the cheque!).[68]

So what do you think? Is Universal Energy's marketing approach unethical? In offering the cheques, was it trying to take advantage of selective distortion or did it simply run into it?

SOURCE: DAVID MENZIES, "CHEQUE MATES," MARKETING, AUG 27, 2007, 30; FEEDBACK, "UNIVERSAL ENERGY 'SET UP' BY MENZIES," MARKETING, OCTOBER 29, 2007, 4; ELLEN ROSEMAN, "ENERGY MARKETING NEEDS CURBS," TORONTO STAR, OCT 18, 2008, B.2; SCOTT SIMPSON, "GAS MARKETER FIGHTING BCUC RULING," THE VANCOUVER SUN, FEB 10, 2009, C.3; GORDON JAREMKO, "WE'LL FIRE WRONGDOERS, CHAIRMAN SAYS," EDMONTON JOURNAL, MAY 23, 2004, D.5; AND TONY COTE, "SAFEGUARD ENBRIDGE ACCOUNT NUMBER, MAN WARNS," THE OTTAWA CITIZEN, JUNE 17, 2002, B.8.

selective retention
A process whereby a consumer remembers only that information which supports his or her personal beliefs.

Selective retention is remembering only information that supports personal feelings or beliefs. The consumer forgets all information that may be inconsistent. For example, ads for over-the-counter and prescription drugs frequently disclose information on side effects and risks but most people forget about these and only remember the main benefit of the drug.

Which stimuli will be perceived often depends on the individual. People can be exposed to the same stimuli under identical conditions but perceive them very differently. Two people viewing a TV commercial may have different interpretations of the advertising message. One person may be thoroughly engrossed by the message and become highly motivated to buy the product. Thirty seconds after the ad ends, the second person may not be able to recall the content of the message or even the product advertised.

MARKETING IMPLICATIONS OF PERCEPTION

Marketers must recognize the importance of cues, or signals, in consumers' perception of products. Marketing managers first identify the important attributes, such as price or quality, that the targeted consumers want in a product and then design signals to communicate these attributes. For example, consumers will pay more for candy wrapped in expensive-looking foil packages. But shiny labels on wine bottles signify less expensive wines; dull labels indicate more expensive wines. Marketers also often use price as a signal to consumers that the product is of higher quality than competing products. Gibson Guitar Corporation briefly cut prices on many of its guitars to compete with Japanese rivals Yamaha and Ibanez; it found that it actually sold *more* guitars when it charged more for them. Consumers perceived that the higher price indicated a better quality instrument.[69]

Of course, brand names send signals to consumers. The brand names of Close-Up toothpaste, Eliminator batteries, and Caress moisturizing soap identify important product qualities. Names chosen for search engines and sites on the Internet, such as Yahoo! and Google, are intended to convey excitement, intensity, and vastness. Companies can even change their names to send a message to consumers. As today's electric utility companies increasingly enter nonregulated markets to sell power, natural gas, and other energy-related products and services, they are finding that their old company names may hold some negative perceptions with consumers. Consequently, some are shedding their stodgy "Power & Light & Electric" names in favour of ones that let consumers know they are not just about electricity any more. Two examples are Alberta-based Enmax (formerly the City of Calgary Electric System) and Ontario-based Reliance Home Comfort (which used to be called Union Energy).

Consumers also associate quality and reliability with certain brand names. Companies watch their brand identity closely, in large part because a strong link has been established between perceived brand value and customer loyalty. Some Canadian brand names that consistently enjoy high perceived value from consumers are Canadian Tire, Telus, Roots, Molson, Weston, Tim Hortons, and President's Choice. Naming a product after a place can also add perceived value by association. Brand names using the words Banff, Whistler, and Yukon convey a sense of openness, freedom, and youth.

SOURCE: © LEIGH PRATHER/SHUTTERSTOCK

" *Consumers will likely notice a 20 percent price decrease more quickly than a 15 percent decrease* "

Marketing managers are also interested in the *threshold level of perception*: the minimum difference in a stimulus that the consumer will notice. This concept is sometimes referred to as the "just noticeable difference." For example, how much would Apple have to drop the price of its iPhone before consumers recognized it as a bargain—$25? $50? more? One study found that the just noticeable difference in a stimulus is about a 20 percent change. Thus consumers will likely notice a 20 percent price decrease more quickly than a 15 percent decrease. This marketing principle can be applied to other marketing variables as well, such as package size or loudness of a broadcast advertisement.[70]

Another study found that the bargain-price threshold for a name brand is lower than that for a store brand. In other words, consumers perceive a bargain more readily when stores offer a small discount on a name-brand item than when they offer the same discount on a store brand; a larger discount is needed to achieve a similar effect for a store brand.[71] Researchers also found that for low-cost grocery items, consumers typically do not see past the second digit in the price. For instance, consumers do not perceive any real difference between two comparable cans of tuna, one priced at $1.52 and the other at $1.59, because they ignore the last digit.[72]

Besides changing such stimuli as price, package size, and volume, marketers can change the product or attempt to reposition its image. Listerine is a well-known brand of mouthwash that has been on retailer's shelves for more than 125 years! A very strong-tasting mouthwash, for nearly a century it was positioned as a brand that "kills germs that cause bad breath." In the 1970s and 1980s, sweet-tasting mouthwashes took hold and Listerine lost market share. In addition, the cosmetic-focused "bad breath" appeal was losing strength and consumers were becoming more concerned with health-related factors such as plaque, tartar, and gingivitis, and most recently, people have become interested in whitening their teeth as well. Listerine has adjusted its product line and now offers a wide variety of products to cater to these needs, including Listerine Total Care, which describes the following user benefits: kills germs that cause gingivitis; strengthens teeth to prevent cavities; reduces plaque; prevents gingivitis to maintain healthy gums; helps keep teeth white; and freshens the breath.[73] But marketers must be careful when adding features. How many new services will discounter Zellers need to add before consumers perceive it as a full-service department store? How many sporty features will Chrysler have to add to a basic two-door sedan before consumers start perceiving it as a sports car?

Marketing managers who intend to do business in global markets should be aware of how foreign consumers perceive their products. For instance, in Japan, product labels are often written in English or French, even though they may not translate into anything meaningful. Many Japanese associate foreign words on product labels with the exotic, the expensive, and high quality.

Marketers have often been suspected of sending advertising messages subconsciously to consumers in what is known as *subliminal perception*. The controversy began when a researcher claimed to have increased popcorn and Coca-Cola sales at a movie theatre after flashing "Eat Popcorn" and "Drink Coca-Cola" on the screen every five seconds for 1/300th of a second, although the audience did not consciously recognize the messages. Almost immediately, consumer protection groups became concerned that advertisers were brainwashing consumers, and this practice was promptly made illegal in Canada and California. Although the researcher later admitted to making up the data and scientists have been unable to replicate the study since, consumers are still wary of hidden messages that advertisers may be sending.

MOTIVATION

By studying motivation, marketers can analyze the major forces influencing consumers to buy or not buy products. When you buy a product, you usually do so to fulfill some kind of need. These needs become motives when aroused sufficiently. For instance, suppose this morning you felt so drowsy that you needed something to perk you up. In response to that need, you stopped at Tim Hortons for an extra-large double-cream double-sugar coffee. In other words, you were motivated by drowsiness to stop at Tim Hortons. **Motives** are the driving forces that cause a person to take action to satisfy specific needs.

Why are people driven by particular needs at particular times? One popular theory is **Maslow's hierarchy of needs**, shown in Exhibit 4.10, which arranges needs in ascending order of importance: physiological, safety, social, esteem, and self-actualization. As a person fulfills one need, a higher-level need becomes more important.

The most basic human needs are *physiological*—that is, the needs for food, water, and shelter. Because they are essential to survival, these needs must be satisfied first. Ads showing how a Harvey's hamburger is made or a runner gulping down Gatorade after a marathon are examples of appeals to satisfy the physiological needs of hunger and thirst.

Safety needs include security and freedom from pain and discomfort. Marketers often exploit consumers' fears and anxieties about safety to sell their products. Michelin has long positioned its products on an appeal to safety. In one media

motive
A driving force that causes a person to take action to satisfy specific needs.

Maslow's hierarchy of needs
A method of classifying human needs and motivations into five categories in ascending order of importance: physiological, safety, social, esteem, and self-actualization.

EXHIBIT 4.10

Maslow's Hierarchy of Needs

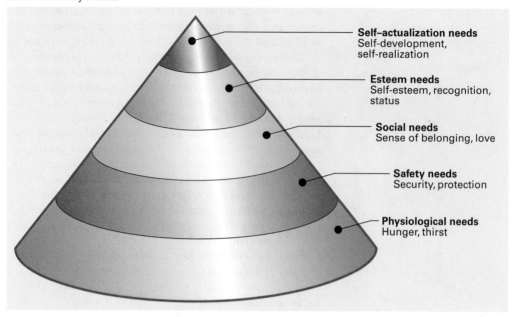

campaign, the Michelin Man—his name is Bibendum, by the way—lies in the snow making snow angels. Several consumers wrote letters to Michelin expressing how nice it was to think of Michelin tires as "guardian angels." Michelin was pleased to discover that consumers were getting the point of the campaign, which was "to make consumers feel warm and safe with Michelin."[74] On the other hand, some companies or industries advertise to allay consumer fears. For example, in the wake of its massive recall in 2010 to fix accelerator pedal problems in popular models such as the Corolla, Camry, Matrix, and RAV4, Toyota found itself having to conduct an image campaign to reassure consumers about the safety of its cars.[75]

After physiological and safety needs have been fulfilled, *social needs*—especially love and a sense of belonging—become the focus. Love includes acceptance by one's peers, as well as sex and romantic love. Marketing managers probably appeal more to this need than to any other. Ads for clothes, cosmetics, and vacation packages suggest that buying the product can bring love. The need to belong is also a favourite of marketers, especially those marketing products to teens. Teens consider the iPod to be not only their favourite brand but also as defining their generation. Other such brands include Axe, Facebook, Google, and YouTube.[76]

Love is acceptance without regard to one's contribution. Esteem is acceptance based on one's contribution to the group. *Self-esteem needs* include self-respect and a sense of accomplishment. Esteem needs also include prestige, fame, and recognition of one's accomplishments. Mont Blanc pens, Mercedes-Benz automobiles, and Holt Renfrew stores all appeal to esteem needs. Colgate-Palmolive's Dove brand has embarked on an international campaign to challenge societal notions of beauty. The company says the "Campaign for Real Beauty" is targeted at average female consumers. Its mission statement points out that it uses real women "of various ages, shapes and sizes to provoke discussion and debate about today's typecast beauty images."[77]

Asian consumers, in particular, are strongly motivated by status and appearance. Asians tend to be strongly conscious of their place in a group, institution, and society as a whole. The importance of gaining social recognition makes Asians some of the most image-conscious consumers in the world. Status-conscious Asians will not hesitate to spend freely on premium brands such as BMW, Mercedes-Benz, and the best Scotch whisky and French cognac. Indeed, marketers of luxury products such as Gucci, Louis Vuitton, and Prada find that demand for their products is so strong among image-conscious consumers that their sales are generally unaffected by economic downturns.

In some cases, companies have been able to make up for sluggish European and North American sales by raising prices and volumes in Asia.[78]

The highest human need is *self-actualization*. This refers to finding self-fulfillment and self-expression, reaching the point in life at which "people are what they feel they should be." Maslow felt that very few people ever attain this level. Even so, advertisements may focus on this type of need. In its ads, American Express Canada conveys the message that acquiring its card is one of the highest attainments in life with campaign slogans like "Realize the Potential."[79]

LEARNING

Almost all consumer behaviour results from **learning**, which is the process that creates changes in behaviour, immediate or expected, through experience and practice. It is not possible to observe learning directly, but we can infer when it has occurred by a person's actions. Suppose you see an ad for a new and improved cold medicine. If you go to the store that day and buy that remedy, we infer that you have learned something about the cold medicine.

There are two types of learning: experiential and conceptual. *Experiential learning* occurs when an experience changes your behaviour. For example, if the new cold medicine does not relieve your symptoms, you may not buy that brand again. *Conceptual learning*, which is not acquired through direct experience, is the second type of learning. Assume, for example, that you are standing at a soft drink machine and notice a new diet flavour with an artificial sweetener. Because someone has told you that diet beverages leave an aftertaste, you choose a different drink. You have learned that you would not like this new diet drink without ever trying it.

Reinforcement and repetition boost learning. Reinforcement can be positive or negative. If you see a vendor selling frozen yogurt (stimulus), buy it (response), and find the yogurt to be quite refreshing (reward), your behaviour has been positively reinforced. On the other hand, if you buy a new flavour of yogurt and it does not taste good (negative reinforcement), you will not buy that flavour of yogurt again (response). Without positive or negative reinforcement, a person will not be motivated to repeat the behaviour pattern or to avoid it. Thus if a new brand evokes neutral feelings, some marketing activity, such as a price change or an increase in promotion, may be required to induce further consumption. Learning theory is helpful in reminding marketers that concrete and timely actions are what reinforce desired consumer behaviour.

Repetition is a key strategy in promotional campaigns because it can lead to increased learning. Most marketers use repetitious advertising so that consumers will learn what their unique advantage is over the competition. Generally, to heighten learning, advertising messages should be spread over time rather than clustered together.

A related learning concept useful to marketing managers is stimulus generalization. In theory, **stimulus generalization** occurs when one response is extended to a second stimulus similar to the first. Marketers often use a successful, well-known brand name for a family of products because it gives consumers familiarity with and knowledge about each product in the family. Such brand-name families spur the introduction of new products and facilitate the sale of existing items. Microsoft entered the video game industry, hoping that the Microsoft brand would guarantee sales for the Xbox. Initial response to the Xbox was strong based on Microsoft's reputation. Since then, Microsoft has worked hard to be successful in an industry dominated by other brand giants, Sony and Nintendo. The latest generation Xbox 360 has high-definition graphics, on-line play, and compelling digital entertainment; it plays music and movies stored in an array of devices, including MP3 players, and displays photos from digital cameras. Branding is examined in more detail in Chapter 8.

Another form of stimulus generalization occurs when retailers or wholesalers design their packages to resemble well-known manufacturers' brands. Such imitation often confuses consumers, who buy the imitator thinking that it's the original. Canadian manufacturers in foreign markets have sometimes found little if any brand protection. The Cowichan First Nations people found a market for their hand-knit sweaters among Japanese tourists in British Columbia. Hoping to capitalize on this interest by selling in Japan, they were shocked to find that machine-made Cowichan knockoffs were being exported to Japan from New Zealand![80] BMW and Chrysler recently sued Chinese car manufacturers for creating near-exact replicas of their cars. Counterfeit products are those which are manufactured to look exactly like the original. Cosmetic giant L'Oréal, maker of Gucci and other luxury brands, threatened legal action against eBay unless the auction site cracked down on sales of counterfeit L'Oréal products on its site. DVD piracy is rampant in China, so much so that special DVD-counterfeit-sniffing dogs have become a common sight at international airports. Because of the threats of terrorism, stepped-up security regulations and authentication technologies have been used successfully in identifying fake passports, currency, and credit cards. Those same technologies—and others, such as embedded microchips, holographic symbols, and tamperproof packaging—are now being used in everyday products such as clothing, footwear, computers, mobile phones, video games, jewellery, software, pharmaceuticals, and medical devices, making it easier for importers and retailers to spot fakes.[81]

The opposite of stimulus generalization is **stimulus discrimination**, which means learning to differentiate among similar products. Consumers usually prefer one product as more rewarding or stimulating. Some consumers prefer Coca-Cola and others prefer Pepsi. Many consumers insist they can taste a difference between the two brands.

With some types of products—such as aspirin, gasoline, bleach, and paper towels—marketers rely on promotion to point out brand differences that consumers would otherwise not recognize. This process, called *product differentiation*, is discussed in more detail in Chapter 6. Usually, product differentiation is based on superficial differences. For example, Bayer tells consumers that it's the aspirin "doctors recommend most."

BELIEFS AND ATTITUDES

Beliefs and attitudes are closely linked to values. A **belief** is an organized pattern of knowledge that an individual holds as true about his or her world. A consumer may believe that Apple iPods are the best MP3 players—they interface best with computer software, tolerate hard use, and are reasonably priced. These beliefs may be based on knowledge, faith, or hearsay. Consumers tend to develop a set of beliefs about a product's attributes and then, through these beliefs, form a *brand image*—a set of beliefs about a particular brand. In turn, the brand image shapes consumers' attitudes toward the product.

An **attitude** is a learned tendency to respond consistently toward a given object, such as a brand. Attitudes rest on an individual's value system, which represents personal standards of good and bad, right and wrong, and so forth; therefore, attitudes tend to be more enduring and complex than beliefs.

For an example of the nature of attitudes, consider the differing attitudes of consumers around the world toward the practice of purchasing on credit. Canadians and Americans are known to be enthusiastic about charging goods and services and are willing to pay high interest rates for the privilege of postponing payment. For many European consumers, doing what amounts to taking out a loan—even a small one—to pay for anything seems absurd. Germans in particular are reluctant to buy on credit. Italy has a sophisticated credit and banking system well suited to handling credit cards, but Italians prefer to carry cash, often huge wads of it. Although most Japanese consumers have credit cards, card purchases amount to less than 1 percent of all consumer transactions. The Japanese have long looked down on credit purchases but will acquire cards to use while travelling abroad.[82]

If a good or service is meeting its profit goals, positive attitudes toward the product merely need to be reinforced. If the brand is not succeeding, however, the marketing manager must strive to change target consumers' attitudes toward it. Changes in attitude tend to grow out of an individual's efforts to reconcile long-held values with a constant stream of new information. This change can be accomplished

stimulus discrimination
A learned ability to differentiate among similar products.

belief
An organized pattern of knowledge that an individual holds as true about his or her world.

attitude
A learned tendency to respond consistently toward a given object.

in three ways: by changing beliefs about the brand's attributes, by changing the relative importance of these beliefs, and by adding new beliefs.

CHANGING BELIEFS ABOUT ATTRIBUTES

The first technique is to turn neutral or negative beliefs about product attributes into positive ones. Quebec-based Canadelle, maker of Wonderbra, celebrated 70 years of business in 2009 but wants to reach more youthful customers. The company is trying to change women's beliefs about Wonderbra products. Research indicated that women viewed the Wonderbra brand as "their grandmother's bra" and that they were not receptive to purchasing it. Too counter this image, the company "has introduced more fashionable underwear, like a leopard-print set."[83]

Changing beliefs about a service can be more difficult because service attributes are intangible. Convincing consumers to switch hairstylists or lawyers or to go to a mall dental clinic can be much more difficult than getting them to change brands of razor blades. Image, which is also largely intangible, significantly determines service patronage. When WestJet Airlines started up, it was perceived as a "folksy airline that could" by many people. The airline offered low prices and served mainly western Canada. WestJet has been a tremendous success and is now Canada's second largest airline. The company wanted to change its "folksy" regional carrier image to one that says "WestJet is a national airline carrier." So in 2005 it developed a national promotional campaign under the theme "It's Nicer Up Here" to establish the WestJet brand in eastern Canada. The result was a 35 percent return on investment for the airline. WestJet has since followed up this image change campaign with a new approach that focuses on the fact that its employees are equity owners who care for customers "Because Owners Care."[84] Service marketing is explored in detail in Chapter 10.

CHANGING THE IMPORTANCE OF BELIEFS

The second approach to modifying attitudes is to change the relative importance of beliefs about an attribute. For years, consumers have known that bran cereals are high in natural fibre. The primary belief associated with this attribute is that the fibre tends to act as a mild, natural laxative. Today, however, cereal marketers promote the high fibre content of bran cereals as a possible factor in preventing certain types of cancer. This shift has vastly increased the importance of this attribute in the minds of consumers.

Marketers can also emphasize the importance of some beliefs over others. For example, when consumers think of SUVs, they do not equate them with good fuel economy. General Motors of Canada has had great success in promoting its new

In order to increase sales, a company must change negative attitudes about its product held by those who are not buying it. One way to accomplish this is by changing the beliefs about the product's attributes, such as taste. This ad for Silk soymilk does just that by focusing on good taste.

SOURCE: COURTESY OF WHITE WAVE FOOD PRODUCTS

Chevrolet Equinox SUV. The vehicle, which is assembled in Ingersoll, Ontario, is being promoted as the most fuel-efficient SUV on the Canadian market. GM Canada's promotion states: "The All New Chevrolet Equinox. At 6.1 L/100 km fuel efficiency and over 1,100 kilometres between fillups, the Chevrolet Equinox has better highway fuel efficiency than Honda CR-V, Toyota RAV4 and even Ford Escape Hybrid."[85]

ADDING NEW BELIEFS

The third approach to transforming attitudes is to add new beliefs. Kellogg's was amazed to discover that "sales of its All-Bran cereal jumped 74 percent in six months after it claimed a high-fibre diet reduced the risk of cancer." Kellogg's learned that consumers were willing to pay a premium for healthy foods; however, despite the sales increases the consumers also let them know that All-Bran was not the most flavourful cereal. Kellogg's responded to both these facts by developing some new products. Kellogg's of Canada is now promoting All-Bran Honey Nut Flavour and All Bran Strawberry Bites cereals and its line of All-Bran Bars using the theme that people "won't believe a high-fibre food can taste so good." Commercials for these products show people trying these foods and commenting on how great they taste; nonbelieving friends and co-workers collapse with laughter on being told that All-Bran tastes good.[86]

North American companies attempting to market their goods overseas may need to help consumers add new beliefs about a product in general. For example, both Coca-Cola and PepsiCo have found it challenging to sell their diet cola brands to consumers in India. Part of the reason is that diet foods of any kind are a new concept in a country where malnutrition was widespread not too many years ago. Indians also have deeply rooted attitudes that anything labelled "diet" is meant for a sick person, such as a diabetic. As a general rule, most Indians are not diet conscious, preferring foods that taste good and are prepared in the traditional manner. Indians are also suspicious of the artificial sweeteners used in diet colas. India's Health Ministry requires warning labels on cans and bottles of Diet Coke and Diet Pepsi that say: "Not Recommended for Children."[87]

REVIEW LEARNING OUTCOME 8

8 | **Identify and understand the psychological factors that affect consumer buying decisions**

Perception	Selective Exposure	
	Selective Retention	Selective Distortion

Motivation	Needs				
	Physiological	Safety	Social	Esteem	Self-Actualization

Learning	Stimulus Generalization	Stimulus Discrimination

Beliefs & Attitudes	Changing Beliefs about Attributes	Changing Importance of Beliefs	Adding New Beliefs

REVIEW AND APPLICATIONS

1 **Explain why marketing managers should understand consumer behaviour.** Consumer behaviour describes how consumers make purchase decisions and how they use and dispose of the products they buy. An understanding of consumer behaviour reduces marketing managers' uncertainty when they are defining a target market and designing a marketing mix.

1.1 The type of decision making a consumer uses for a product does not necessarily remain constant. Why? Support your answer with an example from your own experience.

2 Analyze the components of the consumer decision-making process. The consumer decision-making process begins with need recognition, when stimuli trigger awareness of an unfulfilled want. If additional information is required to make a purchase decision, the consumer may engage in an internal or external information search. The consumer then evaluates the additional information and establishes purchase guidelines. Finally, a purchase decision is made.

2.1 **ONLINE** Visit the Auto Traders website at **www.autotrader.ca**. How does the site assist consumers in the evaluation stage of choosing a new car? Develop your own hypothetical evoked set of three or four car models and present your comparisons. Which vehicle attributes would be the most important in your purchase decision?

3 Explain the consumer's postpurchase evaluation process. Consumer postpurchase evaluation is influenced by prepurchase expectations, the prepurchase information search, and the consumer's general level of self-confidence. Cognitive dissonance is the inner tension that a consumer experiences after recognizing a purchased product's disadvantages. When a purchase creates cognitive dissonance, consumers tend to react by seeking positive reinforcement for the purchase decision, avoiding negative information about the purchase decision, or revoking the purchase decision by returning the product.

3.1 **WRITING** Recall an occasion when you experienced cognitive dissonance about a purchase. In a letter to a friend, describe the event and explain what you did about it.

4 **TEAM** Identify the types of consumer buying decisions and discuss the significance of consumer involvement. Consumer decision making falls into three broad categories. First, consumers exhibit routine response behaviour for frequently purchased, low-cost items that require very little decision effort; routine response behaviour is typically characterized by brand loyalty. Second, consumers engage in limited decision making for occasional purchases or for unfamiliar brands in familiar product categories. Third, consumers practise extensive decision making when making unfamiliar, expensive, or infrequent purchases. High-involvement decisions usually include an extensive information search and a thorough evaluation of alternatives. In contrast, low-involvement decisions are characterized by brand loyalty and a lack of personal identification with the product. The main factors affecting the level of consumer involvement are previous experience, interest, perceived risk of negative consequences (financial, social, and psychological), situation, and social visibility.

4.1 Describe the three categories of consumer decision-making behaviour. Name typical products for which each type of consumer behaviour is used.

4.2 **ONLINE** Describe the level of involvement and the involvement factors likely to be associated with purchasing a new computer. Do you think The Apple Store's website at **store.apple.com/ca** simplifies or complicates the process for the average consumer? Explain.

5 Identify and understand the cultural factors that affect consumer buying decisions. Cultural influences on consumer buying decisions include culture and values, subculture, and social class. Culture is the essential character of a society that distinguishes it from other cultural groups. The underlying elements of every culture are its values, language, myths, customs, rituals, and laws, as well as its artifacts or products, which are transmitted from one generation to the next. The most defining element of a culture is its values—the enduring belief shared by a society that a specific mode of conduct is personally or socially preferable to another mode of conduct. A culture can be divided into subcultures on the basis of demographic characteristics, geographic regions, national and ethnic background, political beliefs, and religious beliefs. Subcultures share elements of the overall culture as well as cultural elements unique to their own group. A social class is a group of people who are considered nearly equal in status or community esteem, who regularly socialize among themselves both formally and informally, and who share behavioural norms.

5.1 ✏ WRITING You are a new marketing manager for a company that produces a line of athletic shoes to be targeted to the college and university student subculture. In a memo to your boss, list some product attributes that might appeal to this subculture and the steps in your customers' purchase processes, and recommend some marketing strategies that can influence their decisions.

6 Identify and understand the social factors that affect consumer buying decisions. Social factors include external influences such as reference groups, opinion leaders, and family. Consumers seek out others' opinions for guidance on new products or services, and products with image-related attributes because the available attribute information is lacking or uninformative. Consumers may use products or brands to identify with or become a member of a reference group. Opinion leaders are members of reference groups who influence others' purchase decisions. Family members also influence purchase decisions; children tend to shop in patterns similar to those of their parents.

6.1 ✏ WRITING Family members play many different roles in the buying process: initiator, influencer, decision maker, purchaser, and consumer. In your family, name who might play each of these roles in the purchase of the following products or services: a dinner at Swiss Chalet; a summer vacation; Fruit Loops breakfast cereal; a Canadian Olympic team jacket; golf clubs; an Internet service provider; and a new car.

7 Identify and understand the individual factors that affect consumer buying decisions. Individual factors that affect consumer buying decisions include gender; age and family life-cycle stage; and personality, self-concept, and lifestyle. Beyond obvious physiological differences, men and women differ in their social and economic roles, and that affects consumer buying decisions. How old a consumer is generally indicates what products he or she may be interested in purchasing. Marketers often define their target markets in terms of consumers' life-cycle stage, following changes in consumers' attitudes and behavioural tendencies as they mature. Finally, certain products and brands reflect consumers' personality, self-concept, and lifestyle.

7.1 ✏ WRITING Assume that you are involved in the following consumer decision situations: (a) renting a video to watch with your roommates, (b) choosing a restaurant to go to with a new friend, (c) buying a new video game, (d) buying jeans to wear to class. List the individual factors that would influence your decision in each situation and explain your responses.

8 Identify and understand the psychological factors that affect consumer buying decisions. Psychological factors include perception, motivation, learning, values, beliefs, and attitudes. These factors allow consumers to interact with the world around them, recognize their feelings, gather and analyze information, formulate thoughts and opinions, and take action. Perception allows consumers to recognize their consumption problems. Motivation is what drives consumers to take action to satisfy specific consumption needs. Almost all consumer behaviour results from learning, which is the process that creates changes in behaviour through experience. Consumers with similar beliefs and attitudes tend to react alike to marketing-related inducements.

8.1 How do beliefs and attitudes influence consumer behaviour? How can negative attitudes toward a product be changed? How can marketers alter beliefs about a product? Give some examples of how marketers have changed negative attitudes about a product or added or altered beliefs about a product.

TERMS

aspirational reference group 108
attitude 122
belief 122
brand extensions 95
cognitive dissonance 96
consumer behaviour 90
consumer decision-making process 90

culture 102
evoked set (consideration set) 94
extensive decision making 99
external information search 92
ideal self-image 114
internal information search 92
involvement 98

learning 121
lifestyle 115
limited decision making 98
marketing-controlled information
    source 93
Maslow's hierarchy of needs 119
motive 119

EXERCISES

APPLICATION EXERCISE

Principles of consumer behaviour are evident in many areas of marketing. Perhaps the easiest place to see this critical foundation of marketing activity is in print ads.[88]

Activities

1. **WRITING** Review the main concepts in this chapter and create a checklist that itemizes them. Then comb through your favourite magazines and newspapers for ads that illustrate each concept. To get a wide variety of ads, you will need to look through several magazines. If you don't have many magazines at your disposal, go to the campus library periodical room. Photocopy the ads you select to support this chapter.

2. Because pictures can help reinforce understanding, consider doing this exercise for each chapter in the book. At the end of the semester, you will have a portfolio of ads that illustrate the concepts in the entire book, which can help you study. Simply look through your portfolio and try to recall the concepts at work in each advertisement.

ETHICS EXERCISE

EyeOnU operates a web filter service for public schools and libraries to protect students from inappropriate material on the Internet. Like the industry as a whole, the company's market share has been stagnant for the past two years. Looking for new sources of revenue, the company is considering selling the data it has collected about student surfing habits to marketers trying to learn more about students' behaviour on the web. The data are anonymous but privacy advocates are concerned about the precedent of selling information about the children to marketers.

Activities

1. What should EyeOnU do? Should it protect the students' data, or should it take the opportunity to create new revenues?

2. **ONLINE** Does the CMA Code of Ethics for marketing to children address this issue? Go to **www.the-cma.org** and locate the Code of Ethics under the Regulatory Affairs category and review the section on marketing to children. Then write a brief paragraph on how the CMA Code of Ethics for marketing to children relates to the activities of EyeOnU.

CASE STUDY

RETAILING CLOTHING TO MEN

When it comes to retailing men's clothing in Canada, it is anything but a "man's world." One retail consultant has been quoted as saying "most men's stores are just modified versions of a space that was really designed for women, rather than a space that men truly feel comfortable in." What is it about the shopping behaviour of men that clothing retailers just don't seem to understand and how can they adapt?

Consider the comments of 37-year-old Torontonian, Sean Kondra, who told writer Susan Mohammad that he insists his girlfriend can shop with him only under the condition that "she shops like a man." This means picking out clothing as fast as possible and getting in and out of the mall as fast as possible. Kondra says, "I hate malls. You have dance beats emanating from different stores like it's a competition to see who can annoy me the most. There are lost souls wandering aimlessly in front of me, and I know what socks and what pants I want—but instead of finding them in one place, I have to go foraging around a 10,000-foot store on four different levels."

Retailing experts in touch with male buying behaviour observe that men don't like malls and they don't like the process of shopping for clothing very much. Still, they want to buy clothing that makes them look good. According to retail consultant Bertrand Pellegrin, who has helped launch concept stores for Louis Vuitton and Gucci, male clothing shoppers in North America are becoming more vain about their looks but he comments they "would still prefer a lobotomy to an afternoon of shopping." Pellegrin believes that male clothing shoppers "need a place where they truly feel masculine."

Pellegrin is of the opinion that male clothing retailers need to take a lesson from traditionally male-oriented retailers like sports bars, electronics stores, and yes, strip clubs! He believes clothing retailers need to offer a lounge area for men so they can hang out like they do in sports bars. This will give them a level of comfort. These lounges should have some distractions and reinforce the idea that the shopper is not forced to have an immediate interaction with sales staff or anyone else. Electronics stores work well for male shoppers because they put products on display so that men can play with them. Pellerin told Mohammad, "It's the interactivity with the product itself that's appealing. If you go on any given day, you see guys exploring a new product, trying to understand it and very often explaining to his girlfriend what it can do and why this one is better than the other. That's a very masculine thing to do." When it comes to learning from strip clubs, men's clothing retailers need to realize that they should remind men about their masculinity. "I think men do struggle with wondering whether people see them as masculine enough in both personal and business relationships. I think guys really respond to a person who acts like their buddy. Of course, a hot but approachable female doesn't hurt either."

Finally, men do not like to be pestered. GotStyle menswear store in the heart of Toronto is a loft store rather like a clubhouse, with its leather chairs, barber shop, in-house tailor, and even a Burmese mountain dog. Owner Melissa Austria has told her staff that they need to educate their clients rather than pressure them to make immediate purchases. Austria instructs her employees to approach clients by saying hello followed by asking them if they have been in the store before and then offering to give a tour. She explicitly comments that asking "Can I help you," is a forbidden manner of greeting. Pellegrin comments that men are a long-term investment. It will take time, but unlike women, men are far more loyal as a consumer. When they find something they like—they stick to it."[89]

Questions

1. Is the shopping behaviour of men really different from that of women? Review the chapter models on buyer behaviour. What process do you think would apply to the purchase of men's clothing?

2. Discuss the approaches that Pellegrin recommends that men's retail stores copy from other retailers. Do you think they would really work as well for clothing? Discuss.

3. Visit (or recall a visit) to a men's clothing store in your local mall and then visit (or recall a visit) to a stand-alone men's store. Evaluate the atmospheres. Are they truly "men's" stores? Now look at the comments of Melissa Austria. If you were going to make your local men's clothing stores more appealing to men, what other touches might you recommend that they add?

VIDEO CASE

THE PSYCHOLOGY OF CONSUMER SPENDING

As Howard Green of Business News Network prepares to interview Priya Raghubir, professor, New York University, Stern School of Business, on the psychology of consumer spending, he discusses buying a chocolate bar with his co-host Linda Nazareth and mentions if all he had was $20 he probably wouldn't buy. Linda professes a love of chocolate and says she would break the $20 bill and get the chocolate bar.

Priya Raghubir has been looking at the subjective value of money for many years along with other researchers at the Stern School of Business. She has learned that people's spending habits differ depending on the form of money they carry whether it is credit cards, debit cards, cash, small bills or large bills, domestic currency or foreign currency. The key finding of her research is that people vary in their "fear" of spending. Some people have a strong "fear" of spending while others do not.

Raghubir comments that a person's level of fear is affected by the form of money they carry. For example, spending using credit cards is easier for people with high levels of fear than using cash, especially large bills. The reason for this difference is that most people don't think of credit cards as a form of "real" money. People think of it as being more like monopoly money and will actually spend more when they use credit cards than if they use cash. Raghubir's research indicates that debit cards are treated more like credit cards when it comes to spending behaviour despite the fact that the money comes directly from a person's bank account, a transaction that is virtually the same as cash. She says that when consumers make purchases using credit or debit cards, they suffer less angst because they don't see their money supply "shrink" before their eyes as they do when they pay with cash.

When people use foreign currencies, they often go one of two ways. They are either paralyzed and will not spend at all, or they will spend freely. In both cases, Raghubir says the explanation of the behaviour is that the person does not really know the "value" of the money and this affects their buying behaviour. She says that Internet buyers purchase quite freely because it is so easy for a person to simply "click" to make a purchase. Unless you shop like you do in a physical store you don't have other products and other prices to make immediate comparisons, and when people are on the Internet many of them don't shop for price even though they could.

What is it about cash that affects people's spending so much, Raghubir is asked. If people carried larger bills, they were less likely to make impulse buys when compared to people who had smaller bills. In her research, Raghubir actually gave buyers the same amounts of money but simply used different denominations, so that one group of people was given single $5 bills and a second group of people was given five loonies. The purchasing behaviour of the two groups was then observed to see how they spent the money. Similarly, one group of people was given single $20 bills and another group was given four $5 bills, and once again, the spending behaviour of the two groups was monitored. The findings in all these cases were that people with the larger bills tended to spend less.

When Raghubir and her co-researchers examined the reasons behind this behaviour, they found that people with larger bills didn't spend because they were afraid of losing self-control. People with large bills don't spend because they are afraid they will spend the whole amount. When Raghubir was asked whether the experience of a recession would change people's spending habits, she replied, "Absolutely not." Raghubir believes that because the current generation has most often used credit cards, debit cards, and gift cards and they will continue to spend with them because they do not think of them as money.[90]

Questions

1. The opening of the video discusses buying a chocolate bar. Outline the steps of the consumer decision-making process for this purchase. What kind of decision-making process do you think is involved?

2. Consider your own buying behaviour. Review some of your recent purchases, what you bought, and how much it cost, and write down how you paid. Be sure to note down how often you used cash, debit, credit cards, gift cards, or some other purchasing method. Did your behaviour mirror what was discussed in the video? Did you spend more when you used "plastic" than when you used cash?

3. Do you agree with Raghubir's assessment that consumers' spending will not be affected by having gone through a recession? Discuss the ways in which a recession might affect consumer buying behaviour.

MARKETING & YOU RESULTS

High scores suggest that you tend to shop for value, whereas lower score indicate compulsive buying, or excessive shopping relative to your disposable income. Lower scores also suggest that you may use excessive shopping to deal with undesirable moods or negative feelings. Even though your mood might improve afterward, beware: the change is temporary, compulsive shopping behaviour is very difficult to stop, and you can experience harmful consequences as a result.

⑤ Business Marketing

SOURCE: COURTESY OF ANCHOR DANLY

LEARNING OUTCOMES

1 Describe business marketing

2 Describe the role of the Internet in business marketing

3 Discuss the role of relationship marketing and strategic alliances in business marketing

4 Identify the four major categories of business market customers

5 Explain the North American Industry Classification System

6 Explain the major differences between business and consumer markets

7 Describe the seven types of business goods and services

8 Discuss the unique aspects of business buying behaviour

MARKETING & YOU

Think about the last time you dealt with a salesperson when making a major purchase. Then using the following scale below, enter your answers or record them on a separate page.

1	2	3	4	5	6	7
Strongly agree						Strongly disagree

___ This salesperson was frank in dealing with me.
___ This salesperson did not make false claims.
___ I do not think this salesperson was completely open in dealing with me.*
___ This salesperson was concerned only about himself/herself.*

___ This salesperson did not seem to be concerned with my needs.*
___ I did not trust this salesperson.*
___ This salesperson was not trustworthy.*

Now total your score, reversing your answers for the items followed by an asterisk. That is, if you put a 2, change it to a 6; if you put a 3, change it to a 5, and so forth. Read the chapter and find out what your score means at the end.

SOURCE: REPRINTED WITH PERMISSION FROM *MARKETING SCALES HANDBOOK* VOL. III, PUBLISHED BY THE AMERICAN MARKETING ASSOCIATION, G. BRUNER, K. JAMES, H. HENSEL, EDS. SCALE #920, P. 166.

Consider Anchor Danly (www .anchordanly.com), one of the most successful tool and die companies in the world! The Anchor Danly Company is the result of a merger between Anchor Lamina and Danly IEM that took place in March 2005. Prior to the merger, Anchor Lamina was founded in 1975 in Windsor, Ontario. Anchor Lamina started out very small and then grew tremendously from 1975 with sales of $400,000 to the most recent reports indicating that Anchor Danly as a company now has sales well over $100 million and employs 661 people. In addition to the Windsor location, Anchor Danly also has Canadian facilities in Montreal, Cambridge and Tilbury; American facilities in the Michigan communities of Bellaire, Grand Rapids and Ithaca, Beaver Dam, WI, Los Angeles, CA, and an international presence in Chemnitz, Germany, Shanghai,

China and Shiyan, China. The company's mission is stated as follows: "Our mission is to be the "customer focused" world class supplier of choice to the metal working and plastic forming industries. Anchor Danly will provide innovative value added products and services to allow our customers to effectively compete in the global marketplace.

Anchor Danly describes its served market as follows: "The automotive and automotive parts industries constitute Anchor Danly's largest single market. Other important markets include manufacturers of industrial machinery, aerospace, household appliances, office furniture, agricultural equipment, and general machinery." Their vast breadth of products manufactured under the brand names of Anchor Lamina, Danly IEM, Lempco, Punchrite and Reliance Fabrications assures quality, innovative

solutions and service. The products manufactured include die sets, machined plate, guide posts and bushings, mold components, wear products, die accessories, springs, cams, punches and retainers, Accu-Bend rotary benders, urethane springs, in-die tapping units, hydraulic drills, hydraulic motors, steel fabrications and fixture bases.[1]

Now that you have become acquainted with Anchor Danly, a successful B2B firm that was founded in Canada, what other kinds of important industries do you think Canadian B2B marketers are competing in? In this chapter, you will be introduced to the topic of Business Marketing and will discover the importance of this area of marketing and be exposed to some of the unique aspects of business buying behaviour that differ from consumer buying behaviour.

SOURCE: ANCHOR LAMINA CORPORATE WEBSITE, WWW.ANCHORLAMINA.COM, ACCESSED APRIL 8, 2010, HTTP://WWW.ANSWERS.COM/TOPIC/ANCHOR-LAMINA-INC, ACCESSED APRIL 8, 2010; HTTP://INVESTING.BUSINESSWEEK.COM/RESEARCH/STOCKS/PRIVATE/SNAPSHOT.ASP?PRIVCAPID=96885, ACCESSED APRIL 8, 2010.

1 WHAT IS BUSINESS MARKETING?

Describe business marketing

business marketing
The marketing of goods and services to individuals and organizations for purposes other than personal consumption. Often referred to as B2B or B-to-B.

Business marketing is the marketing of goods and services to individuals and organizations for purposes other than personal consumption. The sale of a digital data projector to your college or university is an example of business marketing. Business products include those that are used to manufacture other products, become part of another product, or aid the normal operations of an organization, or that are acquired for resale without any substantial change in form. The key characteristic distinguishing business products from consumer products is intended use, not physical characteristics. A product that is purchased for personal or family consumption or as a gift is a consumer good. If that same product, such as a personal computer or a wireless phone, is bought for use in a business, it is a business product. Hence, this activity is called business-to-business marketing (B2B) when the intended product use is for business, and business-to-consumers marketing (B2C) when the intended product use is for consumers. A survey reported by *B to B Marketing* revealed that the three primary marketing goals of business marketers are customer acquisition (62 percent of respondents), creating brand awareness (19 percent of respondents), and customer retention (12 percent of respondents).[2]

The size of the business market in Canada and most other countries substantially exceeds that of the consumer market. In the business market, a single customer can account for a huge volume of purchases. For example, Via Rail recently awarded a $100-million contract to CAD Industries in Lachine, Quebec, to upgrade 54 locomotives that VIA Rail had been using. The Canadian Army planned to spend $1 billion to upgrade its fleet of light military vehicles, and the Manitoba government was investing $345 million in a wind farm near St. Joseph in southern Manitoba to supply renewable-energy power to 50,000 homes.[3]

REVIEW LEARNING OUTCOME 1

1   **Describe business marketing**

SOURCE: Terry Vine/Blend Images/Jupiter Images

SOURCE: Ryan McVay/Photodisc/Jupiter Images

2 BUSINESS MARKETING ON THE INTERNET

Describe the role of the Internet in business marketing

business-to-business electronic commerce
The use of the Internet to facilitate the exchange of goods, services, and information between organizations

The use of the Internet to facilitate activities between organizations is called **business-to-business electronic commerce** (B-to-B or B2B e-commerce). This method of conducting business has evolved and grown rapidly throughout its short history. In 1995, those commercial websites that did exist were static. Only a few had data retrieval capabilities. Frames, tables, and styles were not available. Security of any sort was rare, and streaming video did not exist. In 2005, there were over 1 billion Internet users worldwide. Today's Internet environment is vastly different! The worldwide purchase of business goods and services runs into the trillions of dollars annually. In Canada, on-line transactions were valued at $62.5 billion in 2007. Of this amount, public-sector sales were $4.5 billion and $58 billion was from the private sector, of which B-to-B sales represented 62 percent of the volume (about $36 billion), and Business-to-Consumer sales were about $22 billion.[4]

Business marketing on the Internet offers tremendous opportunities for companies to increase efficiency, reduce costs, improve customer service, create one-to-one relationships, introduce new products, and expand markets. The e-commerce market has grown tremendously, but there are still some barriers to growth. The most recent data (2006) on Internet use by Canadian businesses show that nearly 87 percent of private Canadian enterprises use the Internet (82 percent among the retail trade) but only 41 percent of them have websites (46 percent among retailers). Nearly 49 percent of private Canadian enterprises buy goods over the Internet (51 percent among retailers) but a shockingly low 8 percent of private Canadian enterprises reported "selling goods" over the Internet (only 13 percent among retailers). In contrast, virtually 100 percent of public-sector organizations in Canada use the Internet, 93 percent of them have websites, and 82 percent of them purchase goods but only 16 percent of public-sector organizations sell goods and services over the Internet.[5] When Canadian business people were asked about resistance toward the use of e-commerce, 39 percent of companies felt that their products did not lend themselves to marketing on the Internet and 35 percent did not want to change their business model.[6]

Leading-edge business marketers are using the Internet to transform the way they do business. The Internet provides a powerful platform for conveying information, conducting transactions, delivering innovative services, building customer and supplier relationships, gathering marketing research data, reducing costs and prices, and integrating the entire supply chain from suppliers to end users.[7]

MEASURING ONLINE SUCCESS

Three of the most important measurements of on-line success are recency, frequency, and monetary value. Recency relates to the fact that customers who have made a purchase recently are more likely to purchase again in the near future than customers who haven't purchased for a while. Frequency data help marketers identify frequent purchasers who are definitely more likely to repeat their purchasing behaviour in the future. The monetary value of sales is important because big spenders can be the most profitable customers for a business.

NetGenesis developed a number of equations that can help on-line marketers better understand their data. For example, combining frequency data with the length of time a visitor spent on the website (duration) and the number of site pages viewed during each visit (total site reach) can provide an analytical measure of a site's **stickiness** factor:

stickiness
A measure of a website's effectiveness calculated by multiplying the frequency of visits times the duration of a visit times the number of pages viewed during each visit (site reach).

$$\text{Stickiness} = \text{Frequency} \times \text{Duration} \times \text{Site Reach}$$

By measuring the stickiness factor of a website before and after a design or function change, the marketer can quickly determine whether visitors embraced the change. By adding purchase information to determine the level of stickiness needed to provide a desired purchase volume, the marketer gains an even more precise understanding of how a site change affected business. An almost endless number of factor combinations can be created to provide a quantitative method for determining buyer behaviour on-line. First, though, the marketer must determine what measures are required and which factors can be combined to arrive at those measurements.[8]

TRENDS IN B2B INTERNET MARKETING

According to James Soto, president of the business marketing agency Industrial Strength Marketing, "The number one thing to keep in mind in terms of trends in BtoB Internet marketing is the shift of sourcing to the Net." His firm has found that

90 percent of business buyers go to the Internet at some point during the buying process, and over 50 percent start the buying process on-line.[9]

An Internet marketing technique that hasn't yet lived up to its potential is RSS (Real Simple Syndication) feeds. RSS feeds are used to publish frequently updated materials such as blogs, news headlines, audio, and video in a standard format. Web feeds benefit publishers by letting them syndicate content automatically. They benefit readers who want to subscribe to timely updates or aggregated information from various sources.[10]

A recent survey revealed that 7 out of 10 business marketers do not consider RSS feeds in their campaigns. However, 71 percent of technology buyers reported using feeds.[11] W.W. Grainger Inc., a distributor of facility maintenance supplies, provides RSS feeds on its website, supplylink.com, to help maintenance professionals identify and solve facility issues such as security, productivity, and energy efficiency. The site features industry articles and resources as well as information on new products that Grainger has recently added.[12]

Over the last decade, marketers have become more and more sophisticated in their use of the Internet. Exhibit 5.1 compares three prominent Internet business-marketing strategy initiatives from the late 1990s to five that are currently being pursued. Companies have had to transition from "We have a website because our customer does" to having a store that attracts, interests, satisfies, and retains customers. New applications that provide additional information about current and potential customers, increase efficiency, lower costs, increase supply-chain efficiency, or enhance customer retention, loyalty, and trust are being developed each year. Chapter 18 on customer relationship management describes several of these applications.

One term in Exhibit 5.1 that may be unfamiliar is **disintermediation**, which means eliminating intermediaries such as wholesalers or distributors from a marketing channel.

A prime example of disintermediation is Dell, Inc., which sells directly to business buyers and consumers. Large retailers such as Walmart use a disintermediation strategy to help reduce costs and prices.[13]

A few years ago, many people thought that the Internet would eliminate the need for distributors. Why would customers pay for distributor markups when they

disintermediation
The elimination of intermediaries such as wholesalers or distributors from a marketing channel.

EXHIBIT 5.1

Evolution of E-Business Initiatives

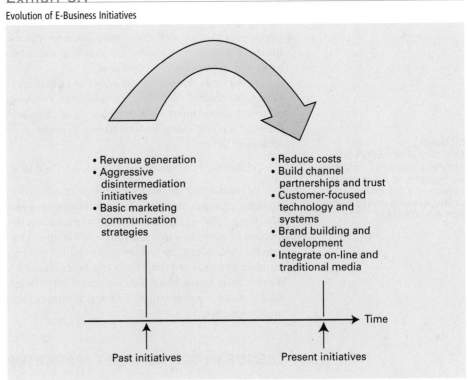

- Revenue generation
- Aggressive disintermediation initiatives
- Basic marketing communication strategies

- Reduce costs
- Build channel partnerships and trust
- Customer-focused technology and systems
- Brand building and development
- Integrate on-line and traditional media

Time

Past initiatives

Present initiatives

SOURCE: Reprinted with permission from *Marketing Management*, published by the American Marketing Association, Andrew J. Rohm and Fareena Sultan, "The Evolution of E-Business", January/February 2004, p. 35.

could buy directly from the manufacturers with a few mouse clicks? Yet Internet disintermediation has occurred less frequently than many expected. The reason is that distributors often perform important functions such as providing credit, aggregation of supplies from multiple sources, delivery, and processing returns. Many business customers, especially small firms, depend on knowledgeable distributors for information and advice that are not available to them on-line. You will notice in Exhibit 5.1 that building channel partnerships and trust has replaced aggressive disintermediation initiatives as a priority for most firms. Some firms have followed disintermediation with **reintermediation**, the reintroduction of an intermediary between producers and users. They realized that providing direct on-line purchasing only was similar to having only one store in a city selling a popular brand.[14]

reintermediation
The reintroduction of an intermediary between producers and users.

2 Describe the role of the Internet in business marketing

Business Internet Uses

THEN   Revenue Generation
        Basic Marketing Communication

and

NOW   Reduce costs
        Build partnerships and alliances
        Build and support branding

3 RELATIONSHIP MARKETING AND STRATEGIC ALLIANCES

Discuss the role of relationship marketing and strategic alliances in business marketing

As Chapter 1 explained, relationship marketing involves seeking and establishing ongoing partnerships with customers. Relationship marketing has become an important business marketing strategy as customers have become more demanding and competition has become more intense. Loyal customers are also more profitable than those who are price sensitive and perceive little or no difference among brands or suppliers. That is why firms such as Bridor Inc. of Boucherville, Quebec, a manufacturer of frozen breads and Viennese pastries for grocery and food service markets, focuses on the importance of partnerships to achieve success. The company states this awareness on its website: "We pride ourselves in developing working partnerships with our suppliers and world-class chefs and bakers. We continually go above and beyond the limits of our equipment by adapting their technological capabilities to our clients' specific needs." Bridor goes beyond simply stating its philosophy to providing specific information on how it caters to its customers' individual needs: "Our flexibility is reflected on every level: in the product itself, packaging, logistics considerations such as size and frequency of shipments tailored to suit our customers' inventory strategy and to maximize freight cost efficiency, as well as administration & billing. Once we've evaluated your specific needs, we'll use your information and feedback to build a proposal that meets your needs."[15]

Customer Experience

 ## INCREASING CUSTOMER RETENTION

Customer relationships are important in both consumer and business-to-business markets. However, business-to-business buying often involves very large volumes of goods and services and if one is dealing with a producer or reseller type of organization, then frequent purchasers are also very common. Consequently, business-to-business marketers must not only focus on making sure that they have good relationships with their customers but also pay attention to retaining existing customers. A recent study by the Chief Marketing Officer Council (CMOC) reported that the majority of B-to-B marketing firms do not have strategies in place to retrieve business from lost or inactive customers. The study reported that only a third of the surveyed businesses indicated they had strategies to reanimate past clients and only 50 percent of the respondents had marketing strategies to develop more business with their current customers.

Most businesses tend to concentrate on finding new customers to develop more demand. This approach is necessary but many firms pursue new customer development to the extreme and may overlook the potential of their existing customers. For example, if marketers were to look at their current customers that are most profitable to them, they might be able to increase the number or size of their transactions by improving the experience of these customers. This means, of course, the marketer must really know their customers well. Knowing your customers well means

having detailed data on customer demographics, buyer behaviour and also the psychographic profile of the buyers for the various business organizations your firm sells to. The study by CMOC also reports that only 6.8 percent of the marketers surveyed reported having customer knowledge that could be classified as excellent. In contrast, 51.9 percent of the business firms surveyed reported that their customer knowledge was only fair.

Fujitsu, serves the telecommunications industry as a service provider of software, hardware, and other services. This firm uses a customer relationship management (CRM) approach (discussed in Chapter 18) with its customers but has decided to manage their system differently. The company has changed the purpose of their CRM system from being a just a selling support tool into more of an asset management tool. Jim Hintze, senior VP-marketing at Fujitsu, comments on the problems of how inbound calls are handled and on managing customer information with their new CRM system approach. Hintze comments, "A customer might call in to an 800-number for warranty support and get turned off because the call isn't handled properly. There is so much information out there that even for a company as sophisticated as Fujitsu, managing it intelligently is really, really difficult."[16]

What ways can you think of that companies like Fujitsu could implement to improve the quality of customer experience? What else might they do to increase customer retention?

SOURCE: KATE MADDOX, "MARKETERS LOOK TO BOOST CUSTOMER RETENTION," BTOB MAGAZINE, ONLINE, MAY 5, 2008.

STRATEGIC ALLIANCES

strategic alliance (strategic partnership)
A cooperative agreement between business companies.

A **strategic alliance**, sometimes called a **strategic partnership**, is a cooperative agreement between business companies. Strategic alliances can take the form of licensing or distribution agreements, joint ventures, research and development consortia, or partnerships. They can be between manufacturers, manufacturers and customers, manufacturers and suppliers, or manufacturers and channel intermediaries.

Business marketers form strategic alliances to leverage what they have (technology, financial resources, access to markets) by combining these assets with those of other companies. Sometimes the alliance partners' assets are complementary. For example, in 2010, Canadian paint manufacturer Para Paints formed a strategic alliance to supply its paint products and paint colouring system to Lowes, an American-based home-improvement retailer that entered the Canadian market in 2009. Bob Sherwood, vice-president of merchandising for Lowe's, made the following comments about the alliance: "Partnering with well-established Canadian paint brands like Para allows us to continue our efforts to offer Canadians the best products at the best prices. By partnering with a trusted brand, we are ensuring that our customers have even more choice when it comes to choosing the right product to complement their design and home improvement needs."[17]

Some alliances are formed with multiple partners to achieve increased productivity and lower costs for all participants. For example, ProMetic Life Sciences Inc. of Montreal formed a strategic alliance with Novozymes, a Danish biotechnology company. ProMetic assumed the role of becoming the exclusive manufacturer of AlbuPure, a product used in drug development to purify albumin and albumin-fusion proteins. The product was developed with both companies' technologies and was to be marketed by both companies.[18]

Sometimes alliance partners are also fierce competitors. For instance, in the face of rising fuel prices, the express delivery service DHL has formed an alliance with rival company UPS. Under the agreement, UPS provides airlift services for DHL. According to one DHL executive, "The customer doesn't actually see a difference at all . . . unless they pay attention to the color of the partner's planes."[19]

Other alliances are formed between companies that operate in completely different industries. Choice Hotels and 1-800-Flowers share call-centre employees because doing so is a cheaper alternative than outsourcing. When one company experiences increased demand for its products and services, it can call on its partner's employees rather than add staff or use a temporary agency. At a given time, as many as 100 call-centre agents may be taking orders for the other company. Both companies report higher employee retention and better recruitment.[20]

For an alliance to succeed in the long term, it must be built on commitment and trust. **Relationship commitment** means that a firm believes an ongoing relationship with some other firm is so important that it warrants maximum efforts at maintaining it indefinitely.[21] A perceived reduction in commitment by one of the parties often leads to a breakdown in the relationship. **Trust** exists when one party has confidence in an exchange partner's reliability and integrity.[22] Some alliances fail when participants lack trust in their trading partners and benefits are not shared. GM, Ford, Chrysler, Nissan Motor Company, and Renault SA created an Internet automobile parts exchange, called Covisint, that was expected to account for $300 billion in sales per year. The auto manufacturers assumed that if they built a website, trading volume would follow. But the industry is characterized by mistrust between buyers and sellers. After a decade of being forced to accept price concessions, suppliers were in no hurry to participate. The manufacturers didn't help by boasting that Covisint would squeeze an additional 30 percent in savings out of vendors.[23]

relationship commitment
A firm's belief that an ongoing relationship with another firm is so important that the relationship warrants maximum efforts at maintaining it indefinitely.

trust
The condition that exists when one party has confidence in an exchange partner's reliability and integrity.

keiretsu
A network of interlocking corporate affiliates.

SOURCE: © AP IMAGES/ DOUGLAS C. PIZAC

Japanese *keiretsu* are powerful combinations of companies—manufacturers, suppliers, and finance companies—that are cemented by family ties or strong financial connections. The North American version of a *keiretsu* is an alliance of suppliers and customers bound by the goods of mutual success. Harley-Davidson borrowed from the *keiretsu* model by making suppliers into partners. Those partners commit to annual cost reductions (even if materials and labour costs are rising) and participate in the company's product development program to help improve quality. In return, those partners participate in Harley's success.

RELATIONSHIPS IN OTHER CULTURES

The concepts of "relationship marketing" and "strategic alliances" are still being implemented by many North American business executives although both concepts have long been familiar in other cultures. Businesses in Mexico, China, Japan, and Korea, and much of Europe, rely heavily on personal relationships. Chapter 18 explores customer relationship management in detail.

In Japan, the basis of exchange between companies is personal relationships, which are developed through what is called *amae*, or indulgent dependency. *Amae* is the feeling of nurturing concern for, and dependence on, another. Reciprocity and personal relationships contribute to *amae*. Relationships between companies can develop into a *keiretsu*—a network of interlocking corporate affiliates. Within a *keiretsu*, executives may sit on the boards of their customers or their suppliers. Members of a *keiretsu* trade with one another whenever possible and often engage in joint product development, financing, and marketing activities. For example, the Toyota Group *keiretsu* includes 14 core companies and another 170 that receive preferential treatment. Toyota holds an equity position in many of these 170 member companies and is represented on many of their boards of directors.

Many Canadian companies have found that the best way to compete in Asian countries is to form relationships with Asian companies. For example, Waterloo-based RIM (Research In Motion) and China Mobile, a state-owned enterprise, formed a strategic alliance to provide mobile PDA service in China for users of RIM's BlackBerry devices.[24]

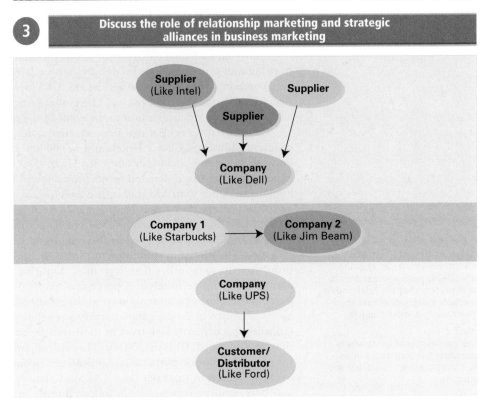

3 | **Discuss the role of relationship marketing and strategic alliances in business marketing**

Global Perspectives

 BOMBARDIER SELLS TO THE "CAPITAL OF CULTURE"

Many consumers continue to associate the Bombardier name with the sales and marketing of Ski-Doo snowmobiles and Sea-Doo personal watercraft. What they don't know is that Bombardier sold off these properties in 2003 to focus on the business of being a Canadian-based manufacturer of aircraft and railway vehicles. The company has sales in the $20-billion range and has been very successful in selling its products to international markets.

In 2009, Bombardier received an order worth $100 million from LINZ LINIEN GmbH, the local railway in Linz, Austria, to supply 23 Bombardier Flexity Outlook trams. Linz is a well-known cultural centre located very close to Vienna, and its transportation company, LINZ AG, serves 105 communities not including Linz. These communities cover an area of nearly 2,300 square kilometres. In the press release announcing the deal, Bombardier said, "The FLEXITY Outlook vehicles are 40 m long, 2.3 m wide and are able to accommodate 224 passengers. The functional interior design elements of the new vehicle integrate many years of day-to-day operational experience. The vehicles are reliable and suitable for people with special needs. . . . The exterior design of the new vehicles corresponds to the Corporate Design of the LINZ AG."

The most recent order followed an earlier order of 33 Flexity trams, which began operating in Linz in 2001. At that time, these

vehicles "were the first 100% low-floor trams with conventional wheel-set bogies. They offer an entirely step-less interior and therefore increased passenger comfort. At the same time, they are easy to maintain," Bombardier said in the press release. The company has had great success selling trams of this type in the European market. More than 450 of them were developed for Brussels, Belgium; Innsbruck, Austria; Marseille, France; Geneva, Switzerland, Alicante and Valencia, Spain; Eskisehir, Turkey; Palermo, Italy; and Krefeld, Germany.

The relationship of Bombardier and LINZ AG is described as a partnership rather than a buyer and seller relationship. The president of Light Rail Vehicles, Bombardier Transportation, Grego Peters, commented on the relationship between the two firms saying: "The design of the new vehicle was developed together with LINZ LINIEN GmbH and is based on operating experience gained with the existing tram fleet. Linz chose Bombardier once again, which makes us very proud. It shows that the customer is satisfied with our products and marks the continuation of our long-term and successful cooperation."[25]

How would you characterize the kind of relationship that Bombardier and LINZ-AG have developed? How can Bombardier use its experience with LINZ-AG to develop relationships with other customers?

SOURCE: ANONYMOUS, "BOMBARDIER TO SUPPLY 23 FLEXITY OUTLOOK TRAMS TO LINZ, AUSTRIA; THE 2009 EUROPEAN CAPITAL OF CULTURE SELECTS BOMBARDIER ONCE AGAIN," MARKETWIRE, JULY 3, 2009. HTTP://WWW.MARKETWIRE.COM/PRESS-RELEASE/BOMBARDIER-TO-SUPPLY-23-FLEXITY-OUTLOOK-TRAMS-TO-LINZ-AUSTRIA-TSX-BBD.A-1012726.HTM

Identify the four major categories of business market customers

The business market consists of four major categories of customers: producers, resellers, governments, and institutions.

PRODUCERS

The producer segment of the business market includes profit-oriented individuals and organizations that use purchased goods and services to produce other products, to incorporate into other products, or to facilitate the daily operations of the organization. Examples of producers include construction, manufacturing, transportation, finance, real estate, and food service companies.

In Canada in 2009–10, producers shipped approximately $1,217 billion worth of goods. Some of these producers were small; others, such as Encana of Calgary (US $30.1 billion in sales), Onex of Toronto (US $25.2 billion in sales), Magna International of Aurora (US$23.7 billion in sales), and Bombardier of Montreal (US$19.7 billion in sales), were in the top 500 of the world's largest businesses. Individual producers such as these often buy large quantities of goods and services.[26]

Producers are often called **original equipment manufacturers** or **OEMs**. This term includes all individuals and organizations that buy business goods and incorporate them into the products they produce for eventual sale to other producers or to consumers. Companies such as GM of Canada that buy steel, paint, tires, and batteries are said to be OEMs.

original equipment manufacturer (OEM)
A company that buys business goods, which it then incorporates into the products it produces for eventual sale to other producers or to consumers.

RESELLERS

The reseller market includes retail and wholesale businesses that buy finished goods and resell them for a profit. A retailer sells mainly to final consumers; wholesalers sell mostly to retailers and other organizational customers.

In 2009, approximately 210,000 retail outlets existed in Canada with combined sales of about $413.3 billion. Also, the retail sector employs more than 2 million Canadians—nearly 12 percent of the labour force. Food retailing is the largest single category of retailing, accounting for 17.2 percent of all retail sales. Chain retailers such as Loblaws and Sobeys dominate the Canadian food retailing market, but Walmart and Costco are also important players in this sector.[27]

The Canadian wholesale sector had 110,247 outlets, had sales of $746.2 billion, and employed approximately 600,000 people in 2008. Wholesale merchant sales were $494 billion and they carried inventories valued at over $52 billion in 2009.[28] The sales revenues of wholesalers are split up among customers in the following proportions: retailers, 33 percent; industry, 29 percent; other wholesalers, 19 percent; exporters, 10 percent; household consumers, 5 percent; and farmers, 4 percent.[29] Retailing and wholesaling are explored in more detail in Chapters 11 and 12.

Business product distributors are wholesalers that buy business products and resell them to business customers. They often carry thousands of items in stock and employ sales forces to call on business customers. Businesses that wish to buy a gross of pencils or a hundred pounds of fertilizer typically purchase these items from local distributors rather than directly from manufacturers such as Empire Pencil or Dow Chemical.

GOVERNMENTS

A third major segment of the business market is governments. Senior government organizations are represented by one federal, ten provincial, and three territorial units. The MASH sector (Municipal, Academic, Social, Hospitals) includes around 6,000 municipal buying units as well as thousands more academic, social, and hospital purchasing units. Together, these government buyers make up the largest single market for goods and services in Canada, with expenditures in 2008–09 of around $631 billion.[30]

Procurement lawyer and author Paul Emanuelli comments, "In government procurement, public institutions seek to achieve value-for-money through open tendering. Open tendering allows purchasers to predetermine the terms of engagement with potential suppliers, set out requirements and terms of the potential deal and bind competing suppliers to their offers for a predetermined amount of time while competing offers are compared. This process can result in an organization getting a deal tailored to its needs, on its terms, and at potentially lower costs."[31]

Government purchasing by Canada's federal, provincial, and territorial governments is subject to the Agreement on Internal Trade (AIT), which came into effect on July 1, 1995. The specific rules for procurement are set out in Chapter 5 of the AIT, whose purpose is "to establish a framework that will ensure equal access to procurement for all Canadian suppliers in order to contribute to a reduction in purchasing costs and the development of a strong economy in a context of transparency and efficiency." The critical provision for marketers is that purchases over $25,000 for goods and over $100,000 for services and construction by government are subject to AIT's provisions.[32]

Senior Government

Name just about any good or service and chances are that someone in the federal government uses it. The Canadian federal government is the country's largest customer; in 2009 it spent about $236 billion. That same year the provincial and territorial governments spent about $350 billion. Health, social services, and education expenses represented the lion's share of these expenditures.[33]

Much of the federal government's buying is centralized. However, no single federal agency contracts for all of the government's requirements, and no single buyer in any agency purchases all the agency needs. The federal government can be viewed as a combination of several large purchasing agencies and Crown corporations with overlapping responsibilities and thousands of small, independent units. Major purchases (expenditures exceeding $100,000 for goods and $250,000 for services and construction) must go through Supply and Services Canada and Public Works and Government Services.

One popular source of information about government procurement is Contracts Canada (**www.contractscanada.gc.ca**). Information about bidding for federal, provincial, and even MASH contracts can be obtained directly from **www.contractscanada.gc.ca** or from **www.merx.com**.

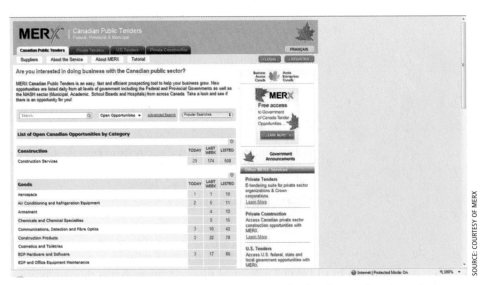

For doing business with buyers from all levels of Canadian governments, there is no better on-line resource than www.merx.com. Users can access government public tenders and order tender documents through MERX.

Municipal, Academic, Social, and Hospitals (MASH)

Municipal governments in Canada spent $123 billion in 2009, colleges and universities spent $37 billion, schools spent $49 billion, and health care organizations spent $81 billion.[34] For both small and large vendors, selling to the MASH sector can be less frustrating than selling to the federal and provincial governments. Many contracts are valued at levels below the AIT agreement threshold, so the paperwork is typically simpler and more manageable. On the other hand, vendors must decide which of these diverse sectors to serve. There are more than 6,000 municipal clients alone that are available to buy their wares.

INSTITUTIONS

The fourth major segment of the business market is institutions that seek to achieve goals other than the standard business goals of profit, market share, and return on investment. Excluding the MASH sector, this segment includes churches, labour unions, fraternal organizations, civic clubs, foundations, not-for-profit organizations, and other nonbusiness organizations. Statistics Canada has labelled this sector as the "core non-profit institutions" and reports the following:

> Total income of the core non-profit sector reached $77.9 billion in 2007. Total expenses for the core non-profit sector increased 3.9% to $68.2 billion. Core non-profit institutions rely on diverse sources of revenue. Sales of goods and services were, by far, the most important source of revenue for the core non-profit group in 2007, accounting for 45.6% of the total income. Government transfers were also significant at 19.7%. In addition to these funds, core non-profit institutions derived roughly one-third of their revenue from three additional sources: membership fees (15.9%), donations from households (12.0%) and investment income (4.9%).[35]

There are estimated to be 78,000 registered charities in Canada, and in 2009 the Canada Revenue Agency (CRA) reported that they were supported by 5,795,210 Canadians whose average age was 53 years and who claimed $8.2 billion in charitable donations on their 2008 tax returns.[36]

REVIEW LEARNING OUTCOME 4

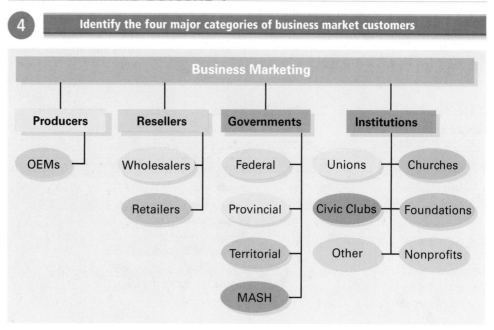

Business Marketing Chapter 5 **141**

THE NORTH AMERICAN INDUSTRY CLASSIFICATION SYSTEM

Explain the North American Industry Classification System

North American Industry Classification System (NAICS)
A detailed numbering system developed by Canada, the United States, and Mexico to classify North American business establishments by their main production processes.

The **North American Industry Classification System (NAICS)** is an industry classification system introduced in 1997 to replace the standard industrial classification system (SIC). Updated in 2007, the NAICS (pronounced *nakes*) is a system for classifying North American business establishments. The system, developed jointly by Canada, the United States, and Mexico, provides a common industry classification system for the North American Free Trade Association (NAFTA). Goods- or service-producing companies that use identical or similar production processes are grouped together.

NAICS 2007 is an extremely valuable tool for business marketers engaged in analyzing, segmenting, and targeting markets. It classifies Canada's economic activity into "20 sectors, 102 subsectors, 324 industry groups, 718 industries and 928 national industries."[37] Each classification group is relatively homogenous with respect to the raw materials required, components used, manufacturing processes employed, and problems faced. The more digits that are contained in a code, the more homogenous the group. Therefore, once a supplier understands the needs and requirements of a few companies within a classification, those requirements can be projected for all companies in that category. The number, size, and geographic dispersion of companies can also be identified. This information can be converted to market potential estimates, market share estimates, and sales forecasts. It can also be used for identifying potential new customers. NAICS codes can help identify companies that may be prospective users of a supplier's goods and services.

Exhibit 5.2 provides an overview of the 20 NAICS economic sectors. Exhibit 5.3 illustrates the six-digit classification system for two of these sectors: manufacturing and information. The hierarchical structure of NAICS allows industry data to be summarized at several levels of detail. To illustrate:

- The first two digits designate a major economic sector such as agriculture (11) or manufacturing (31–33).
- The third digit designates an economic subsector such as crop production or apparel manufacturing.
- The fourth digit designates an industry group, such as grain and oil seed farming or fibre, yarn, and thread mills.

EXHIBIT 5.2

2007 NAICS Two-Digit Codes and Corresponding Economic Sectors

NAICS code	Economic sector
11	Agriculture, forestry, fishing, and hunting
21	Mining, quarrying, and oil and gas extraction
22	Utilities
23	Construction
31–33	Manufacturing
41	Wholesale trade
44–45	Retail trade
48–49	Transportation and warehousing
51	Information and cultural industries
52	Finance and insurance
53	Real estate and rental and leasing
54	Professional, scientific, and technical services
55	Management of companies and enterprises
56	Administrative and support, waste management and remediation services
61	Educational services
62	Health care and social assistance
71	Arts, entertainment, and recreation
72	Accommodation and food services
81	Other services (except public administration)
91	Public administration

EXHIBIT 5.3

Examples of 2007 NAICS Hierarchy

| NAICS level | Example 1 | | Example 2 | |
	NAICS code	Description	NAICS Code	Description
Sector	31–33	Manufacturing	51	Information
Subsector	334	Computer and electronic product manufacturing	517	Broadcasting and telecommunications
Industry group	3346	Magnetic and optical recording media manufacturing	5172	Telecommunications
Industry media	33461	Manufacturing and reproducing magnetic and optical media	51721	Cellular and other wireless telecommunications
Industry services	334611	Software reproducing	517211	Paging services

SOURCE: Adapted from Statistics Canada North American Industry Classification System (NAICS)—Canada 12-501-XIE 2007001 2007 Released April 11, 2007.

- The fifth digit designates the NAICS industry, such as wheat farming or broadwoven fabric mills.
- The sixth digit, when used, identifies subdivisions of NAICS industries that accommodate user needs in individual countries.[38]

For a complete listing of all 2007 NAICS codes, visit the NAICS Association website **www.naics.com**, or visit Statistics Canada's website, **www.statcan.gc.ca**.

5 Explain the North American Industry Classification System

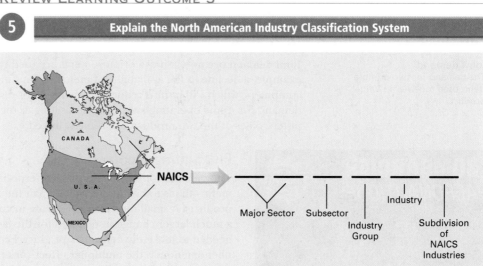

6 BUSINESS VERSUS CONSUMER MARKETS

Explain the major differences between business and consumer markets

The basic philosophy and practices of marketing are the same whether the customer is a business organization or a consumer. Business markets do, however, have characteristics different from consumer markets. Review Learning Outcome 6 summarizes the main differences between business and consumer markets.

DEMAND

Consumer demand for products is quite different from demand in the business market. Unlike consumer demand, business demand is derived, inelastic, joint, and fluctuating.

Derived Demand

derived demand
The demand for business products.

The demand for business products is called **derived demand** because organizations buy products to be used in producing their customers' products. For instance, the number of drills or lathes that a wood furniture manufacturing firm needs is derived from the demand for wooden furniture. Demand for these items rises and falls with the demand for the products they are used to produce.

Because demand is derived, business marketers must carefully monitor demand patterns and changing preferences in final consumer markets, even though their customers are not in those markets. Moreover, business marketers must carefully monitor their customers' forecasts, because derived demand is based on expectations of future demand for those customers' products.

Some business marketers not only monitor final consumer demand and customer forecasts but also try to influence final consumer demand. Aluminum producers use television and magazine advertisements to point out the convenience and recycling opportunities that aluminum offers to consumers, who can choose to purchase soft drinks in either aluminum or plastic containers.

Inelastic Demand

The demand for many business products is inelastic with regard to price. *Inelastic demand* means that an increase or decrease in the price of the product will not significantly affect demand for the product. The concept of inelastic demand will be discussed further in Chapter 16.

The price of a product used in the production of or as part of a final product is often a minor portion of the final product's total price. Therefore, demand for the final consumer product is not affected. If the price of automobile paint or spark plugs rose significantly—say, 200 percent in one year—do you think the number of new automobiles sold that year will be affected? Probably not.

Joint Demand

joint demand
The demand for two or more items used together in a final product.

Joint demand occurs when two or more items are used together in a final product. For example, a decline in the availability of memory chips will slow production of microcomputers, which will in turn reduce the demand for disk drives. Likewise, the demand for Apple operating systems exists as long as there is demand for Apple computers. Sales of the two products are directly linked.

Fluctuating Demand

The demand for business products—especially new plants and equipment—tends to be more unstable than the demand for consumer products. A small increase or decrease in consumer demand can produce a much larger change in demand for the facilities and equipment needed to make the consumer product. Economists refer to this phenomenon as the **multiplier effect** (or **accelerator principle**).

Cummins Engine Company, a producer of heavy-duty diesel engines, uses sophisticated surface grinders to make parts. Suppose Cummins is using 20 surface grinders. Each machine lasts about 10 years. Purchases have been timed so that two machines will wear out and be replaced annually. If the demand for engine parts does not change, two grinders will be bought this year. If the demand for parts declines slightly, only 18 grinders may be needed and Cummins won't replace the worn ones. However, suppose that in the following year demand returns to previous levels plus a little more. To meet the new level of demand, Cummins will need to replace the two machines that wore out in the first year, and the two that wore out in the second year, plus one or more additional machines. The multiplier effect works this way in many industries, which results in highly fluctuating demand for business products.

Bombardier is the leading Canadian aerospace company. Business customers tend to be much more geographically concentrated than consumers. The Canadian aircraft industry is concentrated in Quebec and Ontario.

multiplier effect (accelerator principle)
Phenomenon in which a small increase or decrease in consumer demand can produce a much larger change in demand for the facilities and equipment needed to make the consumer product.

PURCHASE VOLUME

Business customers buy in much larger quantities than consumers. Just think how large an order Molson's Brewery places for the yeast and hops used in brewing Molson's Canadian. Imagine the number of tires that Chrysler Canada buys for its Minivans manufactured in Windsor, Ontario.

NUMBER OF CUSTOMERS

Business marketers usually have far fewer customers than consumer marketers. The advantage is that it is a lot easier to identify prospective buyers, monitor current customers' needs and levels of satisfaction, and personally attend to existing customers. The main disadvantage is that each customer becomes crucial—especially for those manufacturers that have only one or two customers. For example, suppliers of secret military equipment and systems may have one customer, such as NATO (the North Atlantic Treaty Organization). The success or failure of one bid can make the difference between prosperity and bankruptcy. CAE Inc. of Montreal, Quebec, has experienced both immediate ups and immediate downs in its stock price as a result of market reactions to contract bids. CAE designs and manufactures civil flight simulators and visual systems used to train airline and business jet pilots. CAE also operates 29 civil and military aviation training centres where they train more than 75,000 crew members each year. The company employs over 6,500 people at its 90 training sites and reports annual revenues in the $1.6-billion range. It also provides aviation military training services to NATO countries. In the fall of 2003, CAE's share price dropped in value by 18 percent when it was announced that a $1-billion contract bid to provide training services to the U.S. Army had been lost to a rival bidder. In 2010, the stock price jumped up to a 52-week high in response to the announcement that CAE was adding a new simulator to its C-130 Tampa training centre.[39]

LOCATION OF BUYERS

Business customers tend to be much more geographically concentrated than consumers. For instance, most of Canada's buyers are located in the major metropolitan urban areas of Toronto, Montreal, and Vancouver. The oil and gas industry is centred in Alberta, the shoe industry in Quebec, the aircraft industry in Quebec and Ontario. Many of the companies that supply the auto-making industry are located in southwestern Ontario.

DISTRIBUTION STRUCTURE

Unlike consumer products, which may pass through a distribution system that includes the producer, one or more wholesalers, and a retailer, distribution channels are typically shorter in business marketing. Because of many of the characteristics already mentioned, business marketers use direct channels, where manufacturers market directly to users, more frequently. The use of direct channels has increased dramatically in the past decade with the introduction of various Internet buying and selling schemes.

business-to-business on-line exchange
An electronic trading floor that provides companies with integrated links to their customers and suppliers.

One such technique is a **"business-to-business" on-line exchange**, which is an electronic trading floor that provides companies with integrated links to their customers and suppliers. The goal of a B-to-B on-line exchange is to simplify business purchasing and make it more efficient. For example, the SAQ (Société des alcools du Québec) operates SAQ-B2B.com, which SAQ describes as "a private, business-to-business, transactional portal owned and operated by the SAQ's E-commerce Division. The SAQ is the only buyer on the portal (only approved SAQ products are traded there) and any SAQ supplier with a product registered on the SAQ database, or accepted for registration, is eligible to become a member and trade on the portal. There are no membership fees. SAQ-B2B.com enables SAQ suppliers to do business with the SAQ on-line, saving time, effort and money. Transactions related to purchasing, shipping and receiving all take place on-line. There are no product list or per-transaction fees to pay. The only equipment required is a computer and Internet access. If a supplier does not have access to the Internet, but his agent does, the supplier can share his authorized access to the portal (user name and password) with his agent."[40]

NATURE OF BUYING

Unlike consumers, business buyers usually approach purchasing rather formally. Businesses use professionally trained purchasing agents or buyers, who spend their entire careers purchasing a limited number of items. They get to know the items and the sellers well. In Canada, the Purchasing Management Association of Canada (**www.pmac.ca**) enables professional purchasers to earn the designation of Certified Professional Purchaser (CPP) after participating in a rigorous certification program.[41]

NATURE OF BUYING INFLUENCE

Typically, more people are involved in a single business purchase decision than in a consumer purchase. Experts from fields as varied as quality control, marketing, and finance, as well as professional buyers and users, may be grouped in a buying centre (discussed later in this chapter).

TYPE OF NEGOTIATIONS

Consumers are accustomed to negotiating price on automobiles and real estate. However, in most cases consumers expect sellers to set the price and other conditions of sale, such as time of delivery and credit terms. In contrast, negotiating is common in business marketing. Buyers and sellers negotiate product specifications, delivery dates, payment terms, and other pricing matters. Sometimes these negotiations occur during many meetings over several months. Final contracts are often very long and detailed.

USE OF RECIPROCITY

reciprocity
A practice in which business purchasers choose to buy from their own customers.

Business purchasers often choose to buy from their own customers, a practice known as **reciprocity**. For example, GM buys engines for use in its automobiles and trucks from Borg Warner, which in turn buys many of the automobiles and trucks it needs from GM. This practice is neither unethical nor illegal unless one party coerces the other and the result is unfair competition. Reciprocity is generally considered a reasonable business practice. If all possible suppliers sell a similar product for about the same price, doesn't it make sense to buy from those companies that buy from you?

USE OF LEASING

Consumers normally buy products rather than lease them. But businesses commonly lease expensive equipment such as computers, construction equipment and vehicles, and automobiles. Leasing allows companies to reduce capital outflow, acquire a seller's latest products, receive better service, and gain tax advantages.

The lessor, the company providing the product, may be either the manufacturer or an independent company. The benefits to the lessor include greater total revenue from leasing compared to selling and an opportunity to do business with customers who cannot afford to buy.

PRIMARY PROMOTIONAL METHOD

Business marketers tend to emphasize personal selling in their promotion efforts, especially for expensive items, custom-designed products, large-volume purchases, and situations requiring negotiations. For many business products, selling requires a great deal of personal contact. Personal selling is discussed in more detail in Chapter 15.

REVIEW LEARNING OUTCOME 6

6 Explain the major differences between business and consumer markets

Characteristic	Business market	Consumer market
Demand	Organizational	Individual
Purchase volume	Larger	Smaller
Number of customers	Fewer	Many
Location of buyers	Geographically concentrated	Dispersed
Distribution structure	More direct	More indirect
Nature of buying	More professional	More personal
Nature of buying influence	Multiple	Single
Type of negotiations	More complex	Simpler
Use of reciprocity	Yes	No
Use of leasing	Greater	Lesser
Primary promotional method	Personal selling	Advertising

Describe the seven types of business goods and services

Business products generally fall into one of the following seven categories, depending on their use: major equipment, accessory equipment, raw materials, component parts, processed materials, supplies, and business services.

MAJOR EQUIPMENT

major equipment (installations)
Capital goods such as large or expensive machines, blast furnaces, generators, airplanes, and buildings.

Major equipment includes such capital goods such as as large or expensive machines, blast furnaces, generators, airplanes, large earthmoving equipment, road milling machines, and buildings. (These items are also commonly called **installations**.) Major equipment is depreciated over time rather than charged as an expense in the year of purchase. In addition, major equipment is often custom designed for each customer. Personal selling is an important part of the marketing strategy for major equipment because distribution channels are almost always direct from the producer to the business user.

ACCESSORY EQUIPMENT

accessory equipment
Goods, such as portable tools and office equipment, that are less expensive and shorter lived than major equipment.

Accessory equipment is generally less expensive and shorter lived than major equipment. Examples include power tools, data projectors, computer servers, and photocopiers. Accessory equipment is often charged as an expense in the year it is bought rather than depreciated over its useful life. In contrast to major equipment, accessories tend to be standardized. Also, they are usually bought by more customers. These customers tend to be widely dispersed.

Local industrial distributors (wholesalers) play an important role in the marketing of accessory equipment because business buyers often purchase accessories from them. Regardless of where accessories are bought, advertising is a more vital promotional tool for accessory equipment than for major equipment.

RAW MATERIALS

raw materials
Unprocessed extractive or agricultural products, such as mineral ore, lumber, wheat, corn, fruits, vegetables, and fish.

Raw materials are unprocessed extractive or agricultural products—for example, mineral ore, lumber, wheat, corn, fruits, vegetables, and fish. Raw materials become part of finished products. Extensive users, such as steel or lumber mills and food canners, generally buy huge quantities of raw materials. Because there are often many relatively small sellers of raw materials, no single one can greatly influence price or supply. Thus the market tends to set the price of raw materials, and individual producers have little pricing flexibility. Promotion is almost always through personal selling, and distribution channels are usually direct from producer to business user.

COMPONENT PARTS

component parts
Either finished items ready for assembly or products that need very little processing before becoming part of some other product.

Component parts are either finished items ready for assembly or products that need very little processing before becoming part of some other product. The Canadian automotive industry is composed of many automotive suppliers who make component parts such as intake manifolds, spark plugs, tires, and windshield wipers for automobiles. A special feature of component parts is that they can retain their identity after becoming part of the final product. For example, the brand of the automobile's tires is clearly recognizable as part of a car. Moreover, because component parts often wear out, they may need to be replaced several times during the life of the final product. Thus there are two important markets for many component parts: the original equipment manufacturer (OEM) market and the replacement market.

Many of the business features listed in Review Learning Outcome 6 characterize the OEM market. The difference between unit cost and selling price in the OEM market is often small, but profits can be substantial because of volume buying.

The replacement market is composed of organizations and individuals buying component parts to replace worn-out parts. Because components often retain their

SOURCE: © RICHARD HULL

Magna International of Aurora, Ontario, produces and ships automotive parts to original equipment manufacturers (OEMs) of cars and trucks in Canada, the United States, Mexico, Europe, Asia, and South America.

identity in final products, users may choose to replace a component part with the same brand used by the manufacturer—for example, the same brand of automobile tires or battery. The replacement market operates differently from the OEM market, however. Whether replacement buyers are organizations or individuals, they tend to demonstrate the characteristics of consumer markets (see Review Learning Outcome 6). Consider the case of an automobile replacement part. Purchase volume is usually small, and there are many customers, geographically dispersed, who typically buy from car dealers or parts stores. Negotiations do not occur, and neither reciprocity nor leasing is usually an issue. Manufacturers of component parts often direct their advertising toward replacement buyers.

PROCESSED MATERIALS

processed materials
Products used directly in manufacturing other products.

Processed materials are products used directly in manufacturing other products. Unlike raw materials, they have had some processing. Examples include sheet metal, chemicals, specialty steel, lumber, corn syrup, and plastics. Unlike component parts, processed materials do not retain their identity in final products.

Most processed materials are marketed to OEMs or to distributors servicing the OEM market. Processed materials are generally bought according to customer specifications or to some industry standard, as is the case with steel and lumber. Price and service are important factors in choosing a vendor.

SUPPLIES

supplies
Consumable items that do not become part of the final product.

Supplies are consumable items that do not become part of the final product—for example, lubricants, detergents, paper towels, pencils, and paper. Supplies are normally standardized items that purchasing agents routinely buy. Supplies typically have relatively short lives and are inexpensive compared to other business goods. Because supplies generally fall into one of three categories—maintenance, repair, or operating supplies—this category is often referred to as MRO.

Competition in the MRO market is intense. Office product retailers Staples and Grand & Toy battle each other constantly for the office supply purchases of Canadian businesses.

BUSINESS SERVICES

business services
Expense items that do not become part of a final product.

Business services are expense items that do not become part of a final product. Businesses often retain outside providers to perform janitorial, advertising, legal, management consulting, marketing research, maintenance, and other services. Hiring an outside provider makes sense when it costs less than hiring or assigning an employee to perform the task or when an outside provider is needed for particular expertise.

REVIEW LEARNING OUTCOME 7

7 | **Describe the seven types of business goods and services**

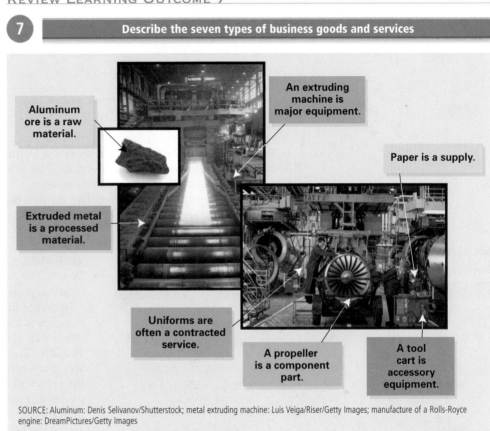

Aluminum ore is a raw material.

An extruding machine is major equipment.

Paper is a supply.

Extruded metal is a processed material.

Uniforms are often a contracted service.

A propeller is a component part.

A tool cart is accessory equipment.

SOURCE: Aluminum: Denis Selivanov/Shutterstock; metal extruding machine: Luis Veiga/Riser/Getty Images; manufacture of a Rolls-Royce engine: DreamPictures/Getty Images

8 BUSINESS BUYING BEHAVIOUR

Discuss the unique aspects of business buying behaviour

As you probably have already concluded, business buyers behave differently from consumers. Understanding how purchase decisions are made in organizations is a first step in developing a business selling strategy. Business buying behaviour has five important aspects: buying centres, evaluative criteria, buying situations, business ethics, and customer service.

BUYING CENTRES

In many cases, more than one person is involved in the purchase decision of a business. Identifying who these people are and the roles they play in the purchasing decision greatly enhances a salesperson's chances for success.[42]

buying centre
All those people in an organization who become involved in the purchase decision.

A **buying centre** includes all those people in an organization who become involved in the purchase decision. Membership and influence vary from company to company. In engineering-dominated companies like Bell Helicopter of Mirabel, Quebec, the buying centre may consist almost entirely of engineers. In marketing-oriented companies like Toyota and IBM, marketing and engineering have almost equal authority. In consumer goods companies like Procter & Gamble, product managers and other marketing decision makers may dominate the buying centre. In a small manufacturing company, almost everyone may be a member.

The number of people involved in a buying centre varies with the complexity and importance of a purchase decision. The composition of the buying group will usually change from one purchase to another and sometimes even during various stages of the buying process. To make matters more complicated, buying centres do not appear on formal organization charts.

For example, even though a formal committee may have been set up to choose a new plant site, it is only part of the buying centre. Other people, like the company president, often play informal yet powerful roles. In a lengthy decision-making process, such as finding a new plant location, some members may drop out of the buying centre when they can no longer play a useful role. Others whose talents are needed then become part of the centre. No formal announcement of "who is in" and "who is out" is ever made.

Roles in the Buying Centre

As in family purchasing decisions, several people may play a role in the business purchase process:

- *Initiator.* The person who first suggests making a purchase.
- *Influencers/evaluators.* People who influence the buying decision. They often help define specifications and provide information for evaluating options. Technical personnel are especially important as influencers.
- *Gatekeepers.* Group members who regulate the flow of information. Frequently, the purchasing agent views the gate-keeping role as a source of his or her power. A secretary may also act as a gatekeeper by determining which vendors get an appointment with a buyer.
- *Decider.* The person who has the formal or informal power to choose or approve the selection of the supplier or brand. In complex situations, it is often difficult to determine who makes the final decision.
- *Purchaser.* The person who actually negotiates the purchase. It could be anyone from the president of the company to the purchasing agent, depending on the importance of the decision.
- *Users.* Members of the organization who will actually use the product. Users often initiate the buying process and help define product specifications.

An example illustrating these basic roles is shown in Exhibit 5.4.

EXHIBIT 5.4

Buying Centre Roles for Computer Purchases

Role	Illustration
Initiator	Division general manager proposes to replace company's computer network.
Influencers/evaluators	Corporate controller's office and vice-president of data processing have an important say about which system and vendor the company will deal with.
Gate keepers	Corporate departments for purchasing and data processing analyze company's needs and recommend likely matches with potential vendors.
Decider	Vice-president of administration, with advice from others, selects the vendor the company will deal with and the system it will buy.
Purchaser	Purchasing agent negotiates terms of sale.
Users	All division employees use the computers.

Implications of Buying Centres for the Marketing Manager

Successful vendors realize the importance of identifying who is in the decision-making unit, each member's relative influence in the buying decision, and each member's evaluative criteria. Successful selling strategies often focus on determining the most important buying influences and then tailoring sales presentations to the evaluative criteria that are most important to these buying-centre members.

For example, Amex Canada Inc., a provider of corporate credit cards used for business travel, found that in order to control travel costs, many companies had travel managers who were corporate procurement professionals. Amex noted that these managers "increasingly have a role to play in controlling these costs as policies become more consistent and companies adopt the same approach to travel buying that they already employ in more 'traditional' purchases."[43]

Marketers are often frustrated by their inability to directly reach c-level (chief) executives who play important roles in many buying centres. To circumvent gate keepers, FedEx Corp. has initiated a marketing effort called "access," aimed at the c-suite. It includes direct mail, e-mail, and a custom magazine prepared exclusively for c-level executives. It also hosts exclusive leadership events for these senior executives.[44] Other firms, such as Motorola Corp., Intel Corp., SAS, and Xerox Corp., have developed programs utilizing a combination of print, on-line, and events to reach the elusive c-level audience.[45]

EVALUATIVE CRITERIA

Business buyers evaluate products and suppliers against three important criteria: quality, service, and price—in that order.

Quality

In this case, quality refers to technical suitability. A superior tool can do a better job in the production process, and superior packaging can increase dealer and consumer acceptance of a brand. Evaluation of quality also applies to the salesperson and the salesperson's company. Business buyers want to deal with reputable salespeople and with companies that are financially responsible. Quality improvement should be part of every organization's marketing strategy.

Service

Almost as much as they want satisfactory products, business buyers want satisfactory service. A purchase offers several opportunities for service. Suppose a vendor is selling heavy equipment. Prepurchase service could include a survey of the buyer's needs. After a thorough analysis of the survey findings, the vendor could prepare a report and recommendations in the form of a purchasing proposal. If a purchase results, postpurchase service might consist of installing the equipment and training those who will be using it. Postsale services may also include maintenance and repairs. Another service that business buyers seek is dependability of supply. They must be able to count on delivery of what was ordered according to the delivery schedule that was agreed upon. Buyers also welcome services that help them sell their finished products. Services of this sort are especially appropriate when the seller's product is an identifiable part of the buyer's end product.

> 9:32 am. Martha Watson fills an order for one of CDW's 360,000 business customers using her own, signature style.

SOURCE: © JOE PACZKOWSKI, LLC

Customer service is not just an issue for retailers of consumer products and services. CDW pairs each of its 360,000 business customers with an experienced account manager who can match the right technology products to the right needs. CDW sells more technology products from more manufacturers than anyone.

Price

Business buyers want to buy at low prices—at the lowest prices, in most circumstances. However, a buyer who pressures a supplier to cut prices to the point where the supplier loses money on the sale almost forces shortcuts on quality and compromises service dependability. The buyer also may, in effect, force the supplier to quit selling to the buyer's firm. Then a new source of supply will have to be found.

BUYING SITUATIONS

Often business firms, especially manufacturers, must decide whether to make something or buy it from an outside supplier. The decision is essentially one of economics. Can an

SOURCE: © ISTOCKPHOTO.COM/JAMIE SHIELDS

new buy
A situation requiring the purchase of a product for the first time.

modified rebuy
A situation in which the purchaser wants some change in the original good or service.

straight rebuy
A situation in which the purchaser reorders the same goods or services without looking for new information or investigating other suppliers.

item of similar quality be bought at a lower price elsewhere? If not, is manufacturing it in-house the best use of limited company resources? For example, Briggs & Stratton Corporation, a major manufacturer of four-cycle engines, might be able to save $150,000 annually on outside purchases by spending $500,000 on the equipment needed to produce gas throttles internally. Yet Briggs & Stratton could also use that $500,000 to upgrade its carburetor assembly line, which would save $225,000 annually. If a company does decide to buy a product instead of making it, the purchase will be a new buy, a modified rebuy, or a straight rebuy.

New Buy

A **new buy** is a situation requiring the purchase of a product for the first time. Suppose a manufacturing company needs a better way to page managers while they are working on the shop floor. Currently, each of the several managers has a distinct ring (e.g., two short and one long), which sounds over the plant intercom whenever he or she is being paged by anyone in the factory. The company decides to replace its buzzer system of paging with handheld wireless radio technology that will allow managers to communicate immediately with the department initiating the page. This situation represents the greatest opportunity for new vendors. No long-term relationship has been established for this product, specifications may be somewhat fluid, and buyers are generally more open to new vendors.

If the new item is a raw material or a critical component part, the buyer cannot afford to run out of supply. The seller must be able to convince the buyer that the seller's company can consistently deliver a high-quality product on time.

Modified Rebuy

A **modified rebuy** is normally less critical and less time-consuming than a new buy. In a modified-rebuy situation, the purchaser wants some change in the original good or service. It may be a new colour, greater tensile strength in a component part, more respondents in a marketing research study, or additional services in a janitorial contract.

Because the two parties are familiar with each other and credibility has been established, buyer and seller can focus on the specifics of the modification. But in some cases, modified rebuys are open to outside bidders. The purchaser uses this strategy to ensure that the new terms are competitive. An example would be a manufacturing company buying radios with a vibrating feature for managers who have trouble hearing the ring over the factory noise. This company may open the bidding to examine the price and quality offerings of several suppliers.

Straight Rebuy

A **straight rebuy** is a situation vendors prefer. The purchaser is not looking for new information or other suppliers. An order is placed and the product is provided as in previous orders. Usually, a straight rebuy is routine because the terms of the purchase have been agreed to in earlier negotiations. An example would be the previously cited manufacturing company purchasing additional radios for new managers from the same supplier on a regular basis.

One common instrument used in straight-rebuy situations is the purchasing contract. Purchasing contracts are used with products that are bought often and in high volume. In essence, the purchasing contract makes the buyer's decision making routine and promises the salesperson a sure sale. The advantage to the buyer is a quick, confident decision; the advantage to the salesperson is reduced or eliminated competition.

Suppliers must remember not to take straight-rebuy relationships for granted. Retaining existing customers is much easier than attracting new ones.

Business Ethics

As we noted in Chapter 3, ethics refers to the moral principles or values that generally govern the conduct of an individual or a group. Ethics can also be viewed as the standard of behaviour by which conduct is judged.

The ethics of business buyer and seller relationships are often scrutinized and sometimes criticized by superiors, associates, other prospective suppliers, the general public, and the news media. There has been a lot of publicity in recent years over corporate misbehaviour although most people and most companies follow ethical practices. More than half of all major corporations offer ethics training to their employees, and many companies have published codes of ethics to guide their managers. The Purchasing Management Association of Canada has developed a code of ethics to guide purchasing agents in their dealings with vendors; see the "Ethics in Marketing" box.

Customer Service

Business marketers need to recognize the benefits of developing a formal system for monitoring customer opinions and perceptions of the quality of customer service. Consumer-oriented companies like McDonald's and Lexus build their strategies not only around products but also around a few highly developed service skills. These companies understand that keeping current customers satisfied is just as important as attracting new ones, if not more so. These leading-edge firms are obsessed not only with delivering high-quality customer service, but also with measuring satisfaction, loyalty, relationship quality, and other indicators of nonfinancial performance.

Most firms find it necessary to develop measures unique to their own strategy, value propositions, and target market. For example, Andersen Corporation assesses the loyalty of its trade customers by their willingness to continue carrying its windows and doors, recommend its products to colleagues and customers, increase their volume with the company, and put its products in their own homes. Basically, each firm's measures should not only ask "What are your expectations?" and "How are we doing?" but should also reflect what the firm wants its customers to do.

Some customers are more valuable than others. They may have greater value because they spend more, buy higher-margin products, have a well-known name, or have the potential of becoming a bigger customer in the future. Some companies selectively provide different levels of service to customers based on their value to the business. By giving the most valuable customers superior service, a firm is more likely to keep them happy, hopefully increasing retention of these high-value customers and maximizing the total business value they generate over time.

To achieve this goal, the firm must be able to divide customers into two or more groups based on their value. It must also create and apply policies that govern how service will be allocated among groups. Policies might establish which customers' phone calls get "fast-tracked" and which customers are directed to use the Web and/or voice self-service, how specific e-mail questions are routed, and who is given access to on-line chat and who isn't.[46]

Providing different customers with different levels of service is a very sensitive matter. It must be handled very carefully and very discreetly to avoid offending lesser value, but still important customers.

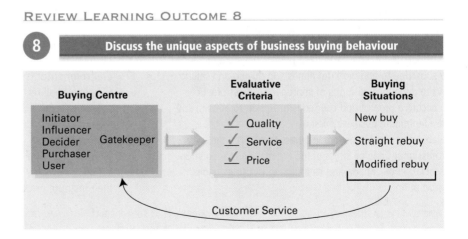

REVIEW LEARNING OUTCOME 8

8 | Discuss the unique aspects of business buying behaviour

Buying Centre	Evaluative Criteria	Buying Situations
Initiator Influencer Decider Purchaser User Gatekeeper	✓ Quality ✓ Service ✓ Price	New buy Straight rebuy Modified rebuy

Customer Service

Ethics in Marketing

 THE CODE OF ETHICS OF THE PURCHASING MANAGEMENT ASSOCIATION OF CANADA

Values and Norms of Ethical Behaviour
A. Values
Members will operate and conduct their decisions and actions based on the following values:

1. **Honesty/Integrity**
   Maintaining an unimpeachable standard of integrity in all their business relationships both inside and outside the organizations in which they are employed;
2. **Professionalism**
   Fostering the highest standards of professional competence amongst those for whom they are responsible;
3. **Responsible Management**
   Optimizing the use of resources for which they are responsible so as to provide the maximum benefit to their employers;
4. **Serving the Public Interest**
   Not using their authority of office for personal benefit, rejecting and denouncing any business practice that is improper;
5. **Conformity to the Laws**
   In terms of:
   - A. The laws of the country in which they practice;
   - B. The Institute's or Corporation's Rules and Regulations;
   - C. Contractual obligations.

B. Norms of Ethical Behaviour

1. To consider first, the interest of one's organization in all transactions and to carry out and believe in its established policies.
2. To be receptive to competent counsel from one's colleagues and be guided by such counsel without impairing the responsibility of one's office.
3. To buy without prejudice, seeking to obtain the maximum value for each dollar of expenditure.
4. To strive for increased knowledge of the materials and processes of manufacture, and to establish practical procedures for the performance of one's responsibilities.
5. To participate in professional development programs so that one's purchasing knowledge and performance are enhanced.
6. To subscribe to and work for honesty in buying and selling and to denounce all forms of improper business practice.
7. To accord a prompt and courteous reception to all who call on a legitimate business mission.
8. To abide by and to encourage others to practice the Professional Code of Ethics of the Purchasing Management Association of Canada and its affiliated Institutes and Corporation.
9. To counsel and assist fellow purchasers in the performance of their duties.
10. To cooperate with all organizations and individuals engaged in activities which enhance the development and standing of purchasing and materials management.

Rules of Conduct
In applying these rules of conduct, members should follow guidance set out below:

A. Declaration of Interest
Any personal interest which may impinge or might reasonably be deemed by others to impinge on a member's impartiality in any matter relevant to his or her duties should be immediately declared to his or her employer.

B. Confidentiality and Accuracy of Information
The confidentiality of information received in the course of duty must be respected and should not be used for personal gain; information given in the course of duty should be true and fair and not designed to mislead.

C. Competition
While considering the advantages to the member's employer of maintaining a continuing relationship with a supplier, any arrangement which might prevent the effective operation of fair competition should be avoided.

D. Business Gifts and Hospitality
To preserve the image and integrity of the member, employer and the profession, business gifts other than items of small intrinsic value should not be accepted. Reasonable hospitality is an accepted courtesy of a business relationship. The frequency and nature of gifts or hospitality accepted should not be allowed whereby the recipient might be or might be deemed by others to have been influenced in making a business decision as a consequence of accepting such hospitality or gifts.

E. Discrimination and Harassment
No member shall knowingly participate in acts of discrimination or harassment towards any person that he or she has business relations with.

F. Environmental Issues
Members shall recognize their responsibility to environmental issues consistent with their corporate goals or missions.

G. Interpretation
When in doubt on the interpretation of these rules of conduct, members should refer to the Ethics Committee of their Institute or Corporation.[47]

SOURCE: PURCHASING MANAGEMENT ASSOCIATION OF CANADA CORPORATE WEBSITE, "PMAC CODE OF ETHICS," HTTP://WWW.PMAC.CA/ABOUT/ETHICS.ASP, ACCESSED APRIL 11, 2010.

1 **Describe business marketing.** Business marketing provides goods and services that are bought for use in business rather than for personal consumption. Intended use, not physical characteristics, distinguishes a business product from a consumer product.

1.1 **WRITING** As the marketing manager for Huggies diapers made by Kimberly-Clark, you are constantly going head to head with Pampers, produced by rival Procter & Gamble. You are considering unlocking the potential of the business market to increase your share of the disposable diaper market, but how? Write an outline of several ways you could transform this quintessentially consumer product into a successful business product as well.

2 **Describe the role of the Internet in business marketing.** The rapid expansion and adoption of the Internet have made business markets more competitive than ever before. The number of business buyers and sellers using the Internet is increasing rapidly. Firms are seeking new and better ways to expand markets and sources of supply, increase sales and decrease costs, and better serve customers. Marketers are becoming more sophisticated in their use of the Internet and are developing quantitative methods that be used to better measure on-line success.

2.1 **ONLINE** How could you use the website **strategis.ic.gc.ca** to help define a target market and develop a marketing plan?

2.2 **ONLINE** Visit the website **BtoBonline.com**. Discuss some of the articles and information you find at this website that can help B-to-B marketers with their marketing efforts.

3  **Discuss the role of relationship marketing and strategic alliances in business marketing.** Relationship marketing entails seeking and establishing long-term alliances or partnerships with customers. A strategic alliance is a cooperative agreement among business companies. Firms form alliances to leverage what they do well by partnering with others who have complementary skills.

3.1 Why is relationship or personal selling the best way to promote in business marketing?

4 **Identify the four major categories of business market customers.** Producer markets consist of for-profit organizations and individuals that buy products to use in producing other products, as components of other products, or in facilitating business operations. Reseller markets consist of wholesalers and retailers that buy finished products to resell for profit. Government markets include federal, provincial, territorial, and municipal governments that buy goods and services to support their own operations. Institutional markets consist of highly diverse nonbusiness institutions whose main goals do not include profit.

4.1 **ONLINE** Understanding businesses is the key to business marketing. Use Canada Business (**www.canadabusiness.ca/eng/**) to learn about all the government services and information available to help you start a business. Examine the sources of business statistics available to you. Read about e-business and describe some of the issues you would have to deal with to set up an e-business. Access the information on selling to government. What kinds of contracts are listed?

4.2 **ONLINE** What do you have to do to get a government contract? Check out the websites **www.contractscanada.gc.ca** and **www.merx.com** to find out. Does it seem worth the effort?

5 **Explain the North American Industry Classification System.** The 2007 NAICS provides a way to identify, analyze, segment, and target business and government markets. Organizations can be identified and compared by a numeric code indicating business sector, subsector, industry group, industry, and country industry. NAICS is a valuable tool for analyzing, segmenting, and targeting business markets.

5.1 Explain how a marketer can use the website **www.naics.com** to convert SIC data to the 2007 NAICS.

5.2 Pick a product and determine its NAICS code. How easy was it to trace the groups and sectors?

6 **Explain the major differences between business and consumer markets.** In business markets, demand is derived, price-inelastic, joint, and fluctuating. Purchase volumes are much larger than in consumer markets, customers are fewer in number and more geographically concentrated, and distribution channels are more direct. Buying is approached more formally using professional purchasing agents, more people are involved in the buying process, negotiations are more complex, and reciprocity and leasing are more common. Finally, selling strategies in business markets normally focus on personal contact rather than on advertising.

6.1   How might derived demand affect the manufacturing of an automobile?

6.2   You are the company's purchasing manager. Your supervisor has asked you to buy new computers for an entire department. Since you have just recently purchased a new home computer, you are well educated about the various products available. How will your buying process for the company differ from your recent purchase for yourself?

7 **Describe the seven types of business goods and services.** Major equipment includes capital goods, such as heavy machinery. Accessory equipment is typically less expensive and shorter lived than major equipment. Raw materials are extractive or agricultural products that have not been processed. Component parts are finished or near-finished items to be used as parts of other products. Processed materials are used to manufacture other products. Supplies are consumable and are not used as part of a final product. Business services are intangible products that many firms use in their operations.

7.1   *TEAM*   In small groups, brainstorm examples of companies that feature the products in different business categories. (Avoid examples already listed in the chapter.) Compile a list of 10 specific business products, including at least one in each category. Then match up with another group. Have each group take turns naming a product and have the other group identify its appropriate category. Try to resolve all discrepancies by discussion. Some identified products might appropriately fit into more than one category.

8 **Discuss the unique aspects of business buying behaviour.** Business buying behaviour is distinguished by five fundamental characteristics. First, buying is normally undertaken by a buying centre consisting of many people who range widely in authority level. Second, business buyers typically evaluate alternative products and suppliers based on quality, service, and price—in that order. Third, business buying falls into three general categories: new buys, modified rebuys, and straight rebuys. Fourth, the ethics of business buyers and sellers are often scrutinized. Fifth, customer service before, during, and after the sale plays a big role in business purchase decisions.

8.1   *WRITING*   A colleague of yours has sent you an e-mail seeking your advice as she attempts to sell a new voice-mail system to a local business. Send her a return e-mail describing the various people who might influence the customer's buying decision. Be sure to include suggestions for dealing with the needs of each of these individuals.

8.2   Intel Corporation supplies microprocessors to Hewlett-Packard for use in its computers. Describe the buying situation in this relationship, keeping in mind the rapid advance of technology in this industry.

TERMS

accessory equipment 147
business marketing 132
business services 149
business-to-business electronic
  commerce 132
business-to-business on-line exchange 145
buying centre 149
component parts 147
derived demand 143
disintermediation 134

joint demand 144
keiretsu 137
major equipment (installations) 147
modified rebuy 152
multiplier effect (accelerator principle) 144
new buy 152
North American Industry Classification
  System (NAICS) 142
original equipment manufacturer (OEM) 139
processed materials 148

raw materials 147
reciprocity 146
reintermediation 135
relationship commitment 137
stickiness 133
straight rebuy 152
strategic alliance (strategic
  partnership) 136
supplies 148
trust 137

EXERCISES

APPLICATION EXERCISE

Purchasing agents are often offered gifts and gratuities. Increasingly, though, companies are restricting the amount and value of gifts that their purchasing managers can accept from vendors. The idea is that purchasing managers should consider all qualified vendors during a buying decision instead of only those who pass out great event tickets. This exercise asks you to consider whether accepting various types of gifts is ethical.[48]

Activities

1. Review the following list of common types of gifts and favours. Put a checkmark next to the items that you think it would be acceptable for a purchasing manager to receive from a vendor.

   ___ Advertising souvenirs   ___ Automobiles

   ___ Clothing   ___ Dinners

   ___ Discounts on personal purchases   ___ Food and liquor

   ___ Golf outings   ___ Holiday gifts

   ___ Large appliances   ___ Loans of money

   ___ Lunches   ___ Small-value appliances

   ___ Tickets (sports, theatre, amusement ___ Trips to vendor plants
       parks, etc.)

   ___ Vacation trips

2. Now look at your list of acceptable gifts through various lenses. Would your list change if the purchasing manager's buying decision involved a low-cost item (say, pens)? Why or why not? What if the decision involved a very expensive purchase (such as a major installation)?

3. Form a team and compare your lists. Discuss (or debate) any discrepancies.

ETHICS EXERCISE

Cameron Stock, a purchasing manager for a sports equipment manufacturer, is responsible for buying $5 million of supplies every year. He has a preferred list of certified suppliers, many of which are awarded a large percentage of this business annually. Cameron has been offered an all-expense-paid weekend for two in Las Vegas as a Christmas present from a major supplier with whom he has done business for close to a decade and with whom he has built a very good relationship.

Questions

1. Would it be legal and ethical for Cameron Stock to accept this gift?

2. How is this situation addressed in the PMAC Code of Ethics? Go to the "Ethics in Marketing" box in the chapter and review the PMAC Code of Ethics. Also visit the CMA website at **www.the-cma.org** and read the CMA's Code of Ethics. Write a brief paragraph summarizing where PMAC and the CMA stand on the issue of supplier gifts.

CASE STUDY

CAMELBAK: THEY'VE GOT YOUR 'BAK

In 1989, Michael Eidson probably never imagined that his homemade, do-it-yourself fix for dehydration during long cycling races would evolve into the world's premier hydration device for outdoor enthusiasts, soldiers, and law-enforcement personnel. That is exactly what happened to the CamelBak backpack, however.

The first version, which used medical tubing to carry water from an intravenous drip bag that was insulated by a sock and strapped to the back of his shirt, was born as most inventions are—out of necessity. The special pack made it possible for Eidson to take in fluids while sitting upright without having to sacrifice speed by reaching down for a water bottle during a race. The packs gained fame during the 1991 Gulf War as extreme sports enthusiasts in the U.S. Special Forces carried their personal CamelBaks into combat during Desert Storm. Thereafter, the CamelBak name would be forever associated with extreme performance and the U.S. Armed Forces.

By 1995, Eidsen sold the company for $4 million. Its buyer, Kransco, introduced the first camouflaged models, and the packs continued to gain acclaim. In 1999, two years after buying his first CamelBak pack, cyclist Chuck Hunter left Lockheed Martin to join the upstart company in hopes of growing its military business. He promptly moved the company to the Sonoma Valley, built a research and development centre, and leveraged his experience in the defence industry to launch a military-specific line of packs.

Hunter partnered with DuPont to help CamelBak develop the Low Infrared Reflective (LIRR) system. LIRR applies specially developed materials to a pack's compartments, buckles, and straps to shield soldiers from enemy detection systems. As advanced identification and kill technologies are increasingly being deployed on the battlefield, individual protection applications like the LIRR will be the camouflage of tomorrow.

Other CamelBak innovations include the WaterBeast reservoir, a fluid storage system that boasts 30 percent more rigidity than other packs on the market. The WaterBeast has the ability to withstand lengthy field engagements, aided by its silver-ion reservoir and tube linings that eliminate 99.99 percent of all fungus and bacteria in the water-delivery system. The WaterBeast reservoir is now a standard feature on all CamelBak packs, as is the company's proprietary drinking nozzle, or bite valve, which must withstand 10,000 compressions to guarantee it will last through three years of combat use.

Another CamelBak first is its CBR 4.0 pack system, which is specially designed to perform under chemical or biological weapons attack. The CBR 4.0 took five years to develop, and like all CamelBak military and law enforcement products, it was created to meet the specific requests and requirements of the target market. Since its introduction in 2005, the Canadian Armed Forces, the U.S. Special Forces, New York Police Department, U.S. Secret Service, Department of Health and Human Services, and a myriad of HAZMAT, law-enforcement, and government agencies from around the world have adopted and deployed the CBR 4.0.

Though CamelBak specializes in offering extreme performance packs for the military, industrial, and professional markets, it also sells a variety of products for hunting, extreme sports, recreational, and "light" law-enforcement applications. Having claimed more than 90 percent of the military market for hydration packs, product manager Shawn Cullen likens CamelBak to Kleenex: "Everyone calls a hydration system a CamelBak," he says. Ironically, the company's biggest customer is its biggest competitor. While it continues to use CamelBaks, the U.S. Army is working with a former supplier to develop its own version, most likely in an attempt to reduce costs.

At prices up to $200 for combat-ready systems, one thing CamelBaks aren't is cheap. But then again, neither is CamelBak itself. Its strong product lines, history of innovation, secure strategic relationships, and dominance in government and institutional markets drove its value to over $200 million when investment bank Bear Stearns Company bought the outfit from Kransco in 2003—not bad for a product that started life as an intravenous fluid bag wrapped in a sock.[49]

Questions

1. Discuss how business relationships and strategic partnerships have helped to increase the value of CamelBak's products and the business itself.

2. What type(s) of business market customers does CamelBak sell to?

3. Review the types of demand that most influence business markets. Which ones are most important for CamelBak to consider in its marketing strategy? Why?

4. What type of business product is a CamelBak backpack?

SOURCE: © PR NEWSFOTO/CAMELBAK PRODUCTS, LLC

VIDEO CASE

CBC

SMED: THE FALKRIDGE MARKETING AND RETREAT CENTRE

Smed Office Furniture is a Calgary-based manufacturer of modular office furniture with sales in the $250-million range. The company was founded as a private company in 1983 by Mogens Smed and went public in 1996. It was acquired by Haworth Office furniture in 2000. Smed currently operates a 72,000-square-metre manufacturing and office facility in Calgary.

Smed approaches office furniture manufacturing and marketing with a unique approach. The Calgary production facility is ISO 9001 registered and features modern equipment and innovative work processes that enable Smed to offer one of the shortest lead times in the office furniture business. Smed is environmentally conscious and employs "recycling programs, efficient lighting, processes that minimize material use and waste, carpooling and water conservation" in its factory. The factory itself is designed to make employees and visitors feel comfortable. It features "a workout facility and gym, an excellent restaurant called 'The Bridge,' and Lake Smed, which has a path around it for walking and is used for skating in the winter." It is part of Smed's approach to see that every day the employees "work in a landscape of leading-edge technology, efficient space, total flexibility, and aesthetically, ergonomically, and environmentally pleasing surroundings."

As pleasing and innovative as Smed's factory is, the Marketing Centre at Falkridge is even more impressive. Smed refers to it as "our ode to architectural detail. Every sense is indulged in textures, lines and colours, all surrounded by the beautiful scenery of the Canadian Rocky Mountains. Spectacular architecture and design is coupled with superior craftsmanship provided by local trades."

Falkridge is a small resort reserved specifically for Smed clients and employees. It features two main buildings that have 13 guest suites designed for "comfort, amenities, and style." Each suite (single or double accommodation) offers its guests Jacuzzi tubs, snack fridges, luxurious beds, automatic blinds, and forest and valley views. In addition to the 13 suites, there is also a three-bedroom apartment with kitchen and laundry facilities. The accommodations support a 22-seat presentation room and a smaller, eight-seat training room, both of which are equipped with state-of-the art audiovisual equipment. Falkridge has an informal kitchen–dining area that serves for breakfast and a larger dining room that offers sit-down service. Both the kitchen and the dining room present exquisite architectural surroundings and a cozy fireplace. Virtually all the furniture and systems in Falkridge are Smed designs and samples of Smed products.

Smed employs the Falkridge Marketing Centre for four purposes. It serves as a product training centre for Smed's employees. It is also a place where important clients are brought for Smed product demonstrations and to see examples of Smed's design capabilities in practice. It is also a way to "thank" clients for taking time to consider Smed's products and services. In Mogens Smed's words, "While visiting us we want clients to have firsthand exposure to our people, our culture, and our company. Falkridge celebrates what we're all about: our style, our commitment to quality and design, and of course our ongoing relationships with our clients." Finally, Falkridge is also available to rent for corporate retreats.

Training aside, the real power of Falkridge lies in its appeal to potential clients and purchase influencers. As CBC reporter Colin King states: "A visit to Falkridge closes many deals." When Smed clients come to Falkridge, they live among Smed products for several days. Mogens Smed likens it to fishing. The clients are the "fish" he is hoping to catch, and Falkridge and its attractive and compelling displays are the bait. Clients can enjoy the view and the luxury of the mountain resort while they live and work among Smed's products. After this, if they can say no to a deal, they are resistant clients indeed!

Smed is not using Falkridge to impress buyers alone. The company is also aware of the importance of key influencers in the purchase of office furniture. That is why it sponsored a retreat for the Northern Pacific Chapter of the International Interior Design Association. A report on the retreat included the following commentary about Falkridge: "The facility was beautiful with architectural textures, lines, and colours all surrounded by the beautiful scenery of the Canadian Rocky Mountains. Though snowing and chilly outside, we were toasty warm inside and enjoyed some productive and quality time among approximately 20 board members. We were also very privileged to have a special dinner at Mogens Smed's log home with beautiful interior detailing all by local craftsmen."

Smed has encountered only two problems with Falkridge: it has only 13 rooms (plus one apartment); and there are only 52 weekends in the year. So there are only so many clients and so many retreats that Smed can fit in. Falkridge will have to produce a lot of million-dollar deals to justify its existence, but so far it seems to be up to the task.[50]

Questions

1. How do you think a facility like Falkridge helps Smed improve its business marketing?

2. What kinds of "clients" would mostly likely be interested in a facility like Falkridge for their "corporate retreats"?

3. What kinds of "ethical" issues might arise around the use of Falkridge to entertain and educate Smed's customers? (Review the PMAC Code of Conduct in the "Ethics in Marketing" box in the chapter, and review the CMA's Code of Ethics on the CMA website, **www.the-cma.org**, to help you answer this question.)

4. The case mentions the four purposes for Falkridge. Advise Smed on how to "ration" the four purposes for Falkridge so that it can maximize the centre's impact as a marketing tool.

MARKETING & YOU RESULTS

A high score indicates that you found the salesperson to be credible and concerned about your needs. Because you found the salesperson to be open and concerned, you had a higher level of trust in the salesperson than did someone with a lower score. As you read in this chapter, trust is an important element in building strategic alliances and in cultivating business clients.

6 Segmenting and Targeting Markets

SOURCE: COURTESY OF THE GEORGIAN COURT HOTEL

LEARNING OUTCOMES

1 Describe the characteristics of markets and market segments

2 Explain the importance of market segmentation

3 Discuss criteria for successful market segmentation

4 Describe the bases commonly used to segment consumer markets

5 Describe the bases for segmenting business markets

6 List the steps involved in segmenting markets

7 Discuss alternative strategies for selecting target markets

8 Explain one-to-one marketing

9 Explain how and why companies implement positioning strategies and how product differentiation plays a role

MARKETING & YOU

Please note your opinion on each of the following questions by using the following scale, enter your answers or record them on a separate page.

1	2	3	4	5	6
Strongly agree					Strongly disagree

___ I frequently have problems making ends meet.
___ My budgeting is always right.
___ I often have to spend more money than I have available.

___ I do not consider myself financially well off.
___ I am generally on a tight budget.
___ Meeting an unexpected expense of $1,000 would be a financial hardship.

Total your score. Now read the chapter and find out what your score means at the end.

SOURCE: REPRINTED WITH PERMISSION FROM *MARKETING SCALES HANDBOOK* VOL. III, PUBLISHED BY THE AMERICAN MARKETING ASSOCIATION, G. BRUNER, K. JAMES, H. HENSEL, EDS. SCALE #646.

Marketers who subscribe to the marketing concept—the basic business philosophy that says marketers should cater to the needs and wants of their customers as the first step in developing products and services—also know discovering these needs and wants is the first step in designing a market segmentation and target marketing strategy. Consider the long-recognized rising economic power of women consumers and the need to understand the nature of these consumers when designing target marketing strategies. This is what a number of hoteliers throughout the world have done, and the result is an offering of "women-only" floors in their hotels to cater specifically to women business travellers.

According to writer Julie Harrison, hoteliers have discovered that "businesswomen are a lucrative market: high income, fiercely loyal and willing to pay more to have their needs met." These are some of the characteristics marketers look for when designing a segmentation and target marketing strategy. However, before developing any offering, marketers need to know the size of their market, its sales potential, and specifically what needs and wants the market has. According to Mary Beth Bond, a women's travel expert, throughout the world 32 million women travel annually, and they spend an estimated $125 billion! In Canada, it is predicted that business travel will be increasing over the next few years, a trend that should balance the downturn predicted for leisure travel.

However, what are the different needs and wants of male travellers and female travellers that a hotel would have to address to attract this market? According to frequent business traveller Penelope Trunk, the CEO of Brazen Careerist, "Men want their room to be something where they dump their stuff, they go out drinking, and they come back and watch porn. . . . The women want it to be a spa. Women use treadmills and men use weight machines, so if there are only two treadmills in a big hotel, it's catering to men. But almost every woman I know who travels a lot works out a lot." Male-oriented hotels have better bars than they do gyms. Women want their hotel room to provide a complementary robe—"Nobody packs pajamas," because space is at a premium when you are travelling. "You want to take off all your clothes and not put them on again until your next meeting. If you get up in the morning and there's no robe, it's totally annoying." Finally, women tend to order room service for breakfast more often than men do. This means hotels need to have enough room-service waiters at breakfast to serve this market.

Women travellers are demanding of hotels to meet their needs, but when they find a hotel that caters to them they are extremely loyal patrons. Penelope Trunk says if she had a good stay in a hotel in a particular city, she will stay there again. Female travellers who are loyal to their hotels expect to be rewarded for this loyalty, though. They prefer to patronize hotels that have loyalty programs, cater to their needs, and respond quickly to their requests. Ann Crombie of Re-Think Strategic Consulting values safety in her hotel choices. "I don't want to get there and find out that it's a shady place."

How have hotels responded to the special needs of the women's travellers segment? Harrison observes that most hotels have added more feminine touches to all their rooms. They offer special shampoos and lotions. Rooms come equipped with "everything from thick bathrobes, curved shower-rods, vanity mirrors, yoga mats, gourmet coffees and teas and satin-covered hangers." However, the creation of women-only floors is the sign of a true commitment to this market segment. For example, the Georgian Court Hotel in Vancouver, British Columbia, has created the 18-room Orchid Floor, where the rooms are reserved for women only. According to Susan Leung, director of sales for the Georgian Court, the hotel was undergoing a major renovation so it was decided to make the hotel more welcoming to women by having a floor dedicated solely to them. Each room on the Orchid Floor comes with Aveda bath products, yoga mats, slippers, robes, flat irons, curling irons, satin padded hangers, lifestyle magazines, a ladies' emergency kit, and of course, fresh orchids! According to Leung, the response to the concept of a floor for women only has been "positive, positive, positive."[1]

Based on the preceding information, how would you define market segmentation and targeting? What type of targeting strategy is involved in attracting women business travellers? What kinds of issues do you think marketers will have to pay attention to in order to market to this segment? This chapter will help you answer these questions and more.

SOURCES: JULIE HARRISON, "WOMEN ONLY," THE WINDSOR STAR, SATURDAY, APRIL 3, 2010, F1–2; HTTP://WWW.WINDSORSTAR.COM/TRAVEL/WOMEN+ONLY/2758806/STORY.HTML AND GEORGIAN COURT HOTEL VANCOUVER WEBSITE, HTTP://WWW.GEORGIANCOURTHOTELVANCOUVER.COM/DOWNTOWN-VANCOUVER-HOTEL-ORCHID-FLOOR.HTML, ACCESSED APRIL 13, 2010

Describe the characteristics of markets and market segments

market
People or organizations with needs or wants and the ability and willingness to buy.

market segment
A subgroup of people or organizations sharing one or more characteristics that cause them to have similar product needs.

market segmentation
The process of dividing a market into meaningful, relatively similar, and identifiable segments or groups.

The term *market* means different things to different people. We are all familiar with the supermarket, stock market, labour market, fish market, and flea market. All these types of markets share several characteristics. First, they are composed of people (consumer markets) or organizations (business markets). Second, these people or organizations have wants and needs that can be satisfied by particular product categories. Third, they have the ability to buy the products they seek. Fourth, they are willing to exchange their resources—usually money or credit—for desired products. In sum, a **market** is (1) people or organizations with (2) needs or wants and with (3) the ability and (4) the willingness to buy. A group of people or an organization that lacks any one of these characteristics is not a market.

Within a market, a **market segment** is a subgroup of people or organizations sharing one or more characteristics that cause them to have similar product needs. At one extreme, we can define every person and every organization in the world as a market segment because each is unique. At the other extreme, we can define the entire consumer market as one large market segment and the business market as another large segment. All people have some similar characteristics and needs, as do all organizations.

From a marketing perspective, market segments can be described as somewhere between the two extremes. The process of dividing a market into meaningful, relatively similar, and identifiable segments or groups is called **market segmentation**. The purpose of market segmentation is to enable the marketer to tailor marketing mixes to meet the needs of one or more specific segments.

Exhibit 6.1 illustrates the concept of market segmentation. Each box represents a market consisting of seven persons. This market might vary as follows: one homogeneous market of seven people; a market consisting of seven individual segments; a

EXHIBIT 6.1

Concept of Market Segmentation

No market segmentation

Fully segmented market

Market segmentation by gender: M, F

Market segmentation by age group: 1, 2, 3

Market segmentation by gender and age group

SOURCE: **CLOCKWISE FROM TOP:** (3M) GWIMAGES/SHUTTERSTOCK; (3M) FOUR OAKS/SHUTTERSTOCK; (1F) WAVEBREAKMEDIA LTD/SHUTTERSTOCK; (1M) RUI VALE DE SOUSA/SHUTTERSTOCK; (2M) AJAY BHASKAR/SHUTTERSTOCK. **CENTRE TOP:** (2F) YURI ARCURS/SHUTTERSTOCK. **CENTRE BOTTOM:** (2F) TRACY WHITESIDE/SHUTTERSTOCK

Describe the characteristics of markets and market segments

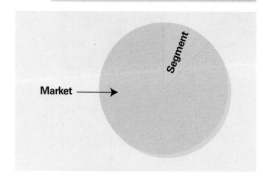

Market →

Segment

market composed of two segments based on gender; a market composed of three age segments; or a market composed of five age and gender market segments. Age and gender and many other bases for segmenting markets are examined later in this chapter.

② THE IMPORTANCE OF MARKET SEGMENTATION

Explain the importance of market segmentation

Up until about 50 years ago, few companies practised market segmentation. When they did, it was more likely a haphazard effort than a formal marketing strategy. For example, before 1960 the Coca-Cola Company produced only one beverage and aimed it at the entire soft drink market. Today, Coca-Cola offers more than a dozen different products to market segments based on diverse consumer preferences for flavours and calorie and caffeine content. Coca-Cola offers traditional soft drinks, energy drinks (such as PowerAde), flavoured teas, fruit drinks (Fruitopia), and water (Dasani).

Market segmentation plays a key role in the marketing strategy of almost all successful organizations and is a powerful marketing tool for several reasons. Most important, nearly all markets include groups of people or organizations with different product needs and preferences. Market segmentation helps marketers define customer needs and wants more precisely. Because market segments differ in size and potential, segmentation helps decision makers define marketing objectives more accurately so as to better allocate resources. Also, performance can be better evaluated when objectives are more precise.

Seneca College in Toronto has developed a segmentation strategy to reach out to different youth groups. The college describes how it is using "transit and outdoor ads designed to position the school as the key to a successful future." Martha Lowrie, Seneca's director of marketing and communications, explains the strategy this way: "We're trying to reach different segments in the youth demographic. That's why we went to transit. We're reaching those just finishing high school, those whom we call nondirect, because they don't go directly from high school into post-secondary, and also those with a college diploma or university undergraduate degree looking to specialize their post-graduate experience." The strategy encourages interested students to visit Seneca through the ExploreChange.ca website, which takes them directly to a Seneca College page. There they will find a number of banner choices that cater to different youth segments: high school student, individual returning to education, someone graduating from college or university, an international student, or a part-time student.[2]

SOURCE: © VICKI BEAVER

How many ways can you slice the market for beverages? Coca-Cola has over a dozen beverages on the market with loyal fans for each one.

2 | **Explain the importance of market segmentation**

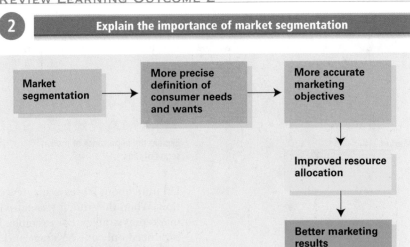

3 CRITERIA FOR SUCCESSFUL SEGMENTATION

Discuss criteria for successful market segmentation

Marketers segment markets for three important reasons. First, segmentation enables marketers to identify groups of customers with similar needs and to analyze the characteristics and buying behaviours of these groups. Second, segmentation provides marketers with information to help them design marketing mixes specifically matched with the characteristics and desires of one or more segments. Third, segmentation is consistent with the marketing concept of satisfying customer wants and needs while meeting the organization's objectives.

To be useful, a segmentation scheme must produce segments that meet four basic criteria:

- *Substantiality.* A segment must be large enough to warrant developing and maintaining a special marketing mix. This criterion does not necessarily mean that a segment must have many potential customers. Marketers of custom-designed homes and business buildings, commercial airplanes, and large computer systems typically develop marketing programs tailored to each potential customer's needs. In most cases, however, a market segment needs many potential customers to make commercial sense. When it was first attempted in the 1980s, home banking failed because not enough people owned personal computers; also, the software to enable home banking was cumbersome and difficult to use. Today, home banking is thriving because a larger number of people have access to high-speed Internet service through web-enabled devices such as computers and smartphones through which they can access their bank's website which is both easy to use and secure.

- *Identifiability and measurability.* Segments must be identifiable and their size measurable. Data about the population within geographic boundaries, the number of people in various age categories, and other social and demographic characteristics are often easy to get, and they provide fairly concrete measures of segment size. Suppose a social service agency wants to identify segments by their readiness to participate in a problem gambling program or in prenatal care. Unless the agency can measure how many people are willing, indifferent, or unwilling to participate, it will have trouble gauging whether there are enough people to justify setting up the service.

- *Accessibility.* An organization must be able to reach members of targeted segments with customized marketing mixes. Some market segments are hard to reach—for example, senior citizens (especially those with reading or hearing disabilities), individuals who don't speak the language being used in the marketing campaign, and people who are illiterate.

- *Responsiveness.* As previously presented in Exhibit 6.1, markets can be segmented using any criteria that seem logical. Unless one market segment responds to a marketing mix differently from other segments, however, that segment need not be treated separately. For instance, if all customers are equally price conscious about a product, there is no need to offer high-, medium-, and low-priced versions to different segments.

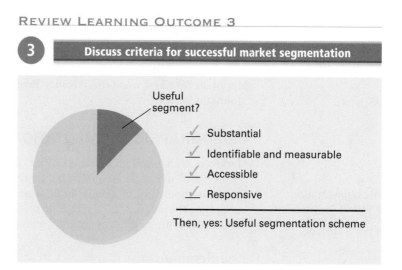

3 | Discuss criteria for successful market segmentation

Useful segment?

✓ Substantial

✓ Identifiable and measurable

✓ Accessible

✓ Responsive

Then, yes: Useful segmentation scheme

 # BASES FOR SEGMENTING CONSUMER MARKETS

Describe the bases commonly used to segment consumer markets

segmentation bases (variables)
Characteristics of individuals, groups, or organizations.

Marketers use **segmentation bases**, or **variables**, which are characteristics of individuals, groups, or organizations, to divide a total market into segments. The choice of segmentation bases is crucial because an inappropriate segmentation strategy may lead to lost sales and missed profit opportunities. The key is to identify bases that will produce substantial, measurable, and accessible segments that exhibit different response patterns to marketing mixes.

Markets can be segmented using a single variable, such as age group, or several variables, such as age group, gender, and education. Multiple-variable segmentation is more precise than single-variable segmentation but single-variable segmentation has the advantage of being simpler and easier to use. The disadvantages of multiple-variable segmentation are that it is often harder to use than single-variable segmentation; usable secondary data are less likely to be available; and as the number of segmentation bases increases, the size of individual segments decreases. Nevertheless, the current trend is toward using more rather than fewer variables to segment most markets.

Consumer goods marketers commonly use one or more of the following characteristics to segment markets: geography, demographics, psychographics, benefits sought, and usage rate.

GEOGRAPHIC SEGMENTATION

geographic segmentation
Segmenting markets by region of a country or the world, market size, market density, or climate.

Geographic segmentation refers to segmenting markets by region of a country or the world, market size, market density (e.g., rural or urban), or climate. Market density refers to the number of people within a unit of land, such as a census tract. Climate is commonly used for geographic segmentation because of its dramatic impact on residents' needs and purchasing behaviours. Snowmobiles, personal watercraft, water and snow skis, clothing, and air conditioning and heating systems are products whose appeal varies depending on climate.

Consumer goods companies take a regional approach to marketing for four reasons. First, many companies need to find new ways to generate sales because of sluggish and intensely competitive markets. Second, computerized checkout stations with scanners enable retailers to assess accurately which brands sell best in their region. Third, many packaged-goods manufacturers are introducing new regional brands intended to appeal to local preferences. Fourth, a more regional approach allows consumer goods companies to react more quickly to competition. Kokanee beer, brewed in the Columbia Brewery in Creston, B. C., has taken a regional approach to marketing its beer. The company has targeted the western provinces of Canada based on their proximity to British Columbia. Kokanee presents itself as one of the "best-selling beers in Western Canada." The brewery's promotional campaign uses the tag line "It's All About Now" and features people travelling and undertaking activities in the mountains and talks about Kokanee beer as being "Glacier Fresh." The firm has sponsored a number of promotional events that are set in the mountains of British Columbia, including the Telus World Ski and Snowboard Festival, the Kokanee Crankworx Mountain Bike Festival at the Whistler Bike Park, and the Kokanee Whiteout Ultimate Mountain Party.[3]

DEMOGRAPHIC SEGMENTATION

demographic segmentation
Segmenting markets by age, gender, income, ethnic background, and family life cycle.

Marketers often segment markets on the basis of demographic information because it is widely available and often related to consumers' buying and consuming behaviour. Some common bases of **demographic segmentation** are age, gender, income, ethnic background, and family life cycle. The discussion here provides some important information about the main demographic segments.

Age Segmentation[4]

Marketers use a variety of terms to refer to different age groups. Examples include newborns, infants, young children, tweens, teens and young adults (Generation Y or Millennials), adults (Generation X), baby boomers, and seniors. Age segmentation can be an important tool, as a brief exploration of several age segments will illustrate.

The data used in age segmentation in Canada are mainly sourced from the Census of Canada (regularly undertaken at five-year intervals, with 2011 as the most recent census year). In between the years when a census has been taken and its information released, estimates of population are made. Based on the most recent information, Canada's population is estimated to be 33.9 million and is divided into 19 different age groups for statistical purposes. Marketers use these statistical age groups, often combining them with other information, in order to estimate demand potentials for products that are age related.

Attracting children is a popular strategy for many companies hoping to instill brand loyalty early. Furthermore, children influence a great deal of family consumption. There are three subsegments in the children's market: young children (9 and under), "tweens" (10 to 14), and teens (15 to 19). Statistics Canada data indicate that there were more than 3.6 million children under nine in Canada in 2009; this group represented 10.7 percent of the total population—an important market. Recently a number of research articles and reports have shown that brand-name recognition among young children is fairly high.[5] For example, a news report on one study distilled the findings this way: "The average 10-year-old is thought to be familiar with approximately 400 brands. The average kindergarten student can recognize some 300 logos. And at just six weeks, a baby can form mental images of corporate logos and mascots."[6]

Marketing to children is a very controversial topic at best, but children are still consumers and have needs and wants that must be fulfilled. Marketers have traditionally marketed toys, cereal, food, and clothing to this age group. For example, recently SpinMaster, well-known maker of Air Hogs™ toys, developed a new line of Liv™ dolls: "four engaging teenage friends—Daniela, Sophie, Katie and Alexis—who live the same life as any average teenagers." They are targeted at girls six to ten years of age. A press released reported, "Accompanying the retail launch of Liv is the launch of **www.livworld.com**, the first website of its kind to deliver an engaging daily narrative of each doll's life to anyone who's purchased the doll. . . . Each Liv product purchase, including accessories, playsets, and fashion packs, [unlocks] additional play features online."[7] Marketers communicate directly with these age group through a number of specialty television networks (BBC Kids, Family Channel, YTV Canada, Teletoon English, Teletoon French, Teletoon Retro, and Tree House)[8] that carry programming for this group and that have developed websites associated with their networks. These sites have interactive capability and activities specifically designed for children.

Older children, dubbed "tweens," number about 1.97 million, represent 5.9 percent of the population, and have an estimated spending power of over $2.9 billion.[9] Tweens desire to be kids but also want some of the fun and glamour of being a teenager.[10] The Family Channel has acquired the rights to the Disney Channel's programming in Canada. Disney has developed a successful strategy to capture the tween market by re-creating the old Hollywood star system with its tween actors and actresses, such as Miley Cyrus (*Hannah Montana*), Selena Gomez (*Wizards of Waverly Place*), and, of course, the Jonas Brothers. Disney makes little-known kids into big names and then directs their talents into every corner of its empire—TV shows, movies, records, and merchandise. Read the "Global Perspectives" box to see how Disney is learning about European tweens.

Teens, sometimes referred to as Generation Y or millennials, number 2.25 million and represent 6.7 percent of the population. Canada's Print Measurement Bureau (PMB) reports: "Canadian teenagers earn an average of $5,255 every year and they spend about 90 percent of it on entertainment and leisure, including clothes, fragrances, hair care and cologne." Marketers are trying very hard to reach out to this market, and a number of specialty magazines have been developed specifically to reach Canadian teens. For example, Youth Culture Group has developed *Vervegirl* as a specialty magazine with a reported circulation of 151,000. It is targeted specifically at teenage girls who live in Canada. Famous Players theatres publishes *Teen Tribute* magazine, which is distributed to 400,000 teenage moviegoers.[11]

Global Perspectives

 ## DISNEY STUDIES EUROPEAN TWEENS

Today's tweens are not familiar with a world in which the Internet and portable wireless communication did not exist. Disney is very interested in marketing to European tweens so they wanted to know how tweens in this market see their place in the world and, more importantly for Disney, how they consume media. The firm recently undertook a detailed study involving a poll of over 3,000 children in the age range of 8 to 14 years in the six European countries of France, Germany, Italy, Poland, Spain, and the United Kingdom. The results of the poll suggest that today's 8- to 14-year-olds use digital media often and have "a heightened awareness of their future and that of the planet. . . . Kids are using the internet to enhance their social interaction, rather than replace it altogether—preferring face-to-face interaction, while using social networks, emailing and texting as other means of keeping up with their friends."

The poll found, as may be expected, that tweens use the Internet for entertainment but they also use it to do their homework. "In fact, homework (59%) scored second only to gaming (74%) as the most common use" of the Internet. Disney also learned that tweens prefer face-to-face interactions and they use the Internet to enhance these interactions rather than as a replacement for face-to-face. Tweens keep up with their friends closely by using social networks, and by sending both e-mails and text messages. Another finding was that although the European youth culture seemed to have a focus on celebrities, most tweens aren't looking for fame but are actually considering more typical careers like teaching, veterinary medicine, and law enforcement. Perhaps one of the most interesting findings was that "in every single country, respondents said the person they admire most in the world is their mom, at 43%, with dad coming second at 30%."

If being sentimental about their parents is a surprise, the poll also found that these tweens are in touch with global issues like managing the environment. An impressive 97 percent said they "believe it is important to look after the planet" and they back this up with action: "74% said they recycle regularly." European tweens are also looking to their future from a financial standpoint as well; 70 percent of the respondents said they "are saving their pocket money rather than spending it immediately, while 64% said they would much rather work for themselves than for someone else when they grow up." The most interesting finding was that despite the fact that the poll was undertaken in six different countries, the values of the tweens were remarkably similar across all the countries.

How is Disney using this information that it collected? Disney has developed a unique television channel for Europe entitled Disney XD. An executive director of EMEA Research, Disney Channels, Victoria Hardy, says the project is helping the company "develop and deliver relevant entertainment that incorporates themes important to tweens' lives."[12]

SOURCE: KATE CALDER, "DISNEY XD UNVEILS RESULTS OF PAN-EURO TWEEN STUDY," KIDSCREEN, FEBRUARY, 2010, 22. © 2010 BRUNICO COMMUNICATIONS LTD. REPRINTED WITH PERMISSION.

Other age segments are also appealing targets for marketers. The approximately 6.9 million Canadians classified as young adults (between 20 and 34) represent 20.6 percent of the population. Many beer, wine, and spirits companies are targeting this group. Bacardi, which uses a bat as a logo, has identified people between legal drinking age and 29 as its "core" market. To reach this market, it has launched a website built around the theme of "The Spirit of Bacardi" and supported this with an advertising campaign. This website is customized by country and asks visitors to indicate their birth date and country of residence before allowing entry to the site. When you enter the site, you are greeted with party music and can access a video of the most recent commercial. One of these videos featured a bunch of boaters throwing rocks into a bay to build an island. After building the island, they stock it with trees, lights, and Bacardi and then have a huge party. In addition to video commercials, the website offers drink mix recipes with videos showing how to make them. The site has a "responsible drinking" tab that promises to find you a taxi if you provide your location. This would be very convenient for someone who had a Web-enabled wireless phone. Computer-literate Gen X-ers are a large and viable market for the Internet, and Bacardi is hoping to tap into this.[13]

The baby boom generation, born between 1946 and 1964, makes up the largest age segment, with 9.5 million people—about 28.0 percent of the Canadian population. The majority of people in this group are now over 50 years old but are continuing to lead active, fully involved lives. Over-50 boomers are changing the way people look at aging, and this presents an opportunity for brands to reposition themselves and for marketers to be more lifestyle-oriented. Agneta Owen, a consultant to Toronto-based Lavalife Corporation, helped the company develop a website specifically for baby boomers called LavalifePRIME. Owen talked with boomer friends who told her that most dating sites were designed for 20-somethings and just weren't very good at producing matches for people in their age group. Owen undertook both survey and focus-group research to come up with the right website concept. According to Calvin Leung of *Canadian Business*, the result was "LavalifePrime, where Singles 45+ Click." Its concept was to allow its visitors to "use videos, audio clips, photos and words to give a more well-rounded representation of themselves. The fonts would be slightly larger than on the lavalife.com site, to make the text easier for older users to read, and other features had to be especially user-friendly. The site would include tips on topics such as dating etiquette and safe-sex techniques." The result was that the plan to spend $1 million to attract 25,000 members resulted in a response that turned out to be double what had been expected.[14]

Seniors (65 and over) are especially attracted to companies that build relationships by taking the time to get to know them and their preferences. Canadian seniors number about 4.7 million and represent 13.9 percent of the population. Older customers say they prefer catalogue shopping over retail outlets because of their dissatisfaction with customer service at retail stores. People of this age group are more likely than most to have the combination of free time, money, and health that lets them pursue leisure activities, especially education and travel. However, they do not think of themselves as old or as seniors, despite their demands for traditional "senior" products.

Marketers and society in general have not paid a lot of attention to seniors but this population group is growing so rapidly that one writer recently stated, "As a generation, we are about to form a grey tsunami!"[15] This tsunami is going to demand a large increase in a variety of services. The City of Toronto is looking at 17 percent of its population being over the age of 65 in the next 20 years and the accommodations for this group need to be built now. The same writer reported that the city is considering "salting the GTA's shops and banks with many more benches, expanding priority seating on public transport, making buildings more wheelchair accessible, and creating more services to enable" seniors to "age in place," meaning serving them where they live now rather than relocating them to assisted living quarters. Arnica Mature Lifestyles is a Canadian company catering to this market by opening unique seniors' residences. Described as "service-oriented seniors' utopias," the Bayview Gardens Arnica property "has a spa, an English style pub and 24-hour concierge." Arnica's competitor, Signature Living Corporation, has a residence that "offers Town Car service (don't have to hope for good seats on the bus) and personal massages."[16]

Gender Segmentation

Marketers of products such as clothing, cosmetics, personal care items, magazines, jewellery, and footwear commonly segment markets by gender. The population breakdown by gender in Canada is 49.6 percent men and 50.4 percent women. However, the ratio of men to women is not equal for all of the age distributions. The number of men exceeds the number of women in every age group under age 50. Over age 50, the number of women exceeds the number of men in every age group.[17]

Globally, women undertake $12 billion of the total of $18.4 billion of consumer spending! In Canada, women purchase 68 percent of the new cars, 56 percent of new home computers, and 51 percent of the new electronics sold.[18] This means that women are making decisions when it comes to the purchase of a huge variety of goods and services, not just the packaged goods that have traditionally been marketed to them. Women are buying and playing video games in rapidly increasing numbers. Forty percent of gamers are women and they outnumber under-17 males by nearly two to one in the gaming world. The video game industry has been forced to respond by developing more games with female protagonists and changing its advertising strategy. A recent commercial for EA Sports featured real video gamers—some of them women—instead of actors, and presented video game playing as an interactive social activity.[19] Other marketers that traditionally focused most of their attention on males are also recognizing the potential of the female market segment. Home Depot undertook a survey that indicated "80 percent of women prefer to do projects themselves because it gives them a sense of accomplishment, price and expression, and helps them save money while improving the value of their home. Additionally 73 percent said doing home improvement projects is just plain fun."[20] Consequently, Home Depot has developed "Do It Herself" workshops where women customers learn from women instructors who demonstrate how to tile floors and walls, install light fixtures, and undertake interior painting and other home improvement projects.[21]

Of course, to reverse the old saying, what's good for the gander may be good for the goose too! Cosmetic companies that have traditionally targeted women are trying to expand their sales by targeting men. Lancôme is a well-known cosmetics company that has traditionally targeted women for anti-aging skin creams. Lancôme has realized that men may be just as interested as women are in looking younger. It has launched a line of skin products for men that "have also targeted specific age groups. For the younger man (25 to 30 years) there's Hydrix Gel, for the established male (30 to 40 years) there's Age Fight, and for the silvered man (40+) there's Renergy 3D, and for every man there's The Essentials, an exfoliating microdermabrasion."[22]

Income Segmentation

Income is a popular demographic variable for segmenting markets because income level influences consumers' wants and determines their buying power. In Canada, Statistics Canada measures income as "economic family income. An economic family is a group of individuals sharing a common dwelling unit who are related by blood, marriage (including common-law relationships) or adoption." In 2007, the average family income for Canadians was $86,300. However, marketers can learn more about consumers by looking at their expenditures, which were an average of $71,360 per family in 2008. The expenditure breakdown that year was as follows: income taxes, 20.5 percent; shelter, 19.9 percent; transportation, 13.6 percent; food, 10.4 percent; recreation, 5.9 percent; insurance and pensions, 5.6 percent; household operation, 4.7 percent; clothing, 4.0 percent; health care, 2.9 percent; household furnishings and equipment, 2.8 percent; charity, 2.3 percent; alcohol and tobacco products, 2.1 percent; personal care, 1.7 percent; education, 1.7 percent; reading (printed material), 0.4 percent; and gambling, 0.4 percent.[23]

Many markets are segmented by income, including the markets for housing, clothing, automobiles, and food. Value retailers, like The Dollar Store, appeal to low- and fixed-income customers with their easy access, small stores, and rock-bottom pricing. Procter & Gamble, best known for its detergent brands, recently lowered the price on its Cheer detergents line in Canada to reposition it as a bargain brand to

EXHIBIT 6.2

Profile of Ethnic Origins and Visible Minorities in Canada, 2006

Ethnic origin	Total number	% of population
Canadian	10,066,290	32.2
English	6,570,015	21.0
French	4,941,210	15.8
Scottish	4,719,850	15.1
Irish	4,354,155	13.9
German	3,179,425	10.2
Italian	1,445,335	4.6
Chinese	1,346,510	4.3
North American Indian	1,253,615	4.0
Ukrainian	1,209,085	3.9
Dutch	1,035,965	3.3
Polish	984,565	3.2
East Indian	962,665	3.1
Russian	500,600	1.6
Welsh	440,965	1.4
Filipino	436,190	1.4
Norwegian	432,515	1.4
Portuguese	410,850	1.3
Metis	409,065	1.3
British Isles	403,915	1.3
Swedish	334,765	1.1
Spanish	325,730	1.0
American	316,350	1.0
Hungarian	315,510	1.0
Jewish	315,120	1.0
Greek	242,685	0.8
Jamaican	231,110	0.7
Danish	200,035	0.6

	Total number	% of population
Total visible minority	5,068,095	16.2
South Asian	1,262,865	4.0
Chinese	1,216,565	3.9
Black	783,795	2.5
Filipino	410,700	1.3
Latin American	304,245	1.0
Arab	265,550	0.9
Southeast Asian	239,935	0.8
West Asian	156,695	0.5
Korean	141,890	0.5
Japanese	81,300	0.3

Note: Total Canadian population was 31,241,030 in 2006.

SOURCES: Adapted from Statistics Canada publication "Ethnocultural Portrait of Canada: Highlight Tables, 2006 Census," Catalogue 97F0024XIE2001006, URL: http://www.statcan.bsolc/english/bsolc?catno=97F0024XIE2001006; and "Visible minority population, by age group" (2006 Census), http://www40.statcan.gc.ca/l01/cst01/demo50a-eng.htm

appeal to price-conscious consumers. To balance this, the firm is offering Tide anti-stain products at a premium price to attract higher-income consumers.[24]

Ethnic Segmentation

Many companies are segmenting their markets by ethnicity. The gathering of such data can raise sensitivity concerns among respondents. Canadian data on ethnic groups were first collected as part of the 1996 census; this was done again in the 2001 and 2006 censuses. An overview of Canada's ethnic makeup is provided in Exhibit 6.2.

Canada is a highly diverse country. In reaching out to ethnic markets, marketers must first choose a language for communication in addition to, or instead of, English or French (Canada's two official languages). The most recent data indicate the following languages spoken in the home for Canadians: English, 65.9 percent; French, 21.2 percent; non-official language, 11.1 percent; English and French, 0.3 percent; English plus one other language, 1.3 percent; French plus one other language, 0.2 percent; English and French and one other language, 0.05 percent. The most common other language was Chinese (2.5 percent).[25]

Canadian marketers are strongly aware of Canada's multicultural makeup. The Toronto Symphony Orchestra found that Chinese families had higher levels of musical literacy than the average for North America. The TSO has been targeting the half a million ethnic Chinese people living in the greater Toronto area with a long-running Chinese-language promotional campaign that includes season brochures in Chinese and a Chinese-language page on its website. It also runs advertising in Chinese newspapers and on Chinese radio stations. In addition, the TSO has a customer service hotline with both Cantonese and Mandarin speakers to handle inquiries.[26]

Family Life-Cycle Segmentation

The demographic factors of gender, age, and income often do not sufficiently explain why consumer buying behaviour varies. Frequently, consumption patterns among people of the same age and gender differ because they are at different stages of the family life cycle. The **family life cycle (FLC)** is a series of stages determined by a combination of age, marital status, and the presence or absence of children.

The life-cycle stage consisting of the married-couple household used be considered the traditional family in Canada. However, according to the most recently available data, traditional families—married couples with children—constitute 35 percent of families. Families have been shrinking in size over the years. In 1961, the average household size was 3.9; by 1971, it was 3.5; by 1981, 2.9; by 1991, 2.7; by 2001, 2.6 and in 2006 it was 2.5.[27] Exhibit 6.3 illustrates both traditional and contemporary FLC patterns and shows how families' needs, incomes, resources, and expenditures differ at each

SOURCE: COURTESY OF THE TORONTO SYMPHONY ORCHESTRA

This ad for the Toronto Symphony Orchestra targets Asians who enjoy classical music.

family life cycle (FLC)
A series of stages determined by a combination of age, marital status, and the presence or absence of children.

stage. The horizontal flow shows the traditional family life cycle. The lower part of the exhibit provides some of the characteristics and purchase patterns of families at each stage of the traditional life cycle. The exhibit also acknowledges that about half of all first marriages end in divorce. When young marrieds move into the young divorced stage, their consumption patterns often revert to those of the young single stage of the cycle. Divorced persons frequently remarry by middle age and re-enter the traditional life cycle, as indicated by the "recycled flow" in the exhibit.

The Dove For Men advertising campaign launched during the 2010 Super Bowl features a humorous advertisement of a man going through all the early stages of the traditional family life cycle and into middle age. The ad features a fast track of the William Tell Overture music (also known as the theme from the Lone Ranger) with lyrics about a man's conception, childhood, adolescence, dating, marriage and then through to married with children. The lyrics conclude "Because you're a man" and then a narrator says "Dove for men. Be comfortable in your skin."[28]

PSYCHOGRAPHIC SEGMENTATION

Age, gender, income, ethnicity, family life-cycle stage, and other demographic variables are usually helpful in developing segmentation strategies, but often they don't paint the entire picture. Demographics provide the skeleton; psychographics add the meat to the bones. **Psychographic segmentation** is market segmentation on the basis of the following variables:

psychographic segmentation
Market segmentation on the basis of personality, motives, lifestyles, and geodemographics.

- *Personality.* Personality reflects a person's traits, attitudes, and habits. Future Now Incorporated (**www.futurenowinc.com**), an Internet tracking service, has identified four basic on-line personality types that marketers can use to develop their websites. Universal Studios Orlando has used this approach to develop eight different personas on their website for which they offer different appeals and packages. One

EXHIBIT 6.3

Family Life Cycle

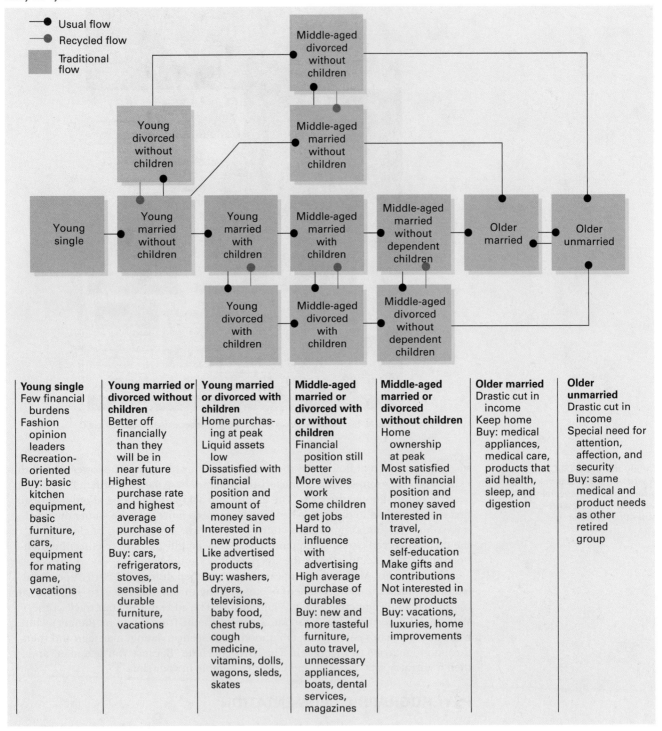

Legend:
- ●— Usual flow
- —● Recycled flow
- (shaded box) Traditional flow

Young single
Few financial
burdens
Fashion
opinion
leaders
Recreation-
oriented
Buy: basic
kitchen
equipment,
basic
furniture,
cars,
equipment
for mating
game,
vacations

Young married or divorced without children
Better off
financially
than they
will be in
near future
Highest
purchase rate
and highest
average
purchase of
durables
Buy: cars,
refrigerators,
stoves,
sensible and
durable
furniture,
vacations

Young married or divorced with children
Home purchas-
ing at peak
Liquid assets
low
Dissatisfied with
financial
position and
amount of
money saved
Interested in
new products
Like advertised
products
Buy: washers,
dryers,
televisions,
baby food,
chest rubs,
cough
medicine,
vitamins, dolls,
wagons, sleds,
skates

Middle-aged married or divorced with or without children
Financial
position still
better
More wives
work
Some children
get jobs
Hard to
influence
with
advertising
High average
purchase of
durables
Buy: new and
more tasteful
furniture,
auto travel,
unnecessary
appliances,
boats, dental
services,
magazines

Middle-aged married or divorced without children
Home
ownership
at peak
Most satisfied
with financial
position and
money saved
Interested in
travel,
recreation,
self-education
Make gifts and
contributions
Not interested in
new products
Buy: vacations,
luxuries, home
improvements

Older married
Drastic cut in
income
Keep home
Buy: medical
appliances,
medical care,
products that
aid health,
sleep, and
digestion

Older unmarried
Drastic cut in
income
Special need for
attention,
affection, and
security
Buy: same
medical and
product needs
as other
retired
group

of the personas is a family: "Pam and Doug Heller (she is spontaneous/he is methodical), married with two kids, 6 and 9. Doug wants the most value for his dollar—a structured plan, cost breakdown per day/activity, and to know the best deal is on-line and whether activities justify ticket prices. Pam wants lots of options. She wants it easy and fun and hip. First Pam will start seeking if this will fit into her budget. The conversion goal is to get Pam to send info to Doug." The result of this approach: on-line ticket purchases rose almost 80 percent! Exhibit 6.4 describes the four personality types.[29]

EXHIBIT 6.4

Basic On-line Personality Types

Type	Description
Competitive visitors	Like to be in control and enjoy challenges. Goal-oriented and impatient. Quick to make a decision once you can answer, "What's in it for me?"
Spontaneous visitors	Prefer a personal touch. Value opinions rather than hard facts. Need to be spoken to within the first two or three paragraphs. They ask, "Why should I buy what you have to offer?" and want you to help them choose.
Humanistic visitors	Relationship-oriented. Slow to make a decision, and read a lot of the content. They like details and are very interested in who you are, and in who your customers are and what they think of you.
Methodical visitors	Need the most information. They do not want to be surprised at any point in the buying process and read the majority of the content. Need to see the value in what you do; most likely to buy the cheapest item. Speak to them last on the page and answer this question: "How can your solution solve the problem?" They will want to learn more.

SOURCE: Melissa Burdon, "The Power of Personas", *Marketing Magazine*, August 28, 2006

geodemographic segmentation
Segmenting potential customers into neighbourhood lifestyle categories.

- *Motives.* Marketers of baby products and life insurance appeal to consumers' emotional motives—namely, to care for their loved ones. Using appeals to economy, reliability, dependability, and safety, carmakers like Volvo and Volkswagen target customers with rational motives. Carmakers like Mercedes-Benz, Lexus, and Infiniti appeal to customers with status-related motives.

- *Lifestyles.* Lifestyle segmentation divides people into groups according to the way they spend their time, the importance of the things around them, their beliefs, and socioeconomic characteristics such as income and education. For example, in Quebec the market for wines is much stronger than the rest of Canada, and despite recessionary pressures in 2008 and 2009 the Société des alcools du Québec (SAQ) reported sales increases of wines approaching 7.9 percent; in Ontario sales had a modest increase of 1.1 percent. The reason for these differences according to SAQ spokesperson Isabelle Mirizzi, is that "Quebecers like their wine and have long adapted it to their way of life."[30]

- *Geodemographics.* **Geodemographic segmentation** clusters potential customers into neighbourhood lifestyle categories. It combines geographic, demographic, and lifestyle segmentations. Geodemographic segmentation helps marketers develop marketing programs tailored to prospective buyers who live in small geographic regions, such as neighbourhoods or who have very specific lifestyle and demographic characteristics. Chain store retailers have a strong affinity for geodemographic segmentation data, which help them make physical store location decisions. Also, database marketers such as magazine publishers, charities, and financial institutions find this form of segmentation very useful for identifying prospective customers.[31] In Canada, geodemographic data are commercially available from census information at the enumeration area (EA) level, which involves surveys of 250 to 300 households. It is also available according to postal code information, which is subdivided into 20,000 assigned postal walks (PWK), with each walk comprising 200 to 400 households; or into 1,500 forward sortation areas (FSAs), which are made up of between 6,000 and 10,000 households. Ken Jones and Michael Pearce of the *Ivey Business Journal* comment that "these three systems are the foundation of the various services that supply data to retailers. For example, Taxfiler data is at the Postal Walk level but not EA, while Compusearch's PSYTE data is available for either the census geography, at the EA levels or, for postal geography, at the FSA unit. Geomedia's system focuses on the FSA level."[32]

Psychographic variables can be used individually to segment markets, or they can be combined with other variables to provide more detailed descriptions of market segments. One combination approach, offered by the marketing and research consulting firm Environics Analytics, offers geodemographics-based segmentation, site evaluation modelling, and custom analytics. According to the Environics website, **www.environicsanalytics.ca**, "PRIZMCE is a new consumer segmentation system that classifies all Canadians into one of 66 lifestyle types—with names like Cosmopolitan Elite, Electric Avenues, Les Chics and Lunch at Tim's. The system marks the first time that a Canadian segmentation model has linked geodemographics to psychographics, incorporating 'Social Values' data from Environics Research with demographics and product preferences to explain consumer behaviour." Through geodemographics, marketers can target e-mail, flyers, and direct mail campaigns. Using PRIZM, Hyundai chose postal codes with a high percentage of promising clusters and sent test-drive offers only to those areas (instead of blanketing entire cities). In those markets, Hyundai not only increased the number of people showing up for a test drive but also increased its sales and halved its costs per vehicle sold.[33]

BENEFIT SEGMENTATION

benefit segmentation
The process of grouping customers into market segments according to the benefits they seek from the product.

Benefit segmentation is the process of grouping customers into market segments according to the benefits they seek from the product. Most types of market segmentation are based on the assumption that this variable and customers' needs are related. Benefit segmentation is different because it groups potential customers on the basis of their needs or wants rather than some other characteristic, such as age or gender. The snack-food market, for example, can be divided into six benefit segments, as shown in Exhibit 6.5.

Marketers need to be aware that customers, when they choose an offering, may be seeking benefits beyond satisfying their own basic needs. For example, green products promise to fulfill consumer needs and societal needs simultaneously. Loblaws has been offering PC Green products for more than 20 years! In April 2007, Loblaws made a stronger commitment to this product line when it "relaunched PC Green with 26 products." [34] By 2010, they had expanded the line to 32 products, including rain barrels, fluorescent lights, diapers, dishwasher rinse, fire logs made of used coffee grounds, toilet tissue and paper towels made of 100 percent recycled paper, and lawn compost made of recycled leaves.[35]

usage-rate segmentation
Dividing a market by the amount of product bought or consumed.

80/20 principle
A principle holding that 20 percent of all customers generate 80 percent of the demand.

Benefit segmentation can be enriched by developing customer profiles employing demographic information that is associated with people seeking certain benefits. This information can be used to match marketing strategies with selected target markets. The many different types of performance energy bars with various combinations of nutrients are aimed at consumers looking for different benefits. For example, PowerBar is designed for athletes looking for long-lasting fuel, while PowerBar Protein Plus is aimed at those who want extra protein for replenishing muscles after strength training. Carb Solutions High Protein Bars are for those on low-carb diets; Luna Bars are targeted to women who want a bar with fewer calories but that includes soy protein and calcium; and Clif Bars are for people who want a natural bar with ingredients like rolled oats, soybeans, and organic soy flour. Dannon introduced its Activia probiotic yogurt as a daily health booster by highlighting its benefits for the digestive tract and immune system.

USAGE-RATE SEGMENTATION

Usage-rate segmentation divides a market by the amount of product bought or consumed. Categories vary with the product, but they are likely to include some combination of the following: former users, potential users, first-time users, light or irregular users, medium users, and heavy users. Segmenting by usage rate enables marketers to focus their efforts on heavy users or to develop multiple marketing mixes aimed at different segments. Because heavy users often account for a sizable portion of all product sales, some marketers focus on the heavy-user segment.

The **80/20 principle** holds that 20 percent of all customers generate 80 percent of the

Loblaws knows that selling its President's Choice Green Products is all about the benefits. Their labels say, "Check your President's Choice® G.R.E.E.N™ Product for one of these symbols to learn its environmental benefit."

EXHIBIT 6.5

Benefit and Lifestyle Segmentation of the Snack-Food Market

	Nutritional Snackers	Weight Watchers	Guilty Snackers	Party Snackers	Indiscriminate Snackers	Economical Snackers
% of Snackers	22%	14%	9%	15%	15%	18%
Lifestyle Characteristics	Self-assured, controlled	Outdoorsy, influential, venturesome	Highly anxious, isolated	Sociable	Hedonistic	Self-assured, price-oriented
Benefits Sought	Nutritious, without artificial ingredients, natural	Low in calories, quick energy	Low in calories, good tasting	Good to serve guests, served with pride, go well with beverages	Good tasting, satisfies hunger	Low in price, best value
Consumption Level of Snacks	Light	Light	Heavy	Average	Heavy	Average
Type of Snacks Usually Eaten	Fruits, vegetables, cheese	Yogurt, vegetables	Yogurt, cookies, crackers, candy	Nuts, potato chips, crackers, pretzels	Candy, ice cream, cookies, potato chips, pretzels, popcorn	No specific products
Demographics	Better educated, have younger children	Younger, single	Younger or older, female, lower socioeconomic status	Middle-aged, nonurban	Teenager	Have large family, better educated

demand. Although the percentages usually are not exact, the general idea often holds true. In the fast-food industry, heavy users account for only one in five fast-food patrons but make about 60 percent of all visits to fast-food restaurants. Thus heavy users (most of whom are single males) account for roughly $11.2 billion of the $18.6 billion that Statistics Canada reports is spent on fast food at Canada's 33,000 limited-service (fast-food) restaurants.[36]

Developing customers into heavy users is the goal behind many frequency and loyalty programs, such as the airlines' frequent flyer programs. Many supermarkets and drugstores have designed loyalty programs that reward heavy users with deals available only to them, such as in-store coupon dispensing systems, loyalty card programs, and special price deals on selected merchandise.

The "Ethics in Marketing" box describes a different type of usage-rate segmentation, relating to "boycotting" behaviours.

REVIEW LEARNING OUTCOME 4

4 **Describe the bases commonly used to segment consumer markets**

Geography	Demographics	Psychographics	Benefits	Usage Rate
• Region • Market size • Market density • Climate	• Age • Gender • Income • Race/Ethnicity • Family life cycle	• Personality • Motives • Lifestyle • Geodemographics	• Benefits sought	• Former • Potential • 1st time • Light or irregular • Medium • Heavy

Ethics in Marketing

 ## SEGMENTING BOYCOTTERS

While all companies need to spend considerable time and effort understanding their markets and developing segmentation and targeting strategies, they also need to spend some time making sure they don't end up being targeted by consumers. Specifically, they have to make sure they don't become the target of a consumer backlash by way of boycotting. Understanding boycott behaviour is one way that businesses can reduce the likelihood of being boycotted.

A recent survey of more than 1,000 consumers looked at how companies can develop strong relationships with their customers but also looked at how companies can damage the relationships they are trying to develop. The survey, conducted by Decima Research, found four key factors that contribute to a strong relationship between a company and consumers: excellent customer service (36 percent of respondents); excellent quality products (30 percent); ethics, integrity, honesty (19 percent); and treatment of employees (17 percent). Respondents were also asked about boycott behaviour. Specifically, they were asked this question: "Some people say that only a few companies exhibit bad behaviour; the kind that results in a boycott. Other people say that most companies exhibit bad behaviour, they just don't get boycotted. Which of these two views best represents your own?"

The answer to this question broke down as follows: 47 percent of respondents said that only a few companies exhibit bad behaviour, while 44 percent of respondents felt that most companies exhibited bad behaviour, they just didn't get boycotted. The study also found that one-third of Canadian households had boycotted a company in the past year. When asked why they did, the respondents indicated the following: poor service (23 percent); treatment of employees (17 percent); product quality (13 percent); and bad ethics (13 percent). The profile of people who are more likely to take part in a boycott was found to be as follows: self-employed (46 percent boycotted); university educated (45 percent); $100,000-plus annual household income (45 percent); and 45 to 54 years old (41 percent). The study identified baby boomers as "the most militant or likely to boycott of all Canadian consumers." In contrast, those least likely to boycott were under 25 (27 percent) or 55 years and over (27 percent).

The survey also examined companies that were most likely to be boycotted. It turned out that two American-based retailers headed the list. Walmart was targeted by the most people (28 percent of Canadian households); the second most boycotted company was McDonald's, which was boycotted by only 5 percent of Canadian households. Walmart has had a very high profile in the Canadian labour market because of its heavily publicized resistance to unionization. The company closed a store in Jonquière, Quebec, after it became unionized. Walmart said it had to close the store because it was unprofitable. Walmart scores high on customer service and product quality. However, boycotters say, "the most frequent reasons for boycotting Walmart are treatment of employees (60 percent) and bad ethics (28 percent)."[37]

What are the ethical implications of boycotts for marketers? What can any company do about a boycott? Explain your answer.

SOURCE: GREG WHITE, "BOYCOTTING BOOMERS," *MARKETING MAGAZINE*, OCTOBER 3, 2005; CBC NEWS ONLINE, "QUEBEC WAL-MART CLOSES EARLIER THAN PLANNED," APRIL 29, 2005, WWW.CBC.CA.

5 BASES FOR SEGMENTING BUSINESS MARKETS

Describe the bases for segmenting business markets

The business market consists of four broad segments: producers, resellers, institutions, and governments (for a detailed discussion of these segments, see Chapter 5). Whether marketers focus on only one or on all four of these segments, they are likely to find diversity among potential customers. Thus further market segmentation offers just as many benefits to business marketers as it does to consumer-product marketers.

COMPANY CHARACTERISTICS

Company characteristics, such as geographic location, type of company, company size, and product use, can be important segmentation variables. Some markets tend to be regional because buyers prefer to purchase from local suppliers; distant suppliers may have difficulty competing on price and service. It follows that companies selling to geographically concentrated industries benefit by locating close to their markets.

Segmenting by customer type allows business marketers to tailor their marketing mixes to the unique needs of particular types of organizations or industries. Many companies are finding this form of segmentation to be quite effective. RONA, one of Canada's big-box do-it-yourself retail businesses, has targeted professional repair and remodelling contractors in addition to consumers. Procter & Gamble is best known as a consumer products firm but it is now targeting business customers by focusing on janitors, fast-food workers, maids, and launderers with products that are specific to each group's cleaning needs.[38]

Volume of purchase (heavy, moderate, light) is a commonly used basis for business segmentation. Another is the buying organization's size, which may affect its purchasing procedures, the types and quantities of products it needs, and its responses to different marketing mixes. Banks frequently offer different services, lines of credit, and overall attention to commercial customers based on their size.

Many products, especially raw materials like steel, wood, and petroleum, have diverse applications. How customers use a product may influence the amount they buy, their buying criteria, and their selection of vendors. Thus a producer of springs may have customers who use the product in applications as diverse as machine tools, bicycles, surgical devices, office equipment, telephones, and pens.

BUYING PROCESSES

Many business marketers find it helpful to segment customers and prospective customers on the basis of *how* they buy. Companies can segment some business markets by ranking key purchasing criteria, such as price, quality, technical support, and service. Atlas Corporation developed a commanding position in the industrial door market by providing customized products in just four weeks—much faster than the industry average of 12 to 15 weeks. Atlas's primary market is companies with an immediate need for customized doors.

The purchasing strategies of buyers may provide useful segments. Two purchasing profiles that have been identified are satisficers and optimizers. **Satisficers** contact familiar suppliers and place the order with the first one to satisfy product and delivery requirements. **Optimizers** consider numerous suppliers (both familiar and unfamiliar), solicit bids, and study all proposals carefully before selecting one.

The personal characteristics of the buyers themselves (their demographic characteristics, decision styles, tolerance for risk, confidence level, job responsibilities, etc.) influence their buying behaviour and thus offer a viable basis for segmenting some business markets. IBM computer buyers, for example, are sometimes characterized as being more risk averse than buyers of less expensive computers that perform essentially the same functions. In advertising, therefore, IBM has stressed its reputation for high quality and reliability.

satisficers
Business customers who place an order with the first familiar supplier to satisfy product and delivery requirements.

optimizers
Business customers who consider numerous suppliers, both familiar and unfamiliar, solicit bids and study all proposals carefully before selecting one.

REVIEW LEARNING OUTCOME 5

 5 | Describe the bases for segmenting business markets

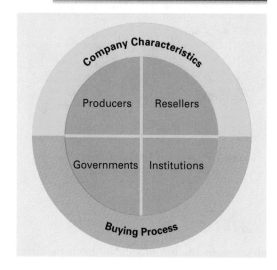

6 STEPS IN SEGMENTING A MARKET

List the steps involved in segmenting markets

The purpose of market segmentation, in both consumer and business markets, is to identify marketing opportunities. Review Learning Objective 6 traces the following steps in segmenting a market. Note that steps 5 and 6 are actually marketing activities that follow market segmentation (steps 1 through 4).

1. *Select a market or product category for study.* Define the overall market or product category to be studied. It may be a market in which the company already competes, a new but related market or product category, or a totally new one. Twinings Tea is trying to encourage 18- to 34-year-old Canadians to drink more tea. It changed its packaging to provide information about its teas, such as Darjeeling and Oolong. Twinings also marketed a special package with five tea leaves as a "strength meter. One coloured leaf indicates a very mild tea while five is very strong."[39]

2. *Choose a basis or bases for segmenting the market.* This step requires managerial insight, creativity, and market knowledge. There are no scientific procedures for selecting segmentation variables. That said, a successful segmentation scheme must produce segments that meet the four basic criteria discussed earlier in this chapter.

3. *Select segmentation descriptors.* After choosing one or more bases, the marketer must select the segmentation descriptors. Descriptors identify the specific segmentation variables to use. For example, if a company selects demographics as a basis of segmentation, it may use age, occupation, and income as descriptors. A company that selects usage segmentation needs to decide whether to go after heavy users, nonusers, or light users.

4. *Profile and analyze segments.* The profile should include the segments' size, expected growth, purchase frequency, current brand usage, brand loyalty, and long-term sales and profit potential. This information can then be used to rank potential market segments by profit opportunity, risk, consistency with organizational mission and objectives, and other factors important to the firm.

5. *Select target markets.* Selecting target markets is not a part of but rather a natural outcome of the segmentation process. It is a major decision that influences and often directly determines the firm's marketing mix. This topic is examined in greater detail later in this chapter.

6. *Design, implement, and maintain appropriate marketing mixes.* The marketing mix has been described as product, place (distribution), promotion, and pricing strategies intended to bring about mutually satisfying exchange relationships with target markets. Chapters 8 through 17 explore these topics in detail.

6 | **List the steps involved in segmenting markets**

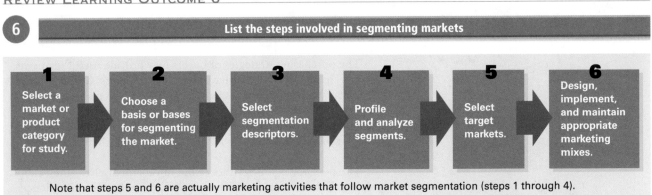

Note that steps 5 and 6 are actually marketing activities that follow market segmentation (steps 1 through 4).

7 STRATEGIES FOR SELECTING TARGET MARKETS

Discuss alternative strategies for selecting target markets

target market
A group of people or organizations for which an organization designs, implements, and maintains a marketing mix intended to meet the needs of that group, resulting in mutually satisfying exchanges.

So far this chapter has focused on the market segmentation process, which is the first consideration when deciding whom to approach about buying a product. The next task is to choose one or more target markets. A **target market** is a group of people or organizations for which an organization designs, implements, and maintains a marketing mix intended to meet the needs of that group, resulting in mutually satisfying exchanges. Because most markets will include customers with different characteristics, lifestyles, backgrounds, and income levels, it is unlikely that a single marketing mix will attract all segments of the market. Thus if a marketer wishes to appeal to more than one segment of the market, it must develop different marketing mixes. For example, Buick targets people in their 60s with the Lucerne sedan, a luxury car with a V8 engine and extras like OnStar service. The company also targets younger, Generation Y customers with the Enclave, a crossover SUV. The three general strategies for selecting target markets—undifferentiated, concentrated, and multisegment targeting—are illustrated in Exhibit 6.6, while Exhibit 6.7 presents the advantages and disadvantages of each of them.

UNDIFFERENTIATED TARGETING

undifferentiated targeting strategy
Marketing approach that views the market as one big market with no individual segments and thus requires a single marketing mix.

A firm using an **undifferentiated targeting strategy** essentially adopts a mass-market philosophy, viewing the market as one big market with no individual segments. The

EXHIBIT 6.6

Three Strategies for Selecting Target Markets

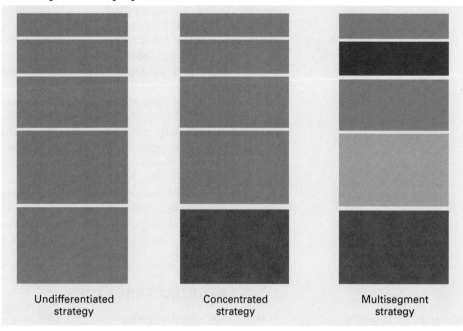

| Undifferentiated strategy | Concentrated strategy | Multisegment strategy |

firm uses one marketing mix for the entire market. A company that adopts an undifferentiated targeting strategy assumes that individual customers have similar needs that can be met with a common marketing mix.

The first company in an industry sometimes uses an undifferentiated targeting strategy. With no competition, the company may not need to tailor marketing mixes to the preferences of market segments. Henry Ford's famous comment about the Model T is a classic example of an undifferentiated targeting strategy: "They can have their car in any color they want, as long as it's black." At one time, Coca-Cola used this strategy with a single product and a single size of its familiar uniquely shaped green bottle. Marketers of commodity products, such as flour and sugar, are also likely to use an undifferentiated targeting strategy.

One advantage of undifferentiated marketing is the potential for saving on production and marketing. Because only one item is produced, the company should be able to achieve economies of mass production. Also, marketing costs may be lower when there is only one product to promote and a single channel of distribution. Too often, however, an undifferentiated strategy emerges by default rather than by design,

EXHIBIT 6.7

Advantages and Disadvantages of Target Marketing Strategies

Targeting strategy	Advantages	Disadvantages
Undifferentiated targeting	Potential savings on production/marketing costs Company more susceptible to competition	Unimaginative product offerings

Concentrated targeting	Concentration of resources
	Can better meet the needs of a narrowly
	    defined segment
	Allows some small companies to better
	    compete with larger companies
	Strong positioning
		Segments too small, or changing
		Large competitors may more effectively market to
		    niche segment

Multisegment targeting	Greater financial success Economies of scale in production/marketing	High costs Cannibalization

reflecting a failure to consider the advantages of a segmented approach. The result is often sterile, unimaginative product offerings that have little appeal to anyone.

Another problem associated with undifferentiated targeting is that it makes the company more susceptible to competitive inroads. Coca-Cola forfeited its position as the leading seller of cola drinks in supermarkets to Pepsi-Cola in the late 1950s, when Pepsi began offering consumers a choice of several sizes of containers.

You might think a company producing a standard product like toilet tissue would adopt an undifferentiated strategy. However, this market has industrial segments and consumer segments. Industrial buyers want an economical, single-ply product sold in boxes of a hundred rolls. The consumer market demands a more versatile product in smaller quantities. Within the consumer market, the product is differentiated with designer print or no print, cushioned or noncushioned, and economy priced or luxury priced. Fort Howard Corporation, the market share leader in industrial toilet paper, does not even sell to the consumer market.

Undifferentiated marketing can succeed in certain situations, though. A small grocery store in a small, isolated town may define all the people who live in the town as its target market. It may offer one marketing mix and generally satisfy everyone in town. This strategy is not likely to be as effective if there are three or four grocery stores in the town.

CONCENTRATED TARGETING

With a **concentrated targeting strategy**, a company selects a market **niche** (one segment of a market) for targeting its marketing efforts. Because the firm is appealing to a single segment, it can concentrate on understanding the needs, motives, and satisfactions of that segment's members and on developing and maintaining a highly specialized marketing mix. Some firms find that concentrating resources and meeting the needs of a narrowly defined market segment is more profitable than spreading resources over several different segments.

For example, Starbucks became successful by focusing on consumers who wanted gourmet coffee products. Watchmakers Patek Philippe, Rolex, and Breguet, which sell watches priced at $200,000 or more, are definitely pursuing a concentrated targeting strategy. The Canadian Association of Retired Persons (CARP) pursues a concentrated strategy if you consider people over 50 years old to be a single market segment of the overall population. It offers *Zoomer Magazine*, which presents lifestyle articles of interest to people who are 45 years of age and older.[40] Fatburger, which has opened 12 stores located in British Columbia and Alberta, describes itself as "the last great hamburger stand."[41]

Small firms often adopt a concentrated targeting strategy to compete effectively with much larger companies. Fashion retailer Winners was developed to attract working women who wanted to buy designer fashions at discounted prices. On the other hand, some companies use a concentrated strategy to establish a strong position in a desirable market segment. Lululemon athletica, which was founded in British Columbia in 1998, opened its first retail outlet in a yoga studio to offer clothing specifically for yoga practitioners. The retailer has grown to more than 100 stores in Canada, the United States, Australia, and Hong Kong. The firm describes its market offerings as "technical clothing for yoga, dancing, running, and most other sweaty pursuits. We create components for people to live longer, healthier, more fun lives."[42]

Concentrated targeting violates the old adage "Don't put all your eggs in one basket." If the chosen segment is too small or if it shrinks because of environmental changes, the company may suffer negative consequences. Lewiscraft, which was founded in Toronto in 1913 as a supplier of leather accessories, expanded into the retail "crafts" market in 1970. The retail craft market has been declining in recent years. After many years of losing money, the company declared bankruptcy in 2006.[43]

Also, a concentrated strategy can be disastrous for a firm that fails in its narrowly defined target market. When Procter & Gamble introduced Head and Shoulders shampoo, several other small firms were already selling anti-dandruff shampoos. Head and Shoulders was introduced with a large promotional campaign, and the new brand captured more than half the market immediately. Within a year, several of the firms that had been concentrating on this market segment went out of business.

MULTISEGMENT TARGETING

multisegment targeting strategy
A strategy that chooses two or more well-defined market segments and develops a distinct marketing mix for each.

A firm that chooses to serve two or more well-defined market segments and then develops a distinct marketing mix for each has a **multisegment targeting strategy**. Maple Leaf Foods offers many different kinds of bacon, such as regular bacon, thick sliced bacon, maple-flavoured bacon, and salt-reduced bacon. For convenience-demanding people it has developed Ready Crisp Bacon, a microwaveable bacon. Finally, for health-conscious segments it has turkey bacon and chicken bacon. Cosmetics companies seek to increase sales and market share by targeting multiple age and ethnic groups. Maybelline and Cover Girl, for example, market different lines to tween girls, teenage women, young adult women, older women, and visible minority women. Mattel targets multiple markets with its Barbie dolls. There are two websites relating to Barbie dolls. **Barbie.everythinggirl.com** is intended for young girls who are interested in Barbie and for parents who want to buy Barbie dolls for their children. This site features trendy products such as Barbie in a Mermaid's Tail doll, Barbie I Can Be a Computer Engineer doll, and Barbie Fashionistas dolls. Then there is also **Barbiecollector.com**, which has a completely different target market. This site features collectable Barbies such as the Wizard of Oz Collection (all of the major characters are featured), Twilight Edward and Bella dolls, and an Alice in Wonderland Mad Hatter doll. This site is aimed at people who want to "invest" in Barbie, not play with her.

Sometimes organizations use different promotional appeals, rather than completely different marketing mixes, as the basis for a multisegment strategy. This can lead to mixed results. Labatt has used two completely different approaches to promoting its Labatt 50 beer in Quebec and Ontario over the years. In the early days of promotion for Labatt 50, the advertising themes in Quebec played to Quebec patriotism and used characters and celebrities who were well known in Quebec. In contrast, Ontario drinkers were exposed to "slice of life with beer" advertising that showed people singing about Labatt 50 and travelling about the country. As a result, in Quebec, beer drinkers think of the product as a Quebec-only brand and the product has a strong customer base, whereas in Ontario, the current drinkers think of Labatt 50 as an Ontario-only brand—and are a lot fewer in number.[44]

Multisegment targeting offers many potential benefits to firms, including greater sales volume, higher profits, larger market share, and economies of scale in manufacturing and marketing. Yet it may also involve greater costs for product design, production, promotion, inventory, marketing research, and management. Before deciding to use this strategy, firms should compare the benefits and costs of multisegment targeting to those of undifferentiated and concentrated targeting.

Mattel targets multiple markets with its Barbie doll. There are two different websites targeting two different audiences. Barbie.everythinggirl.com is for girls and their parents who want to buy the latest "toy" dolls. Barbiecollector.com is for serious collectors who want to "invest" in Barbie dolls.

cannibalization
A situation that occurs when sales of a new product cut into sales of a company's existing products.

Another potential cost of multisegment targeting is **cannibalization**, which occurs when sales of a new product cut into sales of a company's existing products. In many cases, however, companies prefer to steal sales from their own brands rather than lose sales to a competitor. Also, in today's fast-paced world of e-business, some companies are willing to cannibalize existing business in order to build new business. When Future Shop launched FutureShop.ca as a retail website, it was intended as a distribution outlet to build business in cities and towns where the firm didn't have bricks-and-mortar stores. However, a lot of the visitors to the website turned out to be customers who had received flyers in the local papers of cities where Future Shop already had locations. So Future Shop developed an inventory system that allows customers to locate stores that carry the on-line items. Customers can now order on-line and have the product shipped to them, order on-line and pick up the product in the store, or simply go to the nearest store and buy the item in person.[45]

REVIEW LEARNING OUTCOME 7

7 **Discuss alternative strategies for selecting target markets**

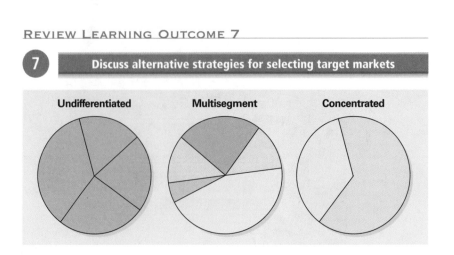

Undifferentiated   Multisegment   Concentrated

ONE-TO-ONE MARKETING

Explain one-to-one marketing

one-to-one marketing
An individualized marketing method that utilizes customer information to build long-term, personalized, and profitable relationships with each customer.

Most businesses today use a mass-marketing approach designed to increase *market share* by selling products to the greatest number of people. For many businesses, however, it is more efficient and profitable to use one-to-one marketing to increase *share of customer*—in other words, to sell more products to each customer. **One-to-one marketing** is an individualized marketing method that utilizes customer information to build long-term, personalized, and profitable relationships with each customer. The goal is to reduce costs through customer retention and increase revenue through customer loyalty. For example, Tesco, the British supermarket chain, sends out a mailing each quarter to 11 million households—but it produces 4 million different versions, tailored to the interests of its diverse customer base.

The difference between one-to-one marketing and the traditional mass-marketing approach can be compared to shooting a rifle versus a firing a shotgun. If you have good aim, a rifle is the most efficient weapon to use. On the other hand, a shotgun increases your odds of hitting the target when it is more difficult to focus. Instead of scattering messages far and wide across the spectrum of mass media (the shotgun approach), one-to-one marketers are homing in on ways to communicate with each individual customer (the rifle approach).

One of the best-known examples of one-to-one product customization is Dell Computer through its Dell.ca website. Dell's system allows customers to choose prepackaged computer systems or to build their own system from the ground up. Blinds-To-Go has both bricks-and-mortar and website locations that allow buyers to shop the way they feel most comfortable yet enable them to fully customize their choice of blinds according to a wide variety of sizes, styles, and colour schemes. Customers are given detailed instructions either on-line or instore on how to measure their windows and then they can select from what Blinds-To-Go pledges is the widest selection of blinds available in the world and at the lowest prices.[46]

Several factors suggest that personalized communications and product customization will continue to expand as more companies understand why and how their customers make and execute purchase decisions. At least four trends will lead to the continuing growth of one-to-one marketing.

First, the one-size-fits-all marketing is no longer relevant. Consumers want to be treated as the individuals they are, with their own unique sets of needs and wants. By its personalized nature, one-to-one marketing can fulfill this desire.

Second, direct and personal marketing efforts will continue to grow to meet the needs of consumers who no longer have the time to spend shopping and making purchase decisions. With the personal and targeted nature of one-to-one marketing, consumers can spend less time making purchase decisions and more time doing the things that are important.

Third, consumers will be loyal only to those companies and brands that have earned their loyalty and reinforced it at every purchase occasion. One-to-one marketing techniques focus on finding a firm's best customers, rewarding them for their loyalty, and thanking them for their business.

Fourth, mass-media approaches will decline in importance as advances in market research and database technology allow marketers to collect detailed information on their customers. New technology offers one-to-one marketers a more cost-effective way to reach customers and enables businesses to personalize their messages. For example, Vancouver-based Photo Gift Cards (**www.photogiftcards.com**) has developed a method of supplying personalized gift cards, which can contain any photograph a person wants. Merchants that sell reloadable gift cards can now provide customers with cards they will take care of and use over and over instead of tossing them away.[47] With the help of database technology, one-to-one marketers can track their customers as individuals, even if they number in the millions.

One-to-one marketing is a huge commitment and often requires a 180-degree turnaround for marketers who spent the last half of the 20th century developing and implementing mass-marketing efforts. Although mass marketing will probably continue to be used, especially to create brand awareness or to remind consumers of a product, the advantages of one-to-one marketing cannot be ignored.

8   **Explain one-to-one marketing**

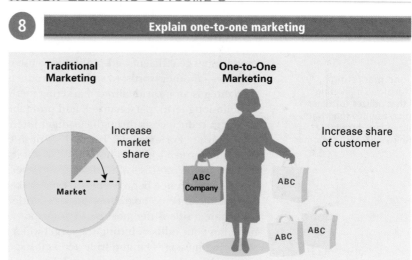

9   POSITIONING

Explain how and why companies implement positioning strategies and how product differentiation plays a role

positioning
Developing a specific marketing mix to influence potential customers' overall perception of a brand, product line, or organization in general.

position
The place a product, brand, or group of products occupies in consumers' minds relative to competing offerings.

product differentiation
A positioning strategy that some companies use to distinguish their products from those of competitors.

The link between the target marketing strategy decision and the development of the marketing mix for the target market depends on **positioning**, a process that influences potential customers' overall perception of a brand, product line, or organization in general. **Position** is the place a product, brand, or group of products occupies in consumers' minds relative to competing offerings. Consumer goods marketers are particularly concerned with positioning. Johnnie Walker, for example, markets five different Scotch whiskies, each with a unique position, as illustrated in Exhibit 6.8.

Positioning assumes that consumers compare products on the basis of important features. Marketing efforts that emphasize irrelevant features are therefore likely to misfire. Crystal Pepsi and a clear version of Coca-Cola's Tab failed because consumers perceived the "clear" positioning as more of a marketing gimmick than a benefit.

Effective positioning involves assessing the positions occupied by competing products, determining the important dimensions underlying these positions, and choosing a position in the market where the organization's marketing efforts will have the greatest impact. Callaway Golf positions its new line of clubs and balls as innovative and technologically superior, using the tagline "A better game by design."[48] Rogers Wireless positions its phone service as "Canada's Reliable Network." Rogers is aware that wireless phone users do not like to experience service interruptions or dead areas when they make phone calls. Rogers believes that its service can deliver the most reliable signals in comparison to Telus and Bell Mobility, which are their major competitors, and that consumers place a lot of importance on this attribute when choosing a wireless phone service provider.[49]

As the previous examples illustrates, many firms use **product differentiation** to distinguish their products from those of competitors. The distinctions can be real or perceived. Toyota of Canada presents a philosophy of "make things better" and positions itself as environmentally friendly. It sells its cars with a "warranty" on the emission components that declares they will meet emissions standards for 130,000 kilometres or 96 months, whichever comes first.[50] Here, Toyota is using product differentiation to create a product with very real advantages for the target market. However, many everyday products, such as bleaches, aspirin, unleaded regular gasoline, and some soaps are differentiated by such trivial means as brand names, packaging, colour, smell, or "secret" additives. The marketer

EXHIBIT 6.8

Positioning of Johnnie Walker Scotch Whiskies

Brand	Positioning	Price for 750 mL
Johnnie Walker Red	The Vibrant Blend	$30
Johnnie Walker Black	The Definitive Blend	$45
Johnnie Walker Green	Discover the Signature Malts	$60
Johnnie Walker Gold	The Sensual Blend	$100
Johnnie Walker Blue	Our Rarest Blend	$246

SOURCES: http://www.johnniewalker.com and http://www.lcbo.ca

attempts to convince consumers that a particular brand is distinctive and that they should demand it over competing brands.

Some firms, instead of using product differentiation, position their products as *similar* to competing products or brands. Artificial sweeteners advertised as tasting like sugar and margarine advertised as tasting like butter are two examples.

PERCEPTUAL MAPPING

Perceptual mapping is a means of displaying or graphing, in two or more dimensions, the locations of products, brands, or groups of products in customers' minds. After several years of decreasing market share as its luxury car buyers aged and literally "stopped" driving, Cadillac knew it needed to look at how the marketplace was changing and how its brand was perceived in the minds of its customers. It discovered that the up-and-coming generation of new buyers that it was counting on to purchase its products saw its brand as conservative black limousine-like vehicles driven by "older" people. At the same time, these buyers were shifting their interest from "large" full-size black limousines to midsize, brightly coloured, sportier luxury vehicles. Cadillac realized it needed to attract a younger generation of luxury car buyers than the typical 50+ age group that it had been historically dependent on. In order to do this, the company would have to change its image, which also meant redesigning the product offerings. As a result, the Cadillac line was changed from the traditional offering of luxury full-size cars to a line of vehicles that included midsize luxury vehicles like the Cadillac CTS and STS and also SUVs like the Escalade and SRX. Of course, you can still buy the full-size Cadillac DTS, but it does have a sporty design! The perceptual map in Review Learning Objective 9 shows how the old Cadillac image and the new Cadillac image fit into the car market in North America.

POSITIONING BASES

Companies use a variety of bases for positioning, including the following:

- *Attribute.* A product is associated with an attribute, product feature, or customer benefit. Kleenex offers an anti-viral tissue that contains substances to kill both viruses and germs in an effort to differentiate its product from competing tissues.[51]
- *Price and quality.* This positioning base may stress high price as a signal of quality or emphasize low price as an indication of value. Denmark-based Lego Building Blocks uses the high-price strategy, whereas Montreal-based Ritvik's Mega Bloks brand uses a low-price and value strategy.[52]
- *Use or application.* Stressing uses or applications can be an effective means of positioning a product with buyers. Kahlua liquor used advertising to point out 228 ways to consume the product. Snapple offers an Acai Mixed Berry Red Tea flavour as a source of vitamin C and acai berry that is positioned to support a healthy immune system.
- *Product user.* This positioning base focuses on a personality or type of user. Canadian Tire is Canada's number-one hardware retailer, in large part because it has positioned itself as a one-stop source for Canadian families while offering its customers discounting practices, such as Canadian Tire Money for cash purchases and Canadian-Tire-Money-on-the card for credit card transactions. Forty percent of Canadians make at least one trip a week to a Canadian Tire store.[53]
- *Product class.* The objective here is to position the product as associated with a particular category of products—for example, positioning a margarine brand with butter.
- *Competitor.* Positioning against competitors is part of any positioning strategy. The Chevrolet Equinox Compact SUV positions itself as both the most powerful and also most fuel-efficient compact crossover vehicle against its main competitors the Honda CRV and Toyota RAV4.
- *Emotion.* Positioning using emotion focuses on how the product makes customers feel. A number of companies use this approach. For example, Nike's "Just Do It" campaign didn't tell consumers what "it" was, but most got the emotional message of achievement and courage. Tim Hortons has embedded itself as part of Canadian

culture with its Tim Hortons "true stories" advertising campaign, which featured Canadians who were overseas but retained their Canadian identities with memorable stories of Tim Hortons. Tim Hortons also sponsors sports that are important to Canadians, such as the Tim Hortons Briar for men's curling, the National Hockey League, minor hockey with the Timbits program, and the Canadian Football League.[54]

REPOSITIONING

Sometimes products or companies are repositioned in order to sustain growth in slow markets or to correct positioning mistakes. **Repositioning** involves changing consumers' perceptions of a brand in relation to competing brands. Brands can be repositioned by their functional characteristics, their symbolic characteristics, or both. When a brand is repositioned on the basis of a change in its functional characteristics, it is called "rational repositioning." When a brand is repositioned based on symbolic characteristics, it is referred to as "emotional repositioning," and if a brand is repositioned on both functional and symbolic characteristics, it is referred to as "complete repositioning."[55] For example, the earlier discussion about how Cadillac decided to reposition its brand involved both symbolic and functional changes so this was a case of complete repositioning. BMW acquired the ownership of the Mini-Cooper automotive brand and modified the vehicles to modernize them but maintained the basic image of the Mini in undertaking "functional" repositioning. Many companies use "emotional" repositioning, where they simply attach different values to their existing products. For example, Procter & Gamble repositioned Olay from being a pink liquid that moisturizes to helping women look better and feel better as they age.[56] Scott Paper had to change the name of its Cottonelle brand toilet tissue to Cashmere brand, which represents a symbolic change leading to emotional repositioning. The reason for the change was the company was losing its licence on the brand name. The new brand name, Cashmere, was developed from a marketing study of women who were asked, "What's softer than cotton?" The most common response was "cashmere." This is the most demanding "repositioning" approach a company can undertake. Scott Paper developed a multimedia campaign involving TV ads, radio ads, magazines, and point-of-purchase materials. The message strategy of the campaign was "We've changed Cottonelle over the years. Now we're giving it a softer name. Cottonelle is changing its name to Cashmere."[57]

Repositioning can be risky and may not even take hold, forcing marketers to reconsider their decision. Consider the well-known near disaster (some say complete disaster) of the introduction of "New" Coke in the 1980s. In response to the highly successful Pepsi Challenge taste-test advertising campaign, the Coca-Cola Company undertook some involved and lengthy taste-testing research to develop a new formulation for a sweeter-tasting product. It developed a formulation based on these taste tests and then publicly announced a major change in its formulation of Coca-Cola and introduced the product as "New Coke." However, after several generations of advertising where the company had established its brand image as the "Real

Nothing feels like Cashmere.

SOURCE: COURTESY OF KRUGER PRODUCTS

Scott Paper Company had to rebrand and reposition its well-known Cottonelle brand bathroom tissue, which for years was advertised with the positioning "cottony soft." The firm decided on the new brand name of "Cashmere" with the new positioning statement "Nothing feels like cashmere."

9 | **Explain how and why companies implement positioning strategies and how product differentiation plays a role**

Each car occupies a position in consumers' minds.
Cars can be positioned according to attribute (sporty, conservative, etc.),
price and quality (affordable, classy, etc.), or other bases.
Cadillac has repositioned itself as a car for younger drivers with edgier ads.

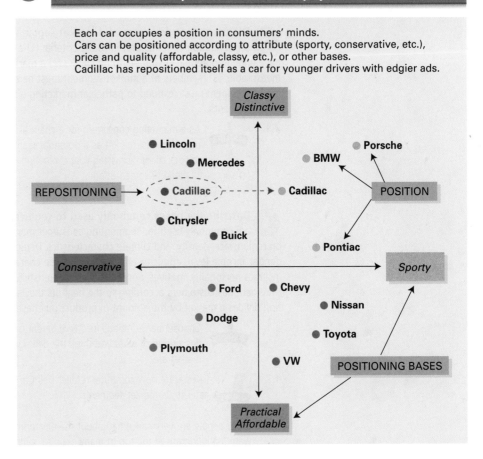

Thing," the firm found it was alienating its most avid customers "so emphatically that Coke was forced to bring back the original recipe, relaunching it as 'the real thing,' Coca-Cola Classic."[58]

REVIEW AND APPLICATIONS

1 **Describe the characteristics of markets and market segments.** A market is composed of individuals or organizations with the ability and willingness to make purchases to fulfill their needs or wants. A market segment is a group of individuals or organizations with similar product needs as a result of one or more common characteristics.

1.1 Mercedes-Benz is thinking about advertising its cars to college and university students. Do you think these students are a viable potential market for Mercedes? Why or why not?

1.2 Go to the website **www.monster.ca**. How are visitors to the website segmented when seeking relevant job openings? Report your results.

2 **Explain the importance of market segmentation.** Before the 1960s, few businesses targeted specific market segments. Today, segmentation is a crucial marketing strategy for nearly all successful organizations. Market segmentation enables marketers to tailor marketing mixes to meet the needs of particular population segments. Segmentation helps marketers identify consumer needs and preferences, areas of declining demand, and new marketing opportunities.

2.1 Describe market segmentation in terms of the historical evolution of marketing.

3 **Discuss criteria for successful market segmentation.** Successful market segmentation depends on four basic criteria: (1) a market segment must be substantial and have enough potential customers to be viable; (2) a market segment must be identifiable and measurable; (3) members of a market segment must be accessible to marketing efforts; and (4) a market segment must respond to particular marketing efforts in a way that distinguishes it from other segments.

3.1 *WRITING* As a marketing consultant for a chain of hair salons, you have been asked to evaluate the kids' market as a potential segment for the chain to target. Write a memo to your client discussing your evaluation of the kids' segment using the four criteria for successful market segmentation.

4 **Describe the bases commonly used to segment consumer markets.** Five bases are commonly used for segmenting consumer markets. Geographic segmentation is based on region, size, density, and climate characteristics. Demographic segmentation is based on age, gender, income level, ethnicity, and family life-cycle characteristics. Psychographic segmentation includes personality, motives, and lifestyle characteristics. Benefits sought is a type of segmentation that identifies customers according to the benefits they seek in a product. Finally, usage segmentation divides a market by the amount of product purchased or consumed.

4.1 *WRITING* Choose magazine ads for five different consumer products. For each ad, write a description of what you think the demographic characteristics of the targeted market are.

4.2 *ONLINE* Investigate how computer retailer Dell Canada (**www.dell.ca**) uses its website to cater to its market segments.

4.3 Many people are very concerned about the environment, and issues like global warming and water pollution are at the top of many people's minds. The chapter discusses a line of PC Green products offered by Loblaws. Research these products. What kinds of products are they, and what benefit do they offer? Would you consider buying some of them? Explain why or why not.

5 **Describe the bases for segmenting business markets.** Business markets can be segmented on two general bases. First, businesses segment markets based on company characteristics, such as customers' geographic location, type of company, company size, and product use. Second, companies may segment customers based on the buying processes those customers use.

5.1 *WRITING* Choose five ads from business publications such as *Marketing Magazine, Canadian Business, Financial Post,* and the *Globe and Mail.* For each ad, write a description of how you think the company has segmented its business market.

6 **List the steps involved in segmenting markets.** Six steps are involved when segmenting markets: (1) selecting a market or product category for study; (2) choosing a basis or bases for segmenting the market; (3) selecting segmentation descriptors; (4) profiling and evaluating segments; (5) selecting target markets; and (6) designing, implementing, and maintaining appropriate marketing mixes.

6.1 *WRITING* Write a letter to the president of your bank or trust company suggesting ideas for increasing profits and enhancing customer service by improving segmentation and targeting strategies.

7 **Discuss alternative strategies for selecting target markets.** Marketers select target markets using three different strategies: undifferentiated targeting, concentrated targeting, and multisegment targeting. An undifferentiated targeting strategy assumes that all members of a market have similar needs that can be met with a single marketing mix. A concentrated targeting strategy focuses all marketing efforts on a single market segment. Multisegment targeting uses two or more marketing mixes to target two or more market segments.

7.1 Form a team with two or three other students. Create an idea for a new product. Describe the segment (or segments) you are going to target with the product, and explain why you chose the targeting strategy you did.

8 **Explain one-to-one marketing.** One-to-one marketing is an individualized marketing method that uses customer information to build long-term, personalized, and profitable relationships with each customer. Successful one-to-one marketing comes from understanding customers and collaborating with them, rather than using them as targets for generic messages. Database technology makes it possible for companies to interact with customers on a personal, one-to-one basis.

8.1 WRITING You are the marketing manager for a specialty retailer that sells customized hand-bags. Write a memo to your boss describing how the company could benefit from one-to-one marketing.

9 **Explain how and why companies implement positioning strategies and how product differentiation plays a role.** Positioning is used to influence consumer percep-tions of a particular brand, product line, or organization in relation to competitors. The term *position* refers to the place the offering occupies in consumers' minds. To establish a unique position, many companies use product differentiation, emphasizing the real or perceived differ-ences among competing offerings. Products may be differentiated on the basis of attribute, price and quality, use or application, product user, product class, competitor or emotion.

9.1 Choose a product category (e.g., pickup trucks), and identify at least three different brands and their respective positioning strategies. How is each position communicated to the target audience?

Terms

Exercises

APPLICATION EXERCISE

How tightly do you fit into a particular market segment? Do you think you can be neatly classified? If you think your purchasing habits make you an enigma to marketers, you may need to think again.[59]

Activities

1. Form a group, then go to the VALs website (**www.strategicbusinessinsights.com/ vals/presurvey.shtml**) and read about VALs and its uses.

2. Now look at the VALs types: innovators, thinkers, believers, achievers, strivers, experiencers, makers, and survivors. Which "type" do you think you fall into? Which type do you think your

other group members fall into? Categorize yourself and your group members before conferring with them. What category did you put them into? What category did they put themselves into? What category did they put you into?

3. Now take the VALs survey and see where VALs put all of you. Were you at all surprised? Do you agree? Write a short statement evaluating the VALs scheme and discuss why, as a marketing manager, you would or would not use it.

ETHICS EXERCISE

Alcoholic beverage marketers, including breweries, wineries, and liquor and spirits distillers, are frequently criticized for targeting potential customers below the legal drinking age to purchase and use their products. Critics cite the kinds of promotions and contests found on the websites of these companies and the sponsorship of professional sports that interests many younger viewers. If alcoholic beverage marketers were actually following this particular demographic targeting strategy, most would agree that it is unethical if not illegal.

Questions

1. Is the sponsorship of programs and events that attract younger consumers unethical?

2. Many are beginning to argue that fast-food companies, such as McDonald's and Burger King, are knowingly marketing unhealthy food to consumers. Is it unethical for fast-food companies to market kids' meals to children?

3. What does the CMA Code of Ethics have to say about marketing unhealthy or harmful products to consumers, particularly children and young adults? Go to the CMA website at **www.the-cma.org/public.asp?WCE=C=32|K=s223391** to review the code. Write a brief paragraph summarizing where the CMA stands on this important issue.

CASE STUDY

COKE ZERO

When a couple of marketing managers for Coca-Cola told lawyer Elizabeth Finn Johnson that they wanted to sue their Coke Zero colleagues for "taste infringement," she was baffled. She tried to talk them out of it, but they were determined. They argued that Coca-Cola Classic should be protected from the age discrimination it would suffer with the introduction of a newer, younger soft drink that tasted exactly the same as the original. Frustrated, Finn Johnson held up the Coke can and shouted, "It's not a person! Title VII doesn't cover these things!"

What she didn't know was that the marketing managers were actors. Hidden cameras had been planted around the meeting room to capture the reactions of several unsuspecting lawyers who had been asked to consider the case, including an immigration lawyer who was asked if he could get the Coke Zero marketing head deported back to Canada. The short videos were strategically placed on websites such as **www.youtube.com** to promote Coke Zero as the hip, new alternative to Diet Coke for men.

The Coca-Cola Company knows it has to be creative if it's going to sell more pop after sales dropped two years in a row in 2005 and 2006. Morgan Stanley analyst Bill Pecoriello explains, "Consumers are becoming ever more health-conscious, and the image of regular carbonated soft drinks is deteriorating rapidly." In an attempt to appeal to consumers concerned with nutrition, Coke introduced Diet Coke Plus in 2007, a sweeter version of Diet Coke fortified with vitamins and minerals. But what the company really needed was a way to reach young male consumers, and Diet Coke Plus, marketed with taglines like "Your Best Friend Just Got Friendlier!" wasn't going to do it.

A few new products appealed to certain male demographics, such as Coca-Cola Blak, a cola with coffee essence created for older, more sophisticated consumers who are willing to pay more, and Full Throttle Blue Demon, an energy drink with an agave azule flavour (think margaritas) designed to appeal to Hispanic men. However, research showed that there was still a big demographic hole to fill as young men between the ages of 18 and 34 were abandoning the Coca-Cola brand altogether. They didn't want all the calories of regular Coke, but they weren't willing to make the move to Diet Coke, either, which has traditionally been marketed to women who want to lose weight.

SOURCE: © VICKI BEAVER

Katie Bayne, chief marketing officer for Coca-Cola North America, says that the men who weren't put off by the "feminine stigma" of Diet Coke often rejected it anyway because of its aspartame-sweetened aftertaste. "What we were seeing before Zero launched was that more and more younger people were interested in no-calorie beverages but weren't going to sacrifice taste," Bayne said. "So when they got interested in no-calorie, they were like 'Forget it, I'm not going to Diet Coke.'"

Testing showed that the name "Coke Zero" would be an effective way to sell a low-calorie cola to men without using the word "diet." And advances in artificial sweeteners made it possible for Coke to finally create a product that tasted more like the Real Thing. So expectations were high when Coke Zero was introduced in 2005 with a big marketing push, including a commercial that remade the famous 1971 "Hilltop/I'd Like to Teach the World to Sing" ad—this time with rapper G. Love on a rooftop singing that he'd like to teach the world to "chill." Unfortunately, the commercial didn't catch on, and neither did the product it was selling.

Despite disappointing sales in North America, however, Coke Zero was an immediate hit in Australia, selling more than three times the number of cases expected during its first year on the market. In North America, the packaging was white and silver, making it difficult for consumers to see the difference between Coke Zero and Diet Coke. In Australia, the bottles and cans were black, making the product stand out on the shelves and look more like the "bloke's Coke" it was intended to be.

The North American marketing team took notice and reintroduced Coke Zero with a black and silver label in 2007. Coca-Cola is now investing more money in Coke Zero than any other brand its size, hoping it will someday be a megabrand for the company alongside Coca-Cola Classic and Diet Coke. Chief marketing officer Bayne is enthusiastic about the impact it may have on the company. "We do see this as potentially a bit of a white knight. There's huge opportunity to grow here."[60]

Questions

1. Describe the specific type of consumer the Coca-Cola Company is targeting with each of the following products: Diet Coke, Coke Zero, Diet Coke Plus, Coca-Cola Blak, and Full Throttle Blue Demon. What types of demographic segmentation is each product's marketing most likely to include?

2. Some industry analysts think soft-drink companies should develop products that will bring new customers into the market rather than just creating variants on the old. They warn that products like Coke Zero will cannibalize lost market share from other soft drink categories instead of increasing the number of consumers overall. Which Coca-Cola products are most likely to lose customers to Coke Zero?

3. Why do you think that the hidden-camera videos used to promote Coke Zero were an effective way to reach its target market? Do you think a similar strategy with a viral marketing campaign on the Internet would appeal to the target market for Diet Coke Plus?

4. Could Diet Coke have been repositioned to change consumers' perceptions of it enough to be considered a drink equally appealing to men?

MARKETING TO BOOMERS

The importance of understanding demographic trends and their economic and business impact is critical for all decision makers. The group of 9 million Canadians born just after World War II (between 1947 and 1966) have been called the baby boom generation or boomers and their arrival has been described as a demographic tsunami. University of Toronto economist David Foot describes the impact in the book *Boom, Bust, and Echo.* He makes the point that many trends can be predicted from an understanding of population demographics. Shifts in population will affect Canada's economy, debt levels, taxation policies, labour market, social programs, education system, and health care policies, as well as Canadians' attitudes. When it comes to marketing, baby boomers have been a key audience for marketing firms for over 60 years, and with Canadian life expectancies in the range of 80 years, this group promises to continue to dominate for yet another generation!

Andrea Mandell-Campbell and Howard Green of Business News Network's *Midday Markets* discussed marketing to boomers with Jeremy Gutsche, the chief trend hunter for Trendhunter.com, and Lina Ko, who authors a weblog entitled Boomerwatch.ca and is also a partner in the firm National Public Relations. The first question of the discussion was how the boomers were different from previous generations.

Lina Ko commented first, stating that although they were born in the same generational span, in fact, boomers are not a homogeneous group. There are several segments within the boomers, and she labels the oldest of them as "leading"-edge boomers. Boomers are different from previous generations in a number of ways. First, boomers hate to age, and they actually think they are ten years younger than they are (or maybe they simply wish they were). The fact is, boomers tend to do their best to be both more physically and mentally fit than previous generations so because of their health and their appearance, they seem ten years younger! Unlike the previous generations, who accepted retirement at 65 years of age and then went to the golf course, did housework, or just sat around, the boomers have chosen to redefine retirement. They have decided to reinvent themselves and are doing things they didn't do when they were employed. For example, boomers are volunteering and giving back to their communities and many are continuing to work since mandatory retirement rules have changed. Others are retiring but going back to work as consultants on flex time.

The next question debated was whether boomers were simply in denial about their age. Jeremy Gutsche commented, "Age isn't cool" and then he described one characteristic of boomers as being "ageless inspiration." Gutsche describes how 41-year-old American swimmer Dara Torres was a boomer Olympian who won an Olympic silver medal in the 2008 Olympic Games. In fact, Torres had won Olympic medals in 1984, 1988, 1992, 2000, and finally in 2008! Gutsche says that pop culture is fascinated with age. For boomers, how you act as a 60-year-old today is not at all like the way people of that age behaved 60 years ago. For example, he mentions the fashion items of brand "Not At Your Age." Gutsche talks about marketing research that has identified what are called "boomer potentialists"—boomers who are trying out new things to get the most out of life. He mentions that boomers are looking to travel and develop hobbies and some are actually choosing to go back to work.

Finally, the discussion question was how to market to boomers. Lina Ko suggests a very basic approach. She advised marketers that they needed to "do the research to understand the group." Ko says, "Target them. Don't talk down to them or call them old." She says that boomers respond to appeals about self-esteem and youthfulness. Marketers need to research this group to understand their "mindset, [and] what keeps them excited every day." Another issue was how to communicate with boomers at the retail level. Gutsche comments that boomers are very technologically savvy. They use social media like Facebook and Twitter. In fact, many Twitter users are over 25 years of age and many boomers are heavy users.

Gutsche agrees with Ko that it is important not to lump the whole generation together. In fact, it is possible that a boomer parent (born in 1947) could have a boomer child (born in 1966 or 1967). The younger boomers are part of what is called the sandwich generation—people who are looking after elderly parents while still having to look after kids living at home. Marketers need to realize that the priorities are different for the leading-edge boomers who are close to 63 years of age and are on the verge of the historical age of retirement—65 years. A lot of people in this age group are still in the workforce but they would like to pursue flex time in their working environment and not have to retire abruptly. When they design their strategies, marketers need to realize that boomers want it all. Boomers are some of the best communicators, and Gutsche describes them as possessing "ageless inspiration." He mentions that one of the best trend hunters in his firm is actually 60 years old. Finally, the comment was made that other generations are probably sick of the baby boomers having been in their shadow for so long. Both Ko and Gutsche believe that younger people can share their experiences with boomers and that boomers love to both work with and even for younger people. After all, the boomers have learned that part of staying young is thinking young and if you work with younger people, you are forced to think that way![61]

Questions

1. Review the kinds of formats and programming on radio stations and TV stations. Do you think that marketers are catering more to boomers than to anyone else? Discuss your impressions, and support your conclusion with facts.

2. Look at your own family situation and then review the case and the chapter's description of the various age groups. What "generation" do you fit into? What about your parents? Do you agree with the generalizations made in this case and the chapter? Comment.

3. Discuss how demographics can affect "attitudes" of people. What kinds of things should marketers consider in trying to make the connection between demographics and attitudes in developing their segmentation strategies?

MARKETING & YOU RESULTS

A high score indicates that you operate within budget constraints. Living on a budget doesn't necessarily mean that you change your shopping behaviour, however. Low scores relate to financial health and a tendency to be brand loyal. After reading Chapter 6, you can see why income and financial situation can be an important segmentation variable!

CHAPTER 7

Decision Support Systems and Marketing Research

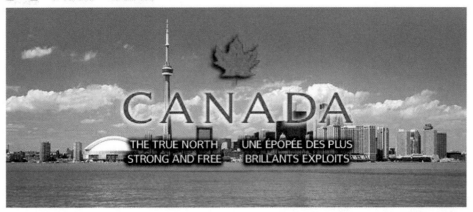

LEARNING OUTCOMES

1 Explain the concept and purpose of a marketing decision support system

2 Define marketing research and explain its importance to marketing decision making

3 Describe the steps involved in conducting a marketing research project

4 Discuss the profound impact of the Internet on marketing research

5 Discuss the growing importance of scanner-based research

6 Explain the concept of competitive intelligence

7 Describe sales forecasting and sales forecasting methods

MARKETING & YOU

Please note your opinion on each of the following questions.
Using the following scale, enter your answers or record them on a separate page.

| 1 | 2 | 3 | 4 | 5 | 6 | 7 |
Strongly disagree   Strongly agree

During a marketing project, a marketing manager should have formal or informal processes for continuously

__ collecting information from customers.
__ collecting information about competitors' activities.
__ collecting information about relevant publics other than customers and competitors.
__ re-examining the value of information collected in previous studies.
__ collecting information from external experts, such as consultants.

Total your score. Now read the chapter and find out what your score means at the end.

When you need information for marketing decision making, who should you turn to first? Have no doubt: it is the "True North Strong and Free" that you need, also known as the Government of Canada. The Canadian government provides Canadian businesses and organizations and, yes, our foreign competitors too, with some of the most important sources of marketing decision-making information available. No matter what your business or organization wants to do, it would do better if it started its research initiatives by visiting Canada.gc.ca on the Web!

What will you find when you visit? Not surprisingly, you will be greeted with an expression of Canadian culture such as the Canadian flag, the Parliament buildings, perhaps a picture of the latest prime minister, and likely all three. As expected, the cultural and political structure of the country comes first. However, one of the critical links for a marketer is offered with the "Popular Services" heading that includes "Starting a Business." If you click on this link, you will be led to a wealth of information (hopefully leading to other wealth), including a link saying "Market Research and Statistics." A quick click on this link presents the following statement: "Discover what market research is and how to create an effective market research campaign. You will also find numerous information resources and statistics that you can use to learn more about your industry, your customers and the markets you serve. This information can ultimately help you to make informed decisions that can maximize the potential of your business."

The promise is fulfilled with helpful links with the following titles: Conducting marketing research; Labour and employment data; Demographics; Industry sector data; Canadian economy; International markets; Importing and exporting; Environment; Science and technology; and General research and statistics. If you start at the beginning, you would select "Conducting marketing research." The topics offered will help you undertake market research. You will find a "Guide to Market Research and Analysis," which will allow you to "discover how market research can help your business succeed and learn how to conduct a variety of market research activities." After you have read this guide, you can choose "Designing a Questionnaire," which allows you to "get advice on how to design a survey questionnaire in order to gather market research data." Since many researchers use the Internet to survey their markets, you will find the "Online Survey Design Guide" from which you can "get tips and guidelines on the design and implementation of web-based surveys." You will also find advice on the "Types of Survey Questions" you can ask and you will be able to "examine different kinds of closed and open-ended questions that can be used in surveys." The Government of Canada can advise you on "Market Research Approaches," which involve helping you "find information on commonly used research approaches that can support your market research efforts." Finally, the government is fully aware that Canadian businesses operate in a global marketplace so they have a set of "Steps to International Market Research" that assists you to "learn some of the basic steps to follow when researching foreign markets."

Any businessperson planning a new business venture would be foolish not to begin his or her quest for information with government sources. And if your business or organization has ongoing operations, you would be well advised to continue to visit the Government of Canada website to keep on top of the change that is inevitable. Here is one of your best opportunities to recover some of the value from your tax dollars![1]

If you have thoroughly explored the information on the Government of Canada website, you may find some of the topics you are about to study redundant. However, the chapter will proceed because looking at government sources of information is only part of one step of undertaking marketing research. What are the various techniques for conducting marketing research? Should managers always do marketing research before they make a decision? How does marketing research relate to decision support systems? We will explore all these topics and others in Chapter 7.

SOURCE: GOVERNMENT OF CANADA WEBSITE, CANADA.GC.CA, ACCESSED APRIL 30, 2010

MARKETING DECISION SUPPORT SYSTEMS

Explain the concept and purpose of
a marketing decision support system

marketing information
Everyday information about
developments in the marketing
environment that managers use
to prepare and adjust marketing
plans.

**decision support system
(DSS)**
An interactive, flexible, computerized information system that
enables managers to obtain and
manipulate information as they
are making decisions.

Accurate and timely information is the lifeblood of marketing decision making. Good information can help an organization maximize its sales and use scarce resources efficiently. To prepare and adjust marketing plans, managers need a system for gathering everyday information about developments in the marketing environment—that is, for gathering **marketing information**. The system most commonly used these days for gathering marketing information is called a *marketing decision support system.*

A marketing **decision support system (DSS)** is an interactive, flexible, computerized information system that enables managers to obtain and manipulate information while they are making decisions. A DSS bypasses the information-processing specialist and provides managers with access to useful data from their own desks. The following are characteristics of a true DSS:

- *Interactive.* Managers give simple instructions and see immediate results. The process is under their direct control; no computer programmer is needed. Managers don't have to wait for scheduled reports.
- *Flexible.* A DSS can sort, regroup, total, average, and manipulate the data in various ways. It can shift gears as the user changes topics, matching information to the problem at hand. For example, a CEO can see highly aggregated figures, while a marketing analyst can view highly detailed breakouts.
- *Discovery-oriented.* Managers can probe for trends, isolate problems, and ask "what if" questions.
- *Accessible.* Managers who aren't skilled with computers can easily learn how to use a DSS. Novice users should be able to choose a standard, or default, method of using the system. They can bypass optional features so that they can work with the basic system right away while gradually learning to apply its advanced features.

As a hypothetical example of how a DSS can be used, consider Renée Smith, vice-president and manager of new products for Central Corporation. To evaluate sales of a recently introduced product, Renée can "call up" sales by the week, then by the month, breaking them out at her option by, say, customer segments. Working from both her mobile computer and her G4 enabled smartphone, she can send her inquiries in several directions, depending on the decision under consideration. If she wants to know about monthly sales last quarter compared to forecasts, she can use her DSS to analyze problems immediately. She might see that her new product's sales were significantly below forecasts. Were her forecasts too optimistic? She compares other products' sales to her forecasts and finds that the targets were accurate. Was something wrong with the product? Is her sales department getting insufficient

database marketing
The creation of a large
computerized file of customers'
and potential customers' profiles
and purchase patterns.

leads, or is it not putting leads to good use? Thinking for a minute about how to examine that question, she checks ratios of leads converted to sales, product by product. The results disturb her. Only 5 percent of the new product's leads generated orders, compared to the company's 12 percent all-product average. Why? Renée guesses that the sales force is not supporting the new product vigorously enough. Quantitative information from the DSS could perhaps provide more evidence to back that suspicion. But already having enough quantitative knowledge to satisfy herself, Renée decides to have a chat with her sales manager.

Perhaps the fastest-growing use of DSSs is for **database marketing**, which involves creating a large computerized file of customers' and potential customers' profiles and purchase patterns. It is usually the key tool for successful micromarketing, which relies on highly specific information about a market.

REVIEW LEARNING OUTCOME 1

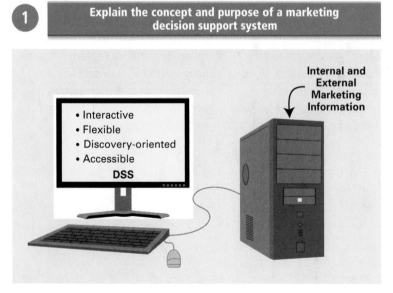

1

Explain the concept and purpose of a marketing decision support system

- Interactive
- Flexible
- Discovery-oriented
- Accessible

DSS

Internal and
External
Marketing
Information

THE ROLE OF MARKETING RESEARCH

Define marketing research and explain its importance to marketing decision making

marketing research
The process of planning, collecting, and analyzing data relevant to a marketing decision.

Marketing research is the process of planning, collecting, and analyzing data relevant to a marketing decision. The results of this analysis are then communicated to management. Marketing research plays a key role in the marketing system. It provides decision makers with data on the effectiveness of the current marketing mix and also with the insights to make necessary changes. Furthermore, marketing research is a main source of data for both management information systems and DSS. In other words, the findings of a marketing research project become data in a DSS.

Each year over $23 billion is spent by the global market research and polling industry to study products, advertising, prices, packages, names, logos, services, buying habits, taglines, colours, uses, awareness, familiarity, new concepts, traffic patterns, wants, needs, and politics.[2]

Marketing research has three roles: descriptive, diagnostic, and predictive. Its *descriptive* role includes gathering and presenting factual statements. For example, what is the historic sales trend in the industry? What are consumers' attitudes toward a product and its advertising? Its *diagnostic* role includes explaining data. For instance, what was the impact on sales of a change in the design of the package? Its *predictive* function is to address "what if" questions. For example, how can the researcher use the descriptive and diagnostic research to predict the results of a planned marketing decision?

MANAGEMENT USES OF MARKETING RESEARCH

Marketing research can help managers in several ways. It improves the quality of decision making and helps managers trace problems. Most important, sound marketing research helps managers focus on the paramount importance of keeping existing customers, aids them in better understanding the marketplace, and alerts them to marketplace trends.

Marketing research also helps managers gauge the perceived value of their goods and services as well as the level of customer satisfaction.

Improving the Quality of Decision Making

Managers can sharpen their decision making by using marketing research to explore the desirability of various marketing alternatives. For example, the Cruise Lines International Association (**www.cruising.org**) collects data and assesses the information to help Cruise Line managers make marketing management decisions. The Cruise Line Industry Association reports that the cruise line industry is responsible for $19 billion in direct sales on an annual basis, with an additional $40 billion in spin-off sales (airline flights for getting to the cruise ships, as well as the hotel stays and meals). The passenger traffic was 13.4 million passengers worldwide in 2009, and 10.29 million of these passengers sailed from North America and stayed for an average of 7.1 days on their cruise vacations.[3] Cruises are relatively expensive and only account for a small proportion of vacation time. Research shows that only 5 percent of people who take vacations longer than five days take cruise vacations.[4]

Despite appealing to a limited and high-end market, the cruise line industry has been adding to its "passenger" capacity at an annual rate of 4 percent per year in response to steadily rising demand. For example, since 2005, cruise line capacity increased from 225,000 beds to nearly 300,000 beds at the end of 2009, and many cruise lines were planning to add even more capacity in 2010 and 2011. The industry noted that the world economy was very weak in 2009 but it responded by adapting quickly to the market changes and by redeploying vessels to serve stronger markets. In addition, the lines offered a number of value-based vacations, managed expenses carefully, sourced passengers on a global basis, encouraged travel agents to go on the ships, and finally brought out new ships with unique products.[5]

Leading the way in bringing out new ships was Royal Caribbean Cruise Lines. It responded to the Cruise Lines International Association's research showing that cruisers feel they get tremendous value from their vacations. The association has

SOURCE: THE CANADIAN PRESS (REX FEATURES)

Marketing research can help managers in several ways. For example, the Cruise Lines International Association is forecasting tremendous growth in cruise ship passenger traffic for the future. Based on optimistic forecasts of increasing demand, Royal Caribbean Cruise Lines has built ships like the *Oasis of the Seas*, which is virtually a floating city capable of carrying over 6,000 passengers.

forecasted that demand for cruises is going to increase by more than 10 percent a year, mainly driven by the baby boomer market. On the strength of these kinds of projections, in 2009 Royal Caribbean International Cruise Lines added the *Oasis of the Seas*, the world's largest cruise ship, displacing 220,000 tons with a maximum capacity of 6,300 passengers and a crew of 1,800! The Oasis of the Seas is a uniquely designed ship which is organized into the seven neighbourhoods identified as: Central Park, Boardwalk, the Royal Promenade, Pool and Sports Zone, Vitality as Sea Spa and Fitness Center, Entertainment Place and the Youth Zone. Each of these neighborhoods is designed to appeal to different guest preferences and desires. One other unique touch on the ship is "the AquaTheatre that serves as a pool by day and a dazzling ocean front theatre by night."[6]

Tracing Problems

Managers also use marketing research to find out why a plan backfired. Was the initial decision faulty? Did an unforeseen change in the external environment cause the plan to fail? How can the same mistake be avoided in the future?

After a series of incidents involving the recalls of contaminated and tainted food products, food marketers are grappling with the problem that "people don't know what products they can trust anymore."[7] This had led to a recent trend in the Canadian food market where consumers are insisting on knowing how their food was made and where it comes from. Market research has found that "today's health-conscious consumer is looking for foods that are rich in nutrients, have added value and feature back-to-basics ingredients. Added to this wish list, consumers are looking at making socially responsible purchases that decrease their carbon footprint and benefit their health and well-being. Families are seeking value, eating out less often and getting back to basics through to fund-friendly tactics such as stocking pantries with homemade goodness."[8]

As a result of all these changes in the external environment, food marketers have been responding with a number of initiatives. For example, Campbell Canada has introduced Campbell's Créations, which is a soup product line positioned as being made "with authentic ingredients" including "vegetables . . . sourced from just outside Toronto." Nestlé Canada is "focusing on offering health, wellness and nutritional choices" and the firm uses a "unique testing process . . . to improve the taste and nutritional advantage of our products." Because of consumer concerns about their food ingredients, Nestlé has reduced the amount of sodium and removed preservatives from at least one of its products.[9]

The Paramount Importance of Keeping Existing Customers

An inextricable link exists between customer satisfaction and customer loyalty. Long-term relationships don't just happen; they are grounded in the delivery of service and value by the company. Customer retention pays big dividends for organizations. Powered by repeat sales and referrals, revenues and market share grow. Costs fall because companies spend less money and energy attempting to replace defectors. Steady customers are easy to serve because they understand the modus operandi and make fewer demands on employees' time. Increased customer retention also drives job satisfaction and pride, both of which lead to higher employee retention. In turn, the knowledge employees acquire as they stay longer increases productivity. A study done by Bain & Co., a global business strategy consulting firm, estimated that a 5 percent decrease in the customer defection rate can boost profits by 25 to 95 percent.[10] Another study found that the customer retention rate has a major impact on the value of the firm.[11]

The ability to retain customers is based on an intimate understanding of their needs. This knowledge comes primarily from marketing research. Burger King Canada is constantly researching its customer needs, and the company has identified a customer type it calls the "super fan," a customer who visits often and has a constant hunger for something new. Jason Keown is the senior director of marketing for Burger King Canada, and he comments as follows about super fan customers: "Because they are going regularly, they are looking for new tastes and new promotions, and that's why it's important that we have something [new] every couple of months."[12]

SOURCE: TONY BOCK/GETSTOCK.COM

Burger King Canada brings out new products often to satisfy its "super fan" customers who visit its restaurants often but have cravings for something new.

Burger King Canada has been employing a dual approach to keep its customers coming back while giving them something different. It has developed what it calls its "dual premium and value" approach. The premium approach revolves around offering different variations of the flagship brand, the Whopper, and charging significantly more for these burger meals. For example, Burger King Canada has brought out burgers with different flavour and dressing approaches like the "Angry Whopper, topped with spicy crispy onions, jalapeños, pepper jack cheese, bacon, tomatoes, lettuce, mayonnaise, and spicy Angry Sauce,"[13] and the Bourbon Whopper, which is made with "nonalcoholic, sweet & tangy, bourbon-flavoured sauce that partners with onion rings, crispy bacon and Cheddar cheese on the burger."[14] A slightly different variation on the premium approach focuses on the meat patty and not just the

Customer Experience

WESTJET'S CARE-ANTEE

Canada's WestJet Airlines is devoted to its customers' experience. Its website even has a headline entitled "The Experience." The airline claims to have the "best customer service" and it publishes its "on-time" performance numbers even though it is not a requirement in Canada for airlines to do this (unlike in the United States, where airlines are required to do so). In addition, in 2008 the airline was recognized by Waterstone Human Capital, a leading Canadian human resource consulting firm, as one of Canada's most admired corporate cultures.

WestJet publishes a list of nearly 20 promises that they refer to as their "Care-antee." Some of the key statements in the "Care-antee" credit the success of the airline to the support of its guests, and promise to publish its rates of on-time flights, cancellations, and baggage delays—along with examples. At the end of any list of promises, there is always fine print but WestJet eschews formal

rules and conditions, simply pledging that the airline's employees will do their best for their guests—and do it happily.[15]

In essence, WestJet Airlines is presenting a very detailed and specific set of promises it communicate to both its customers and its employees. These promises communicate what customers can expect to receive when they book a WestJet flight and also represent the benchmarks by which WestJet can evaluate the services the airline delivers. The airline can conduct research surveys asking questions related to its "Care-antees" to see if it is really delivering on its promises and also if consumers are responding favourably to them.

Do you think WestJet Airlines could live up to any of its Care-antees without undertaking marketing research? Discuss the kinds of marketing research the airline would have to undertake to keep its promises.

SOURCE: WESTJET CORPORATE WEBSITE, "THE EXPERIENCE," WWW.WESTJET.COM, ACCESSED 6 MAY 2010 [HTTP://WWW.WESTJET.COM/GUEST/EN/EXPERIENCE/CAREANTEE.SHTML]

toppings with the offering of a 5.5 oz. "Steakhouse XT" Whopper, which is positioned as an "expensive steakhouse burger." The value approach is focused on Burger King Canada's "King Deals" program: every day a different regular menu item was featured for $1.99. This differed from the approach of offering a separate value menu at a reduced price. The result was that same-store restaurant sales rose to a 15-year high.[16]

Understanding the Ever-Changing Marketplace

Marketing research also helps managers understand what is going on in the marketplace and take advantage of opportunities.

Michelle Halpern, writing in *Marketing Magazine* about the changing marketplace, comments as follows on a shift in attitudes among the youth market: "Today's youth may be more ambitious and goal-oriented than any generation before them."[17] This market has always been difficult for marketers to predict and understand; in this effort, focused research companies such as Youthography and Youth Culture Group can really help Canadian marketers. For example, Canadian universities and colleges used to target teenagers when they were in Grade 12 and close to their decision making about postsecondary education. This approach is still important, but studies by these companies have found that Canadian teens are thinking about university and college at a far earlier age. Consequently, postsecondary institutions are targeting teens at a much younger age in the hope of building brand awareness among them before these teens need to make their concrete decisions on postsecondary institutions and programs. This adjustment recognizes that teens' values are changing. Studies by Youth Culture Group and Youthography have discovered a number of key facts about Canadian teens: "85% of teens and young adults identify themselves as goal-oriented; the number one thing youth 12 to 24 are saving for is tuition; the number one thing young people want from corporations are job opportunities and next is scholarships and student loans."[18]

REVIEW LEARNING OUTCOME 2

 2 Define marketing research and explain its importance to marketing decision making

Why marketing research?

☑ Improve quality of decision making

☑ Trace problems

☑ Focus on keeping existing customers

☑ Understand changes in marketplace

3 STEPS IN A MARKETING RESEARCH PROJECT

Describe the steps involved in conducting a marketing research project

Virtually all companies that have adopted the marketing concept engage in some marketing research, which offers decision makers many benefits. Some companies spend millions on marketing research; others, particularly smaller companies, conduct informal, limited-scale research studies. Recently, a Canadian specialty magazine devoted to history decided to change its name when it conducted some limited research to confirm a number of beliefs developed from informal research. The magazine was founded in 1920 as a Hudson's Bay Company newsletter, which was entitled *The Beaver*. The magazine title was taken over by Canada's Historical Society, who became its publisher and also changed it into a history magazine so that its content and brand clearly separated it from the Hudson's Bay Company.

Deborah Morrison, president and CEO of Canada's National History Society, says that the society was aware there were "sexual" connotations associated with the magazine's name. However, the magazine didn't fully appreciate the magnitude of its "brand name" problem until it began publishing on-line. Subscribers complained they weren't getting their on-line versions because the e-mails the magazine was sending out were going into their spam folders. In addition, traffic counts on *The Beaver's* website showed a large number of hits but visit times were extremely short for the majority of the visits. The obvious conclusion was that history content was not what these visitors were expecting to find. In addition, the society received calls from subscribers suggesting that the name needed to change.

In response, *The Beaver* conducted some focused research on its readers and discovered that women readers and readers under 45 years of age had a negative impression of the title. As a result, *The Beaver* has been rebranded as *Canada's History* magazine so that it more accurately reflects the content and its audience's interests.[19]

Whether a research project costs $200 or $2 million, the same general process should be followed. The marketing research process is a scientific approach to decision making that maximizes the chances of getting accurate and meaningful results. Exhibit 7.1 traces the steps: (1) identifying and formulating the problem or opportunity, (2) planning the research design and gathering primary data, (3) specifying the sampling procedures, (4) collecting the data, (5) analyzing the data, (6) preparing and presenting the report, and (7) following up.

The research process begins with the recognition of a marketing problem or opportunity. As changes occur in the company's external environment, marketing managers are faced with these two questions: "Should we change the existing marketing mix?" "If we should, how?" Marketing research can be used to evaluate product, promotion, distribution, and pricing alternatives. It can also be used to find and evaluate new market opportunities.

Though famous for its well-known line of household lubricants, WD-40 Co. has repositioned one of its product lines as essential bathroom cleaners—the result of a research process. Sales of the company's six household product brand lines (of which X-14 is one) make up a sizable percentage—more than 31 percent—of the overall portfolio. However, rival brands were more popular. Which elements in the company's marketing mix could be adjusted to gain more share of the cleaning products market?

SOURCE: © 2008 WD-40 COMPANY. ALL RIGHTS RESERVED

Using marketing research helped the WD-40 Company successfully reposition its X-14 cleaning products in the marketplace. The research also identified opportunities to extend the X-14 brand.

The repositioning of WD-40's X-14 line helped the $287-million company find the brand's niche. "We previously had products that focused on the bathroom, but there wasn't a unified line in its positioning. We had a line of cleaning products that were not meeting their potential in the marketplace," says Heidi Noorany, director of marketing. The marketing research indicated that there was a need for a "bathroom expert" line of products. "We knew we had the positioning and the quality of products within the current line, but we had to communicate it," Noorany adds. That would be translated through the line's more cohesive packaging design characterized by a variety of pinks, oranges, and blues as well as several bottle designs.

Consumer research was also used to measure product effectiveness versus competitors' products. It found that the X-14 Foaming Bathroom Cleaner scored 4.5 on a scale of 1 to 5, and that its Trigger Bathroom Cleaner scored a 91 percent approval rating, placing it higher than four other competing brands. The research also found that consumers engage in two types of cleaning—weekly deep cleanings and quick daily cleanings. "We saw an opportunity for a bathroom expert line of products," says Noorany. Not only did WD-40 learn how to best reposition the X-14 line, but it garnered enough insight from the research process that it could use the data in future product development.[20]

The WD-40 story illustrates an important point about problem or opportunity definition. The **marketing research problem** is information oriented. It involves determining what information is needed and how that information can be obtained efficiently and effectively. The **marketing research objective**, then, is to provide insightful decision-making information. This requires specific pieces of information needed to answer the marketing research problem. Managers must combine this information with their own experience and other information to make a proper decision. WD-40's marketing research problem was to gather information on how

marketing research problem Determining what information is needed and how that information can be obtained efficiently and effectively.

marketing research objective The specific information needed to solve a marketing research problem; the objective should be to provide insightful decision-making information.

management decision problem
A broad-based problem that requires marketing research in order for managers to take proper actions.

secondary data
Data previously collected for any purpose other than the one at hand.

consumers clean and how they shop for cleaning products. The marketing research objective was several-fold: identify a better positioning strategy for X-14 and identify opportunities to add new items to the X-14 brand.

Whereas the marketing research problem is information oriented, the **management decision problem** is action oriented. Management problems tend to be much broader in scope and far more general than marketing research problems, which must be narrowly defined and specific if the research effort is to be successful. Sometimes several research studies must be conducted to solve a broad management problem. The management decision problem was "How do we grow sales of X-14 family brand?" Management then decided to reposition X-14 as The Bathroom Expert—the centre-piece around which its new product line re-enters the market. Completely redesigned, the line provides a family look for the set of products rather than a disjointed set of similar products. Yet it also includes two additions: Foaming Bathroom Cleaner and Bathroom Cleaner, which combines oxy and citrus (hydrogen peroxide with citric acid) for general bathroom cleaning. Additionally, several future products are expected to be released soon.[21]

SECONDARY DATA

A valuable tool throughout the research process but especially in the problem or opportunity identification stage is **secondary data**—data previously collected for any purpose other than the one at hand. Secondary information originating within the firm includes documents such as annual reports, reports to shareholders, product testing results perhaps made available to the news media, and house periodicals composed by the company's personnel for communication to employees, customers, or others. Often this information is incorporated into a company's internal database.

Innumerable outside sources of secondary information also exist, principally in the forms of government (federal, provincial, municipal) departments and agencies that compile and publish summaries of business data. Trade and industry associations also publish secondary data. Still more data are available in business periodicals and other news media that regularly publish studies and articles on the economy, specific industries, and even individual companies. The unpublished summarized secondary information from these sources corresponds to internal reports, memos, or special-purpose analyses with limited circulation. Economic considerations or priorities in the organization may preclude publication of these summaries. Most of the sources listed above can be found on the Internet.

Secondary data save time and money if they help solve the researcher's problem. Even if the problem is not solved, secondary data have other advantages. They can aid in formulating the problem statement and suggest research methods and other types of data needed for solving the problem. In addition, secondary data can pin-point the kinds of people to approach and their locations and serve as a basis of comparison for other data. The disadvantages of secondary data stem mainly from a mismatch between the researcher's unique problem and the purpose for which the secondary data were originally gathered, which typically are different. For example, a major consumer-products manufacturer wanted to determine the market potential for a fireplace log made of coal rather than compressed wood byproducts. The researcher found plenty of secondary data about total wood consumed as fuel, quantities consumed in each province, and types of wood burned. Secondary data were also available about consumer attitudes and purchase patterns of wood byproduct fireplace logs. The wealth of secondary data provided the researcher with many insights into the artificial log market. Yet nowhere was there any information that would tell the company whether consumers would buy artificial logs made of coal.

The quality of secondary data may also pose a problem, especially in its timeliness. Often secondary data sources do not give detailed information that would enable a researcher to assess their quality or relevance. Whenever possible, a researcher needs to address these important questions: Who gathered the data? Why were the data obtained? What methodology was used? How were classifications (such as heavy users versus light users) developed and defined? Finally, when was the

EXHIBIT 7.1

The Marketing Research Process

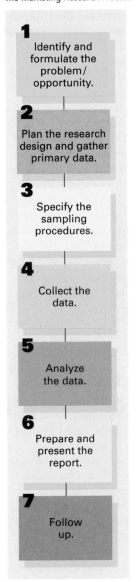

1 Identify and formulate the problem/opportunity.

2 Plan the research design and gather primary data.

3 Specify the sampling procedures.

4 Collect the data.

5 Analyze the data.

6 Prepare and present the report.

7 Follow up.

information gathered? Census data are gathered only every five years, and even though the 2011 Census of Canada precedes the publication date of this text, the first of the data (in the form of basic population counts) will not likely be released until well into 2012. Most of the detailed information and breakdowns are unlikely to be released until more than two years after being collected![22]

THE NEW AGE OF SECONDARY INFORMATION: THE INTERNET

Gathering secondary data, while necessary in almost any research project, has traditionally been a tedious and boring job. The researcher often had to write to government agencies, trade associations, or other secondary data providers and then wait days or weeks for a reply that might never come. Often, one or more trips to the library were required, and the researcher might find that needed reports were checked out or missing. Now, however, the rapid development of the Internet has eliminated much of the drudgery associated with the collection of secondary data.

Finding Secondary Data on the Internet

Virtually all Internet users have a Web browser that is enabled with powerful search engines like Google, Yahoo!, or Ask.com. If you don't know the address of a particular website that contains the secondary data you are searching for, you can type a description of what you are looking for directly into your Web browser's search engine. Each search engine uses its own indexing system to locate relevant information. All of them allow users to enter one or more keywords, which then initiate a search of website databases for all occurrences of those words. They then return listings that allow users to go immediately to the sites described. Remember that the Internet is a self-publishing medium. Your visits to search engines will yield files with a wide range of quality from a variety of sources. So remember to try out multiple sites when you are investigating a topic. A selection of popular sites used by marketing researchers is presented in Exhibit 7.2.

MARKETING RESEARCH AGGREGATORS

marketing research aggregator
A company that acquires, catalogues, reformats, segments, and resells reports already published by marketing research firms.

The **marketing research aggregator** industry is a $120-million business that is growing by about 6 percent a year. Companies in this field acquire, catalogue, reformat, segment, and resell reports already published by large and small marketing research firms. Even Amazon.com has added a marketing research aggregation area to its high-profile e-commerce site.

The role of aggregator firms is growing because their databases of research reports are getting bigger and more comprehensive—and more useful—as marketing research firms get more comfortable using resellers as a sales channel. Meanwhile, advances in Web technology are making the databases easier to search and deliveries speedier. Research aggregators are also indirectly tapping new markets for traditional research firms. By slicing and repackaging research reports into narrower, more specialized sections for resale to small- and medium-sized clients that often cannot afford to commission their own studies or buy full reports, the aggregators are nurturing a new target market for the information.

Prior to the emergence of research aggregators, a lot of marketing research was available only as premium-priced subscription services. Using a market aggregator service, marketing managers can purchase what they need on an à la carte basis and at various prices. For example, Market Research.com recently listed 1,745 reports for various Canadian industry sectors with a wide variety of price ranges. Examples of the segments and costs associated are Lighting Equipment in Canada ($20); Renewable Energy ($250); Mobile Telephones ($500); and Segmenting the Canadian Technology Consumer: Hipsters to Functionalists and Everyone in Between ($3,500). Other aggregators firms include Aarkstore.com, which had 201 reports on the Canadian market, and GDSourcing.com, which had reports on 700 NAFTA industry sectors but also had profile reports on all 10 Canadian provinces at $99 each!

EXHIBIT 7.2

Some Notable Sources of Secondary Data for Marketing Researchers on the Web

Organization	URL	Description
American Marketing Association	www.marketingpower.org	Searches all of the AMA's publications by using keywords.
Building Brands	www.buildingbrands.com	A resource for anyone interested in brands and how to build them.
Canada Business	www.canadabusiness.ca	Provides a wide range of information on government services, programs, and regulations; can answer questions about starting a new business or improving an existing one.
Canada One	www.canadaone.com	Provides access to 1,000+ small business articles, business news, and free business tools. Contains a free Canadian business directory integrated with Google maps that has over 15,000+ verified listings.
Canadian Advertising Rates & Data (CARD)	www.cardmedia.com	CARDonline provides critical advertising rates, data and media planning information for advertising, marketing, PR, and communications professionals in Canada.
Canadian Business	www.canadianbusiness.com	News, opinion, and community for business leaders, entrepreneurs, and investors.
Canadian Institute of Marketing	www.cinstmarketing.ca	Members hold several years of experience at a senior level (with marketing staff supervision responsibilities), or corporate strategic and/or tactical marketing planning positions, or teaching positions in the marketing programs of colleges and universities.
Canadian Marketing Association	www.the-cma.org	The Canadian Marketing Association (CMA) is the largest marketing association in Canada with over 800 members. The CMA serves major business sectors and all marketing disciplines, channels, and technologies in Canada.
Canadian Trade Index	www.ctidirectory.com	Provides detailed information on over 30,000 Canadian companies, featuring nearly 100,000 product listings under more than 20,000 headings.
Click Z Network	www.clickz.com/stats	ClickZ describes itself as "the largest resource of interactive marketing news, information, commentary, advice, opinion, research, and reference in the world, online or off-."
The Dismal Scientist	www.economy.com/dismal	An authoritative site offering timely Global global economic information, including Country country-specific information on Canada such as Canada Business Outlook, Canada Forecast Table, Economic Calendar, and Bank of Canada Coverage.
Equifax	www.equifax.ca	A global provider of consumer and commercial data, along with advanced analytics and proprietary technology.
Financial Post	www.financialpost.com	Provides a broad range of relevant data to help with key business decisions, including the following: magazines and newswires, current financials, data on Canadian companies, and a section on marketing.
Frasers Canadian Trade Directory	www.frasers.com	Provides industrial news and information through on-line publication of the 10 most-read industrial magazines. Also includes Buyer's Guides' and the Fraser's Directory, Canada's largest on-line database of industrial firms.
Government of Canada	canada.gc.ca	Provides a listing of and links to all major Canadian government agencies and departments.
Industry Canada	www.ic.gc.ca	Mission is to foster a growing competitive, knowledge-based Canadian economy. Works with Canadians throughout the economy and in all parts of the country to improve conditions for investment, improve Canada's innovation performance, increase Canada's share of global trade, and build a fair, efficient, and competitive marketplace.
Marketing Magazine	www.marketingmag.ca	Current articles on marketing and advertising in Canada covering media planning and buying, digital marketing, and television, to reports on multicultural marketing, agency rankings, and the out-of-home industry.
Marketing Research Association	www.mra-net.org	An association of the opinion and market research profession with 3,000 members internationally who benefit from programs to assist their professional development, are able to connect with other researchers and the market research community, and can stay abreast of trends occurring in the industry.

EXHIBIT 7.2 (CONTINUED)

Some Notable Sources of Secondary Data for Marketing Researchers on the Web

Organization	URL	Description
Nielsen Media Research	ca.nielsen.com/	One of the world's leading marketing and media information firms; they measure and analyze how people interact with digital platforms, traditional media, and in-store environments, locally as well as globally.
Purchasing Management Association of Canada	www.pmac.ca	Dedicated to serving the needs of the supply management practitioner and the business community by advancing the strategic value of supply management, through continuous learning, standards of practice, advocacy and promotion, research, partnerships, and networking.
Scott's Directories	www.scottsinfo.com	Provides information on 189,000 Canadian organizations including product or service, revenue, year established, square footage, company executives, ISO number, and number of employees.
Standards Council of Canada	www.scc.ca	A Crown corporation, this organization offers programs and services for organizations and individuals that deal directly or indirectly with standardization issues.
Statistics Canada	www.statscan.ca	Provides a wealth of Canadian statistical data, including the Census of Canada and other statistics on the economy, the population, health, education, families, households, culture, leisure and travel, and many other kinds of information.
Strategy Magazine	www.strategymag.com	Current articles on marketing and advertising in Canada.
Transport Canada	www.tc.gc.ca	Statistics and information on Canada's transportation systems and infrastructure.
United Nations	www.un.org	One of the UN's central mandates is the promotion of higher standards of living, full employment, and conditions of economic and social progress and development.
U.S. Census Bureau	www.census.gov	The leading source of quality data about the people and the economy of the United States.
World Trade Organization	www.wto.org	The only global international organization dealing with the rules of trade between nations. Helps producers of goods and services, exporters, and importers conduct their business.

PLANNING THE RESEARCH DESIGN AND GATHERING PRIMARY DATA

research design
Specifies which research questions must be answered, how and when the data will be gathered, and how the data will be analyzed.

primary data
Information collected for the first time; used for solving the particular problem under investigation.

Good secondary data can help researchers conduct a thorough situation analysis. With that information, researchers can list their unanswered questions and rank them. They must then decide on the exact information required to answer the questions. The **research design** specifies which research questions must be answered, how and when the data will be gathered, and how the data will be analyzed. Typically, the project budget is finalized after the research design has been approved.

Sometimes research questions can be answered by gathering more secondary data; otherwise, primary data may be needed. **Primary data**, or information collected for the first time, can be used for solving the particular problem under investigation. The main advantage of primary data is that they will answer a specific research question that secondary data cannot answer. Suppose that fast-food chain Harvey's wants to add a new taco meal to its menu and that it has to decide between a hard or a soft taco. Which one will consumers like better? Secondary data will not help answer this question. Instead, targeted consumers must try each taco meal and evaluate the tastes, textures, appearance, and nutritional value of each. Moreover, primary data are current, and researchers know the source. Sometimes researchers gather the data themselves instead of assigning projects to outside companies. Researchers also specify the methodology of the research. Secrecy can be maintained because the information is proprietary. In contrast, much secondary data are available to all interested parties for relatively small fees or even for free!

Gathering primary data is expensive; costs can range from a few thousand dollars for a limited survey to several million for a nationwide study. For instance, a nationwide, 15-minute telephone interview with 1,000 adult males can cost $50,000 for everything, including a data analysis and report. Because primary data gathering in person is so expensive, many firms now use Internet studies instead. Larger companies that conduct many research projects use another cost-saving technique: they piggy-back studies, or gather data on two different projects using one questionnaire. The drawback is that answering questions about, say, dog food and gourmet coffee may be confusing to respondents. Piggybacking also requires a longer interview (sometimes a half hour or longer), which tires respondents. The quality of the answers typically declines, with people giving curt replies and thinking, "When will this end?" A lengthy interview also makes people less likely to participate in other research surveys.

Nevertheless, the disadvantages of primary data gathering are usually offset by the advantages. It is often the only way of solving a research problem. And with a variety of techniques available for research—including surveys, observations, and experiments—primary research can address almost any marketing question.

Survey Research

The most popular technique for gathering primary data is **survey research**, in which a researcher interacts with people to obtain facts, opinions, and attitudes. Exhibit 7.3 summarizes the characteristics of traditional forms of survey research.

In-Home Personal Interviews. Although in-home personal interviews often provide high-quality information, they tend to be very expensive because of the interviewers' travel time and costs. So they are rapidly disappearing from the marketing researcher's survey toolbox in both North America and Europe. They are, however, still popular in many other countries around the globe.

Mall Intercept Interviews. The **mall intercept interview** is conducted in the common areas of shopping malls or in a market research office within the mall. It is the economy version of the door-to-door interview with personal contact between interviewer and respondent, because the interviewer saves on time and travel costs. To conduct this type of interview, the research company rents office space in the mall or pays a significant daily fee. One drawback is that it is hard to get a representative sample of the population this way.

However, an interviewer can also probe when necessary—a technique used to clarify a person's response. An interviewer might ask, "What did you like best about the salad dressing you just tried?" The respondent might reply, "Taste." This answer doesn't provide a lot of information, so the interviewer could probe by saying, "Can you tell me a little bit more about the taste?" The respondent then elaborates: "Yes, it's not too sweet, it has the right amount of pepper, and I love that hint of garlic."

EXHIBIT 7.3

Characteristics of Traditional Forms of Survey Research

Characteristic	In-Home Personal Interviews	Mall Intercept Interviews	Central-Location Telephone Interviews	Self-Administered and One-Time Mail Surveys	Mail Panel Surveys	Executive Interviews	Focus Groups
Cost	High	Moderate	Moderate	Low	Moderate	High	Low
Time span	Moderate	Moderate	Fast	Slow	Relatively slow	Moderate	Fast
Use of interviewer probes	Yes	Yes	Yes	No	Yes	Yes	Yes
Ability to show concepts to respondent	Yes (also taste tests)	Yes (also taste tests)	No	Yes	Yes	Yes	Yes
Management control over interviewer	Low	Moderate	High	n/a	n/a	Moderate	High
General data quality	High	Moderate	High to moderate	Moderate to low	Moderate	High	Moderate
Ability to collect large amounts of data	High	Moderate	Moderate to low	Low to moderate	Moderate	Moderate	Moderate
Ability to handle complex questionnaires	High	Moderate	High if computer-aided	Low	Low	High	N/A

In the Space Food Systems Laboratory at Johnson Space Center, Canadian astronaut Chris Hadfield tests some rehydrated chocolate cake with journalists. NASA food scientist Vickie Kloeris (back) waits for a reaction. Taste test results are a type of primary data.

computer-assisted personal interviewing
An interviewing method in which the interviewer reads the questions from a computer screen and enters the respondent's data directly into the computer.

computer-assisted self-interviewing
An interviewing method in which a mall interviewer intercepts and directs willing respondents to nearby computers, where the respondent reads questions off a computer screen and directly keys his or her answers into a computer.

central-location telephone (CLT) facility
A specially designed phone room used to conduct telephone interviewing

executive interviews
A type of survey that involves interviewing businesspeople at their offices concerning industrial products or services.

Mall intercept interviews must be brief. Only the shortest ones are conducted while respondents are standing. Usually, researchers invite respondents to their office for interviews, which are still generally less than 15 minutes long. The researchers often show respondents concepts for new products or a test commercial or have them taste a new food product. The overall quality of mall intercept interviews is about the same as telephone interviews.

Marketing researchers are applying computer technology in mall interviewing. The first technique is **computer-assisted personal interviewing**. The researcher conducts in-person interviews, reads questions to the respondent off a computer screen, and directly keys the respondent's answers into the computer. A second approach is **computer-assisted self-interviewing**. A mall interviewer intercepts and directs willing respondents to nearby computers. Each respondent reads questions off a computer screen and directly keys his or her answers into a computer. The third use of technology is fully automated self-interviewing. Respondents are guided by interviewers or independently approach a centrally located computer station or kiosk, read questions off a screen, and directly key their answers into the station's computer.

Telephone Interviews. Compared to the personal interview, the telephone interview costs less, but cost is rapidly increasing due to respondent refusals to participate. Most telephone interviewing is conducted from a specially designed phone room called a **central-location telephone (CLT) facility**. A phone room has many phone lines, individual interviewing stations, sometimes monitoring equipment, and headsets. The research company typically will interview people nationwide from a single location. Canada's National Do Not Call legislation exempts telemarketing calls for survey and opinion research purposes.

Many CLT facilities offer computer-assisted interviewing. The interviewer reads the questions from a computer screen and enters the respondent's data directly into the computer. The researcher can stop the survey at any point and immediately print out the survey results. Thus a researcher can get a sense of the project as it unfolds and fine-tune the research design as necessary. An on-line interviewing system can also save time and money because data entry occurs as the response is recorded rather than as a separate process after the interview. Hallmark Cards found that an interviewer administered a printed questionnaire for its Shoebox Greeting cards in 28 minutes. The same questionnaire administered with computer assistance took only 18 minutes.

Mail Surveys. Mail surveys have several benefits: relatively low cost, elimination of interviewers and field supervisors, centralized control, and actual or promised anonymity for respondents (which may draw more candid responses). Some researchers feel that mail questionnaires give the respondent a chance to reply more thoughtfully and to check records, talk to family members, and so forth. A disadvantage is that mail questionnaires usually produce low response rates.

Low response rates pose a problem because certain elements of the population tend to respond more than others. The resulting sample may therefore not represent the surveyed population. For example, the sample may have too many retired people and too few working people. In this instance, answers to a question about attitudes toward the Canada Pension Plan might indicate a much more favourable overall view of the system than is actually the case. Another serious problem with mail surveys is that no one probes respondents to clarify or elaborate on their answers.

Mail panels like those operated by Toronto-based Ipsos-Reid offer an alternative to the one-shot mail survey. A mail panel consists of a sample of households recruited to participate by mail for a given period. Panel members often receive gifts in return for their participation. Essentially, the panel is a sample used several times. In contrast to one-time mail surveys, the response rates from mail panels are high. Rates of 70 percent (of those who agree to participate) are not uncommon.

Executive Interviews. Marketing researchers use **executive interviews** to conduct the industrial equivalent of door-to-door interviewing. This type of survey involves interviewing businesspeople, at their offices, concerning industrial products or services. For example, if MDG Computers wanted information regarding user preferences for different features that might be offered in a new line of desktop office computers, it would need to interview prospective user-purchasers of office computers. It is appropriate to locate and interview these people at their offices.

This type of interviewing is very expensive. First, individuals involved in the purchase decision for the product in question must be identified and located. Sometimes lists can be obtained from various sources; more frequently, though, screening must be conducted over the telephone. A particular company is likely to have individuals of the type being sought, but locating those people within a large organization can be expensive and time-consuming. Once a qualified person is located, the next step is to get that person to agree to be interviewed and to set a time for the interview. This is not as hard as it might seem because most professionals seem to enjoy talking about their work.

Finally, an interviewer must go to the particular place at the appointed time. Long waits are frequently encountered; cancellations are not uncommon. This type of survey requires the very best interviewers because they are often interviewing on topics they know very little about. Executive interviewing has essentially the same advantages and disadvantages as in-home interviewing.

Focus Groups. A **focus group** is a type of personal interviewing. Often recruited by random telephone screening, seven to ten people with certain desired characteristics form a focus group. These qualified consumers are usually offered an incentive (typically $50 to $75) to participate in a group discussion. The meeting place (sometimes resembling a living room, sometimes featuring a conference table) has audiotaping and perhaps videotaping equipment. It also likely has a viewing room with a one-way mirror so that clients (manufacturers or retailers) can watch the session. During the session, a moderator, hired by the research company, leads the group discussion.

Focus groups are much more than question-and-answer interviews. Market researchers draw a distinction between "group dynamics" and "group interviewing." The interaction provided in **group dynamics** is essential to the success of focus group research; this interaction is the reason for conducting group rather than individual research. One of the essential notions behind group sessions is the idea that a response from one person may become a stimulus for another, thereby generating an interplay of responses that may yield more information than if the same number of people had contributed independently.

Focus groups are occasionally used to brainstorm new product ideas or to screen concepts for new products. Ford Motor Company, for example, asked consumers to drive several automobile prototypes. These "test drivers" were then brought together in focus groups. During the discussions, consumers complained that they were scuffing their shoes because the rear seats lacked foot room. In response, Ford sloped the floor underneath the front seats, widened the space between the seat adjustment

focus group
Seven to ten people who participate in a group discussion led by a moderator.

group dynamics
Group interaction essential to the success of focus group research.

SOURCE: © PURESTOCK/JUPITER IMAGES

Focus groups can be used to gauge consumer response to a product or promotion and are occasionally used to brainstorm new product ideas.

tracks, and made the tracks in the Taurus and Sable models out of smooth plastic instead of metal.

Lewis Stone, former manager of Colgate-Palmolive's research and development division, says the following about focus groups:

"If it weren't for focus groups, Colgate-Palmolive Co. might never know that some women squeeze their bottles of dishwashing soap, others squeeeeeze them, and still others squeeeeeeeeeeze out the desired amount. Then there are the ones who use the soap "neat." That is, they put the product directly on a sponge or washcloth and wash the dishes under running water until the suds run out. Then they apply more detergent."

Stone was explaining how body language, exhibited during focus groups, provides insights into a product that are not apparent from reading questionnaires on habits and practices. Focus groups represent a most efficient way of learning how one's products are actually used in the home. By drawing out the panelists to describe in detail how they do certain tasks, you can learn a great deal about possible need-gaps that could be filled by new or improved products, and also how a new product might be received. It is estimated that over 600,000 focus groups are conducted around the world each year.[23]

A new system by FocusVision Network allows client companies and advertising agencies to view live focus groups from distant locations. For example, the private satellite network would allow a researcher in Toronto to observe an Edmonton focus group and control two cameras in the viewing room. The researcher can get a full-group view or a close-up, and zoom in on or pan across the participants. The researcher can also communicate directly with the moderator using an ear receiver. Ogilvy Mather, a large advertising agency whose clients include StarKist SeaFoods, Seagram's, MasterCard, and Burger King, has installed this system.

Increasingly, focus groups are being conducted on-line. On-line focus groups are examined in detail later in the chapter.

Questionnaire Design

All forms of survey research require a questionnaire. Questionnaires ensure that all respondents will be asked the same series of questions. Questionnaires include three basic types of questions: open-ended, closed-ended, and scaled-response (see Exhibit 7.4). An **open-ended question** encourages an answer phrased in the respondent's own words. Researchers get a rich array of information based on the respondent's frame of reference. In contrast, a **closed-ended question** asks the respondent to make a selection from a limited list of responses. Traditionally, marketing researchers separate the two-choice question (called *dichotomous*) from the many-item type (often called *multiple choice*). A **scaled-response question** is a closed-ended question designed to measure the intensity of a respondent's answer.

Closed-ended and scaled-response questions are easier to tabulate than open-ended questions because response choices are fixed. On the other hand, unless the researcher designs the closed-ended question very carefully, an important choice may be omitted.

Suppose a food study asked this question: "Besides meat, which of the following items do you normally add to a taco that you prepare at home?"

Avocado	1	Olives (black/ or green)	6
Cheese (Monterey Jack/cheddar)	2	Onions (red/ or white)	7
Guacamole	3	Peppers (red/ or green)	8
Lettuce	4	Pimento	9
Mexican hot sauce	5	Sour cream	0

The list seems complete, doesn't it? However, consider the following responses: "I usually add a green, avocado-tasting hot sauce"; "I cut up a mixture of lettuce and spinach"; "I'm a vegetarian; I don't use meat at all. My taco is filled only with guacamole." How would you code these replies? As you can see, the question needs an "other" category.

A good question must also be clear and concise, and ambiguous language must be avoided. Take the question "Do you live within 10 minutes of here?" The answer depends on the mode of transportation (maybe the

open-ended question
An interview question that encourages an answer phrased in the respondent's own words.

closed-ended question
An interview question that asks the respondent to make a selection from a limited list of responses.

scaled-response question
A closed-ended question designed to measure the intensity of a respondent's answer.

EXHIBIT 7.4

Types of Questions Found on Questionnaires for National Market Research

Open-Ended Questions	Closed-Ended Questions	Scaled-Response Question
1. What advantages, if any, do you think ordering from a mail-order catalogue offers compared to shopping at a local retail outlet? (*Probe:* What else?)	Dichotomous 1. Did you heat the Danish product before serving it? Yes. . . . . 1 No. . . . . 2 2. The federal government doesn't care what people like me think. Agree. . . . . 1 Disagree 2	Now that you have used the rug cleaner, would you say that you . . . *(Circle one.)* Would definitely buy it . . . . 1 Would probably buy it . . . . .2 Might or might not buy it. . . . . 3 Probably would not buy it . . . . 4 Definitely would not buy it 5
2. Why do you have one or more of your rugs or carpets professionally cleaned rather than cleaning them yourself or having someone else in the household clean them?	**Multiple choice**	
3. What is there about the colour of the eye shadow that makes you like it the best?	3. I'd like you to think back to the last footwear of any kind that you bought. I'll read you a list of descriptions and would like you to tell me which category they fall into. *(Read list and circle proper category.)* Dress and/or formal . . . . 1 Casual . . . . 2 Canvas/trainer/gym shoes. . . . . 3 Specialized athletic shoes . . . . 4 Boots. 5	
	4. In the last three months, have you used Noxzema skin cream . . . *(Circle all that apply.)* As a facial wash. . . . . 1 For moisturizing the skin . . . . 2 For treating blemishes . . . . 3 For cleansing the skin. . . . . 4 For treating dry skin . . . . 5 For softening skin. . . . . 6 For sunburn . . . . 7 For making the facial skin smooth 8	

person walks), driving speed, perceived time, and other factors. Instead, respondents should see a map with certain areas highlighted and be asked whether they live in one of those areas.

Clarity also implies using reasonable terminology. A questionnaire is not intended to be a vocabulary test so jargon should be avoided, and language use should be geared to the target audience. A question such as "What is the level of efficacy of your preponderant dishwasher powder?" would probably be greeted by a lot of blank stares. It would be much simpler to say: "Are you (1) very satisfied, (2) somewhat satisfied, or (3) not satisfied with your current brand of dishwasher powder?"

Stating the survey's purpose at the beginning of the interview also improves clarity. The respondents should understand the study's intentions and the interviewer's expectations. Sometimes, of course, to get an unbiased response, the interviewer must disguise the true purpose of the study. If an interviewer says, "We're conducting an image study for the Bank of Nova Scotia," and then proceeds to ask a series of questions about the bank, chances are that the responses will be biased. Many times respondents will try to provide answers they believe are "correct" or that the interviewer wants to hear.

A question should also be unbiased. A question such as "Have you purchased any quality Canadian Tire Mastercraft tools in the past six months?" biases respondents to think of the topic in a certain way (in this case, to link quality with Canadian Tire Mastercraft tools). Questions can also be leading: "Weren't you pleased with the good service you received last night at the Chateau Laurier Hotel?" (The respondent is all but instructed to say "yes.") These examples are quite obvious; unfortunately, bias is usually subtler. Even an interviewer's clothing or gestures can create bias.

Finally, to ensure clarity, the interviewer should avoid asking two questions in one—for example, "How did you like the taste and texture of your chocolate-flavoured McCain Triple Chill cake?" This question should be divided into two questions, one concerning taste and the other texture.

Observation Research

In contrast to survey research, **observation research** depends on watching what people do. Specifically, it can be defined as the systematic process of recording the behavioural patterns of people, objects, and occurrences without questioning or communicating with them. A market researcher using the observation technique witnesses and records information as events occur or compiles evidence from records of past events. Carried a step further, observation may involve watching people or phenomena and may be conducted by human observers or machines. Examples of these various observational situations are shown in Exhibit 7.5.

Two common forms of people-watching-people research are one-way mirror observations and mystery shoppers.

At the Fisher-Price Play Laboratory, children are invited to spend 12 sessions playing with toys. Toy designers watch through one-way mirrors to see how children react to Fisher-Price's and other makers' toys. Fisher-Price had difficulty designing a toy lawn mower that children would play with. A designer, observing behind the mirror, noticed the children's fascination with soap bubbles. He then created a lawn mower that spewed soap bubbles. It sold more than a million units in the first year.

Mystery shoppers are researchers posing as customers who gather observational data about a store (i.e., are the shelves neatly stocked?) and collect data about customer–employee interactions. In the latter case, of course, there is communication between the mystery shopper and the employee. The mystery shopper may ask, "How much is this item?" "Do you have this in blue?" "Can you deliver this by Friday?" The interaction is not an interview, and communication occurs only so that the mystery shopper can observe the actions and comments of the employee. Mystery shopping is, therefore, classified as an observational marketing research method even though communication is often involved.

Mystery shopping can provide a variety of benefits and insights, including the following:

- Enabling an organization to monitor compliance with product or service delivery standards and specifications (many clothing retailers require their sales staff to make three attempts to sell "add-ons" to each customer—would you like a bracelet, belt, and hat to go with that blouse?).
- Enabling marketers to examine the gap between promises made through advertising or sales promotion and actual service delivery.
- Helping monitor the impact of training and performance improvement initiatives.
- Identifying differences in the customer experience across different times of day, locations, product or service types, and other potential sources of variation in product or service quality.[24]

Mystery shopping typically has three different levels:

Level 1—The mystery shopper either makes a phone call or shops on-line. The mystery shopper follows a fixed script or set of instructions and evaluates the level of service. The scenario would involve a live on-line conversation with a service representative. For example, the mystery shopper claims that she is having a problem with some software that she recently purchased from the firm.

Hundreds of children tested hundreds of toys at a recent Toys"R"Us opening to come up with a list of the season's favourites.

SOURCE: © AP IMAGES/RICHARD DREW

EXHIBIT 7.5

Situation	Example
People watching people	Observers stationed in supermarkets watch consumers select frozen Mexican dinners; the purpose is to see how much comparison shopping people do at the point of purchase.
People watching phenomena	Observer stationed at an intersection counts traffic moving in various directions.
Machines watching people	Movie or videotape cameras record behaviour as in the people-watching-people example above.
Machines watching phenomena	Traffic-counting machines monitor traffic flow.

Level 2—The mystery shopper visits an establishment and makes a quick purchase with very little, if any, customer-service employee interaction. For example, buying gasoline at a Petro-Canada service station or going to a movie at a Cineplex-Odeon movie theatre. The shopper evaluates the purchase and the image of the facility.

Level 3—The mystery shopper visits a business and has significant interaction with the personnel. Recently, the Automobile Protection Association of Canada (APA) undertook an evaluation of the sales and marketing tactics of 34 used-car dealers in Vancouver and Toronto using mystery shoppers. The mystery shoppers posed as typical car buyers and asked the used-car dealerships to disclose the histories of the vehicles they were buying. The APA found that only one-third of the dealerships provided complete and truthful information about the used vehicles they were selling. The remaining two-thirds either failed to disclose vehicle history information or actually misrepresented the information. For example, some dealers represented cars as "one owner" vehicles when they were in fact "daily" rental vehicles that had been driven by hundreds of different drivers. Another car was presented as having been in a minor accident when in fact it was actually made up of two completely different vehicles, the front half of one welded to the rear half of the other to make one whole car.[25]

Although consumer protection is one purpose behind mystery shopping, most marketers use mystery shopping as a motivator for employees but also as a coaching tool when results are not meeting standards. Thus mystery shopping is ultimately a monitor of quality assurance.

Ethnographic Research

Ethnographic research comes to marketing from the field of anthropology. The technique is becoming increasingly popular in commercial marketing research. **Ethnographic research**, or the study of human behaviour in its natural context, involves observation of behaviour and physical setting. Ethnographers directly observe the population they are studying. As "participant observers," ethnographers can use their intimacy with the people they are studying to gain richer, deeper insights into culture and behaviour—in short, what makes people do what they do. Ethnographers often question those being observed to gain a fuller understanding of what they are seeing.

ethnographic research
The study of human behaviour in its natural context; involves observation of behaviour and physical setting.

Ethnographers can record

- what is happening, including what objects are being created or manipulated.
- where it is happening.
- flow of what is happening.
- order of what is happening.
- time spent on what is happening.
- who is doing what.
- what is being communicated verbally and nonverbally.
- reactions of the various participants (which are critical).[26]

Advertising agency Ogilvy Canada used an ethnographic research approach to develop a promotional campaign for Unilever Canada's Dove Soap brand. Ogilvy employees, along with client representatives, went into consumers' homes and talked to them about how they used Unilever brands including Dove, how they were using competitors' brands, and how the various products fit into their daily lives. Nancy Vonk of Ogilvy comments: "People quickly lose their inhibitions and just start doing their own thing. If [they] feel comfortable with [you], people are pretty forthcoming, and I think they appreciate being asked about their lives." When they returned to the workplace, the agency and client researchers reviewed their experiences and came up with ideas that became part of the Dove promotional campaign.

As a result of the research findings, Ogilvy developed two objectives for Dove. It wanted to invite women and their daughters to workshops on self-esteem held across Canada, and it wanted to make the Dove Self-Esteem Fund visible. To accomplish these objectives, Ogilvy created a series of short on-line films. One of the films, entitled "Daughters," showed young women from Halifax and Toronto talking "about the effect of unrealistic beauty standards in their lives." The second film, called "Evolution," presented "a demonstration of the simple truth that models only look like models after hairstylists, make-up artists, lighting guys and retouchers have created the illusion of beauty." The outcome of the campaign efforts greatly exceeded expectations. Carey Toane, writing in *Strategy* magazine. comments, "The workshops sold out. Within two weeks, over two million people had seen the films on the web. 'Evolution' appeared globally on talk shows and news programs, including BBC Breakfast, Good Morning America, Today and Ellen. It made the front page of the Toronto Star. Ad Age wrote that the YouTube posting generated three times more responses than the previous year's Super Bowl commercial. . . . Dove sales are up and . . . the ads were seen by over 300 million people around the world and with an estimated media value of over $150 million."[27]

Observation Research and Virtual Shopping

Advances in computer technology have enabled researchers to simulate an actual retail store environment on a computer screen. Depending on the type of simulation, a shopper can "pick up" a package by touching its image on the monitor and rotate it to examine all sides. Like buying from most on-line retailers, the shopper touches the shopping cart to add an item to the basket. During the shopping process, the computer unobtrusively records the amount of time the consumer spends shopping in each product category, the time the consumer spends examining each side of a package, the quantity of product the consumer purchases, and the order in which items are purchased.

Computer-simulated environments like this one offer a number of advantages over older research methods. First, unlike focus groups, concept tests, and other laboratory approaches, the virtual store duplicates the distracting clutter of an actual market. Consumers can shop in an environment with a realistic level of complexity and variety. Second, researchers can set up and alter the tests very quickly. Once images of the product are scanned into the computer, the researcher can make changes in the assortment of brands, product packaging, pricing, promotions, and shelf space within minutes. Data collection is also fast and error-free because the information generated by the purchase is automatically tabulated and stored by the computer. Third, production costs are low because displays are created electronically. Once the hardware and software are in place, the cost of a test is largely a function of the number of respondents, who generally are given a small incentive to participate. Fourth, the simulation has a high degree of flexibility. It can be used to test entirely new marketing concepts or to fine-tune existing programs. The simulation also makes it possible to eliminate much of the noise that exists in field experiments.[28]

Kimberly-Clark has refined the virtual shopping experience even more. Located in Appleton, Wisconsin, the firm's virtual testing lab has a woman standing in a room surrounded by three screens showing a store aisle, a retina-tracking device recording her every glance. Asked by a Kimberly-Clark researcher to find a "big box" of Huggies Natural Fit diapers in size three, she pushed forward on a handle like that of a shopping cart, and the video simulated her progress down the aisle. Spotting Huggies' red packages, she turned the handle to the right to face a dizzying array of diapers. After pushing a button to get a kneeling view of the shelves, she reached forward and tapped the screen to put the box she wanted in her virtual cart. Kimberly-Clark hopes these virtual shopping aisles will help it better understand consumer behaviour and make the testing of new products faster, more convenient, and more precise.[29]

Kimberly-Clark's lab also features a U-shaped floor-to-ceiling screen that recreates in vivid detail interiors of the big retailers that sell the company's products—a tool that the company will use in presentations to executives in bids to win shelf space. A separate area is reserved for real replicas of store interiors, which can be customized to match the flooring, light fixtures and shelves of retailers such as Target Corp. and Walmart Stores, Inc.[30]

Kimberly-Clark says its studio allows researchers and designers to get a fast read on new product designs and displays without having to stage real-life tests in the early stages of development. Doing the research in a windowless basement, rather than an actual test market, also avoids tipping off competitors early in the development process. "We're trying to test ideas faster, cheaper, and better," says Ramin Eivaz, a vice-president at Kimberly-Clark focusing on strategy. Before, new product testing typically took eight months to two years. Now, that time is cut in half, he says. Projects that test well with the virtual-reality tools will be fast-tracked to real-store trials.[31]

Experiments

experiment
A method a researcher can use to gather primary data.

An **experiment** is a method a researcher can use to gather primary data. The researcher alters one or more variables—price, package design, shelf space, advertising theme, advertising expenditures—while observing the effects of those alterations on another variable (usually sales). The best experiments are those in which all factors are held constant except the ones being manipulated. The researcher can then observe that changes in sales, for example, result from changes in the amount of money spent on advertising.

Holding all other factors constant in the external environment is a monumental and costly, if not impossible, task. Such factors as competitors' actions, weather, and economic conditions are beyond the researcher's control. Yet market researchers have ways to account for the ever-changing external environment. Mars, the candy company, was losing sales to other candy companies. Traditional surveys showed that the shrinking candy bar was not perceived as a good value. Mars wondered whether a bigger bar sold at the same price would increase sales enough to offset the higher ingredient costs. The company designed an experiment in which the marketing mix stayed the same in different markets but the size of the candy bar varied. The substantial increase in sales of the bigger bar quickly proved that the additional costs would be more than covered by the additional revenue. Mars increased the bar size—and its market share and profits.

Specifying the Sampling Procedures

Once the researchers decide how they will collect primary data, their next step is to select the sampling procedures they will use. A firm can seldom take a census of all possible users of a new product, nor can they all be interviewed. So a company must select a sample of the group to be interviewed. A **sample** is a subset from a larger population.

Several questions must be answered before a sampling plan is chosen. First, the population, or **universe**, of interest must be defined. This is the group from which the sample will be drawn. It should include all the people whose opinions, behaviour, preferences, attitudes, and so on are of interest to the marketer. For example, in a study whose purpose is to determine the market for a new canned dog food, the universe might be defined to include all current buyers of canned dog food.

After the universe has been defined, the next question is whether the sample must be representative of the population. If the answer is yes, a probability sample is needed. Otherwise, a nonprobability sample might be considered.

sample
A subset from a large population.

universe
The population from which a sample will be drawn.

Probability Samples

A **probability sample** is a sample in which every element in the population has a known statistical likelihood of being selected. Its most desirable feature is that scientific rules can be used to ensure that the sample represents the population.

One type of probability sample is a **random sample**—a sample arranged in such a way that every element of the population has an equal chance of being selected as part of the sample. For example, suppose a university is interested in getting a cross-section of student opinions on a proposed sports complex to be built using student

probability sample
A sample in which every element in the population has a known statistical likelihood of being selected.

random sample
A sample arranged in such a way that every element of the population has an equal chance of being selected as part of the sample.

EXHIBIT 7.6

Types of Samples

Probability Samples	
Simple Random Sample	Every member of the population has a known and equal chance of selection.
Stratified Sample	The population is divided into mutually exclusive groups (such as gender or age); then random samples are drawn from each group.
Cluster Sample	The population is divided into mutually exclusive groups (such as geographic areas); then a random sample of clusters is selected. The researcher then collects data from all the elements in the selected clusters or from a probability sample of elements within each selected cluster.
Systematic Sample	A list of the population is obtained—e.g., all persons with a chequing account at the local branch of XYZ Bank—and a *skip interval* is obtained by dividing the sample size by the population size. If the sample size is 100 and the bank branch has 1,000 customers, the skip interval is 10. The beginning number is randomly chosen within the skip interval. If the beginning number is 8, then the skip pattern would be 8, 18, 28. . . .
Nonprobability Sample	
Convenience Sample	The researcher selects the easiest population members from which to obtain information.
Judgement Sample	The researcher's selection criteria are based on personal judgment that the elements (persons) chosen will likely give accurate information.
Quota Sample	The researcher finds a prescribed number of people in several categories—e.g., owners of large dogs versus owners of small dogs. Respondents are not selected on probability sampling criteria.
Snowball Sample	Additional respondents are selected on the basis of referrals from the initial respondents. This method is used when a desired type of respondent is hard to fine—e.g., persons who have taken round-the-world cruises in the last three years. This technique employs the old adage "Birds of a feather flock together."

activity fees. If the university can acquire an up-to-date list of all the enrolled students, it can draw a random sample by using random numbers from a table (found in most statistics books) to select students from the list. Common forms of probability and nonprobability samples are shown in Exhibit 7.6.

NONPROBABILITY SAMPLES

Any sample in which little or no attempt is made to get a representative cross-section of the population can be considered a **nonprobability sample**. Therefore, the probability of selection of each sampling unit is not known. A common form of a nonprobability sample is the **convenience sample**, which uses respondents who are convenient or readily accessible to the researcher—for instance, employees, friends, or relatives. Nonprobability samples are acceptable as long as the researcher understands their nonrepresentative nature. Because of their lower cost, nonprobability samples are the basis of much marketing research.

TYPES OF ERRORS

Whenever a sample is used in marketing research, two major types of error may occur: measurement error and sampling error. **Measurement error** occurs when there is a difference between the information desired by the researcher and the information provided by the measurement process. For example, people may tell an interviewer that they drink milk daily when they do not. Measurement error generally tends to be larger than sampling error.

Sampling error occurs when a sample somehow does not represent the target population. Sampling error can be of several types. **Nonresponse error** occurs when the sample actually interviewed differs from the sample drawn. This error happens because the original people selected to be interviewed either refused to cooperate or were inaccessible. For example, people who feel embarrassed about their weight may refuse to talk about weight loss programs.

Frame error, another type of sampling error, arises when the sample drawn from a population differs from the target population. Suppose a telephone survey is conducted to find out Toronto milk drinkers' attitudes toward milk consumption. If a

nonprobability sample
Any sample in which little or no attempt is made to get a representative cross-section of the population.

convenience sample
A form of nonprobability sample using respondents who are convenient or readily accessible to the researcher—for example, employees, friends, or relatives.

measurement error
An error that occurs when there is a difference between the information desired by the researcher and the information provided by the measurement process.

sampling error
An error that occurs when a sample somehow does not represent the target population.

nonresponse error
An error that occurs when the sample that responds is different from the sample that was selected.

frame error
An error that occurs when a sample drawn from a population differs from the target population.

Toronto telephone directory is used as the *frame* (the device or list from which the respondents are selected), the survey will contain a frame error. Not all Toronto milk drinkers have a phone, and many phone numbers are unlisted. An ideal sample (for example, a sample with no frame error) matches all important characteristics of the target population to be surveyed. Could you find a perfect frame for Toronto milk drinkers?

random error
An error that occurs when the selected sample is an imperfect representation of the overall population.

Random error occurs when the selected sample is an imperfect representation of the overall population. Random error represents how accurately the chosen sample's true average (mean) value reflects the population's true average (mean) value. For example, we might take a random sample of milk drinkers in Toronto and find that 16% regularly drink chocolate milk. The next day we might repeat the same sampling procedure and discover that 14% regularly drink chocolate milk. The difference is due to random error.

Error is common to all surveys, yet it is often not reported or is under-reported. Typically, the only error mentioned in a written report is sampling error (e.g., the poll results will be correct 19 out of 20 times). When errors are ignored, misleading results produce poor information, which can lead to bad decision making.

Collecting the Data

field service firm
A company that specializes in interviewing respondents on a subcontracted basis.

Marketing research field service companies collect most primary data. A **field service firm** specializes in interviewing respondents on a subcontracted basis. Many have offices, often in malls, throughout the country. A typical marketing research study

Global Perspectives

THE CHALLENGES OF GLOBAL MARKETING RESEARCH

Karl Feld, research manager at marketing research firm D3 Systems Incorporated, explains how global research can create unique problems. The story is told in his words.

Imagine you're driving a vehicle of unknown manufacture with dials you can't read down a muddy or dusty dirt track with no name to find a house with no number to make sure your contractor's employee interviewed the right respondent in a language you don't speak. You've been doing this for days, maybe even weeks. There's no running water, no electricity, no telephones, no mail service and possibly no food other than what you've brought with you. Welcome to collecting research data from most of the world's people.

Questionnaire design in multicultural, multilingual research must use both the proper language and cultural context to elicit the desired responses. Context applies both to the language in the survey and the way it is administered, which is often more important than the questionnaire design itself. People in some cultures better relate to conversational interviewing styles than fixed questionnaire order. Some cultures require sensitive questions to be in a different order than others. In some places, people will only talk in particular settings. In research that I conducted in Bosnia-Herzegovina, for example, questionnaires had to be administered in a neutral location not affiliated with any local ethnic group.

Similarly, research in Arabic Muslim countries that involves women generally must be conducted under the watchful eyes of the responsible male family leader, as social custom requires women not meet with outsiders without male presence. In Russia,

it used to be extremely difficult to get face-to-face interviews inside people's homes. Public places were preferred. In Japan, it is only in private places like the home that face-to-face interviews will capture meaningful data.

In my experience in yesterday's Russia and Moldova, and in today's China, respondents asked questions of substance often will refuse to provide meaningful answers without approval from another authority. This is especially the case when interviewing professionals. Appropriate lag time or preapproval needs to be factored into timelines and interviewing environment to allow for this phenomenon.

I was also involved in a research study completed in South Africa. The study's sample frame was to draw from all adults in South Africa. Given that many South African villages lack building addresses, roads, and convenient grid layouts, sampling had to be designed using satellite maps to select dwelling units using an interval formula.

A similar problem exists in Mexico, where streets are unidentified and houses unnumbered, compounded by walls and servants who keep strangers out. In Saudi Arabia, there is no officially recognized census of population and there are no elections and therefore no voter registration records or maps of population centres.[32]

Do you think that conducting research in developing countries is worth the effort? Do you think that doing marketing research in Western Europe is the same as in Canada?

SOURCE: KARL FELD, "DO YOU KNOW WHERE YOUR DATA CAME FROM?" QUIRK'S MARKETING RESEARCH REVIEW, NOVEMBER 2007, 24–31.

involves data collection in several cities and possibly different countries, requiring the marketer to work with a comparable number of field service firms. The Global Perspectives Box reports on some of the situations that arise for marketing researchers who work for field service firms that undertake research on international markets. Besides conducting interviews, field service firms provide focus group facilities, mall intercept locations, test product storage, and kitchen facilities to prepare test food products.

Analyzing the Data

After collecting the data, the marketing researcher proceeds to the next step in the research process: data analysis. The purpose of this analysis is to interpret and draw conclusions from the mass of collected data. The marketing researcher tries to organize and analyze those data by applying one or more techniques common to marketing research: one-way frequency counts, cross-tabulations, and more sophisticated statistical analyses. Of these three techniques, one-way frequency counts are the simplest. One-way frequency tables record the responses to a question. For example, the answers to the question "What brand of microwave popcorn do you buy most often?" would provide a one-way frequency distribution. One-way frequency tables are always done in data analysis, at least as a first step, because they provide the researcher with a general picture of the study's results.

A **cross-tabulation**, or "cross-tab," lets the analyst look at the responses to one question in relation to the responses to one or more other questions. For example, what is the association between gender and the brand of microwave popcorn bought most frequently? Hypothetical answers to this question are shown in Exhibit 7.7.

cross-tabulation
A method of analyzing data that lets the analyst look at the responses to one question in relation to the responses to one or more other questions.

EXHIBIT 7.7

Hypothetical Cross-Tabulation Between Gender and Brand of Microwave Popcorn Purchased Most Frequently

Brand	Purchase by Gender (%)	
	Male	Female
Orville Redenbacher	31	48
T.V. Time	12	6
Pop Rite	38	4
Act II	7	23
Weight Watchers	4	18
Other	8	0

Although the Orville Redenbacher brand was popular with both males and females, it was more popular with females. Compared to females, males strongly preferred Pop Rite; females were more likely than males to buy Weight Watchers popcorn.

Researchers can use many other more powerful and sophisticated statistical techniques, such as hypothesis testing, measures of association, and regression analysis. A description of these techniques goes beyond the scope of this book but can be found in any good marketing research textbook. The use of sophisticated statistical techniques depends on the researchers' objectives and the nature of the data gathered.

PREPARING AND PRESENTING THE REPORT

After data analysis has been completed, the researcher must prepare the report and communicate the conclusions and recommendations to management. This is a key step in the process. If the marketing researcher wants managers to carry out the recommendations, he or she must convince them that the results are credible, as well as justified by the data collected.

Researchers are usually required to present both written and oral reports on the project. Today the written report is no more than a copy of the Microsoft PowerPoint slides used in the oral presentation. Both reports, though, should be tailored to the audience. They should begin with a clear, concise statement of the research objectives, followed by a complete, but brief and simple, explanation of the research design or methodology employed. A summary of major findings should come next. The conclusion of the report should also present recommendations to management.

Most people who enter marketing will become research users rather than research suppliers. Thus they must know what to notice in a report. As with many other items we purchase, quality is not always readily apparent. Nor does a high price guarantee superior quality. The basis for measuring the quality of a marketing research report is the research proposal. Did the report meet the objectives established in the proposal? Was the methodology outlined in the proposal followed? Are the conclusions based on logical deductions from the data analysis? Do the recommendations seem prudent, given the conclusions?

FOLLOWING UP

The final step in the marketing research process is to follow up. The researcher should determine why management did or did not carry out the recommendations in the report. Was sufficient decision-making information included? What could have

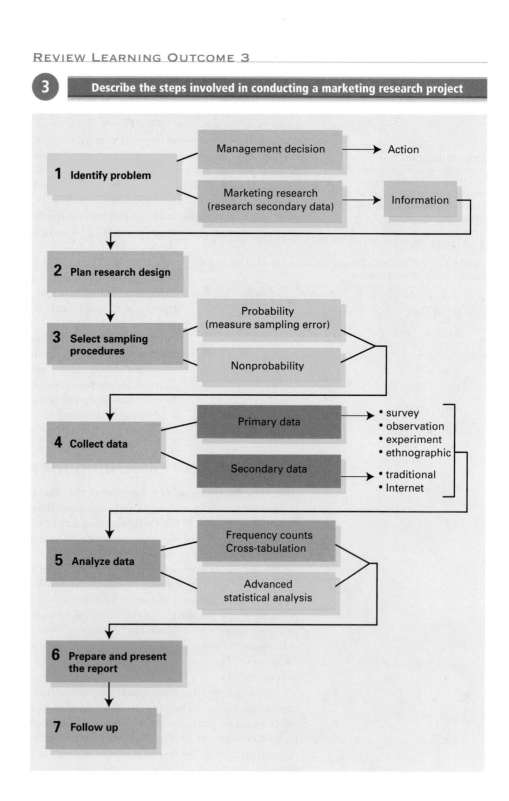

3 Describe the steps involved in conducting a marketing research project

been done to make the report more useful to management? A good rapport between the product manager, or whoever authorized the project, and the market researcher is essential. Often they must work together on many studies throughout the year.

THE PROFOUND IMPACT OF THE INTERNET ON MARKETING RESEARCH

Discuss the profound impact of the Internet on marketing research

The way that survey research is conducted has changed forever because of the Internet. Worldwide, the penetration among the population of Internet usage continues to increase at triple-digit rates. The most recent estimates place it at 26.6 percent among the world population; North America has the highest level of population penetration at over 76 percent. As the number of users grows worldwide, the characteristics of a country's population and of Internet users tend to meld.[33] Consequently, new techniques and new ways of conducting traditional marketing research are coming on-line in increasing numbers every day. In Canada, Internet marketing research revenues have been growing steadily. It has been estimated that the portion of revenue derived from marketing research is approaching 40 percent for some of Canada's largest research companies.[34] Today, on-line survey research has replaced computer-assisted telephone interviewing (CATI) as the most popular mode of data collection.[35] Internet data collection is also rated as having the greatest potential for further growth. Having said this, we must also report that there is no sign that other types of surveys are disappearing—two-thirds of the market research companies are still relying on them.[36] There are several reasons for the success of Internet marketing research:

- It allows for better and faster decision making through rapid access to business intelligence.
- It improves the ability to respond quickly to customer needs and market shifts.
- It makes follow-up studies and longitudinal research much easier to conduct and more fruitful.
- It slashes labour- and time-intensive research activities (and associated costs), including mailing, telephone solicitation, data entry, data tabulation, and reporting.

ADVANTAGES OF INTERNET SURVEYS

The huge growth in the popularity of Internet (see Exhibit 7.8) surveys is the result of the many advantages offered by the Internet. The specific advantages of Internet surveys are related to many factors:

- *Rapid development, real-time reporting.* Internet surveys can be broadcast to thousands of potential respondents simultaneously. Respondents complete surveys simultaneously, then results are tabulated and posted for corporate clients to view as the returns arrive. The survey results can be in a client's hands in significantly less time than would be required for traditional surveys.
- *Dramatically reduced costs.* The Internet can cut costs by 25 to 40 percent and provide results in half the time it takes to do traditional telephone surveys. Data collection costs account for a large proportion of any traditional market research budget. Telephone surveys are labour-intensive efforts incurring training, telecommunications, and management costs. Electronic methods eliminate these completely. Costs for traditional survey techniques rise proportionally with the number of interviews desired; by contrast, e-solicitations can grow in volume with little increase in project costs.
- *Personalized questions and data.* Internet surveys can be highly personalized for greater relevance to each respondent's own situation, thus speeding the response process. Respondents enjoy a personalized survey because they are being asked to

EXHIBIT 7.8

Internet Usage Worldwide, 2009

	% Population	(millions)
North America	76.2	260
(Canada)	(74.9)	(25)
Oceana/Australia	60.8	21
Europe	53.0	426
Latin America/Caribbean	31.9	18
Asia	20.1	764
Middle East	28.8	58
Africa	8.7	86
Total	26.6	1,802

SOURCE: www.internetworldstats.com, accessed May 11, 2010. Copyright © 2000–2010, Miniwatts Marketing Group. All rights reserved worldwide.

answer only pertinent questions, can pause and resume the survey as needed, and can see previous responses and correct inconsistencies.

- *Improved respondent participation.* Busy respondents may be growing increasingly intolerant of "snail mail" and telephone-based surveys. Internet surveys take half as much time to complete as phone interviews, can be accomplished at the respondent's convenience (i.e., after work), and are much more stimulating and engaging. Graphics, interactivity, links to incentive sites, and real-time summary reports make the interview enjoyable. The result? Much higher response rates.
- *Contact with the hard to reach.* Certain groups—doctors, high-income professionals, top management in Global 2000 companies—are among the most surveyed on the planet and the most difficult to reach. Many of these groups are well represented on-line. Internet surveys provide convenient access that is not dependent on time of day or location so they make it easy for busy professionals to participate.

Lee Smith, the chief operating officer of the digital marketing research company Insight Express, conducted a side-by-side comparison of on-line research and mail surveys. He found that on-line research delivered data of the same quality as mail surveys in one-eighth the time and at one-eighth the cost.[37] Other research has shown that in most countries where the Internet penetration rate exceeds 20 percent, on-line surveys tend to yield very similar results to those found in traditional forums such as telephone or paper-and-pencil survey research.[38]

SOURCE: COURTESY OF IPSOS CANADA

The Internet is becoming a powerful tool in marketing research with an average of 25 million Canadians visiting the Web each month and 75 percent of Canadians on-line. Ipsos-Reid, a leading Canadian market research company, uses the Internet to gather data about customers and their opinions.

USES OF THE INTERNET BY MARKETING RESEARCHERS

Marketing researchers are using the Internet to administer surveys, conduct focus groups and observation research, and perform a variety of other types of marketing research.

Methods of Conducting On-line Surveys

There are several basic methods for conducting on-line surveys: Web survey systems, survey design websites, and Web hosting. Each of these methods is briefly discussed.

Web Survey Systems. Web survey systems are software systems specifically designed for Web questionnaire construction and delivery. They consist of an integrated questionnaire designer, Web server, database, and data delivery program, designed for use by nonprogrammers. In a typical use, the questionnaire is constructed with an easy-to-use edit feature, using a visual interface, and then automatically transmitted to the Web server system. The Web server distributes the questionnaire and files responses in a database. The user can query the server at any time via the Web for completion statistics, descriptive statistics on responses, and graphical displays of data. Several popular on-line survey research software packages are Hosted in Canada Surveys, SPSS Quanquest, Inquisite, Sawtooth CiW, Web Survent, Infopoll, SurveyMonkey, and SurveyPro.

Survey Design and Web Hosting Sites. Several websites allow the researcher to design a survey on-line without loading design software. The survey is then administered on the design site's server. Some offer tabulation and analysis packages as well. Two Canadian sites that offer Web hosting are Survey-Hosting.ca and Nooro Online research. Several of the other firms mentioned in the previous paragraph also offer Web hosting.

On-line Panel Providers

Designing a questionnaire is one step in the on-line survey process, and another is procuring a sample to survey. Sometimes do-it-yourself researchers already have a sample or census of those they wish to survey, so sampling is not a problem. Examples would be members of a country club, persons who just purchased a new Ford, students at a university, or customers at Future Shop. Often, however, researchers don't have a sample available, so they turn to on-line panel providers. Canadian on-line panel providers such as Fresh Intelligence, Harris/Decima, Ipsos Canada, and Opinion Search recruit people who agree to opt in to participate in on-line market research surveys whenever they are asked to.

Some on-line panels are created for specific industries such as construction, medical, or technology and may have a few thousand panel members, while the large commercial on-line panels have millions of people worldwide who have opted in to participate in on-line surveys of varying topics. When people join most on-line panels, they answer an extensive profiling questionnaire that records demographic, lifestyle, and psychographic information, typically with hundreds of dimensions. This profiling information enables the panel provider to record detailed information on every panel member. Using this information, the panel provider can then target research efforts to panel members who meet specific criteria. For example, a research study may require surveying avid golfers who play golf at least once a week, people who own an HDTV, or people who make decisions regarding information technology and work in organizations with over 500 employees. Finding people who meet these criteria can be difficult, but on-line panel providers may be able to more easily identify these people based on their profiling information.

By having thousands of people already recruited and engaged in the research process, on-line panels help reduce recruitment cost and field time needed to complete a research project. For the really low-incidence groups, many of the larger panel providers, such as Harris/Decima and Ipsos-Reid, are able to develop specialty panels for hard-to-reach audiences, such as small business owners, affluent consumers, and health care providers.

On-line Focus Groups

A recent development in qualitative research is the on-line focus group. A number of Canadian organizations such as Consumer Vision, Opinion Search, Harris/Decima, and Ipsos Reid are currently offering this new means of conducting focus groups. The process is fairly simple.

- The research firm builds a database of respondents via a screening questionnaire on its website.
- When a client comes to a firm with a need for a particular focus group, the firm goes to its database and identifies individuals who appear to qualify. It sends an e-mail message to these individuals, asking them to log on to a particular site at a particular time scheduled for the group. The firm pays them an incentive for their participation.
- The firm develops a discussion guide similar to the one used for a conventional focus group.
- A moderator runs the group by typing in questions on-line for all to see. The group operates in an environment similar to that of a chat room so that all participants see all questions and all responses.
- The firm captures the complete text of the focus group and makes it available for review after the group has finished.

Types of On-line Focus Groups. Two types of on-line focus groups are typically offered by market research firms that apply Internet technology to marketing research:

1. Real-time on-line focus groups: These are live, interactive sessions with four to six participants and a moderator in a chat-room format. The typical session does not last longer than 45 to 50 minutes. This technique is best for simple, straightforward issues that can be covered in limited time. The results tend to be superficial compared to in-person focus groups—but this is acceptable for certain types of projects. Typically, three to four groups are recommended as a minimum. Clients can view the chat room as the session unfolds and communicate with the moderator.

2. Time-extended on-line focus groups: These sessions follow a message-board format and usually last five to ten days. The 15 to 20 participants must comment at least two or three times per day and spend 15 minutes a day logged in to the discussion. The moderator reviews respondents' comments several times per day (and night) and probes or redirects the discussion as needed. This technique provides three to four times as much content as the average in-person focus group. Time-extended on-line focus groups give participants time to reflect, talk to others, visit a store, or check the pantry. This extra time translates into richer content and deeper insights. Clients can view the on-line content as it is posted and may communicate with the moderator at any time.[39]

Advantages of On-line Focus Groups. Many advantages are claimed for cyber groups. Cyber Dialogue, a marketing research company specializing in cyber groups, lists the following benefits of on-line focus groups on its website:

- Speed: Typically, focus groups can be recruited and conducted, with delivery of results, within five days of client approval.
- Cost-effectiveness: Off-line focus groups incur costs for facility rental, airfare, hotel, and food. None of these costs is incurred with on-line focus groups.
- Broad geographic scope: In a given focus group, you can speak to people in different cities and provinces at the same time.
- Accessibility: On-line focus groups give you access to individuals who otherwise might be difficult to recruit (e.g., business travellers, doctors, mothers with infants).
- Honesty: From behind their screen names, respondents are anonymous to other respondents and tend to talk more freely about issues that might create inhibitions in a face-to-face group.

Web Community Research

A **Web community** is a carefully selected group of consumers who agree to participate in an ongoing dialogue with a particular corporation.[40] All community interaction takes place on a custom-designed website. During the life of the community—which may last anywhere from six months to a year or more—community members respond to questions posed by the corporation on a regular basis. These discussions, which typically take the form of qualitative "dialogues," are augmented by the ability of community members to talk to one another about topics that are of interest to them as well.

The popularity and power of Web communities initially came from several key benefits such as their ability to

- engage customers in a space where they are most comfortable, allowing clients to interact with them on a deeper level;
- uncover "exciters" and "eureka moments," resulting in customer-derived innovations;
- establish brand advocates who are emotionally invested in a company's success;
- offer real-time results, enabling clients to explore ideas that normal time constraints prohibit;
- create a forum where natural dialogue allows customers to initiate topics important to them.[41]

Additionally, Web communities help companies create a customer-focused organization by putting employees into direct contact with consumers from the comfort of their own desks. Since communities provide advantages in speed, flexibility and 24/7 access to consumers, they let the organization be agile in its research decision-making and prudent in its spending.

By adding a research focus to the Web community, it becomes a way to

- map the thinking of consumer segments;
- brainstorm new ideas;
- create and test new products; and
- observe natural consumer behaviour.[42]

The Role of Consumer-Generated Media in Marketing Research

consumer-generated media (CGM)
Media that consumers generate and share among themselves.

Consumer-generated media (CGM) is media that consumers generate themselves and share among themselves. Because it is consumer-based, it is trusted more than traditional forms of advertising and promotion.[43] CGM originates from

- blogs
- message boards and forums
- public discussions (Usenet newsgroups)
- discussions and forums on large e-mail portals (Yahoo! and Gmail)
- on-line opinion or review sites and services
- on-line feedback or complaint sites
- shared videos and photos
- podcasts

It is estimated that billions of CGM comments are archived on the Web today, with nearly 100 million content creators active. Those numbers grow by about 30 percent annually.[44]

CGM can be influenced but not controlled by marketers. To influence CGM, one must first understand what is being said or shown. Nielsen BuzzMetrics is the leading marketing research firm tracking CGM. The firm uses sophisticated data mining and other technologies to help marketers understand what is being said about their company and brands on the Web. BrandPulse is BuzzMetrics' most popular product. BrandPulse can tell a company about the spread and influence of CGM. How much "buzz" exists? Where is on-line discussion taking place, and by whom? What issues are most important? Is the tone of discussion negative or positive?

BrandPulse enables clients to listen in on unaided consumer conversations that take place on Internet forums, boards, Usenet newsgroups, and blogs, providing timely understanding of the opinions and trends affecting a company or brand.

A second product, BrandPulse Insight reports, focuses on specific issues and concerns such as

- What's the buzz about a certain issue, trend, product, or piece of news?
- Who's active on-line, and what are these on-line consumers saying?
- Are current trends building or waning?
- Can any emerging trends be detected early, before they catch fire (or fizzle out prematurely)?
- What key motivators influence and affect consumer behaviour?
- What are consumer or customer moods and emotions on a particular topic or about a specific brand?
- Which on-line consumers are likely candidates for influencer panels and relationship marketing programs?[45]

A marketer wanting to know about the latest diet trend, technological gadget, automotive perceptions, or health-related concerns can tap into BrandPulse Insights to understand what's being said.

Nielsen BuzzMetrics offers a free service entitled BlogPulse, **www.blogpulse.com**, which is a blog search engine and a trend tracker. You can easily create your own graphs to plot blog buzz by entering a search term. Alternatively, you can check out popular blog trends, follow a story trail between two bloggers, or see profiles of popular bloggers.

Behavioural Targeting

behavioural targeting
A form of observation marketing research that uses data mining coupled with identifying Web surfers by their IP addresses.

Behavioural targeting (BT) is fairly new. BT began as a simple process by placing "cookies" on users' browsers to track which websites they visited. Researchers could determine pages visited, time at each page, and the number and type of searches made. The objective is to match the Internet user with ads for products and services that they will most likely purchase. Today, the more sophisticated forms of BT combine a consumer's on-line activity with psychographic and demographic profiles inferred from databases. Thus the BT firms claim that they use IP addresses and not an individual's actual name and address. Because of the potential effectiveness of BT advertising, its popularity is skyrocketing. Over 24 percent of all on-line advertisers have used BT.[46]

The most exciting growth area of BT is in the area of social networking, where users share personal information with "friends." The information that a member of MySpace, Facebook, or Friendslator shares plus marrying the information with demographic and psychographic databases becomes a very powerful tool for ad placement. Critics have called this form of BT "conversational eavesdropping analysis." Tom Kendall, a Facebook executive, counters by saying that it is simply "user-declared information targeting."[47] This is because much of it is derived from what members provide in their profile such as gender, age, political views, hobbies, university or college, and occupation. This type of data is much more powerful for marketers than clickstream information. For example, if a member says that she has a strong interest in kayaking, this is much more useful than knowing that someone using the same computer went to the kayaking site, Kayakonline.com. It could have been a friend using the computer.

BT has raised a number of privacy issues, particularly with regard to the latest forms of the technology that is integrated with social networking sites. Yet, according to the latest research, only 7 percent of the respondents in a recent survey were concerned about their ISP tracking their activity; 54 percent were worried about viruses; and 52 percent about identity theft or fraud.[48] Also, 29 percent claimed that they would rather receive appropriately targeted ads than random ones.

Other Uses of the Internet by Marketing Researchers

The Internet revolution in marketing research has had an impact on more than just the way surveys are conducted. The management of the research process and the dissemination of information have also been greatly enhanced by the Internet. Several key areas have been affected by the Internet:

- *The distribution of requests for proposals (RFPs) and proposals.* Companies can now quickly and efficiently send RFPs to a select e-mail list of research suppliers. In turn, research suppliers can develop proposals and e-mail them back to clients. A process that used to take days using snail mail now occurs in a matter of hours.
- *Collaboration between the client and the research supplier in the management of a research project.* Now a researcher and client may both be looking at a proposal, RFP, report, or some type of statistical analysis at the same time on their respective computer screens while discussing it over the telephone. This setup is very powerful and efficient. Changes in the sample size, quotas, and other aspects of the research plan can be discussed and made immediately.
- *Data management and on-line analysis.* Clients can access their survey via the research supplier's secure website and monitor the data gathering in real time. The client can use sophisticated tools to do data analysis as the survey develops. This real-time analysis may result in changes in the questionnaire, the sample size, or the types of respondents being interviewed. The research supplier and the client become partners in "just in time" marketing research.
- *Publication and distribution of reports.* Reports can be published to the Web directly from programs such as Microsoft PowerPoint and all the latest versions of leading word-processing, spreadsheet, and presentation software packages. This means that results are available to appropriate managers worldwide on an almost instantaneous basis. Reports can be searched for the content of interest using the same Web browser used to view the report.

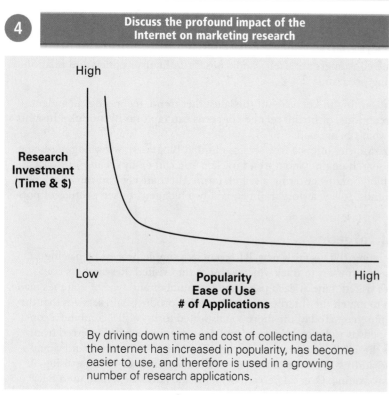

REVIEW LEARNING OUTCOME 4

4 Discuss the profound impact of the Internet on marketing research

High

Research Investment (Time & $)

Low   **Popularity Ease of Use # of Applications**   High

By driving down time and cost of collecting data, the Internet has increased in popularity, has become easier to use, and therefore is used in a growing number of research applications.

- *Viewing of oral presentations of marketing research surveys by widely scattered audiences.* By placing oral presentations on password-protected websites, managers throughout the world can see and hear the actual client presentation. This saves time and money by avoiding the need for managers to travel to a central meeting site.[49]

5 SCANNER-BASED RESEARCH

Discuss the growing importance of scanner-based research

scanner-based research
A system for gathering information from a single group of respondents by continuously monitoring the advertising, promotion, and pricing they are exposed to and the things they buy.

BehaviourScan
A scanner-based research program that tracks the purchases of 3,000 households through store scanners.

InfoScan
A scanner-based sales-tracking service for the consumer packaged-goods industry.

Scanner-based research is a system for gathering information from a single group of respondents by continuously monitoring the advertising, promotion, and pricing they are exposed to and the things they buy. The variables measured are advertising campaigns, coupons, displays, and product prices. The result is a huge database of marketing efforts and consumer behaviour. Scanner-based research is bringing ever closer the Holy Grail of marketing research: an accurate, objective picture of the direct causal relationship between different kinds of marketing efforts and actual sales.

The two major scanner-based suppliers are Information Resources, Inc. (IRI) and the ACNielsen Company. Each has about half the market. However, IRI is the founder of scanner-based research.

IRI's first product is called **BehaviourScan**. A household panel (a group of 3,000 long-term participants in the research project) has been recruited and maintained in each BehaviourScan town. Panel members shop with an ID card, which is presented at the checkout in scanner-equipped grocery stores and drugstores, allowing IRI to track electronically each household's purchases, item by item, over time. It uses microcomputers to measure TV viewing in each panel household and can send special commercials to panel members' TV sets. With such a measure of household purchasing, it is possible to manipulate marketing variables, such as TV advertising and consumer promotions, and to introduce a new product and analyze real changes in consumer buying behaviour.

IRI's most successful product is **InfoScan**—a scanner-based sales-tracking service for the consumer packaged-goods industry. Retail sales, detailed consumer purchasing information (including measurement of store loyalty and total grocery basket expenditures), and promotional activities by manufacturers and retailers are monitored and evaluated for all bar-coded products. Data are collected weekly from more than 34,000 supermarkets, drugstores, and mass merchandisers in North America.[50]

IRI's BehaviorScan product allows IRI to track individual household purchases over time. Participants in the household panel present an ID card at the checkout of a scanner-equipped grocery store.

SOURCE: © PHOTODISC/JUPITERIMAGES

WHEN SHOULD MARKETING RESEARCH BE CONDUCTED?

When managers have several possible solutions to a problem, they should not instinctively call for marketing research. In fact, the first decision to make is whether to conduct marketing research at all.

Some companies have been conducting research in certain markets for many years. Such companies understand the characteristics of target customers and their likes and dislikes regarding existing products. Under these circumstances, further research would be repetitive and waste money. Procter & Gamble has extensive knowledge of the coffee market. After it conducted initial taste tests with Folgers Instant Coffee, P&G went into national distribution without further research. Sara Lee Bakery followed the same strategy with its frozen croissants, as did Quaker Oats with Chewy Granola Bars. This tactic, however, does not always work. Clairol felt it understood the hair care market very well when it launched "Look of Buttermilk" shampoo, only to find that consumers rejected the product because of negative perceptions of buttermilk. Undaunted, Clairol followed up with "Touch of Yogurt" shampoo, which also failed, indicating low acceptance for "dairy-based" shampoos.[51]

5 **Discuss the growing importance of scanner-based research**

BehaviourScan

Panel information from specific groups of people, enables researchers to manipulate variables and see real results

InfoScan

Aggregate consumer information on all bar-coded products

Managers rarely have such great trust in their judgment that they would refuse more information if it were available and free. But they may have enough confidence that they are unwilling to pay very much for the information or to wait a long time to receive it. The willingness to acquire additional decision-making information depends on managers' perceptions of its quality, price, and timing. Of course, if perfect information were available—that is, the data conclusively showed which alternative to choose—decision makers would be willing to pay more for it than for information that still left uncertainty. In summary, research should be undertaken only when the expected value of the information is greater than the cost of obtaining it.

6 COMPETITIVE INTELLIGENCE

Explain the concept of competitive intelligence

competitive intelligence (CI)
An intelligence system that helps managers assesses their competition and vendors in order to become more efficient and effective competitors.

Derived from military intelligence, competitive intelligence is an important tool for helping a company overcome a competitor's advantage. Competitive intelligence can help identify the advantage; it can also provide insights regarding how that advantage was achieved.

Competitive intelligence (CI) helps managers assess their competitors and their vendors in order to become a more efficient and effective competitor. Intelligence is analyzed information. It becomes decision-making intelligence when it has implications for the organization. For example, one of your firm's primary competitors may have plans to introduce a product with performance standards equal to those of your own but with a 15 percent cost advantage. The new product will reach the market in eight months. This intelligence has important decision-making and policy consequences for management. Competitive intelligence and environmental scanning (where management gathers data about the external environment—see Chapter 3) combine to create marketing intelligence. Marketing intelligence is then used as input into a marketing decision support system. Nine out of ten large companies have employees dedicated to the CI function.

Competitive intelligence helps managers assess their competition and their vendors; this in turn means fewer surprises. Competitive intelligence allows managers to predict changes in business relationships, identify marketplace opportunities, guard against threats, forecast a competitor's strategy, discover new or potential competitors, learn from the success or failure of others, learn about new technologies that can affect the company, and learn about the impact of government regulations on the competition. In summary, CI promotes effective and efficient decision making, which should lead to greater profitability. Sheena Sharp, principal of Sharp Market Intelligence, says: "CI gives the company the competitive advantage of foresight and allows it to learn today what will be discovered by others tomorrow."[52]

SOURCES OF COMPETITIVE INTELLIGENCE

The Internet and its databases are an excellent source of competitive intelligence. A CI researcher can use Internet databases to answer these and other questions:

- What articles have been written about this market?
- What companies are associated with this product group?
- What patents have been filed for this technology?
- What are the major magazines or texts in this industry?
- What are the chances that I will find something in print on the target company?
- How many companies are in the same industry as the target company?
- Who are the reporters studying this industry?
- How can I be updated on industry and company events without having to constantly request the information?
- How can I compile a list of the leading experts in the industry and the key institutions they are associated with?

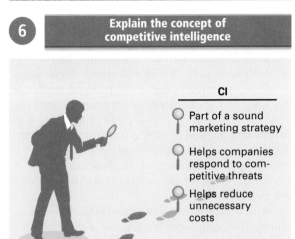

6 | **Explain the concept of competitive intelligence**

CI

○ Part of a sound marketing strategy

○ Helps companies respond to competitive threats

○ Helps reduce unnecessary costs

Noncomputer-based sources of CI can be found in a variety of areas:

- A company's salespeople, who can directly observe and ask questions about the competition.
- Experts with in-depth knowledge of a subject or activity.
- CI consultants, who can use their knowledge and experience to gather needed information quickly and efficiently.
- Government agencies, a valuable source of all types of data.
- Suppliers, a group that may offer information on products shipped to a competitor.
- Periodicals, a good source for timely articles on successes, failures, opportunities, and threats.
- The Yellow Pages, which often provide data on the number of competitors, trading areas, and special offerings.
- Trade shows, official gatherings where competitors display their latest offerings.

This list is not exhaustive but it does provide an idea of how CI can be gathered.

⑦ SALES FORECASTING

Describe sales forecasting and sales forecasting methods

sales forecasts
An estimate of a firm's sales for a specific product or service to a specific market over a specific period of time.

One of the most important routine marketing research activities undertaken by marketing managers involves making **sales forecasts**. A sales forecast involves making an estimate of a firm's sales for a specific product or service to a specific market over a specific period of time. Sales forecasting is critical to virtually all aspects of marketing decision making including objective setting, target market selection, marketing mix strategy development, and finally, the evaluation and control process.

There are essentially three methods used to make sales forecasts: correlational, opinion-based, and finally research-based methods. Each one of these approaches has its strengths and weaknesses depending on the product and market situation (see Exhibit 7.9 for a description of the various methods). Regardless, each one of the methods depends on obtaining decision-making information for analysis upon which to make an estimate.

CORRELATIONAL METHODS

trend analysis
Estimating future sales based on past sales.

complex trend analysis
Estimating future sales based on past sales while accounting for cyclical variations, competitor activity, and other impacts.

time series analysis
Estimating future sales while accounting for changes in key economic variables over time.

chain-ratio method
A method of forecasting by which a firm's sales are estimated by relating them in proportion to larger trends.

Correlational methods involve estimating future sales based on the relationship of a firm's sales to some type of benchmark. This benchmark could be based on historical sales experience, industry sales forecasts, and even economic forecasts. Virtually all of the methodologies employ the use of "secondary" data. Many firms use a form of **trend analysis** sales forecasting to estimate their future sales. In simple trend analysis, a firm looks at its past sales and then estimates future sales from their historical performance. It is a very easy approach to take but it assumes that there have been no fundamental changes in any of the firm's uncontrollable environments and, most notably, no changes in the competitive environment. In a dynamic and changing world, this is most often an unwarranted assumption. Many firms choose a "more dynamic" benchmark upon which to relate the trends in their sales and this involves **complex trend analysis** sales forecasting methods (cyclical variations are considered, competitive activity and other impacts are accounted for) and **time series** sales forecasting methods (the impact of changes in key economic variables over time are accounted for). The details of these techniques are far beyond the scope of this text, but suffice it to say, a sales forecast is determined in relation to industry trends or even the larger economic trends that have been occurring.

The **chain-ratio method** of sales forecasting is one in which a firm's sales are estimated by relating them in proportion to larger trends like the GDP growth or the industry growth. These latter trends have already taken many of the uncontrollable variables into account. The firm acquires future estimates of these trends from "expert" sources and then relates them to its own sales.

Similarly, the **market share method** of sales forecasting looks at the firm's long-term market share in an industry and then considers industry growth and the industry sales potential. The firm relates this information to the likelihood of its maintaining, increasing, or losing market share based on historical patterns and planned marketing actions. Based on the firm's expected share of the estimated industry sales, a dollar or unit sales forecast can be made.

The **market aggregation sales forecasting method** is really just a variation of the market share method. However, the difference is in the level of analysis. In market aggregation the firm looks at their market shares and sales potentials across their various market segments and makes a series of small estimates which are then added together to come up with a total sales estimate.

All these approaches depend on correlating the firm's potential sales performance to some other benchmark estimate. The accuracy of the forecast is therefore heavily dependent on how accurate the benchmark estimate is and how valid the "correlation" is between the firm's sales and the benchmark being used.

OPINION-BASED METHODS

In opinion-based methods, the marketing firm confers with people who are knowledgeable about the business and its industry and asks them what they believe the firm's sales will be for the upcoming period. The fundamental basis of these opinions would normally be expected to come from an expert analysis of both secondary and primary data. However, they are opinions and there is the possibility that they are based on no data at all! Thus it is very important that those whose opinions are being sought are truly "expert" about what they are talking about. In addition, before seeking opinions, you might want to review the track record of the experts. How accurate have their predictions been in the past?

For example, one might get a sales estimate by **jury of executive opinion**. This is a sales forecast based on the opinion of a combined group of the firm's executives. In this method, the firm's executives meet and, through consensus, come up with a sales forecast for the coming year. A firm's executives usually have considerable experience and knowledge and are often able to make good judgments.

Likewise, the executives might undertake a **sales force survey**, which is a sales forecast based on the combined estimates of sales provided by a firm's sales force. In this method, the salespeople are asked to estimate the firm's sales for next year. A firm's salespeople are out in the market every day dealing with both customers and competitors and keeping their fingers on the pulse of the local markets they are serving. They are capable of making good "on the ground" judgments. However, whether one is an executive or a salesperson, employees within any organization are subject to group thinking and personal bias in making their estimates. In addition, they may not be as aware of external forces or trends that are outside their industry and that may have an impact. Executives tend to be very optimistic in what they expect for the future. In contrast, salespeople often consider their own self interests and know that a high sales forecast will likely result in a high sales quota that they may not be able to meet.

Another method of forecasting sales is to use **outside experts** who follow an industry closely and report on it. These experts tend to be more objective in their views and do not have the inherent bias of people within competing firms of an industry. In addition, they usually take a much wider view of an industry and see it within a larger context. Experts may follow an industry while working as analysts: as part of the government, such as Industry Canada; as part of the general media, such as reporters from the *Globe and Mail*, the *Financial Post*, Business News Network, and the CBC; as part of investment firms, like TDWaterhouse; as part of independent research firms, like A.C. Nielsen; as part of independent consulting firms, like Desrosiers Automotive Consultants; as part of academic institutions, like business professors; as part of think tanks, like the Fraser Institute; and finally, they may even

market share method
A method of forecasting that derives a sales estimate based on a firm's long term-market share in relation to the total industry sales potential.

market aggregation sales forecasting method
A method of forecasting that occurs when a firm looks at its market shares and sales potentials across the various market segments and adds them together to make a total sales estimate.

jury of executive opinion sales forecast
A sales forecast based on the opinion of a combined group of the firm's executives.

sales force survey
A sales forecast based on the combined estimates of sales provided by a firm's sales force.

outside experts sales forecast
A sales forecast based on the opinions of expert people who follow an industry closely and report on it.

be part of a union organization, like Jim Stanford, an economist employed by the Canadian Auto Workers (CAW). In all these instances, the judgment of these individuals is based on attempting to understand the dynamics of an industry and the impact on the industry of the larger economy.

It must be understood that all outside experts have their own philosophies and points of view, and they may work for organizations that have specific agendas, all of which may affect their analysis and estimates. Ultimately, these experts will normally develop and communicate a forecast for the industry. The manner in which the forecasts are developed may be more or less transparent depending on the organization. For example, independent investment, research, or consulting firms are not very willing to reveal their trade secrets so they may not reveal their methods of estimation. In contrast, government organizations and university researchers might be more open about their methodologies. In the end, an opinion is what is received, regardless of its basis.

RESEARCH-BASED METHODS

The marketing research methodologies presented in this chapter are all ultimately designed to enable firms to develop a final sales forecast. All the research-based methods use primary data as the basis of their forecasting information.

customer buyer intention survey forecasting
Surveying buyer intentions to determine how many customers plan to buy the firm's products in the future.

Many firms undertake **customer buyer intention surveys** to determine whether consumers intend to purchase their products in the future but also to discover customer needs and wants and their motivations for purchasing. Buyer intention surveys are often undertaken as part of marketing mix development but they don't tap into actual behaviour but intended behaviour. Thus there is considerable doubt as to whether intentions will result in actual behaviour. These types of surveys often precede marketing mix development and normally would be undertaken to determine if a test market is worthwhile. They can be sent to a fully representative group of people so marketers can gauge the response potential of the total market. However, they are a one-time measure so even if you can estimate first-time purchasing, you can't measure repeat buying, which is why many firms use test markets to make sales estimates.

test market sales forecasting
Occurs when a firm introduces some new aspect of its marketing strategy into a limited market to gauge the behavioural response of customers.

In **test market sales forecasting,** a firm introduces some new aspect of its marketing strategy into a limited market to gauge the behavioural response of customers. Very often firms test new products with approaches like Burger King's. Burger King operates soda bar–style restaurants called Whopper bars, which are located in Munich, Germany, and Orlando, Florida. Their specific purpose is to test new products before offering them to Burger King franchises for sales and promotion.[53] Although firms often test new products, they also test other aspects of their marketing mixes, including new advertising campaigns, new promotional contests, new forms of packaging, new prices, and a new distribution channel. Based on the test market response, the firm will decide whether to make the change in its marketing strategy and estimate its impact on total sales. Test markets have the virtue of discovering what the actual response behaviour of consumers is, but they must be viewed with some caution because they often do not run long enough to accurately gauge long-term purchasing behaviour and they may not be representative enough of the total market to provide an accurate estimate of total market response.

simulation sales forecasting method
Building and using a computer simulation model of a company and its industry to estimate future sales.

In the **simulation sales forecasting method,** a company will build a computer simulation model of its firm and industry. Simulation models are usually based on the past experiences of a firm, but they can be designed to incorporate the future expectations of what the business environment will be. Simulation models allow for both controllable and uncontrollable environmental variables to be added. They can be made dynamic so that new variables can be incorporated into the model as they arise. For example, if a new competitor enters the industry or the company undergoes a merger, the model can be adjusted to reflect this change. Simulation models allow the firm to make real-time adjustments to its particular situations and receive a real-time forecast of expected sales in response. For example, the impact of interest rate changes on sales of homes and automobiles can be significant. A simulation model would allow an automotive manufacturer to model the impact of interest rate increases or decreases on its sales. This would allow it to readjust its sales forecasts in response to changes or perhaps to adjust its financing policies to ensure sales stability in the face of unstable rates. The virtual shopping research discussed earlier in the chapter is a form of simulation modelling as well.

The accuracy of sales forecasts from simulation models depends on the validity of the simulation model, that is, how well does it capture the reality of the marketplace? Simulation models allow for the anticipation of relationship changes but they take a lot of time and expense to build and maintain.

COMPARISON OF METHODS

The correlational methods depend heavily on secondary data so firms need to look more at past behaviours and relate them to the future. In the same way that secondary data can be acquired quickly and inexpensively, sales forecasts can be developed quickly and inexpensively.

The opinion methods have the strength of being based on the experience and judgment of experts who may have had access to both secondary and primary data and have been able to assess and interpret the information. In this regard, they may take into account a change in the relationship between past and future sales potentials. The problem is that there may be considerable bias in the estimates, and the underlying information upon which they are truly based may be unknown and, at worst, absent.

Finally, the research methods of forecasting are based on primary data and have the virtue of enabling researchers to uncover the current state of the market and explore its future trends. Buyer intention surveys and test markets are in step with the current environments the marketing firm is facing. Simulations allow the firm to try to model the current market situation and to adjust the parameters to reflect both current and future situations. All the research methods of forecasting can enable researchers to develop accurate forecasts, but they take time to develop and implement. In addition, the research methods are generally very expensive. Firms need to make ongoing forecasts, but it may prove too costly and too difficult to continue to undertake primary research for this purpose. However, many of the on-line research panels discussed earlier in the chapter were recruited to enable business firms to overcome this problem. Still, as timely as Internet panel-based research might be, whether a firm's customers will carry out the intentions they express is uncertain and may be no more accurate as a means to forecast sales than looking at past sales.

In conclusion, all three methods of sales forecasting have their strengths and weaknesses and marketing managers would be well advised to use a mix of sales forecasting approaches rather than relying on one single method.

REVIEW LEARNING OUTCOME 7

7	Describe sales forecasting and sales forecasting methods

A sales forecast involves making an estimate of a firm's sales for a specific product or service to a specific market over a specific period of time.

There are three basic methods of sales forecasting, and marketing managers are advised to use a mix of these methods rather than rely on one particular type.

Correlational Methods	Opinion Based Methods	Research Based Methods
Trend analysis—simple, complex, time series	Jury of executive opinions	Test market
Chain ratio analysis	Jury of expert opinions	Customer buyer intention surveys
Market share analysis	Sales force survey	Simulations
Market aggregation		

EXHIBIT 7.9

Methods of Sales Forecasting

Correlational Methods	Example	Weaknesses
Trend analysis—simple, complex, time- series	Simple: Current sales $1 million and have been growing at 5% per year. Estimate next year's sales = 1.05 x $1 million = $1,050,000	Assumes all future market conditions will remain the same as the past.
Chain-ratio analysis	GDP is forecasted to be $1,000 billion, industry sales are traditionally 0.05% of GDP, and company sales are traditionally 20% of industry sales = $1,000 billion x 0.0005 x 0.2 = $100 million	Like trend analysis, assumes all market conditions and relationships remain the same. Depends on accuracy of GDP forecast.
Market share analysis	Current market share is 20% and will remain stable, industry sales are forecasted at $80 million for the year. Sales forecast = 0.2 x $80 million or $16 million	Assumes industry sales forecast is accurate, and firm sales in relation to competitor sales will remain the same.
Market aggregation	Three market segments are analyzed and their estimated sales growth levels for next year are determined. The firm's market share in each segment is expected to remain the same—e.g., Ontario sales are $10 million and estimated growth is 5%, market share remains 20%; Quebec sales are $6 million and estimated growth is 4%, market share remains 15%; B.C. sales are $8 million, and estimated growth is 8%, market share remains 25%. Sales estimate = ($10 million x 1.05 x 0.2) + ($6 million x 1.04 x .15) + ($8 million x 1.08 x .25) = $2.1 million + $936,000 + $2.16 million = $5,196,000.	Assumes segment forecasts are accurate and firm's sales in relation to competitor sales will remain the same.

Opinion-Based Methods	Example	Weaknesses
Jury of executive opinions	The eight members of the board of directors meet. Four directors believe the firm's sales will increase by 7% next year; three members predict sales will increase by 4%; one member feels sales will actually decline by 1%. The board reaches a consensus prediction that sales will increase by 5%. Current sales are $100 million. Future sales are forecasted to be $105 million.	The basis of the opinions cannot be verified. It is strictly a qualitative assessment based on subjective judgments. Internal politics and bias towards the firm can cloud the judgments.
Jury of expert opinions	Four auto industry analysts put out their annual market outlook reports. One analyst works for TD Investments, one owns his own consulting firm, a third is a university professor, and the fourth is employed by Industry Canada. All four agree that the industry will experience sales growth, and their estimates range from a low of 2% to a high of 7% with an average of 4%. Based on current Canadian auto sales of 1,500,000 vehicles, the experts estimate next year's sales will be 1,560,000.	The basis of the opinions can be known. It is strictly a qualitative assessment based on subjective reporting. The analysts are less likely to have any bias in their assessments in comparison with industry executives.
Sales force survey	The firm's sales force of 80 people are asked to estimate what customer demand will be in their territories during the coming year, and based on this, what they expect to sell? The firm sold $40 million last year. When the 80 separate estimates are added together, the total adds to $44 million for the coming year.	The same weaknesses as executive opinions plus one other: salespeople are more likely to "underestimate" sales because their compensation plans usually reward them for exceeding sales forecasts but punish them for falling short.

Research-Based Methods	Example	Weaknesses
Test market	A new flavour of potato chips is introduced in 10 stores located in Halifax, N.S. After 6 months, average sales per store are $300 per month. The company plans to launch the new product with coverage in a total of 1,000 stores throughout Canada next year. Sales are estimated to be $300 x 1,000 stores x 12 months, or $3.6 million.	Test markets may not have run long enough to ensure repurchase rates are stable. Flavour preferences in Halifax may not be typical of people across the rest of Canada.
Customer buyer intention surveys	A representative consumer panel is shown a new food product concept and asked how many would be interested in buying the new food product at a retail price of $10? The panel represents the entire Canadian population, and .03% say they would buy 4 times a year. The company estimates annual retail sales to be $10 x 4 x .0003 x 34.5 million Canadians = $414,000.	Buyer intentions and actual buyer behaviour may not be the same. People are more likely to overestimate their likelihood of purchasing rather than underestimate it.
Simulations	A firm builds a simulation model of its industry based on its past experiences and the future expectations of what the business environment will become. Both controllable and uncontrollable environmental variables have been accounted for in the model. The expected future changes in both the controllable and uncontrollable environments are inputted into the model and a sales prediction results. As conditions change, the inputs can be adjusted to provide a real-time forecast of expected sales for each quarterly period.	The accuracy of the forecast depends on the validity of the simulation model. Simulation models allow for the anticipation of relationship changes but they take a lot of time and expense to build and may not be more accurate than less costly techniques.

REVIEW AND APPLICATIONS

1 **Explain the concept and purpose of a marketing decision support system.** A decision support system (DSS) makes data instantly available to marketing managers and allows them to manipulate the data themselves to make marketing decisions. Four characteristics make DSSs especially useful to marketing managers: they are interactive, flexible, discovery oriented, and accessible. A DSS gives managers access to information immediately and without outside assistance. A DSS allows users to manipulate data in a variety of ways and to answer "what if" questions. And, finally, a DSS is accessible to novice computer users.

1.1 In the absence of company problems, is there any reason to develop a marketing DSS?

1.2 Explain the difference between marketing research and a DSS.

2 **Define marketing research and explain its importance to marketing decision making.** Marketing research is a process of collecting and analyzing data for the purpose of solving specific marketing problems. Marketers use marketing research to explore the profitability of marketing strategies. They can examine why particular strategies failed and analyze characteristics of specific market segments. Managers can use research findings to help keep current customers. Moreover, marketing research allows management to behave proactively, rather than reactively, by identifying newly emerging patterns in society and the economy.

2.1 The task of marketing is to create exchanges. What role might marketing research play in the facilitation of the exchange process?

2.2 **WRITING** Marketing research has traditionally been associated with manufacturers of consumer goods. Today, however, an increasing number of organizations, both profit and nonprofit, are using marketing research. Why do you think this trend exists? Give some examples of specific reasons why organizations might use marketing research.

2.3 **WRITING** Write a reply to the following statement: "I own a restaurant in the downtown area. I see customers every day whom I know on a first-name basis. I understand their likes and dislikes. If I put something on the menu and it doesn't sell, I know they didn't like it. I also read *Hospitality Magazine*, so I know what the trends are in the industry. This is all the marketing research I need to do."

2.4 Give an example of (a) the descriptive role of marketing research, (b) its diagnostic role, and (c) its predictive function.

3 **Describe the steps involved in conducting a marketing research project.** The marketing research process involves several basic steps. First, the researcher and the decision maker must agree on a problem statement or set of research objectives. The researcher then creates an overall research design to specify how primary data will be gathered and analyzed. Before collecting data, the researcher decides whether the group to be interviewed will be a probability or nonprobability sample. Field service companies are often hired to carry out data collection. Once data have been collected, the researcher analyzes them using statistical analysis. The researcher then prepares and presents oral and written reports, with conclusions and recommendations, to management. As a final step, the researcher determines whether the recommendations were implemented and what could have been done to make the project more successful.

3.1 Critique the following methodologies and suggest more appropriate alternatives:

    a. A supermarket was interested in determining its image. It dropped a short questionnaire into the grocery bag of each customer before putting in the groceries.

    b. To assess the extent of its trade area, a shopping mall stationed interviewers in the parking lot every Monday and Friday evening. Interviewers walked up to people after they had parked their cars and asked them for their postal codes.

    c. To assess the popularity of a new movie, a major studio invited people to call a 900 number and vote either yes, they would see it again, or no, they would not. Each caller was billed a $2 charge.

3.2 You have been asked to determine how to attract more business majors to your school. Write an outline of the steps you would take, including the sampling procedures, to accomplish the task.

3.3 Why are secondary data sometimes preferable to primary data?

3.4 Discuss when focus groups should and should not be used.

3.5 Divide the class into teams of eight. Each group will conduct a focus group on the quality and number of services your college or university is providing its students. One person from each group should be chosen to act as moderator. Remember, it is the moderator's job to facilitate discussion, not to lead the discussion. These group discussions should last approximately 45 minutes. If possible, the groups should be videotaped or recorded. On completion, each group should write a brief report of its results. Consider offering to meet with the dean of students to share the results of your research.

4 **Discuss the profound impact of the Internet on marketing research.** The Internet has vastly simplified the secondary data search process, placing more sources of information in front of researchers than ever before. Internet survey research is surging in popularity. Internet surveys can be created rapidly and reported in real time. They are also relatively inexpensive and can easily be personalized. Often researchers can use the Internet to contact respondents who are difficult to reach by other means. The Internet can also be used to distribute research proposals and reports and to facilitate collaboration between the client and the research supplier. Clients can access real-time data and analyze the information as the collection process continues.

4.1 Open a Web search engine such as Google or Yahoo! and type "marketing research." Thousands of options will appear. Pick a website you find interesting and report on its content to the class.

4.2 Why has the Internet been of such great value to researchers seeking secondary data?

4.3 Do you see traditional forms of marketing research disappearing? Discuss.

5 **Discuss the growing importance of scanner-based research.** A scanner-based research system enables marketers to monitor a market panel's exposure and reaction to such variables as advertising, coupons, store displays, packaging, and price. By analyzing these variables in relation to the panel's subsequent buying behaviour, marketers gain useful insights into sales and marketing strategies.

5.1 Why has scanner-based research been seen as "the ultimate answer" for marketing researchers? Do you see any disadvantages to this methodology?

5.2 Detractors argue that scanner-based research is like "driving a car down the road looking only in the rear-view mirror." What does this mean? Do you agree?

6 **Explain the concept of competitive intelligence.** Competitive intelligence (CI) is the creation of an intelligence system that helps managers assess their competition and their vendors in order to become more efficient and effective. Intelligence is analyzed information; it becomes decision-making intelligence when it has implications for the organization.

By helping managers assess their competition and vendors, CI prevents surprises. CI allows managers to predict changes in business relationships, guard against threats, forecast a competitor's strategy, and develop a successful marketing plan.

The Internet and databases accessed via the Internet are excellent sources of CI. Company personnel, particularly sales and service representatives, are usually good sources of CI. Many companies require their salespeople to routinely fill out CI reports. Other external sources of CI include experts, CI consultants, government agencies, suppliers, newspapers and other publications, Yellow Pages, and trade shows.

6.1 Why is CI growing in today's environment?

6.2 Prepare a memo to your boss at TD Canada Trust and outline why the organization needs a CI unit.

6.3 Form a team with three other students. Each team must choose a company in the PC manufacturing industry and then go to the website of the company and acquire as much CI as possible. Each team will then prepare a five-minute oral presentation on its findings.

7 **Describe sales forecasting and sales forecasting methods.** Sales forecasting is one of the most important routine marketing research activities undertaken by marketing managers. A sales forecast involves making an estimate of a firm's sales for a specific product or service to a specific market over a specific period of time. There are essentially three methods used to make sales forecasts: (1) correlational methods, which usually depend on secondary data and include trend analysis, complex trend analysis, time series analysis, chain-ratio, market share, and market aggregation sales forecasting; (2) expert opinion estimates, which may have an uncertain data basis and involve jury of executive opinion, sales force surveys, and outside expert sales forecasting; and finally, (3) research based methods that usually involve primary data collection to undertake test marketing, customer buyer intention survey, and simulation sales forecasting. Marketing managers are advised to use a mix of sales forecasting approaches rather than relying on one single method.

7.1 List the three basic forecasting approaches and discuss the advantages and disadvantages of each methodology.

7.2 Marketing managers are advised to use a mix of sales forecasting approaches and not to rely on any particular method. Review the methods and the examples in Exhibit 7.9. Which methods would you recommend for use and why? Be sure to justify your choices well.

TERMS

EXERCISES

APPLICATION EXERCISE

 For its study Teens and Healthy Eating: Oxymoron or Trend?, BuzzBack Market Research focused on snacking. Among its findings: teens eat an average of three snacks per day; breakfast is the meal they skip most often. Though scads of snacks are stacked on store shelves, when it comes to healthier treats targeting adolescents, it's a bit of a teenage wasteland. BuzzBack asked 532 teen respondents to conjure up new foods they'd gobble up. The following are some of their ideas:

- "Travel fruit. Why can't fruit be in travel bags like chips or cookies? Canned fruit is too messy. Maybe have a dip or something sold with it, too."—Female, age 17.
- "A drink that contains five servings of fruits and vegetables."—Male, age 16.
- "I would invent all natural and fat-free, vitamin-enhanced cookies and chips that had great flavour."—Female, age 16.
- "I would make fruit-based cookies."—Male, age 16.
- "Low-carb trail mix, because trail mix is easy to eat but it has a lot of fat/carbs."—Female, age 15.
- "I would create some sort of microwavable spaghetti."—Male, age 16.
- "Something quick and easy to make that's also cheap. I'll be in university next year, and I'm trying to find things that are affordable, healthier than cafeteria food, and easy to make."—Female, age 17.
- "Good vegan mac 'n' cheese."—Female, age 18.
- "A smoothie where you could get all the nutrients you need, that tastes good, helps you stay in shape, and is good for you. Has vitamins A, B3, B12, C, ginkgo. Packaging would be bright."—Female, age 16.
- "A breakfast shake for teens. Something easy that tastes good, not necessarily for dieters like SlimFast, etc. Something to balance you off in the morning."—Male, age 18.

Activities

1. You are a new-product development specialist at Kraft Canada. What guidance can you get from the BuzzBack study?

2. Choose one of the suggestions from the above list of healthy snack concepts. Imagine that your company is interested in turning the idea into a new product but wants to conduct market research before investing in product development. Design a marketing research plan that will give company managers the information they need before engaging in new-product development of the idea. (Hint: Use steps 1–3 in Exhibit 7.1 as a guide.)

3. Once you have finished your plan, collect the data. Depending on the data collection methods you have outlined in your plan, you may need to make adjustments so that you can collect actual data to analyze.

4. Analyze the data you collected and create a report for your company either recommending that the company pursue the idea you chose or investigate another.

ETHICS EXERCISE

John Michael Smythe owns a small marketing research firm in Newmarket, Ontario, that employs 25 people. Most of his employees are sole breadwinners in their families. John's firm has not fared well for the past two years and is on the verge of bankruptcy. The company recently surveyed more than 2,500 people in the Greater Toronto Area about new car purchase plans as part of a study on car emissions sponsored by the Ontario Ministry of Transportation. Because the study identified many hot prospects for new cars, a new car dealer has offered John $8,000 for the names and phone numbers of people saying they are likely or very likely to buy a new car within the next 12 months. John needs the money to avoid laying off a number of employees.

Questions

1. Should John Smythe sell the names?

2. Does the CMA *Code of Ethics* address this issue? Go to **www.the-cma.org** and review the code. Then write a brief paragraph on what that code contains that relates to John Smythe's dilemma.

SOURCE: © PRNEWSFOTO/
RED LOBSTER

RED LOBSTER: MARKET RESEARCH REVEALS WHAT'S FRESH TODAY

Remember the Red Lobster commercials featuring lots of fried shrimp bouncing around and lobster claws dripping with butter? They've been replaced by scenes of steaming fresh fish, rice, and vegetables. The old slogan "For the Seafood Lover in You" has also been canned. Now Red Lobster wants you to "Come See What's Fresh Today." The restaurants themselves will soon look different, too, with a more streamlined, contemporary decor that downplays the traditional nautical themes.

These changes and more are part of an effort to make over the seafood chain after marketing research revealed that the restaurant was considered outdated and unappealing to potential customers. Red Lobster president Kim Lodrup says that in the first stage of the makeover, the chain improved operations so that customers wouldn't have to wait so long for the food to reach their table. The second phase focused on improving the restaurant's image and shifting the focus from low prices to freshness. The third and final challenge will be to increase sales. Lodrup says, "We are positioning Red Lobster to be the best seafood restaurant on the planet."

Lodrup was originally hired as a marketing specialist to revive the sagging brand's image in 2003 when sales were falling and customer satisfaction was at an all-time low. He immediately put the kibosh on promotions like the All-You-Can-Eat Crab Legs Specials that had lost money for the company in the past and emphasized Red Lobster's seafood expertise instead. After sales increased in 2004, he was promoted to president, but he still relies on marketing research to keep his finger on the pulse of customer preferences.

"We find out what they want from idealized dining service and research how to deliver value to guests," Lodrup says. "To do that, Red Lobster follows changing consumer habits and pays attention to which dishes patrons prefer. They use phone and Internet surveys to learn about guest attitudes toward the food they've tried and try to determine how well they might respond to new menu items or concept changes before instituting them. The guest-relations department catalogues the nature of guest contact so we can see if there are changes in trends," Lodrup explains. "Emerging concerns or requests from consumers get captured weekly and recorded for our executives."

More in-depth research measures attitudes and trends that could affect the brand in the future. Before a promotion is launched, featured menu items are chosen through extensive consumer testing. Beginning with a large number of possible dishes, they narrow it down to the one that testers deem most appealing.

After studies indicated that freshness is the single biggest criteria consumers use to judge a seafood restaurant, the chain knew it was vital to get word out that fresh fish is delivered to Red Lobster restaurants six days a week. Interviews with former customers revealed that many still believed that Red Lobster's fish was frozen despite the company's extensive global connections and rapid seafood delivery system.

"It's really important to signal to people food is freshly prepared," says marketing V.P. Salli Setta, who created the Culinary Institute of Tuscany for Olive Garden before being hired by Red Lobster. The company is considering opening a similar seafood-related school on the East Coast to add authenticity to Red Lobster's menu. In the meantime, Setta hired a new team of executive chefs to create updated recipes with the herbs that customers said had fresher connotations than the traditional lemon and butter sauces.

They also introduced a separate Fresh Fish Menu that is updated twice a day at the restaurants. Even though fresh fin fish had been on the regular menu for years, it had never really been promoted. Research showed that this could make the restaurant more appealing to its lapsed customers, who tend to be affluent, educated, and over 50. Households with an annual income of more than $70,000 account for half of all food eaten in restaurants and have been shown to be most interested in seafood dining. Reeling these customers back in has become a top priority in the chain's turnaround.

So far the makeover is working. Red Lobster has been reporting same-store sales increases since 2004. Improvements in operations and other cost controls led to the highest operating margin in Red Lobster history and, Lodrup reports, "every measure of guest satisfaction is at a record level." However, it continues to be a challenge for the chain to change old perceptions of itself. As one surveyed customer put it, "My wife swears by the fish. She just can't get her friends to try it."[54]

Questions

1. Why do you think Red Lobster relies on Internet surveys to track customer opinions, preferences, and criticisms? What are the advantages of on-line questionnaires versus traditional surveys conducted over the phone or through the mail?

2. Go to **www.redlobster.ca** and click around. How well do you think the site appeals to the educated, affluent, and over-50 crowd that the chain wants to attract? What are the primary messages that it communicates about the restaurant, and how effective are they? How does the site attempt to capture information about its customers?

3. One of Red Lobster's competitors in the Canadian seafood-dining business is Joey's Seafood Restaurants. Check out its website at **www.joeys.ca** and compare it to Red Lobster's. How does their marketing approach differ? Do you think they're appealing to the same types of customers? How does the website try to get information from its customers?

4. Suppose Red Lobster was wondering how well its new interior design was being received by customers at a redecorated restaurant in Edmonton, Alberta, and hired you to create a questionnaire. Write one of each: an open-ended question, a closed-ended question (either dichotomous or multiple choice), and a scaled-response question.

VIDEO CASE

FORECASTING CANADIAN AUTOMOBILE SALES: ADJUSTING TO CHANGING TIMES

Andrew Bell of BNN interviews Dennis DesRosiers of DesRosiers Automotive Consultants to get an outlook on the future of the Canadian automotive industry. One of Canada's foremost experts on the Canadian automobile industry, Dennis DesRosiers grew up in Windsor, Ontario, the "Automotive Capital of Canada" and then attended the University of Windsor, where he was trained as an economist. His connection to the automotive industry was established early on, and he has been following the automotive market in Canada ever since founding his company in 1985.

DesRosiers' firm specializes in the Canadian automotive industry and offers a number of services, including consulting, consumer market research, aftermarket analysis, publishing, and forecast services. One of the publications that DesRosiers puts out as part of his forecasting services is the *DesRosiers AutoWatch*. According to the company website, "The *DesRosiers AutoWatch* was created to keep you informed of month to month developments in the Canadian new vehicle sales market. Here are a few items that you will find in the DesRosiers AutoWatch:

- In-depth monthly Canadian sales analysis and commentary

- Monthly sales update and top-ten models

- Incentive tracking

- Gasoline pricing tracking

- New model launches and reviews

- Economic analysis that includes core economic indicators."

In his interview on BNN, DesRosiers comments on the current state of the Canadian automotive industry and makes a number of predictions for the future. He notes that small car sales in Canada are down and he is predicting a tough decade for the auto industry. For example, he mentions that all the top-selling small cars in Canada have had major declines in sales through 2009, including the number-one-selling car, the Honda Civic, which is down 26 percent, the Toyota Corolla down 17 percent, the Mazda 3 down 12 percent, and the Hyundai Accent, down 13 percent. The one bright spot was the Hyundai Elantra, whose sales were actually up 134 percent. DesRosiers attributes this one increase to strong styling combined with attractive pricing. DesRosiers indicates the reason for the decline in this segment is due to the fact that people in the bottom end of the economy are feeling the most impact of the economic downturn. In contrast, large luxury vehicle sales are down the least relative to the market. DesRosiers comments that people who have money are spending it!

Andrew Bell asks DesRosiers to speculate on the future for the Canadian automotive market. DesRosiers makes the general comment that in the future, there will be more drivers on the road. However, these drivers will be driving less than in the past and their cars will be lasting longer. He describes the concept of the vehicle intensity level, which he says is at saturation. According to Desrosiers, the vehicle intensity level is determined by the number of eligible drivers who own a car. He says that in the 1960s about 50 percent of people who were of driving age owned a car in North America. Currently, the rate is close to 70 percent in Canada and over 100 percent in the United States! DesRosiers comments that there is no room for growing the vehicle intensity and he believes the United States will come down a bit.

DesRosiers notes that increasing vehicle durability dampens new vehicle sales, meaning that long-term auto sales will fall. In the 1980s, North American auto sales averaged 15.3 million vehicles per year, climbing to 16.7 million during the 1990s and peaking at an average of 18.7 million vehicles per year during the first decade of the 21st century. He is predicting a slide back to levels of the 1990s for the 2010 to 2019 decade, with an average of 16.3 million new vehicles sold per year. In essence, North Americans will be buying 2 million vehicles less per year for the whole decade and this means fewer auto plants will be needed, fewer auto suppliers and fewer jobs. DesRosiers doesn't mince words: the new car market is in trouble and will likely not return to peak levels!

Although a number of doors in the new car market are going to be shut, and shut permanently, a window is opening in the used car market. DesRosiers predicts that the used car market will boom. The negative image of the sector—when used cars were sold in back alleys—is changing, and this specialized market is moving to centre stage. The quality that has been built into new cars in recent years is now carrying over to the used car market and this market will see growth. The adage used to be that "a used car was somebody else's problem." Now there are fewer problems than ever before, even in 8- and 10-year-old vehicles. Used cars now account for nearly 60 percent of sales in Canada compared to the past, when it was half that amount.

A dramatic illustration of the quality difference between the cars made today versus the cars of yesterday was provided by the Insurance Institute for Highway Safety in the United States. The institute released a YouTube video showing a crash test between a modern 2009 Chevy Malibu and a 1958 Chevy. The 1958 Chevy is totally destroyed. DesRosiers comments that today's vehicles are far more crashworthy and more soundly built. In the 1960s, vehicles lasted only about 100,000 kilometres while on average today's vehicles will last up to 350,000 kilometres and many will last even longer.

Auto retailers are discovering that they are selling more used cars, which have much higher profit margins than new ones! DesRosiers says that the profit margin on new vehicles is typically $1,500 while on used cars it is $2,000. The reason for the difference is that the dealer does not have to satisfy the manufacturers when they sell a used car. In Canada, a few used car "superstore" dealers have been opening up to take advantage of this market opportunity. In turn, this adds to consumer confidence in buying used cars because many of the superstores are offering warranties. The used car market is not totally foolproof because there are still curbsiders or grey-market guys who sell cars that have had accidents or other major problems. DesRosiers' opinion is that private sales are very risky for consumers. However, both new and used car dealers will provide quality used cars. As long as they haven't been in an accident, cars that are only two or three years old are very safe bets, according to DesRosiers.[55]

Questions

1. In reference to the various methods of forecasting presented in Exhibit 7.9, how would you categorize the forecasting services and methods of Dennis DesRosiers? Discuss the kinds of data sources he presents as he discusses his forecasts for the future. What types of data do you think he is using?

2. Go to the DesRosiers Automotive Consulting website (**www.desrosiers.ca**) and review some of the reports that are presented. Describe some of them and discuss how they would help you understand the automotive market.

3. Characterize the kinds of clients that DesRosiers Automotive Consulting might have. What kinds of decision-making information would they be looking for? Based on the website presentation (**www.desrosiers.ca**), does the firm supply all the types of information services that potential clients might be seeking? What other information services might the firm be able to provide?

4. So what do you think, are you convinced that "used" is better than "new"? Write down your initial feeling about whether you would prefer to buy a new or used car. Now do some of your own research into the new versus used car markets. List the advantages and disadvantages of each type of purchase. Did your feelings change at all? Why or why not?

MARKETING & YOU RESULTS

Higher scores indicate that you place greater importance on collecting primary and secondary information when developing marketing campaigns or projects. A lower score means you would be less aggressive in collecting information and might plow ahead regardless of how much information you do (or don't) have. After reading Chapter 7, you can see how involved gathering and analyzing market information can be, but also how critical it is to success.

MARKETING MISCUE

A MARKETING OPPORTUNITY MISFIRE BETWEEN DR. PEPPER AND GUNS N' ROSES

Guns N' Roses is a hard rock band that formed in the mid-1980s. Having sold over 100 million albums worldwide, Guns N' Roses was one of the world's biggest rock bands in the early 1990s. Recording for a new album, *Chinese Democracy*, began in 1994. Recording expenses for the album were said to top $13 million, yet the album had not been released by early 2008.

In March of 2008, Dr. Pepper announced that it would give every man, woman, and child in the United States a free can of Dr. Pepper if the *Chinese Democracy* album was released by the end of 2008. The planned promotion involved some sort of on-line coupon system in which consumers would go to Dr. Pepper's website to request a coupon for one free can of Dr. Pepper if the album was released in 2008. At the time of the announcement, Axl Rose, lead vocalist of the band, supposedly posted his opinion about the Dr. Pepper promotion on the Guns N' Roses' website (**www.gunsnroses.com**). Axl Rose noted that the band was both surprised and happy to have Dr. Pepper's support.

SOURCE: © MEDIABLITZIMAGES (UK) LIMITED / ALAMY

In general, the marketing idea sounded easy to implement, yet most thought this was a promise that Dr. Pepper would not have to keep. This might be why a Dr. Pepper spokesperson said that the details of the plan would not be released until the band stated a specific release date for the album. In October of 2008, however, a confirmed release date of November 23, 2008, was announced for the *Chinese Democracy* album.

The album was released as planned, and Dr. Pepper followed through on its marketing promise. The company posted the coupon for a can of pop on its website. The catch was that fans had a 24-hour window of opportunity to visit the site and print out the coupon. Unfortunately, traffic on the site, with so many people flocking to it, caused it to crash. Rather than blaming Dr. Pepper for the malfunction, some disgruntled fans (bloggers) blamed Axl Rose!

Although Dr. Pepper tried to appease angry website visitors by extending the promotion, adding a toll-free line to handle disgruntled consumers and setting up an interactive voice recorder to accept coupon requests, Axl Rose was not satisfied. Via his lawyers, Rose also demanded that Dr. Pepper place a full-page apology in the *New York Times*, the *Los Angeles Times*, *USA Today*, and the *Wall Street Journal*. Additionally, the lawyer sought payment for the "unauthorized use of and abuse of their [Guns N' Roses] publicity and intellectual property rights." Basically, the accusation was that Dr. Pepper had profited from the band's name and then failed in its promised giveaway. Just prior to this accusation, rapper 50 Cent had sued Taco Bell for using his name in its advertising without his permission. Taco Bell had run a print ad asking 50 Cent to change his name to 79 Cent, 89 Cent, or 99 Cent so as to help publicize the chain's value menu.

All the while, *Chinese Democracy* did not receive the reception that had been hoped for. Some sources blamed Axl Rose, saying that he had not done necessary promotional work on the album. As though the album's less-than-stellar reception and Dr. Pepper's promotional snafu were not enough, the Chinese Communist Party described the album as a venomous attack on China. So, was it the fact that the promotion ran into implementation problems or the fact that the album was not faring as well as hoped that was the root of the problem?[1]

Questions

1. Who is the consumer in this situation—Dr. Pepper consumers or Guns N' Roses fans? Are they one and the same? Explain.

2. Would any type of marketing research have helped prepare Dr. Pepper for the amount of activity on its website? Explain your answer.

CRITICAL THINKING CASE

HOW CAN BROKERS COPE WITH THE CHANGING PERSONAL INSURANCE MARKET?

Insurance providers in Ontario have a guaranteed market because the law requires anyone who operates an automobile in the province to have automobile insurance. In addition, insurance providers are also able to offer homeowners and renters insurance to go with automobile insurance. The sales and distribution of home and automobile insurance services has traditionally been through independent insurance brokers who formed an industry association to help them manage this business. The Insurance Brokers Association of Ontario (IBAO) describes itself as "a voluntary membership organization serving the interests of more than 10,000 independent insurance brokers across Ontario." The mission of this organization is "to preserve and enhance the value and integrity of the independent broker insurance distribution system and to be recognized as an invaluable resource to and by member brokers."

Recently, the consumer market for insurance products in Ontario has been undergoing significant changes because banks have started offering both automobile and home insurance products. In addition, a number of auto insurance firms are now bypassing insurance brokers and offering direct distribution of home and auto insurance through the Internet too. The result has been a form of market fragmentation that has resulted in a loss of business for the brokers. In order to understand the market and how it was changing, the Insurance Brokers Association of Ontario (IBAO) hired Navicom Incorporated, a consulting firm that specializes in predictive intelligence, to assist it in understanding where the market was going. The application of predictive intelligence is summed up by this quote from Navicom's chief statistician: "The objective of statistics is to make an inference about a population based on information contained in a sample and to provide an associated measure of goodness for the inference. It is the only method to deal with uncertainty, explanation and prediction."

Navicom undertook "an in-depth market study that focused on the buying behaviors of consumers that purchase personal lines insurance from non-broker distribution channels." The IBAO had seen a shift in consumer buying patterns but wasn't sure what the reasons were so it didn't know how to respond. The IBAO confirmed that "the Ontario personal lines insurance market" was becoming fragmented. Consumers were using different criteria to make purchase decisions and this was at odds with the way that traditional "broker" firms were operating.

The research indicated that the brokers were "facing new customer segments that did not previously exist. These segments include customers who are new to the market, as well as current broker customers who are starting to see the market in a new way." The research also showed that consumers were changing the way they wanted to communicate. Communication via regular mail was losing its lustre. Also, people wanted to be able to do business after 5:00 p.m. and to be able to contact their insurance providers via the Internet as well as by telephone. The IBAO realized that its brokers needed to change their communication approaches. In addition, the research showed many insurance buyers were affected by inertia. Specifically, once a consumer had adopted a way of doing business, he or she preferred to stay with it. For those customers who had been with a broker, this was a plus. However, in the case of new customers who had decided to buy from their banks or had selected firms that sold via the Internet, inertia meant that these customers would likely stay with these new distribution channels.

As a result of the research findings, the IBAO realized that it had to make changes in its business model. The organization concluded that "simply getting better at what many brokers already do well is not enough to help them win back some of the new customer segments who are not necessarily dissatisfied, but are increasingly aware of insurance options elsewhere." Consequently, brokers needed to adopt technology to be competitive with the Internet sellers and the banks. The IBAO realized that this would require many of its members to make investments in equipment and would lead to changes in their current business processes. The IBAO also realized it needed to reinvigorate its brand to counter the advertising of the Internet sellers and the customer information and contacts that the banks had available to them. Consequently, the IBAO was recommending that brokers do a better job of reaching out to their customers and engaging them.[2]

Questions

1. Do the consumers to which the IBAO members are targeting their services satisfy the definition of a market, a market segment, or both? Explain.

2. Outline the decision process of the buying behaviour of consumers for purchasing auto and home insurance.

3. Visit the IBAO website at **www.ibao.org**. Evaluate the website and describe the positioning strategy for the IBAO as an organization.

4. Using Exhibit 7.1 as a guide, outline and describe the marketing research process that Navicom undertook for the IBAO.

SOURCE: © FRANK CHMURA/ALAMY

Product ③
Decisions

8 Product Concepts

SOURCE: LYNN MCLEOD

LEARNING OUTCOMES

1 Define the term *product*

2 Classify consumer products

3 Define the terms *product item*, *product line*, and *product mix*

4 Describe marketing uses of branding

5 Describe marketing uses of packaging and labelling

6 Discuss global issues in branding and packaging

7 Describe how and why product warranties are important marketing tools

Ⓥ MARKETING & YOU

Using the following scale, indicate your opinion on the line before each item.

1	2	3	4	5
Strongly disagree	Disagree	Neutral	Agree	Strongly agree

__ I usually purchase brand-name products.
__ Store brands are of poor quality.*
__ All brands are about the same.*
__ The well-known national brands are best for me.

__ The more expensive brands are usually my choices.
__ The higher the price of a product, the better its quality.
__ Nice department and specialty stores offer me the best products.

Total your score, reversing your scores for the items followed by an asterisk. That is, if you answered 1, change it to 5 and vice versa. Read the chapter and find out what your score means at the end.

SOURCE: REPRINTED WITH PERMISSION FROM *MARKETING SCALES HANDBOOK* VOL. III, PUBLISHED BY THE AMERICAN MARKETING ASSOCIATION, G. BRUNER, K. JAMES, H. HENSEL, EDS. SCALE #230.

While it might be tempting to flood the market with new flavours of Canada's best-selling chocolate bar, even Bob Leonidas, president of Nestlé Canada Inc., concedes that there can be too many kinds of Kit Kats. This is what happened to Nestlé in the United Kingdom. "They went way overboard. They had 'Christmas Pudding' and they had 'Blood Orange' for Halloween," Leonidas says. As for Canada, where Nestlé is headquartered in Toronto and has been selling its products since 1922, Leonidas says, "We're sticking to the fundamentals." That's not to say Nestlé Canada won't be introducing more brand extensions for its top-selling Kit Kat candy bar.

Kit Kat Peanut Butter was the first brand extension in Canada for the popular product. "Peanut butter is a big segment," according to Leonidas. In fact, peanuts and peanut butter with chocolate make up about 10 percent of the $3-billion chocolate market in Canada. Kit Kat also comes in Chunky, Chunky Cinnamon, Xtra Chocolate, and dark chocolate versions in Canada, and there are Kit Kat bites for the calorie-conscious and Kit Kat ice cream.

The practice of introducing new varieties, flavours, formats, or products under a brand name that is already well established in the market is called *brand extension*. Extending brands, to take advantage of well-known and accepted names, has become a popular marketing tactic for consumer products companies. It is far less expensive to use an already established brand name than to introduce, and have to build recognition for, a new name. It is also less risky. Consumers are more likely to buy a product that bears a name they are already familiar with. Nearly 95 percent of new food and household products introduced in Canada each year are brand extensions.

Kellogg's has revitalized sales for the Eggo brand waffle, which has been on breakfast tables in Canada since 1936, through numerous extensions. Nearly a dozen new Eggo flavours, including strawberry and chocolate chip for kids and Nutri-Grain and Low Fat lines for adults, were introduced. The Eggo name was then added to toaster muffins, cinnamon rolls, pancakes, and maple syrup. Limited-edition Scooby-Doo, Spider-Man, and Sponge Bob Eggos were also marketed. With these extensions, Eggo sales grew by over 12 percent over each of the three years after the brand extensions.

Although it was successful for Eggo, brand extensions can go too far. The over-extension of the Kit Kat brand in the United Kingdom is an example. No fewer than ten new Kit Kat flavours were launched in a single year. Beyond the Christmas Pudding and Blood Orange extensions already mentioned, the new flavours included lemon, yoghurt, mango, passion fruit, tiramisu, and lime crush. Sales increased for a short time but the quick introduction of so many Kit Kat flavours ended up confusing and tiring consumers. After the flood of brand extensions, Kit Kat sales in the United Kingdom fell. This is unlikely to happen in Canada as Leonidas believes that brand extensions should not change the fundamentals of what made the original product successful.

Many of the Nestlé Canada brand extensions are aimed directly at the competition. The Kit Kat Peanut Butter bar was aimed directly at Reese's Peanut Butter Cups. Aero, Nestlé Canada's second-biggest-selling chocolate bar, was extended to include a caramel flavour to take on Cadbury Adams Canada's Caramilk bar. Peanut butter and fruity flavours of Nestlé Canada's Smarties brand have been added. The company has used the same brand-extension strategy with its Nestea, Lean Cuisine, and Häagen-Dazs brands. According to Leonidas, "Nestlé uses its well-known names for new products for the same reason that General Motors decided to bring back the Camaro [which is built in Oshawa, Ontario] instead of launching a new name. These brand names are strong. It costs a fortune to launch brand names. The best brand launch is a brand you already own."[1]

Think about some of your favourite products. How many varieties or extensions of these products are being sold?

SOURCE: ANDY HOFFMAN, "MORE KIT KATS IS GOOD, TOO MANY IS NOT," GLOBE AND MAIL, SEPTEMBER 9, 2006, B3; "EGGO LESSON: EXPAND YOUR PRODUCT CATEGORY," FORTUNE, OCTOBER 31, 2005, 166–68; WWW.NESTLE.CA; WWW.LEGGOMYEGGO.COM

1 WHAT IS A PRODUCT?

The product offering, the heart of an organization's marketing program, is usually the starting point in creating a marketing mix. A marketing manager cannot determine a price, design a promotion strategy, or create a distribution channel until the firm has a product to sell. Moreover, an excellent distribution channel, a persuasive promotion campaign, and a fair price will not be enough if a company has a poor or inadequate product offering.

product
Everything, both favourable and unfavourable, that a person receives in an exchange.

A **product** may be defined as everything, both favourable and unfavourable, that a person receives in an exchange. A product may be a tangible good like a pair of shoes, a service like a haircut, an idea like "don't litter," or any combination of these. Packaging, style, colour, options, and size are some typical product features. Just as important are intangibles such as service, the seller's image, the manufacturer's reputation, and the way consumers believe others will view the product.

REVIEW LEARNING OUTCOME 1

To most people, the term *product* means a tangible good. However, services and ideas are also products. Chapter 10 focuses specifically on the unique aspects of marketing services. The marketing process identified in Chapter 1 is the same whether the product marketed is a good, a service, an idea, or some combination of these.

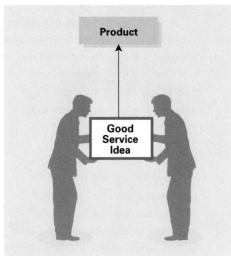

2 TYPES OF CONSUMER PRODUCTS

Classify consumer products

business product (industrial product)
A product used to manufacture other goods or services, to facilitate an organization's operations, or to resell to other customers.

consumer product
A product bought to satisfy an individual's personal wants.

Products can be classified as either business (industrial) or consumer products, depending on the buyer's intentions. The key distinction between the two types of products is their intended use. If the intended use is a business purpose, the product is classified as a business or industrial product. As explained in Chapter 5, a **business product** is used to manufacture other goods or services, to facilitate an organization's operations, or to resell to other customers. A **consumer product** is bought to satisfy an individual's personal wants. Sometimes the same item can be classified as either a business or a consumer product, depending on its intended use. Examples include light bulbs, pencils and paper, and computers.

We need to know about product classifications because business and consumer products are marketed differently. They are marketed to different target markets and use different distribution channels, promotion, and pricing strategies.

Chapter 5 examined seven categories of business products: major equipment, accessory equipment, component parts, processed materials, raw materials, supplies, and services. The current chapter examines an effective way of categorizing consumer products. Although there are several ways to classify them, the most popular approach includes these four types: convenience products, shopping products, specialty products, and unsought products (see Exhibit 8.1). This approach classifies products according to how much effort is normally used to shop for them.

CONVENIENCE PRODUCTS

convenience product
A relatively inexpensive item that merits little shopping effort.

A **convenience product** is a relatively inexpensive item that merits little shopping effort—that is, a consumer is unwilling to shop extensively for such an item. Candy, soft drinks, combs, aspirin, bread and milk, small hardware items, dry cleaning, and car washes fall into the convenience product category.

Consumers buy convenience products regularly, usually without much planning. Nevertheless, consumers do know the brand names of popular convenience products, such as Coca-Cola, Bayer aspirin, and Right Guard deodorant. Convenience products normally require wide distribution in order to sell sufficient quantities to meet profit

EXHIBIT 8.1

Classification of Consumer Products

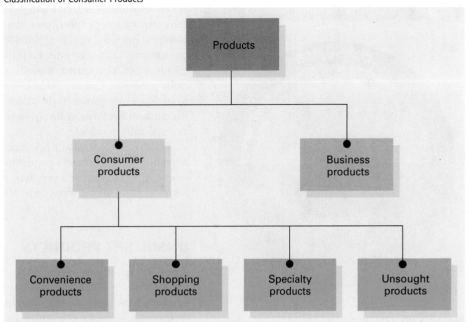

SOURCE: COURTESY OF LG APPLIANCES

shopping product
A product that requires comparison shopping because it is usually more expensive than a convenience product and is found in fewer stores.

The LG Tromm Front Panel Washer and Dryer.
Introducing the newest laundry combination from LG. Incredible style and performance to match. Features convenient upfront electronic control panels and a Sensor Dry system for intelligent fabric care and energy efficiency. Easy to use side by side, or stack them to save space. Either way, you'll not only like it, you'll love it. Don't be surprised if you look for excuses to do the wash! Great design. Great technology. Great for the way you live. Discover the full line of LG premium home appliances at www.LGusa.com, or call 1-800-243-0000.

©2004 LG Electronics, Inc. LG Design and Life's Good are trademarks of LG Electronics, Inc.

Although major appliances, like washers and dryers, are usually considered homogeneous shopping goods, the high-efficiency front-loaders that boast many more features than standard machines are gaining in popularity. Do you think high efficiency is enough to make washers and dryers heterogeneous shopping goods?

goals. For example, Kit Kat candy bars are available everywhere, including Walmart, Zellers, 7-Eleven, supermarkets, drug stores, vending machines, gas stations, newsstands, and many other places.

SHOPPING PRODUCTS

A **shopping product** is usually more expensive than a convenience product and is found in fewer stores. Consumers usually buy a shopping product only after comparing several brands or stores on style, practicality, price, and lifestyle compatibility. Consumers are willing to invest some effort into the shopping process to get the desired benefits.

There are two types of shopping products: homogeneous and heterogeneous. Consumers perceive *homogeneous* shopping products as basically similar—for example, washers, dryers, refrigerators, and televisions. With homogeneous shopping products, consumers typically look for the lowest-priced brand that has the desired features. For example, consumers might compare power lawn mowers at Canadian Tire, Sears, Walmart, and Home Depot before buying.

In contrast, consumers perceive *heterogeneous* shopping products as essentially different—for example, furniture, clothing, housing, and universities. Consumers often have trouble comparing heterogeneous shopping products because the prices, quality, and features vary so much. The benefit of comparing heterogeneous shopping products is "finding the best product or brand for me"—a decision that is often highly individual and very important because you may have the shopping product for a long time.

2   **Classify consumer products**

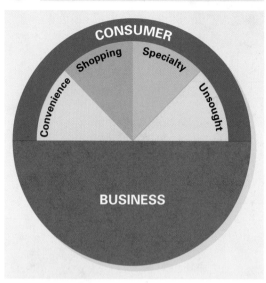

specialty product
A particular item for which consumers search extensively and for which they are very reluctant to accept substitutes.

unsought product
A product unknown to the potential buyer or a known product that the buyer does not actively seek.

SPECIALTY PRODUCTS

When consumers search extensively for a particular item and are very reluctant to accept substitutes, that item is known as a **specialty product**. Breitling watches, Rolls-Royce automobiles, Simaudio stereo equipment, Leica cameras, Laguiole knives, gourmet restaurants, and highly specialized forms of medical care are generally considered specialty products. Guitars made one at a time for rock stars such as Keith Richards, James Taylor, Peter Gabriel, and Sting by George Rizsanyi on his farm in Bridgewater, Nova Scotia, would also qualify as a specialty product.[2]

Marketers of specialty products often use selective, status-conscious advertising to maintain their product's exclusive image. Distribution is often limited to one or a very few outlets in a geographic area. Brand names and quality of service are often very important.

UNSOUGHT PRODUCTS

A product unknown to the potential buyer or a known product that the buyer does not actively seek is referred to as an **unsought product**. New products fall into this category until advertising and distribution increase consumer awareness of them.

Some goods are always marketed as unsought items, especially needed products that we do not like to think about or care to spend money on. Insurance, burial plots, encyclopedias, and similar items require aggressive personal selling and highly persuasive advertising. Salespeople actively seek leads to potential buyers. Because consumers usually do not seek out this type of product, the company must go directly to them through a salesperson, direct mail, or direct-response advertising.

 PRODUCT ITEMS, LINES, AND MIXES

Define the terms product item, product line, and product mix

product item
A specific version of a product that can be designated as a distinct offering among an organization's products.

product line
A group of closely related product items.

Rarely does a company sell a single product. More often, it sells a variety of things. A **product item** is a specific version of a product that can be designated as a distinct offering among an organization's products. Campbell's Chicken Noodle soup is an example of a product item (see Exhibit 8.2).

A group of closely related product items forms a **product line**. For example, the column in Exhibit 8.2 titled "Canned Soups" represents one of Campbell's product lines with the different brands representing the many product items in this line. "Gravies" would represent another product line for Campbell's. Different container

EXHIBIT 8.2

Campbell's Product Lines and Product Mix

	Width of the Product Mix			
	Canned Soups	**Microwave Soups**	**Gravies**	**Tomato Juice**
Depth of the Product Lines	Chicken Noodle	Creamy Tomato	Beef	Regular
	Tomato	Vegetable	Turkey	Low Sodium
	Vegetable Beef	Chicken Noodle	Mushroom	Organic
	French Onion	Creamy Chicken	Chicken	Healthy Request
	Chicken & Stars	Tomato Parmesan	Country Sausage	
	Minestrone	Cream of Broccoli	Golden Pork	
	Hearty Beef Barley	Vegetable with	Au Jus	
	Sirloin Burger	Noodles	Brown Gravy with	
	Chunky Beef with	New England	Onions	
	Vegetable	Clam Chowder		
	And More	And More		

SOURCE: Campbell's Web site: http//www.campbellsoup.com, June 2010

sizes and shapes also distinguish items in a product line. Diet Coke, for example, is available in cans and various plastic containers. Each size and each container are separate product items.

product mix
All products that an organization sells.

An organization's **product mix** includes all the products it sells. Together, all of Campbell's products—canned soups, microwave soups, gravies, and tomato juice—constitute its product mix. Each product item in the product mix may require a separate marketing strategy. In some cases, however, product lines and even entire product mixes share some marketing strategy components. Nike has promoted all its product items and lines with the theme "Just Do It."

Companies derive several benefits from organizing related items into product lines, including the following:

- *Advertising economies*: Product lines provide economies of scale in advertising. Several products can be advertised under the umbrella of the line. Campbell's can talk about its soup being "Mm! Mm! Good!" and promote the entire line.
- *Package uniformity*: A product line can benefit from package uniformity. All packages in the line may have a common look and still keep their individual identities. Again, Campbell's soup is a good example.
- *Standardized components*: Product lines allow firms to standardize components, thus reducing manufacturing and inventory costs. For example, many of the components Samsonite uses in its folding tables and chairs are also used in its patio furniture. General Motors and Toyota use the same parts on many different automobile makes and models.
- *Efficient sales and distribution*: A product line enables sales personnel for companies like Procter & Gamble to provide a full range of choices to customers. Distributors and retailers are often more inclined to stock the company's products when the company offers a full line. Transportation and warehousing costs are likely to be lower for a product line than for a collection of individual items.
- *Equivalent quality*: Purchasers usually expect and believe that all products in a line are about equal in quality. Consumers expect that all Campbell's soups and all President's Choice cookies will be of similar quality.

product mix width
The number of product lines an organization offers.

product line depth
The number of product items in a product line.

Product mix width (or breadth) refers to the number of product lines an organization offers. In Exhibit 8.2, for example, the width of Campbell's product mix shown would be four product lines. **Product line depth** is the number of product items in a product line. As shown in Exhibit 8.2, the canned soup line has more product items than the tomato juice line.

Firms increase the *width* of their product mix to diversify risk. To generate sales and boost profits, firms spread risk across many product lines rather than depend on only one or two. Firms also widen their product mix to capitalize on established reputations. By introducing new product lines, Levi's Dockers brand capitalized on its image of casual style and comfort. Dockers started as a casual apparel brand for men but extended into women's apparel with Dockers for Her. Recently, Dockers moved its comfort image from clothing to bedroom and bath products with its Dockers Home line. The Oreo Cookie brand has been extended to include items such as breakfast cereal, ice cream, Jell-O Pudding, and cake mix.

Firms increase the *depth* of product lines to attract buyers with different preferences, to increase sales and profits by further segmenting the market, to capitalize on economies of scale in production and marketing, and to even out seasonal sales patterns. Marriott International has 14 different lodging brands. Coca-Cola and Pepsi are introducing soft drinks using the natural plant-based sweetener stevia. These line extensions are targeting consumers looking for healthier alternatives. Oreo Cookies now come in a variety of flavours, including Double Delight Mint Crème, Chocolate Crème, Uh-Oh Oreos (chocolate filling with vanilla cookie), Double Delight Peanut Butter, and Chocolate Fudge Sundae Creme.

The Oreos Cookies product line is quite deep including the original Oreo cookie flavour plus Double Delight Mint Creme, Chocolate Creme, Uh-Oh Oreos, Double Delight Peanut Butter, and Chocolate Fudge Sundae Creme.

SOURCE: RICHARD LEVINE/GETSTOCK.COM

Product Concepts **Chapter 8**

ADJUSTMENTS TO PRODUCT ITEMS, LINES, AND MIXES

Over time, firms change product items, lines, and mixes to take advantage of new technical or product developments or to respond to changes in the environment. They may adjust by modifying products, repositioning products, or extending or contracting product lines.

Product Modification

product modification
Changing one or more of a product's characteristics.

Marketing managers must decide if and when to modify existing products. **Product modification** changes one or more of a product's characteristics:

- *Quality modification*: change in a product's dependability or durability. Reducing a product's quality may let the manufacturer lower the price and appeal to target markets unable to afford the original product. On the other hand, increasing quality can help the firm compete with rival firms. Increasing quality can also result in increased brand loyalty, greater ability to raise prices, or new opportunities for market segmentation. Inexpensive ink-jet printers have improved in quality to the point that they produce photo-quality images. These printers are now competing with camera film. Michelin has added a higher-quality, higher-priced "run-flat" tire to its product mix. This tire will travel up to 70 kilometres after suffering total air loss.

planned obsolescence
The practice of modifying products so those that have already been sold become obsolete before they actually need replacement.

- *Functional modification*: change in a product's versatility, effectiveness, convenience, or safety. Oral-B introduced Stages toothbrushes, a line of toothbrushes for children. For example, Stage 2, designed for toddlers, has an easy-to-grip handle and a narrow brush that makes it easier to reach all teeth.[3] Lea & Perrins offers its steak sauce in a value-priced squeeze bottle with a "no mess, stay clean" cap.
- *Style modification*: aesthetic product change, rather than a quality or functional change. Procter & Gamble has added Febreze scents to its Tide liquid detergent, Downy liquid fabric softener, and Bounce dryer sheets. These products all promise their usual function with a touch of scent to improve the aesthetics of each brand.[4] Clothing and auto manufacturers also commonly use style modifications to motivate customers to replace products before they are worn out. **Planned obsolescence** is a term commonly used to describe the practice of modifying products so those that have already been sold become obsolete before they actually need replacement. Some products become obsolete because technology changes so rapidly. Some argue that planned obsolescence is wasteful; some claim it is unethical. Marketers respond that consumers favour style modifications because they like changes in the appearance of goods like clothing and cars. Marketers also contend that consumers, not manufacturers and marketers, decide when styles are obsolete.

Repositioning

Repositioning involves changing consumers' perceptions of a brand. Kool-Aid, the soft drink brand that has stood for fun and refreshment for many years, is adding better-for-you options by introducing new and reformulated products. The company is repositioning the brand as supporting a healthier family lifestyle.[5]

Changing demographics, declining sales, or changes in the social environment often motivate firms to reposition established brands. The clothing retailer Banana Republic started out selling safari-style clothing, but the concept soon became outdated. Gap acquired the chain and repositioned it as a more upscale retailer offering business casual clothing. Procter & Gamble is redesigning its Dawn liquid detergent line, including adding new products, sizes

EVERY KID GOES THROUGH STAGES. FORTUNATELY, SO DO OUR NEW BRUSHES.

SOURCE: COURTESY THE GILLETTE COMPANY

Oral-B's Stages toothbrushes represent a functional modification to adult toothbrushes. Numerous colours and designs of a single-stage toothbrush would be a style modification.

Product extensions enable a company to compete more broadly in an industry. Coca-Cola's Minute Maid was successful building on its original Premium orange juice brand with Premium Blends, which mix orange juice with cranberry, passion fruit, strawberry and banana, or tangerine juice. Other product extensions include Minute Maid Coolers, Minute Maid Smoothies, and Minute Maid Frozen Fruit Bars.

and graphics. For example, the Dawn Plus line will be positioned as a tough cleaning brand, reformulated with an added enzyme to fight stuck-on foods.[6]

Product Line Extensions

product line extension
Adding products to an existing product line in order to compete more broadly in the industry.

A **product line extension** occurs when a company's management decides to add products to an existing product line in order to compete more broadly in the industry. Minute Maid has added two calcium-fortified juices—Premium HomeSqueezed Style orange juice and Ruby Red Grapefruit Blend—to attract health-conscious baby boomers.[7] Jolly Rancher launched Fruit Chews to compete in the chewy candy product category.[8] Procter & Gamble extended its Febreze odour freshener line with Febreze to Go aimed at travellers.[9] Kraft extended a number of its popular Nabisco brands by adding small-portioned packages. Campbell's offers its soups in cans and in microwavable containers.[10]

Product Line Contraction

Does the world really need 31 varieties of Head & Shoulders shampoo? Or 52 versions of Crest? When Steve Jobs took over Apple, the company sold over 40 products. He immediately simplified by cutting the product line down to four computers—two desktop and two laptops that Apple could focus on perfecting. This move helped Apple double its market share. Symptoms of product line overextension include the following:

- Some products in the line do not contribute to profits because of low sales or they cannibalize sales of other items in the line.
- Manufacturing or marketing resources are disproportionately allocated to slow-moving products.
- Some items in the line are obsolete because of new product entries in the line or new products offered by competitors.

> BIG MACS TAKE ON A LOCAL FLAVOUR

The next time you're in Brazil, Italy, or Portugal and want something familiar, stop off at a local McDonald's and order a Big Tasty burger. As the name suggests, it's a giant sandwich consisting of a 5.5-ounce beef patty slathered in smoky barbecue sauce. Once you include the square-chopped lettuce, tomatoes, and three slices of cheese, it all adds up to a whopping 840 calories. Just don't try looking for the Big Tasty here in Canada. The Big Tasty was dreamed up in a test kitchen in Germany and then tweaked, trialled, and launched in Sweden.

McDonald's worldwide operations are now far bigger than its North American business, and the international business is growing faster. And as the world has become the principal revenue engine for the company, it has turned this iconic brand upside down. These days new ideas come from anywhere.

Walk out of London's Cannon Street Station and turn right, leaving St. Paul's Cathedral behind you, and you'll come across a restaurant with three giant green swivel armchairs in the window that look like the modernist Egg chair created by the late Danish designer Arne Jacobsen. Inside, lime-green slats partition several seating zones. The pillars are orange. Funky murals hang on the walls, covered in green and red striped wallpaper. The scene is light-years removed from the red-and-white vinyl seats and Formica tabletops that have long served as McDonald's standard decor. If it wasn't for the golden arches over the door, you might not realize that it was a McDonald's restaurant at all. In fact, the furnishings come from a catalogue of different decor types that a team of McDonald's designers in Paris has worked up with the help of an architect named Philippe Avanzi, who is based in Grenoble, France.

It's not just the decor that varies. McDonald's in Britain added freshly ground fair-trade coffee to its menu, along with organic milk. It boasts that its eggs are free range. Naturally, the Brits serve up McDonald's classics such as Big Macs, Happy Meals, and Double Cheeseburgers. But you can also order porridge for breakfast and a range of other items customized for British tastes, including a variant of a French chicken sandwich—with salsa dressing.

Such variation has become the norm, belying McDonald's image that it serves the same standard fare around the world. In India, where eating beef is a religious taboo, the Big Mac equivalent is the Maharaja Mac, made from chicken, and there's a plethora of vegetarian dishes on the menu. And even some of the classics are now tweaked from market to market. In Germany, less coriander is used in SouthWest salads, while Britain puts less salt on its Chicken McNuggets.[11]

Do you think that McDonald's made the right move in letting global managers design their own stores and products? What if a manager wanted to change the McDonald's logo? Do you think that we will see the Big Tasty in Canada? Why or why not?

SOURCE: PETER GUMBEL, "BIG MAC'S LOCAL FLAVOR," FORTUNE, MAY 5, 2008, 115–121

REVIEW LEARNING OUTCOME 3

3   Define the terms *product item*, *product line*, and *product mix*

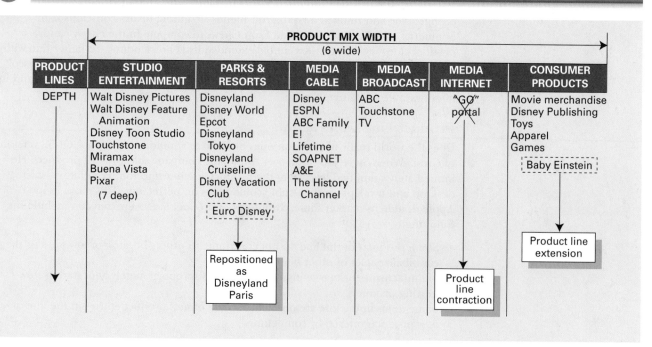

PRODUCT MIX WIDTH (6 wide)						
PRODUCT LINES	STUDIO ENTERTAINMENT	PARKS & RESORTS	MEDIA CABLE	MEDIA BROADCAST	MEDIA INTERNET	CONSUMER PRODUCTS
DEPTH	Walt Disney Pictures Walt Disney Feature Animation Disney Toon Studio Touchstone Miramax Buena Vista Pixar (7 deep)	Disneyland Disney World Epcot Disneyland Tokyo Disneyland Cruiseline Disney Vacation Club Euro Disney ↓ Repositioned as Disneyland Paris	Disney ESPN ABC Family E! Lifetime SOAPNET A&E The History Channel	ABC Touchstone TV	"GO" portal ↓ Product line contraction	Movie merchandise Disney Publishing Toys Apparel Games Baby Einstein ↓ Product line extension

Three major benefits are likely when a firm eliminates items from overextended product lines. First, resources become concentrated on the most important products. Second, managers no longer waste resources trying to improve the sales and profits of poorly performing products. Third, new product items have a greater chance of being successful because more financial and human resources are available to manage them.

4 BRANDING

Describe marketing uses of branding

brand
A name, term, symbol, design, or combination that identifies a seller's products and differentiates them from competitors' products.

brand name
That part of a brand that can be spoken, including letters, words, and numbers.

brand mark
The elements of a brand that cannot be spoken.

brand equity
The value of company and brand names.

global brand
A brand where at least one-third of the product sales are outside its home country or region.

EXHIBIT 8.3

The World's Top 10 Global Brands (2009)

Rank	Brand
1	Coca-Cola
2	IBM
3	Microsoft
4	General Electric
5	Nokia
6	McDonald's
7	Google
8	Toyota
9	Intel
10	Disney

SOURCE: Reprinted from the September 17, 2009 issue of Bloomberg Businessweek by special permission, copyright © 2009 by Bloomberg L.P. "The 100 Best Global Brands 2009," www.businessweek.com; accessed June 7, 2010.

brand loyalty
A consistent preference for one brand over all others.

The success of any business or consumer product depends in part on the target market's ability to distinguish one product from another. Branding is the main tool marketers use to distinguish their products from the competition's.

A **brand** is a name, term, symbol, design, or combination of these that identifies a seller's products and differentiates them from competitors' products. A **brand name** is that part of a brand that can be spoken, including letters (GM, YMCA), words (Mastercraft and MotoMaster), and numbers (WD-40, 7-Eleven, Ford F-150). The elements of a brand that cannot be spoken are called the **brand mark**—for example, the well-known Mercedes-Benz, Nike, and McDonald's symbols.

BENEFITS OF BRANDING

Branding has three main purposes: product identification, repeat sales, and new-product sales. The most important purpose is *product identification*. Branding allows marketers to distinguish their products from all others. Many brand names are familiar to consumers and may indicate quality because they are so readily recognized.

The term **brand equity** refers to the value of company and brand names. A brand that has high awareness, perceived quality, and brand loyalty among customers has high brand equity. A brand with strong brand equity is a valuable asset.

The term **global brand** has been used to refer to brands where at least one-third of the product sales are outside the home country or region. A strong global brand acts as an ambassador when companies enter new markets or offer new products. It also helps guide corporate strategy decisions by indicating which new ideas fit within the brand concept and which do not.[12] Yum Brands, which owns Pizza Hut, KFC, and Taco Bell, is a good example of a company that has developed strong global brands. Yum believes that it has to adapt its restaurants to local tastes and different cultural and political climates. In Japan, for instance, KFC sells tempura crispy strips. In northern England, KFC focuses on gravy and potatoes, while in Thailand it offers rice with soy or sweet chili sauce. In China, the company recruits employees who balance an understanding of the Chinese mindset with Western business training.[13]

What constitutes a good brand name? Exhibit 8.3 lists the world's 10 best global brands. Most effective brand names have several of the following features:

- Easy to pronounce (by both domestic and foreign buyers)
- Easy to recognize
- Easy to remember
- Short
- Distinctive, unique
- Describes the product
- Describes the product use
- Describes product benefits
- Has a positive connotation
- Reinforces the desired product image
- Is legally protectable in home and foreign markets of interest

The best generator of *repeat sales* is a satisfied customer. Branding helps consumers identify products they wish to buy again and avoid those they do not. **Brand loyalty**, a consistent preference for one brand over all others, is quite high in some product categories. Over half the users in product categories such as cigarettes, mayonnaise, toothpaste, coffee, headache remedies, photographic film, bath soap, and ketchup are loyal to one brand. Brand identity is essential to developing brand loyalty.

The third main purpose of branding is to *facilitate new-product sales.* Company and brand names like those listed in Exhibit 8.3 are extremely useful when introducing new products.

The Internet has provided firms with a new alternative for generating brand awareness, promoting a desired brand image, stimulating new and repeat brand sales, enhancing brand loyalty, and building brand equity. Nearly all packaged-goods firms, such as Procter & Gamble, Campbell's soup, and Gerber, have a presence on-line. Tide.com offers a useful feature called Stain Detective, a digital tip sheet on how to remove almost any substance from almost any fabric.

BRANDING STRATEGIES

Firms face complex branding decisions. As Exhibit 8.4 illustrates, the first decision is whether to brand at all. Some firms actually use the lack of a brand name as a selling point. These unbranded products are called generic products. Firms that decide to brand their products may choose to follow a policy of using manufacturers' brands, private (distributor) brands, or both. In either case, they must then decide between individual branding (different brands for different products) or family branding (common names for different products) or a combination of the two.

Manufacturers' Brands versus Private Brands

manufacturer's brand
The brand name of a manufacturer.

The brand name of a manufacturer—such as Kodak, Nike, or Fruit of the Loom—is called a **manufacturer's brand**. Sometimes "national brand" is used as a synonym for "manufacturer's brand." This term is not always accurate, however, because many manufacturers serve only regional markets. Using "manufacturer's brand" more precisely defines the brand's owner.

private brand
A brand name owned by a wholesaler or a retailer.

A **private brand**, also known as a private label or store brand, is a brand name owned by a wholesaler or a retailer. Craftsman (a Sears brand), President's Choice (Loblaws), Mastercraft (Canadian Tire), Beaumark (The Bay), Big Eight and Compliments (Sobeys), Select (Safeway), Kirkland (Costco Canada), and Life Brand (Shoppers Drug Mart) are all private brands. A survey conducted by the Private Manufacturers' Association indicated that 41 percent of respondents identify themselves as frequent buyers of store brands. At some stores, such as Canadian Tire and Walmart, sales of store brands exceed 40 percent.[14] Ol' Roy, Walmart's private brand of dog food, is not only the largest-selling dog food in Canada but also the largest-selling brand of dog food in the world. Private-label sales are higher in Ontario

Exhibit 8.4

Major Branding Decisions

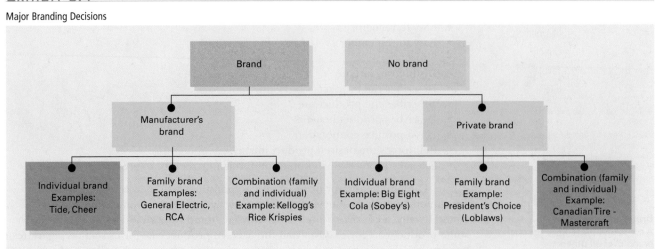

where's the one place all our brands hang out together?

introducing the **PG.com** network

The new pg.com lets you **do more,** **learn more** and **get more** from P&G and our brands than ever before...

Discover the surprising number of online resources our brands have to offer.

Try and buy products before they're available in stores.

Share your ideas for improving our products and creating new ones.

and coming soon... Take advantage of new tools to help manage your P&G shareholder account.

www.pg.com

SOURCE: © THE PROCTER & GAMBLE COMPANY. USED BY PERMISSION.

Procter & Gamble has an extensive Web presence to support its complete slate of brands. P&G has launched the pg.com network, touting it as "the one place where all our brands hang out together."

individual branding
Using different brand names for different products.

family brand
Marketing several different products under the same brand name.

(25.2 percent of sales) and lower in Quebec (11.4 percent of sales). Across the board, store brands are growing faster than national brands.[15]

Retailers love consumers' acceptance of private brands as they earn, on average, 10 percent higher margins than on manufacturers' brands. In addition, a trusted store brand helps to differentiate one retailer from all others and creates loyalty to the store. Exhibit 8.5 illustrates key issues that wholesalers and retailers should consider in deciding whether to sell manufacturers' brands or private brands. Many firms, such as Zellers, Walmart, and Loblaws, offer a combination of both. In fact, Walmart and Sears have turned their low-priced, private-label jeans into some of the most popular brands around. Loblaws has moved some of its private labels upmarket by emphasizing the quality of the product (e.g., President's Choice Decadent Chocolate Chip Cookies). Zellers carries many brands that are exclusive to Zellers in Canada but are carried by other retailers in other countries. Examples include Cherokee (casual clothes), Mossimo (designer clothes and home decor), Sportek (sports clothing), and Wabasso (linens and home accessories).[16]

Individual Brands versus Family Brands

Many companies use different brand names for different products, a practice referred to as **individual branding**. Companies use individual brands when their products vary greatly in use or performance. For instance, it would not make sense to use the same brand name for a pair of dress socks and a hockey stick. Canada Packers sells its food products under the names Maple Leaf, York, Domestic, Dial, and Devon. Procter & Gamble targets different segments of the laundry-detergent market with Bold, Cheer, Dash, Dreft, Era, Gain, Ivory Snow, Oxydol, Solo, and Tide. Marriott International targets different market segments with Courtyard by Marriott, Residence Inn, and Fairfield Inn.

In contrast, a company that markets several different products under the same brand name is using a **family brand**. Sony's family brand includes radios, television sets, stereos, and other electronic products. Roots is another family brand, applied to a wide range of clothing items. The Heinz brand name is attached to products such as ketchup, mustard, and pickles. A brand name can be stretched only so far, however. Do you know the differences among Holiday Inn, Holiday Inn Express, Holiday Inn Select, Holiday Inn Sun Spree Resort, Holiday Inn Garden Court, and Holiday Inn Hotel & Suites? Neither do most travellers.

EXHIBIT 8.5

Comparing Manufacturers' and Private Brands from the Reseller's Perspective

Key Advantages of Carrying Manufacturers' Brands	Key Advantages of Carrying Private Brands
• Heavy advertising to the consumer by manufacturers like Procter & Gamble helps develop strong consumer loyalties.	• A wholesaler or retailer can usually earn higher profits on its own brand. In addition, because the private brand is exclusive, there is less pressure to mark the price down to meet competition.
• Well-known manufacturers' brands, such as Kodak and Fisher-Price, can attract new customers and enhance the dealer's (wholesaler's or retailer's) prestige.	• A manufacturer can decide to drop a brand or a reseller at any time or even to become a direct competitor to its dealers.
• Many manufacturers offer rapid delivery, enabling the dealer to carry lower inventories.	• A private brand ties the customer to the wholesaler or retailer. A person who wants a DieHard battery must go to Sears.
• If a dealer happens to sell a manufacturer's brand of poor quality, the customer may simply switch brands and remain loyal to the dealer.	• Wholesalers and retailers have no control over the intensity of distribution of manufacturers' brands. Canadian Tire store managers don't have to worry about competing with other sellers of Mastercraft or MotoMaster products. They know that these brands are sold only in Canadian Tire stores.

Cobranding

Cobranding involves placing two or more brand names on a product or its package. There are three types of cobranding. *Ingredient branding* identifies the brand of a part that makes up the product. Examples of ingredient branding are a microprocessor (Intel) in a personal computer such as Dell, a satellite system (OnStar) in an automobile (Cadillac), or the Clodhoppers (candy) Blizzard that can be purchased at Dairy Queen Canada. *Cooperative branding* occurs when two brands receiving equal treatment (in the context of an advertisement) borrow on each other's brand equity. An example would be Air Canada promoting the Second Cup coffee that is served on its planes. Another example of cooperative branding is SpongeBob Eggo waffles. Finally, there is *complementary branding*, where products are advertised or marketed together to suggest common usage, such as a spirits brand (Seagram's) and a compatible mixer (7 Up).

Cobranding is a useful strategy when a combination of brand names enhances the prestige or perceived value of a product or when it benefits brand owners and users. Toyota Motor's luxury division introduced a Platinum version of its Lexus brand. For a premium of as much as 10 percent above the base sticker prices, buyers get upgraded paint, leathers, and accessories and a free two-year subscription to the $300-a-year American Express Platinum Card. Both companies say that the Platinum Series models will reinforce their brands while delivering added value.[17] American Express also cobranded with Costco outlets in Canada to allow shoppers to benefit from dollars off on their purchases when they used the American Express card.

Cobranding may be used to increase a company's presence in markets in which it has little or no market share. For example, Coach, a company that makes accessories such as handbags, was able to build a presence in a whole new category when its leather upholstery with logo was used in Lexus automobiles.

TRADEMARKS

A **trademark** is the exclusive right to use a brand or part of a brand. Others are prohibited from using the brand without permission. A **service mark** performs the same function for services, such as H&R Block and Weight Watchers. Parts of a brand or other product identification may qualify for trademark protection. Some examples are the following:

- Shapes, such as the Jeep front grille and the Coca-Cola bottle
- Ornamental colour or design, such as the decoration on Nike tennis shoes, the black-and-copper colour combination of a Duracell battery, Levi's small tag on the left side of the rear pocket of its jeans, and the cutoff black cone on the top of Cross pens
- Catchy phrases, such as Prudential's "Own a piece of the rock," Timex's "Takes a licking and keeps on ticking," Mountain Dew's "Do the Dew," Nike's "Just Do It," and Tim Hortons' "Roll Up the Rim to Win"
- Abbreviations, such as Blue, Coke, or CN
- Sounds, such as General Electric Broadcasting Company's ship's bell clock sound and the MGM lion's roar

In Canada, trademarks are registered under the Trade-marks Act. Rights to a trademark last as long as the mark is used. Usually, if a firm does not use a trademark for two years, the trademark is considered abandoned. If a new user picks up the abandoned trademark, that new user can claim exclusive ownership of the mark. The Trade-marks Act specifies the types of marks that can be protected and the remedies available for trademark violations. Businesses planning to introduce new brands, trademarks, or packages should consider the following:

- Check carefully before adopting a trademark or packaging style to make sure you're not infringing on someone else's.
- After a thorough search, consider registering your trademark.
- Make your packaging as distinctive as possible.
- Police your trademark.

Companies that fail to protect their trademarks face the possibility that their product names will become generic. A **generic product name** identifies a product by class or type and cannot be trademarked. Former brand names that were not sufficiently protected by their owners and subsequently became generic product names include aspirin, cellophane, linoleum, thermos, kerosene, monopoly, cola, and shredded wheat.

Companies like Rolls-Royce, Cross, Xerox, Levi Strauss, Frigidaire, and McDonald's aggressively enforce their trademarks. Rolls-Royce, Coca-Cola, and Xerox even run newspaper and magazine ads stating that their names are trademarks and should not be used as descriptive or generic terms. Some ads threaten lawsuits against competitors that violate trademarks. In some cases, it is hard to say whether a trademark has been infringed or not. A few years ago, GolfGear International began marketing the Ti-Gear driver. The company claimed that it had been using the name Titanium Gear since 1990 and simply shortened it to Ti-Gear. Representatives for Tiger Woods, however, felt that this was an unauthorized attempt to play off the Tiger Woods name.[18] What do you think? For a look at another trademark case, and how trademark law might differ between Canada and other countries, read the "Global Perspectives" box.

Despite severe penalties for trademark violations, trademark infringement lawsuits are not uncommon. One of the major battles is over brand names that closely resemble another brand name. Donna Karan filed a lawsuit against Donnkenny Inc., whose Nasdaq trading symbol—DNKY—was too close to Karan's DKNY trademark.

Companies must also contend with fake or unauthorized brands, such as fake Levi's jeans, Microsoft software, Rolex watches, Reebok and Nike footwear, and Louis Vuitton handbags. Sales of copycat golf clubs, such as Big Bursa, a knockoff of Callaway's popular Big Bertha, are common. Hasbro sued the makers of the on-line game Scrabulous for copyright infringement on its Scrabble game. Scrabulous was an obvious copy of Scrabble, including the rules, game pieces, and board colours.[19]

In Europe, you can sue counterfeiters only if your brand, logo, or trademark is formally registered. Until recently, formal registration was required in each country in which a company sought protection. A company can now register its trademark in all European Union (EU) member countries with one application.

REVIEW LEARNING OUTCOME 4

4	Describe marketing uses of branding

Brand name: MGM

Brand mark:

SOURCE: © AP IMAGES/PRNEWSFOTO/METRO-GOLDWYN-MAYER INC.

BRANDING

Benefits	Strategies
Brand equity (from being able to identify product)	Generic Brand Trademark — Manufacturer ⟨ Individual / Family / Combination⟩ — Private
Brand loyalty (from repeat sales)	
Brand recognition (to generate new product sales)	

COURTROOM BARBIE

As a further brand extension for America's top fashion doll, how about Barbie in her court robes appearing before the Supreme Court of Canada? Mattel Inc., the giant U.S. owner of the Barbie doll trademark, recently appealed two Federal Court judgments allowing a Montreal restaurant and bar owner to use the "Barbie's" name and logo for the sale of food and catering services in Canada. Despite the fact that Mattel had registered the Barbie name in Canada under the Trade-marks Act more than 30 years ago, the Trade-marks Opposition Board, a federal court, and the Federal Court of Appeal, all ruled that the restaurant and bar owner could use the Barbie's name. Now Barbie was on her way to the top court in Canada.

Mattel, with over $1.4 billion in Barbie sales globally and $80 million in annual Barbie sales in Canada, argued that allowing the Montreal company to use and register the Barbie's name for restaurant services would confuse consumers. The Montreal restaurant and bar owner, in business since 1992, responded that its menu features barbecue dishes and argued that people are well aware that the term "barbie" refers to barbecue as in "Throw some shrimp or chicken on the barbie." Mattel responded that some brand names are "so famous that marks such as Barbie may not now be used in Canada on most consumer products and services without the average consumer being led to infer the existence of a trade connection with the owners of the famous brand." In fact, Mattel presented findings from a Canadian survey it conducted that showed 99.3 percent of the respondents were familiar with Barbie dolls, 57 percent said Barbie dolls came to mind when they saw the Barbie's restaurant logo, and 36 percent believed that the company that manufactured the Barbie doll might have something to do with the Barbie's restaurant.

The stakes in the court case were high for not just Mattel but for other holders of globally famous brand names who have also had problems convincing Canadian courts to grant them broad exclusive rights to the use of their trademarks. The issue is whether Canada's Trade-marks Act gives monopoly protection to companies like Mattel. Monopoly protection would give Mattel exclusive use not only of the Barbie name for all doll and doll-related products but, essentially, for a wide range of non-doll–related products and services.

Under the Trade-marks Act in Canada, use or registration of a trademark isn't allowed if it could reasonably be confused with an already registered trademark. Mattel argued to the Supreme Court of Canada that the decisions of the lower courts "may open Canada to widespread, even wholesale, appropriation of existing famous trademarks. To illustrate the consequences of the lower courts' decisions, famous marks such as Kodak, Cutty Sark, Vogue or 007 would have no recourse in Canada to prevent a third party from using their famous marks in association with, or to promote sales of an unrelated product such as Kodak bicycles, Cutty Sark tobacco, Vogue jewelry or 007 pizza."

Mattel's arguments likely would have been more successful in the United States and Europe where courts have generally granted wide protection to famous trademarks. However, as at the lower court level, the Supreme Court of Canada denied Mattel's appeal, thus allowing the Montreal restaurant and bar to use the Barbie's name. The Supreme Court ruled that "the Barbie trademark is not famous for anything but dolls and doll accessories and there is no evidence that using the Barbie name for restaurant services is likely to confuse the casual consumer."

The Mattel ruling is consistent with earlier Supreme Court of Canada rulings involving the Pink Panther and Lexus trademarks. In the Pink Panther case, a majority of the court ruled in favour of allowing the registration of "Pink Panther" as a trademark for a line of hair care and beauty products over the opposition of United Artists' studios, the holder of an existing trademark representing a very successful series of films of the same name starring Peter Sellers as Inspector Clouseau. In the Lexus case, the court ruled to allow the registration of the "Lexus" trademark for a line of canned foods and canned fruit juice over the objections of Toyota, the owner of the Lexus name used on a line of upscale automobiles. In both cases, the court ruled that the new trademarks would not cause confusion as they were being used on substantially different products.[20]

Do you agree with the ruling of the Supreme Court of Canada to allow the registration and use of the Barbie's name, a name legally registered under the Trade-marks Act of Canada by Mattel for over 30 years, by a restaurant and bar in Montreal? Why or why not? Why do you think courts in other countries around the world have provided wider-ranging trademark protection than has been the case in Canada? Who is right? What is too much versus too little protection for a trademark? What do you think the ruling of the Supreme Court of Canada would have been if the business wishing to register and use the Barbie's name was a retailer of girl's clothing instead of a restaurant and bar?

SOURCE: CRISTIN SCHMITZ, "COURTROOM BARBIE," FINANCIAL POST, MAY 26, 2005, FP3; SUPREME COURT OF CANADA, CITATION: MATTEL, INC. V. 3894207 CANADA, INC., 2006 SCC, DOCKET: 30839, JUNE 2, 2006, SCC.LEXUM.UMONTREAL.CA/EN/2006/2006 SCC22/2006SCC22.HTML.

 ## 5 PACKAGING

Describe marketing uses of packaging and labelling

Packages have always served a practical function—that is, they hold contents together and protect goods as they move through the distribution channel. Today, however, packaging is also a container for promoting the product and making it easier and safer to use.

PACKAGING FUNCTIONS

The three most important functions of packaging are to contain and protect products, promote products, and facilitate the storage, use, and convenience of products. A fourth function of packaging that is becoming increasingly important is to facilitate recycling and reduce environmental damage.

Containing and Protecting Products

The most obvious function of packaging is to contain products that are liquid, granular, or otherwise divisible. Packaging also enables manufacturers, wholesalers, and retailers to market products in specific quantities, such as grams.

Physical protection is another obvious function of packaging. Most products are handled several times between the time they are manufactured, harvested, or otherwise produced and the time they are consumed or used. Many products are shipped, stored, and inspected several times between production and consumption. Some products, like milk or ice cream, need to be refrigerated or frozen. Others, like beer, are sensitive to light. Still others, like medicines and bandages, need to be kept sterile. Packages protect products from breakage, evaporation, spillage, spoilage, light, heat, cold, infestation, and many other conditions.

Promoting Products

Packaging does more than identify the brand, list the ingredients, specify features, and provide directions. A package differentiates a product from competing products and may associate a new product with a family of other products from the same manufacturer. Welch's repackaged its line of grape juice-based jams, jellies, and juices to unify the line and get more impact on the shelf.

Packages use designs, colours, shapes, and materials to try to influence consumers' perceptions and buying behaviour. For example, marketing research shows that health-conscious consumers are likely to think that any food is probably good for them as long as it comes in green packaging. Two top brands of low-fat foods—Snackwell and Healthy Choice—use green packaging. Packaging can have a major effect on sales. Quaker Oats revised the package for Rice-A-Roni without making any other changes in marketing strategy and experienced a 44 percent sales increase in one year.

Facilitating Storage, Use, and Convenience

Wholesalers and retailers prefer packages that are easy to ship, store, and stock on shelves. They also like packages that protect products, prevent spoilage or breakage, and extend the product's shelf life.

Consumers' requirements for storage, use, and convenience cover many dimensions. Consumers are constantly seeking items that are easy to handle, open, and reclose, while some consumers want packages that are tamperproof or childproof. Hard-to-open packages are among consumers' top complaints. Consumers also want reusable and disposable packages. Quaker State oil, packaged in easy-to-open and easy-to-reseal twist-off tops, makes the product more convenient to customers at self-serve gas stations. Such packaging innovations as zipper tear strips, hinged lids, tab slots, screw-on tops, and pour spouts were introduced to solve these and other problems. H. J. Heinz Company developed a new container for ketchup designed to fit the hands of children and encourage extra squeezing, which facilitates use for this target market.[21] Miracle-Gro's packages have pictures on the front of the plants for which the products are formulated, so gardeners can more easily identify which product best fits their needs.[22]

Some firms use packaging to segment markets. For example, a sugar carton with an easy-to-pour, reclosable top is targeted to consumers who don't do a lot of baking and are willing to pay at least 20 cents more for the package. Different-size packages appeal to heavy, moderate, and light users. Salt is sold in package sizes ranging from single serving to picnic size to giant economy size. Campbell's soup is packaged in single-serving cans aimed at the elderly and singles market segments. Beer and soft

One way marketers design packaging is to facilitate use of the product. Recent innovations in this area include Hungary Jack's microwaveable syrup bottle, Pringles' Lunch Buddies single-serving containers, and now lightweight, easy-to-carry, plastic paint cans with a pourable spout by Sherwin Williams.

drinks are similarly marketed in various package sizes and types. Packaging convenience can increase a product's utility and, therefore, its market share and profits. Guinness Bass Import recently introduced a packaged-draft system that allows consumers to drink nitrogenated Guinness Stout right out of the bottle.[23] Tim Hortons sells ten-cup containers of coffee in packaging that is easy to carry and keeps the coffee hot for home or party consumption.

The Internet will soon give consumers more packaging options. Indeed, the Internet may significantly change the purpose and appearance of packaging. Packaging for products sold on the Internet will be more under the customer's control and will be customized by consumers to fit their needs. Some designers are already offering to personalize, for a fee, packages such as wine bottle and soft drink labels. Jones Soda can be purchased over the Internet in any flavour or flavours desired and with any picture desired on the label.

Facilitating Recycling and Reducing Environmental Damage

One of the most important packaging issues today is compatibility with the environment. Research has shown that consumers are willing to give up many packaging conveniences if it would benefit the environment.[24] Brocato International markets shampoo and hair conditioner in bottles that are biodegradable in landfills. Procter & Gamble markets Sure Pro and Old Spice in "eco-friendly" pump-spray packages that do not rely on aerosol propellants. The French winery Boisset Family Estates introduced TetraPak cartons of its French Rabbit chardonnay to offer consumers a playful and eco-friendly alternative to glass bottles.[25] As described in the video case at the end of Chapter 1, Terracycle packages its organic fertilizer products only in recycled bottles. Clearly, all these companies promote the "eco-friendly" nature of their packages.

LABELLING

persuasive labelling
A type of package labelling that focuses on a promotional theme or logo with consumer information being secondary.

informational labelling
A type of package labelling designed to help consumers make proper product selections and lower their cognitive dissonance after the purchase.

An integral part of any package is its label. Labelling generally takes one of two forms: persuasive or informational. **Persuasive labelling** focuses on a promotional theme or logo, and consumer information is secondary. Price Pfister, a producer of plumbing products, among other things, developed a new, persuasive label—featuring a picture of a faucet, the brand name, and the logo—with the goal of strengthening brand identity and becoming known as a brand instead of as a manufacturer. Note that the standard promotional claims on labels—such as "new," "improved," and "super"—are no longer very persuasive. Consumers have been saturated with "newness" and thus discount these claims.

Informational labelling, in contrast, is designed to help consumers make proper product selections and lower their cognitive dissonance after the purchase. Sears attaches a "label of confidence" to all its floor coverings. This label gives such product information as durability, colour, features, cleanability, care instructions, and construction standards. Most major furniture manufacturers affix labels to their wares that explain the products' construction features, such as type of frame, number of coils, and fabric characteristics. The Consumer Packaging and Labelling Act, the Food and Drug Act, and the Weights and Measures Act state the minimum information that must appear on food products, set the standards for health claims on food packaging, and regulate the units of measurement information on labels. An important outcome of this legislation is that guidelines now exist for using terms like *low fat, light, reduced cholesterol, low sodium, low calorie,* and *fresh.* Getting the right information is very important to consumers—so much so that nearly 75 percent of consumers say they are willing to pay extra to have products display country of origin information.[26] And all of this has to be done in both of Canada's official languages.

UNIVERSAL PRODUCT CODES

universal product codes (UPCs)
Series of thick and thin vertical lines (bar codes), readable by computerized optical scanners that represent numbers used to track products.

The **universal product codes (UPCs)** that appear on most items in supermarkets and other high-volume outlets were first introduced in 1974. Because the numerical codes appear as a series of thick and thin vertical lines, they are often called *bar codes.* The lines are read by computerized optical scanners that match codes with brand names, package sizes, and prices. They also print information on cash register tapes and help retailers rapidly and accurately prepare records of customer purchases, control inventories, and track sales. Radio-frequency identification tags (RFID), discussed in Chapter 11, are also used for product shipment tracking and inventory control.

REVIEW LEARNING OUTCOME 5

5 **Describe marketing uses of packaging and labelling**

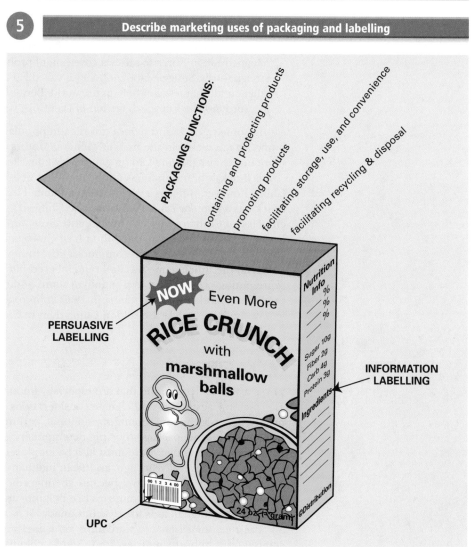

GLOBAL ISSUES IN BRANDING AND PACKAGING

International marketers must address several concerns regarding branding and packaging.

BRANDING

When planning to enter a foreign market with an existing product, a firm has three options for handling the brand name:

- *One brand name everywhere*: This strategy is useful when the company markets mainly one product and the brand name does not have negative connotations in any local market. The Coca-Cola Company uses a one-brand-name strategy in 195 countries around the world. The advantages of a one-brand-name strategy are greater identification of the product from market to market and ease of coordinating promotion from market to market.
- *Adaptations and modifications*: A one-brand-name strategy is not possible when the name cannot be pronounced in the local language, when the brand name is owned by someone else, or when the brand name has a negative or vulgar connotation in the local language. The Iranian detergent "Barf," for example, might encounter some problems in the Canadian market, as would a Mexican bread named Bimbo or a Japanese coffee creamer named Creap.
- *Different brand names in different markets*: Local brand names are often used when translation or pronunciation problems occur, when the marketer wants the brand to appear to be a local brand, or when regulations require localization. Gillette's Silkience hair conditioner is called Soyance in France and Sientel in Italy. The adaptations were deemed to be more appealing in the local markets. Coca-Cola's Sprite brand had to be renamed Kin in Korea to satisfy a government prohibition on the unnecessary use of foreign words. Snuggle fabric softener is called FaFa in Japan, Cajoline in France, and other cuddly names elsewhere in the world. Because of the feminine connotations of the word *diet*, the European version of Diet Coke is Coca-Cola Light.

In some cases, brand names can remain popular for many years, even when the brand isn't available in the market. General Motors currently has a leading market share in the fast-growing Chinese automotive market. One of the reasons for its success is Buick, a brand that has not been selling well in Canada in recent years. In China, however, Buick is a well-respected name. First appearing in China in 1912, Buick was a popular car for high-ranking Chinese government officials. The last emperor of China owned two Buicks, and these were the first cars to enter the Forbidden City. Buick remained the car of choice among China's elite from the late 1920s to 1949 when the then communist government closed its market to outsiders. However, the Buick name was well remembered in China and is still seen as a name representing prestige and as a symbol of status and upward mobility. As such, when the Buick brand re-entered China in 1995, it immediately became a top-selling car. Currently, more Buicks are sold in China than in Canada and the United States combined.[27]

PACKAGING

Three aspects of packaging that are especially important in international marketing are labelling, aesthetics, and climate considerations. The major *labelling* concern is properly translating ingredient, promotional, and instructional information on labels. In Eastern Europe, packages of Ariel detergent are printed in 14 languages, such as Latvian and Lithuanian. Care must also be employed in meeting all local labelling requirements. Several years ago, an Italian judge ordered that all bottles of Coca-Cola be removed from retail shelves because the ingredients were not properly labelled. Labelling is also harder in countries like Belgium and Finland, which require the labels to be bilingual, as is the case in Canada.

Package *aesthetics* may also require some attention. The key is to stay attuned to cultural traits in host countries. For example, colours may have different connotations.

Coca-Cola uses a one-brand-name strategy in 195 countries around the world. Its product and positive image are recognizable almost everywhere.

SOURCE: JEFF GREENBERG/PHOTO EDIT

Red is associated with witchcraft in some countries, green may be a sign of danger, and white may be symbolic of death. Aesthetics also influence package size. Soft drinks are not sold in six-packs in countries that lack refrigeration. In some countries, products like detergent may be bought only in small quantities because of a lack of storage space. Other products, like cigarettes, may be bought in small quantities, and even single units, because of the low purchasing power of buyers.

Extreme *climates* and long-distance shipping necessitate sturdier and more durable packages for goods sold overseas. Spillage, spoilage, and breakage are all more important concerns when products are shipped long distances or frequently handled during shipping and storage. Packages may also have to ensure a longer product life if the time between production and consumption lengthens significantly.

A number of automotive assemblers in Europe, including BMW, Rolls-Royce, Volkswagen, and Volvo, are using shrink wrapping on vehicles being shipped long distances from their assembly plants. The vehicles are covered with a tight-fitting protective plastic fabric called Transhield. The cost of the Transhield covering is approximately $60 per car. Normally auto makers apply a wax coating to protect cars during shipment to market. The cost of applying the wax coating and removing it at the destination is about $50 per car. The advantages of the plastic shrink wrapping over waxing include being easier to remove, the vehicle can be driven and fuelled without removing the wrapping, the shrink wrapping better protects the vehicle from scratches, and the shrink wrapping reduces the amount of dust and dirt that can get on the vehicle during transport.[28]

REVIEW LEARNING OUTCOME 6

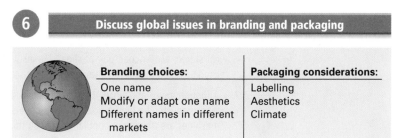

6 | Discuss global issues in branding and packaging

Branding choices:	Packaging considerations:
One name	Labelling
Modify or adapt one name	Aesthetics
Different names in different markets	Climate

7 PRODUCT WARRANTIES

Describe how and why product warranties are important marketing tools

warranty
A confirmation of the quality or performance of a good or service.

express warranty
A written guarantee.

implied warranty
An unwritten guarantee that the good or service is fit for the purpose for which it was sold.

Just as a package is designed to protect the product, a **warranty** protects the buyer and provides essential information about the product. A warranty confirms the quality or performance of a good or service. An **express warranty** is a written guarantee. Express warranties range from simple statements—such as "100 percent cotton" (a guarantee of quality) and "complete satisfaction guaranteed" (a statement of performance)—to extensive documents written in technical language. In contrast, an **implied warranty** is an unwritten guarantee that the good or service is fit for the purpose for which it was sold.

While court rulings would suggest that all products sold in Canada carry an implied warranty, warranties do vary from province to province. At the federal level, protection against misleading warranties is provided under the Competition Act. In general, products sold must be free from encumbrances (the seller has clear title),

7 **Describe how and why product warranties are important marketing tools**

| Express warranty | = | written guarantee |
| Implied warranty | = | unwritten guarantee |

descriptions of the product on the package must be accurate, the product must be fit for its purpose, and the product must be of reasonable durability.

Warranties can be important marketing promotion tools. To overcome perceptions of poor quality, Mitsubishi extended its warranty coverage from seven years and 100,000 kilometres to ten years and 160,000 kilometres.

REVIEW AND APPLICATIONS

1 **Define the term *product*.** A product is anything, desired or not, that a person or organization receives in an exchange. The basic goal of purchasing decisions is to receive the tangible and intangible benefits associated with a product. Tangible aspects include packaging, style, colour, size, and features. Intangible qualities include service, the retailer's image, the manufacturer's reputation, and the social status associated with a product. An organization's product offering is the crucial element in any marketing mix.

1.1 Form a team of four or five. Have the team determine what the tangible and intangible benefits are for a computer, a tube of toothpaste, a beauty salon, and a dentist.

2 **Classify consumer products.** Consumer products are classified into four categories: convenience products, shopping products, specialty products, and unsought products. Convenience products are relatively inexpensive and require limited shopping effort. Shopping products are of two types: homogeneous and heterogeneous. Because of the similarity of homogeneous products, price and features are the main differences between them. In contrast, heterogeneous products appeal to consumers because of their distinct characteristics. Specialty products possess unique benefits that are highly desirable to certain customers. Finally, unsought products are either new products or products that require aggressive selling because they are generally avoided or overlooked by consumers.

2.1 Break into groups of four or five. Have the members of each group classify each of the following products into the category (convenience, shopping, specialty, unsought) that they think fits best from their perspective as consumers (i.e., if they were buying the product): Coca-Cola (brand), car stereo, winter coat, pair of shoes, life insurance, blue jeans, fast-food hamburgers, shampoo, canned vegetables, and curtains.

2.2 Although major appliances, like washers and dryers, are usually considered homogeneous shopping products, the high-efficiency front-loaders that boast many more features than standard machines are gaining in popularity. Do you think high-efficiency technology is enough to make washers and dryers heterogeneous shopping products? Explain.

3 **Define the terms *product item*, *product line*, and *product mix*.** A product item is a specific version of a product that can be designated as a distinct offering among an organization's products. A product line is a group of closely related products offered by an organization. An organization's product mix is made up of all the products it sells. Product mix width refers to the number of product lines an organization offers. Product line depth is the number of product items in a product line. Firms modify existing products by changing their quality, functional characteristics, or style. Product line extension occurs when a firm adds new products to existing product lines.

3.1 A local civic organization has asked you to give a luncheon presentation about planned obsolescence. Rather than pursuing a negative approach by talking about how businesses exploit customers through planned obsolescence, you have decided to talk about the benefits of producing products that do not last forever. Prepare a one-page outline of your presentation.

3.2 Go to Unilever's website at **www.unilever.com**. Can Unilever delete anything from its product lines? Visit the company's product category pages on its "Brands" Web page to see the number of existing products and new products planned. Write a proposal for contracting one of Unilever's product lines.

4 **Describe marketing uses of branding.** A brand is a name, term, or symbol that identifies and differentiates a firm's products. Established brands encourage customer loyalty and help new products succeed. Branding strategies require decisions about individual, family, manufacturers', and private brands.

4.1 A local supermarket would like to introduce its own brand of paper goods (i.e., paper towels, facial tissue, etc.) to sell alongside its current inventory. The company has hired you to generate a report outlining the advantages and disadvantages of doing so. Write the report.

4.2 How does Hormel use its website (**www.hormel.com)** to promote its store brands? Is the site designed more to promote the company or its brands? Check out the Spam website at **www.spam.com**. How do you think Hormel is able to successfully sustain this brand that is often the punch line to a joke?

5 **Describe marketing uses of packaging and labelling.** Packaging has four functions: containing and protecting products; promoting products; facilitating product storage, use, and convenience; and facilitating recycling and reducing environmental damage. As a tool for promotion, packaging identifies the brand and its features. It also serves the critical function of differentiating a product from competing products and linking it with related products from the same manufacturer. The label is an integral part of the package, with persuasive and informational functions. In essence, the package is the marketer's last chance to influence buyers before they make a purchase decision.

5.1 Find a product at home that has a distinctive package. Write a paragraph evaluating that package based on the four functions of packaging discussed in this chapter.

6 **Discuss global issues in branding and packaging.** In addition to brand piracy, international marketers must address a variety of concerns regarding branding and packaging, including choosing a brand name policy, translating labels and meeting host-country labelling requirements, making packages aesthetically compatible with host-country cultures, and offering the sizes of packages preferred in host countries.

6.1 List the countries to which Levi Strauss & Company markets through the website **www.levi.com**. How do the product offerings differ between the Canadian and European selections?

7 **Describe how and why product warranties are important marketing tools.** Product warranties are important tools because they offer consumers protection and help them gauge product quality.

7.1 Lands' End and L.L. Bean are renowned for their product guarantees. Find and read the exact wording of their guarantees on their websites (**www.landsend.com** and **www.llbean.com**). Do you think that a company could successfully compete against either without offering the same guarantee?

TERMS

brand 253
brand equity 253
brand loyalty 253
brand mark 253

brand name 253
business product (industrial product) 246
cobranding 256
consumer product 246

convenience product 246
express warranty 263
family brand 255
generic product name 256

EXERCISES

APPLICATION EXERCISE

What is your favourite brand of sandwich cookie? If you're like most others, there's a good chance it's Oreo. In fact, Oreos are so popular that many people think Oreo was the original sandwich cookie. They're wrong. Sunshine Biscuits first marketed its Hydrox sandwich cookie in 1908. Hydrox thrived until 1912 when Nabisco (now a part of Kraft) introduced the Oreo cookie. Nabisco's superior marketing, distribution, and advertising quickly made Oreo the more popular sandwich cookie. Today, Oreo outsells Hydrox by a margin of more than 25 to 1. In 1998, the Hydrox brand was purchased by Keebler and Keebler was later purchased by Kellogg. The Keebler elves, with the help of Kellogg, are now trying to decide how to reinvigorate the Hydrox brand.

Activities

1. Some people think that Hydrox sounds more like a cleaning product than a cookie. What would be a better brand name to compete with Oreo? Make a list of three to five possible names.

2. **WRITING** What type of innovative packaging might you create for the new Hydrox product to make it more attractive than the Oreo package? Draft a packaging plan for the product.

3. What type of product modifications or extensions would help Hydrox to compete with Oreo?

ETHICS EXERCISE

A product that a potential buyer knows about but that he or she is not actively seeking is called an unsought product. If a product is unsought, doesn't that suggest that consumers don't want it? Is the marketing of unsought products unethical? Discuss your answer in terms of the CMA Code of Ethics found at **www.the-cma.org**.

CASE STUDY

TERRACYCLE: TERRACYCLE'S WORM POOP TRADEMARK PROBLEMS

Environmentally friendly products are hot sellers today and the number of products touting their "green" credentials is growing but TerraCycle Plant Food may be the ultimate organic product to come to market. A college student from Toronto named Tom Szaky founded TerraCycle after some buddies showed him how worm droppings could be used as a cheap and eco-friendly fertilizer (see Chapter 1 Video Case "Wormboy" for complete background information on TerraCycle).

Szaky based his business model on recycling, starting with the trash that TerraCycle turns into compost and feeds to millions of red worms. The worm castings are then liquefied and put into previously used plastic water and soda bottles. Even the company's shipping cartons come from recycled materials.

TerraCycles's organic plant food hit store shelves in 2004 with labels boasting that it "Contains Liquefied Worm Poop!" Within two years company sales passed $1 million and the company snagged shelf space in retail giants like Walmart Canada and Home Depot Canada. Founder and president Tom Szaky liked to refer to his company as "the anti-Miracle-Gro." But Scotts, the industry giant and maker of Miracle-Gro, thought that TerraCycle was encroaching too closely on its territory. In 2007, Scotts sued Szaky's young company for trademark infringement and for making "false claims" that its organic products were superior to synthetic versions.

Small companies can easily fold under the weight of such a lawsuit. Even if they win, the legal costs can cripple them. So TerraCycle took its case to the Internet with a blog, hoping to stir public support and raise contributions for its legal fees. "I knew there was no way I could out-lawyer Scotts," Tom Szaky says. "So as I thought about it, I wondered what core competency our company had that we could exploit. Guerrilla marketing seemed to be the obvious answer." He adds that they hoped to get so much public support for their cause that Scotts would drop its suit.

The blog offered a comparison chart titled "David vs. Goliath" that illustrated the differences between the two companies. A photo of TerraCycles's modest headquarters behind a chain-link fence was in stark contrast to Scott's grand, pillared entryway. The blog listed TerraCycles's CEO's "major perquisite" as "unlimited free worm poop," whereas Scott's CEO enjoys "personal use of company-owned aircraft."

The blog also countered Scott's claims that consumers might be confused by its "overly similar yellow and green packaging" by posting photographs of TerraCycle's wacky and unusual bottles in their variety of shapes and sizes beside Miracle-Gro's uniform and professional-looking ones. Scotts continued to insist that TerraCycle change its labels, but TerraCycle's general counsel, Rickard Ober Jr., stated that changing packaging would hurt the sales momentum.

Su Lok, a Scott's spokesperson, argued that the blog was just one of TerraCycle's PR tactics and insisted that none of its arguments had merit. "We've spent a lot of time building up brands that consumers trust," she says, "and we are going to protect those brands." Ira J. Levy, an intellectual property lawyer, warned that Scotts could have had more to lose by pursuing TerraCycle than it was worth. "By pursuing a trade dress case," Levy says, "they can allow a small player to promote itself on the national stage. When word gets out that the mega-conglomerate is suing the little guy, you risk having bloggers launching boycotts, and the plaintiff ends up injuring his own business."

Which is precisely what Tom Szaky hoped would happen. The lawsuit wasn't something he wanted to fight, he said, but it was a chance to generate buzz. "It's like *The Art of War*," he explained. "You need to have a villain to be up against, and for us, that's Scotts."

The fight is now over. TerraCycle reached a settlement with Scotts and agreed to change its packaging and its advertising claims. In its time, the blog gained massive media attention, leading major newspapers and magazines to cover the story, and hundreds of bloggers to defend TerraCycle's cause. Although on-line donations totalled less than $1,000, overall company sales surged 122 percent within weeks of the blog's launch. And TerraCycle's main website, which averaged about 1,000 visitors a day, spiked to as high as 13,000.[29]

Questions

1. What type of consumer product is TerraCycle's plant food: convenience, shopping, specialty, or unsought? Why?

2. Go to **www.terracycle.net** and look at the types of products the company sells. Describe its product mix. How wide is it? Which basic product lines does it sell? How long are the product lines?

3. Do you think that product line extension or product line contraction would make more sense for TerraCycle at this stage of the company's growth? Why?

4. How well do TerraCycle's bottles perform the four packaging functions discussed in this chapter? Compare TerraCycle's products to Miracle-Gro's (**www.scotts.com**). Do you think TerraCycle's package design distinguishes its products well enough from those of the industry giant, or are they similar enough to cause customer confusion?

CBC

FAKE MERCHANDISE

In May 2010, the Canada Border Services Agency and the Royal Canadian Mounted Police seized counterfeit cigarettes with a street value of $3.4 million from a marine container at the Port of Vancouver. The container, from China, was destined for an address in Richmond, B.C. In Calgary, police discovered shipping containers with hundreds of thousands of counterfeit products in a rail yard. The counterfeit products included Armani and Hugo Boss suits and Versace, Chanel, and Prada accessories. The containers had been shipped from Hong Kong. The retail value of the counterfeit merchandise was into the millions of dollars.

A few years ago, police seized merchandise from a string of retail stores in St. John's, Newfoundland. Leather goods, clothing, and sunglasses, bearing bogus labels with such well-known names as Gucci and Louis Vuitton, were among the hundreds of thousands of dollars of counterfeit merchandise seized. Louis Vuitton counterfeit wallets, which normally retail for $500, were being sold for $88. As for the retailers, police say that most were unaware they were selling counterfeit items, although the unusually low prices should have been a giveaway. Charges, though, are pending against one St. John's store.

In June 2007, Health Canada warned consumers that counterfeit toothpaste products, falsely labelled as Colgate Fluoride Toothpaste Herbal and Colgate Toothpaste Maximum Cavity Protection and containing high levels of harmful bacteria, were discovered on store shelves. These products could be particularly dangerous to young children. In the same year, a Calgary man was arrested and charged with manufacturing and distributing counterfeit merchandise. A search of the man's home turned up $50,000 worth of counterfeit DVDs, software, and video games. A few months earlier, Toronto police seized 150,000 counterfeit DVDs, worth millions of dollars, from three shopping malls in Toronto. Police also closed a lab in Scarborough, Ontario, where the counterfeit DVDs were made. The movie industry estimates that $35 million in counterfeit DVDs are sold in the Toronto area alone. Also in that year, an airline pilot was caught flying counterfeit Viagra, Cialis, and Levitra pills, worth an estimated $2.5 million, into Toronto.

These are just a few examples of the counterfeiting activity that goes on across Canada every day. Counterfeit products are being brought into Canada and counterfeit merchandise is being produced in Canada, leaving many unsuspecting consumers with counterfeit items. Some consumers, like Julia Kenny, a grandmother from Newfoundland, do something about it. Julia bought a lamp with a counterfeit safety label on it. The lamp caught fire the first time it was used. When the retailer who sold the lamp refused to give Julia Kenny a refund, she took the lamp to the fire commissioner for Newfoundland and Labrador. The retailer ultimately received a hefty fine. According to the International Chamber of Commerce, counterfeit merchandise accounts for between 5 and 7 percent of all commerce. The problem is particularly acute in Canada.

Why is the problem so big in Canada? Essentially there are two reasons: (1) it is easy and (2) the penalties are light. For example, when an owner of four retail stores in Ontario travelled to China, he was able to purchase counterfeit merchandise with whatever labels he requested from Chinese manufacturers at very low cost. Importing the merchandise into Canada was also easy since Canada Customs does not have the personnel or resources to closely monitor all the merchandise coming across the border. After four years and the sale of an estimated $10 million in counterfeit merchandise at his four stores, the business owner was finally caught. Counterfeit merchandise was seized from the stores and the businessman was fined only $24,000. This businessman left Ontario and is now operating a clothing store in Vancouver!

According to the RCMP, the typical penalty for selling counterfeit merchandise is so minimal that it provides an incentive for criminals to deal in counterfeit goods. The sale of counterfeit goods, however, does much harm to companies that spend millions of dollars to develop new products and well-known brand names, only to lose sales to counterfeiters. The government, of course, loses billions in tax revenue. In addition, some counterfeit products, such as batteries that explode in children's toys and cellphones or power cords that are not up to Canadian safety standards, are dangerous. Under the Copyright Act, counterfeiters can be fined up to $1 million and sentenced to five years in jail. Sentencing, however, is usually much lighter.

Angry at losing millions of dollars in sales from Chinese companies counterfeiting his products, Garry Peters, owner of Art in Motion of Coquitlam, B.C., spent three years and over $100,000 of his own money to track down the counterfeiters and put them out of business. Lawyers and others are tracking down counterfeiters in Canada every day. The major countries of origin for counterfeit products in Canada are China, Pakistan, India, and Singapore. A recent CTV news report showed counterfeit Arc'teryx (company headquartered in Vancouver) and Canada Goose (headquartered in Toronto) winter jackets being sold at the famous Silk Market in Beijing, China.[30]

Questions

1. Why is counterfeiting such a big problem in Canada?

2. What should Canada Customs and the RCMP be doing to reduce the size of this problem?

3. What are the safety issues when it comes to counterfeit electrical products that don't meet Canadian safety standards? As many of these products are winding up in reputable Canadian stores with counterfeit safety labelling, how great are the risks to consumers?

4. Should business owners like Garry Peters have to spend considerable amounts of time and money policing the counterfeiting of their companies' products?

MARKETING & YOU RESULTS

A higher score on this scale indicates that you are very brand conscious when you shop. You prefer to buy brands that are nationally known rather than private brands or generics. Conversely, a lower score suggests that you are not so brand conscious and tend to choose lower-priced, lesser-known brands.

Developing and Managing Products

SOURCE: COURTESY OF THE POP SHOPPE

LEARNING OUTCOMES

1 Explain the importance of developing new products and describe the six categories of new products

2 Explain the steps in the new-product development process

3 Explain why some products succeed and others fail

4 Discuss global issues in new-product development

5 Explain the diffusion process through which new products are adopted

6 Explain the concept of product life cycles

ⓥ MARKETING & YOU

Using the following scale, indicate your opinion on the line before each item.

1	2	3	4	5	6
Strongly disagree					Strongly agree

___ I like introducing new brands and products to my friends.

___ I like helping people by providing them with information about many kinds of products.

___ People ask me for information about products, places to shop, or sales.

___ If someone asked where to get the best buy on several types of products, I could tell him or her where to shop.

___ My friends think of me as a good source of information when it comes to new products or sales.

___ I know a lot of different products, stores, and sales, and I like sharing this information.

Total your score. Read the chapter and find out what your score means at the end.

SOURCE: REPRINTED WITH PERMISSION FROM *MARKETING SCALES HANDBOOK* VOL. III, PUBLISHED BY THE AMERICAN MARKETING ASSOCIATION, G. BRUNER, K. JAMES, H. HENSEL, EDS. SCALE #18.

Brian Alger has every right to smile as he watches bottles of Pop Shoppe soft drinks roll along the production line. "It was touch and go if we could do the run," Brian says, "because we weren't sure we'd get the bottles in time." The clear "stubbie" bottles were custom-designed at a cost of over a quarter of a million dollars to resemble those used by the original Pop Shoppe in the 1970s.

From 1969 to 1983, the original Canadian discount soft drinks were a household staple, with families making weekend runs to their neighbourhood Pop Shoppe depots to return empty bottles and pick up Pop Shoppe favourites like Lime Ricky and Cream Soda for 10 cents a bottle. At its peak, the original Pop Shoppe was selling more than a million bottles a day. Unfortunately, price competition from the industry giants Coca-Cola and Pepsi and the coming of low-priced store brands eventually put the Pop Shoppe out of business.

Believing that there was a market among baby boomers and Gen-Xers who had fond memories of the product, Brian Alger re-registered the lapsed trademarks for the Pop Shoppe in 2004. Although it's been a struggle, by 2010 the Pop Shoppe brand was selling more than six million bottles a year, making it the second-largest-selling premium soft drink in Canada behind only Jones Soda and ahead of Dad's and Stewart's, both of which are U.S. brands. Of course, all these brands are a mere drop in the bucket compared to the sales of Coke and Pepsi.

The Pop Shoppe product is manufactured and bottled in a 60-year-old facility in North Toronto and managed out of Brian Alger's home in Grimsby, Ontario. To get the product started, Brian obtained flavour formulas from a supplier to the original Pop Shoppe. In addition, he purchased unopened Pop Shoppe bottles from collectors and had them reverse-engineered to determine the ingredients. After several tries, an acceptable-looking label was designed, and Brian decided to go with glass bottles like the original product. In today's environmentally conscious market, the refillable bottles may be a marketing plus.

The original Pop Shoppe product was discount priced, but with no economies of scale, Brian knew he couldn't make a profit at the low price end of the soft drink market. The only alternative was the premium end of the market with a 355-millilitre bottle that would be priced around $1.59—a price that would provide a reasonable margin. One downside to the premium market: the entire premium soft drink segment in Canada is only a $25-million market.

Distribution is one of the toughest challenges for a new product, and Brian certainly didn't have the funds to set up warehousing and retail outlets like the original Pop Shoppe had. Brian, instead, personally contacted supermarkets, convenience stores, and gas stations and just about any other logical place to sell soft drinks but got only "no" as an answer. Finally, Brian met one of the owners of Beverage World, a wholesaler/distributor based in Hamilton, Ontario. The owner remembered Pop Shoppe and, as luck would have it, was also looking for a premium-priced soft drink that it could exclusively handle. Beverage World would take over the warehousing, shipping, accounts receivable, and other functions for the Pop Shoppe brand and Brian would have to deal with only one customer. Beverage World was able to get the Pop Shoppe product into Costco, Zellers, Canadian Tire, regional and local chains like Kitchen Table and Hasty Market, many convenience stores and independent markets, and a number of restaurants.

Shortly after setting up the distribution deal with Beverage World, Brian received a call from a new Toronto design company that had heard of the attempt to revive the Pop Shoppe brand. For a very small fee, it agreed to update the label and develop some grassroots marketing tactics, such as having Brian drive around Toronto in a 1978 VW van handing out pop on the streets. Brian also enlisted the services of former Maple Leaf player Eddie Shack who had served as a pitchman for the original company.

With a complete marketing mix package now in place and sales of over six million bottles a year, Brian is considering other options for Pop Shoppe. These include taking the product into the United States, where the premium soft drink segment is significantly larger than in Canada; taking the Pop Shoppe public with a stock sale; or looking to form a joint venture with a company that can help to expand the Pop Shoppe's distribution.

Whatever happens with the Pop Shoppe, Brian Alger has his next project lined up. Brian has acquired the rights to the Mother's Pizza Parlour & Spaghetti House name whose trademark, like that of the Pop Shoppe, had lapsed.[1]

Do you consider Pop Shoppe to be a new product? If so, what kind? Once the nostalgia of Pop Shoppe wears off, what must Brian do to continue to grow the sales of the product? What can Pop Shoppe do to appeal to a younger market, the biggest soft drink consumers, who don't remember the original product?

SOURCE: JOANNA PACHNER, "RETRO COOL: ENTREPRENEUR REVIVES THE POP SHOPPE," THE GLOBE AND MAIL, JUNE 3, 2010, 16; JOANNA PACHNER, "OTHER BRANDS THAT HAVE BEEN RESURRECTED," YOUR BUSINESS, JUNE 3, 2010, 5.

Explain the importance of developing new products and describe the six categories of new products

New products are important to sustain company growth and profits and to replace obsolete products. Research by the Boston Consulting Group revealed that the world's most innovative companies (including Apple Inc., RIM, Nintendo Corporation, Boeing Company, Nokia, and Microsoft Corporation) have higher stock returns and higher revenue growth than less innovative companies.[2] These firms are known for innovative products as well as innovative business models, innovative customer experiences, and innovative processes.

In this chapter we focus on new products, processes for developing new products, and how new products spread among consumers or business users. Being first into the market with a new product offers a number of advantages, including the following:

- *Increased sales through longer sales life*: The earlier the product reaches the market, relative to the competition, the longer its life can be.
- *Increased margins*: The more innovative the product (i.e., the longer it remains unchallenged on the market), the longer consumers will accept a premium price.
- *Increased product loyalty*: Early adopters are likely to upgrade, customize, or purchase companion products.
- *More resale opportunities*: For components, commodities, or products that other companies can private-label, being first to market can often help ensure sales in other channels.
- *Greater market responsiveness*: The faster that companies can bring products to market that satisfy new or changing customer needs, the greater the opportunity to capitalize on those products for high margins and to increase brand recognition.
- *A sustained leadership position*: Being first is a market position that a competitor can't take away. And repeated firsts establish companies as innovators and leaders in the market.[3]

CATEGORIES OF NEW PRODUCTS

new product
A product new to the world, the market, the producer, the seller, or some combination of these.

The term **new product** is somewhat confusing because its meaning varies widely. Actually, the term has several "correct" definitions. A product can be new to the world, to the market, to the producer or seller, or to some combination of these. There are six categories of new products:

- *New-to-the-world products* (also called *discontinuous innovations*): These products create an entirely new market. The telephone, transistor radio, television, computer, microprocessor, microwave oven, and the Internet are commonly cited examples of new-to-the-world products. New-to-the-world products represent the smallest category of new products.
- *New product lines*: These are products that the firm has not previously offered that allow it to enter an established market. Bombardier was formed in 1942 to manufacture enclosed multipassenger snowmobiles for military use. In 1959, Bombardier introduced the Ski-Doo snowmobile. Later the Sea-Doo, a watercraft product, was introduced. In 1974, Bombardier won a contract to supply cars for the Montreal subway. Since then, the company has added corporate jets, regional jets for major airlines, surface-to-air defence systems, and golf carts, among other products. Each of these additions represents a new product line for Bombardier.
- *Additions to existing product lines*: This category includes new products that supplement a firm's established line. Examples of product line additions include Tide detergent in tablet form, Huggies Pull-Ups and Pampers Easy-Up brands of disposable training pants, Downy Wrinkle Releaser fabric softener, and Yoplait's Go-GURT. Each time Nintendo introduces a new Wii game, it is adding to an existing product line. NSF International of Toronto added a new product to its existing lines as a result of the *Escherichia coli* outbreak in the drinking water of Walkerton, Ontario, which resulted in seven deaths. The product, called the

SOURCE: PRNEWSFOTO/GLAXOSMITHKLINE CONSUMER HEALTHCARE

Into what category of new products do you think the Breathe Right Nasal Strip falls? It could fall into more than one: additions to existing product lines and repositioned products. How?

UVD8.40—Ultra Violet Sterilizing Water Purification & Water Filtration System—is based on the Ultra Light technology that the company already possessed. The product, marketed to builders, attaches to the main water line outside the home and purifies all water before it enters the home.

- *Improvements or revisions of existing products*: The "new and improved" product may be significantly changed or only slightly changed. For example, Breyers Soft 'n Creamy! ice cream "scoops right out without bending the spoon." Anyone who has ever sat around for 15 minutes waiting for an ice-cream container to thaw would certainly agree that this is a product improvement. Tide Coldwater laundry detergent is concentrated and does not require hot water so less energy is used when doing the laundry. Another type of revision is package improvement. The Heinz EZ Squirt Ketchup bottle is short, is made from easy-to-squeeze plastic, and has a needle-shaped nozzle that lets small hands use it to decorate food.[4]
- *Repositioned products*: These are existing products targeted at new markets or market segments or repositioned to change the current market's perception of the product. The bottle for Beefeater gin was totally redesigned in an effort to appeal

Tide Coldwater detergent is concentrated and does not require hot water—a definite product improvement for consumers concerned about their levels of energy consumption.

Into what category of new products do you think the Adidas 1 computerized "intelligent" shoe falls? The new running shoe comes with magnetic sensors located in the heel to provide intelligent cushioning by automatically adjusting the positioning of the shoe. The computerized shoes might be considered a new product line, an addition to an existing product line, an improvement of an existing product, or a repositioned product.

to a younger, more upscale market.[5] Following a decline in sales, Diet Dr. Pepper was repositioned as an alternative to a dessert instead of comparing it to other diet drinks.

- *Lower-priced products*: This category refers to products that provide performance similar to competing brands but at a lower price. The Hewlett-Packard Laser Jet 3100 is a scanner, copier, printer, and fax machine combined. This new product is priced lower than many conventional colour copiers and much lower than the combined price of the four items purchased separately. The Aveo is the lowest-priced car that General Motors sells in Canada. It is manufactured by GM Daewoo in South Korea to keep assembly costs as low as possible.

REVIEW LEARNING OUTCOME 1

1   **Explain the importance of developing new products and describe the six categories of new products**

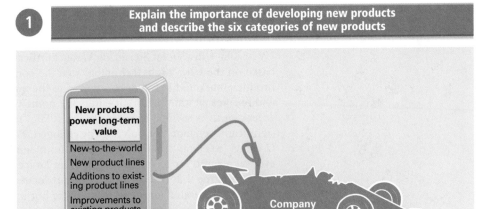

New products power long-term value

New-to-the-world

New product lines

Additions to existing product lines

Improvements to existing products

Repositioned products

Lower-priced products

Company

Long-term value →

NEW-PRODUCT DEVELOPMENT USING WEB 2.0 TOOLS

Web 2.0 offers marketers a great new way to engage consumers. How can companies use these new tools to build relationships and collaborate with consumers on-line? But first, what is Web 2.0? Essentially, it encompasses the set of tools that allow people to build social and business connections, share information, and collaborate on projects on-line. This includes blogs, wikis, social-networking sites, and other on-line communities and virtual worlds.

Millions of people have become familiar with these tools through sites like Facebook, Wikipedia, and Second Life, or by writing their own blogs. And a growing number of marketers are using Web 2.0 tools to collaborate with consumers on product development, service enhancement, and promotion. But most companies still don't appear to be well versed in this area.

Many marketers have been trained to bludgeon consumers with advertising—to sell anytime and anywhere consumers can be found. In an on-line community, it pays to resist that temptation. When consumers are invited to participate in on-line communities, they expect marketers to listen and to consider their ideas. They don't want to feel like they're simply a captive audience for advertising, and if they do, they're likely to abandon the community.

The head of consumer research for a leading consumer electronics company created an on-line community of nearly 50,000 consumers to discuss product development and marketing issues. One of the key principles of the community, she says, was "not to do anything about marketing, because we weren't about selling; we were about conversing."

In short order, community members not only identified what it was they were looking for in the company's products, but also suggested innovations to satisfy those needs. The company quickly developed prototypes based on those suggestions and got an enthusiastic response: Community members asked when they would be able to buy the products and if they would get the first opportunity to buy them. They didn't have to be sold on anything.[6]

Suggest other ideas that companies might use to generate and/or improve new product ideas using Web 2.0 tools. Briefly describe a positive or negative experience you have had visiting a Web 2.0 site.

SOURCE: MELANIE WARNER, "P&G'S CHEMISTRY TEST," FAST COMPANY, JULY/AUGUST 2008, 71.

2 THE NEW-PRODUCT DEVELOPMENT PROCESS

Explain the steps in the new-product development process

The management and technology consulting firm Booz, Allen, & Hamilton has studied the new-product development process for over 30 years. Analyzing five major studies undertaken during this period, the firm has concluded that the companies most likely to succeed in developing and introducing new products are those that take the following actions:

- Make the long-term commitment needed to support innovation and new-product development
- Use a company-specific approach, driven by corporate objectives and strategies, with a well-defined new-product strategy at its core
- Capitalize on experience to achieve and maintain competitive advantage
- Establish an environment—a management style, organizational structure, and degree of top-management support—conducive to achieving company-specific new-product and corporate objectives

Most companies follow a formal new-product development process, usually starting with a new-product strategy. Exhibit 9.1 traces the seven-step process that is discussed in detail in this section. The exhibit is funnel-shaped to highlight the fact that each stage acts as a screen, screening out ideas that should not move on to the next stage.

NEW-PRODUCT STRATEGY

new-product strategy
A plan that links the new-product development process with the objectives of the marketing department, the business unit, and the corporation.

A **new-product strategy** links the new-product development process with the objectives of the marketing department, the business unit, and the corporation. A new-product strategy must be compatible with these objectives, and in turn, objectives at all three levels of the company must be consistent with one another.

EXHIBIT 9.1

Product Development Process

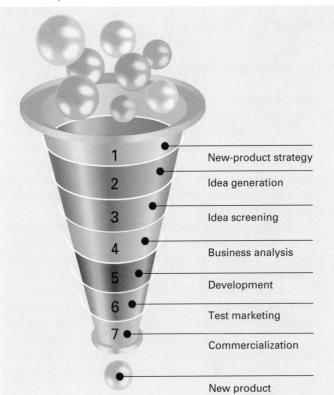

1	New-product strategy
2	Idea generation
3	Idea screening
4	Business analysis
5	Development
6	Test marketing
7	Commercialization
	New product

A new-product strategy is part of the organization's overall marketing strategy. It sharpens the focus and provides guidelines for generating, screening, and evaluating new-product ideas. The new-product strategy specifies the roles that new products must play in the organization's overall plan and describes the characteristics of products the organization wants to offer and the markets it wants to serve. The importance of having a well-thought-out new-product strategy is illustrated by a Dun & Bradstreet finding that for each successful new product introduced, a company needs between 50 and 60 other new-product ideas somewhere in the new-product development process.[7]

IDEA GENERATION

New-product ideas come from many sources, including customers, employees, distributors, competitors, suppliers, research and development (R&D), and consultants.

- *Customers*: The marketing concept suggests that customers' wants and needs should be the springboard for developing new products. Many of today's most innovative and successful marketers are introducing fewer new products, but they are taking steps to ensure that these "chosen few" are truly unique and better and, above all, really do address unmet consumer needs. How do they do that? Many firms rely on "co-creation," inventing new products along with their customers.[8] At **www.MyStarbucksIdea.com**, customers can make suggestions, other customers can vote on and discuss them, and Starbucks can see which ideas gain support.[9] Dell Computers has a similar site, called IdeaStorm.com. As the Customer Experience box illustrates, some companies are using Web 2.0 tools to get consumers more involved in new-product development.
- *Employees*: Marketing personnel—advertising and marketing research employees, as well as salespeople—often create new-product ideas because they analyze and are involved in the marketplace. The very successful introduction of Post-it Notes started with an employee's idea. The R&D department of 3M's commercial tape division developed and patented the adhesive component of Post-it Notes. However, it was a year before an employee in the commercial tape division, who sang in a church choir, identified a use for the adhesive. He had been using paper clips and slips of paper to mark places in hymn books. But the paper clips damaged his books, and the slips of paper fell out. The solution, as we now all know, was to apply the adhesive to small pieces of paper and sell them in packages. The idea for Heinz's coloured ketchups came from an employee at the company's Leamington, Ontario, plant. Toyota claims that its employees, worldwide, submit over two million product ideas each year. Many companies, like Kindred Industries, the largest manufacturer of stainless steel sinks in Canada, located in Midland, Ontario, routinely offer financial awards to employees who suggest new-product ideas or ideas for product improvements.
- *Distributors*: A well-trained sales force routinely asks distributors about needs that are not being met. Because they are closer to end users, distributors are often more aware of customer needs than are manufacturers. The inspiration for Rubbermaid's litter-free lunch box, named Sidekick, came from a distributor. The distributor suggested that Rubbermaid place some of its plastic containers inside a lunch box and sell the box as an alternative to plastic wrap and paper bags.
- *Competitors*: No firms rely solely on internally generated ideas for new products. A big part of any organization's marketing intelligence system should be monitoring

the performance of competitors' products. One purpose of competitive monitoring is to determine which, if any, of the competitors' products should be copied. Tim Hortons' breakfast sandwiches are, of course, a copy of the successful McDonald's breakfast sandwiches. There is plenty of information about competitors on the Internet. For example, AltaVista (**www.altavista.com**) is a powerful index tool that can be used to locate information about products and companies.

- *Suppliers*: Sometimes a company can work with its suppliers to develop a new offering. 7-Eleven worked with one of its suppliers to come up with the Candy Gulp (a plastic cup filled with gummies) and with another supplier (Nestlé) to come up with the Blue Vanilla Laffy Taffre Rope candy that is sold exclusively in 7-Eleven stores. Krave's Candy Company of Winnipeg, which markets Cloddhoppers candy, worked with Dairy Queen Canada to develop the Cloddhoppers Blizzard and with Breyers to develop a line of Breyers ice cream with Cloddhoppers pieces.

- *Research and development*: R&D is carried out in four distinct ways. Basic research is scientific research aimed at discovering new technologies. Applied research takes these new technologies and tries to find useful applications for them. **Product development** goes one step further by converting applications into marketable products. *Product modification* makes cosmetic or functional changes to existing products. Many new-product breakthroughs come from R&D activities. Pert Plus, Procter & Gamble's combination shampoo and conditioner, was invented in the company's laboratory. Nokia, with an R&D budget of $3 billion, has over 20,000 employees working in R&D around the globe. Nokia's Mobile Phone division alone averages more than 30 new product launches each year.[10]

- *Consultants*: Outside consultants are always available to examine a business and recommend product ideas. Examples of these consultants include the Weston Group; Booz, Allen, & Hamilton; and Management Decisions. Traditionally, consultants determine whether a company has a balanced portfolio of products and, if not, what new-product ideas are needed to offset the imbalance. For instance, an outside consultant conceived Airwick's highly successful Carpet Fresh carpet cleaner. In some cases, outside companies will develop new product ideas and then bring them to your firm for marketing.

Creativity is the wellspring of new-product ideas, regardless of who comes up with them. A variety of approaches and techniques have been developed to stimulate creative thinking. The two considered most useful for generating new-product ideas are brainstorming and focus group exercises. The goal of **brainstorming** is to get a group to think of unlimited ways to vary a product or solve a problem. Group members avoid criticism of an idea, no matter how ridiculous it may seem. Objective evaluation is postponed. The sheer quantity of ideas is what matters. The more ideas generated at this stage, the more likely a successful new product will ultimately be developed.

As noted in Chapter 7, an objective of focus group interviews is to stimulate insightful comments through group interaction. Focus groups usually consist of seven to ten people. Sometimes consumer focus groups generate excellent new product ideas—for example, Cycle dog food, Stick-Up room deodorizers, Dustbuster vacuum cleaners, and Wendy's salad bar. In the industrial market, machine tools, keyboard designs, aircraft interiors, and backhoe accessories have evolved from focus groups. One marketing research firm uses high-IQ Mensa Society members in its focus groups to generate new product ideas.[11]

IDEA SCREENING

After new ideas have been generated, they pass through the first filter in the product development process. This stage, called **screening**, eliminates ideas that are inconsistent with the organization's new-product strategy or are obviously inappropriate for some other reason. A company's new-product committee, new-product department, or some other formally appointed group performs the screening review. General Motors' Advanced Portfolio Exploration Group (APEx) knows that only one out of every 20 new car concepts developed by the group will ever become a reality. That's not a

product development
A marketing strategy that entails the creation of marketable new products; the process of converting applications for new technologies into marketable products.

brainstorming
The process of getting a group to think of unlimited ways to vary a product or solve a problem.

screening
The first filter in the product development process; it eliminates ideas that are inconsistent with the organization's new-product strategy or are obviously inappropriate for some other reason.

bad percentage. In the pharmaceutical business, one new product out of 5,000 ideas is not uncommon. Most new-product ideas are rejected at the screening stage in order to minimize the costs associated with developing new products and to make the most productive use of company time.

Concept tests are often used at the screening stage to rate concept (or product) alternatives. A **concept test** involves presenting the product idea to target consumers and getting their reaction, usually before any prototype has been created. Typically, researchers get consumer reactions to descriptions and visual representations of a proposed product.

Concept tests are considered fairly good predictors of success for line extensions. They have also been relatively precise predictors of success for new products that are not copycat items, are not easily classified into existing product categories, and do not require major changes in consumer behaviour—such as Betty Crocker Tuna Helper, Cycle dog food, and Libby's Fruit Float. However, concept tests are usually inaccurate in predicting the success of new products that create new consumption patterns or require major changes in consumer behaviour—such as microwave ovens, videocassette recorders, computers, and word processors.

concept test
A test to evaluate a new-product idea, usually before any prototype has been created.

BUSINESS ANALYSIS

business analysis
The second stage of the screening process, where preliminary figures for demand, cost, sales and profitability are calculated.

New-product ideas that survive the initial screening process move to the **business analysis** stage, where preliminary figures for demand, cost, sales, and profitability are calculated. For the first time, costs and revenues are estimated and compared. Depending on the nature of the product and the company, this process may be simple or complex.

The newness of the product, the size of the market, and the nature of the competition all affect the accuracy of revenue projections. In an established market like soft drinks, industry estimates of total market size are available. Forecasting sales for a new-to-the-world entry is a big challenge.

Analyzing overall economic trends and their impact on estimated sales is especially important in product categories that are sensitive to fluctuations in the business cycle. If consumers view the economy as uncertain and risky, they will put off buying durable goods like major home appliances, automobiles, and homes. Likewise, business buyers postpone major equipment purchases if they expect a recession.

These questions are commonly asked during the business analysis stage:

- What is the likely demand for the product?
- What impact would the new product have on company sales, profits, market share, and return on investment?
- How would the introduction of the product affect existing products? Would the new product cannibalize existing products?
- Would current customers benefit from the product?
- Would the product enhance the image of the company's overall product mix?
- Would the new product affect current employees in any way? Would it lead to hiring more people or reducing the size of the workforce?
- What new facilities, if any, would be needed?
- How might competitors respond?
- What is the risk of failure? Is the company willing to take the risk?

Answering these and related questions may require studies of markets, competition, costs, and technical capabilities. But at the end of this stage, management should have a good understanding of the product's market potential. This full understanding is important because costs increase dramatically once a product idea enters the development stage.

A visitor at the China International Software Product Expo in Nanjing, China, tries the infrared sensing keyboard developed by a Korean mobile phone company

DEVELOPMENT

development
The stage in the product development process in which a prototype is developed and a marketing strategy is outlined.

In the early stage of **development**, the firm's R&D or engineering department may develop a prototype of the product. During this stage, the firm should start sketching a marketing strategy. The marketing department should decide on the product's packaging, branding, labelling, and so forth. In addition, it should map out preliminary promotion, price, and distribution strategies. The feasibility of manufacturing the product at an acceptable cost should also be thoroughly examined.

The development stage can last a long time and thus be very expensive. Crest toothpaste was in the development stage for 10 years. It took 18 years to develop Minute Rice, 15 years to develop the Polaroid Colorpack camera, 15 years to develop the Xerox copy machine, and 51 years to develop television. Gillette developed three shaving systems over a 27-year period (TracII, Atra, and Sensor) before introducing the Mach 3 in 1998 and Fusion in 2006. Not only is the development stage long, it can be very costly. The development of a new model of automobile can cost up to $2 billion.

simultaneous product development
A team-oriented approach to new-product development.

The development process works best when all the involved areas (R&D, marketing, engineering, production, and even suppliers) work together rather than sequentially, a process called **simultaneous product development**. This approach allows firms to shorten the development process and reduce costs. With simultaneous product development, all relevant functional areas and outside suppliers participate in all stages of the development process. Rather than proceeding through highly structured stages, the cross-functional team operates in unison. Involving key suppliers early in the process capitalizes on their specialized knowledge and enables them to design and develop critical component parts.

The Internet is a useful tool for implementing simultaneous product development. On the Net, multiple partners from a variety of locations can meet regularly to assess new-product ideas, analyze markets and demographics, and review cost information. Ideas judged to be feasible can quickly be converted into new products. Without the Internet, it would be impossible to conduct simultaneous product development from different parts of the world. Global R&D is important for two reasons. First, large companies have become global and are no longer focused only on one market. Second, companies want to tap into the world's best talent.

Some firms use on-line brain trusts to solve technical problems. InnoCentive, Inc. is a network of 80,000 self-selected science problem solvers in 173 countries. Its clients include Boeing, DuPont, and Procter & Gamble. Procter & Gamble has another program called the Connect-and-Develop Model. When the company selects an idea for development, it no longer tries to develop it from the ground up with its own resources and time. Instead, it issues a brief to its network of thinkers, researchers, technology entrepreneurs, and inventors around the world, hoping to generate dialogue, suggestions, and solutions. Olay Regenerist Eye Derma Pods, a top-selling skin care item, was developed through Connect-and-Develop.[12]

Innovative firms are also gathering a variety of R&D input from customers on-line. Google polls millions of Web page creators to determine the most relevant search results. LEGO Group uses the Internet to identify its most enthusiastic customers and to help design and market products. Threadless, a T-shirt company, and Ryz, an athletic shoe manufacturer, ask consumers to vote on-line for their favourites. The companies use these results to determine the products they will sell over the Internet.

Laboratory tests are often conducted on prototype models during the development stage. User safety is an important aspect of laboratory testing, which actually subjects products to much more severe treatment than is expected by end users. Kindred Industries of Midland, Ontario, tests kitchen faucets by

SOURCE: LUCAS SCHIFRES/LANDOV

Danone chose to test-market its successful European product Actimel (name changed to Activia in Canada) before rolling out the bacteria-loaded dairy product North America-wide. Test marketing for two years allowed the company to refine its marketing strategy and determine customer reaction.

running water through them at much higher pressure and for much longer than would ever occur in someone's kitchen.

Many products that test well in the laboratory are also tried out in homes or businesses. Product categories well suited for such tests include human and pet food products, household cleaning products, and industrial chemicals and supplies. These products are all relatively inexpensive and their performance characteristics are apparent to users. Procter & Gamble tests many of its personal and home-care products in the communities around its plants. For example, Procter & Gamble invited 500 women to the lab at one of its plants every morning to apply lipstick. At the end of the day, the women returned, identified what they had done during the day, and Procter & Gamble measured the lipstick remaining. The result was the introduction of the highly successful Cover Girl Outlast all-day lip product. Red Lobster routinely uses its restaurants to test new recipes and food dishes with the dining public.

TEST MARKETING

test marketing
The limited introduction of a product and a marketing program to determine the reactions of potential customers in a market situation.

After products and marketing programs have been developed, they are usually tested in the marketplace. **Test marketing** is the limited introduction of a product and a marketing program into one or two test cities to determine the reactions of potential customers in a market situation. Test marketing allows management to evaluate alternative strategies and to assess how well the various aspects of the marketing mix fit together. Even established products are test-marketed to assess new marketing strategies. Bottles of chocolate, strawberry, and coffee-flavoured milk, distributed through vending machines, were offered in schools to assess this alternative distribution strategy. Initial weekly sales ran about 200 bottles per machine.[13]

The cities chosen as test sites should reflect market conditions in the new product's projected market area. There is no perfect test city that can universally represent all market conditions, and a product's success in one city doesn't guarantee that it will be a nationwide hit. When selecting test-market cities, researchers should select locations where the demographics and consumer purchasing habits mirror the overall market. The company should also have good distribution in test cities. Moreover, test locations should have little media spread. If the TV stations in a particular market reach a very large area outside that market, the advertising used for the test product may pull in many consumers from outside the market. The product may then appear more successful than it really is. Exhibit 9.2 provides a useful checklist of criteria for selecting test markets. Winnipeg is a popular test market city. Canada, being only one-tenth the size of the United States, is sometimes used as a test market before products are introduced into the United States.

EXHIBIT 9.2

Checklist for Selecting Test Markets

In choosing a test market, many criteria need to be considered, especially the following:

- Similarity to planned distribution outlets
- Relative isolation from other cities
- Availability of advertising media that will cooperate
- Diversified cross-section of ages, religions, cultural-societal preferences, etc.
- No atypical purchasing habits
- Representative population size
- Typical per capita income
- Good record as a test city, but not overly used
- Not easily "jammed" by competitors
- Stability of year-round sales
- No dominant television station; multiple newspapers, magazines, and radio stations
- Availability of research and audit services
- Availability of retailers that will cooperate
- Freedom from unusual influences, such as one industry's dominance or heavy tourism

The High Costs of Test Marketing

Test marketing frequently takes one year or longer and costs can easily exceed $1 million. Some products remain in test markets even longer. McDonald's spent 12 years developing and testing salads before introducing them. Despite the cost, many firms believe it is a lot better to fail in a test market than in a national introduction.

Because test marketing is so expensive, some companies do not test line extensions of well-known brands. For example, because the Folgers brand is well known, Procter & Gamble faced little risk in distributing its instant decaffeinated version nationally. Consolidated Foods Kitchen of Sara Lee followed the same approach with its frozen croissants. Other products introduced without being test-marketed include General Foods'

International Coffees, Quaker Oats' Chewy Granola Bars and Granola Dipps, and Pillsbury's Milk Break Bars.

The high cost of test marketing is not just financial. One unavoidable problem is that test marketing exposes the new product and its marketing mix to competitors before its introduction. Thus the element of surprise is lost. Competitors can also sabotage or "jam" a testing program by introducing their own sales promotion, pricing, or advertising campaigns. The purpose is to hide or distort the normal conditions that the testing firm might expect in the market.

Alternatives to Test Marketing

Many firms are looking for cheaper, faster, safer alternatives to traditional test marketing. Information Resources, Inc. pioneered one alternative: single-source research using supermarket scanner data. A typical supermarket scanner test costs about $300,000. Another alternative to traditional test marketing is **simulated (laboratory) market testing**. Advertising and other promotional materials for several products, including the test product, are shown to members of the product's target market. These people are then taken to shop at a mock or real store, where their purchases are recorded. Shopper behaviour, including repeat purchasing, is monitored to assess the test product's likely performance under true market conditions. Research firms offer simulated market tests for $25,000 to $100,000, compared to $1 million or more for full-scale test marketing.

On-Line Test Marketing

Despite these alternatives, most firms still consider test marketing essential for new products. The high cost of failure simply prohibits the widespread introduction of most new products without testing. Many firms are finding that the Internet offers a fast, cost-effective way to conduct test marketing.

Procter & Gamble is an avid proponent of using the Internet as a means for gauging customer demand for potential new products. Many products that are not available in grocery stores or drugstores can be sampled from P&G's corporate website. The company's home tooth-bleaching kit Crest Whitestrips provides an illustration. When Procter & Gamble was ready to launch Crest Whitestrips, management wasn't sure that consumers would pay the proposed $44 retail price. P&G then began an eight-month campaign selling the strips exclusively on **www.whitestrips.com**. TV spots and magazine ads were run to promote the on-line sale. In eight months, 144,000 whitening kits were sold on-line. The product was introduced in retail outlets and $50 million worth of kits were sold in the first three months at the initial $44 per kit price.[14] Other consumer goods firms that use on-line test marketing include General Mills and Quaker Oats.

COMMERCIALIZATION

The final stage in the new-product development process is **commercialization**, the decision to market a product. The decision to commercialize the product sets several tasks in motion: ordering production materials and equipment, starting production, building inventories, shipping the product to field distribution points, training the sales force, announcing the new product to the trade, and advertising to potential customers.

The time from the initial commercialization decision to the product's actual introduction varies. It can range from a few weeks for simple products that use existing equipment to several years for technical products that require custom manufacturing equipment. The total cost of development and initial introduction can be staggering. Gillette spent $750 million developing the Mach3, and the first-year marketing budget for the new three-bladed razor was $300 million. Marketing expenditures for new products often run as high as 60 percent of the product's first-year sales.

For some products, a well-planned Internet campaign can provide new-product information for people who are looking for the solutions that a particular new

simulated (laboratory) market testing
The presentation of advertising and other promotion materials for several products, including a test product, to members of the product's target market.

commercialization
The decision to market a product.

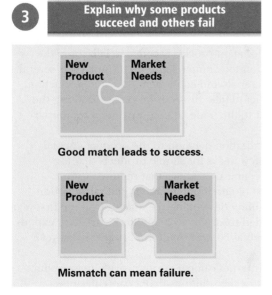

2 Explain the steps in the new-product development process

Number of new product ideas

New-product strategy
Idea generation
Idea screening
Business analysis
Development
Test marketing
Commercialization

0   Time

product offers. Attempting to reach customers just when they need a product is much more cost-effective and efficient than communicating with a target market that may eventually have a need for the product.

At commercialization, companies can use "crash" or "roll-out" programs. A crash program involves attempting to get the new product introduced everywhere as fast as possible. A crash program might be used when company management feels that a competitor is close behind. For example, Gillette attempting to beat Schick into the market with a new shaving system. A roll-out program involves a gradual, market-by-market introduction of the new product until national distribution is achieved. Roll-outs permit more market testing while the product is being "rolled" into the market and adjustments made to the marketing program. With a roll-out program, company management must decide when the new product will be introduced (best selling season, for example) and where the roll-out will begin (most favourable markets, for example).

3 WHY SOME PRODUCTS SUCCEED AND OTHERS FAIL

Explain why some products succeed and others fail

Despite a company's best efforts in developing and testing new products, a proportion of all new-product introductions fail. Estimates of new-product failure rates range to 50 percent and higher. Products fail for a number of reasons. One common reason is that they simply do not offer any discernible benefit compared to existing products. Another commonly cited factor in new product failures is a poor match between product features and customer desires. For example, there are telephone systems on the market with over 700 different functions, although the average user is happy with just 10 functions. Other reasons for failure include overestimation of market size, incorrect positioning, a price too high or too low, inadequate distribution, poor promotion, or simply an inferior product compared to those of competitors. One survey reported that nearly 70 percent of consumers could not identify one new product introduced in the previous year.[15]

Failure can be a matter of degree. Absolute failure occurs when a company cannot recoup its development, marketing, and production costs. The product actually loses money for the company. A relative product failure results when the product returns a profit but fails to achieve sales, profit, or market share goals.

3 Explain why some products succeed and others fail

New Product   Market Needs

Good match leads to success.

New Product   Market Needs

Mismatch can mean failure.

The most important factor in a successful new-product introduction is a good match between the product and market needs—as the marketing concept would predict. Pete Mateja, president of Home & Park Motorhomes in Kitchener, Ontario, the largest builder of camper vans in Canada, says that it is his company's goal to deliver to customers what they want even before they realize that they want it.[16] Successful new products deliver a meaningful and perceivable benefit to a sizable number of people or organizations and are different in some meaningful way from competitive products. Firms that routinely experience success in new-product introductions tend to share the following characteristics:

- A history of carefully listening to customers
- An obsession with producing the best product possible
- A vision of what the market will be like in the future
- Strong leadership
- A commitment to new-product development
- A project-based team approach to new-product development
- Getting every aspect of the product development process right

Discuss global issues in new-product development

The increasing globalization of markets and of competition provides a reason for multinational firms to consider new product development from a worldwide perspective. That perspective includes developing countries as well as more established markets. As the Global Perspectives box illustrates, Canadian firms are sometimes dependent on products developed for the unique needs of consumers in foreign markets.

A firm that starts with a global strategy is better able to develop products that are marketable worldwide. In many multinational corporations, every product is developed for potential worldwide distribution. Procter & Gamble introduced Pampers Phases into global markets within one month of first getting the product on the market in North America. P&G's goal was to have the product on store shelves in 90 countries within one year. The objective was to establish brand loyalty among dealers and consumers before foreign competitors could react.

Some global marketers first design their products to meet regulations and other key requirements in their major markets and then, if necessary, meet smaller markets' requirements country by country. Nissan develops lead-country car models that, with minor changes, can be sold in most other countries. With this approach, Nissan has been able to reduce the number of its basic models from 48 to 18.

Developing countries represent huge automobile markets but not at the same prices we see in Canada. Renault SA introduced the Dacia Logan, a low-priced car with exposed screws, a coarse fabric interior, and a 90-horsepower motor. The Logan sells for about $7,300 in Eastern Europe and the Middle East and has become very successful in these markets. India's Tata Motors Ltd. has introduced a new automobile called the Nano that sells for $2,500 in that country.[17]

Some companies could not sell their products at affordable prices and still make an adequate profit in many countries. GE Healthcare engineers figured out a way to develop the MAC 400, a portable electrocardiograph machine that GE is able to sell for $1,500 in India. The MAC 400 was based on technology developed in North America for a product that sells in Canada for over $5 million!

In some cases, lower-cost-country competitors can't be beaten on price, so some other way is sought. For Gérard Vroomen, the only similarity between the bikes found at a typical Canadian Tire store (and often made in China) and the ones produced at his plant in Toronto is that they are both called bikes. In 1995, Vroomen and a partner founded Cervélo to manufacture racing bike frames using high-tech engineering. He says, "Manufacturing in Canada will always be more expensive than manufacturing in China. So you have to figure out the best way to compete."[18] In the case of Cervélo, it was through building high-quality carbon-fibre racing bikes that are priced from $2,000 to $11,000. The strategy has worked—Cervélo's sales have grown from $800,000 in 1999 to over $15 million by 2010.

We often hear about how popular North American products are in foreign countries. Recently, companies such as Levi Strauss, Roots, Coca-Cola, RJR Nabisco, and Nike have been finding that products popular in foreign markets can become hits here. An example is Häagen-Dazs's new ice-cream flavour *dulce de leche,* originally introduced in Buenos Aires. The brand is named after a caramelized milk spread that is popular in Argentina. *Dulce de leche* became an instant success in Argentina. The brand has since been successfully introduced in North America. Enova, a cooking oil that helps to reduce weight and body fat, was the top-selling brand in Japan before being introduced in Canada.

In other cases, former alliance partners have become competitors. Shanghai Automotive Industry Corp. (SAIC) has assembled cars with General Motors and Volkswagen in China for the Chinese market for a number of years. Now SAIC is assembling its own vehicles in other countries, competing with both General Motors and Volkswagen.

SOURCE: MICHAEL NEWMAN/PHOTOEDIT

Insights for new products are coming increasingly from around the world. An Argentine success, Häagen-Dazs's *dulce de leche* is gaining popularity in North America where in-store displays promote the new flavour.

REVIEW LEARNING OUTCOME 4

4 Discuss global issues in new-product development

- Single product worldwide
- Modification of products
- Multiple products in multiple countries

FRUGAL ENGINEERING

The world is becoming one big R&D lab. Companies increasingly are finding that their international operations are coming up with ideas that resonate far beyond local markets. Case in point: Deere & Co. is now pursuing a new market in Canada—recreational farmers—thanks to innovations hatched at its research facility in Pune, India.

Deere opened the Pune centre in 2001 as a way of entering the Indian market. The move was unexpected as Deere is known for its heavy-duty farm equipment and big construction gear. Many of India's 300 million-plus farmers still use oxen-pulled plows. But Deere saw potential, and its engineers in Pune responded with four no-frills models that were sturdy enough to handle the rigours of commercial farming.

The tractors, which cost $8,000 to $11,000 in India, were so basic that Deere never even contemplated selling them here. Then Indian tractor maker Mahindra & Mahindra began selling its wares here, targeting a market Deere had largely ignored—hobby farmers. These customers didn't need advanced features, and it turns out they coveted the same qualities as Indian farmers: affordability and manoeuvrability. Deere, taking a cue from Mahindra, brought a slightly modified version (with softer seats

and higher horsepower) of the Indian line of tractors here and markets it as the 5003 series at a starting price of under $15,000. Today, half of the tractors that Deere manufactures in India are exported to other countries.

The Indian-made tractor was perfect for hobby farmers who have full-time jobs but farm on weekends. Even full-time farmers who were skeptical of the streamlined product ultimately were convinced that the product was durable enough for everyday farm work.

Deere doesn't disclose margins for specific machines but the company surely sees financial benefits from transplanting Indian innovations back to North America. Raj Kalathur, the managing director of Deere's Indian division, says the 5003 tractors were born out of "frugal engineering." Many of Deere's Indian employees witness poverty daily, he explains, and they took great care to minimize costs. That kind of innovation isn't just global— it's good business.[19]

What other products might be candidates for frugal engineering? Write a memo to the director of marketing research for a Canadian manufacturer proposing and justifying your favourite idea.

SOURCE: JENNY MERO, "JOHN DEERE'S FARM TEAM," FORTUNE, APRIL 14, 2008, 121, 126.

 5 THE SPREAD OF NEW PRODUCTS

Explain the diffusion process through which new products are adopted

adopter
A consumer who was happy enough with his or her trial experience with a product to use it again.

innovation
A product perceived as new by a potential adopter.

diffusion
The process by which the adoption of an innovation spreads.

Managers have a better chance of successfully marketing new products if they understand how consumers learn about and adopt products. A person who buys a new product, a product never before tried, may ultimately become an adopter. An **adopter** is a consumer who was happy enough with his or her trial experience with a product to use it again.

DIFFUSION OF INNOVATION

An **innovation** is a product perceived as new by a potential adopter. It really doesn't matter whether the product is "new to the world" or some other category of new product. If it is new to a potential adopter, it is an innovation as far as this purchaser is concerned. **Diffusion** is the process by which the adoption of an innovation spreads.

The diffusion process proceeds through five categories of adopters:

- *Innovators*: the first 2.5 percent of all those who adopt the product. Innovators are eager to try new ideas and products. In addition to having higher incomes, they are worldlier and more active outside their community than non-innovators. They rely less on group norms and are more self-confident. Because they are well educated, they are more likely to get their information from scientific sources and experts. Innovators are characterized as being venturesome.
- *Early adopters*: the next 13.5 percent to adopt the product. Although early adopters are not the very first, they do adopt early in the product's life cycle. Compared to innovators, they rely much more on group norms and values. They are also more oriented to the local community, in contrast to the innovators' worldly outlook. Early adopters are more likely than innovators to be opinion leaders because of

Coca-Cola is a company that seems to need little help with the global penetration of its products. In fact, despite adapting its product formula and product mix to various cultures, Coke is one of the world's most recognized brands.

their closer relationship with many different groups. Early adopters are a new product's best friends. Apple Computer spends its entire marketing budget attempting to appeal to early adopters. Joe Bates, research director for the Consumer Electronics Association, has noted that early adopters spend up to three times more money on consumer electronics devices than other categories of adopters and are two to five times more likely to spread the word about new products.[20] The respect of others is a dominant characteristic of early adopters.

• *Early majority*: the next 34 percent to adopt. The early majority weighs the pros and cons before adopting a new product. They are likely to collect more information and evaluate more brands than early adopters. They rely on others for information but are unlikely to be opinion leaders themselves. Instead, they tend to be opinion leaders' friends and neighbours. The early majority is an important link in the process of diffusing new ideas because they are positioned between earlier and later adopters. A dominant characteristic of the early majority is deliberateness.

• *Late majority*: the next 34 percent to adopt. The late majority adopts a new product because most of their friends have already adopted it. Because they rely on group norms, their adoption stems from pressure to conform. This group tends to be older and below average in income and education. They depend mainly on word-of-mouth communication rather than on the mass media. The dominant characteristic of the late majority is skepticism.

• *Laggards*: the final 16 percent to adopt. Like innovators, laggards do not rely on group norms. Their independence is rooted in their ties to tradition. Thus the past heavily influences their decisions. By the time laggards adopt an innovation, it has probably been outmoded and replaced by something else. For example, this group will still be using 35 mm cameras and video cassettes long after the market has moved to more advanced technologies. Laggards have the longest adoption time and the lowest socioeconomic status. They tend to be suspicious of new products and alienated from a rapidly advancing society. The dominant value of laggards is tradition. Marketers typically ignore laggards, who do not seem to be motivated by advertising or personal selling and are virtually impossible to reach on-line.

Exhibit 9.3 illustrates the diffusion of digital TVs in Canada. Digital TVs exceeded 50 percent household penetration in 2009, only 11 years after being introduced to the market. As a comparison, it took personal computers 20 years to exceed 50 percent household penetration. Based on the characteristics of these two products, why do you believe that digital TVs seem to be penetrating the market faster? Notice how slow the initial penetration of digital TV was and how fast it took off after 2004. How would you account for this? Note that for most product categories, household penetration may never reach 100 percent. The adopter categories refer to all of those who will eventually adopt a product, not the entire population.

EXHIBIT 9.3

Consumer Adoption Line Graph

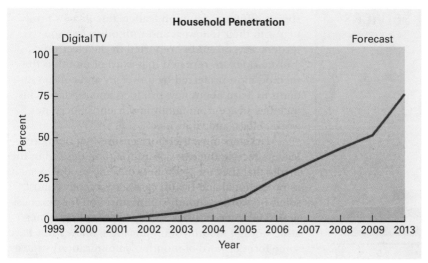

SOURCE: Media Trends Track, "TV Basics: Personal Computer & Digital TV Sales," http://www.tvb.org/rcentral/MediaTrendsTrack; Digital TV Business, Technology & Market Research News, "Half the world's homes to have digital TV by 2013," http://www.digitalTVnews.net; Forrester Research; Consumer Electronics Association.

PRODUCT CHARACTERISTICS AND THE RATE OF ADOPTION

Five product characteristics can be used to predict and explain the rate of acceptance and diffusion of a new product:

- *Complexity*: the degree of difficulty involved in understanding and using a new product. The more complex the product, the slower is its diffusion. For instance, DVD recorders have been around for a number of years now. To date, they have been purchased mostly by early adopters willing to go to the trouble of linking the recorders to their PCs or by those willing to pay high prices for the stand-alone units that connect to a TV.
- *Compatibility*: the degree to which the new product is consistent with existing values and product knowledge, past experiences, and current needs. Incompatible products diffuse more slowly than compatible products. For example, the introduction of contraceptives is incompatible in countries where religious beliefs discourage the use of birth control devices.
- *Relative advantage*: the degree to which a product is perceived as superior to existing substitutes. For example, because it reduces cooking time, the microwave oven has a clear relative advantage over a conventional oven.
- *Observability*: the degree to which the benefits or other results of using the product can be observed by others and communicated to target customers. For instance, fashion items and automobiles are highly visible and more observable than personal care items.
- *"Trialability"*: the degree to which a product can be tried on a limited basis. It is much easier to try a new toothpaste or breakfast cereal than a new automobile or microcomputer. While demonstrations in showrooms and test drives can be used, they are different from in-home trial use. To stimulate trials, marketers often use free-sampling programs, tasting displays, and small package sizes.

Now that you've just read this section of the text, can you better explain the rate of adoption exhibited by digital TVs as shown in Exhibit 9.3? Exhibit 9.4 shows the time it took for various audio and video products to reach sales of one million units. Note how long it took for some products.

MARKETING IMPLICATIONS OF THE ADOPTION PROCESS

Two types of communication aid the diffusion process: *word-of-mouth communication* among consumers and communication from marketers to consumers. Word-of-mouth communication within and across groups speeds diffusion. Opinion leaders discuss new products with their followers and with other opinion leaders. Several studies reported in the electronic journal *eMarketer* revealed that word of mouth is the method most preferred by university and college students to learn about new products and services. This includes advice from family and friends, social networks, blogs, and viral video.

Marketers must therefore ensure that opinion leaders receive the types of information desired in the media that they use. Suppliers of some products, such as professional and health care services, rely almost solely on word-of-mouth communication for new business. The Internet plays an important role in generating word-of-mouth communication. Many firms have some form of word-of-mouth communications strategy, often referred to as buzz marketing. Marketers will sometimes recruit a core group of opinion leaders to get the buzz going.

EXHIBIT 9.4

Sales of New Audio Products

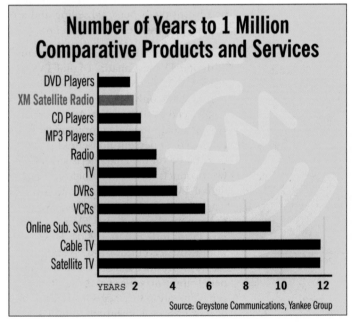

SOURCE: © PR NEWSFOTO/XM SATELLITE RADIO

5 **Explain the diffusion process through which new products are adopted**

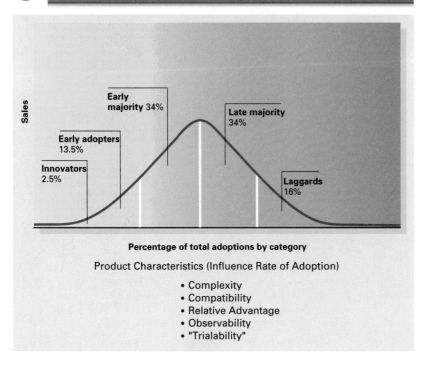

Sales

Innovators 2.5%

Early adopters 13.5%

Early majority 34%

Late majority 34%

Laggards 16%

Percentage of total adoptions by category

Product Characteristics (Influence Rate of Adoption)

- Complexity
- Compatibility
- Relative Advantage
- Observability
- "Trialability"

The second type of communication aiding the diffusion process is *communication directly from the marketer to potential adopters.* Messages directed toward early adopters should normally use different appeals than messages directed toward the early majority, the late majority, or the laggards. Early adopters are more important than innovators because they make up a larger group, are more socially active, and are usually opinion leaders. Early adopters spend five or more hours each day on-line, use websites to learn about products, and use on-line advertising as an important information source.

As the focus of a promotional campaign shifts from early adopters to the early majority and the late majority, marketers should study the dominant characteristics, buying behaviour, and media characteristics of these target markets. Then they should revise messages and media strategy to fit. The diffusion model helps guide marketers in developing and implementing promotion strategies.

6 PRODUCT LIFE CYCLES

Explain the concept of product life cycles

product life cycle (PLC)
A concept that provides a way to trace the stages of a product's acceptance, from its introduction (birth) to its decline (death).

product category
All brands that satisfy a particular type of need.

The **product life cycle (PLC)** is one of the most familiar concepts in marketing. Few other general concepts have been so widely discussed. Although some researchers have challenged the theoretical basis and managerial value of the PLC, most believe it has great value as a marketing management tool and guide. The product life cycle provides a way to trace the stages of a product's acceptance, from its introduction (birth) to its decline (death). As Exhibit 9.5 shows, a product progresses through four major stages: introduction, growth, maturity, and decline.

The product life cycle concept can be used to analyze a brand or a product category. Brands such as Intuition, Quattro, and Mach3 will each have a product life cycle. Each of these brands is part of the product category that might be called razors or shaving systems, which also has a PLC. A **product category** includes all brands that satisfy a particular type of need. Product categories include shaving products, passenger cars, soft drinks, and coffee. Product categories would generally have longer life cycles than any of the individual brands that make up the product category. When we trace the product life cycle of a product category such as DVD players, we are including the aggregate sales of all brands of DVD players, not just a single brand.

The time a product spends in any one stage of the life cycle may vary dramatically. Some products, such as fad items, move through the entire cycle in weeks. Others, such as electric clothes washers and dryers, stay in the maturity stage for decades. Exhibit 9.5 illustrates the typical life cycle for a consumer durable good, such as a washer or dryer. In contrast, Exhibit 9.6 illustrates typical life cycles for styles (such as formal, business, or casual clothing), fashions (such as miniskirts or baggy jeans), and fads (such as leopard-print clothing). Changes in a product, its uses, its image, or its positioning can extend that product's life cycle.

As product life cycles continue to decrease, compressing development cycles and accelerating new-product developments are critical. The product life cycle concept does not tell managers the length of a product's life cycle or its duration in any stage.

EXHIBIT 9.5

Four Stages of the Product Life Cycle

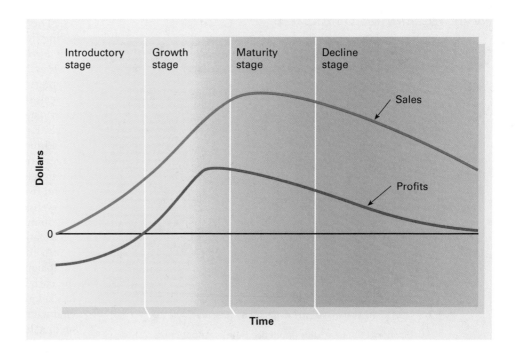

EXHIBIT 9.6

Product Life Cycles for Styles, Fashions, and Fads

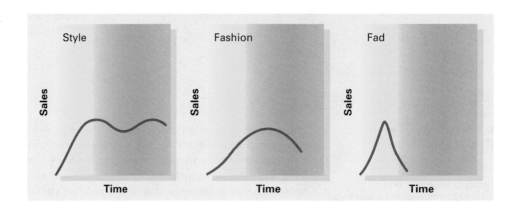

It does not dictate marketing strategy. It is simply a tool to help marketers forecast future events and suggest appropriate strategies.

INTRODUCTORY STAGE

introductory stage
The first stage of the product life cycle in which the full-scale launch of a new product into the marketplace occurs.

The **introductory stage** of the product life cycle represents the full-scale launch of a new product into the marketplace. Computer databases for personal use, room-deodorizing air-conditioning filters, and wind-powered home electric generators are all product categories that have recently entered the product life cycle. A high failure rate, little competition, frequent product modification, and limited distribution typify the introduction stage of the PLC.

Marketing costs in the introductory stage are normally high for several reasons. High dealer margins are often needed to obtain adequate distribution, and incentives are needed to get consumers to try the new product. Advertising expenses are high because of the need to educate consumers about the new product's benefits. Production costs are also often high in this stage, as product and manufacturing flaws are identified and corrected and efforts are undertaken to develop mass-production economies.

As Exhibit 9.5 illustrates, sales normally increase slowly during the introductory stage. Moreover, profits are usually negative because of R&D costs, factory tooling, and

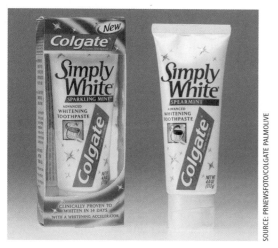

Development and use of tooth-whitening products have exploded in recent years. Crest Whitestrips, Colgate Simply White Gel, and Colgate's Simply White toothpaste are some of the big new products in this market. Do you think that tooth whitening is a style, fashion, or fad?

SOURCE: PRNEWSFOTO/COLGATE PALMOLIVE

growth stage
The second stage of the product life cycle, when sales typically grow at an increasing rate, many competitors enter the market, large companies may start acquiring small pioneering firms, and profits are healthy.

maturity stage
The third stage of the product life cycle during which sales increase at a decreasing rate.

Styles, fashions, and fads tend to follow different product life cycles. Based on what you see in Exhibits 9.5 and 9.6, what might be the life cycle for Vitaballs, a new vitamin-infused bubblegum? Do you think it will be adopted by the mainstream of the population? If so, how quickly?

SOURCE: COURTESY AMERIFIT NUTRITION, INC.

high introduction costs. The length of the introductory phase is largely determined by product characteristics, such as the product's advantages over substitute products, the educational effort required to make the product known, and management's commitment of resources to the new item. A short introductory period is usually preferred to help reduce the impact of negative earnings and cash flows. As soon as the product gets off the ground, the financial burden should begin to diminish. Also, a short introduction helps dispel some of the uncertainty as to whether the new product will be successful.

Promotion strategy in the introductory stage focuses on developing product awareness and informing consumers about the product category's potential benefits. At this stage, the communication challenge is to stimulate primary demand—demand for the product in general rather than for a specific brand. Intensive personal selling is often required to gain acceptance for the product among wholesalers and retailers. The promotion of convenience products often requires heavy consumer sampling and couponing. Shopping and specialty products demand educational advertising and personal selling to the final consumer.

The introductory stage of the PLC varies from country to country. According to research undertaken in Europe, the range for the introductory stage varies from under four years in Denmark and Norway to nearly nine years in Great Britain and Greece. Finland and Sweden are under the six-year average for all European countries while Germany, Italy, Spain, and France are countries above the six-year average.[21] Cultural factors likely play a role in how long it takes to get a new product accepted. Scandinavians seem to be more open to new products as shown by the fact that product introductory times are lowest in Denmark, Norway, Sweden, and Finland. Are you surprised at how long typical product introductory periods are (average of six years in Europe)? What do you think the average introductory period in Canada might be?

GROWTH STAGE

If a product category survives the introductory stage, and many don't, it advances to the **growth stage** of the life cycle. In this stage, sales typically grow at an increasing rate, many competitors enter the market, and large companies may start to acquire small pioneering firms. Profits rise rapidly in the growth stage, reach their peak, and begin declining as competition intensifies. Emphasis switches from primary demand promotion (for example, promoting personal digital assistants or PDAs) to aggressive brand advertising and communication of the differences between brands (for example, promoting Casio versus Palm and Visor).

Distribution becomes a major key to success during the growth stage, as well as in later stages. Manufacturers scramble to sign up dealers and distributors and to build long-term relationships. Without adequate distribution, it is impossible to establish a strong market position. It is important to recognize at this stage that competition will increase and firms must work hard to hold on to their position in the market.

MATURITY STAGE

A period during which sales increase, but at a decreasing rate, signals the beginning of the **maturity stage** of the life cycle. New users cannot be added indefinitely and sooner or later the market approaches saturation. Normally, this is the longest stage of the product life cycle. Many major household appliances are in the maturity stage of their life cycles.

Coffee is an example of a product in the maturity stage where niche marketers have emerged. Starbucks, for example, targets its gourmet products at newer, younger, more affluent coffee drinkers.

For shopping products and many specialty products, annual models begin to appear during the maturity stage. Product lines are lengthened to appeal to additional market segments. Service and repair assume more important roles as manufacturers strive to distinguish their products from others. Product design changes tend to become stylistic (i.e., how can the product be made different?) rather than functional (i.e., how can the product be made better?).

As prices and profits continue to fall, marginal competitors start dropping out of the market. Dealer margins also shrink, resulting in less shelf space for mature items, lower dealer inventories, and a general reluctance to promote the product. Thus promotion to dealers often intensifies during this stage in order to retain loyalty.

Heavy consumer promotion by the manufacturer is also required to maintain market share. Consider these well-known examples of competition in the maturity stage: the "cola war" featuring Coke and Pepsi, the "beer war" featuring Molson's and Labatt's, and the "burger wars" pitting leader McDonald's against challengers like Burger King, Wendy's, and Harvey's.

Another characteristic of the maturity stage is the emergence of "niche marketers" that target narrow, well-defined, underserved segments of a market. Starbucks Coffee targets its gourmet line at the only segment of the coffee market that is growing: newer, younger, more affluent coffee drinkers. Globally, with new car sales expected to be about the same in North America in 2015 as in 1998, the auto companies are all targeting China, India, Russia, and Brazil—countries where automobile sales are growing.

DECLINE STAGE

decline stage
The fourth stage of the product life cycle, characterized by a long-run drop in sales.

A long-run drop in sales signals the beginning of the **decline stage**. The rate of decline is governed by how rapidly consumer tastes change or substitute products are adopted. Many convenience products and fad items lose their market overnight, leaving large inventories of unsold items, such as designer jeans. Others die more slowly—CD sales fell by about 10 percent a year from 2005 through 2009.

Some firms have developed successful strategies for marketing products in the decline stage of the product life cycle. They eliminate all nonessential marketing expenses and let sales decline as more and more customers stop purchasing the products. Eventually, the product is withdrawn from the market.

Management sage Peter Drucker says that all companies should practise "organized abandonment," which entails reviewing every product, service, and policy every two or three years and asking the critical question: "If we didn't do this already, would we launch it now?" Would we introduce the product, service, or policy now? If the answer is no, it's time to begin the abandonment process.[22]

IMPLICATIONS FOR MARKETING MANAGEMENT

The product life cycle concept encourages marketing managers to plan so that they can take the initiative instead of reacting to past events. The product life cycle is especially useful as a predicting or forecasting tool. Because products pass through distinctive stages, it is often possible to estimate a product's location on the curve using historical data. Profits, like sales, tend to follow a predictable path over a product's life cycle.

Exhibit 9.7 shows the relationship between the adopter categories and the stages of the product life cycle. Note that the various categories of adopters first buy products during different stages of the product life cycle. Almost all sales in the maturity and decline stages represent repeat purchasing.

EXHIBIT 9.7

Relationship between the Diffusion
Process and the Product Life Cycle

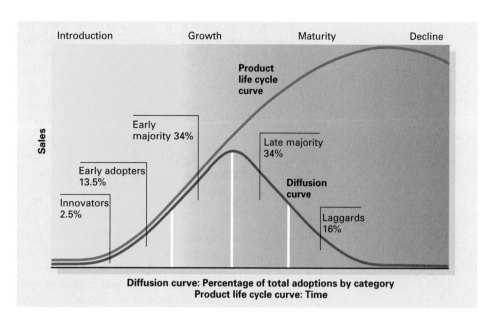

Diffusion curve: Percentage of total adoptions by category
Product life cycle curve: Time

REVIEW LEARNING OUTCOME 6

6 | **Explain the concept of product life cycles**

Typical Marketing Strategies During the Product Life Cycle

Marketing Mix Strategy	Product Life Cycle Stage			
	Introductory	Growth	Maturity	Decline
Product Strategy	Limited number of models; frequent product modifications	Expanded number of models; frequent product modifications	Large number of models	Elimination of unprofitable models and brands
Distribution Strategy	Distribution usually limited, depending on product; intensive efforts and high margins often needed to attract wholesalers and retailers	Expanded number of dealers; intensive efforts to establish long-term relationships with wholesalers and retailers	Extensive number of dealers; margins declining; intensive efforts to retain distributors and shelf space	Unprofitable outlets phased out
Promotion Strategy	Develop product awareness; stimulate primary demand; use intensive personal selling to distributors; use sampling and couponing for consumers	Stimulate selective demand; advertise brand aggressively	Stimulate selective demand; advertise brand aggressively; promote heavily to retain dealers and customers	Phase out all promotion
Pricing Strategy	Prices are usually high to recover development costs (see Chapter 17)	Prices begin to fall toward end of growth stage as result of competitive pressure	Prices continue to fall	Prices stabilize at relatively low level; small price rises are possible if competition is negligible

Sales

Time

REVIEW AND APPLICATIONS

1 **Explain the importance of developing new products and describe the six categories of new products.** New products are important to sustain growth and profits and to replace obsolete items. New products can be classified as new-to-the-world products (discontinuous innovations), new product lines, additions to existing product lines, improvements or revisions of existing products, repositioned products, or lower-cost products. To sustain or increase profits, a firm must introduce at least one new successful product before a previous product advances to the maturity stage and profit levels begin to drop. Several factors make it more important than ever for firms to consistently introduce new products: shortened product life cycles, rapidly changing technology and consumer priorities, the high rate of new-product failures, and the length of time needed to implement new-product ideas.

1.1   **WRITING**   How many new products can you identify? Visit a supermarket and make a list of at least 15 items with the word "New" on the label. Include on your list anything that looks like a new product. Next to each item on your list, write the category of new product that best describes the item. Share your results with the class.

1.2   **TEAM**   New entertainment products aren't necessarily media products. Form a team of three or four students and brainstorm new nonmedia entertainment products. Try to identify one item for each of the categories of new products discussed in this chapter.

2 **Explain the steps in the new-product development process.** First, a firm forms a new-product strategy by outlining the characteristics and roles of future products. Then new-product ideas are generated by customers, employees, distributors, competitors, suppliers, and internal R&D personnel. Once a product idea has survived initial screening by an appointed screening group, it undergoes business analysis to determine its potential profitability. If a product concept seems viable, it progresses into the development phase, in which the technical and economic feasibility of the manufacturing process is evaluated. The development phase also includes laboratory and use testing of a product for performance and safety. Following initial testing and refinement, most products are introduced in a test market to evaluate consumer response and marketing strategies. Finally, test market successes are propelled into full commercialization. The commercialization process involves starting up production, building inventories, shipping to distributors, training a sales force, announcing the product to the trade, and advertising to consumers.

2.1   **WRITING**   List the advantages of simultaneous product development.

2.2   **WRITING**   You are a marketing manager for Nike. Your department has come up with the idea of manufacturing a baseball bat for use by amateur teams around the country. Assuming you are in the business analysis stage, write a brief analysis based on the questions in the "Business Analysis" section of this chapter.

2.3   What are the major disadvantages to test marketing and how might they be avoided?

2.4   **ONLINE**   How could information from customer orders at **www.pizzahut.ca** help the company's marketers plan new product developments?

3 **Explain why some products succeed and others fail.** The most important factor in determining the success of a new product is the extent to which the product matches the needs of the market. Good matches are frequently successful. Poor matches are not.

3.1   **TEAM**   In small groups, brainstorm ideas for a new wet-weather clothing line. What type of product would potential customers want and need? Prepare and deliver a brief presentation to your class.

4 **Discuss global issues in new-product development.** A marketer with global vision seeks to develop products that can easily be adapted to suit local needs. The goal is not simply to develop a standard product that can be sold worldwide. Smart global marketers also look for good product ideas worldwide.

4.1   **ONLINE**   Visit **www.pg.com** and look at the brands Procter & Gamble offers around the world. What conclusions can you draw about Procter & Gamble's global new-product development strategy?

5 **Explain the diffusion process through which new products are adopted.** The diffusion process is the spread of a new product from its producer to ultimate adopters. Adopters in the diffusion process belong to one of five categories: innovators, early adopters, the early majority, the late majority, and laggards. Product characteristics that affect the rate of adoption include product complexity, compatibility with existing social values, relative advantage over existing substitutes, visibility, and "trialability." The diffusion process is facilitated by word-of-mouth communication and communication from marketers to consumers.

5.1 Describe some products whose adoption rates have been affected by complexity, compatibility, relative advantage, observability, and/or "trialability."

5.2 What type of adopter behaviour do you typically follow? Explain.

5.3 **WRITING** Review Exhibit 9.4. Analyze each product on the graph according to the characteristics that influence the rate of adoption. For example, what can you conclude from the data about the relative advantage of DVD audio? Write one to two pages explaining your analysis.

6 Explain the concept of product life cycles. All brands and product categories undergo a life cycle with four stages: introduction, growth, maturity, and decline. The rate at which products move through these stages varies dramatically. Marketing managers use the product life cycle concept as an analytical tool to forecast a product's future and devise effective marketing strategies.

6.1 What is Cheerios doing to compete successfully in the maturity stage? Go to its website (**www.cheerios.com**) to find out.

TERMS

EXERCISES

APPLICATION EXERCISE

A simple statistical analysis will help you to better understand the types of new products. As in an earlier Application Exercise, you will be using print advertisements but you will also be adding information from other sources (TV ads, trips to the store, and the like).

Activities

1. **WRITING** Compile a list of 100 new products. If you are building a portfolio of ads, you can generate part of this list as you collect print advertisements for the topics in this chapter. Consider tabulating television ads for new products that are aired during programs you normally watch. A trip to the grocery store could probably yield your entire list but then your list would be limited to consumer products.

2. **WRITING** Make a table with six columns labelled as follows: new-to-the world products, new product line, additions to existing product line, improvement or revision of existing product line, repositioned product, and lower-priced product.

3. Place each of your 100 new products into one of the six categories. Tabulate your results at the bottom of each column. What conclusions can you draw from the distribution of your products? Consider adding your results together with the rest of the class to get a larger and more random sample. Do you see any changes from your sample to the larger sample?

ETHICS EXERCISE

One source of new product ideas is competitors. Steven Fischer recently joined Frankie and Alex Specialty Products as a brand manager. His new boss told him, "We don't have a budget for new product development. We just monitor our competitors' new product introductions and offer 'knock-offs' or copies of any that look like they will be successful."

Questions

1. Is this practice ethical?

2. Does the CMA Code of Ethics address this issue? Go to **www.the-cma.org/ consumer/ethics.cfm** and review the code. Then write a brief paragraph on what the CMA Code of Ethics contains that relates to knock-off products.

CASE STUDY

NINTENDO: A CONSOLE IN EVERY HOME

When Nintendo released its latest video gaming console, the Wii, many industry analysts thought the machine would quickly go by the wayside. At the time, the prevailing philosophy was that success in the video-game industry depended on being able to produce the fastest, most powerful machine on the market. Faced with competition from Microsoft's Xbox 360 and Sony's PlayStation 3 (PS3) gaming consoles, both of which fit the bill, Nintendo's strategy of building a console around much simpler and less powerful hardware raised many questions about the Wii's viability.

Now move forward to 2009 and consider the numbers. Nintendo Wii sales were double those of the Xbox 360 and four times higher than the PS3. That's right—Nintendo sold more consoles than both of its major competitors combined! In year-over-year sales growth, Xbox experienced a modest increase while PS3 sales declined. As for the Wii, sales in 2009 doubled. On the software front, the video-game industry as a whole saw software sales increase by 26 percent. With that in mind, consider that the four top-selling games were all exclusively for the Wii. The top seller, *Wii Play*, sold more than the combined Xbox and PS3 sales of *Grand Theft Auto4*. Consider as well that Nintendo's staggering hardware and software sales growth occurred in the middle of a deep economic slowdown.

So what exactly has given Nintendo such an edge? Part of it certainly goes back to its hardware design. When designing their next-generation consoles, both Sony and Microsoft invested considerable time and funding into designing entirely new processing systems and new features to make their machines more versatile. For instance, the PS3 included a Blu-ray player. The hardware for the original PS3 model cost almost $700 per unit, and while Sony has managed to pull its costs on the current model down 35 percent from the previous model, it remains in the red and has yet to make a profit on console sales. Furthermore, after several reductions, the current PS3 model still sells for $399, at least $150 more than its two competitors. Microsoft has not had nearly the same difficulties as Sony in making its console profitable; however, it has recently had to introduce price cuts to its consoles. Nintendo, on the other hand, chose to use a simpler and much less expensive processing system and has yet to introduce a price reduction to the system.

The Wii's overall game play generally varies from its competitors' as well. While the Xbox 360 and PS3 in many ways appear to be bigger, stronger, faster versions of their predecessors, the Wii—with a much more integrated motion capture system—in many ways has offered gamers something new.

Nintendo isn't looking at just gamers either. Traditionally the core market for video games has been dominated by teen and early-adult male action gamers. With the Wii, Nintendo has been pushing titles that it hopes will have a more casual family-friendly appeal—titles such as *Wii Fit* and *Wii Music*. The top-selling game, *Wii Play*, includes basic games like pool, ping-pong, and target shooting. With offerings like these, the Wii provides relatively inexpensive in-home whole-family entertainment.

Nintendo's vision also extends beyond just providing video-game entertainment. For example, the Nintendo DS, a portable gaming system, can also be used as a book reader. By purchasing its book cartridge, users can take advantage of the Nintendo DS's touchscreen to flip a page by swiping a finger (or a stylus) across the screen. Adaptation as an e-reader reflects just one of the ways that Nintendo is looking to make its hardware more versatile. The *Wii Fit* was designed to bring fitness activities into the family room and make it a communal activity. Nintendo, however, hasn't abandoned its core audience. Two of the top-selling games, *Mario Cart Wii* and *Super Smash Bros. Brawl*, were the latest releases in two longstanding Nintendo game franchises.

When asked about the future direction of Nintendo's software, its chief game designer Shigeru Miyamoto commented that his goal was for the Wii to become "a necessity for every home." Based on Wii's recent success, it looks like Nintendo is off to a pretty good start.[23]

Questions

1. Imagine that you are responsible for designing a successor to the Wii. Briefly describe the new-product strategy you might use.

2. How might the diffusion process differ between the Wii and its competitors?

3. Compare the life cycle of Nintendo's video-game consoles as a whole to a particular console, such as the Wii.

VIDEO CASE

CBC

IDEAFETCH

As you know from reading this chapter, companies are always in search of new-product ideas. The more new-product ideas that a company has to work with, the more likely one or more of them will actually be developed into a new-product offering.

Idea generation is an important early step in the new-product development process. Idea generation includes identifying sources for new-product ideas and encouraging idea submissions from each of these sources. Some of the major sources for new-product ideas include the company's customers, employees, distributors, competitors, suppliers, R&D labs, and consultants. Brainstorming and focus group sessions are among the methods used with these groups to encourage ideas. Let's look at an interesting approach used by Doug Grindstaff.

Doug Grindstaff is vice-president of marketing for PetSafe. PetSafe is an industry leader in pet training, pet containment, and pet safety products. PetSafe introduced the first do-it-yourself electronic fence to the pet market in 1991 and the first wireless fence in 1998. PetSafe's product line includes kennels and electronic underground fences; pet feeder products; bark control systems; remote training products; pet doors; pet identification and specialty collars; heated wellness products and pet waste removal products that are sold under the PetSafe, Guardian, and SportDOG brands.

As vice-president of marketing for PetSafe, Doug Grindstaff is responsible for new product development. A few years ago, Doug got the thought that most pet owners probably get a pet product idea from time to time but, not being in the pet business, simply forget about it. What if, Doug thought, he could harness all these ideas? Surely, there would be some good ones. The result was a contest called IdeaFetch.

IdeaFetch was launched in London, Ontario. The contest was sponsored by PetSafe and Canadian Tire and was open to all Canadian residents 18 years of age and over. Potential contestants were directed to go to a website set up for the IdeaFetch contest and describe their pet product idea. The general public was invited to help select the IdeaFetch contest winner by voting on-line for the ideas submitted. Consumer votes would determine the top 100 ideas from which a panel of judges would select the best. The top idea winner would receive $25,000, the second-place winner $5,000 and the third-place winner $2,500. PetSafe would develop and manufacture the first-place idea concept and the product would be sold through Canadian Tire stores.

Let's watch as the IdeaFetch contest finalists pitch their ideas to Doug for the $25,000 prize and the opportunity to see their idea developed into a product and sold at Canadian Tire stores.[24]

Questions

1. What do you think of the IdeaFetch contest for new-product ideas and what do you think of the four finalist ideas?

2. How new and innovative were the finalist ideas that were presented? Did you agree with the winning idea selected? Why or why not?

3. What if the winning idea sells really well? Should the person who conceived of the idea get more than $25,000? Why do you feel the way you do?

4. Do you think that the new product arising from the IdeaFetch contest will be successful? Why or why not?

MARKETING & YOU RESULTS

If your score is high, you are most likely a "market maven." You are aware of new products earlier and talk about a variety of products with your friends. High scores also indicate a greater interest in and attentiveness to the market. Conversely, the lower your score, the less interested you are in the market and new products.

10 Services and Nonprofit
Organization Marketing

LEARNING OUTCOMES

1 Discuss the importance of services to the economy

2 Discuss the differences between services and goods

3 Describe the components of service quality and the gap model of service quality

4 Develop marketing mixes for services

5 Discuss relationship marketing in services

6 Explain internal marketing in services

7 Discuss global issues in services marketing

8 Describe nonprofit organization marketing

ⓥ MARKETING & YOU

What do you think about charities?

Using the following scale, enter your answers on the lines provided.

1	2	3	4	5
Strongly agree	Moderately agree	Agree	Moderately disagree	Strongly disagree

__ The money given to charities goes for good causes.
__ Much of the money donated to charity is wasted.*
__ My image of charitable organizations is positive.

__ Charitable organizations have been quite successful in helping the needy.
__ Charitable organizations perform a useful function for society.

Total your score, reversing your answer for the item followed by an asterisk. That is, if you answered 2, change it to 4, and vice versa. Read the chapter, and find out what your score means at the end.

The previous two chapters talked about products. But some companies don't sell physical products. Instead, they sell services. One such company is PlentyOfFish. Until recently, PlentyOfFish was run out of the apartment of Markus Frind, but it is now located on the 26th floor of a downtown Vancouver skyscraper. This means that Markus now has to walk a couple of blocks to work each morning instead of just going from his bedroom to the living room of his apartment.

Markus grew up in Hudson's Hope in northern British Columbia, moved to Vancouver in 1997, and obtained a diploma in computer programming at the British Columbia Institute of Technology. He created plentyoffish.com in 2003.

The idea to create plentyoffish.com came to Markus after a friend showed him the website for LavaLife, a well-established player in the on-line dating business. On-line dating seemed like a good idea to Markus but he was surprised to discover that the dating sites charged fees to users. "I thought it was ridiculous," he says. "It was this rinky-dink little site charging money for something anyone could make. I was like, I can beat these guys."

After earning his diploma in computer programming from BCIT in 1999, Frind got a job at an on-line shopping mall. Soon after, the dot-com bubble burst and Markus spent two years going through jobs at six different dot-com start-ups. By early 2003, the technology economy in Vancouver had yet to pick up and Frind's current employer was laying off half its workforce. Markus decided that he needed to upgrade his qualifications. He would devote a few weeks to mastering Microsoft's new tool for building websites, ASP.net, and he would do it by building a website for an on-line dating service.

Working a few hours each evening for several weeks, Marcus built a crude dating site, which he named PlentyOfFish. It was quite simple, including only plain-text personal ads and a few pictures. But it was different from larger, more established dating sites in one important respect: it was free.

The first thing about PlentyOfFish that a user will notice is its very simple interface. Members can sign up and create a profile very easily, then upload digital photos of themselves, up to a maximum of eight pictures. PlentyOfFish gives its new members a bit of a personality test that helps in setting up appropriate matches on the site. Another feature of POF is that you can set the preferences for who can and can't contact you. You can choose distance (such as only people within 50 kilometres of your postal code) and age ranges; you can stop people who are looking for intimate relationships from contacting you or those who do not include a photo. You can also browse for other members based on age, location, ethnicity, and other preferences.

PlentyOfFish first became popular in Canada and later spread to the United States, the United Kingdom, Australia, and Ireland. POF receives more than 2.1 billion page views and 90 million visitors every month. It is the number one dating service in Canada and the United Kingdom and number two in the United States. According to the research firm Hitwise, POF might be the largest on-line dating service in the world.

As Markus Frind does not charge a fee to users of PlentyOfFish, he has to make money in other ways. With an audience as large as PlentyOfFish has, Markus is able to earn money from Google's small text ads, through larger banner ads, and through "affiliate marketing," where other on-line sites pay you for sending them customers. And Markus Frind does well at all three. On a recent morning, for example, there was a $180,000 order waiting for his signature. It was from VideoEgg, a company that is paying Frind to run a series of Budweiser commercials in Canada. Like most of his advertising deals, this one found Frind. He hadn't heard of VideoEgg until a week earlier but when you serve a large audience, you attract advertisers' attention.

When asked how much he's making, Markus just says it's "north of $5 million annually." Industry sources say it is considerably north of $10 million—not bad for a free dating service that took Markus all of three weeks to develop.[1]

How do services, such as those offered by PlentyOfFish, differ from physical products? How does the marketing of services differ from the marketing of physical products? Is there any secret to the success of Markus Frind and POF? What are other on-line services that Markus Frind, or anyone eles, might be successful with?

SOURCE: MAX CHAFKIN, "AND THE MONEY COMES ROLLING IN," INC.COM, JANUARY 1, 2009, HTTP://WWW.INC.COM/MAGAZINE; "MAKING MONEY MAKING DATES," NATIONAL POST, CANADA.COM, JULY 20, 2007, HTTP://WWW.CANADA.COM; LEE GOMES, "PLENTYOFFISH OWNER HAS THE PERFECT BAIT FOR A HUGH SUCCESS," THE WALL STREET JOURNAL, MAY 23, 2007, B1; "PLENTYOFFISH.COM DATING SITE REVIEW," STRATEGY, JULY 15, 2009, 22; HTTP://WWW.PLENTYOFFISH.COM.

1 THE IMPORTANCE OF SERVICES

Discuss the importance of services to the economy

service
The result of applying human or mechanical efforts to people or objects.

A **service** is the result of applying human or mechanical efforts to people or objects. Services involve a deed, a performance, or an effort that cannot be physically possessed. Today, the service sector substantially influences the Canadian economy. The service sector accounts for 72.3 percent of the Canadian gross domestic product and 77.8 percent of employment, including 89.7 percent of female employment in Canada.[2] The demand for services is expected to continue to grow. According to Statistics Canada, service occupations will be responsible for nearly all net job growth in Canada through 2016. Over the period from December 2008 to December 2009, manufacturing employment in Canada fell by 4 percent while service employment grew by 1 percent.[3] As can be seen in Exhibit 10.1, the service labour force continues to grow at a pace well beyond that of the goods sector. Much of this demand results from demographics. An aging population will need nurses, home health care, physical therapists, and social workers. Two-earner families need child-care, house-cleaning, and lawn-care services. Also increasing will be the demand for information managers, such as computer engineers and systems analysts. In 2009, 56.3 percent of all household spending was on services.[4] There is also a growing market for service companies worldwide. Canada's exports of services has grown by over 9 percent since 2001.[5]

The marketing process described in Chapter 1 is the same for all types of products, whether they are goods or services. Many ideas and strategies discussed throughout this book have been illustrated with service examples. In many ways, marketing is marketing, regardless of the product's characteristics. In addition, although a comparison of goods and services marketing can be beneficial, in reality it is hard to distinguish clearly between manufacturing and service firms. Indeed, many manufacturing firms can point to service as a major factor in their success. For example, the maintenance and repair services offered by manufacturers are important to buyers of a wide range of products. Many large companies, like IBM and General Electric, earn most of their revenue from services. Nevertheless, services have some characteristics that distinguish them from goods and marketing strategies need to be adjusted for these characteristics.

REVIEW LEARNING OUTCOME 1

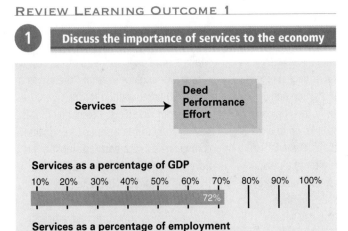

1 Discuss the importance of services to the economy

Services ⟶ Deed Performance Effort

Services as a percentage of GDP

10% 20% 30% 40% 50% 60% 70% 80% 90% 100%

72%

Services as a percentage of employment

10% 20% 30% 40% 50% 60% 70% 80% 90% 100%

78%

EXHIBIT 10.1

The Impact of the Service Sector on Job Growth

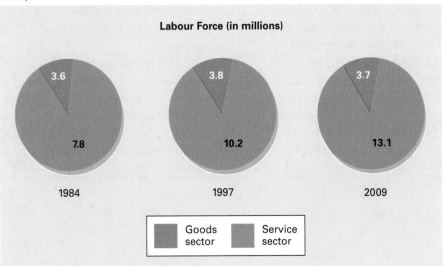

Labour Force (in millions)

3.6

7.8

1984

3.8

10.2

1997

3.7

13.1

2009

Goods sector | Service sector

SOURCE: Statistics Canada, Employment by Industry, Table 282-0008, January 29, 2010.

Discuss the differences between services and goods

Services have four unique characteristics that distinguish them from goods. Services are intangible, they are produced and consumed simultaneously, they have greater variability in inputs and outputs than goods, and they are perishable.

INTANGIBILITY

intangibility
The inability of services to be touched, seen, tasted, heard, or felt in the same manner that goods can be sensed.

search quality
A characteristic that can be easily assessed before purchase.

experience quality
A characteristic that can be assessed only after use.

credence quality
A characteristic that consumers may have difficulty assessing even after purchase because they do not have the necessary knowledge or experience.

The basic difference between services and goods is that services are intangible. Because of their **intangibility**, services cannot be touched, seen, tasted, heard, or felt in the same manner as goods. Services cannot be stored and are often easy to duplicate.

Evaluating the quality of services before or even after making a purchase is harder than evaluating the quality of goods because, compared to goods, services tend to exhibit fewer search qualities. A **search quality** is a characteristic that can be easily assessed before purchase—for instance, the colour of an appliance or automobile. At the same time, services tend to exhibit more experience and credence qualities. An **experience quality** is a characteristic that can be assessed only after use, such as the quality of a meal in a restaurant or the actual experience of a vacation. A **credence quality** is a characteristic that consumers may have difficulty assessing even after purchase because they do not have the necessary knowledge or experience. Medical and consulting services are examples of services that exhibit credence qualities.

These service characteristics also make it harder for marketers to communicate the benefits of an intangible service than to communicate the benefits of tangible goods. Thus marketers often rely on tangible cues to communicate a service's nature and quality. For example, Travelers Insurance Company's use of the umbrella symbol helps make tangible the benefit of protection that insurance provides.

The facilities that customers visit, or from which services are delivered, are a critical tangible part of the total service offering. Messages about the service provider are communicated to customers through such elements as the decor, the clutter or neatness of service areas, and the staff's manners and dress. Reflecting this idea, the design and development team at Bass Pro Shops believes that in-store displays are not just fixtures, but marketing tools that will attract customers if designed to reflect local culture. Each store in the chain has pictures and decorations, including indigenous fish and wildlife reflecting the region in which it is located.[6]

GRAB LIFE BY THE UMBRELLA.

Look to the red umbrella company for life insurance to protect your family, your estate, and your business.

When protecting what's important to you, get everything you expect from life: a well-respected company, extraordinary corporate stability, and affordable rates. For term, universal, and variable universal life insurance, look to Travelers.

Travelers Life & Annuity
A member of citigroup

The Travelers Insurance Company and Its Affiliates • One Tower Square • Hartford, CT 06183
(800) 842-7794 • www.travelersla.com

Variable universal life insurance is offered by prospectus only. Read the prospectus carefully before you invest or send money.

SOURCE: COURTESY OF TRAVELERS LIFE & ANNUITY

To communicate the benefits of intangible services, marketers often rely on concrete symbols. The umbrella symbol used by Travelers Insurance signifies protection. This helps to give substance to the company's service.

INSEPARABILITY

Goods are produced, sold, and then consumed. In contrast, services are often sold, produced, and consumed at the same time. In other words, their production and consumption are inseparable activities. This inseparability means that, because consumers must be present during the production of services like haircuts or surgery, they are actually involved in the production of the services they buy. That type of consumer involvement is rare in goods manufacturing. Inseparability also means that customers have an opportunity to provide input into their service experience and outcome. For example, individuals getting a haircut can provide feedback during the process so that their hair looks the way they want it to look.

Simultaneous production and consumption also means that services normally cannot be produced in a centralized location and consumed in decentralized locations, as goods typically are. Services are also inseparable from the perspective of the service provider. Thus the quality of service that firms are able to deliver depends on the quality of their employees.

HETEROGENEITY

Consistency is one of the great strengths of McDonald's. Whether customers order a Big Mac and french fries in Halifax, Vancouver, Tokyo, or Moscow, they know exactly what they are going to get. This is

heterogeneity
The variability of the inputs and outputs of services, which cause services to tend to be less standardized and uniform than goods.

perishability
The inability of services to be stored, warehoused, or inventoried.

REVIEW LEARNING OUTCOME 2

Discuss the difference between services and goods

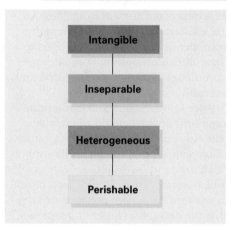

Intangible

Inseparable

Heterogeneous

Perishable

not the case, however, with many service providers. Because services have greater **heterogeneity**, they tend to be less standardized and uniform than goods. For example, physicians in a group practice or barbers in a barbershop differ within each group in their technical and interpersonal skills. A given physician's or barber's performance may even vary depending on time of day, physical health, or some other factor. Because services tend to be labour-intensive and production and consumption are inseparable, consistency and quality control can be hard to achieve.

Standardization and training help increase consistency and reliability. Limited-menu restaurants like Harvey's, Pizza Hut, and KFC offer their customers high consistency from one visit to the next because of standardized preparation procedures.

Another way to increase consistency is to mechanize the process. Banks have reduced the inconsistency of teller services by providing automated teller machines (ATMs). Automatic coin receptacles and electronic toll collection systems such as E-Z Pass have replaced human collectors. Internet banking, like Mbanx (**www.bmo.com/banking**) from the Bank of Montreal, also results in greater service consistency.

PERISHABILITY

Another characteristic of services is their **perishability**, which means that they cannot be stored, warehoused, or inventoried. An empty hotel room or airplane seat produces no revenue that day. Yet service organizations are often forced to turn away full-price customers during peak periods.

One of the most important challenges in many service industries is finding ways to synchronize supply and demand. The philosophy that some revenue is better than none has prompted many hotels to offer deep discounts on weekends and during the off-season and has prompted airlines to adopt similar pricing strategies during off-peak hours. Car rental agencies, movie theatres, and restaurants also use discounts to encourage demand during nonpeak periods.

3 SERVICE QUALITY

Describe the components of service quality and the gap model of service quality

Because of the four unique characteristics of services, service quality is more difficult to define and measure than is the quality of tangible goods. Business executives rank the improvement of service quality as one of the most critical challenges facing them today.

Research has shown that customers evaluate service quality by the following five components:[7]

reliability
The ability to perform a service dependably, accurately, and consistently.

- *Reliability*: the ability to perform the service dependably, accurately, and consistently. Reliability is performing the service right the first time. An air traveller who gets to the destination on time with his or her luggage intact has experienced reliable service. This component has been found to be the one most important to consumers.

responsiveness
The ability to provide prompt service.

- *Responsiveness*: the ability to provide prompt service. Examples of responsiveness include calling the customer back quickly, serving lunch quickly to someone who is in a hurry, or mailing a transaction slip immediately. The ultimate in responsiveness is offering service 24 hours a day, 7 days a week. For example, Zappos.com, a successful on-line shoe company, keeps its warehouse open 24/7 so that customers can order shoes at 11 p.m. and still get next-day delivery.[8]

assurance
The knowledge and courtesy of employees and their ability to convey trust.

- *Assurance*: the knowledge and courtesy of employees and their ability to convey trust. Skilled employees who treat customers with respect and make customers feel that they can trust the firm exemplify assurance.

empathy
Caring, individualized attention to customers.

- *Empathy*: caring, individualized attention to customers. Firms whose employees recognize customers, call them by name, and learn their customers' specific requirements are providing empathy. When taking your car in for servicing at Windsor (Ontario) Nissan, the Nissan dealership personnel will address you by name, drive you to work, call when your car is ready, and come back to your place

tangibles
The physical evidence of a service, including the physical facilities, tools, and equipment used to provide the service.

of employment to drive you back to your car. As well, when you pick up your car, it will have been cleaned outside and in. Getting customer feedback and listening to that feedback is a critical aspect of implementing empathy.

- *Tangibles*: the physical evidence of the service. The tangible parts of a service include the physical facilities, tools, and equipment used to provide the service, and the appearance of personnel. For example, Enterprise Rent-A-Car has strict dress codes for its employees. Hospitals have found that improving their layouts and looks can translate into better health for their patients.

Overall service quality is measured by combining customers' evaluations for all five components.

THE GAP MODEL OF SERVICE QUALITY

gap model
A model identifying five gaps that can cause problems in service delivery and influence customer evaluations of service quality.

A model of service quality called the **gap model** identifies five gaps that can cause problems in service delivery and influence customer evaluations of service quality.[9] These gaps are illustrated in Exhibit 10.2.

- *Gap 1*: the gap between what customers want and what management thinks customers want. This gap results from a lack of understanding or a misinterpretation

EXHIBIT 10.2

Gap Model of Service Quality

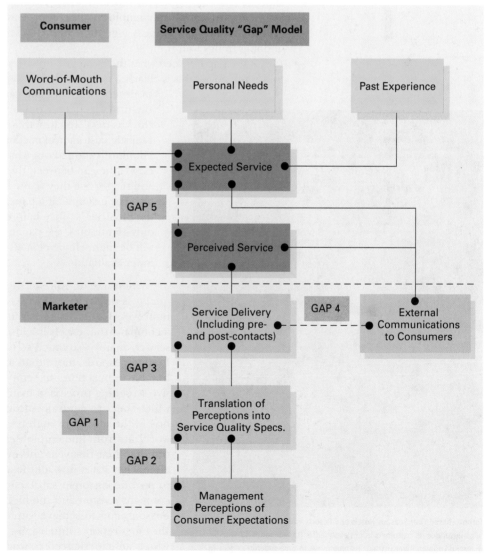

SOURCE: From Valarie A. Zeithaml, Mary Jo Bitner, and Dwayne Gremler, "Services Marketing" 4/e, © 2006 The McGraw-Hill Companies, Inc.

of the customers' needs, wants, or desires. A firm that does little or no customer satisfaction research is likely to experience this gap. An important step in closing Gap 1 is to keep in touch with what customers want by doing research on customer needs and customer satisfaction. Every two years, FrankeKindred Industries of Midland, Ontario, distributor of kitchen and bathroom accessories and recipient of a Canadian Business Best Practices Award in the category of Customer Satisfaction, undertakes thousands of interviews with its customers to determine how well the company is satisfying its customers' needs.

- *Gap 2*: the gap between what management thinks, or knows, customers want and the quality specifications that management develops to provide the service. Essentially, this gap is the result of management's inability to translate customers' needs into delivery systems within the firm. For example, KFC once rated its managers' success according to "chicken efficiency," or how much chicken they threw away at the end of the night. Consumers who came in late at night would either have to wait for chicken to be cooked or settle for chicken several hours old. The "chicken efficiency" measurement did not take customers into account.

- *Gap 3*: the gap between the service quality specifications and the service that is actually provided. If both Gaps 1 and 2 have been closed, then Gap 3 is due to the inability of management and employees to do what should be done. Poorly trained or poorly motivated workers can cause this gap. Management needs to ensure that employees have the skills and proper tools to perform their jobs. Other techniques that help to close Gap 3 are training employees so they know what management expects, encouraging teamwork, and hiring employees with the proper attitude. For example, when hiring employees, the Four Seasons looks for attitudes that reflect kindness, helpfulness, a genuine desire to see other people happy, and pride in doing things well.[10]

- *Gap 4*: the gap between what the company provides and what the customer is told it provides. This is clearly a communication gap. It may include misleading or deceptive advertising campaigns promising more than the firm can deliver or doing "whatever it takes" to get the business. To close this gap, companies need to create realistic customer expectations through honest, accurate communication about what their companies can provide.

- *Gap 5*: the gap between the service that customers receive and the service they want. This gap can be positive or negative. For example, if a patient expects to wait 20 minutes in the physician's office before seeing the physician but waits only 10 minutes, the patient's evaluation of service quality will be high. However, a 40-minute wait would result in a lower evaluation.

When one or more of these gaps are large, service quality is perceived as low. As the gaps shrink, service quality improves. Toronto-based Four Seasons Hotels and Resorts is a company that excels in closing gaps to offer superior service quality—so much so that it has won 17 Five Diamond Lodging Awards, more than any other hotel operator. This hotel firm puts potential employees through a comprehensive screening process to match their skills with positions for which they are naturally inclined. Four Seasons also sponsors one of the most thorough training programs in the business world. Its front-line employees undergo many weeks of training their first year and over 100 hours per year thereafter. They learn how all the areas in the hotel work together to provide customer satisfaction. They also learn about the company's vision and the high service standards Four Seasons aims to achieve with each guest experience. When they first report to their jobs, they are paired with a trainer, who is an experienced co-worker. The company also recognizes and rewards employee contributions by listing them in

Toronto-based Four Seasons Hotels and Resorts works hard to close any gaps in service its customers might experience. The winner of 17 Five Diamond Lodging Awards trains its employees to give superior service in one of the most thorough training programs in the business world.

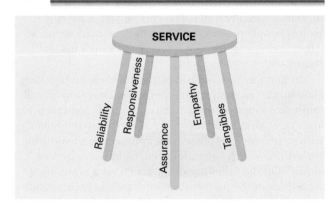

its newsletter, by paying cash bonuses, and by highlighting the employee's deeds during staff meetings. What has been the result of this high level of service? The Four Seasons has expanded from 22 hotels in three countries in 1990 to 83 hotels in 35 countries today.[11]

4 # MARKETING MIXES FOR SERVICES

Develop marketing mixes for services

The unique characteristics of services—intangibility, inseparability of production and consumption, hetero-geneity, and perishability—make the marketing task more challenging. Elements of the marketing mix (product, place, promotion, and pricing) need to be adjusted to meet the special needs created by these characteristics.

PRODUCT (SERVICE) STRATEGY

A product, as described in the previous chapter, is everything that a person receives in an exchange. In the case of a service organization, the product offering is intangible and consists in large part of a process or a series of processes. Product strategies for services include decisions on the type of service process to be used, core and supplementary services, standardization or customization of the service, and the service mix.

Service as a Process

People and objects are part of the service process. In some cases the process is physical, or tangible, while in others the process is intangible. Based on these possibilities, service processes fall into one of four categories.[12]

* *People processing* takes place when the service is directed at a customer. Examples are transportation services, hairstyling, health clubs, and dental and health care.
* *Possession processing* occurs when the service is directed at customers' physical possessions. Examples are lawn care, car repair, dry cleaning, and veterinary services.
* *Mental stimulus processing* refers to services directed at people's minds. Examples are entertainment, spectator sports events, theatre performances, and education.
* *Information processing* describes services that use technology or brainpower directed at a customer's assets. Examples are insurance, banking, and consulting.

SOURCE: © SPENCER GRANT/PHOTO EDIT

Dry cleaning is an example of possession-processing services. These types of services require less focus on attractive physical environments and customer service training than people-processing services like hairdressers and airlines.

Because customers' experiences and involvement differ for each of these types of services, marketing strategies may also differ. For example, people-processing services require customers to enter the *service factory*, which is a physical location, such as an aircraft, a physician's office, or a hair salon. In contrast, possession-processing services typically do not require the presence of the customer in the service factory; the customer may simply leave the car at the garage for repairs, for example. Marketing strategies for the former would therefore focus more on an attractive, comfortable physical environment and employee training than would strategies for the latter.

Core and Supplementary Services

core service
The most basic benefit the consumer is buying.

supplementary services
A group of services that support or enhance the core service.

The service offering can be viewed as a bundle of activities that includes the **core service**, which is the most basic benefit the customer is buying, and a group of **supplementary services** that support or enhance the core service. Exhibit 10.3 illustrates concepts for an overnight stay at a luxury hotel. The core service is overnight rental of a bedroom, which involves people processing. The supplementary services, some of which involve information processing, include reservations, check-ins and check-outs, room service, and meals.

In many service industries, the core service becomes a commodity as competition increases. Thus firms usually emphasize supplementary services to create a competitive advantage. Virgin Atlantic, Malaysia Airlines, and Japan Airlines provide complimentary limo service to and from the airport. Virgin's chauffeurs check in passengers en route.[13] On the other hand, some firms are positioning themselves in the marketplace by greatly reducing supplementary services. For example, Microtel Inn is an amenity-free hotel concept known as "fast lodging." These low-cost hotels have one- and two-bedroom accommodations and a swimming pool but no meeting rooms or other services.

EXHIBIT 10.3

Core and Supplementary Services for a Luxury Hotel

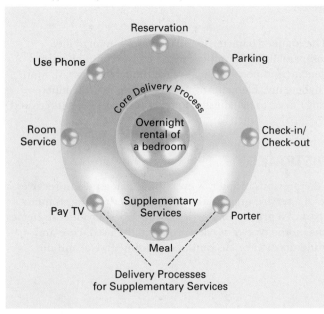

SOURCE: From Christopher H. Lovelock/Jochen Wirtz JOCHEN, SERVICES MARKETING, 6th, © 2007. Printed and Electronically reproduced by permission of Pearson Education, Inc., Upper Saddle River, New Jersey.

Customization/Standardization

An important issue in developing the service offering is whether to customize or standardize it. Customized services are more flexible and respond to individual customers' needs. They also usually command a higher price. The traditional law firm, which treats each case differently according to the client's situation, offers customized services. Standardized services are more efficient and cost less. Unlike the traditional law firm, Walk-In Law Firm of Canada offers low-cost, standardized service "packages" for those with uncomplicated legal needs, such as drawing up a will or mediating an uncontested divorce.

mass customization
A strategy that uses technology to deliver customized services on a mass basis.

Instead of choosing to either standardize or customize a service, a firm may incorporate elements of both by adopting an emerging strategy called **mass customization**. Mass customization uses technology to deliver customized services on a mass basis; the result is that each customer receives whatever he or she asks for. For example, a feature on the Lands' End website allows women to define their figures on-line, receive advice on what swimsuits will flatter their shapes, and mix and match more than 216 combinations of colours and styles. Several airlines are designing services to cater to travellers' individual needs and preferences. Some will serve dinner to passengers when they want to eat it, rather than when the airline wants to serve it. More airlines are offering video-on-demand systems, which let passengers start or stop their movie anytime they want.

The Service Mix

Most service organizations market more than one service. For example, TruGreen offers lawn care, shrub care, carpet cleaning, and industrial lawn services. Each organization's service mix represents a set of opportunities, risks, and challenges. Each part of the service mix should make a different contribution to achieving the firm's goals. To succeed, each service may also need a different level of financial and marketing support.

Designing a service strategy therefore means deciding which new services to introduce to which target market, which existing services to maintain, and which services to eliminate. For example, to increase membership, the CAA added financial services, credit cards, and travel perks. Organic, a company that designs websites for clients,

Making services more personalized is the goal of mass customization. For example, airlines are rolling out personal interactive entertainment systems on airplanes so that passengers can watch movies when they want.

SOURCE: ©PRNEWSFOTO/NORTHWEST AIRLINES

has set up two new service divisions: Organic Communications, a full-service public relations department; and Organic Logistics, which helps clients figure out how to get products ordered on-line into customers' hands.

PLACE (DISTRIBUTION) STRATEGY

Distribution strategies for service organizations must focus on such issues as convenience, number of outlets, direct versus indirect distribution, location, and scheduling. A key factor influencing the selection of a service provider is *convenience*. Therefore, service firms must offer convenience. Many Shoppers Drug Mart outlets, especially those in downtown locations, have late-night hours, and some are even open 24 hours a day to provide maximum customer convenience. Walk-in clinics are being opened in neighbourhood Rexall Drug Stores. Applebee's restaurants will bring take-out meals to customers waiting in their cars. Banks have opened small branches in places like Walmart stores to make banking more convenient.

An important distribution objective for many service firms is the *number of outlets* to use or the number of outlets to open during a certain time. Generally, the intensity of distribution should meet, but not exceed, the target market's needs and preferences. Having too few outlets may inconvenience customers; having too many outlets may boost costs unnecessarily. Intensity of distribution may also depend on the image desired. Having only a few outlets may make the service seem more exclusive or selective.

The next service distribution decision is whether to distribute services to end users *directly* or *indirectly* through other firms. Because of the intangible nature of services, many service firms have to use direct distribution or franchising. Examples include legal, medical, accounting, real estate, and personal-care services. The newest form of direct distribution is the Internet. Most of the major airlines are now using on-line services to sell tickets directly to consumers, a practice that results in lower distribution costs for the airline companies. Merrill Lynch offers Merrill Lynch OnLine, an Internet-based service that connects clients with company representatives. Most of Canada's retail banks now offer on-line banking services.

The *location* of a service most clearly reveals the relationship between its target market strategy and its distribution strategy. Reportedly, Conrad Hilton claimed that the three most important factors in determining a hotel's success are "location, location, and location." An interesting location trend has started in the banking industry. In the past few years, banks have aggressively directed customers away from branches and toward ATMs and the Internet. In a recent about-face, banks are trying to entice customers back into the branches. For example, CIBC is designing new branches and remodelling old ones to provide a brighter, more open atmosphere.

For time-dependent service providers like airlines, physicians, and dentists, scheduling is an important factor. Scheduling is sometimes the most important factor in a customer's choice of airline.

PROMOTION STRATEGY

Consumers and business users have more trouble evaluating services than goods because services are less tangible. In turn, marketers have more trouble promoting intangible services than tangible goods. Here are four promotion strategies they can try:

- *Stressing tangible cues*: A tangible cue is a concrete symbol of the service offering. To make their intangible services more tangible, hotels turn down the bedcovers and put mints on the pillows. Insurance companies use symbols like rocks, blankets, umbrellas, and hands to help make their intangible services appear tangible. Merrill Lynch uses a bull to help give substance to its services.

- *Using personal information sources*: A personal information source is someone consumers are familiar with (such as a celebrity) or someone they know or can relate to personally. Celebrity endorsements are sometimes used to reduce customers' perceived risk in choosing a service. Service firms may also seek to simulate positive word-of-mouth communication among present and prospective customers by using real customers in their ads.
- *Creating a strong organizational image*: One way to create an image is to manage the physical environment of the service facility, the appearance of the service employees, and the tangible items associated with a service (like stationery, bills, and business cards). For example, McDonald's has created a strong organizational image with its Golden Arches, standardized interiors, and employee uniforms. Another way to create an image is through branding. MCI Communications has grown by creating and promoting brands in the commodity business of common-carrier long-distance service. An example of an MCI brand is 1-800-COLLECT.
- *Engaging in postpurchase communication*: Postpurchase communication refers to the follow-up activities that a service firm might engage in after a customer transaction. Postcard surveys, telephone calls, brochures, and various other types of follow-up show customers that their feedback matters and that their patronage is appreciated.

PRICE STRATEGY

Considerations in pricing a service are similar to product pricing as will be discussed in Chapters 16 and 17. However, the unique characteristics of services present two special pricing challenges.

First, in order to price a service, it is important to define the unit of service consumption. For example, should pricing be based on completing a specific service task (cutting a customer's hair), or should it be time-based (how long it takes to cut a customer's hair)? Some services include the consumption of goods, such as food and beverages. Restaurants charge customers for food and drink rather than the use of a table and chairs. Some transportation firms charge by distance; others charge a flat rate.

Second, for services that are composed of several elements, the issue is whether pricing should be based on a "bundle" of elements or whether each element should be priced separately. A bundled price may be preferable when consumers dislike having to pay "extra" for every part of the service (for example, paying extra for baggage or food on an airplane). Further, a bundled price may be simpler to administer. For instance, many wireless firms offer basic communications packages that include telephone time, Internet access, and text messaging, all for one price. Alternatively, customers may not want to pay for service elements they do not use. Many furniture stores now have "unbundled" delivery charges from the price of the furniture. Customers who wish to can pick up the furniture at the store to save on the delivery fee.

Marketers should set performance objectives when pricing each service. Three categories of pricing objectives have been suggested:[14]

- *Revenue-oriented pricing* focuses on maximizing the surplus of income over costs. A limitation of this approach is that determining costs can be difficult for many services.
- *Operations-oriented pricing* seeks to match supply and demand by varying prices. For example, matching hotel demand to the number of available rooms can be achieved by raising prices at peak times and decreasing them during slow times.

Using real customers can be a successful promotion strategy. One of the more successful of recent memory has been Jared Fogle, spokesperson for Subway. When Subway executives heard that Fogle went from 425 pounds to 180 pounds eating their product, they put him in TV commercials.

- *Patronage-oriented pricing* tries to maximize the number of customers using the service. Thus prices vary with different market segments' ability to pay and methods of payment (such as credit). Patronage-oriented pricing is offered to increase the likelihood of a purchase.

A firm may need to use more than one type of pricing objective. In fact, all three objectives probably need to be included to some degree in a pricing strategy, although the importance of each type may vary depending on the type of service provided, the prices that competitors are charging, the differing ability of various customer segments to pay, and the opportunity to negotiate price. For customized services (for example, legal services and construction services), customers may also have the ability to negotiate a price.

REVIEW LEARNING OUTCOME 4

4 Develop marketing mixes for services

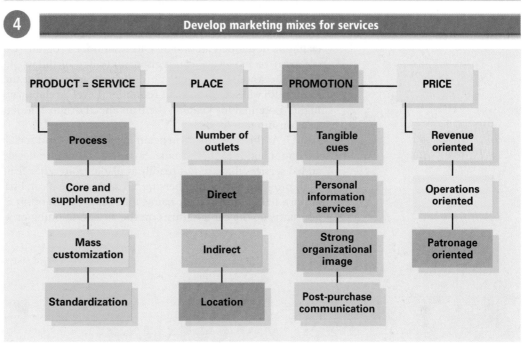

5 RELATIONSHIP MARKETING IN SERVICES

Discuss relationship marketing in services

Many services involve ongoing interaction between the service organization and the customer. Thus they can benefit from relationship marketing, the strategy described in Chapter 1, as a means of attracting, developing, and retaining customer relationships. The idea is to develop strong loyalty by creating satisfied customers who will buy additional services from the firm and who are unlikely to switch to a competitor. Satisfied customers are also likely to engage in positive word-of-mouth communication, thereby helping bring in new customers.

Many businesses have found that it is more cost-effective to hang on to the customers they have than to focus only on attracting new ones. A study of machinery, tool and die, and mould maker companies in southern Ontario determined that the cost of retaining an existing customer was less than 10 percent of the cost of acquiring a new customer.[15]

Services that purchasers receive on a continuing basis (for example, cable TV, banking, insurance) can be considered membership services. This type of service naturally lends itself to relationship marketing. When services involve discrete transactions (any one-at-a-time sale such as at a movie theatre or restaurant, or on public transportation), it may be more difficult to build membership-type relationships with customers. Nevertheless, services involving discrete transactions can be transformed into membership relationships using marketing tools. For example, the service could be sold in bulk (a theatre series subscription or a commuter ticket on public transportation). Or a service firm could offer special benefits to customers who choose to register with the firm (for example, loyalty programs for hotels, airlines, and car rental firms). The service firm that has a more formalized relationship with its customers has an advantage because it knows who its customers are and how and when they use the services offered.

Relationship marketing can be practised at three levels:

- *Level 1*: The firm uses pricing incentives to encourage customers to continue doing business with it. Examples include the frequent flyer programs offered by many airlines and the free or discounted travel services given to frequent hotel guests. This level of relationship marketing is the least effective in the long term as other firms can easily imitate its price-based advantage.
- *Level 2*: This level of relationship marketing also uses pricing incentives but seeks to build social bonds with customers. The firm stays in touch with customers, learns about their needs, and designs services to meet those needs. 1-800-FLOWERS, for example, developed an on-line Gift Reminder Program. Customers who reach the company via its website can register unlimited birthdays, anniversaries, or other special occasions. Five days before each occasion and at their request, 1-800-FLOWERS will send an e-mail reminder. Level 2 relationship marketing has a higher potential for keeping the firm ahead of the competition than does Level 1 relationship marketing.
- *Level 3*: At this level, the firm again uses financial and social bonds but adds structural bonds to the formula. Structural bonds are developed by offering value-added services that are not readily available from other firms. Hertz No. 1 Gold Club program allows members to call and reserve a car, board a courtesy bus at the airport, tell the driver their name, and get dropped off in front of their car. Hertz also starts up the car and turns on the air conditioning or heat, depending on the

Ethics in Marketing

 ## SOON, THE DESK CLERK WILL KNOW ALL ABOUT YOU

Hilton Hotels has developed a sophisticated customer and hotel-management system for use in its 2,100 hotels, including the hundreds of Hiltons and Hilton-owned hotels in Canada. The $50-million Hilton computer network can amass a sizable marketing database of customer habits and spending, in addition to running the hotels' other operating systems. The system extends across all Hilton chains and has set the company apart from its major competitors. But the new technology may mean that Hilton customers have a bit less privacy.

The system ranks customers in order of their value to Hilton—how often they stay at Hilton hotels and how much they spend. Once guests are identified at the front desk, the clerk will be prompted with the correct way to greet them: "I see that this is your first time staying at an Embassy Suites. Let me tell you about our made-to-order breakfasts," for instance. A clerk may be prompted to apologize that a guest's room wasn't made up on time during a visit to a Hampton Inn in Ottawa last month. The clerk will also be able to see the guests' bar tab last week at a Hilton in Toronto and whether the guest used the high-speed Internet there. All this information is collected and can be used to personalize the marketing program for a guest's next visit to a Hilton property.

Personalized information of this nature is routinely gathered by most major hotel operations. However, the information is generally maintained by the general manager of a specific hotel and not shared among other units of the hotel chain. Hilton anticipates that its new technology will help the company to market more effectively to the over 15 million Hilton hotel guests each year. It also hopes that the new technology will help all the Hilton hotels to operate more efficiently and at a lower cost. The system is already helping Hilton to eliminate booking errors across its units.[16]

Is it always ethical to collect and use customer database information to better customize services for your customers?

SOURCE: CHRISTINA BINKLEY, "SOON, THE DESK CLERK WILL KNOW ALL ABOUT YOU," WALL STREET JOURNAL, MAY 8, 2003, D4.

temperature. Marketing programs like this one have the strongest potential for sustaining long-term relationships with customers.

Building relationships with customers sometimes requires using data collected from your customers. However, this practice may not always be welcomed by customers, as the "Ethics in Marketing" box illustrates.

5 | **Discuss relationship marketing in services**

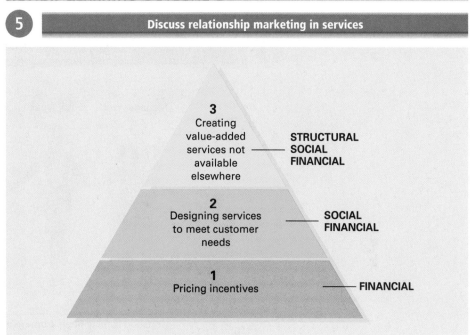

3
Creating
value-added
services not —— **STRUCTURAL**
available **SOCIAL**
elsewhere **FINANCIAL**

2
Designing services —— **SOCIAL**
to meet customer **FINANCIAL**
needs

1
Pricing incentives —— **FINANCIAL**

internal marketing
Treating employees as customers and developing systems and benefits that satisfy their needs.

6 INTERNAL MARKETING IN SERVICE FIRMS

Explain internal marketing in services

Services are performances, so the quality of a firm's employees is an important part of building long-term relationships with customers. Employees who like their jobs and are satisfied with the firm they work for are more likely to deliver superior service to customers. In other words, a firm that makes its employees happy has a better chance of keeping its customers coming back. Studies show that replacing an employee costs roughly 1.5 times a year's pay. Also, companies with highly committed employees have been found to post sharply higher shareholder returns.[17] Thus it is critical that service firms practise **internal marketing**, which means treating employees as customers and developing systems and benefits that satisfy their needs. Internal marketing involves the following activities: competing for talent, offering a vision, training employees, stressing teamwork, giving employees more freedom to make decisions, measuring and rewarding good service performance, and knowing employees' needs.

Companies have instituted a wide variety of programs designed to satisfy employees. Some companies are trying to retain happy employees by offering concierges who run errands to help ease the lives of time-strapped, stressed-out workers. Starbucks claims to be in the people business rather than the coffee business and prides itself

SOURCE: COURTESY LASALLE BANK N.A., CHICAGO, ILLINOIS

Corporate concierge services are one way companies are beginning to market themselves to their own employees. Internal marketing efforts like this can help employers attract and retain valuable employees.

on its stellar customer service. Its top executives believe that the key to great service is to create an environment of respect and appreciation for all employees. Travelocity keeps its employees engaged in their work by sending them weekly e-mails and hosting a monthly lunch where employees can express their concerns.[18] These examples illustrate how service firms can invest in their most important resources—their employees.

REVIEW LEARNING OUTCOME 6

6   **Explain internal marketing in services**

Good service flows from management to customers through employees.

Customer Experience

 STARBUCKS

Starbucks, an international coffeehouse chain with hundreds of locations in Canada, is the largest coffeehouse company in the world. Starbucks' success is based on its quality and variety of coffee drinks and its distinctive European-style coffeehouse experience. Stores offered comfortable stuffed sofas and chairs as well as tables with hard-backed chairs. Most stores provided free electricity and wireless Internet access. The aroma of freshly ground coffee beans permeated the air, and hand-pulled espresso shots added a sense of theatre. Customers were willing to pay a premium for the product and the coffeehouse experience. In the late 1990s and early 2000s, Starbucks was opening a new store every day.

As the company grew and customer traffic increased, the company added new food products and began introducing more efficient operations, like automated espresso machines and preground coffee. The sofas and large chairs were removed to make room for more customers.

Customers complained that Starbucks was starting to feel more like a fast-food restaurant than a coffeehouse. The customer experience that was an integral part of the Starbucks brand, and that kept customers loyal, had been watered down. Howard Schultz, the man who built the chain and recently returned as CEO, said, "Stores no longer have the soul of the past." At the same time, competitors such as Tim Hortons, Dunkin' Donuts, and McDonald's were introducing gourmet coffee drinks for less money and gradually started wooing Starbucks' customers away. Starbucks closed 600 stores in 2008.[19]

What does Starbucks need to do to turn the company around? How can it compete against Tim Hortons, Dunkin' Donuts and McDonalds?

SOURCE: ROBERT PASSIKOFF, "WHY STARBUCKS HAS GROUND TO A HALT," BRANDWEEK, NOVEMBER 10, 2008, 16.

7 GLOBAL ISSUES IN SERVICES MARKETING

Discuss global issues in services marketing

The international marketing of services is a major part of global business, and Canada is a growing exporter of services. According to Statistics Canada, Canada's export of services exceeded $70 billion in 2007. Competition in international services is increasing rapidly, however, as many mature economies like Canada's are moving from manufacturing jobs to service jobs.

To succeed in the global marketplace, service firms must first determine the nature of their core product. Then the marketing mix elements (additional services, pricing, promotion, distribution) should be designed to take into account each country's cultural, technological, and political environment.

Because of their competitive advantages, many Canadian service industries have been able to enter the global marketplace. Canadian banks, for example, have advantages in customer service and collections management. The field of construction and engineering services offers great global potential; Canadian companies have vast experience in this industry, so economies of scale are possible for machinery and materials, human resource management, and project management. The Canadian insurance industry has substantial knowledge about underwriting, risk evaluation, and insurance operations that it can export to other countries. In fact, a current survey of top executives of Canadian service companies by Ipsos-Reid shows that 87 percent of the CEOs feel that their companies have what it takes to compete in the global market.[20]

REVIEW LEARNING OUTCOME 7

7 Discuss global issues in services marketing

CANADA

Canadian exports of services are growing by $2 billion each year.

 ## 8 NONPROFIT ORGANIZATION MARKETING

Describe nonprofit organization marketing

nonprofit organization
An organization that exists to achieve some goal other than the usual business goals of profit, market share, or return on investment.

A **nonprofit organization** is an organization that exists to achieve some goal other than the usual business goals of profit, market share, or return on investment. Nonprofit organizations share important characteristics with private-sector service firms. Both market intangible products. Both often require the customer to be present during the production process. Both for-profit and nonprofit services vary greatly from producer to producer and from day to day, even from the same producer. Neither for-profit nor nonprofit services can be stored in the way that tangible goods can be produced, saved, and sold at a later date.

Few people realize that nonprofit organizations account for 20 percent of the economic activity in Canada. The cost of government, the predominant form of nonprofit organization, has become the biggest single item in the Canadian family budget—more than housing, food, or transportation. Together, federal, provincial, and local governments collect tax revenues that amount to 41.5 percent of the Canadian gross domestic product. Moreover, they employ 19.9 percent of nonagricultural civilian workers.[21] In addition to government entities, nonprofit organizations include thousands of private museums, theatres, schools, churches, and so on.

WHAT IS NONPROFIT ORGANIZATION MARKETING?

Nonprofit organization marketing is the effort by nonprofit organizations to bring about mutually satisfying exchanges with target markets. Although these organizations vary substantially in size and purpose and operate in different environments, most perform the following marketing activities:

• Identify and target the customers they wish to serve or attract (although they usually use another term, such as *clients, patients, members,* or *sponsors*)
• Explicitly or implicitly specify objectives
• Develop, manage, and eliminate programs and services
• Decide on prices to charge (although they use other terms, such as *fees, donations, tuition, fares, fines,* or *rates*)
• Schedule events or programs and determine where they will be held or where services will be offered
• Communicate their availability through brochures, signs, public service announcements, or advertisements

Often, the nonprofit organizations that carry out these functions do not realize they are engaged in marketing.

UNIQUE ASPECTS OF NONPROFIT ORGANIZATION MARKETING STRATEGIES

Like their counterparts in business organizations, nonprofit managers develop marketing strategies to bring about mutually satisfying exchanges with target markets. However, marketing in nonprofit organizations is unique in many ways—including the setting of marketing objectives, the selection of target markets, and the development of appropriate marketing mixes.

Objectives

In the private sector, the profit motive is both an objective for guiding decisions and a criterion for evaluating results. Nonprofit organizations do not seek to make a profit for redistribution to owners or shareholders. Rather, their focus is often on generating enough funds to cover expenses. The Methodist Church does not gauge its success by the amount of money collected in offering plates. The Canadian Film Centre does not base its performance evaluations on the dollars of revenue it brings in.

Most nonprofit organizations are expected to provide equitable, effective, and efficient services that respond to the wants and preferences of multiple constituencies. These include users, payers, donors, politicians, appointed officials, the media, and the general public. Nonprofit organizations cannot measure their success or failure in strictly financial terms.

The lack of a financial "bottom line" and the existence of multiple, diverse, intangible, and sometimes vague or conflicting objectives make prioritizing objectives, making decisions, and evaluating performance hard for nonprofit managers. They must often use approaches different from the ones commonly used in the private sector. For example, the Art Gallery of Windsor has devised a system for basing salary increases on how employees perform in relation to the objectives set for them each year.

Target Markets

Three issues relating to target markets are unique to nonprofit organizations:

- *Apathetic or strongly opposed targets*: Private-sector organizations usually give priority to developing those market segments that are most likely to respond to particular offerings. In contrast, nonprofit organizations must often target those who are apathetic about or strongly opposed to receiving their services, such as vaccinations, family-planning guidance, help for problems of drug or alcohol abuse, and psychological counselling.
- *Pressure to adopt undifferentiated segmentation strategies*: Nonprofit organizations often adopt undifferentiated strategies by default. Sometimes they fail to recognize the advantages of targeting, or an undifferentiated approach may appear to offer economies of scale and low per capita costs. In other instances, nonprofit organizations are pressured or required to serve the maximum number of people by targeting the average user. The problem with developing services targeted at the average user is that there are few "average" users. Therefore, such strategies typically fail to fully satisfy any market segment.
- *Complementary positioning*: The main role of many nonprofit organizations is to provide services, with available resources, to those who are not adequately served by private-sector organizations. As a result, the nonprofit organization must often complement, rather than compete with, the efforts of others. The positioning task is to identify underserved market segments and to develop marketing programs that match their needs rather than to target the niches that may be most profitable. For example, a university library may see itself as complementing the services of the public library, rather than as competing with it.

Product Decisions

There are three product-related distinctions between business and nonprofit organizations:

- *Benefit complexity*: Rather than simple product concepts, like "Freedom 55" or "We earn money the old-fashioned way," nonprofit organizations often market complex behaviours or ideas. Examples include the need to exercise or eat right, not to drink and drive, and not to smoke tobacco. The benefits that a person receives are complex, long-term, and intangible and therefore are more difficult to communicate to consumers.
- *Benefit strength*: The benefit strength of many nonprofit offerings is quite weak or indirect. What are the direct, personal benefits to you of driving under the speed limit, donating blood, or asking your neighbours to contribute money to a charity? In contrast, most private-sector service organizations can offer customers direct, personal benefits in an exchange relationship.
- *Involvement*: Many nonprofit organizations market products that elicit very low involvement ("Prevent forest fires" or "Don't litter") or very high involvement ("Buy only Canadian-made vehicles" or "Stop smoking"). The typical range for private-sector goods is much narrower. Traditional promotional tools may be inadequate to motivate adoption of either low- or high-involvement products.

Place (Distribution) Decisions

A nonprofit organization's capacity for distributing its service offerings to potential customer groups when and where they want them is typically a key variable in determining the success of those service offerings. For example, many universities have one or more satellite campus locations to provide easier access for students in other geographic areas. Some educational institutions also offer classes to students at off-campus locations via interactive video technology.

The extent to which a service depends on fixed facilities has important implications for distribution decisions. Obviously, services like rail transit and lake fishing can be delivered only at specific points. Many nonprofit services, however, do not depend on special facilities. Counselling, for example, need not take place in agency offices; it may occur wherever counsellors and clients can meet. Probation services, outreach youth programs, and educational courses taught on commuter trains are other examples of deliverable services.

Promotion Decisions

Some nonprofit organizations are explicitly or implicitly prohibited from advertising; other nonprofit organizations simply do not have the resources to retain advertising agencies, promotion consultants, or marketing staff. However, nonprofit organizations have a few special promotion resources to call on:

- *Professional volunteers*: Nonprofit organizations often seek out marketing, sales, and advertising professionals to help them develop and implement promotion strategies. In some instances, an advertising agency donates its services in exchange for potential long-term benefits. One advertising agency donated its services to a major symphony because the symphony had a blue-ribbon board of directors. Donated services create goodwill, personal contacts, and general awareness of the donor's organization, reputation, and competency.
- *Sales promotion activities*: Sales promotion activities that make use of existing services or other resources are increasingly being used to draw attention to the offerings of nonprofit organizations. Sometimes nonprofit charities even team up with other companies for promotional activities. For example, Rainbow Cinemas, the *Toronto Star*, and Cadillac Fairview Shopping Centres all teamed up with United Way to run a Movie Marathon at the Galleria Cinemas. All proceeds during the 12-hour movie marathon at the Toronto theatres went to the United Way.[22]

- *Public service advertising*: A **public service advertisement (PSA)** is an announcement that promotes a program of a federal, provincial, or local government or of a nonprofit organization. Unlike a commercial advertiser, the sponsor of the PSA does not pay for the time or space. Instead, it is donated by the medium.
- *Peer-to-peer communications*: Some nonprofit agencies have been successful in offering forums for people to share experiences. For example, the March of Dimes Birth Defect Foundation created an on-line forum at **www .shareyourstory.org** to gather real-life stories that help spread the word about its mission to prevent birth defects, premature birth, and infant mortality. Families can share their experiences in the form of short stories and blogs.

Pricing Decisions

Five key characteristics distinguish the pricing decisions of nonprofit organizations from those of the profit sector:

- *Pricing objectives*: The main pricing objective in the profit sector is revenue or, more specifically, profit maximization, sales maximization, or target return on sales or investment. Many nonprofit organizations must also be concerned about revenue. Often, however, nonprofit organizations seek to either partially or fully defray costs rather than to achieve a profit for distribution to stockholders. Nonprofit organizations also seek to redistribute income—for instance, through taxation and sliding-scale fees. Moreover, they strive to allocate resources fairly among individuals or households or across geographic or political boundaries.
- *Nonfinancial prices*: In many nonprofit situations, consumers are not charged a monetary price but instead must absorb nonmonetary costs. The importance of those costs is illustrated by the large number of eligible

SOURCE: COURTESY NEWMAN'S OWN

Cause-related marketing can be a controversial marketing technique because not all companies are as scrupulous as they should be about their intentions. A company like Newman's Own, however, which donates all after-tax profits to charity, is clear in its mission. By not profiting from using causes as a marketing tool, its motives are beyond reproach.

citizens who do not take advantage of so-called free services for the poor. In many public assistance programs, about half the people who are eligible don't participate. Nonmonetary costs consist of the opportunity cost of time, embarrassment costs, and effort costs.

- *Indirect payment*: Indirect payment through taxes is common to marketers of "free" services, such as libraries, fire protection, and police protection. Indirect payment is not a common practice in the profit sector.

- *Separation between payers and users*: By design, the services of many charitable organizations are provided for those who are relatively poor and largely paid for by those who are better off financially. Although examples of separation between payers and users can be found in the profit sector (such as insurance claims), the practice is much less prevalent.

- *Below-cost pricing*: University tuition is an example of below-cost pricing. Virtually all colleges and universities price their services below full cost.

REVIEW LEARNING OUTCOME 8

8 | **Describe nonprofit organization marketing**

Nonprofit Organization Marketing

- **PRODUCT**
  - Benefit complexity
  - Benefit strength
  - Involvement

- **PLACE**
  - Special facilities

- **TARGET**
  - Apathetic or strongly opposed
  - Undifferentiated segmentation
  - Complementary positioning

- **PROMOTION**
  - Professional volunteers
  - Sales
  - Public service advertising

- **PRICE**
  - Nonfinancial
  - Indirect payment
  - Separation between payers and users
  - Below-cost pricing

REVIEW AND APPLICATIONS

1 **Discuss the importance of services to the economy.** The service sector plays a crucial role in the Canadian economy, employing over three-quarters of the workforce and accounting for nearly three-quarters of Canada's gross domestic product.

1.1 What services can you find at the website **www.servicecanada.gc.ca**? Are you surprised at some of the services offered by the government?

2 Discuss the differences between services and goods. Services are distinguished by four characteristics. Services are intangible performances in that they lack clearly identifiable physical characteristics, making it difficult for marketers to communicate their specific benefits to potential customers. The production and consumption of services occur simultaneously. Services are heterogeneous because their quality depends on such elements as the service provider, individual consumer, location, and so on. Finally, services are perishable in the sense that they cannot be stored or saved. As a result, synchronizing supply with demand is particularly challenging in the service industry.

2.1 *WRITING* Assume you are the manager of a bank branch. Write a list of the implications of intangibility for your firm.

2.2 *ONLINE* Over 25 years ago, Tim and Nina Zagat began publishing leisure guides containing reviews of restaurants. Today, the renowned Zagat guides still contain reviews of restaurants, but they also rate hotels, entertainment, nightlife, movies, shopping, and even music. Go to **www.zagat.com**. In your opinion, are Zagat survey guides goods or services? Explain your reasoning.

3 Describe the components of service quality and the gap model of service quality. Service quality has five components: reliability (ability to perform the service dependably, accurately, and consistently), responsiveness (providing prompt service), assurance (knowledge and courtesy of employees and their ability to convey trust), empathy (caring, individualized attention), and tangibles (physical evidence of the service).

The gap model identifies five key discrepancies that can influence customer evaluations of service quality. When the gaps are large, service quality is low. As the gaps shrink, service quality improves. Gap 1 is found between customers' expectations and management's perceptions of those expectations. Gap 2 is found between management's perception of what the customer wants and specifications for service quality. Gap 3 is found between service quality specifications and delivery of the service. Gap 4 is found between service delivery and what the company promises to the customer through external communication. Gap 5 is found between customers' service expectations and their perceptions of service performance.

3.1 Analyze a recent experience that you have had with a service business (for example, hairdresser, movie theatre, dentist, restaurant, car repair) based on your expectations and perceptions about each of the five components of service quality.

4 Develop marketing mixes for services. "Product" (service) strategy issues include what is being processed (people, possessions, mental stimulus, information), core and supplementary services, customization versus standardization, and the service mix or portfolio. Place decisions involve convenience, number of outlets, direct versus indirect distribution, and scheduling. Stressing tangible cues, using personal sources of information, creating strong organizational images, and engaging in postpurchase communication are effective promotion strategies. Pricing objectives for services can be revenue oriented, operations oriented, patronage oriented, or any combination of the three.

4.1 *TEAM* Form a team with at least two other classmates and come up with an idea for a new service. Develop a marketing mix strategy for the new service.

5 Discuss relationship marketing in services. Relationship marketing in services involves attracting, developing, and retaining customer relationships. There are three levels of relationship marketing: Level 1 focuses on pricing incentives; Level 2 uses pricing incentives and social bonds with customers; and Level 3 uses pricing, social bonds, and structural bonds to build long-term relationships.

5.1 *TEAM* For the new service developed for question 4.1, have the members of your team discuss how they would implement a relationship marketing strategy.

6 **Explain internal marketing in services.** Internal marketing means treating employees as customers and developing systems and benefits that satisfy their needs. Employees who like their jobs and are happy with the firm they work for are more likely to deliver good service. Internal marketing activities include competing for talent, offering a vision, training employees, stressing teamwork, giving employees freedom to make decisions, measuring and rewarding good service performance, and knowing employees' needs.

6.1 Choose a service firm with which you do a lot of business. Write a memo to the manager explaining the importance of internal marketing and outlining the factors that internal marketing includes.

6.2 Return to **www.zagat.com** and investigate what the site offers. How does Zagat propose to help companies with internal services marketing?

7 **Discuss global issues in services marketing.** Canada is a growing exporter of services. Although competition is keen, Canada has been able to grow its service businesses due to the experience this country has in many service industries. To be successful globally, service firms must adjust their marketing mix for the environment of each target country.

7.1 What issues would you have to think about in going global with the new service that you developed in the questions above? How would you change your marketing mix to address those issues?

8 **Describe nonprofit organization marketing.** Nonprofit organizations pursue goals other than profit, market share, and return on investment. Nonprofit organization marketing facilitates mutually satisfying exchanges between nonprofit organizations and their target markets. Several unique characteristics distinguish nonbusiness marketing strategy, including a concern with services and social behaviours rather than manufactured goods and profit; a difficult, undifferentiated, and in some ways marginal target market; a complex product that may have only indirect benefits and elicit very low involvement; a short, direct, immediate distribution channel; a relative lack of resources for promotion; and prices only indirectly related to the exchange between the producer and the consumer of the services.

8.1 Form a team with two or three classmates. Using the promotion strategies discussed in the nonprofit section of this chapter, develop a promotion strategy for your college or university.

TERMS

assurance 300
core service 304
credence quality 299
empathy 300
experience quality 299
gap model 301
heterogeneity 300

intangibility 299
internal marketing 309
mass customization 304
nonprofit organization 311
nonprofit organization marketing 312
perishability 300
public service advertisement (PSA) 314

reliability 300
responsiveness 300
search quality 299
service 298
supplementary services 304
tangibles 301

EXERCISES

APPLICATION EXERCISE

 Most people know quality when they see it—or do they? Let's take a look at some goods and services and then think about assessing their quality. For this exercise, work in teams of two or three and discuss each item before determining its final placement.

Activities

1. Using the abbreviations in parentheses, place each of the following products and services along the continuum below: a new car (C), designer jeans (J), car oil change (O), dry cleaning (D), haircut (H), tax preparation software (T), college or university education (E).

   100% physical good _____ 100% service

2. Once you have placed the items along the continuum, consider how easy it is to assess the quality of each item.

   Easy to assess quality _____ Difficult to assess quality

3. What assumptions can you make about the ability to assess the quality of goods compared to services? Is it easier to assess the quality of some goods than others? What about the services?

ETHICS EXERCISE

Websites such as **Oncology.com** and **cancerpage.com** offer cancer patients sophisticated medical data and advice in exchange for personal information that is then sold to advertisers and business partners and used by the websites to create products to sell back to patients. Some argue that cancer patients visiting these sites are willingly exchanging their personal information for the sites' medical information. Others would contend that this kind of exchange is unethical.

Questions

1. Is this practice ethical?

2. Does the CMA Code of Ethics have anything to say about this issue? Go to **www.the-cma.org/consumer/ethics.cfm** and review the code. Then write a brief paragraph on what the CMA Code of Ethics contains that relates to this scenario.

CASE STUDY

TRIBUTE MAGAZINE: *TRIBUTE* PLAYS A LEADING ROLE IN MOVIE THEATRES ACROSS CANADA

Anyone who has gone to see a movie anywhere across Canada has probably flipped through the pages of *Tribute* magazine. Founded in 1979, Tribute Entertainment Media Group Inc. publishes *Tribute* magazine nine times a year. *Tribute* is distributed in Cineplex Galaxy Cinemas, AMC Theatres, Empire Theatres, Cinemas Guzzo, Cine Enterprise, Landmark Cinemas, Ontario Theatre Group, Stinson Theatres, Rainbow Cinemas, Cinemark, and Odeon and independent theatres across Canada. According to the Print Measurement Bureau, over 1.8 million adults read each issue of *Tribute*. In 2004, *Teen Tribute* magazine was added to its list by Tribute Entertainment Media Group and, most recently, *Kids Tribute* magazine was added.

Each issue of *Tribute* contains articles about current movies playing across the country, movie reviews, celebrity interviews, behind-the-scenes coverage of upcoming movies, movie gossip, movie trivia, fashion tips, reviews of movie books and music, and celebrity fashions and photos. In addition to the movie and celebrity coverage found in *Tribute* magazine, *Teen Tribute* covers TV programs and video games and has advice columns. *Kids Tribute*, which is geared to the 6 to 11 age group, includes games, puzzles, and learning experiences based on kids' movies. And best of all for the readers, *Tribute* is free—it comes with your purchase of a ticket to the movie. You can find *Tribute*, *Teen Tribute*, and *Kids Tribute* in racks in the lobbies of the movie theatre. For yet more movie details, there is also a *Tribute* website (**www.tribute.ca**).

Your ticket purchase, of course, doesn't really cover the cost of *Tribute* magazine. *Tribute* earns its revenue from the sale of advertising space within the magazine. A one-page ad in *Tribute* will cost the advertiser $20,000. Why do advertisers pay so much? *Tribute* reaches an audience that is young (over 70 percent of the readers are under age 49 with a full 54 percent being under 34 years of age), educated (over 41 percent of the readers have a college or university degree), and high earning (nearly 60 percent of readers earn over $60,000 per year).[23] Of course, *Teen Tribute* and *Kids Tribute* reach younger audiences.

Questions

1. Is *Tribute* a good, a service, or both? Explain.

2. Using what you have learned in this chapter, outline *Tribute*'s marketing mix. Discuss its product, core and supplementary services, mass customization, service mix, distribution, promotion, and pricing.

3. What kinds of companies are most likely to advertise in each of the *Tribute* magazines?

VIDEO CASE

CBC

CREDIT LIFE INSURANCE: IS THIS REALLY A CUSTOMER SERVICE?

Automotive dealerships sell credit life insurance to cover car loan payments in cases where the car purchaser dies. It's offered when someone buys a new car or truck as an assurance that family members won't be stuck with the payments remaining on the deceased purchaser's vehicle. Sounds pretty good, but let's look at some examples in which new vehicle purchasers died and what happened to the families trying to file a credit life insurance claim on the purchased vehicle.

Automotive dealers sometimes sell credit life insurance policies to customers without asking any health questions. In some cases, even when the credit life insurance purchaser raises health issues and admits to existing health problems, the dealership sells the customer a policy anyway. However, if the policy holder dies, and the cause of death is related to even a minor pre-existing health problem, the policy claim will be denied. Commissions on the sale of credit life insurance can range from 15 percent to 48 percent of the policy amount. This is often an amount greater than the dealership makes on the sale of the new car or truck.

Industrial Alliance Pacific is the insurance carrier for each of the three policies discussed in the video you are about to watch. IAP is located in Vancouver and is the fifth-largest insurance company in Canada with nearly $4 billion in assets. IAP issues approximately $150 million of credit life insurance each year. IAP's website indicates that they are Canada's leading provider of credit life insurance for the automotive industry in this country. The company, however, will not disclose how much it pays out in credit life insurance claims or how many claims it denies.[24]

Questions

1. Across the three examples you watched in this video, do you feel that the automotive dealerships, salespeople, or insurance company did anything illegal or unethical in the offering of the credit life insurance service? Explain.

2. How much responsibility does the purchaser have to ask detailed and specific questions and read the fine print before signing a contract? Do you feel that reading the fine print and asking questions would have made a difference in any of the three cases profiled in this video?

3. The United States has stronger laws governing "post-claim underwriting." Do you feel that Canada needs stronger laws? What can you find out about the U.S. laws?

4. IAP does refund the insurance premiums when a claim is denied because of a pre-existing condition. Is this adequate? Why or why not? What can you find out about how to make an insurance claim complaint?

MARKETING & YOU RESULTS

A high score means that you have a positive attitude about charitable operations and most likely think that nonprofit organizations fulfill an important role in society. However, a high score does not necessarily mean you give more to charity.

MARKETING MISCUE

MOBILEME FAILED ON THE "ME"

July 9, 2008, is a date that Apple Computer would like to forget. At 8 p.m. on that date, the company was taking its existing .Mac service offline to launch the .Mac successor, MobileMe. The outage was scheduled to last until approximately 2 a.m. on July 10, 2008. Unfortunately, according to published sources, there were an estimated 20,000 loyal Apple customers still without e-mail service a week later. How could a product and service error such as this happen at Apple—an error that was said to result in the worst product launch in the ten years since Steve Jobs had returned to Apple?

At the World Wide Developers Conference in June of 2008, a senior vice-president for product marketing at Apple touted MobileMe as a product that would push contact and calendar changes nearly instantaneously among various communication and electronic products. Steve Jobs was noted as saying that MobileMe was the "exchange for the rest of us," indicating, for example, that the service would synchronize with features offered to iPhone users. For a $99 annual fee, MobileMe was the replacement for .Mac, Apple's on-line sync and data storage service.

Communication outages due to maintenance occur on most servers, but companies such as Apple schedule these outages for times that will be the least disruptive to customers. An 8 p.m. outage start time on the West Coast would mean a later outage start time for customers on the East Coast, with the 2 a.m. Pacific time meaning that East Coast customers would be able to be on-line at normal morning hours. Thus, an 8 p.m. to 2 a.m. outage window on the West Coast should have been nondisruptive to a majority of Apple customers. Unfortunately, that was not the case.

Over time, more than 96,000 messages appeared on MobileMe discussion boards, with 340,000 views. Comments such as the following appeared in various locations:

- MAC.COM BLOWS! It has been down for over 12 hours!!!

- . . . did a big earthquake just drop Apple in the sea?

- I don't really feel like for $100/yr I should have to play roulette with different methods of accessing e-mail

Media reviewers were not going any easier on Apple and MobileMe. Walt Mossberg gave it a "can't recommend" as the product had too many flaws to keep its promises. David Pogue focused more on Apple's response (or lack thereof) as the real problem and said that Apple, while good at marketing, had no clue about crisis management.

Word even got out about an internal e-mail that Steve Jobs supposedly wrote about the botched launch of MobileMe. Excerpts from this e-mail purported that Jobs had made comments along the following lines:

- MobileMe was simply not up to Apple's standards.

- Rather than launch MobileMe as a monolithic service, we could have launched (components in phases).

- It was a mistake to launch MobileMe at the same time as iPhone 3G, iPhone 2.0 software, and the AppStore. . . . MobileMe could have been delayed without consequence.

- The MobileMe launch clearly demonstrates that we have more to learn about Internet services.

Of course, there is always the chance of problems with any product launch. Unfortunately, technology-related product launches are fraught with concerns and fears that products, en masse, will not work as planned. Thus most technology-consumers have a smidgen of understanding for technology product flaws. However, the e-mail excerpts from Steve Jobs suggest that the flawed launch was not necessarily just a product-related launch problem. Sure, the comment that the product was not up to Apple's standards implies a product-specific concern. But other comments attributed to Jobs imply that the company as a whole was not ready for, and behind, the MobileMe launch. Was Apple trying to do too much too quickly, with managers not able to dedicate the necessary time to the company's various and sundry products and projects?

Questions

1. Where would MobileMe be in the categories of new products?

2. Is MobileMe a product or service? Explain your answer.

3. What can you find out about how Apple responded to the over-week-long outages that some Apple customers experienced?

4. How would you have handled the Apple MobileMe problem?

CRITICAL THINKING CASE

TIC TAC REFRESHES YOUR BREATH AND ITS PACKAGING

Launched in 1969, Tic Tac is one of the market's leading breath mints. The Tic Tac product line is owned by one of the largest confectionery companies in the world, the Ferrero Group, which has 36 operating companies, 15 manufacturing plants, and almost 20,000 employees worldwide. The Tic Tac line is sold around the world, with large sales volumes in North America, Italy, Australia, Ireland, England, France, Germany, and South America. In 1969, the catchy jingle "Put a Tic Tac in your mouth and get a BANG out of life!" was a huge success for the company.

In the 1970s, the original Tic Tac tiny white mints were joined by the first line extension, cinnamon-flavoured red mints. This was followed closely by the next extension—tangerine-flavoured orange mints. The product was repositioned in 1980 as "The 1½ Calorie Breath Mint" so as to fit the growing health craze in Canada, and wintergreen and spearmint flavours were added to the product line. With a strong line of breath mints, the company began to make Tic Tac into an icon with its little flip-top packaging.

The product's 25th birthday was celebrated with a cake made with thousands of Tic Tac packages, and a lime flavour was also introduced. Ferraro introduced Tic Tac Bold! mints in the early 2000s, along with mixed fruit flavours, and Tic Tac continued to enjoy its position as the number-one breath mint in Canada.

It was around this time that Altoids, the "curiously strong" mints in the metal container from Callard & Bowser-Suchard, overtook Tic Tac for the lead position in the mint marketplace. Other breath mint competitors (Everest, Cool Chews, Icefresh, Blitz, Ice Chips, Cool Blast, Ice Breakers) were also entering the market. All the while, the packaging for Tic Tac remained unchanged.

In 2008, the Ferrero Group decided to modernize the Tic Tac brand, introducing Tic Tac Chill with new packaging. The Chill mints are larger than the traditional Tic Tac mint and are the first Tic Tac mint to be completely sugar-free. The mints are sweetened with xylitol, an all-natural sweetener that has proven popular with people following diabetic diets. In introducing the new Chill mint, Tic Tac tapped into two fast-growing product segments in the mint marketplace—sugar-free and strong flavouring. Both of these product segments have experienced keen interest from customers.

Not only did Tic Tac introduce new flavours—Paradise Mint and Exotic Cherry—and new mint sizing, the Chill mint was introduced in a new package that maintained the iconic nature of the original packaging. Tic Tac Chill mints are available in a dual-use package. The package is the familiar Tic Tac see-through, flip-top packaging. Yet it also has a new, wide, slide-top opening that enables one-handed access.

The target market for Tic Tac Chill is consumers in the 25- to 45-year-old age group. The product is positioned as recognizing that consumers in this age group rarely take the time to just relax or "chill." The product rollout was accompanied by an on-line campaign in which the first 50,000 visitors to the **www.TicTac.com** website could choose four free downloads from 20 different "chill" songs. The first 1,000 visitors also received the added bonus of free Tic Tac Chill mints. With new flavours and new packaging, the goal is to modernize the brand while giving it a personality.

Questions

1. Why would Ferrero change the packaging of Tic Tac after making it such an icon?

2. Profile the Tic Tac Chill consumer.

3. What does the term *brand equity* mean in relation to Tic Tac?

4. Take a look at the Tic Tac website (**www.Ferrero.com**). How many product lines does Ferrero offer? How many Tic Tac brand extensions (or product items) can you count?

SOURCE: © TERRI MILLER/E-VISUAL COMMUNICATIONS, INC.

PART

4

Distribution
Decisions

11 Marketing Channels and Supply Chain Management

SOURCE: JUTTA KLEE/PHOTOLIBRARY

LEARNING OUTCOMES

1 Explain what a marketing channel is and why intermediaries are needed

2 Define the types of channel intermediaries and describe their functions and activities

3 Describe the channel structures for consumer and business products and discuss alternative channel arrangements

4 Define supply chain management and discuss its benefits

5 Discuss the issues that influence channel strategy

6 Explain channel leadership, conflict, and partnering

7 Describe the logistical components of the supply chain

8 Explain why supply chain performance measurement is necessary and important

9 Discuss new technology and emerging trends in supply chain management

10 Discuss channels and distribution decisions in global markets

11 Identify the special problems and opportunities associated with distribution in service organizations

ⓥ MARKETING & YOU

Using the following scale, indicate your opinions on the lines before the items.

1	2	3	4	5
Strongly disagree				Strongly agree

__ I would prefer to be a leader.
__ I see myself as a good leader
__ I will be a success.
__ People always seem to recognize my authority.

__ I have a natural talent for influencing people.
__ I am assertive.
__ I like to have authority over other people.
__ I am a born leader.

Now, total your score. Read the chapter and find out what your score means at the end.

SOURCE: REPRINTED WITH PERMISSION FROM *MARKETING SCALES HANDBOOK* VOL. III, PUBLISHED BY THE AMERICAN MARKETING ASSOCIATION, G. BRUNER, K. JAMES, H. HENSEL, EDS. SCALE #119.

Nancy is looking over two silver bracelets on a recent evening. She's looking for gifts for her sisters and maybe something for herself. "I love silver jewellery," Nancy says as she sips on a lemonade. Nearby, other women drink red wine while looking over bracelets, necklaces, and rings. The women are not at a mall or in a trendy boutique. They're in the home of a friend, Debra, in Calgary, Alberta.

Ranging in age from under 30 to over 50, the women include Debra's friends, neighbours, fellow book clubbers, co-workers, and some hockey moms. They've come together for an evening of cocktails, fig and goat cheese crostini, conversation, a bit of fun, and some shopping. The women, about 30 of them, at Debra's Calgary home are part of the $2.2-billion direct sales industry in Canada. Direct sales are a growing part of the distribution structure in Canada these days. This party at Debra's home is sponsored by jewellery maker Stella & Dot, one of many companies engaged in sales directly to consumers.

Many well-known companies are engaged in direct sales across Canada, including Mary Kay, Avon, and Tupperware. It is estimated that 1.2 million people are actively engaged in direct sales across Canada today. Nearly 90 percent of them are women, including Jody Robbins, age 38, who has hosted a number of home parties at which Usborne children's books are sold, and Dana King, age 43, an accountant by day,

who hosts parties selling Silpada jewellery. Over the past year, Dana, who lives in Vancouver, has earned over 125 pieces of free jewellery and has received commission cheques as high as $800 from her direct sales parties.

Mother and daughter Sylvie Rochette and Amelia Warren began their own direct sales company in North Saanich, British Columbia, in 1997. The company, Epicure Selections, started out selling four unique spice blends made in Sylvie's home and initially sold in local markets and trade shows around southern Vancouver Island. Within a few years, Epicure Selections' product mix had grown to seven dip mixes, nine spice blends, and a line of teas. Today, Epicure Selections sells more than 200 spice blends and a line of gourmet food products. The company has been growing by 40 percent a year over the past ten years, has a direct sales network of 6,000 part-time home party hosts, and its sales have now passed $40 million!

There are many other successful direct sales companies in Canada. Examples include PartyLite, which was started in 1992 and now has 6,500 direct sales consultants; Pampered Chef Canada, which was started in 1996 by Janice Gerol; Steeped Tea Inc., started as a hobby by Tonia Jahshan in Nova Scotia in 2006; and Herbal Magic Inc., started in London, Ontario, in 1996 and which now boasts sales of nearly $20 million. The Direct Sellers Association of Canada lists

nearly 50 member companies—all of whom sell products directly to household consumers—and new direct selling companies continue to sprout up.

A recent study by the Direct Sellers Association found that 50 percent of Canadians could name four or more direct selling companies and that 80 percent of households had bought a product from a direct seller in the past year. The University of Calgary hosts Entrepreneurship Days on its campus each year, and part of the program features speakers from the direct sales industry.[1]

Direct selling, of course, is only one way of getting products to consumers. Direct selling, as its name suggests, means getting a product directly from the producer to the consumer with no middlemen in-between. Most consumer and business products, though, go through longer channels of distribution. This chapter will take a look at the channels through which products flow as they move from where they are produced to where they are needed in the market. The many types of middlemen and supporting businesses that facilitate this flow of billions of dollars of products into the hands of buyers will be explored. You will be able to see the advantages and disadvantages of direct and indirect distribution of products into the market and reach some conclusions on what you think are the most efficient ways of getting products to market.

SOURCE: LISA KADANE, "THE NEW PARTYANIMALS; DIRECT SELLERS DELIVER COCKTAILS AND CROSTINI WITH A SIDE OF SHOPPING," EDMONTON JOURNAL, JANUARY 2, 2010, F7; MARY TERESA BITTI, "LAID OFF? WHY NOT THROW A PARTY? DIRECT SELLING FIRMS DOING WELL IN ECONOMIC DOWNTURN," NATIONAL POST, MAY 25, 2009, FP4; "COMPANY'S PLAN FOR WAREHOUSE AT AIRPORT NIXED," TIMES—COLONIST, JANUARY 31, 2008, B3.

MARKETING CHANNELS

marketing channel (channel of distribution)
A set of interdependent organizations that ease the transfer of ownership as products move from producer to business user or consumer.

channel members
All parties in the marketing channel that negotiate with one another, buy and sell products, and facilitate the change of ownership between buyer and seller in the course of moving the product from the manufacturer into the hands of the final consumer.

supply chain
The connected chain of all the business entities, both internal and external to the company, that perform or support the logistics function.

The term *channel* comes from the Latin word *canalis*, which means canal. A marketing channel can be viewed as a large canal or pipeline through which products, their ownership, communication, financing, payment, and the accompanying risk, flow from their origin to the consumer. Formally, a **marketing channel** (also called a **channel of distribution**) is a business structure of interdependent organizations that reach from the point of product origin to the consumer with the purpose of moving products to their final consumption destination. Marketing channels facilitate the physical movement of goods through the supply chain, representing the "place" element in the marketing mix (product, price, promotion, and place) and encompassing the processes involved in getting the right product to the right place at the right time.

Many different types of organizations participate in marketing channels. **Channel members** (wholesalers, distributors, and retailers, also called *intermediaries*, *resellers*, and *middlemen*) negotiate with one another, buy and sell products, and facilitate the change of ownership between buyer and seller in the course of moving the product from the manufacturer into the hands of the final consumer. An important aspect of marketing channels is the joint effort of all channel members to create a continuous and seamless supply chain. The **supply chain** is the connected chain of all the business entities, both internal and external to the company, that perform or support the marketing channel functions. As products move through the supply chain, channel members facilitate the distribution process by providing specialization and division of labour, overcoming discrepancies, and providing contact efficiency.

PROVIDING SPECIALIZATION AND DIVISION OF LABOUR

According to the concept of specialization and division of labour, breaking down a complex task into smaller, simpler ones and allocating them to specialists will create greater efficiency and lower average production costs. Manufacturers achieve economies of scale through the use of efficient equipment capable of producing large quantities of a single product.

Marketing channels can also attain economies of scale through specialization and division of labour by aiding producers who lack the motivation, financing, or expertise to market directly to end users or consumers. In some cases, as with most consumer convenience goods, such as soft drinks, the cost of marketing directly to millions of consumers—taking and shipping individual orders—is prohibitive. For this reason, producers hire channel members, such as wholesalers and retailers, to do what the producers are not equipped to do or what channel members are better prepared to do. Channel members can do some things more efficiently than producers because they have built good relationships with their customers. Therefore, their specialized expertise enhances the overall performance of the channel.

OVERCOMING DISCREPANCIES

discrepancy of quantity
The difference between the amount of product produced and the amount an end user wants to buy.

discrepancy of assortment
The lack of all the items a customer needs to receive full satisfaction from a product or products.

Marketing channels aid in overcoming the discrepancies of quantity, assortment, time, and space created by economies of scale in production. For example, assume that the H. J. Heinz Co. can most efficiently produce its Heinz ketchup at rates of 20,000 or more units in a typical day at its Leamington, Ontario, plant. Not even the most ardent ketchup user could consume that amount. The quantity produced to achieve low unit costs has created a **discrepancy of quantity**, which is the difference between the amount of product produced and the amount an end user wants to buy. By storing the product and distributing it in the appropriate amounts, marketing channels overcome quantity discrepancies by making products available in the quantities that consumers desire.

Mass production creates not only discrepancies of quantity but also discrepancies of assortment. A **discrepancy of assortment** occurs when a consumer does not have all the items needed to receive full satisfaction from a product. For Heinz ketchup to provide maximum satisfaction, several other products are required to complete the assortment. At the very least, most people want a knife, fork, plate, and various foods to put the ketchup on. Even though Heinz is a large consumer-products company, it does not come close to providing the optimal assortment to go with its ketchup. To overcome discrepancies of assortment, marketing channels assemble in one place many of the products necessary to complete a consumer's needed assortment.

A **temporal discrepancy** is created when a product is produced but a consumer is not ready to buy it. Marketing channels overcome temporal discrepancies by maintaining inventories in anticipation of demand. For example, manufacturers of seasonal merchandise, such as Christmas decorations, are in operation all year even though consumer demand is concentrated during certain months of the year.

Furthermore, because mass production requires many potential buyers, markets are usually scattered over large geographic areas, creating a **spatial discrepancy**. Often global, or at least nationwide, large markets are needed to absorb the output of mass producers. Marketing channels overcome spatial discrepancies by making products available in locations convenient to consumers. For example, Heinz ketchup is made available in supermarkets and convenience stores across Canada so that consumers don't have to travel to Leamington to buy it.

PROVIDING CONTACT EFFICIENCY

The third need fulfilled by marketing channels is that they provide contact efficiency. Marketing channels provide contact efficiencies by reducing the number of locations buyers have to visit to complete their shopping. Consider your extra time and costs if supermarkets, department stores, and shopping centres or malls did not exist. Suppose you had to buy your milk at a dairy and your meat at a stockyard. Imagine buying your eggs and chicken at a hatchery and your fruits and vegetables at various farms. You would spend a great deal of time, money, and energy just shopping for a few groceries. Supply chains simplify distribution by cutting the number of transactions required to get products from manufacturers to consumers and making an assortment of goods available at one location.

Consider the example illustrated in Exhibit 11.1. Four consumers each want to buy a television set. Without a retail intermediary like Future Shop, television

EXHIBIT 11.1

Marketing Channels

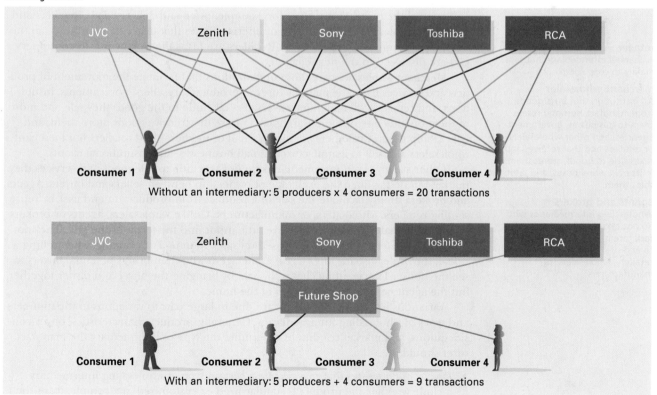

Without an intermediary: 5 producers x 4 consumers = 20 transactions

With an intermediary: 5 producers + 4 consumers = 9 transactions

1 | **Explain what a marketing channel is and why intermediaries are needed**

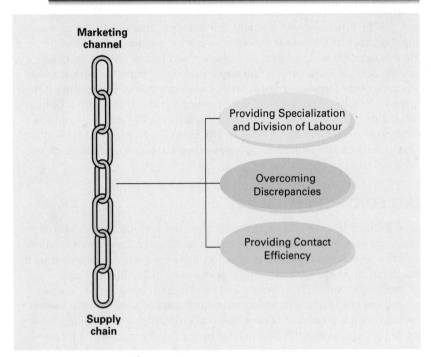

Marketing channel

- Providing Specialization and Division of Labour
- Overcoming Discrepancies
- Providing Contact Efficiency

Supply chain

manufacturers JVC, Zenith, Sony, Toshiba, and RCA would each have to make four contacts to reach the four buyers who are in the target market, totalling 20 transactions. However, when Future Shop acts as an intermediary between the producers and consumers, each producer has to make only one contact, reducing the number of transactions to nine. Each producer sells to one retailer rather than to four consumers. In turn, consumers buy from one retailer instead of from five producers.

Contact efficiency is being enhanced even more by information technology. Better information on product availability and pricing increasingly is reducing the need for consumers to actually shop for bargains or view ads in a traditional manner. By making information on products and services easily accessible over the Internet, Google, Yahoo, and similar information assemblers are becoming the starting points for finding and buying products and services.

2 CHANNEL INTERMEDIARIES AND THEIR FUNCTIONS

Define the types of channel intermediaries and describe their functions and activities

retailer
A channel intermediary that sells mainly to consumers.

merchant wholesaler
An institution that buys goods from manufacturers and resells them to businesses, government agencies, and other wholesalers or retailers and that receives and takes title to goods, stores them in its own warehouses, and later ships them.

agents and brokers
Wholesaling intermediaries who do not take title to a product but facilitate its sale from producer to end user by representing retailers, wholesalers, or manufacturers.

Intermediaries in a channel negotiate with one another, facilitate the change of ownership between buyers and sellers, and physically move products from the manufacturer to the final consumer. The most prominent difference separating intermediaries is whether they take title to the product. *Taking title* means they own the merchandise and control the terms of the sale—for example, price and delivery date. Retailers and merchant wholesalers are examples of intermediaries that take title to products in the marketing channel and resell them. **Retailers** are firms that sell mainly to consumers and are discussed in the next chapter.

Merchant wholesalers are those organizations that facilitate the movement of products and services from the manufacturer to producers, resellers, governments, institutions, and retailers. All merchant wholesalers take title to the goods they sell, and most of them operate one or more warehouses where they receive goods, store them, and later reship them. Customers are mostly small or medium-sized retailers but merchant wholesalers also sell to manufacturers, small businesses, and institutional clients.

Other supply chain intermediaries do not take title to the goods and services they market but do facilitate the exchange of ownership between sellers and buyers. **Agents and brokers** simply facilitate the sale of a product from producer to end user by representing retailers, wholesalers, or manufacturers. Unlike wholesalers, agents or brokers only facilitate sales and generally have little input into the terms of the sale. They do, however, get a fee or commission based on sales volume. For example, when selling a home, the owner usually hires a real estate agent who then brings potential buyers to see the house. The agent facilitates the sale by bringing the buyer and owner together, but the agent never takes ownership of the home.

Variations in channel structures are due in large part to variations in the numbers and types of wholesaling intermediaries. Generally, product characteristics, buyer considerations, and market conditions determine the type of intermediary the manufacturer should use.

- *Product characteristics* that may dictate a certain type of wholesaling intermediary include whether the product is standardized or customized, the complexity of the product, and the gross margin of the product. For example, a customized product such as insurance is sold through an insurance agent or broker who may represent several companies. In contrast, a standardized product such as gum is sold through a merchant wholesaler that takes possession of the gum and reships it to the appropriate retailers.

- *Buyer considerations* affecting the wholesaler choice include how often the product is purchased and how long the buyer is willing to wait to receive the product. For example, at the beginning of a school term, a student may be willing to wait a few days for a textbook to get a lower price by ordering on-line. Thus the product can be distributed directly. But if the student waits to buy the book until right before an exam and needs the book immediately, it will have to be purchased at the school bookstore.
- *Market characteristics* determining the wholesaler type include how many buyers are in the market and whether they are concentrated in a general location or are widely dispersed. Gum and ketchup, for example, are produced in one location and consumed in many locations; therefore, a merchant wholesaler is needed to distribute the products. In contrast, in a home sale, the buyer and seller are localized in one area, which facilitates the use of an agent/broker relationship.

logistics
The process of strategically managing the efficient flow and storage of raw materials, in-process inventory, and finished goods from point of origin to point of consumption.

Exhibit 11.2 shows the factors determining the type of wholesaling intermediary that will be used.

EXHIBIT 11.2

Factors Suggesting Type of Wholesaling Intermediary to Use

Factor	Merchant Wholesalers	Agents or Brokers
Nature of Product	Standard	Nonstandard, custom
Technicality of Product	Complex	Simple
Product's Gross Margin	High	Low
Frequency of Ordering	Frequent	Infrequent
Time between Order and Receipt of Shipment	Buyer desires shorter lead time	Buyer satisfied with long lead time
Number of Customers	Many	Few
Concentration of Customers	Dispersed	Concentrated

SOURCE: This article was published in "Products and Markets Served by Distributors and Agents", Donald M. Jackson and Michael F. D'Amico, Industrial Marketing Management, 27–33, Copyright Elsevier (1989).

CHANNEL FUNCTIONS PERFORMED BY INTERMEDIARIES

Retailing and wholesaling intermediaries in marketing channels perform several essential functions that make the flow of goods between producer and buyer possible. The three basic functions that intermediaries perform are summarized in Exhibit 11.3.

Transactional functions involve contacting and communicating with prospective buyers to make them aware of existing products and explain their features, advantages, and benefits. Intermediaries in the supply chain also provide *logistical* functions. **Logistics** is the process of strategically managing the efficient flow and storage of raw materials, in-process inventory, and finished goods from point of origin to point of consumption. Logistical functions include transporting,

EXHIBIT 11.3

Marketing Channel Functions Performed by Intermediaries

Type of Function	Description
Transactional Functions	**Contacting and promoting:** Contacting potential customers, promoting products, and soliciting orders
	Negotiating: Determining how many goods or services to buy and sell, type of transportation to use, when to deliver, and method and timing of payment
	Risk Taking: Assuming the risk of owning inventory
Logistical Functions	**Physically distributing:** Transporting and sorting goods to overcome temporal and spatial discrepancies
	Storing: Maintaining inventories and protecting goods
	Sorting: Overcoming discrepancies of quantity and assortment by
	Sorting out: Breaking down a heterogeneous supply into separate homogeneous stocks
	Accumulation: Combining similar stocks into a larger homogeneous supply
	Allocation: Breaking a homogeneous supply into smaller and smaller lots ("breaking bulk")
	Assorting: Combining products into collections or assortments that buyers want available at one place
Facilitating Functions	**Researching:** Gathering information about other channel members and consumers
	Financing: Extending credit and other financial services to facilitate the flow of goods through the channel to the final consumer

storing, sorting out, accumulating, allocating, and assorting products for the purpose of serving customer requirements. For example, grading agricultural products typifies the sorting-out process while consolidation of many lots of grade A eggs from different sources into one lot illustrates the accumulation process. Supermarkets or other retailers perform the assorting function by assembling thousands of different items that match their customers' desires. Similarly, while many large companies have direct channels, many small companies depend on wholesalers to distribute their products. For example, small beverage manufacturers like Jones Soda or Pop Shoppe depend on wholesalers to distribute their products in a marketplace dominated by large competitors like Coca-Cola and Pepsi.

The third basic channel function, *facilitating*, includes research and financing. Research provides information about channel members and consumers by getting answers to key questions: Who are the buyers? Where are they located? Why do they buy? Financing ensures that channel members have the money to keep products moving through the channel to the ultimate consumer.

A single company may provide one, two, or all three functions. Consider Dominion Citrus Limited, a fresh produce and food processing distributor located in Markham, Ontario. Dominion provides transactional, logistical, and facilitating channel functions as it procures, processes, repacks, warehouses, and distributes fresh produce to grocery chains and independent grocery outlets in Ontario and Quebec.

Although individual channel members can be added to or deleted from a channel, someone must still perform the essential channel functions. They can be performed by producers, end users, channel intermediaries, and even non-member channel participants. For example, if a manufacturer decides to eliminate its fleet of delivery trucks, it must still have a way to move goods to its customers. The transportation function may be taken on by a wholesaler or an independent trucking company. Other nonchannel member companies may take on the research function (a market research company), the promoting function (an advertising agency), the storage function (a warehouse operator), or the financing function (a bank).

Define the types of channel intermediaries and describe their functions and activities

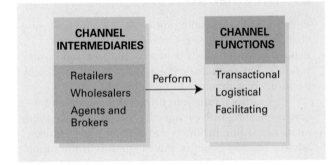

CHANNEL INTERMEDIARIES		CHANNEL FUNCTIONS
Retailers	Perform →	Transactional
Wholesalers		Logistical
Agents and Brokers		Facilitating

③ CHANNEL STRUCTURES

Describe the channel structures for consumer and business products and discuss alternative channel arrangements

A product can take many routes to reach its final consumer. Marketers search for the most efficient channel from the many alternatives available. Marketing a consumer convenience good like gum or candy differs from marketing a specialty good like a Mercedes-Benz. The two products require very different distribution channels. Likewise, the appropriate channel for a major equipment supplier like Bombardier would be unsuitable for an accessory equipment producer like Black & Decker.

CHANNELS FOR CONSUMER PRODUCTS

Exhibit 11.4 illustrates the four ways manufacturers can route products to consumers. Producers use the **direct channel** to sell directly to consumers. Direct marketing activities—including telemarketing, mail-order and catalogue shopping, and forms of electronic retailing like on-line shopping and shop-at-home television networks—are good examples of this type of channel structure. For example, home computer users can purchase Dell computers directly over the telephone or directly from Dell's website. There are no intermediaries. Producer-owned stores and factory outlet stores—like Sherwin-Williams, Polo Ralph Lauren, Nike, Club Monaco, Tilley, Lululemon Athletica, Mountain Equipment Co-Op, and Body Shop—are other examples of direct channels. Farmers' markets are also direct channels.

At the other end of the spectrum, an *agent/broker channel* involves a fairly complicated process. Agent/broker channels are typically used in markets with many small manufacturers and many retailers that lack the resources to find each other. Agents or

direct channel
A distribution channel in which producers sell directly to consumers.

EXHIBIT 11.4

Marketing Channels for Consumer Products

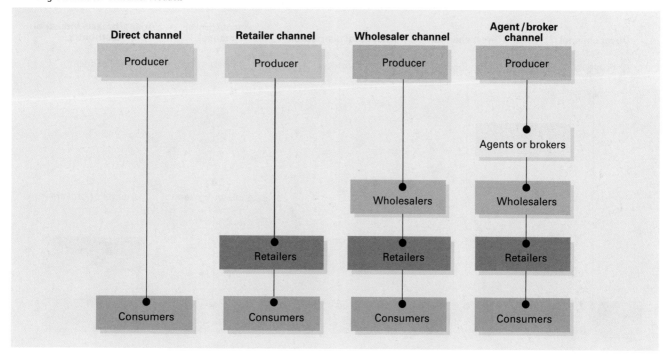

brokers bring manufacturers and wholesalers together for negotiations, but they do not take title to merchandise. Ownership passes directly to one or more wholesalers and then to retailers. Finally, retailers sell to the ultimate consumer of the product. For example, a food broker may represent buyers or sellers of grocery products. The broker acts on behalf of many different producers and negotiates the sale of their products to wholesalers that specialize in foodstuffs. These wholesalers in turn sell to grocers and convenience stores.

Most consumer products are sold through distribution channels similar to the other two alternatives: the retailer channel and the wholesaler channel. A *retailer channel* is most common when the retailer is large and can buy in large quantities directly from the manufacturer. Walmart, Zellers, Canadian Tire, and car dealers are examples of retailers that often bypass a wholesaler. A *wholesaler channel* is generally used for low-cost items that are frequently purchased, such as candy, cigarettes, and magazines—especially when these products are sold to smaller outlets like convenience stores. For example, M&M/Mars sells candies and chocolates to wholesalers in large quantities. The wholesalers then break these quantities into smaller amounts for sale to individual retailers.

CHANNELS FOR BUSINESS-TO-BUSINESS AND INDUSTRIAL PRODUCTS

As Exhibit 11.5 illustrates, five channel structures are common in business-to-business and industrial markets. First, direct channels are very common in business-to-business and industrial markets. For example, manufacturers buy large quantities of raw materials, major equipment, processed materials, and supplies directly from other manufacturers. Manufacturers that require suppliers to meet detailed technical specifications often prefer direct channels. The direct communication required between Ford Motor Company and its suppliers, for example, along with the tremendous size of the orders, makes anything but a direct channel impractical. The channel from producer to government buyers is also a direct channel. Since much of government buying is done through bidding, a direct channel is attractive. Dell Computer

EXHIBIT 11.5

Channels for Business and Industrial Products

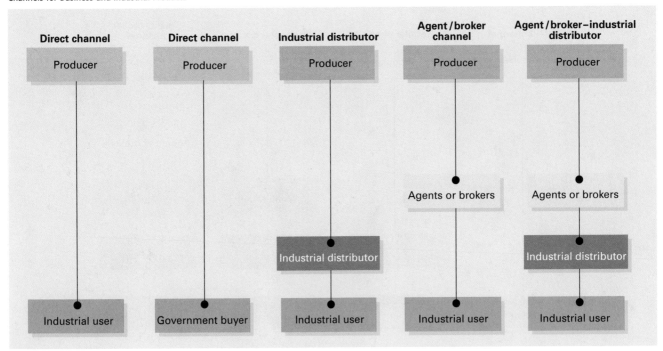

Corporation, for example, a top seller of desktop computers to federal, provincial, and local governments, sells its computers through direct channels.

Companies selling standardized items of moderate or low value often rely on *industrial distributors*. In many ways, an industrial distributor is like a supermarket for organizations. Industrial distributors are wholesalers and channel members that buy and take title to products. Moreover, they usually keep inventories of their products and sell and service them. Often small manufacturers cannot afford to employ their own sales forces. Instead, they rely on manufacturers' representatives or selling agents to sell to either industrial distributors or users.

Today, the traditional industrial distributor is facing many challenges. Manufacturers are getting bigger due to growth and mergers. Through technology, manufacturers and customers have access to information that wasn't previously available. Increasingly, companies are using the Internet to create more direct and efficient business-to-business channels. The Internet has enabled virtual distributors to emerge. An example is **www.pumpbiz.com**, which sells pumps for chemicals, wastewater, sumps, water, coolants, and all other industrial process fluids. The site offers 24/7 purchasing and provides access to information on major manufacturers of pumps, including side-by-side comparisons and reviews.

The Internet has also led to the emergence of three other new forms of industrial distribution. Some companies serve as agents that link buyers and sellers and charge a fee. For example, Expedia.com links business travellers to airlines, hotels, and car rental companies. A second form of marketplace has been developed by existing companies looking for ways to drop the intermediary from the supply chain. For example, the WorldWide Retail Exchange is a marketplace created by major retailers in North America, Europe, and Asia. Retailers use the exchange to make purchases that in the past would have required telephone, fax, or face-to-face sales calls. Combined sales through the WorldWide Retail Exchange are over $800 billion, and retailers using the exchange estimate they have saved approximately 15 percent on their purchasing costs. Finally, the third type of Internet marketplace is a "private exchange." Private exchanges allow companies to automate their supply chains while sharing information only with select suppliers. Home Hardware and Hewlett-Packard, for example, use private exchanges to manage their inventory supplies.[2]

dual distribution (multiple distribution)
The use of two or more channels to distribute the same product to target markets.

ALTERNATIVE CHANNEL ARRANGEMENTS

Rarely does a producer use just one type of channel to move its product. It usually employs several different or alternative channels, which include multiple channels, nontraditional channels, and strategic channel alliances.

Multiple Channels

When a producer selects two or more channels to distribute the same product to target markets, this is called **dual distribution** (or **multiple distribution**). For example, Whirlpool sells its washers, dryers, and refrigerators directly to home and apartment builders and contractors, but it also sells these same appliances to retail stores that sell to consumers. Avon, which has traditionally sold its products only through a company sales force, now sells on-line and through retail stores.[3] Similarly, Dell Computer Corporation made a radical departure from its direct channel sales model by opening retail kiosks in shopping malls as a way to increase its market share of home computers. Dell has also tried selling computers directly to home users through cable shopping channels. Most recently, Dell has reached an agreement with Walmart to sell Dell Computers through Walmart retail outlets.

Adding a new supply chain can renew a company's image. Such is the case with Avon, the leading company in direct selling, which broke its own mould with the launch of beComing, the company's first brand distributed exclusively in retail outlets.

SOURCE: COURTESY OF BECOMING

Nontraditional Channels

Often nontraditional channel arrangements help differentiate a firm's product from the competition. For example, manufacturers may decide to use nontraditional channels such as the Internet, mail-order channels, or infomercials to sell products instead of going through traditional retailer channels. Although nontraditional channels may limit a brand's coverage, they can give a producer serving a niche market a way to gain market access and customer attention without having to establish channel intermediaries. Nontraditional channels can also provide another avenue for sales. For example, a London publisher has begun selling short stories through a vending machine in the London Underground. Instead of the traditional book format, the stories are printed like folded maps, which makes them an easy-to-read alternative for commuters.[4]

Strategic Channel Alliances

Companies often form **strategic channel alliances**, which enable them to use another manufacturer's already established channel. Alliances are used most often when the creation of marketing channel relationships may be too expensive and time-consuming. Starbucks and Kraft signed a long-term licensing arrangement to stock Starbucks coffee on supermarket shelves. Under the arrangement, Starbucks will roast and package the coffee and Kraft will market and distribute it in supermarkets. The Starbucks coffee will be sold by Kraft's sales force. Later, when Starbucks developed a ready-to-drink (RTD) coffee beverage, it signed an agreement with Pepsi to bottle and distribute its RTD coffee wherever Pepsi products were sold.[5]

Strategic channel alliances are proving to be more successful for growing businesses than mergers and acquisitions.

Why Just Collapse The Supply Chain When You Can Flatten The Competition?

Rockwell Automation can link your manufacturing operations to your business goals.

e-Manufacturing isn't a new way to make a product. It's the advanced way to link your resources together to achieve significantly greater efficiencies.

Rockwell Automation integrated plant-floor architecture, with seamless connectivity to your information systems, can enable your enterprise for build-to-order production and nonstop operation. Helping you gain the flexibility to adjust to changing market conditions.

By creating an e-Manufacturing strategy, which links your manufacturing environment to your business environment, you share critical information across your enterprise. And synchronize your supply chain.

e-Manufacturing solutions from Rockwell Automation, your Complete Automation™ provider. Helping you build a streamlined model of competitive strength. For more information, visit our web site: **www.rockwellautomation.com.**

Rockwell Automation

SOURCE: COURTESY OF ROCKWELL AUTOMATION

Supply chain management is the key to competitiveness, and many companies market tools to help other businesses manage their supply chains effectively. Rockwell Automation is one such solutions provider, helping companies share critical production information across the business enterprise.

strategic channel alliance
A cooperative agreement between business firms to use the other's already established distribution channel.

This is especially true in global markets where cultural differences, distance, and other barriers can prove challenging. For example, Heinz has a strategic alliance with Kagome, one of Japan's largest food companies. The companies are working together to find ways to reduce operating costs while expanding both brands' market presence globally.[6]

REVIEW LEARNING OUTCOME 3

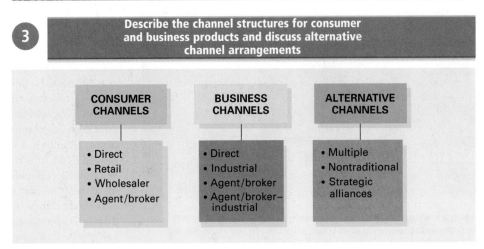

3 Describe the channel structures for consumer and business products and discuss alternative channel arrangements

CONSUMER CHANNELS	BUSINESS CHANNELS	ALTERNATIVE CHANNELS
• Direct • Retail • Wholesaler • Agent/broker	• Direct • Industrial • Agent/broker • Agent/broker–industrial	• Multiple • Nontraditional • Strategic alliances

4 SUPPLY CHAIN MANAGEMENT

Define supply chain management and discuss its benefits

supply chain management
A management system that coordinates and integrates all of the activities performed by supply chain members into a seamless process, from the source to the point of consumption, resulting in enhanced customer and economic value.

In today's sophisticated marketplace, many companies are focusing on their supply chain and turning to supply chain management for competitive advantages. The goal of **supply chain management** is to coordinate and integrate all the activities performed by supply chain members into a seamless process from the source to the point of consumption, ultimately giving supply chain managers "total visibility" of the supply chain both inside and outside the firm. The philosophy behind supply chain management is that by visualizing the entire supply chain, supply chain managers can maximize strengths and efficiencies at each level of the process to create a highly competitive, customer-driven supply system that is able to respond immediately to changes in supply and demand.

An important element of supply chain management is that it is completely customer-driven. During the mass-production era, manufacturers produced standardized products that were "pushed" down through the supply channel to the consumer. In contrast, in today's marketplace, customers expect to receive product configurations and services matched to their unique needs. Dell, for example, builds computers according to its customers' precise specifications, such as the amount of RAM memory; type of monitor, modem, or optical drive; and amount of hard disk space. Similarly, car companies offer customers the option to customize even economy-priced cars. For less than $25,000, customers can order a Ford Mustang with a V-6 engine, a six-disc CD changer, MP3 player, and eight speakers. The focus is on pulling products into the marketplace and partnering with members of the supply chain to enhance customer value. Customizing an automobile is now possible because of new supply chain relationships between the automobile manufacturers and the after-market auto-parts industry.[7]

This reversal of the flow of demand from a "push" to a "pull" system has resulted in a radical reformulation of market expectations as well as traditional marketing, production, and distribution functions. Through the coordinated partnership of suppliers, manufacturers, wholesalers, and retailers working together along the entire supply chain, supply chain management allows companies to respond with the unique product configurations and mix of services demanded by the customer. Today, supply chain management plays a dual role: first, as a *communicator* of customer demand that extends from the point of sale all the way back to the supplier, and second, as a

334 Part 4 Distribution Decisions

physical flow process that engineers the timely and cost-effective movement of goods through the entire source-to-consumer supply pipeline.

Supply chain managers are responsible for making strategic channel decisions such as coordinating the sourcing and procurement of raw materials, scheduling production, processing orders, managing inventory, transporting and storing supplies and finished goods, dealing with returns, and coordinating customer service activities. Supply chain managers are also responsible for the management of information that flows through the supply chain. Coordinating the relationships between the company and its external partners, such as vendors, carriers, and third-party companies, is also a critical function of supply chain management. Because supply chain managers play such a major role in both cost control and customer satisfaction, they are more valuable than ever.[8]

In summary, supply chain managers are responsible for directing raw materials and parts to the production department and the finished or semifinished product through warehouses and eventually to the intermediary or end user. Above all, supply chain management begins and ends with the customer. Instead of forcing into the market a product that may or may not sell quickly, supply chain managers react to actual customer demand. By doing so, they minimize the flow of raw materials, finished product, and packaging materials at every point in the supply chain, resulting in lower costs and increased customer value. Exhibit 11.6 depicts a typical supply chain model that managers attempt to optimize for their firm and customer benefit.

EXHIBIT 11.6

A Typical Supply Chain Management Process

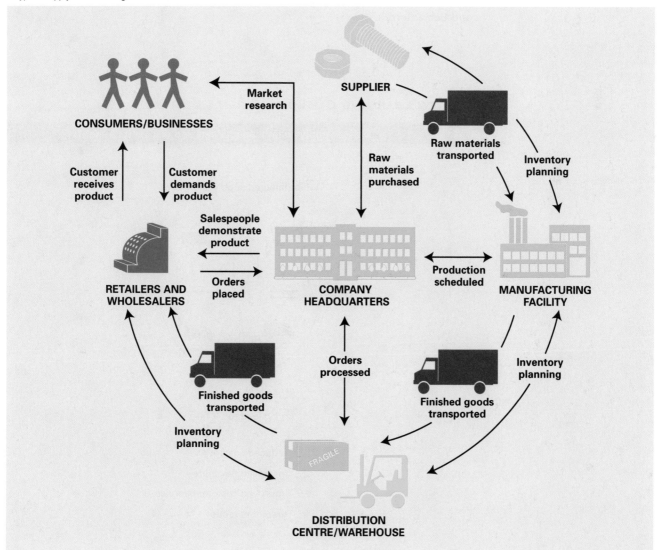

Dreyer's Ice Cream's successful logistics system starts with its state-of-the-art manufacturing facility. The return on investment the company experienced subsequent to its supply chain upgrades was extremely impressive.

SOURCE: ASSOCIATED PRESS

BENEFITS OF SUPPLY CHAIN MANAGEMENT

Supply chain management is a key means of differentiation for a firm and a critical component in marketing and corporate strategy. Supply chain–oriented companies commonly report lower inventory, transportation, warehousing, and packaging costs; greater supply chain flexibility; improved customer service; and higher revenues. Research has shown a clear relationship between supply chain performance and profitability. Specific benefits from effective implementation of supply chain procedures include an almost 20 percent increase in cash flow, a more than 50 percent increase in flexibility of supply chain activities, and a reduction of 5 to 10 percent in supply chain costs.[9]

Dreyer's ice cream has built its success on its logistics system. The company invested $150 million in a new fleet of trucks, manufacturing centres, and a computerized delivery system that enables dispatchers to design delivery routes around sales volume, distance, traffic patterns, road conditions, and a store's hours of operation. As a return on its investment, the company has experienced a 33 percent increase in sales accounts, eliminated many unnecessary stops, saved $11 million in gas and labour hours, and increased its net income. In fact, the system provides such strong customer service capability and cost savings that nearly one-third of Dreyer's revenue comes from deals to distribute its competitors' brands such as Häagen-Dazs and Ben & Jerry's.[10]

REVIEW LEARNING OUTCOME 4

4   **Define supply chain management and discuss its benefits**

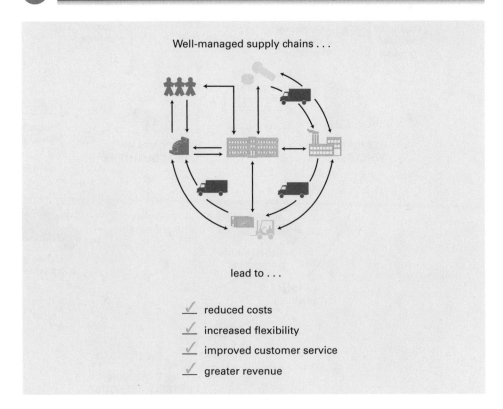

Well-managed supply chains . . .

lead to . . .

✓ reduced costs

✓ increased flexibility

✓ improved customer service

✓ greater revenue

Customer Experience

> RESPONSE TO CUSTOMER UNPREDICTABILITY IN THE AUTOMOTIVE INDUSTRY

In the ultra-competitive automobile industry, delivering the right car to the customer, in the right colour, with the right features, at the right price, and in the shortest amount of time possible, is a critical determinant of customer satisfaction. Automobile makers both domestic and foreign know this but are faced with a competing goal as well—minimizing inventory costs. Auto makers need to sell as many cars as possible but they also need to be sure to make only as many cars as customers will demand in order to be profitable. A big reason for the bankruptcies of General Motors and Chrysler in 2009 was the fact that both companies had well over 100 days of inventory of their cars and had to steeply discount their products to move them off dealers' lots. This led to very small margins or losses on many of the car sales.

The companies that build cars in Canada (Chrysler, General Motors, Ford, Toyota, and Honda) as well as the companies that import cars into Canada for sale (Hyundai, Mazda, Nissan, Volkswagen, Mercedes-Benz, Kia, and others), are turning to lean supply chain management principles in order to get the job done. A lean supply chain is one that has been streamlined to reduce waste and other non-value-added activities, minimizes unnecessary inventory, reduces time delays, and lowers production costs.

Auto makers have adopted lean supply chain principles as a method for improving customer outcomes. For example, General Motors is using technologies such as radio-frequency identification (RFID) to track parts and finished automobiles' locations. Using RFID, managers can view the locations of components or finished goods on an electronic colour-coded map that tracks in real time,

so the company has constant, complete visibility of inventories and avoids unnecessary ordering of parts and/or manufacturing of models that are already represented within a shipment or geographic area. The company can then reinvest these savings into parts and finished cars that are actually needed at dealerships and/or manufacturing and service facilities. Tracking parts is especially important at the General Motors plant in Ingersoll, Ontario, where GM assembles the Equinox and Terrain models with parts coming to the plant from Mexico, Japan, South Korea, the Philippines, and China. The parts are travelling different distances and take different amounts of time to arrive, but can't be delayed as a parts shortage will stop production and result in significant lost sales.

Executives at Toyota Canada also point out another key benefit of lean supply chain management: nothing is manufactured until the customer places an order. Then and only then does the company place a replacement unit into production. As one manager at Toyota states, "Most production schedules are based on (sales forecasts). . . . Production should be based on sold end-customer orders, not forecasts. . . . (This allows us to) eliminate just-in-case ordering and the 'noise' in the supply chain." By ordering and manufacturing on a lean, just-in-time basis, everyone in the supply chain holds less unwanted inventory and customers get the car they wanted quickly and at the lowest possible price. In other words, a lean supply chain enables customers to buy exactly what they wanted, and the automobile company saves money at the same time by making only what they sell. Isn't that what is best for everyone?[11]

SOURCE: DAVID HANNON, "LEVERAGE RFID FOR STREAMLINED LOGISTICS," PURCHASING MAGAZINE, APRIL 2008, 20; BILL VLASIC, "GLOBAL SUV FUELS GM'S REVOLUTION," DETROIT NEWS, AUGUST 1, 2004, 1A, 8A.

 5 MAKING CHANNEL STRATEGY DECISIONS

Discuss the issues that influence channel strategy

Devising a marketing channel strategy requires several critical decisions. Supply chain managers must decide what role distribution will play in the overall marketing strategy. In addition, they must be sure that the channel strategy chosen is consistent with product, promotion, and pricing strategies. In making these decisions, marketing managers must analyze what factors will influence the choice of channel and what level of distribution intensity will be appropriate.

FACTORS AFFECTING CHANNEL CHOICE

Supply chain managers must answer many questions before choosing a marketing channel. The final choice depends on the analysis of several factors that often interact. These factors can be grouped as market factors, product factors, and producer factors.

Market Factors

Among the most important market factors affecting the choice of distribution channel are target customer considerations. Specifically, supply chain managers should answer the following questions: Who are the potential customers? What do they buy? Where do they buy? When do they buy? How do they buy? Additionally, the choice of channel depends on whether the producer is selling to consumers or to industrial customers. Industrial customers' buying habits are very different from those of consumers. Industrial customers tend to buy in larger quantities and require more customer service. Consumers usually buy in very small quantities and sometimes do not mind if they get little or no service, such as in discount stores like Walmart or Zellers.

The geographic location and size of the market are also important to channel selection. As a rule, if the target market is concentrated in one or more specific areas, direct selling through a sales force is appropriate. When markets are more widely dispersed, intermediaries will be less expensive. The size of the market also influences channel choice. Generally, a very large market requires more intermediaries. For instance, Procter & Gamble has to reach millions of consumers with its many brands of household goods. It needs many intermediaries, including wholesalers and retailers, to do this.

Product Factors

Products that are more complex, customized, and expensive tend to benefit from shorter and more direct marketing channels. These types of products sell better through a direct sales force. Examples include pharmaceuticals, scientific instruments, airplanes, and mainframe computer systems. On the other hand, the more standardized a product is, the longer its distribution channel can be and the greater the number of intermediaries that can be involved. For example, chewing gum is about the same from producer to producer. Chewing gum is also very inexpensive. As a result, the distribution channel for gum tends to involve many wholesalers and retailers.

The product's life cycle is also an important factor in choosing a marketing channel. In fact, the choice of channel may change over the life of the product. For example, when photocopiers were first available, a direct sales force typically sold them. Now, however, photocopiers can be found in several places, including warehouse clubs, electronics superstores, and mail-order catalogues. As products become more common and less intimidating to users, producers tend to look for alternative channels. Gatorade was originally sold to sports teams, gyms, and fitness clubs. As the drink became more popular, supermarket channels were added, followed by convenience stores and drugstores. Now Gatorade can be found in vending machines and fast-food restaurants.

Another factor is the delicacy of the product. Perishable products like vegetables and milk have a relatively short life span. Fragile products like china and crystal require a minimum amount of handling. Therefore, both require fairly short marketing channels. On-line retailers such as eBay facilitate the sale of unusual or difficult-to-find products that benefit from a direct channel.

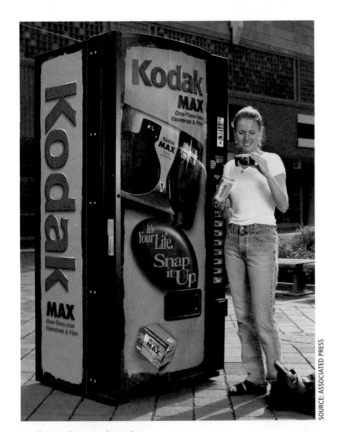

Vending machines are becoming a popular way to sell everything from boxer shorts to cameras. Kodak teamed up with Maytag to roll out thousands of camera-and-film vending machines. Kodak wants to satisfy instant cravings for a must-have snapshot in places like amusement parks, resorts, and the beach.

SOURCE: ASSOCIATED PRESS

Producer Factors

Several factors pertaining to the producer are important to the selection of a marketing channel. In general, producers with large financial, managerial, and marketing resources are better able to use more direct channels. These producers have the ability to hire and train their own sales forces, warehouse their own goods, and extend credit to their customers. Smaller or weaker firms, on the other hand, must rely on intermediaries to provide these services for them. Compared to producers with only one or two product lines, producers that sell many products in a related area are able to choose channels that are more direct. Sales expenses then can be spread over more products.

EXHIBIT 11.7

Intensity of Distribution Levels

Intensity Level	Distribution Intensity Objective	Number of Intermediaries in Each Market	Examples
Intensive	Achieve mass-market selling; popular with health and beauty aids and convenience goods that must be available everywhere	Many	Pepsi-Cola, Frito-Lay potato chips, Huggies diapers, Alpo dog food, Crayola crayons
Selective	Work closely with selected intermediaries who meet certain criteria; typically used for shopping goods and some specialty goods	Several	Donna Karan clothing, Hewlett-Packard printers, Burton snowboards, Aveda aromatherapy products
Exclusive	Work with a single intermediary for products that require special resources or positioning; typically used for specialty goods and major industrial equipment	One	BMW cars, Rolex watches, Valiant industrial robotics

A producer's desire to control pricing, positioning, brand image, and customer support also tends to influence channel selection. For instance, firms that sell products with exclusive brand images, such as designer perfumes and clothing, usually avoid channels in which discount retailers are present. Manufacturers of upscale products, such as Gucci (handbags) and Godiva (chocolates), may sell their wares only in expensive stores in order to maintain an image of exclusivity.

LEVELS OF DISTRIBUTION INTENSITY

Organizations have three options with regard to intensity of distribution: intensive distribution, selective distribution, or exclusive distribution (see Exhibit 11.7).

Intensive Distribution

intensive distribution
A form of distribution aimed at having a product available in every outlet where target customers might want to buy it.

Intensive distribution is a form of distribution aimed at maximum market coverage. The manufacturer tries to have the product available in every outlet where potential customers might want to buy it. If buyers are unwilling to search for a product (as is true of convenience goods and operating supplies), the product must be very accessible to buyers, which often means using a lengthy channel. For example, candy, chips, and other snack foods are found in almost every type of retail store imaginable. These foods are typically sold to retailers in small quantities by a food or candy wholesaler. Concord Confections, which manufactures Dubble Bubble chewing gum in Canada, could not afford to sell its gum directly to every service station, drugstore, supermarket, and discount store across the country. The cost would be too high. But wholesalers, selling gum along with many other products, can reach all of these retail outlets.

Selective Distribution

selective distribution
A form of distribution achieved by screening dealers to eliminate all but a few in any single area.

Selective distribution is achieved by screening dealers and retailers to eliminate all but a few in any single area. Because only a few are chosen, the consumer must seek out the product. For example, when Heeling Sports Ltd. launched Heelys, thick-soled sneakers with a wheel embedded in each heel, the company hired a group of teens to perform Heelys exhibitions in targeted malls, skate parks, and on university and college campuses across the country. Then the company made the decision to avoid large stores and to distribute the shoes only through selected mall retailers and skate shops in order to position the product as "cool and kind of irreverent."

Selective distribution strategies often hinge on a manufacturer's desire to maintain a superior product image so as to be able to charge a premium price. Tilley clothing, for instance, is sold only in select retail outlets, mainly full-price department stores, while Devinci bicycles are sold only through bicycle retailers and not in large

exclusive distribution
A form of distribution that establishes one or very few dealers within a given area.

REVIEW LEARNING OUTCOME 5

 5 Discuss the issues that influence channel strategy

Factors	Distribution
Market	Intensive
Product	Selective
Producer	Exclusive

Channel Strategy

stores like Sears, Canadian Tire, or Walmart. Likewise, premium pet food brands such as Hill's Pet Nutrition Canada and Ralston Purina's Pro Plan are distributed chiefly through specialty pet food stores and veterinarians, rather than mass retailers, so that a premium price can be charged. On the other hand, when Procter & Gamble purchased premium pet food brand Iams, it expanded Iams's selective distribution strategy to include mass retailers. This change in distribution strategy created channel conflict with the breeders and veterinarians who had been the brand's primary source of strength.

Exclusive Distribution

The most restrictive form of market coverage is **exclusive distribution**, which entails only one or very few dealers within a given area. Because buyers may have to search or travel extensively to buy the product, exclusive distribution is usually confined to consumer specialty goods, a few shopping goods, and major industrial equipment. Products such as Rolls-Royce automobiles, Chris-Craft powerboats, Swift Canoes, and Pettibone tower cranes are distributed under exclusive arrangements. Sometimes exclusive territories are granted by new companies (such as franchisers) to obtain market coverage in a particular area. Limited distribution may also serve to project an exclusive image for the product.

Retailers and wholesalers may be unwilling to commit the time and money necessary to promote and service a product unless the manufacturer guarantees them an exclusive territory. This arrangement shields the dealer from direct competition and enables it to be the main beneficiary of the manufacturer's promotion efforts in that geographic area. With exclusive distribution, channels of communication are usually well established as the manufacturer works with a limited number of dealers. Exclusive distribution also takes place within a retailer's store rather than a geographic area. Toys are often made exclusively for certain retailers and cannot be found elsewhere. In return, the retailer agrees not to carry competing brands from other manufacturers.

6 MANAGING CHANNEL RELATIONSHIPS

Explain channel leadership, conflict, and partnering

A marketing channel is more than a set of institutions linked by economic ties. Social relationships play an important role in building unity among channel members. A critical aspect of supply chain management, therefore, is managing the social relationships among channel members to achieve synergy. The basic social dimensions of channels are power, control, leadership, conflict, and partnering.

CHANNEL POWER, CONTROL, AND LEADERSHIP

channel power
The capacity of a particular marketing channel member to control or influence the behaviour of other channel members.

channel control
A situation that occurs when one marketing channel member intentionally affects another member's behaviour.

channel leader (channel captain)
A member of a marketing channel that exercises authority and power over the activities of other channel members.

Channel power is a channel member's capacity to control or influence the behaviour of other channel members. **Channel control** occurs when one channel member affects another member's behaviour. To achieve control, a channel member assumes channel leadership and exercises authority and power. This member is termed the **channel leader**, or **channel captain**. In one marketing channel, a manufacturer may be the leader because it controls new-product designs and product availability. In another, a retailer may be the channel leader because it wields power and control over the retail price, inventory levels, and postsale service.

The exercise of channel power is a routine element of many business activities in which the outcome is who has control over various elements of a company's brands. For example, the Sheraton Hotel chain operates hundreds of hotels across North America and around the globe, most of which are owned by franchisees. As with many franchises, it is in the best interest of the parent company to closely monitor and control operations to prevent the brand name from being devalued. However, when the company asked its franchisees to invest nearly $4 billion of their own money to make improvements (such as redesigned lobbies and bathrooms), many franchise owners balked and a power struggle ensued. Eventually, the parent company and franchise group came to an agreement detailing the hotel features Sheraton would control, such as lobby design, room layout, and even which coffee brand would be provided in the rooms, and which would be controlled by the owners (including number of sheets provided for each bed).[12]

CHANNEL CONFLICT

channel conflict
A clash of goals and methods between distribution channel members.

Inequitable channel relationships often lead to **channel conflict**, which is a clash of goals and methods among the members of a distribution channel. Channel conflict is not always bad. Conflict can arise when some traditional channel members refuse to keep pace with the times. Removing an outdated channel intermediary may result in lower costs for the entire channel. The Internet has forced many intermediaries to offer services such as merchandise tracking and inventory availability on-line.

Conflicts among channel members can be due to many different situations and factors. Often, conflict arises because channel members have conflicting goals. For instance, athletic footwear retailers want to sell as many different shoes as possible in order to maximize profits, regardless of whether the shoe is manufactured by Nike, Adidas, or Saucony. But as a manufacturer, Nike would like to have the retailer concentrate on its brand and achieve desired levels of Nike sales.

Conflict can also arise when channel members fail to fulfill the expectations of other channel members—for example, when a franchisee does not follow the rules set down by the franchiser, or when communications channels break down between channel members. As an example, if a manufacturer reduces the length of warranty coverage and fails to communicate this change to dealers, conflict may occur when dealers make repairs with the expectation that they will be reimbursed by the manufacturer. Furthermore, ideological differences and different perceptions of reality can cause conflict among channel members. For instance, retailers may believe "the customer is always right" and offer very liberal return policies. Wholesalers and manufacturers may feel that people "try to get something for nothing" or don't follow product instructions carefully. These differing views of allowable returns will undoubtedly cause some conflict.

horizontal conflict
A channel conflict that occurs among channel members on the same level.

Conflict within a channel can be either horizontal or vertical. **Horizontal conflict** occurs among channel members on the same level, such as two or more different wholesalers or two or more different retailers that handle the same manufacturer's brands. This type of channel conflict is found most often when manufacturers practise dual or multiple distribution strategies. For instance, there was considerable channel conflict after computer manufacturers began distributing their computers beyond the traditional computer resellers, through discount stores, department stores, warehouse clubs, and giant electronics superstores such as Future Shop. Horizontal conflict may also occur when channel members on the same level feel they are being treated differently by a manufacturer.

vertical conflict
A channel conflict that occurs between different levels in a marketing channel, most typically between the manufacturer and wholesaler or between the manufacturer and retailer.

While many regard horizontal conflict as healthy competition, more serious is **vertical conflict**, which occurs between different levels in a marketing channel, most typically between the manufacturer and wholesaler or the manufacturer and retailer. Producer-versus-wholesaler conflict occurs when the producer chooses to bypass the wholesaler and deal directly with the consumer or retailer. For example, conflict arose when several producers agreed to Walmart's request to deal with it directly, bypassing intermediaries altogether.

Dual distribution strategies can also cause vertical conflict in the channel. For example, high-end fashion designers have traditionally sold their products through luxury retailers. Interested in increasing sales and gaining additional presentation control, many designers such as Giorgio Armani, Donna Karan, and Louis Vuitton began opening their own boutiques in the same shopping centres with specialty retailers carrying their products. Similarly, manufacturers that are experimenting with selling to customers directly over the Internet are creating conflict with their traditional retailing intermediaries. For example, Baby Jogger worked closely with retailers to build a business with $15 million in sales. But when numerous look-alike products began appearing on the market, the company decided to try to increase sales by selling directly to consumers on the Internet. Angry retailers responded by promoting other brands. Recognizing how important the retailers were to its success, Baby Jogger halted Internet sales.[13]

Producers and retailers may also disagree over the terms of the sale or other aspects of the business relationship. When Procter & Gamble introduced "everyday low pricing" to its retail channel members, a strategy designed to standardize wholesale prices and eliminate most trade promotions, many retailers retaliated. Some cut the variety of P&G sizes they carried or eliminated marginal brands. Others moved P&G brands from prime shelf space to less visible shelves.

CHANNEL PARTNERING

Regardless of the locus of power, channel members rely heavily on one another. Even the most powerful manufacturers depend on dealers to sell their products; even the most powerful retailers require the products provided by suppliers. In sharp contrast

Ethics in Marketing

 THE BATTLE OF PORT ELGIN

For better than two years, lawyers for Walmart Canada and its Canadian real estate partner, SmartCentres, battled with lawyers from Loblaw to build a shopping centre to be anchored by a 120,000-square-foot Walmart store on a parcel of land Walmart and SmartCentres had purchased in Port Elgin, Ontario. Loblaw, the largest supermarket operator in Canada and the owner of the only supermarket in Port Elgin, strongly opposed the Walmart development. The Walmart store would have a major grocery section to compete with Loblaw.

Port Elgin is on the shore of Lake Huron, a drive of a little more than two hours from Toronto. Port Elgin has a population of more than 8,000, with nearly 13,000 in surrounding Saugeen Shores, and this population grows to over 40,000 with the arrival of cottagers in the summer. The Port Elgin market is high income and is expected to grow by more than 50 percent over the next 20 years. Loblaw would like to keep this market to itself and strongly opposed the rezoning application made by SmartCentres. This case of horizontal channel conflict between the two retail giants did not involve the typical price cuts we see in retail battles but, instead, a battle between lawyers and consultants.

Loblaw spokesman Geoffrey Wilson stated that the grocer didn't object just for the sake of objecting. Loblaw objected because there wasn't enough business in Port Elgin to support two large grocery retailers. Andrew Pelletier, a Walmart Canada spokesman disagreed: "We find it very unfortunate that they would resort to these tactics to try to maintain what amounts to monopolies in these markets. They're ultimately trying to limit competition." Townspeople already were driving 45 minutes to shop at Walmart stores in nearby towns, said Saugeen Shores' mayor Mark Kraemer. While away on these shopping trips, they patronized other businesses too. "We need the dollars retained in our community," Mayor Kraemer said.

SmartCentres' director of land development, Joshua Kaufman, spent many months studying the Port Elgin market. Based on his own work and studies from a number of other consultants, Kaufman recommended that SmartCentres buy a parcel of land just off Highway 21 leading into town. Once the land was acquired, SmartCentres applied for a zoning change to allow for larger retail space than was currently permitted. This zoning application was approved by Port Elgin town staff and a public meeting was called.

Loblaw hired a consultant of its own to review Walmart's market analysis. The Loblaw consultant advised the Port Elgin town council that it was setting itself up for an overabundance of grocery store space, and a Loblaw lawyer submitted a letter expressing Loblaw's concerns. Further, Loblaw management indicated that it might be expanding its own supermarket in the town. Loblaw recommended that Port Elgin undertake its own studies before allowing for any zoning changes or, at a minimum, limit the size of the grocery section in any new Walmart store.

"It's unrealistic to presume that you can retain a monopoly in a community forever," Mayor Kraemer said. "It's nothing but a delay tactic to keep Walmart out as long as they can." The Port Elgin town council approved the zoning changes as requested by Walmart. The final go-ahead for the Walmart development was further delayed, however. Loblaw appealed the zoning change to the Ontario Municipal Board.[14]

What do you think of Loblaw's fight to keep Walmart and SmartCentres from developing their property? Should Loblaw appeal a zoning change approved by the Port Elgin town council? Does Loblaw have only its own interests at heart or could the company truly be concerned about too much grocery retailing in the area and the subsequent business failures that could result?

SOURCE: MARINA STRAUSS, "IN SMALL-TOWN ONTARIO, STORE WARS FOUGHT WITH LAWYERS AND LOBBYISTS, NOT COUPONS," GLOBE AND MAIL, AUGUST 28, 2006, B1, B11.

to the adversarial relationships of the past between buyers and sellers, contemporary management thought emphasizes the development of close working partnerships among channel members. **Channel partnering**, or **channel cooperation**, is the joint effort of all channel members to create a supply chain that best serves customers and creates a competitive advantage. Channel partnering is vital if each member is to gain something from the others. By cooperating, retailers, wholesalers, manufacturers, and suppliers can speed up inventory replenishment, improve customer service, and reduce the total costs of the marketing channel.

Channel alliances and partnerships help supply chain managers create the parallel flow of materials and information required to leverage the supply chains' intellectual, material, and marketing resources. The rapid growth in channel partnering is due to new enabling technology and the need to lower costs. A comparison between companies that approach the marketplace unilaterally and those that engage in channel cooperation and form partnerships is detailed in Exhibit 11.8. Collaborating channel partners meet the needs of consumers more effectively by ensuring that the right products are available at the right time and at a lower cost.

REVIEW LEARNING OUTCOME 6

6 Explain channel leadership, conflict, and partnering

Channel power, control, leadership

Channel partnering

Channel relationship synergy

Channel conflict

horizontal   vertical

EXHIBIT 11.8
Transaction-Based versus Partnership-Based Firms

	Transaction-Based	Partnership-Based
Relationships between manufacturer and supplier	• Short-term • Adversarial • Independent • Price more important	• Long-term • Cooperative • Dependent • Value-added services more important
Number of suppliers	Many	Few
Level of information sharing	Minimal	High
Investment required	Minimal	High

SOURCE: Creating Market-Winning Stategies Throught Supply Chain Partnerships (New York: Chapman & Hall, 1998), 61, Table 2.2. With kind permission from Springer Science+Business Media B.V.

7 MANAGING THE LOGISTICS FUNCTION IN THE SUPPLY CHAIN

Describe the logistical components of the supply chain

Now that you are familiar with the structure and strategy of marketing channels and the role of supply chain management, it is important to also understand the physical means by which products move through the supply chain. As described, supply chain management coordinates and integrates all the activities performed by supply chain members into a seamless process. The logistics function of the supply chain is responsible for the movement and delivery of goods and services into, through, and out of each firm in the supply chain network. The logistics function consists of several interrelated and integrated logistical components: (1) sourcing and procurement of raw materials and supplies, (2) production scheduling, (3) order processing, (4) inventory management and control, (5) warehousing and materials-handling, and (6) transportation.

Integrating and linking all the logistics components of the supply chain is the **logistics information system**. The components of the system include software for

logistics information system
The link that connects all the logistics components of the supply chain.

materials acquisition and handling, warehouse-management and enterprise-wide solutions, data storage and integration in data warehouses, mobile communications, electronic data interchange, on-board computers, radio-frequency identification (RFID) chips, and the Internet. Working together, the components of the logistics information system are the fundamental enablers of successful supply chain management.

The **supply chain team**, leveraging the capabilities of the logistics information system, orchestrates the movement of goods, services, and information from the source to the consumer. Supply chain teams typically cut across organizational boundaries, embracing all parties who participate in moving the product to market. The best supply chain teams also move beyond the organization to include the external participants in the chain, such as suppliers, transportation carriers, and third-party logistics suppliers. Members of the supply chain communicate, coordinate, and cooperate extensively to make the logistics function as efficient and effective as possible.

SOURCING AND PROCUREMENT

One of the most important links in the supply chain is the one between the manufacturer and the supplier. Purchasing professionals are on the front lines of supply chain management. Purchasing departments plan purchasing strategies, develop specifications, select suppliers, and negotiate price and service levels. Often, goods are procured for use in local manufacturing processes from suppliers halfway around the world.

The goal of most sourcing and procurement activities is to reduce the costs of raw materials and supplies. Purchasing professionals have traditionally relied on tough negotiations to get the lowest price possible from suppliers. Perhaps the biggest contribution purchasing can make to supply chain management, however, is in the area of vendor relations. Companies can use the purchasing function to strategically manage suppliers in order to reduce the total cost of materials and services. Through enhanced vendor relations, buyers and sellers can develop cooperative relationships that reduce costs and improve efficiency with the aim of lowering prices and enhancing profits. By integrating suppliers into their companies' businesses, purchasing managers have become better able to streamline purchasing processes, manage inventory levels, and reduce overall costs of the sourcing and procurement operations.

ORDER PROCESSING

The order is often the catalyst that sets the supply chain in motion, especially in the build-to-order environments of leading computer manufacturers such as Dell. The **order processing system** processes the requirements of the customer and sends the information into the supply chain via the logistics information system. The order goes to the manufacturer's warehouse. If the product is in stock, the order is filled and arrangements are made to ship it. If the product is not in stock, it triggers a replenishment request that finds its way to the factory floor.

The role of proper order processing in providing good service cannot be overemphasized. As an order enters the system, management must monitor two flows: the flow of goods and the flow of information. Often the best-laid plans of marketers can get entangled in the order processing system. Obviously, good communication among sales representatives, office personnel, and warehouse and shipping personnel is essential to correct order processing. Shipping incorrect merchandise or partially filled orders can create just as much dissatisfaction as stockouts or slow deliveries. The flow of goods and information must be continually monitored so that mistakes can be corrected before an invoice is prepared and the merchandise shipped.

Order processing is becoming more automated through the use of computer technology known as **electronic data interchange (EDI)**. The basic idea of EDI is to replace the paper documents that usually accompany business transactions, such as purchase orders and invoices, with electronic transmission of the needed information. A typical EDI message includes all the information that would traditionally be included on a paper invoice such as product code, quantity, and transportation details. The information is usually sent via private networks, which are more secure and reliable than the networks used for standard e-mail messages. Most importantly, the information can be

---

supply chain team
An entire group of individuals who orchestrate the movement of goods, services, and information from the source to the consumer.

order processing system
A system whereby orders are entered into the supply chain and filled.

electronic data interchange (EDI)
Information technology that replaces the paper documents that usually accompany business transactions, such as purchase orders and invoices, with electronic transmission of the needed information to reduce inventory levels, improve cash flow, streamline operations, and increase the speed and accuracy of information transmission.

read and processed by computers, significantly reducing costs and increasing efficiency. Companies that use EDI can reduce inventory levels, improve cash flow, streamline operations, and increase the speed and accuracy of information transmission. EDI also creates a closer relationship between buyers and sellers.

It should not be surprising that retailers have become major users of EDI. For Walmart, Canadian Tire, and the like, logistics speed and accuracy are crucial competitive tools. Many big retailers are helping their suppliers acquire EDI technology so that they can be linked into the system. EDI works hand in hand with retailers' *efficient consumer response* programs, which are designed to have the right products on the shelf, in the right styles and colours, through improved inventory, ordering, and distribution techniques.

INVENTORY MANAGEMENT AND CONTROL

inventory control system
A method of developing and maintaining an adequate assortment of materials or products to meet a manufacturer's or a customer's demand.

Closely interrelated with the procurement, manufacturing, and ordering processes is the **inventory control system**—a method that develops and maintains an adequate assortment of materials or products to meet a manufacturer's or a customer's demands.

Inventory decisions, for both raw materials and finished goods, have a big impact on supply chain costs and the level of service provided. If too many products are kept in inventory, costs increase—as do the risks of obsolescence, theft, and damage. If too few products are kept on hand, the company risks product shortages and angry customers, and ultimately lost sales. For example, when CN rail went on strike, many car dealers across Canada were left short of product. The goal of inventory management, therefore, is to keep inventory levels as low as possible while maintaining an adequate supply of goods to meet customer demand.

materials requirement planning (MRP) (materials management)
An inventory control system that manages the replenishment of raw materials, supplies, and components from the supplier to the manufacturer.

distribution resource planning (DRP)
An inventory control system that manages the replenishment of goods from the manufacturer to the final consumer.

Managing inventory from the supplier to the manufacturer is called **materials requirement planning (MRP)**, or **materials management**. This system also encompasses the sourcing and procurement operations, signalling purchasing when raw materials, supplies, or components need to be replenished. The system that manages the finished goods inventory from manufacturer to end user is commonly referred to as **distribution resource planning (DRP)**. Both inventory systems use various inputs, such as sales forecasts, available inventory, outstanding orders, lead times, and mode of transportation to be used, to determine what actions must be taken to replenish goods at all points in the supply chain. Demand in the system is collected at each level in the supply chain from the retailer back up to the manufacturer. With the use of electronic data interchange, the information can be transmitted much faster to meet the quick-response needs of today's competitive marketplace. Exhibit 11.9 provides an example of inventory replenishment using DRP from the retailer to the manufacturer.

automatic replenishment program
An inventory management system that triggers shipments only once a good is sold to the customer; the program uses an EDI linkage connected with bar-code scanners at the point of purchase, so the supplier can view the inventory being held at the next tier of the supply chain in real time.

Other inventory management systems that have gained in popularity in recent years, however, use few or no forecasts at all during the scheduling of shipments. Known as **automatic replenishment programs**, these systems trigger shipments only once a good (usually something with a relatively predictable demand pattern) is sold to the customer. Using an EDI linkage connected with bar-code scanners at the point of purchase, the supplier can view the inventory being held at the next tier of the supply chain in real time. When stock of a good at the customer location falls below pre-established safety levels, orders are automatically packed and shipped from the supplier location. Thus, in this type of system, the supplier takes responsibility for keeping inventory on the shelves or in the customer's warehouse; this usually results in reduced stockouts and lowers overall inventory levels.

WAREHOUSING AND MATERIALS-HANDLING

Supply chain logisticians oversee the constant flow of raw materials from suppliers to manufacturers and finished goods from the manufacturer to the ultimate consumer. Although build-to-order manufacturing processes may eliminate the need to warehouse many raw materials, manufacturers may often keep some safety stock on hand in the event of an emergency, such as a strike at a supplier's plant or a catastrophic event that temporarily stops the flow of raw materials to the production line. Likewise, the final user may not need or want the goods at the same time the manufacturer

EXHIBIT 11.9

Inventory Replenishment Example

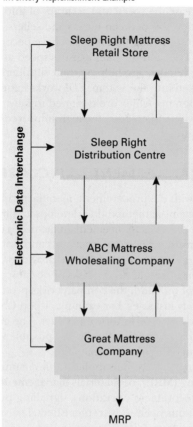

Electronic Data Interchange

Sleep Right Mattress Retail Store → Sleep Right Distribution Centre → ABC Mattress Wholesaling Company → Great Mattress Company → MRP

Sleep Right is planning a promotion on the Great Mattress Company's Gentle Rest mattress. Sales forecast is for 50 units to be sold. Sleep Right has 10 open Gentle Rest orders with its distribution centre. New mattresses must be delivered in two weeks in time for the promotion.

Sleep Right's Distribution Centre is electronically notified of the order of 50 new Gentle Rest mattresses. It currently has 20 Gentle Rest mattresses in inventory and begins putting together the transportation plans to deliver these to the Sleep Right Store. Delivery takes one day. It orders 40 new mattresses from its mattress wholesaler to make up the difference.

ABC Mattress Wholesaling Company is electronically notified of Sleep Right DC's order of 40 new Gentle Rest mattresses. It currently does not have any of these in stock but electronically orders 40 from the Great Mattress Company's factory. Once it receives the new mattresses, it can have them delivered to the Sleep Right DC in two days.

The Great Mattress Company electronically receives ABC's order and forwards it to the factory floor. Production of a new mattress takes 20 minutes. The total order of 40 mattresses can be ready to be shipped to ABC in two days. Delivery takes one day. Raw material supplies for this order are electronically requested from Great Mattress's supply partners, who deliver the needed materials just-in-time to its stitching machines.

produces and wants to sell them. Products like grain and corn are produced seasonally, but consumers demand them year-round. Other products, such as Christmas ornaments and turkeys, are produced year-round, but consumers do not want them until autumn or winter. Therefore, management must have a storage system to hold these products until they are shipped.

Storage is what helps manufacturers manage supply and demand, or production and consumption. It provides time utility to buyers and sellers, which means that the seller stores the product until the buyer wants or needs it. Even when products are used regularly, not seasonally, many manufacturers store excess products in case the demand surpasses the amount produced at a given time. Storing additional product does have disadvantages, however, including the costs of insurance on the stored product, taxes, obsolescence or spoilage, theft, and warehouse operating costs. Another drawback is opportunity costs—that is, the opportunities lost because money is tied up in stored product instead of being used for something else.

Because businesses are focusing on cutting supply chain costs, the warehousing industry is also changing to better serve its customers. For example, many warehouses are placing greater emphasis on more efficient unloading and reloading layouts and on customized services that move merchandise through the warehouse faster—often in the same day. They also are investing in services that use sophisticated tracking technology such as materials-handling systems.

A **materials-handling system** moves inventory into, within, and out of the warehouse. Materials-handling includes these functions:

- Receiving goods into the warehouse or distribution centre
- Identifying, sorting, and labelling the goods
- Dispatching the goods to a temporary storage area
- Recalling, selecting, or picking the goods for shipment (may include packaging the product in a protective container for shipping)

materials-handling system
A method of moving inventory into, within, and out of the warehouse.

The goal of the materials-handling system is to move items quickly with minimal handling. With a manual, nonautomated materials-handling system, a product may be handled more than a dozen times. Each time it is handled, cost and the risk of damage increase. Consequently, most manufacturers today have moved to automated systems. Scanners quickly identify goods entering and leaving a warehouse through bar-coded labels affixed to the packaging. Electronic storage and retrieval systems store and pick goods in the warehouse or distribution centre. Automated materials-handling systems decrease product handling, ensure accurate placement of product, and improve the accuracy of order picking and the rates of on-time shipment. In fact, many firms are relying on materials handling systems operated either partially, or fully, by robots. For example, at office supply giant Staples, over 150 robots collect materials, process, and pack up to 9,000 orders daily.[15]

Dell Computer uses the OptiPlex system to run its plants. The computer software receives orders, sends requests for parts to suppliers, orders components, organizes assembly of the product, and arranges for its shipment. An order for hundreds of computers can be processed in hours. With the OptiPlex system, productivity at Dell plants has increased by160 percent.[16]

TRANSPORTATION

Transportation typically accounts for 5 to 10 percent of the price of goods. Supply chain logisticians must decide which mode of transportation to use to move products from supplier to producer and from producer to buyer. These decisions are, of course, related to all other logistics decisions. The five major modes of transportation are railroads, motor carriers, pipelines, water transportation, and airways. Supply chain managers generally choose a mode of transportation on the basis of several criteria:

- *Cost*: The total amount a specific carrier charges to move the product from the point of origin to the destination
- *Transit time*: The total time a carrier has possession of goods, including the time required for pickup and delivery, handling, and movement between the point of origin and the destination
- *Reliability*: The consistency with which the carrier delivers goods on time and in acceptable condition
- *Capability*: The ability of the carrier to provide the appropriate equipment and conditions for moving specific kinds of goods, such as those that must be transported in a controlled environment (for example, under refrigeration)
- *Accessibility*: A carrier's ability to move goods over a specific route or network
- *Traceability*: The relative ease with which a shipment can be located and transferred

The mode of transportation used depends on the needs of the shipper, as they relate to these six criteria. Exhibit 11.10 compares the basic modes of transportation on these criteria.

The importance of transportation is difficult to overstate. Many industry experts regard on-time delivery and shipment of products as the single most important supply chain management criteria leading to customer satisfaction. This perspective is reflected in companies' investment in transportation management systems—software applications designed to optimize transportation modes' routing, loading, unloading, and other functions. In many cases, especially in a build-to-order manufacturing environment, the transportation network replaces the warehouse or eliminates the expense of storing inventories, since goods are timed to arrive the moment they're needed on the assembly line or for shipment to customers. Toyota is so committed to build-to-order that it has no parts warehouses in Canada or the United States. Instead, it works closely with its suppliers to make sure that parts will be delivered on time.

EXHIBIT 11.10

Criteria for Ranking Modes of Transportation

	Highest				Lowest
Relative Cost	Air	Truck	Rail	Pipe	Water
Transit Time	Water	Rail	Pipe	Truck	Air
Reliability	Pipe	Truck	Rail	Air	Water
Capability	Water	Rail	Truck	Air	Pipe
Accessibility	Truck	Rail	Air	Water	Pipe
Traceability	Air	Truck	Rail	Water	Pipe

7 | **Describe the logistical components of the supply chain**

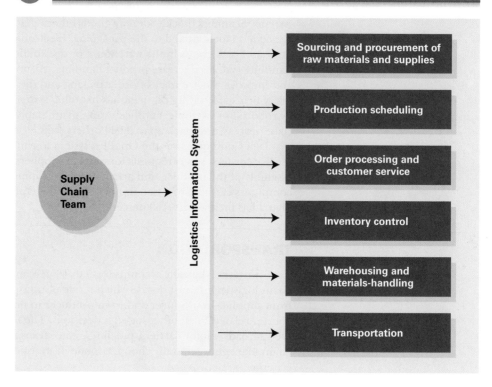

8 SUPPLY CHAIN PERFORMANCE MEASUREMENT

Explain why supply chain performance measurement is necessary and important

A commonly repeated saying in business is "That which cannot be measured cannot be managed." This adage is especially true in the case of supply chain management, where multiple processes, each composed of different types of activities, are operated simultaneously with the goal of enhancing the performance of the business. Firms that are able to develop a well-thought-out system of procedures to measure the supply chain are able to constantly monitor their processes, and see where they are doing well in addition to where they are failing, and are best able to gain a competitive advantage through better service and lower cost.

Because supply chains can be very complex and information is not always visible across firms operating in the same supply chain, many of the ways that managers try to measure their success or failure are not always reflective of the supply chain as a whole; many firms use measures of logistics performance for their own firm (such as on-time delivery rates, order cycle time, or inventory turnover) as proxies for the performance of the whole supply chain. However, recalling that a primary goal of supply chain management is the optimization of the entire system rather than any single firm within it, many companies are seeking to develop new metrics that will allow them a broader and more comprehensive viewpoint from which to study their supply chain's efficiency and effectiveness. **Metrics** are standard measures that can be used repeatedly to assess performance on a supply chain–related process. Common examples of metrics might include customer satisfaction ratings, orders picked from the warehouse per hour, or the ratio of operating assets to income. From the perspective of the supply chain manager, a good metric is characterized by five qualities:

metrics
Standard measures that can be used repeatedly to assess performance on a supply chain–related process.

- It creates understanding of strategic objectives and tactical plans.
- It promotes behaviours that are consistent with achieving these objectives.
- It allows for the recording of actual results and outcomes; therefore, the firm can monitor progress toward objectives.

- It allows companies to compare themselves to competitors (or benchmarks) and customer expectations.
- It motivates continuous improvement.

For firms using the logistics-proxy approach to supply chain measurement, several measures are often used across four unique categories of performance. The performance categories are customer satisfaction, time, cost, and asset utilization. Customer satisfaction measures often include metrics such as order fulfillment, satisfaction ratings taken from questionnaires, on-time deliveries, number of returned products, or length of delay in executing customer service activities. Time measures often employ metrics such as order-to-receipt time or source-to-make cycle time. Cost measures are often calculated as the total aggregate costs of the supply chain (on an activity basis) for a good or service, from creation through delivery. Asset utilization metrics frequently include days of inventory supply, asset performance ratios, or forecast accuracy, to name a few.

THE BALANCED SCORECARD APPROACH

Balanced Scorecard Approach
A measurement system used to evaluate overall supply chain performance.

Because supply chain management is concerned with the performance of all firms in the system simultaneously, any performance measurement system used to evaluate a supply chain must address both the chain itself and all the processes and firms that make it up. One method developed for this purpose is known as the **Balanced Scorecard Approach**. This approach, invented by Robert S. Kaplan and David P. Norton of the Harvard Business School, combines many different categories of measurements that can be used at all levels of the supply chain. The Balanced Scorecard Approach is shown pictorially in Exhibit 11.11.

The Balanced Scorecard Approach is an effective method for assessing overall supply chain performance because it implicitly includes the linkage between the supply chain strategy adopted by the firm in conjunction with the processes undertaken to fulfill it. By using the Balanced Scorecard, firms gain different types of feedback related to their supply chain operations, including strategic data for high-level decision makers, diagnostic feedback to guide process improvement, knowledge of trends in important metrics over time, feedback on the effectiveness of the performance measures themselves, and data that can be used for forecasting future business activities.[17]

At each tier of the supply chain, the Balanced Scorecard addresses four areas of performance that are reflective of supply chain operations: customer-related performance metrics, financial metrics, learning and growth metrics, and business process metrics. Firms take repeated measurements in each of these categories and then alternate through a system whereby they do things to improve lagging performance in weak areas, check the results following implementation of changes, and act again based on new measurements.

EXHIBIT 11.11

Balanced Scorecard Approach to Performance Measurement

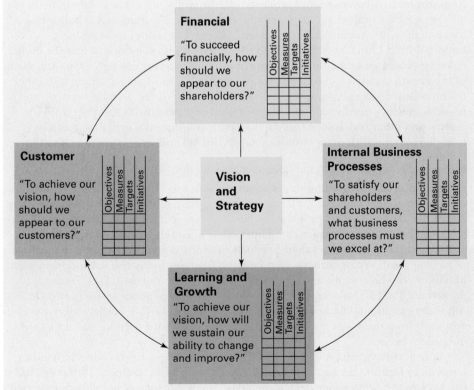

SOURCE: Balanced Scorecard Institute www.balancedscorcard.org, Adapted from Robert S. Kaplan and David P. Norton, "Using the Balanced Scorecard as a Strategic Management System," Harvard Business Review (January-February 1996): 76.

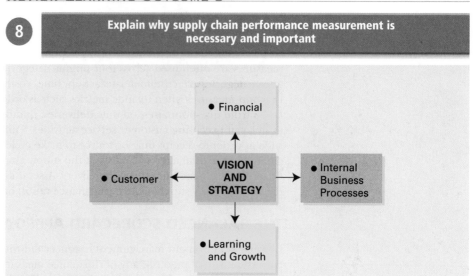

8 Explain why supply chain performance measurement is necessary and important

9 TRENDS IN SUPPLY CHAIN MANAGEMENT

Discuss new technology and emerging trends in supply chain management

Several technological advances and business trends are affecting the job of the supply chain manager today. Four of the most important trends are the globalization of supply chain management, advanced computer technology, outsourcing of logistics functions, and electronic distribution.

GLOBAL SUPPLY CHAIN MANAGEMENT

As global trade becomes a more important factor in the success or failure of firms of all sizes, global supply chain management increases in importance. A Windsor-based tool and die firm, Anchor Danly, reported a 40 percent savings on machinery imported from China. Further, a supply chain research firm estimated that the global economy would grow at a rate of 3 percent or more per year through 2030 with much of the growth occurring outside of North America.[18] Thus Canada's trade with other countries will be increasing. Companies must be aware of the permits, licences, and registrations they need to acquire supplies from other countries and the tariffs, quotas, and other regulations that apply to each country. As Canada reaches new trade agreements with other countries, tariffs will fall and international trade will continue to grow.

Transportation can be a major issue for companies dealing with global supply chains. Uncertainty regarding shipping usually tops the list of reasons that companies resist international markets. Even companies that have scored overseas successes often are vulnerable to logistical problems. While large companies have the capital to create global logistics systems, smaller companies often must rely on the services of carriers and freight forwarders to get their products to overseas markets. Further, the process of moving goods across borders, even between the most industrialized and friendliest of nations, can be complicated. For example, the North American Free Trade Agreement (NAFTA) was supposed to improve the flow of goods across the North American continent, but moving goods across the Canada–U.S. border still requires approvals from dozens of government agencies, broker intervention, and hours spent in border checks.

Busy border crossings, such as the Ambassador Bridge, which connects Windsor, Ontario, to Detroit, Michigan, can still be real problems for shippers. Well over 10,000 trucks cross the Ambassador Bridge each day. The yearly total of merchandise carried by these trucks amounts to over $130 billion, representing nearly 25 percent of the merchandise trade between Canada and the United States. Massive border delays at this one crossing alone are estimated to cost Canadian exporting companies over $140 million each year.[19]

ADVANCED COMPUTER TECHNOLOGY

Advanced computer technology has boosted the efficiency of logistics dramatically with tools such as automatic identification systems (auto ID) using bar-coding and radio frequency technology, communications technology, and supply chain software systems that help synchronize the flow of goods and information with customer demand. Amazon.com's state-of-the-art distribution centres, for instance, use sophisticated order-picking systems that use computer terminals to guide workers through the picking and packing process. Radio frequency technology, which uses radio signals that work with scanned bar codes identifying products, directs Amazon's workers to the precise locations in the warehouse where the product is stored. Warehouse management software examines pick rates, location, and picking and storage patterns, and builds combinations of customer orders for shipping. After installing these supply chain technology tools, Amazon saw a 70 percent improvement in operational efficiency.

Procter & Gamble and many other major companies use radio-frequency identification tags (RFID) for shipments to customers. RFID are chips attached to a pallet of goods that allow the goods to be tracked from the time they are shipped until they reach the customer. Benefits include increased revenue as products arrive when they are needed and reduced inventory management costs. Best Buy is currently using an RFID-enabled payment system to reduce and eventually eliminate checkout lines at the front of their stores—customers with a personalized Best Buy RFID shopping card could simply load up their carts and walk out the front door with their chequing or credit card account debited.[20]

One of the major goals of technology is to bring up-to-date information to the supply chain manager's desk. The transportation system has long been referred to as a "black hole" where products and materials fall out of sight until they reappear some time later in a plant, store, or warehouse. Now carriers have systems that track freight, monitor the speed and location of carriers, and make routing decisions on the spur of the moment. For instance, Roadway Express handles more than 70,000 shipments a day, many for large retailers like Walmart and Home Depot. Information technology allows each package to be tracked from the minute it is received at one of Roadway's terminals until it is delivered. Customers can check on the progress of their shipment anytime by using the company's password-protected website.[21] Swedish-based communications giant Ericsson, whose operations span the globe, uses specialized supply chain software to gain visibility over the 50,000 outbound shipments it makes each year. As products leave its manufacturing facilities, transportation providers transmit status information at specified intervals to Ericsson's information system, which is accessible to management using a standard Web browser.[22]

SOURCE: © DAVID SAMUEL ROBBINS/CORBIS SYGMA

Matt Spangler and others are pictured here picking orders from the media cage at one of Amazon.com's distribution centres. Amazon's command of the supply chain has translated into increased sales and customer satisfaction.

outsourcing (contract logistics)
A manufacturer's or supplier's use of an independent third party to manage an entire function of the logistics system, such as transportation, warehousing, or order processing.

OUTSOURCING LOGISTICS FUNCTIONS

External partners are becoming increasingly important in the efficient deployment of supply chain management. **Outsourcing**, or **contract logistics**, is a rapidly growing

Electronic distribution has become a viable channel for many products, from financial services to postage to software. The Canada Revenue Agency is also realizing gains by accepting tax returns on-line.

segment of the distribution industry in which a manufacturer or supplier turns over an entire function of the logistics system, such as buying and managing transportation or warehousing, to an independent third party. Many manufacturers are turning to outside partners for their logistics expertise in an effort to focus on their core competencies. Partners create and manage entire programs for getting products where they need to be and when they need to be there. Logistics partners offer staff, an infrastructure, and services that reach consumers virtually anywhere in the world. Because a logistics provider is focused, clients receive service in a timely, efficient manner, thereby increasing customers' satisfaction levels and boosting their perception of the company's offerings.[23]

Third-party contract logistics allow companies to cut inventories, locate stock at fewer plants and distribution centres, and still provide the same service level or even better. Companies then can refocus investment on their core business. The Ford Motor Company uses third-party logistics provider UPS Worldwide Logistics to manage the delivery of Ford and Lincoln cars and trucks in Canada, the United States, and Mexico. The alliance between Ford and UPS has substantially reduced the time it takes to move vehicles from Ford's assembly plants to dealers. Moreover, Ford and its dealers can easily track where a car is at any time.[24]

Many firms are taking outsourcing one step further by allowing business partners to take over the final assembly of their product or its packaging in an effort to reduce inventory costs, speed up delivery, or meet customer requirements better. Ryder Truck Lines assembles and packages 22 different combinations of shrink-wrapped boxes that contain the ice trays, drawers, shelves, doors, and other accessories for the various refrigerator models Whirlpool sells. Similarly, the outsourcing firm StarTek, Inc., packages and ships products for Microsoft.

ELECTRONIC DISTRIBUTION

electronic distribution
A distribution technique that includes any kind of product or service that can be distributed electronically, whether over traditional forms such as fibre-optic cable or through satellite transmission of electronic signals

Electronic distribution is the most recent development in the logistics arena. Broadly defined, **electronic distribution** includes any kind of product or service that can be distributed electronically, whether over traditional forms such as fibre-optic cable or through satellite transmission of electronic signals. For instance, instead of buying and installing software from stores, computer users increasingly can purchase software over the Internet and download it electronically to their personal computers or rent the same software from Internet services that have the program available for use on their servers. For example, accounting and financing firm Intuit, Inc. allows people to fill out their tax returns on its website rather than buying its TurboTax software. Similarly, consumers can purchase tickets to sporting events, concerts, and movies via the Internet and print the tickets at home. Music, television shows, and movies have long been delivered to consumers through electronic pipelines. Apple sells over 20 million songs and TV shows annually through iTunes.[25]

9 | Discuss new technology and emerging trends in supply chain management

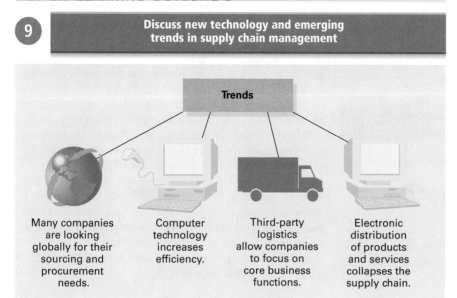

Trends

Many companies are looking globally for their sourcing and procurement needs.

Computer technology increases efficiency.

Third-party logistics allow companies to focus on core business functions.

Electronic distribution of products and services collapses the supply chain.

One of the most innovative electronic distribution ventures of late has come from ESPN. The sports broadcaster offers free access on the iPhone to the most comprehensive sports coverage available in a mobile format. Using an iPhone App, ESPN Mobile Web broadcasts a multimedia-rich sports information package unlike anything else, including breaking news and analysis, up-to-the-minute scores, ESPN Fantasy teams, ESPN columnists, ESPN Podcenter, and more. There's also a special section where users can choose to receive news and stats about their favourite players and teams.[26]

10 CHANNELS AND DISTRIBUTION DECISIONS FOR GLOBAL MARKETS

Discuss channels and distribution decisions in global markets

With the spread of free-trade agreements and treaties, such as the European Union and the North American Free Trade Agreement (NAFTA), global marketing channels and management of the supply chain have become increasingly important to Canadian corporations that export their products or manufacture abroad.

DEVELOPING GLOBAL MARKETING CHANNELS

Executives must recognize the unique cultural, economic, institutional, and legal aspects of each market before trying to develop marketing channels in foreign countries. Manufacturers introducing products in global markets face a tough decision when trying to determine what type of channel structure to use. Specifically, should the product be marketed directly, by company salespeople, or through independent foreign intermediaries, such as agents and distributors? Using company salespeople generally provides more control and is less risky than using foreign intermediaries. However, setting up a sales force in a foreign country also entails a greater commitment, both financially and organizationally.

Marketers should be aware that channel structures and types abroad might differ from those in Canada. For instance, the more highly developed a nation is economically, the more specialized its channel types. Therefore, a marketer wishing to sell in Germany or Japan will have several channel types to choose from. Conversely, developing countries like India, Ethiopia, and Venezuela have limited channel types available; there are typically few mail-order channels, vending machines, or specialized retailers and wholesalers. Some countries also regulate channel choices, such as requiring foreign firms to have a local partner.

Developing effective marketing channels in emerging nations is further complicated due to different retail format preferences. In many emerging nations, consumers shun the supercentre and other big-box formats that are popular here and, instead, buy from tiny, independently operated street-side retailers. These small retailers provide small packages of goods intended to fulfill customer needs for only a day or two. Shoppers will visit these small stores many times per week.

Marketers must also be aware that many foreign countries have "grey" marketing channels, in which products are distributed through unauthorized channel intermediaries. It is estimated that sales of counterfeit luxury items like Prada handbags and Big

Bertha golf clubs exceed $2 billion a year. The new fakes are harder to detect and hit the market almost instantly. For instance, a fake Christian Dior saddlebag was available just weeks after the original arrived on retailers' shelves. Similarly, Chinese companies are producing so many knockoffs of Yamaha, Honda, and Suzuki motorcycles that the Japanese companies are seeing a drop in sales. What's more, many companies are getting so good at design piracy that they are beginning to launch their own new products.[27]

The Internet has also proved to be a way for pirates to circumvent authorized distribution channels, especially in the case of popular prescription drugs. In recent years, millions of dollars worth of prescription drugs, most of which were purchased from foreign Internet sites, have been seized. Some were seized because they had not been approved for use, others because they did not comply with Canadian labelling laws. Most sites offer just a handful of the most popular drugs, such as Viagra. Consumers can get the drugs after obtaining the approval of a doctor who is affiliated with the site and who never sees the patient.

10 | Discuss channels and distribution decisions in global markets

- Distribute directly or through foreign partners
- Different channel structures than in domestic markets
- Illegitimate "grey" marketing channels
- Legal and infrastructure differences

11 CHANNELS AND DISTRIBUTION DECISIONS FOR SERVICES

Identify the special problems and opportunities associated with distribution in service organizations

The fastest-growing part of our economy is the service sector. Although distribution in the service sector is difficult to visualize, the same skills, techniques, and strategies used to manage inventory can also be used to manage service inventory—for instance, hospital beds, bank accounts, or airline seats. The quality of the planning and execution of distribution can have a major impact on costs and customer satisfaction.

One thing that sets service distribution apart from manufacturing distribution is that, in a service environment, production and consumption are simultaneous. In manufacturing, a production setback can often be remedied by using safety stock or a faster mode of transportation. Such substitution is not possible with a service. The benefits of a service are also intangible—that is, you can't normally see the benefits of a service, such as a doctor's physical exam. But a consumer can see the benefits provided by a product—for example, a vacuum cleaner removing dirt from the carpet.

Because service industries are so customer-oriented, customer service is a priority. To manage customer relationships, many service providers use technology to schedule appointments, manage accounts, and distribute information. Service distribution focuses on three main areas:

- *Minimizing wait times*: Minimizing the amount of time customers wait in line to deposit a cheque, wait for food at a restaurant, or wait in a doctor's office for an appointment is a key factor in maintaining the quality of service. People tend to overestimate the amount of time they spend waiting in line, researchers report, and unexplained waiting seems longer than explained waits. To reduce anxiety among waiting customers, some restaurants give patrons pagers that allow them to roam around or go to the bar. Banks sometimes install electronic boards displaying stock

Modelled after successful programs like ExxonMobil's Speedpass, McDonald's is testing a program to minimize the time customers spend at the register. Customers run a small wand over the electronic reader to pay for food they order. People can load the wand electronically with dollars by using a credit or debit card. Reduced time paying for food means that McDonald's can sell hamburgers almost as fast as customers can order them.

SOURCE: ASSOCIATED PRESS

quotes or sports scores. Car rental companies reward repeat customers by eliminating their waits altogether. Airports have designed comfortable sitting areas with televisions and children's play areas for those waiting to board planes. Many hotels and airlines are using electronic check-in kiosks. Travellers can insert their credit cards to check in upon arrival and receive their room key, get directions and print maps to restaurants and attractions, and print out their hotel bills.

- *Managing service capacity*: For product manufacturers, inventory acts as a buffer, enabling them to provide the product during periods of peak demand without extraordinary efforts. Service firms don't have this luxury. If they don't have the capacity to meet demand, they must either turn down some prospective customers, let service levels slip, or expand capacity. For instance, at tax time a tax preparation firm may have so many customers desiring its services that it has to either turn business away or add temporary offices and preparers. Restaurants risk losing business when seating is unavailable and the wait is too long. To better manage capacity, travel websites allow users to find last-minute deals to fill empty airline seats and hotel rooms.

- *Improving service delivery*: Like manufacturers, service firms are now experimenting with different distribution channels for their services. Choosing the right distribution channel can increase the times that services are available (such as using the Internet to disseminate information and services 24/7) or add to customer convenience (like pizza delivery, walk-in medical clinics, or a dry cleaner located in a supermarket). The airline industry has found that using the Internet for ticket sales both reduces distribution costs and raises the level of customer service by making it easier for customers to plan their own travel.[28] In the real estate industry, realtors are placing kiosks in local malls that enable consumers to directly access listings.

REVIEW LEARNING OUTCOME 11

11 | Identify the special problems and opportunities associated with distribution in service organizations

Minimizing wait times is a key factor in maintaining service quality.

Managing service capability is critical to successful service distribution.

Improving service delivery makes it easier and more convenient for consumers to use the service.

The Internet is fast becoming an alternative channel for delivering services. Consumers can now purchase plane tickets, plan a vacation cruise, reserve a hotel room, pay bills, purchase mutual funds, and receive electronic newspapers in cyberspace. Insurance giant Allstate Canada sells auto and home insurance directly to consumers in some provinces through the Internet in addition to its traditional network of agents. The effort reduces costs so that Allstate can stay competitive with rival insurance companies. Similarly, several new residential real estate websites are making it easier for customers to shop for a new home on the Web. Traditionally, the only way for customers to gain access to realtors' listings was to work through a real estate agent, who would search the listings and then show homes to customers that met their requirements. The new companies offer direct access to the listings, enabling customers to review properties for sale on their own and choose which ones they would like to visit.

REVIEW AND APPLICATIONS

1 **Explain what a marketing channel is and why intermediaries are needed.** A marketing channel is a business structure of interdependent organizations that reach from the point of product origin to the consumer with the purpose of physically moving products to their final consumption destination, representing "place" in the marketing mix and encompassing the processes involved in getting the right product to the right place at the right time. Members of a marketing channel create a continuous and seamless supply chain that performs or supports the marketing channel functions. Channel members provide economies to the distribution process in the form of specialization and division of labour; overcoming discrepancies in quantity, assortment, time, and space; and providing contact efficiency.

1.1 Your family runs a specialty ice cream parlour that manufactures its own ice cream in small batches and sells it only in small 750 mL containers. Recently, someone not affiliated with your company sent six containers of your ice cream to Oprah Winfrey, who proclaimed on her national TV show that it was the best ice cream she had ever eaten. Immediately after the broadcast, orders came flooding in, overwhelming your small-batch production schedule and your rudimentary distribution system. Your company's shipping manager thinks she can handle it, but you disagree. List the reasons why you need to restructure your supply chain.

2 **Define the types of channel intermediaries and describe their functions and activities.** The most prominent difference separating intermediaries is whether they take title to the product. Retailers and merchant wholesalers take title, but agents and brokers do not. Retailers are firms that sell mainly to consumers. Merchant wholesalers are those organizations that facilitate the movement of products and services from the manufacturer to producers, resellers, governments, institutions, and retailers. Agents and brokers do not take title to the goods and services they market, but do facilitate the exchange of ownership between sellers and buyers. Channel intermediaries perform three basic types of functions. Transactional functions include contacting and promoting, negotiating, and risk taking. Logistical functions performed by channel members include physical distribution, storing, and sorting functions. Finally, channel members may perform facilitating functions, such as researching and financing.

2.1 What kind of marketing channel functions can be performed over the Internet? Why do you think so?

3 **Describe the channel structures for consumer and business products and discuss alternative channel arrangements.** Marketing channels for consumer and business products vary in degree of complexity. The simplest consumer-product channel involves direct selling from producers to consumers. Businesses may sell directly to business or government buyers. Marketing channels grow more complex as intermediaries become involved. Consumer-product channel intermediaries include agents, brokers, wholesalers, and retailers. Business-product channel intermediaries include agents, brokers, and industrial distributors. Marketers often use alternative channel arrangements to move their products to the consumer. With dual distribution or multiple distribution, they choose two or more different channels to distribute the same product. Nontraditional channels help differentiate a firm's product from the competitor's or provide a manufacturer with another avenue for sales. Finally, strategic channel alliances are arrangements that use another manufacturer's already established channel.

3.1 Describe the most likely marketing channel structure for each of these consumer products: candy bars, Tupperware products, nonfiction books, new automobiles, farmers' market produce, and stereo equipment. Now, construct alternative channels for these same products.

3.2 You have been hired to design an alternative marketing channel for a firm specializing in the manufacturing and marketing of novelties for college and university student organizations. In a memo to the president of the firm, describe how the channel operates.

3.3 Building on question 1.1, determine a new channel structure for the ice cream company. Write a proposal to present to your key managers.

4 **Define supply chain management and discuss its benefits.** Supply chain management coordinates and integrates all the activities performed by supply chain members into a seamless process from the source to the point of consumption. The responsibilities of a supply chain manager include developing channel design strategies, managing the relationships of supply chain members, sourcing and procuring raw materials, scheduling production, processing orders, managing inventory and storing product, and selecting transportation modes. The supply chain manager is also responsible for managing customer service and the information that flows through the supply chain. The benefits of supply chain management include reduced costs in inventory management, transportation, warehousing, and packaging; improved service through techniques like time-based delivery and make-to-order; and enhanced revenues, which result from such supply chain-related achievements as higher product availability and more customized products.

4.1 Discuss the benefits of supply chain management. How does the implementation of supply chain management result in enhanced customer value?

5 **Discuss the issues that influence channel strategy.** When determining marketing channel strategy, the supply chain manager must determine what market, product, and producer factors will influence the choice of channel. The manager must also determine the appropriate level of distribution intensity. Intensive distribution is distribution aimed at maximum market coverage. Selective distribution is achieved by screening dealers to eliminate all but a few in any single area. The most restrictive form of market coverage is exclusive distribution, which entails only one or a few dealers within a given area.

5.1 Decide which distribution intensity level—intensive, selective, or exclusive—is used for each of the following products, and explain why: Piaget watches, Land Rover sport utility vehicles, M&Ms, special-edition Barbie dolls, and Crest toothpaste.

5.2 Now that you have a basic channel structure for the ice cream company (from question 3.3), form a team of three to four students and list the market, product, and producer factors that will affect your final channel structure.

6 **Explain channel leadership, conflict, and partnering.** Power, control, leadership, conflict, and partnering are the main social dimensions of marketing channel relationships. Channel power refers to the capacity of one channel member to control or influence other channel members. Channel control occurs when one channel member intentionally affects another member's behaviour. Channel leadership is the exercise of authority and power. Channel conflict occurs when there is a clash of goals and methods among the members of a distribution channel. Channel conflict can be either horizontal, among channel members at the same level, or vertical, among channel members at different levels of the channel. Channel partnering is the joint effort of all channel members to create a supply chain that serves customers and creates a competitive advantage. Collaborating channel partners meet the needs of consumers more effectively by ensuring that the right products reach shelves at the right time and at a lower cost, boosting sales and profits.

6.1 Procter & Gamble and Walmart are key partners in a shared supply chain. P&G is one of Walmart's biggest suppliers, and Walmart provides extremely detailed scanner data about customer purchases of P&G products. Walmart has begun selling its own brand of Sam's Choice laundry detergent in bright orange containers alongside P&G's Tide but for a greatly reduced price. What do you think will be the impact of this new product on what has been a stable channel relationship?

7 **Describe the logistical components of the supply chain.** The logistics supply chain consists of several interrelated and integrated logistical components: (1) sourcing and procurement of raw materials and supplies, (2) production scheduling, (3) order processing, (4) inventory control, (5) warehousing and materials-handling systems, and (6) transportation. Integrating and linking all the logistics functions of the supply chain is the logistics information system. Information technology connects the various components and partners of the supply chain into an integrated whole. The supply chain team, in concert with the logistics information system, orchestrates the movement of goods, services, and information from the source to the consumer. Supply chain teams typically cut across organizational boundaries, embracing all parties that participate in moving product to market. Procurement deals with the purchase of raw materials, supplies, and components according to production scheduling. Order processing monitors the flow of goods and information (order entry and order handling). Inventory control systems regulate when and how much to buy (order timing and order quantity). Warehousing provides storage of goods until needed by the customer while the materials-handling system moves inventory into, within, and out of the warehouse. Finally, the major modes of transportation include railroads, motor carriers, pipelines, waterways, and airways.

7.1 Assume that you are the supply chain manager for a producer of expensive, high-tech computer components. Identify the most suitable method(s) of transporting your product with regard to cost, transit time, reliability, capability, accessibility, and traceability. Now, assume that you are the supply chain manager for a producer of milk. How does this assumption change your choice of transportation?

8 **Explain why supply chain performance measurement is necessary and important.** Because supply chains are often very complex, with each firm in the chain seeking to fulfill its own goals, it is sometimes difficult to determine whether the supply chain as a whole is functioning well. Firms in the best supply chains develop and use common metrics to assess whether customers are satisfied and whether operations are completed in a timely fashion, at an acceptable level of cost, and with good asset utilization. Often, this includes the use of the Balanced Scorecard methodology, which ensures that not only will customers be satisfied, but also that the firm will execute its tasks with process efficiency, with financially acceptable returns, and in a way that allows for learning and growth for the company.

8.1 Why is supply chain performance measurement necessary and important?

8.2 How does the Balanced Scorecard Approach help firms within the supply chain to establish and meet common goals?

9 **Discuss new technology and emerging trends in supply chain management.** Several trends are emerging that affect the job of today's supply chain manager. Technology and automation are bringing up-to-date distribution information to the decision maker's desk. Technology is also linking suppliers, buyers, and carriers for joint decision making, and it has created a new electronic distribution channel. Many companies are saving money and time by outsourcing third-party carriers to handle some or all aspects of the distribution process.

9.1 Visit the website of Menlo Logistics at **www.menlolog.com**. What logistics functions can this third-party logistics supplier provide? How does its mission fit in with the supply chain management philosophy?

10 **Discuss channels and distribution decisions in global markets.** Global marketing channels are becoming more important to companies seeking growth abroad. Manufacturers introducing products in foreign countries must decide what type of channel structure to use—in particular, whether the product should be marketed through direct channels or through foreign intermediaries. Marketers should be aware that channel structures in foreign markets might be very different from those they are accustomed to in Canada. Global distribution expertise is emerging as an important skill for supply chain managers now that many countries are removing trade barriers.

10.1 Go to the World Trade Organization's website at **www.wto.org**. What can you learn at the site about how globalization affects channel management and other aspects of business?

11 **Identify the special problems and opportunities associated with distribution in service organizations.** Managers in service industries use the same skills, techniques, and strategies to manage logistics functions as managers in goods-producing industries. The distribution of services focuses on three main areas: minimizing wait times, managing service capacity, and improving service delivery.

11.1 Assume that you are the marketing manager of a hospital. Write a report indicating the distribution functions that concern you. Discuss the similarities and dissimilarities of distribution for services and for goods.

TERMS

agents and brokers 328
automatic replenishment program 345
Balanced Scorecard Approach 349
channel conflict 341
channel control 340

channel leader (channel captain) 340
channel members 326
channel partnering (channel
   cooperation) 343
channel power 340

direct channel 330
discrepancy of assortment 326
discrepancy of quantity 326
distribution resource planning
   (DRP) 345

EXERCISES

APPLICATION EXERCISE

It may be easy to understand how distribution channels work just from reading, but you may not appreciate their broad scope. This exercise will help you see for yourself how complex a single distribution channel is. Then, when you think of the number of products and services available on the market at any one time, you will understand how tremendous the national (and international) distribution network actually is.

Activities

1. Create a list of approximately 20 products that you often purchase for personal use and/or that are present in your home.

2. For each of the products that you listed, speculate whether the product was routed through the marketing channel using (a) exclusive, (b) selective, or (c) intensive distribution.

3. Now, for each product-distribution strategy combination, speculate as to the product, market, or producer factors that lead to this distribution strategy.

4. Finally, identify any potential alternative distribution channel options through which you might have purchased this product. Would the alternative channel choice have changed the way (location, timing, price) you purchased this good? Why or why not?

ETHICS EXERCISE

For years, labour and environmental groups have criticized and pressured companies whose suppliers pay low wages, run sweatshops, use child labour, or use other illicit labour practices. More recently, companies have come under fire for sourcing materials from foreign companies that are contributing to massive pollution problems in their local environments. When it was discovered that Fuan Textiles, a major fabric supplier to companies such as Nike and Liz Claiborne, had been dumping large quantities of untreated wastewater into Chinese lakes and streams, many companies in the Fuan supply chain were forced to take notice. As Daryl Brown, VP for ethics and compliance at Liz Claiborne noted, "The environment is the new frontier. We certainly don't want to be associated with a company that's polluting the waters."

Questions

1. Should companies such as Nike and Liz Claiborne avoid purchasing from companies like Fuan Textiles that are polluting lakes and streams, even if the pollution is occurring in another part of the world?

2. What are the pros and cons associated with using supplies and/or labour sourced from supply chain partners based in countries that do not have strict pollution standards?

3. Does the CMA Code of Ethics address the issue of environmental protection in supply chain management? Go to **www.the-cma.org** and review the code. Then write a brief paragraph on what you have found.

CAN THE ICON OF THE LOGISTICS INDUSTRY SUCCEED IN INDIA?

Michael Dell had the idea of selling computer systems directly to customers when he was a university student. In 1985, his new company designed its first computer system and soon began offering next-day, on-site product service. Dell entered Canada in 1988 and has major facilities in Toronto, Ottawa, and Montreal. By 1996, Dell was selling computers on the Internet and by 2000 the company's website was pulling in $50 million a day in direct sales.

Today Dell is well established as an icon of the logistics industry. Its lean business model has influenced countless other companies to follow its lead. Dell's 300,000-square-foot manufacturing centre serves as the base for the build-to-order (or "just-in-time") manufacturing process it's famous for. Dell assembles hundreds of computers every hour, taking orders as they come in and making them to the customers' specifications. In the computer industry, technological equipment quickly becomes outdated so Dell wants everything that goes out the door to be fresh off the assembly line—not losing value in a warehouse.

Dell's revolutionary supply chain is characterized by its minimum levels of inventory, a policy of paying suppliers only after the customers have paid Dell, and direct sales. Industry analysts say that these strategies have changed high-tech manufacturing the way Walmart changed retailing.

The question for Dell now is how to plan for future growth in emerging global markets such as China and India. Can Dell's business model, which is based on information, efficiency, and speed, work as well in parts of the world where the economic and social contexts are so different from what they are in North America?

Dell has planned a major capital investment and expansion in its Indian operation, which would employ 20,000 people in a new manufacturing facility. Analysts predict that if Dell is successful in bringing its build-to-order model to India, it could spur a movement of manufacturing-focused foreign investment in that country.

A recent report by KPMG International concluded that China and India will be the world's two biggest economies by mid-century, and, "although India has underperformed in the last lap of the growth race, there is a strong possibility that India may well move ahead." Dell appears to agree. CEO Kevin Rollins explained, "India currently sells over four million computers per year and this is projected to rise to ten million units annually in the next three to five years. Our workforce here is capable and the time is right for the second phase of expansion in contact centre activities, research and development and . . . a manufacturing site."

Critics are skeptical that India will be as profitable as Dell hopes, however, citing the country's lack of reliable roads, power, and telecommunications. Although telecommunications have improved with an 87,000-kilometre fibre-optic network, India maintains only 4,000 kilometres of highways (Canada has 20 times that). Delivery chains rely almost exclusively on small vehicles with only three wheels that navigate on dirt roads. As for India's power supply, business owners experience nearly 20 significant outages every month. Add to this the hassle of endless red tape required of businesses in India, labour regulations that force businesses to get government permission to lay off workers, and laws that require unanimous worker approval before companies can reorganize, and it becomes clear why critics wonder whether Dell can succeed there.

Dell counters that its computers are lightweight enough to be transported in the three-wheeled trucks that are the backbone of the Indian supply chain. And industry observer Clay Risen adds, "Dell's requirement that suppliers locate warehouses nearby suddenly seems an advantage—after all, the less the supply chain has to deal with the Indian transportation system, the better." Dell can concentrate on the urban middle class with the money to buy computers in major cities like New Delhi, where the country's infrastructure, power, and telecommunication systems are more reliable.

Even with the risks involved with doing business there, Dell has decided that India is too large and full of possibilities to ignore. The industry is watching and waiting to see how the computer giant fares. Dell's success—or failure—could determine whether more manufacturing companies follow its example.[29]

Questions

1. Describe how Dell's manufacturing processes represent a change in supply chain management from how things were done during the mass-production era. What does it mean that there has been a reversal of the flow of demand from a "push" to a "pull" system?

2. Describe the order processing system. How does it work in a company like Dell? As an order enters the system, what must management monitor? Why is it so important that the order processing system be executed well?

3. Describe the role that a supply chain manager at Dell might play. What would his or her responsibilities be? Why is there such high demand for supply chain managers in companies like Dell today?

4. Describe the benefits that Dell and other companies receive from supply chain management. What benefits do supply chain–oriented companies commonly report?

VIDEO CASE

CBC

CARGOJET: CANADA'S LEADING CARGO AIRLINE

Cargojet, Canada's leading cargo-only airline, was formed in 2002, a year in which the passenger side of the airline industry was experiencing considerable difficulty. Both the largest passenger carrier in Canada (Air Canada) and the largest air passenger carrier in the United States (American Airlines) were operating under bankruptcy protection. By 2009, Cargojet was carrying over 600,000 pounds of cargo every day while generating over $200 million per year in revenue and $16 million in profits.

Ajay Virmani, the founder of Cargojet, had owned a freight forwarding business for over 20 years. "I was frustrated because I never had a reliable carrier I could use in Canada on a consistent basis," said Virmani. "Cargo was always added onto passenger operations."

Cargojet itself is partially the result of a bankruptcy in the passenger airline business. Virmani had invested $10 million in Canada 3000 to operate the cargo end of the passenger airline. Shortly after Virmani's investment came the infamous 9/11 disaster in the United States, and passenger bookings on Canada 3000 dropped by over 70 percent. Canada 3000 went into bankruptcy and never re-emerged as a passenger carrier. Ajay Virmani, however, invested additional funds in the cargo end of the business, and Cargojet has become a leader in this part of the airline business in Canada.

In the months after 9/11, Virmani was able to buy a number of unneeded passenger planes at very low prices and convert them into cargo planes. He was also able to hire hundreds of laid-off Canada 3000 employees to give Cargojet an experienced workforce.

As opposed to passenger transportation, which takes place mostly during the day, Cargojet's busy time is at night. Cargojet loads its planes from 10:00 p.m. to 12:30 a.m. each night to ensure delivery of its cargo to its destination by 8:00 a.m. As a tribute to its efficiency in doing this, Cargojet has set on-time performance records in the airline cargo business with 99 percent on-time deliveries. Cargojet makes nearly 7,000 deliveries each year with its 10 planes while operating coast to coast across Canada.

Might you be interested in a career in the transportation industry? Visit Cargojet's website (**www.cargojet.com**) and learn about careers at this company. Want to see how easy it is to ship something? Check under "Route Network," "Locations," or "Flight Schedule" on the website. Cargojet states that its mission is "to be the dominant, most reliable air cargo company in Canada." To learn even more about Cargojet, its operations, and its founder, there are five videos on the Cargojet website you can watch.

Air Canada, by the way, hasn't ignored the cargo end of the airline industry. Air Canada fills the bellies of its passenger planes with cargo such as fresh seafood, vegetables and fruits, and auto parts being flown for Chrysler from Canada to Germany. In fact, the cargo portion of Air Canada's business has been growing so rapidly, and becoming so profitable, that Air Canada is investing in 32 new Boeing 777 freighters that will solely be dedicated to cargo service.[30]

Questions

1. What do you think of the cargo end of the airline business? Does it match your perceptions of it? How is it different?

2. Why has Cargojet succeeded when Canada 3000 failed?

3. What are your views of the future of the airline cargo industry in Canada?

MARKETING & YOU RESULTS

A higher score indicates that you like to be a leader and use authority. Studies have linked authority to vanity, so a high score also suggests a high level of vanity. In particular, you have "achievement view vanity." That means you have very high opinions of your accomplishments and think that others consider you successful as well.

CHAPTER

12 Retailing

SOURCE: THE CANADIAN PRESS (RICHARD LAM)

LEARNING OUTCOMES

1 Discuss the importance of retailing in the Canadian economy

2 Explain the dimensions by which retailers can be classified

3 Describe the major types of retail operations

4 Discuss nonstore retailing techniques

5 Define franchising and describe its two basic forms

6 List the major tasks involved in developing a retail marketing strategy

7 Describe new developments in retailing

MARKETING & YOU

How much do you enjoy shopping? Using the scales below, enter your answers or record them on a separate page.

1	2	3	4	5
Strongly disagree		Neutral		Strongly agree

___ I shop because buying things makes me happy.
___ Shopping is fun.
___ I get a real "high" from shopping.
___ I enjoy talking with salespeople and other shoppers who are interested in the same things I am.

___ I like having a salesperson bring merchandise out for me to choose from.
___ I enjoy seeing mall exhibits while shopping.

Total your score, and find out what it means after you read the chapter.

SOURCE: REPRINTED WITH PERMISSION FROM *MARKETING SCALES HANDBOOK* VOL. III, PUBLISHED BY THE AMERICAN MARKETING ASSOCIATION, G. BRUNER, K. JAMES, H. HENSEL, EDS. SCALE #715.

When you think of clothing and retailing in association with cities throughout the world, the names New York, Paris, Milan, and Hong Kong come to mind. If you think Canadian clothing and retailing, you would likely start with Montreal and Toronto. This may have to change in light of the success of Vancouver-based Lululemon Athletica. This Canadian-based retailer operates more than 125 stores throughout Canada, the United States, Australia, and Hong Kong. The firm was founded in British Columbia in 1998 to offer clothing specifically for yoga practitioners. The firm's mission is presented as "Creating components for people to live longer, healthier, more fun lives." Lululemon describes its market offerings as "technical clothing for yoga, dancing, running, and most other sweaty pursuits."

The first thing you notice about a Lululemon store is that most of the entrance doorways are actually archways depicting the retailer's brand symbol which is supposed to be a stylized letter A standing for athletica (although it looks a lot like a horseshoe to the authors). The atmosphere of the stores is relaxing, just like yoga. Each store offers shoppers filtered water to drink and there are comfortable chairs to sit in. Typical of most apparel retail stores, there are large pictures throughout showing people using the active wear, as well as display mannequins wearing the clothing.

The sales associates in the stores are trim and fit and practise yoga or some form of athletic activity. They both wear and use the clothing they are selling. The stores have a strong service orientation so a sales associate assists each customer quickly and efficiently. However, their sales techniques are very soft-sell in that they ask people lots of questions and focus on helping you buy rather than pushing products or specials. They want your purchase experience to be as comfortable as the clothing you are buying.

The employees of Lululemon are expected to live what they are selling: a balanced lifestyle. The company website says, "It's also important for our team to embody a balanced lifestyle. To help facilitate this, Lululemon pays for all employees to attend yoga classes in the community. For the head office folks, there is also a yoga studio in the Store Support Centre with daily classes. In the summer, staff are encouraged to hike one of Vancouver's local mountains before heading into the office or the stores. Staff are also encouraged to jog/bike/walk to work and there is filtered water in all of our stores for our staff and guests. In the communities, we work with local athletes and yogis for their feedback on our products and often hold in-store community classes."[1]

Were you aware of Lululemon Athletica before? What factors have made the firm a success so far? Will the firm be able to continue to have success with its international expansion? This chapter seeks to provide you with the background to answer these questions and many more by discussing retailers' important role in moving products and services to consumers. We begin with a discussion of the importance of retailing and the ways in which retail operations can be classified. We will then describe the decisions involved in developing a retail marketing strategy.

SOURCE: SUNNY FREEMAN, "LULULEMON TARGETING 45 MARKETS FOR SHOWROOM OPENINGS TO CREATE BRAND BUZZ," THE CANADIAN PRESS, MAR 25, 2010; LULULEMON CORPORATE WEBSITE, WWW.LULULEMON.COM, ACCESSED MAY 16, 2010; CANADIAN PRESS, "LULULEMON GOES FROM MINORITY TO MAJORITY SHAREHOLDER IN AUSSIE YOGA BRAND," THE CANADIAN PRESS, MAY 12, 2010

Discuss the importance of retailing in the Canadian economy

retailing
All the activities directly related to the sale of goods and services to the ultimate consumer for personal, nonbusiness use.

Retailing—all the activities directly related to the sale of goods and services to the ultimate consumer for personal, nonbusiness use—has enhanced the quality of our daily lives. When we shop for groceries, hairstyling, clothes, books, and countless other products and services, we are involved in retailing. The millions of goods and services provided by retailers mirror the needs and styles of Canadian society.

Retailing affects all of us directly or indirectly. The retailing industry is one of Canada's largest employers; approximately 210,000 Canadian retail locations employ over 2.15 million people, which accounts for 12 percent of total Canadian employment. At the store level, retailing is still considered a mom-and-pop business. Almost 8 out of 10 retail establishments employ fewer than ten employees and, according to Statistics Canada, 97 percent of all retail establishments have fewer than 50 employees.[2]

The Canadian economy is heavily dependent on retailing. Retailers rang up more than $413 billion in sales in 2009, representing over 32 percent of the country's GDP.[3] However, most retailers are quite small; a few large retail chains tend to dominate their categories. Who are these dominant retailers? Exhibit 12.1 lists the top 10 Canadian-based retailers.

EXHIBIT 12.1

Top 10 Canadian-Based Retailers

Retailer	Business	Canadian dollar sales (billions)	Number of Canadian stores
Loblaws	Supercentre/Superstore	30.7	1,000
Alimentation Couche-Tard Inc.	Convenience/Forecourt Store	15.8	2000
Empire Co. (Sobeys)	Supermarket	13.3	1300
Metro Inc.	Supermarket	10.6	923
Shoppers Drug Mart	Drug Store/Pharmacy	8.9	1132
Canadian Tire	Specialty/Department Stores	8.6	1100
Katz Group Inc. (Rexall)	Drug Store/Pharmacy	6.3	500
Jim Pattison Group (Overwaitea)	Supermarket	6.3	449
Sears Canada	Department Store	6.2	386
Rona Inc.	Home Improvement/Hardware	4.6	700

SOURCES: *Canadian Business Investor 500*, list.canadianbusiness.com/rankings/investor500/2009; Report by Deloitte Touche Tohmatsu, (2009), "Emerging from the Downturn: Global Powers of Retailing 2010,"; and corporate websites of the top 10.

REVIEW LEARNING OUTCOME 1

1 | **Discuss the importance of retailing in the Canadian economy**

Explain the dimensions by which retailers can be classified

A retail establishment can be classified according to its ownership, level of service, product assortment, price, and place of business. Retailers use the latter four variables to position themselves in the marketplace. (As noted in Chapter 6, positioning is the strategy used to influence how consumers perceive one product in relation to all competing products.) These four variables can be combined in several ways to create distinctly different retail operations. Exhibit 12.2 lists the major types of retail stores discussed in this chapter and classifies them by type of retailer, level of service, product assortment, price, and gross margin.

OWNERSHIP

Retailers can be classified broadly by form of ownership: independent, chain member, or franchise. Retailers owned by a single person or partnership and not operated as part of a larger retail institution are **independent retailers**. Around the world, most retailers are independent, operating one or a few stores in their community. Local florists, shoe stores, and ethnic food markets typically fit this classification.

   Chain stores are owned and operated as a group by a single organization. Under this form of ownership, the home office handles many administrative tasks for the entire chain. The home office also buys most of the merchandise sold in the stores.

   Franchises are owned and operated by individuals but are licensed by a larger supporting organization. An example is Tim Hortons. Franchising combines the advantages of independent ownership with those of the chain store organization. Franchising is discussed in more detail later in the chapter.

independent retailers
Retailers owned by a single person or partnership and not operated as part of a larger retail institution.

chain stores
Stores owned and operated as a group by a single organization.

franchise
The right to operate a business or to sell a product.

LEVEL OF SERVICE

The level of service ranges from full service to self-service. Some retailers, such as exclusive clothing stores, offer high levels of service. They provide alterations, credit, delivery, consulting, liberal return policies, layaway, gift wrapping, and personal shopping. Discount stores usually offer fewer services. Retailers such as factory outlets and warehouse clubs offer virtually no services.

EXHIBIT 12.2

Types of Stores and Their Characteristics

Type of Retailer	Level of Service	Product Assortment	Price	Gross Margin
Department store	Moderately high to high	Broad	Moderate to high	Moderately high
Specialty store	High	Narrow	Moderate to high	High
Supermarket	Low	Broad	Moderate	Low
Convenience store	Low	Medium to narrow	Moderately high	Moderately high
Drugstore	Low to moderate	Medium	Moderate	Low
Full-line discount store	Moderate to low	Medium to broad	Moderately Low	Moderately Low
Discount specialty store	Moderate to low	Medium to broad	Moderately low to low	Moderately Low
Warehouse clubs	Low	Broad	Low to very low	Low
Off-price retailer	Low	Medium to narrow	Low	Low
Restaurant	Low to high	Narrow	Low to high	Low to high

PRODUCT ASSORTMENT

The third basis for positioning or classifying stores is according to the breadth and depth of the products they offer. Specialty stores—for example, Lululemon Athletica, Laura Secord, Aldo Shoes, and Harvey's Hamburgers—have the most concentrated product assortments, usually carrying single or narrow product lines but in considerable depth. At the other end of the spectrum, full-line discounters typically carry broad assortments of merchandise with limited depth. For example, Zellers carries automotive supplies, household cleaning products, and pet food. However, Zellers may carry only four or five brands of canned dog food; a Loblaws supermarket may carry as many as twenty.

Other retailers, such as factory outlet stores, may carry only part of a single line. Nike, a major manufacturer of sporting goods and clothing, sells only certain items of its own brand in its many outlet stores. Discount specialty stores like Rona or Toys "R" Us carry a broad assortment in concentrated product lines, such as building and home supplies or toys.

PRICE

Price is a fourth way to position retail stores. Traditional department stores and specialty stores typically charge the full "suggested retail price." In contrast, discounters, factory outlets, and off-price retailers use low prices as a major lure for shoppers.

The last column in Exhibit 12.2 shows the typical **gross margin**—how much the retailer makes as a percentage of sales after the cost of goods sold is subtracted. The level of gross margin and the price level generally match. A traditional jewellery store has high prices and high gross margins. A factory outlet has low prices and low gross margins. Markdowns on merchandise during sale periods and price wars among competitors, in which stores lower prices on certain items in an effort to win customers, cause gross margins to decline. According to Statistics Canada, the average gross margin for a Canadian retail operation is 27.1 percent, ranging from a low of 15.1 percent for new car dealers to near the average at 27.2 percent for department stores to a high of 51.1 percent for clothing stores.[4] When Walmart entered the pharmacy business in Newfoundland, a fierce price war ensued between it and Shoppers Drug Mart. By the time the price war was in full swing, the dispensing fee for a prescription had plummeted to zero, a price at which no pharmacist could claim value added for the service and no pharmacy retailer could make a profit on its prescription business.

PLACE OF BUSINESS

Traditionally, most retailers have conducted business using in-store methods at fixed sites (referred to as bricks-and-mortar stores, or **in-store retailing**), with consumers coming in to shop. However, retailers can also engage in nonstore retailing, with consumers "shopping in place" by means of a direct visit from a retailer or through communications technology. A recent survey by Statistics Canada indicated that retailers owning fixed locations generated about 97 percent of retail revenues and nonstore retailing the remaining 3 percent.[5] Clearly, in-store retailers are dominant, as is this form of retailing. However, the growth potential of nonstore retailing—a result of Internet expansion and mobile telecommunications—cannot be ignored. Many retailers employ both in-store and nonstore retailing approaches to satisfy their customers. The true level of nonstore sales may be greatly underestimated, since retailers using combination forms often do not publicize the breakdown of sales between the two approaches.

gross margin
The amount of money the retailer makes as a percentage of sales after the cost of goods sold is subtracted.

place of business
Whether a retailer primarily sells using an in-store method through a physical (bricks-and-mortar) store location method or sells using a nonstore method.

in-store retailing
Customers must physically shop at stores to make a purchase.

REVIEW LEARNING OUTCOME 2

2 | **Explain the dimensions by which retailers can be classified**

STORE
OPEN

- Ownership
- Level of service
- Product assortment
- Price
- Place of business

MAJOR TYPES OF RETAIL OPERATIONS

Describe the major types of retail operations

Traditionally, there have been several distinct types of retail stores, with each offering a different product assortment, type of service, and price level, according to its customers' shopping preferences.

In a recent trend, however, retailers are experimenting with alternative formats that make it harder to classify them. Supermarkets are expanding their nonfood items and services, discounters are adding groceries, drugstores are becoming more like convenience stores, and department stores are experimenting with smaller stores. Nevertheless, many stores still fall into the basic types.

DEPARTMENT STORES

department store
A store housing several departments under one roof.

buyer
A department head who selects the merchandise for his or her department and who may also be responsible for promotion and personnel.

Housing several departments under one roof, a **department store** carries a wide variety of shopping and specialty goods, including apparel, cosmetics, housewares, electronics, and sometimes furniture. Purchases are generally made within each department rather than at one central checkout area. Each department is treated as a separate buying centre to achieve economies in promotion, buying, service, and control. Each department is usually headed by a **buyer**, a department head who not only selects the merchandise for his or her department but may also be responsible for promotion and personnel. For a consistent, uniform store image, central management sets broad policies regarding the types of merchandise carried and price ranges. Central management is also responsible for the overall advertising program, credit policies, store expansion, customer service, and so on.

Large, independent department stores such as Honest Ed's in downtown Toronto are rare in Canada and becoming even rarer. For example, the S&R Department Store in Kingston closed in 2009 after 50 years in business. There are a few regional chains, such as two Winnipeg-based chains—The North West Company and V&S Department Stores—plus the Quebec-based Hart Stores/Bargain Giant Department Stores, which operate in Quebec and the Maritimes.[6] However, most department store sales are

Independent department store Honest Ed's in Toronto has been in business for over 60 years. Independent department stores are becoming very rare in Canada

made by national chains. Canada's department store market is dominated by two chains: Sears and The Bay.

In recent years, consumers have become more cost conscious and value oriented. Discounters, catalogue outlets, specialty retailers like Lululemon Athletica, and even on-line shopping alternatives are offering superior merchandise selection and presentation, sharper pricing, and greater convenience, with the goal of taking sales away from traditional department stores like Sears and The Bay. They have also been quicker to adopt new technologies and to invest in labour-saving strategies. In addition, their leaner cost structures translate into lower prices. Meanwhile, manufacturers like Columbia Sportswear, Nike, Liz Claiborne, Bass, Calvin Klein, and Ralph Lauren have opened outlet stores of their own, and discount department stores, such as Walmart and Zellers, have been upgrading their apparel assortments, taking still more sales away from the traditional department stores.

Department store managers are using several strategies to preserve their market share. One is to reposition department stores as specialty outlets. They are adding separate stores that are specialized, such as Home Outfitters, which is part of the Bay. They are also dividing departments into mini-boutiques, each catering to a distinct fashion taste, just as specialty stores do. For example, The Bay has Ralph Lauren and Lacoste Home boutiques. Department stores are also enhancing customer service to shift the focus away from price. Services include complimentary alterations, longer store hours, personalized attention, after-sale follow-up, and personal wardrobe planning. Finally, department stores are expanding, remodelling, and revitalizing to show off new merchandising directions and to reflect the growth in their marketing areas.

SPECIALTY STORES

specialty store
A retail store specializing in a given type of merchandise.

Specialty store formats allow retailers to refine their segmentation strategies and tailor their merchandise to specific target markets. A **specialty store** is not only a type of store but also a method of retail operation—namely, specializing in a given type of merchandise. Examples include children's clothing, men's clothing, candy, baked goods, gourmet coffee, sporting goods, and pet supplies. A typical specialty store carries a deeper but narrower assortment of specialty merchandise than does a department store. Generally, specialty stores' knowledgeable sales clerks offer more attentive customer service. The format has become very powerful in the apparel market and other areas. Studies indicate that consumers buy more clothing from specialty stores than from any other type of retailer.[7] Mountain Equipment Co-op, Athletes World, Aldo Shoes, Tim Hortons, and M&M Meat Shops are examples of successful chain specialty retailers.

Consumers usually consider price to be secondary in specialty outlets. Instead, the distinctive merchandise, the store's physical appearance, and the calibre of the staff determine its popularity. Moores, a national retail chain, has grown quickly by offering a large selection of quality men's clothing with the positioning "Moores Clothing for Men." Moores offers shoppers "on-premise tailoring" in its stores, with a promise of "while-you-wait hemming." Moores's retail strategy is summed up in the following company statement: "Well Made. Well Priced. Well Dressed."[8] Because small specialty stores such as Moores pay attention to their customers and offer limited product lines, manufacturers often favour introducing new products in these small specialty stores before moving on to larger retail and department stores.

SUPERMARKETS

supermarket
A large, departmentalized, self-service retailer that specializes in food and nonfood items.

Canadian consumers made 10.4 percent of their household expenditures on food, according to the most recent data. Total food expenditures were estimated to be $73.2 billion in 2009. Most of these sales were made in **supermarkets**—large, departmentalized, self-service retailers that specialize in food and some nonfood items.[9]

A decade ago, industry experts predicted the decline of the supermarket industry, whose slim profit margins of just 1 to 2 percent of sales left it vulnerable. These experts contended that supermarkets would need an ever-growing customer base to sustain volume and compensate for low margins. The population did in fact keep growing, albeit at less than 1 percent a year, yet supermarkets continued to experience declining sales. This compelled experts to examine not only population trends but also demographic and lifestyle changes. They discovered several trends affecting the supermarket industry.

There are more dual-income and single-parent families than ever before; as a result, consumers are eating out more or are too busy to prepare meals at home. According to the most recent data from Statistics Canada, Canadians were spending 70 percent of their food money in retail grocery stores, compared to 30 percent for food away from home. In comparison, Canadians spent over 80 percent of their food money in grocery stores in 1961.[10] The growth in the away-from-home food market has been driven by the entry of more women into the workforce and their need for convenience and time-saving products. Working couples need one-stop shopping, and increasing numbers of affluent customers are willing to pay for specialty and prepared foods.

As stores seek to meet consumer demand for one-stop shopping, conventional supermarkets are being replaced by *superstores*, which are usually twice the size of supermarkets. Superstores meet the needs of today's customers for convenience, variety, and service. Superstores offer one-stop shopping for many food and nonfood needs, as well as many services—including pharmacies, flower shops, salad bars, in-store bakeries, take-out food sections, sit-down restaurants, health food sections, video rentals, dry-cleaning services, shoe repair, photo processing, and banking. Some even offer family dentistry and opticians. This tendency to offer a wide variety of nontraditional goods and services under one roof is called **scrambled merchandising**. Canada's largest supermarket chain, Loblaws, exemplifies this trend: at one location, along with a dry cleaner, a liquor store, a coffee shop, a pharmacy, and a banking centre, it offers video-game and mobile-phone sales outlets and leases space to a clothing chain and a fitness club complete with a sauna, a tanning salon, and a day-care centre. Loblaws's ancillary services aim to attract today's time-strapped customers by providing one-stop shopping.[11]

A recent trend in supermarket diversification is the addition of store-owned gas stations. The gas stations not only are a new revenue source for the supermarkets and a convenience for customers, but also attract customers to the location by offering lower prices than can usually be found at a traditional gas station. It is estimated that these stores will account for approximately 20 percent of overall gasoline sales in the future.

Another demographic trend affecting supermarkets is expanding ethnicity. Over the past 10 years, well over 2.3 million immigrants have arrived in Canada, most of them settling in urban areas such as Montreal, Ottawa-Hull, Toronto, Hamilton, Calgary, Edmonton, and Vancouver. These demographic changes promise to have a vast impact on supermarket retailers. Immigrants perceive Canada as a multicultural society and expect to find ethnic foods in the stores. Grocery retailers are aware of the market opportunity that ethnic groups represent, so they stock many ethnic products such as basmati rice, curry powders, and egg noodles. However, it is not enough to simply stock ethnic foods; signage in the language of important ethnic groups and the hiring of multilingual employees are also important considerations for supermarket retailers.[12]

In this increasingly competitive marketplace, many supermarket chains are tailoring their marketing strategies to appeal to specific consumer segments. Most notable is the shift toward *loyalty marketing programs*, which reward loyal customers who carry frequent-shopper cards with discounts or gifts. Once scanned at

scrambled merchandising
The tendency to offer a wide variety of nontraditional goods and services under one roof.

SOURCE: © AP PHOTO/MEL EVANS

For supercentre operators, food is a customer magnet that sharply increases the store's overall volume, while taking customers away from traditional supermarkets.

the checkout, frequent-shopper cards help supermarket retailers electronically track shoppers' buying habits.

DRUGSTORES

drugstore
A retail store that stocks pharmacy-related products and services as its main draw.

Drugstores stock pharmacy-related products and services as their main draw. Consumers are most often attracted to a drugstore by its pharmacy or pharmacist, its convenience, or its policy of honouring third-party prescription drug plans. Drugstores also carry extensive selections of over-the-counter (OTC) medications, cosmetics, health and beauty aids, seasonal merchandise, specialty items such as greeting cards and toys, and nonrefrigerated convenience foods. As competition has increased from mass merchandisers and supermarkets with their own pharmacies, as well as from direct mail prescription services, drugstores have been adding value in the form of 24-hour operations and drive-through pharmacies.

Demographic trends in Canada look favourable for the drugstore industry. As baby boomers continue to age, they will be spending an increasing percentage of their disposable income on health care and wellness. This is good news for the drugstore industry, as the average 60-year-old purchases 15 prescriptions per year—nearly twice as many as the average 30-year-old. Because baby boomers are attentive to their health and keenly sensitive about their looks, increased traffic at pharmacy counters should spur sales in other traditionally strong drugstore merchandise categories, most notably OTC drugs, vitamins, and health and beauty aids.

CONVENIENCE STORES

convenience store
A miniature supermarket, carrying only a limited line of high-turnover convenience goods.

A **convenience store** is a miniature supermarket, carrying only a limited line of high-turnover convenience goods. These self-service stores are typically located near residential areas and are open 24 hours, seven days a week. Convenience stores offer exactly what their name implies: convenient location, long hours, and fast service. However, prices are almost always higher at a convenience store than at a supermarket. Thus the customer pays for the convenience.

When the original convenience stores added self-service gas pumps, full-service gas stations fought back by closing service bays and opening miniature stores of their own, selling convenience items like cigarettes, soft drinks, and snacks. Supermarkets and discount stores also wooed customers with one-stop shopping and quick checkout. To combat the gas stations' and supermarkets' competition, convenience store operators have changed their strategy. They have expanded their offerings of nonfood items with video rentals, health and beauty aids, upscale sandwich and salad lines, and more fresh produce. Some convenience stores are even selling hot foods like pizzas, tacos, and hot dogs, which are prepared in the store.

The Canadian market is dominated by chain store competitors, including North America's market leader, 7-Eleven, and Montreal-based Couche-Tard, which operates nearly 2,000 stores in Canada, mainly under the trade names of Couche-Tard and Mac's. Couche-Tard is the second-largest convenience store operator in North America, employing 53,000 people and generating more than $15.8 billion in sales from a network of 5,800 stores in Canada and the United States.[13]

DISCOUNT STORES

discount store
A retailer that competes on the basis of low prices, high turnover, and high volume.

A **discount store** is a retailer that competes on the basis of low prices, high turnover, and high volume. Discounters can be classified into four major categories: full-line discount stores, specialty discount stores, warehouse clubs, and off-price discount retailers.

Full-Line Discount Stores

full-line discount store
A retailer that offers consumers very limited service and carries a broad assortment of well-known, nationally branded "hard goods."

Compared to traditional department stores, **full-line discount stores** offer consumers very limited service and carry a much broader assortment of well-known, nationally branded "hard goods," including housewares, toys, automotive parts, hardware, sporting goods, and garden items, as well as clothing, bedding, and linens. Some even carry limited nonperishable food items, such as soft drinks, canned goods, and potato chips. As with department stores, national chains dominate the discounters. Full-line discounters are often called mass merchandisers. **Mass merchandising** is a retailing strategy whereby retailers offer reduced service and moderate to low prices on large quantities of merchandise in order to stimulate high turnover of products.

Walmart is the world's largest full-line discount organization, with sales of $405 billion in 2010. Walmart operates more than 8,400 stores in 15 countries, including the United States (4,304), Mexico (1,469), Brazil (434), China (279), Japan (371), the United Kingdom (371), Costa Rica (170), Guatemala (164), El Salvador (77), Puerto Rico (56), Nicaragua (55), Honduras (53), Argentina (43), and India (1). It also operates 317 stores in Canada that employ more than 82,000 people. It has expanded rapidly by locating on the outskirts of small towns, thus absorbing business for kilometres around. Much of Walmart's success has been attributed to its merchandising foresight, cost consciousness, efficient communication and distribution systems, and motivated employees. Walmart is credited with pioneering the retail strategy of "everyday low pricing," which has since been copied by retailers the world over. Walmart has also become formidable in on-line shopping, concentrating on toys and electronics. The company is expected to introduce millions of customers to on-line shopping through in-store kiosks that are able to handle returns and exchanges from Internet sales.[14]

In an attempt to compete against Walmart in Canada, Zellers has been aggressively positioning its chain of over 279 stores as "everyday value." Zellers, which is owned and operated by the Hudson's Bay Company, has developed proprietary labels such as the Jules and James clothing line and has the sole distribution rights for a number of other product labels, including Tres You. Zellers is also distributing a number of celebrity labels, including Alfred Sung and the Creativity Collection by Paris Hilton.[15]

Supercentres combine a full line of groceries and general merchandise with a wide range of other services, including pharmacy, dry cleaning, photo finishing, hair styling, opticians, and restaurants—all in one location. For supercentre operators like Walmart, food is a customer magnet that sharply increases the store's overall volume while taking customers away from traditional supermarkets. Walmart operates more than 1,000 supercentres globally and has 84 such stores in Canada. Loblaws operates supercentres across Canada under names such as The Real Canadian Superstore and Atlantic Superstore. Over and above their full line of President's Choice convenience products, the Loblaws superstores provide photo labs, dry cleaners, garden centres, Joe Fresh clothing boutiques, and various other value-added services.[16]

Supercentres are also threatening to push Europe's traditional small and medium-sized food stores into extinction. Old-fashioned corner stores and family businesses are giving way to larger chains that offer food, drugs, services, and general merchandise all in one place. Today, the largest British food retailer is Tesco, a chain operator that has over 30 percent of the grocery market in the United Kingdom. Tesco is expanding rapidly and now has over 2,033 stores in the United Kingdom and almost 1,376 stores in other parts of the world.[17]

Many European countries, however, are passing legislation to make it more difficult for supercentres to open. In France, for example, laws ban authorizations for new supercentres over 1,000 square metres. Belgium and Portugal have passed similar bans. In Britain and the Netherlands, areas outside towns and cities are off-limits to superstores. By imposing planning and building restrictions for large stores, these countries are trying to accommodate environmental concerns, movements to revive city centres, and the worries of small shopkeepers.

An increasingly popular variation of off-price retailing is *extreme-value retailing*. The most notable examples of this are the Dollar Store, Dollarama, and Buck or Two. Extreme-value retailers have grown in popularity as major discounters continue to shift toward the supercentre format. This has created an opening for extreme-value retailers to entice shoppers from the low-income segment. Low- and fixed-income customers are drawn to extreme-value retailers, whose stores are located in their communities. Extreme-value retailers also build smaller stores (a typical store is about the size of one department in a Loblaws superstore) and offer a narrower selection that emphasizes daily necessities. Rock-bottom prices, though, are the key to their success. The average transaction in these stores is under $10. Extreme-value retailers have found low price to be far more critical to building traffic and loyalty than it is for any other retailing format.[18]

Specialty Discount Stores

Another discount niche is single-line **specialty discount stores**—for example, stores selling sporting goods, electronics, auto parts, office supplies, or toys. These stores offer a nearly complete selection of single-line merchandise and use self-service, discount prices, high volume, and high turnover to their advantage. Specialty discount stores are often termed **category killers** because they so heavily dominate their narrow merchandise segment. Examples include Toys "R" Us in toys, Mountain Equipment Co-op in sporting goods, Future Shop and Best Buy in electronics, Staples and Office Depot in office supplies, Rona and Lowes in home improvement supplies, Ikea in home furnishings, and Bed Bath & Beyond in kitchen and bath accessories.

Category killers have emerged in other specialty segments as well, creating retailing empires in highly fragmented mom-and-pop markets. For instance, the office products industry has been changed dramatically. Once more people began to work from home, replacing their typewriters with personal computers and purchasing fax machines, the local stationery store, with its limited selection of paper and writing materials, quickly became obsolete. The industry is now dominated by Office Depot, Staples, and OfficeMax, each of which stocks almost 7,000 different types of products. Category-dominant retailers like these serve their customers by offering a large selection of merchandise, stores that make shopping easy, and low prices every day—which eliminates the need for time-consuming comparison shopping.

Warehouse Membership Clubs

Warehouse membership clubs sell a limited selection of brand-name appliances, household items, and groceries. These are usually sold in bulk from warehouse outlets

on a cash-and-carry basis to members only. Individual members of warehouse clubs are charged low or no membership fees. Currently, Costco and the Real Canadian Wholesale Club dominate the Canadian market in this category; Walmart actually closed its Canadian Sam's Club stores in 2009.[19]

Warehouse clubs have had a strong impact on supermarkets. At 90,000 square feet or more, warehouse clubs offer 60 to 70 percent general merchandise and health and beauty care products, with grocery-related items making up the difference. Warehouse club members tend to be more educated and more affluent and to have larger households than regular supermarket shoppers. These core customers use warehouse clubs to stock up on staples, then they go to specialty outlets or food stores for perishables.

Off-Price Retailers

An **off-price retailer** sells at prices 25 percent or more below traditional department store prices because it pays cash for its stock and usually doesn't ask for return privileges. Off-price retailers buy manufacturers' overruns at cost or even less. They also absorb goods from bankrupt stores, irregular merchandise, and unsold end-of-season output. Nevertheless, much off-price retailer merchandise is top-quality current goods. Because buyers for off-price retailers purchase only what is available or what they can get a good deal on, merchandise styles and brands often change monthly. Today there are dozens of off-price retailers, one of the best known being Winners.

Factory outlets are an interesting variation on the off-price concept. A **factory outlet** is an off-price retailer owned and operated by a manufacturer. Thus it carries one line of merchandise—its own. Each season, 5 to 10 percent of a manufacturer's output does not sell through

Warehouse clubs, like Costco, are growing in popularity by offering savings on everyday items and luxury products. Costco marks up its inventory only by 10 percent, whether it's a case of toothpaste or a case of Dom Perignon champagne.

SOURCE: ASSOCIATED PRESS

regular distribution channels; this percentage consists of closeouts (merchandise being discontinued), factory seconds, and cancelled orders. With factory outlets, manufacturers can regulate where their surplus is sold, and they can realize higher profit margins than they would by disposing of the goods through independent wholesalers and retailers. Factory outlet malls typically locate in out-of-the-way rural areas or near vacation spots. Most are situated at least 15 to 20 kilometres from urban or suburban shopping areas so that manufacturers don't alienate their department store accounts by selling the same goods virtually next door at a discount.

Several manufacturers reaping the benefits of outlet mall popularity include Aldo Outlet and Nine West (shoes); Roots, Hugo Boss, Jones New York, and Tommy Hilfiger (apparel); The Body Shop (soaps and fragrances); and As Seen On TV (housewares). Sears has opened a series of outlet centres to make final attempts to move merchandise that failed to sell in the department stores. The Canada One Outlet Mall, located near the the busy border crossing in Niagara Falls, Ontario, boasts about its status as the number one outlet mall in Canada, having 40 stores, including Adidas, Coach, Guess, Jones New York, Levis, Nike, Roots, Parasuco, and Tommy Hilfiger.

As outlet malls gain in popularity, they are beginning to act less and less like traditional outlets, in which manufacturers sell surplus or damaged goods. Some manufacturers, such as The Gap, Brooks Brothers, Ann Taylor, and Donna Karan, now make lower-quality lines specifically for their outlet stores. Outlet centres are also becoming less sensitive toward department stores that carry their brands at full retail price, and they are choosing to compete with regional malls by adding high-end amenities and entertainment.

RESTAURANTS

Restaurants straddle the line between retailing establishments and service establishments. Restaurants do sell tangible products—food and drink—but they also provide a valuable service for consumers in the form of food preparation and food service. As a retailing institution, restaurants must deal with many of the same issues as more traditional retailers do, such as personnel, distribution, inventory management, promotion, pricing, and location.

Eating out is an important part of Canadians' daily activities and is growing in popularity. According to data from the Canadian Restaurant and Foodservices Association, on average each Canadian spends $1,828 per year on food and alcohol from restaurants and licensed establishments. There are around 83,800 eating establishments in Canada—that is, 25.2 units per 10,000 Canadians. The food service industry employs more than a million Canadians and enjoyed sales of about $59.6 billion in 2008. This means that Canadians spend an average of $35 per person on commercially prepared meals each week. The trend toward dining out has been fuelled by the increase in working mothers and dual-income families, who have more money to spend and less time to prepare meals at home. Money spent on food away from home at restaurants represents about 25 percent of household food budgets, and this percentage is expected to grow.[20]

The restaurant industry is one of the most entrepreneurial of businesses and one of the most competitive. Because barriers to entry are low, the opportunity appeals to many people. The risks, however, are great. About 50 percent of all new restaurants fail within the first year of operation. Restaurants face competition not only from other restaurants but also from consumers, who can easily choose to cook at home. Competition has fostered innovation and ever-changing menus in most segments of the restaurant industry. Many restaurants are now competing directly with supermarkets by offering take-out and delivery in an effort to capture more of the home-meal replacement market. Seeking out and targeting underserved niches is another way restaurants are competing with one another to reach consumers. Fast-food operators are increasingly looking to provide service at locations such as hospitals, airports, schools, and highway rest stops. Companies like Subway and Tim Hortons are partnering with branded service stations to offer customers one-stop shopping. These partnerships save money on leases, lure more customers, and foster innovation.

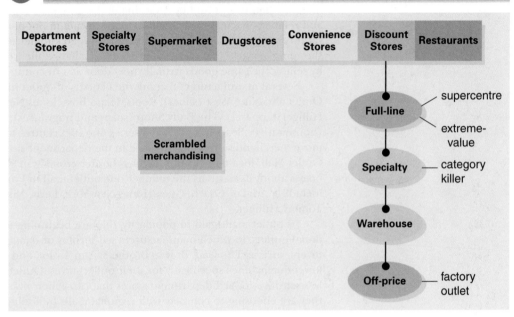

Department Stores	Specialty Stores	Supermarket	Drugstores	Convenience Stores	Discount Stores	Restaurants

Scrambled merchandising

Full-line — supercentre, extreme-value

Specialty — category killer

Warehouse

Off-price — factory outlet

 NONSTORE RETAILING

Discuss nonstore retailing techniques

nonstore retailing
Shopping without visiting a store.

The retailing methods discussed so far have been in-store methods—in other words, customers must physically shop at stores. **Nonstore retailing** is shopping without visiting a store. Because consumers demand convenience, nonstore retailing is currently growing faster than in-store retailing. The major forms of nonstore retailing are automatic vending, direct retailing, direct marketing, and electronic retailing.

AUTOMATIC VENDING

automatic vending
The use of machines to offer goods for sale.

A low-profile yet important form of retailing is **automatic vending**, that is, the use of machines to offer goods for sale—for example, the soft drink, candy, and snack vending machines found in college and university cafeterias and office buildings. In Canada, vending machine and coffee retailers generate annual sales of around $650 million, with most sales coming from food and beverages. Vending machine operators typically have high gross margins, in the over 50 percent range; recently, however, high operating costs have made this form of retailing a break-even proposition in Canada. High gross margins means prices are high; because of the convenience, consumers are willing to pay more for products from a vending machine than for the same products in traditional retail settings.[21]

Retailers are constantly seeking new opportunities to sell via vending (The Global Perspectives box shows how innovative Japanese retailers have been with vending machines). For example, in late 2009 Mark's Work Wearhouse began testing out two vending machines in Ontario to dispense clothing. The first machine was located at the GO Transit bus terminal next to Union Station in Toronto and dispensed items such as umbrellas, mittens, and toques. The second was set up at the William Osler Health Centre in Brampton, Ontario, and dispensed clothing such as loungewear and nurse's scrubs. Mark's partnered with IBM Canada to develop these machines, which are designed to accept only credit and debit cards instead of cash. Another feature of the machines is a set of sensors that sends a wireless signal to indicate that the shelves need more merchandise.[22] Like Mark's Work Warehouse, many vending machines today sell nontraditional kinds of merchandise, such as videos, toys, stickers, sports cards, office-type supplies, film, and disposable cameras. In a sign of the times, shoppers can purchase iPod music players and accessories from specially designed Zoom Store vending machines located in select stores, airports, supermarkets, and other high foot-traffic areas.[23]

TOKYO CONSUMERS EMBRACE VENDING MACHINES

In Tokyo, Japan, vending machines, referred to as *jidoohanbaiki*, are everywhere! In fact, all over Japan you find vending machines, so many that there is one machine for every 23 Japanese citizens.[24] The explosion of vending machines actually had its start in 1964 when Tokyo hosted the summer Olympic Games, and they were needed to feed millions of visitors. The Japanese embraced the machines, and their use grew proportionately so that they have become one of the more important retailing tools in Japan.

Canadians seem to be indifferent when it comes to vending machines. You would think we would be heavier users given we

developed $1 and $2 coins, which were a big advantage for the coin-operated vending machine industry. However, inflation has reached the point where we will soon need $5 and $10 coins to be able to buy what Japanese consumers buy from vending machines! In Japan, consumers are faced with an army of machines dispensing the typical juice, water, and soft drink products we see in Canada but also a whole lot more. For example, green tea comes in dozens of flavours at these machines, and hot coffee and iced coffee in different flavours can be bought from one machine. Food is also available—rice balls, ramen soup, octopus dumplings, and bags of rice. Not only that, but eggs and french fries are offered too. Nonfood items include umbrellas, CDs, DVDS, comic books, hats, shirts, ties, socks, and lingerie. You can even buy flowers and toilet paper! The Japanese sell cigarettes, beer, whiskey, and sake through vending machines. In Japan, the *jidoohanbaiki* are very advanced; they accept credit cards and debit cards and can verify your age and identity with either a special card or a face recognition scanner.

Why have the Japanese embraced vending machines so greatly? There are a number of reasons. Their cultural modesty makes purchasing products like tampons, condoms, and erotica too embarrassing from a "live" sales clerk (North Americans aren't particularly thrilled by live sales of these products, either). It is far more discreet to buy these products from a machine that won't pass any judgment and notice you blushing![25]

SOURCE: OFFWENT.COM/GETSTOCK.COM

SOURCE: DAVID HAYES, "POSTCARD FROM TOKYO: RISE OF THE (VENDING) MACHINES," THIS.ORG/MAGAZINE/2009/06/02, ACCESSED JUNE 6, 2010.

Of course, vending machines are also an important tool in the ongoing cola wars between Coca-Cola and Pepsi. Both companies are constantly looking for new ways to improve vending machine sales. Coca-Cola is implementing "intelligent vending," a cashless payment system. Vending machines with this system accept credit cards, RFID devices, and hotel room keys and can even be accessed via mobile phone (mobile e-commerce, or m-commerce, is discussed later in this chapter).[26]

DIRECT RETAILING

direct retailing
The selling of products by representatives who work door-to-door, office-to-office, or at home parties.

In **direct retailing**, representatives sell products door-to-door, office-to-office, or at home sales parties. Companies like Avon, Mary Kay, Tupperware, Discovery Toys, and Pampered Chef depend on these techniques. Even computers are now being sold this way. Sales by direct retailing in Canada were estimated at more than $1.5 billion in 2008.[27]

Recently the sales of direct retailers have suffered as women have entered the workforce. Working women are not home during the day and have little time to attend selling parties. Although most direct sellers, including cosmetics seller Avon and jewellery seller Silpada, still advocate the party plan method, the realities of the marketplace have forced them to be more creative in reaching their target customers. Direct sales representatives now hold parties in offices, parks, and even parking lots. Others hold informal gatherings where shoppers can drop in at their convenience, or

SOURCE: © PRNEWSFOTO/MOTOROLA INSTANTMOTO

Vending machines have come a long way from accepting coins to sell items like coffee and soda. These days they dispense items as varied as clothing and iPods and accept credit cards and debit cards in payment. They even signal when they need to be restocked!

they offer self-improvement classes. Many direct retailers are also turning to direct mail, telephone, or more traditional retailing venues to find new channels to their customers. Avon has begun opening cosmetics kiosks, called Avon Beauty Centres, in malls and strip centres. Direct retailers are also experimenting with the Internet to reach more buyers and increase sales. Amway's on-line spinoff is called Quixtar.com. Customers access the site using referral numbers unique to each of the Amway reps; this process ensures that the reps earn commissions. Avon, Tupperware, and Mary Kay have followed Amway's lead by setting up Internet retail sites. At Avon's site, individual reps have created home pages that link from Avon's home page so that the sale will still go through them.

In response to the decline in Canadian and U.S. sales growth, many direct retailers are exploring opportunities in other countries. Mary Kay, Avon, and Amway have started successful operations in China by adapting their business models to China's laws. Mary Kay agents in China do not purchase and resell the products; instead, they are paid by sales commission. The company has also changed its slogan from "God First, Family Second, Career Third," to "Faith First, Family Second, Career Third."[28]

DIRECT MARKETING

direct marketing (direct-response marketing)
Techniques used to get consumers to make a purchase from their home, office, or other nonretail setting.

Direct marketing, sometimes called **direct-response marketing**, refers to the techniques used for getting consumers to make a purchase from their home, office, or other nonretail setting. Those techniques include direct mail, catalogue and mail order, telemarketing, and electronic retailing, which together in 2008 represented about $3.7 billion in revenues in Canada.[29] Shoppers using these methods are less bound by traditional shopping situations. Time-strapped consumers and those who live in rural or suburban areas are most likely to be direct-response shoppers because they value the convenience and flexibility that direct marketing provides.

Many retailers employ a direct selling business model as part of a multichannel distribution approach, encompassing electronic retailing, catalogue retailing, and bricks-and-mortar locations. Clothing retailer Justwhiteshirts.com started selling on the Internet but now operates a retail store in Toronto to support its catalogue and e-tailing efforts. Justwhiteshirts.com claims that its retail store holds the greatest selection of dress shirts in Canada. This is the opposite of the usual trend among bricks-and-mortar retailers, many of which have also offered catalogues but are establishing "e-tailing" sites. The multichannel approach has changed the way marketers employ direct marketing techniques.[30]

Direct Mail

Direct mail can be the most efficient or the least efficient retailing method, depending on the quality of the mailing list and the effectiveness of the mailing piece. Promotional expenditures on direct mail were $1.6 billion in 2008.[31] Using direct mail, marketers can precisely target their customers according to demographics, geography, and even psychographics. Good mailing lists come from an internal database or from list brokers for about $35 to $150 per thousand names.

Direct mailers are becoming more sophisticated in targeting the right customers. Using statistical methods to analyze census data, lifestyle and financial information, and past-purchase and credit history, direct mailers can pick out those most likely to buy their products. We'll explore how direct marketers are using customer relationship management (CRM) in Chapter 18.

Catalogues and Mail Order

Canadian consumers can buy just about anything through catalogues and mail order, from the mundane, such as books, music, and polo shirts, to the outlandish, such as the $5-million black diamond fantasy miracle bra offered in the Victoria's Secret catalogue. Catalogue and mail order shopping have been giving way to Internet shopping; one study reported that catalogue and mail order sales have fallen by nearly 50 percent![32] Although most catalogue shoppers are women, the percentage of men has recently soared. As changing demographics have shifted more of the shopping responsibility to men, they are viewing shopping by catalogue, mail order, and the Internet as more sensible than a trip to the mall.

Successful catalogues are usually developed for highly segmented markets. Michelle Warren, writing in *Marketing Magazine*, describes the use of catalogues by Ikea:

> IKEA, which published its first catalogue in 1951, launched in Canada in 1976 and this year will distribute six million books across the country and 160 million worldwide. Cass Hall, marketing manager at Ikea Canada, says, "We've always looked at it as a broader shopping tool. Traditionally it's been to drive people into the store and help plan their visit. More and more it's a branding tool for us." Hall calls it the company's "main marketing tool," adding that the 350-page book features about a third of what its stores offer and highlights specific categories ([one year it was] bedrooms).[33]

Improved customer service and quick delivery policies have boosted consumer confidence in ordering from home. Shoppers can order 24 hours a day and return any merchandise for any reason for a full refund. Successful Canadian mail order catalogues—including Ikea, Mountain Equipment Co-op, and Regal Greetings and Gifts—target hard-working, home-oriented baby boomers who would rather not visit a retail store or don't have time to visit. To remain competitive and save time for customers, catalogue companies are building computer databases containing customer information so that people do not have to repeatedly give their address, credit card information, and so on. They also are working with overnight shippers such as UPS and FedEx to speed up deliveries. Indeed, some products can be ordered as late at 12:30 a.m. and arrive the same day by 10:30 a.m.

Telemarketing

telemarketing
The use of the telephone to sell directly to consumers.

Telemarketing is the use of the telephone to sell directly to consumers. It consists of outbound sales calls, usually unsolicited, and inbound calls—that is, orders through toll-free 800 numbers or fee-based 900 numbers. According to the most recent data, Canadian telemarketing operations employed 270,000 Canadians and produced $16 billion in sales.[34]

Rising postage rates and decreasing long-distance phone rates have made *outbound* telemarketing an attractive direct marketing technique. Skyrocketing field sales costs have also led marketing managers to use outbound telemarketing. Searching for ways to keep costs under control, marketing managers are discovering how to pinpoint prospects quickly, zero in on serious buyers, and keep in close touch with regular customers. Meanwhile, they are reserving expensive, time-consuming, in-person calls for closing sales. Outbound telemarketing is an industry in decline. So many consumers have complained about telemarketing calls that in July 2007, the Canadian Radio-Television and Telecommunications Commission (CRTC) enacted a national "Do Not Call" list to prevent unsolicited telecommunications. Registration for Canadians is via the Internet. It is illegal for marketers to call anyone on this list unless an exception applies. Specifically, the CRTC says that calls may still be made if they are "by or on behalf of registered charities; by or on behalf of political parties; to collect information for a survey; to solicit a subscription for a general-circulation newspaper; and to a consumer that has an existing business relationship with the telemarketer."[35] In addition to putting themselves on the "Do Not Call" registry, consumers can avoid telemarketers by using call display features on their phones and answering machines to screen unwanted calls.

Inbound telemarketing programs, which use 800 and 900 numbers, are mainly used to take orders, generate leads, and provide customer service. Inbound 800 telemarketing has successfully supplemented direct-response TV, radio, and print advertising for more than 25 years.

ELECTRONIC RETAILING

Electronic retailing includes the 24-hour, shop-at-home television networks and on-line retailing.

Shop-at-Home Networks

The shop-at-home television networks are specialized forms of direct-response marketing. These shows display merchandise, with the retail price, to home viewers. Viewers can phone in their orders directly on a toll-free line and shop with a credit card. The shop-at-home industry has quickly grown into a billion-dollar business with a loyal customer following. Shop-at-home networks have the capability of reaching nearly every home that has a television set.

Most TV shopping networks have "converged" their services with the Internet to provide a comprehensive and interactive shopping experience for consumers. The Shopping Channel, based in Toronto, has taken this convergence even further by combining its on-air promotional solicitations with its interactive e-commerce website—**www.theshoppingchannel.com**—a shopping channel blog, a Facebook site, and a Twitter contact, along with a catalogue and an off-air outlet retail store located in Toronto. It even helped consumers finance purchases with the Shopping Channel credit card. This means that customers can stay in contact through Twitter, Blogs, and Facebook and then purchase items they have seen on TV or in the catalogue through the Shopping Channel's website or at the Toronto bricks-and-mortar store. The website ties in with the TV broadcasts by providing daily broadcast schedules. The shows can be viewed through streaming video players.

Home shopping networks attract a broad audience through diverse programming and product offerings. They are now adding new products to appeal to more affluent audiences. On the Shopping Channel, cooking programs attract both men and women, fashion programs attract mostly women, and electronics and coin shows attract primarily men. Since it began broadcasting, the channel has sold a variety of products—Sharp electronics, space savers, and gems and coins.[36]

On-line Retailing

For years, shopping at home meant looking through catalogues and then placing an order over the telephone. For most people today, it means turning on a computer, surfing retail websites, and selecting and ordering products on-line with the click of a mouse. **On-line retailing**, or *e-tailing*, is a type of shopping available to consumers with personal computers and access to the Internet. Canadians are the heaviest Internet users in the world, spending an average of 45.5 hours a month on-line with 75 percent of them accessing the Internet from home; 97 percent of Canadians who use the Internet at home have broadband connections.[37]

On-line retailing has exploded over the past several years; consumers have found this type of shopping convenient and often less costly. Consumers can shop without leaving home, choose from a wide selection of merchants, use shopping comparison services to search the Web for the best price, and then have the items delivered to their doorstep. As a result, on-line shopping continues to grow at a rapid pace. According to Statistics Canada, Canadians in 2007 placed more than 70 million orders on-line and purchased $12.7 billion worth of goods from e-retailers.[38]

Amazon.com is an e-commerce pioneer and represents one of the best examples in the world of how to succeed at e-tailing. Amazon's success is attributed to product selection, customer service, one-click payment methods, and reliable shipping and delivery. Amazon.com was founded in 1995 primarily as an on-line bookseller, but by

on-line retailing
A type of shopping available to consumers with personal computers and access to the Internet.

2010 the company had evolved into a broad-based on-line retailer, and its corporate mission was stated as "We seek to be Earth's most customer-centric company for three primary customer sets: consumer customers, seller customers and developer customers." Amazon's most recent sales were at the $24.5-billion level by selling millions of products to customers all over the world.[39]

Most traditional retailers have jumped on the Internet bandwagon, allowing shoppers to purchase the same merchandise found in their stores from their website. On-line retailing also fits well with traditional catalogue companies, such as the former Winnipeg Fur Exchange. This company started as a fur brokerage in 1970, but the development of a large, Winnipeg-based store along with a catalogue retailing operation in 1978 took the company away from its basic business. The advent of e-tailing, combined with the issue of animal rights, prompted the company to change its name to Winnipeg Outfitters; this change also fit its merchandise mix more appropriately.[40]

REVIEW LEARNING OUTCOME 4

4 | **Discuss nonstore retailing techniques**

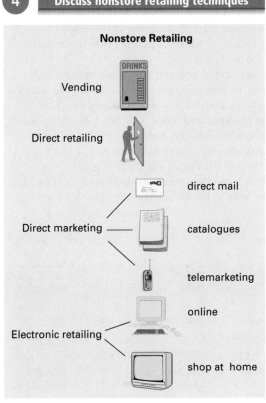

Nonstore Retailing

Vending

Direct retailing

Direct marketing — direct mail

catalogues

telemarketing

online

Electronic retailing

shop at home

As the popularity of on-line retailing grows, it is becoming vital for retailers to go on-line and for their stores, websites, and catalogues to be integrated. Customers expect to find the same brands, products, and prices whether they purchase on-line, on the phone, or in a store. For this reason, retailers are increasingly using in-store kiosks to help tie the channels together for greater customer service. Edmonton-based PharmaPlus is offering Internet-enabled touch-screen kiosks in a number of its stores. The kiosks are multifunctional in that they present TV commercials, point-of-sale advertising, and contests, but they also allow customers to go on-line to access Web portals to get information and even shop. Kiosks are highly useful to pharmacy retailers because they occupy customers who are waiting for their prescriptions. Famous Players Theatres sells tickets through in-theatre kiosks, through its on-line website **www.famousplayers.com**, and of course through its in-theatre box offices. All three ticket venues are linked in order to manage the number of tickets being ordered for a particular showtime in relation to the seating capacity of the theatre. In addition, advanced ticket sales via the Internet enable managers of multiscreen venues to adjust the number of screens and its scheduling based on demand for a particular movie. The linking of information from the websites and kiosks enables Famous Players to conduct data mining; it also provides other management information.[41]

On-line auctions run by Internet companies like eBay.ca and Amazon.ca have enjoyed phenomenal success. With over 90 million users and $60 billion in goods, ranging from antique clocks to car stereos, changing hands each year, eBay is the leader in cyberspace auctions. Internet auction services like eBay run the Web service and collect a token listing fee, plus a commission of 1 to 5 percent when a sale is completed.[42]

5 FRANCHISING

Define franchising and describe its two basic forms

franchiser
The originator of a trade name, product, methods of operation, and so on, that grants operating rights to another party to sell its product.

franchisee
An individual or business that is granted the right to sell another party's product.

A *franchise* is a continuing relationship in which a franchiser grants to a franchisee the business rights to operate or sell a product. The **franchiser** originates the trade name, product, methods of operation, and so on. The **franchisee**, in return, pays the franchiser for the right to use its name, product, or business methods. A franchise agreement between the two parties usually lasts 10 to 20 years, at which time the agreement can be renewed if both parties agree.

To be granted the rights to a franchise, a franchisee usually pays an initial, one-time franchise fee. The amount of this fee depends solely on the individual franchiser, but it generally ranges from $10,000 to $150,000 or more. In addition to this initial franchise fee, the franchisee is expected to pay weekly, biweekly, or monthly royalty fees, usually in the range of 3 to 7 percent of gross revenues. The franchisee may also be expected to pay advertising fees, which usually cover the cost of promotional materials and, if the franchise organization is large enough, regional or national advertising. A McDonald's Canada franchise costs an initial $45,000 per store plus a monthly fee based on the restaurant's sales performance and base rent equal to 20 percent of sales. Franchisees must have $300,000 in "unencumbered" funds. While the dollar amount will vary depending on the type of franchise, fees such as these are typical for all major Canadian franchisers, including Apple Auto Glass, Extreme Pita, Pizza Pizza, and the commercial cleaning company, Jani-King Canada.[43]

Franchising is not new. GM has used this approach since 1898, and Rexall drugstores since 1901. Canadian franchises produce over $100 billion in sales from 76,000 franchised establishments, employ over a million Canadians, and produce about 30 percent of all retail trade sales. Franchised restaurants represent 26 percent of all franchise outlets and attract a lot of those sales; however, hundreds of retail and service franchises, such as Arcadia Academy of Music, Future Stars Photography & Pegasus School Images, and Mathnasium, also are thriving. The Canadian Franchise Association (CFA) identifies 45 different franchise industries, and the *Canadian Franchise Directory* reports Canadian franchise growth to have been over 20 percent since 1993. Industries expected to see real growth in franchising include home repair, business support services, automotive repairs, hair salons, children's services, and telecommunications.[44] Exhibit 12.3 lists some facts about some of the best-known Canadian franchisers and Exhibit 12.4 lists some websites that provide information on franchising.

Two basic forms of franchises are used today: product and trade name franchising, and business format franchising. In *product and trade name franchising*, a dealer agrees to sell certain products provided by a manufacturer or a wholesaler. This approach has been used most widely in the auto and truck, soft drink bottling, tire, and gasoline service industries. A local tire retailer may hold a franchise to sell Michelin tires. Likewise, the Coca-Cola bottler in a particular area is a product and trade name franchisee licensed to bottle and sell Coca-Cola's soft drinks.

Business format franchising is an ongoing business relationship between a franchiser and a franchisee. Typically, a franchiser "sells" a franchisee the rights to use the

EXHIBIT 12.3

Ten Well-Known Canadian Franchisers

Franchiser	Type of Business	Total Units	Initial Investment
Apple Auto Glass Concord, ON	Glass repair and replacement	Franchised units: 118; company-owned units: 4	$100,000–$300,000
Canadian Tire Toronto, ON	Hardware retailing	Franchised units: 475; company-owned units: 0	$125,000+
Harvey's Restaurants Mississauga, ON	Fast food	Franchised units: 151; company-owned units: 111	$450,000–$650,000
Keg Restaurants Richmond, BC	Steakhouse	Franchised units: 52; company-owned units: 32	$2,500,000–$4,000,000
Mr. Sub Toronto, ON	Submarine sandwiches	Franchised units: 400; company-owned units: 2	$15,000+
M&M Meat Shops Kitchener, ON	Frozen food	Franchised units: 469; company-owned units: 4	$260,000–$350,000
Mister Transmission Richmond Hill, ON	Auto transmission repair	Franchised units: 85; company-owned units: 0	$120,000–$150,000
Second Cup Mississauga, ON	Coffee retailer	Franchised units: 360; company-owned units: 0	$100,000–$140,000
Shoeless Joes Vaughan, ON	Restaurant	Franchised units: 40 company-owned units: 0	$550,000–$850,000
Tim Hortons Oakville, ON	Food, baked goods, coffee, doughnuts	Franchised units: 3,000; company-owned units: 18	$194,000

SOURCE: Canadian Franchise Association, www.cfa.ca

EXHIBIT 12.4

Sources of Franchise Information

Some Websites Where People with Questions about Franchising Can Find Answers

- **Buy That Franchise.Ca (www.buythatfranchise.ca):** Describes its service as a "comprehensive and informative franchise directory" that "offers the best in franchise opportunities and expert advice."

- **Canada Business for Entrepreneurs (www.canadabusiness.ca):** Keyword search—franchising; a government agency whose "goal is to help your business grow and succeed through streamlined access to reliable, up-to-date information and services tailored to your needs."

- **Canadian Franchise Association (www.cfa.ca):** "A not-for-profit national trade association [that] represents almost 500 franchise systems and the professionals who support the industry."

- **Canadian Franchise Directory (www.canadianfranchisedirectory.ca):** An "online Web directory solution focused exclusively on making it easier, faster and smarter than ever for Canadians to shop for the perfect franchise opportunity."

- **Franchise Business Review (topfranchises.franchisebusinessreview.com):** A "franchise market research firm that performs independent surveys of franchisee satisfaction."

- **Franchise Direct Canada (www.franchisedirect.ca):** "As one of the leading portals of franchise and business opportunities, Franchise Direct is regarded as a high-quality, efficient company in promoting new franchises and targeting new entrepreneurs worldwide."

- **Franchise Opportunities.Com (canada.franchiseopportunities.com):** Its site says, "As the web's largest directory of franchise opportunities, we aspire to continue giving potential franchisees simple and easy search practices, as well as thorough franchise and business resources."

- **International Franchise Association (www.franchise.org):** Contains information on such topics as buying a franchise and government relations. The site's FAQ section deals with some issues of franchise regulation.

- **American Franchisee Association (www.franchisee.org):** Represents franchisees and has information on legal resources, FTC regulations, and state law.

- **American Association of Franchisees & Dealers (www.aafd.org):** Offers legal and financial information.

franchiser's format or approach to doing business. This form of franchising has expanded rapidly since the 1950s through retailing, restaurant, food service, hotel and motel, printing, and real estate franchises. Fast-food restaurants like McDonald's, Wendy's, and Burger King use this kind of franchising, as do other companies such as Kumon Math & Reading Centres, Supercuts, and Valpak of Canada. To qualify for a Domino's Pizza franchisee, you must have worked in a Domino's pizza store for at least one year. The company believes that after working in an existing location, you will have a better understanding of the company and its values and standards. Then potential franchisees must participate in a series of programs in career development, franchise orientation, presentation skills, and franchise development.[45]

Like other retailers, franchisers are seeking new growth abroad. U.S.-based franchisers have been particularly successful at international expansion and are actively seeking foreign franchisees to open new locations. KFC operates both franchises and company-owned restaurants throughout the world. KFC has 731 franchise restaurants in Canada, around 4,280 franchise and 1,020 company-owned restaurants in the United States, and another 14,000 stores in more than 109 countries around the world, including

SOURCE: PHOTODISC/GETTY IMAGES

Franchising is most frequently thought of with respect to restaurants, but some of the most successful franchises of late are not food related. Kumon Canada Incorporated involves an investment of between $10,000 and $100,000 to start up a math and reading centre.

Japan, Australia, China, Indonesia, and Saudi Arabia. More overseas locations are planned for the near future. KFC's parent company attributes the franchise's success to its ability to adapt to local cultures and tastes without losing control of quality and brand image.[46] The International Franchise Association now lists more than 100 different types of international franchise businesses available in every region of the world.[47]

Franchisers usually allow franchisees to alter their business format slightly in foreign markets. For example, some McDonald's franchisees in Germany sell beer, and in Japan they offer food items that appeal to Japanese tastes, such as steamed dumplings, curry with rice, and roast pork cutlet burgers with melted cheese. McDonald's franchisees in India serve mutton instead of beef because most Indians are Hindu, a religion whose followers believe cows are a sacred symbol of the source of life. The menu also features rice-based vegetable burgers made with peas, carrots, red pepper, beans, and Indian spices, as well as vegetable McNuggets. In spite of menu differences, McDonald's foreign franchisees still maintain the company's standards of service and cleanliness.

REVIEW LEARNING OUTCOME 5

5   **Define franchising and describe its two basic forms**

6 RETAIL MARKETING STRATEGY

List the major tasks involved in developing a retail marketing strategy

Retailers must develop marketing strategies based on overall goals and strategic plans. Retailing goals might include more traffic, higher sales of a specific item, a more upscale image, or heightened public awareness of the retail operation. The strategies retailers use to achieve their goals might include a sale, updated decor, or a new advertising campaign. The key tasks in strategic retailing are defining and selecting a target market and developing the retailing mix to successfully meet the needs of the chosen target market.

DEFINING A TARGET MARKET

The first and foremost task in developing a retail strategy is to define the target market. This process begins with market segmentation, the topic of Chapter 6. Successful retailing has always been based on knowing the customer. Sometimes retailing chains founder when management loses sight of the customers the stores should be serving. For example, after 175 years selling men's shoes in Canada, retail chain Dack's shoes declared bankruptcy. The firm had concentrated on the men's market, selling high-quality and high-priced leather shoes since its founding in 1834 in York, Ontario. In recent times, the firm had begun to lose market share drastically as workplace attire for men became more casual and leather shoes lost ground to less expensive shoe brands like Rockport and Clark's. Dack's went from being known as a quality-shoe retailer to being an "old man's" shoe retailer. A belated attempt to refocus the shoe chain's customer emphasis by bringing in women's shoes was defeated by the recession of 2008–2009, which decreased demand for all retailers and put Dack's into bankruptcy.[48]

Target markets in retailing are often defined by demographics, geography, and psychographics. Quebec-based Croteau has stores everywhere throughout its home province. The company is focusing its marketing effort on the target segment of mothers with young children or teenagers, concentrating on the regions where Croteau has stores. Croteau has studied the shopping habits of its customers and determined that for its offerings, family purchasing is important. It recognizes that Mom is the key purchaser and that children can be key influencers.[49]

Determining a target market is a prerequisite to creating the retailing mix. Walmart Canada has developed a "Store of the Community" program that employs both demographic analysis and market research to ensure local stores stock merchandise that reflects its customer base. Using this information, Walmart Canada placed a line of "Bollywood Signature" women's wear in 16 Canadian stores, including the one in Brampton, Ontario. A marketing journalist reports that the clothing launch was "supported by television ads on local South Asian-language stations, print ads in South Asian publications and a fashion show kick-off" with the result that "the Bollywood clothes sold so well that the line has been expanded to include additional casual and formal options."[50]

CHOOSING THE RETAILING MIX

retailing mix
A combination of the six P's—product, place, promotion, price, presentation, and personnel—to sell goods and services to the ultimate consumer.

Retailers combine the elements of the retailing mix to come up with a single retailing method to attract the target market. The **retailing mix** consists of six P's: the four P's of the marketing mix (product, place, promotion, price) as well as presentation and personnel (see Exhibit 12.5).

EXHIBIT 12.5

The Retailing Mix

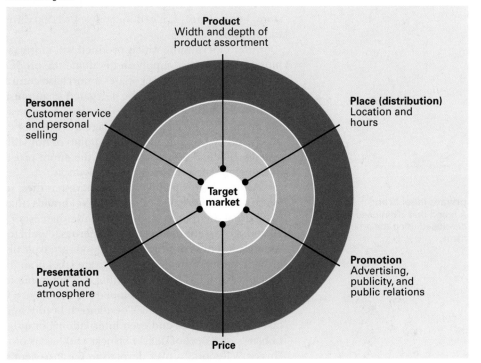

The six P's together project a store's image, which influences consumers' perceptions. Using these impressions of stores, shoppers position one store against another. A retail marketing manager must make sure the store's positioning is compatible with the target customers' expectations. As discussed at the beginning of the chapter, retail stores can be positioned on three broad dimensions: service provided by store personnel, product assortment, and price. Management should use everything else—place, presentation, and promotion—to fine-tune the store's basic positioning.

The Product Offering

product offering
The mix of products offered to the consumer by the retailer; also called the product assortment or merchandise mix.

The first element in the retailing mix is the **product offering**, also called the *product assortment* or *merchandise mix*. Retailers decide what to sell on the basis of what their target market wants to buy. They base their decisions on market research, past sales, fashion trends, customer requests, and other sources. A new technology, called *analytics*, uses complex mathematical models to help retailers make better product-mix decisions. In Canada, The Bay uses this technology to analyze its HBC Rewards customer database, which has approximately 8.5 million members. An example of the power of analytics comes from David Strickland, senior vice-president of marketing at Zellers in Brampton, Ontario, who says: "When someone's buying kids' clothing at either The Bay or at Zellers, we now have the data to tell us that." Using the SKU (stock keeping unit) number within that data, "we actually know what size they're buying, which effectively tells us the sex and age of their kids."[51]

Developing a product offering is essentially a question of the width and depth of the product assortment. *Width* refers to the assortment of products offered; *depth* refers to the number of different brands offered within each assortment. Price, store design, displays, and service are important to consumers in determining where to shop, but the most critical factor is merchandise selection. This reasoning also holds true for on-line retailers. Amazon.com has ambitious plans to build the world's biggest on-line department store so that shoppers can get whatever they want with one click. Like a traditional department store or mass merchandiser, Amazon.ca offers considerable width in its product assortment. The millions of different items it offers include books, music, toys, videos, tools and hardware, health and beauty aids, electronics, and software. Conversely, on-line specialty retailers, such as tigerdirect.ca (electronics) and rugman.com (rugs), focus on a single category of merchandise, hoping to attract loyal customers with a greater depth of products at lower prices as well as with better customer service. Many on-line retailers purposely focus on single-product-line niches that could never garner enough foot traffic to support a traditional bricks-and-mortar store. For instance, Fridgedoor.com sells 1,500 different types of refrigerator magnets to collectors.[52]

After determining which products will satisfy target customers' desires, retailers must find sources of supply and evaluate the products. When the right products are found, the retail buyer negotiates a purchase contract. The buying function can be performed in-house or can be delegated to an outside company. The goods must then be moved from the seller to the retailer, which means shipping, storing, and stocking the inventory. The trick is to manage the inventory by cutting prices to move slow goods and by keeping adequate supplies of hot-selling items in stock. As in all good systems, the final step is to evaluate the entire process to seek more efficient methods and to eliminate problems and bottlenecks.

private label brand
A brand that is designed and developed using the retailer's name.

As margins drop and competition intensifies, retailers are becoming ever more aware of the advantages of **private label brands**, that is, brands designed and developed using the retailer's name. Because the cost of goods typically makes up between 70 and 85 percent of a retailer's expenses, eliminating intermediaries can shave costs. As a result, prices of private label goods are typically lower than for national brands, giving customers greater value. Private label branding is not new. For decades, Canadian Tire has been fashioning its Mastercraft and MotoMaster brands into household names. Loblaw has developed the President's Choice private label brand, which has become one of Canada's best-known brands and has been so successful it has taken on a "national and even international brand status." The brand is plastered on Loblaw's own fleet of delivery trucks and has its own website. Loblaw publishes the "Insider's Report," a flyer devoted to the President's Choice brand, and has even set up its own financial services, President's Choice Financial. Because Loblaw is the nation's largest food retailer, its President's Choice brand worries many major brand marketers, including international giants such as Coca-Cola and PepsiCo. Loblaw was once just an extremely important customer for both Coca-Cola Canada and PepsiCo Canada. With the introduction of President's Choice Cola and President's Choice Diet Cola, Canada's largest food retailer has transformed itself into a major competitor to both Coca-Cola and PepsiCo in the Canadian market. And although President's Choice will not be sending popular brands like Coke and Pepsi to the sidelines anytime soon, in the long run smaller second- and third-tier brands that don't bring consumers to the shelves may have a difficult time surviving.[53]

Promotion Strategy

Retail promotion strategy includes advertising, public relations and publicity, and sales promotion. The goal is to position the store in consumers' minds. Retailers design intriguing ads, stage special events, and develop promotions aimed at their target markets. Today's grand openings are carefully orchestrated blends of advertising, merchandising, goodwill, and glitter. All the elements of an opening—press coverage, special events, media advertising, and store displays—are carefully planned. For example, when Canadian Tire first introduced its Q store concept in Mississauga, Ontario (a Q store is a gasoline station that also sells Canadian Tire convenience items and offers a Starbucks outlet, a Tucker's Kitchen, and a Sobeys store), the firm began by publicizing the opening celebrations. The grand opening featured a half-price sale on gasoline from 6 a.m. to 9 p.m., followed with appearances by former Toronto Maple Leaf star Darryl Sittler, mayor Hazel McCallion, and city councillor Eve Adams. The event blocked traffic and generated local news stories on radio and TV stations and in newspapers.[54]

Retailers' advertising is mostly local, although major retailers like Canadian Tire and HBC advertise nationally. Local retailers' ads usually provide specific information about stores, such as location, merchandise, hours, prices, and special sales. By contrast, national retail ads generally focus on image. Since entering Canada in the mid-1990s, Walmart has conducted a "Watch Out For Falling Prices" ad campaign to position the company as a low-priced retailer.

Many retailers combine their ad campaigns with those of brand-name manufacturers—a popular practice known as cooperative advertising. Traditionally, marketers would pay retailers to feature their products in store mailers, or a marketer would develop a TV campaign for the product and simply tack on several retailers' names at the end. More and more retailers are using co-op ads that integrate brand-name products. Ads linking Adidas Footwear with Athletes World, a Canadian athletic clothing and footwear chain, let everyone know that the latter sells the former's latest styles. In turn, these ads expand the reach of Adidas's advertising. Another common form of co-op advertising involves the promotion of exclusive products. The Martha Stewart product line was exclusive to Zellers when it first came to Canada, and the advertising campaign accomplished the dual role of promoting the products and attracting customers to the store. Now Sears Canada has acquired the distribution rights for the Martha Stewart line and will have to establish a new store relationship for this brand in the minds of Canadian customers. The linking of a store's image to a brand's image is something that retailers *and* manufacturers must consider. See the accompanying "Ethics in Marketing" box regarding British retailer French Connection U.K.

Many retailers nowadays are reducing or even forgoing media ads in favour of direct mail or frequent-shopper programs. Direct mail and catalogue programs are luring many retailers, who hope the programs will be cost-effective means of increasing brand loyalty and spending by core customers. Each quarter, Greenhawk Harness and Equestrian mails a catalogue to the equestrian community across the country. Hardware outlets such as Canadian Tire and Home Hardware have also used direct mail, often around holidays, when people have time off to complete needed repairs. Restaurants and small retailers have successfully used frequent-diner or frequent-shopper programs for years. Many retail chains, including Shoppers Drug Mart and Sears Canada, offer frequent-shopper programs with perks ranging from gift certificates to special "members only" sale prices.

Ethics in Marketing

 RETAILING A CONTROVERSIAL BRAND

As discussed earlier, retailers often like to have their stores associated with new, well-known national brands in order to create customer loyalty and develop new customer relationships. But what if influential people in the marketplace are repelled by your retail concept?

British retailer French Connection U.K., which operates 14 retail stores in major metropolitan areas in Canada, developed a unique customer franchise in Europe for its clothing and fragrance products with a controversial brand name supported by edgy advertising focusing on the company's initials, F.C.U.K. Clearly, the usual "promise of benefit" of clothing and fragrance products is to attract the opposite sex; French Connection U.K.'s brand name takes this promise to its "base" level. In both Canada and the United States, many influential consumer groups are incensed by the company's name as well as by its ad campaigns.

Some examples: A set of transit ads scheduled to run in Vancouver were cancelled after a single bus driver raised concerns that the company's name could lead to "harassing comments." French Connection U.K. developed an ad campaign with two new fragrance brands labelled FCUK Him and FCUK Her. Print ads were placed in magazines such as *Cosmopolitan, Marie Claire, Maxim, Seventeen,* and *Teen People.* These ads featured sexually suggestive photos of a scantily clad couple and used the logo "Scent to Bed." Parental complaints were made to *Seventeen* and *Teen People,* and these magazines immediately dropped the ads. A spokesperson for French Connection U.K.'s distributor in the United States said that she didn't realize the audience for these two magazines was so young.

In Toronto, the retailer set up a window display in its Bloor Street store that had a male mannequin standing with a pair of pants down at his ankles. Two other male mannequins were dressed but looking on. A caption read, "Does this condom make me look fat? FCUK safely." The display generated a strong public reaction, to which the managing director of French Connection Canada, Elizabeth Hardy, replied: "It was about promoting safe sex by using the FC humour that's always applied in our advertisements." F.C.U.K. was using this display as part of a campaign against AIDS timed in conjunction with the Toronto Gay Pride parade. The retailer promised to donate 2 percent of sales revenue from T-shirts promoting these kinds of messages to the Canadian Foundation for AIDS Research. In light of this cause and its event timing, the *Toronto Star,* with great reservations, agreed to accept an ad that used the same caption.[55]

What do you think F.C.U.K. should do? How should it handle the negative publicity? Should it scrap its name and, if so, what name should the company use?

SOURCE: CANADA.FRENCHCONNECTION.COM; STREET TALK, "FCUK'S 'FRONT END,'" MARKETING MAGAZINE, JULY 14, 2003; DAVID MENZIES, "COMPLAIN, COMPLAIN, COMPLAIN," MARKETING MAGAZINE, NOVEMBER 20, 2000; JENNIFER CAMPBELL, "FCUK'S RISQUE ADS GET THE BOOT," CANWEST NEWS, DON MILLS, OCTOBER 20, 2003, 1.

The Proper Location

The retailing axiom "location, location, location" has long emphasized the importance of place to the retail mix. The location decision is important, first, because the retailer is making a large, semi-permanent commitment of resources that can reduce its future flexibility. Second, the location will affect the store's growth and profitability.

Site location begins with choosing a community. Important factors to consider are the area's economic growth potential, the amount of competition, and geography. Retailers like Winners, Walmart, and Toys "R" Us build stores in areas where the population is growing. Often these large retailers build stores in communities that are still under development. While population growth is an important consideration for fast-food restaurants, most also look for an area that already has other fast-food restaurants because clusters draw customers for all restaurants. However, even after careful research, the perfect position can be elusive in the face of changing markets. For example, Wendy's Restaurants found when attempting to enter the competitive breakfast business that its locations weren't positioned on the right side of the road to attract the bulk of commuters looking for breakfast.[56] Finally, for many retailers geography remains the most important factor in choosing a community. Many retailers, such as Starbucks, look for densely populated urban communities; by contrast, the North West Company, a company historically associated with Canada's fur trade, locates in small and remote northern Canadian communities stretching from British Columbia to Labrador.

After settling on a geographic region or community, retailers must choose a specific site. Besides growth potential, the important factors are neighbourhood socioeconomic characteristics, traffic flows, land costs, zoning regulations, and public transportation. A particular site's visibility, parking, entrance and exit locations, accessibility, and safety and security issues are other variables contributing to site selection. Additionally, a retailer should consider how its store would fit into the surrounding environment. Retail decision makers probably would not want to locate a Great Canadian Dollar store next door to a Les Ailes de la Mode department store.

One final decision about location faces retailers: whether to have a freestanding unit or to become a tenant in a shopping centre or mall.

Freestanding Stores

destination stores
Stores that consumers purposely plan to visit.

An isolated, freestanding location can be used by large retailers such as Walmart, Shoppers Drug Mart, and Canadian Tire, and by companies that sell shopping goods such as furniture and cars, because these are "destination" stores. **Destination stores** are stores that consumers seek out and then purposely plan to visit. An isolated store location may have the advantages of low site cost or rent and no nearby competitors. On the other hand, it may be hard to attract customers to a free-standing location, and there are no other retailers around with which to share costs.

Freestanding units are increasing in popularity as retailers strive to make their stores more convenient to access, more enticing to shop in, and more profitable. Freestanding sites are being developed at an increasing rate as more and more retailers are deciding not to locate in pedestrian malls. Perhaps the biggest reason for developing a freestanding site is greater visibility. Retailers often feel that they get lost in huge centres and malls; freestanding units can help stores develop an identity with shoppers. The ability to grow at faster rates through freestanding buildings has also propelled the surge toward standalone units. Retailers like Leon's, Ikea, and Future Shop often choose to be freestanding in order to achieve their expansion objectives. Finally, an aggressive expansion plan may not allow time to wait for shopping centres to be built. Similarly, drugstore chains like Shoppers Drug Mart and Rexall have been aggressively relocating their existing mall and shopping centre stores to freestanding sites, especially street corner sites for drive-through accessibility.

Shopping Centres

Shopping centres began in the 1950s when Canadians started migrating to the suburbs. The first shopping centres were *strip centres*, typically located along a busy street. They usually included a supermarket, a variety store, and perhaps a few specialty stores. Then *community shopping centres* emerged, with one or two small department store branches, more specialty shops, one or two restaurants, and several apparel stores. These community shopping centres provided off-street parking and a broader variety of merchandise.

Regional Malls

Regional malls, which offer a much wider variety of merchandise, started appearing in the mid-1970s. Regional malls are either entirely enclosed or roofed to allow shopping in any weather. Many are landscaped with trees, fountains, sculptures, and the like to enhance the shopping environment. They have hectares of free parking. The *anchor stores* or *generator stores* (e.g., The Bay, Sears, or Zellers) are usually located at opposite ends of the mall to create heavy foot traffic. The West Edmonton Mall in Edmonton, Alberta, has six anchor stores, including The Bay, Sears, Zellers, The Brick, Winners, and London Drugs.[57]

According to shopping centre developers, *lifestyle centres* are now emerging as the newest generation of shopping centres. They offer time-pressed consumers a more convenient alternative to malls. These new, open-air shopping centres are targeted to upper-income shoppers with an aversion to malls and seek to create an atmosphere that is part neighbourhood park and part urban shopping centre. Lifestyle centres have upscale retail space occupied by trendy restaurants and specialty retailers. Other attractions include expensive landscaping and convenient parking. The Heartland Centre in Mississauga, Ontario, is a lifestyle centre featuring specialty stores such as Fairweather, Harry Rosen, Adidas, Golf Town, Bowring, Home Outfitters, XS Cargo,

When not actually browsing or buying, people enjoy a comfortable and memorable experience in a shopping environment. Shopping malls and lifestyle centres now provide shoppers with kids' play towns and parents' rooms for retreating with babies and toddlers.

SOURCE: © PR NEWSFOTO/MALL OF AMERICA

Best Buy, Future Shop, and Tiger Direct; it also includes restaurants such as The Keg, East Side Marios, Swiss Chalet, Krispy Kreme, and virtually all the major fast-food chains.[58]

Locating in a community shopping centre or regional mall offers several advantages. First, the facilities are designed to attract shoppers. Second, the shopping environment, anchor stores, and "village square" activities draw customers. Third, ample parking is available. Fourth, the centre or mall projects a unified image. Fifth, tenants share the expenses of the mall's common area as well as promotions for the whole mall. Finally, malls can target different demographic groups. Some malls are considered upscale; others are aimed at people shopping for bargains.

Locating in a shopping centre or mall does have disadvantages. These include expensive leases, the chance that common promotion efforts will not attract customers to a particular store, lease restrictions on merchandise carried and hours of operation, the anchor stores' domination of the tenants' association, and the possibility of having direct competitors within the same facility. Consumers have also become more pressed for time in recent years and have decreased the number of visits and the time they spend in malls in favour of more convenient standalone stores and neighbourhood centres. Faced with this trend, mall developers have improved the layout of many malls to make it more convenient for customers to shop.

Retail Prices

Another important element in the retailing mix is price. Retailing's ultimate goal is to sell products to consumers, and the right price is critical in ensuring sales. Because retail prices are usually based on the cost of the merchandise, an essential part of pricing is efficient and timely buying.

Price is also a key element in a retail store's positioning strategy and classification. Higher prices often indicate a level of quality and help reinforce the prestigious image of retailers, as they do for Birks, Harry Rosen, Rolex, and Reitman's. On the other hand, discounters and off-price retailers, such as Zellers and Winners, offer good value for the money. There are even stores, such as Dollarama, where the majority of products cost shoppers one dollar. Dollarama's single-price-point strategy is aimed at getting higher-income customers to make impulse purchases through what analysts call the "wow factor"—the excitement of discovering that an item costs only a dollar.

A pricing trend among North American retailers that seems to be here to stay is *everyday low pricing*, or EDLP. Introduced to the retail industry by Walmart, EDLP offers consumers low prices all the time instead of holding periodic sales on merchandise. The Gap reduced prices on denim jeans, denim shirts, socks, and other items to protect and broaden the company's share of the casual clothes market. Supermarket chains such as Loblaws and Sobeys are also featuring EDLP.

Presentation of the Retail Store

The presentation of a retail store helps determine the store's image; it also positions the retail store in consumers' minds. For instance, a retailer that wants to position itself as an upscale store would use a lavish or sophisticated presentation.

The main element of a store's presentation is its **atmosphere**, the overall impression conveyed by its physical layout, decor, and surroundings. The atmosphere might create a relaxed or a busy feeling, a sense of luxury or of efficiency, a friendly or a cold attitude, a sense of organization or of clutter, a fun or a serious mood. HMV music stores have a recording studio feel, with areas for private listening. Roots clothing stores, with their log walls, project a sense of the rustic outdoors. Many Chapters stores have a Starbucks coffee outlet inside so that people can have a coffee and relax while they read.

The layout of retail stores is a key factor in their success. Layout is planned so that all space in the store is used effectively, including aisles, fixtures, merchandise displays, and nonselling areas. Effective store layout ensures the customer's shopping ease and convenience, but it also has a powerful influence on customer traffic patterns and purchasing behaviour.

Layout includes where products are placed in the store (see Anatomy of a Store Layout). Many technologically advanced retailers are using a technique called *market basket analysis* to analyze the huge amounts of data collected through their point-of-purchase scanning equipment. The analysis looks for products that are commonly purchased together to help retailers place products in the right places. Walmart uses market basket analysis to determine where in the store to stock products for customer convenience.[59] Bananas are placed not only in the produce section but also in the cereal aisle. Kleenex tissues are in the paper goods aisle and also mixed in with the cold medicines. Measuring spoons are in housewares and also hanging next to Crisco shortening. During October, flashlights are placed with the Halloween costumes as well as in the hardware aisle.

These are the most influential factors in creating a store's atmosphere:

- *Employee type and density.* Employee type refers to an employee's general characteristics—for instance, neat, friendly, knowledgeable, or service oriented. Density is the number of employees per 100 square metres of selling space. A discounter like Zellers has a low employee density that creates a "do it yourself," casual atmosphere. In contrast, Holt Renfrew's density is much higher, denoting readiness to serve the customer's every whim. Too many employees and not enough customers, however, can convey an air of desperation and intimidate customers.

- *Merchandise type and density.* The type of merchandise carried and how it is displayed add to the atmosphere the retailer is trying to create. A prestigious retailer like Les Ailes de la Mode in Montreal carries the top brand names and displays them in a neat, uncluttered arrangement. Discounters and off-price retailers may sell some well-known brands, but many carry seconds or out-of-season goods. Their merchandise may be stacked so high that it falls into the aisles, helping create the impression that "we've got so much stuff, we're practically giving it away."

- *Fixture type and density.* Fixtures can be elegant (rich woods), or trendy (chrome and smoked glass), or consist of old, beat-up tables, as in an antiques store. The fixtures should be consistent with the general atmosphere the store is trying to create. Apple has let its focus on design inform the look of its retail stores. Many Apple stores contain a signature glass staircase designed in part by CEO Steve Jobs, and all use large open tables to display company products. Because products are not cluttered on store shelves, it is easier for store visitors to play with them.[60]

- *Sound.* Sound can be pleasant or unpleasant for a customer. Classical music at a nice Italian restaurant helps create ambience, just as country-and-western music does at a truck stop. Music can entice customers to stay in the store longer and buy more, or it can encourage them to eat quickly and leave a table for others. For instance, rapid music tends to make people eat more, chew less, and take bigger bites, whereas slow music prompts people to dine more slowly and eat less. Retailers can tailor their musical atmosphere to their shoppers' demographics and the merchandise they are selling. Music can control the pace of the store traffic, create an image, and attract or direct the shopper's attention. In Quebec, Les Ailes de la Mode features piano music by live pianists in the entrances to its stores. Coffee shops are also getting into the music business, as are theme restaurants like Hard Rock Café, Planet Hollywood, Harley-Davidson Café, and Rainforest Café,

1 If a store wants to project a "service" image as well as "fresh food" image, services are placed near the entrance.

2 Vegetables and fruits are placed near beginning of the store's traffic pattern for their inviting, "fresh food" image.

3 Pharmacy + floral shop + restaurant = scrambled merchandizing.

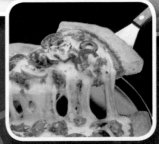

4 "Race track" arrangement keeps customers moving through the store and making purchases.

5 Staples such as meat, eggs, milk, and bakery items are placed farthest from the entrance because the more products a shopper passes by, the more they are likely to purchase.

7 Reduced service (self bagging and self checkout) saves time and reduces costs.

6 Food manufacturers pay "slotting" fees to get aisle end caps and eye-level shelf space. Upper- and lower-level shelf space is reserved for low-margin/low-profit items.

This enormous frog sculpture crowns the entrance to the Rainforest Café. Coupled with the giant toadstools that flank the doors, the sculptures that decorate the outside of the restaurant create an impression of fun and whimsy.

which turn eating a hamburger and fries into an experience. Starbucks and Victoria's Secret sell copies of their background music, hoping that the music will remind consumers of the feeling of being in their stores.

• *Odours.* Smell can either stimulate or detract from sales. The wonderful smell of pastries and breads entices bakery customers. Conversely, customers can be repulsed by bad odours such as cigarette smoke, musty smells, antiseptic odours, and overly powerful room deodorizers. If a grocery store pumps in the smell of baked goods, sales in that department increase threefold. Department stores have pumped in fragrances that are pleasing to their target market, and the response has been favourable. Not surprisingly, retailers are increasingly using fragrance as a key design element, as important as layout, lighting, and background music. Research suggests that people evaluate merchandise more positively, spend more time shopping, and are generally in a better mood when an agreeable odour is present. Retailers use fragrances as an extension of their retail strategy. The Rainforest Café, for instance, pumps fresh-flower extracts into its retail sections.[61]

• *Visual factors.* Colours can create a mood or focus attention and therefore are an important factor in atmosphere. Red, yellow, and orange are considered warm colours and are used when a feeling of warmth and closeness is desired. Cool colours like blue, green, and violet are used to open up closed-in places and create an air of elegance and cleanliness. Some colours are better for display. For instance, diamonds appear most striking against black or dark blue velvet. Lighting can also have an important effect on store atmosphere. Jewellery is best displayed under high-intensity spotlights, cosmetics under more natural lighting. Many retailers have found that natural lighting, either from windows or skylights, can lead to increased sales. Outdoor lighting can also affect consumer patronage. Consumers often are afraid to shop after dark in many areas and prefer strong lighting for safety. The outdoor facade of the store also adds to its ambience. It can help create favourable first impressions among shoppers, as well as help establish a visual identity for the store. Canadian book retailer Chapters has developed stores with unique designs, colours, and facades that identify them to customers at a distance even before customers are close enough for their eyes to read the signage.

Personnel and Customer Service

People are a unique aspect of retailing. Most retail sales involve a customer—salesperson relationship, if only briefly. When customers shop at a grocery store, the cashiers check and bag their groceries. When customers shop at a prestigious clothier, the salesclerks may help select the styles, sizes, and colours. They may also assist in the fitting process, offer alteration services, wrap purchases, and even offer a glass of champagne. Sales personnel provide their customers with the amount of service prescribed in the retail strategy of the store.

Retail salespeople serve another important selling function: they persuade shoppers to buy. They must therefore be able to convince customers that what they are selling is what the customer needs. Salespeople are trained in two common selling techniques: trading up and suggestion selling. Trading up means persuading customers to buy a higher-priced item than they originally intended to buy. To avoid selling customers something they do not need or want, however, salespeople should take care when practising trading-up techniques. Suggestion selling, a common practice among retailers, seeks to broaden customers' original purchases with related

PRODUCT
Width and depth of product assortment

PLACE
Location and hours

PROMOTION
Advertising, publicity, public relations

PRICE

PRESENTATION
Layout and atmosphere

PERSONNEL
Customer service and personal selling

TARGET

items. McDonald's cashiers may ask customers whether they would like dessert with their meal. Suggestion selling and trading up should always help shoppers recognize true needs rather than load them with unwanted merchandise.

Providing great customer service is one of the most challenging elements in the retail mix because customer expectations for service are so varied. What customers expect in a department store is very different from their expectations for a discount store. Customer expectations also change. Ten years ago, shoppers wanted one-on-one attention. Today, most customers are happy to help themselves as long as they can easily find what they need. To respond to this new perspective, some retailers are adding retail sales technologies that maximize salesperson helpfulness while minimizing intrusion. New handheld devices marketed by Motorola enable sales associates to look up product information on the spot and to communicate with other associates in order to facilitate the quick response needed for customer questions.[62]

Customer service is also critical for on-line retailers. On-line shoppers expect a retailer's website to be easy to use, products to be available, and returns to be simple. The Canadian Online Shopping Mall promotes the following virtues of on-line shopping: dependability, 24/7 shopping, privacy and security, immediate access to consumer information, comparative shopping with the use of "shopping agents," clean environment, time savings, access to virtual storefronts of bricks-and-mortar retailers, easy gift buying and shipping, and cross-border shopping. Many on-line retailers have begun including a return envelope with all orders to make returns easier for the customer.[63]

 NEW DEVELOPMENTS IN RETAILING

Describe new developments in retailing

In an effort to better serve their customers and attract new ones, retailers are constantly adopting new strategies. Three recent developments are interactivity, m-commerce, and pop-up shops.

INTERACTIVITY

Adding interactivity to the retail environment has been one of the most popular strategies in retailing over the past few years. Small retailers as well as national chains are using interactivity in stores to differentiate themselves from the competition. For some time, retailers have used "entertainment" retailing in the form of playing music, showing videos, hosting special events, and sponsoring guest appearances; however, the new interactive trend gets customers involved instead of just catching their eye. For example, Build-A-Bear enables customers to make their own stuffed animal by choosing which animal to stuff and then dressing and naming it. You can hold birthday parties at Build-A-Bear, too.

One of the newest concepts in interactivity has been developed by Experticity, a firm based in Seattle, Washington, which specializes in customer-service products for the retail and hospitality industry. The firm has developed a product called Experticity In Store, which is designed to allow "customers to reach a live salesperson at the other end of the technological connection." According to Experticity president, D. L. Baron, "Our customer stations have no keyboard and no mouse. A touch screen routes the customer to a live on-screen person—if I'm in the plumbing department of a store, I'll get a plumber; if I'm in the electric department, I'll get an electrician. In fact, we can make it so easy that you don't need to touch the screen. We can make it motion triggered, so they (the salesperson) can come on and ask if there's anything you need." Experticity has been working with Staples in Canada to develop Video Agent, a version of Experticity In Store that is specific to Staples.[64]

M-COMMERCE

M-commerce (mobile e-commerce) enables consumers using wireless mobile devices to connect to the Internet and shop. Essentially, m-commerce goes beyond text message advertisements to allow consumers to purchase goods and services by using wireless mobile devices, such as mobile telephones, pagers, personal digital assistants (PDAs), and handheld computers. For example, both PepsiCo and Coca-Cola have developed smart vending technologies that use a "cashless" payment system that accepts credit cards, RFID devices, and even hotel room keys. Offices across the country are installing self-serve coffee machines where office workers can buy freshly brewed single-cup gourmet coffee and conveniently pay with their traditional magnetic stripe credit or debit cards. The company AIR-serv plans to install cashless transaction terminals for its coin-operated tire inflation and vacuuming machines at gas stations and convenience stores. Cashless services are also available for the vending industry, laundry facilities, parking and toll booths, photo and video kiosks, hotel business centres, and a variety of other commercial markets.[65] M-commerce enjoyed early success overseas, but has been slower in gaining acceptance and popularity in Canada even though a majority of Canadians have access to mobile devices. For instance, Japan has over 95 million wireless subscribers, of which 27 million are m-commerce users, generating $10 billion in sales. One research company in the United Kingdom, Juniper Research, predicts the global m-commerce market will reach at least $88 billion this decade.[66]

pop-up shops
Temporary retail establishments that allow flexible locations without the long-term commitment of a more expensive retail lease.

7 — **Describe new developments in retailing**

Interactivity gets consumers involved in retail experience.

M-commerce is purchasing goods through mobile devices.

Pop-up shops provide flexible locations without long-term commitment.

Small stores within larger stores—a store-in-a-store—provide shopping convenience.

POP-UP-SHOPS

Companies of all sizes are experimenting with pop-up shops. As the name implies, pop-up shops are temporary retail establishments that allow companies to have flexible locations without the long-term commitment of a more expensive retail lease. For example, Toronto Life.com advertises pop-up shops like the temporary clothing boutique containing clothing from Canadian fashion designers Juma, Aime, Philip Sparks, and Jessica Jensen, which was set up in the Fashion Designers Guild in Toronto during weekends in June 2010. Italian coffee maker Illy opened a pop-up shop at Time Warner Center in New York for ten days. In addition to selling coffee, the Illy shop, created from a shipping container, offered free samples from the company's soon-to-be-released Hyper Espresso System machine.[67]

Wired magazine incorporated interactivity in its holiday pop-up shop. Customers could try out over 100 of the latest techie toys and participate in a SoHo, New York, scavenger hunt (contestants used a Palm Centro to navigate through the game) for a chance at winning a Nintendo Wii.[68]

Another trend in pop-up retailing is the store-in-a-store model. Recently Umbro, known for its soccer sports apparel, opened a pop-up shop in Norml, an Ottawa-based clothing boutique. Umbro wanted to take advantage of the 2010 World Cup and was selling limited-edition soccer apparel. Companies as diverse as Apple, Kolo (an international photo album company), and others have used the store-in-a-store concept throughout the world. Apple has stores in various Best Buy stores in North America and FNAC stores in France; and Kolo opened a 450-square-foot Kolo Boutique inside Kate's Paperie, a famous stationery store in New York.[69]

1 **Discuss the importance of retailing in the Canadian economy.** Retailing plays a vital role in the Canadian economy for two main reasons. First, retail businesses contribute to our high standard of living by providing a vast number and diversity of goods and services. Second, retailing employs a large part of the Canadian working population—2.15 million people.

1.1 To fully appreciate the role retailing plays in the Canadian economy, it may be helpful to visit the website of the Retail Council of Canada, the key trade association representing this vital economic sector. Visit **www.retailcouncil.org** and search for items and information pertaining to retailing in Canada. Read a selection of items and report your findings to the class.

1.2 Keep a shopping journal that details all the retail establishments you visit in a week, how long you spent in each store, how much money you spent, and the reason for your visit. At the end of the week, review your journal and analyze your relationship to retail. As a class, compile your results to get a picture of shopping habits and consumer behaviour.

2 **Explain the dimensions by which retailers can be classified.** Many different kinds of retailers exist. A retail establishment can be classified according to ownership, level of service, product assortment, price, and place of business. On the basis of ownership, retailers can be differentiated broadly as independent retailers, chain stores, or franchise outlets. The level of service retailers provide can be classified along a continuum of high to low. Retailers also classify themselves by the breadth and depth of their product assortments: some retailers have concentrated product assortments, whereas others have extensive product assortments. General price levels also classify a store: from discounters offering low prices, to exclusive specialty stores where high prices are the norm. Lastly, retailers can be classified by place of business: either a physical in-store location where consumers come to shop, or a nonstore location where consumers may shop using communications technologies. Retailers use these latter four variables to position themselves in the marketplace.

2.1 Form a team of three classmates to identify different retail stores in your city where pet supplies are sold. Include nonstore forms of retailing as well, such as catalogues, the Internet, or the local veterinarian. Team members should divide up and visit all the different retailing outlets for pet supplies. Prepare a report describing the differences in brands and products sold at each of the retailing formats and the differences in store characteristics and service levels. For example, which brands are sold via mass merchandiser, independent specialty store, or other type of retailer? Suggest why different products and brands are distributed through different types of stores.

2.2 Identify some popular "entertainment" retailers in your immediate area. Classify them according to the dimensions discussed in the chapter. Do any trends emerge? What conclusions can you draw about entertainment and retailing, if any?

2.3 Identify some retailers in your immediate area that have both an in-store and nonstore "place of business." How many retailers did you identify? Which "place of business" do you find most appealing? Explain your reasoning.

3 **Describe the major types of retail operations.** The major types of retail stores are department stores, specialty retailers, supermarkets, drugstores, convenience stores, discount stores, and restaurants. Department stores carry a wide assortment of shopping and specialty goods, are organized into relatively independent departments, and offset higher prices by emphasizing customer service and decor. Specialty retailers typically carry a narrower but deeper assortment of merchandise, emphasizing distinctive products and a high level of customer service. Supermarkets are large self-service retailers that offer a wide variety of food products and some nonfood items. Drugstores are retail formats that sell mostly prescription and over-the-counter medications, health and beauty aids, cosmetics, and specialty items. Convenience stores carry a limited line of high-turnover convenience goods. Discount stores offer low-priced general merchandise and consist of four types: full-line discounters, specialty discount retailers, warehouse clubs, and off-price retailers. Finally, restaurants straddle the line between the retailing and services industries; although restaurants sell a product, food and drink, to final consumers they can also be considered service marketers because they provide consumers with the service of preparing food and providing table service.

3.1 Discuss the possible marketing implications of the recent trend toward supercentres, which combine a supermarket with a full-line discount store.

3.2 Explain the function of warehouse clubs. Why are they classified as both wholesalers and retailers?

3.3 Would you be interested in buying luxury items, like expensive jewellery, at a warehouse club or a discount department store? Walmart offered a $350,000 diamond solitaire ring during a recent Christmas shopping season. If you could afford such a ring, would you consider buying it at Walmart? Why or why not?

4 **Discuss nonstore retailing techniques.** Nonstore retailing, which is shopping outside a store setting, has three main categories. Automatic vending uses machines to offer products for sale. In direct retailing, the sales transaction occurs in a home setting, typically through door-to-door sales or party plan selling. Direct marketing refers to the techniques used to get consumers to buy from their homes or place of business. Those techniques include direct mail, catalogues and mail order, telemarketing, and electronic retailing, such as home shopping channels and on-line retailing using the Internet.

4.1 Have you or someone you know well ever attended a "direct selling" party for products like Tupperware or Magic Chef? What was the experience like? Discuss the advantages and disadvantages to this approach to retailing.

4.2 How much does the most powerful computer with the fastest processor, most memory, largest monitor, biggest hard drive, and all the available peripherals cost at **www.dell.ca**? Visit a store like Best Buy or Future Shop and price a comparable computer. How can you explain any price differences between the two retail operations? Explain any differences in features that you encountered. What conclusions can you draw from your research?

4.3 Discuss the various reasons that on-line retail sales estimates like those provided by Statistics Canada are probably understated. How might you be able to make an estimate of the actual level of on-line sales?

4.4 Most catalogue companies also offer on-line shopping. Visit the website of one of your favourite catalogues to see if you can buy on-line. If so, surf the on-line catalogue for a few minutes. Then compare the two retailing methods (paper and Internet) for prices, products, and so forth. Which do you prefer—the paper catalogue or on-line shopping? Why?

5 **Define franchising and describe its two basic forms.** Franchising is a continuing relationship in which a franchiser grants to a franchisee the business rights to operate or to sell a product. Modern franchising takes two basic forms. In product and trade name franchising, a dealer agrees to buy or sell certain products or product lines from a particular manufacturer or wholesaler. Business format franchising is an ongoing business relationship in which a franchisee uses a franchiser's name, format, or method of business in return for several types of fees.

5.1 What advantages does franchising provide to franchisers as well as franchisees?

5.2 Pizza Pizza is a well-established Canadian franchise company. What do you need to do to become a Pizza Pizza franchisee? Visit the Canadian Franchise Association website (**www.cfa.ca**) and then visit the Pizza Pizza website (**www.PizzaPizza.ca**) and click on franchising to find out. Does anything surprise you?

6 **List the major tasks involved in developing a retail marketing strategy.** Retail management begins with defining the target market, typically on the basis of demographic, geographic, and psychographic characteristics. After determining the target market, retail managers must develop the six variables of the retailing mix: product, promotion, place, price, presentation, and personnel.

6.1 Identify a successful retail business in your community. What marketing strategies have led to its success?

6.2 **ONLINE** How can a company create an atmosphere on its website? Visit the pages of some of your favourite retailers to see if they have been able to re-create the store atmosphere on the Internet.

7 Describe new developments in retailing. Three major trends are evident in retailing today. First, adding interactivity to the retail environment is one of the most popular strategies in retailing in recent years. Small retailers as well as national chains are using interactivity to involve customers and set themselves apart from the competition. Second, m-commerce (mobile e-commerce) is gaining in popularity. M-commerce enables consumers to purchase goods and services using wireless mobile devices, such as mobile telephones, pagers, PDAs, and handheld computers. Pop-up shops give companies flexible locations without the expense of a long-term lease.

7.1 **WRITING** You have been asked to write a brief article about the way m-commerce is influencing the future of retailing. Write the outline for your article. Once you have written your outline, Google M-commerce and locate several articles on m-commerce. Read a sampling and draft your article.

7.2 **WRITING** Make a list of stores that actively incorporate some kind of interactivity or entertainment into their retailing strategy. Now make a list of stores that do not, such as office supply stores. Compare your two lists. Select a company from your second list and draft a strategy to help it become more interactive.

7.3 What kind of retailers or brands do you think would most benefit from a pop-up shop? Why?

TERMS

atmosphere 389
automatic vending 374
buyer 367
category killers 372
chain stores 365
convenience store 370
department store 367
destination stores 387
direct marketing (direct-response marketing) 376
direct retailing 375
discount store 370
drugstore 370

factory outlet 372
franchise 365
franchisee 379
franchiser 379
full-line discount store 370
gross margin 366
independent retailers 365
in-store retailing 366
mass merchandising 371
nonstore retailing 374
off-price retailer 372
on-line retailing 378
place of business 366

pop-up shops 393
private label brand 384
product offering 384
retailing 364
retailing mix 383
scrambled merchandising 369
specialty discount store 372
specialty store 368
supercentre 371
supermarket 368
telemarketing 377
warehouse membership club 372

EXERCISES

APPLICATION EXERCISE

After reading the chapter, you can see that differences in retailing are the result of strategy. To better understand the relationship between strategic retailing factors and consumer perceptions, you can conduct a simple observation exercise. First, pick a product to shop for; then identify two stores where you have never shopped as places to look for your product. The two stores must be different types of retailers. For example, you can shop for a video game at Future Shop (category killer) and at Roger's Video (specialty retailer). Once you have identified what you are looking for and where you're going to look, visit each store and record your observations of specific strategic retailing factors.[70]

Activities

1. Go through each store and make careful observations on the following:

    *   Location. Where is each store? How congested is the area of town where each store is located? What influence does the neighbourhood have on your impression of the store? Would you travel to this store under normal circumstances to shop? Write a detailed paragraph on the location of each store.

    *   Exterior atmosphere. How convenient and adequate is parking? What kinds of stores are around the store you are visiting? Do you think that being located next to them increases traffic at your store? Are direct competitors nearby? Is the building modern or historic? Is it attractive, clean, and appealing? Is the entrance inviting to shoppers?

    *   Interior atmosphere. Compare the following attributes at each store: aisle width; lighting; number of customers; noise (background music, loudspeakers, etc.); store layout; signage; accessibility of the cashier; number of products available (depth and width of assortment); ability to inspect the product before purchase; quality of the fixtures (shelves, lights, etc.); availability of salespeople and their knowledge about the product; willingness of salespeople to help.

    *   Product. Is your product available? If not, is there a satisfactory substitute? What is your perception of the quality of goods offered? Why do you think as you do?

    *   Price. What is the price of the product or brand at this store? Is the price prominently marked? How do the prices at the two stores compare? How does the price compare to your expectations?

2. From which of these two stores would you actually purchase the item? Why, specifically? List the factors that played a role in your decision. Which factor is most important to you? If you would not purchase the item at either store, why not?

3. What are the three most important differences you observed between the stores?

4. Using the results of your research, write a short paper that outlines your observations. Conclude your paper with your answers to questions 2 and 3.

ETHICS EXERCISE

Andy's Electronics Store is a typical independent small electronics retailer. Andy's has been struggling in recent years trying to compete with electronics retailers like Future Shop, Best Buy, and The Source. To compete, Andy's owner has been buying recently discontinued electronics and factory close-outs and selling them as the latest technology. All products are sold with full factory warranties and support, but when Andy's makes a sale, all the receipts say "final sale" in fine print on the back. Andy's agrees to price-match any of the "exact" products sold by competitors within 30 days, but because of their buying policies, Andy's owner knows his store will rarely have to price-match. Andy's will accept returns but does not grant refunds, opting to offer store credits instead. Andy's offers same-day delivery of merchandise purchased, and the delivery people will set up large-screen televisions or in-home theatre systems and remove old equipment for disposal.

Questions

1. What do you think about Andy's merchandising policies? Are they legal? Ethical? Explain your reasoning.

2. What do you think about Andy's policy of certifying all products as final sales and refusing to give any refunds? Does the CMA Code of Ethics address this issue? Go to **www.the-cma.org** and review the code. Then write a brief paragraph on how the CMA Code of Ethics relates to this issue.

CASE STUDY

MOUNTAIN EQUIPMENT CO-OP (MEC): WHAT DOES IT MEAN TO GO GREEN?

Ryerson University's Centre for the Study of Commercial Activity (CSCA) has commented that retailers deciding to go green "makes good business sense and lessens our carbon footprint." The CSCA has reported that Canadian retailers are "responsible for more than 40 million tonnes

SOURCE: THE CANADIAN PRESS (DON DENTON)

of carbon emissions and producing six million tonnes of waste annually" from their 1.2 billion square feet of retail space.[71] "If just five per cent of retailers and their suppliers reduced their energy consumption by 10 per cent, the estimated energy savings could power every home in Ottawa, which is half a million houses. Greenhouse gas emissions would also be reduced by 1.4 million tonnes, which is equivalent to removing 233,000 cars off the road for one year," says adjunct professor at Ryerson's Ted Rogers School of Retail Management.[72]

The idea of retailers going green runs deeper than merely conserving energy as part of their physical retail operations. There is the offering of environmentally friendly green products as well. However, many stores have taken up this challenge and done it so well that researchers are reporting that "consumers no longer feel they have to pay a premium price for sustainable items" and that although about 80 percent of consumers "are interested in some type of green product" many of them report that "their purchases are primarily determined by price."[73]

One Canadian-based retailer that is well-known for undertaking environmental leadership is Mountain Equipment Co-op (MEC). Mountain Equipment Co-op operates 14 stores across Canada and boasts sales in the $260 million range. Like other Co-op retailers, MEC is a community-owned enterprise whose 3.25 million members are both its customers and owners. Each customer pays a $5 membership fee, which qualifies them as a member and allows them a vote in MEC's governance structures and entitles them to shop at the stores.[74]

Mountain Equipment Co-op summarizes one aspect of its "Green" philosophy with its guiding principle: "At MEC, our aim is to provide quality gear and excellent value. We also want to minimize our environmental impact, by building products that last. To do this, we take the time to test the materials and products we're developing so they will function and endure. If your gear works season after season then we're really getting somewhere."[75]

On the face of it, it sounds like MEC is paying lip service, claiming to be green by simply making a quality product.

Products that are durable and last longer may not go into the landfills as soon as cheaper goods but their manufacturing process could have a major environmental impact to create the quality claimed. This is not the case with MEC. Its commitment goes very deep because MEC has embraced the concept of sustainability (defined in Chapter 3 as the idea that socially responsible companies will outperform their peers by focusing on the world's social problems, viewing them as opportunities to build profits and help the world at the same time). MEC does this by using four key practices: (1) designing products with sustainability in mind. For example, MEC tries to use organically grown cotton and recycled fabrics in as many of their garments as possible; (2) MEC has designed its new stores and renovated older stores to be both more ecologically and energy friendly. A case in point is that MEC has installed solar panels and geothermal heating systems in some of their stores; (3) MEC has developed employee policies geared toward the firm's goal of sustainability. For example, the compensation packages of MEC's senior managers have performance goals based on sustainability. In addition, the firm's staff are constantly encouraged to develop approaches for the company to improve its sustainability; and (4) MEC undertakes community-based philanthropic and environmentally focused activities. Some of these activities have included donating 1 percent of the firm's annual gross sales to important Canadian wilderness conservation and outdoor recreation with its "1 percent for the planet" program. MEC has also worked with the Canadian Parks and Wilderness Society to create "The Big Wild—an organization devoted to keeping at least half of Canada's public land and water wild forever."[76]

Questions

1. What retailer classification does Mountain Equipment Co-op best fit into? Explain your choice.

2. Which of the "six" components of retailing would MEC have to emphasize in its strategy to achieve its being a "green" retailer and accomplish its mission of sustainability? What advantages or disadvantages do you think MEC has as a result of being "green"?

3. Visit the Mountain Equipment Co-op website at **www.mec.ca**. Report on the signs of MEC's commitment to being a "green" retailer based on its website.

VIDEO CASE

CANADIAN TIRE: CANADIAN TIRE'S BACK-TO-BASICS STRATEGY

On April 7, 2010, Canadian Tire held an "investor's" news conference where president and CEO Steven Whetmore outlined the firm's planned strategy for the next three to five years. Whetmore stated that "the strength of our core brand is at the heart of all of our growth strategies. All of our businesses have to be focused on serving one valuable customer as one great company—centred on the Canadian Tire retail business."[77] Business News Network commentators Michael Kane and Paul Bagnell discuss this press release and comment on Canadian Tire's strategy.[78]

In the press release, Whetmore presented the following financial objectives for Canadian Tire:

- Top line growth in Canadian Tire Retail between 3 and 5 percent per year;

- Consolidated operating earnings per share annual growth of 8 to 10 percent;

- A return on invested capital of 10 percent for its retail operations; and

- A return on credit card receivables of 4.5 to 5 percent.

Whetmore stated that Canadian Tire had undertaken significant investments in recent years and the plan for future sales growth was no longer expansion but efforts to "maximize the productivity of the existing retail footprint." This would involve the use of a "racetrack floor plan" which "includes more space for high growth and 'cornerstone' categories and helps customers find products more easily through better signage and more logical product adjacencies."[79]

Another key initiative presented by Whetmore was a refocusing on Canadian Tire's automotive business, which had been ignored for quite a while. Whetmore commented that "Canadian Tire aspires to grow its overall automotive business at 4 to 6 percent per year over the next five years. A core element of the strategy is to implement the Automotive Infrastructure initiative to deliver a much improved customer experience at the parts and service centres through broader inventory assortment, a faster supply chain and a better technology foundation. The Automotive Infrastructure project is expected to grow CTR sales of tires, parts and auto service labour. It will improve the consistency of the customer experience by giving staff the information and training they need to better meet the needs of customers."[80]

Paul Bagnell of Business News Network discusses Canadian Tire's press release. He mentions how Steven Whetmore said the firm had invested billions and needed to drive more return for its shareholders on their assets. Bagnell reports how the company needs to improve the consistency of customer service because Canadian Tire has not been delivering on service and needs to do better. Bagnell mentions that Canadian Tire has fixed its capital spending at its current levels of $280 to $300 million per year. He also describes how the firm wants to do a better job of selling from existing stores.

Michael Kane comments that when he thinks of going to Canadian Tire, he doesn't think customer service is lax. Rather he wonders if the products might be positioned in the store better to make you buy more. Paul Bagnell responds by mentioning how the announcement presented the race-track format as the new store layout approach for Canadian Tire stores. Bagnell explains he is not totally sure what the race-track format means but he understands that Canadian Tire is planning on aligning products more logically beside one another. The idea is to make sure complementary products are lined up together to encourage more impulse purchasing.

Paul Bagnell describes how in earlier stages of Canadian Tire's sales growth, it had expanded floor space to attain more sales. Now the firm is planning to do a better job with the current floor space to increase sales. Michael Kane responds by mentioning that Canada is undergoing an economic recovery so Canadian Tire doesn't "want to get lost in the dust because you have blown the business plan." Paul Bagnell observes that Canadian Tire did well against the recession and has done well against its major competitors, Home Depot and Rona. Bagnell also comments that all retailers struggled in 2009 because consumers were simply not shopping.

Bagnell believes that Steven Whetmore feels that Canadian Tire had become complacent in its operations and this was behind the strategies being proposed. Bagnell interprets the announced Canadian Tire strategy as trying to do better with what it has by taking a back-to-basics approach where the firm would focus on traditional Canadian Tire products.

Michael Kane observes that Canadian Tire is an interesting retail store because it cuts across so many retail lines. For example, it has "sporting goods but it's not a sporting goods store; it's hardware but it's not a hardware store; and it's automotive, but frankly I have never thought of buying my tires at Canadian Tire." Bagnell responds that Canadian Tire wants to get people to come in for automotive parts. It wants people to make a direct link between its gas bars and auto part outlets. Finally, Canadian Tire wants to improve financial services and increase its receivables.[81]

Questions

1. Discuss how the "presentation" of Canadian Tire retail stores is likely to change with the newly proposed "race-track" strategy.

2. Michael Kane wasn't sure what retail category to put Canadian Tire in. How would you classify Canadian Tire as a retailer? Justify your answer.

3. What other aspects of Canadian Tire's retail marketing strategy do you think will be most affected by Steven Whetmore's plans? Discuss.

MARKETING & YOU RESULTS

If your score was on the low side, it means you don't find shopping in stores to be enjoyable. The higher your score, the more likely you are to think shopping is a fun activity. But beware: a high score can also indicate a tendency toward being a compulsive buyer!

MARKETING MISCUE

SPRINGSTEEN AND WALMART: OPPOSITES ATTRACT IN BUSINESS PARTNERSHIP?

Rock and roll legend Bruce Springsteen and Walmart, the world's largest retailer, teamed up in late 2008 to deliver fans Springsteen's hits at Walmart's price. With such a great deal for all, why was Springsteen criticized by his fans for this exclusive distribution partnership?

Bruce Springsteen was very busy in late 2008 and early 2009. In December 2008, he made a surprise appearance at the fourth Hope Concert in New Jersey, performing "Run Run Rudolph" with Bon Jovi and various Christmas songs with the house band. In January 2009, Springsteen headlined an inaugural concert for President Barack Obama at the Lincoln Memorial in Washington, DC. Then on February 1, 2009, Springsteen and his E Street Band performed in the coveted half-time slot at Super Bowl XLIII in Tampa, Florida.

Amid all of this touring, Springsteen was working hard on the release of a couple of albums. Just two weeks prior to the release of *Working on a Dream,* Springsteen and his infamous E Street Band were releasing the group's *Greatest Hits.* The track list for the *Greatest Hits* release included classic material from Springsteen and his band, such as "Born to Run," "Thunder Road," and "Born in the USA."

Bruce Springsteen is known for being a champion of the blue-collar workforce and has been a longtime supporter of workers' rights. Some of his hits, such as "Born to Run," "Glory Days," and "My Hometown," chronicle the struggles of working life. In contrast, Walmart reportedly refuses to recognize unions (the mainstay of the blue-collar workforce) and has been criticized for its labour practices. For example, Walmart Canada closed its Jonquière, Quebec, store in April 2005 just months after it had unionized. The United Food and Commercial Workers Union took Walmart to the Supreme Court of Canada to protest the store closing, arguing that Walmart closed the store to "break" the union. However, in 2009 the Supreme Court ruled that Walmart had every right to close the store. Still, organizations like Human Rights Watch has condemned Walmart for its allegedly poor treatment of low-wage employees. Thus, *Greatest Hits*, which could be considered iconic for blue-collar workers, is available only in Walmart, which many union people perceive to be a nemesis of blue-collar workers. What were Springsteen's and Walmart's rationales for this exclusive distribution arrangement?

From Walmart's perspective, the answer was clear in that the album would be a big seller. The company released a statement that it would continue, as always, to deliver Springsteen's music to his fans. Included in the statement were comments related to the benefits and career opportunities provided to the over one million Walmart employees in the United States. Basically, Walmart was happy to be the sole distributor of *Greatest Hits*. No apologies from Walmart were expected or needed, particularly since Walmart has continually fought the workforce allegations.

Was Springsteen the one, however, who reneged on his reputed blue-collar principles by signing an exclusive distribution agreement with Walmart? Soon after criticisms about the exclusive deal hit the Internet, Springsteen admitted to having made a wrong decision. He reportedly told that the *New York Times* that the exclusive distribution deal with Walmart was a mistake and that the decision was made during a very busy time for the band. Springsteen said that the arrangement was not vetted properly. Yet the band had followed the business example already set by classic rock icons such as the Eagles and AC/DC—both of which had exclusive distribution arrangements with Walmart.[1]

Questions

1. From a values or principles perspective, did Springsteen make a poor decision in giving Walmart an exclusive deal on the distribution of *Greatest Hits*? Explain your answer.

2. From a business perspective, what are the pros and cons of an exclusive distribution deal such as the one between Springsteen and Walmart?

LOBLAW: IMPROVING CUSTOMER SERVICE WITH SUPPLY CHAIN MANAGEMENT

The basic concept of grocery supermarket retailing (and actually what puts the word "super" together with market) is the idea of finding all the groceries you need in one place. This is the basic expectation of all shoppers and when it is not being met the retailer will struggle to maintain both customer satisfaction and loyalty.[2]

As the first decade of the new millennium unfolded, Loblaw was building supercentres to satisfy the basic concept of one-stop shopping and also to position itself to compete with Walmart Canada's plans to begin offering groceries in its own versions of superstores. However, Loblaw discovered that more and more of its shoppers were complaining about merchandise stock-outs and others just simply went elsewhere. While it had been building retail stores and offering more merchandise, Loblaw discovered it had outgrown its distribution system and need to make major changes and upgrades.

Loblaw began with an analysis of its distribution system, and the results were not pleasing. For example, it examined the movement of a container of Yoplait yogurt as it travelled from its processing plant into the firm's regional distribution centre and finally onto store shelves. The best-before date on a typical yogurt product is 30 days from production. As Loblaw examined the movement of this package of yogurt, it found it sat in trucks for a few days, sat in the warehouse for several days, and then sat in the back room of the grocery store for more time before finally making its way onto the store shelves with only 13 days left on the best before date.[3] Discerning shoppers examine these dates carefully and typically pass up merchandise that has short "fridge-life." The impact for a retailer is significant because any product with a short shelf life is likely destined for the garbage bin, which will result in a loss of profits combined with unsatisfied customers who were unable to find acceptably "in-date" merchandise.

Loblaw estimated that the inefficiency of its logistic system was costing the company in the tens of millions of dollars but the more likely situation was this estimate was far below the real costs. In its first move to address the problem, one business journalist reported that Loblaw "shuttered six warehouses and amalgamated a patchwork distribution system into a single network. Alas, Loblaw moved too quickly on too many fronts. It was also cutting staff and merging divisions, as well as moving employees to a new head office. As the remaining 26 distribution centres proved unable to handle the extra capacity, chaos flourished. Surplus inventory crammed warehouses, crews waited to unpack goods that never arrived, and seasonal products missed demand windows and had to be liquidated. According to Brian Yarbrough, an analyst with Edward Jones, store service levels, or 'fill rates,' plunged from around 95% to less than 70%."[4]

In addition to its supply chain system being inadequate, Loblaw also cut store costs with employee lay-offs. The result was that some of the store stock-out issues were simply that stores just did not have enough staff to transfer stock from the delivery and storage areas of the store to the grocery shelves! With the current system being inadequate and the advent of Walmart entering the supercentre business, Loblaw knew it had to re-examine how it was making changes.

One of its most important moves was the development of a new 875,000-square-foot distribution centre in Ajax, Ontario, to serve the Greater Toronto Area, one of the most important food retailing markets in Canada. In addition to a new facility, Loblaw also decided to outsource the operations of the distribution centre to a specialist company, Atlas Logistics Services. Linda Jakowec, who's in charge of the warehouse, comments: "As a third-party logistics operator, Atlas's job is simple. We receive, we count, we put away."[5]

One industry commentator observing the changes said: "As a result, in our analysis, the food retailer has to show strong, continuous improvement in key areas like solving the out-of-stocks problem, increasing service-levels in its stores and other basic functions in the next year in order to not lose thousands more customers to Walmart and other food and grocery retailers."[6]

Questions

1. Discuss how logistics can give a retailer like Loblaw or Walmart a competitive advantage.

2. As an intermediary, what channel functions was Atlas Logistics System taking on for Loblaw?

3. Think of your most recent grocery store trip to a superstore or supermarket. In your opinion, are grocery retailers really doing an effective job of stocking shelves and making sure the products you want are available? Develop an assessment approach to measure customer service for these retailers.

PART

Promotion 5

Decisions

13 Integrated Marketing Communications

HELP KEEP JAMES READY A BUCK.

SHARE OUR BILLBOARD.

MAKE US AN OFFER AT JAMESREADY.COM

SOURCE: COURTESY OF LEO BURNETT AND JAMES READY BREWERY

LEARNING OUTCOMES

1 Discuss the role of promotion in the marketing mix

2 Describe the communication process

3 Explain the goals of promotion

4 Discuss the elements of the promotional mix

5 Discuss the AIDA concept and its relationship to the promotional mix

6 Discuss the concept of integrated marketing communications

7 Describe the factors that affect the promotional mix

MARKETING & YOU

Using the scales below, enter your answers or record them on a separate page.

1	2	3	4	5	6
Strongly disagree					Strongly agree

__ People frequently tell me about themselves.
__ I've been told that I'm a good listener.
__ I'm very accepting of others.
__ People trust me with their secrets.
__ I easily get people to "open up."

__ People feel relaxed around me.
__ I enjoy listening to people.
__ I'm sympathetic to people's problems.
__ I encourage people to tell me how they are feeling.
__ I can keep people talking about themselves.

Total your score, and see what it means after you read the chapter.

SOURCE: REPRINTED WITH PERMISSION FROM *MARKETING SCALES HANDBOOK* VOL. III, PUBLISHED BY THE AMERICAN MARKETING ASSOCIATION, G. BRUNER, K. JAMES, H. HENSEL, EDS. SCALE #455.

MARKETING HAPPENS

An effective marketing promotional campaign communicates the product's positioning statements to the selected target market through a number of communication channels. A successful campaign requires that all marketing communications be integrated to provide consistency in the messages sent so that the product's positioning is properly understood. For example, a promotional campaign for the James Ready Brewing Company recently received a number of international promotional industry awards, including a Silver Pencil at the One Show in New York, two golds at the Andy Awards, and Best in Show at the Obie Awards, sponsored by the Outdoor Advertising Association of America, all for using a unique approach to billboard advertising in an integrated promotional campaign.

James Ready Brewing Company is a microbrewer based in Niagara Falls, Ontario. The company has positioned itself as an economical brand and has been aiming to maintain a $1-a-beer price point throughout Canada. The essence of its promotional strategy is to portray the firm as a focused cost cutter, especially in its use of promotional tools, all in the name of keeping its beer prices at $1.

In a campaign created by its agency, Leo Burnett, Arc Worldwide, of Toronto, James Ready developed a "Share Our Billboard" customer-participation campaign. The company took out 100 billboards in Ontario with a picture of one of their beer bottles on one side flanked by a dotted green "cut-out" area with the caption appeal "Help Keep James Ready

a Buck, Share Our Billboard" and bottom tagline saying "Make Us an Offer at JamesReady.com." According to Jeromy Lloyd of *Marketing Magazine*, the campaign was a major success as many beer drinkers sought their 15 minutes of fame by buying the space, thus lowering the cost of the promotion and making it "very unique."

James Ready followed up the billboard effort with another approach to audience participation, this time using the radio in the Ontario beer markets of Barrie, London, North Bay, Ottawa, St. Catharines, Sudbury, and Toronto. The company offered radio listeners in these markets two things: they could get air time on the radio to use in whatever way they wished, or they could call on the brewer for help for something typical in their life such as, the advertisement suggested, breaking up with a girlfriend, flipping a mattress, or helping pay for a wedding. Listeners were told to visit the web page "HowCanJRHelpYou.ca" where they could fill out a submission to make their case for being able to get air time or receive aid. James Ready set a deadline of mid-July 2009 to receive submissions and promised to make decisions in August. All this activity was designed to drive traffic to the company's web pages, where people would visit often to see what was happening.

Account director Natasha Dagenais of Leo Burnett describes this campaign: "For the last three years, it's been 'How can you help us keep the price as low as possible?' It's tough economic times and everyone is tightening their belts. This was an opportunity for us to reach out

and say thank you in a very JR tone. We're not going to give out five shirts and have a party. That's very beer-ish. We wanted to support what James Ready stands for as the beer of the people. Who better to tell us what they need help with than [the consumer]?"

Russ Martin of *Marketing Magazine* describes how James Ready helped out with a number of small requests and then took on five more costly requests, such as flying one customer to Newfoundland at Christmas to visit his family. Another customer was given a money to fly to a reunion held in British Columbia. One patron was given a James Ready Halloween costume while a mom was provided with an amplifier and guitar to be used as a birthday gift for her son. The most extravagant bequest was made to Dean and Cori-Ann Litster to hold a James Ready wedding. James Ready's advertising agency, Leo Burnett, saw to it that the couple's wedding guests received invitations created from beer labels. The groom was provided cufflinks made from bottle caps and the wedding cake was bottle-topped. Of course, James Ready beer was served at the wedding reception and the newlyweds were treated to a complementary night at a hotel in Toronto.[1]

Promotion is a critical component of a company's marketing mix. What types of promotional tools are available to companies, and what factors influence the choice of tools? Why is consistent integrated marketing important to the promotional plan? These questions, and others, will be answered as you read this chapter.

SOURCE: JEROMY LLOYD, "JAMES READY LENDING A HELPING HAND," MARKETING MAGAZINE, MAY 7, 2009; MARKETING AWARDS: INTEGRATED CAMPAIGN, "SHARE OUR BILLBOARD CAMPAIGN," MARKETING MAGAZINE, JUNE 15, 2009; RUSS MARTIN, "JAMES READY TO PARTY NEAR CAMPUS," MARKETING MAGAZINE, OCTOBER 15, 2009; AND WWW.JAMESREADY.COM.

Discuss the role of promotion in the marketing mix

Few goods or services, no matter how well developed, priced, and distributed, can survive in the marketplace without effective **promotion**—communication by marketers that informs, persuades, and reminds potential buyers of a product in order to influence their opinion or elicit a response.

Promotional strategy is a plan for the optimal use of the elements of promotion: advertising, public relations, personal selling, and sales promotion. As Exhibit 13.1 shows, the marketing manager determines the goals of the company's promotional strategy in light of the company's overall goals for the marketing mix—product, place (distribution), promotion, and price. Using these overall goals, marketers combine the elements of the promotional strategy (the promotional mix) into a coordinated plan. The promotion plan then becomes an integral part of the marketing strategy for reaching the target market.

The main function of a marketer's promotional strategy is to convince target customers that a company's goods and services offer a **competitive advantage** over the competition. A competitive advantage is the set of unique features of a company and its products that are perceived by the target market as significant and superior to the competition. Such features can include high product quality, rapid delivery, low prices, excellent service, or a feature not offered by the competition. For example, fast-food restaurant Subway promises fresh sandwiches that are better for you than a hamburger or pizza. Subway communicates its competitive advantage effectively through ads featuring longtime "spokes-eater" Jared Fogle, who lost weight by eating at Subway every day.[2] Thus promotion is a vital part of the marketing mix, informing consumers of a product's benefits and thereby positioning the product in the marketplace.

EXHIBIT 13.1

Role of Promotion in the Marketing Mix

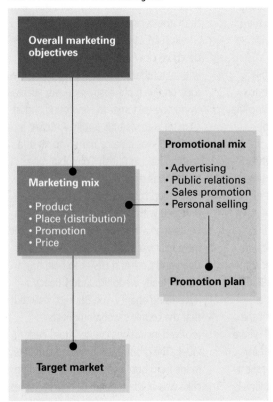

SOURCE: COURTESY OF SUBWAY

Subway effectively communicates its competitive advantage with its "Eat Fresh" campaign.

promotion
Communication by marketers that informs, persuades, and reminds potential buyers of a product in order to influence an opinion or elicit a response.

promotional strategy
A plan for the optimal use of the elements of promotion: advertising, public relations, personal selling, and sales promotion.

competitive advantage
One or more unique aspects of an organization that cause target consumers to patronize that company rather than competitors.

1 Discuss the role of promotion in the marketing mix

Promotional Strategy

Promotional mix
Advertising
Public Relations
Sales Promotion
Personal Selling

Competitive advantage

Marketer

Consumer

MARKETING COMMUNICATION

Describe the communication process

communication
The process by which we exchange or share meanings through a common set of symbols.

Promotional strategy is closely related to the process of communication. As humans, we assign meaning to feelings, ideas, facts, attitudes, and emotions. **Communication** is the process by which we exchange or share meanings through a common set of symbols. When a company develops a new product, changes an old one, or simply tries to increase sales of an existing good or service, it must communicate its selling message to potential customers. Marketers communicate information about the company and its products to the target market and to various segments of the public through promotion programs.

According to the *New York Times*, using effective communication, Pepsi-Cola Canada has developed the strongest market in North America for Pepsi in Quebec, where Pepsi outsells Coke at a ratio of more than two to one. ACNielsen MarketTrack reports that "Pepsi's main brand commands 29.9 percent of the retail soft drink market in Quebec, based on volume, compared with 12.3 percent for Coke."[3] The secret to Pepsi's success in Quebec is strongly related to a "made in Quebec" approach to promotion combined with the use of one of the longest-running promotional campaigns in North America. The campaign, begun in 1984, was a departure from the company's past practice of simply turning campaigns developed for English Canada into Quebec campaigns by dubbing an English theme into French. Rather, the company developed a Quebec-only approach that featured comedian Claude Meunier, who wrote the ads, performed in the TV ads, and lent his voice to the radio ads. In one Christmas campaign, Meunier appeared as "Santa Claude," wearing, of course, a blue Santa suit à la Pepsi rather than the traditional red. Over the years, Meunier developed new ideas to sustain the campaign; he succeeded in this because he was completely plugged into Quebec culture and has an appealing personality that has not worn out the audience. Meunier has switched over to doing Diet Pepsi ads in recent years, a move that befits his age, but he still shows up once in a while in ads for regular Pepsi. Sylvain Charbonneau, vice-president for Pepsi's Canadian bottling group and its director general for Quebec Pepsi, says of Pepsi's promotional strategy: "It's more costly for a population of seven million to do a unique advertising campaign year after year. It costs you more per capita than it would for the U.S. with 300 million people. But it pays out for us and Quebecers don't mind laughing about themselves."[4]

Communication can be divided into two major categories: interpersonal and mass. **Interpersonal communication** is direct, face-to-face communication between two or more people. When communicating face to face, each person can see the other's reaction and respond almost immediately. A salesperson speaking directly with a client is an example of interpersonal communication.

interpersonal communication
Direct, face-to-face communication between two or more people.

mass communication
The communication of a concept or message to large audiences.

Mass communication involves communicating a concept or message to large audiences. A great deal of marketing communication is directed to consumers as a whole, usually through mass media such as TV or newspapers. When a company advertises, it generally does not know the people with whom it is trying to communicate on a personal basis. Furthermore, the company is unable to respond immediately to consumers' reactions to its message. Instead, the marketing manager must wait to see whether people are reacting positively or negatively to the mass-communicated promotion. Any clutter from competitors' messages or other distractions in the environment can reduce the effectiveness of the mass-communication effort.

THE COMMUNICATION PROCESS

Marketers are both senders and receivers of messages. As senders, marketers attempt to inform, persuade, and remind the target market to adopt certain courses of action. As receivers, marketers attune themselves to the target market in order to develop the appropriate messages, adapt existing messages, and spot new communication opportunities. In this fashion, marketing communication is a two-way rather than a one-way process. The two-way nature of the communication process is illustrated in Exhibit 13.2.

EXHIBIT 13.2

Communication Process

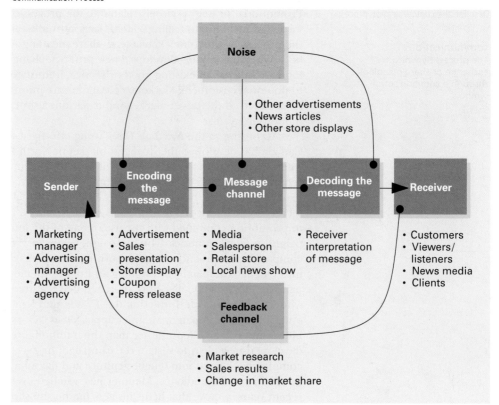

SOURCE: © MEDIABLITZIMAGES (UK) LIMITED/ALAMY

sender
The originator of the message in the communication process.

encoding
The conversion of the sender's ideas and thoughts into a message, usually in the form of words or signs.

The Sender and Encoding

The **sender** is the originator of the message in the communication process. In an interpersonal conversation, the sender may be a parent, a friend, or a salesperson. For an advertisement or press release, the sender is the company or organization itself. For example, the Swedish brand Absolut Vodka launched a marketing campaign using the theme "In an Absolut World." At the outset, the objective of the campaign was to increase Absolut's market share in the crowded and increasingly competitive vodka market. To appeal to this market, Absolut had to differentiate its message from the "rational benefits" (such as best taste or smooth feel) being claimed by so many of the upstarts in the vodka category. Absolut changed its near-legendary super-premium brand strategy—a print campaign pairing the iconic shape of its bottle with equally iconic art figures—to a campaign that would appeal to the "emotional benefits" of the brand.[5] Thus, Absolute launched a new campaign using the phrase "Absolut World" to promote the message that its vodka was the brand to choose if the customer was intelligent and savvy and wanted to challenge the status quo by taking on bold and optimistic new world views. The new ads assert that Absolut vodka is in a class by itself—indeed, in a world of its own, an "Absolut World." The ad campaign also invites Absolut's consumers to visualize a world that appeals to them—even a world that may be idealized or "fantastic."[6]

Encoding is the conversion of the sender's ideas and thoughts into a message, usually in the form of words or signs. A basic principle of encoding is that what matters is not what the source says but what the receiver hears. One way of conveying a message that the receiver will hear properly is to use concrete words and pictures. For example, Absolut's marketers encoded the message by creating a series of life-size outdoor ads, wrapped buildings, and other media that imagined an "Absolut World" where factories emit harmless bubbles instead of smoke, ATMs dispense "free" money, politicians' noses grow if they lie, and people in bars wear buttons labelling their dating status and mindset.[7]

Message Transmission

Transmission of a message requires a **channel**—a voice, radio, newspaper, or other communication medium. A facial expression or gesture can also serve as a channel.

Reception occurs when the message is detected by the receiver and enters his or her frame of reference. In a two-way conversation such as a sales pitch given by a sales representative to a potential client, reception is normally high. In contrast, the desired receivers may or may not detect the message when it is mass-communicated because most media are cluttered with **noise**, defined as anything that interferes with, distorts, or slows down the transmission of information. In some media that are overcrowded with advertisers, such as radio and TV, the noise level is high and the reception level is low. For example, competing network advertisements, other entertainment option advertisements, or other programming on the network itself might hamper reception of the "Absolut World" advertising campaign message. Transmission can also be hindered by situational factors: physical surroundings such as light, sound, location, and weather; the presence of other people; or the temporary moods consumers might bring to the situation. Mass communication may not even reach all the right consumers. Some members of the target audience were likely watching television when Absolut's commercials were shown, but others probably were not.

The Receiver and Decoding

Marketers communicate their message through a channel to customers, or **receivers**, who then decode the message. **Decoding** refers to the interpretation of the language and symbols sent by the source through a channel. Common understanding between two communicators, or a common frame of reference, is required for effective communication. Therefore, marketing managers must ensure a proper match between the message to be conveyed and the target market's attitudes and ideas.

Even though a message has been received, it may not necessarily be properly decoded—or even seen, viewed, or heard—because of selective exposure, distortion, and retention (refer to Chapter 4). Even when people receive a message, they tend to manipulate, alter, and modify it to reflect their own biases, needs, knowledge, and culture. For example, differences in age, social class, education, culture, and ethnicity can lead to miscommunication. Further, because people don't always listen or read carefully, they can easily misinterpret what is said or written. In fact, researchers have found that consumers misunderstand a large proportion of both printed and televised communications. Bright colours and bold graphics have been shown to increase consumers' comprehension of marketing communication. Even these techniques are not foolproof, however. A classic example of miscommunication occurred when Lever Brothers mailed out samples of its then new dishwashing liquid, Sunlight, which contains real lemon juice. The package clearly stated that Sunlight was a household cleaning product. However, many people saw the word sunlight, the large picture of lemons, and the phrase "with real lemon juice," and thought the product was lemon juice.

Marketers targeting consumers in foreign countries must worry about the mistranslation and possible miscommunication of their promotional messages. An important issue for global marketers is whether they should standardize or customize the message for each global market in which they sell. Although Absolut's marketers used the "World" message globally, they tailored the ads to reflect how people in various regions might envision an "Absolut World." For example, in the United States a bus shelter on Second Avenue in New York City was wrapped to look like a subway entrance—a dream of many New York commuters.[8] In Germany, consumers were given a firsthand experience of the "Absolut World." For one week, a fleet of Porsche

<div class="margin-definitions">

channel
A medium of communication, such as a voice, radio, or newspaper, for transmitting a message.

noise
Anything that interferes with, distorts, or slows down the transmission of information.

receiver
The person who decodes a message.

decoding
Interpretation of the language and symbols sent by the source through a channel.

</div>

feedback
The receiver's response to a message.

Would you have used Sunlight detergent to lemon-flavour your baked goods or make lemonade? When it first came on the market showing lemons on the package, some people failed to decode the message on the product and did just that!

taxis chauffeured passengers quickly—and for free—around Hamburg, Munich, and Berlin. By the end of that week, the taxis had generated over 15 million media contacts through TV, print, and on-line news coverage.[9]

Feedback

In interpersonal communication, the receiver's response to a message is direct **feedback** to the source. Feedback can be verbal, as in saying "I agree," or nonverbal, as in nodding, smiling, frowning, or gesturing.

Because mass communicators like Absolut's are often cut off from direct feedback, they must rely on market research or analysis of viewer responses from indirect feedback. Absolut might use such measurements as the percentage of television viewers who recognized, recalled, or stated they were exposed to Absolut's messages. Indirect feedback enables mass communicators to decide whether to continue, modify, or drop a message. Websites also facilitate feedback. For example, Absolut could capture consumer feedback in e-mails, discussion boards, blogs, and other tools from its website.

THE IMPACT OF THE WEB AND ITS SOCIAL MEDIA ON MARKETING COMMUNICATION

The Internet and its social media like Facebook and Twitter are having a profound impact on marketing communication. When companies initially developed websites, the primary formats were either on-line

Global Perspectives

MONTREAL: THE PLACE TO TEST YOUR GLOBAL ADVERTISING!

Global marketing—selling your products and services world-wide—is a huge undertaking. Marketing products or services overseas requires both cultural sensitivity and an understanding of consumers in diverse markets to communicate successfully. In particular, developing advertising campaigns for global markets can be a tremendous communications challenge.

The Association of Quebec Advertising Agencies has been trying to convince North America's multinational companies that Montreal is the place to design and test their international advertising campaigns. The association's chairperson, Sébastien Fauré, has described Montreal an ideal testing ground. The logic behind this belief rests on the fact that Montreal is such a highly multicultural city and its market is receptive to creative advertising efforts that have the potential to be used for global marketing.

One of the major communications challenges being faced by marketers today involves the revolutionary new technologies being developed and the use of social media by consumers. Marketers have realized that social media like Facebook and Twitter are controlled by consumers and that marketers need to learn how to communicate with consumers most effectively through this new media. Fauré notes that Montreal is an ideal location to work out

how to do it. The Association of Quebec Advertisers is convinced that since the experience of marketing with social media is limited companies need to experiment to truly understand how to use this media. Because Montreal is such a cosmopolitan city, its residents offer a representative sample population upon which marketers can carry out media experiments, the results of which would be generalizable to markets all around the world.

The Association of Quebec Advertising Agencies has named this initiative Yul-Lab, in honour of Montreal's three-letter airport code. Some Canadian marketers have either already used Montreal as a test market for promotion or have plans to do so. For example, MasterCard Worldwide has test-marketed its Priceless.Com program, and Level 5, a brand strategy firm in Toronto, plans to use Yul-Lab. Tom Wright of Level 5 comments, "Yul-Lab is a great approach," and describes the market in Montreal as a "petri dish for the world." "I think it's a perfect location," he says.[10]

What challenges do you think the Association of Quebec Advertisers will face while trying to convince multinational marketers to consider Montreal as the laboratory for developing advertising campaigns? What other kinds of research could marketers use when considering advertising in new countries?

brochures, where essentially the corporate brochure or catalogue was put on-line, or e-commerce sites, where the companies could facilitate on-line sales of products. The next generation of the Internet, Web 2.0, facilitated consumer empowerment. For the first time, consumers were able to directly speak to other consumers, the company, and Web communities.

Web 2.0 tools include blogs (on-line journals), podcasting (on-line radio shows), vodcasts (on-line videos and newscasts), and social networks such as Facebook and Twitter. In the beginning, these tools were primarily used by individuals to express themselves. For example, a real estate agent may develop a blog to talk about politics because that is a hobby. Or a first-year university student may develop a profile on Facebook to stay in touch with high school friends. But soon, businesses began to see that these tools could be used to engage with consumers as well. The rise of blogging, for example, has created a completely new way for marketers to manage their image, connect with consumers, and generate interest in and desire for their companies' products.

Despite what could be considered a national obsession with blogs, measuring blogging activity remains challenging. According to Technorati, the first blog search engine, there were more than 28 million blogs on-line in 2006. But by early 2008, there were so many blogs there was not a consistent number. While research companies agree that there are millions of blogs, comScore Media Metrix says that as of August 2008, there were 189 million blogs (counting Facebook); Universal McCann reports there were 184 million blogs, and Blogpulse estimated 186 million blogs as of 2009.[11] As part of its annual State of the Blogosphere, Technorati says the real trend is with the active blogosphere that tends to influence the mainstream media. Brands also permeate the blogosphere. Four of five bloggers post brand or product reviews, so even if a company does not have a formal social media strategy, chances are the brand is still out in the blogosphere thanks to the millions of bloggers. Because of this, companies are reaching out to the most influential bloggers. Indeed, more than one-third of those with a blog have been approached to be a brand advocate.

The question then is whether blogging is a passing fad, representing at best an unreliable means of communicating, or an emerging trend. If it is a fad, why are marketers so interested in blogging as a promotional tool? The answer in part is that blogging alters the marketing communication process for the promotional elements that rely on mass communication—advertising, public relations, and sales promotion—by moving them away from impersonal, indirect communication toward a personalized, direct communication model.

corporate blogs
Blogs that are sponsored by a company or one of its brands and maintained by one or more of the company's employees.

Blogs can be divided into broad categories: corporate blogs and professional blogs versus noncorporate blogs (such as personal blogs). **Corporate blogs** are sponsored by a company or one of its brands and maintained by one or more of the company's employees. Corporate blogs disseminate marketing-controlled information. (Recall from Chapter 4 that marketing-controlled information is a source of product information that originates with marketers promoting the product.) Because blogs are designed to change daily, corporate blogs are dynamic and highly flexible, giving marketers the opportunity to adapt their messages more frequently than with any other communication channel. Initially, blogs were maintained by only the most technology-savvy companies. But today many large Canadian companies such as Molson, Labatt, Tim Hortons, Zellers, Canadian Tire, and multinationals such as Coca-Cola, Starwood Hotels, Honda, Nokia, Benetton, Ducati, Guinness, and HSBC have all launched some form of corporate blogs. Undoubtedly, many more will appear in the near future.

noncorporate blogs
Independent blogs that are not associated with the marketing efforts of any particular company or brand.

In contrast, **noncorporate blogs** are independent and not associated with the marketing efforts of any particular company or brand. As independent offerings, noncorporate blogs function much like nonmarketing-controlled information: they provide a source of information and opinion perceived to be independent and more authentic than a corporate blog.[12] If they offer a positive view of a company, they can create a lot of goodwill. Noncorporate blogs are often part of somebody's hobby or interest so they may not be maintained well or even for long. For example, Michael Marx loved Barq's root beer. He wore Barq's T-shirts, brought the beverage to parties, and called it his "beer." He established a blog dedicated to Barq's, **www.thebarqsman.com**, where he posted news about the brand, Barq's commercials he likes, and musings on why Barq's is superior to other root beers. Thebarqsman.com is not affiliated with Coca-Cola, the owner of the Barq's brand, which had no idea of the blog's existence until a *New York Times* reporter writing a story on brand blogs mentioned it. However, Michael Marx eventually got tired of his hobby and let the blog go with a final tribute by saying "Long Live Barq's."[13]

Both corporate and noncorporate blogs have had an impact on the communication model depicted in Exhibit 13.2. That model shows the feedback channel as primarily impersonal and numbers-driven. In the traditional communication process, marketers can see the results of consumer behaviour (e.g., a drop in sales), but are able to explain them only using their judgment. Even the information generated by market research is not as natural as that gleaned from bloggers. Corporate blogs allow marketers to personalize the feedback channel by opening the door for direct conversation with consumers. However, because there is no control over noncorporate blogs, there is a chance that comments and postings will be negative. Thus, many companies have a crisis communication strategy to deal with negative information in the blogosphere. When marketers launch a corporate blog, they create an unfiltered feedback channel. For example, Enrico Minoli, CEO of Ducati, the Italian motorcycle brand, launched a blog at blog.ducati.com. He vowed to write "openly about what's going on at Ducati." Within three days, his postings had generated 99 responses, from motorcycle enthusiasts from Greece to Daytona Beach, who all seemed most pleased that the CEO himself was a motorbike enthusiast. They began peppering him with questions about when new models would hit production and chatted with each other about their own bikes and biking experiences. Minoli's blog put a face on the impersonal nature of a large corporation.[14]

Noncorporate blogs have also personalized the feedback channel. But while corporate blogs create a direct, personalized feedback channel for masses of consumers, noncorporate blogs represent an indirect, personalized feedback channel. Because noncorporate blogs are independent, they are often perceived as more authentic. Blogging experts offer marketers some solid advice for giving their blogs the honest quality many bloggers associate with noncorporate blogs: open the feedback channel. Todd Copilevitz, a consultant specializing in digital marketing, says, "Blogs are not an environment where you just hold forth opinion and don't accept feedback. You have to have your wits about you to understand it's not the same old PR machine."[15]

REVIEW LEARNING OUTCOME 2

2   **Describe the communication process**

Sender	Feedback channel	Receiver
Message to be conveyed		Message that was understood
Encode message	NOISE NOISE NOISE NOISE	Decode message
Transmit message		Receive message

Message channel

THE GOALS AND TASKS OF PROMOTION

Explain the goals of promotion

People communicate with one another for many reasons. They seek amusement, ask for help, give assistance or instructions, provide information, and express ideas and thoughts. Promotion, on the other hand, seeks to modify behaviour and thoughts in some way. For example, promoters may try to persuade consumers to eat at Harvey's rather than at McDonald's. Promotion also strives to reinforce existing behaviour—for instance, getting consumers to continue to dine at Harvey's once they have switched. The source (the seller) hopes to project a favourable image or to motivate purchase of the company's goods and services.

Effective promotion will achieve one or more of three goals. It will *inform* the target audience, *persuade* the target audience, or *remind* the target audience. Often a marketer will try to achieve two or more of these goals at the same time.

INFORMING

Informative promotion seeks to convert an existing need into a want or to stimulate interest in a new product. It is generally more prevalent in the early stages of the product life cycle. People typically will not buy a product or service or support a non-profit organization until they know its purpose and its benefits to them. Informative messages are important for promoting complex and technical products such as automobiles, computers, and investment services. For example, Philips's original advertisement for the Magnavox flat-screen television showed young, urban consumers trying the flat-screen TV all over the house, including the ceiling. The ad focused on "how to" use the flat-screen TV rather than the Philips Magnavox brand or the technological capabilities.[16] Informative promotion is also important for a new brand being introduced into an old product class. Coke Zero was introduced into the market using ads depicting Coke brand managers trying to hire lawyers to sue their own company for "taste infringement." Coke Zero is being promoted as having the same Coca-Cola taste but with "no calories." Coke Zero will not be able to establish itself against more mature brands like Diet Coke and Diet Pepsi unless potential buyers are aware of it, understand its benefits, and understand its positioning in the marketplace.

PERSUADING

Persuasive promotion is designed to stimulate a purchase or an action—for example, to eat more McCain frozen french fries or to use the banking services of the Royal Bank of Canada (RBC). Persuasion normally becomes the main promotion goal when the product enters the growth stage of its life cycle. By this time, the target market should have general product awareness and some knowledge of how the product can fulfill its wants. For this reason, the promotional task switches from informing consumers about the product category to persuading them to buy the company's brand rather than the competitor's. At this time, the promotional message emphasizes the product's real and perceived differential advantages, often through an appeal to emotional needs such as love, belonging, self-esteem, and ego satisfaction. For example, the latest advertisement for the Philips Magnavox flat-screen television still features young, urban consumers. But the ad focuses on the product's benefits such as lifestyle enhancements, technological features like HDTV and Dolby digital surround sound, and the superiority of the brand.[17]

Persuasion can also be an important goal in highly competitive mature-product categories such as household items, soft drinks, beer, and banking services. In a marketplace characterized by many competitors, the promotional message often encourages brand switching and aims to convert some buyers into loyal users. To persuade new customers to switch their chequing accounts, a bank's marketing manager may offer a year's worth of free cheques with no fees.

Critics believe that some promotional messages and techniques can be too persuasive, causing consumers to buy products and services they really don't need.

REMINDING

Reminder promotion is used to keep the product and brand name in the public's mind. This type of promotion prevails during the maturity stage of the life cycle. It assumes that the target market has already been persuaded of the good's or service's merits. Its purpose is simply to trigger a memory. Crest toothpaste, Sunlight laundry detergent, Cadbury Caramilk chocolate bars, and many other consumer products often use reminder promotion. Similarly, Philips Magnavox could advertise just the brand rather than the benefits of the product.

REVIEW LEARNING OUTCOME 3

 3 | **Explain the goals of promotion**

- **Informative promotion**
  Increasing the awareness of a new brand, product class, or product attribute
  Explaining how the product works
  Suggesting new uses for a product
  Building a company image
- **Persuasive promotion**
  Encouraging brand switching
  Changing customers' perceptions of product attributes
  Influencing customers to buy now
  Persuading customers to call
- **Reminder promotion**
  Reminding consumers that the product may be needed in the near future
  Reminding consumers where to buy the product
  Maintaining consumer awareness

promotional mix
The combination of promotional tools, including advertising, public relations, personal selling, and sales promotion, used to reach the target market and fulfill the organization's overall goals.

advertising
Impersonal, one-way mass communication about a product or organization that is paid for by a marketer.

SOURCE: © AP IMAGES/PRNEWSFOTO/DENTEK ORAL CARE COMPANY

4 THE PROMOTIONAL MIX

Discuss the elements of the promotional mix

As you read earlier, most promotional strategies use several ingredients, including advertising, public relations, sales promotion, and personal selling, to reach a target market. That combination is called the **promotional mix**. The best promotional mix is the one that meets the needs of the target market and fulfills the organization's overall goals. The more funds allocated to each promotional ingredient and the more emphasis managers place on each technique, the more important that element is thought to be in the overall mix.

ADVERTISING

Almost all companies selling goods or services use some form of advertising, whether in the form of a multimillion-dollar campaign illustrated by the DenTek flossing tool ad on this page or a simple classified ad in the local Pennysaver flyer. **Advertising** is any form of paid communication in which the sponsor or company is identified. Chapter 14 examines advertising in greater detail.

One of the primary benefits of advertising is its ability to communicate to a large number of people at one time. Although the cost per contact in advertising is low compared to the other promotional elements, the total cost to advertise is typically very high. This hurdle tends to restrict national ads to only those companies with the financial resources to run national campaigns. When AT&T Canada decided to change its name to Allstream, it launched a $20- to $25-million campaign to inform Canadians about the change.[18] Few small companies can match this level of spending for a national campaign.

Traditional media—such as television, radio, newspapers, magazines, books, direct mail, billboards, and transit cards (advertisements on buses and taxis and at bus stops)—have been most commonly used to transmit advertisements to consumers but they are giving way to electronic media such as websites, e-mail, and even interactive video kiosks located in department stores and supermarkets. This had led to increasing fragmentation of media choices, a change that means advertisers are having more and more difficulty reaching large numbers of people with their messages. Many companies are using Internet ads as a vital component in their marketing mix. Banner ads,

Ethics in Marketing

WHO'S PEEPING AT YOUR FACEBOOK? PRIVACY CONCERNS AND SOCIAL NETWORKS

Hundreds of millions of people have embraced social networking sites such as Facebook (465 million users worldwide with 16 million in Canada) and MySpace (well over 100 million users) and increasingly specialized sites such as LinkedIn. In fact, Canadians have the highest percentage use of Facebook of any nation in the world, with over 47 percent of our population subscribed. While social networks are easy ways to keep in touch with friends and family, there are privacy concerns. A study at Carnegie Mellon found that a large portion of the Facebook users the researchers studied generously supplied plenty of personal data and limited privacy settings. A simple viewing of personal information can make it easier for stalking and identify theft. More insidiously, Facebook and MySpace allow outside developers to create widgets or apps for the sites. Since 2007, 24,000 applications have been created by more than 400,000 developers, and more than 95 percent of Facebook users have downloaded at least one application.

In 2009, the Canadian Internet Policy and Public Interest Clinic complained to the Office of the Privacy Commissioner of Canada (OPC) that Facebook was operating in violation of Canada's Personal Information Protection and Electronic Documents Act (PIPEDA). The OPC determined these concerns to be well-founded. Consequently, the privacy commissioner contacted Facebook and directly asked the firm to answer "how the company deals with deactivated or deceased user accounts, the handling of non-user information that may end up online through Facebook-using friends and how much information is made available to third-party developers, among other issues."

In response to the query by the Privacy Commissioner of Canada, as well as other consumer advocates, Jeromy Lloyd of *Marketing Magazine* reported that in May 2010 "Facebook

founder and CEO Mark Zuckerberg unveiled a new, simplified set of privacy controls for the social networking site." He said, "When people have control over what they share, they want to share more. . . . Today we're starting to roll out changes that will make our controls simpler and easier." These changes included, he said, "a new privacy settings page, which gives users more control on who sees the content they post and makes it easier for users to close off access from websites and third-party applications that may be seeking their information."

A number of interested parties have reviewed the changes made by Facebook. Some were positive, like Leslie Harris, president of the Center for Democracy and Technology (CDT), who commented, "While more work still needs to be done, these changes are the building blocks for giving people what they want and deserve." Chris Conley of the American Civil Liberties Union of Northern California stated, "Today's changes are a major step forward for privacy on Facebook: users simply have more and better controls today than they had yesterday. There are still substantial issues that Facebook needs to address, but they deserve credit for today's release." However, some were negative, like Meg Roggensack, of *The Huffington Post,* who said, "Facebook 'missed the mark' because the company just doesn't get it." The company is not off the hook in Canada, either: Elizabeth Denham, Assistant Privacy Commissioner of Canada, responded, "At first blush, it appears to be that the site is still [leaving information] more open than it was last summer, when we concluded our investigation into Facebook."[19]

As a result of the actions taken by Facebook in response to the Privacy Commissioner of Canada's concerns as well as concerns raised by consumer groups, do you feel more comfortable about using this social network? Why or why not?

SOURCE: KIM HART, "A FLASHY FACEBOOK PAGE AT A COST TO PRIVACY," THE WASHINGTON POST, JUNE 12, 2008, WWW.WASHINGTONPOST.COM, ACCESSED FEBRUARY 2008; WWW.ALLFACEBOOK.COM/2009/FACEBOOK-PRIVACY, ACCESSED FEBRUARY 2009; RALPH GROSS AND ALESSANDRO ACQUISTI, "INFORMATION REVELATION AND PRIVACY IN ONLINE SOCIAL NETWORKS (THE FACEBOOK CASE)," ACM WORKSHOP ON PRIVACY IN THE ELECTRONIC SOCIETY, NOVEMBER 7, 2007; JEROMY LLOYD, "TALKS WITH FACEBOOK 'VERY POSITIVE,' SAYS PRIVACY COMMISSIONER," MARKETING MAGAZINE, AUGUST 18, 2009; AND JORDAN ADLER, "CHATTER: FACEBOOK PRIVACY UPDATES," MARKETING MAGAZINE, MAY 27, 2010

viral marketing, and interactive promotions are all being used to reach target audiences through the Web. As the Internet becomes a more vital component of many companies' promotion and marketing mix, consumers and lawmakers are increasingly concerned about possible violations of consumers' privacy. Read more about this issue in the Ethics in Marketing box, which describes how social networking sites are using all the information that is freely collected.

PUBLIC RELATIONS

public relations
The marketing function that evaluates public attitudes, identifies areas within the organization that the public may be interested in, and executes a program of action to earn public understanding and acceptance.

Concerned about how they are perceived by their target markets, organizations often spend large sums to build a positive public image. **Public relations** is the marketing function that evaluates public attitudes, identifies areas in the organization that may interest the public, and executes a program of action to earn public understanding and acceptance. Public relations helps an organization communicate with customers, suppliers, shareholders, government officials, employees, and the community in which it operates. Marketers use public relations not only to maintain a positive image but also to educate the public about the company's goals and objectives, to introduce new products, and to support the sales effort. Public relations will be covered in more depth in Chapter 14.

SALES PROMOTION

sales promotion
Marketing activities, other than personal selling, advertising, and public relations, which stimulate consumer buying and dealer effectiveness.

Sales promotion consists of all marketing activities, other than personal selling, advertising, and public relations, that stimulate consumer purchasing and dealer effectiveness. Sales promotion is generally a short-run tool used to stimulate immediate increases in demand. Sales promotion can be aimed at end consumers, trade customers, or a company's employees. Sales promotions include free samples, contests, premiums, trade shows, vacation giveaways, and coupons. A major promotional campaign might use several of these sales promotion tools. Sales promotion is discussed in more detail in Chapter 15.

PERSONAL SELLING

personal selling
A purchase situation in which two people communicate in an attempt to influence each other.

Personal selling is a purchase situation in which two people communicate in an attempt to influence each other. Traditional methods of personal selling include a planned presentation to one or more prospective buyers for the purpose of making a sale. More current notions on personal selling emphasize the relationship that develops between a salesperson and a buyer. Recently, both business-to-business and business-to-consumer selling focus on building long-term relationships rather than on making a one-time sale.

Personal selling, like other promotional mix elements, increasingly depends on the Internet. Most companies use their websites to attract potential buyers seeking information on products and services. While some companies sell products direct to consumers on-line, many do not. Instead, they rely on the website to drive customers to their physical locations where personal selling can close the sale. Whether it takes place face-to-face, over the phone, or on-line, personal selling attempts to persuade the buyer to accept a point of view or take some action. Personal selling is discussed further in Chapter 15.

THE COMMUNICATION PROCESS AND THE PROMOTIONAL MIX

The four elements of the promotional mix differ in their ability to affect the target audience. For instance, promotional mix elements may communicate with the consumer directly or indirectly. The message may flow one way or two ways. Feedback may be fast or slow, a little or a lot. Likewise, the communicator may have varying degrees of control over message delivery, content, and flexibility. Exhibit 13.3 outlines differences among the promotional mix elements with respect to mode of communication, marketer's control over the communication process, amount and speed of feedback,

EXHIBIT 13.3

Characteristics of the Elements in the Promotional Mix

	Advertising	Public Relations	Sales Promotion	Personal Selling
Mode of Communication	Indirect and nonpersonal	Usually indirect and nonpersonal	Usually indirect and nonpersonal	Direct and face-to-face
Communicator Control over Situation	Low	Moderate to low	Moderate to low	High
Amount of Feedback	Little	Little	Little to moderate	Much
Speed of Feedback	Delayed	Delayed	Varies	Immediate
Direction of Message Flow	One-way	One-way	Mostly one-way	Two-way
Control over Message Content	Yes	No	Yes	Yes
Identification of Sponsor	Yes	No	Yes	Yes
Speed in Reaching Large Audience	Fast	Usually fast	Fast	Slow
Message Flexibility	Same message to all audiences	Usually no direct control over message	Same message to varied target	Tailored to prospective buyer

direction of message flow, marketer's control over the message, identification of the sender, speed in reaching large audiences, and message flexibility.

Exhibit 13.3 illustrates that most elements of the promotional mix are indirect and impersonal when used to communicate with a target market, providing only one direction of message flow. For example, advertising, public relations, and sales promotion are generally impersonal, one-way means of mass communication. Because they provide no opportunity for direct feedback, they cannot easily adapt to consumers' changing preferences, individual differences, and personal goals. One exception is how a company uses its website, which can provide a forum for some types of feedback.

Personal selling, on the other hand, is personal, two-way communication. The salesperson receives immediate feedback from the consumer and can adjust the message in response. Personal selling, however, is very slow in dispersing the marketer's message to large audiences. Because a salesperson can communicate to only one person or a small group of people at a time, it is a poor choice if the marketer wants to send a message to many potential buyers.

REVIEW LEARNING OUTCOME 4

4   **Discuss the elements of the promotional mix**

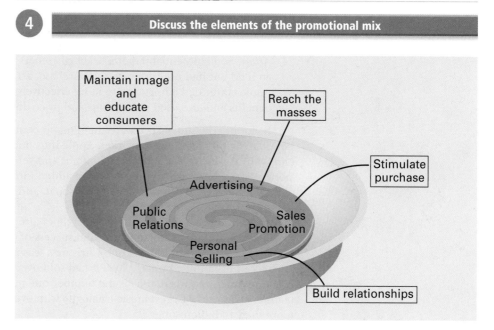

5 PROMOTIONAL GOALS AND THE AIDA CONCEPT

Discuss the AIDA concept and its relationship to the promotional mix

AIDA concept
A model that outlines the process for achieving promotional goals in terms of stages of consumer involvement with the message; the acronym stands for attention, interest, desire, and action.

The ultimate goal of any promotion is to get someone to buy a good or service or, in the case of nonprofit organizations, to take some action (for instance, donate money or volunteer time). A classic model for reaching promotional goals is the **AIDA concept**.[20] The acronym stands for *attention, interest, desire,* and *action*—the stages of consumer involvement with a promotional message.

This model proposes that consumers respond to marketing messages in a cognitive (thinking), affective (feeling), and conative (doing) sequence. First, a promotion manager may focus on attracting a person's *attention* by training a salesperson to use a friendly greeting and approach, or by using loud volume, unusual colour contrasts, bold headlines, movement, bright colours, and the like in an advertisement. Next, a good sales presentation, demonstration, or advertisement creates *interest* in the product and then, by illustrating how the product's features will satisfy the consumer's needs, arouses *desire*. Finally, a special offer or a strong closing sales pitch may be used to obtain purchase *action*.

The AIDA concept assumes that promotion propels consumers along the following four steps in the purchase-decision process:

1. *Attention.* The advertiser must first gain the attention of the target market. A company cannot sell something if the market does not know that the good or service exists. When Apple introduced the iPod, it was a new product for the company. To create awareness and gain attention for the new product, Apple had to advertise and promote it extensively through ads on TV, in magazines, and on the Internet. Because the iPod was a brand extension of the Apple computer, it required less effort than if it had been an entirely new brand. At the same time, because the iPod was an innovative new product line, the promotion had to get customers' attention and create awareness of a new idea from an established company.

2. *Interest.* Simple awareness of a brand seldom leads to a sale. The next step is to create interest in the product. A print ad or TV commercial cannot tell potential customers all the features and benefits of the iPod. Thus Apple had to arrange iPod demonstrations and target messages to innovators and early adopters to create interest in the new portable music players.

3. *Desire.* Potential customers for the Apple iPod may like the concept of a portable music player, but they may not feel it is necessarily better than a Sony Walkman portable radio or a portable music player with fewer features. Therefore, Apple had to create brand preference with its iTunes Music Store, extended-life battery, clock and alarm, calendar and to-do list, photo storage, and other features. Specifically, Apple had to convince potential customers that the iPod was the best solution to meet their desire for a portable digital music player.

4. *Action.* Some potential target market customers may have been convinced to buy an iPod but had not yet made the purchase. To motivate them to take action, Apple continued advertising to more effectively communicate the features and benefits and also used promotions and price discounts.

Following the initial success of the iPod, to continue its market dominance of the portable digital music player market, Apple introduced new models such as the Nano and Shuffle, which were smaller and lighter and yet had longer battery life and more storage. Then podcasting and video were added with access to thousands of network and cable shows and interfaces with auto, boat, and home equipment—and the iPod became a "portable media player."

With each product innovation, the cycle of attention, interest, desire, and action began again. But with the familiarity and success of earlier models, the time frame became shorter. In fact, during one Christmas season, Apple was selling more than 100 iPods per minute; by early 2009 it had sold over 150 million iPods. Moreover, Apple's iTunes, reports that it "is the number one music retailer in the world and features the world's largest music catalogue with over 12 million songs" and has sold more than 10 billion songs.[21]

Most buyers involved in high-involvement purchase situations pass through the four stages of the AIDA model on the way to making a purchase. The promoter's task is to determine where on the purchase ladder most of the target consumers are located and then design a promotion plan to meet their needs. For instance, if Apple learned from its market research that many potential customers were in the desire stage but had not bought an iPod for some reason, Apple could place advertising on Yahoo or Google, and in video games as well, to target younger individuals, who are the primary target market, with specific messages to motivate them to take immediate action and buy an iPod.

The AIDA concept does not explain how all promotions influence purchase decisions. The model does suggest that promotional effectiveness can be measured in terms of consumers progressing from one stage to the next. However, the order of stages in the model, as well as whether consumers go through all steps, has been much debated. For example, a purchase can occur without interest or desire, perhaps when a low-involvement product is bought on impulse. Regardless of the order of the stages or consumers' progression through these stages, the AIDA concept helps marketers by suggesting which promotional strategy will be most effective.[22]

5 | **Discuss the AIDA concept and its relationship to the promotional mix**

	Attention	Interest	Desire	Action
Advertising	✓+	✓+	✓	✓−
Public Relations	✓+	✓+	✓+	✓−
Sales Promotion	✓	✓	✓+	✓
Personal Sell	✓	✓+	✓+	✓+

6 INTEGRATED MARKETING COMMUNICATIONS

Discuss the concept of integrated marketing communications

Ideally, marketing communications from each promotional mix element (personal selling, advertising, sales promotion, and public relations) should be integrated—that is, the message reaching the consumer should be the same regardless of whether it is from an ad, a salesperson in the field, a magazine article, or a coupon in a newspaper insert.

From the consumer's perspective, a company's communications are already integrated. Consumers do not think in terms of the four elements of promotion: advertising, sales promotion, public relations, and personal selling. Instead, everything is an "ad." In general, the only people who recognize the distinctions among these communications elements are the marketers themselves. Unfortunately, many marketers forget this when planning promotional messages and fail to integrate their communication efforts from one element to the next. The most common rift typically occurs between personal selling and the other elements of the promotional mix.

This disjointed approach to promotion has propelled many companies to adopt the concept of **integrated marketing communications (IMC)**. IMC is the careful coordination of all promotional messages—traditional advertising, direct marketing, interactive, public relations, sales promotion, personal selling, event marketing, and other

integrated marketing communications (IMC)
The careful coordination of all promotional messages for a product or a service to ensure the consistency of messages at every contact point where a company meets the consumer.

ANATOMY OF AN **Integrated Marketing Campaign**

Indiana Jones movie

Lucasfilm Ltd. used integrated marketing communications to ensure that *Indiana Jones and the Kingdom of the Crystal Skull* was widely and consistently promoted before its release.

NASCAR cars increase publicity.

Hallmark greeting cards and Scholastic books hold kids' interest even after the movie leaves theaters.

Burger King's "Indy Double Whopper" and Mars M&M's tie the movie to summer fun.

Legos and Kellogg's cereal attracts kids.

NEL

communications—for a product or service to ensure the consistency of messages at every contact point where a company meets the consumer. Following the concept of IMC, marketing managers carefully work out the roles that various promotional elements will play in the marketing mix. Timing of promotional activities is coordinated, and the results of each campaign are closely monitored to improve future use of the promotional mix tools. Typically, a marketing communications director is appointed with responsibility for integrating the company's marketing communications.

Movie marketing campaigns benefit greatly from an IMC approach. Those campaigns that are most integrated generally have more impact and make a deeper impression on potential moviegoers, leading to higher box-office sales. The Anatomy of an Integrated Marketing Campaign shows how Lucasfilm Ltd. used integrated marketing communications for the latest Indiana Jones movie installment, *Indiana Jones and the Kingdom of the Crystal Skull.*

The IMC concept has been growing in popularity for several reasons. First, the proliferation of thousands of media choices beyond traditional television has made promotion a more complicated task. Instead of promoting a product just through mass media options, such as TV and magazines, promotional messages today can appear in many varied sources. Furthermore, the mass market has fragmented—more selectively segmented markets and an increase in niche marketing have replaced the traditional broad market groups that marketers promoted to in years past. For instance, a large number of ethnic media choices exist in Canada to cater to our country's multicultural population. According to the Media Director's Council, Canadian marketers can reach more than 87 cultures through more than 370 media outlets in the 100 different languages spoken.[23] Finally, marketers have slashed their advertising spending in favour of promotional techniques that generate immediate sales responses or that are more easily measured, such as direct marketing. The interest in IMC is largely a reaction to the scrutiny that marketing communications has come under, and especially to suggestions that uncoordinated promotional activity leads to a strategy that is wasteful and inefficient.

6 | **Discuss the concept of integrated marketing communications**

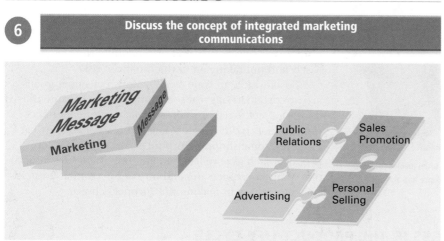

7 FACTORS AFFECTING THE PROMOTIONAL MIX

Describe the factors that affect the promotional mix

Promotional mixes vary a great deal from one product and one industry to the next. Normally, advertising and personal selling are used to promote goods and services, supported and supplemented by sales promotion. Public relations helps develop a positive image for the organization and the product line. However, a company may choose not to use all four promotional elements in its promotional mix, or it may choose to use them in varying degrees. The particular promotional mix chosen by a company for a product or service depends on several factors: the nature of the product, the stage in the product life cycle, target market characteristics, the type of buying decision, funds available for promotion, and whether a push or a pull strategy will be used.

NATURE OF THE PRODUCT

Characteristics of the product itself can influence the promotional mix. For instance, a product can be classified as either a business product or a consumer product (refer to Chapters 5 and 8). As business products are often custom-tailored to the buyer's exact specifications, they are usually not well suited to mass promotion. Therefore, producers of most business goods, such as computer servers and industrial machinery, rely more heavily on personal selling than on advertising. Informative personal selling is common for industrial installations, accessories, and component parts and materials. Advertising, however, still serves a purpose in promoting business goods. Advertisements in the trade media may be used to create general buyer awareness and interest. Moreover, advertising can help locate potential customers for the sales force. For example, print media advertising often includes coupons soliciting the potential customer to "fill this out for more detailed information."

In contrast, because consumer products generally are not custom-made, they do not require the selling efforts of a company representative who can tailor them to the user's needs. Thus consumer goods are promoted mainly through advertising to create brand familiarity. TV and radio, newspapers, and consumer magazines are used extensively to promote consumer goods, especially nondurables. Sales promotion, the brand name, and the product's packaging are about twice as important for consumer goods as for business products. Persuasive personal selling is important at the retail level for shopping goods such as automobiles and appliances.

The costs and risks associated with a product also influence the promotional mix. As a general rule, when the costs or risks of using a product increase, personal selling becomes more important. Items that are a small part of a company's budget (supply items) or of a consumer's budget (convenience products) do not require a salesperson to close the sale. In fact, inexpensive items cannot support the cost of a salesperson's time and effort unless the potential volume is high. On the other hand, expensive and complex machinery, new buildings, cars, and new homes represent a considerable investment. A salesperson must assure buyers that they are spending their money wisely and not taking an undue financial risk.

Social risk is an issue as well. Many consumer goods are not products of great social importance because they do not reflect social position. People do not experience much social risk in buying a loaf of bread or a candy bar. However, some shopping products and many specialty products such as jewellery and clothing do involve a social risk. Many consumers depend on sales personnel for guidance and advice in making the "proper" choice.

SOURCE: © PURESTOCK/JUPITERIMAGES

Buying specialty products such as jewellery and clothing often involves a social risk. Many consumers depend on sales personnel for guidance and advice in making the "proper" choice.

STAGES IN THE PRODUCT LIFE CYCLE

The product's stage in its life cycle is a big factor in designing a promotional mix (see Exhibit 13.4). During the *introduction stage*, the basic goal of promotion is to inform the target audience that the product is available. Initially, the emphasis is on the general product class—for example, mobile phone service. This emphasis gradually changes to gaining attention for a specific brand, such as Telus or Rogers. Typically, both extensive advertising and public relations inform the target audience of the product class or brand and heighten awareness levels. Sales promotion encourages early trial of the product, and personal selling gets retailers to carry the product.

When the product reaches the *growth stage* of the life cycle, the promotion blend may shift. Often a change is necessary because different types of potential buyers are targeted. Although advertising and public relations continue to be major elements of the promotional mix, sales promotion can be reduced because consumers need fewer incentives to purchase. The promotional strategy is to emphasize the product's differential advantage over the competition. Persuasive promotion is used to build and maintain brand loyalty to support the product during the growth stage. By this stage, personal selling has usually succeeded in getting adequate distribution for the product.

As the product reaches the *maturity stage* of its life cycle, competition becomes more intense and thus persuasive, and reminder advertising is more strongly emphasized. Sales promotion comes back into focus as product sellers try to increase their market share.

EXHIBIT 13.4

Product Life Cycle and the Promotional Mix

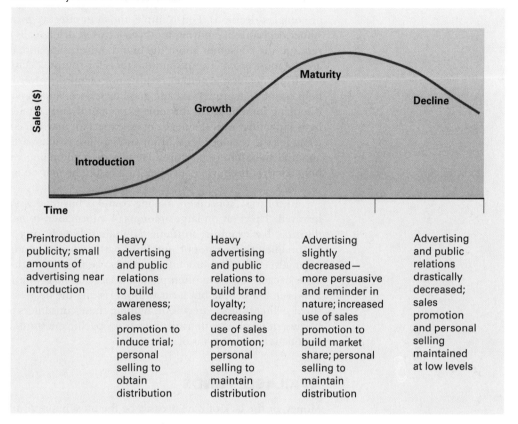

| Preintroduction publicity; small amounts of advertising near introduction | Heavy advertising and public relations to build awareness; sales promotion to induce trial; personal selling to obtain distribution | Heavy advertising and public relations to build brand loyalty; decreasing use of sales promotion; personal selling to maintain distribution | Advertising slightly decreased— more persuasive and reminder in nature; increased use of sales promotion to build market share; personal selling to maintain distribution | Advertising and public relations drastically decreased; sales promotion and personal selling maintained at low levels |

All promotion, especially advertising, is reduced as the product enters the decline stage. Nevertheless, personal selling and sales promotion efforts may be maintained, particularly at the retail level.

TARGET MARKET CHARACTERISTICS

A target market characterized by widely scattered potential customers, highly informed buyers, and brand-loyal repeat purchasers generally requires a promotional mix with more advertising and sales promotion and less personal selling. Sometimes, however, personal selling is required even when buyers are well informed and geographically dispersed. Although industrial installations and component parts may be sold to extremely competent people with extensive education and work experience, salespeople must still be present to explain the product and work out the details of the purchase agreement.

Often companies sell goods and services in markets where potential customers are hard to locate. Print advertising can be used to find them. The reader is invited to go on-line, to phone for more information, or to mail in a reply card for a detailed brochure. As the on-line inquiries, calls, or cards are received, salespeople are sent to visit the potential customers.

Consumers making complex buying decisions often depend on the salesperson to provide important product information. Purchasing a car is one such example. Can you think of others?

SOURCE: © CORBIS

TYPE OF BUYING DECISION

The promotional mix also depends on the type of buying decision (routine decision or complex decision). For example, the most effective promotion for routine consumer decisions like buying toothpaste or soft drinks calls attention to the brand or reminds the consumer about the brand. Advertising and, especially, sales promotion are the most productive promotion tools for routine decisions.

If the decision is neither routine nor complex, advertising and public relations help establish awareness for the good or service. Suppose a single and childless person is looking for a baby gift for some expectant friends. As a single and childless person, he is unfamiliar with the needs of an expectant married couple, yet he has seen advertising for the retailer Please Mum and has also read an article in a business magazine about Please Mum retail stores. He may then go on-line and research this retailer to help confirm his buying decision. As a result, he may be more likely to shop at this retailer.

In contrast, consumers making complex buying decisions are more extensively involved. They rely on large amounts of information to help them reach a purchase decision. For example, consumers thinking about buying a car typically research the car on-line using corporate and third-party websites. In addition to on-line resources, print advertising and brochures may also be used for high-involvement purchase decisions because they can often provide a large amount of information to the consumer. However, few people buy a car without visiting the dealership. In this situation, personal selling is most effective in helping these consumers to reach a final decision because it involves gathering answers to specific questions and also enables a final negotiation of the terms of sale.

AVAILABLE FUNDS

Money, or the lack of it, may easily be the most important factor in determining the promotional mix. A small, undercapitalized manufacturer may rely heavily on free publicity if its product is unique. If the situation warrants a sales force, a financially strained company may turn to manufacturers' agents, who work on a commission basis with no advances or expense accounts. Even well-capitalized organizations may not be able to afford the advertising rates of publications like *Maclean's*, *Reader's Digest*, and the *Globe and Mail* or the cost of running television ads on *Hockey Night in Canada* or the Grey Cup game. The price of a high-profile ad in these media could support one or more salespeople for an entire year.

When funds are available to permit a mix of promotional elements, a company will generally try to optimize its return on promotion dollars while minimizing the *cost per contact*, or the cost of reaching one member of the target market. In general, the cost per contact is very high for personal selling, public relations, and sales promotions like sampling and demonstrations. On the other hand, for the number of people national advertising reaches, it has a very low cost per contact.

Usually there is a tradeoff among the funds available, the number of people in the target market, the quality of communication needed, and the relative costs of the promotional elements. A company may have to forgo a full-page colour ad in *Canadian Business* in order to pay for a personal selling effort. Although the magazine ad will reach more people than personal selling, the high cost of the magazine space is a problem. There are plenty of low-cost options available to companies without a huge budget. Many of these include on-line strategies and public relations efforts, where the company relies on free publicity.

PUSH AND PULL STRATEGIES

push strategy
A marketing strategy that uses aggressive personal selling and trade advertising to convince a wholesaler or a retailer to carry and sell particular merchandise.

The last factor that affects the promotional mix is whether a push or a pull promotional strategy will be used. Manufacturers may use aggressive personal selling and trade advertising to convince a wholesaler or a retailer to carry and sell their merchandise. This approach is known as a **push strategy** (see Exhibit 13.5). The wholesaler, in turn, must often push the merchandise forward by persuading the retailer to handle the goods. The retailer then uses advertising, displays, and other forms of promotion to convince the consumer to buy the "pushed" products. This concept also applies to services. For example, the Jamaican Tourism Board targets promotions to travel agencies, which in turn tell their customers about the benefits of vacationing in Jamaica.

pull strategy
A marketing strategy that stimulates consumer demand to obtain product distribution.

At the other extreme is a **pull strategy**, which stimulates consumer demand to obtain product distribution. Rather than concentrating on the wholesaler, the manufacturer using a pull strategy focuses its promotional efforts on end consumers or opinion leaders. For example, Procter & Gamble spent $100 million in North America on an advertising campaign to promote its new toothpaste, Crest Pro-Health. The toothpaste claims to deliver everything a consumer could want in one tube—it supposedly protects against gingivitis, plaque, cavities, sensitivity, and stains, and it freshens breath. The theme of the campaign, targeted to the information-seeking customer, is "Healthy, beautiful smiles for life."[24] Consumers responded positively to the campaign and began demanding the product from their retailer. The retailer ordered the merchandise from the wholesaler. The wholesaler, confronted with rising demand, then placed an order for the "pulled" merchandise from the manufacturer. Consumer demand pulled the product through the channel of distribution (see Exhibit 13.5). Heavy sampling, introductory consumer advertising, cents-off campaigns, and couponing are part of a pull strategy. P&G flooded dental offices with product samples and informational materials in hopes of generating favourable testimonials from users.

Arguably, the most successful example of a pull strategy is Intel Corporation's "Intel Inside" campaign, which established a brand identity for the Pentium microprocessor, one of the least visible components of a personal computer. When one considers all the critical components that go into a computer and the brand images of the computer manufacturers themselves, it is truly remarkable that many people not only are fully aware of the processors that go into their computers, but also even insist that their computers have Pentium processors. Intel's pull strategy has been so effective that computer retailers and manufacturers cannot even advertise their

EXHIBIT 13.5

Push Strategy versus Pull Strategy

Push strategy

| Manufacturer promotes to wholesaler | Wholesaler promotes to retailer | Retailer promotes to consumer | Consumer buys from retailer |

Orders to manufacturer

Pull strategy

| Manufacturer promotes to consumer | Consumer demands product from retailer | Retailer demands product from wholesaler | Wholesaler demands product from manufacturer |

Orders to manufacturer

7 **Describe the factors that affect the promotional mix**

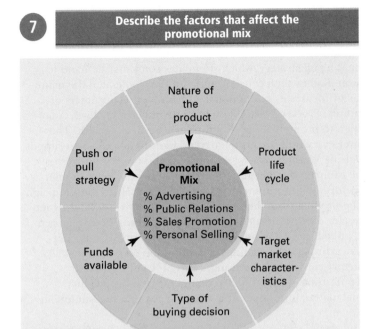

computers without identifying the processor component. Before this, computer manufacturers had a customer franchise and could sell their products based on the brand name of the computer. The computer brands put their choice of microprocessor in the computers and would negotiate for price concessions from a number of microprocessor suppliers. Intel wanted to strengthen its position as a supplier and decided to use a pull strategy. The result: Intel has developed such a strong customer franchise that it now holds a near-monopoly over both computer manufacturers and retailers as a microprocessor supplier.

Rarely does a company use a pull or a push strategy exclusively. Instead, the mix emphasizes one of these strategies. Pharmaceutical companies generally use a push strategy, through personal selling and trade advertising, to promote their drugs and therapies to physicians. Sales presentations and ads in medical journals give physicians the detailed information they need to prescribe medication to their patients. Most pharmaceutical companies supplement their push promotional strategy with a pull strategy targeted directly at potential patients through ads in consumer magazines and on television.

REVIEW AND APPLICATIONS

1 **Discuss the role of promotion in the marketing mix.** Promotion is communication by marketers that informs, persuades, and reminds potential buyers of a product in order to influence an opinion or elicit a response. Promotional strategy is the plan for using the elements of promotion—advertising, public relations, sales promotion, and personal selling—to meet the firm's overall objectives and marketing goals. Based on these objectives, the elements of the promotional strategy become a coordinated promotion plan. The promotion plan then becomes an integral part of the total marketing strategy for reaching the target market, along with product, distribution, and price.

1.1 What is a promotional strategy? Explain the concept of a differential advantage in relation to promotional strategy.

2 **Describe the communication process.** The communication process has several steps. When an individual or organization has a message it wishes to convey to a target audience, it encodes that message using language and symbols familiar to the intended receiver and sends the message through a channel of communication. Noise in the transmission channel distorts the source's intended message. Reception occurs if the message falls within the receiver's frame of reference. The receiver decodes the message and usually provides feedback to the source. Normally, feedback is direct for interpersonal communication and indirect for mass communication.

2.1 Why is understanding the target market a crucial aspect of the communication process?

3 **Explain the goals of promotion.** The fundamental goals of promotion are to induce, modify, or reinforce behaviour by informing, persuading, and reminding. Informative promotion explains a good's or service's purpose and benefits. Promotion that informs the consumer is typically used to increase demand for a general product category or to introduce a new good or service. Persuasive promotion is designed to stimulate a purchase or an action. Promotion that persuades the consumer to buy is essential during the growth stage of the product life cycle, when competition becomes intense. Reminder promotion is used to keep the product and brand name in the public's mind. Promotions that remind are generally used during the maturity stage of the product life cycle.

3.1 Why might a marketing manager choose to promote his or her product using persuasion? Give some current examples of persuasive promotion.

3.2 [TEAM] Choose a partner from class and go together to interview the owners or managers of several small businesses in your community. Ask them what their promotional objectives are and why they selected them. Are they trying to inform, persuade, or remind customers to do business with them? Do they believe they face awareness issues, or do they believe they need to persuade customers to patronize their business instead of those of their competitors? Ask them to list the characteristics of their primary market, the strengths and weaknesses of their competitors, and the steps they are taking to position themselves to compete. Prepare a report to present to the class summarizing your findings.

4 **Discuss the elements of the promotional mix.** The elements of the promotional mix include advertising, public relations, sales promotion, and personal selling. Advertising is a form of impersonal, one-way mass communication paid for by the source. Public relations is the function of promotion concerned with a company's public image. Sales promotion is typically used to back up other components of the promotional mix by stimulating immediate demand. Finally, personal selling typically involves direct communication, in person or by telephone; the seller tries to initiate a purchase by informing and persuading one or more potential buyers.

4.1 [WRITING] As the promotional manager for a new line of cosmetics targeted to preteen girls, you have been assigned the task of deciding which promotional mix elements—advertising, public relations, sales promotion, and personal selling—should be used in promoting it. Your budget for promoting the preteen cosmetics line is limited. Write a promotional plan explaining your choice of promotional mix elements given the nature of the product, the stage in the product life cycle, the target market characteristics, the type of buying decision, available funds, and the use of a pull or push strategy.

5 **Discuss the AIDA concept and its relationship to the promotional mix.** The AIDA model outlines the four basic stages in the purchase decision-making process, which are initiated and propelled by promotional activities: (1) attention, (2) interest, (3) desire, and (4) action. The components of the promotional mix have varying levels of influence at each stage of the AIDA model. Advertising and public relations are good tools for increasing awareness and knowledge of a good or service. Sales promotion is effective when consumers are at the purchase stage of the decision-making process. Personal selling is most effective in developing customer interest and desire.

5.1 Discuss the AIDA concept. How do these different stages of consumer involvement affect the promotional mix?

5.2 [ONLINE] How does a website's ease of use affect its ability to create attention, interest, desire, and action? Visit the kitchen and bath pages of Kohler's website (**www.kohler.com**) and determine how successful the company is at moving consumers through the AIDA process.

6 **Discuss the concept of integrated marketing communications.** Integrated marketing communications (IMC) is the careful coordination of all promotional messages for a product or service to ensure the consistency of messages at every contact point where a company meets the consumer—advertising, sales promotion, personal selling, and public relations, as well as direct marketing, packaging, and other forms of communication. Marketing managers carefully coordinate all promotional activities to ensure that consumers see and hear one message. Integrated Marketing Communications has received more attention in recent years due to the proliferation of media choices, the fragmentation of mass markets into more segmented niches, and the decrease in advertising spending in favour of promotional techniques that generate immediate sales responses.

6.1 Discuss the importance of IMC. Give some current examples of companies that are and are not practising IMC.

6.2 What do you think is the role of Hallmark's website (**www.hallmark.com**) in the company's Integrated Marketing Communications plan? What seems to be the marketing function of the site? Do you think the site is effective?

7 **Describe the factors that affect the promotional mix.** Promotion managers consider many factors when creating promotional mixes. These factors include the nature of the product, product life-cycle stage, target market characteristics, the type of buying decision involved, availability of funds, and the feasibility of push or pull strategies. Because most business products tend to be custom-tailored to the buyer's exact specifications, the marketing manager may choose a promotional mix that relies more heavily on personal selling. On the other hand, consumer products are generally mass produced and lend themselves more to mass promotional efforts such as advertising and sales promotion. As products move through different stages of the product life cycle, marketers will choose to use different promotional elements. For example, advertising is emphasized more in the introductory stage of the product life cycle than in the decline stage. Characteristics of the target market, such as the geographic location of potential buyers and brand loyalty, influence the promotional mix as does whether the buying decision is complex or routine. The amount of funds a company has to allocate to promotion may also help determine the promotional mix. Small firms with limited funds may rely more heavily on public relations, whereas larger firms may be able to afford broadcast or print advertising. Finally, if a firm uses a push strategy to promote the product or service, the marketing manager may choose to use aggressive advertising and personal selling to wholesalers and retailers. If a pull strategy is chosen, the manager often relies on aggressive mass promotion, such as advertising and sales promotion, to stimulate consumer demand.

7.1 Explain the difference between a "pull" and a "push" promotional strategy. Under what conditions should each strategy be used?

7.2 Use Radioguide (**www.radioguide.fm**) to find a listing of radio websites in your area. View several of the stations' sites and compare the promotions featured. What conclusions can you draw about the target market of each station based on the types of promotions they are currently running? Would any of the promotions entice you to tune to a station that you normally don't listen to?

7.3 Visit **www.teenresearch.com**. What research can this company offer about the size and growth of the teen market, the buying power of teenagers, and their buying habits? Why might these statistics be important to a company targeting teenagers through marketing communications and promotion strategy?

TERMS

advertising 414
AIDA concept 418
channel 409
communication 407
competitive advantage 406
corporate blogs 411
decoding 409
encoding 408
feedback 410

integrated marketing
   communications (IMC) 419
interpersonal communication 407
mass communication 407
noise 409
noncorporate blogs 411
personal selling 416
public relations 416
promotion 406

promotional mix 414
promotional strategy 406
pull strategy 425
push strategy 424
receiver 409
sales promotion 416
sender 408

EXERCISES

APPLICATION EXERCISE

Many people don't understand the rationale behind certain advertising messages. "Why do Infiniti ads show rocks and trees instead of automobiles?" "If car safety is so important, why do automobile ads often show cars skidding on wet, shiny surfaces?" "Telus ads are funky, with all the bright colours and exotic animals, but what's the message?"

One way to understand the vagaries of the encoding process is to consider the popular board game Taboo, by Hasbro. In this game, each team tries to get its members to guess a word without using obvious word clues. For example, when getting the team to guess "apple," you aren't allowed to say such words as red, fruit, pie, cider, or core. Sometimes advertising is like Taboo in that advertisers are not allowed to use certain words or descriptions. For example, pharmaceutical companies are not permitted to make certain claims or to say what a drug treats unless the ad also mentions the potential side effects. Language choices are also limited in advertising. To appreciate this, try applying Taboo's rules in an advertising format.[25]

Activities

1. **WRITING** Select a product from the list below, then create a print ad or TV storyboard for that product. As part of the exercise, give your product a brand name. Taboo words, visuals, and concepts are given for each product type. Taboo items cannot be present in your work.

Product	Taboo Words, Visuals, and Concepts
Deodorant	Odour, underarm, perspiration, smell, sweat
Toothpaste	Teeth, smile, breath, clean, plaque
Pain reliever	Pain, aches, fever, childproof cap, gel
Soft drinks	Sugar-free, refreshing, thirst, swimwear, any celebrity

2. **WRITING** Now create a second ad or storyboard for your product. This time, however, you must use all the words, visuals, and concepts that are listed in the right column.

Product	Must-Use Words, Visuals, and Concepts
Deodorant	A romantic couple, monster trucks
Toothpaste	Lips, tongue, flowers
Pain reliever	A mother and child, oatmeal, homework
Soft drinks	A cup of coffee, cookies, birthday cake, wine

APPLICATION EXERCISE 2

An important concept in promotion is semiotics, or the study of meaning and meaning-producing events. An understanding of semiotics can help you not only to identify objects (denotation) but also to grasp the utility of images and associations (connotation). By manipulating connotations of objects in advertising, you can create, change, or reinforce images for products. Thus semiotics is a powerful tool for brand management and promotion.[26]

Activities

1. **WRITING** Make a list of ten images and associations that come to mind for each of the following items: baseball, vinyl record album, spoon, rubber band.

2. Look through magazines and see if you can find print advertisements that include each of the items (baseball, vinyl record album, spoon, rubber band) in a supporting role. What seems to be the message of each ad? How does the item help create or reinforce an image for the product being sold in the ad?

3. **WRITING** Think of an everyday object of your own. What are its likely connotations? For example, a dog in a car might signal a family vehicle, but a dog also connotes loyalty, "man's best friend," and dependability. What images and associations are likely with your item? Make a list of as many as you can.

4. Now use your object and list of associations to create an image for another product. Think of the likely connotations your object will have for a certain target market and how such connotations can support a brand image. For example, if your everyday object is a candle, you might choose lingerie for your product, based on a candle's romantic connotations.

ETHICS EXERCISE

Integrated Marketing Solutions is a consumer-products marketing services firm. Currently, the firm is handling the launch of a new book for one of its publishing clients. The campaign includes advance review copies for key book reviewers, "Coming Soon" posters for booksellers, an author book-signing tour, and several television interviews. Everything has been produced and scheduled for release next week. Today, Jane Kershaw, the account executive, has learned that although the book received numerous favourable reviews, the review quoted on all the promotional materials is fabricated.

Questions

1. What should Jane do?

2. Go to **www.the-cma.org** and review the CMA Code of Ethics. Write a brief paragraph describing how it relates to this issue.

CASE STUDY

SOURCE: © MARK SULLIVAN/WIREIMAGE/GETTY IMAGES

HBO'S BLOOD VIRUS

When prominent occult film bloggers and fans began receiving strange letters written in dead languages and mailed in wax-sealed black envelopes, a shockwave of curiosity and excitement rippled through the horror-film fandom. A legion of bloggers and message-board posters set to work translating the letters from languages like Babylonian and Ugaritic into English, discovering that the missives led them to a mysterious and macabre website featuring an image of a seductive lady vampire. The site advertised a beverage called TruBlood—a synthetic blood developed by the Japanese that vampires could drink as an alternative to feeding on humans. As visitors explored the site, they discovered short webisodes for the then-upcoming HBO television series, which incorporates the TruBlood beverage into its storyline.

The letters and website were developed as part of a viral marketing campaign by HBO and Campfire Media, an independent agency founded by two of the creators of the successful 1999 film *The Blair Witch Project*. Viral marketing is the propagation of brand or product awareness through pre-existing social networks, using unconventional media, with the hope that the campaign spreads as a cultural phenomenon. In addition to the letters, Campfire established a fictional blog and MySpace pages written by characters from the show, launched a human–vampire dating service, advertised TruBlood on vending machines, and strategically leaked tidbits of information and multimedia about the show. Campfire employees closely monitored popular horror blogs and message boards in order to gauge and encourage public interest, as well as orchestrate the release of new materials.

The campaign was an incredible, if somewhat subversive success—not only did Campfire generate momentous interest in the show, but a number of individuals actually tried to locate a TruBlood distributor. "We didn't mean to dupe people," said Zach Enterlin, HBO's vice-president of advertising and promotions. "We just wanted a campaign that breaks through and resonates a little bit. It's a testament to how true to form the ads are. Some people aren't paying close attention." Viral marketing campaigns are ideal for shows like *True Blood*, whose fans fervently share and discuss ideas within Internet communities. In addition, as it's based on the popular Sookie Stackhouse series of books by Charlaine Harris, *True Blood* came with an avid built-in fan base of those already familiar with the story.

Viral marketing has been a successful part of many advertising campaigns, such as those of 2008 films *Cloverfield* and *The Dark Knight*. *Cloverfield* is a film in which gargantuan monsters rampage through New York City, and the action is captured on handheld video cameras. It was introduced to viewers through an untitled, unexplained teaser trailer that played before 2007's *Transformers* movie. As speculation mounted, *Cloverfield* marketers unveiled a number of enigmatic websites, as well as a tie-in campaign for the fictional Slusho! beverage and a Japanese drilling company, both of which play a part in *Cloverfield*'s mythology.

In May of 2007, 42 Entertainment began a viral campaign for *The Dark Knight*, a sequel to 2005's *Batman Begins*. The campaign focused on the film's antagonists: a website titled "I Believe in Harvey Dent" was created as an advertisement for district attorney candidate Harvey Dent (played by Aaron Eckhart), as was a site titled "I Believe in Harvey Dent Too," a defiled version of the former which slowly revealed the first image of the Joker (played by Heath Ledger) as visitors sent e-mails through the site. The Joker's catchphrase "Why so serious?" spread virally on the Internet and was used as the URL of a website that sent visitors on a Joker-themed scavenger hunt.

As *True Blood*'s premier drew near, HBO and Campfire turned to less obtuse, if still unorthodox, methods of advertisement. A prequel comic book about an elder vampire and the development of *True Blood* was handed out for free at 2008's San Diego Comic-Con, the largest pop cultural convention in the world. The first episode of *True Blood* was distributed on DVD for free to thousands of moviegoers at the 2008 Toronto International Film Festival and was made available for rental from Blockbuster Video several days before it aired on television.

True Blood premiered on HBO on September 7, 2008—six months after Campfire's subtle marketing campaign began. According to Nielsen Co., the first three-quarters of 2008 had seen HBO's viewership drop by nearly 23 percent compared with the previous year. However, thanks to interest in new shows such as *True Blood*, HBO saw a 2.4 percent increase in fourth-quarter viewership compared with 2007. Without question, the success of *True Blood* is due in part to the novel marketing developed by Campfire Media.[27]

Questions

1. What is the communication process for viral marketing? Is it different from conventional marketing? How so?

2. What was the initial promotional mix of the *True Blood* campaign, and how might it suggest an observance of IMC?

3. Did *Cloverfield* use a push or pull promotional strategy? What about *The Dark Knight*? Explain.

4. Why did *True Blood* shift its promotional mix as its premier neared? Was this a good or a bad strategy? Explain.

VIDEO CASE

ADVERTISING IN A DIGITAL AGE

Brandon Berger, the vice-president of Digital Innovation for MDC Partners, is on the cutting edge of knowledge for marketing with digital media. He is interviewed by Business News Network commentator Michael Hainsworth, who wants to get a feel for the use of digital advertising and promotion and its ability to engage consumers. Digital advertising refers to the use of the Internet and mobile communications media devices for brand promotion through the use of social networks like Facebook, Twitter, and Google as well as videos on media sites like Youtube. Hainsworth comments that as the digital landscape grows companies feel they need to have a presence there. However, this landscape is fragmented.

Hainsworth opens his conversation with Brandon Berger by asking: "Do companies need to care whether or not they are on Facebook?" Berger replies immediately that the real question is whether companies need to care where their customers are. Berger says, "Their customers are on Facebook, they are on Twitter, they are using all kinds of channels, so companies do need to care." Hainsworth asks Berger, "Do customers want corporations like GM and Pepsi hitting their Facebook pages? Am I taking an old-fashioned advertising model and trying to cram it into a 21st-century world? Are we just thinking about it the wrong way here?"

Berger replies, "I think you are. The reality is that we went from a time of interruption to a time of engagement." Berger comments that the media landscape is fragmented and that customers are now in control. People are demanding these days. They want what they want, and they want to get it when they want it. This means that interruptive advertising isn't as effective as engagement advertising. Michael Hainsworth wonders how you hire a bunch of people to engage in social networking and be sure that they just aren't checking out their own Facebook pages. He asks how a 30-second ad on television compares with a simple corner picture on a social networking page? Berger replies that digital communication "delivers data and that data delivers ROI [return on investment] which is what marketing is moving to." He comments that the 30-second ad has reach and you can get frequency with television advertising but the issue is proving that customers engaged with the advertising. Hainsworth brings up an old advertising industry joke, "that managers know that 50 percent of their advertising works, they just don't know which

50 percent it is." Hainsworth mentions that "in the digital domain you know whether somebody has clicked on your ad." Berger agrees, and comments that you know if someone has seen your ad and whether they have engaged with it, click is just another way to look at it.

Hainsworth asks Berger, "Aside from large multinational companies who have lots of cash to throw around, if you are a small or medium-sized business, how do you engage a customer as opposed to bombarding them with marketing material?" Berger replies, "When you are small and nimble, you can be more effective. You have to think more strategically about how you engage your customer. You can spend more time thinking about how they live and how they engage, what they engage with. You have to figure out how to put your brand into their environment so that you ultimately deliver value. It is more about getting in and understanding your customer versus understanding the media."

Hainsworth is not clear as to what Berger means by "understanding customers." He pointedly asks what he means and adds, "What do we need to understand?" Berger replies, "That they're people, they have needs, that they have behaviours, they do things differently. . . . As media becomes much more focused and much more digital we can understand and target individual audiences." Hainsworth responds by commenting that the era of advertising wouldn't matter for marketers who use demographics as the means to understand their customers. "What's the difference between understanding your demographic and actually communicating with them in a manner that doesn't make them feel like they're being pitched?" Berger replies, "It's understanding where they live" and it's understanding how your brand will fit into their environment. An example of this is moms. He says you can engage not just on iVillage or moms watching *The View*. You participate by fostering the community. Sponsor communities the advertisers care about, not just advertise to. Hainsworth interjects, "So your local soccer association brought to you by Pepsi." Berger replies, "Could be—how about your local soccer uniforms and the field and all that stuff brought to you by Pepsi." In the digital realm, getting involved in the communities that consumers engage with is "using the digital."

Hainsworth asks Berger, "How about Twitter—do you tweet?" Berger says, "I do tweet but I use it differently than most people." Berger discusses how he uses Twitter to find news. He scans hundreds of people who are relevant to him. He reads what they are reading and learns what they are thinking. Hainsworth comments that when Twitter first began, people would "tweet" what they were eating. However, people quickly grew tired of it and now it's become a kind of news bulletin distribution service. Berger says that Twitter has many uses. One is as a news distribution service but it also allows you to simply keep on top of what your community is talking about. It is a way to keep in touch.

Michael Hainsworth talks about his iPhone and how he really likes it. He asks Berger about the GPS facilities in phones like this and about location-based services such as asking his phone, "Where is the nearest Tim Hortons?" Hainsworth asks Berger how the ad industry can leverage the GPS services in mobile phones. Berger replies that location-based services have taken digital from the computer into the real world. The implication of this is that people who are out and about can get information that is relevant to the immediate world around them. Hainsworth asks how it works. Can he get maps from Google? Berger says there are software applications like Google maps, the 4-Square game, and Yelp that allow him to check in. Berger can broadcast his location on his own network if he wishes.

Hainsworth concludes the discussion with Berger by asking him about the future. "Who is the big shot in this business ten years from now? Apple bought a small company for location-based ads. Does Apple take over or Google?" Berger replies, "I think everybody is trying to figure that out. I think the big shot is really marketers that understand where the consumers are going. The device is just the means to get information. I don't think it is a specific in that sense."[28]

Questions

1. How is the effectiveness of digital advertising measured compared to the effectiveness of traditional advertising such as television or radio? Discuss.

2. Berger talks about understanding customers. Isn't this necessary regardless of which promotional approach you employ? Discuss what this means according to him.

3. Both Berger and Hainsworth use the terms *engagement advertising* and *interruptive advertising*. With reference to the chapter material, compare and contrast these two forms of promotion as presented in this case.

4. If you are typical, you are living the digital life (if not, research it on the Internet). Either way, Berger didn't really answer Hainsworth's last question as to who was going to be the "big shot" in the future. Answer for Berger and justify your answer: which company do you think will dominate this area in the future? Explain.

MARKETING & YOU RESULTS

Higher scores on this scale indicate that others perceive you to be responsive, warm, and a good listener. A high score also corresponds to a willingness to mentor others. If your score is low, it indicates that you don't actively encourage other people to share information about themselves with you. That doesn't mean you are a poor listener, however. Rather, you prefer not to take the initiative in the interaction.

14 Advertising
and Public Relations

MasterCard

CENTRE
FOR HOCKEY EXCELLENCE

SOURCE: MASTERCARD INTERNATIONAL INCORPORATED

LEARNING OUTCOMES

1 Discuss the effects of advertising on market share and consumers

2 Identify the major types of advertising

3 Discuss the creative decisions in developing an advertising campaign

4 Describe media evaluation and selection techniques

5 Discuss the role of public relations in the promotional mix

ⓥ MARKETING & YOU

What do you think of television advertising?
Using the scales below, enter your answers or record them on a separate page.

1	2	3	4	5
Strongly disagree	Disagree	Neutral	Agree	Strongly agree

___ TV advertising is a good way to learn what products and services are available.

___ TV advertising results in better products for the public.

___ In general, TV advertising presents a true picture of the product advertised.

___ You can trust brands advertised on TV more than brands not advertised on TV.

___ TV advertising helps raise our standard of living.

___ TV advertisements help me find products that match my personality and interests.

___ TV advertising helps me to know which brands have the features I am looking for.

___ TV advertising gives me a good idea about products by showing the kinds of people who use them.

___ TV advertising helps me buy the best brand for the price.

___ I am willing to pay more for a product that is advertised on TV.

Total your score, and find out what it means at the end of the chapter.

SOURCE: REPRINTED WITH PERMISSION FROM *MARKETING SCALES HANDBOOK* VOL. III, PUBLISHED BY THE AMERICAN MARKETING ASSOCIATION, G. BRUNER, K. JAMES, H. HENSEL, EDS. SCALE #167.

Sponsorships can be a powerful promotional tool as part of a firm's marketing promotional campaign. MasterCard® Canada employs sponsorships as part of an extremely effective integrated marketing communication campaign. For example, MasterCard® has been using the "MasterCard: Priceless" positioning approach on a global basis for well over a decade. Sustaining a positioning theme over this long a time without wearing it out is a significant achievement for any promotional campaign. The power of this positioning resides in its ability to be adapted well to all the promotional elements and to fit well into local markets. The "Priceless" positioning theme crosses all media and all promotional vehicles MasterCard Canada uses. Whenever you view TV ads, listen to radio spots, encounter sponsorships, or even visit MasterCard's website, you are exposed to the following slogan: "There are some things money can't buy. For everything else, there's MasterCard."

MasterCard has undertaken a number of Canadian sponsorships to support its "Priceless" positioning campaign. MasterCard describes its sponsorship approach in Canada this way: "MasterCard Canada is proud to lend its support to a broad range of programs that reflect what matters to Canadians, from grassroots to professional sponsorships." Many things, of course, matter deeply to Canadians but one thing that touches our passionate roots very

strongly is the love for the game of ice hockey. MasterCard understands this and has developed a number of key sponsorships related to this passion.

At the highest level, MasterCard sponsors a number of Canada's professional hockey teams, including the Montreal Canadiens, the Toronto Maple Leafs, and the Vancouver Canucks. At the grassroots level, MasterCard has its Little Fans in Big Seats™ program, which, MasterCard says, "gives kids a chance to see their favourite hockey teams play live from some of the best seats in the house. We've partnered with Big Brothers Big Sisters of Canada as well as other children's organizations to send kids and their mentors to watch their heroes play live—a priceless experience for any child. Starting with the 2009–2010 hockey season, MasterCard is dedicating 100 percent of its hockey sponsorship tickets to Little Fans in Big Seats." This sponsorship provides premium tickets to home games in Canada for all the sponsored professional teams.

At the amateur level, MasterCard has been the title sponsor since 1999 for what it describes as "North America's toughest championship," the annual MasterCard® Memorial Cup, which is emblematic of supremacy among all three regional Junior A leagues that make up the Canadian Hockey League. This annual tournament is rotated among the Ontario Hockey League, the Quebec Major Junior Hockey League, and the

Western Hockey League. Each selects a host team when it is their league's turn to have the tournament. In this way, the Memorial Cup tournament moves across Canada (and sometimes to the United States if one of the American members of the CHL is hosting) and becomes what could be called a nationalized local event.

The love of hockey by Canadians is further recognized in the MasterCard® Centre for Hockey Excellence™, which opened in Toronto in September 2009. It is a community facility with four ice pads and MasterCard says it "provides the opportunity to fulfill hockey dreams, with hundreds of teams from the Greater Toronto Area and beyond making use of this state-of-the-art facility." Aside from being a facility for the wider community, the centre also joins the grassroots level of hockey with its highest level because the MasterCard Centre for Hockey Excellence is also a "permanent training facility for the Toronto Maple Leafs® and Toronto Marlies®, regional office to Canada's national hockey teams, and home to the Lakeshore Lions Hockey Club."[1]

How do sponsorships as part of public relations and publicity benefit marketers' promotional plans? How do marketers like MasterCard Canada decide which sponsorships to undertake and how to fit them into their advertising campaigns? Answers to these questions and many more will be found as you read this chapter.

SOURCES: WWW.MASTERCARD.CA, "SPONSORSHIPS," ACCESSED JUNE 13, 2010; AND CHRIS DANIELS, "PRICELESS PROMOTIONS," MARKETING MAGAZINE, DECEMBER 12, 2005.

THE EFFECTS OF ADVERTISING

Discuss the effects of advertising on market share and consumers

advertising
Impersonal, one-way mass communication about a product or organization that is paid for by a marketer.

Advertising is defined as any form of impersonal, paid communication in which the sponsor or company is identified. It is a popular form of promotion, especially for consumer packaged goods and services. Advertising spending has been increasing annually; at present, Canadian expenditures are roughly $14 billion per year. This spending is allocated to the Canadian media in the following proportions: 23.3 percent to TV, 15.3 percent to daily newspapers, 13.1 percent to the Internet, 11.1 percent to direct mail, 11.1 percent to radio, 9.8 percent to "other," 8.6 percent to phone directories, 4.4 percent to consumer magazines, and 3.1 percent to outdoor and transit. The Internet is growing the most quickly of all media, with its most recent annual growth rate in the 30 percent range.[2]

Total advertising expenditures seem large, yet the industry itself is very small. There are approximately only 68,000 Canadians employed in the advertising industry.[3] The Canadian industry is composed of both Canadian firms and U.S. multinationals.

In 2010, MDC Partners (**www.mdc-partners.com**) of Toronto was Canada's largest ad agency, with 5,651 employees and total Canadian revenues of $546 million. The next largest employer was Cossette Communications, with 1,650 employees. Canada's top 10 marketing communications companies by employment and their reported Canadian billings are listed in Exhibit 14.1.

Spending on advertising varies by industry. The game and toy industry has one of the highest ratios of advertising dollars to sales. For every dollar of merchandise sold in the toy industry, about 12¢ to 15¢ is spent advertising toys. Book publishers spend roughly 27¢ on advertising for every dollar of book revenue. Other consumer goods manufacturers that spend heavily on advertising in relation to total sales are sugar and candy manufacturers, leather manufacturers, watchmakers, perfume and cosmetics manufacturers, detergent makers, and wine and liquor companies.[4]

EXHIBIT 14.1

Top 10 Advertising Agencies in Canada by Employment

Rank	Agency	Est. Canadian revenues (in $millions)	Number of employees
1	MDC Partners	500–1000	6,561
2	Cossette Communications	500–1000	1,650
3	McLaren-McCann	NA	600
4	Palmer Jarvis DDB	200–400	360
5	FCB Canada	100–200	300
6	BBDO	20–50	210
7	Publicis	100–200	153
8	Marketel	50–100	140
9	Bensimon-Byrne	50–100	100
10	Saatchi & Saatchi	50–100	100

SOURCE: "Profile Canada," Advertising Agencies, http://www.profilecanada.com/, accessed June 18, 2010.

ADVERTISING AND MARKET SHARE

Canada's most successful brands today, such as Tim Hortons and President's Choice, were built over the years through heavy advertising and marketing investments. Most companies spend their advertising dollars to maintain brand awareness and market share.

New brands with a small market share tend to spend proportionately more for advertising and sales promotion than those with a large market share. Typically, there are two reasons. First, beyond a certain level of spending for advertising and sales promotion, diminishing returns set in; that is, market share begins to decrease no matter how much is spent on advertising and sales promotion. This phenomenon is referred to as the **advertising response function**. Understanding the advertising response function helps marketers use budgets wisely. A market leader like Johnson & Johnson's Neutrogena typically spends proportionately less on advertising than a newcomer like Jergens's Natural Glow Revitalizing Daily Moisturizer. Jergens spends more on its brand to gain attention and increase market share. Neutrogena, on the other hand, spends only as much as necessary to maintain market share; anything more would produce diminishing benefits. Neutrogena has already captured the attention of most of its target market. It only needs to remind customers of its product.

The second reason new brands tend to require higher spending for advertising and sales promotion is that a certain minimum level of exposure is needed to measurably affect purchase habits. If Jergens advertised Natural Glow Revitalizing Daily Moisturizer in only one or two publications and bought only one or two TV spots, it

advertising response function
A phenomenon in which spending for advertising and sales promotion increases sales or market share up to a certain level but then produces diminishing returns.

certainly would not achieve the exposure required to penetrate consumers' perceptual defences, gain attention, and ultimately affect purchase intentions. Instead, Natural Glow was advertised in many different media for a sustained time.

THE EFFECTS OF ADVERTISING ON CONSUMERS

Advertising affects consumers' daily lives, informing them about products and services and influencing their attitudes, beliefs, and ultimately their purchases. The average Canadian is exposed to hundreds of ads a day from all types of advertising media. In the TV medium alone, the average Canadian watches almost 27 hours of TV a week, and typically 25 percent of that time involves commercials. In addition, that person is probably exposed to countless print ads and promotional messages in other venues.[5] Advertising affects the TV programs people watch, the content of the newspapers they read, the politicians they elect, the medicines they take, and the toys their children play with. Consequently, the influence of advertising on Canada's economy and

Customer Experience

 PEPSI'S NEW LOOK

PEPSI 1898:
PEPSI 1905:
PEPSI 1906:
PEPSI 1940:
PEPSI 1945:
PEPSI 1951:
PEPSI 1962:
PEPSI 1973:
PEPSI 1987:
PEPSI 1991:
PEPSI 1998:
PEPSI 2003:
PEPSI 2007:
PEPSI 2008:

SOURCE: © PEPSI-COLA NORTH AMERICA BEVERAGES

How much does a brand logo makeover cost these days? More than $1 million and five months if you are Pepsi-Cola. Pepsi recently revealed its new logo—only the 11th change since 1898, five changes coming in the last 21 years. According to Pepsi's top executives, part of the strategy was to move the brand from the traditional mass marketing and mass distribution era into the current culture of personalization. "By making the logo more dynamic and more alive . . . it is absolutely a huge step in the right direction," said Pepsi's vice-president of portfolio brands, Frank Cooper. While the $1 million spent on design could be considered hefty, the real costs come in the other changes—on the trucks, vending machines, stadium signage, point of sale materials, and more. This could easily reach into the hundreds of millions of dollars.

So just what does the new logo signify? According to Pepsi, the new logo has a white band in the middle of the Pepsi circle that represents a series of smiles . . . a smile for Pepsi, a grin for Diet Pepsi, and a laugh for Pepsi Max. Branding experts are mixed: some think the new look will make the logo less durable and classic while others feel that it is more adventurous and youthful. Indeed, Pepsi has succeeded in the past by targeting the "new generation."

There are also mixed consumer reviews. Some think the new logo looks like the old Diet Pepsi logo with the identical sans-serif typeface and the red and blue Pepsi wave in a diagonal slope. Others feel the new logo looks similar to the 2008 U.S. presidential campaign of Barack Obama. Regardless, there is a minimalist feel that has captured the attention of the iPod generation—that idea of simple elegance.

Interestingly, Pepsi's new advertising campaign also comes with a dose of optimism that "every generation refreshes the world." However, arch rival Coca-Cola is also dosing out the optimism with its new advertising tagline "Open happiness."[6] Although both companies have embraced this message at various times, never has this happened simultaneously. So the question is whether this helps or hurts the differentiation of each brand.

SOURCE: NATALIE ZMUDA, "WHAT WENT INTO THE UPDATED PEPSI LOGO" ADVERTISING AGE, OCTOBER 27, 2008, WWW.ADAGE.COM, ACCESSED FEBRUARY 2009; NATALIE ZMUDA, "PEPSI, COKE TRY TO OUTDO EACH OTHER WITH RAYS OF SUNSHINE," ADVERTISING AGE, JANUARY 19, 2009, WWW.ADAGE.COM, ACCESSED FEBRUARY 2009; JIM EDWARDS, "PEPSI'S NEW $1 MILLION LOGO LOOKS LIKE OLD DIET PEPSI LOGO," BNET INDUSTRIES, OCTOBER 27, 2008, HTTP://INDUSTRY.BNET.COM/ADVERTISING/1000270.

society has been subject to extensive debate among economists, marketers, sociologists, psychologists, politicians, consumerists, and many others.

Though advertising cannot change consumers' deeply rooted values and attitudes, it may succeed in transforming a person's negative attitude toward a product into a positive one. For instance, serious or dramatic advertisements are more effective at changing consumers' negative attitudes. Humorous ads, in contrast, are more effective at shaping attitudes when consumers already have a positive image of the advertised brand.[7] However, as much as humour in advertising tends to improve brand recognition, it does not necessarily improve product recall, message credibility, or buying intentions. Consumers who find the ad funny may have good feelings about the product, but their purchasing decisions will not be affected unless they can actually recall the brand. The best results with humorous ads are achieved by making the message relevant to the product. For example, Buckley's Cough syrup has consistently run ads showing people taking their cough syrup and then reacting with a sourpuss expression to its strong taste. The Buckley's website (**www.buckleys.com**) even tells the story of the product under the headline, "A History of Bad Taste." The campaign tagline is "It tastes awful and it works." Canadians have been exposed to this promotion for years as Buckley's makes fun of themselves. The use of humour is closely tied to the image and the benefits of the product.[8]

Advertising also reinforces positive attitudes toward brands. When consumers have a neutral or favourable frame of reference toward a product or brand, ads often positively influence them. When consumers are already strongly loyal toward a brand, they may buy more of it when advertising and promotion for that brand increase.[9] This is why market leaders like Loblaw, GM, and Procter & Gamble spend tens of millions of dollars in Canada every year: they are reminding their loyal customers about the benefits of their stores, cars, and household products.

Furthermore, advertising can affect consumers' rankings of a brand's attributes, such as colour, taste, smell, and texture. In years past, car ads emphasized brand attributes such as roominess, speed, low maintenance, and safety. Today, car marketers have been focusing on fuel economy. For example, in its most recent advertising campaigns General Motors has been featuring the fuel economy of all the car models in its Chevrolet product line in comparison to the directly competing models in the product lines of major competitors like Honda, Toyota, and Ford.[10]

REVIEW LEARNING OUTCOME 1

1 | **Discuss the effects of advertising on market share and consumers**

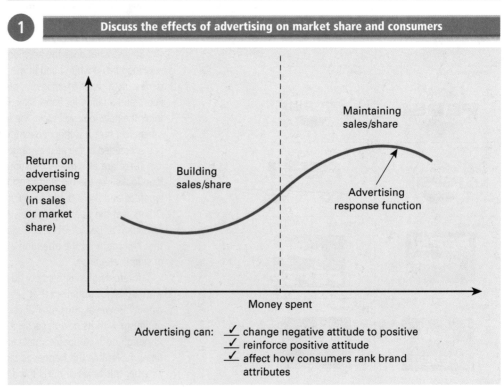

Return on advertising expense (in sales or market share)

Building sales/share

Maintaining sales/share

Advertising response function

Money spent

Advertising can: ✓ change negative attitude to positive
✓ reinforce positive attitude
✓ affect how consumers rank brand attributes

Identify the major types of advertising

institutional advertising
A form of advertising designed to enhance a company's image rather than to promote a particular product.

product advertising
A form of advertising that touts the benefits of a specific good or service.

The firm's promotional objectives determine the type of advertising it uses. If the goal of the promotion plan is to build up the image of the company or the industry, **institutional advertising** may be used. In contrast, if the advertiser wants to enhance the sales of a specific good or service, **product advertising** is used.

INSTITUTIONAL ADVERTISING

Historically, advertising in Canada has been product-oriented. Today, however, companies market many products and need a different type of advertising. Institutional advertising, or corporate advertising, promotes the corporation as a whole and is designed to establish, change, or maintain the corporation's identity. It usually does not ask the audience to do anything but maintain a favourable attitude toward the advertiser and its goods and services. For example, Shell Canada wants to improve how it is perceived by influential Canadians such as business and industry leaders, academics, media people, and elected officials. The firm wants people to be aware of its commitment to sustainable development. It wants people to perceive Shell Canada as a responsible company, a company with strong ethics, and a company that listens to people. Shell's website provides the following statement of values: "Shell is a global group of energy and petrochemical companies. Our aim is to meet the energy needs of society, in ways that are economically, socially and environmentally viable, now and in the future." To support these values, Shell has developed the "New Energy Future series" campaign, which runs in newspapers and on television. The campaign will feature four employees from Shell Canada and will present statements that fit the into predetermined themes.[11]

A form of institutional advertising called **advocacy advertising** is typically used to safeguard against negative consumer attitudes and to enhance the company's credibility among consumers who already favour its position. Often corporations use advocacy advertising to express their views on controversial issues. Other times, firms' advocacy campaigns are a direct response to criticism in the media. Still other advocacy campaigns try to ward off increased regulation, damaging legislation, or an unfavourable outcome in a lawsuit. MADD Canada (Mothers Against Drunk Driving) and #TAXI have combined for a promotional campaign over the years. The focus of these joint campaigns has been to discourage drinking and driving. The interest of #TAXI is very clear—it earns revenue from the use of its service. Using this service, you can call a cab from anywhere in Canada and the service acts as a dispatcher to send you the nearest cab for a charge on your phone service. The service of #TAXI acts directly to prevent drinking and driving and the firm also supports MADD Canada's cause as a sponsor.[12]

NAME OF DECEASED: ASHLEY JEFFREY
AGE: 28
DATE OF DEATH: MARCH 8, 2007
CAUSE OF DEATH: SISTER KILLED BY IMPAIRED DRIVER

A part of you dies when someone you love is killed.
If you are hurting, we can help.

MADD
Mothers Against Drunk Driving
Les mères contre l'alcool au volant

SOURCE: COURTESY OF MADD CANADA

MADD Canada (Mothers Against Drunk Driving) continuously uses ads like the one above as part of an advocacy advertising to discourage drinking and driving.

PRODUCT ADVERTISING

Unlike institutional advertising, product advertising promotes the benefits of a specific good or service. The product's stage in its life cycle often determines which type of product advertising is used: pioneering advertising, competitive advertising, or comparative advertising.

Pioneering Advertising

advocacy advertising
A form of advertising in which an organization expresses its views on controversial issues or responds to media attacks.

pioneering advertising
A form of advertising designed to stimulate primary demand for a new product or product category.

Pioneering advertising is intended to stimulate primary demand for a new product or product category. Heavily used during the introductory stage of the product life cycle, pioneering advertising offers consumers in-depth information about the benefits of the product class. Pioneering advertising also seeks to generate interest. Microsoft used pioneering advertising to introduce its Windows and Office software products. In a move to reposition the products as more "user friendly," the software giant launched Windows 7.0 with the slogan "Your PC, Simplified." Microsoft launched its campaign as part of its $500-million North American promotional budget. The print, outdoor, TV, and on-line campaign carries the tagline "Windows 7.0 was my idea." Microsoft's pioneering campaign hopes to convince PC users to buy this new version because it is "simpler and easier to use . . . Windows 7 has better ways to find and manage files—like Jump Lists and improved taskbar previews—to help you speed through everyday tasks. It's designed for faster and more reliable performance, so your PC just works the way you want it to. With 64-bit support, you can take full advantage of the latest powerful PCs. And great features like HomeGroup, Windows Media Center, and Windows Touch make new things possible."[13]

Competitive Advertising

Firms use competitive or brand advertising when a product enters the growth phase of the product life cycle and other companies begin to enter the marketplace. Instead of building demand for the product category, the goal of **competitive advertising** is to influence demand for a specific brand. Often during this phase, promotion becomes less informative and appeals more to emotions. Ads may begin to stress subtle differences among brands, with heavy emphasis on building recall of a brand name and creating a favourable attitude toward the brand. Automobile advertising has long used highly competitive messages, drawing distinctions based on such factors as quality, safety, performance, and image.

Comparative Advertising

Comparative advertising directly or indirectly compares two or more competing brands on one or more specific attributes. Some advertisers even use comparative advertising against their own brands. Products experiencing sluggish growth or those entering the marketplace against strong competition are more likely to employ comparative claims in their ads. For instance, the Mac versus PC ads for Apple have been masterful. The ads create an image of a stodgy PC battling with a hip, cool Mac. The campaign's success has escalated the battle between the two computer icons with each creating new ads aimed at the other. Chevrolet Canada has been undertaking direct comparisons of its Chevrolet brands versus their main competitors with their "May the Best Car Win" campaign. Anyone who visited **www.gm.ca** and clicked on any Chevrolet vehicle could then choose a "compare" button on the website that would allow them to compare the Chevrolet's features with its main competitors. For example, during the campaign if you compared the Chevrolet Equinox SUV, which is assembled in Ingersoll, Ontario, to the Toyota RAV4, which is assembled just up the road in

Cambridge, Ontario, you would discover that the fuel economy of the Chevy is better as is the horsepower and the warranty. However, the RAV4 is $1,500 less expensive than the Equinox so the comparison was not fully flattering to Chevrolet.[14]

Comparative advertising can lead to litigation if a company feels that its product has been misrepresented or displayed inappropriately. The Federal Competition Act prohibits advertisers from falsely describing competitors' products and allows competitors to sue if ads show their products or mention their brand names in an incorrect or false manner. Bell Aliant has sued Rogers Communications for misleading advertising stating Rogers' advertising is "false and misleading with respect to their claims to having the 'fastest and most reliable' high-speed Internet product." Bell Aliant put out a press release claiming it has "one of the most reliable networks in North America," avoiding absolutist claims to being the "best" or "most reliable." Bell Aliant is not seeking money damages—it simply wants Rogers Communications to cease and desist from using its comparative advertising strategy.[15]

The Mac vs. PC ads for Apple use comparitive advertising by portraying the PC (and everything and everyone associated with it) as "stodgy," and constantly losing to a hip, cool Mac.

SOURCE: © A. MILLER/WENN/NEWSCOM

Companies must be careful with comparative advertising approaches in other countries as well. Germany, Italy, Belgium, and France, for example, do not permit advertisers to claim that their products are the best or better than competitors' products; such claims are both common and acceptable in Canada. In the Netherlands, car manufacturers cannot make claims in their ads about the fuel consumption or environmental aspects of the car. In Italy, Seagram ran an ad claiming that its Absolut vodka was the only vodka made from grain (and thus superior to potato-based vodkas). Rival distributor Aosta Company filed a complaint against Absolut's Italian distributor, Seagram Italia, noting that two of its products were made from grain. Comparative advertising has been legal in Italy since 1999; however, ads cannot make unsubstantiated claims. So authorities ordered the campaign stopped, and Seagram Italia had to pull all ads.[16]

In other countries, hard-hitting comparative advertising will not be effective because it offends cultural values. Muslim cultures generally encourage people not to compete with one another, and the sharing of wealth is common. So comparative advertising is not consistent with social values in Muslim countries.[17] Japanese advertisers have also been reluctant to use comparative advertising because it is considered confrontational and doesn't promote the respectful treatment of consumers or portray other companies in a respectful light. Nevertheless, although the Japanese have traditionally favoured soft-sell advertising approaches, consumers are witnessing a trend toward comparative ads.

REVIEW LEARNING OUTCOME 2

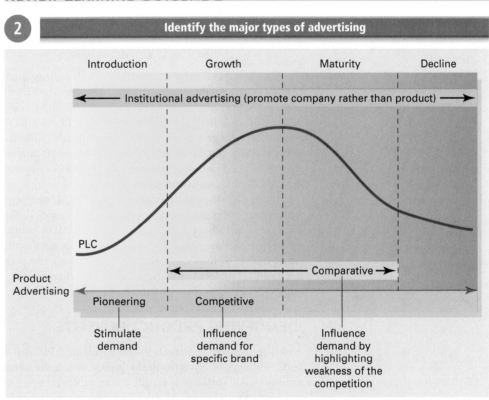

2 Identify the major types of advertising

3 CREATIVE DECISIONS IN ADVERTISING

Discuss the creative decisions in developing an advertising campaign

advertising campaign
A series of related advertisements focusing on a common theme, slogan, and set of advertising appeals.

Advertisements that are seen on TV, in magazines, and on the Internet are typically the result of an **advertising campaign**—a series of related ads focusing on a common theme, slogan, and set of advertising appeals. It is a specific advertising effort for a particular product that extends for a defined period of time. In the years since their founding through to today, Tim Hortons restaurants have focused on essentially one main theme and slogan in their product advertising, "Always Fresh." In addition, the Tim Hortons name has also become a Canadian icon synonymous with Canada, and the company has developed institutional advertising campaigns using this theme. For example, one recent television ad features an African immigrant husband who has lived by himself in Canada for awhile. He is waiting at the airport for his family who are arriving in Canada for the first time. It is during the winter and he has bought them some coats and other winter clothing. The husband orders two Tim Hortons coffees and as his wife and kids arrive, he hugs and kisses them and then hands his wife a coffee as he says, "Welcome to Canada." The scene cuts to cold blowing snow outside the airport and the slogan "A coffee all our own" appears. Tim Hortons has run a number of campaigns that have tied the brand to its Canadian roots. For example, there was a long-running set of ads showing Canadians living overseas and feeling homesick for Canada. They all felt a little less homesick when they were able to have some Tim Hortons coffee. And more recently, Tim Hortons has featured NHL superstar Sidney Crosby in a number of ads focusing on Crosby's hockey beginnings when he started out playing hockey as a child in a Tim Hortons–sponsored "Timbits" hockey league right through to his ascendancy into an NHL superstar. In the most recent campaign, Crosby talks about what hockey means to Canadians, and as we see pictures of Canadian families taking their children to hockey, Tim Hortons coffee and doughnuts are ever present in the rinks and the cars as family members watch their kids.[18]

Before any creative work can begin on an advertising campaign, it is important to determine what goals or objectives the advertising should achieve. An **advertising objective** identifies the specific communication task that a campaign should accomplish for a specified target audience during a specified period. The objectives of a specific advertising campaign often depend on the overall corporate objectives, the firm's marketing objectives, the target market selected, and the positioning strategy designed for the product. Tim Hortons' main campaign objective is to continue to remind Canadians to enjoy Tim Hortons products and to entrench the restaurant as the place to go for coffee.[19]

The DAGMAR approach (defining advertising goals for measured advertising results) is one method for setting advertising objectives. According to this method, all advertising objectives should precisely define the target audience, the desired percentage change in some specified measure of effectiveness, and the time frame in which that change is to occur. For example, the objectives for an ad campaign for Telus Mobility phones might be to encourage 20 percent of current competitor Roger's Wireless subscribers living in Ontario to inquire about switching to a new Telus Mobility plan within six months.

Once objectives are defined, creative work can begin on the campaign. Advertising campaigns often follow the AIDA model, which was discussed in Chapter 13. Depending on where consumers are in the AIDA process, the creative development of an advertising campaign might focus on creating attention, arousing interest, stimulating desire, or leading to the action of buying the product. Specifically, creative decisions relate to identifying product benefits, developing and evaluating advertising appeals, executing the message, and evaluating the effectiveness of the campaign.

IDENTIFYING PRODUCT BENEFITS

A well-known rule of thumb in the advertising industry is "Sell the sizzle, not the steak"—that is, in advertising the goal is to sell the benefits of the product, not its attributes. An attribute is simply a feature of the product such as its easy-open package or special formulation. A benefit is what consumers will receive or achieve by using the product. A benefit should answer this question from consumers: "What's in it for me?" Benefits might be such things as convenience, pleasure, savings, or relief. A quick test to determine whether you are offering attributes or benefits in your advertising is to ask: "So?" Consider this example:

- *Attributes:* "The iPhone 4 is coming soon to Virgin Mobile and all Virgin Mobile phones are available in thousands of stores across Canada including Best Buy, Future Shop, The Source, 7-Eleven, Walmart, London Drugs, etc." "So . . . ?"
- *Benefits:* "We've got the happiest customers in Canada, plans with extra for no extra, award-winning member care, no funny business, more than a mobile phone company, and what they want, where they want it."[20]

Marketing research and intuition are typically used to unearth the perceived benefits of a product and to rank consumers' preferences for these benefits. Virgin's rivals, Roger's Wireless, Bell Mobility, and Telus, all have their own wireless communications offerings, and each positions itself as a leader in providing subscribers with important benefits, such as family rate plans, free calling among family members, international roaming capabilities, downloadable ring tones, phone upgrades, and so on. Virgin is a recent entrant to the Canadian market; with low prices and the "rebel" Virgin image, it is countering efforts by established Canadian competitors to appeal to the underdeveloped youth market.[21]

DEVELOPING AND EVALUATING ADVERTISING APPEALS

advertising appeal
A reason for a person to buy a product.

An **advertising appeal** identifies a reason for a person to buy a product. Developing advertising appeals, a challenging task, is typically the responsibility of the creative people in the ad agency. Advertising appeals typically play off consumers' emotions, such as fear or love, or they address some need or want the consumer has, such as a need for convenience or the desire to save money. For integrated marketing campaigns, it is important to be sure that when the advertising appeal is developed it supports the product positioning strategy that has been chosen.

Advertising campaigns can focus on one or more advertising appeals. Often the appeals are quite general, thus allowing the firm to develop a number of subthemes or minicampaigns using both advertising and sales promotion. Several possible advertising appeals are listed in Exhibit 14.2.

Choosing the best appeal from those developed normally requires market research. Criteria for evaluation include desirability, exclusiveness, and believability. The appeal first must make a positive impression on and be desirable to the target market. It must also be exclusive or unique; consumers must be able to distinguish the advertiser's message from competitors' messages. Most important, the appeal should be believable. An appeal that makes extravagant claims not only wastes promotional dollars but also creates ill will for the advertiser.

unique selling proposition
A desirable, exclusive, and believable advertising appeal selected as the theme for a campaign.

The advertising appeal selected for the campaign becomes what advertisers call its **unique selling proposition**. This proposition usually becomes the campaign's slogan. Telus's unique selling proposition is "future friendly," which is the firm's "commitment to innovation, fresh thinking, and technological progress."[22]

Effective slogans often become so ingrained that consumers can immediately conjure up images of the product just by hearing the slogan. Most consumers can easily name the companies and products behind these memorable slogans and even hum the jingle that goes along with them: "Have it your way" (Burger King), "Tastes great, less filling" (Miller Lite), "Ring around the collar" (Wisk), and "Tum te Tum Tum" (Tums Antacid). Advertisers often revive old slogans or jingles in the hope that the nostalgia will create good feelings with consumers. Maytag refreshed its campaign featuring its appliance pitchman by changing the actor who plays him and giving him an assistant—the third change since the ads originated in 1967. And Hershey's Kit Kat bar's 10-year-old jingle "Gimme a Break" is so etched in consumers' minds that recently the agency hired a film crew to walk around and ask people on the street to sing the jingle for

EXHIBIT 14.2

Common Advertising Appeals

Profit	Lets consumers know whether the product will save them money, make them money, or keep them from losing money
Health	Appeals to those who are body-conscious or who want to be healthy
Love or Romance	Is used often in selling cosmetics and perfumes
Fear	Can centre on social embarrassment, growing old, or losing one's health; because of its power, requires advertiser to exercise care in execution
Admiration	Is the reason that celebrity spokespeople are used so often in advertising
Convenience	Is often used for fast-food restaurants and microwave foods
Fun and Pleasure	Are the key to advertising vacations, beer, amusement parks, and more
Vanity and Egotism	Are used most often for expensive or conspicuous items such as cars and clothing
Environmental Consciousness	Centres on protecting the environment and being considerate of others in the community

A healthy diet low in saturated and trans fats may reduce the risk of heart disease. Becel is low in saturated fat and has no trans fat. It is also non-hydrogenated and is a source of omega-3 polyunsaturates. It is the margarine doctors and dietitians recommend most.

www.becel.ca

Becel
LOVE
YOUR
HEART

SOURCE: COURTESY OF UNILEVER CANADA INC.

Many appeals could be used successfully to advertise margarine. In this print ad, Becel has chosen the health appeal "Love your heart."

use on the Internet, in future ad campaigns, and in its Kit Kat "Gimme a Break" Café.[23]

EXECUTING THE MESSAGE

Message execution is the way an ad portrays its information. In general, the AIDA plan (see Chapter 13) is a good blueprint for executing an advertising message. Any ad should immediately draw the reader's, viewer's, or listener's attention. The advertiser must then use the message to hold consumers' interest, create desire for the good or service, and ultimately motivate action—a purchase.

The style in which the message is executed is one of the most creative elements of an ad. Exhibit 14.3 lists some examples of executional styles used by advertisers. Executional styles often dictate which media are to be employed to convey the message. Scientific executional styles lend themselves well to print advertising, where more information can be conveyed. Demonstration and musical styles are more likely found in broadcast advertising.

Testimonials by athletes are one of the more popular executional styles. Sidney Crosby, Peyton Manning, and Shaquille O'Neal are all successful athlete spokespersons. Read O'Neal's own words about the power of marketing and advertising in Exhibit 14.4.

Injecting humour into an ad is a popular and effective executional style. Selection of a humorous approach is based on the communications goal. Humorous executional styles are more often used in radio and TV advertising than in print and magazine advertising, where humour is less easily communicated. Regardless of the advertising medium, however, humour can be tricky to use because not all people find the

EXHIBIT 14.3

10 Common Executional Styles for Advertising

Slice of life	Depicts people in normal settings, such as at the dinner table or in their cars. McDonald's often uses slice-of-life styles showing youngsters munching french fries and Happy Meals on family outings.
Lifestyle	Shows how well the product will fit in with the consumer's lifestyle. As their Mitsubishi Lancers move through the streets of Toronto, Gen-X drivers listen to techno music and marvel at how the rhythms of the world mimic the vibes inside their vehicles.
Spokesperson/ testimonial	Can feature a celebrity, a company official, or a typical consumer making a testimonial or endorsing a product. During the 2010 winter Olympics, Canadian-born Hollywood actors Michael J. Fox, Kim Catrall, and Eric McCormick all gave endorsements for B.C. Tourism in TV ads saying, "You gotta be here." Film actress Drew Barrymore endorses CoverGirl cosmetics.
Fantasy	Creates a fantasy for the viewer built around use of the product. Car makers often use this style to let viewers fantasize about how they would feel speeding around tight corners or down long country roads in their cars.
Humorous	Snickers's "Not Going Anywhere for a While" campaign featured hundreds of souls waiting, sometimes impatiently, to get into heaven.
Real/animated product symbols	Creates a character to represent the product, such as the Energizer bunny, or General Mills's Betty Crocker, who has been redesigned for the new millennium.
Mood or image	Builds a mood or image around the product, such as peace, love, or beauty. De Beers ads depicting shadowy silhouettes wearing diamond engagement rings and diamond necklaces portray passion and intimacy while extolling that a "diamond is forever."
Demonstration	Shows consumers the expected benefit. Many consumer products use this technique. Laundry detergent spots are famous for demonstrating how their product will clean clothes whiter and brighter.
Musical	Conveys the ad's message through song. Ford Lincoln launched its new MKZ vehicles with ads on the theme of "Light Speed" using the song "Major Tom" by the group Shiny Toy Guns.
Scientific	Uses research or scientific evidence to give a brand superiority over competitors. Shell differentiates its new V-power nitrogen-enriched gasolines from competitors using scientific evidence in their ads.

EXHIBIT 14.4

Dreamful Attraction: Shaquille O'Neal's Thoughts on Marketing and Advertising

While on the outside looking in, I did not realize that marketing was so complicated. I never knew that a person, such as an athlete, could have such a powerful effect on people's thought processes and purchasing behaviour. The use of a well-known athlete in marketing a product or service can have a great impact on the sales of that product or service. Look at Michael Jordan. Almost overnight most every kid either was wearing or wanted to wear Air Jordan shoes.

Why does this happen? Is it the appeal of a great athlete or is it great marketing? The answer is "none of the above." It's both. In my years as a professional basketball player, I have seen firsthand the dramatic appeal that athletes have for the fans and public in general. Top-name athletes are like E. F. Hutton—when they talk, people listen. But why do they listen? I believe they listen to us, the athletes, because we have credibility. The effectiveness of celebrity endorsements depends largely on how credible and attractive the spokesperson is and how familiar people are with him or her. Companies sometimes use sports figures and other celebrities to promote products hoping they are appropriate opinion leaders.

Because of an athlete's fame and fortune, or attraction, the athlete can often have the right credibility to be a successful spokesperson. The best definition of credibility that I could find was by James Gordon in his book *Rhetoric of Western Thought*. He said that attraction "can come from a person's observable talents, achievements, occupational position or status, personality and appearance, and style." That may be why a famous athlete's personality and position can help him or her communicate more effectively than a not-so-famous athlete.

Credibility is a positive force in the persuasive promotion used predominantly by cola marketers like Pepsi because of what I like to call "dreamful attraction." For example, when I was young, I dreamed that I was like Dr. J., the famous basketball player for the Philadelphia 76ers. I would take his head off a poster and put my head on it. I wanted to be Dr. J. That is dreamful attraction. The youth of today are no different. Just the other day a kid stopped me and told me that he wanted to be like me. He had a dreamful attraction. This dreamful attraction can help sell products. In my case, Pepsi, Spalding, Kenner, and Reebok are hoping they are able to package properly and market whatever dreamful attraction I might have for their target audience—kids.

There are many ways to communicate to my target audience. I find that the most effective way for me is through television commercials. This avenue gives me a chance to express myself and show my real feelings about a message we are trying to communicate—either visually or vocally. I feel that I have what Clint Eastwood has—"Sudden Impaq." My impact is revealed through my sense of humour and my nonverbal communication.

Why does Shaq sell? Communication. Although the verbal communication in many of my commercials is slim, the impact is still there. This makes me believe even more in the quote that who you are can almost be as important as what you say. But if you can blend the two together—who you are and what you have to say—then imagine how much more successful the communication message can be in the marketing process. Andre Agassi's favourite quote from his Canon commercial is "Image is everything." If it is not everything, it is almost everything. If you have the right image, match it with the right product, and market it properly, then success should follow.

I have been involved in commercials and the marketing of products for only a short time, but I have learned a great deal. If there is one formula for success in selling products, it would be this: marketing plus credibility and image plus effective communications equals increase in sales—hopefully.

Now, you can call me Dr. Shaq, M.E. (Marketing Expert).

SOURCE: James Gordon, "Rhetoric of Western Thought" (Dubuque, Iowa: Kendall-Hunt Publishing Co., 1976) p 207.

same things funny and marketers have to be sure the humour won't be misconstrued. For example, local FM radio station Rock 100.7 in Windsor, Ontario, put up a series of billboards to promote the morning show of Craig and Matt, two popular male DJs who were known for their humour and off-beat styles. In three of the billboards, the headline was "See They're Nuts." The problem was the billboard showed the two out-of-shape 40-plus-year-old DJs totally naked holding coconuts strategically placed over their genital areas. According to a story in the *Windsor Star*, the local paper that reported on the billboards, many people, parents in particular, found the advertisements both "disgusting and tasteless." The response of the radio station's manager to questions from the *Windsor Star* reporter about the complaints was that similar campaigns had been run elsewhere and that people were being too sensitive. The station's seemingly carefree response brought out even more sensitivity in the community, who complained directly to Pattison Outdoor, the media company who put up the billboards. In response, Pattison took the initiative to remove all three of the offensive billboards irrespective of the radio station's view. The radio station reported that their listeners didn't seem offended by this advertising approach. Regardless, advertisers need to realize that any promotional execution that goes on display to the general public has to meet community standards. Although the radio station didn't seem to know this, clearly media company Pattison Outdoor did.[24]

Executional styles for foreign advertising are often quite different from those we are accustomed to in Canada. Sometimes they are sexually oriented or aesthetically imaginative. The *Financial Times* created the world's biggest newspaper by covering Hong Kong's tallest skyscraper in fabric that showed the front page. The skyscraper is also home to the newspaper's Asian headquarters. The outdoor advertising space is worth about $6 million.[25] European advertising avoids the direct-sell approaches

common in Canadian ads; instead, it is more indirect, more symbolic, and, above all, more visual. For example, Adidas commissioned a German ad company to come up with a "talk-of-the-world, spectacular" outdoor ad to welcome visitors to the FIFA World Cup soccer match. They designed a 65-metre, front-and-back billboard of soccer star Oliver Kahn diving to catch a soccer ball, which stretched across a four-lane highway near the airport in Munich, Germany. Four million cars drove under the installation and it became the global visual that accompanied almost all the foreign news coverage of the World Cup event.[26]

This "talk-of-the-world" outdoor ad welcoming visitors to the 2006 FIFA World Cup soccer match is an example of an aesthetically imaginative executional style.

POST-CAMPAIGN EVALUATION

Evaluating an advertising campaign can be the most demanding task facing advertisers. How do advertisers know whether the campaign led to an increase in sales or market share or elevated awareness of the product? Most ad campaigns aim to create an image for the good or service instead of asking for action, so their real effect is unknown. So many variables shape the effectiveness of an ad that in many cases advertisers must guess whether their money has been well spent. Despite this grey area, marketers spend a considerable amount of time studying advertising's effectiveness and its probable impact on sales, market share, or awareness.

Testing ad effectiveness can be done either before or after the campaign. Before a campaign is released, marketing managers use pretests to determine the best advertising appeal, layout, and media vehicle. After advertisers implement a campaign, they often conduct tests to measure its effectiveness. Several monitoring techniques can be used to determine whether the campaign has met its original goals. Even if a campaign has been highly successful, advertisers still undertake a typical post-campaign analysis. They assess how the campaign might have been more efficient and which factors contributed to its success. Every year, the Institute of Communications and Advertising (ICA), the Association of Quebec Advertising Agencies, and Le Publicité Club de Montreal combine to present the Cassie Awards to honour Canadian ad campaigns. The Cassies were created to recognize, reward, and improve the effectiveness of advertising. Cassie awards involve a thorough case history of advertising success, and the campaigns are published as exemplars for Canadian businesses to learn from. For a sample of award-winning efforts by Canadian advertisers as judged by the industry itself, visit **www.cassies.ca**.

REVIEW LEARNING OUTCOME 3

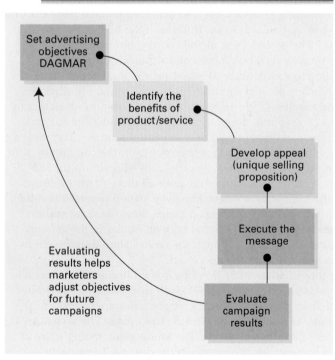

3 — Discuss the creative decisions in developing an advertising campaign

Set advertising objectives DAGMAR

Identify the benefits of product/service

Develop appeal (unique selling proposition)

Execute the message

Evaluate campaign results

Evaluating results helps marketers adjust objectives for future campaigns

4 MEDIA DECISIONS IN ADVERTISING

Describe media evaluation and selection techniques

medium
The channel used to convey a message to a target market.

media planning
The series of decisions advertisers make regarding the selection and use of media, allowing the marketer to optimally and cost-effectively communicate the message to the target audience.

A major decision for advertisers is the choice of **medium**—the channel used to convey a message to a target market. **Media planning**, therefore, is the series of decisions advertisers make regarding the selection and use of media, allowing the marketer to optimally and cost-effectively communicate the message to the target audience.[27] Specifically, advertisers must determine which media will best communicate the benefits of their product or service to the target audience and when and for how long the ad will run.

Promotional objectives and the appeal and executional style of the advertising strongly affect the selection of media. It is important to understand that creative and media decisions are made at the same time. Creative work cannot be completed without knowing which medium will be used to convey the message to the target market. For instance, creative planning will likely differ for an ad to be displayed on a website versus one placed in a print medium, such as a newspaper or magazine. In many cases, the advertising objectives dictate the medium and the creative approach to be used. Thus, if the objective is to demonstrate how fast a product operates, a TV commercial that shows this action may be the best choice.

As mentioned at the beginning of this chapter, Canadian advertisers spend nearly $14 billion on media advertising annually. About 47 percent, or $6.6 billion, is spent in daily and weekly newspapers, radio, and television, and $3.6 billion or roughly 54 percent of this amount is spent on nationally distributed vehicles. This means that local advertisers spend nearly $3.0 billion on local daily or weekly newspapers and local radio and TV stations.[28] Exhibit 14.5 breaks down the $14 billion spent in monitored advertising by media type. As you can see, about 23 percent of every dollar spent in monitored media goes toward purchasing time for TV ads.

 **EXHIBIT 14.5**

Domestic Advertising Spending by Media

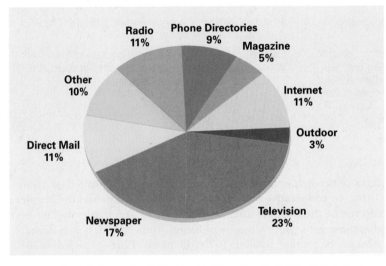

SOURCE: Canadian Media Directors Council, "Net Advertising Volume (Canadian $ Millions)," Media Digest 10/11, 13. Reprinted with permission.

MEDIA TYPES

Advertising media are channels that advertisers use in mass communication. The major advertising media are newspapers, magazines, radio, TV, outdoor media, and the Internet. Exhibit 14.6 summarizes the advantages and disadvantages of these major channels. In recent years, alternative media vehicles have emerged that offer advertisers innovative ways to reach their target audience and avoid advertising clutter. The most comprehensive source of information on the available Canadian media types, media vehicles, their markets, and media costs is available from Canadian Advertising Rates and Data (CARD), at **www.cardmedia.com**.

Newspapers

The advantages of newspaper advertising include geographic flexibility and timeliness. Because copywriters can usually prepare newspaper ads quickly and at a reasonable cost, local merchants can reach their target market almost daily. Because newspapers are generally a mass-market medium, however, they may not be the best vehicle for marketers trying to reach a very narrow market. For example, local newspapers are not the best media vehicles for reaching purchasers of specialty steel products or even tropical fish. These target consumers make up very small, specialized markets. Newspaper advertising also encounters a lot of distractions from competing ads and news stories; thus, one firm's ad may not be particularly visible.

EXHIBIT 14.6

Advantages and Disadvantages of Major Advertising Media

Medium	Advantages	Disadvantages
Printed Newspapers	Geographic selectivity and flexibility; short-term advertiser commitments; news value and immediacy; year-round readership; high individual market coverage; co-op and local tie-in; availability; short lead time	Little demographic selectivity; limited colour capabilities; low pass-along rate; may be expensive
Printed Magazines	Good reproduction, especially for colour; demographic selectivity; regional selectivity; local market selectivity; relatively long advertising life; high pass-along rate	Long-term advertiser commitments; slow audience buildup; limited demonstration capabilities; lack of urgency; long lead time
Broadcast Radio	Low cost; immediacy of message; can be scheduled on short notice; relatively no seasonal change in audience; highly portable; short-term advertiser commitments; entertainment carryover	No visual treatment; short advertising life of message; high frequency required to generate comprehension and retention; distractions from background sound; commercial clutter
Broadcast and Cable Television	Ability to reach a wide, diverse audience; low cost per thousand; creative opportunities for demonstration; immediacy of messages; entertainment carryover; demographic selectivity with cable stations	Short life of message; some consumer skepticism about claims; high campaign cost; little demographic selectivity with network stations; long-term advertiser commitments; long lead times required for production; commercial clutter
Outdoor Media	Repetition; moderate cost; flexibility; geographic selectivity	Short message; lack of demographic selectivity; high "noise" level distracting audience
Internet	Fastest-growing medium; a mobile medium; ability to reach a narrow target audience; relatively short lead time to create ads; moderate cost; most versatile—allows for the same format as all other media; allows more engagement via two-way communication; audience measures are well developed	Extremely cluttered with websites; ad exposure relies on "click through"; many users have pop-up blockers that screen ads; not all consumers have access to the Internet

cooperative advertising
An arrangement in which the manufacturer and the retailer split the costs of advertising the manufacturer's brand.

The main sources of newspaper ad revenue are local retailers, classified ads, and cooperative advertising. In **cooperative advertising**, the manufacturer and the retailer split the costs of advertising the manufacturer's brand. One reason that manufacturers use cooperative advertising is the impracticality of listing all their dealers in national ads. Also, cooperative ads encourage retailers to devote more effort to the manufacturer's lines.

Printed Magazines

Compared to other media, the cost per contact in printed magazine advertising is usually high. The cost per potential customer may be much lower, however, because magazines are often targeted to specialized audiences and thus reach more potential customers. The types of products most frequently advertised in magazines include automobiles, apparel, computers, and personal care products.

One of the main advantages of magazine advertising is its market selectivity. Magazines are published for virtually every market segment. For instance, in Canada there are nearly 1,280 different consumer magazines and 770 trade magazines with a combined circulation level of 770 million. In addition, each magazine has approximately 4.8 readers per issue.[29] For instance, *Maclean's* is a leading current events publication; *Zoomer Magazine* targets one of the largest consumer segments, the baby boomers; *Golf Canada* has one of the highest reported circulations (129,000) for a Canadian-distributed sporting publication; *Marketing Magazine* is a trade magazine for marketing and advertising professionals; and *Canadian Gardening* is a niche publication geared to people interested in gardening.[30]

Radio

Radio has several strengths as an advertising medium: selectivity and audience segmentation, a large out-of-home audience, low unit and production costs, timeliness, and geographic flexibility. In Canada, there are 681 private commercial radio stations (158 AM and 523 FM), which are able to penetrate the 99 percent of Canadian households that have radio receivers; on average, 92 percent of Canadians tune into radio broadcasts each week.[31] Local advertisers are the most frequent users of radio advertising, contributing over three-quarters of all radio ad revenues. Like newspapers, radio also lends itself well to cooperative advertising.

Radio advertising has been enjoying a resurgence in popularity. As Canadians become more mobile and pressed for time, media such as network television and newspapers have lost viewers and readers, particularly in the youth market. Radio listening, however, has grown in step with population increases mainly because its immediate, portable nature meshes so well with a fast-paced lifestyle. The ability to target specific demographic groups is also a major selling point for radio stations; this ability attracts advertisers who are pursuing narrowly defined audiences that are more likely to respond to certain kinds of ads and products. Moreover, radio listeners tend to listen habitually and at predictable times, with the most popular being "drive time," when commuters form a vast captive audience. Finally, satellite radio has attracted new audiences that are exposed to some advertising, although its allure has been to offer mainly commercial-free content.

Television

Because TV is an audiovisual medium, it provides advertisers with many creative opportunities. TV broadcasters include network TV, independent stations, cable TV, and direct broadcast satellite TV. CBC and CTV are the only national English-language networks in Canada, both claiming to have 99 percent of coverage of Canada's English-speaking population. Radio-Canada (French CBC) and TVA are also national networks that broadcast in French. Conversely, regional networks provide excellent coverage of many of Canada's larger population centres. The Global Television Network covers 95 percent of Canada. Subscription TV services through cable systems in Canada, such as Rogers Cable, Shaw Cable, and Cogeco Cable, and also delivered via satellite systems such as Bell ExpressVu and Star Choice, are among the most highly developed in the world. Ninety-two percent of Canadian households are served by at least one of these systems. Both satellite and cable systems are able to distribute the signals of virtually all of the commercial TV networks; they also offer pay TV and specialty channels. The cable TV system has also been able to piggyback high-speed Internet access along many of its lines. Specialty networks abound in Canada, with a multitude of channels devoted exclusively to particular audiences—for example, women, children, Aboriginal people, diverse ethnic groups, nature lovers, food lovers, senior citizens, religious groups, sports fans, music lovers, and fitness enthusiasts.[32] Because of its targeted channels, cable and satellite subscription TV is often characterized as "narrowcasting" by media buyers. Canadian businesses routinely include cable and satellite buys in their marketing mixes.

Advertising time on TV is usually very expensive, especially for network stations, but some cable stations offer good deals. First-run prime-time shows and special events command the highest rates. The average price of a 30-second ad on the CBC full network is $6,500, but depending on the program and the time of day, this cost can range from a low of $100 to a maximum of $52,000. The CTV network is among the priciest, with an average rate of $12,000 per 30-second ad and a range of $2,500 to $80,000! In comparison, specialty channel TV Guide is a good deal, charging $7,500 per week for 150 spots.[33] The most expensive TV advertising in the world is a national ad on the U.S. broadcast of the Super Bowl, which in 2010 commanded a price of US $2.8 million with a viewership of 106.5 million people. Canadian advertisers got a bargain with the price of a 2010 Super Bowl ad on the CTV feed costing only $120,000 and delivering a record average audience of 6.7 million Canadians. In contrast, the CFL's 2009 Grey Cup commanded between $40,000 and $50,000 for a 30-second ad and delivered a record average audience estimated at 6.1 million viewers.[34]

One of the more successful recent television formats that has emerged is the **infomercial**, a 30-minute or longer advertisement. Infomercials are an attractive advertising vehicle for many marketers because of the cheap air time and the lower production costs. Advertisers say the infomercial is an ideal way to present complicated information to potential customers, which other advertising vehicles typically don't allow time to do. Infomercials have been found to be most effective for selling relatively high-priced products ($100 or more) that require explanation. Small appliances

infomercial
A 30-minute or longer advertisement that looks more like a TV talk show than a sales pitch.

(dehydrators, small convection ovens), home improvement products (ladders, home painting systems), self-improvement products (exercise machines or programs), get-rich-quick schemes (financial planning, real estate investing), and entertainment vehicles (DVD sets, CD collections) have all used infomercials. This advertising approach is rapidly gaining favour with some of the more mainstream marketers. Canadian firms that have used direct-response TV in their marketing programs include the Royal Bank, Bell Canada, Liberty Health, Ford, and ING Direct.[35] A shorter direct-retail infomercial is more common in daytime programming, running an average of 120 seconds.[36]

Sponsoring reality shows using a firm's products is another type of infomercial television advertising. For example, in the fall of 2009, West 49 got together with Glassbox television to create West 49 Ambition Skatecamp, an eight-part reality show that prominently displays West 49 products in the programming. The show will also be available for viewing on West 49's commercial website.[37] West 49's approach is similar to the *My Rona Home* show, which has been around since 2004 in one form or another and has most recently been shown on Citytv network stations in Canada. The premise of the show can be described as "Home Improvement meets Family Feud," where families compete with each other to renovate and decorate a home. The prize for the winning family? The home! Along with the program title identifying Rona as the sponsor, there are a number of other promotional ties, including Rona commercials run during the show, Rona's name on the opening and closing program credits, and a number of minutes of programming that expose supplier brands.[38]

Probably the most significant trend to affect television advertising is the rise in popularity of personal video recorders (PVRs). The most recent estimates are that 29 percent of Canadians have PVRs.[39] For every hour of television programming, an average of 15 minutes is dedicated to nonprogram material (ads, public service announcements, and network promotions), so it's hardly surprising that viewers weary of ad breaks have embraced ad-skipping PVR technology as the solution to interruptions during their favourite shows. Marketers of the products featured in those advertisements are not the only ones trying to figure out ways to keep consumers from avoiding them; networks are also concerned about ad skipping. If consumers are not watching advertisements, marketers will spend a greater proportion of their advertising budgets on alternative media, and a critical revenue stream for networks will disappear. For example, American network NBC ran a test to measure the effectiveness of running shorter blocks of advertising and decided it has no intention of changing its business model relative to advertising sales. The full impact of PVR technology on television as an advertising medium has yet to be determined, but research companies such as Nielsen have started to measure the number of people who time-shift—that is, record a show and watch at their convenience.[40]

Outdoor Media

Outdoor or out-of-home advertising is a flexible, low-cost medium that can take a variety of forms. Examples include billboards, skywriting, giant inflatables, minibill-boards in malls and on bus stop shelters, signs in sports arenas, lighted moving signs in bus terminals and airports, and ads painted on the sides of cars, trucks, buses, water towers, and even people (referred to as "living advertising"). Leaseyourbody.com is a promotional broker for people who want to be paid to put "advertising on their bodies." During the 2007 Super Bowl, Jennifer Gordon, a near full-term pregnant mother and a devoted Chicago Bears fan, was desperate to get tickets to the game. She offered to rent advertising space on her belly for two tickets on the 50-yard line at Super Bowl XLI. Amazing as it seems, uBid.com in Chicago took her up on her offer. The payoff was big: Gordon and uBid.com were featured in many stories about the Super Bowl, and yes, Super Bowl broadcaster CBS cooperated by looking for her in the crowd during the broadcast and mentioning her story. Marketers have also been using the plywood scaffolding that often rings downtown construction sites. Think about New York's Times Square, which has an estimated 1.5 million pedestrians every day![41]

Outdoor advertising reaches a broad and diverse market and is, therefore, ideal for promoting convenience products and services as well as directing consumers to

New technology is enabling outdoor ads to become more interactive. As part of Shell's promotion of its sponsorship of an exhibit in the science museum, children such as eight-year-old Sourav Shingare can play a video game on a giant screen projected on the Shell Building in London, England.

SOURCE: DAVID PARRY/ASSOCIATED PRESS

local businesses. One of outdoor's main advantages over other media is that its exposure frequency is very high, yet the amount of clutter from competing ads is very low. Also, outdoor advertising can be customized to local marketing needs. For these reasons, local business establishments such as car dealers, retailers, public transportation services, and hotels and restaurants are the leading outdoor advertisers. Outdoor advertising categories on the rise include telecommunications with a heavy emphasis on wireless services, financial services, and packaged goods.

Canadian advertisers interested in outdoor advertising can join the Out-of-Home Marketing Association of Canada. The Canadian Outdoor Measurement Bureau (COMB, at **www.comb.org**) provides comprehensive, up-to-date, and accurate traffic and audience data for major out-of-home products. The audience data are location-specific, full coverage, and in-market in nature.[42]

Outdoor advertising continues to become more innovative. New technology is enabling outdoor ads to become interactive and to be more like on-line ads. For instance, Mirvish Productions used a series of electronic posterboards in Toronto to promote its stage production of *Lord of the Rings*. Anyone who had a Bluetooth-enabled mobile phone could instantly download a special ringtone from the show by pointing their phone at the billboards.[43] Using this kind of technology, Nike commissioned a 23-storey interactive, digital billboard in New York's Times Square. People passing the display on the sidewalk could use their cell phones to temporarily control the billboard and design their own shoes.[44]

Innovative outdoor advertising campaigns are not limited to North America. Adidas Japan created a "living billboard" in the form of a vertical soccer field on the side of a skyscraper. The billboard featured live players and a ball attached by ropes to the side of the building.[45] Virgin Atlantic painted an ad on the grass next to the runway at South Africa's Johannesburg International Airport to greet arriving and departing passengers. A world's first, the ad required 1,000 litres of paint and nine separate permits from different regulatory authorities due to the sensitive nature of the site.[46]

The Internet

The Internet has dramatically changed the advertising industry. Canadian Internet ad revenues were about $1.8 billion in 2009, representing 13 percent of total advertising revenues. Revenue growth for Internet advertising has been slowing since its early days when it was 100 percent or more each year but it still has an impressive rate of growth of over 9 percent for the most recent year. The Internet now exceeds radio advertising in Canada in revenue generation. Also, 74.9 percent of Canadians have broadband Internet access at home, where they spend an average of 90 minutes on-line each day.[47]

On-line advertising continues to grow as a proportion of companies' advertising budgets. Advertising presentations on the Internet are categorized under search engines, display ads, classified and directory ads, e-mail, and video. Advertisers wishing to purchase on-line promotional vehicles have a number of choices, including e-mail marketing, site-specific placement, sponsorships, social media, on-line video and broadcasting, search engines, and Internet advertising networks. Search engines are becoming extremely important as advertising sources, garnering nearly 38 percent of the promotional revenues.[48] This has prompted a few companies to create special positions to manage search engine promotion alone.[49]

The effectiveness of Internet advertising has been hotly debated, however. Early research on banner ads found response rates as high as 30 percent, but more recent studies indicate much lower response rates. Given the high-speed broadband penetration in Canada, advertisers have switched their on-line advertising approaches from that of a basic on-line delivery of print ads to more use of sound and motion. For example, marketers are using ads that float, sing, or dance; video commercials similar to traditional TV spots; and ads that pop up in another window, use larger, hard-to-miss shapes, and include both on-line and off-line cross-promotions. These new formats are often large enough for marketers to include their entire message so that users don't have to click through to another site.

Go on-line and read Chapter 19 for a more thorough discussion of the marketing implications and uses of the Internet.

Alternative Media

To cut through the clutter of traditional advertising media, advertisers are creating new media vehicles to advertise their products, some ordinary and others quite innovative. Alternative media vehicles can include shopping carts in grocery stores, computer screen savers, DVDs, interactive kiosks in department stores, aerial ads, washroom posters, advertisements run before movies at the cinema and on rented DVDs, and "advertainments"—"mini movies" that promote a product and are shown on the Internet. BMW shows films by recognized directors that run six to eight minutes and that feature its cars in extreme situations.[50] Just about anything can become a vehicle for displaying advertising. Supermarkets are now testing "flooranimation," that is, ads on supermarket floors animated with graphics and sounds. Unanimated floor ads are already in use in a number of Canadian convenience stores. Research has shown that static floor ads increase sales 15 percent to 30 percent. Marketers are hoping that with animation and sound, sales will increase even more.[51] Marketers are also looking for more innovative ways to reach captive and often bored commuters. For instance, subway systems are now showing ads via lighted boxes installed along tunnel walls. As a train passes through the tunnel, the passengers view the illuminated boxes, which create the same kind of illusion as a child's flip book, in which the images appear to move as the pages are flipped rapidly.[52]

Video Game Advertising When trying to reach males aged 18 to 34, video game advertising is emerging as an excellent medium. The medium first attracted attention when Massive, Inc., (**www.massiveincorporated.com**) started a videogame advertising network and later established a partnership with Nielsen Entertainment, Inc., to provide ad ratings. Massive provides the capability to have ads with full motion and sound inserted into games played on Internet-connected computers. This is a big improvement over previous ads, which had to be inserted when the games were made and therefore quickly became obsolete. In 2006, Microsoft acquired Massive, a move that the company says will help it "deliver dynamic, relevant ads" across its on-line services including Xbox Live and MSN Games.[53]

Mobile Phones Mobile phones are among the newest advertising media and are particularly useful for reaching the youth market. Mobile advertising has substantial upside potential when you consider that more than 75 percent of Canadians have mobile phone subscriptions.[54] Canadian spending on mobile advertising is relatively low at $67 million but is expected to grow dramatically in the next few years.[55] Today's data- and video-oriented phones can deliver advertisements and also have GPS capability, so they can receive "location-based" advertising; for example, a nearby restaurant can alert potential customers about specials. McDonald's enjoyed success doing this at locations in California where it gave away free McFlurry desserts. Marketers also are using text and video messages to notify customers of special deals, such as ring tone downloads. Mobile phone advertising is less popular in Canada than in Europe and Asia, where mobile phone owners use text messaging much more heavily. Although there is concern that mobile phone spam will become as much of a problem as Internet spam, mobile phone advertisers are targeting their ads to users who agree to receive the ads in exchange for premium services or who sign up on opt-in lists to learn about items that interest them, such as a particular band's next album or concert.[56]

Stealth (Guerrilla) Marketing The term "stealth" might conjure images of undercover operations, possibly even sneakiness. In marketing, however, stealth has come to

Ethics in Marketing

 WHEN DOES GUERRILLA (STEALTH) MARKETING CROSS THE LINE?

The terms *guerrilla marketing*, *ambush marketing*, and *stealth marketing* are all synonymous and suggest that business is a form of economic warfare. This terminology refers to a range of short-term marketing tactics that are designed to disrupt or take advantage of a competitor's marketing tactics in such a way as to gain some type of publicity or usurp the competitor's intellectual property rights. It is often hard to determine clearly when a company has engaged in an illegal activity or simply operated in a spirit of intense competition. Sports organizations like the International Olympic Committee (IOC), which controls and administers both the Summer and Winter Olympic Games, and the Fédération Internationale de Football Association (FIFA), which controls the rights to soccer's World Cup, are in a continual state of mobilization to protect their intellectual properties from ambush marketing tactics.

For example, during the 2010 Winter Olympics in Vancouver, the Vancouver Organizing Committee (VANOC), which administers the games for the IOC, as host felt considerable concern over the threat of ambush marketing. The IOC has identified ambush marketing and its tactics as follows: "Attempts by competitors of official sponsors to trade on the goodwill of the Olympic Games by creating an association between the non-sponsor and the Olympic Games without authorization from the host organization and without payment of any sponsorship or licensing fees have historically been accomplished by several different non-sponsor marketing strategies including sponsoring the television broadcast of the event, sponsoring sub-categories within the event such as a federation, team or particular athletes, purchasing advertising time on television before, during and after an event, creating promotions that coincide with the event, purchasing advertising on billboards in the vicinity of the site, and handing out merchandise so that spectators effectively become walking billboards for the nonsponsored competing brand at an event."[57]

Almost all countries have some form of trademark laws that may apply to ambush marketing. However, host countries for events like the Olympics and the World Cup may pass temporary trademark laws designed specifically to protect the intellectual property rights for these events. To protect the Vancouver 2010 Winter Olympic Games, in 2007 the Government of Canada passed Bill C-47, which expires on December 31, 2010. Bill C-47 states among other things "that no person shall adopt or use in connection with a business, as a trade-mark or otherwise, an Olympic or Paralympic mark or a mark that so nearly resembles an Olympic or Paralympic mark as to be likely to be mistaken for it."[58] During the 2010 FIFA World Cup in South Africa, the "Contravention of Merchandise Marks Act" was the enforceable law available to FIFA to prevent ambush marketing.[59]

So now that we know how what kinds of ambushes can be set and how sponsoring organizations try to prevent them, what kinds of things have gone on? With a specific reference to Bill C-47, Lululemon Athletica came out with a line of clothing called "Cool Sporting Event That Takes Place in British Columbia Between 2009 & 2011 Edition." The company looked at the law and realized that they couldn't put Vancouver 2010 on anything. They even decided that "2010" alone or "Vancouver" alone on their clothing would likely contravene the law. Spokesperson Eric Peterson of Lululemon commented that "we would never do anything that we felt was ambush marketing." Of course, the Vancouver Organizing Committee would see almost any clothing that had even a remote resemblance to officially sponsored clothing as an ambush. VANOC did consult its lawyers about Lululemon's clothing and found that the firm was within the letter of the law, although VANOC felt the intent of the law had been broken.[60]

In June 2010, Dutch brewer Bavaria NV ambushed Anheuser-Busch, the official beer sponsor of the 2010 FIFA World Cup. Bavaria NV began selling a beer brand named "Dutchy Dress" in April 2010. In order to promote the beer, the firm decided it needed some exposure at the world's most-viewed event, the FIFA World Cup. So during the 2010 World Cup in South Africa, the brewery hired 34 stunningly attractive South African women to dress in bright orange skirts (orange is the national colour of Holland) that had a Dutchy Dress logo on the hem. The women were given tickets to the Holland versus Denmark game but they didn't merely show up in the orange skirts and parade into the stadium. That would be too obvious to the FIFA organizers. Instead, the women came dressed as Danish fans wearing all kinds of different clothing with their orange dresses hidden underneath. Once inside the stadium, the group drew a lot of attention for their attractiveness, then when the game was 25 minutes old, they stripped off their Danish colours and threw them to the rest of the crowd and revealed their true colours as it were. They drew tremendous attention and interest during the game but afterwards FIFA officials surrounded the group and escorted them from the stadium and questioned them. Later, two of the women were charged with violating South Africa's trademark act although FIFA itself did not get involved. As a result, it seemed more people became aware of Bavaria NV's involvement with the 2010 World Cup than that of Anheuser-Busch.[61]

Do you think ambush marketing works? Refer back to the discussion of ethics in Chapter 3 and comment. What level of morality do you think Lululemon and Bavaria NV were operating on?

SOURCES: JEREMY CURTHOYS AND CHRISTOPHER W. KENDALL AMBUSH MARKETING AND THE SYDNEY 2000 GAMES (INDICIA AND IMAGES) PROTECTION ACT: A RETROSPECTIVE AT PARAGRAPHS 14–15 AS QUOTED IN NANCY A. MILLER, "AMBUSH MARKETING AND THE 2010 VANCOUVER-WHISTLER OLYMPIC GAMES: A PROSPECTIVE VIEW," INTELLECTUAL PROPERTY LAW JOURNAL, 22 (1), 2009, 75–86; NANCY A. MILLER, "AMBUSH MARKETING AND THE 2010 VANCOUVER-WHISTLER OLYMPIC GAMES: A PROSPECTIVE VIEW," INTELLECTUAL PROPERTY LAW JOURNAL, 22 (1), 2009, 82; NANCY ARMOUR, "2 DUTCH WOMEN IN COURT FOR WCUP AMBUSH MARKETING," ASSOCIATED PRESS, HTTP://G.SPORTS.YAHOO.COM/SOCCER/WORLD-CUP/NEWS/WORLD-CUP-OFFICIALS-WOMEN-WERE-DRESSED-TO-SHILL--FBINTL_AP-WCUP-ORANGEDRESS.HTML, JUNE 15, 2010, ACCESSED JUNE 15, 2010; DAMIAN INWOOD, "LULULEMON IRKS OLYMPIC OFFICIALS WITH 'ROGUE' CLOTHING LINE," CANWEST NEWS, DECEMBER 16, 2009; NANCY ARMOUR, "WORLD CUP OFFICIALS: WOMEN WERE DRESSED TO SHILL," ASSOCIATED PRESS, HTTP://G.SPORTS.YAHOO.COM/SOCCER/WORLD-CUP/NEWS/WORLD-CUP-OFFICIALS-WOMEN-WERE-DRESSED-TO-SHILL--FBINTL_AP-WCUP-ORANGEDRESS.HTML, JUNE 15, 2010, ACCESSED JUNE 15, 2010.

Dutch brewer Bavaria NV ambushes Anheuser-Busch at the 2010 World Cup in South Africa.

mean a campaign of outsmarting the competition, rather than outspending them. Stealth marketing, also known as guerrilla marketing, ambush marketing, or buzz, is usually just any unconventional way of performing marketing promotions on a low budget. Stealth marketing is often designed to leave the target audience unaware they have been marketed to, but that they have simply participated in something fun, or sometimes shocking. For instance, in a recent guerrilla campaign to promote the film *The Water Horse: Legend of the Deep*, a 50-foot dragon (think Loch Ness monster) was created by way of hologram projection on the water surface of Tokyo bay, in Japan. Conjuring a huge monster practically out of thin air created marketing "buzz" on-line, on the street, and in the media.[62] The Ethics in Marketing box presents some of the ethical issues associated with guerrilla marketing.

MEDIA SELECTION CONSIDERATIONS

media mix
The combination of media to be used for a promotional campaign.

cost per contact
The cost of reaching one member of the target market.

reach
The number of target consumers exposed to a commercial at least once during a specific period, usually four weeks.

frequency
The number of times an individual is exposed to a given message during a specific period.

audience selectivity
The ability of an advertising medium to reach a precisely defined market.

An important element in any advertising campaign is the **media mix**, that is, the combination of media to be used. Media mix decisions are typically based on several factors: cost per contact, reach, frequency, target audience considerations, flexibility of the medium, noise level, and the life span of the medium.

Cost per contact is the cost of reaching one member of the target market. Naturally, as the size of the audience increases, so does the total cost. Cost per contact enables an advertiser to compare media vehicles, such as TV versus radio or magazine versus newspaper, or, even within the same medium, such as *Canadian Family* versus *Today's Parent*. An advertiser debating whether to spend local advertising dollars for TV spots or radio spots could consider the cost per contact of each. The advertiser might then pick the vehicle with the lowest cost per contact to maximize advertising impact for the money spent.

Reach is the number of different target consumers who are exposed to a commercial at least once during a specific period, usually four weeks. Media plans for product introductions and attempts at increasing brand awareness usually emphasize reach. For example, an advertiser might try to reach 70 percent of the target audience during the first three months of the campaign. Reach is related to media ratings, generally referred to in the industry as *gross ratings points*, or GRP. A TV program with a higher GRP means that more people are tuning in to the show and that the reach is therefore higher. Accordingly, as GRP increases for a particular medium, so does cost per contact.

Because the typical ad is short-lived and because often only a small portion of an ad may be perceived at one time, advertisers repeat their ads so that consumers will remember the message. **Frequency** is the number of times an individual is exposed to a message during a specific period. Advertisers use average frequency to measure the intensity of a specific medium's coverage. For example, Telus Mobility might want an average exposure frequency of five for its TV ads featuring its new G4 smartphones. That means that each of the TV viewers who saw the ad viewed it an average of five times.

Media selection is also a matter of matching the advertising medium with the product's target market. If marketers are trying to reach expectant mothers, they could select *Baby Stages Newborn* magazine. If they are trying to reach consumers over 50, they could choose *Good Times* magazine. The ability of a medium to reach a precisely defined market is its **audience selectivity**. Some media vehicles, such as general newspapers and network TV, appeal to a broad cross-section of the population.

EXHIBIT 14.7

Selected Canadian Specialty TV Network Profiles

APTN	Aboriginal Peoples Television Network illustrates the lives of indigenous peoples in Canada and throughout the world; 84% of APTN programming originates in Canada, with 56% of the programs broadcast in English, 16% in French, and 28% in a variety of Aboriginal languages.
Bravo!	Bravo! is an English-language network whose programming focuses on the arts and culture.
CMT	Country Music Television is devoted to country music through videos, concerts, and specials but also offers comedy and drama series, movies, and country music news.
Fairchild Televison	A Chinese-language network serving Canada's larger cities. Airtime may be purchase on a regional or national basis.
MuchMusic	The programming focuses on music industry news and information, international music guests, and many of the latest music videos of popular artists.
YTV	YTV Canada (Youth Television) is targeted to children and teens. The programming is blocked to appeal to specific age groups throughout the day. Early morning programs focus on elementary schoolchildren; a block of commercial-free daytime programming on preschoolers; and lunchtime on elementary school age. Afternoon returns to preschool; then, after school and in the evening, programming shifts demographics again.
ZTELE	This French-language station offers programming devoted to science and technology, multimedia and computers, extreme jobs, paranormal documentaries, and supernatural and mystery fiction.

SOURCE: Canadian Media Directors Council, "Specialty Networks," Media Digest 09/10, 19–25; www.aptn.ca; www.bravo.ca.

Others, such as *Homemakers, Ontario Golfer*, Leafs TV, Telelatino, and CHIN AM and FM radio stations, appeal to very specific groups. Viewer profiles for a sampling of popular cable networks are presented in Exhibit 14.7.

The *flexibility* of a medium can be extremely important to an advertiser. In the past, because of printing timetables, paste-up requirements, and so on, some magazines required final ad copy several months before publication. Therefore, magazine advertising traditionally could not adapt as rapidly to changing market conditions. Although this situation is changing quickly owing to computer technology that creates electronic ad images and layouts, the lead time for magazine advertising is still considerably longer. On the other hand, radio and Internet advertising provide maximum flexibility. Usually, the advertiser can change a radio ad on the day it is aired, if necessary. Similarly, Internet advertisements can be changed in minutes with the click of a few buttons.

Noise level is the level of distraction to the target audience in a medium. To understand a televised promotional message, viewers must watch and listen carefully. But they often watch TV with others, who may well provide distractions. Noise can also be created by competing ads, as when a street is lined with billboards or when a TV program is cluttered with competing ads. About two-thirds of a newspaper's pages are now filled with advertising. Even more space is dedicated to ads in magazines. For example, 85 percent of the space in the February–March issue of *Brides* magazine is typically devoted to ads. In contrast, direct mail is a private medium with a low noise level. Typically, no other advertising media or news stories compete for direct-mail readers' attention.

Media have either a short or long life span. *Life span* means that messages can either fade quickly or persist as tangible copy to be carefully studied. A radio commercial may last less than a minute. Listeners can't replay the commercial unless they have recorded the program. One way advertisers overcome this problem is by repeating radio ads often. In contrast, a printed magazine has a relatively long life span. A person may read several articles, put the magazine down, and pick it up a week later to continue reading. In addition, magazines often have a high pass-along rate. That is, one person will read the publication and then give it to someone else to read.

Media planners have traditionally relied on the above factors for selecting an effective media mix, with reach, frequency, and cost often the overriding criteria. But some experts question the reliance media planners have traditionally placed on reach and frequency. For instance, well-established brands with familiar messages may require fewer exposures to be effective, while newer brands or brands with unfamiliar messages may need more exposures to become familiar.

Additionally, media planners have hundreds more media options today than they had 50 years ago, when network TV reigned. For instance, Canada has 40 TV markets and 148 commercial TV stations to cover them. It also has 681 commercial radio stations, 158 AM and 523 FM, offering a wide variety of formats. There are 123 daily newspapers in Canada with total circulation of 5.9 million. The number of unique magazine titles is impressive: more than 2,000 are listed, of which 1,279 are targeted to consumers.[63] Satellite and cable TV now bring hundreds of channels into viewers' homes. The Internet provides media planners with even more targets for their messages. Alternative media choices are popping up in some very unlikely places. *Media fragmentation* is forcing media planners to pay as much attention to where they place their ads as to how often the ads are to be repeated. Indeed, experts recommend evaluating reach along with frequency when the effectiveness of advertising is assessed. That is, in certain situations it may be more important to reach as many consumers in as many media vehicles as possible. When this approach is considered, however, the budget must be large enough to achieve sufficient levels of frequency to have an impact. In evaluating reach versus frequency, therefore, the media planner ultimately must select an approach that is most likely to result in the ad being understood and remembered when a purchase decision is being made.

Advertisers also evaluate the qualitative factors involved in media selection. These qualitative factors include such things as attention to the commercial and the program, involvement, lack of distractions, how well the viewer likes the program, and other audience behaviours that affect the likelihood that a commercial message is being seen and, hopefully, absorbed. Advertisers can promote their product in as many media as possible and repeat an ad as many times as they like, yet the ad still may not be effective if the audience is not paying attention. For example, research on audience attentiveness for television indicates that the longer viewers stay tuned to a particular program, the more memorable they find the commercials. Holding power, therefore, can be more important than ratings (the number of people tuning in to any part of the program) when selecting media vehicles, challenging the long-held assumption that the higher the rating of a program, the more effective the advertising run during the program, even though it is more costly.

MEDIA SCHEDULING

After choosing the media for the advertising campaign, advertisers must schedule the ads. A **media schedule** designates the medium or media to be used (such as magazines, TV, or radio), the specific vehicles (such as *Hockey News* magazine, *Hockey Night in Canada* TV broadcasts, or sports talk radio stations), and the insertion dates of the advertising. There are three basic types of media schedules:

- Products in the latter stages of the product life cycle, which are advertised on a reminder basis, use a **continuous media schedule**. A continuous schedule allows the advertising to run steadily throughout the advertising period. Examples include President's Choice, Molson Canadian, and The Bay.
- With a **flighted media schedule**, the advertiser may schedule the ads heavily every other month or every two weeks to achieve a greater impact with an increased frequency and reach at those times. Movie studios might schedule TV advertising on Wednesday and Thursday nights, when moviegoers are deciding which films to see that weekend. A variation is the **pulsing media schedule**, which combines continuous scheduling with flighting. Continuous advertising is simply heavier during the best sale periods. A retail department store may advertise on a year-round basis but place more advertising during certain sale periods such as spring and summer, Christmas, and back-to-school.
- Certain times of the year call for a **seasonal media schedule**. Products like Contac cold tablets and Coppertone suntan lotion, which are used more during certain times of the year, tend to follow a seasonal strategy. Advertising for champagne is concentrated during the weeks of Christmas and New Year's, whereas health clubs concentrate their advertising in January to take advantage of New Year's resolutions.

media schedule
Designation of the media, the specific publications or programs, and the insertion dates of advertising.

continuous media schedule
A media scheduling strategy in which advertising is run steadily throughout the advertising period; used for products in the latter stages of the product life cycle.

flighted media schedule
A media scheduling strategy in which ads are run heavily every other month or every two weeks, to achieve a greater impact with an increased frequency and reach at those times.

pulsing media schedule
A media scheduling strategy that uses continuous scheduling throughout the year coupled with a flighted schedule during the best sales periods.

seasonal media schedule
A media scheduling strategy that runs advertising only during times of the year when the product is most likely to be used.

New research comparing continuous media schedules to flighted ones finds that continuous schedules for TV ads are more effective than flighting in driving sales. The research suggests that it may be more important to get exposure as close as possible to the time when someone is going to make a purchase. For example, if a consumer shops on a weekly basis, the best time to reach that person is right before he or she shops. Therefore, the advertiser should maintain a continuous schedule over as long a period of time as possible. Often called *recency planning*, this theory of scheduling is now commonly used for scheduling TV ads for frequently purchased products, such as Molson Canadian and Sunlight detergent. Recency planning's main premise is that advertising works by influencing the brand choice of people who are ready to buy.

4 Describe media evaluation and selection techniques

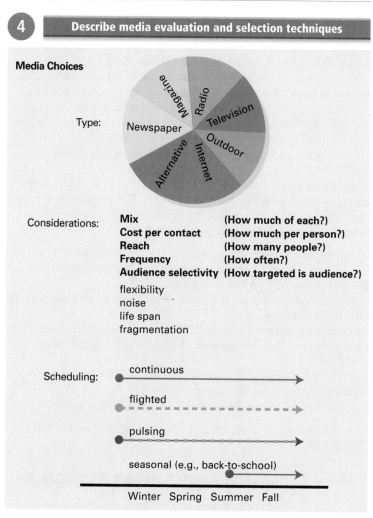

Media Choices

Type:

Magazine / Radio / Television / Outdoor / Internet / Alternative / Newspaper

Considerations:

Mix	**(How much of each?)**
Cost per contact	**(How much per person?)**
Reach	**(How many people?)**
Frequency	**(How often?)**
Audience selectivity	**(How targeted is audience?)**

flexibility
noise
life span
fragmentation

Scheduling:

continuous

flighted

pulsing

seasonal (e.g., back-to-school)

Winter Spring Summer Fall

SOURCE: © THE PROCTER & GAMBLE COMPANY. USED BY PERMISSION.

Laundry detergent is a product in the mature stage of the product life cycle. As such, companies like Procter & Gamble use a continuous media schedule to remind consumers to choose Tide over the competition.

5 PUBLIC RELATIONS

Discuss the role of public relations in the promotional mix

public relations
The marketing function that evaluates public attitudes, identifies areas within the organization that the public may be interested in, and executes a program of action to earn public understanding and acceptance.

Public relations is the element in the promotional mix that evaluates public attitudes, identifies issues that may elicit public concern, and executes programs to gain public understanding and acceptance. Like advertising and sales promotion, public relations is a vital link in a progressive company's marketing communication mix. Marketing managers plan solid public relations campaigns that fit into overall marketing plans and focus on targeted audiences. These campaigns strive to maintain a positive image of the corporation in the eyes of the public. Before launching public relations programs, managers evaluate public attitudes and company actions. Then they create programs to capitalize on the factors that enhance the firm's image and that minimize the factors that could generate a negative image.

A public relations program can generate favourable *publicity*—public information about a company, product, service, or issue appearing in the mass media as a news item. Organizations generally do not pay for the publicity and are not identified as the source of the information, but they can benefit tremendously from it. Corporations usually initiate publicity through press releases that further their public relations plans. A company about to introduce a new product or open a new store may send press releases to the media in the hope that the story will be published or broadcast. Savvy publicity can often create overnight sensations.

Scream TV, a Canadian specialty TV network, had a very small promotional budget to draw attention to its service. It was seeking to interest more subscribers through an innovative publicity campaign. So it hired Toronto-based ad agency Zig's ACDs to come up with a publicity campaign. The agency decided that the stealth approach to publicity using Halloween would be best. The firm came up with a stunt that was publicized in the *National Post*, on YouTube, and throughout the blogosphere. The agency selected a Victorian-style house in the heart of Toronto and set up 3-D special effects to generate a haunted house. A key feature was the image of a spooky child seen in the top-floor window. The agency used the Internet to spread the word that this was a real haunted house. People started coming to see it, and the agency used special effects to make the "ghost child" go from one window to the next. Images of the ghost were seeded on the Internet through weblogs and on YouTube. The stealth publicity event concluded when the ghost held up a sign saying: "Get scared more often on Scream TV."[64]

Again, although organizations do not directly pay for publicity, it should not be viewed as free. Preparing news releases, staging special events, and persuading media personnel to broadcast or print publicity messages costs money. Public relations departments may perform any or all of the following functions:

- *Press relations.* Placing positive, newsworthy information in the news media to attract attention to a product, a service, or a person associated with the firm or institution.
- *Product publicity.* Publicizing specific products or services.
- *Corporate communication.* Creating internal and external messages to promote a positive image of the firm or institution.
- *Public affairs.* Building and maintaining national or local community relations.
- *Lobbying.* Influencing legislators and government officials to promote or defeat legislation and regulation.
- *Employee and investor relations.* Maintaining positive relationships with employees, shareholders, and others in the financial community.
- *Crisis management.* Responding to unfavourable publicity or a negative event.

Public relations is a professional occupation and is supported by a number of organizations. See Exhibit 14.8.

EXHIBIT 14.8

Some Key Public Relations Organizations

The Canadian Public Relations Society (CPRS). "An organization of men and women who practise public relations in Canada and abroad. Members work to maintain the highest standards and to share a uniquely Canadian experience in public relations."

www.cprs.ca

International Association of Business Communicators (IABC). "A professional network of more than 15,000 business communication professionals in over 80 countries."

www.iabc.com

Public Relations Society of America (PRSA). "The world's largest organization for public relations professionals. The society has more than 31,000 professional and student members."

www.prsa.org

Institute for Public Relations. "An independent nonprofit organization that builds and documents research-based knowledge in public relations, and makes this knowledge available and useful to practitioners, educators, researchers, and their clients."

www.instituteforpr.com

MAJOR PUBLIC RELATIONS TOOLS

Public relations professionals commonly use several tools, including new-product publicity, product placement, consumer education, sponsorships, and websites. Although many of these tools require an active role on the part of the public relations professional, such as writing press releases and engaging in proactive media relations, some techniques create their own publicity.

New-Product Publicity

Publicity is instrumental in introducing new products and services. It can help advertisers explain what's different about their new product by prompting free news stories or positive word of mouth. During the introductory period, an especially innovative new product often needs more exposure than conventional, paid advertising affords. Public relations professionals write press releases or develop videos in an effort to generate news about their new product. They also jockey for exposure of their product or service at major events, on popular TV and news shows, and in the hands of influential people. Coincident with the campaign to introduce the new Virgin Mobile service in Canada, Richard Branson, billionaire founder of Virgin Group, dressed up as Captain Canada and leaped from a 15-storey building in Toronto's Dundas Square. After a safe landing, he jumped into a monster truck, which he used to demolish three cars wrapped to resemble Virgin's three major Canadian wireless competitors.[65]

Product Placement

Marketers are increasingly using product placement to reinforce brand awareness and create favourable attitudes. Product placement is a strategy that involves getting one's product, service, or name to appear in a movie, television show, radio program, magazine, newspaper, video game, video or audio clip, book, or commercial for another product; on the Internet; or at special events. Including an actual product such as a can of Pepsi adds a sense of realism to a movie, TV show, video game, book, or similar vehicle that a can simply marked "pop" cannot. Product placements are arranged through barter (trade of product for placement), through paid placements, or at no charge when the product is viewed as enhancing the vehicle where it is placed.

Product placement expenditures are estimated to be approximately $3.6 billion in North America on an annual basis. Though this amount is small relative to other marketing expenditures in North America, it is growing about 30 percent annually due to increasing audience fragmentation and the spread of ad-skipping technology.[66] Philip J. Hart, president of MMI Product Placement in Toronto, provides the following comments on product placement: "When a brand appears within the natural setting of a scene, it cannot be zipped, zapped, skipped or muted. Product placement plays an important role in the marketing mix, working in tandem with print, radio, TV, and other media. It's certainly the only way to provide third-party visibility in a realistic environment. Our most recent ACNeilsen research indicates product placement increases brand loyalty by validating the purchase decisions of the consumer."[67]

Most product placements are for transportation, clothing, food, beverages, home furnishings, travel, and leisure activities. More than two-thirds of product placements are in movies and TV shows, but placements in alternative media are growing, particularly on the Internet and in video games. One example of product placement is Pepsi, which appeared in seven top-ranked films in one year. The television series *Mad Men* is particularly suited for product placement activities. The show is about the advertising industry and thus a focus on brand name products is a legitimate part of the story line. However, given that *Mad Men*'s time setting is in the 1960s, only long-established brands can fit into the storylines. In contrast, the NBC comedy *30 Rock* is about the television business and has a contemporary setting so virtually any product can be fit into the storylines and often is. Finally, the television show *American Idol* was estimated to have had as many as 4,636 instances of product placement during one season.[68] Digital technology now enables companies to "virtually" place their products in any audio or video production. Virtual placement not only reduces the cost of product placement for new productions, but also enables companies to place products in previously produced programs, such as reruns of television shows and movies.

Companies obtain valuable product exposure, brand reinforcement, and increased sales through product placement, often at a much lower cost than in mass media like television ads. However, product placement is rarely an effective method for displaying the true benefits of products.[69]

Consumer Education

Some major firms believe that educated consumers are better, more loyal customers. Financial planning firms often sponsor free educational seminars on money management, retirement planning, and investing in the hope that the seminar participants will choose the sponsoring organization for their future financial needs. Likewise, computer hardware and software firms, realizing that many consumers feel intimidated

Consumer education can influence buying decisions; moreover, it can result in better, more loyal customers. BMW's instructional driving tour is a way for the company to show off its cars' capabilities to prospective purchasers and current owners without mounting expensive advertising campaigns.

SOURCE: © MARK PETERSON/CORBIS

by new technology and recognizing the strong relationship between learning and purchasing patterns, sponsor computer seminars and free in-store demonstrations. BMW Canada, for example, sponsors instructional driving schools in major cities across Canada. Drivers receive a special training session in driving techniques, accident avoidance skills, and traction aid tricks from a professional driver.[70]

Sponsorships

Sponsorships are increasing both in number and as a proportion of companies' marketing budgets, with spending reaching an estimated $1.4 billion annually in Canada. Overall, global spending on sponsorships, including North America, was expected to exceed $44 billion in 2009. Probably the biggest reason for the increasing use of sponsorships is the difficulty of reaching audiences and differentiating a product from competing brands through the mass media. With a **sponsorship**, a company spends money to support an issue, cause, or event that is consistent with corporate objectives, such as improving brand awareness or enhancing corporate image. Although companies have recently been turning to specialized events such as tie-ins with schools, charities, and other community service organizations, the most popular sponsorship events are still those involving sports, music, or the arts. The biggest category is sports, which accounts for almost 70 percent of spending in sponsorships. Nonsports categories include entertainment tours and attractions, causes, arts, festivals, fairs and annual events, and association and membership organizations.[71]

Because corporate objectives are changing, event sponsorships may undergo changes as well. For example, a few years ago the Canadian Women's Open Golf tournament was having a difficult time. It lost its status as one of the majors in the LPGA to the British Women's Open, and then it lost its title sponsor when the Bank of Montreal pulled out. However, the golf tournament was put back on track, almost literally, through the sponsorship of the Canadian National Railway, which has chosen to support women's golf in a big way. When CN first came on board, the firm upped the prize money for the championship and turned it into a high-quality event, which resulted in all 50 of the top 50 ranked LPGA women's players coming to the tournament in 2009. Aside from sponsoring the Canadian Women's Open, CN is also sponsoring the Canadian Women's Tour for developmental players as well as a junior golfers' program called Future Links. To support these sponsorships, CN has recruited highly regarded Canadian LPGA professional Lorie Kane to be a spokesperson.[72]

Marketers can also create their own events tied to their products. For example, Austrian-based Red Bull, maker of Red Bull Energy drink, employs more than 6,900 people in 160 countries and had sales levels in the range of 3.6 billion euros. The company makes a high-energy drink so it sponsors a number of high-energy sports events. However, arguably none is more high energy than the Red Bull Air Race event, which is an annual series of international air races that began in 2005 and was most recently held in eight cities on five continents in 2010, including Windsor, Ontario. Red Bull's website says, "The Red Bull Air Race World Championship features the world's best race pilots in a motor sports competition that combines speed, precision, and skill. The objective is to complete the course, navigating the 20 metre (65 ft) high specially designed inflatable pylons known as 'Air Gates' in the fastest possible time. But it's not just about speed. Pilots must pass between the Air Gates in the correct position (either knife or level flying) taking care not to touch them with their wings. Precision is crucial because any mistakes incur penalty seconds which are then added to the pilot's time." Red Bull has been the force behind this event since 2005 when it

sponsorship
A company spends money to support an issue, cause, or event that is consistent with corporate objectives.

SOURCE: MATTHIAS HANGST/ASSOCIATED PRESS

Red Bull has sponsored its own created event, the Red Bull Air Race, to support its "Red Bull Gives You Wings" promotional theme. The events are held in only a few cities around the world each year. The photograph shown here is from Windsor, Ontario, which has been one setting for this event for a number of years.

developed its key promotional benefit statement, "Red Bull Gives You Wings," hence the direct tie-in to the air race concept.[73]

Corporations sponsor issues as well as events, and they can build public awareness and loyalty by supporting their customers' favourite causes. Sponsorship issues are quite diverse, but the three most popular are education, health care, and social programs. A special type of sponsorship, cause-related marketing, involves the association of a for-profit company with a nonprofit organization. Through the sponsorship, the company's product or service is promoted, and money is raised for the nonprofit. For example, in 2010, Shoppers Drug Mart became the main sponsor of the "Weekend to End Women's Cancers." The company is sponsoring the annual event in cities all across Canada; over two days, participants undertake a 60-kilometre walk to raise funds that will go to cancer foundations for breast or gynecological cancer research.[74] In another common type of cause-related sponsorship, a company agrees to donate a percentage of the purchase price of a particular item to a charity, but some arrangements are more complex. In the United Kingdom, for example, Blockbuster Entertainment Ltd. works with the Starlight Children's Foundation to raise money, and Tesco supermarkets raise money for computers in schools.[75] Canadian Tire has created the Jumpstart program. On certain weekends during the year, the firm donates $1 to the program for every purchase made in the store; the aim is to raise enough money to allow about 20,000 youngsters to participate in an organized sport such as hockey, dance, soccer, or swimming.[76] Findings from several studies suggest that some consumers consider a company's reputation when making purchasing decisions and that a company's community involvement boosts employee morale and loyalty.[77] The Anatomy of an Advertisement for Yoplait provides insight into how advertising and public relations efforts may be combined. The ad highlights Yoplait's sponsorship of breast cancer research.

Internet Web Sites

Public relations professionals are increasingly using the Internet in their public relations strategies. Web sites are used to introduce new products, promote existing products, obtain consumer feedback, post news releases, communicate legislative and regulatory information, showcase upcoming events, provide links to related sites, release financial information, interact with customers and potential customers, and perform many more marketing activities. On-line reviews from opinion leaders and other consumers help marketers sway purchasing decisions in their favour. On its website for PlayStation 3 (**www.playstation.com**), Sony has on-line support, events and promotions, game trailers, and new and updated product releases such as Killzone 3, Red Dead Redemption, Prince of Persia—The Forgotten Sands, and UFC Undisputed 2010. The site also includes message boards where the gaming community posts notes and chats, exchanges tips on games, votes on lifestyle issues like music and videos, and learns about promotional events.[78]

More and more often, companies are also using blogs—both corporate and noncorporate—as a tool to manage their public images. Noncorporate blogs cannot be controlled, but marketers must monitor them to be aware of and respond to negative information and encourage positive content. Walmart has been especially active in

ANATOMY OF AN Advertisement

Yoplait

1 Media type: Magazine

2 Good color reproduction = Advantage of magazine

Even the lid is good for you.
Yoplait
Original
99% Fat Free
French Vanilla
Save Lids to Save Lives
Save Lids to Save Lives℠
For every pink lid you mail back by December 31, 2003, Yoplait will make a 10-cent donation to the Susan G. Komen Breast Cancer Foundation, up to $1.2 million. Combined with Yoplait's guaranteed donation of $830,000, we can raise $2 million. Yoplait and you – partners in the fight against breast cancer. This September and October, look for Yoplait pink lids at a store near you. www.YoplaitUSA.com.
© 2003 General Mills, Inc.

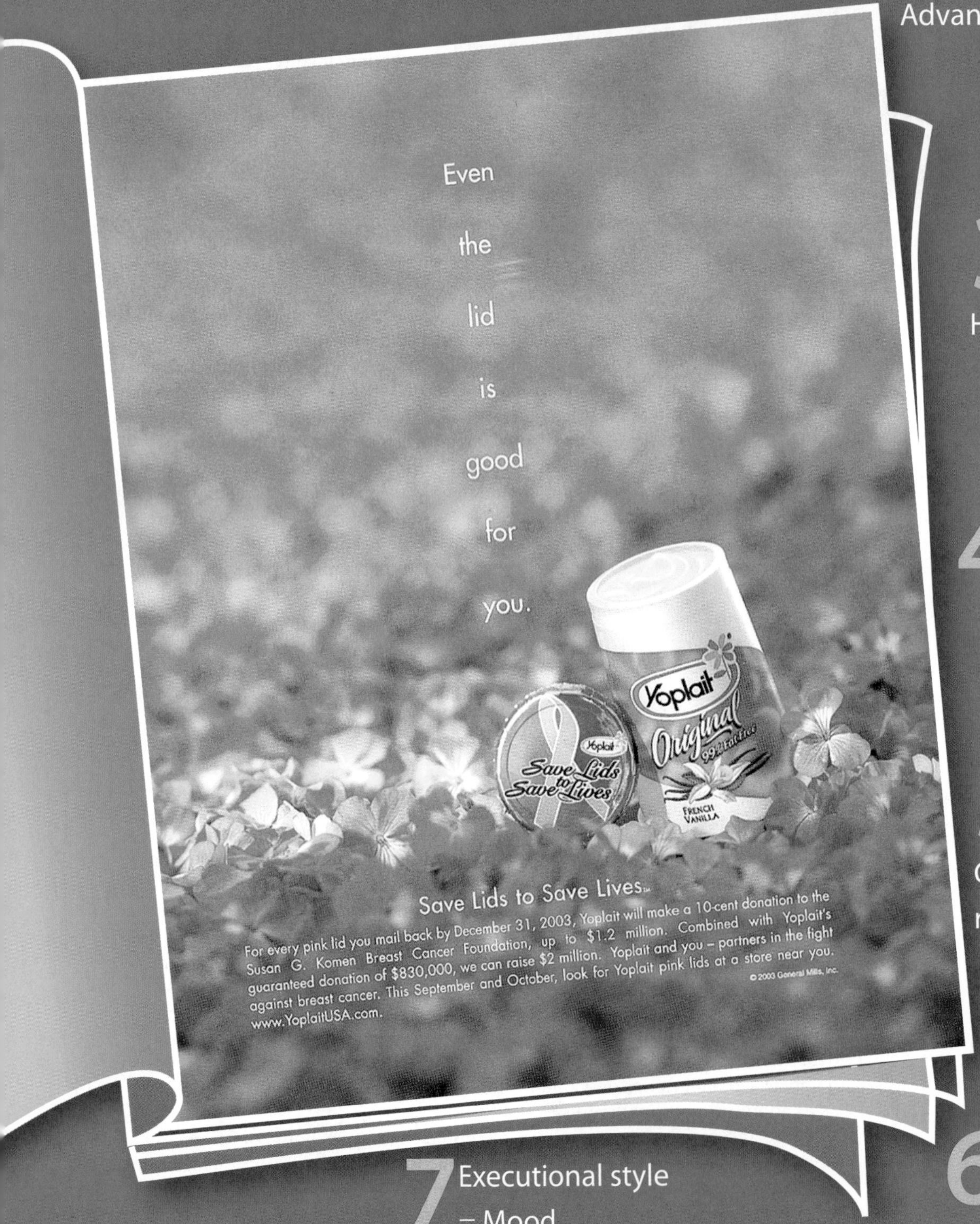

3 Advertising appeal = Health, charity

4 Cause-related marketing

5 Long life span: Campaign still running in 2009

6 Product advertising

7 Executional style = Mood

cultivating bloggers to get the company's message out. Mona Williams, Walmart's spokesperson, says, "We reach out to bloggers in the same way we reach out to reporters. A lot of people are looking to bloggers for their news source, and this is a good way to get our message out."[79] The company hired a public relations firm to combat negative publicity. The publicist assigned to the Walmart account, Marshall Manson, contacts bloggers who write pro-Walmart content and asks if he can send them materials to use in their commentaries. Those who agree become champions for the giant retailer.[80]

In addition to "getting the message out," companies are using blogs to create communities of consumers who feel positively about the brand. The hope is that the positive attitude toward the brand will build into strong word-of-mouth marketing. Companies must exercise caution when diving into corporate blogging, however. Coca-Cola launched a blog authored by a fictional character that did little except parrot the company line. Consumers immediately saw the blog for what it was (a transparent public relations platform) and lambasted Coca-Cola for its insincerity.[81]

MANAGING UNFAVOURABLE PUBLICITY

Although marketers try to avoid unpleasant situations, crises do happen. In Canada's free-press environment, publicity is not easily controlled, especially in a crisis. **Crisis management** is the coordinated effort to handle the effects of unfavourable publicity and to ensure fast and accurate communication in times of emergency.

A good public relations staff is perhaps more important in bad times than in good. Companies must have a communication policy firmly in hand before a disaster occurs, because timing is uncontrollable. A good public relations and crisis management plan helped Internet auctioneer eBay climb its way out of a public relations mess after a computer crash halted its bidding operations for 22 hours. The outage left nearly 2.3 million auctions stranded in the middle of bids, infuriating customers and sellers. To soothe users' frustrations, eBay sent messages apologizing for the disruption and promising to aggressively hire more computer-network experts. The company also refunded users' listing fees, totalling close to $5 million.[82] In contrast, British Petroleum's handling of the undersea oil well leak in the Gulf of Mexico during 2010 has been described as a lesson in disastrous public relations. The oil well leaked for months as British Petroleum (BP) tried every possible approach to stem the leak. In the United States, where tremendous environmental damage was done, the efforts by BP to explain what happened and what the company was doing about the leak were very poorly received, especially as the problem carried on for so long. Although BP's chief executive officer, Tony Hayward, came to the Gulf Coast almost immediately after the firm's oil rig exploded, he did not come across as a confident or able communicator in either interviews or advertisements where he tried to explain what BP was doing about the disaster. The American media covered the disaster heavily, they reported with more and more concern as the leak continued to defy all efforts to stem it, and Hayward's comments became less and less credible in the eyes of the public. Further, every comment he made and every activity he undertook was thoroughly scrutinized and even criticized in the American media and on late-night television programming. For example, Hayward was savaged for making the comment that he "hoped the leak could stop soon so he could have his life back." He was again heavily criticized in June of 2010 for taking a break from the Gulf crisis to watch a yacht race and spend time with his family in Britain. Commentators in the United States were all quick to note that he didn't seem to be anywhere near floating oil.[83]

So what should a firm in crisis do? David Dunne, adjunct professor of marketing at the Joseph L. Rotman School of Management at the University of Toronto, offers the following advice:

- *Have a strong brand to begin with.* Brand crises are all about trust, and having a deep reserve of trust to draw from can be an important factor.
- *Be honest from the beginning.* Evasion and cover-up can quickly erode public trust and greatly exacerbate the problem.

- *Act decisively and quickly.* When the *Exxon Valdez* spilled more than 10 million gallons of oil in Alaska in 1989, it took CEO Lawrence Rawl six days to make a statement to the media, and he did not visit the scene of the accident until nearly three weeks after the spill. Exxon's delay and stonewalling damaged the brand's credentials as an environmentally responsible company.
- *Take responsibility.* Do this even if you don't think you should. In 1982, seven people died in the Chicago area after swallowing cyanide-laced Tylenol. The maker Johnson & Johnson was not responsible for the tampering incident. Yet J&J took full responsibility for preventing such incidents from happening again and gained public confidence as a result.
- *Give customers a reason to trust you again.* When she was in jail, Martha Stewart sent regular messages to her loyal fans (and there are still many of them). She has used this connection to rebuild trust in her brand and to attract back those who have lost faith.

Brand crisis management, fundamentally, is not about "spin." Rather, it is about being forthright and honest and accepting responsibility. It's good advice for all of us, crisis or no crisis.[84]

MEASURING THE IMPACT OF PUBLIC RELATIONS

The use of public relations and publicity as part of an Integrated Marketing Communications program necessitates some measure of its effectiveness. Advertising has a highly developed approach to determining impact; the effectiveness of public relations is much more difficult to measure. Regardless, marketing organizations insist that all elements of their communication strategies be measurable somehow. A number of companies have been developing technological systems for measuring the impact of public relations efforts. For example, iTVx has developed a system the company claims is able to track the effectiveness of product placements on the Web, in movies, and on television shows. The system is proprietary but the television-based system is described as follows: "iTVx measures the quality and media value of a brand integration by assigning a Q ratio that is multiplied by the cost of a 30-second commercial in that same show. Some 50 different factors are assessed to calculate the quality of the integration, as represented by the Q ratio, and determine its dollar value in relation to a TV ad."[85]

Susanne Courtney, president of Courtney Public Relations Group, provides the following guidelines for measuring public relations campaigns:

- Agree at the outset what the critical success factors will be, and measure your success against achieving them. These may be qualitative or quantitative, and linked to marketing and sales, influencing public policy, share valuation, and/or the media coverage.
- For longer-term strategic communications programs, undertake benchmark attitude and awareness research with a sample of your target publics. Follow up at regular intervals to measure progress in effecting changes.
- In measuring publicity, it is common across North America to track media impressions based on Canadian advertising rates and data, for example, and then multiply by 2 or 2.5 to account for the increased influence of editorial over advertising. Some PR agencies also establish and agree to a target range of impressions for marketing campaigns.
- In measuring publicity, track tone (were your messages communicated?) as well as impressions. Although many believe that any publicity is good publicity, Courtney doesn't agree unless a company has a product that thrives on notoriety.
- Each program is different and has different goals and critical success factors. Measurement must reflect this. If 65 percent of the output is not related to media relations, make sure only 35 percent of the program is evaluated by media hits.
- Do not overlook the subjective scorecard. It is just as critical to manage everyone's expectations from the outset and throughout, and to keep deliverables within reach.[86]

5 | **Discuss the role of public relations in the promotional mix**

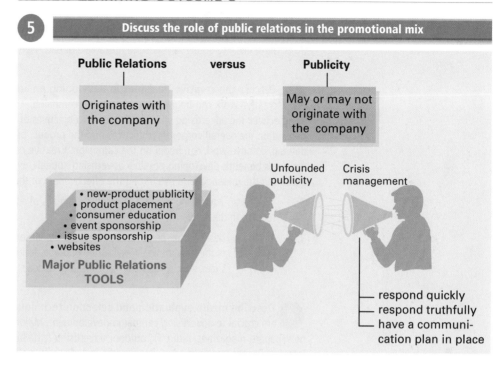

Public Relations versus Publicity

Originates with the company

May or may not originate with the company

Unfounded publicity   Crisis management

- new-product publicity
- product placement
- consumer education
- event sponsorship
- issue sponsorship
- websites

Major Public Relations TOOLS

— respond quickly
— respond truthfully
— have a communication plan in place

REVIEW AND APPLICATIONS

1 **Discuss the effects of advertising on market share and consumers.** Advertising helps marketers increase or maintain brand awareness as well as market share. Typically, more is spent to advertise new brands with a small market share than to advertise older brands. Brands with a large market share use advertising mainly to maintain their share of the market. Advertising affects consumers' daily lives as well as their purchases. Although advertising can seldom change strongly held consumer attitudes and values, it may transform a consumer's negative attitude toward a product into a positive one. Additionally, when consumers are highly loyal to a brand, they may buy more of that brand when advertising is increased. Last, advertising can change the importance of a brand's attributes to consumers. By emphasizing different brand attributes, advertisers can change their appeal in response to consumers' changing needs or try to achieve an advantage over competing brands.

1.1 Discuss the reasons that new brands with a smaller market share spend proportionately more on advertising than brands with a larger market share.

1.2 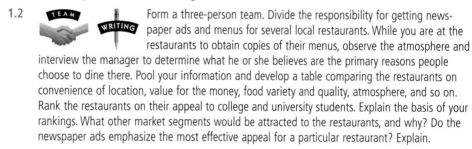 Form a three-person team. Divide the responsibility for getting newspaper ads and menus for several local restaurants. While you are at the restaurants to obtain copies of their menus, observe the atmosphere and interview the manager to determine what he or she believes are the primary reasons people choose to dine there. Pool your information and develop a table comparing the restaurants on convenience of location, value for the money, food variety and quality, atmosphere, and so on. Rank the restaurants on their appeal to college and university students. Explain the basis of your rankings. What other market segments would be attracted to the restaurants, and why? Do the newspaper ads emphasize the most effective appeal for a particular restaurant? Explain.

2 **Identify the major types of advertising.** Advertising is any form of nonpersonal, paid communication in which the sponsor or company is identified. The two major types of advertising are institutional advertising and product advertising. Institutional advertising is not product oriented; rather, its purpose is to foster a positive company image among the general public, investment community, customers, and employees. Product advertising is designed mainly to promote goods and services; it falls under three main categories: pioneering, competitive, and comparative. A product's place in the product life cycle is a major determinant of the type of advertising used to promote it.

2.1　At what stage in a product's life cycle are pioneering, competitive, and comparative advertising most likely to occur? Give a current example of each type of advertising.

3 **Discuss the creative decisions in developing an advertising campaign.** Before any creative work can begin on an advertising campaign, it is important to determine what goals or objectives the advertising should achieve. The objectives of a specific advertising campaign often depend on the overall corporate objectives and the product being advertised. Once objectives are defined, creative work can begin on the campaign. Creative decisions include identifying the product's benefits, developing possible advertising appeals, evaluating and selecting those appeals, executing the message, and evaluating the effectiveness of the campaign.

3.1　What is an advertising appeal? Give some examples of advertising appeals you have observed recently in the media.

3.2　[WRITING] Design a full-page magazine advertisement for a new brand of soft drink. The name of the new drink, as well as the package design, is at your discretion. On a separate sheet, specify the benefits stressed or appeals made in the advertisement.

4 **Describe media evaluation and selection techniques.** Media evaluation and selection are crucial to advertising campaign development. Major types of advertising media include newspapers, magazines, radio, TV, outdoor advertising (e.g., billboards and bus panels), and the Internet. Recent trends in advertising media include mobile phones, DVD advertising, video games, computer screen savers, cinema and video shopping carts. Promotion managers choose the advertising campaign's media mix on the basis of the following variables: cost per contact, reach, frequency, characteristics of the target audience, flexibility of the medium, noise level, and the life span of the medium. After choosing the media mix, a media schedule designates when the advertisements will appear and the specific vehicles they will appear in.

4.1　What are the advantages of radio advertising? Why is radio expanding as an advertising medium?

4.2　[WRITING] You are the advertising manager of a sailing magazine, and one of your biggest potential advertisers has questioned your rates. Write the firm a letter explaining why you believe your audience selectivity is worth the extra expense for advertisers.

4.3　Identify an appropriate media mix for the following products:

　　a.　Chewing gum

　　b.　*Maclean's* magazine

　　c.　Weed Eaters

　　d.　Foot odour killers

　　e.　"Drink responsibly" campaigns by beer brewers

4.4　[ONLINE] How easy is it to find out about advertising options on the Internet? Go to Google's and Yahoo!'s advertiser pages (**www.google.ca/intl/en/ads/** and **www.yahoo.com/info/advertising**). What kind of information do they require from you? Send an e-mail requesting information and compare what you receive.

5 **Discuss the role of public relations in the promotional mix.** Public relations is a vital part of a firm's promotional mix. A company fosters good publicity in order to enhance its image and promote its products. Popular public relations tools include new-product publicity, product placement, consumer education, sponsorship, and the Internet. An equally important aspect of public relations is managing unfavourable publicity in a way that is least damaging to a firm's image. Finally, marketing managers need to try to measure the effectiveness of their public relations efforts.

5.1　How can advertising and publicity work together? Give an example.

5.2　As the new public relations director for a sportswear company, you have been asked to set public relations objectives for a new line of athletic shoes to be introduced to the teen market.

Draft a memo outlining the objectives you propose for the shoe's introduction and your reasons for them.

5.3   As you read in this chapter, event sponsorship is a good way to garner publicity, especially when entering new markets. This type of public relations is not just for national companies and national events. In fact, there are probably many events in your city or region that are sponsored by local, regional, and national brands. Review the newspapers in your area for one week. Try to review several newspapers (local, campus, cultural, countercultural, etc.). During this period, cut out all the event ads that list sponsors. Once you have your collection, spread them out so that you can see them all at once. Identify any patterns or connections between the type of event and its sponsors. Identify companies that sponsor more than one event. What do sponsors tell you about target markets? After analyzing the ads, write a brief paragraph summarizing your discoveries.

TERMS

advertising 436	continuous media schedule 456	media schedule 456
advertising appeal 443	cooperative advertising 448	medium 447
advertising campaign 441	cost per contact 454	pioneering advertising 439
advertising objective 442	crisis management 463	product advertising 439
advertising response	flighted media schedule 456	public relations 457
function 436	frequency 454	pulsing media schedule 456
advocacy advertising 439	infomercial 449	reach 454
audience selectivity 454	institutional advertising 439	seasonal media schedule 456
comparative advertising 440	media mix 454	sponsorship 460
competitive advertising 440	media planning 447	unique selling proposition 443

EXERCISES

APPLICATION EXERCISE 1

You may think that creating advertising is easy. After all, you have a lot of experience with advertising, having been bombarded with ads since you were a child. But creating advertising presents real challenges. In this exercise you will be challenged to create an ad for a new product for animals that is based on a product used by humans. Some examples include snowboots for dogs, claw polish for tigers, and "Minute Mice" for cats. You can pick any product and any animal, but the combination must make sense.[87]

Activities

1.   You have been hired by the purveyor of your chosen product to create a print advertisement. Lay out your ad on a piece of paper that is no smaller than 8.5 by 11 inches and no larger than 11 by 14 inches. Include a headline, illustration, logo, and body copy. Your illustration can be hand-drawn or clipped from a magazine.

2.   Include the copy for your ad directly on the front of the ad unless your copy blocks are too large for you to be legible or neat. If that is the case, label your copy blocks with letters, put them on the back of your ad, and write the corresponding letter in the appropriate place on the front of the ad.

3.   Don't forget to pick your own brand name for the product or service (like "Minute Mice").

APPLICATION EXERCISE 2

In this age of 24-hour cable news channels, tabloid news shows, and aggressive local and national news reporters intent on exposing corporate wrongdoing, one of the most important skills for a manager to learn is how to deal effectively with the press. Test your ability to deal effectively with the press by placing yourself in the following situation. To make the situation more realistic, read the scenario and then give yourself two minutes to write a response to each question.[88]

Activity

Today, in Ottawa, the nation's capital, a public interest group held a press conference to release the results of a study that found that the food sold in most Chinese restaurants is high in fat. The group claims that the most popular Chinese dishes, including orange chicken, pork fried rice, and Hunan beef, contain nearly as much fat as the food you get from fast-food chains like Harvey's, McDonald's, Wendy's, and Burger King. (Much of it is fried or is covered with heavy sauces.) Furthermore, the group says that customers who hope to keep their cholesterol and blood pressure low by eating Chinese food are just fooling themselves.

A TV reporter from Channel 5 has called you at Szechuan Palace, your Szechuan-style Chinese restaurant, to get your response to this study. When she arrives with her camera crew, she asks you the following questions:

1. "A new study released today claims that food sold in Chinese restaurants is on average nearly as fattening as that sold at fast food restaurants. How healthy is the food you serve at Szechuan?"

2. "Get the camera in close here [camera closes in to get the shot] because I want the audience at home to see that you don't provide any information on your menu about calories, calories from fat, or cholesterol. Without this information [camera pulls back to get a picture of you and the reporter], how can your customers know whether the food you serve is healthy for them?"

3. "These new studies were based on lunches and dinners sampled from Chinese restaurants across the nation. A local company, Huntington Labs, has agreed to test foods from local restaurants so that we can provide accurate information to our viewers. Would you agree to let us sample the main dishes in your restaurant to test the number of calories, as well as the calories from fat and cholesterol? Furthermore, can we take the cameras into your restaurant so that we can get your customers' reactions to these studies?"

ETHICS EXERCISE

Sony Corporation wanted to cut through the clutter and reach the urban youth market to advertise its PlayStation Portable system during the holiday season. It decided to use a stealth marketing approach by hiring artists to create graffiti ads on inner-city buildings in large American cities. The graffiti did not mention Sony or PlayStation by name, but the graffiti did display cartoon characters riding the PlayStation products. A number of critics were incensed—in particular, the Society Created to Reduce Urban Blight (SCRUB), a community group that opposes illegal and ill-advised billboards in Philadelphia. One of the "ads" was placed on an abandoned Philadelphia building, so SCRUB director Pedro Ramos faxed a cease-and-desist request to Sony Corporation. Antiblight organizations in other cities were also upset with Sony. However, Sony actually didn't break any laws. In fact, it had obtained permits for the sites where its hired artists were working. Still, if copycat graffiti were to spread around the cities, Sony would have to bear some moral responsibility.

As word spread that Sony was behind the ads, some of them were defaced. One ad in San Francisco had the messages "Fony" and "Get out of my city" written on it. Not everyone was negative, though; Philadelphia resident Leslie Griggs commented that the Sony ad was actually an improvement over the handbills and other graffiti it was replacing. She went so far as to say, "I don't think that's graffiti, that's art."[89]

Questions

1. Although Sony obtained permits for the graffiti campaign, a number of people were still offended. Should Sony conduct a damage control campaign, or should it simply leave things the way they are? Explain.

2. It is possible that copycat artists could reproduce the Sony art on buildings and structures that do not permit advertising. Does Sony have any ethical responsibility if this happens? Discuss.

3. What is your opinion about the ethics behind stealth marketing in general? Go to **www.adstandards.com** and review the code. Then write a brief paragraph describing how the Canadian Code of Advertising Standards relates to this issue.

BURGER KING: HAVING IT THEIR WAY FOR A CHANGE

So how do you get your name out when you're the number two burger joint in the country? By the turn of the millennium, in the minds of many, Burger King had been relegated to sitting the bench in the fast-food industry. And in a way, after having changed owners and being rebranded so many times, it might come as no surprise. Then in 2003 Burger King hired the advertising agency Crispin Porter + Bogusky, which brought in some major brand changes for the fast-food franchise. At the time, Burger King was viewed as a boring brand with very little personality and identity. Crispin Porter + Bogusky quickly took steps to give Burger King a new image, an image that would be fun and that people would want to be associated with. Over the last few years, Burger King's new advertising campaigns have certainly caught people's attention.

Attention, however, is not necessarily a positive thing. The Crispin Porter + Bogusky agency has been known for edgy and controversial advertising, and its work for Burger King has been no exception. It certainly gave Burger King a new face. Early promotions included Burger King's "subservient chicken" website, where a man in a chicken suit sitting in front of a video camera would respond to commands put in by viewers. BK spun off the subservient chicken theme in 2005 with a faux metal band called Coq Roq to promote its new Chicken Fries. The campaign included commercials featuring the band—a group of six musicians wearing chicken masks—along with a website and music videos for four songs praising subservient chickens and Chicken Fries. If the name of the band itself did not set the tone (never mind the lead singer: Fowl Mouth), the website launched with a photo gallery containing pictures of young women with captions like "Groupies love the Coq." The images set off a major controversy, with many viewers claiming the images were demeaning to women and inappropriate for children. The captions quickly came down. The company blamed the captions on malfunctions in Flash and XML programming. The innuendo of Coq Roq was not an anomaly in BK's new advertising messages either; about the same time, BK released a series of commercials featuring former Hootie and the Blowfish frontman Darius Rucker singing a rewritten version of "Have It Your Way" with suggestive lyrics while travelling through a fantasy land of food and provocatively dressed women. Though controversial, Crispin Porter + Bogusky was setting Burger King apart, and sales began to improve.

BK's advertising, however, has not just relied on sex to sell its products. While it has established the 18- to 34-year-old male as a major target demographic, many of BK's latest advertising campaigns have been simply designed to surprise consumers and shake things up. One of Crispin's early moves was a resurrection of Burger King's stale old mascot: the King. But rather than give him a hip contemporary makeover, they kept the crown, red beard, and kingly apparel topped with a creepy smiling immobile mask. The King has since been featured in many of Burger King's recent campaigns, such as its "Waking up with the King" feature in which a confused young man wakes up to find the King in bed right next to him. The King then gives him a breakfast sandwich. In 2007, Burger King launched its "Whopper Freakout" hoax campaign, where they pulled the Whopper off the menu at a couple of select Burger King locations and filmed customers' reactions on hidden cameras.

In late 2008, Burger King advertisers stoked further controversy with their "Whopper Virgins" commercials. The campaign focused on taste tests between the Whopper and McDonald's Big Mac, similar to Pepsi-Cola's "Pepsi Challenge" against Coca-Cola, but as ever, Burger King added a twist. The ad firm hired an independent research team to perform the tests among three separate groups (the Inuit tribes of Greenland, the Hmong of Thailand, and a group of rural farmers in Transylvania) who they identified as having no exposure to either the McDonald's or Burger King brands or marketing (or fast food at all). The taste testers appeared in their traditional garb, and according to the filming by the research team, the majority chose the Whopper. And while the research team and the advertisers at Crispin claimed that the project was undertaken with the utmost care and respect for the people and their cultures, the ads (again) set off a flurry of controversy with accusations that Burger King's campaign was exploitative and culturally degrading.

Whether their advertising crosses the line or not, BK's promotions have certainly been successful. The subservient chicken website drew 439 million visitors, the Coq Roq website drew substantial traffic as well, and the Chicken Fries proved a success on the BK menu. When Burger King released an Xbox video game featuring the King, the game sold several million copies. Burger King caught significant attention as well with its latest stunt, titled "Whopper Sacrifice." The campaign, featuring the tagline "Friendship is strong, but the Whopper is stronger," was run on Facebook, where the company created an application that would send out a message every time the user defriended someone. For every ten people users defriended, BK offered them a coupon for a free Whopper. Shortly after the launch, Facebook banned the application. BK responded by posting the following message on the campaign's website: "Facebook has disabled Whopper Sacrifice after your love for the Whopper proved to be stronger than 233,906 friendships."[90]

Questions

1. What do you think of Burger King's advertising tactics? Is it okay to attract new customers while alienating others? Is Burger King's advertising ethical? Explain.

2. How did Burger King manage the negative publicity it received over the content of its Coq Roq website?

VIDEO CASE

SPORTS SPONSORSHIPS

Michael Kane and Patricia Lovett-Reid of Business News Network interviewed Keith McIntyre of KMAC and Associates about the value and impact of sports sponsorships in the context of the 2010 Vancouver Olympic Winter Games. Michael Kane opened the segment by discussing how research by Joyce-Julius Associates placed the value of Sun Life's sponsorship of the Miami Stadium for the Super Bowl at $27 million dollars. He told Keith McIntyre it bothers him that at one time the Olympics was the Olympics because it wasn't tied to professional athletes, but now that has changed. Kane asked whether the sport has been degraded because corporate sponsorships have become so big. McIntyre agreed that corporate sponsorships are huge and that the Olympic Games were for amateur athletes and, although that has changed, for the most part Olympic athletes in the Winter Olympics are still basically amateurs, as are most of the athletes who compete in the Summer Games.

Lovett-Reid asked McIntyre about the many categories of sponsors and advertisers and who was paying the "big bucks." McIntyre replied that "overall the International Olympic Committee (IOC) owns the rights to the rings." The IOC owns the broadcast rights, which they sell to 11 international organizations such as NBC and the CTV consortium. McIntyre mentioned that there are corporate sponsorships at the worldwide level with sponsors like Coca-Cola, Visa, McDonald's, Panasonic, Acer, Samsung, General Electric, Omega, and Atos Origin. On the domestic side, the Vancouver Organizing Committee (VANOC) stages the games. VANOC is able to sell sponsorships to national partners in Canada such as Bell Canada, HBC, the Royal Bank of Canada, Chevrolet, Rona, and Petro-Canada. McIntyre said that you can also have national supporters and suppliers who may have sponsorship positions. McIntyre stated that these partners at all levels are paying from $500,000 to $130 million.

Michael Kane disclosed that CTV is the owner of BNN and bought the broadcast rights for $90 million and then sold the space for advertising. Kane asked McIntyre if he knew how the selling was going. McIntyre began by saying that the true costs of the rights needed to include production costs, meaning they would run about $170 million. CTV sold about 85 percent of the inventory to 102 advertisers but there were actually only a couple of major advertisers, so 80 percent of revenue was coming from about 20 percent of the sponsors. McIntyre emphasized that when a company buys a sponsorship, it doesn't include advertising dollars, which are an extra expense that is over and above the sponsorship.

Lovett-Reid asked how the 2010 games compared to past games on money spent. McIntyre replied that the difference is phenomenal, with sponsorship money in the $750- to $850-million range in Vancouver; in comparison, the 1988 Calgary Olympics were a tenth of this level. Lovett-Reid asked McIntyre how you can evaluate return on investment for this. McIntyre said that sponsorship should be part of a strategic plan. You need to have your own corporate marketing position and you have to continue to market that throughout the year. You don't create an Olympic marketing platform, rather you use the Olympic medium for your current campaign. Because the Olympics delivers such a large audience it can be a springboard to launch a new product. McIntyre explained that Coca-Cola's "Open Happiness" and Visa's "Gold World" campaigns were well in place before the Olympics. He commented that if companies simply create an Olympics-only message it may not pay for itself. McIntyre said that the key is to create what he called "a holistic program" (really an integrated marketing program) that is marketed at all touch points such as advertising, sport body sponsorship, building it together, using it internally, and on the Internet.

Michael Kane raised the point that some sponsors have been abandoning the Olympic Games. He said that Eastman Kodak, a longtime sponsor—since the modern games began—stopped its sponsorship, although Kane mused that it might be due to its financial position. Kane also pointed out that both Home Depot and Manulife had also dropped out. He wondered what these actions say to us. McIntyre replied that companies often change their strategies and this affects sponsorship. For example, Beijing was a great entry into the Asian market. If you are looking to grow your business, sponsorship is a good approach. When a company pulls out, it means that sponsorship is not part of its core marketing mix and it id not seeing the payback from the Olympics.

Lovett-Reid asked which companies are doing well with sponsorship of the Olympics. She wanted to know which company had a strategy "with legs to it." McIntyre responded that Visa has been very effective as the exclusive credit card, and that people were using their Visa card at the Olympics. Visa was able to see a return on its investment and consequently it had sponsorship at all levels. Similarly, Bell Canada had a good fit with its mobile phones and its Internet and high-definition TV services. McIntyre observed that Coca-Cola works very well with activation—getting participation in their promotions—across all their retail stores outlets from convenience stores to grocery retailers. McIntyre commented that these companies invest in the Olympics, they set metrics for performance, they follow the sales results, and they measure their return on investment and payback.[91]

Questions

1. Discuss some of the considerations marketers need to take into account in making a decision to sponsor a large and visible event like the Olympics.

2. McIntyre highlighted the importance of having an integrated marketing strategy (he called it holistic) into which you would fit sponsorship rather than the other way around. Do you agree with him? Can you think of any situations where the sponsorship might dictate the strategy rather than the strategy the sponsorship?

3. Discuss what kinds of products you think go well with Olympic sponsorship and then discuss the kinds of products that might not do so well. What are the similarities or differences among the products you put into each of these categories? Comment.

MARKETING & YOU RESULTS

High scores indicate that you like television advertising. Not only do you like it, you think television ads have informational benefits. Low scores correspond to a more skeptical attitude toward television advertising. If you are skeptical about television ads, are you also skeptical about print ads and other forms of advertising? How much do you tune out (or tune in)?

CHAPTER

15 Sales Promotion and Personal Selling

CARS
car allowance rebate system

REGISTERED DEALER

SOURCE: TOBY TALBOT/ASSOCIATED PRESS

LEARNING OUTCOMES

1 Define and state the objectives of sales promotion

2 Discuss the most common forms of consumer sales promotion

3 List the most common forms of trade sales promotion

4 Describe personal selling

5 Discuss the key differences between relationship selling and traditional selling

6 List the steps in the selling process

7 Describe the functions of sales management

ⓥ MARKETING & YOU

What do you think of coupons? Using the scales below, enter your answers or record them on a separate page.

1	2	3	4	5
Strongly agree				Strongly disagree

___ Coupons can save a person a lot of money.

___ The money I can save by using coupons does not amount to much.*

___ I believe that people can help their families financially by using coupons.

___ Overall, I like coupons.

___ Personally for me, using coupons for supermarket products is or would be useless.*

___ Taking everything into account, using coupons for supermarket shopping is wise.

Now, total your score, reversing your answers for the items followed by an asterisk (for example, if you answered 4, change it to 2). Find out what your score means after you read the chapter.

SOURCE: REPRINTED WITH PERMISSION FROM *MARKETING SCALES HANDBOOK* VOL. III, PUBLISHED BY THE AMERICAN MARKETING ASSOCIATION, G. BRUNER, K. JAMES, H. HENSEL, EDS. SCALE #115.

The Canadian automotive industry has typically used a push marketing strategy for its products, a policy that tends to make marketers more reliant on sales promotion and personal selling as promotional tools. Consequently, auto makers and their dealers are among the heaviest users of sales promotion incentives when marketing their products. Consumers shopping for automobiles are often faced with a wide variety of different incentive programs to consider when they are choosing from among the various auto makers' models.

Canadian auto dealers have either invented or used virtually every kind of sales promotion technique imaginable at one time or another, including trade-ins, rebates, credit cards, loyalty programs, preferred financing, zero percent financing offers, coupons, premiums, contests, point-of-purchase promotions, recent graduate programs, trade shows, and the list goes on. Recently, because of the major economic downturn that occurred in the industry in 2008 through 2009, all the world's auto makers, assisted by governments, have taken their sales promotion efforts to levels never before seen. For example, Hyundai offered an incentive they described as an "assurance program, which allows buyers who lose their jobs to return cars within a year of purchase." Ford brought out a

similar program it called "Job Loss Protection" and General Motors responded with the "Total Confidence program." In all cases, to qualify you had to be eligible for unemployment benefits to enact the programs.[1] General Motors adopted an approach that amounted to a form of sampling with a 60-day return program. Buyers who purchased certain General Motors vehicles between September 2009 and January 2010 could drive a new car for up to 5,000 kilometres and return it if they didn't like it. They had to keep the car for a minimum of 30 days and could not return it after 60 days. In addition, buyers would forgo cash rebates of $500 and the applicable sales taxes if they returned the cars. If the cars sustained damage in excess of $200, the offer was void as well.[2] Honda Canada adopted low financing and offered incentive discounts on virtually all their models for one of the few times in their history.[3]

However, one creative promotional tool had to be the involvement of governments around the world who subsidized the auto industry using programs like Cash for Clunkers. These innovative programs gave consumers cash subsidies if they traded in automobiles that were made prior to 1995 for new cars. In the United States, 690,000 cars were sold under the Cash for Clunkers program,

although the auto industry publication Edmunds.com estimates that 565,000 of them would have sold even if the program didn't exist.[4] Canada's federal government offered the Retire Your Ride scrapage program but the offer was a modest $300 cash or $500 rebate savings for consumers and was limited to fuel inefficient vehicles that were 15 years or older. Canadian auto makers and dealers realized that a $300 cash incentive was insufficient to generate the level of interest needed so they piggybacked their own "cash for clunkers" programs on the government offer. For example, Ford Motor Company had offers as high as $3,000, and GM offered rebates from $500 to $3,000 toward the purchase of its new car models. Hyundai Auto Canada was offering up to $1,000 for clunkers and was one of the first companies to adopt this approach. As a result of these incentive programs, many Canadian auto makers reported sales increases in early 2010, and, perhaps not surprisingly, the firms who used the cash-for-clunkers programs seemed to be leading the pack.[5]

How do marketers decide which sales promotional tools to use to influence consumers? How does personal selling benefit a marketer's promotional plan? Answers to these questions and many more will be found as you read through this chapter.

SOURCE: NO FORECASTS—JUST LESSONS LEARNED IN A TOUGH YEAR," AUTOMOTIVE NEWS, JANUARY 4, 2010, 84: 12; AND WWW.GM.CA, ACCESSED JUNE 25, 2010; WWW.GM.COM, ACCESSED JUNE 25, 2010; MARK RECHTIN, "MENDEL: HONDA ON TRACK DESPITE LOST SHARE," AUTOMOTIVE NEWS, MAY 24, 2010, 84: 4; JEANNINE FALLON AND CHINTAN TALATI, "CASH FOR CLUNKERS RESULTS FINALLY IN: TAXPAYERS PAID $24,000 PER VEHICLE SOLD, REPORTS EDMUNDS.COM," PRESS RELEASE, OCTOBER 28, 2009 HTTP://WWW.EDMUNDS.COM/HELP/ABOUT/PRESS/159446/ARTICLE.HTML; TONY VAN ALPHEN, "GM HAS CASH FOR CUSTOMERS' OLD CARS," TORONTO STAR, SEPTEMBER 17, 2009, B2; AND GOOD CAR BAD CAR, "CANADA AUTO SALES BY BRAND MAY 2010," WWW.GOODCARBADCAR.NET/2010/06/CANADA-AUTO-SALES-MAY-2010.HTML, ACCESSED JUNE 26, 2010.

① SALES PROMOTION

sales promotion
Marketing activities, other than personal selling, advertising, and public relations, which stimulate consumer buying and dealer effectiveness.

consumer sales promotion
Sales promotion activities targeting the ultimate consumer.

trade sales promotion
Sales promotion activities targeting a channel member, such as a wholesaler or retailer.

In addition to using advertising, public relations, and personal selling, marketing managers can use sales promotion to increase the effectiveness of their promotional efforts. **Sales promotion** is marketing communication activities, other than advertising, personal selling, and public relations, in which a short-term incentive motivates consumers or members of the distribution channel to purchase a good or service immediately, either by lowering the price or by adding value.

Advertising offers consumers a reason to buy; sales promotion offers an incentive to buy. Both are important, but sales promotion is usually cheaper than advertising and easier to measure. A major national TV advertising campaign may cost more than $2 million to create, produce, and place. In contrast, promotional campaigns using the Internet or direct marketing methods can cost less than half that amount. It is also very difficult to determine how many people buy a product or a service as a result of radio or TV advertisements. But with sales promotion, marketers know the precise number of responses to their activities through Internet registrations, coupons redeemed, or the number of contest entries.

Sales promotion is usually targeted at one of two distinctly different markets. **Consumer sales promotion** is directed to the ultimate consumer market. **Trade sales promotion** is directed to members of the marketing channel, such as wholesalers and retailers. Sales promotion has become an important element in a marketer's integrated marketing communications program (see Chapter 13). Sales promotion expenditures have been steadily increasing over the past several years as a result of increased competition, the ever-expanding array of available media choices, consumers and retailers demanding more deals from manufacturers, and the ongoing reliance on accountable and measurable marketing strategies. In addition, product and service marketers that have traditionally ignored sales promotion activities, such as power companies and restaurants, have discovered the marketing power of sales promotion. In fact, annual expenditures on promotional activities in North America now exceed $400 billion a year. Direct mail is the most widely used promotional approach, accounting for 50 percent of annual promotional expenditures.[6] The next two most widely used promotional approaches are sampling and in-store promotions. Examples of these include point-of-purchase promotions (17 percent of expenditures), events and sponsorships (14 percent), and promotions via Internet and mobile devices (7 percent).[7]

THE OBJECTIVES OF SALES PROMOTION

Sales promotion usually has more effect on behaviour than on attitudes. Immediate purchase is the goal of sales promotion, regardless of the form it takes. Therefore, it seems to make more sense when planning a sales promotion campaign to target customers according to their general behaviour. For instance, is the consumer loyal to your product or to your competitor's? Does the consumer switch brands readily in favour of the best deal? Does the consumer buy only the least expensive product, no matter what? Does the consumer buy any products in your category at all?

The objectives of a promotion depend on the general behaviour of target consumers (see Exhibit 15.1). For example, marketers targeting loyal users of their product do not want to change behaviour. Instead, they need to reinforce existing behaviour or increase product usage. An effective tool for strengthening brand loyalty is the *frequent-buyer program*, which rewards consumers for repeat purchases. Other types of promotions are more effective with customers who are prone to switch brands, or with those who are loyal to a competitor's product. A cents-off coupon, free sample, or eye-catching display in a store will often entice shoppers to try a different brand. Consumers who do not use the product may be enticed to try it through the distribution of free samples.

Once marketers understand the dynamics occurring within their product category and have determined the particular consumers and consumer behaviours they want to influence, they can then go about selecting promotional tools to achieve these goals. Sometimes if marketers aren't careful about the choice of promotional tools to achieve their objectives, their efforts might produce unintended results. See the Ethics in Marketing Box to learn how sports marketers have discovered this.

Ethics in Marketing

 MACARONI AND CHEESE: SPORTS PROMOTIONS GONE WILD!

It has often be said, and usually with profanity included, that "the road to ruin is paved with good intentions." Marketers who design special promotions for sporting events need to heed this more than anybody. No matter what kind of special promotional feature a marketer comes up with, they have to carefully consider all the potential behavioural responses, not just the intended ones! It is important to realize that some consumers just won't buy into the premise, and when you give out "free stuff" you have to expect that consumers will then put their own value on it—some people will use it in a different way than the marketer expects or they may simply throw it away. When it's a coupon or rebate offer or free item contained in the package, the expectation is that if they don't want it, it will be passed on to someone else or properly deposited in the nearest garbage receptacle. But what should marketers do if there is a risk that some of the consumers might almost immediately throw the promotion back at the marketer, literally?

For the opening game of the 2010 Ontario Hockey League Championship playoffs between the Barrie Colts and defending 2009 Memorial Cup champion Windsor Spitfires, the Barrie Colts' marketers came up with a marvellous promotional idea. They gave all the fans who attended the game a box of macaroni and cheese dinner. The idea was that the fans would shake the boxes to make noise during the hockey game and then at the conclusion, they could take it home or, preferably, deposit the macaroni and cheese in any of a number of food bank collection bins provided around the arena. On the surface, a wonderful idea—whip up the fans, feed them later, and, most likely, benefit charity. What could go wrong?

There were two considerations that weren't taken into account: (1) buy-in by all the participants into the noble premise, and (2) the possibility of a highly charged competitive sports environment coupled with the heartbreaking loss of the opening game of the series. These two considerations were joined when the Barrie Colts gave up a late tying goal to the Windsor Spitfires, sending the game into overtime and upsetting the partying fans who were rattling away with their macaroni and cheese anticipating victory in regulation time. This was followed up by an overtime penalty to the home team that led to a rattle-hushing sudden victory goal off the stick of Windsor Spitfire scoring star Taylor Hall.

The disappointment of some fans could not be contained as they rained down boxes of macaroni and cheese onto the ice and the Windsor Spitfires to show their displeasure at the outcome. The Spitfires hastily left the ice under the barrage of macaroni and cheese missiles. In the press conference after the game, Spitfires overtime hero Taylor Hall, a truly unassuming young

man, commented that he didn't know why people were throwing away good food. He said that he wished he had picked up a few boxes to take home to his billet. For the most part, the fans were well behaved and did deposit the food as intended, but the televised game drew a fair amount of publicity and the announcers wondered aloud, "What were the promotional managers thinking?"

Indeed, what were they thinking, given all the precedents of fans behaving badly in response to well-intended but not fully thought out promotions. For example, in 1974, the Cleveland Indians decided to attract fans with a 10-cent beer night with virtually no limit on beer purchases. The result was a stadium filled with thousands of fans who quickly became inebriated, then unruly, resulting in a riot that caused Cleveland to suspend and then forfeit the game. In 1979, the Chicago White Sox baseball team had a "disco demolition" night where fans were given a discount for bringing a disco-style vinyl record to be demolished in between the parts of a double-header baseball game. The fans showed up in droves, and when they demolished their discs in a giant explosion on the baseball field between the first and second game, they made it unplayable, leading to the cancellation of the second baseball game. In 1995, the L.A. Dodgers had "souvenir ball" night and gave away thousands of baseballs, of which a few hundred were then returned, striking umpires and players as fans threw them on the field to show their displeasure with a controversial late game call. The Dodgers had to forfeit the baseball game. In 2009, the Chicago Blackhawks gave out souvenir hard hats to the first 1,000 fans at one game. Of course, nobody working as a marketer for an NHL hockey team could be expected to be aware of a hockey tradition known as the "hat trick"! Imagine both the surprise and the irony when Blackhawk player Jonathan Toews scored three goals in the game, resulting in a rain of the souvenir hats. The litany of "arming fans who throw things" goes on—ice scraper night, Frisbee night, seat cushion night, water bottle night, card night, etc.

Even when the promotion manager has given it some thought and doesn't see what could go wrong, it can. The Minnesota Twins gave their fans commemorative Minnesota road maps only to discover that thousands of fans felt they made wonderful paper airplanes and created their own event of whose plane can fly farthest on to the field, resulting in a massive disruption as thousands of paper airplanes floated down. The bottom-line lesson for sports marketers: if you are going to give your fans something to take away from the game, and it is something they could throw (which seems to be virtually everything), consider a way to do it when the game is over.[8]

SOURCE: BOB DUFF, "FINE DINING FOR SPITS," THE WINDSOR STAR, APRIL 28, 2010; WILLIAM J. WELLINGTON, WITNESSED TELECAST OF:, "WINDSOR SPITFIRES VERSUS BARRIE COLTS," COGECO CABLE WINDSOR, LOCAL STATION CABLE 11, APRIL 27, 2010; "ITS THE 35TH ANNIVERSARY OF THE WORST PROMOTION IDEA IN SPORTS HISTORY," WWW.FARK.COM/CGI/COMMENTS.PL?IDLINK=4428597&HL=ITS-35TH-ANNIVERSARY-OF-WORST-PROMOTION-IDEA-IN-SPORTS-HISTORY, ACCESSED JUNE 24, 2010; AND "14 REGRETTABLE PROFESSIONAL SPORTS PROMOTIONS," WWW.SLOSHSPOT.COM/BLOG/07-13-2009/14-REGRETTABLE-PROFESSIONAL-SPORTS-PROMOTIONS-187, ACCESSED JUNE 24, 2010.

EXHIBIT 15.1

Types of Consumers and Sales Promotion Goals

Type of buyer	Desired results	Sales promotion examples
Loyal customers People who buy your product most or all of the time	Reinforce behaviour, increase consumption, change purchase timing	• Loyalty marketing programs, such as frequent-buyer cards or frequent-shopper clubs • Bonus packs that give loyal consumers an incentive to stock up or premiums offered in return for proofs of purchase
	Break loyalty, persuade to switch to your brand	• Sampling to introduce your product's superior qualities compared to their brand • Sweepstakes, contests, or premiums that create interest in the product
Brand switchers People who buy a variety of products in the category	Persuade to buy your brand more often	• Any promotion that lowers the price of the product, such as coupons, price-off packages, and bonus packs • Trade deals that help make the product more readily available than competing products
Price buyers People who consistently buy the least expensive brand	Appeal with low prices or supply added value that makes price less important	• Coupons, price-off packages, refunds, or trade deals that reduce the price of the brand to match that of the brand that would have been purchased

SOURCE: From Sales Promotion Essentials, 2nd ed., by Don E. Schultz, William A Robinson, and Lisa A. Petrison. © 1998 The McGraw-Hill Companies, Inc.

REVIEW LEARNING OUTCOME 1

1 Define and state the objectives of sales promotion

2 TOOLS FOR CONSUMER SALES PROMOTION

Discuss the most common forms of consumer sales promotion

Marketing managers must decide which consumer sales promotion devices to use in a specific campaign. The methods chosen must suit the objectives in order to ensure the success of the overall promotion plan. Popular tools for consumer sales promotion are coupons and rebates, premiums, loyalty marketing programs, contests and sweepstakes, sampling, and point-of-purchase promotion. Consumer sales promotion tools have also been easily transferred to on-line versions to entice Internet users to visit sites, purchase products, or use services on the Web.

Although coupons are a high-cost promotion alternative, they are still an important incentive. Since coupons tend to be redeemed by customers who would have bought the product anyway, using coupon sites like Save.ca or fabuloussavings.ca is an efficient way to distribute coupons. They also allow marketers to get information on coupon users. Can you argue that coupons are really more of a loyalty marketing program? Why or why not?

COUPONS AND REBATES

coupon
A certificate that entitles consumers to an immediate price reduction when they buy the product.

A **coupon** is a certificate that entitles consumers to an immediate price reduction when they buy the product. Coupons are an especially good way to encourage product trial and repurchase. They are also likely to increase the amount of a product bought.

According to CouponsCanada.Org, approximately 3.6 billion coupons are distributed to consumers in Canada in each year but only about 100 million are redeemed, representing a 2.8 percent redemption rate. The average face value of coupons redeemed was $1.35, meaning that consumers saved $135 million. Although coupon distribution has been going up, redemption rates have not, they have remained steady.[9] Part of the problem is that coupons are often wasted on consumers who have no interest in the product—for example, pet food products coupons that reach pet-less people. This is owing to the fact that coupons are still commonly distributed in mass-media newspaper inserts or general mail. Also, coupons are more likely to encourage repeat purchases by regular users and have less power to stimulate product trial by nonusers.

Because of coupons' high cost and disappointing redemption rates, many marketers are reevaluating their use of them. Some marketers have increased redemption rates by shortening the time the coupon can be redeemed, thus creating a greater sense of urgency to redeem the coupon. Distributing coupons through the Internet reduces expenses because the marketer does not have to pay for printing or physical distribution and because the coupons go only to those who are truly interested. Some marketers are de-emphasizing their use of coupons in favour of everyday low prices, while others are distributing single, all-purpose coupons that can be redeemed for several brands.

In-store coupons are becoming more popular as it has been proved that they are more likely to affect customers' buying decisions. Instant coupons on product packages, coupons distributed from on-shelf coupon-dispensing machines, and e-coupons issued at the checkout counter are achieving much higher redemption rates. Indeed, coupons distributed in stores represented 40 percent of the coupons redeemed. Studies have found that in-store coupons are used 15 times more frequently than traditional newspaper coupons, indicating that consumers are making more in-store purchase decisions. As marketing tactics grow more sophisticated, coupons are no longer being viewed as a stand-alone tactic, but rather as an integral component of a broader promotional campaign.

Retailer Jean Machine, an Ontario-based retail chain of 29 clothing stores, developed one of the most innovative coupon campaigns ever seen. The retailer developed a "Picture This" promotion for August and September 2009 that involved turning the retailer's magazine and outdoor ads into e-coupons. Customers were simply asked to take a picture of either an outdoor Jean Machine ad or an ad from the retailer's magazine with their mobile phone camera or a digital camera. They only had to bring their phone or camera into the store and show the picture to a sales associate to receive a 10 percent merchandise discount on regular-priced merchandise.[10]

rebate
A cash refund given for the purchase of a product during a specific period.

Rebates are similar to coupons in that they offer the purchaser a price reduction; many of them require the purchaser to mail in a rebate form and usually some proof of purchase, so the reward is not as immediate as a coupon. Traditionally used by food and car manufacturers, rebates now appear on all types of products, from computers and software to baby seats. Electronics retailer Future Shop routinely promotes products with rebates and often quotes "prices after savings" in its flyers. However, Future Shop and its sister company, Best Buy Canada, have been trying to phase out mail-in rebates among their suppliers in favour of instant rebates.[11] It is almost standard practice to offer cell phone handsets for free after an instant rebate combined with an agreement to sign a multiyear service plan.

Manufacturers prefer rebates for several reasons. Rebates allow manufacturers to offer price cuts to consumers directly. Manufacturers have more control over rebate promotions because they can be rolled out and shut off quickly. Furthermore, because buyers must fill out forms with their names, addresses, and other data, manufacturers can use rebate programs to build customer databases. Mail-in rebates are especially popular because they entice purchase even though most consumers never bother to redeem them. Studies show that only about one-half of customers eligible for rebates actually collect them.[12]

PREMIUMS

premium
An extra item offered to the consumer, usually in exchange for some proof of purchase of the promoted product.

A **premium** is an extra item offered to the consumer, usually in exchange for some proof that the promoted product has been purchased. Premiums reinforce the consumer's purchase decision, increase consumption, and persuade nonusers to switch brands. Premiums such as telephones, tote bags, and umbrellas are available when consumers buy cosmetics, magazines, bank services, rental cars, and so on. Probably the best example of a premium is the McDonald's Happy Meal, which rewards children with a small toy. McDonald's has had agreements with firm's like Disney and Dreamworks, as well as with Ty, Inc., marketer of Beanie Babies, all of which resulted

in high demand among children for Happy Meals. Most recently, McDonald's has a deal with Dreamworks to promote its animated films with Happy Meal toys, and they had a lot of success with *Shrek 3*, which was released in 2007. Implementing premium programs can also be risky as McDonald's found in the spring of 2010 when it came up with a special four-piece glassware offer associated with the fourth Shrek movie, *Shrek Forever and After.* McDonald's discovered that the glasses had high levels of the metal cadmium in them, which could be potentially toxic to people who drank from them. McDonald's had to recall 1.4 million of the glasses in Canada and 12 million in the United States.[13]

Premiums can also involve more products for the regular price, as with two-for-one bonus packs or packages that include more of the

SOURCE: © AP IMAGES/PRNEWSFOTO

product. Kellogg's added two more pastries and waffles to its Pop-Tarts and Eggo waffles packages without increasing the price in an effort to boost market share lost to private label brands and new competitors. The promotion was so successful that the company decided to keep the additional product in its regular packaging. Another possibility is to attach a premium to the product's package or even make the package itself a premium. For example, Absolut Vodka brought out a special commemorative bottle designed by Vancouver illustrator and graphic artist Douglas Fraser especially for the 2010 Vancouver Olympics.[14]

LOYALTY MARKETING PROGRAMS

loyalty marketing programs
A promotional program designed to build long-term, mutually beneficial relationships between a company and its key customers.

frequent-buyer program
A loyalty program in which loyal consumers are rewarded for making recurring purchases of a particular good or service.

Loyalty marketing programs, or **frequent-buyer programs**, reward loyal consumers for making recurring purchases. One of the longest-running loyalty programs in Canada was instituted by Canadian Tire in 1958 when it introduced Canadian Tire Money to its gasoline retail outlets as a redemption for cash purchases. The company quickly spread the program into its retail stores. The program has remained highly popular ever since, with nearly $100 million in Canadian Tire Money distributed every year. According to current company information, over 90 percent of Canadians shop at Canadian Tire every year and 40 percent of Canadians shop there weekly. In Canada, Canadian Tire Money is arguably the most popular discount program in use, with a redemption rate of over 90 percent.[15] Loyalty marketing enables companies to invest sales promotion dollars in activities designed to capture greater profits from customers already loyal to the product or company. This is critical, as studies indicate that consumer loyalty is on the decline. Forrester Research found that the percentage of consumers ranking price as more important than brand rose from 41 percent to 47 percent over three years. According to the *Building Loyalty Handbook*, recent studies indicate that as loyalty increases, consumers buy more, with the most loyal consumers buying 20 times more than an average consumer.[16]

The objective of loyalty marketing programs is to build long-term, mutually beneficial relationships between a company and its key customers. Frequent-shopper programs offered by many supermarkets and other retailers have exploded in popularity. A recent survey of Canadians found that 93.6 percent of them are enrolled in at least one loyalty program, they hold a total of 114,655,300 loyalty memberships, and the average Canadian household is enrolled in 9.2 programs. The leading loyalty programs in which Canadians are enrolled are Air Miles (9.5 million), Aeroplan (4 million), other Mulitplan programs (1.7 million), financial services (24.3 million), retail (57.9 million), and travel, gaming, dining, and entertainment (17.3 million).[17] Although most Canadian consumers have enrolled in loyalty programs, one survey found that only 27 percent said they really liked these programs and that the programs influenced their behaviour. In contrast, 26 percent indicated they disliked the programs and would not use them at all. An additional 41 percent said they used loyalty programs but didn't like them. (The remaining 6 percent of people surveyed refused to answer.)[18]

Through loyalty programs, shoppers receive discounts, alerts on new products, and other enticing offers. In exchange, retailers are able to build customer databases that help them better understand customer preferences. For example, the Shoppers Drug Mart's Optimum Card loyalty program has nearly 10 million members and one commentator observes that: "Optimum members visit the store more frequently and spend more money—the average basket size of Optimum members is 60 per cent greater than non-members—that's not the real value for Shoppers Drug Mart. Rather, the chain banks on using the cards to learn more about how their customers spend money in the store, through tracking their purchases."[19]

Cobranded credit cards are another popular loyalty marketing tool. They allow consumers to spend their money at any participating retail outlet but also build up rewards at particular retail organizations they like to patronize. For example, Canadians can acquire a TD-GM Visa card that builds up credit toward the purchase of a new General Motors car (maximum of $3,000) or they can acquire other types of cards, including the Shoppers Drug Mart Optimum MasterCard, which builds up Optimum Points with each purchase; the CAA Quebec Platinum MasterCard, which is available only to current Canadian Automobile Association members; the Sony Card MasterCard, which allows points to be used to purchase items from Sony retail outlets in Canada.[20]

CONTESTS AND SWEEPSTAKES CONTESTS

Contests and sweepstakes contests are generally designed to create interest in a good or service and often to encourage brand switching. *Contests* are promotions in which participants use skill or ability to compete for prizes. A consumer contest usually requires entrants to answer questions, complete sentences, or write a paragraph about the product and submit proof of purchase. In contrast, winning a *sweepstakes contest* depends more on chance or luck, participation is free but winners must answer mathematical skill-testing questions. Sweepstakes contests usually draw about 10 times more participation than contests.

Contests and sweepstakes contests may draw considerable interest and publicity; generally, though, they are not effective tools for generating long-term sales. To increase their effectiveness, sales promotion managers must make certain the award will appeal to the target market.[21] Over the summer in 2010, Cadbury-Adams ran a sweepstakes contest mimicking the *Willy Wonka and the Chocolate Factory* movie's Golden Ticket giveaway, only in this case it was a "Golden Key" inside one of ten Cadbury Caramilk Bars with a $250,000 prize for the one key that would unlock the treasure box.[22]

A recent trend in contests is to combine in-store and on-line promotions. For example, Harvey's ran a "Name the Burger Contest" with a prize of $10,000 for the

SOURCE: THE CANADIAN PRESS (STEVE WHITE)

winner. The contest required contestants to visit a Facebook site that presented the contest activity. Contestants were first asked to try Harvey's Premium Burger and then "offer us a name befitting of its flame-grilled perfection along with a compelling reason why." Harvey's said that all names would go to a panel of judges who would select three names to be voted on by the public. If the contestant's name won the vote, he or she would receive a prize of $10,000 cash and free Premium Burgers for a year (awarded in the form of a $2,000 Harvey's gift card).[23]

The effectiveness of a promotion can often be increased by offering several smaller prizes to many winners instead of one huge prize to just one person and also by running it as an annual contest or sweepstakes contest. Tim Hortons "Roll Up the Rim To Win" sweepstakes contest has been ongoing for 25 years and still continues. The contest involves a chance to win a prize ranging from hot drinks or doughnuts to the grand prize of a new automobile. Patrons enter by purchasing large or extra-large hot beverages that come in specially marked cups that may have a prize named under the rim. The contest is so popular that patrons are warned to finish their beverages before checking for their prizes so they don't spill hot beverages on themselves. Tim Hortons produced approximately 280 million contest cups in 2010 and the prize odds were calculated at 1 in 9, which are very good odds considering the number of times people patronize Tim Hortons. At an average of a coffee a day during the 67-day contest period, you could win a prize 7 times. In addition, Tim Hortons reports that 80 percent of the prizes are redeemed—so there are a lot of winning cups that end up being recycled or sent to landfills.[24]

SAMPLING

Distributing samples can often mitigate the risks consumers perceive in trying a new product. As part of its global marketing strategy, Starbucks has aggressively expanded into Asia. A woman in Hong Kong samples a cup of coffee from "Mercury Man," a Starbucks employee who walks around with a pot of coffee on his back.

sampling
A promotional program that allows the consumer to try a product or service for free.

Consumers generally perceive a certain amount of risk in trying new products. Many are afraid of trying something they will not like (such as a new food item) or spending too much money and getting little reward. **Sampling** allows the customer to try a product without risk. Sampling can increase retail sales by as much as 40 percent, and according to one recent survey, 81 percent of Canadians reported that they were more likely buy something they have sampled.[25] Marketers' spending on sampling in North America is significant, with some $2.2 billion spent on this activity in 2009.[26]

Sampling can be accomplished by directly mailing the sample to the customer, delivering the sample door-to-door, packaging the sample with another product, or demonstrating or handing out samples of the product at a retail store or service outlet. Inventa Sales and Promotions was hired by Nestlé Canada to hand out coffee flavoured with liquid Coffee Mate (a new product) to nearly 325,000 Canadian commuters. Nestlé felt that sampling was the key to changing the perception that Coffee Mate was simply a milk substitute. Nestlé wanted to convince people that Coffee Mate was a flavour enhancer on its own and offered a choice of flavours. Innovative research was conducted to measure the effectiveness of the sampling campaign. The research revealed that 64 percent of the people sampled would consider buying Coffee Mate. In contrast, only 22 percent of people who had been exposed to a print campaign but had not tasted a sample said they would consider buying it.[27]

Sampling at special events is a popular, effective, and high-profile distribution method that permits marketers to piggyback onto fun-based consumer activities, including sporting events, campus fests, fairs, festivals, beach events, and chili cook-offs. During the summer of 2010, Riceworks, which makes snacks from natural brown rice, embarked on sampling tour of Ontario to introduce its whole-grain gluten-free Gourmet Brown Rice Crisps. The company decided to take a logo-branded snack trailer to give out samples at summer events like the Taste of Danforth in Toronto and the Burlington Jazz 'n Blues Festival.[28] This method of distributing samples is working. One study found that sampling events produced an average 36 percent increase in sales soon afterward.[29]

Distributing samples to specific types of locations where consumers regularly meet for a common objective or interest, such as health clubs, churches, and doctors' offices, is one of the most efficient methods of sampling. What better way to get consumers to try a product than to offer a sample exactly when it is needed most? Marketers agree that companies must be much more precise in what, where, and how samples are delivered. For example, Banana Boat, which makes sun-protection products, worked with Mama Media Inc., a firm that has developed what it calls its "Campling sampling program, a summer-long campaign that provides free samples to day camps throughout Ontario."[30] The Campling program allowed Banana Boat to distribute samples of full-size bottles of a sunscreen for children, as well as sample sachets, brochures, and coupons.[31] On-line sampling is gaining momentum as Web communities bring together people with common interests in trying new products, often using blogs to spread the word. John Frieda Haircare products used a social-media approach to stage an "Exclusive Sheer Blonde Experience" in 2010. The blonde experience allowed participants to learn how to use the company's products to increase their blondeness, be pampered by a team of hair stylists, and receive free John Frieda products. The firm arranged for street teams to visit shopping malls, commuter collection points, night clubs, and movie premieres to convince blondes to visit the firm's Facebook site to sign up for the event. In addition to the street teams, the company also sponsored on-line banner ads. Blondes who visited the firm's "Canadian Sheer Blonde Facebook" site could participate in the sampling program and enter a contest to win a trip to New York. More than 330 women accepted the invitation.[32]

POINT-OF-PURCHASE PROMOTION

A **point-of-purchase (P-O-P) display** is any display set up at the retailer's location to build traffic, advertise the product, or induce impulse buying. Point-of-purchase promotions include shelf "talkers" (signs attached to store shelves), shelf extenders (attachments that extend shelves so that products stand out), ads on grocery carts and bags, end-aisle and floor-stand displays, TV monitors at supermarket checkout counters, in-store audio messages, and AV displays such as digital signage. One big advantage of P-O-P promotion is that it offers manufacturers a captive audience in retail stores. Another advantage is that about 75 percent of all retail purchase decisions are made in-store, so P-O-P promotions have the potential to be highly effective. In spite of this, only 5 percent of advertising spending is made in-store.[33] P-O-P promotions can increase sales by as much as 65 percent. Strategies to increase sales include adding header or riser cards, changing messages on base or case wraps, adding inflatable or mobile displays, and using signs that advertise the brand's sports, movie, or charity tie-in.[34]

Companies are cashing in on in-store purchasing decisions through more sophisticated P-O-P promotions and by planning new technologies to further increase their effectiveness. Bell Canada developed its own in-store digital signage system in partnership with Convergent Media Systems of Atlanta, Georgia, and Sony of Canada. Bell ran system tests at 12 stores in and around Toronto and discovered that the stores using the digital signage system experienced a 12 percent increase in sales. The digital signs presented a number of ads promoting subscription plans for wireless and home Internet services. The test was judged so successful that Bell Canada decided to install the system in all its stores. Besides promoting its own offerings, Bell also plans to sell ad space on the system to its suppliers.[35]

Digital signage can do much more than simply show ads. Radio frequency identification tags (RFIDs) in products are becoming very common as a means for manufacturers, distributors, and retailers to manage their supply chains. But the RFIDs can also be tied in with in-store digital signage systems for promotional purposes. Say that a person goes through a store with a shopping cart that has a digital sign device and decides to buy a particular brand of cereal. As the person places the cereal in the shopping cart, an instant coupon pops up for the cereal and the digital display presents a reminder that milk goes with cereal. The cereal coupon has been triggered by the RFID tag in the cereal box being purchased. The choice of cereal is being recorded, the cereal's maker is being informed of the choice, and a grocery tally and bill are being recorded for the shopper that already includes all digital coupons presented. Consider the convenience and labour savings as the shopping cart records all your purchases, totals the bill, and even accepts payment. The power of P-O-P promotion is only beginning to approach its zenith.[36]

ON-LINE SALES PROMOTION

On-line sales promotions have been continuing to expand in recent years even as the growth rate of Internet penetration has begun to slow in Canada. Marketers are spending billions of dollars each year on on-line promotions. Sales promotions on-line have proven to be both effective and cost-efficient, generating response rates three to five times higher than their off-line counterparts. The most effective types of on-line sales promotions are free merchandise, sweepstakes contests, free shipping with purchases, and coupons.

Eager to boost traffic, Internet retailers are busy giving away free services, such as travel, or equipment, such as personal computers, to lure consumers not only to their own websites, but to the Internet in general. Another goal is to add potential customers to their databases. For example, East Side Mario's restaurant launched a "Budda Boom Budda Ching" contest for its Canadian patrons that ran from January through March of 2010. The contest was advertised on radio and in magazines and, of course, promoted in the stores and on the firm's Web page. Diners could win instant prizes such as free appetizers or desserts; gift cards from promotion partners; trips; TVs; and minivans. In addition, a PIN code on the bottom of the bill could be entered at Eastsidemarios.com, where patrons were invited to join the firm's Facebook page, which enabled East Side Marios to build its customer database. In fact, this goal was so important that the company set up kiosks in ten of its restaurants so that patrons could enter their PIN codes immediately after dinner, and if the person had a winning code, the kiosks would react like Vegas slot machines so that everyone in the restaurant would know what had happened.[37]

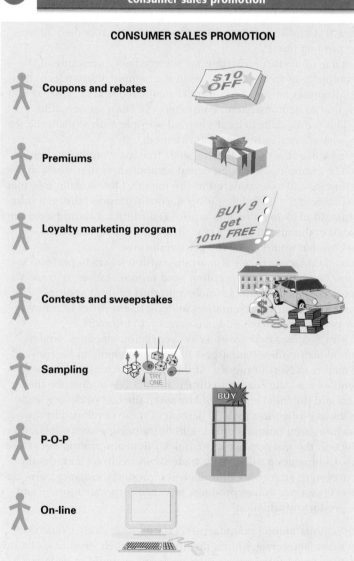

2 Discuss the most common forms of consumer sales promotion

CONSUMER SALES PROMOTION

Coupons and rebates

Premiums

Loyalty marketing program

Contests and sweepstakes

Sampling

P-O-P

On-line

Marketers have discovered that on-line coupon distribution provides another vehicle for promoting their products. On-line coupons often have a redemption rate of more than 20 percent, as much as 10 times higher than for traditional coupons.[38] In fact, nearly 50 percent of consumers who purchase something on-line use a coupon or discount promotional code.[39] The most recent report on Canadian consumers indicates that Canadians visited on-line coupon sites almost 2.6 million times in 2009 and that the following percentages of consumers said they would be likely to download coupons for regularly purchased products such as gasoline (58 percent); groceries (54 percent), on-line restaurants (44 percent), food delivery services (38 percent), consumer electronics (35 percent), hotels (34 percent), and airline flights (34 percent).[40]

On-line versions of loyalty programs are also popping up, and although many types of companies have these programs, the most successful are those run by hotel and airline companies. But other programs such as Cineplex Entertainment's Scene rewards program allows people to earn movie ticket rewards through their movie-going behaviour and their Scotiabank account usage. People can join the program on-line and get a rewards card that allows them to save 10 percent on movie concessions and access to exclusive movie and music promotions. On top of this, members earn points for free movies, free popcorn and concessions, free music, and contest entries for prizes and concert tickets.[41]

More discussion of on-line promotions in marketing is presented later in Chapter 19, Internet Marketing which is found, naturally, on-line.

3 TOOLS FOR TRADE SALES PROMOTION

List the most common forms of trade sales promotion

Whereas consumer promotions *pull* a product through the channel by creating demand, trade promotions *push* a product through the distribution channel (see Chapter 11). When selling to members of the distribution channel, manufacturers use many of the same sales promotion tools used in consumer promotions—such as sales contests, premiums, point-of-purchase displays, and so forth. Several tools, however, are unique to manufacturers and intermediaries:

- *Trade allowances.* A **trade allowance** is a price reduction offered by manufacturers to intermediaries such as wholesalers and retailers. The price reduction or rebate is given in exchange for doing something specific, such as allocating space for a new product or buying something during special periods. A local dealer could receive a special discount for running its own promotion on Telus Mobility phones.
- *Push money.* Intermediaries receive **push money** as a bonus for pushing the manufacturer's brand through the distribution channel. Often the push money is directed toward a retailer's salespeople. LinoColor, the leading high-end scanner company, produces a Picture Perfect Rewards catalogue filled with merchandise that retailers can purchase with points accrued for every LinoColor scanner they sell. The cover of the catalogue features a personal watercraft that was brought to three industry trade shows and given away in a sweepstakes to one of the dealers who had visited all the product displays and passed a quiz. The program resulted in a 26 percent increase in LinoColor sales, and the manufacturer recruited 32 new dealers to carry the product line.[42]
- *Training.* Sometimes a manufacturer will train an intermediary's personnel if the product is rather complex—as frequently occurs in the computer and telecommunications industries. Representatives of a computer manufacturer like Toshiba may train salespeople in how to demonstrate to consumers the latest models of its laptop computers. This is especially helpful when salespeople must explain the features to consumers who are not technologically oriented.
- *Free merchandise.* Often a manufacturer offers retailers free merchandise in lieu of quantity discounts. For example, a breakfast cereal manufacturer may throw in one case of free cereal for every 20 cases ordered by the retailer. Occasionally, free merchandise is used as payment for trade allowances normally provided through other sales promotions. Instead of giving a retailer a price reduction for buying a certain quantity of merchandise, the manufacturer may throw in extra merchandise "free"—that is, at a cost that would equal the price reduction.
- *Instore demonstrations.* Manufacturers can also arrange with retailers to perform instore demonstrations. Food manufacturers often send representatives to grocery stores and supermarkets to let customers sample a product while shopping. Cosmetics companies send their representatives to department stores to promote their beauty aids by performing facials and makeovers for customers.
- *Business meetings, conventions, and trade shows.* Trade association meetings, conferences, and conventions are an important aspect of sales promotion and a growing, multibillion-dollar market in North America. At these shows, manufacturers, distributors, and other vendors have the chance to display their goods or describe their services to customers and potential customers. Moreover, the cost of closing leads generated at trade shows is often less than 50 percent of those developed in the field.[43] Trade shows have been uniquely effective in introducing new products; they can establish products in the marketplace more quickly than advertising, direct marketing, or sales calls. Companies participate in trade shows to attract and identify new prospects, serve current customers, introduce new products, enhance corporate image, test the market response to new products, enhance corporate morale, and gather competitive product information.

Trade promotions are popular among manufacturers for many reasons. Trade sales promotion tools help manufacturers gain new distributors for their products, obtain wholesaler and retailer support for consumer sales promotions, build or reduce dealer inventories, and improve trade relations. Car manufacturers annually sponsor dozens of auto shows for consumers. Many of the displays feature interactive computer stations where consumers enter vehicle specifications and get a printout of prices and local dealer names. In return, the local car dealers get the names of good prospects. The shows attract millions of consumers, providing dealers with increased store traffic as well as good leads. Read the case about the annual North American International Auto Show at the end of this chapter to get a feel for the impact of auto shows.

3 **List the most common forms of trade sales promotion**

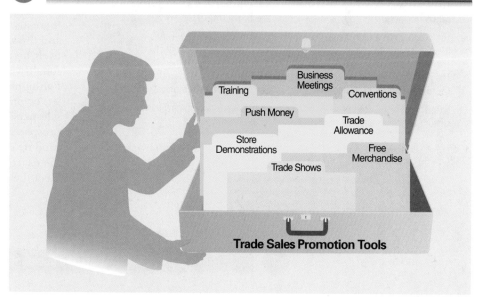

Trade Sales Promotion Tools

4 PERSONAL SELLING

Describe personal selling

personal selling
A purchase situation in which two people communicate in an attempt to influence each other.

Personal selling is direct communication between a sales representative and one or more prospective buyers in which each attempts to influence the other.

In a sense, all businesspeople are salespeople. An individual may become a plant manager, a chemist, an engineer, or a member of any profession and yet still have to sell. During a job search, applicants must "sell" themselves to prospective employers in an interview. To reach the top in most organizations, individuals need to sell ideas to peers, superiors, and subordinates. Most important, people must sell themselves and their ideas to just about everyone with whom they have a continuing relationship and to many other people they see only once or twice. Chances are that students majoring in business or marketing will start their professional careers in sales. Even students in nonbusiness majors may pursue a sales career.

Personal selling offers several advantages over other forms of promotion:

- Personal selling provides a detailed explanation or demonstration of the product. This capability is especially needed for complex or new goods and services.
- The sales message can be varied according to the motivations and interests of each prospective customer. Moreover, when the prospect has questions or raises objections, the salesperson is there to provide explanations. In contrast, advertising and sales promotion can respond only to the objections the copywriter thinks are important to customers.
- Personal selling can be directed only at qualified prospects. Other forms of promotion include some unavoidable waste because many people in the audience are not prospective customers.
- Personal selling costs can be controlled by adjusting the size of the sales force (and resulting expenses) in one-person increments. On the other hand, advertising and sales promotion must often be purchased in fairly large amounts.
- Perhaps the most important advantage is that personal selling is considerably more effective than other forms of promotion in obtaining a sale and gaining a satisfied customer.

Personal selling may often work better than other forms of promotion given certain customer and product characteristics. Generally, personal selling becomes more

Exhibit 15.2

Comparison of Personal Selling and Advertising/Sales Promotion

Personal selling is more important if . . .	Advertising and sales promotion are more important if . . .
The product has a high value. It is a custom-made product. There are few customers. The product is technically complex. Customers are concentrated.	The product has a low value. It is a standardized product. There are many customers. The product is easy to understand. Customers are geographically dispersed.
Examples: insurance policies, custom windows, airplane engines	**Examples:** soap, magazine subscriptions, cotton T-shirts

SOURCE: From Sales Promotion Essentials, 2nd ed., by Don E. Schultz, William A. Robinson, and Lisa A. Petrison. © 1998 The McGraw-Hill Companies, Inc.

important as the number of potential customers decreases, as the complexity of the product increases, and as the value of the product grows (see Exhibit 15.2). When there are relatively few potential customers and the value of the good or service is relatively high, the time and travel costs of personally visiting each prospect are justifiable. For highly complex goods, such as business jets or private communication systems, a salesperson is needed to determine the prospective customer's needs, explain the product's basic advantages, and propose the exact features and accessories that will meet the client's needs.

REVIEW LEARNING OUTCOME 4

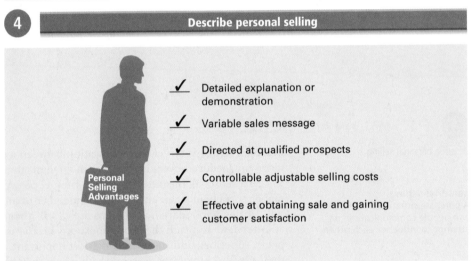

4 Describe personal selling

Personal Selling Advantages

✓ Detailed explanation or demonstration

✓ Variable sales message

✓ Directed at qualified prospects

✓ Controllable adjustable selling costs

✓ Effective at obtaining sale and gaining customer satisfaction

5 RELATIONSHIP SELLING

Discuss the key differences between relationship selling and traditional selling

relationship selling (consultative selling)
A sales practice that involves building, maintaining, and enhancing interactions with customers in order to develop long-term satisfaction through mutually beneficial partnerships.

Until recently, marketing theory and practice concerning personal selling focused almost entirely on a planned presentation to prospective customers for the sole purpose of making the sale. In contrast, modern views of personal selling emphasize the relationship that develops between a salesperson and a buyer. **Relationship selling**, or **consultative selling**, is a multistage process that emphasizes personalization and empathy as key ingredients in identifying prospects and developing them as long-term, satisfied customers. The old way was all about "selling a product," but with relationship selling the objective is to build long-term branded relationships with consumers and buyers.[44] Thus, the focus is on building mutual trust between the buyer and seller through the delivery of anticipated, long-term, value-added benefits to the buyer.

Relationship or consultative salespeople, therefore, become consultants, partners, and problem solvers for their customers. They strive to build long-term relationships with key accounts by developing trust over time. The emphasis shifts from a one-time sale to a long-term relationship in which the salesperson works with the customer to develop solutions for enhancing the customer's bottom line. Moreover, research has shown that a positive customer–salesperson relationship contributes to trust, increased customer loyalty, and the customer's intention to continue the relationship with the salesperson.[45] Thus relationship selling promotes a win–win situation for both buyer and seller.

Acclivus (**www.acclivus.com**) provides training in consultative selling, a multistage process focusing on developing trust over time; relationship selling emphasizes a win–win outcome.

The result of relationship selling tends to be loyal customers who purchase from the company time after time. Because a relationship-selling strategy focuses on retaining customers, it costs a firm less than when the firm is constantly prospecting and selling to new customers. Companies that focus on customer retention through high customer service gain 6 percent market share per year, while companies that offer low customer service *lose* 2 percent market share per year. In fact, it typically costs businesses six times more to gain a new customer than to retain a current one.[46]

Relationship selling is more typical with selling situations for industrial-type goods such as heavy machinery or computer systems, and services, such as airlines and insurance, than for consumer goods.[47] "Webinars" (on-line seminars lasting about an hour) are becoming an increasingly popular way to support relationship selling tasks such as lead generation, client support, sales training, and corporate meetings. 3Com, a computer data networking system, held a webinar that was attended by 1,300 executives in 80 countries; the session generated 60 percent of 3Com's five-month lead generation goals.[48]

Exhibit 15.3 lists the key differences between traditional personal selling and relationship or consultative selling. These differences will become more apparent as we explore the personal selling process later in the chapter.

EXHIBIT 15.3

Key Differences Between Traditional Selling and Relationship Selling

Traditional personal selling	Relationship or consultative selling
Sell products (goods and services)	Sell advice, assistance, and counsel
Focus on closing sales	Focus on improving the customer's bottom line
Limited sales planning	Consider sales planning as top priority
Spend most contact time telling customers about product	Spend most contact time attempting to build a problem-solving environment with the customer
Conduct "product specific" needs assessment	Conduct discovery in the full scope of the customer's operations
"Lone wolf" approach to the account	Team approach to the account
Proposals and presentations based on pricing and product features	Proposals and presentations based on profit impact and strategic benefits to the customer
Sales follow-up is short term, focused on product delivery	Sales follow-up is long term, focused on long-term relationship enhancement

SOURCE: Robert M. Peterson, Patrick L. Schul, and George H. Lucas, Jr., "Consultative Selling: Walking the Walk in the New Selling Environment," National Conference on Sales Management, Proceedings, March 1996

REVIEW LEARNING OUTCOME 5

5 **Discuss the key differences between relationship selling and traditional selling**

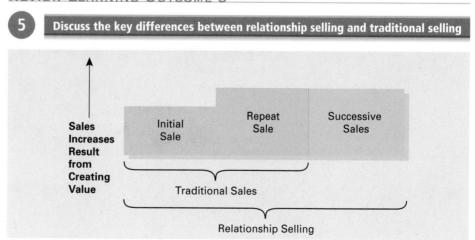

6 STEPS IN THE SELLING PROCESS

List the steps in the selling process

sales process (sales cycle)
The set of steps a salesperson goes through in a particular organization to sell a particular product or service.

Although personal selling may sound like a relatively simple task, completing a sale actually requires several steps. The **sales process**, or **sales cycle**, is simply the set of steps a salesperson goes through to sell a particular product or service. The sales process or cycle can be unique for each product or service depending on the features of the product or service, characteristics of customer segments, and internal processes in place within the firm, such as how leads are gathered.

Some sales take only a few minutes; others may take much longer to complete. Sales of technical products, such as a Boeing or Airbus airplane, and of customized goods and services typically take many months, perhaps even years, to complete. On the other end of the spectrum, sales of less technical products such as copy machines and office supplies are generally more routine and may take only a few days. Whether a salesperson spends a few minutes or a few years on a sale, these are the seven basic steps in the personal selling process:

1. Generating leads

2. Qualifying leads

3. Approaching the customer and probing needs

4. Developing and proposing solutions

5. Handling objections

6. Closing the sale

7. Following up

Like other forms of promotion, these steps of selling follow the AIDA concept discussed in Chapter 13. Once a salesperson has located a prospect with the authority to buy, he or she tries to get the prospect's attention. A thorough needs assessment turned into an effective sales proposal and presentation should generate interest. After developing the customer's initial desire (preferably during the presentation of the sales proposal), the salesperson seeks action at the close by trying to get an agreement to buy. Following up after the sale, the final step in the selling process, not only lowers cognitive dissonance (refer to Chapter 4) but may also open up opportunities to discuss future sales. Effective follow-up will also lead to repeat business, at which time the process may start all over again at the needs assessment step.

Traditional selling and relationship selling follow the same basic steps. They differ in the relative importance placed on key steps in the process (see Exhibit 15.4). Traditional selling efforts are transaction oriented, focusing on generating as many leads as possible, making as many presentations as possible, and closing as many sales as possible. Minimal effort is placed on asking questions to identify customer needs and wants or on matching those needs and wants to the benefits of the product or

EXHIBIT 15.4

Relative Amount of Time Spent in Key Steps of the Selling Process

Key Selling Steps	Traditional Selling	Relationship/Consultative Selling
Generating leads	High	Low
Qualifying leads	Low	High
Approaching the customer and probing needs	Low	High
Developing and proposing solutions	Low	High
Handling objections	High	Low
Closing the sale	High	Low
Following up	Low	High

Customer Experience

 THE SEVEN SINS OF SALESPEOPLE?

Virtually every consumer and every business buyer has a negative story about an encounter with a salesperson to tell. It may go something like this: "So many salespeople are idiots these days. I went to this car dealership and this salesperson walked by and just ignored me even though I asked her for help to take a test drive. She said she was waiting on another customer and would be right back to help me soon. I waited over 20 minutes and she didn't come back. Naturally, I left the showroom and went to another car dealer where they weren't too busy to sell me a car!"

On the other side, virtually every salesperson has story about an unpleasant customer they had to deal with. It might go something like this: "Some customers are so rude and difficult to deal with. I was working in the car dealership and checking some inventory for a customer who was ready to make a deal. She wanted to know if I could get her a sky-blue colour in the model she wanted to buy. I left my office cubicle to check our central computer when I was suddenly approached by another customer on the floor. The person said they were in a hurry and wanted to go for a test drive. He just expected me to drop everything I was doing and give him the keys to a car. I told the gentleman that I was currently working with another customer and that I would be happy to find another sales associate to help him. He just huffed at me, then made some remark that nobody cares anymore and walked away. I actually felt threatened and went to see my sales manager to report the problem."

You can probably think of a couple of your own stories of negative encounters with salespeople. No matter what perspective you take, buyer or seller, almost all of these stories have one theme in common: the sale did not work out very well for either of the parties. As long as humans are involved in selling, it is likely there will be be some negative stories to tell. Maura Schreier-Fleming of Best@Selling (http://www.bestatselling.com) has identified a list of seven common mistakes that salespeople make, all of which could become the topic of the latest watercooler discussion of why salespeople are idiots.

The seven mistakes made by salespeople are these:

1. *Thinking you can do it all by yourself.* Schreier-Fleming observes that teamwork in selling is very common these days. Organized salespeople know that each step in the sales process is a specialized task that could be delegated or shared with others.
2. *Talking too much.* Salespeople need to listen far more than they talk. How can you determine what a person wants or needs unless you listen? Salespeople need to be good communicators and this requires the ability to speak well. Good communication is two-way and you need to let the customer do the talking to start with.
3. *Doing the same thing in all situations.* Many salespeople have developed a specific selling routine for their products. This might be appropriate for the majority of the customers but a salesperson needs to adapt. They need to read the situation and the personality of the customer they are dealing with.

Some customers are assertive and know what they want while others are more shy and reserved. You can't use the same selling approach and opening with these different kinds of people. Even your greeting may have to be different depending on the person. Saying good day to a person who appears emotionally upset might be the wrong thing.

4. *Expecting things to happen now.* Many salespeople are paid on commissions and their incentive programs are tied to monthly or weekly sales programs. This means they are encouraged to concentrate on buyers who are close to making a purchase. Buyers who are deliberating will demand a lot of time right now but won't be buying till later. Many salespeople lack the patience to understand that some processes just can't be rushed. They may not want to invest the time in a buyer who is in the early stage of information search, much preferring to deal with a customer who is in the final stage of making a decision.
5. *Not telling the truth.* It goes without saying that salespeople need to be honest with customers and provide complete and proper information. A good reputation is essential for any salesperson who wants a long career. Customers aside, salespeople need to be honest with themselves. Very often a salesperson may impose their wishful thinking on how close a prospect is to making a purchase. They may spend an inordinate amount of time trying to convince a customer to buy or chasing down potential customers who provided weak signals in an earlier sales encounter. Pressure from their sales managers may cause them to indicate they are close to making a sale when they are not. They need to move on to prospects who have real potential.
6. *Not taking good care of customers.* A great deal of successful selling comes from repeat business with customers who have bought from you before. You need to stay in touch with them and follow up with them after they have made a purchase. If you don't follow up when they have a problem, they will feel you don't care about them and they will feel like victims and not customers. In addition, during the selling process, you need to subordinate your desire to make a sale in favour of meeting the customer's needs for making the purchase. When customers raise objections, you need to listen and address them and not tell them that they are being silly.
7. *Thinking it's easy to sell.* Selling is a process that must be planned out and involves a great deal of preparation. It involves learning about your own products and also about your competitor's products. It means researching the market and the needs and wants of your customers. It means looking at the selling process and relating it to the business you are working in. Finally, it means reviewing your experiences as a salesperson so that you can learn what worked and what didn't.[49]

So how can salespeople avoid making these kinds of mistakes? Discuss what good can come from customers' and salespeople's "horror" stories.

SOURCE: MAURA SCHREIER-FLEMING, "7 HABITS OF LESS SUCCESSFUL SALESPEOPLE," MLM KNOWHOW, HTTP://WWW.MLMKNOWHOW.COM/ARTICLES/MARKETING/7HABITSLESS.HTM, ACCESSED NOVEMBER 5, 2010.

service. In contrast, salespeople who practise relationship selling emphasize an up-front investment in the time and effort needed to uncover each customer's specific needs and wants and match them as closely as possible to the product or service offering. By doing their homework up front, relationship salespeople create the conditions necessary for a relatively straightforward close. Let's look at each step of the selling process individually.

GENERATING LEADS

lead generation (prospecting)
Identification of those companies and people most likely to buy the seller's offerings.

Initial groundwork must precede communication between the potential buyer and the salesperson. **Lead generation**, or **prospecting**, involves identifying those companies and people most likely to buy the seller's offerings. These firms or people become "sales leads" or "prospects."

Sales leads can be obtained in several different ways, most notably through advertising, trade shows and conventions, or direct mail and telemarketing programs. One accounting firm used direct mail, telephone, sales visits, and seminars in a four-step process aimed at generating business-to-business leads. The initial step was a direct-mail piece, in the form of an introductory letter from a firm partner. The second piece, sent one month later, was a black and white direct-mail circular with company contact information. The third step was a follow-up call from a firm partner to arrange a meeting. In the last stage, partners contacted prospects who had initially declined appointments and invited them to attend a free tax seminar the following month. Of the 1,100 businesses targeted, 200 prospects set up meetings. Favourable publicity also helps create leads. Company records of past client purchases are another excellent source of leads. Many sales professionals also secure valuable leads from their company's website. For example, Chrysler's use of interactive media to create ongoing interaction with on-line consumers is paying off. The company recently sponsored 42 on-line video games featuring Chrysler, Jeep, and Dodge vehicles, generating more than 10,000 sales leads among the estimated 3.5 million consumers who downloaded the games. The company generates an estimated 40,000 sales leads monthly through its website and other on-line venues.[50]

referral
A recommendation to a salesperson from a customer or business associate.

networking
A process of finding out about potential clients from friends, business contacts, co-workers, acquaintances, and fellow members in professional and civic organizations.

Another way to gather a lead is through a **referral**—a recommendation from a customer or business associate. The advantages of referrals over other forms of prospecting include highly qualified leads, higher closing rates, larger initial transactions, and shorter sales cycles. Simply put, the salesperson and the company can earn more money in less time when prospecting using referrals. Referrals typically are as much as ten times more productive in generating sales than are cold calls. Unfortunately, although most clients are willing to give referrals, many salespeople do not ask for them. Effective sales training can help overcome this reluctance to ask for referrals. To increase the number of referrals they receive, some firms pay or send small gifts to customers or suppliers who provide referrals.

Networking is using friends, business contacts, co-workers, acquaintances, and fellow members in professional and civic organizations to identify potential clients. Indeed, a number of national networking clubs have been started for the sole purpose of generating leads and providing valuable business advice. The networking clubs usually have between 15 and 30 members in noncompeting business categories. During weekly breakfast or lunch meetings, each member is allowed to talk about the company he or she represents for an allotted period of time. Then members exchange lead cards. Research suggests that on average, chapter members see an increase in business volume between 16 and 25 percent after they've been with their group for three to six months. Increasingly, sales professionals are also using on-line networking sites such as Ryze, LinkedIn, and The Ladders to connect with targeted leads and clients around the world 24 hours a day. Some of LinkedIn's estimated 4.8 million

Networking is being transformed by the Internet. Sites like LinkedIn connect the contact lists of thousands of users, creating easily navigable networks made up of millions of people working in nearly every industry.

users have reported response rates between 50 and 60 percent, versus 3 percent from direct marketing efforts.[51]

Before the advent of more sophisticated methods of lead generation, such as direct mail and telemarketing, most prospecting was done through **cold calling**—a form of lead generation in which the salesperson approaches potential buyers without any prior knowledge of the prospects' needs or financial status. Although this method is still used, many sales managers have realized the inefficiencies of having their top salespeople use their valuable selling time searching for the proverbial needle in a haystack. Passing the job of cold calling to a lower cost employee—typically an internal sales support person—allows salespeople to spend more time with and use their relationship-building skills on prospects that have already been identified. Sales experts note that the days of cold calls and unannounced office visits have given way to referral-based and relationship selling.[52]

QUALIFYING LEADS

When a prospect shows interest in learning more about a product, the salesperson has the opportunity to follow up, or qualify, the lead. Personally visiting unqualified prospects wastes valuable time and company resources. Often many leads go unanswered because salespeople are given no indication as to how qualified the leads are with regard to interest and ability to purchase. Unqualified prospects give vague or incomplete answers to a salesperson's specific questions, try to evade questions on budgets, and request changes in standard procedures like prices or terms of sale. In contrast, qualified leads are strong prospects that answer questions, value your time, and are realistic about money and when they are prepared to buy. Salespeople who are given accurate information on qualified leads are more than twice as likely to follow up.[53]

Lead qualification consists of determining whether the prospect has three things: a recognized need, willingness to see a salesperson, and buying power. Lead qualification is often handled by a telemarketing group or a sales support person who prequalifies the lead for the salesperson. But companies are increasingly using websites to qualify leads. When leads are qualified on-line, companies want visitors to register, indicate the products and services they are interested in, and provide information on their time frame and resources. Leads from the Internet can then be prioritized (those indicating a short time frame, for instance, given a higher priority) and then transferred to salespeople. Often website visitors can be enticed to answer questions with offers of free merchandise or information. Enticing visitors to register also enables companies to customize future electronic interactions—for example, by giving prospects who visit the website their choice from a menu of products tailored specifically to their needs.

APPROACHING THE CUSTOMER AND PROBING NEEDS

Before approaching the customer, the salesperson should learn as much as possible about the prospect's organization and its buyers. This process, called the **preapproach**, describes the "homework" that must be done by the salesperson before contacting the prospect. This may include consulting standard reference sources, such as company websites, websites like Profile Canada, and sources like *Fraser's Canadian Trade Directory*, the *Canadian Trade Index*, or D&B Canada (formerly Dun & Bradstreet Canada), or contacting acquaintances or others who may have information about the prospect. Another preapproach task is to determine whether the actual approach should be a personal visit, a phone call, a letter, an e-mail, or some other form of communication.

During the sales approach, the salesperson either talks to the prospect or secures an appointment for a future time in which to probe the prospect further as to his or her needs. Relationship selling theorists suggest that salespeople should begin developing mutual trust with their prospect during the approach. Salespeople should use the approach to introduce themselves and their company and products. They must sell themselves before they can sell the product. Small talk that introduces sincerity and some suggestion of friendship is encouraged because it builds rapport with the prospect, but remarks that could be construed as insincere should be avoided.

needs assessment
A determination of the customer's specific needs and wants and the range of options the customer has for satisfying them.

The salesperson's ultimate goal during the approach is to conduct a **needs assessment** in order to learn as much as possible about the prospect's situation. This involves interviewing the customer to determine his or her specific needs and wants and the range of options the customer has for satisfying them. The salesperson should be determining how to maximize the fit between what he or she can offer and what the prospective customer wants. In conducting a needs assessment, consultative salespeople learn about the product or service, the customers and their needs, the competition, and the industry. Using this information, the salesperson can create a customer profile.

Creating a *customer profile* during the approach helps salespeople optimize their time and resources. This profile is then used to develop an intelligent analysis of the prospect's needs in preparation for the next step, developing and proposing solutions. Customer profile information is typically stored and manipulated using sales force automation software packages designed for use on laptop computers. Sales force automation software provides sales reps with a computerized and efficient method of collecting customer information for use during the entire sales process. Further, customer and sales data stored in a computer database can be easily shared among sales team members. The information can be appended with industry statistics, sales or meeting notes, billing data, and other information that may be pertinent to the prospect or the prospect's company. The more salespeople know about their prospects, the better they can meet their needs.

DEVELOPING AND PROPOSING SOLUTIONS

Once the salesperson has gathered the appropriate information about the client's needs and wants, the next step is to determine whether his or her company's products or services match the needs of the prospective customer. The salesperson then develops a solution, or possibly several solutions, in which the salesperson's product or service solves the client's problems or meets a specific need.

sales proposal
A formal written document or professional presentation that outlines how the salesperson's product or service will meet or exceed the prospect's needs.

sales presentation
A formal meeting in which the salesperson presents a sales proposal to a prospective buyer.

These solutions are typically presented to the client in the form of a **sales proposal** presented at a **sales presentation**. A sales proposal is a written document or professional presentation that outlines how the company's product or service will meet or exceed the client's needs. The sales presentation is the formal meeting during which the salesperson has the opportunity to present the sales proposal. The presentation should be explicitly tied to the prospect's expressed needs. Further, the prospect should be involved in the presentation by being encouraged to participate in demonstrations or by exposure to computer exercises, slides, video or audio, flipcharts, photographs, and the like.

Technology has become an important part of presenting solutions. Pen manufacturer Bic uses the Internet to connect with its wholesale and convenience store customers. Before launching **BIClink.com**, Bic received 80 percent of its order volume by fax. Processing these orders was time consuming, and the orders often were filled with errors. BIClink.com has eliminated the potential for errors and made it easier and faster to validate purchase order numbers, ship dates, case quantities, and pricing. When customers sign on (through a secure, password-protected system), the welcome screen is personalized with their company's name and the name of their Bic rep. On placing an order, customers receive both hard copy and an e-mail confirmation, complete with the salesperson's name and contact information, including e-mail, voice-mail, phone, and fax numbers. Virtually all of Bic's customers now order on-line.[54]

Because the salesperson often has only one opportunity to present solutions, the quality of both the sales proposal and presentation can make or break the sale. Salespeople must be able to present the proposal and handle any customer objections confidently and professionally. For a powerful presentation, salespeople must be well prepared, use direct eye contact, ask open-ended questions, be poised, use hand gestures and voice inflection, focus on the customer's needs, incorporate visual elements that impart valuable information, know how to operate the audio/visual or computer equipment being used for the presentation, make sure the equipment works, and practise, practise, practise.[55] Nothing turns a potential customer off faster than a boring presentation. If the salesperson doesn't have a convincing and confident manner, the prospect will very often forget the information. Prospects take in body

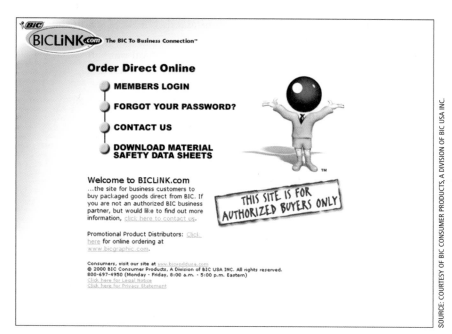

Part of the selling process involves proposing solutions to resolve difficulties customers are having. Bic used the Internet to streamline the order process for its wholesale and convenience store customers. The result was BICLink.com.

language, voice patterns, dress, and body type. Customers are more likely to remember how salespeople present themselves rather than what they say.

HANDLING OBJECTIONS

Rarely does a prospect say "I'll buy it" right after a presentation. Instead, the prospect often raises objections or asks questions about the proposal and the product. The potential buyer may insist that the price is too high, that he or she does not have enough information to make a decision, or that the good or service will not satisfy the present need. The buyer may also lack confidence in the seller's organization or product.

One of the first lessons every salesperson learns is that objections to the product should not be taken personally as confrontations or insults. Rather, salespeople should view objections as requests for information. A good salesperson considers objections a legitimate part of the purchase decision. To handle objections effectively, the salesperson should anticipate specific objections, such as concerns about price, fully investigate the objection with the customer, be aware of what the competition is offering, and, above all, stay calm. For example, ever since the release of the 2006 film *Blood Diamond* (a story of how diamond sales are used to buy arms to fund African warlords), jewellery salespeople in Canada have been trained to handle concerns about the source of the diamonds in the products they sell. South African diamond producer De Beers provides advice to salespeople. One business journalist reports the company does this "by offering an organized chart of positive messages that completely removes the words conflict or blood from the discussion. . . . 'Revenues from the diamond trade,' De Beers states, 'have helped fund the construction of hospitals, medical centres and hospices, ensuring that more than five million people in Southern Africa have access to appropriate healthcare.'"[56]

Zig Ziglar, a renowned sales trainer, created a popular method for handling objections: "When an objection occurs, always use the fundamentals of FEEL, FELT, FOUND. It gives you an extra cushion of time and allows the prospect to identify with others." For example: "I see how you FEEL! Others have FELT the same way too until they FOUND. . . ." Imagine a copy machine salesperson pitching a new copier to a doctor. The doctor might say, "The copy machine seems to be very expensive." Using the Zig Ziglar method, the salesperson would respond: "I see how you feel. Other doctors have felt the same way until they found out how much money they were saving after the first year."[57]

Often the salesperson can use the objection to close the sale. If the customer tries to pit suppliers against one another to drive down the price, the salesperson should be prepared to point out weaknesses in the competitor's offer and stand by the quality in his or her own proposal.

CLOSING THE SALE

At the end of the presentation, the salesperson should ask the customer how he or she wants to proceed. If the customer exhibits signs that he or she is ready to purchase and that all questions have been answered and objections have been met, the salesperson can try to close the sale. Customers often give signals during or after the presentation that they are either ready to buy or are not interested. Examples include changes in facial expression, gestures, and questions asked. The salesperson should look for these signals and respond appropriately.

Closing requires courage and skill. Naturally, the salesperson wants to avoid rejection, and asking for a sale carries with it the risk of a negative answer. A salesperson should keep an open mind when asking for the sale and be prepared for either a yes or a no answer. Rarely is a sale closed on the first call. In fact, the typical salesperson makes several hundred sales calls a year, many of which are repeat calls to the same client in an attempt to make the sale. Some salespeople may negotiate with large accounts for several years before closing a sale. As you can see, building a good relationship with the customer is very important. Often, if the salesperson has developed a strong relationship with the customer, only minimal efforts are needed to close a sale.

Negotiation often plays a key role in the closing of the sale. Negotiation is the process during which both the salesperson and the prospect offer special concessions in an attempt to arrive at a sales agreement. For example, the salesperson may offer a price cut, free installation, free service, or a trial order. Effective negotiators, however, avoid using price as a negotiation tool because cutting price directly affects a company's profitability. Because companies spend millions on advertising and product development to create value, when salespeople give in to price negotiations too quickly it decreases the value of the product. Instead, effective salespeople should emphasize value to the customer, rendering price a nonissue. Salespeople should also be prepared to ask for tradeoffs and try to avoid giving unilateral concessions. If you're making only a 30 percent margin on a product, and you need at least a 40 percent margin, raise your prices or drop the product. Moreover, if the customer asks for a 5 percent discount, the salesperson should ask for something in return, such as higher volume or more flexibility in delivery schedules.

FOLLOWING UP

Unfortunately, many salespeople hold the attitude that making the sale is all that's important. Once the sale is made, they think, they can forget about their customers. They are wrong. Salespeople's responsibilities do not end with making the sale and placing the order. One of the most important aspects of their jobs is **follow-up**—the final step in the delivery process, in which they must ensure that delivery schedules are met, that the goods or services perform as promised, and that the buyers' employees are properly trained to use the products.

In the traditional sales approach, follow-up is generally limited to successful product delivery and performance. A basic goal of relationship selling is to motivate customers to return again and again, by developing and nurturing long-term relationships. Most businesses depend on repeat sales, and repeat sales depend on thorough and continued follow-up by the salesperson. Finding a new customer is far more expensive than retaining an existing customer. When customers feel abandoned, cognitive dissonance arises and repeat sales decline. Today, this issue is more pertinent than ever because customers are far less loyal to brands and vendors. Buyers are more inclined to look for the best deal, especially in the case of poor after-the-sale follow-up. More and more buyers favour building a relationship with sellers.

Automated e-mail follow-up marketing—a combination of sales automation and Internet technology—is enhancing customer satisfaction as well as bringing in more business for some marketers. Here's how it works: After the initial contact with a prospect, a software program automatically sends a series of personalized e-mails over a period of time. For example, after a person books a trip with on-line travel agency Expedia.ca, they get an immediate e-mail contact. The e-mail thanks the person for the booking, provides them with details of the trip, and provides a link to an itinerary page to check for changes. The e-mail also contains information asking what else the travel agency can help with and presents services like shuttles from the airport or attraction tickets. Expedia.ca also monitors the booking arrangements from the airlines, hotels, and car rental agencies that have been selected and automatically updates their clients if there has been any change in travel times or other arrangements. Finally, the service will keep track of your favourite destinations and send you e-mails when there are any special trips available.[58]

negotiation
The process during which both the salesperson and the prospect offer special concessions in an attempt to arrive at a sales agreement.

follow-up
The final step of the selling process, in which the salesperson ensures that delivery schedules are met, that the goods or services perform as promised, and that the buyers' employees are properly trained to use the products.

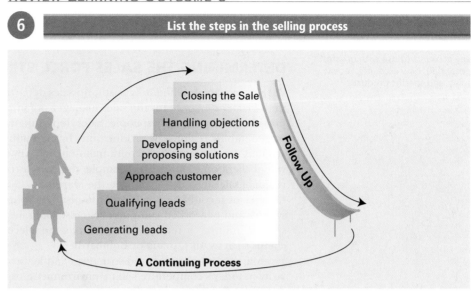

6   List the steps in the selling process

Closing the Sale

Handling objections

Developing and proposing solutions

Approach customer

Qualifying leads

Generating leads

Follow Up

A Continuing Process

7 SALES MANAGEMENT

Describe the functions of sales management

There is an old adage in business that nothing happens until a sale is made. Without sales there is no need for accountants, production workers, or even a company president. Sales provide the fuel that keeps the corporate engines humming. Companies like Bombardier, Magna Corporation, and Cisco Systems Canada, and hundreds of other large Canadian manufacturers, would cease to exist without successful salespeople. Even companies like Procter & Gamble Canada and Kraft General Foods Canada, which mainly sell consumer goods and use extensive advertising campaigns, still rely on salespeople to move products through the channel of distribution. Thus sales management is one of marketing's most critical specialties. Effective sales management stems from a highly success-oriented sales force that accomplishes its mission economically and efficiently. Poor sales management can lead to unmet profit objectives or even to the downfall of the company.

Just as selling is a personal relationship, so is sales management. Although the sales manager's basic job is to maximize sales at a reasonable cost while also maximizing profits, he or she has many other important responsibilities and decisions:

1. Defining sales goals and the sales process

2. Determining the sales force structure

3. Recruiting and training the sales force

4. Compensating and motivating the sales force

5. Supervising the sales force

6. Evaluating the sales force

DEFINING SALES GOALS AND THE SALES PROCESS

Effective sales management begins with a determination of sales goals. Without goals to achieve, a salesperson's performance will be mediocre at best, and the company will likely fail. Like any marketing objective, sales goals should be stated in clear, precise, and measurable terms and should always specify a time frame for their fulfillment. Overall sales force goals are usually stated in terms of desired dollar sales volume, market share, or profit level. For example, a life insurance company may have a goal to sell $50 million in life insurance policies annually, to attain a 12 percent market share, or to achieve $1 million in profits. Individual salespeople are also assigned goals

quota
A statement of the individual salesperson's sales objectives, usually based on sales volume alone but sometimes including key accounts (those with greatest potential), new accounts, repeat sales, and specific products.

in the form of quotas. A **quota** is simply a statement of the salesperson's sales goals, usually based on sales volume alone but sometimes including key accounts (those with greatest potential), new accounts, repeat sales, and specific products.

DETERMINING THE SALES FORCE STRUCTURE

Because personal selling is so costly, no sales department can afford to be disorganized. Proper design helps the sales manager organize and delegate sales duties and provide direction for salespeople. Sales departments are most commonly organized by geographic regions, by product line, by marketing function performed (such as account development or account maintenance), by market or industry, or by individual client or account. For example, the sales force for IBM could be organized into regional sales territories covering the Maritimes, Quebec, Ontario, and Western Canada, or it could be organized into distinct groups selling personal computer systems and networked computer systems. IBM salespeople may also be assigned to a specific industry or market—for example, the telecommunications industry—or to key clients such as Air Canada or Bombardier.

Market- or industry-based structures and key account structures are gaining popularity in today's competitive selling environment, especially with the emphasis on relationship selling. Being familiar with one industry or market allows sales reps to become experts in their fields and thereby offer better solutions and service. Further, by organizing the sales force around specific customer types, many companies hope to improve customer service, encourage collaboration with other arms of the company, and unite salespeople in customer-focused sales teams. The Royal Bank of Canada provides a variety of products and services under the categories of creditor, life, health, travel, home, auto, and reinsurance and serves more than 1 million clients worldwide. Consequently, the Royal Bank uses a number of sales and distribution channels such as the telephone, independent brokers, travel agents, an in-house sales force, and the Internet to better serve the diverse needs of its many clients.[59]

RECRUITING AND TRAINING THE SALES FORCE

Sales force recruitment should be based on an accurate, detailed description of the sales task as defined by the sales manager. Besides the usual characteristics such as level of experience and education, what traits should sales managers look for in applicants? One of the most important traits of top performers is ego strength, or having a strong, healthy self-esteem and the ability to bounce back from rejection. Great salespeople also have a sense of urgency and competitiveness that pushes their sales to completion. Moreover, they have a desire to persuade people and close the sale. Effective salespeople are also assertive; they have the ability to be firm in one-to-one negotiations, to lead the sales process, and to get their point across confidently, without being overbearing or aggressive. They are sociable, willing to take risks, and capable of understanding complex concepts and ideas. Additionally, great salespeople are creative in developing client solutions, and they possess empathy—the ability to place oneself in someone else's shoes. Not surprisingly, in a recent study of top salespeople, almost 95 percent stated that their sales style was relationship oriented rather than transaction oriented.[60]

After the sales recruit has been hired and given a brief orientation, training begins. A new salesperson generally receives instruction in company policies and practices, selling techniques, product knowledge, industry and customer characteristics, and nonselling duties such as filling out sales and market information reports or using a sales automation computer program. Companies that sell complex products generally offer the most extensive training programs. Once applicants are hired at GE, for example, they enter one of many "rotational" training programs depending on their interest and major. One program, the Communications Leadership Development Program (CDLP), is geared toward public relations, marketing, communications, and organizational development. This 21-month program includes three six-month rotations and a project. Once they have completed the program, the new employees can decide whether they want to enter GE's sales force. At this point they will be better able to sell GE products because of their high level of product knowledge and on-the-job experience interacting with customers.[61]

Most successful sales organizations have learned that training is not just for newly hired salespeople. Instead, training is offered to all salespeople in an ongoing effort to hone selling skills and relationship building. In pursuit of solid salesperson–client relationships, training programs now seek to improve salespeople's consultative selling and listening skills and to broaden their product and customer knowledge. In addition, training programs stress the interpersonal skills needed to become the contact person for customers. Because negotiation is increasingly important in closing a sale, salespeople are also trained to negotiate effectively without risking profits. A recent international study predicts that the corporate on-line learning market will soon surpass the $7 billion mark as more companies re-evaluate the high cost of sending one or two employees to a central training classroom. Biovail, a pharmaceutical company in Mississauga, Ontario, used a computer-based system to train its sales force to sell its antihypertension drug Tiazac. The system, called Interactive Training Tree, uses animated role-play scenarios to train employees on-line. It was developed by Redwood E-Learning Systems, a Toronto-based company.[62]

COMPENSATING AND MOTIVATING THE SALES FORCE

Compensation planning is one of the sales manager's toughest jobs. Only good planning will ensure that compensation attracts, motivates, and retains good salespeople. Generally, companies and industries with lower levels of compensation suffer higher turnover rates, which increase costs and decrease effectiveness. Therefore, compensation needs to be competitive enough to attract and motivate the best salespeople. Firms sometimes take profit into account when developing their compensation plans. Instead of paying salespeople on overall volume, they pay according to the profitability achieved from selling each product. Still other companies tie a part of the salesperson's total compensation to customer satisfaction assessed through periodic customer surveys.

The three basic compensation methods for salespeople are commission, salary, and combination plans. A typical commission plan gives salespeople a specified percentage of their sales revenue. A **straight commission** system compensates the salesperson only when a sale is made. At the other end of the spectrum, a **straight salary** system compensates a salesperson with a stated salary regardless of sales productivity. Most companies, however, offer a compromise between straight commission and straight salary plans. A *combination system* offers a base salary plus an incentive—usually a commission or a bonus for achieving some specified goals or objectives. Combination systems have benefits for both the sales manager and the salesperson. The salary portion of the plan helps the manager control the sales force; the incentive provides motivation to accomplish goals and objectives. For the salesperson, a combination plan offers an incentive to excel while minimizing the extremely wide swings in earnings that may occur when the economy surges or contracts.

As the emphasis on relationship selling increases, many sales managers are coming to feel that tying a portion of a salesperson's compensation to a client's satisfaction with the salesperson and the company encourages relationship building. To determine this, sales managers can survey clients on a salesperson's ability to create realistic expectations and his or her responsiveness to customer needs. At PeopleSoft (recently acquired by Oracle), once one of the world's largest application software companies, structure, culture, and strategies are built around customer satisfaction. Sales force compensation was tied to both sales quotas and a satisfaction metric that allows clients to voice their opinions on the service provided.[63]

Although the compensation plan motivates a salesperson to sell, sometimes it is not enough to produce the volume of sales or the profit margins required by the firm's management. Sales managers, therefore, often offer rewards or incentives, such as recognition at

straight commission
A method of compensation in which the salesperson is paid some percentage when a sale is made.

straight salary
A method of compensation in which the salesperson receives a salary regardless of sales productivity.

SOURCE: © DYNAMIC GRAPHICS/CREATAS IMAGES/ JUPITERIMAGES

A highly motivated sales force is essential to a firm's success. Here a salesperson receives a plaque in front of her peers in recognition of a sales achievement.

ceremonies, plaques, vacations, merchandise, and pay raises or cash bonuses. The most popular incentives are cash rewards, which are in use by some 60 percent of sales organizations.[64] Rewards may help increase overall sales volume, add new accounts, improve morale and goodwill, move slow items, and bolster slow sales. They can be used to achieve long-term or short-term objectives, such as unloading overstocked inventory and meeting a monthly or quarterly sales goal.

Motivation also takes the form of effective sales leadership on the part of the sales manager. An effective sales manager is inspirational to his or her salespeople, encouraging them to achieve their goals through clear and enthusiastic communications. He or she has a clear vision, a commitment to the organization's mission, and the ability to instill pride and earn the respect of employees. Effective sales leaders are constantly increasing their knowledge and skills and encouraging others to do so. A recent study that assessed the attributes of sales leaders found that the best ones share a number of key personality traits (see Exhibit 15.5), such as assertiveness, a sense of urgency, an ability to handle rejection, drive, openness to new ideas, empathy toward customers, and a willingness to take risks. These traits separate motivational sales leaders from mere sales managers.[65]

SUPERVISING THE SALES FORCE

Most salespeople function with a great deal of independence and autonomy in managing their sales territories and scheduling their time. In fact, this is something that attracts many people to this type of career. One life-long salesperson jokingly commented to one of the authors when the author was seeking a promotion from sales into marketing management: "It's back to Saturday haircuts." On the downside, many salespeople find their job to be lonely. So a personal visit from the sales manager can improve their morale while simultaneously keeping them on their toes.

Effective sales managers realize that they need to visit their salespeople to keep them sharp and to help them with their selling tasks, such as developing written sales plans, keeping proper records of the calls they have made, reporting on the results of those calls, keeping lists of prospects, and, of course, placing sales orders. Salespeople also carry out a number of **nonselling tasks** that are important to the company, which need to be monitored as well. They need to maintain their sales aids and materials, properly maintain their vehicles, keep adequate supplies of samples, prepare proper sales expense reports, and, most important, maintain their personal appearance and hygiene. Direct visits from the sales manager to observe the physical state of things is often necessary to encourage salespeople to keep up with their nonselling responsibilities.

Sales managers need to be aware of the activities and condition of all their salespeople at all times. A salesperson holds a customer franchise on behalf of the company. A sales manager must be sure that the company's equity is protected in case something happens to the salesperson. This means ensuring that records are kept up to date and communicated to the company so that the company can maintain its

nonselling tasks
Salespeople need to maintain their appearance, their vehicles, their sales aids and materials, and also prepare their expense reports to perform effectively.

EXHIBIT 15.5

Seven Key Leadership Traits of Effective Sales Leaders

Effective sales leaders . . .	
Are assertive	Assertive sales leaders know when and how to get tough and how to assert their authority.
Possess ego drive	Sales leaders with ego drive have the desire and ability to persuade their reps to take action.
Possess ego strength	Sales leaders with ego strength are able to make sure not only that they bounce back from rejection but also that their reps rebound, too.
Take risks	Risk-taking sales leaders are willing to go out on a limb in an effort to make a sale or enhance a relationship.
Are innovative	Innovative sales leaders stay open to new ideas and new ways of conducting business.
Have a sense of urgency	Urgent sales leaders understand that getting things done now is critical to winning and keeping business.
Are empathetic	Empathetic sales leaders help their reps grow by listening and understanding.

SOURCE: Table adapted from "The 7 Traits of Great Sales Leaders" by Geoffrey Brewer, Sales & Marketing Management, July 1997, 38–46. Reprinted with permission.

customer relationships in the event a salesperson becomes incapacitated or resigns. Sales force automation tools, mentioned earlier in the chapter, are the means by which most sales managers supervise their salespeople on a daily basis.

EVALUATING THE SALES FORCE

The final task of sales managers is evaluating the effectiveness and performance of the sales force. To evaluate the sales force, the sales manager needs feedback—that is, regular information from salespeople. Typical performance measures include sales volume, contribution to profit, calls per order, sales or profits per call, or percentage of calls achieving specific goals such as sales of products that the company is heavily promoting.

Performance information helps the sales manager monitor a salesperson's progress through the sales cycle and pinpoint where breakdowns may be occurring. For example, by learning the number of prospects an individual salesperson has in each step of the sales cycle process and determining where prospects are falling out of the sales cycle, a manager can determine how effective a salesperson may be at lead generation, needs assessment, proposal generation, presenting, closing, and follow-up stages. This information can then tell a manager what sales skills may need to be reassessed or retrained. For example, if a sales manager notices that a sales representative seems to be letting too many prospects slip away after presenting proposals, it may mean that he or she needs help with developing proposals, handling objections, or closing sales.

7 | Describe the functions of sales management

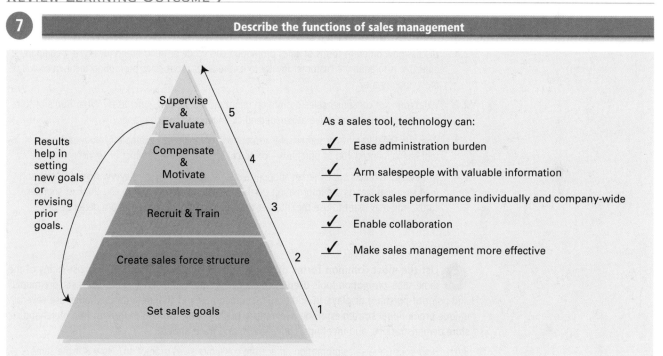

REVIEW AND APPLICATIONS

1 **Define and state the objectives of sales promotion.** Sales promotion consists of those marketing communication activities, other than advertising, personal selling, and public relations, in which a short-term incentive motivates consumers or members of the distribution channel to purchase a good or service immediately, either by lowering the price or by adding value. The main objectives of sales promotion are to increase trial purchases, consumer inventories, and repeat purchases. Sales promotion is also used to encourage brand switching and to build brand loyalty. Sales promotion supports advertising activities.

1.1 What is the primary factor that determines sales promotion objectives? Name some different types of sales promotion techniques, and explain the type of customer they are intended to influence.

1.2 You have recently been assigned the task of developing promotional techniques to introduce your company's new product, a spicy-hot chicken sandwich. Advertising spending is limited, so the introduction will include only some low-budget sales promotion techniques. Write a sales promotion plan that will increase awareness of your new spicy hot chicken sandwich and allow your customer base to try it risk-free.

2 **Discuss the most common forms of consumer sales promotion.** Consumer forms of sales promotion include coupons and rebates, premiums, loyalty marketing programs, contests and sweepstakes, sampling, and point-of-purchase displays. Coupons are certificates entitling consumers to an immediate price reduction when they purchase a product or service. Coupons are a particularly good way to encourage product trial and brand switching. Similar to coupons, rebates provide purchasers with a price reduction, which may or may not be immediate. To receive a rebate, consumers generally must complete a rebate form that the retailer handles or that they have to mail in later with a proof of purchase. Premiums offer an extra item or incentive to the consumer for buying a product or service. Premiums reinforce the consumer's purchase decision, increase consumption, and persuade nonusers to switch brands. Rewarding loyal customers is the basis of loyalty marketing programs. Loyalty programs are extremely effective at building long-term, mutually beneficial relationships between a company and its key customers. Contests and sweepstakes are generally designed to create interest, often to encourage brand switching. Because consumers perceive risk in trying new products, sampling is an effective method for gaining new customers. Finally, point-of-purchase displays set up at the retailer's location build traffic, advertise the product, and induce impulse buying.

2.1 Discuss how different forms of sales promotion can erode or build brand loyalty. If a company's objective is to enhance customer loyalty to its products, what sales promotion techniques will be most appropriate?

2.2 What forms of consumer sales promotion might induce impulse purchases? What forms of sales promotion are more effective at persuading consumers to switch brands?

2.3 Consider the different consumer sales promotion tools. Give an example of how each type of tool has influenced you to purchase—or purchase more of—a product or service.

2.4 Not everyone thinks supermarket shopper cards are a bargain. Go to **www.nocards.org** and read several pages. Is the information on the site compelling? What do you think of shopper cards? You may want to use the Internet to research shopper cards in more detail before forming an opinion.

3 **List the most common forms of trade sales promotion.** Manufacturers use many of the same sales promotion tools used in consumer promotions, such as sales contests, premiums, and point-of-purchase displays. In addition, manufacturers and channel intermediaries use several unique promotional strategies: trade allowances, push money, training programs, free merchandise, store demonstrations, and meetings, conventions, and trade shows.

3.1 How does trade sales promotion differ from consumer sales promotion? How is it the same?

3.2 Form a team of three to five students. As marketing managers, you are in charge of selling Popsicles. Design a consumer sales promotion plan and trade sales promotion plan for your product. Incorporate at least three different promotion tools into each plan. Share your results with the other teams in the class.

3.3 What are the main forms of trade sales promotion? Which type might be most enticing to a grocery store manager? To a buyer for a major electronics chain?

4 **Describe personal selling.** Personal selling is direct communication between a sales representative and one or more prospective buyers in an attempt to influence each other in a purchase situation. Broadly speaking, all businesspeople use personal selling to promote themselves and their ideas. Personal selling offers several advantages over other forms of promotion. Personal selling allows salespeople to thoroughly explain and demonstrate a product. Salespeople have the flexibility to tailor a sales proposal to the needs and preferences of individual customers. Personal selling can be more efficient than other forms of promotion because salespeople target qualified prospects and avoid wasting efforts on unlikely buyers. Personal selling affords greater managerial control over promotion costs. Finally, personal selling is the most effective method of closing a sale and producing satisfied customers.

4.1 Discuss the role of personal selling in promoting products. What advantages does personal selling offer over other forms of promotion?

4.2 What are the major advantages of personal selling to the company selling a product? What are the advantages to the person or company buying the product?

5 **Discuss the key differences between relationship selling and traditional selling.** Relationship selling is the practice of building, maintaining, and enhancing interactions with customers in order to develop long-term satisfaction through mutually beneficial partnerships. Traditional selling, on the other hand, is transaction focused. That is, the salesperson is most concerned with making one-time sales and moving on to the next prospect. Salespeople practising relationship selling spend more time understanding a prospect's needs and developing solutions to meet those needs.

5.1 What are the key differences between relationship selling and traditional methods of selling? What types of products or services do you think would be conducive to relationship selling?

5.2 Based on the key differences between traditional and relationship selling, which type of sales approach would you use as a salesperson? Do the different approaches require different personal strengths or attributes?

6 **List the steps in the selling process.** The selling process is composed of seven basic steps: (1) generating leads, (2) qualifying leads, (3) approaching the customer and probing needs, (4) developing and proposing solutions, (5) handling objections, (6) closing the sale, and (7) following up.

6.1 You are a new salesperson for a well-known medical software company, and one of your clients is a large group of physicians. You have just arranged an initial meeting with the office manager. Develop a list of questions you might ask at this meeting to uncover the group's specific needs.

6.2 What does sales follow-up entail? Why is it an essential step in the selling process, especially from the perspective of relationship selling? How does it relate to cognitive dissonance?

6.3 Consider each step in the selling process. Which steps could be conducted through technology (Internet, webinars, etc.)? Which are most important to handle "face-to-face"?

7 **Describe the functions of sales management.** Sales management is a critical area of marketing that performs several important functions. Sales managers set overall company sales goals and define the sales process most effective for achieving those goals. They determine sales force structure based on geographic, product, functional, or customer variables. Managers develop the sales force through recruiting and training. Sales management motivates the sales force through compensation planning, motivational tools, and effective sales leadership. Sales managers supervise their salespeople on both selling and nonselling tasks. Finally, sales managers evaluate the sales force through salesperson feedback and other methods of determining their performance.

7.1 With two classmates, select a company or business near your campus that has a sales force. Use a search engine to research how to use the Internet to support personal selling; then list all the things the company would need to do to create an e-savvy sales force.

7.2 Without revenue, a company cannot survive, and sales are the means to that end. How does each of the sales management functions contribute to a successful, high-performing sales force?

TERMS

cold calling 491
consumer sales promotion 474
coupon 477
follow-up 494
frequent buyer program 479
lead generation (prospecting) 490
lead qualification 491
loyalty marketing programs 479
needs assessment 492
negotiation 494

networking 490
nonselling tasks 498
personal selling 485
point-of-purchase display (P-O-P) 482
preapproach 491
premium 478
push money 484
quota 496
rebate 478
referral 490

relationship selling (consultative selling) 486
sales presentation 492
sales process (sales cycle) 488
sales promotion 474
sales proposal 492
sampling 481
straight commission 497
straight salary 497
trade allowance 484
trade sales promotion 474

EXERCISES

APPLICATION EXERCISE

WRITING

Have you ever been left to languish in the dressing room of a clothing store by a salesperson who promised to help you with your clothing but then seemingly disappeared? Have you waited forever for some assistance and advice regarding a product you wanted to buy? Have you even been abandoned by a salesperson who left you to serve another customer before you were finished with your transaction? If so, you already know that sales and customer service are integral parts of marketing. While you are working on this chapter, keep a journal of your personal sales and/or customer service experiences with local merchants. Don't ignore the details. Even such things as how crowded a store or restaurant is when you visit may affect your perceptions of the service you receive.[66]

Activities

1. Keep your journal for a week, recording all sales and service transactions, if possible, on the day they occur.

2. At the end of the week, examine your journal and pick the most noteworthy entry. Provide the basic information about the transaction: company where it occurred, type of transaction (purchase, return, complaint, etc.), type of good or service involved, and so forth.

3. Once you have the outlined situation, evaluate the experience. Use the information about selling in this chapter as support for your evaluation. For example, did the salesperson seem to treat the situation as an individual, discrete transaction, or did he or she seem interested in building a relationship?

4. Finally, make recommendations as to how the company can improve its sales and/or service. Your ideas on this should be logical and achievable (meaning you have to consider the cost of implementing your suggestions).

ETHICS EXERCISE

Sally Burke works for Hi-Tech Electronics. Her responsibilities include selecting items to advertise in her company's weekly regular Thursday newspaper flyers. One hot item is a 60-inch flat-panel LED 3 Dimensional TV. The list price is $3,999, but her manager tells her to advertise it at $2,999, since customers can apply for a $1,000 mail-in rebate. The advertised price has attracted many people to buy the TV; however, Sally has heard several complaints from customers who found the rebate process unusually complex and were denied a rebate because the manufacturer claimed they hadn't provided the required information. She would prefer to advertise the "real" list price, knowing that customers are not guaranteed to receive a rebate.

Questions

1. Is it unethical to advertise products at their post-rebate price in order to increase sales? Why or why not? What is another sales promotion method Hi-Tech Electronics could use to persuade customers to buy their LED 3 Dimensional TV at the store?

2. Rebate programs are commonly used by electronics manufacturers because the rebates arouse consumers' interest in buying products, yet only half of purchasers ultimately claim their rebates.

Is a rebate program itself unethical if the manufacturer knows consumers are unlikely to receive their money?

3. Visit a local electronics store—or website—and find a product being sold with a mail-in rebate offer. Are the rebate instructions clear? Would you take the time to complete the process?

CASE STUDY

MCDONALD'S: MCDONALD'S SAMPLES ITS PREMIUM ROAST COFFEE

Canadians love coffee, especially their morning coffee! According to Statistics Canada, on an annual basis Canadians consumed 90 litres of coffee per person in 2009, which nicely works out to be about a cup of coffee per day for every person in Canada or 33.5 million per day, which adds up to about 12 billion coffees a year.[67] McDonald's Canada has been battling Tim Hortons, the market leader for out-of-home coffee consumption in Canada, without much success for many years. Consequently, in 2009 McDonald's decided to launch a major coffee offensive using the theme "Let's Start Fresh," whose major thrust was an in-store sampling of a new coffee product.

McDonald's Canada hired Cossette Communications of Montreal to manage the integrated promotional campaign. In April 2009, McDonald's Canada initiated a two-week Canada-wide free coffee give-away of its new premium roast coffee at breakfast time. Customers didn't have to buy any other breakfast items to get the coffee, all they had to do was show up during the breakfast hour at McDonald's and ask for a coffee. Of course, if a customer shows up for coffee, breakfast is likely to go with it, so sales of breakfast items were expected to offset some of the expense of the promotion.

McDonald's Canada spared no expense with the effort. Aside from the direct cost of giving away coffee, it developed a new cup for the product. The "fire-roasted coloured cup" was insulated so it would not be too hot to touch. The promotion was integrated with a number of other supporting media. For example, there was billboard advertising, new outdoor promotions, and, of course, radio and television ads.

The television advertisement had a tag line tie-in to a phrase made famous in the movie *Jerry McGuire*. The scene shows a young female McDonald's employee moving through a McDonald's restaurant with a tray full of coffees. She offers one of them to a man, asking if he would like to try a free cup of coffee. She goes on to describe how "McDonald's Premium Roast Coffee is made with 100 percent arabica beans, hand-picked and fire-roasted for a full-bodied flavour." As the employee carries on with her description, the man's friends sitting at a nearby table stare with interest when suddenly the man raises his hand and says, "You had me at free," at which point he takes a coffee and joins his friends.[68]

Another part of the promotion involved a "Mug Shot" contest where restaurant patrons could have themselves photographed drinking a McDonald's coffee and then have this picture uploaded to the McDonaldsMugShots.ca contest website. Five finalists were selected and then on-line voters would choose a winner who would receive 500 gift cards for medium-size coffees. Along with the website for the Mug Shot contest, McDonald's also created a Facebook page for coffee drinkers.[69]

McDonald's advertising agency, Cossette, developed a number of localized promotional stunts in Canada's major markets, including skywriting in Montreal, giant steaming cups of coffee and a superboard of a three-dimensional steaming cup of coffee in Toronto. In Vancouver, the agency dressed up a streetlight so it looked like a coffee pot pouring coffee into a coffee cup. In Edmonton, the agency arranged for a "sleep-walking" stunt where actors dressed in pyjamas and carrying teddy bears walked into McDonald's restaurants.[70]

The result of this was that McDonald's reported coffee consumption was up by 1.3 million cups in one month. And how about Tim Hortons, how did the promotion affect them? When asked whether business had been affected, the CEO of Tim Hortons, Don Schroeder, replied, "McDonald's promotional campaign was hardly noticed. . . . The fact is that we actually grew [in] transactions over the two weeks of this competitive activity, demonstrating the tremendous loyalty of our customers, and the entrenchment of our competitive position in Canada."[71]

Questions

1. What do you think the key motivation is behind the choice of a breakfast restaurant? How does a promotion like free coffee affect this motivation?

2. Evaluate some of the ideas presented in the case for promoting McDonald's coffee. What do you think of them? Can you think of any other sales promotion ideas to add to them?

3. Compare Tim Horton's "Roll Up the Rim To Win" promotion, which is discussed in the chapter, to McDonald's free coffee promotion, which is presented in this case. Which do you find more alluring? Explain your reasoning.

VIDEO CASE

THE NORTH AMERICAN INTERNATIONAL AUTO SHOW

The North American International Auto Show in Detroit has a history of over 100 years behind it. The auto show began in 1907 with the formation of the Detroit Area Dealers Association, which put on a regional effort to display the automobiles they had to sell. The show had displays for 17 auto makers when it first began and has grown to include more than 60 auto makers today. The show was suspended during the Second World War and through the Korean War (1950–1953) but reappeared in 1954. The first international vehicles to be displayed came in 1957 with the appearance of European brands such as Volvo, German Isetta, Mercedes-Benz, Jaguar, and Porsche. However, it wasn't until 1987 that the Detroit Auto Dealers Association got together and sought to make the show the best in the United States, and for that matter, the best in the world. Now, according to its website, "the North American International Auto Show pursues a vision of continually redefining what it means to be the auto industry's indispensable North American event. To achieve this goal, the Auto Show continually introduces bold new ways to enhance attendees' experience and deliver exceptional value to media, industry and the public."[72]

During the 2010 show, nearly 5,000 members of the international media attended the show to witness 40 new vehicle unveilings. In addition, the show was attended by over 700,000 members of the public, interested to see the latest and greatest automobiles available.[73] In 2010, Pat Bolland of Business News Network (BNN), interviewed Bob Carter, the group vice-president and general manager for the Toyota Division at Toyota U.S.A. at the 2010 North American International Auto Show in Detroit, Michigan.

Pat Bolland tells his BNN viewers that "it's been a tough year for the auto industry, somewhat boosted by cash for clunkers." To find out what the future will hold, he interviews Toyota U.S.A.'s Bob Carter to see if Bob can provide some insights on the pulse of the industry. Pat begins by asking, "What is the pulse? Are people happy? Are they enthused or are they still worried about the past?" Carter responds by saying, "The mood of everybody at the auto show is very positive, Pat. The industry in the U.S. closed on a high in November and December 2009 and so not only Toyota but every manufacturer and the vendors and the dealers that are here at the show are very positive that the improvements that we've seen in the retail industry . . . are going to continue on into 2010."

Bolland asks Carter to take off his Toyota "hat" for a moment and comment on what he thinks is the most exciting vehicle at this year's show. Bob gives a mild chuckle and naturally responds that he has to talk about the new concept that Toyota has just introduced to the market—the FTCH—which stands for "future Toyota compact hybrid." Carter discusses how Toyota has had a lot of past success introducing new hybrids into the U.S. market. He mentions that consumers have said they love the Prius but they would like a little smaller version and some have said they would like a slightly larger version. Carter says Toyota is trying to gauge the reaction of consumers to the idea of an entire Prius brand line-up of cars. He adds there are a lot of interesting cars at the show and mentions that Ford has brought out a new Focus model, Volkswagen has unveiled a new hybrid concept, Honda just introduced its new CRZ, and that there is a lot of fresh product and new cars for consumers to choose from.

Bolland comments, "I used to live in the United States and Americans love their cars." He observes that when gas prices went down, it seemed that Americans wanted gas guzzlers, so manufacturers like GM met this demand. Bolland says that Toyota is going against this with two things, compacts and hybrids. He asks Carter, "Do you think that the psychology in the United States is going to flip quickly?" Carter replies that consumers are showing a trend to smaller vehicles like light trucks and smaller cars. He notes that people are moving from midsize SUVs to compact SUVs like the RAV4, which is produced in Canada. Demand is so high the company plans to add a second production shift in Canada. Carter adds that the industry is seeing this downsizing trend on the car side too. He says it's not just with Toyota but the entire industry is going small. For example, Ford's big news is the introduction of two small cars, the Ford Focus and Ford Fiesta. "The industry is seeing where the consumer wants us to go," Carter says, adding that the consumer wants smaller vehicles that are comfortable and more efficient. At least he's finding that's what consumers who attend the show are saying.

Bolland says he once owned a massive 1976 Cadillac that he loved. However, he knows that the job market in the United States is unsure. He asks Carter if the economic environment is stable enough to sustain the industry without major incentives like Cash for Clunkers. Carter replies that the industry is convinced the worst is behind them, saying that 2009 was the toughest year since 1982, maybe even the toughest year ever for the automobile industry. He comments that there is improved consumer confidence, low interest rates, and other factors like pent-up demand, so Toyota is expecting an extra 1 million vehicles will be sold in the industry in 2010. In 2009, industry sales were 10.4 million but Toyota is expecting 11.5 million units will be sold by the North American auto industry in 2010. Carter says that this is a suppressed level by historic standards but it is still an encouraging market relative to 2009. He adds that other manufacturers seem to be in agreement with Toyota that the industry will grow by about 1 million vehicles.

Bolland asks Carter for his opinion on the impact of the cost of technology to make hybrids and electric batteries: "What does that do to margins in the industry and Toyota in particular?" Carter says that Toyota has had a lot of experience making hybrids—they have been making them since 1999 and each new generation gets better in performance, provides more energy, is smaller, is lighter weight, and has lower costs. Toyota still has a lot of challenges to improve but if you compare where the industry is now versus five years ago, Carter is expecting even more advances in the future.

Bolland notes that Bob Carter used to manage Toyota's Lexus luxury car division. He asks Carter to comment on how the luxury car market is doing compared to the rest of the car market. Carter says that in the short term the luxury market has had a tough time in the United States. During the 1990s, the luxury car market represented 8 to 9 percent of the volume but now the market share of luxury cars has climbed into the 11 to 12 percent range. Carter says the long-term trend in sales is going up but luxury manufacturers are looking to see what consumers in the luxury market will be looking for in the future. He believes the luxury car market is showing the same trend as that of the general markets, smaller and more fuel-efficient cars.

The interview concludes with one final question: "What is the market focus for Toyota going to be—North America or Asia?" Carter responds that North America is the most important market in world. Toyota was the number one automobile brand in the United States during 2009 with about 20 percent of the U.S. market. Toyota knows it can do better. It is going to bring out new concepts and is launching a new Sienna minivan in 2010. What is driving Toyota is that it is listening to its customers and developing the products that customers want to see—this is what is giving Toyota confidence over the next couple of years.[74]

Questions

1. Have you ever attended an auto show? Whether you have or not, what is your opinion of this kind of event?

2. For the most part, trade shows are targeted to channel members rather than final consumers. Why might an auto show be more effective as a consumer promotional event as opposed to a trade promotional event? Discuss.

3. One of the most interesting comments during the interview between Pat Bolland and Bob Carter was the importance of the show to manufacturers in learning what consumers are looking for. How could a trade show better assist an auto marketer in learning what consumers want as opposed to simply talking to them when they visit the manufacturer's dealer showrooms?

4. Do you think Toyota has the pulse of the market with its plans to bring out more hybrids and smaller cars? Do you agree that fuel efficiency is going to be the driving force in the auto market in the future or are there some other forces that are important to consumers? Discuss.

MARKETING & YOU

High scores on this poll indicate a preference for using coupons, which may indicate that you are a comparison shopper. If your score was low, you probably don't see any economic benefits to using coupons, and you're likely not a comparison shopper. Instead, you probably prefer to buy what you want regardless of any coupon promotion.

MARKETING MISCUE

MOTRIN GETS TWITTERED!

Motrin got caught in the net of social networking in the fall of 2008. Its new, edgy ad for Motrin was a source of a huge headache for Johnson & Johnson's McNeil Consumer Healthcare unit executives—yes, an ad for a product that was intended to relieve pain, not cause it!

In late September of 2008 as part of its "We Feel Your Pain" marketing campaign, McNeil launched a print and on-line advertising campaign targeting new moms. The ad was about (and for) moms who carry their babies either in the front or to the side in baby carriers, referred to as slings, swings, wraps, or pouches. The ad said that these baby carriers put a ton of strain on the mother's back, neck, and shoulders. While this may or may not be a fact, the Motrin ad suggested that mothers were carrying their babies to be fashionable and seemed to make light of the bonding experience between mother and baby that occurred when a mother carried her baby close to her body. Then, to top it all off, the ad gave the idea that moms who did this looked tired and crazy.

Did baby-carrying mothers rush out and buy Motrin to relieve the pain induced by all of this baby lugging? No. Instead, much to McNeil's chagrin, these late-GenX and early-GenY moms picked up their mobile devices. These mommy-bloggers were offended by the ad and hit their popular social networking site Twitter. Here is some of the tweet:

- Picking on new mothers is vile, it's as vulnerable as we will ever be and they should know better.

- I credit a large portion of my children's happiness to baby wearing.

- I can't even count the ways I'm offended right now.

- And wearing my son never gave me back pain.

- Note to self . . . never piss off moms . . . especially twitter moms. . . they can be a nasty bunch.

It took only a few hours for the Motrin ad to become the most tweeted subject on Twitter. Within a day, there was a nine-minute video on YouTube, to the tune of "Danny Boy," with screen shots of the twitter posts and mothers carrying babies in their carriers. Additionally, these mommy-bloggers and, by then, other offended bloggers began calling for a boycott of Motrin.

Within 48 hours of the all-out viral attack, McNeil's marketing vice-president issued an apology on the Motrin website. She stated that Johnson & Johnson and McNeil took the feedback from moms very seriously and that the company was in the process of removing the ad from all media. While the on-line ad was easy to remove, the print ads were already in distribution in magazines that were at the newsstands. The print ads appeared in *Cookie*, the lifestyle magazine that celebrates the joys of parenthood,; *Lucky*, the magazine about shopping and style; and *Nylon*, a fashion and beauty magazine.

Social networking sites, such as Twitter, have dramatically increased the feedback and word-of-mouth about ads. Regular posters on these sites could have thousands of followers. Thus it takes only seconds for opinions to spread, and mommy-bloggers are one of the most vocal and quickest-to-blog groups of consumers. While "MotrinGate" might not hurt the estimated $1 billion annual Motrin profit, it certainly made many high-level executives realize that they had to pay more attention to social media.[1]

Questions

1. How could McNeil have predicted the negative impact of the Motrin ad?

2. What is the impact of Web 2.0 on marketing communications?

SOURCE: © TETRA IMAGES / JUPITERIMAGES

CRITICAL THINKING CASE

COKE'S "OPEN HAPPINESS": AN INTEGRATED MARKETING COMMUNICATIONS CAMPAIGN

For decades, Coca-Cola has been listed as the brand with the highest brand equity in the world. In 2009, Interbrand ranked Coca-Cola as the world's best global brand, assigning a brand equity value of $68.7 billion.[2] In 2009, Coke sales were $30.9 billion, which was down about $1 billion from the previous year but the company made up for the decline by offsetting it with a $1-billion earnings increase from $5.8 billion in 2008 to $6.8 billion in 2009.[3] Coca-Cola has done a masterful job of maintaining its brand as the most valuable in the world. One of the keys to its success has been the ongoing effectiveness of its promotional efforts and the company's ability to make changes to keep its brand image as refreshing as its drink.

In 2009, the Coca-Cola Company introduced its latest promotional campaign for its Coca-Cola flagship brand, using the theme "Open Happiness." Over the years, Coca-Cola has used a number of themes, averaging one about every 20 months. Some of the most memorable include "Delicious and Refreshing," which was used at the turn of the century, (the 20th century that is); "Drink Coca-Cola" (1886); "Pause and Refresh Yourself" (1924); "Coca-Cola Goes Along" (1939); "It's the Real Thing" (1948); "Things Go Better With Coke" (1963); "Coke Adds Life" (1976); "Have a Coke and a Smile" (1979); "Coke Is It" (1982); "Can't Beat the Feeling" (1989); "Always Coca-Cola" (1993); "Real" (2000); "Life Tastes Good" (2001); and "The Coke Side of Life" (2006). In earlier times, Coca-Cola seemed to introduce a new theme almost every year. However, in recent times, slogan changes have been less frequent.[4]

The "Open Happiness" campaign was unveiled in Canada to fit with the company's sponsorship of the 2010 Winter Olympic Games in Vancouver. Coca-Cola had developed a campaign song titled "Open Happiness," which was used worldwide but the company had three Canadian artists— Kardinal Offishall, Jay Malinowski of Bedouin Soundclash, and Coeur de pirate (Béatrice Martin), a singer-songwriter from Quebec—record a version just for Canada.[5] The "Open Happiness Song" was integrated into the advertising campaign through Coke's consumer website, **iCoke.ca**, where it was available in English and French versions for downloading. It was also made available as a mobile phone ringtone and the three musical artists were contracted to give a live performance during the Olympic Games. Coca-Cola Canada also launched a "win a trip to the Olympics" contest that asked Coca-Cola drinkers to look under the cap or the flap of specially marked packages of Coca-Cola.[6]

Coca-Cola also sponsored its own pavilion at the Vancouver Olympics. The company described it as "a multi-sensory, interactive experience that will inspire more than 275,000 visitors, while highlighting Coca-Cola's past and present involvement with the Olympic Games as well as the company's current and future commitments to environmental sustainability. . . . The pavilion will bring Coca-Cola's sustainability efforts to life as guests learn about efforts to protect the polar bear, recycle in unique ways, and meet the 'bottle of the future,' the PlantBottle. Of course, they will be able to enjoy Coca-Cola and Coke Zero, served perfectly chilled at four degrees."[7]

The Olympic sponsorship by Coca-Cola involved a wide number of efforts that were integrated into the promotional campaign. For example, Coca-Cola hosted three official Pin Trading Centres,

where people could trade Vancouver 2010 lapel pins. The company donated a part of the proceeds from the sale of these pins to WWF-Canada. Every night in Yaletown, there was the Coca-Cola After Dark Parade, featuring musicians, performers, and buskers that the company boasted would "energize and invigorate crowds, sharing smiles, Olympic Spirit and above all . . . happiness!" A Gold Medal contest was operated through iCoke.ca; consumers could win $25,000 each time Canada won a gold medal. (Coca-Cola likely exceeded the planned budget on this promotion given Canada's record 14 gold medals.) Another form of celebration of Canada's performance described in the press release involved a "gigantic maple leaf billboard in Vancouver (at Hastings and Vernon). The maple leaf represents a podium, and every time a Canadian athlete makes it to the real podium, a medal will be hung on the billboard." During the Olympics the company also ran television advertising to salute the torchbearers.

Coca-Cola undertook a number of pure public relations activities as well. For example, in the Athletes' Village, the company installed an interactive screen for "securing pledges to personal sustainability and environmental action from former and current Olympic Games athletes, who will become environmental ambassadors." The company presented "Live Positively Awards," which were given to celebrate "those who make positive choices and strive to better themselves, their communities and others in their everyday lives." The company also sponsored the Coca-Cola Post-Olympic Games Legacy Project, an outdoor sports court for Vancouver's inner-city young people. In addition, Coca-Cola Canada asked some First Nations, Inuit, and Métis artists to use plastic Coca-Cola bottles to create artpieces that celebrated their heritage and the 2010 Olympic Games. The art was put on display during the Winter Olympics and then auctioned off at icoke.ca with all proceeds donated to the Aboriginal Youth Legacy Fund.[8]

Questions

1. Discuss some of the problems that Coca-Cola would face in developing and implementing their new "Open Happiness" promotional campaign as part of an Integrated Marketing Communications program. As you consider this issue, keep in mind the many channels of communication that Coca-Cola typically uses.

2. When you think of Coca-Cola, what slogan or theme comes to mind? Go on-line and Google "Coca-Cola Slogans" and check out some of the websites that list historical themes. Review some of Coca-Cola's promotional themes over time. What do you think makes a good promotional theme for a product like Coke? Evaluate some of these past themes with your criteria for what makes a good theme. Do you think "Open Happiness" will be as well remembered as some of the others?

3. Coca-Cola has reused a number of themes over time (e.g., "Pause and Refresh"; "The Real Thing"). If you could bring back an old theme, which one would it be and why?

PART

Pricing
Decisions

6

16 Pricing Concepts

SOURCE: LYNN MCLEOD

LEARNING OUTCOMES

1 Discuss the importance of pricing decisions to the economy and to the individual firm

2 List and explain a variety of pricing objectives

3 Explain the role of demand in price determination

4 Understand the concept of yield management systems

5 Describe cost-oriented pricing strategies

6 Demonstrate how the product life cycle, competition, distribution and promotion strategies, guaranteed price matching, customer demands, the Internet and extranets, and perceptions of quality can affect price

(Ÿ) MARKETING & YOU

Using the following scale, enter your opinion of the following items on the lines provided.

1	2	3	4	5	6	7
Strongly disagree						Strongly agree

__ People notice when you buy the most expensive brand of a product.

__ Buying the most expensive brand of a product makes me feel classy.

__ I enjoy the prestige of buying a high-priced brand.

__ It says something to people when you buy the high-priced version of a product.

__ I have purchased the most expensive brand of a product just because I knew other people would notice.

__ Even for a relatively inexpensive product, I think that buying a costly brand is impressive.

Total your score, and find out what it means after you read the chapter.

SOURCE: REPRINTED WITH PERMISSION FROM *MARKETING SCALES HANDBOOK* VOL. III, PUBLISHED BY THE AMERICAN MARKETING ASSOCIATION, G. BRUNER, K. JAMES, H. HENSEL, EDS. SCALE #265.

C. J. Sinnott, a 12-year-old avid reader, and his mom, Lara, were extremely happy to find the 22nd book in the Roy MacGregor Screech Owl series, *Trouble at the Top of the World*, and the first five books in Hockey Hall of Fame announcer Brain McFarlane's Mitchell Brothers Series for $1 each at the All Dollars store on Lauzon Road in Windsor, Ontario. These books would normally cost $9.99 each at the nearby Indigo Bookstore. Dollar stores offer quite a bargain on a wide variety of products and are growing by leaps and bounds. According to ACNeilson Canada, 77 percent of all Canadians shop at dollar stores.

Price lining (discussed in the next chapter) is the practice of selling products at well-defined price points. For example, a men's clothing store could price all suits at $199, $299, and $399 with no prices in between. Dollar stores have taken price lining to an extreme and made price the central focus of their whole marketing program.

Anna McGaw is another dollar-store regular and goes out of her way to shop at her favourite dollar stores in Toronto for greeting cards, gifts, and many household items. Anna really likes the prices: "There's such a variety and the price is right. Why pay $5 if you can pay $1 and get just as nice a card?" Janet Foster is also hooked on dollar stores. Janet recently paid $10 for a pad of paper, a pencil case, glue, and arts and crafts supplies for her three daughters—items she would have bought at Zellers before she started shopping at Dollarama.

The dollar stores are getting bigger, carrying more merchandise, offering wider aisles and nicer furnishings, moving into malls, and increasing their sales. ACNielsen Canada reports that sales at dollar stores are growing at a rate double that of all retail establishments and now account for well over $1.5 billion in yearly sales. That's a lot of transactions at $1 each! There are over 1,000 dollar stores across the country—about one for every 33,000 Canadians.

Dollarama, Buck or Two, Great Canadian Dollar Stores, Your Dollar Store With More, Dollar Giant, Dollar Blitz, All Dollars, Dollarland Plus, Buck N Change, Mighty Dollar, Everything for a Dollar, and A Buck & More are among the many dollar-store chains in Canada. These companies alone operate over 2,000 dollar stores across Canada. As the dollar stores grow, they are adding merchandise that, in the past, was unthinkable at $1. "We're selling at a dollar what 15 or 20 years ago we could not have come close to selling at a dollar," says Larry Rossy, president of Montreal-based S. Rossy Inc., which operates over 350 dollar stores from the Maritimes to Manitoba. Many dollar-store products are sourced overseas, with Dollarama stores buying over 70 percent of its goods from outside the country. Dollarama is even offering its own private label brands such as Duramax hardware goods and Celebration party supplies.

The dollar stores are adding more clothing items, name-brand cosmetics, and other items to continue to attract shoppers. In addition, dollar stores are always hunting for special deals. Ed Sivitille, president of Sivex Housewares Inc. in Concord, Ontario, which owns over 30 dollar stores, proudly pointed out that he was able to offer ceramic dinnerware at his stores for $1 a piece and a $1 girls' kit filled with a sponge, body gel, hair brush, and accessories—something that might sell for $9.95 at a drugstore.

The dollar stores are also exerting an impact on other retailers. Loblaws Cos. Ltd., Food Basics, Zellers, and Walmart Canada have all introduced, or are experimenting with, dollar aisles in their stores. "The dollar-store phenomenon is growing and consumers have accepted that," said Doug Brummer, senior vice-president of marketing at A&P Canada's Food Basics stores. "We wanted to get a piece of that action."

Food Basics stores and Loblaw's No Frills already have very prominent aisles of dollar goods in store sections labelled Under a Buck in Food Basics and Dollar Zone in No Frills. The merchandise carried in these aisles, similar to the wide range of goods found in the dollar stores, includes toys, party supplies, housewares, kitchen utensils, stationery, candles, hair accessories, greeting cards, and gift items. Geoffrey Wilson of Loblaw reported that "the consumer response [had] been very strong."

"The new competition speaks well for the business," said Dennis Klein, CEO of Denninghouse, the parent company of Buck or Two.[1]

THE IMPORTANCE OF PRICE

Discuss the importance of pricing decisions to the economy and to the individual firm

Price means one thing to the consumer and something else to the seller. To the consumer, it is the cost of something. To the seller, price is revenue, the primary source of profits. In the broadest sense, price allocates resources in a free-market economy. With so many ways of looking at price, it's no wonder that marketing managers find the task of setting prices a challenge.

WHAT IS PRICE?

price
That which is given up in an exchange to acquire a good or service.

Price is that which is given up in an exchange to acquire a good or service. Price plays two roles in the evaluation of product alternatives: as a measure of sacrifice and as an information cue. To some degree, these two are opposing effects.[2]

The Sacrifice Effect of Price

Price is typically the money exchanged for the good or service. It may also be time lost while waiting to acquire the good or service. Standing in long lines at the airport first to check in and then to get through the new security checkpoint procedures is a cost. In fact, these delays are one reason more people are selecting alternative modes of transportation for relatively short trips. Price might also include "lost dignity" for individuals who lose their jobs and must rely on charity to obtain food and clothing.

The Information Effect of Price

Consumers do not always choose the lowest price. One explanation of this is that we infer quality information from price. The information effect of price may also extend to favourable price perceptions by others because higher prices can convey the prominence and status of the purchaser to other people. Thus, a Swatch and a Rolex both can accurately tell time but convey different meanings. Similarly, a Buick Enclave and the Lexus 450LX are both SUVs and both can take you from point A to B. However, the two vehicles convey different meanings.

Value Is Based upon Perceived Satisfaction

Consumers are interested in obtaining a "reasonable price." "Reasonable price" really means "perceived reasonable value" at the time of the transaction. One of the authors of this textbook bought a fancy European-designed toaster for about $45. The toaster's wide mouth made it possible to toast a bagel, warm a muffin, and, with a special $15 attachment, make a grilled sandwich. The author felt that a toaster with all these features surely must be worth the total price of $60. But after three months of using the device, toast that burned around the edges and remained raw in the middle lost its appeal. The disappointed buyer put the toaster in the attic. Why didn't he return it to the retailer? Because the boutique had gone out of business and no other local retailer carried the brand. Also, there was no local service centre. Remember, the price paid is based on the satisfaction consumers *expect* to receive from a product and not necessarily the satisfaction they *actually* receive.

Price can relate to anything with perceived value, not just money. When goods and services are exchanged, the trade is called *barter*. For example, if you exchange this book for a chemistry book at the end of the term, you have engaged in barter. The price you paid for the chemistry book was this textbook.

THE IMPORTANCE OF PRICE TO MARKETING MANAGERS

revenue
The price charged to customers multiplied by the number of units sold.

profit
Revenue minus expenses.

Prices are the key to revenues, which in turn are the key to profits for an organization. **Revenue** is the price charged to customers multiplied by the number of units sold. Revenue is what pays for every activity of the company: production, finance, sales, distribution, and so on. What's left over (if anything) is **profit**. Managers usually strive to charge a price that will earn a fair profit.

To earn a profit, managers must choose a price that is not too high or too low, a price that equals the perceived value to target consumers. If, in consumers' minds, a price is set too high, the perceived value will be less than the cost, and sales opportunities will be lost. Many mainstream purchasers of cars, sporting goods, CDs, tools, wedding gowns, and computers are buying "used or preowned" items to get a better deal. Pricing a new product too high may give some shoppers an incentive to go to a "preowned" or consignment retailer. Lost sales mean lost revenue. Conversely, if a price is too low, it may be perceived as a great value for the consumer, but the firm loses revenue it could have earned.

Trying to set the right price is one of the most difficult tasks of the marketing manager, as trends in the consumer market attest:

- The Internet has made comparison shopping easier.
- The increased availability of bargain-priced private and generic brands has put downward pressure on overall prices.
- Many firms are trying to maintain or regain their market share by cutting prices. For example, Ikea has gained market share in the furniture industry by aggressively cutting prices. General Motors Canada increased sales of pickups by offering cash rebates of nearly $10,000.

REVIEW LEARNING OUTCOME 1

1 Discuss the importance of pricing decisions to the economy and to the individual firm

Price × Sales Units = Revenue

Revenue − Cost = Profit

Profit drives growth, salary increases, and corporate investment.

In the organizational market, where customers include both governments and businesses, buyers are also becoming more price sensitive and better informed. In the consumer market, consumers are using the Internet to make wiser purchasing decisions. Computerized information systems enable the organizational buyer to compare price and performance with great ease and accuracy. Improved communication and the increased use of telemarketing and computer-aided selling have also opened up many markets to new competitors. Finally, competition in general is increasing, so some installations, accessories, and component parts are being marketed like indistinguishable commodities.

2 PRICING OBJECTIVES

List and explain a variety of pricing objectives

To survive in today's highly competitive marketplace, companies need pricing objectives that are specific, attainable, and measurable. Realistic pricing goals then require periodic monitoring to determine the effectiveness of the company's strategy. For convenience, pricing objectives can be divided into three categories: profit oriented, sales oriented, and status quo.

PROFIT-ORIENTED PRICING OBJECTIVES

Profit-oriented objectives include profit maximization, satisfactory profits, and target return on investment. A brief discussion of each of these objectives follows.

Profit Maximization

Profit maximization means setting prices so that total revenue is as large as possible relative to total costs. Profit maximization does not always mean high prices. Both price and profits depend on the type of competitive environment a firm faces, such as whether it is in a monopoly position (being the only seller) or in a much more competitive situation. Also, remember that a firm cannot charge a price higher than the product's perceived value. Many firms do not have the accounting data they need for maximizing profits. It is easy to say that a company should keep producing and selling goods or services as long as revenues exceed costs. Yet it is often hard to set up an accounting system that can accurately determine the point of profit maximization.

In attempting to maximize profits, managers can try to expand revenue by increasing customer satisfaction or they can attempt to reduce costs by operating more efficiently. A third possibility is to attempt to do both. Recent research has shown that striving to enhance customer satisfaction leads to greater profitability

Setting the right price on a product is extremely critical and so is a source of much stress for the marketing manager. Part of the reason is the continuous flood of new products that encourages shoppers to carefully compare prices.

(and customer satisfaction) than following a cost reduction strategy or attempting to do both.[3] This means that companies should consider allocating more resources to customer service initiatives, loyalty programs, and customer relationship management programs and allocating fewer resources to programs that are designed to improve efficiency and reduce costs. Both types of programs, of course, are critical to the success of the firm.

Satisfactory Profits

Satisfactory profits are a reasonable level of profits. Rather than maximizing profits, many organizations strive for profits that are satisfactory to the stockholders and management—in other words, a level of profits consistent with the level of risk an organization faces. In a risky industry, a satisfactory profit may be 35 percent. In a low-risk industry, it might be 7 percent. To maximize profits, a small-business owner might have to keep his or her store open seven days a week. However, the owner might not want to work that hard and might be satisfied with less profit and more leisure time.

Target Return on Investment

return on investment (ROI)
Net profit after taxes divided by total assets.

The most common profit objective is a target **return on investment (ROI)**, sometimes called the firm's return on total assets. ROI measures management's overall effectiveness in generating profits with the available assets. The higher the firm's return on investment, the better off the firm is. Many companies, including DuPont Canada, General Motors, Navistar International, ExxonMobil, and Magna, use target return on investment as their main pricing goal. In summary, ROI is a percentage that puts a firm's profits into perspective by showing profits relative to investment. Return on investment is calculated as follows:

$$\text{Return on investment} = \frac{\text{Net profits after taxes}}{\text{Total assets}}$$

Assume that in 2011 Johnson Controls had assets of $4.5 million, net profits of $550,000, and a target ROI of 10 percent. This was the actual ROI:

$$\text{ROI} = \frac{\$550,000}{\$4,500,000}$$
$$= 12.2\%$$

As you can see, the actual ROI for Johnson Controls exceeded its target. Comparing the 12.2 percent ROI of Johnson Controls with the industry average provides a yet more meaningful picture. Any ROI needs to be evaluated in relation to the competitive environment, risks in the industry, and economic conditions. Generally speaking, firms seek ROIs in the 10 to 30 percent range. For example, General Electric seeks a 25 percent ROI, whereas Alcoa, Rubbermaid, and most major pharmaceutical companies strive for a 20 percent ROI. In some industries, such as the grocery industry, a return of less than 5 percent is common and acceptable.

A company with a target ROI can predetermine its desired level of profitability. The marketing manager can use the standard, such as 10 percent ROI, to determine whether a particular price and marketing mix are feasible. In addition, however, the manager must weigh the risk of a given strategy even if the return is in the acceptable range.

SALES-ORIENTED PRICING OBJECTIVES

Sales-oriented pricing objectives are based either on market share or on dollar or unit sales. Alternatively, a marketing manager could strive for sales maximization.

Market Share

Market share is a company's product sales as a percentage of total sales for that industry. Sales can be reported in dollars or in units of product. It is very important to know whether market share is expressed in revenue or units because the results may be different. Consider four companies competing in an industry with 2,000,000 total unit sales and total industry revenue of $4 million (see Exhibit 16.1). Company A has the largest unit market share at 50 percent, but it has only 25 percent of the revenue market share. In contrast, company D has only a 15 percent unit share but the largest revenue share at 30 percent. Market share may be expressed in terms of revenue or units.

Many companies believe that maintaining or increasing market share is an indicator of the effectiveness of their marketing mix. Larger market shares have indeed often meant higher profits, thanks to greater economies of scale, market power, and ability to compensate top-quality management. Conventional wisdom also says that market share and return on investment are strongly related. For the most part they are; however, many companies with low market share survive and even prosper.

Conventional wisdom about market share and profitability isn't always reliable. Because of extreme competition in some industries, many market share leaders either do not reach their target ROI or actually lose money. Air Canada, the largest air carrier in the country, has exhibited poor financial performance in recent years. General Motors Canada, the leading market share automotive company in the country, needed government bailouts in 2009 to pay its bills. Freightliner grew its market share to 36 percent to become the market share leader in the heavy truck market but lost hundreds of millions of dollars and had to close plants and slash jobs. Procter & Gamble switched from market share to ROI objectives after realizing that profits don't automatically follow from a large market share. PepsiCo says its new Pepsi challenge is to be No. 1 in share of industry profit, not in share of sales volume.

Still, the struggle for market share can be all-consuming for some companies. For years, Intel Corporation has had a "monopoly grip" on the chip market. Advanced Micro Devices (AMD) has had a singular focus of breaking that grip. Through acquisitions, advanced technology, and aggressive pricing, AMD attained 23 percent market share. Together, the two companies account for 99 percent of the chip market for the X86 processor. AMD's objective is to grow its total chip market share to 30 percent over the next several years.[4]

Research organizations like ACNielsen and Information Resources, Inc., provide excellent market share reports for many different industries. These reports enable companies to track their performance in various product categories over time. And many times, market share and profits do work out the way they're expected to. Magna, the largest automotive parts company in Canada, was, as usual, the highest-profit automotive parts company in Canada for 2009.

EXHIBIT 16.1

Two Ways to Measure Market Share (Units and Revenue)

Company	Units Sold	Unit Price	Total Revenue	Unit Market Share	Revenue Market Share
A	1,000,000	$1.00	$1,000,000	50%	25%
B	200,000	4.00	800,000	10	20
C	500,000	2.00	1,000,000	25	25
D	300,000	4.00	1,200,000	15	30
Total	2,000,000		$4,000,000		

Sales Maximization

Rather than strive for market share, sometimes companies try to maximize sales. A firm with the objective of maximizing sales ignores profits, competition, and the marketing environment as long as sales are rising.

If a company is strapped for funds or faces an uncertain future, it may try to generate a maximum amount of cash in the short run. Management's task when using this objective is to calculate which price–quantity relationship generates the greatest cash revenue. Sales maximization can also be used effectively on a temporary basis to sell off excess inventory. It is not uncommon to find Christmas cards, ornaments, and so on discounted at 50 to 70 percent off retail prices after the holiday season. In addition, management can use sales maximization for year-end sales to clear out old models before introducing the new ones.

Maximization of cash should never be a long-run objective because cash maximization may mean little or no profitability. Without profits, a company cannot survive.

STATUS QUO PRICING OBJECTIVES

status quo pricing
A pricing objective that maintains existing prices or meets the competition's prices.

Status quo pricing seeks to maintain existing prices or to meet the competition's prices. This third category of pricing objectives has the major advantage of requiring little planning. It is essentially a passive policy.

Often firms competing in an industry with an established price leader simply meet the competition's prices. These industries typically have fewer price wars than those with direct price competition. In other cases, managers regularly shop competitors' stores to ensure that their prices are comparable. Fast-food chains regularly monitor one another's prices. Middle managers of Zellers may visit competing Walmart stores to compare prices and make adjustments.

REVIEW LEARNING OUTCOME 2

2 | List and explain a variety of pricing objectives

Profit-Oriented			Sales-Oriented		Status Quo
Profit maximization	Satisfactory Profits	Target ROI	Market Share	Sales Maximization	Maintain Existing Price
• Drive down costs • Increase revenue		Net profit after tax ÷ Total assets	• Unit • Revenue	• Generate cash	• Meet the competition • Passive policy

3 THE DEMAND DETERMINANT OF PRICE

Explain the role of demand in price determination

After marketing managers establish pricing goals, they must set specific prices to reach those goals. The price they set for each product depends mostly on two factors: the demand for the good or service and the cost to the seller for that good or service. When pricing goals are mainly sales oriented, demand considerations usually dominate. Other factors, such as distribution and promotion strategies, perceived quality, demands of large customers, the Internet, and stage of the product life cycle, can also influence price.

THE NATURE OF DEMAND

demand
The quantity of a product that will be sold in the market at various prices for a specified period.

Demand is the quantity of a product that will be sold in the market at various prices for a specified period. The quantity of a product that people will buy depends on its

EXHIBIT 16.2

Demand Curve and Demand Schedule for Fruit Smoothies

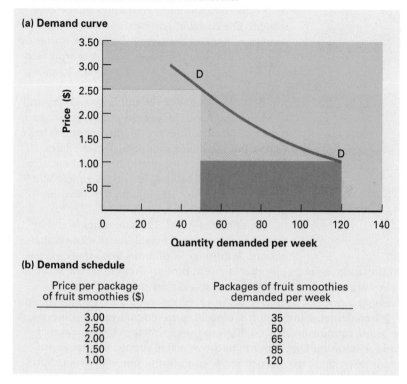

(a) Demand curve

(b) Demand schedule

Price per package of fruit smoothies ($)	Packages of fruit smoothies demanded per week
3.00	35
2.50	50
2.00	65
1.50	85
1.00	120

EXHIBIT 16.3

Supply Curve and Supply Schedule for Fruit Smoothies

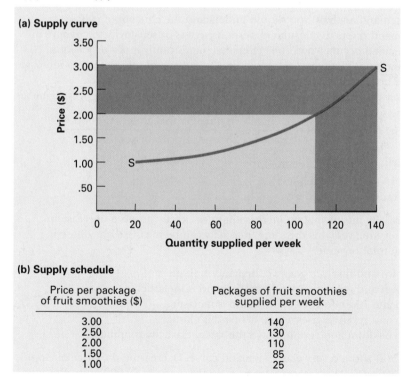

(a) Supply curve

(b) Supply schedule

Price per package of fruit smoothies ($)	Packages of fruit smoothies supplied per week
3.00	140
2.50	130
2.00	110
1.50	85
1.00	25

supply
The quantity of a product that will be offered to the market by a supplier at various prices for a specified period.

price. The higher the price, the fewer goods or services consumers will demand. Conversely, the lower the price, the more goods or services they will demand.

This trend is illustrated in Exhibit 16.2(a), which graphs the demand per week for fruit smoothies at various prices. This graph is called a *demand curve*. The vertical axis of the graph shows different prices of fruit smoothies, measured in dollars per package. The horizontal axis measures the quantity of fruit smoothies that will be demanded per week at each price. For example, at a price of $2.50, 50 smoothies will be sold per week; at $1.00, consumers will demand 120 smoothies, as the *demand schedule* in Exhibit 16.2(b) shows.

The demand curve in Exhibit 16.2 slopes downward and to the right. This indicates that more fruit smoothies are demanded as the price is lowered. In other words, if smoothie makers put a greater quantity on the market, then their hope of selling all of it will be realized only by selling it at a lower price.

One reason more is sold at lower prices than at higher prices is that lower prices bring in new buyers. This fact might not be so obvious with fruit smoothies, but consider the example of steak. As the price of steak drops lower and lower, some people who have not been eating steak will probably start buying it rather than hamburger. With each reduction in price, existing customers may also buy extra amounts. Similarly, if the price of fruit smoothies falls low enough, some people will buy more than they have bought in the past.

Supply is the quantity of a product that will be offered to the market by a supplier or suppliers at various prices for a specified period. Exhibit 16.3(a) illustrates the resulting *supply curve* for fruit smoothies. Unlike the falling demand curve, the supply curve for fruit smoothies slopes upward and to the right. At higher prices, smoothie makers will obtain more resources (apples, peaches, strawberries) and make more smoothies. If the price consumers are willing to pay for smoothies increases, producers can afford to buy more ingredients and offer more for sale.

Output tends to increase at higher prices because makers can earn greater profits. The *supply schedule* in Exhibit 16.3(b) shows that at $2.00 suppliers are willing to place 110 smoothies on the market, but they will offer 140 packages at a price of $3.00.

HOW DEMAND AND SUPPLY ESTABLISH PRICES

At this point, let's combine the concepts of demand and supply to see how market prices are determined. So far, the premise is that if the price is X, then consumers will

EXHIBIT 16.4

Equilibrium Price for Fruit Smoothies

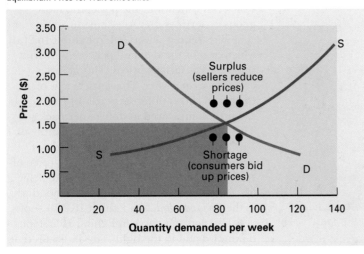

purchase Y amount of smoothies. How high or low will prices actually go? How many smoothies will be produced? How many smoothies will be consumed? The demand curve cannot predict consumption, nor can the supply curve alone forecast production. Instead, we need to look at what happens when supply and demand interact, as shown in Exhibit 16.4.

At a price of $3.00, the public would demand only 35 smoothies. However, suppliers stand ready to place 140 smoothies on the market at this price (data from the demand and supply schedules). If 140 smoothies were supplied, this would create a surplus of 105 smoothies. How does a merchant eliminate a surplus? The merchant lowers the price.

At a price of $1.00, 120 smoothies would be demanded, but only 25 would be placed on the market. A shortage of 95 units would be created.

If a product is in short supply and consumers want it, how do they entice the seller to provide more? They offer more money—that is, pay a higher price.

Now let's examine a price of $1.50. At this price, 85 smoothies are demanded and 85 are supplied. When demand and supply are equal, **price equilibrium** is achieved. A temporary price below equilibrium, say, $1.00, results in a shortage because at that price the demand for smoothies is greater than the available supply. Shortages put upward pressure on price. Similarly, a price above equilibrium puts a downward pressure on price. At equilibrium, there is no inclination for prices to rise or fall.

price equilibrium
The price at which demand and supply are equal.

ELASTICITY OF DEMAND

To appreciate demand analysis, you should understand the concept of elasticity. **Elasticity of demand** refers to consumers' responsiveness or sensitivity to changes in price. **Elastic demand** occurs when consumers buy significantly more or less of a product when the price changes. Conversely, **inelastic demand** means that an increase or a decrease in price will not significantly affect demand for the product.

Elasticity over the range of a demand curve can be measured by using this formula:

elasticity of demand
Consumers' responsiveness or sensitivity to changes in price.

elastic demand
A situation in which consumer demand is sensitive to changes in price.

inelastic demand
A situation in which an increase or a decrease in price will not significantly affect demand for the product.

$$\text{Elasticity } (E) = \frac{\text{Percentage change in quantity demanded of good A}}{\text{Percentage change in price of good A}}$$

If E is greater than 1, demand is elastic.
If E is less than 1, demand is inelastic.
If E is equal to 1, demand is unitary.

unitary elasticity
A situation in which total revenue remains the same when prices change.

Unitary elasticity means that an increase in sales exactly offsets a decrease in prices, so total revenue remains the same. Elasticity can be measured by observing these changes in total revenue:

If price goes down and revenue goes up, demand is elastic.
If price goes down and revenue goes down, demand is inelastic.
If price goes up and revenue goes up, demand is inelastic.
If price goes up and revenue goes down, demand is elastic.
If price goes up or down and revenue stays the same, elasticity is unitary.

Exhibit 16.5(a) shows a very elastic demand curve. Decreasing the price of Apple iPhones from $300 to $200 increases sales from 18,000 units to 59,000 units. Revenue increases from $5.4 million ($300 × 18,000) to $11.8 million ($200 × 59,000). The price decrease results in a large increase in unit sales and revenue.

Exhibit 16.5(b) shows a completely inelastic demand curve. Let's assume that Ontario dropped its vehicle licence plate renewal fee from $70 to $60. There is no change in the number of vehicle licence renewals in Ontario. Decreasing the price

EXHIBIT 16.5

Elasticity of Demand for Apple iPhones and Vehicle Licence Plate Renewals

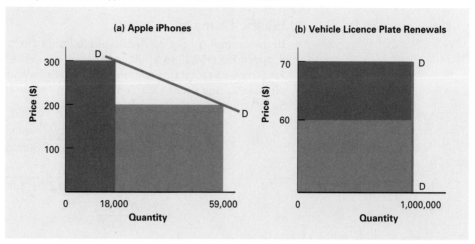

did not cause people to increase licence renewals. Demand is completely inelastic for licence renewals as they are required by law. Thus it also follows that Ontario could double the fee to $140 and double the province's licence renewal revenues.

Exhibit 16.6 presents the demand curve and demand schedule for bottles of Spring Break suntan lotion. Let's follow the demand curve from the highest price to the lowest and examine what happens to elasticity as the price decreases.

Inelastic Demand

The initial decrease in the price of Spring Break suntan lotion, from $5.00 to $2.25, results in a decrease in total revenue of $969 ($5,075 − $4,106). When price and total revenue fall, demand is inelastic. The decrease in price is much greater than the increase in suntan lotion sales (810 bottles). Demand is therefore not very flexible in the price range from $5.00 to $2.25. When demand is inelastic, sellers can raise prices

EXHIBIT 16.6

Demand for Bottles of Spring Break Suntan Lotion

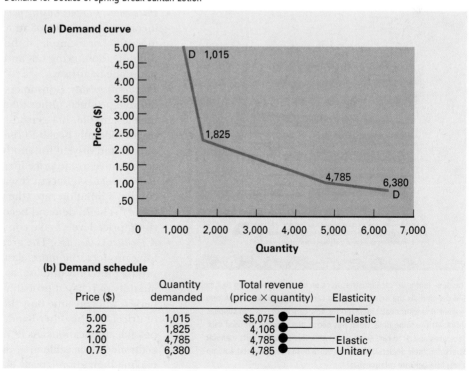

and increase total revenue. Often items that are relatively inexpensive but convenient tend to have inelastic demand.

Elastic Demand

In the example of Spring Break suntan lotion (Exhibit 16.6), when the price is dropped from $2.25 to $1.00, total revenue increases by $679 ($4,785 − $4,106). An increase in total revenue when price falls indicates that demand is elastic. Let's measure Spring Break's elasticity of demand when the price drops from $2.25 to $1.00 by applying the formula presented earlier:

$$E = \frac{\text{Change in quantity}/(\text{Sum of quantities}/2)}{\text{Change in price}/(\text{Sum of prices}/2)}$$

$$= \frac{(4,785 - 1,825)/[(1,825 + 4,785)/2]}{(2.25 - 1)/[(2.25 + 1.00)/2]}$$

$$= \frac{2,960/3,305}{1.25/1.63}$$

$$= \frac{.896}{.767}$$

$$= 1.17$$

Because E is greater than 1, demand is elastic.

Factors That Affect Elasticity

Several factors affect elasticity of demand, including the following:

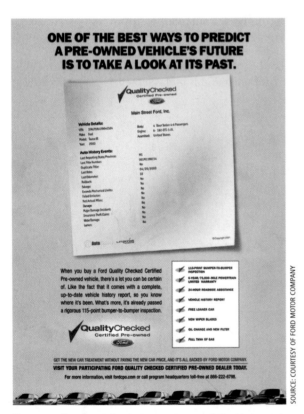

ONE OF THE BEST WAYS TO PREDICT A PRE-OWNED VEHICLE'S FUTURE IS TO TAKE A LOOK AT ITS PAST.

When you buy a Ford Quality Checked Certified Pre-owned vehicle, there's a lot you can be certain of. Like the fact that it comes with a complete, up-to-date vehicle history report, so you know where it's been. What's more, it's already passed a rigorous 115-point bumper-to-bumper inspection.

QualityChecked
Certified Pre-owned

GET THE NEW CAR TREATMENT WITHOUT PAYING THE NEW CAR PRICE, AND IT'S ALL BACKED BY FORD MOTOR COMPANY.
VISIT YOUR PARTICIPATING FORD QUALITY CHECKED CERTIFIED PRE-OWNED DEALER TODAY.
For more information, visit fordcpo.com or call program headquarters toll-free at 866-222-6798.

The new- and used-car industries have an inverse relationship to supply and demand. As the demand for new cars rises (such as with the zero percent financing deals), demand for new cars increases and supplies shrink. At the same time, when this occurs, the demand for used cars decreases and used-car inventories swell. This situation puts manufacturers and their dealers (who often stock both new and used automobiles) in a delicate relationship.

- *Availability of substitutes:* When many substitute products are available, the consumer can easily switch from one product to another, making demand elastic. The same is true in reverse. When there are no substitutes, a person will pay whatever price is charged. Bose Stereo equipment is priced 300 to 500 percent higher than other stereo brands. Yet consumers are willing to pay the higher price because they perceive the Bose equipment as being so superior to other brands that there is no acceptable substitute.
- *Price relative to purchasing power:* If a price is so low that it is an inconsequential part of an individual's budget, demand will be inelastic. For example, if the price of salt doubles, consumers will not stop putting salt and pepper on their eggs, because salt is cheap anyway.
- *Product durability:* Consumers often have the option of repairing durable products rather than replacing them, thus prolonging their useful life. If a person had planned to buy a new car and prices suddenly began to rise, he or she might elect to fix the old car and drive it for another year. In other words, people are sensitive to the price increase, and demand is elastic.
- *Rate of inflation:* Recent research has found that when a country's inflation rate (the rate at which the price level is rising) is high, demand becomes more elastic. In other words, rising price levels make consumers more price sensitive.[5]
- *A product's other uses:* The greater the number of different uses for a product, the more elastic demand tends to be. If a product has only one use, as may be true of a medicine, the quantity purchased probably will not vary as price varies. A person will consume only the prescribed quantity, regardless of price. On the other hand, a product like steel has many possible applications. As its price falls, steel becomes more economically feasible in a wider variety of applications, thereby making demand relatively elastic.

Examples of both elastic and inelastic demand abound in everyday life. For example, as the cell phone rate in India fell from 16.8 rupees per minute to 4.5 rupees per minute, the number of cell phone subscribers tripled.[6] When car manufacturers first began offering zero percent financing, sales of new vehicles jumped 35 percent over the same period a year earlier. Sales of so many new cars resulted in a huge surplus of used vehicles. When demand remains constant and supply increases, prices fall. In this case, the price of a used Lexus fell 12 percent from the price for a comparable vehicle a year earlier; the price of a used Chevrolet Tahoe fell 14 percent, and the price of a used Ford F-series pickup truck fell 11 percent.[7] This is simply supply and demand at work.

3   Explain the role of demand in price determination

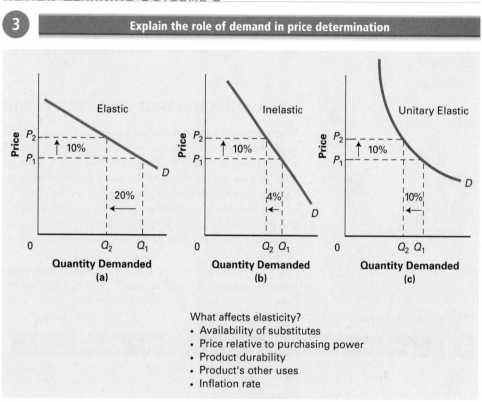

What affects elasticity?
- Availability of substitutes
- Price relative to purchasing power
- Product durability
- Product's other uses
- Inflation rate

4   THE POWER OF YIELD MANAGEMENT SYSTEMS AND TARGETING TECHNOLOGY

Understand the concept of yield management systems

yield management systems (YMS)
A technique for adjusting prices that uses complex mathematical software to profitably fill unused capacity by discounting early purchases, limiting early sales at these discounted prices, and overbooking capacity.

Another important tool for gaining pricing power is the yield management system. More and more companies are turning to yield management systems to help fine-tune prices. First developed in the airline industry, **yield management systems (YMS)** use complex mathematical software to profitably fill unused capacity. The software employs techniques such as discounting early purchases, limiting early sales at these discounted prices, and overbooking capacity. YMSs now are appearing in other services such as lodging, other forms of transportation, rental firms, and retailing.

Yield management systems are spreading beyond service industries as their popularity increases. The lessons of airlines and hotels aren't entirely applicable to other industries, however, because plane seats and hotel rooms are perishable—if they go empty, the revenue opportunity is lost forever. So it makes sense to slash prices to move toward capacity if it's possible to do so without reducing the prices that other customers pay. Cars and steel aren't so perishable. Still, the capacity to make these goods is perishable. An underused factory or mill is a lost revenue opportunity. So it makes sense to cut prices to use up capacity if it's possible to do so while getting other customers to pay full price.

Yield management systems have helped customers such as Gymboree, retailer Ann Taylor, and Gap to determine the best markdown price. The software has boosted profit margins from 5 to 18 percent. A YMS used by Buy.com analyzes dozens of factors such as a product's life cycle, competitors' prices, and past sales data at various price points before churning out a list of possible prices and calculating the best ones. New sales data are fed back into the formulae daily to refine the process. Systems such as this aren't cheap, however, costing from $200,000 to $500,000.[8]

Some companies, such as Omni Hotels, are creating their own YMS software. Omni CHARM (Centralized Hotel Automated Revenue Management), created by Omni Hotels, predicts demand and indicates when to discount rooms and when to charge the maximum. Marriott Hotels & Resorts, with a similar system, earns an additional estimated $400 million per year.[9]

BEHAVIOURAL TARGETING TECHNOLOGY

Internet retailers are now offering different prices and promotional offers to different customers based on their Internet shopping and browsing habits. Using Internet cookies and new targeting software, Internet retailers can identify you each time you visit, and e-stores can gather reams of preferences as you shop. "It's as if we had a little camera that can watch you flip through a catalogue. We can see where you stopped, what pages you dog-eared, what pages you ripped out and what made you pick up the phone to buy," says John Squire, vice-president of product strategy at Coremetrics, a software company that helps on-line retailers analyze and act on consumer behaviour.[10]

At Overstock.com, the company watches how long you linger on the site and how much you spend. That alone could determine whether you'll see an ad for a liquidation sale on last year's sweatshirts or a notice about a new shipment of pricey freshwater pearls. Watchmaker Fossil sometimes offers discounts and deals to first-time site visitors that it hides from repeat customers. Targeted offers can also boost the effectiveness of e-mail campaigns. Consumers typically open one out of five e-mail offers from retailers and only 20 percent of those views lead to a site visit. When e-mail is customized with anything from the customer's name to a discount for something they've bought before, conversion rates double.[11] No wonder, then, that high-profile e-commerce sites like Travelocity.com and eBay.com, along with the on-line arms of big retailers like Best Buy and Petco, are pouring resources into targeting technology.

REVIEW LEARNING OUTCOME 4

4 | Understand the concept of yield management systems

Price = $x

YMS varies price to fill capacity (adjusts price to increase demand to meet supply)

Discounted Price = $x − y%$

5 THE COST DETERMINANT OF PRICE

Describe cost-oriented pricing strategies

Sometimes companies minimize or ignore the importance of demand and decide to price their products largely or solely on the basis of costs. Prices determined strictly on the basis of costs may be too high for the target market, thereby reducing or eliminating sales. On the other hand, cost-based prices may be too low, causing the firm to earn a lower return than it should. Nevertheless, costs should generally be part of any price determination, if only as a floor below which a good or service must not be priced in the long run.

The idea of cost may seem simple, but it is actually a multifaceted concept, especially for producers. A **variable cost** is a cost that varies with changes in the level of output. An example of a variable cost is the cost of materials. In contrast, a **fixed cost** does not change as output is increased or decreased. Examples include rent and executives' salaries.

To compare the cost of production to the selling price of a product, it is helpful to calculate costs per unit, or average costs. **Average variable cost (AVC)** equals total variable costs divided by quantity of output. **Average total cost (ATC)** equals total costs divided by output. As the graph in Exhibit 16.7(a) shows, AVC and ATC are basically U-shaped curves. In contrast, average fixed costs (AFC) decline continually as output increases because total fixed costs are constant.

Marginal cost (MC) is the change in total costs associated with a one-unit change in output. Exhibit 16.7(b) shows that when output rises from seven to eight units, the change in total cost is from $640 to $750; therefore, the marginal cost is $110.

All the curves illustrated in Exhibit 16.7(a) have definite relationships:

- AVC plus AFC equals ATC.
- MC falls for a while and then turns upward, in this case after the fourth unit. At that point diminishing returns set in, meaning that less output is produced for every additional dollar spent on variable input.
- MC intersects both AVC and ATC at their lowest possible points.
- When MC is less than AVC or ATC, the incremental cost will continue to pull the averages down. Conversely, when MC is greater than AVC or ATC, it pulls the averages up, and ATC and AVC begin to rise.
- The minimum point on the ATC curve is the least cost point for a fixed-capacity firm, although it is not necessarily the most profitable point.

Costs can be used to set prices in a variety of ways. Markup pricing is relatively simple to use. Profit maximization pricing and break-even pricing make use of the more complicated concepts of cost.

Sidebar definitions

variable cost
A cost that varies with changes in the level of output.

fixed cost
A cost that does not change as output is increased or decreased.

average variable cost (AVC)
Total variable costs divided by quantity of output.

average total cost (ATC)
Total costs divided by quantity of output.

marginal cost (MC)
The change in total costs associated with a one-unit change in output.

markup pricing
The cost of buying the product from the producer plus amounts for profit and for expenses.

Although yield management is being implemented across diverse and multiple industries, it continues to be the hallmark of the travel industry. Often hotels like Omni offer different weekend specials each week to encourage the kind of spontaneous travel that will maximize company revenues.

SOURCE: COURTESY OF OMNI HOTELS

MARKUP PRICING

Markup pricing is the most popular method used by wholesalers and retailers to establish a selling price. **Markup pricing** uses the cost of buying the product from the producer and adds amounts for profit and for expenses. The total is the selling price.

A retailer, for example, adds a certain percentage to the cost of the merchandise received to arrive at the retail price. An item that costs the retailer $1.80 and is sold for $2.20 carries a markup of 40 cents, which is a markup of 22 percent over the cost (40¢/$1.80). Retailers, however, tend to discuss markup in terms of its percentage of the retail price—in this example, 18 percent (40¢/$2.20). The difference between the retailer's cost and the selling price (40 cents) is the gross margin.

EXHIBIT 16.7

Hypothetical Set of Cost Curves and a Cost Schedule

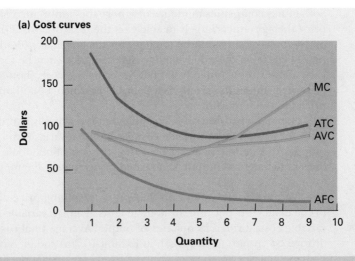

(a) Cost curves

(b) Cost schedule

	Total-cost data, per week			Average-cost data, per week			
(1) Total product (Q)	(2) Total fixed cost (TFC)	(3) Total variable cost (TVC)	(4) Total cost (TC)	(5) Average fixed cost (AFC)	(6) Average variable cost (AVC)	(7) Average total cost (ATC)	(8) Marginal cost (MC)
			$TC = TFC + TVC$	$AFC = \dfrac{TFC}{Q}$	$AVC = \dfrac{TVC}{Q}$	$ATC = \dfrac{TC}{Q}$	$MC = \dfrac{\text{change in TC}}{\text{change in Q}}$
0	$100	$ 0	$ 100	—	—	—	—
1	100	90	190	$100.00	$90.00	$190.00	$ 90
2	100	170	270	50.00	85.00	135.00	80
3	100	240	340	33.33	80.00	113.33	70
4	100	300	400	25.00	75.00	100.00	60
5	100	370	470	20.00	74.00	94.00	70
6	100	450	550	16.67	75.00	91.67	80
7	100	540	640	14.29	77.14	91.43	90
8	100	650	750	12.50	81.25	93.75	110
9	100	780	880	11.11	86.67	97.78	130
10	100	930	1,030	10.00	93.00	103.00	150

The formula for calculating the retail price given a certain desired markup is as follows:

$$\text{Retail price} = \frac{\text{Cost}}{1 - \text{Desired return on sales}}$$

Using the previous example, if a retailer purchases an item for $1.80 and desires a return on sales of 18 percent, the selling price becomes $2.20:

$$\text{Retail price} = \frac{\$1.80}{1 - .18} = \$2.20$$

If the retailer wants a 30 percent return on sales, then

$$\text{Retail price} = \frac{\$1.80}{1 - .30} = \$2.57$$

To use markup based on cost or selling price effectively, the marketing manager must calculate an adequate gross margin—the amount added to cost to determine price. The margin must provide adequate funds to cover selling expenses and the desired profit. Once an appropriate margin has been determined, the markup approach has the advantage of being easy to use. Walmart, for example, strives for a gross margin of around 16 percent.

Markups are often based on experience. For example, many small retailers mark up merchandise 100 percent over cost. In other words, they double the cost. This practice is called **keystoning**. Some other factors that influence markups are the merchandise's appeal to customers, past response to the markup (an implicit demand consideration), the item's promotional value, the seasonality of the goods, their fashion appeal, the product's traditional selling price, and competition. The biggest advantage of markup pricing is its simplicity. The primary disadvantage is that it ignores demand and may result in overpricing or underpricing the merchandise. What if you let your customers determine the markup as the Customer Experience box indicates?

PROFIT MAXIMIZATION PRICING

Producers tend to use more complicated methods of setting prices than distributors use. One is **profit maximization**, which occurs when marginal revenue equals marginal cost. You learned earlier that marginal cost is the change in total costs associated with a one-unit change in output. Similarly, **marginal revenue (MR)** is the extra revenue

keystoning
The practice of marking up prices by 100 percent, or doubling the cost.

profit maximization
A method of setting prices that occurs when marginal revenue equals marginal cost.

marginal revenue (MR)
The extra revenue associated with selling an extra unit of output or the change in total revenue with a one-unit change in output.

Customer Experience

 ## PAY WHAT IT'S WORTH

In pay-what-you-want restaurants, you decide how much your meal is worth. And from Vienna to London, Berlin to Melbourne, restaurants are reeling customers in with this unique format.

"The point is to attract people and to bring back some joie-de-vivre to the city," says George Pappas, co-owner of Montreal's Taverne Crescent, where the three owners introduced the pay-what-you-want system from Monday to Friday. They got the idea from a friend who had dined at a Little Bay restaurant in London, England. Little Bay, a popular London chain, first introduced the idea at its Central London location and attracted 10,000 customers in one month and a media frenzy. With this success, the idea was expanded to all of the Little Bay locations.

The pay-what-you-want restaurant model has had similar success around the world. Vienna, Austria, is home to Der Wiener Deewan, a pay-what-you-want Pakistani curry buffet. In Berlin, Germany, three restaurants known as the Berlin Weinerei are pay-what-you-want. Nearly 15 years ago owner Jurgen Stumpf started inviting friends to dine at his wine shop once a week. Neighbour Mariano Goni would cook. Folks coughed up what they wanted for their meals and the concept stuck. Other pay-what-you-want restaurants are Lentil as Anything, a chain of six organic vegetarian restaurants in Melbourne, Australia, and the Terra Bit Lounge (Kirkland, Washington) and One World Café (Salt Lake City, Utah) in the United States.

Marketing professor Robert Soroka of McGill University explains how consumer confidence is a factor in the pay-what-you-want trend: "People spend less on what they deem to be luxuries. In a recessionary period, these restaurants are eliminating what they perceive to be the critical block from getting the sale." Also important is the media hype. Montreal has more than 6,000 restaurants. "So you have to figure out ways to differentiate yourself from everyone else," says Professor Soroka.

Madeline Dube, a recent customer at Montreal's Taverne Crescent paid $20 for her calamari appetizer and chicken Caesar salad. Her friend, Gabrielle Gagne, paid $20 for her mushroom soup and pasta.

"All in all, this is not too risky an approach," said Jean-Francois Ouellet, an associate marketing professor at HEC Montreal. "Research shows that consumers, when given the option of paying whatever they want for a good or service, will actually pay more than what providers would have elected to charge. This is due to social desirability: consumers don't want to be perceived as cheap."

"I've really seen some good-hearted people," said Taverne Crescent server Gary Mathieu, who shares with the rest of the wait staff 15 percent of the restaurant's daily take. "People don't take advantage."[12]

Would the pay-what-you-want concept work in an upscale restaurant? Why or why not? Could this model be applied to other types of businesses? Give an example.

EXHIBIT 16.8

Point of Profit Maximization

Quantity	Marginal Revenue (MR)	Marginal Cost (MC)	Cumulative Total Profit
0	—	—	—
1	$140	$90	$50
2	130	80	100
3	105	70	135
4	95	60	170
5	85	70	185
*6	80	80	185
7	75	90	170
8	60	110	120
9	50	130	40
10	40	150	(70)

*Profit maximization

break-even analysis
A method of determining what sales volume must be reached before total revenue equals total costs.

associated with selling an extra unit of output. As long as the revenue of the last unit produced and sold is greater than the cost of the last unit produced and sold, the firm should continue manufacturing and selling the product.

Exhibit 16.8 shows the marginal revenues and marginal costs for a hypothetical firm, using the cost data from Exhibit 16.7(b). The profit-maximizing quantity, where MR = MC, is six units. You might say, "If profit is zero, why produce the sixth unit? Why not stop at five?" In fact, you would be right. The firm, however, would not know that the sixth unit would produce zero profits until it determined that profits were no longer increasing. Economists suggest producing up to the point where MR = MC. If marginal revenue is just one penny greater than marginal costs, it will still increase total profits.

BREAK-EVEN PRICING

Now let's take a closer look at the relationship between sales and cost. **Break-even analysis** determines what sales volume must be reached before the company breaks even (its total revenue equals total costs).

The typical break-even model assumes a given fixed cost and a constant average variable cost. Suppose that Universal Sportswear, a hypothetical firm, has fixed costs of $2,000 and that the cost of labour and materials for each unit produced is 50 cents. Assume that it can sell up to 6,000 units of its product at $1.00 without having to lower its price.

Exhibit 16.9(a) illustrates Universal Sportswear's break-even point. As Exhibit 16.9(b) indicates, Universal Sportswear's total variable costs increase by 50 cents every time a new unit is produced and total fixed costs remain constant at $2,000 regardless of the level of output. Therefore, for 4,000 units of output, Universal Sportswear has $2,000 in fixed costs and $2,000 in total variable costs (4,000 units × 50¢), or $4,000 in total costs.

Revenue is also $4,000 (4,000 units × $1.00), resulting in a net profit of zero dollars at the break-even point of 4,000 units. Notice that once the firm gets past the break-even point, the gap between total revenue and total costs gets wider and wider because both functions are assumed to be linear.

The formula for calculating break-even quantities is simple:

$$\text{Break-even quantity} = \frac{\text{Total fixed costs}}{\text{Fixed cost contribution}}$$

Fixed cost contribution is the price minus the average variable cost. Therefore, for Universal Sportswear,

$$\text{Break-even quantity} = \frac{\$2,000}{(\$1.00 - 50¢)} = \frac{\$2,000}{50¢} = 4,000 \text{ units}$$

The advantage of break-even analysis is that it provides a quick estimate of how much the firm must sell to break even and how much profit can be earned if a higher sales volume is obtained. If a firm is operating close to the break-even point, it may want to see what can be done to reduce costs or increase sales.

Break-even analysis is not without several important limitations. Sometimes it is hard to know whether a cost is fixed or variable. If labour wins a tough guaranteed-employment

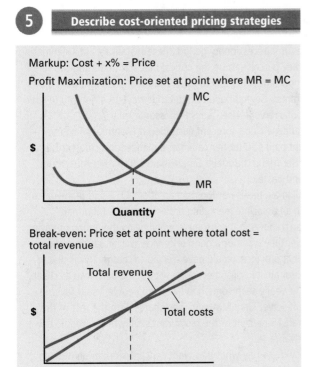

REVIEW LEARNING OUTCOME 5

5 | **Describe cost-oriented pricing strategies**

Markup: Cost + x% = Price

Profit Maximization: Price set at point where MR = MC

MC

$

MR

Quantity

Break-even: Price set at point where total cost = total revenue

Total revenue

$

Total costs

Quantity

EXHIBIT 16.9

Costs, Revenues, and Break-Even Point for Universal Sportswear

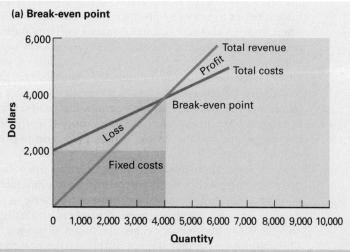

(a) Break-even point

(b) Costs and revenues

Output	Total fixed costs	Average variable costs	Total variable costs	Average total costs	Average revenue (price)	Total revenue	Total costs	Profit or loss
500	$2,000	$0.50	$ 250	$4.50	$1.00	$ 500	$2,250	($1,750)
1,000	2,000	0.50	500	2.50	1.00	1,000	2,500	(1,500)
1,500	2,000	0.50	750	1.83	1.00	1,500	2,750	(1,250)
2,000	2,000	0.50	1,000	1.50	1.00	2,000	3,000	(1,000)
2,500	2,000	0.50	1,250	1.30	1.00	2,500	3,250	(750)
3,000	2,000	0.50	1,500	1.17	1.00	3,000	3,500	(500)
3,500	2,000	0.50	1,750	1.07	1.00	3,500	3,750	(250)
*4,000	2,000	0.50	2,000	1.00	1.00	4,000	4,000	(0)
4,500	2,000	0.50	2,250	.94	1.00	4,500	4,250	250
5,000	2,000	0.50	2,500	.90	1.00	5,000	4,500	500
5,500	2,000	0.50	2,750	.86	1.00	5,500	4,750	750
6,000	2,000	0.50	3,000	.83	1.00	6,000	5,000	1,000

*Break-even point

contract, are the resulting expenses a fixed cost? Are middle-level executives' salaries fixed costs? More important than cost determination is the fact that simple break-even analysis ignores demand. How does Universal Sportswear know it can sell 4,000 units at $1.00? Could it sell the same 4,000 units at $2.00 or even $5.00? Obviously, this information would profoundly affect the firm's pricing decisions.

 OTHER DETERMINANTS OF PRICE

Demonstrate how the product life cycle, competition, distribution and promotion strategies, guaranteed price matching, customer demands, the Internet and extranets, and perceptions of quality can affect price

Other factors besides demand and costs can influence price. For example, the stages in the product life cycle, competition, the product distribution strategy, promotion strategy, and perceived quality can all affect pricing.

STAGES IN THE PRODUCT LIFE CYCLE

As a product moves through its life cycle, the demand for the product and the competitive conditions tend to change:

- *Introductory stage:* Management usually sets prices high during the introductory stage. One reason is that it hopes to recover its development costs quickly. In addition, demand originates in the core of the market (the customers whose needs ideally match the product's attributes) and thus is relatively inelastic. On the other hand, if the target market is highly price sensitive, management often finds it better to price the product at the market level or lower. For example, when Kraft Foods brought out Country Time lemonade, it was priced like similar products in the highly competitive beverage market because the market was price sensitive.

- *Growth stage:* As the product enters the growth stage, prices generally begin to stabilize for several reasons. First, competitors have entered the market, increasing the available supply. Second, the product has begun to appeal to a broader market, often lower income groups. Finally, economies of scale are lowering costs, and the savings can be passed on to the consumer in the form of lower prices.

- *Maturity stage:* Maturity usually brings further price decreases as competition increases and inefficient, high-cost firms are eliminated. Distribution channels become a significant cost factor, however, because of the need to offer wide product lines for highly segmented markets, extensive service requirements, and the sheer number of dealers necessary to absorb high-volume production. The manufacturers that remain in the market toward the end of the maturity stage typically offer similar prices. Usually, only the most efficient remain, and they have comparable costs. At this stage, price increases are usually cost initiated, not demand initiated. Nor do price reductions in the late phase of maturity stimulate much demand. Because demand is limited and producers have similar cost structures, the remaining competitors will probably match price reductions.

- *Decline stage:* The final stage of the life cycle may see further price decreases as the few remaining competitors try to salvage the last vestiges of demand. When only one firm is left in the market, prices begin to stabilize. In fact, prices may eventually rise dramatically if the product survives and moves into the specialty goods category, as horse-drawn carriages and vinyl records have.

THE COMPETITION

Competition varies during the product life cycle and so does its effect on pricing decisions. Although a firm may not have any competition at first, the high prices it charges may eventually induce another firm to enter the market. A number of Internet auto sellers, such as Autobytel.com, have sprung up in response to the perceived high profit margins earned by car dealers.

On the other hand, intense competition can sometimes lead to price wars. What pulls companies into such self-defeating price wars? Often they make the mistake of measuring their success by market share rather than by profitability—but something more is at play. Michael Marn, a partner at McKinsey & Company, the worldwide management consulting firm, says that price wars are often caused by companies misreading or misunderstanding competitors. Marn tells of one McKinsey client, a company that dominated the market for adhesive labels. After a small competitor built a tiny factory with no prospects for further expansion, the company reacted with a price cut of 15 percent and, says Marn, "gave away profitability for two years." Typically, concludes Marn, price wars are "overreactions to threats that either aren't there at all or are not as big as they seem."[13]

Sometimes companies choose to price above the competition, as the Global Perspectives box demonstrates.

DISTRIBUTION STRATEGY

An effective distribution network can often overcome minor flaws in the marketing mix. For example, although consumers may perceive a price as being higher than normal, they may buy the product anyway if it is being sold at a convenient retail outlet.

L'ORÉAL PLAYS THE PRICE-QUALITY CARD IN INDIA

In India most beauty products sell for less than a dollar. L'Oréal SA is betting its future there on products costing three to twenty times as much. The French cosmetics giant has embarked on a strategy that sharply differs from that of its rivals. Having failed to earn a profit selling low-priced shampoo in India, it now hopes to capture the growing ranks of middle-class Indian women by luring them upscale. In shops across the country, L'Oréal's offerings include a $5.60 Garnier Nutrisse hair dye, a $17 L'Oréal Paris face powder, and a $25 Vichy sunscreen. Jaya Sethi says she's willing to splurge. The office assistant in New Delhi recently bought two bottles of the Garnier hair dye. Sethi used to buy cheaper dyes made of henna plant extract but says the foreign brand is "good quality."

Racing to expand in a competitive global market, L'Oréal is tapping into a powerful demographic force: India's emerging middle class, estimated at over 200 million people. Over the past decade, foreign brands, from Tommy Hilfiger jeans to Absolut Vodka, have moved in to capture a slice of the market. At the heart of the transformation in consumer spending is a cultural shift among Indian women. Decades of poverty instilled a strong sense of price-consciousness in women, which was passed on from mothers to daughters. But the generation that came of age during the market liberalization of the early 1990s is more willing to splurge on luxuries. "For these people, consumption is a way of life," says Neelesh Hundekari, principal at AT Kearney Inc., a management consulting firm in Mumbai.

L'Oréal's strategy stands out as particularly aggressive compared with its competitors. Most Western cosmetics companies stock grocery stores in India with low-priced basic shampoo and cold creams that compete with an array of local brands. For example, market leader Hindustan Unilever Ltd. sells 70-cent bottles of body lotion and 90-cent shampoo. Its target audience includes the more than 800 million people in India who live on less than $2 a day. In contrast, L'Oréal's biggest seller in India is its Excellence Crème hair colour—priced at $11 a bottle. "We don't do poor products for poor people," says Alain Evrard, managing director for L'Oréal's Africa, Orient, and Pacific zone.

Evrard says his first step was to understand what products would best resonate with middle-class working women. He spent months speaking with advertising executives and editors of fashion magazines including *Elle*, which had launched in India in 1996. He quizzed L'Oréal's local employees on their families' consumer habits, focusing on hair care. He says the breakthrough came when some of these employees complained that they and their peers were getting grey hairs—and they were still only in their 20s. At the time, Western-style, do-it-yourself hair-colouring kits barely existed in India. Women used henna and other ammonia-based liquids and powders to cover their grey but said ammonia dried out their hair while henna faded quickly.

So L'Oréal introduced Excellence Crème into India. Excellence Crème was one of the French company's most innovative and pricey mass-market products in Europe. In cream form, dye is considered more gentle on hair than liquid products. In India, it cost $9 at introduction—about the same as in France. L'Oréal set out to market it as a luxury purchase. The company signed on Diana Hayden, a Miss World contest winner, as L'Oréal's first Indian advertising face. "For me, beauty starts with beautiful hair," Ms. Hayden cooed in television commercials.[14]

What pricing effects is L'Oréal appealing to with Indian women? Do you think that L'Oréal can use the same strategy in China? Why or why not?

SOURCE: CHRISTINA PASSARIELLO, "BEAUTY FIX: BEHIND L'OREAL'S MAKEOVER IN INDIA: GOING UPSCALE … WHEN CHEAP SHAMPOO DIDN'T SELL, COMPANY TAPPED THE RISING CLASS," WALL STREET JOURNAL, JULY 13, 2007, A1, A8.

Adequate distribution for a new product can often be attained by offering a larger-than-usual profit margin to distributors. A variation on this strategy is to give dealers a large trade allowance to help offset the costs of promotion and further stimulate demand at the retail level.

Manufacturers have gradually been losing control within the distribution channel to wholesalers and retailers who often adopt pricing strategies that serve their own purposes. For instance, some distributors are **selling against the brand**: they place well-known brands on their shelves at high prices while offering other brands—typically, their private-label brands, such as Craftsman tools, Mastercraft auto parts, or Life Brand cosmetics—at lower prices. Of course, sales of the higher-priced brands decline.

Manufacturers can regain some control over price by using an exclusive distribution system by franchising or by avoiding doing business with price-cutting

selling against the brand
Stocking well-known branded items at high prices in order to sell store brands at discounted prices.

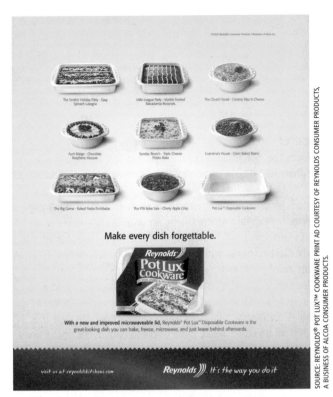

Management usually sets prices higher during the introductory stage of the product life cycle. Still, it must be careful not to set the price so high that it turns customers off. For a product innovation like Reynold's PotLux disposable cookware, how do you think marketing managers decide on a base price?

discounters. Manufacturers can also package merchandise with the selling price marked on it or place goods on consignment. The best way for manufacturers to control prices, however, is to develop brand loyalty in consumers by delivering quality and value.

THE IMPACT OF THE INTERNET

The Internet, corporate networks, and wireless setups are linking people, machines, and companies around the globe—and connecting sellers and buyers as never before. This link is enabling buyers to quickly and easily compare products and prices, putting them in a better bargaining position. At the same time, the technology allows sellers to collect detailed data about customers' buying habits, preferences, and even spending limits so that they can tailor their products and prices.

Picking a Product to Buy Online

The online shopping process begins with selecting a product. If you want a pet, camera, electronics product, or computer but don't know which brand, try **www.activebuyersguide.com,** which will help you narrow your choice. If you want help with outdoor gear, try **http://outside.away.com**. Once you select a brand, you can always get a second opinion at **www.consumersearch.com**. This is an expert site that aggregates reviews from many sources such as *Consumer*

Competition can be a significant factor in pricing. Microsoft's Xbox and Sony's PlayStation are continuing to go head-to-head, much like Coke and Pepsi. Such intense competition has a definite impact on pricing.

Digest, Consumer Reports, and *PC World.* For example, a quick click on sleeping bags led to reviews from *Backpacker* and *Outside* magazines. The problem with expert reviews is that each judgment reflects the views of a few people at most. Many shoppers find **www.consumerreview.com** or **www.epinions.com** helpful. These sites provide user opinions of hundreds of different products. Unfortunately, consumer reviews vary widely in quality. Some are quite terse whereas others tend to ramble on and on.

Using Shopping Bots

A shopping bot is a program that searches the Web for the best price for a particular item that you wish to purchase. *Bot* is short for *robot.* Shopping bots theoretically give pricing power to the consumer. The more information the shopper has, the more efficient his or her purchase decision will be. When consumers use their money wisely, they can raise their standard of living. This applies not only to purchasing but to the wise use of credit as well.

There are two general types of shopping bots. The first is the broad-based type that searches a wide range of product categories such as **mySimon.com, DealTime.com, Bizmate.com, pricegrabber.com,** and **PriceSCAN.com**. These sites operate using a Yellow Pages type of model, in that they list every retailer they can find. The second is the niche-oriented type that searches for only one type of product such as computer equipment (**cnet.com**), books (**BookFinder.com**), or CDs (**CDPriceShop.com**).

Most shopping bots give preferential listings to those e-retailers that pay for the privilege. These so-called merchant partners receive about 60 percent of the click-throughs. Typically, the bot lists its merchant partners first, not the retailer that offers the lowest price.

Internet Auctions

The Internet auction business is huge. Part of the lure of buying on-line is that shoppers don't have to go to a flea market, use up a coveted weekend day, or worry about the weather. Plus, bidding itself can be fun and exciting. A few of the most popular consumer auction sites are the following:

- **www.sothebys.com**: Links to Sotheby's for qualified sellers of high-end items.
- **www.ebay.ca**: The most popular auction site.
- **http://bidz.ca/**: Bidz.ca buys closeout deals in very large lots and offers them on-line in its no-reserve auctions.

Even though consumers are spending billions on Internet auctions, B2B auctions are likely to be the dominant form in the future. FreeMarkets, Inc., a publicly traded B2B exchange, has hosted on-line reverse auctions, in which suppliers bid for a factory's component orders, involving $5.4 billion of transactions. Among the companies using FreeMarkets are Owens Corning, GlaxoSmithKline PLC, and Magna, the largest auto-parts company in Canada.[15] As an example of the benefits of using **FreeMarkets.com**, one company paid $175,000 for a batch of plastic auto parts—before turning to auctions. With an auction, after 33 minutes of frenzied bidding by 25 competing suppliers, the price came down to $118,000.[16]

Recently, Whirlpool began holding on-line auctions. Participants bid on the price of the items that they would supply to Whirlpool, but with a twist: they had to include the date when Whirlpool would have to pay for the items. The company wanted to see which suppliers would offer the longest grace period before requiring payment. Five auctions held over five months helped Whirlpool uncover savings of close to $2 million and more than doubled the grace period. Whirlpool's success is a sign that the B2B auction world is shifting from haggling over prices to hammering out the parameters of the deal. Warranties, delivery dates, transportation methods, customer support, financing options, and quality have all become bargaining chips.

PROMOTION STRATEGY

Price is often used as a promotional tool to increase consumer interest. The weekly flyers sent out by grocery stores, for instance, advertise many products with special low prices. The Palace Theatre in downtown Windsor has recently begun promoting $2 movie tickets all week long for 2:00 p.m. matinee shows that are normally not well attended. How do they make money on $2 movie tickets? Popcorn, soft drinks, candy, and other concession items go for over $5 per item.

Pricing can be a tool for trade promotions as well. For example, Levi's Dockers (casual men's pants) are very popular with men between 25 and 45, a lucrative market. Sensing an opportunity, rival pants maker Bugle Boy began offering similar pants at cheaper wholesale prices, which gave retailers a bigger gross margin than they were getting with Dockers. Levi Strauss had to either lower prices or risk its $400-million annual Docker sales. Although Levi Strauss intended its cheapest Dockers to retail for $35, it started selling Dockers to retailers for $18 a pair. Retailers could then advertise Dockers at a very attractive retail price of $25.

GUARANTEED PRICE MATCHING

Closely related to promotion pricing is the price guarantee. In its most basic form, a firm promotes the fact that it will match any competitor's price. Other firms claim that they will refund double the difference if you find a lower price. WestJet recently guaranteed to refund the difference for tickets already purchased if the same seats later went on sale. Research shows that when a retailer offers a price-matching guarantee, it is signalling that it is positioned as a low-price dealer. Conversely, a lack of a price-matching guarantee signals a high-service positioning.[17]

DEMANDS OF LARGE CUSTOMERS

Manufacturers often find that large customers such as Walmart, Zellers, Canadian Tire, and others make specific pricing demands that the suppliers must agree to. Large retailers are making greater-than-ever demands on their suppliers to cover the heavy discounts and markdowns on their own selling floors. They want suppliers to guarantee their stores' profit margins and they insist on cash rebates if the guarantee isn't met. They are also exacting fines for violations of ticketing, packing, and shipping rules. Cumulatively, the demands are nearly wiping out profits for all but the very biggest suppliers.

When customers are as large as Walmart, with sales approaching $400 billion, they expect suppliers to offer them their best prices, always. And there is no later negotiation to raise prices. When suppliers have attempted to raise prices, Walmart has been known to keep paying at the old price levels. Suppliers who object lose their biggest customer.[18]

THE RELATIONSHIP OF PRICE TO QUALITY

When a purchase decision involves great uncertainty, consumers tend to rely on a high price as a predictor of good quality. Reliance on price as an indicator of quality seems to occur for all products, but it reveals itself more strongly for some items than for others.[19]

Among the products that benefit from this phenomenon are coffee, stockings, aspirin, salt, floor wax, shampoo, clothing, furniture, perfume, whisky, and many services. In the absence of other information, people typically assume that prices are higher because the products contain better

SOURCE: COURTESY OF TIGI

Hair-care products benefit from the customer perception that higher prices mean higher quality. Salon products, like Bed Head and Paul Mitchell, convey the message of quality through high prices and exclusive distribution. In fact, customers may assume that the products are better because of the expertise of the hairdresser in whose salon the products are sold.

materials, because they are made more carefully, or, in the case of professional services, because the provider has more expertise. In other words, consumers assume that "you get what you pay for."

Research shows that products perceived to be of high quality tend to benefit more from price promotions than products perceived to be of lower quality. Knowledgeable merchants take these consumer attitudes into account when devising their pricing strategies. **Prestige pricing** is charging a high price to help promote a high-quality image. A successful prestige pricing strategy requires a retail price that is reasonably consistent with consumers' expectations. No one goes shopping at Gucci in Toronto and expects to pay $9.95 for a pair of loafers. In fact, demand would fall drastically at such a low price. Bayer Aspirin would probably lose market share over the long run if it lowered its price.

Consumers also expect private or store brands to be cheaper than national brands. However, if the price difference between a private brand and a nationally distributed manufacturer's brand is *too* great, consumers tend to believe that the private brand is inferior. On the other hand, if the savings aren't big enough, there is little incentive to buy the private brand.

Research on consumer durable goods has shown that the dimensions of quality are (1) ease of use; (2) versatility; (3) durability; (4) serviceability (ease of obtaining quality repairs); (5) performance; and (6) prestige. The research showed that when consumers focused on prestige or durability to assess quality, price was a strong indicator of quality. Price was less an indicator of quality if the consumer was focusing on one of the other four dimensions of quality.[20]

prestige pricing
Charging a high price to help promote a high-quality image.

REVIEW LEARNING OUTCOME 6

6 Demonstrate how the product life cycle, competition, distribution and promotion strategies, guaranteed price matching, customer demands, the Internet and extranets, and perceptions of quality can affect price

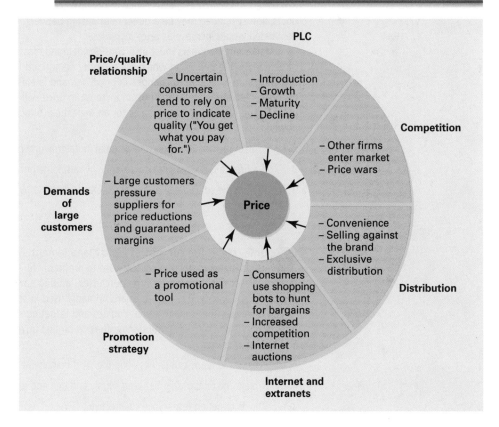

Pricing Concepts Chapter 16 **533**

REVIEW AND APPLICATIONS

1 **Discuss the importance of pricing decisions to the economy and to the individual firm.** Pricing plays an integral role in the Canadian economy by allocating goods and services among consumers, governments, and businesses. Pricing is essential in business because it creates revenue, which is the basis of all business activity. In setting prices, marketing managers strive to find a level high enough to produce a satisfactory profit.

1.1 Why is pricing so important to the marketing manager?

1.2 How does price allocate goods and services?

2 **WRITING** **List and explain a variety of pricing objectives.** Establishing realistic and measurable pricing objectives is a critical part of any firm's marketing strategy. Pricing objectives are commonly classified into three categories: profit oriented, sales oriented, and status quo. Profit-oriented pricing is based on profit maximization, a satisfactory level of profit, or a target return on investment. The goal of profit maximization is to generate as much revenue as possible in relation to cost. Often, a more practical approach than profit maximization is setting prices to produce profits that will satisfy management and stockholders. The most common profit-oriented strategy is pricing for a specific return on investment relative to a firm's assets. The second type of pricing objective is sales oriented, and focuses on either maintaining a percentage share of the market or maximizing dollar or unit sales. The third type of pricing objective aims to maintain the status quo by matching competitors' prices.

2.1 Give an example of each major type of pricing objective.

2.2 Why do so many firms not maximize profits?

3 **Explain the role of demand in price determination.** Demand is a key determinant of price. When establishing prices, a firm must first determine demand for its product. A typical demand schedule shows an inverse relationship between quantity demanded and price: when price is lowered, sales increase; when price is increased, the quantity demanded falls. For prestige products, however, there may be a direct relationship between demand and price: the quantity demanded would increase as price increases.

Marketing managers must also consider demand elasticity when setting prices. Elasticity of demand is the degree to which the quantity demanded fluctuates with changes in price. If consumers are sensitive to changes in price, demand is elastic; if they are insensitive to price changes, demand is inelastic. Thus an increase in price will result in lower sales for an elastic product and little or no loss in sales for an inelastic product. Inelastic demand creates pricing power.

3.1 Explain the role of supply and demand in determining price.

3.2 If a firm can increase its total revenue by raising its price, shouldn't it do so?

3.3 Explain the concepts of elastic and inelastic demand. Why should managers understand these concepts?

4 **Understand the concept of yield management systems.** Yield management systems use complex mathematical software to profitably fill unused capacity. The software uses techniques such as discounting early purchases, limiting early sales at these discounted prices, and overbooking capacity. These systems are primarily used in service businesses and are substantially raising revenues. The use of Internet cookies and targeting software enables on-line retailers to offer different pricing and promotional offers to on-line buyers based on their on-line shopping and browsing habits.

4.1 Why are so many companies adopting yield management systems?

4.2 Explain the relationship between supply and demand and yield management systems.

4.3 Why is targeting technology so effective?

5 **Describe cost-oriented pricing strategies.** The other major determinant of price is cost. Marketers use several cost-oriented pricing strategies. To cover their own expenses and obtain a profit, wholesalers and retailers commonly use markup pricing: they tack an extra amount onto the manufacturer's original price. Another pricing technique is to maximize profits by setting price where marginal revenue equals marginal cost. Still another pricing strategy determines how much a firm must sell to break even and uses this amount as a reference point for adjusting price.

5.1 Your firm has based its pricing strictly on cost in the past. As the newly hired marketing manager, you believe this policy should change. Write the president a memo explaining your reasons.

5.2 Why is it important for managers to understand the concept of break-even points? Are there any drawbacks?

6 **Demonstrate how the product life cycle, competition, distribution and promotion strategies, customer demands, guaranteed price matching, the Internet and extranets, and perceptions of quality can affect price.** The price of a product normally changes as it moves through the life cycle and as demand for the product and competitive conditions change. Management often sets a high price at the introductory stage, and the high price tends to attract competition. The competition usually drives prices down because individual competitors lower prices to gain market share.

Adequate distribution for a new product can sometimes be obtained by offering a larger-than-usual profit margin to wholesalers and retailers. The Internet enables consumers to compare products and prices quickly and efficiently. Price is also used as a promotional tool to attract customers. Special low prices often attract new customers and entice existing customers to buy more. Price matching positions the retailer as a low-price vender. Firms that don't match prices are perceived as offering a higher level of service. Demands of large customers can squeeze the profit margins of suppliers.

Perceptions of quality can also influence pricing strategies. A firm trying to project a prestigious image often charges a premium price for a product. Consumers tend to equate high prices with high quality.

6.1 Divide the class into teams of five. Each team will be assigned a different grocery store from a different chain or an independent store. Appoint a group leader. The group leaders should meet as a group and pick 15 nationally branded grocery items. Each item should be specifically described as to brand name and size of the package. Each team will then proceed to its assigned store and collect price data on the 15 items. The team should also gather price data on 15 similar store brands and 15 generics, if possible.

Each team should present its results to the class and discuss why there are price variations between stores, national brands, store brands, and generics.

As a next step, go back to your assigned store and share the overall results with the store manager. Bring back the manager's comments and share them with the class.

6.2 How does the stage of a product's life cycle affect price? Give some examples.

6.3 Go to **Priceline.com**. Can you research a ticket's price before purchasing it? What products and services are available for purchasing? How comfortable are you with naming your own price? Relate the supply and demand curves to customer-determined pricing.

TERMS

APPLICATION EXERCISE

Reliance on price as a predictor of quality seems to occur for all products. Does this mean that high-priced products are superior? Well, sometimes. Price can be a good predictor of quality for some products, but for others, price is not always the best way to determine the quality of a product or service. This exercise (and worksheet) will help you examine the price-quality relationship for a simple product: canned goods.

Activity

1. *WRITING* Take a trip to a local supermarket where you are certain to find multiple brands of canned fruits and vegetables. Pick a single type of fruit or vegetable that you like and list six or more brands on the worksheet below:

| (1) Brand | (2) Quality Rank (y) | Price | | | (6) $d(y - x)$ | (7) d^2 |
		(3) Price/ Weight	(4) Price per ml	(5) Price Rank (x)		
TOTAL						

2. Once the brands are listed in the worksheet above, rank the brands according to which you think is the highest quality (1) to the lowest quality (6 or lower). This ranking will be y.

3. Record the price and the volume of each brand. For example, if a 355 mL can costs $2.89, you would list $2.89/355 mL.

4. Translate the price per volume into price per mL. The $2.89 can costs $.00814 per mL.

5. Now rank the price per mL (which we will call x) from the highest (1) to the lowest.

6. We'll now begin calculating the coefficient of correlation between the price and quality rankings. The first step is to subtract x from y. Enter the result, d, in column 6.

7. Now calculate d^2 and enter the value in column 7. Sum all of the entries in column 7 in the bottom row.

8. The formula for calculating a price-quality coefficient r is as follows:

$$R_s = \frac{1 - 6\Sigma d^2}{(n^3 - n)}$$

In the formula, r_s is the coefficient of correlation, 6 is a constant, and n is the number of items ranked.

9. What does the result of your calculation tell you about the correlation between the price and the quality of the canned vegetable or fruit you selected? Now that you know this, will it change your buying habits?

ETHICS EXERCISE

Advanced Bio Medics (ABM) has invented a new stem cell-based drug that will arrest even advanced forms of lung cancer. Development costs were actually quite low because the drug was an accidental discovery by scientists working on a different project. To stop the disease requires a regimen of taking one pill per week for 20 weeks. There is no substitute offered by competitors.

ABM is thinking that it could maximize its profits by charging $10,000 per pill. Of course, many people will die because they can't afford the medicine at this price.

Questions

1. Should ABM maximize its profits?

2.   Does the CMA Code of Ethics address this issue? Go to **http://www.the-cma.org/ consumer/ethics.cfm** and review the code. Then write a brief paragraph on what the CMA Code of Ethics contains that relates to ABM's situation.

CASE STUDY

APPLE IPHONE: LIFE IN THE TECHNOLOGY LANE

Before Apple introduced the iPhone, it was hard for most people to imagine that they'd ever pay as much as $599 for a cell phone. But in June 2007, Apple customers stood in line for hours to do just that, eager to be among the first to get their hands on the sleek new device dubbed "the God machine." *Newsweek* columnist Steven Levy described how the proud new owners were "lofting their newly acquired iPhones in the air like they'd won the Stanley Cup." Within the first three days alone, Apple sold 270,000 iPhones at premium prices ($499 for a 4GB model and $599 for 8GB) and CEO Steve Jobs was predicting that they'd cross the 10-million mark by the end of 2008.

Industry analyst Lev Grossman says that Jobs, who had already revolutionized the portable music player market with the iPod, turned his attention to mobile phones because he believed they were "broken." And Jobs likes things that are broken, Grossman says. "It means he can make something that isn't and sell it to you for a premium price." And members of the "Apple Nation" have proven that they are willing to pay.

In a company of 20,000 employees, Apple has only one committee, and its job is to establish prices. In September 2007, Jobs announced the decision to slash the price of the iPhone, even though it had been only 68 days since its launch. Company research had shown that it was priced too high for holiday shoppers. "If we don't take that chance, we wait a whole year," Jobs explained. "We're willing to make less money to get more iPhones out there." The same iPhone that had sold for $599 would now cost $399. At the same press conference, Jobs introduced the new iPod Classic and the iPod Touch. The only thing that made headlines, however, was the unexpected iPhone price cut and stories of the consumer outrage that followed.

Elaine Soloway, a longtime Mac user, said, "Apple really infuriated their fans, the people who urge other people to buy Apple products. We are ambassadors for them." Like Soloway, thousands of iPhone early adopters expressed their disappointment.

"This is life in the technology lane," Jobs said in an attempt to defend the company's decision to drop the price so soon. "There is always something better and less expensive on the horizon." Some call it the curse of the early adopter. But usually they get bragging rights for more than two months before the masses can afford to buy the same product they paid a premium for. In an attempt to appease his angry customers, Jobs announced that those who paid the original price would now be eligible for a $100 refund in the form of a store credit.

The store credit pleased some but wasn't enough for others. One customer, who bought his iPhone only weeks before the price drop, said the $100 was merely a pay-off for being a sucker. "Steve Jobs actually put a price tag on my suckerdom—$200—and now he's trying to drain off some of that embarrassment."

The price cut didn't just disappoint Apple's core customers. Investors were concerned as well, suspecting that the iPhone wasn't selling as well as expected. Apple shares immediately fell $1.75 after the announcement. Industry analysts suggested that the price change could indicate that Apple, which had long been immune to the pricing wars among other personal computer companies, may have found the cell phone business more competitive than anticipated. Whatever the reasons, Jobs acknowledged, "We need to do a better job of taking care of our early iPhone customers as we aggressively go after new ones with a lower price."

The Cult Mac showed no sign of waning in the aftermath of the company's rare misstep, however. Customers love their iPhones, they say, and remain devoted to Apple as the arbiter of cutting-edge technology that is intuitively and beautifully designed. "Sure," admits one loyal customer, "it sucks. But if they had told me they were going to drop the price in a few months, I still would have bought it. I was obsessed."[21]

Questions

1. Apple CEO Steve Jobs alluded to the price a customer may have to pay to own an iPhone when he said that the steep and sudden price change was simply part of "life in the technology lane." What did he mean? Beyond the simple exchange of money, what else might the price of such a product include?

2. Discuss the role that product demand played in pricing the iPhone. How did this demand influence Apple's decision to price it high in the beginning and then lower the price two months later?

3. Discuss how the availability of substitutes affects elasticity of demand for Apple products such as the iPhone.

4. How do you think the relationship of price to quality affects how customers perceive Apple products?

VIDEO CASE

CBC

BUSTED: EASYHOME

There are over 240 easyhome outlets across the country and, when you walk in the door, each looks much like any other furniture store that you might have visited. One thing, though, is likely to catch your attention. It's the prices—they're remarkably low. Then you notice that the price shown isn't the full price for the object, it's the price per week.

Many Canadians with low incomes or who are temporarily out of work are unable to buy with cash or credit. Young parents like Matt and Cindy Perry, who live in Arnprior, just outside of Ottawa, and who have two young children, fall into this group. They needed some home furnishings and a laptop computer. With limited income, they couldn't buy with cash or on credit. Easyhome sounded perfect for them. Like all other easyhome customers, they were told that there would be no credit checks and no down payments, and that they were pre-approved for up to $5,000 of credit. It seemed too good to be true to the Perrys—and you know what they say about things that are too good to be true.

Visit the easyhome website (**www.easyhome.ca**) to listen to the company's sales pitch. Look at some of the seemingly amazing prices on the site. You could easily be enticed like the Perrys were. A laptop computer for $19 a week, a kitchen table set with four chairs for $9 per week, a stove or refrigerator for $12 a week, or living room furniture for $17 a week.

After you get over the seemingly attractive weekly prices, try multiplying the weekly payment times the number of weeks you'll be paying. You might find that a TV set that would normally retail for $759 will end up costing you $2,261; a refrigerator that would normally retail for $639 will cost you $1,233; or you could end up paying $3,266.64 for a used laptop computer, like the Perrys did, when you are finished making all the payments.

Products purchased through lease-to-own or rent-to-own outlets like easyhome normally end up costing customers anywhere from two to five times as much as the item would cost at a regular retail outlet. Given normal retail prices, customers of rent-to-own stores are paying interest rates ranging from 148 percent to 512 percent! Let's watch as we see customers like the Perrys astonished at the prices they are paying at rent-to-own outlets.[22]

Questions

1. How can a company like easyhome get away with the prices and seemingly high interest rates on the products they are selling?

2. What do you think of the ethics of a company like easyhome?

3. What alternatives are there for families like the Perrys? If they don't have the cash or can't get credit at regular retail outlets, doesn't easyhome at least provide a way for the Perrys to get the products they need now?

MARKETING & YOU RESULTS

High scores on this poll relate to a belief that you'll get more enjoyment and make better impressions if you buy high-priced brands. That is, you have a higher prestige sensitivity than someone with a lower score. If your score was low, compare it with your score for the Chapter 15 poll, which was probably high. That's because people with lower prestige sensitivities are more likely to use coupons!

CHAPTER

17 Setting the Right Price

SOURCE: DAISY DAISY/SHUTTERSTOCK

LEARNING OUTCOMES

1 Describe the procedure for setting the right price

2 Identify the legal and ethical constraints on pricing decisions

3 Explain how discounts, geographic pricing, and other special pricing tactics can be used to fine-tune the base price

4 Discuss product line pricing

5 Describe the role of pricing during periods of inflation and recession

ⓥ MARKETING & YOU

How price conscious are you?
Enter your answers on the lines provided.

1	2	3	4	5	6	7
Strongly disagree						Strongly agree

__ I shop a lot for "specials."
__ I find myself checking the prices in the grocery store even for small items.
__ I usually watch the advertisements for announcements of sales.
__ A person can save a lot of money by shopping around for bargains.

__ I check the prices even for inexpensive items.
__ I pay attention to sales and specials.
__ Clothing, furniture, appliances—whatever I buy, I shop around to get the best prices.
__ I usually purchase the cheapest item.
__ I usually purchase items on sale only.

Total your score, and find out what it means at the end of the chapter.

SOURCE: REPRINTED WITH PERMISSION FROM *MARKETING SCALES HANDBOOK* VOL. III, PUBLISHED BY THE AMERICAN MARKETING ASSOCIATION, G. BRUNER, K. JAMES, H. HENSEL, EDS. SCALE #29.

Jane Walter, founder of Calgary-based organicKidz (**www.organickidz.ca**), was thrilled. It was September 2008 and Walter was in the second day of a major trade show for children's products. She hadn't expected to be at this show. OrganicKidz was still in start-up mode and Walter had heard of the trade show only a few weeks earlier. A last-minute cancellation by another vendor had opened up a spot at the otherwise fully booked show.

As luck would have it, organicKidz was given a spot in the show's "natural products" section, a good fit for Walter's product—a stainless-steel baby bottle that was shatterproof, bacterial-resistant, and free of a chemical called BPA, found in plastic baby bottles, which had been drawing criticism from government regulators as a potential health risk. Trade show visitors were impressed with the product and Walter was writing up potential sales.

Jane Walter had come up with the idea for a stainless-steel bottle while gift shopping for a family member who was expecting. Baby bottles were on her shopping list, and Walter was aware of the BPA issue. This looked like an opportunity. She undertook a little research and came up with the idea for stainless steel bottles in various colours. Having come from an entrepreneurial family, Walter was able to use some family connections to locate suppliers who could make the bottle moulds and produce some prototypes. A few weeks later, Jane was at the trade show talking with potential customers.

The interest shown by potential buyers stopping at Walter's booth raised some questions, however. Specifically, what form of distribution and pricing strategies should she use? Should Walter market her product through baby boutiques where prices and margins would be higher but sales might be limited? Or should she go after mass merchandisers where prices and margins would be lower but sales volumes could be much higher? Could she pursue both? If she went after both baby boutiques and mass merchandisers, would the product have to be different to reflect higher and lower prices?

The baby boutiques targeted upscale customers and tended to be owner-operated. These outlets would be good for Walter's product in that the customers of the boutiques would not be very price-sensitive. Volumes, however, might be low and it would be time-consuming to service the many small accounts. The smaller volumes, though, might be easier for a new start-up company to handle. Further, Walter felt that a retail price of between $19 and $24 a bottle could be charged through the baby boutiques.

The mass retailers were a very different situation. Could Walter supply the large volumes that a few large customers might request, sometimes at short notice? Then there was the issue of price.

Walter felt that prices through mass merchandisers would have to be in the range of $12 to $15 a bottle. If she went after both types of outlets, would the very low mass merchandiser prices be a serious problem for her boutique customers? There was also the possibility of selling the product through the on-line stores of some mass merchandisers. Walter wasn't sure what pricing on-line should be or what volumes might be. Would on-line prices be highly elastic?

Could Walter simply offer her product at the same price and same margins to all customers? She also toyed with the idea of offering a line of products that were visually different to the mass merchandisers from those offered to the baby boutiques. It was going to be hard enough to offer the first product for a new start-up company. Could Walter afford to invest in a second set of moulds and have a second product designed before any sales came in? Could she sell to the baby boutiques first and hold off for a year on selling to the mass merchandisers? If she waited for a year to sell to the mass merchandisers, would the opportunity that is present now be lost?[1]

As you can see, pricing a new product and developing a strategy for market introduction is difficult. What would you do if you were Jane Walter? This chapter will help you to develop some guidelines on how to establish the right price for a product—not an easy decision.

SOURCE: STEWART THORNHILL, "GO BIG OR GO BOUTIQUE?" FINANCIAL POST MAGAZINE, OCTOBER 2009, 55.

Describe the procedure for setting the right price

Setting the right price on a product is a four-step process (see Exhibit 17.1):

1. Establish pricing goals.

2. Estimate demand, costs, and profits.

3. Choose a price strategy to help determine a base price.

4. Fine-tune the base price with pricing tactics.

ESTABLISH PRICING GOALS

The first step in setting the right price is to establish pricing goals. Recall from Chapter 16 that pricing objectives fall into three categories: profit oriented, sales oriented, and status quo. These goals are derived from the firm's overall objectives. If, for example, a firm's objective is to be the market share leader in an industry, it will pursue a sales-oriented pricing goal. A firm interested in maximizing shareholder value might use a profit-oriented pricing goal. A conservative, risk-averse firm might adopt a status quo pricing objective.

A good understanding of the marketplace and of the consumer can sometimes tell a manager very quickly whether a goal is realistic. For example, if firm A has an objective of a 20 percent target return on investment (ROI), and its product development and implementation costs are $5 million, the market must be rather large or must support the price required to earn a 20 percent ROI. Assume that company B has a pricing objective that all new products must reach at least 15 percent market share within three years after their introduction. A thorough study of the environment may convince the marketing manager that the competition is too strong and the market share goal can't be met.

All pricing objectives have tradeoffs that managers must weigh. A profit maximization objective may require a bigger initial investment than the firm can commit or wants to commit. Reaching the desired market share often means sacrificing short-term profit because without careful management, long-term profit goals may not be met. Meeting the competition is the easiest pricing goal to implement. But can managers really afford to ignore demand and costs, the life-cycle stage, and other considerations? When creating pricing objectives, managers must consider these tradeoffs in light of the target customer, the environment, and the company's overall objectives.

ESTIMATE DEMAND, COSTS, AND PROFITS

Chapter 16 explained that total revenue is a function of price and quantity demanded and that quantity demanded depends on elasticity. Some key questions that a manager might consider when conducting marketing research on demand and elasticity are these:

-   What price is so low that customers would question quality?
-   What is the highest price at which the product would still be a bargain?
-   What is the price at which the product is becoming too expensive?
-   What is the price at which the product becomes too expensive to consider buying?

After establishing pricing goals, managers should estimate total revenue at a variety of prices. Next, they should determine corresponding costs for each price. They are then ready to estimate how much profit, if any, and how much market share can be earned at

EXHIBIT 17.1

Steps in Setting the Right Price

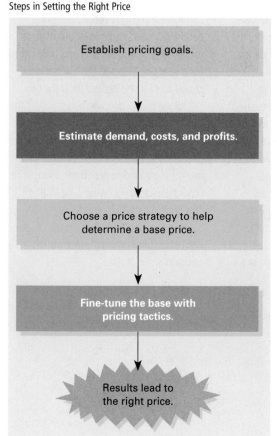

SEND THE KIDS TO **YOUR ROOM!**

Introducing Ceiva. The digital picture frame that lets you share photos over the internet. It's easy to set up. Easy to use. You don't even need a computer to receive photos. And anyone you want can send photos to your Ceiva frame from just about anywhere. Set your sights on one. And get one for your parents. So you can send the kids to their house whenever you want. **SHARE photos** EVERYDAY

©2000 Ceiva Logic, Inc. All rights reserved. Ceiva is a trademark of Ceiva Logic, Inc. Patents pending.   ceiva.com

SOURCE: COURTESY OF CEIVA LOGIC, INC.

Companies with new products with no close substitutes are less restricted in the pricing strategies they can pursue. How do you think Ceiva will price this Internet-connected digital picture frame? Keep in mind that other factors besides novelty may affect the pricing strategy.

price strategy
A basic, long-term pricing framework, which establishes the initial price for a product and the intended direction for price movements over the product life cycle.

price skimming
A pricing policy whereby a firm charges a high introductory price, often coupled with heavy promotion.

each possible price. These data become the heart of developing price policy. Managers can study their pricing options in light of revenues, costs, and profits. In turn, this information can help determine which price can best meet the firm's pricing goals.

CHOOSE A PRICE STRATEGY

The basic, long-term pricing framework for a good or service should be a logical extension of the firm's pricing objectives. The marketing manager's chosen **price strategy** defines the initial price and gives direction for price movements over the product life cycle.

The price strategy sets a competitive price in a specific market segment, based on a well-defined positioning strategy. Changing a price level from premium to super-premium may require a change in the product itself, the target customers served, the promotional strategy, and distribution channels. Thus changing a price strategy can require dramatic alterations in the marketing mix. A car-maker cannot successfully compete in the superpremium category if the car looks and drives like an economy car.

A company's freedom in pricing a new product and devising a price strategy depends on the market conditions and the other elements of the marketing mix. If a firm launches a new product resembling several others already on the market, its pricing freedom will be restricted. To succeed, the company will probably have to charge a price close to the average market price. In contrast, a firm that introduces a totally new product with no close substitutes will have considerable pricing freedom.

Most companies do not undertake adequate research into their price strategy. McKinsey & Company's Pricing Benchmark Survey estimated that only about 15 percent of companies do serious pricing research. A Coopers & Lybrand study found that 87 percent of the surveyed companies had changed prices in the previous year. Only 13 percent of the price changes, however, came after a careful review of pricing strategy.[2]

These numbers indicate that strategic pricing decisions tend to be made without an understanding of the likely buyer or the likely competitive response. Further, the research shows that managers often make tactical pricing decisions without reviewing how they may fit into the firm's overall pricing or marketing strategy. The data suggest that many companies make pricing decisions and changes without an existing process for managing the pricing activity. As a result, many companies do not have a serious pricing strategy and do not conduct pricing research to develop their strategy.[3]

Companies that do serious planning in advance of developing a price strategy can select from three basic approaches: price skimming, penetration pricing, and status quo pricing.

Price Skimming

Price skimming is sometimes called a "market-plus" approach to pricing because it denotes a high price relative to the prices of competing products. BMW and Porsche have focused on the premium end of the new car market. This focus has allowed the companies to price their cars at the high end of the new vehicle market.

The term **price skimming** is derived from the phrase "skimming the cream off the top." Companies often use this strategy for new products when the product is perceived by the target market as having unique advantages. For example, Caterpillar sets premium prices on its construction equipment to support and reflect its high-perceived value. Genzyme Corporation introduced Ceredase as the first effective treatment for Gaucher's disease. This medication allows patients to avoid years of painful physical deterioration and lead normal lives. A year's supply for one patient can exceed $300,000.

Often companies will use skimming initially and then lower prices over time. This is called "sliding down the demand curve." Hardcover book publishers lower their prices when the books come out in paperback. Calloway lowers the price of its older-model golf clubs as new models hit the market. Chanel, on the other hand, takes back unsold inventory of its purses and destroys them rather than selling at a discount.

Price skimming works best when the market is willing to buy the product even though it carries an above-average price. If, for example, some purchasing agents feel that Caterpillar equipment is far superior to competitors' products, then Caterpillar can charge premium prices successfully. Firms can also effectively use price skimming when a product is well protected legally, when it represents a technological breakthrough, or when it has in some other way blocked the entry of competitors. Managers may follow a skimming strategy when production cannot be expanded rapidly because of technological difficulties, shortages, or constraints imposed by the skill and time required to produce a product. As long as demand is greater than supply, skimming is a viable strategy.

A successful skimming strategy enables management to recover its product development or "educational" costs quickly. Even if the market perceives an introductory price as too high, managers can easily correct the problem by lowering the price. Firms often feel it is better to test the market at a high price and then lower the price if sales are too slow. They are tacitly saying, "If there are any premium-price buyers in the market, let's reach them first and maximize our revenue per unit." Successful skimming strategies are not limited to products. Well-known athletes, entertainers, lawyers, and hairstylists are experts at price skimming. A skimming strategy, though, will often encourage competitors to enter the market. Above all, if price skimming is to be successful, customers must perceive a high value for the product or service.

Penetration Pricing

Penetration pricing is at the opposite end of the spectrum from skimming. **Penetration pricing** means charging a relatively low price for a product as a way to reach the mass market. The low price is designed to capture a large share of a substantial market, resulting in lower production costs. If a marketing manager has made obtaining a large market share the firm's pricing objective, penetration pricing is a logical choice.

penetration pricing
A pricing policy whereby a firm charges a relatively low price for a product initially as a way to reach the mass market.

Penetration pricing does mean lower profit per unit. Therefore, to reach the break-even point, it requires a higher volume of sales than would a skimming policy. If reaching a high volume of sales takes a long time, the recovery of product development costs will also be slow. As you might expect, penetration pricing tends to discourage competition.

Procter & Gamble examined the electric toothbrush market and noted that most electric brushes cost over $50. The company brought out the Crest Spinbrush, which works on batteries and sells for under $7. It has become a leading seller and has helped the Crest brand of products to become P&G's twelfth billion-dollar brand.[4] A penetration strategy tends to be effective in a price-sensitive market. Price should decline more rapidly when demand is elastic because the market will be expanded through the lower price.

Although Walmart is associated with penetration pricing, other chains have done an excellent job of following this strategy. Dollar stores, those bare-bones, strip-mall chains that sell staples at cut-rate prices, are now the fastest-growing retailers in the country. Salvage or surplus grocers are also growing in popularity. Salvage stores sell "close-outs" which include products that manufacturers

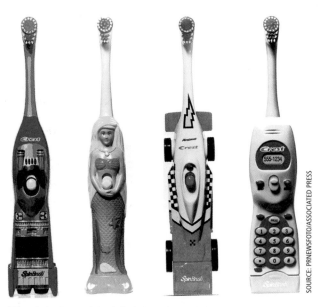

Although the Crest Spinbrush for kids is a low-priced electric toothbrush, it costs about 200 percent more than a traditional kid's toothbrush. Do you think that the Spinbrush pricing strategy is a penetration strategy or a skimming strategy?

SOURCE: PRNEWSFOTO/ASSOCIATED PRESS

have discounted, seasonal items that are outdated, goods that are near the date when manufacturers expect freshness to wane, and damaged goods.

If a firm has a low fixed-cost structure and each sale provides a large contribution to those fixed costs, penetration pricing can boost sales and provide large increases to profits—but only if the market size grows or if competitors choose not to respond. Low prices can draw additional buyers to enter the market. The increased sales can justify production expansion or the adoption of new technologies, both of which can reduce costs. And if firms have excess capacity, even low-priced business can provide incremental dollars toward fixed costs.

Penetration pricing can also be effective if an experience curve will cause costs per unit to drop significantly. The experience curve suggests that per-unit costs will go down as a firm's production experience increases. On average, for each doubling of production, a firm can expect per-unit costs to decline by roughly 20 percent. Cost declines can be significant in the early stages of production. Manufacturers that fail to take advantage of these effects will find themselves at a competitive cost disadvantage relative to others that are further along the curve.

The big advantage of penetration pricing is that it typically discourages or blocks competition from entering a market. The disadvantage is that penetration means gearing up for mass production to sell a large volume at a low price. What if the volume fails to materialize? The company will face huge losses from building or converting a factory to produce the failed product. Skimming, in contrast, lets a firm "stick its toe in the water" and see whether limited demand exists at the high price. If not, the firm can simply lower the price. Skimming lets a company start out with a small production facility and expand it gradually as price falls and demand increases.

Penetration pricing can also prove disastrous for a prestige brand that adopts the strategy in an effort to gain market share and fails. When Omega—once a more prestigious brand than Rolex—was trying to improve the market share of its watches, it adopted a penetration pricing strategy that succeeded in destroying the watches'

1 Describe the procedure for setting the right price

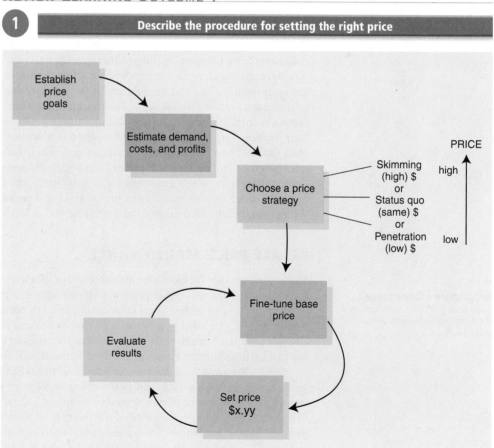

brand image by flooding the market with lower-priced products. Omega never gained sufficient share on its lower-priced/lower-image competitors to justify destroying its brand image and high-priced position with upscale buyers. The failed Cadillac Cimarron and Lacoste clothing experienced similar outcomes from a penetration pricing strategy.

Status Quo Pricing

The third basic price strategy a firm may choose is status quo pricing, also called *meeting the competition* or *going rate pricing*. Status quo pricing means charging a price identical to or very close to the competition's price. Although status quo pricing has the advantage of simplicity, its disadvantage is that the strategy may ignore demand or cost or both. If the firm is comparatively small, however, meeting the competition may be the safest route to long-term survival.

2 THE LEGALITY AND ETHICS OF PRICE STRATEGY

Identify the legal and ethical constraints on pricing decisions

It is important to note that companies are not always free to charge whatever prices they wish. As was mentioned in Chapter 3, some pricing decisions are subject to government regulation. Before marketing managers establish any price strategy, they should know the laws that limit their decision making. Most of the legal issues with regard to pricing are covered in Sections 36, 45, 47, 50, 61, and 74 of the Competition Act. Among the pricing issues covered by the Competition Act are deceptive pricing, resale price maintenance, price fixing, price discrimination, and predatory pricing.

DECEPTIVE PRICING

deceptive pricing
Promoting a price or price saving that is not actually available.

Deceptive pricing takes place when a seller promotes a price or price saving that is not actually available to consumers. For example, if a retailer promotes a very low price on a product, but the product is not in stock or is available in only very small quantities, and then encourages customers to buy a higher-priced product, this form of "bait and switch" is illegal. Sellers must carry adequate stocks of price-promoted items or offer customers "rain cheques" if the product quickly sells out.

Deceptive pricing also occurs when a seller promotes a price as being a significant discount from the normal price when, in fact, the product has never, or rarely, been sold at the so-called normal price. For example, the Forzani Group Ltd. was recently fined a record $1.7 million by the Competition Bureau (which enforces the Competition Act) for exactly this form of price deception at its Sport Chek and Sport Mart stores. The Competition Bureau charged Forzani with advertising "misleading sales based on inflated regular prices." According to Section 36 of the Competition Act, retailers have to sell a product for a "substantial amount of time at a certain price" in order to then mark down the product and promote the discounted price. While Forzani admitted no wrongdoing, it agreed to pay the fine.[5]

RESALE PRICE MAINTENANCE

resale price maintenance
Laws that prohibit manufacturers from controlling prices at the retail level.

Most producers would like to be able to control the price of their products on retail store shelves. However, **resale price maintenance**, as this practice is called, is illegal in Canada. Section 61 of the Competition Act prohibits a manufacturer from requiring a retailer to sell a product at a particular price or below a particular price. The act allows a manufacturer to set a *suggested retail price* as long as it is clear that the retailer will not be discriminated against if it does not maintain that suggested price.

Labatt Brewing Co. Ltd. was convicted and fined $250,000 after Labatt sales representatives in Quebec were found to have illegally offered up to $2,000 and free beer to convenience store owners who agreed to maintain Labatt beer prices at certain levels. "They tried to influence the price of the beer up or prevent price drops from happening," said Competition Bureau assistant deputy commissioner Madeleine Dussault, "and this is contrary to the provisions of the Competition Act."[6]

PRICE FIXING

price fixing
An agreement between two or more firms on the price they will charge for a product.

Sellers must set prices without talking to competitors. **Price fixing** is an agreement between two or more firms on the price they will charge for a product. Suppose two or more executives from competing firms meet to decide how much to charge for a product or to decide which of them will submit the lowest bid on a certain contract. Such practices are illegal under the Competition Act. Offenders have received fines and sometimes prison terms. Domtar Inc. of Montreal, Cascades Inc. of Kingsey Falls, Quebec, and Unisource Canada Inc. of Richmond Hill, Ontario, were each fined $12.5 million in a price-fixing case involving the sale of carbonless paper in Ontario and Quebec. The Competition Bureau's investigation showed that the three companies colluded to maintain artificially high prices in the carbonless paper market in violation of Section 45 of the Competition Act. In addition to the fines, it was reported that "key personnel involved in the conspiracy were removed from their positions in the companies."[7]

PRICE DISCRIMINATION

The Competition Act prohibits any firm from selling to two or more different buyers, within a reasonably short time, commodities (not services) of like grade and quality at different prices where the result would be to substantially lessen competition. The act also makes it illegal for a seller to offer two buyers different supplementary services and for buyers to use their purchasing power to force sellers into granting discriminatory prices or services. Note that not all price differences represent price discrimination. For example, children and senior citizens pay lower prices for movie tickets.

Six elements are needed for price discrimination to occur:

SOURCE: EDDY RISCH/ASSOCIATED PRESS

In a scandal that rocked the art world, Sotheby's and Christie's, two of the industry's most venerable auction houses, were caught in a price-fixing scheme. The CEOs of both companies received substantial fines and prison time.

- The seller must charge different prices to different customers for the same product.
- The two customers must be competitors.
- The seller must discriminate by price among two or more purchasers; that is, the seller must make two or more actual sales within a reasonably short time.
- The products sold must be commodities or other tangible goods.
- The products sold must be of like grade and quality, not necessarily identical. If the goods are truly interchangeable and substitutable, they are of like grade and quality.
- The act of discrimination must be part of an ongoing practice of discrimination.

PREDATORY PRICING

predatory pricing
The practice of charging a very low price for a product with the intent of driving competitors out of business or out of a market.

Predatory pricing is the practice of charging a very low price for a product with the intent of driving competitors out of business or out of a market. Once competitors have been driven out, the firm raises its prices. This practice is illegal under section 51(1)(c) of the Competition Act. Proving the use of the practice is difficult, however. It must be shown that the predator, the destructive company, explicitly tried to ruin a competitor and that the predatory price was below the predator's average variable cost. Some provinces, such as British Columbia, Alberta, and Manitoba, have provincial legislation that prohibits companies from selling below cost plus some reasonable markup, such as 5 percent.

Under the Competition Act, pricing below cost to sell off excess inventory is not considered predatory, but pricing below cost to drive a competitor out of business *is*. A few years ago, both WestJet and Hawkair (a discount B.C. airline) accused Air Canada of predatory pricing.[8] In the case of Hawkair, Air Canada lowered fares between Terrace, B.C., and Vancouver to $126. The Hawkair price over this route was $149. Yet Air Canada was charging $275 for a flight from Sandpit, B.C., to Vancouver (a comparable distance but a route not covered by Hawkair). In the case of WestJet, after WestJet moved many of its flights from Hamilton to Toronto Pearson International Airport, Air Canada lowered one-way fares from Toronto to Ottawa to $12. Are these cases of selling off excess inventory (empty seats) or predatory pricing? Proving predatory pricing in the courts is often very difficult.

ETHICAL ISSUES IN PRICING

At a minimum, of course, marketing managers must be in compliance with the law when prices are set. Beyond this, there are many ethical considerations when it comes to setting prices. What are the ethics of setting a very high price for patented drug products that are needed by severely ill people? What are the ethics of prices based on nearly impossible to understand leasing or purchase contracts? What about when prices are not fixed but are negotiated? Is it ethical to charge higher prices to customers who are unable to bargain as well as others? Is it okay to charge higher prices in poor neighbourhoods where shoppers may not own the necessary transportation to be able to shop elsewhere? What's your view of the situation described in the "Ethics in Marketing" box? It isn't always clear what is ethical or unethical when it comes to pricing decisions.

Ethics in Marketing

 ### PRICING FOR THE POOR IN BRAZIL

Maria Pereira visited a Casas Bahia store in Sao Paulo recently to pay a $38 monthly instalment on a music system that she bought a year earlier. On her way out, a set of five cooking pots on sale for $25 caught the housewife's attention and Pereira purchased it. The cooking pots would be paid in four instalments. "I hadn't thought of buying anything," says Pereira, whose husband earns $167 a month as a security guard.

That is the secret of how Samuel Klein has unlocked the buying power of the poor in Latin America's biggest country and how Klein has become Brazil's version of Sam Walton (founder of Walmart). By selling in instalments, Klein makes products accessible to people like Maria Pereira. And by requiring customers to return to the store each month to pay, he induces two-thirds of them to make another purchase. About 90 percent of sales at Klein's stores are on credit. Klein's Casas Bahia chain is Brazil's biggest non-food retailer, with $2 billion in annual sales of furniture, household goods, and appliances—including about one-third of all TV sets sold in Brazil.

While mainstream Brazilian retailers shun the poor, Klein aggressively courts them. Klein's stripped-down stores are located in some of the most deprived neighbourhoods of Sao Paulo and Rio de Janeiro. His customers include bricklayers, hot-dog vendors, and other blue-collar workers whose average monthly income is $190, below Brazil's national average of $290. Surprisingly, their default rates are lower than the national average and their loyalty is intense—a combination that has turned Klein into a billionaire. "The poorer the customer, the more punctual the payments," says Klein. "The poor know they need to guard their reputations, or they jeopardize buying on credit."

In a country where annual credit card rates surpass 200 percent for the minority of Brazilians who qualify, Casas Bahia's policies are not unusual. The retailer charges monthly interest payments of 3 to 5 percent, depending on the payment plan. For a higher initial price, customers can get "interest-free" loans. The average monthly instalment at Casas Bahia is about $14. Only a permanent mailing address is required to get credit approval. About 10 percent of credit applicants are turned down, generally because their names appear on a government list of defaulters.

Many customers say they are aware that they pay more at Casas Bahia. But "the terms are good for me," says Maria Nogueira, a building superintendent, after making a $13 instalment payment on a sofa. Plus, she notes, Casas Bahia has a five-day grace period and slightly discounts early instalment payments.[9]

Is Klein serving the poor or taking advantage of them? If Klein's customers didn't shop at Casas Bahia, where would they shop? Would the customers have a higher or lower standard of living without Casas Bahia? Would it be better for the poor to save their money and pay with cash?

SOURCE: MIRIAM JORDAN, "A RETAILER IN BRAZIL HAS BECOME RICH BY COURTING THE POOR," WALL STREET JOURNAL, JUNE 11, 2002, A1, A8.

2   **Identify the legal and ethical constraints on pricing decisions**

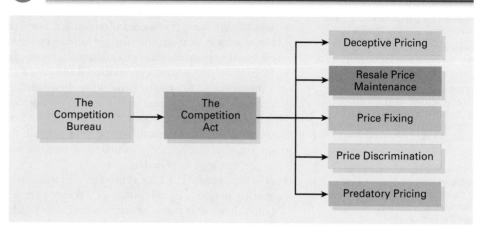

3 TACTICS FOR FINE-TUNING THE BASE PRICE

Explain how discounts, geographic pricing, and other special pricing tactics can be used to fine-tune the base price.

base price
The general price level at which the company expects to sell the good or service.

After managers understand both the legal and the marketing consequences of price strategies, they should set a **base price**, the general price level at which the company expects to sell the good or service. The general price level is correlated with the pricing policy: above the market (price skimming), at the market (status quo pricing), or below the market (penetration pricing). The final step, then, is to fine-tune the base price.

Fine-tuning techniques are short-run approaches that do not change the general price level. They do, however, result in changes within a general price level. These pricing tactics allow the firm to adjust for competition in certain markets, meet ever-changing government regulations, take advantage of unique demand situations, and meet promotional and positioning goals. Fine-tuning pricing tactics include various sorts of discounts, geographic pricing, and special pricing tactics.

DISCOUNTS, ALLOWANCES, REBATES, AND VALUE-BASED PRICING

quantity discount
A price reduction offered for buying in multiple units or above a specified dollar amount.

cumulative quantity discount
A deduction from list price that applies to the buyer's total purchases made during a specific time period.

noncumulative quantity discount
A deduction from list price that applies to a single order rather than to the total volume of orders placed during a certain period.

cash discount
A price reduction offered to a consumer, an industrial user, or a marketing intermediary in return for prompt payment of a bill.

A base price can be lowered through the use of discounts and the related tactics of allowances, rebates, low or zero percent financing, and value-based pricing. Managers use the various forms of discounts to encourage customers to do what they would not ordinarily do, such as paying cash rather than using credit, taking delivery out of season, or performing certain functions within a distribution channel. The following are the most common tactics:

- *Quantity discounts:* When buyers get a lower price for buying in multiple units or above a specified dollar amount, they are receiving a **quantity discount**. A **cumulative quantity discount** is a deduction from list price that applies to the buyer's total purchases made during a specific period; it is intended to encourage customer loyalty. In contrast, a **noncumulative quantity discount** is a deduction from list price that applies to a single order rather than to the total volume of orders placed during a certain period. It is intended to encourage orders in large quantities.
- *Cash discounts:* A **cash discount** is a price reduction offered to a consumer, an industrial user, or a marketing intermediary in return for prompt payment of a bill. Prompt payment saves the seller carrying charges and billing expenses and allows the seller to avoid bad debt.
- *Functional discounts:* When distribution channel intermediaries, such as wholesalers or retailers, perform a service or function for the manufacturer, they must be

functional discount (trade discount)
A discount to wholesalers and retailers for performing channel functions.

seasonal discount
A price reduction for buying merchandise out of season.

promotional allowance (trade allowance)
A payment to a dealer for promoting the manufacturer's products.

rebate
A cash refund given for the purchase of a product during a specific period.

markdown money
Money or discounts provided by vendors to department stores to help cover end-of-season discounts offered by department stores to customers.

value-based pricing
Setting the price at a level that seems to the customer to be a good price compared to the prices of other options.

compensated. This compensation, typically a percentage discount from the base price, is called a **functional discount** (or **trade discount**). Functional discounts vary greatly from channel to channel, depending on the tasks performed by the intermediary.

- *Seasonal discounts*: A **seasonal discount** is a price reduction for buying merchandise out of season. It shifts the storage function to the purchaser. Seasonal discounts also enable manufacturers to maintain a steady production schedule year-round.
- *Promotional allowances*: A **promotional allowance** (also known as a **trade allowance**) is a payment to a dealer for promoting the manufacturer's products. It is both a pricing tool and a promotional device. As a pricing tool, a promotional allowance is like a functional discount. If, for example, a retailer runs an ad for a manufacturer's product, the manufacturer may pay half the cost of the ad. If a retailer sets up a special display, the manufacturer may include a certain quantity of free goods in the retailer's next order.
- *Rebates*: A **rebate** is a cash refund given for the purchase of a product during a specific period. The advantage of a rebate over a simple price reduction for stimulating demand is that a rebate is a temporary inducement that can be taken away without altering the basic price structure. A manufacturer that uses a simple price reduction for a short time may meet resistance when trying to restore the price to its original, higher level. Car manufacturers have been adding significant rebates to boost the sales of slower-selling vehicles.
- *Zero percent financing*: After record sales years in 1999 and 2000, new-car sales in Canada fell. To get people back into the automobile showrooms, manufacturers offered zero percent financing, which enabled purchasers to borrow money to pay for new cars with no interest charges. The tactic did increase sales but not without a cost to the manufacturers. A five-year interest-free car loan represented a cost of over $3,000 on a typical vehicle sold with zero percent financing. And auto makers are still offering such incentives over ten years later!
- *Markdown money*: For decades, department stores have expected clothing companies and other merchandise suppliers to share in their sales risk. Whenever a suit or a sweater doesn't sell at full price, it is marked down. Department stores have required vendors to absorb some of the cost by paying the retailer **markdown money** at the end of the season. While many vendors would like to stop paying markdown money, big retailers with big buying power can always go to other suppliers who are willing to pay.

Recently, Chinese consumers have found a new way to get discounts by ganging up on retailers. This phenomenon is explored in the Customer Experience box.

Value-Based Pricing

Value-based pricing (also called *value pricing*) is a pricing strategy that has grown out of the quality movement. Instead of figuring prices based on costs or competitors' prices, it starts with the customer, considers the competition, and then determines the appropriate price. The basic assumption is that the firm is customer driven, seeking to understand the attributes customers want in the goods and services they buy and the value of that bundle of attributes to customers. Because very few firms operate in a pure monopoly, however, a marketer using value-based pricing must also determine the value of competitive offerings to customers. Customers determine the value of a product (not just its price) relative to the value of alternatives. In value-based pricing, therefore, the price of the product is set at a level that seems to the customer to be a good price compared with the prices of other options.

Shoppers are seeing prices fall as Walmart pushes rivals to match its value prices. With Walmart's aggressive move into grocery retailing, Canadian shoppers have been reaping the benefits of the grocery price wars. Led by food sales leader Loblaw, grocery chains are working to sharpen their operations and keep prices as competitive as possible. To fend off the Walmart Super Centres, Loblaw is expanding Real Canadian Superstores, which carry everything from steaks to stereos at very low prices. Sobeys and Metro have joined the battle by lowering prices. After the opening of one new Walmart Super Centre, nearby Loblaw stores dropped the

GANGING UP FOR DISCOUNTS

Chinese shoppers have long been known as hard-nosed bargainers. Now, to the dismay of merchants, some have started shopping in teams to haggle for bigger markdowns. The practice, called *tuangou*, or team purchase, begins in Internet chat rooms, where like-minded consumers hatch plans to buy appliances, furnishings, food, even cars, in bulk. Next they show up en masse at stores like Suzhou Zhongyi Kitchen Co. to demand discounts.

On a recent Saturday, Zhang Qinyong, who owns the kitchen-cabinetry shop in Suzhou, found himself cornered against his display cabinets by a team of more than a dozen shoppers. "In Suzhou, no other products are better than ours," he told the crowd. He insisted that craftsmanship and German materials made his cabinets worth more. "Forget quality. Let's talk about price," snapped one member of the buying group, 36-year-old Guo Yong, an electrical engineer. For the next hour, the shoppers turned aside Zhang's sales pitches with an unbending response: "Thirty-five percent off!"

Group purchasing is catching on in booming cities across China. On a website with a name that in Chinese sounds like "I want to team buy," consumer teams formulate plans to bargain for products ranging from Buick automobiles to Panasonic television sets and refrigerators.

In Shanghai, when Cai Kun decided to buy a new General Motors subcompact, the Chevrolet Aveo, he logged on to a website where others were chatting about staging a team purchase. On a Saturday morning, 28-year-old Cai and 17 others met for the first time at Anji Mingmen Car Services Co., a Chevy showroom in downtown Shanghai. As planned, they told the dealership's manager they would buy 18 Aveos in one pop—but only if he would cut roughly 10 percent off sticker prices as high as $12,862.

Negotiations went on for six hours. Group members broke away occasionally for private meetings. The dealer tried unsuccessfully to negotiate separately with buyers who wanted the more expensive SX model and those who didn't. In the end, the group extracted a discount of nearly 9 percent on a fleet of 18 Aveo cars, along with gifts such as car-wash vouchers.[10]

Is group purchasing by consumers ethical? Would this practice work in Canada? Why or why not? Many multinational firms such as Kohler (plumbing fixtures), Estée Lauder, and Cartier have refused to meet with team buyers in China. Is this unethical? Why?

SOURCE: JAMES AREDDY, "CHINESE CUSTOMERS OVERWHELM RETAILERS WITH TEAM TACTICS", WALL STREET JOURNAL, FEBRUARY 28, 2006.

price of a four-litre package of milk from $4.99 to $3.99 and Sobeys furthered lowered the price to $3.89.[11]

The economic slowdown of 2008–2009 has given food companies an opportunity to push value pricing on certain lines. Just because a product is value-priced does not mean it is low profit margin. For example, powdered Kool-Aid beverages are inexpensive to make and are extremely profitable. For the first time in years, Kraft is advertising Kool-Aid on TV. Kraft and Campbell soup are promoting soup and grilled cheese sandwiches as a wallet-friendly meal "your family will love."[12]

Pricing Products Too Low

Sometimes managers price their products too low, thereby reducing company profits.[13] This seems to happen for two reasons. First, managers attempt to buy market share through aggressive pricing. Usually, however, competitors quickly meet these price cuts. Thus any gain in market share is short-lived, and overall industry profits end up falling. Second, managers have a natural tendency to want to make decisions that can be justified objectively. The problem is that companies often lack hard data on the complex determinants of profitability, such as the relationship between price changes and sales volumes, the link between demand levels and costs, and the likely responses of competitors to price changes. In contrast, companies usually have rich, unambiguous information on costs, sales, market share, and competitors' prices. As a result, managers tend to make pricing decisions based on current costs, projected short-term share gains, or current competitor prices rather than on long-term profitability.

GEOGRAPHIC PRICING

Because many sellers ship their wares to a nationwide or even a worldwide market, the cost of freight can greatly affect the total cost of a product. Sellers may use several

You read in Chapter 16 how the Internet is affecting pricing strategies, and that extends to the world of coupons and rebates. Many sites, like ebates.com, catalogue rebate opportunities and pass information along to consumers who are willing to sign up.

FOB origin pricing
A price tactic that requires the buyer to absorb the freight costs from the shipping point ("free on board").

uniform delivered pricing
A price tactic in which the seller pays the actual freight charges and bills every purchaser an identical, flat freight charge.

zone pricing
A modification of uniform delivered pricing that divides the country (or the total market) into segments or zones and charges a flat freight rate to all customers in a given zone.

freight absorption pricing
A price tactic in which the seller pays all or part of the actual freight charges and does not pass them on to the buyer.

basing-point pricing
A price tactic that charges freight from a given (basing) point, regardless of the city from which the goods are shipped.

single-price tactic
A price tactic that offers all goods and services at the same price (or perhaps two or three prices).

different geographic pricing tactics to moderate the impact of freight costs on distant customers. The following methods of geographic pricing are the most common:

- *FOB origin pricing*: **FOB origin pricing**, also called FOB factory or FOB shipping point, is a price tactic that requires the buyer to absorb the freight costs from the shipping point ("free on board"). The farther buyers are from sellers, the more they pay because transportation costs generally increase with the distance merchandise is shipped.

- *Uniform delivered pricing*: If the marketing manager wants total costs, including freight, to be equal for all purchasers of identical products, the firm will adopt uniform delivered pricing, or "postage stamp" pricing. With **uniform delivered pricing**, the seller pays the actual freight charges and bills every purchaser an identical, flat freight charge.

- *Zone pricing*: A marketing manager who wants to equalize total costs among buyers within large geographic areas—but not necessarily all of the seller's market area—may modify the base price with a zone-pricing tactic. **Zone pricing** is a modification of uniform delivered pricing. Rather than placing the entire country (or its total market) under a uniform freight rate, the firm divides the market into segments or zones and charges a flat freight rate to all customers in a given zone. Canada Post's package rate structure is probably the best-known zone-pricing system in the country.

- *Freight absorption pricing*: In **freight absorption pricing**, the seller pays all or part of the actual freight charges and does not pass them on to the buyer. This tactic might be used in intensely competitive areas or as a way to break into new market areas.

- *Basing-point pricing*: With **basing-point pricing**, the seller designates a location as a basing point and charges all buyers the freight cost from that point, regardless of the city from which the goods are shipped.

OTHER PRICING TACTICS

Unlike geographic pricing, special pricing tactics are unique and defy neat categorization. Managers use these tactics for various reasons—for example, to stimulate demand for specific products, to increase store patronage, and to offer a wider variety of merchandise at a specific price point. Other pricing tactics include a single-price tactic, flexible pricing, professional services pricing, price lining, leader pricing, odd–even pricing, price bundling, and two-part pricing. A brief overview of each of these tactics follows, along with a manager's reasons for using the tactic or a combination of tactics to change the base price.

Single-Price Tactic

A merchant using a **single-price tactic** offers all goods and services at the same price (or perhaps two or three prices). Retailers using this tactic include Buck or Two, Dollarama, Dollar Blitz, Dre$$ to the Nine$, Your $10 Store, and Fashions $9.99. The Great Canadian Dollar Store, Your Dollar Store with More, and A Buck & More, all located in malls across Canada, sell all products at a price of one or two dollars.

Single-price selling removes price comparisons from the buyer's decision-making process. The consumer just looks for suitability and the highest perceived quality. The retailer enjoys the benefits of a simplified pricing system and minimal clerical errors. However, continually rising costs are a headache for retailers following this strategy.

Flexible Pricing

flexible pricing
(variable pricing)
A price tactic in which different
customers pay different prices for
essentially the same merchandise
bought in equal quantities.

Flexible pricing (or **variable pricing**) means that different customers pay different prices for essentially the same merchandise bought in equal quantities. This tactic is often found in the sale of shopping goods, specialty merchandise, and most industrial goods except supply items. Car dealers, many appliance retailers, and manufacturers of industrial installations, accessories, and component parts commonly follow this practice. It allows the seller to adjust for competition by meeting another seller's price. Thus a marketing manager with a status quo pricing objective might readily adopt the tactic. Flexible pricing also enables the seller to close a sale with price-conscious consumers. If buyers show promise of becoming large-volume shoppers, flexible pricing can be used to lure their business.

The obvious disadvantages of flexible pricing are the lack of consistent profit margins, the potential ill will among high-paying purchasers, the tendency for salespeople to automatically lower the price to make a sale, and the possibility of a price war among sellers. The disadvantages of flexible pricing have led many companies to stay with a single-price strategy. On the other hand, General Motors attempted a one-price tactic for some of its models but has generally gone back to flexible pricing.

Trade-Ins

Flexible pricing and trade-ins often go hand-in-hand. The majority of new car purchases, for example, involve trade-ins. Trade-ins occur for other products as well, such as musical instruments, sporting goods, jewellery, and some appliances. If a trade-in is involved, the consumer must negotiate two prices, one for the new product and one for the existing product. The existence of a trade-in raises several questions for the purchaser. Will the new product's price differ depending on whether there is a trade-in? Are consumers better off trading in their used product toward the purchase of the new one from the same retailer or should they keep the two transactions separate by dealing with different retailers? Several car-buying guides, such as edmunds.com and AutoTrader.com, advise consumers to keep the two transactions separate.[14]

Recent research found that trade-in customers tend to care more about the trade-in value they receive than the price they pay for the new product. Thus, these buyers tend to pay more than purchasers without a trade-in. Analysis of data from the automobile market found that, on average, trade-in customers end up paying nearly $500 more than customers who simply buy a new car from a dealer.[15]

Professional Services Pricing

Professional services pricing is used by people with lengthy experience, training, and often certification through a licensing board—for example, lawyers, dentists, and family counsellors. Professionals sometimes charge customers at an hourly rate, but sometimes fees are based on the solution to a problem or the performance of an act (such as an eye examination) rather than on the actual time involved. A lawyer may charge $1,000 for completing a divorce but only $200 for handling a traffic violation.

Price Lining

price lining
The practice of offering a product
line with several items at specific
price points.

When a seller establishes a series of prices for a type of merchandise, it creates a price line. **Price lining** is the practice of offering a product line with several items at specific price points. For example, HON, an office furniture manufacturer, may offer its four-drawer file cabinets at $125, $250, and $400. The Limited may offer women's dresses at $40, $70, and $100, with no merchandise marked at prices between those figures. Instead of a normal demand curve running from $40 to $100, The Limited has three demand points (prices).

Price lining reduces confusion for both the salesperson and the consumer. The buyer may be offered a wider variety of merchandise at each established price. Price lines may also enable a seller to reach several market segments. For buyers, the question of price may be quite simple: all they have to do is find a suitable product at the predetermined price. Moreover, price lining is a valuable tactic for the marketing manager because the firm may be able to carry a smaller total inventory than it could without price lines. The results may include fewer markdowns, simplified purchasing, and lower inventory carrying charges.

Price lines also present drawbacks, especially if costs are continually rising. Sellers can offset rising costs in three ways. First, they can begin stocking lower-quality merchandise at each price point. Second, sellers can change the prices, although frequent price line changes confuse buyers. Third, sellers can accept lower profit margins and hold quality and prices constant. This third alternative has short-run benefits, but its long-run handicaps may drive sellers out of business.

Leader Pricing

leader pricing (loss-leader pricing)
A price tactic in which a product is sold near or even below cost in the hope that shoppers will buy other items once they are in the store.

Leader pricing (or **loss-leader pricing**) is an attempt by the marketing manager to attract customers by selling a product near or even below cost in the hope that shoppers will buy other items once they are in the store. This type of pricing appears weekly in the newspaper advertising of supermarkets, specialty stores, and department stores. Leader pricing is normally used on well-known items that consumers can easily recognize as bargains at the special price. The goal is not necessarily to sell large quantities of leader items, but to try to appeal to customers who might shop elsewhere.

Leader pricing is not limited to products. Health clubs offer a one-month free trial as a loss leader. Lawyers give a free initial consultation. Restaurants may distribute two-for-one coupons. When Quizno's opened its first outlets in Windsor, Ontario, all sandwiches were half-priced for the first week.

Odd–Even Pricing

odd–even pricing (psychological pricing)
A price tactic that uses odd-numbered prices to connote bargains and even-numbered prices to imply quality.

Odd–even pricing (or **psychological pricing**) means pricing at odd-numbered prices to connote a bargain and pricing at even-numbered prices to imply quality. For years, many retailers have priced their products in odd numbers—for example, $99.95 or $49.95—to make consumers feel they are paying a lower price for the product.

Some retailers favour odd-numbered prices because they believe that $9.99 sounds less imposing to customers than $10.00. Other retailers believe that an odd-numbered price signals to consumers that the price is at the lowest level possible, thereby encouraging them to buy more units. Neither theory has ever been conclusively proven, although some research has shown that consumers perceive odd-priced products as being on sale and consumers may buy more at odd prices.[16]

Even-numbered pricing is sometimes used to denote quality. Examples include a fine perfume at $100 a bottle, a good watch at $500, or a mink coat at $3,000.

Price Bundling

price bundling
Marketing two or more products in a single package for a special price.

Price bundling involves marketing two or more products in a single package for a special price. Examples include the sale of maintenance contracts with computer hardware and other office equipment, packages of stereo equipment, packages of options on cars, weekend hotel packages that include a room and several meals, and airline vacation packages. Microsoft offers "suites" of software that bundle spreadsheets, word processing, graphics, electronic mail, Internet access, and groupware for networks of microcomputers. Price bundling can stimulate demand for the bundled items if the target market perceives the price as a good value.

Services like hotels and airlines sell a perishable commodity (hotel rooms and airline seats) with relatively constant fixed costs. Bundling can be an important income stream for these businesses because the variable cost tends to be low—for instance, the cost of cleaning a hotel room or putting one more passenger on an airplane. Therefore, the added revenue can help cover fixed costs and generate profits.

The automobile industry has a different motive for bundling. People buy cars only every three to five years. Thus selling options is a somewhat rare opportunity for the car dealer. Price bundling can help the dealer sell a maximum number of options.

unbundling
Reducing the bundle of services that comes with the basic product.

Bundling has also been used in the telecommunications industry. Companies offer local service, long distance, DSL Internet service, wireless, and even cable TV in various menus of bundling. Such bundling is not necessarily consumer-focused. Telecom companies use bundling as a way to protect their market share and fight off competition by

Club Med

Imagine a paradise where kids play all day and parents can relax. At Club Med Family Villages, you'll enjoy a fun-filled vacation where one price includes it all. With Children's Clubs available for kids from 4 months and up, they can enjoy exciting activities such as circus school, in-line skating, soccer camp, and more. Of course, you can stop by and see your kids any time you want, but chances are, they'll be having too much fun to even notice. Which gives you time for something you rarely get a chance to do. Kick back and relax.

Now THIS is a sandbox!

one week all-inclusive from $899
1-800-CLUB MED
OR CALL YOUR TRAVEL AGENT
clubmed.com

Re-new

SOURCE: COURTESY OF CLUB MED

Club Med advertises an all-inclusive vacation for one from $899 in this humorous ad. Included in the price are the airfare, room, meals, sports, and children's clubs. However, several contingencies are placed on this bundled vacation—listed in the ad's fine print.

two-part pricing
A price tactic that charges two separate amounts to consume a single good or service.

SOURCE: NBAE/GETTY IMAGES

In order to maximize revenue, managers could oversell tickets to an event for which season ticket subscriptions are high. This is because people who buy season tickets for an event are less likely to use all the tickets they purchase.

locking customers into a group of services. For consumers, comparison shopping may be difficult since they may not be able to determine how much they are really paying for each component of the bundle.

A related price tactic is **unbundling**, or reducing the bundle of services that comes with the basic product. Rather than raise the price of hotel rooms, some hotel chains have started charging registered guests for parking. To help hold the line on costs, some stores require customers to pay for gift wrapping. Airlines have unbundled in a dramatic fashion. Now everything from checking luggage to soft drinks and food to pillows and blankets comes at a price.

Some research has focused on how people consume certain bundled services. Studies show that when people buy season tickets to a concert series, sporting event, or other activity, the sunk costs (price of the bundle) and the pending benefit (going to see an event) become decoupled, which reduces the likelihood of consumption of the event over time. For example, researchers found that theatregoers who purchased tickets to four plays were only 84 percent likely to use their first-play tickets and only 78 percent likely to use any given ticket across the four plays.[17] In contrast, theatregoers who purchased tickets to a single play were almost certain to use those tickets.

In practice, these findings mean that a theatre manager might expect a no-show rate of 20 percent when the percentage of season ticket holders is high, but a no-show rate of only 5 percent when the percentage of season ticket holders is low. With a high number of season ticket holders, a manager could oversell performances and maximize the revenue for the theatre. Airlines routinely overbook in anticipation of a predictable percentage of no-shows.

While the price bundling of services can result in a lower rate of total consumption of that service, the same is not necessarily true for products. Consider the purchase of an expensive bottle of wine, which can be inventoried until needed. When the wine is purchased as a single unit, its cost and eventual benefit are tightly coupled. As a result, the cost of the wine will be quite important, and a person will likely reserve that wine for a special occasion. When purchased as part of a bundle (e.g., as part of a case of wine), however, the cost and benefit of that individual bottle of wine will likely become decoupled, reducing the impact of the cost on eventual consumption. As a result, a person will likely find the wine appropriate for many more (not-so-special) occasions. Thus, in contrast to the price bundling of services, the price bundling of physical goods could lead to an increase in product consumption.

Two-Part Pricing

Two-part pricing means establishing two separate charges to consume a single good or service. Tennis clubs and health clubs charge a membership fee and a flat fee each time a person uses certain equipment or facilities. In other cases, they charge a base rate for a certain level of usage, such as 10 racquetball games per month, and a surcharge for anything over that amount.

Consumers sometimes prefer two-part pricing because they are uncertain about the number and the types of activities they might use at places like an amusement park. Also, the people who use a service most often pay a higher total price. Two-part pricing can increase a seller's revenue by attracting consumers who would not pay a high fee even for unlimited use. For example, a health club might be able to sell only 100 memberships at $700 annually with unlimited use of facilities, for total revenue of $70,000. However, perhaps it could sell 900 memberships at $200 with a guarantee of using the racquetball courts 10 times a month. Every use over 10 would require the member to pay a $5 fee. Thus membership revenue would provide a base of $180,000, with some additional usage fees coming in throughout the year.

CONSUMER PENALTIES

consumer penalty
An extra fee paid by the consumer for violating the terms of the purchase agreement.

More and more businesses are adopting **consumer penalties**—extra fees paid by consumers for violating the terms of a purchase agreement (see Exhibit 17.2).

Businesses will impose consumer penalties for two reasons: the business will allegedly (1) suffer an irrevocable revenue loss and/or (2) incur significant additional transaction costs should customers be unable or unwilling to complete their purchase obligations. For the company, these customer payments are part of doing business in a highly competitive marketplace. With profit margins in many companies increasingly coming under pressure, organizations are looking to stem losses resulting from customers not meeting their obligations. However, the perceived unfairness of a penalty may affect some consumers' willingness to patronize a business in the future.

EXHIBIT 17.2

Common Consumer Penalties

1. **Airlines**
   - Most airlines charge a penalty for changing reservations on discount tickets; many airlines charge for overweight bags or checking a second bag.

2. **Automobiles**
   - Penalties are imposed for early terminations of car leases. In some cases, deposits on cancelled leases can be subject to penalties.
   - Car owners in England pay penalties, administration fees, and commissions if they cancel an insurance policy early.

3. **Banks**
   - Penalties are often associated with early withdrawal of certificates of deposit.
   - Some banks charge penalties for too many withdrawals in a month.
   - Some have monthly penalties of $5 to $10 if a client's balance falls below a minimum level.
   - Banks can charge late fees, in addition to interest, for tardy payments.
   - Banks might charge penalty fees to ATM users who are customers of another bank.

4. **Car Rentals**
   - Rental companies often have $25 to $100 penalties for no-shows for specialty vehicles. Budget, National, and Dollar/Thrifty are experimenting with no-show fees on all rentals.

5. **Child Daycare**
   - Many daycare centres charge a penalty of up to $5 a minute when parents are late in picking up their children.

6. **Cellular Phones**
   - Companies have cancellation penalties, often in the small print on the back of a contract, which can run as high as $525.

7. **Credit and Debit Cards**
   - Some vendors now charge late fees (beyond normal interest).
   - GE Rewards MasterCard charges $25 a year for those who pay their bill each month, in full, on time. Advanta credit card company may charge $25 for six-month inactivity on an account and $25 to close an account.

8. **Cruises**
   - If a cruise is sailing, even though there are hurricane warnings, some cruise lines will assess penalties if a passenger cancels.
   - Even trip cancellation insurance will not ensure a refund if the traveller has embarked on the trip.
   - Britain is trying to crack down on executive cancellation penalties on package holidays.
   - The *Carnival Paradise* will disembark passengers found smoking.

9. **Hotels**
   - Some hotels require 72 hours' cancellation notice, or the client must pay a penalty of one day's room cost.
   - Most hotels have high charges for using in-room long-distance service.
   - Hilton, Hyatt, and Westin have early departure fees ranging from $25 to $50.

10. **Restaurants**
    - Some now charge up to $50 per person for no-show parties.

11. **Retail Stores**
    - Some retailers are charging a 15-percent restocking fee on certain items. A restocking fee is for putting a returned item back in inventory.

12. **Trains**
    - Via Rail Canada has a penalty for a returned ticket and charges a fee for changing a ticket.

13. **Universities**
    - Universities will give only a partial tuition refund after a course begins.

SOURCE: Eugene Fram and Michael McCarthy, "The True Price of Penalties", *Marketing Management*, Fall 1999, 51.

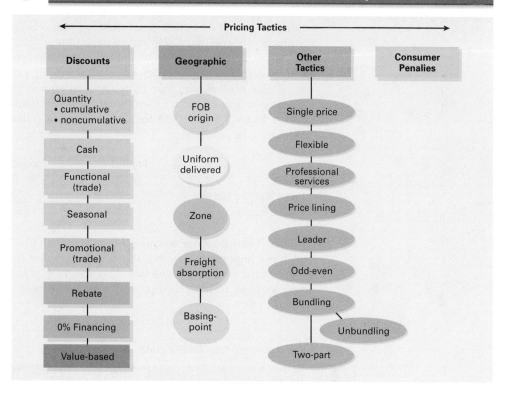

3 Explain how discounts, geographic pricing, and other pricing tactics can be used to fine-tune the base price

Pricing Tactics

Discounts	Geographic	Other Tactics	Consumer Penalies
Quantity • cumulative • noncumulative	FOB origin	Single price	
Cash	Uniform delivered	Flexible	
Functional (trade)	Zone	Professional services	
Seasonal	Freight absorption	Price lining	
Promotional (trade)	Basing-point	Leader	
Rebate		Odd-even	
0% Financing		Bundling	Unbundling
Value-based		Two-part	

4 PRODUCT LINE PRICING

Discuss product line pricing

product line pricing
Setting prices for an entire line of products.

Product line pricing is the practice of setting prices for an entire line of products. Compared to setting the right price on a single product, product line pricing encompasses broader concerns. In product line pricing, the marketing manager tries to achieve maximum profits or other goals for the entire line rather than for a single component of the line.

RELATIONSHIPS AMONG PRODUCTS

A marketing manager must determine the type of relationship that exists among the various products in the line:

The demand curve is influenced by the relationship among products. For example, the demand for bindings depends on the demand for skis. This kind of relationship is described as complementary.

SOURCE: © PHOTOLIBRARY/TOM STILLO

- If items are *complementary,* an increase in the sale of one good causes an increase in demand for the complementary product, and vice versa. For example, the sale of ski poles depends on the demand for skis, making these two items complementary.
- Two products in a line can also be *substitutes* for each other. If buyers buy one item in the line, they are less likely to buy a second item in the line. For example, if someone goes to an automotive supply store and buys paste Turtle Wax for a car, it is very unlikely that he or she will buy liquid Turtle Wax in the near future.
- A *neutral* relationship can also exist between two products. In other words, demand for one of the products is unrelated to demand for the other. For instance, Ralston Purina sells chicken feed and Wheat Chex, but the sale of one of these products has no known impact on demand for the other.

JOINT COSTS

joint costs
Costs that are shared in the manufacturing and marketing of several products in a product line.

Joint costs are costs that are shared in the manufacturing and marketing of several products in a product line. These costs pose a unique problem in product pricing. In oil refining, for example, fuel oil, gasoline, kerosene, naphtha, paraffin, and lubricating oils are all derived from a common production process. Another example is the production of compact discs that combine photos and music.

Any assignment of joint costs must be somewhat subjective because costs are actually shared. Suppose a company produces two products, X and Y, in a common production process, with joint costs allocated on a weight basis. Product X weighs 100 kilograms and product Y weighs 50 kilograms. Thus costs are allocated on the basis of $2 for X for every $1 for Y. Gross margins (sales less the cost of goods sold) might then be as follows:

	Product X	Product Y	Total
Sales	$20,000	$6,000	$26,000
Less: cost of goods sold	15,000	7,500	22,500
Gross margin	$ 5,000	($1,500)	$ 3,500

The example above reveals a loss of $1,500 on product Y. Is that important? Yes, any loss is important. However, the firm must realize that overall it earned a $3,500 profit on the two items in the line. Also, weight may not be the right way to allocate the joint costs. Instead, the firm might use other bases, such as market value or quantity sold.

REVIEW LEARNING OUTCOME 4

4 | **Discuss product line pricing**

5 PRICING DURING DIFFICULT ECONOMIC TIMES

Describe the role of pricing during periods of inflation and recession

Pricing is always an important aspect of marketing, but it is especially crucial in times of inflation and recession. The firm that does not adjust to economic trends may lose ground that it can never make up.

INFLATION

When the economy is characterized by high inflation, special pricing tactics are often necessary. They can be subdivided into cost-oriented and demand-oriented tactics.

Cost-Oriented Tactics

One popular cost-oriented tactic is *culling products with a low profit margin* from the product line. However, this tactic may backfire for three reasons:

- A high volume of sales on an item with a low profit margin may still make the item highly profitable.
- Eliminating a product from a product line may reduce economies of scale, thereby lowering the margins on other items.
- Eliminating the product may affect the price–quality image of the entire line.

Another popular cost-oriented tactic is **delayed-quotation pricing**, which is used for industrial installations and many accessory items. Price is not set on the product until the item is either finished or delivered. Long production lead times force many firms to adopt this policy during periods of inflation. Builders of nuclear power plants, ships, airports, and office towers sometimes use delayed-quotation tactics.

Escalator pricing is similar to delayed-quotation pricing in that the final selling price reflects cost increases incurred between the time an order is placed and the time delivery is made. An escalator clause allows for price increases (usually across the board) based on the cost-of-living index or some other formula. As with any price increase, management's ability to implement such a policy is based on inelastic demand for the product. About a third of all industrial product manufacturers now use escalator clauses. Many companies do not apply the clause in every sale, however. Often it is used only for extremely complex products that take a long time to produce or with new customers.

Any cost-oriented pricing policy that tries to maintain a fixed gross margin under all conditions can lead to a vicious circle. For example, a price increase will result in decreased demand, which in turn will increase production costs (because of lost economies of scale). Increased production costs require a further price increase, leading to further diminished demand, and so on.

Demand-Oriented Tactics

Demand-oriented pricing tactics use price to reflect changing patterns of demand caused by inflation or high interest rates. Cost changes are considered, of course, but mostly in the context of how increased prices will affect demand.

Price shading is the use of discounts by salespeople to increase demand for one or more products in a line. Often shading becomes habitual and is done routinely without much forethought. Ducommun, a metals producer, is among the major companies that have succeeded in eliminating the practice. Ducommun has told its salespeople not to deviate from book price without management authorization.

To make the demand for a good or service more inelastic and to create buyer dependency, a company can use several strategies:

- *Cultivate selected demand*: Marketing managers can target prosperous customers who will pay extra for convenience or service. Harry Rosen, for example, stresses quality and service. As a result, the luxury retailer is more lenient with suppliers and their price increases than are discount retailers. In cultivating close relationships with affluent organizational customers, marketing managers should avoid putting themselves at the mercy of a dominant firm. They can more easily raise prices when an account is readily replaceable. Finally, in companies where engineers exert more influence than purchasing departments do, performance is favoured over price. Often a preferred vendor's pricing range expands if other suppliers prove technically unsatisfactory.
- *Create unique offerings*: Marketing managers should study buyers' needs. If the seller can design distinctive goods or services uniquely fitting buyers' activities, equipment, and procedures, a mutually beneficial relationship will evolve. Buyers would incur high changeover costs in switching to another supplier. By satisfying targeted buyers in a superior way, marketing managers can make them dependent. Cereal manufacturers have been able to accomplish this by marketing unique value-added or multi-ingredient cereals, increasing the perceived quality of the cereals, and allowing the companies to raise prices. These cereals include General Mills' Basic 4,

delayed-quotation pricing
A price tactic used for industrial installations and many accessory items, in which a firm price is not set until the item is either finished or delivered.

escalator pricing
A price tactic in which the final selling price reflects cost increases incurred between the time the order is placed and the time delivery is made.

price shading
The use of discounts by salespeople to increase demand for one or more products in a line.

Clusters, and Oatmeal Crisp; Post's Banana Nut Crunch and Blueberry Morning; and Kellogg's Mueslix, Nutri-Grain, and Temptations.

- *Change the package design*: Another way companies pass on higher costs is to shrink product sizes but keep prices the same. Scott Paper Company reduced the number of sheets in the smallest roll of Scott paper towels from 96 to 60 and actually lowered the price by 10¢ a roll. The company also changed the names of the paper roll sizes to de-emphasize the size of the rolls. When Wrigley introduced its "Slim Pack" to replace its traditional packages of Juicy Fruit, Big Red, and other brands, it reduced the number of sticks per pack from 17 to 15 but left price the same.
- *Heighten buyer dependence*: Owens-Corning Fiberglas supplies an integrated insulation service (from feasibility studies to installation) that includes commercial and scientific training for distributors and seminars for end users. This practice freezes out competition and supports higher prices.

RECESSION

A recession is a period of reduced economic activity, such as the 2008 and 2009 period in Canada. Reduced demand for goods and services, along with higher rates of unemployment, is a common trait of a recession. Yet astute marketers can often find opportunities during recessions. A recession is an excellent time to build market share because competitors are struggling to make ends meet.

Two effective pricing tactics to hold or build market share during a recession are value-based pricing and bundling. *Value-based pricing*, discussed earlier in the chapter, stresses to customers that they are getting a good value for their money. Charles of the Ritz, usually known for its pricey products, introduced the Express Bar during a recession. A collection of affordable cosmetics and skin treatment products, the Express Bar sold alongside regular Ritz products in department stores. Although lower-priced products offer lower profit margins, Ritz found that increases in volume could offset slimmer margins. For example, the company found that consumers would buy two to three Express Bar lipsticks at a time.

Sony created a value-priced TV called the Bravia M series for sale in Mexico where incomes are much lower. It was created by Sony engineers in Mexico using mostly off-the-shelf parts. The Bravia M series is $200 cheaper than comparable Sony TV sets.

Bundling or *unbundling* can also stimulate demand during a recession. If features are added to a bundle, consumers may perceive the offering as having greater value. For example, suppose that Hyatt offers a "great escape" weekend for $149. The package includes two nights' lodging and a continental breakfast. Hyatt could add a massage and a dinner for two to create more value for this price. Conversely, companies can unbundle offerings and reduce base prices to stimulate demand. A furniture store, for example, could start charging separately for design consultation, delivery, credit, setup, and hauling away old furniture.

Recessions are a good time for marketing managers to study the demand for individual items in a product line and the revenue they produce. Pruning unprofitable items can save resources to be better used elsewhere. Borden, for example, found that it made about 3,200 sizes, brands, types, and flavours of snacks—but got 95 percent of its revenues from just half of them.

Retailers also use recessions to drop or reduce shelf space for manufacturers' brands and introduce more store brands. Consumers increase their consumption of store brands during recessions because these products are typically less expensive.

Prices often fall during a recession as competitors try desperately to maintain demand for their wares. Even if demand remains constant, falling prices mean lower profits or no profits. Falling prices, therefore, are a natural incentive to lower costs. During the recent recession, companies implemented new technologies to improve efficiency and then slashed payrolls. Whereas it took nearly 7,000 workers to assemble 350,000 vehicles at Chrysler's minivan plant in Windsor, Ontario, in 2000, the same number of vehicles can now be assembled with fewer than 5,000 employees. Companies also discovered that suppliers are an excellent source of cost savings; the cost of purchased materials accounts for slightly more than half of most manufacturers' expenses. General Electric's appliance division told 300 key suppliers that they had to reduce prices 10 percent or risk losing GE's business. The automobile assemblers have been demanding price reductions of 5 percent each year from their suppliers. Specific strategies that companies use with suppliers include the following:

- *Renegotiating contracts*: Sending suppliers letters demanding price cuts of 5 percent or more and putting out for rebid the contracts of those that refuse to cut costs.
- *Offering help*: Dispatching teams of experts to suppliers' plants to help them reorganize and suggest other productivity-boosting changes; working with suppliers to make parts simpler and cheaper to produce.
- *Keeping the pressure on*: To make sure that improvements continue, setting annual, across-the-board cost-reduction targets, often of 5 percent or more a year.
- *Paring down suppliers*: To improve economies of scale, slashing the overall number of suppliers, sometimes by up to 80 percent, and boosting purchases from those that remain.

Tough tactics like these help keep companies afloat during economic downturns.

REVIEW LEARNING OUTCOME 5

5   **Describe the role of pricing during periods of inflation and recession**

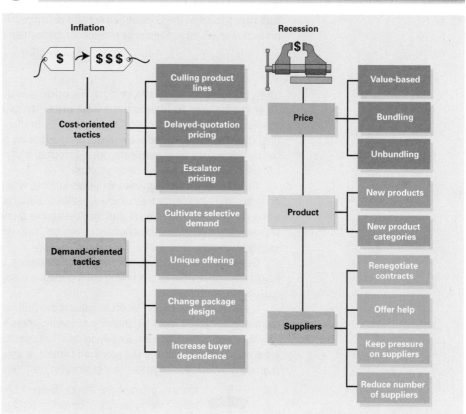

REVIEW AND APPLICATIONS

1 **Describe the procedure for setting the right price.** The process of setting the right price on a product involves four major steps: (1) establishing pricing goals; (2) estimating demand, costs, and profits; (3) choosing a price policy to help determine a base price; and (4) fine-tuning the base price with pricing tactics.

A price strategy establishes a long-term pricing framework for a good or service. The three main types of price policies are price skimming, penetration pricing, and status quo pricing. A price-skimming policy charges a high introductory price, often followed by a gradual reduction. Penetration pricing offers a low introductory price to capture a large market share and attain economies of scale. Finally, status quo pricing strives to match competitors' prices.

1.1 A manufacturer of office furniture decides to produce antique-style rolltop desks reconfigured to accommodate personal computers. The desks will have built-in surge protectors, a platform for raising or lowering the monitor, and a number of other features. The quality, solid-oak desks will be priced far below comparable products. The marketing manager says, "We'll charge a low price and plan on a high volume to reduce our risks." Comment.

1.2 Janet Oliver, owner of a mid-priced dress shop, notes, "My pricing objectives are simple: I just charge what my competitors charge. I'm happy because I'm making money." React to Janet's statement.

1.3 What is the difference between a price policy and a price tactic? Give an example.

2 **Identify the legal and ethical constraints on pricing decisions.** Government regulation helps monitor five major areas of pricing: deceptive pricing, resale price maintenance, price fixing, predatory pricing, and price discrimination. Some provinces have enacted unfair trade practice acts that protect small businesses from large firms that operate efficiently on extremely thin profit margins; the acts prohibit charging below-cost prices. The Competition Act prohibits price fixing, which is an agreement between two or more firms on a particular price, and predatory pricing, in which a firm undercuts its competitors with extremely low prices to drive them out of business, and makes it illegal for firms to discriminate between two or more buyers with regard to price. The Competition Act also describes what constitutes deceptive prices and protects resellers from manufacturer demands to maintain desired price levels.

2.1 What are the basic defences that a seller can use if accused under the Competition Act?

3 **Explain how discounts, geographic pricing, and other special pricing tactics can be used to fine-tune the base price.** Several techniques enable marketing managers to adjust prices within a general range in response to changes in competition, government regulation, consumer demand, and promotional and positioning goals. Techniques for fine-tuning a price can be divided into three main categories: discounts, allowances, rebates, and value-based pricing; geographic pricing; and other pricing tactics.

The first type of tactic gives lower prices to those who pay promptly, order a large quantity, or perform some function for the manufacturer. Value-based pricing starts with the customer, considers the competition and costs, and then determines a price. Other tactics in this category include seasonal discounts, promotion allowances, rebates (cash refunds), zero percent financing, and markdown money.

Geographic pricing tactics, such as FOB origin pricing, uniform delivered pricing, zone pricing, freight absorption pricing, and basing-point pricing, are ways of moderating the impact of shipping costs on distant customers.

A variety of other pricing tactics stimulates demand for certain products, increases store patronage, and offers more merchandise at specific prices.

More and more customers are paying price penalties, which are extra fees for violating the terms of a purchase contract. The perceived fairness or unfairness of a penalty may affect some consumers' willingness to patronize a business in the future.

3.1 **WRITING** You are contemplating a price change for an established product sold by your firm. Write a memo analyzing the factors you need to consider in your decision.

3.2 Columnist Dave Barry jokes that federal law requires this message under the sticker price of new cars: "Warning to stupid people: Do not pay this amount." Discuss why the sticker price is generally higher than the actual selling price of a car. Tell how you think car dealers set the actual prices of the cars they sell.

3.3 **TEAM** Divide into teams of four persons. Each team should choose one of the following topics: skimming, penetration pricing, status quo pricing, price fixing, geographic pricing, adopting a single-price tactic, flexible pricing, or professional services pricing. Each team should then pick a retailer that it feels most closely follows the team's chosen pricing strategy. Go to the store and write down examples of the strategy. Interview the store manager and get his or her views on the advantages and disadvantages of the strategy. Each team should then make an oral report in class.

3.4 Canada Post regularly raises the price of a first-class stamp but has difficulty making a profit. Is uniform delivered pricing the best choice for first-class mail? Explain your reasoning.

3.5 How is the "information age" changing the nature of pricing?

3.6 Have you ever paid a price penalty? How did it affect your attitude toward that company?

3.7 ![WRITING] Imagine that you are a marketing manager for a mid-sized amusement park. You have attended an industry-wide meeting where a colleague gave a talk about new pricing strategies for amusement parks. You were very motivated by the seminar. On your return to work, write a memo to your boss outlining the pros and cons of the new pricing strategy. End your memo with a recommendation either for or against à la carte pricing of attractions (pricing each attraction separately rather than charging a single high entrance fee).

4 **Discuss product line pricing.** Product line pricing maximizes profits for an entire product line. When setting product line prices, marketing managers determine what type of relationship exists among the products in the line: complementary, substitute, or neutral. Managers also consider joint (shared) costs among products in the same line.

4.1 Develop a price line strategy for each of these firms:

    a. a university bookstore

    b. a restaurant

    c. a video-rental store

5 **Describe the role of pricing during periods of inflation and recession.** Marketing managers employ cost-oriented and demand-oriented tactics during periods of economic inflation. Cost-oriented tactics include dropping products with a low profit margin, delayed-quotation pricing, and escalator pricing. Demand-oriented pricing methods include price shading and increasing demand through cultivating selected customers, creating unique offerings, changing the package size, and heightening buyer dependence.

To stimulate demand during a recession, marketers use value-based pricing, bundling, and unbundling. Recessions are also a good time to prune unprofitable items from product lines. Managers strive to cut costs during recessions in order to maintain profits as revenues decline. Implementing new technology, cutting payrolls, and pressuring suppliers for reduced prices are common techniques used to cut costs. Companies also create new value-added products.

5.1 During a recession, what pricing strategies would you consider using to gain or maintain market share? Explain your answer.

5.2 ![ONLINE] After a period of growth and prosperity, Canadians were challenged by the economic downturn of 2008 and 2009. As a result, pricing became an issue for many consumers looking to pinch pennies. This was also true in areas where penny-pinching isn't a common occurrence, like high-end retailers. Search *the Globe and Mail*'s on-line archives (**www.theglobeandmail.com**) to find articles on price-cutting. Make a list of pricing tactics that are illustrated in the articles.

TERMS

base price 549
basing-point pricing 552
cash discount 549
consumer penalty 556
cumulative quantity discount 549
deceptive pricing 546
delayed-quotation pricing 559
escalator pricing 559
flexible pricing (variable pricing) 553
FOB origin pricing 552
freight absorption pricing 552
functional discount (trade discount) 550
joint costs 558

leader pricing (loss-leader pricing) 554
markdown money 550
noncumulative quantity discount 549
odd–even pricing (psychological pricing) 554
penetration pricing 544
predatory pricing 547
price bundling 554
price fixing 547
price lining 553
price shading 559
price skimming 543
price strategy 543

product line pricing 557
promotional allowance (trade allowance) 550
quantity discount 549
rebate 550
resale price maintenance 546
seasonal discount 550
single-price tactic 552
two-part pricing 555
unbundling 554
uniform delivered pricing 552
value-based pricing 550
zone pricing 552

APPLICATION EXERCISE

You read in this chapter about the dangers of pricing products too low. Do you really think that companies sometimes price their products so low that they don't make any money? After all, companies are in business to make money, and if they don't, they won't be in business long. Let's take a closer look at the effects of pricing products too low or creating excessive discounts during sale periods.

Activity

1. The average markup in the produce department of a local supermarket is 28 percent on selling price. When sold at a 28 percent markup on selling price, bananas usually account for 25 percent of the department's sales and 25 percent of the department markup. This week, assume that bananas were put on sale at cost. The department sold twice as many bananas as normal. However, they were sold at zero markup. If all other things remain the same, what is the average markup on selling price for the entire produce department this week?

ETHICS EXERCISE

People feel better when they think that they are getting a great bargain when they shop. Knowing this, some retailers mark up items above the traditional retail price and then offer a 60 percent discount. If they had simply discounted the normal retail price by 20 percent, the resulting "sale price" would have been the same. One retailer says that he is just making shoppers happy that they got a great deal when he inflates the retail price before discounting.

Questions

1. What do you think?

2. Does the CMA Code of Ethics address this issue? Go to **http://the-cma.org/consumer/ethics.cfm** and review the code. Then write a brief paragraph summarizing what the CMA Code of Ethics contains that relates to retail pricing.

CASE STUDY

SOURCE: © JIM LOTT/SEATTLE TIMES

BUNDLED PRICING: DISCONNECTING CABLE CHANNELS FROM PRICING BUNDLES

When people go shopping, the grocery store doesn't make them buy broccoli if they are buying milk; the department store doesn't make them buy socks when they're buying shoes. Why, then, do cable and satellite TV companies make people pay for channels they don't watch? Try counting how many channels you have that you never watch. Why don't cable companies offer à la carte service, or individual channels, in lieu of traditional packages of channels?

Adding to consumer frustration with having to subscribe to gardening and cooking channels when all they want is A&E is the spiralling price of cable TV. According to a recent report, cable rates have jumped far more than the rate of inflation over the past five years. Cable companies claim that the rate increases are necessary in order to invest in original programming, to upgrade technology, and to cover the costs of rapidly increasing sports programming.

Unbundling cable channels appeals to many consumers who hope that it would lower monthly bills and provide more control over what their families are watching. Further, the average household with 50 or more channels watches only 12 to 17 of them. However, the thought of changing how cable service is priced alarms the industry.

Cable operators say that their entire business model is predicated on packaged offerings. That setup gives cable networks two revenue streams: advertising revenue and per-subscriber fees. Each of these revenue sources could be hurt. Further, a move to individual channel selection would severely limit an individual network's ability to generate original programming. Cable operators also say that selling channels separately presents technological problems. Some consumers still have older, analog systems in which it is more difficult to break down individual channel signals for each household. Given the technological costs of implementing an individualized system and the likelihood that fees would increase to make up for lost subscribers, subscribers could end up getting only a dozen or so channels for the same price they are currently paying for a bundle.

Questions

1. What other pricing strategies could cable operators use that would maintain their revenue stream and check the escalating price of cable service?

2. Should the government step in and do something about cable pricing? Why or why not?

3. What would happen to the cable industry if it was deregulated in the same way as the telecommunications industry?

4. Would you prefer à la carte or a bundle pricing strategy for your cable service?

VIDEO CASE

CBC

AIR WARS: AIR CANADA'S PRICING WOES

Since its establishment as a Crown corporation by an act of the Parliament of Canada in 1937, Air Canada has been Canada's largest airline. After being privatized and taking over Canadian Airlines, Air Canada controlled over 90 percent of airline passenger travel in Canada. By 2010, Air Canada had grown to the 14th-largest airline in the world, was carrying over 32 million passengers a year to over 700 destinations in 128 countries, and generating nearly $11 billion in revenue while still controlling nearly 50 percent of all Canadian airline passenger travel. Sound good to you? Well, being large can bring on many different types of problems. Among them, how would you like to have every move you make closely watched by the government and your competition?

Many aspects of Air Canada's operations are closely scrutinized to ensure that the company is in compliance with all federal legislation, but one of the areas most closely monitored by the government is Air Canada's pricing. Because Air Canada is Canada's largest air passenger carrier, the government wants to ensure that Air Canada charges "fair" prices to Canadian air travellers. Generally, of course, Air Canada would like to comply with the wishes of the government. What do you do, however, when different government agencies send different signals?

Let's watch as Air Canada and its president and CEO, Robert Milton, battle with two government departments over Air Canada's prices. On the one hand, the Ministry of Transport has accused Air Canada of charging monopoly prices on some of its routes and wants Air Canada to lower its fares. On the other hand, the Competition Bureau of Industry Canada has accused Air Canada of charging predatory prices, making it difficult for other air carriers to compete with the airline. The Competition Bureau wants Air Canada to raise its fares. What's a company to do?[18]

Questions

1. How would you handle Air Canada's pricing problems if you were in Robert Milton's shoes?

2. Is the current level of government regulation of business good or bad for consumers? What is too much government regulation?

3. What sort of pricing policy do you feel Air Canada is following?

MARKETING & YOU RESULTS

High scores on this poll indicate that you are very sensitive to prices and that your price consciousness affects how you shop. Conversely, a lower score suggests that you are not very price conscious.

MARKETING MISCUE

RYANAIR'S PRICING RAISES EYEBROWS

Started in 1985 with a single 15-seat aircraft flying one daily run between Waterford Airport in Ireland and Gatwick Airport in London, Ryanair now ranks as one of the largest airlines in terms of passengers. In 2010, the airline was on target to haul over 72 million passengers, generate $4.7 billion in revenue, and earn $680 million in after-tax profits. But has its low-cost model and obsessive focus on the bottom line pushed it over the edge on frugality?

According to one report, Ryanair had at least 15 separate taxes and charges that could be assessed on passengers—and sometimes these extra charges would total more than the ticket itself. In 2009, the company reported that money raised from these extra charges rose over 25 per-cent to nearly $740 million. All the while, however, the airline reduced actual seat ticket prices by 4 percent. Ryanair's ticket prices average less than $60 but the airline charges for everything, including check-in, baggage, peanuts, beverages, and infants who sit on an adult's lap.

Savings through reduced airport and aircraft costs are supposedly passed on to Ryanair passengers via lower fares. Airport costs include such amenities as the airline check-in desk—something Ryanair hopes to abolish. By late 2010, Ryanair indicated that all passengers will have to check in on-line in order to confirm their flight. According to the carrier, over 75 percent of passengers already do this. Thus doing away with check-in desks would reduce the overall costs to the 75 percent who are covering the cost of the desk but not using it. Another major airport cost relates to the handling of luggage. The goal is for only one in five Ryanair passengers to check luggage. Reduced luggage handling results in lower costs, which the airline has said it can pass on to the consumer via lower seat prices. Additionally, there was a report that the company was planning to charge a $12 fee per return flight even if the passenger checked in on-line, printed out his or her own boarding pass, and did not carry a bag.

Like many airlines, Ryanair charges for on-board extras such as food and drinks. An idea that Ryanair's chief executive has pondered is that of instituting a toilet charge. Similar to some public restrooms, coin slots could be retrofitted to toilet doors so passengers would have to pay to visit the toilet. There is no legal requirement to provide toilets onboard, so a toilet fee would be legal. Another suggested on-board cost reduction, however, raised the ire of many of the Ryanair pilots. In 2008, the company began to curb the discretionary rights of pilots to request extra fuel for safety reserves. From many pilots' perspective, the restriction was a compromise on safety.

The chairman of the Air Transport Users Council has said that Ryanair is not doing anything illegal with respect to the ancillary or optional charges as long as the company is transparent about them. Ryanair's website does have a table of fees that includes such items as on-line check-in, payment handling, airport check-in, priority boarding, infant under two years in the same seat, checked baggage, excess baggage, infant equipment, sports equipment, musical instruments, flight change, and name change. Thus the ancillary fee charges are transparent and noted for the passenger who navigates the website to identify the additional charges.

One area in which Ryanair did run into some pricing problems in late 2008 was with respect to non-optional costs, such as taxes. The Office of Fair Trading (OFT) mandated that all U.K. airlines should include "fixed non-optional" costs in their headline fares. Ryanair's website, however, was displaying prices excluding taxes and charges. This made Ryanair's seat prices appear to be consid-erably more appealing to a price-comparison shopper. While the airline attributed the pricing error to a "system performance issue," which they were working with their software partner to rectify, the fact that the airline was breaking the law did not go unnoticed by competitors and the busi-ness media, which have had many ups and downs with the company, both praising it and criti-cizing it. While many can empathize with system performance problems, Ryanair and its pricing tactics had angered too many to let the problem go unresolved, with some suggesting that the airline was, yet again, attempting to hide pricing charges.[1]

Questions

1. What is the relationship between demand and price for airline tickets?

2. Ryanair is not violating any laws with the ancillary or optional charges, but do you think the airline is pricing ethically?

KINDLE KEEPS SAME PRICE EVEN DURING RECESSION

In October 2008, talk-show host Oprah Winfrey gave her endorsement to Amazon.com's e-reader, the Kindle. An endorsement by Oprah Winfrey has proven to be a gold mine for consumer product companies and, in difficult economic times, this endorsement was critical to Kindle's ability to ride out recessionary times.

The Amazon Kindle is a portable reader that downloads books, blogs, magazines, and newspapers wirelessly. The material is then displayed on a high-resolution display that looks and reads like the real thing (even in sunlight).

The Kindle was first launched in late 2007 and, due to the wireless partnership with Sprint required for product downloads, was initially available only in the U.S. market. Retailing at $399, Amazon.com's first offering of the Kindle reportedly sold out in five and a half hours. Eventually, the price was dropped to $359. Upon introduction of the Kindle, Amazon.com had upwards of 90,000 digital titles available for downloading. Although Amazon did not report sales figures for the Kindle, one analyst reported that about 500,000 Kindles had been sold prior to the launch of the Kindle 2.

Initially, the Kindle had one major competitor, the Reader by Sony. Sony launched the Reader, priced at $299, in 2006 and made it available in the United States, Canada, and the United Kingdom. Later versions of the Reader sold for between $299 and $400. Product downloads to the Reader require that the Reader be attached to a computer to download material from a special website. As of early 2009, Sony had reportedly shipped just over 400,000 Readers since its launch.

In February of 2009, Amazon.com released the Kindle 2 in the United States at a price of $359. Rather than lowering the price of this next-generation Kindle, Amazon opted to provide upgrades and keep the price constant. The new Kindle offered several product improvements over the original Kindle, which was now available in Canada. These improvements included the following:

- Slimmer

- Lighter

- 3G wireless allowing downloads from anywhere, anytime

- Improved display

- Longer battery life

- Greater storage capacity

- Faster page turns

- New text-to-speech feature allowing the device to read out loud

- Larger selection of reading material

An additional incentive to buy the Kindle 2 was that famed author Stephen King wrote a novella available exclusively for the new device.

Although there was considerable interest in learning about the new and improved Kindle 2, bloggers were focusing a lot of attention on its price. The general consensus among the bloggers was that the price was too high given the difficult economic times during which it was introduced. However, according to Amazon's CEO and founder, Jeff Bezos, there was no way to simultaneously provide upgrades and reduce price.

The maintenance of the $359 price tag for the Kindle 2 has led some to question the pricing strategy and ultimate business model for the Kindle. From a price perspective, many wonder if the somewhat high price point is practical in a recessionary economy. Will consumers part with $359 for an unnecessary electronic gadget? With respect to the business model, the focus is on where money is to be made in this market. At the start of 2010, e-books were only around 1 percent of overall book sales. With such huge untapped market potential, it seemed that there was considerable money to be made in the sale of e-books.

Making money in the e-book marketplace would mean that consumers had to first have an electronic reader such as Amazon's Kindle or Sony's Reader. Driving down the price of the electronic readers would mean more sales of the readers and, thus, more sales of e-books. With the Kindle Store offering over 250,000 books, newspapers, magazines, and blogs available for downloading, many wondered about the rationale behind the pricing of the Kindle 2.[2]

Questions

1. What pricing objective is driving Amazon.com with its Kindle product offering?

2. What is the company's pricing strategy?

PART

7

Managing
Marketing-Created
Relationships

(18) Customer Relationship Management (CRM)

SOURCE: BAYNE STANLEY/GETSTOCK.COM

LEARNING OUTCOMES

1 Define customer relationship management

2 Explain how to identify customer relationships with the organization

3 Understand interactions with the current customer base

4 Outline the process of capturing customer data

5 Describe the use of technology to store and integrate customer data

6 Describe how to identify the best customers

7 Explain the process of leveraging customer information throughout the organization

(Y) MARKETING & YOU

How do you feel about complaining?
Using the scales below, enter your answers or record them on a separate page.

1	2	3	4	5	6
Strongly agree		Agree	Disagree		Strongly disagree

__ People are bound to end up with an unsatisfactory product once in a while, so they shouldn't complain to the store or the manufacturer about it.*

__ It bothers me quite a bit if I don't complain about an unsatisfactory product.

__ It sometimes feels good to get my dissatisfaction and frustration with a product off my chest by complaining.

__ I often complain when I'm dissatisfied with a business or a product because I feel it is my duty to do so.

__ I don't like people who complain to stores because usually their complaints are unreasonable.*

Now total your score, reversing your answers for the items followed by an asterisk (for example, if you answered 3, enter 4). Find out what your score means after reading the chapter.

SOURCE: REPRINTED WITH PERMISSION FROM MARKETING SCALES HANDBOOK VOL. III, PUBLISHED BY THE AMERICAN MARKETING ASSOCIATION, G. BRUNER, K. JAMES, H. HENSEL, EDS. SCALE #264.

Marketers of travel and tourism products have discovered that knowing who their customers are and what they like is critical to a successful marketing strategy. Consequently, customer relationship management (CRM) is a key marketing concept for travel and tourism marketing companies like WestJet Vacations whose promotional line is "We take fun seriously."[1] For example, WestJet Vacations has teamed up with Vancouver-based Contac to personalize the vacations of their clients using a technology system called "eConcierge." Virtually all on-line vacation providers send their clients e-mail confirmations with their trip itineraries. However, eConcierge goes one step further. Along with the e-mail confirmation, clients who have made booking also get a PURL (personalized URL—universal resource locator) which resides on the

my.westjetvacations.com website. Clients' PURL allows them to find information on flights, transfers, hotels, tours, destinations, and attractions and discount coupons that are tailored specifically to them.

In essence, WestJet Vacations is giving its clients their own page where they can "upload photos, share their vacation details on social networks and email their PURL to friends and family."[2] In addition to the content based on the trips a client has booked, the PURL is also designed to reflect the demographic and psychographic profile of the client. For example, WestJet vacation puts different images into each PURL. The kinds of pictures in a university student's PURL would be vastly different from those found in the PURL of someone who is about to retire.

WestJet Vacations hopes that the eConcierge system will help it increase its revenues and get customers to purchase more of its services. In addition, since it is a customer relationship management system, the company expects to be able to build relationships with its clients, gain repeat business, and also acquire referrals. The eConcierge software tool will also allow WestJet Vacations to track on-line activity, compile data for its marketing programs, enable it to sell on-line ads, and capitalize "on impulse purchases such as trip add-ons."[3]

How does a company go about setting up a CRM program like WestJet Vacations? And once such a program is in place, how does a company use the information it collects to its advantage? In this chapter we answer these questions and more.

SOURCES: WWW.WESTJETVACATIONS.COM, ACCESSED JUNE 30, 2010; GARIN TCHOLAKIAN AND EMILY WEXLER, "WESTJET VACATIONS GET PERSONAL," STRATEGY, JUNE 2009, 7.

Define customer relationship management

Customer relationship management (CRM) focuses on understanding customers as individuals instead of as part of a group. To do so, marketers make their communications more customer-specific, like the personalized marketing efforts used by WestJet Vacations. It is as much a philosophy of doing business as well as a marketing strategy and some marketers believe in it so strongly that they incorporate CRM into everything they do.

Customer relationship management (CRM) is a company-wide business strategy designed to optimize profitability, revenue, and customer satisfaction by focusing on precisely defined customer groups. This is accomplished by organizing the company around customer segments, establishing and tracking customer interactions with the firm, fostering customer-satisfying behaviours, and linking all the firm's processes from its customers through to its suppliers. For example, **Listen.com**'s Rhapsody player targets consumers who listen to streaming audio. Then, by requiring users to log in, Rhapsody tracks their musical preferences and usage. Listen.com can leverage this information to offer special promotions and make recommendations to specific target markets and individuals.

The difference between CRM and traditional mass marketing can be compared to shooting a rifle versus a shotgun. If you have good aim, a rifle is the more efficient weapon to use. A shotgun, on the other hand, increases your odds of hitting the target when it is more difficult to focus your aim. Instead of scattering messages far and wide across the spectrum of mass media (the shotgun approach), CRM marketers are able to focus their efforts to more effectively communicate with each individual customer (the rifle approach).

If only you **knew** the **REAL me**...

SOURCE: COURTESY OF SURADO SOLUTIONS, INC. ALL RIGHTS RESERVED.

CRM is a strategy designed to optimize business performance by focusing on highly defined customer groups. This Surado ad for SCM SQL is a perfect example of what CRM systems seek to know: the real customer.

customer relationship management (CRM)
A company-wide business strategy designed to optimize profitability, revenue, and customer satisfaction by focusing on precisely defined customer groups.

THE CRM CYCLE

On the surface, CRM may appear to be a rather simplistic customer service strategy. But while customer service is part of the CRM process, it is only a small part of a totally integrated, holistic approach to building customer relationships. CRM is often described as a closed-loop system that builds relationships with customers. Exhibit 18.1 illustrates this closed-looped system, one that is continuous and circular and that has no predefined starting or end point.[4]

To initiate the CRM cycle, a company must first *establish customer relationships within the organization.* This may simply entail learning who the customers are and where they are located, or it may require more complex information on the products and services they are using. Bridgestone/Firestone, a tire manufacturer and tire service company, uses a CRM system called OnDemand5.[5] OnDemand5 initially gathers information from a point-of-sale interaction. The types of information gathered include basic demographic information, how frequently consumers purchase goods, how much they purchase, and how far they drive.

Next, the company must understand the interactions with current customers. Companies accomplish this by collecting data on all types of communications a customer has with the company. Using its OnDemand5 system, Bridgestone/Firestone can add information based on additional interactions with the consumer, such as several visits to a physical store location and purchasing history. In this phase, companies build on the initial information collected and develop a more useful database.

Customer Experience

SOURCE: BRIAN CLIFTON, "ADVANCED WEB METRICS WITH GOOGLE ANALYTICS," 2008: WWW.GOOGLE.COM/ANALYTICS/ FEATURES.HTM; WWW.GOOGLE.COM/ANALYTICS/BENEFITS.HTM; WWW.GOOGLE.COM/ANALYTICS/CASE_STUDY.

> TRACKING CONSUMER EXPERIENCES WITH GOOGLE ANALYTICS

Since the early days of the Internet, companies have known a good Web presence is essential to brand image. But with the growing importance of an on-line presence, it also became clear that measuring the effectiveness of the website is crucial. Web analytics, and specifically Google Analytics, enables companies to measure on-line and off-line marketing effectiveness in visitor attraction, conversion rate, user experiences, and an ROI for the web-site. As an on-line measurement tool, at a basic level, Google Analytics can show companies the number of daily visitors to the site, the average conversion rates on a variety of outcomes, the most visited pages, the average time spent on each page, the average visit depth, the geographic dispersion of visitors, the amount of revenue the site is producing, its top-selling products, and many other metrics. At a deeper level, Google Analytics can show companies the value of each customer, the value of the Web page, the difference in ROI between new and returning customers, variations of conversion rates, variations in bounce rate, the effectiveness of internal search tools, and how many visits it takes a noncustomer to become a new customer. Using Google Analytics, a company can even use search engine optimization methods and Google AdWords to identify profitable key terms. And best of all, most of it is free. Here are some of the results:

- Global realtor RE/MAX gets more than 2 million visits a month. Google Analytics showed the company that 90 percent came from search engines and used the search term "remax," and that 70 percent of people searched for properties on its site. It also found that moving the property search function to the home page was important.
- The American Cancer Society needed to get the most bang for its fundraising buck. With Google Analytics, it was able to improve site design, functionality, and technology. For example, it was able to optimize its AdWords keywords around content so it could measure ROI on this tool. Google Analytics also helped it develop cancer education programs on-line by using search engine optimization for clinical trial information.
- Discount Tires found the Internet was one of its most successful distribution channels. Using Google Analytics and AdWords, the company increased on-line sales 14 percent in the first week. It also learned how to revise the wording on its website, which reduced the abandonment rate by 36 percent.[6]

How can marketers use Google Analytics (think about building brand loyalty, e-mail campaigns, retaining customer, targeting the marketing message, etc.)? It's free; what's in this for Google?

EXHIBIT 18.1

A Simple Flow Model of the Customer Relationship Management System

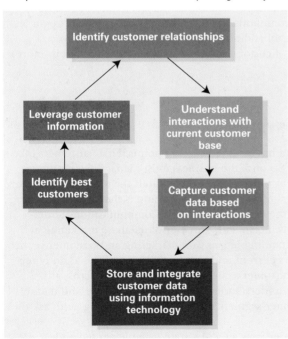

Using this knowledge of its customers and their interactions, the company then captures relevant customer data on interactions. As an example, Bridgestone/Firestone can collect information such as the date of the last communication with a customer, how often the customer makes purchases, and whether the customer redeemed coupons sent through direct mail.

How can marketers analyze and communicate with individual customers? How can huge corporations like Rogers Communications and the Bank of Montreal manage relationships with each and every one of their millions of customers on a personal level? The answer lies in how information technology is used to implement the CRM system. For example, software expenditures on CRM technology were expected to be in the $10.9-billion range in North America in 2010.[7] Although dependent on technology for effective implementation, fundamentally, a CRM approach is no more than the relationship cultivated by a salesperson with the customer. A successful salesperson builds a relationship over time, constantly thinks about what the customer needs and wants, and is mindful of the trends and patterns in the customer's purchase history. A good salesperson often knows what the customer needs even before the customer knows. The salesperson may also inform, educate, and instruct the customer about new products, technology, or applications in anticipation of the customer's future needs or requirements.

Thoughtful attention is the basis of all successful CRM systems. Information technology is used not only to enhance the collection of customer data, but also to store and integrate customer data throughout the company and, ultimately, to "get to know" customers on a personal basis. Customer data are the firsthand responses that are obtained from customers through investigation or by asking direct questions. These initial data, which might include individual answers to questionnaires, responses on warranty cards, or lists of purchases recorded by electronic cash registers, are waiting to be analyzed and interpreted.

The value of customer data depends on the system that stores the data and the consistency and accuracy of the data captured. Obtaining high-quality, actionable data from various sources is a key element in any CRM system. Bridgestone/Firestone accomplishes this by managing all information in a central database accessible by marketers. Different kinds of database management software tools are available ranging from extremely high-tech, expensive, custom-designed databases to standardized programs. Oracle is the world's largest CRM software company; it offers customized software for virtually any type of CRM application. In contrast, NetERP offers users database software in a standardized format that is available off the shelf at a much lower cost.[8]

Every customer wants to be a company's main priority. Yet not all customers are equally important in the eyes of a business. Some customers are simply more profitable for the company than others. Consequently, the company must identify its profitable and unprofitable customers. Data mining is an analytical process that compiles actionable data about the purchase habits of a company's current and potential customers. Essentially, data mining transforms customer data into customer information a company can use to make managerial decisions. The NetERP software allows managers to customize their "dashboard" to obtain real-time reports on top-selling items and gross sales over a given period. Similarly, Bridgestone/Firestone uses OnDemand5 to analyze its data to determine which customers qualify for the MasterCare Select program. It also identifies customers who have not made a purchase in the past 8 to 12 months.

Once customer data are analyzed and transformed into usable information, the information must be leveraged. The CRM system sends the customer information to all areas of a business because the customer interacts with all aspects of the business (e.g., sales or marketing, operations, production, and accounting). Essentially, the company is trying to enhance customer relationships by getting the right information to the right person in the right place at the right time.

Bridgestone/Firestone uses the information in its database to develop different marketing campaigns for each type of customer. For example, MasterCare Select customers receive free tire rotation, maps, roadside assistance, and lost-key service. Customers are also targeted by promotions aimed at increasing store visits, upgrades to higher-end tires, and purchases of additional services. Since the company customized its mailings to each type of customer, visits to stores have increased by more than 50 percent.[9]

IMPLEMENTING A CRM SYSTEM

Our discussion of the CRM system has assumed two key points. First, customers take centre stage in any organization. Second, the business must manage the customer relationship across all points of customer contact throughout the entire organization. This factor is critical to the success of any CRM initiative and is the whole point of sharing information throughout the organization. Telus Communications understands these two points completely. Lorne Hill, director of database marketing at Telus, says that "customer understanding lets us vary marketing and customer service investments based on a customer's current and potential value to Telus as an enterprise. We need to understand a customer's current and future value across all product lines. At Telus, customer understanding depends on customer and market profiles, predictive models, customer segmentation, campaign tracking, and 'ask the customer' data."[10]

In the next sections, we examine how a CRM system is implemented and follow the progression depicted in Exhibit 18.1 as we explain each step in greater detail.

1   Define customer relationship management

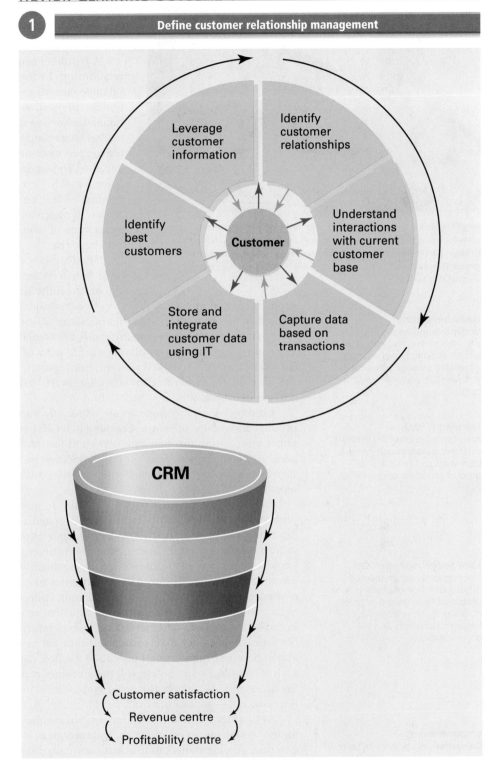

IDENTIFY CUSTOMER RELATIONSHIPS

2

Explain how to identify customer relationships with the organization

Companies that have a CRM system follow a customer-centric focus or model. **Customer-centric** is an internal management philosophy similar to the marketing concept discussed in Chapter 1. Under this philosophy, the company customizes its product and service offering based on data generated through interactions between the customer and the company. This philosophy transcends all functional areas of the

SOURCE: © AP PHOTO/NICK UT

Sony's PlayStation system is one of the leaders in the video-game market. To increase customer loyalty and ensure that the company's products meet the needs and wants of its target market, Sony designed a website that feels like an exclusive club for video gamers. Through player feedback, Sony can refine its site to match its customers' exact wants as they evolve.

business (production, operations, accounting, etc.), producing an internal system where all of the company's decisions and actions are a direct result of customer information.

A customer-centric company builds long-lasting relationships by focusing on what satisfies and retains valuable customers. For example, Sony's PlayStation website, **playstation.com**, focuses on learning, customer knowledge management, and empowerment to market its gaming entertainment system. The website is designed to create a community of users who can join the PlayStation®Network*, which is described as "your home for exclusive entertainment and online gaming." A free sign-up allows customers to download games, movies, and TV shows, with the additional enticement of "some exclusive games you can't play anywhere else."[11]

The PlayStation is designed to support Sony's CRM system. When PlayStation users wish to access amenities on the site, they are required to log in and supply information such as their name, e-mail address, and date of birth. Also, users can opt to fill out a survey that asks questions about the types of computer entertainment systems they own, how many games are owned for each console, expected future game purchases, time spent playing games, types of games played, and level of Internet connectivity. Armed with this information, Sony marketers can then tailor the site, new games, and even PlayStation hardware based on players' replies to the survey and use of the website.[12]

Customer-centric companies are constantly learning ways to enhance their product and service offerings. **Learning** in a CRM environment involves collecting customer information through comments and feedback on product and service performance. As just described, Sony uses its PlayStation website to gather information from surveys and message boards so that it can offer more customer-friendly products and services.

Each unit of a business typically has its own way of recording what it learns and perhaps even its own customer information system. The departments' different interests make it difficult to pull all of the customer information together in one place using a common format. To overcome this problem, companies using CRM rely on knowledge management. **Knowledge management** is a process by which customer information is centralized and shared in order to enhance the relationship between customers and the organization. Information collected includes experiential observations, comments, customer actions, and qualitative facts about the customer. For example, PlayStation marketers gather survey information and generate a computer file for each customer that is available to the call centre as well as on the website. If a PlayStation user registers and purchases a yellow console but then wants to change to a silver console, he or she can call the customer service line, and the representative on the other end will change the order and indicate its availability, which brings us to the next concept—empowerment.[13]

As Chapter 1 explained, empowerment involves delegating authority to solve customers' problems. In other words, **empowerment** is the latitude that organizations give their representatives to negotiate mutually satisfying commitments with customers. At Sony's PlayStation call centre, a representative can change an order over the phone without having to wait for management's approval. Usually, organizational representatives are able to make such changes during interactions with customers through phone, fax, e-mail, or Web communication, or face to face.

An **interaction** is a touch point at which a customer and a company representative exchange information and develop learning relationships. With CRM the customer, not the organization, defines the terms of the interaction, often by stating his or her preferences. The organization responds by designing products and services that align with customers' desired experiences. For example, students can purchase the Student

customer-centric
Under this philosophy, the company customizes its product and service offering based on data generated through interactions between the customer and the company.

learning (CRM)
An informal process of collecting customer data through customer comments and feedback on product or service performance.

knowledge management
The process by which learned information from customers is centralized and shared in order to enhance the relationship between customers and the organization.

empowerment
Delegation of authority to solve customers' problems quickly—usually by the first person the customer notifies regarding the problem.

interaction
The point at which a customer and a company representative exchange information and develop learning relationships.

Price Discount Card (SPC) for a nominal fee and use it to obtain discounts from affiliated retailers, such as Aldo, Fairweather, Harveys, Sport Check, The Bay, and Zellers. SPC can track the cardholders' spending patterns and behaviours to gain a better understanding of what the students want. SPC can then communicate this information to the affiliated retailers, who then tailor their discounts on products that best meet students' needs. Ultimately, everyone benefits from this program: cardholders get relevant discounts, and retailers enjoy increased sales.[14]

The success of CRM—building lasting and profitable relationships—can be directly measured by the effectiveness of the interaction between the customer and the organization. In fact, what further differentiates CRM from other strategic initiatives is the organization's ability to establish and manage interactions with its current customer base. The more latitude (empowerment) a company gives its representatives, the more likely the interaction will conclude in a way that satisfies the customer.

REVIEW LEARNING OUTCOME 2

2   **Explain how to identify customer relationships with the organization**

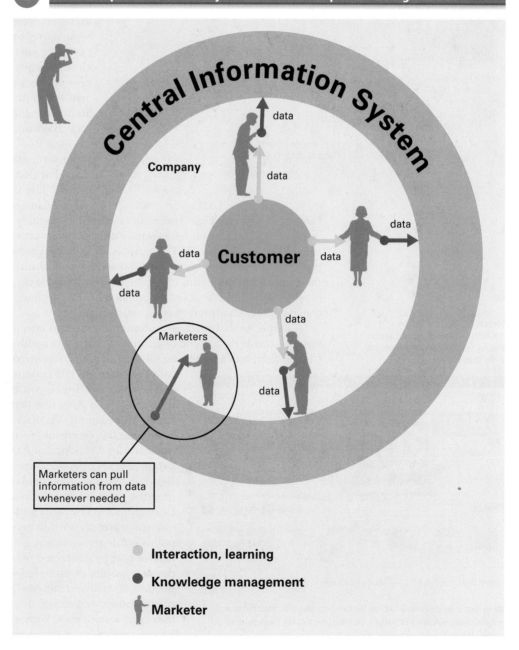

- Interaction, learning
- Knowledge management
- Marketer

③ UNDERSTAND INTERACTIONS WITH THE CURRENT CUSTOMER BASE

Understand interactions with the current customer base

The interaction between the customer and the organization is the foundation on which a CRM system is built. Only through effective interactions can organizations learn about the expectations of their customers, generate and manage knowledge about them, negotiate mutually satisfying commitments, and build long-term relationships.

EXHIBIT 18.2

Customer-Centric Approach for Managing Customer Interactions

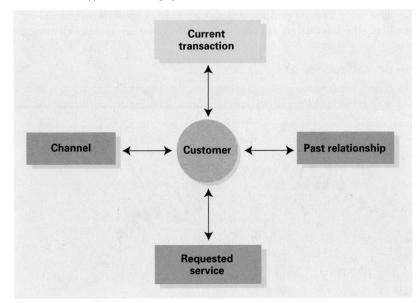

Exhibit 18.2 illustrates the customer-centric approach for managing customer interactions. Following a consumer-centric approach, an interaction can occur through a formal or direct communication channel, such as the Internet, a phone, or a salesperson. Interactions also occur through a previous relationship a customer has had with the organization, such as a past purchase or a survey response to a marketing research request; or through some current transaction or request by the customer, such as an actual product purchase, a request for repair service, or a response to a coupon offer. In short, any activity or touch point a customer has with an organization, either directly or indirectly, constitutes an interaction.

Best Buy Canada, an electronic retail superstore, offers its Performance Service Plan (PSP) on products bought in-store or on-line. The PSP guarantees products against damage and malfunctioning. Customers who need assistance can contact the company in-store, on-line, or by mail or phone. All initial-purchase contact information is kept in the customer database, along with copies of the PSP. If a customer calls the Customer Care 1-800 number, the representative will have access to all this information and will be able to either help the customer or refer him or her to another representative. Thus any form of communication with Best Buy, whether initiated by the customer or by a company representative, qualifies as an interaction or touch point.[15]

Companies that manage customer interactions effectively understand that customers provide data to the organization that affect a wide variety of touch points. In a CRM system, **touch points** are all areas of a business where customers have contact with the company, either personally or virtually, and data can be collected. Touch points might include a customer registering for a particular service, a customer communicating with customer service for product information, a customer completing and returning the warranty information card for a product, or a customer talking with salespeople, delivery personnel, and product installers. In the Best Buy example, touch points include the customer-initiated purchase and the customer-initiated call to the Customer Care line. Data gathered at these touch points, once interpreted, provide information that affects touch points inside the company. For example, interpreted information may be redirected to marketing research, to develop profiles of extended warranty purchasers; to production, to analyze recurring problems and repair components; and to accounting, to establish cost-control models for repair service calls. With a CRM system, touch points become critical parts of the service delivery process.

touch point
All possible areas of a business where customers communicate with that business.

SOURCE: COURTESY OF BEST BUY CANADA

When customers create accounts on the Bestbuy.ca website, their orders and purchases are recorded and tracked. Best Buy uses this key touch point to provide the best customer service possible.

Web-based interactions are an increasingly popular touch point for customers to communicate with companies on their own terms. Instead of wasting time with phone numbers and mail surveys, companies are beginning to publicize their websites as the first touch point for customer interactions. Web users can evaluate and purchase products, make reservations, input preferential data, and provide feedback on services and products. Data from these **web-based interactions** are then captured, compiled, and used to segment customers, refine marketing efforts, develop new products, and deliver a degree of individual customization to improve customer relationships.

Mars, maker of Pedigree dog food and Whiskas cat food, has designed a website called **mypedigree.ca**, targeted at Canadian dog lovers. This site provides an on-line collection of content about pets and combines it with personalized information and tools; it also offers merchandise that is both relevant and timely for the individual pet owners. The dog owner portion of the site features a "puppy milestones" information section; visitors need to sign up for it to receive information on topics such as puppy selection, puppy nutrition, puppy preparation, and puppy's first night. When visitors join the Pedigree Club, they will enter details about their breed of dog and the website will provide information about the breed and its age-specific needs.[16]

Another touch point is through **point-of-sale interactions** in stores or at information kiosks. Many point-of-sale software programs enable customers to easily provide information about themselves without feeling their privacy has been violated. The information is then used for marketing and merchandising activities, and to accurately identify the store's best customers and the types of products they buy. Data collected at point-of-sale interactions are also used to increase customer satisfaction through the development of in-store services and customer recognition promotions. Chapters offers its customers an iRewards membership card for $25 that can be purchased either in-store or on-line. Members can get discounts of up to 40 percent on bestsellers, 10 percent on all books, and 5 percent on all on-line purchases. Chapters can identify its best customers and track their purchases with the membership information.[17]

web-based interactions
Communications between customers and organizations using Web vehicles.

point-of-sale interactions
Communications between customers and organizations that occur at the point of sale, normally in a store.

REVIEW LEARNING OUTCOME 3

 3 | Understand interactions with the current customer base

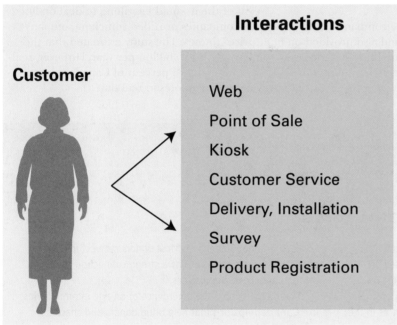

Customer

Interactions

Web

Point of Sale

Kiosk

Customer Service

Delivery, Installation

Survey

Product Registration

4 CAPTURE CUSTOMER DATA

Outline the process of capturing customer data

Vast amounts of data can be obtained from the interactions between an organization and its customers. Therefore, in a CRM system, the issue is not how much data can be obtained, but rather what types of data should be acquired and how they can be used effectively for relationship enhancement.

The traditional approach for acquiring data from customers is through distribution channel interactions such as store visits, conversations with salespeople, interactions via the Internet, phone conversations, and satellite communications. In a CRM system, distribution channel interactions are viewed as primary information sources based on the channel selected to initiate the interaction rather than on the data acquired. For example, if a consumer logs on to the Sony website to find out why a Sony device is not functioning properly and the answer is not available on-line, the consumer is referred to a page where he or she can describe the problem. The website then e-mails the problem description to a company representative, who will

Customer data are captured through interactions with customers, which can happen in a wide variety of ways, including store visits, interactions with salespeople, the Internet, wireless phone conversations, and satellite communications.

SOURCE: COMSTOCK/JUPITERIMAGES

research the problem and reply via e-mail. Furthermore, Sony will follow up with a brief satisfaction survey also sent via e-mail. Sony continues to use the e-mail mode of communication because the customer has established this as the preferred method of contact.[18]

Interactions between the company and the customer facilitate the collection of large amounts of data. Companies can obtain not only simple contact information (name, address, phone number), but also data pertaining to the customer's current relationship with the organization—past purchase history, quantity and frequency of purchases, average amount spent on purchases, sensitivity to promotional activities, and so forth. Many companies using a CRM system also view the transaction as an opportunity to collect behavioural data on customers. A recent study of Canadian consumers found that nearly 25 percent of them would be willing to deal on-line with insurance companies as long as these companies provided sufficient company information and also provided on-line "price" quotes. The study estimated that the potential for on-line insurance sales was as high as $10 billion per year. However, realizing this potential is going to be hard, because only 18 percent of Canadian insurance company websites are able to provide on-line quotes in real time.[19]

Global Perspectives

 ## ON-LINE CHARITIES USE CRM TOOLS

A new type of nonprofit organization has emerged recently that takes on-line technology to a completely new level. Based on theories of customer relationship management in the for-profit world, organizations such as **Globalgiving.com** and **Kiva.org** are enabling ordinary people to make extraordinary differences in the lives of people across the globe. For example, Globalgiving.com has a database of small international projects that donors can select to participate in by making a donation directly to the project. One of the most popular gifts is to send a child in India to school for a year—for a donation of $40. The organization uses database technology and the Internet to enable people to choose a project—based on cause type such as education or social issues or location like India or Brazil—and make a direct donation that has an immediate effect. The website is an on-line marketplace that connects people with causes around the world. In addition, the donor gets regular updates, in some cases from the individual that was helped, about the progress of the project. Kiva.org, which is similar in its global mission, enables donors to make zero-interest loans to aspiring business owners in developing countries. The organization combines the principles of microfinance and poverty reduction along with a strong database and Internet presence to create results. Indeed, the payback rate for donors to

Kiva.org is about 90 percent. Most donors reinvest in another project. Kiva.org also maintains a strong connection to donors through messages and updates.[20]

Another change is the emergence of on-line intermediaries like **Canadahelps.org** that help bring donors and charities together for both global and domestic markets. According to the Canadahelps.org website, the virtues of using its service include the following:

- Giving on-line is easier than writing a cheque.
- Giving is personal. Through CanadaHelps, you decided how much, which charity to support, and how often to give.
- You can give to all your charities in one place.
- Get your tax receipts immediately, and store them to download at tax time.
- The site is safe and secure.
- On-line donations require less administration and oversight by charities.[21]

According to Keith Taylor, the founder of an on-line charity called Modest Needs, "The e-commerce model has changed philanthropy. Donors expect the same level of interaction they get from Amazon.com."[22]

SOURCE: BEN GOSE, "GIVE AND TAKE: DIRECT GIVING WEBSITES RELY ON FEES TO HELP COVER COSTS," CHRONICLE OF PHILANTHROPY, AUGUST 7, 2008, WWW.PHILANTHROPY.COM, ACCESSED FEBRUARY 2009; SUE HOYE AND ELIZABETH SCHWINN, "COMPETITION FOR DONATIONS IS GOING GLOBAL, FUND RAISER PREDICTS," CHRONICLE OF PHILANTHROPY, AUGUST 7, 2008, WWW.PHILANTHROPY.COM, ACCESSED FEBRUARY 2009; RACHEL EMMA SILVERMAN "A NEW GENERATION REINVENTS PHILANTHROPY," THE WALL STREET JOURNAL, AUGUST 21, 2007, WWW.ONLINE.WSJ.COM, ACCESSED FEBRUARY 2009; WWW.KIVA.ORG; WWW.CANADAHELPS.ORG/INFO/3/16/41/SS, ACCESSED JULY 3, 2010; WWW.MODESTNEEDS.ORG.

It should be clear at this point that a voluminous amount of information can be captured from one individual customer across several external touch points. Multiply this by the thousands of customers across all the touch points (both internal and external) within the organization, and the volume of data can rapidly become unmanageable for company personnel. The large volumes of data resulting from a CRM initiative can be managed effectively only through the use of technology.

4 | Outline the process of capturing customer data

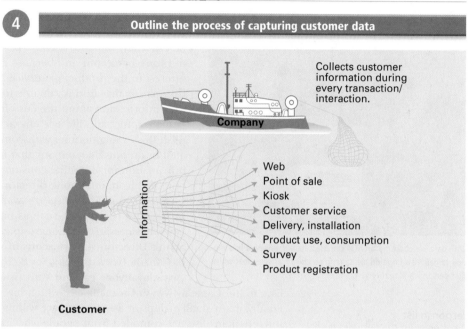

5 STORE AND INTEGRATE CUSTOMER DATA

Describe the use of technology to store and integrate customer data

Customer data are only as valuable as the system in which the data are stored and the consistency and accuracy of the data captured. Customer data gathering is further complicated by the fact that the data needed by one unit of the organization, such as sales and marketing, are often generated by another area of the business, or even a third-party supplier such as an independent marketing research firm. Thus companies must use information technology to capture, store, and integrate strategically important customer information. This process of centralizing data in a CRM system is referred to as data warehousing.

data warehouse
A central repository for data from various functional areas of the organization that are stored and inventoried on a centralized computer system so that the information can be shared across all functional departments of the business.

A **data warehouse** is a central repository (database) of customer data collected by an organization. Essentially, it is a large computerized file of all information collected in the previous phase of the CRM process—for example, information collected in the distribution channel, transaction, and product or service touch points. The core of the data warehouse is the **database**, "a collection of data, especially one that can be accessed and manipulated by computer software."[23] The CRM database focuses on collecting vital statistics on consumers, their purchasing habits, transaction methods, and product usage in a centralized repository that is accessible by all functional areas of a company. Traditionally, this information was stored in separate computer systems throughout the company. By using a data warehouse, however, marketing managers can quickly access vast amounts of information required to make decisions. For example, Canadian real estate agents can better advise potential buyers on home purchasing decisions by accessing resources stored in a number of data warehouses designed for the Canadian real estate market. They can access the Teranet GeoWarehouse database and find information on what the street looks like, which houses have been sold in the neighbourhood, and what the average local income is. For buyers who are looking for new homes in Toronto, agents across Canada can

database
A collection of data, especially one that can be accessed and manipulated by computer software.

With data warehousing, an ATM can use a bank's database information to deliver a targeted message to an individual consumer while that person waits to receive cash.

response list
A customer list that includes the names and addresses of individuals who have responded to an offer of some kind, such as through the Internet, e-mail, mail, telephone, direct-response TV, product rebates, contests or sweepstakes, or billing inserts.

compiled list
A customer list that was developed by gathering names and addresses from telephone directories and membership rosters, usually enhanced with information from public records, such as census data, auto registrations, birth announcements, business start-ups, or bankruptcies.

database enhancement
Purchasing information on customers or prospects to better describe their needs or determine how responsive they might be to marketing programs.

access the RealNet Canada database to get information on real estate developments in Toronto. In addition, agents are able to get information for their clients on government programs such as the EnerGuide retrofit grant, rebate programs for the land transfer tax, and a plan that allows RRSP holders to use some of their funds to finance a house purchase.[24]

When a company builds its database, the first step is to develop a list. A **response list** is based on customers who have indicated an interest in a product or service. They may have responded to a direct mail offer, an e-mail, an on-line advertisement, a print ad in a magazine or newspaper, or a TV commercial. Response lists tend to be especially valuable because past behaviour is a strong predictor of future behaviour and because consumers who have indicated interest in the product or service are more prone to purchase. Companies may find it valuable to enhance their customer records with information about the customers' or prospective customers' demographics and lifestyle characteristics. They can often accomplish this by augmenting with compiled lists. **Compiled lists** are created by an outside company that has collected names and contact information for potential consumers. This information is usually obtained from telephone directories and membership rosters of various groups. Many lists are available, ranging from those owned by large list companies, such as Business Information Group (**www.businessinformationgroup.ca**), CLB Media (**www.clbmedia.ca**), Scott's Directories (**www.scottsinfo.com**), and the D&B Companies of Canada (**www.dnb.ca**), for B2B data; to Loyalty One (**www.loyaltyone.ca**) and Watt (**www.wattintl.com**) for consumer lists; to infoCanada (**www.infocanada.ca**), which has both business and consumer lists. Finally, many small groups or associations are willing to sell their membership lists. Indeed, many lists are compiled from people who have opted in to the list after they have purchased a related product. Data compiled by large data-gathering companies are usually very accurate.

In this phase, companies typically are collecting distribution channel, transaction, and product or service information such as store, salesperson, communication channel, contact information, relationship, and brands. For example, when Philips wanted to determine how to best sell its Cool Skin Shaver accessories, it used existing information to expand its database. By sending an e-mail to registered users, Philips was able to collect information, including whether consumers purchased on-line; if so, the "landing page" on the website; the number of "unsubscribes" when sent an e-mail; and the timeliness of response.[25]

A customer database becomes even more useful to marketing managers when it is enhanced to include more than simply a customer's or prospect's name, address, telephone number, and transaction history. **Database enhancement** involves purchasing information on customers or prospects to better describe their needs or determine how responsive they might be to marketing programs. Types of enhancement data typically include demographic, lifestyle, or behavioural information. Database enhancement can increase the effectiveness of marketing programs. By learning more about their best and most profitable customers, marketers can maximize the effectiveness of marketing communications and cross-selling. Shoppers Drug Mart, working with Schering Canada, mined its Optimum Card database to identify allergy sufferers, who were then targeted with a specific promotion for the antihistamine Claritin. By looking at information on past purchasing behaviour for antihistamines in the Optimum database, Shoppers Drug Mart identified 180,000 potential buyers. These buyers were sent a direct mail communication with an outdoor theme containing information about allergies as well as a special offer of 3,000 Optimum bonus points, which would be awarded for a purchase of Claritin. Schering Canada believes that targeting consumers who have demonstrated a specific need for its products, and then providing them with a bonus like Optimum points, will give it a competitive advantage. Franco Di Clemente, senior brand manager for Claritin, made the following comment on the promotional effort: "As we move forward on this brand, it is these kinds of programs that will help us grow."[26]

5 | **Describe the use of technology to store and integrate customer data**

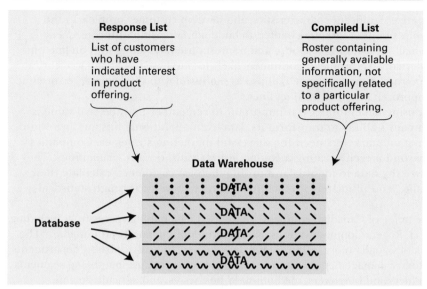

Response List

List of customers who have indicated interest in product offering.

Compiled List

Roster containing generally available information, not specifically related to a particular product offering.

Data Warehouse

DATA
DATA
DATA
DATA

Database

Multinational corporations building worldwide databases often face difficult problems when pulling together internal data about their customers. Differences in language, computer systems, and data collection methods can be huge obstacles to overcome. In spite of the challenges, many global companies are committed to building databases. Unilever is using the Internet not only to educate consumers about its brands but also to develop relationships with its customers by providing helpful information. Website visitors can get information on removing stubborn stains and solving similar consumer problems. They also receive a discount on their next purchase in exchange for completing an on-line questionnaire. With diligent effort, Unilever has collected information on more than 30 million loyal customers from numerous countries.[27]

6 IDENTIFYING THE BEST CUSTOMERS

Describe how to identify the best customers

CRM manages the interactions between a company and its customers. To be successful, firms must identify customers who will yield either high profits or have the potential for high profits. To do so, significant amounts of data must be gathered from customers, stored and integrated in the data warehouse, and then analyzed and interpreted for common patterns that can identify homogeneous customers who are different from other customer segments. Because all customers are not the same, firms need to develop interactions that target *individual* customer needs and wants. Likewise, all customers do not generate the same revenue for the firm. Recall, from Chapter 6, the 80/20 principle—80 percent of a company's revenue is generated by 20 percent of its customers. Therefore, the question becomes "How do we identify the 20 percent of our customer base that contributes 80 percent to our revenue?" In a CRM framework, the answer is data mining.

DATA MINING

data mining
A data analysis procedure that identifies significant patterns of variables and characteristics that pertain to particular customers or customer groups.

Data mining is used to find hidden patterns and relationships in the customer data stored in the data warehouse. It is a data analysis procedure that identifies significant patterns of variables and characteristics that pertain to particular customers or customer groups. Although businesses have been conducting such analyses for many years, typically, the procedures were performed on small data sets containing as few as 300 to 400 customers. Today, it is not uncommon for companies to have to analyze billions of customer shopping patterns stored in their data warehouses. For example, Nokia examined over 6 billion pieces of data to develop its N-Series mobile phone. The Bank of Montreal has implemented a CRM strategy that involves data mining of its massive transaction databases, which record more than 100 million transactions a month. Besides these transactions, the bank's databases contain other data such as personal information, liability, income, and net assets for over 7 million customers. BMO's CRM software undertakes calculations that determine the fees and costs of all those transactions per customer. Based on these calculations, one-third of the bank's customers have been identified as valuable or profitable, and as such have been chosen to become the focus of BMO's marketing efforts. This group has been analyzed and divided into segments of customers with similar profiles. These segments are being targeted with direct communications. According to David Moxley, vice-president of customer knowledge management for BMO, the effort has "produced response rates north of 20 percent. It's not unlikely our return on investment is in excess of 1,000 percent."[28]

Using data mining, marketers can search the data warehouse, capture relevant data, categorize significant characteristics, and develop customer profiles. In the Philips razor example, marketers wanted to build a relationship with consumers through e-mail. By assessing response and nonresponse rates along with on-line purchases, it developed a profile of consumers likely to purchase Cool Skin accessories over the Internet. Moreover, once Philips was successful with Cool Skin accessories, it used this approach on other product lines.[29]

When using data mining, it is important to remember that the real value is in the company's ability to transform its data from operational bits and bytes into the information marketers need for successful marketing strategies. Companies must go beyond merely creating a contact list for calls, e-mails, or mailings. They must analyze the data to identify and profile the best customers, calculate their lifetime value, and ultimately predict purchasing behaviour through statistical modelling.

A wide range of Canadian companies have used data mining successfully, including Bell Canada, Rogers Communications, Research in Motion, and Kraft Canada.[30] The Royal Bank of Canada reorganized itself from product- and service-based departments into a customer management team focusing on 14 different customer-based segments such as builders and borrowers, medium-sized businesses, and agriculture and agribusiness.[31]

Data mining is applicable to most companies looking to leverage a large data warehouse to better manage customer relationships. The two critical factors for success with data mining are (1) a large, well-integrated data warehouse and (2) a well-defined understanding of how the result of the mining activities will be used and leveraged throughout the organization. Before the information is leveraged, several types of analysis are often run on the data. These analyses include customer segmentation, recency–frequency–monetary analysis (RFM), lifetime value analysis (LTV), and predictive modelling.

Customer Segmentation

Recall that *customer segmentation* is the process of breaking large groups of customers into smaller, more homogenous groups. This type of analysis generates a "profile" or picture of the customers' similar demographic, geographic, and psychographic traits as well as their previous purchase behaviour; it focuses particularly on the best customers. Profiles of the best customers can be compared and contrasted with other customer segments. For example, a bank could segment consumers on frequency of use, credit, age, and turnover. Once a profile of the best customer is developed using these criteria, it can be used to screen other potential consumers. Similarly, customer profiles can be used to introduce customers selectively to specific marketing actions. For example, consulting firm Right Sleeve Marketing specializes in developing promotions but is very particular about the clients it works with. The firm says it wants to "build a relationship with customers so deep they won't even be tempted to switch to anyone else." Recently the company "weeded out low-margin, unstable customers, focusing instead on brand-conscious clients that valued more than just a source of cheap stuff." For example, Right Sleeve landed the Red Bull account in Canada for special promotions in 2004 to specifically produce some special coolers. Right Sleeve quickly realized that unless it could develop value for this prestigious client, it might lose future business to low-price bidders. It did this in a number of ways. Right Sleeve developed a custom-made-in-Canada uniform to outfit Red Bull's Canadian distributor sales force and street-marketing teams. Next, Right Sleeve developed an on-line fulfillment system so that Red Bull could sell its uniforms to distributors across Canada and the United States as well. Now Red Bull views Right Sleeve as being more part of its business rather than a "firm" it hired to make "Red Bull Coolers."[32] See Chapter 6 for a detailed discussion of segmentation.

EXHIBIT 18.3

RFM Analysis: All Customers Are Not the Same

Best Customers	Average Customers	Poor Customers
High profit	Average profit	Low profit
Spent >$1,500	Spent approximately $400	Spent <$100
Multiple purchases	Two purchases	One purchase
Purchase in past 6 months	Purchase in past 18 months	Purchase in past two years
Lifetime value = high	Lifetime value = average	Lifetime value = low
N = 2,500 (18.5%)*	N = 4,000 (29.6%)*	N = 7,000 (51.9%)*
Total annual sales = $2.4 million	Total annual sales = $1.1 million	Total annual sales = $800,000

*N = number of customers in a category. The total number of customers is 13,500, and total annual sales are $4.3 million.

Recency–Frequency–Monetary Analysis (RFM)

recency–frequency–monetary analysis (RFM)
A data manipulation technique that determines the company's best customers by identifying those customers who have purchased most recently, most frequently, and who have spent the most money.

Customers who have purchased recently and often, and have spent considerable money, are more likely to purchase again. **Recency–frequency–monetary analysis (RFM)** identifies those customers most likely to purchase again because they have bought most recently, bought most frequently, or have spent a specified amount of money with the company. Firms develop equations to identify the "best customers" (often the top 20 percent of the customer base) by assigning a score to customer records in the database on how often, how recently, and how much they have spent. Customers are then ranked to determine which ones move to the top of the list and which ones fall to the bottom. The ranking provides the basis for maximizing profits because it enables the company to use the information in its customer database to select those individuals who have proved to be good sources of revenue. As an example of RFM analysis, Exhibit 18.3 depicts the breakdown of customers in categories that describe their value.

Many marketers take RFM analysis one step further by introducing *profitability* into the equation. For instance, based on the monetary value of purchases, a customer may float to the top of the RFM list. If this customer buys only items on sale, however, he or she is less profitable for the company than a customer who purchases the identical items at full price. One major retailer discovered that 3 percent of shoppers accounted for 40 percent of its sales volume. Using RFM, the retailer determined that each year the "best customers" charged more than $1,000 on the private label credit card and shopped at least five times in at least four product categories. With this analysis, a marketing campaign was designed to reach the "best customers," the top 10 percent of cardholders. The campaign resulted in a 21 percent increase in the "best customer" retention rate and an annual purchase increase of $100 per customer. The same information was used to move other consumers into the "best customer" category. Each of these steps had a significant impact on increasing the company's profitability.[33]

Lifetime Value Analysis (LTV)

lifetime value analysis (LTV)
A data manipulation technique that projects the future value of the customer over a period of years, using the assumption that marketing to repeat customers is more profitable than marketing to first-time buyers.

Recency, frequency, and monetary data can also be used to create a lifetime value model on customers in the database. Whereas RFM looks at how valuable a customer is currently to a company, **lifetime value analysis (LTV)** projects the future value of the customer over a period of years. One of the basic assumptions in any lifetime value calculation is that marketing to repeat customers is more profitable than marketing to first-time buyers. That is, it costs more to find a new customer with regard to promotion and gaining trust than to sell more to a customer who is already loyal.

Customer lifetime value has a number of benefits. It shows marketers how much they can spend to *acquire* a new customer, it tells them the level of spending to *retain* customers, and it facilitates targeting new customers who look as though they will be profitable customers. Cadillac has calculated the lifetime value of its top customers at $332,000. Similarly, Pizza Hut figures its customers are worth $8,000 in bottom-line lifetime value.

Predictive Modelling

The ability to reasonably predict future customer behaviour gives marketers a significant competitive advantage. Through **predictive modelling**, marketers try to determine, based on some past set of occurrences, what the odds are that some other occurrence, such as an Internet inquiry or purchase, will take place in the future. SPSS Predictive Marketing software is one tool that marketers can use to answer questions about their customers. The software requires minimal knowledge of statistical analysis. Users operate from a prebuilt model, which generates profiles in three to four days. SPSS also has an on-line product that predicts website users' behaviour. Gaming enterprise Harrah's Entertainment Inc. uses predictive modelling to attract millions of customers. Its models include the ages, gender, postal codes, amount of time spent gambling, and how much individuals have won or lost. Analysis of the data allows Harrah's to target individuals with special offers, like getaway weekends and gourmet restaurant meals, to attract them back to the casinos to gamble more. Predictive modelling enabled Harrah's to average 22 percent growth for five years recently while its stock price tripled.[34] Harrah's management uses predictive modelling to develop long-term, personalized, and profitable relationships with each of their customers.

REVIEW LEARNING OUTCOME 6

6 **Describe how to identify the best customers**

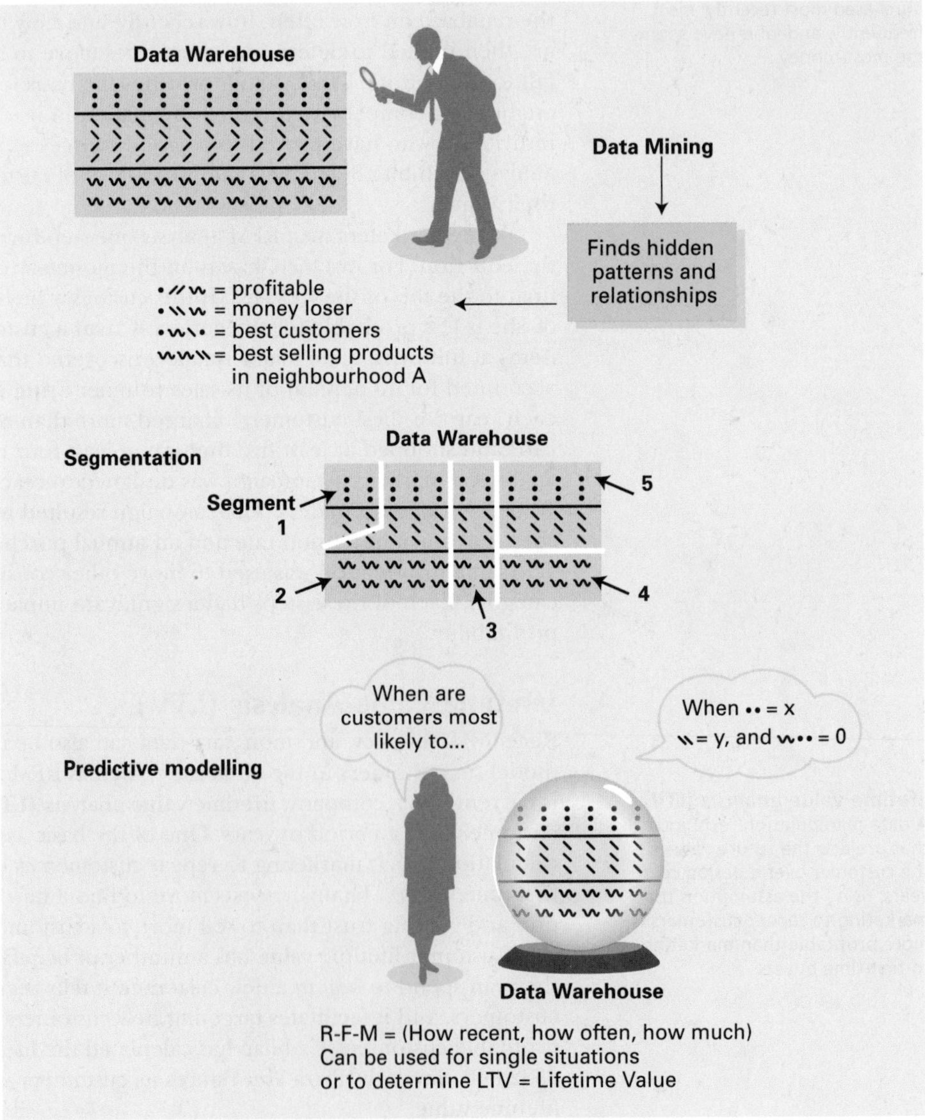

Data Warehouse

Data Mining

Finds hidden patterns and relationships

- •∕∕ᴧ = profitable
- •∖∖ᴧ = money loser
- •ᴧᴧ∖• = best customers
- ᴧᴧᴧ∖ = best selling products in neighbourhood A

Segmentation

Data Warehouse

Segment 1

5

2

3

4

Predictive modelling

When are customers most likely to...

When •• = x
ᴧ = y, and ᴧ•• = 0

Data Warehouse

R-F-M = (How recent, how often, how much)
Can be used for single situations
or to determine LTV = Lifetime Value

LEVERAGE CUSTOMER INFORMATION

Explain the process of leveraging customer information throughout the organization

Data mining identifies the most profitable customers and prospects. Managers can then design tailored marketing strategies to best appeal to the identified segments. In CRM this is commonly referred to as leveraging customer information to facilitate enhanced relationships with customers. Exhibit 18.4 shows some common CRM marketing database applications.

CAMPAIGN MANAGEMENT

campaign management
Developing product or service offerings customized for the appropriate customer segment and then pricing and communicating these offerings for the purpose of enhancing customer relationships.

Through campaign management, all areas of an organization participate in the development of programs targeted to its customers. **Campaign management** involves monitoring and leveraging customer interactions to sell a company's products and to increase customer service. Campaigns are based directly on data obtained from customers through various interactions. Campaign management includes monitoring the success of the communications based on customer reactions through sales, orders, callbacks to the company, and the like. If a campaign seems unsuccessful, it must be evaluated and possibly changed in order to achieve the company's desired objective. Consider Stave Puzzles, producer of handcrafted wood puzzles that are the "Rolls-Royce" of puzzles. Each puzzle is unique and can be customized as the customer desires. Steve Richardson, the company's co-founder, has narrowed his customer base to his "Hot Hundred" most valuable customers. To manage his customer base and ensure they are receiving optimal service, he tracks not only standard information, such as contact data and orders, but also birthdays, anniversaries, relationships between customers, phone conversations, inquiries, and workshop visits.[35]

Campaign management involves developing customized product and service offerings for the appropriate customer segment, pricing these offerings attractively, and communicating these offers in a manner that enhances customer relationships. Customizing product and service offerings requires managing multiple interactions with customers, as well as giving priority to those products and services that are viewed as most desirable for a specifically designated customer. Even within a highly defined market segment, individual customer differences will emerge. Therefore, interactions among customers must focus on individual experiences, expectations, and desires. Stave Puzzles customizes its marketing campaigns by tailoring mail contacts to eight different segments. For example, the monthly buyers and top 10 percent of the customers receive individual reminder notes about special occasions and previous purchases.

EXHIBIT 18.4

Common CRM Marketing Database Applications

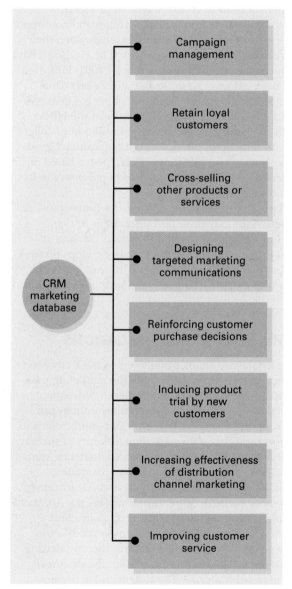

RETAINING LOYAL CUSTOMERS

Once a company has identified its best customers, it should make every effort to maintain and increase their loyalty. When a company retains an additional 5 percent of its customers each year, it will increase its profits by at least 25 percent. What's more, improving customer retention by a mere 2 percent can decrease costs by as much as 10 percent.[36]

Loyalty programs reward loyal consumers for making many purchases with the objective of building long-term, mutually beneficial relationships between a company and its key customers. These programs employ database technology in order to identify a company's best customers. Quebec-based Laurentian Bank of Canada has developed the "Passport" reward program for holders of its Visa Gold credit card. This program differs from typical reward programs

VISA GOLD PASSPORT PROGRAM

Travel Chic – Bianca
À la Carte – "Chef" Michel
Outdoor Passions – David and Marie-Paul
Techno Fun – Sylvain

LAURENTIAN BANK OF CANADA

SOURCE: COURTESY OF LAURENTIAN BANK

The Laurentian Bank of Canada is building customer loyalty through its innovative Passport rewards program for customers who use its Gold Visa Card. The Passport program's four different reward categories provide Laurentian Bank customers with the ability to choose an African safari or a week of spa relaxation in the Alps.

in that it offers its members personalized experiences referred to as "Oomphs," which are a way to use reward points "to make your dreams come true." It offers typical reward merchandise, but the exotic as well. The Passport program has four different reward categories: Travel Chic, Outdoor Passions, Techno Fun, and À la carte. People can choose an African safari or a week of spa relaxation in the Alps. In addition, customers can add a unique activity to their trip, such as having the use of a Lamborghini for a weekend. Customers also have the freedom to combine points and money as part of their packages. For example, customers can use reward points to buy a digital camera, which they can then use to commemorate a weekend vacation acquired with other rewards points. Laurentian Bank wants to position itself uniquely from other banks by offering an innovative difference in how its customers can use credit card reward points.[37]

Besides rewarding good customers, loyalty programs provide businesses with a wealth of information about those customers and their shopping trends; these data can then be used when making business decisions.

CROSS-SELLING OTHER PRODUCTS OR SERVICES

CRM provides many opportunities to cross-sell related products. Marketers can use the database to match product profiles and consumer profiles so that they can cross-sell customers products that match their demographic, lifestyle, or behavioural characteristics. The Hudson's Bay Company is a Canadian retail leader in cross-selling. By 2001, HBC had merged its Zellers and Bay credit cards and its Bay and Zellers Club Z loyalty programs under one banner, HBC Rewards, which has grown to be a database of over 8.1 million Canadians. The power of the HBC database was tested with the launch of the Mossimo fashion line. Zellers used the HBC database to target customers who bought fashions goods at The Bay but not at Zellers. These customers were sent direct mail pieces based on their past purchasing behaviour. Zellers noted an increase in fashion purchases in its stores among the members of this customer group.[38]

Marketers rely heavily on related purchase behaviour to stimulate future purchases. For instance, past purchase behaviour may show that subscribers to *Golf Canada* may also be interested in business magazines such as *Canadian Business* or *Profit Magazine*. Similarly, the Internet music retailer **Puretracks.com** develops profiles of music buyers who have purchased similar selections. A buyer who searches for or purchases music titles that match a profile can later be presented with titles that other buyers in the profile have bought.

DESIGNING TARGETED MARKETING COMMUNICATIONS

Using transaction and purchase data, a database enables marketers to track customers' relationships to the company's products and services and modify the marketing message accordingly. For instance, a company can segment its customers as infrequent users, moderate users, and heavy users. A segmented communications strategy can then be developed based on which group the customer falls into. Communications to infrequent users might encourage repeat purchases through direct incentives such as a limited-time price discount for ordering again. Communications to moderate users might use fewer incentives and more reinforcement of past purchase decisions. Communications to heavy users would be designed around loyalty and reinforcement of the purchase rather than price promotions. Nike Store Toronto offers the Air Max Club (AMC), a loyalty club for customers. Club members can collect points and redeem them for gift certificates, movies, and books. Customers considered "most valuable" are identified when they swipe their card to collect points, thereby alerting the salesperson. A message on the salesperson's screen indicates that the customer should receive a special thank you and possibly a prize. The system also generates customized coupons based on purchase history. The company has found that club members spend about 50 percent more than the average customer.[39]

REINFORCING CUSTOMER PURCHASE DECISIONS

As you learned in the consumer behaviour chapter, *cognitive dissonance* is the feeling consumers experience when they recognize an inconsistency between their values and opinions and their behaviour. In other words, they begin to doubt the soundness of their purchase decision and feel anxious. CRM offers marketers an excellent opportunity to reach out to customers to reinforce the purchase decision. By thanking customers for their purchase and telling them they are important, marketers can help cement a profitable, long-term relationship. A survey of business travellers who stay often at Canada's Fairmont Hotels and Resorts found that instead of extra stays in a Fairmont hotel for being loyal, they actually preferred to receive special recognition of their individual preferences, extraordinary efforts to make their stays more pleasant, and more flexible check-in and check-out times. Fairmont responded by developing a frequent-guest club that was committed to satisfying customers with extraordinary efforts. For example, if customers preferred a twin rather than a king-sized bed, they would get it. Likewise, if they wanted Mountain Dew to drink instead of Pepsi, the staff would provide it. The value of reinforcing consumer purchases was significant for Fairmont; the chain saw its share of the market among Canadian business travellers increase by 16 percent.[40]

Updating customers periodically about the status of their order also reinforces purchase decisions. Minutes after customers order merchandise from **Chapters.Indigo.ca**, they receive an e-mail acknowledging their order. Every few days afterwards, customers receive updates that allow them to track the shipment of their order, from ship date to receipt.

INDUCING PRODUCT TRIAL BY NEW CUSTOMERS

Although significant time and money are largely expended on encouraging repeat purchases by a company's best customers, a marketing database is also used to identify new customers. Because a firm using a marketing database already has a profile of its best customers, it can easily use the results of modelling to profile potential customers.

Marketing managers generally use demographic and behavioural data overlaid on existing customer data to develop a detailed customer profile that is a powerful tool for evaluating lists of prospects. For instance, if a firm's best customers are between 35 and 50 years of age, live in suburban areas, own luxury cars, like to eat at Thai restaurants, and enjoy mountain climbing, then the company can find prospects already in its database or customers who currently are identified as using a competitor's product who match this profile. Whiskas uses its website, **www.whiskas.ca**, to introduce new products and to develop relationships with its customers. Cat owners can become "Whiskas members," allowing them to be informed of any new products or promotions that the company is making available.[41]

INCREASING THE EFFECTIVENESS OF DISTRIBUTION CHANNEL MARKETING

In Chapter 11 you learned that a *marketing channel* is a business structure of interdependent organizations, such as wholesalers and retailers that move a product from the producer to the ultimate consumer. Most marketers rely on indirect channels to move their products to the end user. Thus marketers often lose touch with the customer as an individual since the relationship is really between the retailer and the consumer. Marketers facing this predicament tend to view their customers as aggregate statistics because specific customer information is hard to gather.

With CRM databases, manufacturers now have a tool to gain insight into who is buying their products. Instead of simply unloading products into the distribution channel and leaving marketing and relationship building to dealers, auto manufacturers today are using websites to keep in touch with customers and prospects, learn about

One of the major benefits of CRM is that it enables companies to customize product and service offerings for each customer. Rogers Communications allows its customers to log into "My Rogers" so they can access their account information and communicate and do transactions with Rogers on-line.

their lifestyles and hobbies, understand their vehicle needs, and develop relationships in the hope that these consumers will reward them with brand loyalty in the future. BMW and Mercedes-Benz, as well as other vehicle manufacturers, have databases containing the names of millions of consumers who have expressed an interest. The Coca-Cola company has created **iCoke.ca** to develop a personal relationship with the millions of customers who buy their products from the wide variety of distribution channels they employ.

With many bricks-and-mortar stores setting up shop on-line, companies are being challenged to monitor the purchases made by customers who shop both in-store and on-line. This concept is referred to as multichannel marketing. Companies are also using radio frequency identification (RFID) technology to improve distribution. The technology uses a microchip with an antenna that tracks anything from a soda can to a car. A computer can locate the product anywhere. The main implication of this technology is that companies will enjoy a reduction in theft and loss of merchandise shipments and will always know where merchandise is in the distribution channel. Moreover, as this technology develops further, marketers will be able to gather essential information relating to product use and consumption.[42]

IMPROVING CUSTOMER SERVICE

customer retention
The percentage of customers that repeatedly purchase products from a company.

CRM marketing techniques are being used more and more to improve the customer service experience for customers. The level of customer service provided by companies is influential in customer retention. **Customer retention** is the percentage of customers that repeatedly purchase products from a company. Rogers Communications employs CRM to improve customer service with its shared call centre for its cable, wireless, and Web customers. The idea is to allow customers to have multichannel contact with the company via toll-free numbers, e-mail, Web chat, and fax machines. In addition, Rogers offers a single point of contact to handle questions and issues for four different consumer products: Rogers cable TV, Rogers Internet service, Rogers wireless telephone customers, and Rogers Home Phone, all of which are often used by the same customers. This approach is designed to allow Rogers to improve customer service, to focus the skills of its employees, and to reduce costs.[43]

However, staff turnover among call centre employees is generally very high— typically 20 percent or more—which adds to the difficulty of maintaining consistent and excellent customer service. In order to deliver strong customer service, Rogers's staff are trained to provide "just in time" service. The representatives are trained to use all the communication equipment, and telephone calls are recorded and computer screen interactions are photographed in order to monitor service quality and allow for continuous training. The call centre is staffed by representatives with different skill levels in handling inbound and outbound calls, as well as by specialists in handling specific types of service calls. This variety enables Rogers to route its calls on a skill basis so that customers talk with representatives who have the knowledge to deal with their problems. In order to reduce staff turnover, and thereby field experienced agents and reduce training costs, Rogers is trying to shake the image that call centres are dead-end jobs for the poorly educated. The company offers career paths to other areas of the organization that are based on experience within the call centre.[44]

CRM, PRIVACY CONCERNS, AND PRIVACY LEGISLATION

Before rushing out to invest in a CRM system and build a database, marketers should consider consumers' reactions to the growing use of databases. Many Canadians are

ANATOMY OF a Customer Relations Decision: Zane's Cycles

SOURCE: © ISTOCKPHOTO.COM/BRASIL2

SOURCE: COURTESY OF ZANE'S CYCLES

Zane's Cycles' best customers? The ones it keeps.

1 Gather data

Zane's offers its customers free bicycle maintenance in exchange for answering survey questions.

2 Leverage data

Zane's uses the data supplied by each customer to draw up a profile of each customer, which guides its one-to-one marketing efforts.

4 Capitalize on the data

Zane's best employees understand "CLV" and focus on long-term customer experience and relationships. The company has grown an average of 23.5 percent/year.

3 Analyze data

How much to acquire a new customer or retain one? Zane's calculates its Customer Lifetime Value as $12,500.

If a customer leaves disappointed or unhappy, Zane's Cycles doesn't just lose the profit from that single transaction, it risks $12,500.

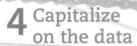

SOURCE: © ISTOCKPHOTO.COM/DARRAN BARTON

reluctant to provide personal information because of the potential for invasion of privacy. A specific concern is the sheer volume of information that databases aggregate and the vulnerability of this information to unauthorized access and use. Consider these two heavily publicized incidents involving theft and hacking into Canadian business databases: in 2007, Homesense and Winners stores suffered theft from their computer databases; the hackers then used the information to commit identity theft. The CIBC's Talvest Mutual Funds had a computer hard drive stolen that contained information on the mutual funds of 470,000 customers.[45] Fundamental to CRM marketing is the idea of providing valuable services to customers based on knowledge of what they really value. It is critical, however, for marketers to remember that these relationships must be built on trust. Database technology is allowing marketers to compile ever richer information about their customers in order to build and manage relationships, but if these customers feel their privacy is being violated, that relationship can become a liability.

Privacy Issues Must Be Resolved for CRM's Success

Once customer data have been collected, the question of who has custody of this information and the obligations of the collectors with respect to its use becomes extremely important. Marketers need to be highly aware that one of the key obligations associated with customer data gathering involves maintaining customer and client privacy. Organizations that use CRM strategies must include privacy relationship management as part of their business practices in order to remain compliant with Canadian federal and provincial privacy legislation. In Canada, Bill C-6, the Personal Information Protection and Electronic Documents Act (PIPEDA), came into force on January 1, 2004. By then, similar provincial legislation had been passed in British Columbia, Alberta, and Quebec. The implication of all this privacy legislation is that organizations across Canada must follow rules designed to protect the personal information of both their employees and their customers and clients. It follows that any organization using CRM will need to appoint a privacy specialist to ensure that it is in compliance with privacy legislation. PIPEDA requires organizations to have systems in place to ensure that their customer and client information is gathered with the consent of the customers and clients, and that once gathered, the information is secure, accurate, and not used except for the stated purpose for which it was collected and stored.

The legislation means that companies must develop and state privacy policies regarding how they collect, use, share, and protect the personal information of consumers and employees. There is widespread debate, however, as to how consumers' rights to privacy can be protected. To a large extent, this debate revolves around opt-in/opt-out options. Canadian marketers are required to state explicitly the reasons why they are collecting customer information and how they plan to use this information. When customers fill out a sign-in form (referred to as an opt-in page), the company is bound to use the information collected only for the purpose originally stated and for no other unless it obtains a further consent. One issue that arises revolves around what constitutes "consent." Canada's privacy laws give customers the right to request copies of their files. Marketing companies need to be able to demonstrate that the customer did in fact opt in by providing information on the date and location where the customer signed up. In addition, a stated privacy policy must be linked to the opt-in page. Furthermore, marketing companies that are operating as third parties to gather information or build databases for other marketers must disclose this fact as well. Many marketers rely on companies that are specialists in CRM to assist them, but unless they have told their customers that these third parties will have access to their personal data, the marketers will be in violation of PIPEDA if they share this information.[46]

Explain the process of leveraging customer information throughout the organization

Marketing Information

CRM Database

Applications

✓ Campaign management

✓ Retaining loyal customers

✓ Cross-selling other products and services

✓ Designing targeted marketing communications

✓ Reinforcing customer purchase decisions

✓ Introducing product trial by new customers

✓ Increasing effectiveness of distribution channel marketing

✓ Improving customer service

In addition to PIPEDA, marketers need to be aware that in July 2007, the Canadian Radio-Television and Telecommunications Commission (CRTC) enacted a national "Do Not Call" list to prevent unsolicited telecommunications. When enacting a CRM program, marketers still need to comply with the "Do Not Call" list. They need to seek and gain permission to contact their customers at all their touch points. The "Do Not Call" regulations provide a further impetus for the use of CRM systems because the rules provide an exemption for calls related to ongoing business relationships.[47]

REVIEW AND APPLICATIONS

1 **Define customer relationship management.** Customer relationship management (CRM) is a company-wide business strategy designed to optimize profitability, revenue, and customer satisfaction by focusing on precisely defined customer groups. This is accomplished by organizing the company around customer segments, encouraging and tracking customer interaction with the company, fostering customer-satisfying behaviours, and linking all processes of a company from its customers through its suppliers.

1.1 Identify the six components of CRM.

1.2 Form a team and identify several local businesses that would benefit from a CRM strategy. Select one business and outline a plan for implementing a CRM strategy for that business. You may want to visit the company and interview managers about their current initiatives. When you have completed your CRM plan, share it with the class—and the company.

1.3 OnStar is a location, information, and communication system available to drivers who wish to subscribe to the service. GM installs the OnStar system in many of its vehicles. Go to the OnStar website, **www.onstar.com**, and read about some of the services that are offered to consumers. Based on your discovery, write a short report describing the various ways that OnStar can be used as a CRM tool, specifically in the context of creating interactions, gathering customer data, and customizing service offerings to customers.

2 **Explain how to identify customer relationships with the organization.** Companies that implement a CRM system adhere to a customer-centric focus or model. A customer-centric company focuses on learning the factors that build long-lasting relationships with valuable customers and then builds its system on what satisfies and retains those customers. Building relationships through CRM is a strategic process that focuses on learning, managing customer knowledge, and empowerment.

2.1 Briefly explain the concept of a customer-centric focus. Why is this so important in a CRM process?

2.2 What is meant by knowledge management? Why is it so important in a CRM system?

3 **Understand interactions with the current customer base.** The interaction between the customer and the organization is considered to be the foundation on which a CRM system is built. Only through effective interactions can organizations learn about the expectations of their customers, generate and manage knowledge about them, negotiate mutually satisfying commitments, and build long-term relationships. Effective management of customer interactions recognizes that customers provide information to organizations across a wide variety of touch points. Customer-centric organizations are implementing new and unique approaches for establishing interactions specifically for this purpose. They include Web-based interactions, point-of-sale interactions, and transaction-based interactions.

3.1 Develop a plan for establishing and managing interactions with a business's customers. In this plan, identify the key touch points for customers, explain how the data warehouse would be designed, and indicate the main interaction methods that would be promoted to the customer.

4 **Outline the process of capturing customer data.** Based on the interaction between the organization and its customers, vast amounts of information can be obtained. In a CRM system, the issue is not how much data can be obtained, but rather what type of data should be acquired and how those data can be used effectively for relationship enhancement. The channel, transaction, and the product or service consumed, all constitute touch points between a customer and the organization. These touch points represent possible areas within a business where customer interactions can take place and, hence, the opportunity for acquiring data from the customer.

4.1   Assume you are the manager for Caesars Windsor. Your boss has asked you to evaluate how the company is using its various touch points (such as its website) to gather customer data. Go to the website for Caesars Windsor (**www.caesarswindsor.com**) and provide a detailed critique of how the site is being used to capture customer data. Comment on the types of customer data the website is designed to capture, and explain how those data would benefit Caesars Windsor's operations.

5 **Describe the use of technology to store and integrate customer data.** Customer data gathering is complicated because information needed by one unit of the organization (e.g., sales and marketing) is often generated by another area of the business or even a third-party supplier (e.g., an independent marketing research firm). Because of the lack of a standard structure and interface, organizations are relying on technology to capture, store, and integrate strategically important customer information. The process of centralizing data in a CRM system is referred to as data warehousing. A data warehouse is a central repository of customer information collected by an organization.

5.1   Briefly explain the concept of a data warehouse. In the context of a CRM framework, why is a data warehouse such an important tool?

5.2   What is being written about customer data in today's periodicals? Visit the library or access Google and search your favourite database of articles using keywords such as "customer data" and "data warehousing." Are certain industries better represented in the citation list generated by your search? Are certain issues more prevalent? Read three or four articles and write a brief analysis of what is being discussed in the press regarding these CRM topics.

6 **Describe how to identify the best customers.** CRM attempts to manage the interactions between a company and its customers. To succeed, organizations must identify customers who currently yield high profitability or have a high potential for profitability. To accomplish this task, significant amounts of information must be gathered from customers, stored and integrated in the data warehouse, and then analyzed to generate customer segments. A useful approach to identifying the best customers is recency–frequency–monetary (RFM) analysis. Data mining uses RFM, predictive modelling, and other approaches to identify significant relationships among several customer dimensions within vast data warehouses. These significant relationships enable marketers to better define the most profitable customers and prospects.

6.1   Explain the concept of data mining. Provide five examples of companies that are currently using data mining, and explain why each is using it.

7 **Explain the process of leveraging customer information throughout the organization.** One of the benefits of a CRM system is that it enables a company to share information throughout the organization. This allows all functional areas within the company to interact in developing marketing programs. This process is commonly referred to as campaign management. Campaign management involves developing customized product and service offerings for appropriate customer segments and then pricing and communicating these offerings for the purpose of enhancing customer relationships.

7.1 Campaign management is the benefit derived when a company is able to leverage and disseminate information throughout its departments. Briefly define campaign management and explain how a business can apply it to its daily operations. In your answer, select a particular business as an example of effective campaign management.

TERMS

campaign management 587
compiled list 582
customer relationship
    management (CRM) 572
customer retention 590
customer-centric 576
data mining 583
data warehouse 581

database 581
database enhancement 582
empowerment 576
interaction 576
knowledge management 576
learning (CRM) 576
lifetime value analysis (LTV) 585
point-of-sale interactions 579

predictive modelling 586
recency–frequency–monetary analysis
    (RFM) 585
response list 582
touch point 578
web-based interactions 579

EXERCISES

APPLICATION EXERCISE

Understanding how companies use consumer information can be difficult if you have never had a job or internship that required you to use databases or customer profiles.[48]

Activity

Save all the direct mail advertising that comes to your mailbox for at least a week. You could ask your parents or friends to collect their direct mail as well.

1. Once you have your stack of mail, organize it according to the household that received it. That is, if friends and family helped you collect mail, keep mail sent to each address together. Make a list of all material in each group.

2. To what kind of customer is each piece of mail targeted? What makes you think as you do?

3. Based on the content of the mail pieces, determine what kind of information the various companies have about you, your friends, or your family in their databases. Are there indications on the mailers about what kinds of interactions the recipient has had with the sender of the marketing piece?

4. **WRITING** Write out an aggregate profile for each address. If you were a direct marketer, what kind of products and services would you market to each? What kinds of offers would you create?

ETHICS EXERCISE

Having combined several of its databases about parental purchasing behaviour and the results of its market research, Play Company believes it has the tools to launch a CRM campaign with messages for the six- to nine-year-old fans of its JoyMax educational products without violating the law. In spite of potential parental backlash, the company believes the approach will help customize new children's products and increase the company's share of these profitable young customers.

Questions

1. Should Play Company use CRM marketing tools to communicate with children?

2. **ONLINE** Does the CMA Code of Ethics address marketing to children in its Code of Ethics? Go to **www.the-cma.org/consumer/ethics.cfm** and review the code. Then write a brief paragraph on how the CMA Code of Ethics relates to Play Company's dilemma.

PETCO.COM: TURNING NEGATIVE REVIEWS INTO POSITIVE SALES

On **Petco.com** you can buy a soft-sided travel carrier for your cat for only $19.99. You might think twice, though, after seeing that customers gave it only two "paws" out of five overall for pet satisfaction, appearance, and quality. The reviews reveal more serious reasons to hesitate before adding the product to your cart. A customer with the screen name "Disgruntled Bunny" reports: "The mesh on the sides was such poor quality that my cat was able to rip it to shreds and escape in a matter of seconds!" Another customer recommends buying a carrier with stronger sides, adding, "It costs more but is safer for your pet, so it's worth it."

Products have long been rated on sites like **Amazon.com** and those like **CNET.Com** that exist entirely for customer reviews, but Petco was one of the first mainstream retailers to create a forum on its own website for criticism. The risk was obvious: customers could pan products and send buyers running. But Petco reports that business is booming, even with bad reviews like Disgruntled Bunny's.

New research is proving what Petco already learned: peer reviews work. Shoppers are turning to everyday people for product advice. The 2007 Edelman Trust Barometer reports that over half the population said they trust "a person like me" for information about a company or product. David Brain, CEO of Edelman, urges companies to stop relying on "top-down communications delivered to an elite audience and move to peer-to-peer dialogue."

Making customer reviews public has an immediate impact on sales and brand loyalty. Data from ForeSee Results in 2007 revealed that 40 percent of on-line shoppers said peer ratings on websites influenced their purchasing decisions. Furthermore, this group was 21 percent more satisfied with its purchases than other buyers and was 18 percent more likely to buy from the same site again.

According to Petco executive John Lazarchic, most users who search for products by customer ratings shop longer, buy more, and return less: "The savings in returns alone pays for all the technology involved in the review and ratings feature." And if one product gets too many bad reviews, it usually prompts customers to buy higher-rated, more expensive merchandise instead.

Other advantages? Reviews build camaraderie with an on-line community where shoppers can connect. They can boost a site's ratings on search sites. And they establish credibility. As long as the reviews aren't overwhelmingly negative, positive reviews have been shown to outweigh the negatives in shoppers' minds. For example, a four-paw review on Petco.com would outnumber one-paw ratings by seven to one.

Lazarchic insists that reviews provide valuable feedback. Critical comments are shared within the company and can instigate changes. In fact, it's finding that the risk is not in receiving too many negative comments on a product, but too few. When no one is responding, it looks like no one is buying it. Or, if they are, they don't care enough about it to talk about it. Petco had that problem at first. In the beginning, when the company posted a small link for users to click and write a review, the silence was deafening. So it added promotional banners to the site and advertised drawings in which lucky reviewers would receive cash prizes. Within a couple of weeks, the company had received 4,500 new comments.

Analysts warn that to maintain credibility, reviews shouldn't be edited unless necessary. Petco removes the names of rival brands, URLs, and personal information, but less than 10 percent of the reviews it receives are deleted. Now it's experimenting with the idea of using customer comments as marketing tools in print catalogues, off-line ads, e-mail messages, and point-of-purchase displays. In print circulars, for example, Petco highlights its five-paw-rated products.

Many of its customers' e-mail addresses are collected through a loyalty program in Petco stores, which means those shoppers may not have visited the website. By including customer comments in e-mail ads, it expands the reach of the review program and boosts sales of products those shoppers may not have considered in the store. According to a Nielsen BuzzMetrics study, the customers most likely to write reviews on websites are empty-nesters and "young transitionals" without children. Petco found that on its site, reviewers tend to be women with higher levels of education and income who are passionate about their pets. It is generally someone who wants to be helpful, share her opinion, and feel important. Someone, perhaps, like Disgruntled Bunny, who wants to warn others of the dangers of defective travel carriers before another cat escapes.[49]

Questions

1. A customer-centric company builds long-lasting relationships by focusing on what satisfies and retains valuable customers. Discuss how Petco follows this customer-centric philosophy.

2. Go to petco.com and read some of the customer reviews for various types of products. Do the one- and two-paw ratings tend to outnumber those with four and five paws, or the other way around? Can you find a customer review that Petco could use to market a product in a company circular or e-mail ad?

3. Now that Petco has identified the type of customer most likely to write reviews of its products, discuss the kinds of promotions that might encourage continued loyalty and response on-line from them in the future. What could it do to appeal to these customers?

4. Many mainstream retailers are still hesitant to post customer reviews on their websites. If you were consulting with one of these companies, what arguments would you use to convince management to try them?

VIDEO CASE

CBC

GIFT CARDS, NOT AS GOOD AS CASH

Retailers are constantly looking for ways to develop customer franchises and encourage consumer loyalty. Combine this with consumers who have the generosity of wanting to give but who are not sure what to give, and presto, technology has provided the solution: the gift card. They would seem to be perfect. The giver need only know what the recipient's favourite store or restaurant is. You go to the preferred retailer, buy a gift card in an amount you can reasonably afford, and give it to the recipient. Recipients then go at their own convenience and purchase whatever they want using the gift card (and perhaps some of their own money). As a consumer, you have given a person the freedom to get what he or she wants. A gift card is thoughtful (I know where you like to shop) and is not perceived to be as "crass" as cash.

Gift cards are a major win for retailers. They get cash now against a promise to buy merchandise later (possibly at inflated prices) as well as the potential for some incremental sales if the person decides to spend more than what is on the gift card. Statistics indicate that in 2004, 47 percent of Canadians did in fact spend more than the face value of the gift card they received. Even if people spend less than what is on the gift card, no problem, they will return later and perhaps spend more at that time. Finally, some people don't redeem their gift cards at all, so for the retailer, it's free money. Even when the merchant redeems the cards, it doesn't give cash; instead it provides merchandise, which includes the mark-up. One estimate indicates that Canadians spent $6 billion on gift cards in 2006.

With all this going for them, it is hard to fathom why some retailers have placed expiry dates and depreciation expenses on their gift cards. In addition, they do not go out of their way to inform the buyers of these cards that there are expiry dates and depreciation rates. One could argue that since retailers have accepted money in advance, they have taken on a form of promissory note. Some cards expire after two years, others as soon as one year, and some have depreciation fees that kick in after six months. Add to this, some cards simply get ruined because they have been damaged or demagnetized. Regardless, about 10 percent of gift cards go unredeemed before their expiry dates. Many retailers report income from unredeemed cards at astonishing levels. In 2005, Home Depot recorded a company-wide $52 million income from cards that expired between 1998 and 2001; in 2006, Best Buy earned $16 million from unredeemed cards.

In Canada, gift cards are widely distributed. They are offered by 100 percent of department stores, 93 percent of home electronics and appliance stores, 85 percent of furniture stores, 71 percent of supermarkets, and 54 percent of clothing, shoe, and accessory stores. There are costs of distribution for retailers. For example, the magnetized cards alone can cost from 50 cents to three dollars to produce. Gift card programs can cost up to $50,000 to set up, and then there are administrative expenses associated with managing them. However, the costs are less than those associated with credit cards, which virtually all retailers accept in some form these days. Clearly, gift card programs are a marketing expense to develop customer loyalty. Besides generating revenue, they represent an expense item in retail operations.

In light of all of the benefits to retailers and the evidence of "windfall profits," consumers are rightfully upset when gift cards expire; after all, they are supposed to be a substitute for cash. This issue has been brought to the attention of provincial governments. In 2006, Manitoba and Ontario passed laws banning expiry dates on gift cards.[50]

Questions

1. Describe the advantages and disadvantages of gift card programs for retailers and consumers.

2. What impact do you think the nonexpiration date legislation will have on gift card use? Will consumers be more willing to buy and use gift cards now that they are the same as cash, or do you think use will remain unchanged? Discuss.

3. Retailers will now have to keep closer track of gift card redemptions than ever before. Discuss some of the possible issues that retailers will have to contend with because of the nonexpiration date laws.

MARKETING & YOU RESULTS

A low score on this poll suggests that you think it is acceptable to complain, whereas a high score suggests you think it is inappropriate to complain, even when you receive a bad product or service. People who perceive complaining to be most acceptable also tend to be aggressive, and those who regard complaining as inappropriate tend to be unassertive and generally passive.

MARKETING MISCUE

GOOGLE STREET VIEW AND PRIVACY CONCERNS

Google Street View, a feature of Google Maps and Google Earth, was launched in May 2007 in the United States and, by 2009, also provided street shots from cities in the United Kingdom, Australia, and Japan and numerous other countries and cities in Europe. According to Google, the goal is to provide street views of every place in the world. Google Street View displays photos taken by Google Street View cameras mounted on Google Street View cars driving on the roads around the world (or Google Street bikes if access cannot be gained by car).

Some residents in the United States were angered over the posting of private residential sites on the Internet. A Pittsburg, Pennsylvania, couple sued Google for its Street View drivers going down a private driveway (uninvited) and taking pictures of their home, including house, swimming pool, and outbuildings. In California, it was reported that Street View drivers traversed over 100 private roads in Sonoma County, went past many "no trespassing" signs, and even drove through someone's yard in order to gather photographs to post on Google's site. Numerous blogs appeared soon after the United States launch. Top bizarre sights in Google Street View (such as images of Borat, the Hot Babes, headless figures next to a newly dug grave, an alien invasion) clogged cyberspace airwaves.

Google Street View debuted in the United Kingdom in March 2009, stirring up many complaints about the invasion of privacy and raising concerns about security. One privacy organization, Privacy International, planned a legal challenge to Street View since individuals had not given prior consent for the photos. The British newspaper the *Daily Mail* attacked Street View, branding it a "burglar's charter." According to one source, U.K. citizens could take action under the U.K. Data Protection Act if they suffered as a consequence of the Street View posting.

The taking of photographs, even on the scale that Google has undertaken, has always aroused controversy, but the right to take them has been pretty well protected. However, Google also collected some information whose privacy protection falls into a different category. Subsequent to taking the photos in 2009, in June 2010, it was discovered that the Google Street View vehicles had taken more than pictures, "they had also gathered unsecured Wi-Fi data while scanning neighbourhoods."[1] Authorities in the United Kingdom and the United States were pondering whether criminal charges should be brought for this action.

Responding to privacy concerns about their photographs, Google Street View began to include imagery that would be visible only from the street, and the newer version of the program included technology that automatically blurred faces and licence plates. However, the blurring technology did not always work as planned and many memorable sights were posted on the Internet. These sights included a man throwing up between his knees outside a London bar, youths with traffic cones on their heads in Edinburgh, someone coming out of a sex shop in Soho, and a man being arrested by police. The Internet was once again fair game for bloggers and picture postings.

In situations in which the technology did not work to protect privacy, Street View offered a "Report a Concern" link with every photograph posted on the Google site. Anyone who thought they could be identified in a photo or who wanted their property removed only had to notify Google via the link. The notification needed to single out areas of the photo that needed to be removed and Google, when updating photos, would leave those areas blank in later versions of the posting. This removal request tool enabled Google Street View to receive the support of the Information Commissioner's Office in the United Kingdom.

As with many services, it was in the hands of the consumer to be proactive and check the Google Street View site for any possible invasion of privacy. It was unclear how the person throwing up outside a bar or the one leaving a sex shop would know to check those particular sites for personal photos. But, as noted by one blogger, Google Street View is not meant to protect privacy. It is meant to help Google sell ads. According to another blogger, new technology necessitates new laws and new rules of etiquette. These laws and rules of etiquette will have a huge impact on the way marketers, such as Google, do business in the 21st century.

With respect to privacy issues associated with the unsecured Wi-Fi data collected, on June 4, 2010, Google claimed the data collected from unsecured wireless networks was acquired by mistake. The company agreed to give this data to European regulators and discontinued using vehicles that had equipment that could locate wireless data hubs. The company was awaiting any contacts from the U.S. Federal Trade Commission on the matter as well. As far as anyone knew, the Wi-Fi information collected was not publicized in any fashion and only Google would have had access to its content.[2]

Questions

1. Identify the customer relationships inherent in a product offering such as Google Street View.

2. Is Google Street View basically a forum for on-line advertising? Explain.

3. How are the privacy issues surrounding the taking of pictures and the collection of Wi-Fi data similar? How are these issues different? Discuss.

CRITICAL THINKING CASE

HOW KRAFT CANADA ENGAGES CUSTOMERS

With all the technology available, sometimes marketers lose sight of what is most important—fulfilling the needs of their customers better than their competitors. Kraft Canada is a firm that has avoided this pitfall by keeping its purpose front and centre, using technology to engage its customers and then offering simple food solutions.

Kraft Canada accomplishes its purpose with a number of tools. The first tool is "Kraft Kitchens Experts," which consumers can reach through the Kraft Canada website (**www.kraftcanada.com**) and ask questions about food offerings and recipes. It is not just the name of a contact centre either. It is a real kitchen where, for a fee, Canadians can take cooking lessons or attend workshops. Kraft Kitchens publishes *What's Cooking* magazine, which is mailed to over 1.4 million Canadians. Kraft Canada believes in using all the available communication technology. Kraft Kitchens uses the telephone and the mail and provides on-line assistance to its cooks with thousands of food recipes on its website. The firm also sends out recipes via weekly e-mails.

Kraft's latest efforts have involved the development of a television show called *What's Cooking*, clearly named after its magazine, which is a 30-minute program broadcast on CITY TV on Saturday nights at 7:00 p.m. The show is hosted by Richard Cazeau (a former MuchMoreMusic personality), along with Jack Hourigan, formerly of Second City, and Warren Assaly, a graduate of the Cordon Bleu Culinary Institute, who is the cooking expert. The show is designed as another way to reach out to consumers, but it is part of a multimedia effort too. According to Sandra Ciferons, the director of media at Kraft Canada, "We will be driving to on-line—all of the recipes will be housed there. There will be streamed video as well, and you'll be able to download the show if you can't watch it in its scheduled time, you can watch it at your convenience." The show is a typical kind of cooking show and features three recipes per show that will be made available on the Kraft Canada website.[3]

In addition to the cooking show, Kraft has also developed a set of Kraft Canada mobile applications called the iFood Assistant, which is a mobile app accompanied by a mobile site and is accessible by smart phones like the iPhone and iPod Touch, as well as the Blackberry. According to Edward Kaczmarek, the director of innovation, consumer experiences at Kraft Foods, "It's the ultimate engagement tool. We tried to design something that answers an unmet consumer need but that also enables us to connect with the user closer to the point of purchase."[4]

All these efforts are part of Kraft's strategy to implement a customer relationship management strategy with its customers, to understand them better, and to support their needs as they buy Kraft brands such as Miracle Whip, Philadelphia Cream Cheese, Shake 'n Bake, and, of course, Kraft Dinner Macaroni and Cheese (a.k.a. KD). The development of a direct customer relationship management program with so many customers is not usually considered financially feasible, but Kraft Canada decided that the current technology would give it the means. The number of Canadian households with access to the Web, e-mail, and mobile phones, combined with the availability of CRM tools and technology, makes it easier than ever for firms like Kraft Canada to engage their customers.

Kraft has a variety of content in its CRM communication channels, including recipes, food and entertainment ideas, and basic cooking skills. The theme of Kraft's CRM program is "Family. Food. Simple." In addition, Kraft is interested in helping its consumers, so its service offerings focus on a few simple steps, a few dishes, and recipes requiring products that are currently in the kitchen whether they are Kraft brands or not.

Kraft's direct marketing campaign begins by sending out *What's Cooking* magazine in both English and French versions with coverage to 1.4 million Canadians. Every three months Kraft mails hundreds of thousands of direct-mail pieces, which are targeted in Canada's official languages but also include ethnic languages such as Mandarin. Kraft Canada sends out weekly e-mails to its customers who have opted into its e-mail list; this communication is combined with asking people to visit **www.kraftcanada.com**, the firm's website. People are responding. Kraft's website is ranked number one in Canada among packaged foods manufacturers. The website has a couple of key personalized features such as "My Recipe Box" and "My Profile," which allow users to customize the site.

Consumers who sign into Kraft Kitchens' cooking classes and workshops are greeted by cooking experts who know their subject and who have featured roles in Kraft's promotional communications. Many consumers feel they already know these people and are delighted to discover that they are "real-life," down-to-earth people, not just "models, actors, or professional talking heads." The personal and helpful approach is the objective of the program, so the Kraft brand presence is not overdone in the cooking classes or the *What's Cooking* magazine.

As much as possible, Kraft Canada personalizes all its communications. Along with the website data collection, surveys are conducted in *What's Cooking* magazine, in the direct mail pieces, and in the e-mails to discover needs and wants, preferences, key demographics like family size, and product usage rates. However, Kraft is careful to use the information to design communications focused on responding to customer needs rather than on making a "hard sell pitch."

One of the prime reasons that Kraft has been successful with this approach is the depth and width of its product line. Packaged goods products are usually low purchase involvement, low margin, and high turnover products. These kinds of products are usually not conducive to CRM programs. However, given Kraft's wide product line combined with its ability to build loyalty and cross-sell its products, a typical household's weekly purchase value in Kraft products can easily approach $10 to $20, an amount that will lower the costs of a CRM program.[5]

Questions

1. How does Kraft Canada's CRM approach differ from many of the CRM approaches that you have read about so far in this textbook? With reference to some of these other programs you have encountered, do you have any suggestions that might improve Kraft's CRM program?

2. Kraft's CRM program is relatively new and, as described, fairly expensive. Often companies start these programs without being sure where they will lead or how much they will cost. Usually when these evaluations are finally made, a lot of customers have become involved with the program. What are some of the negative effects that a firm like Kraft might face if it had to close down its CRM program because of expense?

3. Do you think people will really embrace the mobile phone applications that Kraft has developed or are they just tapping into a fad with mobile technology? Discuss.

19 Marketing on the Web

LEARNING OUTCOMES

1 Describe the impact of the Web on business

2 Discuss the effects of the Web on marketing objectives and strategy

3 Describe buyer behaviour on the Web

4 Explain how the Web affects the traditional marketing mix

5 Describe how marketers are leveraging the power of Web technology

6 Name the critical factors involved in measuring Web marketing success

7 Discuss the privacy and regulatory issues surrounding Web-based marketing

ⓥ MARKETING & YOU

How concerned are you about using the Web because of privacy concerns?
Using the scales below, enter your answers or record them on a separate page.

1	2	3	4	5
Strongly disagree	Disagree	Agree	Strongly	Agree

__ I detest the fact that the Web is becoming a haven for electronic junk mail.

__ I wish I had more control over unwanted messages sent by businesses on the Web.

__ I dislike the fact that marketers are able to find out personal information of on-line shoppers.

Now total your score by adding all the scores together. Find out what your score means after reading the chapter.

SOURCE: REPRINTED WITH PERMISSION FROM *MARKETING SCALES HANDBOOK* VOL. IV, PUBLISHED BY THE AMERICAN MARKETING ASSOCIATION, G. BRUNER, K. JAMES, H. HENSEL, EDS. SCALE #216.

Many years ago, electronics retailer Radio Shack used the promotional theme "This Place Is Completely Wired" to refer to its status as a high-technology service provider. In the modern world of Web marketing, the new theme is "This place is completely wireless." We now live in a world of mobile high-technology devices based on digital data communications via both wired and wireless digital networks. Because of this, the wireless smartphone is the cutting-edge communications device that marketers are focusing their efforts on these days. Syndicated writer Jamie Sturgeon reports on an address given by Nadir Mohamed, CEO of Rogers Communications, at the Canadian Telecom summit. Sturgeon reports that Mohamed says that "Canadians' appetite to communicate, access information and entertainment, and even make transactions through their wireless device is becoming insatiable. . . . Rogers is moving quickly to bring mobile Internet to the masses." Sturgeon writes that Mohamed estimates that more than 3 million Canadians will be using smartphones like the BlackBerry or iPhone by 2014 so they can surf the Web and access their e-mail.

Mohamed also commented that there were over 50,000 apps that had a wide focus of activity from communications programs for business to video games for fun. All these applications could be downloaded from other phones or from Apple's virtual store. Mohamed believes that the future for smartphones is good but goes on to say, "You need a network, you need devices, you need applications, and you need pricing to be right to actually foster customers embracing it."[1]

Mike Lazaridis is the president of Research In Motion (RIM), the maker of BlackBerry devices, which were the first mobile devices capable of allowing access to e-mail. Lazaridis is considered a guru of the technology world, and this status is reinforced by the fact that he is often asked to autograph BlackBerry devices whenever he makes public appearances. Lazaridis agrees with Mohamed that the success of smartphones is going to be phenomenal. However, he worries that service carriers like Rogers are going to be in trouble as demand for the devices continues to grow. Lazaridis comments: "As an industry, we need to think of a way to conserve this precious resource just like we're trying to conserve other things today. Believe it or not, [wireless] spectrum is a physically limited resource. We only have so much electromagnetic spectrum left in the cellular usage class . . . so we're getting to the point where we're starting to understand that data is not free. We're starting to use these devices as credit cards, we're starting to use these things for transactions, we're starting to have them connected to a banking account. . . . [G]overnments are starting to look at these and say, 'Think of how much money we could save and how well we could control things like passports and passport counterfeiting. How about licences for cars? For insurance?'"[2]

The world of wireless digital communications that can access the World Wide Web is a rapidly evolving one. How do companies operate in this world to market their products and communicate with customers? How might they operate in the future? In this chapter, you will learn about Web marketing and how marketers can use this interactive medium.

SOURCES: JAMIE STURGEON, "ROGERS TARGETING RESTRUCTURED INTERNET; SMARTPHONE FUTURE," *THE GAZETTE*, JUNE 16, 2009, B.7; THERESA TEDESCO, "FUTURE PHONES," *NATIONAL POST*, DECEMBER 29, 2009, 1.

Find the whole chapter online at
www.lamb5e.nelson.com.

Glossary

(Numbers in parentheses refer to the chapter(s) containing the main discussion of the term.)

A

accessory equipment Goods, such as portable tools and office equipment, that are less expensive and shorter lived than major equipment. (5)

adopter A consumer who is happy enough with his or her trial experience with a product to use it again. (9)

advertising Impersonal, one-way mass communication about a product or organization that is paid for by a marketer. (13)

advertising appeal A reason for a person to buy a product. (14)

advertising campaign A series of related advertisements focusing on a common theme, slogan, and set of advertising appeals. (14)

advertising objective A specific communication task that a campaign should accomplish for a specified target audience during a specified period. (14)

advertising response function A phenomenon in which spending for advertising and sales promotion increases sales or market share up to a certain level but then produces diminishing returns. (14)

advocacy advertising A form of advertising in which an organization expresses its views on controversial issues or responds to media attacks. (14)

affiliate program A form of advertising on the World Wide Web that rewards self-selected advertisers (called affiliates) for driving traffic to the advertiser or for subsequent transactions. (web 19)

agents and brokers Wholesaling intermediaries that do not take title to a product but facilitate its sale from producer to end user by representing retailers, wholesalers, or manufacturers. (11)

AIDA concept A model that outlines the process for achieving promotional goals in terms of stages of consumer involvement with the message; the acronym stands for *attention, interest, desire,* and *action.* (13)

applied research An attempt to develop new or improved products. (3)

aspirational reference group A group that someone would like to join. (4)

assurance The knowledge and courtesy of employees and their ability to convey trust. (10)

ATC *See* average total cost.

atmosphere The overall impression conveyed by a store's physical layout, decor, and surroundings. (12)

attitude A learned tendency to respond consistently toward a given object. (4)

audience selectivity The ability of an advertising medium to reach a precisely defined market. (14)

automatic replenishment program An inventory management system that triggers shipments only once a good is sold to the customer; the program uses an EDI linkage connected with bar-code scanners at the point of purchase, so the supplier can view the inventory being held at the next tier of the supply chain in real time. (11)

automatic vending The use of machines to offer goods for sale. (12)

AVC *See* average variable cost.

average total cost (ATC) Total costs divided by quantity of output. (16)

average variable cost (AVC) Total variable costs divided by quantity of output. (16)

B

baby boomers People born between 1946 and 1964. (3)

Balanced Scorecard Approach A measurement system used to evaluate overall supply chain performance. (11)

banner advertisement A paid advertisement that runs the entire width of the Web page, usually placed near the top or bottom of the page. (web 19)

base price The general price level at which the company expects to sell the good or service. (17)

basic research Pure research that aims to confirm an existing theory or to learn more about a concept or phenomenon. (3)

basing-point pricing A price tactic that charges freight from a given (basing) point, regardless of the city from which the goods are shipped. (17)

BehaviorScan A scanner-based research program that tracks the purchases of 3,000 households through store scanners. (7)

behavioural targeting A form of observation marketing research that uses data mining coupled with identifying Web surfers by their IP addresses. (7)

belief An organized pattern of knowledge that an individual holds as true about his or her world. (4)

benefit segmentation The process of grouping customers into market segments according to the benefits they seek from the product. (6)

brainstorming The process of getting a group to think of unlimited ways to vary a product or solve a problem. (9)

brand A name, term, symbol, design, or combination thereof that identifies a seller's products and differentiates them from competitors' products. (8)

brand equity The value of company and brand names. (8)

brand extension The practice of introducing new varieties, flavours, formats, or products under a brand name that is already well established in the market. (4, 8)

brand loyalty A consistent preference for one brand over all others. (8)

brand mark The elements of a brand that cannot be spoken. (8)

brand name That part of a brand that can be spoken, including letters, words, and numbers. (8)

break-even analysis A method of determining what sales volume must be reached before total revenue equals total costs. (16)

business analysis The second stage of the screening process, where preliminary figures for demand, cost, sales, and profitability are calculated. (9)

business marketing The marketing of goods and services to individuals and organizations for purposes other than personal consumption. Often referred to as B2B or B-to-B. (5)

business product (industrial product) A product used to manufacture other goods or services, to facilitate an organization's operations, or to resell to other customers. (8)

business services Expense items that do not become part of a final product. (5)

business-to-business (B2B) electronic commerce The use of the Internet to facilitate the exchange of goods, services, and information between organizations. (5, web 19)

business-to-business on-line exchange An electronic trading floor that provides companies with integrated links to their customers and suppliers. (5, web 19)

business-to-consumer (B2C) electronic commerce Using the Internet to conduct business between an organization and individual consumers. (web 19)

buyer A department head who selects the merchandise for his or her department and who may also be responsible for promotion and personnel. (12)

buying centre All those people in an organization who become involved in the purchase decision. (5)

C

campaign management Developing product or service offerings customized for the appropriate customer segment and then pricing and communicating these offerings for the purpose of enhancing customer relationships. (18)

cannibalization When sales of a new product cut into sales of a company's existing products. (6)

cash cow In the portfolio matrix, a business unit that usually generates more cash than it needs to maintain its market share. (2)

cash discount A price reduction offered to a consumer, an industrial user, or a marketing intermediary in return for prompt payment of a bill. (17)

category killers Specialty discount stores that heavily dominate their narrow merchandise segment. (12)

central-location telephone (CLT) facility A specially designed phone room used to conduct telephone interviewing. (7)

chain stores Stores owned and operated as a group by a single organization. (12)

chain-ratio sales forecasting A method of forecasting by which a firm's sales

are estimated by relating them in proportion to larger trends. (7)

channel A medium of communication, such as a voice, radio, or newspaper, for transmitting a message. (13)

channel conflict A clash of goals and methods between distribution channel members. (11)

channel control When one marketing channel member intentionally affects another member's behaviour. (11)

channel leader (channel captain) A member of a marketing channel that exercises authority and power over the activities of other channel members. (11)

channel members All parties in the marketing channel that negotiate with one another, buy and sell products, and facilitate the change of ownership between buyer and seller in the course of moving the product from the manufacturer into the hands of the final consumer. (11)

channel partnering (channel cooperation) The joint effort of all channel members to create a supply chain that serves customers and creates a competitive advantage. (11)

channel power The capacity of a particular marketing channel member to control or influence the behaviour of other channel members. (11)

CLT *See* central-location telephone facility.

closed-ended question An interview question that asks the respondent to make a selection from a limited list of responses. (7)

cobranding Placing two or more brand names on a product or its package. (8)

code of ethics A guideline to help marketing managers and other employees make better decisions. (3)

cognitive dissonance Inner tension that a consumer experiences after recognizing an inconsistency between behaviour and values or opinions. (4)

cold calling A form of lead generation in which the salesperson approaches potential buyers without any prior knowledge of the prospects' needs or financial status. (15)

commercialization The decision to market a product. (9)

communication The process by which we exchange or share meanings through a common set of symbols. (13)

comparative advertising A form of advertising that compares two or more specifically named or shown competing brands on one or more specific attributes. (14)

Competition Bureau The federal department charged with

administering most marketplace laws. (3)

competitive advantage The set of unique features of a company and its products that are perceived by the target market as significant and superior to the competition (2); One or more unique aspects of an organization that cause target consumers to patronize that company rather than competitors. (2, 13)

competitive advertising A form of advertising designed to influence demand for a specific brand. (14)

competitive intelligence (CI) An intelligence system that helps managers assess their competition and vendors in order to become more efficient and effective competitors. (7)

compiled list A customer list that was developed by gathering names and addresses from telephone directories and membership rosters, usually enhanced with information from public records, such as census data, auto registrations, birth announcements, business start-ups, and bankruptcies. (18)

complex trend analysis sales forecasting Estimating future sales based on past sales while accounting for cyclical variations, competitor activity, and other impacts. (7)

component lifestyles The practice of choosing goods and services that meet one's diverse needs and interests rather than conforming to a single, traditional lifestyle. (3)

component parts Either finished items ready for assembly or products that need very little processing before becoming part of some other product. (5)

computer-assisted personal interviewing An interviewing method in which the interviewer reads the questions from a computer screen and enters the respondent's data directly into the computer. (7)

computer-assisted self-interviewing An interviewing method in which a mall interviewer intercepts and directs willing respondents to nearby computers, where the respondent reads questions off a computer screen and directly keys his or her answers into the computer. (7)

concentrated targeting strategy A strategy used to select one segment of a market for targeting marketing efforts. (6)

concept test A test to evaluate a new product idea, usually before any prototype has been created. (9)

consumer behaviour Processes a consumer uses to make purchase decisions, as well as to use and dispose of purchased goods or services; also includes factors that influence purchase decisions and product use. (4)

consumer decision-making process A five-step process used by consumers when buying goods or services. (4)

consumer-generated media (CGM) Media that consumers generate and share among themselves. (7)

consumer penalty An extra fee paid by the consumer for violating the terms of the purchase agreement. (17)

consumer product A product bought to satisfy an individual's personal wants. (8)

consumer sales promotion Sales promotion activities targeting the ultimate consumer. (15)

consumer-to-consumer (C2C) electronic commerce Using the Internet to conduct business with another consumer or consumers. (web 19)

continuous media schedule A media scheduling strategy in which advertising is run steadily throughout the advertising period; used for products in the latter stages of the product life cycle. (14)

control Provides the mechanisms for evaluating marketing results in light of the plan's goals and for correcting actions that do not help the organization reach those goals within budget guidelines. (2)

convenience product A relatively inexpensive item that merits little shopping effort. (8)

convenience sample A form of non-probability sample using respondents who are convenient or readily accessible to the researcher—for example, employees, friends, or relatives. (7)

convenience store A miniature supermarket, carrying only a limited line of high-turnover convenience goods. (12)

conversion rate The percentage of website visitors or e-mail recipients who take a desired action, such as purchasing a product or requesting additional information. (web 19)

cookie A digital tag written to the user's local hard drive that is keyed to a specific server (e.g., a Web page) and passed back to the server when the user's browser again accesses the server. (web 19)

cooperative advertising An arrangement in which the manufacturer and the retailer split the costs of advertising the manufacturer's brand. (14)

core service The most basic benefit the consumer is buying. (10)

corporate blogs Blogs that are sponsored by a company or one of its brands and maintained by one or more of the company's employees. (13)

corporate social responsibility Business's concern for society's welfare. (3)

cost competitive advantage Being the low-cost competitor in an industry while maintaining satisfactory profit margins. (2)

cost per contact The cost of reaching one member of the target market. (14)

coupon A certificate that entitles consumers to an immediate price reduction when they buy the product. (15)

credence quality A characteristic that consumers may have difficulty assessing even after purchase because they do not have the necessary knowledge or experience. (10)

crisis management A coordinated effort to handle the effects of unfavourable publicity or of another unexpected, unfavourable event. (14)

CRM *See* customer relationship management.

cross-tabulation A method of analyzing data that lets the analyst look at the responses to one question in relation to the responses to one or more other questions. (7)

culture The set of values, norms, attitudes, and other meaningful symbols that shape human behaviour and the artifacts, or products, of that behaviour as they are transmitted from one generation to the next. (4)

cumulative quantity discount A deduction from list price that applies to the buyer's total purchases made during a specific time period. (17)

customer buyer intention survey forecasting Surveying buyer intentions to determine how many customers plan to buy the firm's products in the future. (7)

customer-centric Under this philosophy, the company customizes its product and service offering based on data generated through interactions between the customer and the company. (18)

customer relationship management (CRM) A company-wide business strategy designed to optimize profitability, revenue, and customer satisfaction by focusing on highly defined and precise customer groups. (18)

customer retention The percentage of customers that repeatedly purchase products from a company. (18)

customer satisfaction Customers' evaluation of a good or service based on whether it has met their needs and expectations. (1)

customer value The ratio of benefits to the sacrifice necessary to obtain those benefits. (1)

D

data mining A data analysis procedure that identifies significant patterns of variables and characteristics that pertain to particular customers or customer groups. (18)

data warehouse A central repository for data from various functional areas of the organization that are stored and inventoried on a centralized computer system so that the information can be shared across all functional departments of the business. (18)

database A collection of data, especially one that can be accessed and manipulated by computer software. (18)

database enhancement Purchasing information on customers or prospects to better describe their needs or determine how responsive they might be to marketing programs. (18)

database marketing The creation of a large computerized file of customers' and potential customers' profiles and purchase patterns. (7)

deceptive pricing Promoting a price or price saving that is not actually available. (17)

decision support system (DSS) An interactive, flexible, computerized information system that enables managers to obtain and manipulate information as they are making decisions. (7)

decline stage A long-run drop in sales. (9)

decoding Interpretation of the language and symbols sent by the source through a channel. (13)

delayed-quotation pricing A price tactic used for industrial installations and many accessory items, in which a firm price is not set until the item is either finished or delivered. (17)

demand The quantity of a product that will be sold in the market at various prices for a specified period. (16)

demographic segmentation Segmenting markets by age, gender, income, ethnic background, and family life cycle. (6)

demography The study of people's vital statistics, such as their age, ethnicity, and location. (3)

department store A store housing several departments under one roof. (12)

derived demand The demand for business products. (5)

destination stores Stores that consumers purposely plan to visit. (12)

development The stage in the product development process during which a prototype is developed and a marketing strategy is outlined. (9)

diffusion The process by which the adoption of an innovation spreads. (9)

direct channel A distribution channel in which producers sell directly to consumers. (11)

direct marketing (direct-response marketing) Techniques used to get consumers to make a purchase from their home, office, or other non-retail setting. (12)

direct retailing The selling of products by representatives who work door-to-door, office-to-office, or at home parties. (12)

discount store A retailer that competes on the basis of low prices, high turnover, and high volume. (12)

discrepancy of assortment The lack of all the items a customer needs to receive full satisfaction from a product or products. (11)

discrepancy of quantity The difference between the amount of product produced and the amount an end user wants to buy. (11)

disintermediation The elimination of intermediaries such as wholesalers or distributors from a marketing channel. (5)

distribution resource planning (DRP) An inventory control system that manages the replenishment of goods from the manufacturer to the final consumer. (11)

diversification A strategy of increasing sales by introducing new products into new markets. (2)

dog In the portfolio matrix, a business unit that has low growth potential and a small market share. (2)

DRP *See* distribution resource planning.

drugstore A retail store that stocks pharmacy-related products and services as its main draw. (12)

DSS *See* decision support system.

dual distribution (multiple distribution) The use of two or more channels to distribute the same product to target markets. (11)

E

e-tailing Using the Internet to sell retail products and services. (web 19)

e-WOM (word-of-mouse) Marketer use of Web communications to encourage their customers to send personal messages to their friends to refer them to products or services. (web 19)

EDI *See* electronic data interchange.

80/20 principle A principle holding that 20 percent of all customers generate 80 percent of the demand. (6)

elastic demand A situation in which consumer demand is sensitive to changes in price. (16)

elasticity of demand Consumers' responsiveness or sensitivity to changes in price. (16)

electronic data interchange (EDI) Information technology that replaces the paper documents that usually accompany business transactions, such as purchase orders and invoices, with electronic transmission of the needed information to reduce inventory levels, improve cash flow, streamline operations, and increase the speed and accuracy of information transmission. (11)

electronic distribution A distribution technique that includes any kind of product or service that can be distributed electronically, whether over traditional forms such as fibre-optic cable or through satellite transmission of electronic signals. (11)

empathy Caring, individualized attention to customers. (10)

empowerment Delegation of authority to solve customers' problems quickly—usually by the first person the customer notifies regarding the problem. (1, 18)

encoding The conversion of the sender's ideas and thoughts into a message, usually in the form of words or signs. (13)

environmental management When a company implements strategies that attempt to shape the external environment within which it operates. (3)

environmental scanning Collection and interpretation of information about forces, events, and relationships in the external environment that may affect the future of the organization or the implementation of the marketing plan. (2)

escalator pricing A price tactic in which the final selling price reflects cost increases incurred between the time the order is placed and the time delivery is made. (17)

ethics The moral principles or values that generally govern the conduct of an individual or a group. (3)

ethnographic research The study of human behaviour in its natural context; involves observation of behaviour and physical setting. (7)

evaluation Gauging the extent to which the marketing objectives have been achieved during the specified time period. (2)

evoked set (consideration set) Group of brands, resulting from an information search, from which a buyer can choose. (4)

exchange The idea that people give up something to receive something they would rather have. (1)

exclusive distribution A form of distribution that establishes one or a few dealers within a given area. (11)

executive interviews A type of survey that involves interviewing business-people at their offices concerning industrial products or services. (7)

experience curves Curves that show costs declining at a predictable rate as experience with a product increases. (2)

experience quality A characteristic that can be assessed only after use. (10)

experiment A method for gathering primary data; the researcher alters one or more variables while observing the effects on another variable (usually sales). (7)

expert opinion sales forecasting A sales forecast based on the opinions of expert people who are knowledge-able about an industry. (7)

express warranty A written guarantee. (8)

extensive decision making The most complex type of consumer decision making, used when buying an unfamiliar, expensive product or an infrequently bought item; requires use of several criteria for evaluating options and much time for seeking information. (4)

external information search The process of seeking information in the outside environment. (4)

F

factory outlet An off-price retailer that is owned and operated by a manufacturer. (12)

family brand Marketing several different products under the same brand name. (8)

family life cycle (FLC) A series of stages determined by a combination of age, marital status, and the presence or absence of children. (6)

feedback The receiver's response to a message. (13)

field service firm A firm that specializes in interviewing respondents on a subcontracted basis. (7)

Fighting Internet and Wireless Spam Act Legislation that covers spam, spyware, malware (malicious software), spoofing, e-mail phishing, and identity theft. (web 19)

fixed cost A cost that does not change as output is increased or decreased. (16)

FLC *See* family life cycle.

flexible pricing (variable pricing) A price tactic in which different customers pay different prices for essentially the same merchandise bought in equal quantities. (17)

flighted media schedule A media scheduling strategy in which ads are run heavily every other month or every two weeks, to achieve a greater impact with an increased frequency and reach at those times. (14)

FOB origin pricing A price tactic that requires the buyer to absorb the freight costs from the shipping point ("free on board"). (17)

focus group Seven to ten people who participate in a group discussion led by a moderator. (7)

follow-up The final step of the selling process, in which the salesperson ensures that delivery schedules are met, that the goods or services perform as promised, and that the buyers' employees are properly trained to use the products. (15)

four Ps Product, place, promotion, and price, which together make up the marketing mix. (2)

frame error An error that occurs when a sample drawn from a population differs from the target population. (7)

franchise The right to operate a business or to sell a product. (12)

franchisee An individual or business that is granted the right to sell another party's product. (12)

franchiser The originator of a trade name, product, methods of operation, and so on, that grants operating rights to another party to sell its product. (12)

freight absorption pricing A price tactic in which the seller pays all or part of the actual freight charges and does not pass them on to the buyer. (17)

frequency The number of times an individual is exposed to a given message during a specific period. (14)

frequent buyer program A loyalty program in which loyal consumers are rewarded for making recurring purchases of a particular good or service. (15)

full-line discount store A retailer that offers consumers very limited service and carries a broad assortment of well-known, nationally branded "hard goods." (12)

functional discount (trade discount) A discount to wholesalers and retailers for performing channel functions. (17)

G

gap model A model identifying five gaps that can cause problems in service delivery and influence customer evaluations of service quality. (10)

Generation X People born between 1965 and 1978. (3)

Generation Y People born between 1979 and 1994. (3)

generic product name Identifies a product by class or type and cannot be trademarked. (8)

geodemographic segmentation Segmenting potential customers into neighbourhood lifestyle categories. (6)

geographic segmentation Segmenting markets by region of a country or the world, market size, market density, or climate. (6)

global brand A brand where at least 20 percent of the product is sold outside its home country or region. (8)

green marketing The development and marketing of products designed to minimize negative effects on the physical environment or to improve the environment. (3)

gross margin The amount of money the retailer makes as a percentage of sales after the cost of goods sold is subtracted. (12)

group dynamics Group interaction essential to the success of focus-group research. (7)

growth stage The second stage of the product life cycle, when sales typically grow at an increasing rate, many competitors enter the market, large companies may start acquiring small pioneering companies, and profits are healthy. (9)

H

heterogeneity The variability of the inputs and outputs of services, which cause services to tend to be less standardized and uniform than goods. (10)

hit A record that a file was requested from a website. (web 19)

horizontal conflict A channel conflict that occurs among channel members on the same level. (11)

I

ideal self-image The way an individual would like to be. (4)

IMC *See* integrated marketing communications.

implementation The process that turns marketing plans into action assignments and that ensures these assignments are executed in a way that accomplishes the plan's objectives. (2)

implied warranty An unwritten guarantee that the good or service is fit for the purpose for which it was sold. (8)

independent retailers Retailers owned by a single person or partnership and not operated as part of a larger retail institution. (12)

individual branding Using different brand names for different products. (8)

inelastic demand A situation in which an increase or a decrease in price will not significantly affect demand for the product. (16)

inflation A general rise in prices, often without a corresponding increase in wages, that results in decreased purchasing power. (3)

infomercial A 10-to 30-minute or longer advertisement that looks more like a TV talk show than a sales pitch. (14)

informational labelling A type of package labelling designed to help consumers make proper product selections and lower their cognitive dissonance after the purchase. (8)

InfoScan A scanner-based sales-tracking service for the consumer packaged-goods industry. (7)

innovation A product perceived as new by a potential adopter. (9)

inseparability The fact that services are produced and consumed at the same time. (10)

institutional advertising A form of advertising designed to enhance a company's image rather than to promote a particular product. (14)

in-store retailing Customers must physically shop at stores to make a purchase. (12)

intangibility The inability of services to be touched, seen, tasted, heard, or felt in the same manner that goods can be sensed. (10)

integrated marketing communications (IMC) The careful coordination of all promotional messages for a product or a service to ensure the consistency of messages at every contact point where a company meets the consumer. (13)

intensive distribution A form of distribution aimed at having a product available in every outlet where target customers might want to buy it. (11)

interaction The point at which a customer and a company representative exchange information and develop learning relationships. (18)

internal information search The process of recalling past information stored in the memory. (4)

internal marketing Treating employees as customers and developing systems and benefits that satisfy their needs. (10)

interpersonal communication Direct, face-to-face communication between two or more people. (13)

introductory stage The full-scale launch of a new product into the marketplace. (9)

inventory control system A method of developing and maintaining an adequate assortment of materials or products to meet a manufacturer's or a customer's demand. (11)

involvement The amount of time and effort a buyer invests in the search, evaluation, and decision processes of consumer behaviour. (4)

J

joint costs Costs that are shared in the manufacturing and marketing of several products in a product line. (17)

joint demand The demand for two or more items used together in a final product. (5)

jury of executive opinion sales forecast A sales forecast based on the opinion of a combined group of the firm's executives. (7)

K

keiretsu A network of interlocking corporate affiliates. (5)

keystoning The practice of setting prices by doubling the cost. (16)

knowledge management The process by which learned information from customers is centralized and shared in order to enhance the relationship between customers and the organization. (18)

L

laws The values and standards enforceable by the courts. (3)

lead generation (prospecting) Identification of those companies and people most likely to buy the seller's offerings. (15)

lead qualification Determination of a sales prospect's (1) recognized need, (2) buying power, and (3) receptivity and accessibility. (15)

leader pricing (loss-leader pricing) A price tactic in which a product is sold near or even below cost in the hope that shoppers will buy other items once they are in the store. (17)

learning A process that creates changes in behaviour, immediate or expected, through experience and practice. (4)

learning (CRM) An informal process of collecting customer data through customer comments and feedback on product or service performance. (18)

lifestyle A mode of living as identified by a person's activities, interests, and opinions. (4)

lifetime value analysis (LTV) A data manipulation technique that projects the future value of the customer over a period of years, using the assumption that marketing to repeat customers is more profitable than marketing to first-time buyers. (18)

limited decision making The type of decision making that requires a moderate amount of time for gathering information and deliberating about an unfamiliar brand in a familiar product category. (4)

logistics The process of strategically managing the efficient flow and storage of raw materials, in-process inventory, and finished goods from point of origin to point of consumption. (11)

logistics information system Information technology that integrates and links all the logistics functions of the supply chain. (11)

loyalty marketing programs A promotional program designed to build long-term, mutually beneficial relationships between a company and its key customers. (15)

LTV *See* lifetime value analysis.

M

major equipment (installations) Capital goods such as large or expensive machines, mainframe computers, blast furnaces, generators, airplanes, and buildings. (5)

mall intercept interview A survey research method that involves interviewing people in the common areas of shopping malls. (7)

management decision problem A broad-based problem that requires marketing research in order for managers to take proper actions. (7)

manufacturer's brand The brand name of a manufacturer. (8)

marginal cost (MC) The change in total costs associated with a one-unit change in output. (16)

marginal revenue (MR) The extra revenue associated with selling an extra unit of output, or the change in total revenue with a one-unit change in output. (16)

markdown money Money or discounts provided by vendors to department stores to help cover end-of-season discounts offered by department stores to customers. (17)

market People or organizations with needs or wants and the ability and willingness to buy. (6)

market aggregation sales forecasting A method of forecasting that occurs when a firm looks at its market shares and sales potentials across the various market segments and adds them together to make a total sales estimate. (7)

market development A marketing strategy that entails attracting new customers to existing products. (2)

market opportunity analysis (MOA) The description and estimation of the size and sales potential of market segments that are of interest to the company and the assessment of key competitors in these market segments. (2)

market orientation A philosophy that assumes that a sale does not depend on an aggressive sales force but rather on a customer's decision to purchase a product. Synonymous with the marketing concept. (1)

market penetration A marketing strategy that tries to increase market share among existing customers. (2)

market segment A subgroup of people or organizations sharing one or more characteristics that cause them to have similar product needs. (6)

market segmentation The process of dividing a market into meaningful, relatively similar, and identifiable segments or groups. (6)

market share A company's product sales as a percentage of total sales for that industry. (16)

market share sales forecasting A method of forecasting that derives a sales estimate based on a firm's long term-market share in relation to the total industry sales potential. (7)

marketing An organizational function and a set of processes for creating, communicating, and delivering value to customers and for managing customer relationships in ways that benefit the organization and its stakeholders. (1)

marketing audit A thorough, systematic, periodic evaluation of the goals, strategies, structure, and performance of the marketing organization. (2)

marketing channel (channel of distribution) A set of interdependent organizations that ease the transfer of ownership as products move from producer to business user or consumer. (11)

marketing concept The idea that the social and economic justification for an organization's existence is the satisfaction of customer wants and needs while meeting organizational objectives. (1)

marketing-controlled information source A product information source that originates with marketers promoting the product. (4)

marketing information Everyday information about developments in the marketing environment that managers use to prepare and adjust marketing plans. (7)

marketing mix A unique blend of product, distribution, promotion, and pricing strategies designed to produce mutually satisfying exchanges with a target market. (2)

marketing myopia Defining a business in terms of goods and services rather than in terms of the benefits that customers seek. (2)

marketing objective A statement of what is to be accomplished through marketing activities. (2)

marketing performance metrics Marketing performance metrics are measures that tell us how well a business is performing in the market. (2)

marketing plan A written document that acts as a guidebook of marketing activities for the marketing manager. (2)

marketing planning Designing activities relating to marketing objectives and the changing marketing environment. (2)

marketing research The process of planning, collecting, and analyzing data relevant to a marketing decision. (7)

marketing research aggregator A company that acquires, catalogues, reformats, segments, and resells reports already published by marketing research firms. (7)

marketing research objective The specific information needed to solve a marketing research problem; the objective should be to provide insightful decision-making information. (7)

marketing research problem Determining what information is needed and how that information can be obtained efficiently and effectively. (7)

marketing strategy The activities of selecting and describing one or more target markets and developing and maintaining a marketing mix that will produce mutually satisfying exchanges with target markets. (2)

markup pricing The cost of buying the product from the producer plus amounts for profit and for expenses not otherwise accounted for. (16)

Maslow's hierarchy of needs A method of classifying human needs and motivations into five categories in ascending order of importance: physiological, safety, social, esteem, and self-actualization. (4)

mass communication The communication of a concept or message to large audiences. (13)

mass customization (build-to-order) A strategy that uses technology to deliver customized services on a mass basis; a production method whereby products are not made until an order is placed by the customer, and products are made according to customer specifications. (10)

mass merchandising A retailing strategy whereby retailers offer reduced service and moderate to low prices on large quantities of merchandise in order to stimulate high turnover of products. (12)

materials-handling system A method of moving inventory into, within, and out of the warehouse. (11)

materials requirement planning (MRP) (materials management) An inventory control system that manages the replenishment of raw materials, supplies, and components from the supplier to the manufacturer. (11)

maturity stage A period during which sales increase at a decreasing rate. (9)

MC *See* marginal cost.

measurement error An error that occurs when there is a difference between the information desired by the researcher and the information provided by the measurement process. (7)

media mix The combination of media to be used for a promotional campaign. (14)

media planning The series of decisions advertisers make regarding the selection and use of media, allowing the marketer to optimally and cost-effectively communicate the message to the target audience. (14)

media schedule Designation of the media, the specific publications or programs, and the insertion dates of advertising. (14)

medium The channel used to convey a message to a target market. (14)

merchant wholesaler Institution that buys goods from manufacturers and resells them to businesses, government agencies, and other wholesalers or retailers and that receives and takes title to goods, stores them in its own warehouses, and later ships them. (11)

metrics Standard measures that can be used repeatedly to assess performance on a supply chain–related process. (11)

mission statement A statement of the company's business based on a careful analysis of benefits sought by present and potential customers and analysis of existing and anticipated environmental conditions. (2)

modified rebuy A situation where the purchaser wants some change in the original good or service. (5)

morals The rules people develop as a result of cultural values and norms. (3)

motive A driving force that causes a person to take action to satisfy specific needs. (4)

MR *See* marginal revenue.

MRP *See* materials requirement planning.

multiculturalism When all major ethnic groups in an area—such as a city, county, or census metropolitan area—are roughly equally represented. (3)

multiplier effect (accelerator principle) Phenomenon in which a small increase or decrease in consumer demand can produce a much larger change in demand for the facilities and equipment needed to make the consumer product. (5)

multisegment targeting strategy A strategy that chooses two or more well-defined market segments and develops a distinct marketing mix for each. (6)

mystery shoppers Researchers posing as customers who gather observational data about a store. (7)

N

need recognition Result of an imbalance between actual and desired states. (4)

needs assessment A determination of the customer's specific needs and wants and the range of options the customer has for satisfying them. (15)

negotiation The process during which both the salesperson and the prospect offer special concessions in an attempt to arrive at a sales agreement. (15)

networking A process of finding out about potential clients from friends, business contacts, co-workers, acquaintances, and fellow members in professional and civic organizations. (15)

new buy A situation requiring the purchase of a product for the first time. (5)

new product A product new to the world, the market, the producer, the seller, or some combination of these. (9)

new-product strategy A plan that links the new-product development process with the objectives of the marketing department, the business unit, and the corporation. (9)

niche One segment of a market. (6)

niche competitive advantage The advantage achieved when a company seeks to target and serve effectively a small segment of the market. (2)

noise Anything that interferes with, distorts, or slows down the transmission of information. (13)

nonaspirational reference group A group with which an individual does not want to associate. (4)

noncorporate blogs Independent blogs that are not associated with the marketing efforts of any particular company or brand. (13)

noncumulative quantity discount A deduction from list price that applies to a single order rather than to the total volume of orders placed during a certain period. (17)

nonmarketing-controlled information source A product information source that is not associated with advertising or promotion. (4)

nonprobability sample Any sample in which little or no attempt is made to get a representative cross-section of the population. (7)

nonprofit organization An organization that exists to achieve some goal other than the usual business goals of profit, market share, or return on investment. (10)

nonprofit organization marketing The effort by nonprofit organizations to bring about mutually satisfying exchanges with target markets. (10)

nonresponse error An error that occurs when the sample that responds is different from the sample that was selected. (7)

nonselling tasks Salespeople need to maintain their appearance, their vehicles, their sales aids and materials, and also prepare their expense reports to perform effectively. (15)

nonstore retailing Shopping without visiting a store. (12)

norm A value or attitude deemed acceptable by a group. (4)

North American Industry Classification System (NAICS) A detailed numbering system developed by Canada, the United States, and Mexico to classify North American business establishments by their main production processes. (5)

O

observation research A research method that relies on three types of observation: people watching people, people watching an activity, and machines watching people. (7)

odd–even pricing (psychological pricing) A price tactic that uses odd-numbered prices to connote bargains and even-numbered prices to imply quality. (17)

off-price retailer A retailer that sells at prices 25 percent or more below traditional department store prices because it pays cash for its stock and usually doesn't ask for return privileges. (12)

one-to-one marketing An individualized marketing method that uses customer information to build long-term, personalized, and profitable relationships with each customer. (6)

on-line retailing A type of shopping available to consumers with personal computers and access to the Internet. (12)

open-ended question An interview question that encourages an answer phrased in the respondent's own words. (7)

opinion leader An individual who influences the opinions of others. (4)

optimizers Business customers who consider numerous suppliers, both familiar and unfamiliar, solicit bids, and study all proposals carefully before selecting one. (6)

order processing system A system whereby orders are entered into the supply chain and filled. (11)

original equipment manufacturer (OEM) A company that buys business goods, which it then incorporates into the products it produces for eventual sale to other producers or to consumers. (5)

outside expert sales forecast A sales forecast based on the opinions of expert people who follow an industry closely and report on it. (7)

outsourcing (contract logistics) A manufacturer's or supplier's use of an independent third party to manage an entire function of the logistics system, such as transportation, warehousing, or order processing. (11)

P

penetration pricing A pricing policy whereby a company charges a relatively low price for a product initially as a way to reach the mass market. (17)

perception The process by which people select, organize, and interpret stimuli into a meaningful and coherent picture. (4)

perceptual mapping A means of displaying or graphing, in two or more dimensions, the location of products, brands, or groups of products in customers' minds. (6)

perishability The inability of services to be stored, warehoused, or inventoried. (10)

personal selling A purchase situation in which two people communicate in an attempt to influence each other. (13)

personality A way of organizing and grouping the consistencies of an individual's reactions to situations. (4)

persuasive labelling A type of package labelling that focuses on a promotional theme or logo; consumer information is secondary. (8)

pioneering advertising A form of advertising designed to stimulate primary demand for a new product or product category. (14)

place of business A physical in-store location where consumers come to shop, or a nonstore location where consumers may shop using communications technologies. (12)

planned obsolescence The practice of modifying products so that those that have already been sold become obsolete before they actually need replacement. (8)

planning The process of anticipating future events and determining strategies to achieve organizational objectives in the future. (2)

PLC *See* product life cycle.

point-of-purchase (POP) display A promotional display set up at the retailer's location to build traffic, advertise the product, or induce impulse buying. (15)

point-of-sale interactions Communications between customers and organizations that occur at the point of sale, normally in a store. (18)

pop-up shop Temporary retail establishments that allow flexible locations without the long-term commitment of a more expensive retail lease. (12)

portfolio matrix A tool for allocating resources among products or SBUs on the basis of relative market share and market growth rate. (2)

position The place a product, brand, or group of products occupies in consumers' minds relative to competing offerings. (6)

positioning Developing a specific marketing mix to influence potential customers' overall perception of a brand, product line, or organization in general. (6)

preapproach A process that describes the "homework" that must be done by the salesperson before he or she contacts a prospect. (15)

predatory pricing The practice of charging a very low price for a product with the intent of driving competitors out of business or out of a market. (17)

predictive modelling A data manipulation technique in which marketers try to determine, based on some past set of occurrences, what the odds are that some other occurrence, such as a response or purchase, will take place in the future. (18)

premium An extra item offered to the consumer, usually in exchange for some proof of purchase of the promoted product. (15)

prestige pricing Charging a high price to help promote a high-quality image. (16)

price That which is given up in an exchange to acquire a good or service. (16)

price bundling Marketing two or more products in a single package for a special price. (17)

price equilibrium The price at which demand and supply are equal. (16)

price fixing An agreement between two or more companies on the price they will charge for a product. (17)

price lining The practice of offering a product line with several items at specific price points. (17)

price shading The use of discounts by salespeople to increase demand for one or more products in a line. (17)

price skimming A pricing policy whereby a company charges a high introductory price, often coupled with heavy promotion. (17)

price strategy A basic, long-term pricing framework that establishes the initial price for a product and the intended direction for price movements over the product life cycle. (17)

primary data Information collected for the first time. Can be used for solving the particular problem under investigation. (7)

primary membership group A reference group with which people interact regularly in an informal, face-to-face manner, such as family, friends, and fellow employees. (4)

private brand A brand name owned by a wholesaler or a retailer. (8)

private label brand A brand that is designed and developed using the retailer's name. (12)

probability sample A sample in which every element in the population has a known statistical likelihood of being selected. (7)

problem child (question mark) In the portfolio matrix, a business unit that shows rapid growth but poor profit margins. (2)

processed materials Products used directly in manufacturing other products. (5)

product Everything, both favourable and unfavourable, that a person receives in an exchange. (8)

product advertising A form of advertising that touts the benefits of a specific good or service. (14)

product category All brands that satisfy a particular type of need. (9)

product development A marketing strategy that entails the creation of marketable new products; the process of converting applications for new technologies into marketable products. (2, 9)

product differentiation A positioning strategy that some companies use to distinguish their products from those of competitors. (6)

product item A specific version of a product that can be designated as a distinct offering among an organization's products. (8)

product life cycle (PLC) A concept that provides a way to trace the stages of a product's acceptance, from its introduction (birth) to its decline (death). (9)

product line A group of closely related product items. (8)

product line depth The number of product items in a product line. (8)

product line extension Adding additional products to an existing product line in order to compete more broadly in the industry. (8)

product line pricing Setting prices for an entire line of products. (17)

product mix All products that an organization sells. (8)

product mix width The number of product lines an organization offers. (8)

product modification Changing one or more of a product's characteristics. (8)

product offering The mix of products offered to the consumer by the retailer; also called the *product assortment* or *merchandise mix*. (12)

product/service differentiation competitive advantage The provision of something that is unique and valuable to buyers beyond simply offering a lower price than the competition. (2)

production orientation A philosophy that focuses on the internal capabilities of the company rather than on the desires and needs of the marketplace. (1)

profit Revenue minus expenses. (16)

profit maximization A method of setting prices that occurs when marginal revenue equals marginal cost. (16)

promotion Communication by marketers that informs, persuades, and reminds potential buyers of a product in order to influence an opinion or elicit a response. (13)

promotional allowance (trade allowance) A payment to a dealer for promoting the manufacturer's products. (17)

promotional mix The combination of promotional tools, including advertising, public relations, personal selling, and sales promotion, used to reach the target market and fulfill the organization's overall goals. (13)

promotional strategy A plan for the optimal use of the elements of promotion: advertising, public relations, personal selling, and sales promotion. (13)

PSA *See* public service advertisement.

psychographic segmentation Market segmentation on the basis of personality, motives, lifestyles, and geodemographics. (6)

public relations The marketing function that evaluates public attitudes, identifies areas within the organization that the public may be interested in, and executes a program of action to earn public understanding and acceptance. (13)

public service advertisement (PSA) An announcement that promotes a program of a federal, provincial, or local government or of a not-for-profit organization. (10)

pull strategy A marketing strategy that stimulates consumer demand to obtain product distribution. (13)

pulsing media schedule A media scheduling strategy that uses continuous scheduling throughout the year coupled with a flighted schedule during the best sales periods. (14)

purchasing power A comparison of income versus the relative cost of a set standard of goods and services in different geographic areas. (3)

push money Money offered to channel intermediaries to encourage them to "push" products, that is, to encourage other members of the channel to sell the products. (15)

push strategy A marketing strategy that uses aggressive personal selling and trade advertising to convince a wholesaler or a retailer to carry and sell particular merchandise. (13)

pyramid of corporate social responsibility A model that suggests that corporate social responsibility is composed of economic, legal, ethical, and philanthropic responsibilities and that the company's economic performance supports the entire structure. (3)

Q

quantity discount A price reduction offered for buying in multiple units or above a specified dollar amount. (17)

quota A statement of the individual salesperson's sales objectives, usually based on sales volume alone but sometimes including key accounts (those with greatest potential), new accounts, repeat sales, and specific products. (15)

R

random error An error that occurs when the selected sample is an imperfect representation of the overall population. (7)

random sample A sample arranged in such a way that every element of the population has an equal chance of being selected as part of the sample. (7)

raw materials Unprocessed extractive or agricultural products, such as mineral ore, lumber, wheat, corn, fruits, vegetables, and fish. (5)

reach The number of target consumers exposed to a commercial at least once during a specific period, usually four weeks. (14)

real self-image The way an individual actually perceives himself or herself. (4)

rebate A cash refund given for the purchase of a product during a specific period. (15, 17)

receiver The person who decodes a message. (13)

recency–frequency–monetary analysis (RFM) A data manipulation technique that determines the company's best customers by identifying those customers who have purchased most recently, most frequently, and who have spent the most money. (18)

recession A period of economic activity characterized by negative growth, which reduces demand for goods and services. (3)

reciprocity A practice where business purchasers choose to buy from their own customers. (5)

reference group A group in society that influences an individual's purchasing behaviour. (4)

referral A recommendation to a salesperson from a customer or business associate. (15)

reintermediation The reintroduction of an intermediary between producers and users. (5)

relationship commitment A firm's belief that an ongoing relationship with another firm is so important that the relationship warrants maximum efforts at maintaining it indefinitely. (5)

relationship marketing A strategy that entails forging long-term partnerships with customers. (1)

relationship selling (consultative selling) A sales practice that involves building, maintaining, and enhancing interactions with customers in order to develop long-term satisfaction

through mutually beneficial partnerships. (15)

reliability The ability to perform a service dependably, accurately, and consistently. (10)

repositioning Changing consumers' perceptions of a brand in relation to competing brands. (6)

resale price maintenance Relates to laws that prohibit manufacturers from controlling prices at the retail level. (17)

research-based sales forecasting methods Research methods that use primary data as the basis of their sales forecasting information. (7)

research design Specifies which research questions must be answered, how and when the data will be gathered, and how the data will be analyzed. (7)

response list A customer list that includes the names and addresses of individuals who have responded to an offer of some kind, such as through mail, telephone, direct-response TV, product rebates, contests or sweepstakes, or billing inserts. (18)

responsiveness The ability to provide prompt service. (10)

retailer A channel intermediary that sells mainly to consumers. (11)

retailing All the activities directly related to the sale of goods and services to the ultimate consumer for personal, nonbusiness use. (12)

retailing mix A combination of the six P's—product, place, promotion, price, presentation, and personnel—to sell goods and services to the ultimate consumer. (12)

return on investment (ROI) Net profit after taxes divided by total assets. (16)

revenue The price charged to customers multiplied by the number of units sold. (16)

RFM *See* recency–frequency–monetary analysis.

ROI *See* return on investment.

routine response behaviour The type of decision making exhibited by consumers buying frequently purchased, low-cost goods and services; requires little search and decision time. (4)

S

sales force survey A sales forecast based on the combined estimates of sales provided by a firm's sales force. (7)

sales forecasts An estimate of a firm's sales for a specific product or service to a specific market over a specific period of time. (7)

sales orientation The idea that people will buy more goods and services if aggressive sales techniques are used and that high sales result in high profits. (1)

sales presentation A formal meeting in which the salesperson presents a sales proposal to a prospective buyer. (15)

sales process (sales cycle) The set of steps a salesperson goes through in a particular organization to sell a particular product or service. (15)

sales promotion Marketing activities, other than personal selling, advertising, and public relations, which stimulate consumer buying and dealer effectiveness. (13, 15)

sales proposal A formal written document or professional presentation that outlines how the salesperson's product or service will meet or exceed the prospect's needs. (15)

sample A subset from a large population. (7)

sampling A promotional program that allows the consumer the opportunity to try a product or service for free. (15)

sampling error An error that occurs when a sample somehow does not represent the target population. (7)

satisficers Business customers who place an order with the first familiar supplier to satisfy product and delivery requirements. (6)

scaled-response question A closed-ended question designed to measure the intensity of a respondent's answer. (7)

scanner-based research A system for gathering information from a single group of respondents by continuously monitoring the advertising, promotion, and pricing they are exposed to and the things they buy. (7)

scrambled merchandising The tendency to offer a wide variety of nontraditional goods and services under one roof. (12)

screening The first filter in the product development process; it eliminates ideas that are inconsistent with the organization's new-product strategy or are obviously inappropriate for some other reason. (9)

search quality A characteristic that can be easily assessed before purchase. (10)

seasonal discount A price reduction for buying merchandise out of season. (17)

seasonal media schedule A media scheduling strategy that runs advertising only during times of the year when the product is most likely to be used. (14)

secondary data Data previously collected for any purpose other than the one at hand. (7)

secondary membership group A reference group with which people associate less consistently and more formally than a primary membership group, such as a club, professional group, or religious group. (4)

secured sockets layer (SSL) A protocol that transmits communications via the Internet in an encrypted format. SSL ensures that the information is sent, unchanged, to the server you intended to send it to. (web 19)

segmentation bases (variables) Characteristics of individuals, groups, or organizations. (6)

selective distortion A process whereby a consumer changes or distorts information that conflicts with his or her feelings or beliefs. (4)

selective distribution A form of distribution achieved by screening dealers to eliminate all but a few in any single area. (11)

selective exposure The process by which a consumer notices certain stimuli and ignores others. (4)

selective retention A process whereby a consumer remembers only that information which supports his or her personal beliefs. (4)

self-concept How consumers perceive themselves in terms of attitudes, perceptions, beliefs, and self-evaluations. (4)

self-regulation Programs voluntarily adopted by business groups to regulate the activities of their members. (3)

selling against the brand Stocking well-known branded items at high prices in order to sell store brands at discounted prices. (16)

sender The originator of the message in the communication process. (13)

service The result of applying human or mechanical efforts to people or objects. (10)

service mark A trademark for a service. (8)

shopping product A product that requires comparison shopping because it is usually more expensive than a convenience product and is found in fewer stores. (8)

simulated (laboratory) market testing The presentation of advertising and other promotion materials for several products, including a test product, to members of the product's target market. (9)

simulation sales forecasting Building and using a computer simulation model of a company and its industry to estimate future sales. (7)

simultaneous product development A team-oriented approach to new-product development. (9)

single-price tactic A price tactic that offers all goods and services at the same price (or perhaps two or three prices). (17)

social class A group of people in a society who are considered nearly equal in status or community esteem, who regularly socialize among themselves both formally and informally, and who share behavioural norms. (4)

socialization process How cultural values and norms are passed down to children. (4)

societal marketing orientation The idea that an organization exists not only to satisfy customer wants and needs and to meet organizational objectives but also to preserve or enhance individuals' and society's long-term best interests. (1)

spatial discrepancy The difference between the location of the producer and the location of widely scattered markets. (11)

specialty discount store A retail store that offers a nearly complete selection of single-line merchandise and uses self-service, discount prices, high volume, and high turnover. (12)

specialty product A particular item for which consumers search extensively and for which they are very reluctant to accept substitutes. (8)

specialty store A retail store specializing in a given type of merchandise. (12)

sponsorship When a company spends money to support an issue, cause, or event that is consistent with corporate objectives, such as improving brand awareness or enhancing corporate image. (14)

star In the portfolio matrix, a business unit that is a fast-growing market leader. (2)

status quo pricing A pricing objective that maintains existing prices or meets the competition's prices. (16)

stickiness A measure of a website's effectiveness calculated by multiplying the frequency of visits times the duration of a visit times the number of pages viewed during each visit (site reach). (5, web 19)

stimulus Any unit of input affecting one or more of the five senses: sight, smell, taste, touch, hearing. (4)

stimulus discrimination A learned ability to differentiate among similar products. (4)

stimulus generalization A form of learning that occurs when one response is extended to a second stimulus similar to the first. (4)

straight commission A method of compensation in which the salesperson is paid some percentage when a sale is made. (15)

straight rebuy A situation in which the purchaser reorders the same goods or services without looking for new information or investigating other suppliers. (5)

straight salary A method of compensation in which the salesperson receives a salary regardless of sales productivity. (15)

strategic alliance (strategic partnership) A cooperative agreement between business companies. (5)

strategic business unit (SBU) A subgroup of a single business or collection of related businesses within the larger organization. (2)

strategic channel alliance A cooperative agreement between business companies to use the other's already established distribution channel. (11)

strategic planning The managerial process of creating and maintaining a fit between the organization's objectives and resources and evolving market opportunities. (2)

subculture A homogeneous group of people who share elements of the overall culture as well as unique elements of their own group. (4)

supercentre A retail store that combines groceries and general merchandise goods with a wide range of services. (12)

supermarket A large, departmentalized, self-service retailer that specializes in food and nonfood items. (12)

supplementary services A group of services that support or enhance the core service. (10)

supplies Consumable items that do not become part of the final product. (5)

supply The quantity of a product that will be offered to the market by a supplier at various prices for a specified period. (16)

supply chain The connected chain of all the business entities, both internal and external to the company, that perform or support the logistics function. (11)

supply chain management A management system that coordinates and integrates all the activities performed by supply chain members into a seamless process, from the source to the point of consumption, resulting in enhanced customer and economic value. (11)

supply chain team An entire group of individuals who orchestrate the movement of goods, services, and information from the source to the consumer. (11)

survey research The most popular technique for gathering primary data; a researcher interacts with people to obtain facts, opinions, and attitudes. (7)

sustainability The idea that socially responsible companies will outperform their peers by focusing on the world's social problems, viewing them as opportunities to build profits and help the world at the same time. (3)

sustainable competitive advantage An advantage that cannot be copied by the competition. (2)

SWOT analysis Identifying internal strengths (S) and weaknesses (W) and also examining external opportunities (O) and threats (T). (2)

T

tangibles The physical evidence of a service, including the physical facilities, tools, and equipment used to provide the service. (10)

target market A defined group most likely to buy a company's products; a group of people or organizations for which an organization designs, implements, and maintains a marketing mix intended to meet the needs of that group, resulting in mutually satisfying exchanges. (3, 6)

teamwork Collaborative efforts of people to accomplish common objectives. (1)

teens With some overlap, those between tweens and Generation Y, roughly 13 to 19 years of age. (3)

telemarketing The use of the telephone to sell directly to consumers. (12)

temporal discrepancy When a product is produced but a customer is not ready to buy it. (11)

test marketing The limited introduction of a product and a marketing program to determine the reactions of potential customers in a market situation. (9)

test market sales forecasting Occurs when a firm introduces some new aspect of its marketing strategy into a limited market to gauge the behavioural response of customers. (7)

time series analysis forecasting Estimating future sales while accounting for changes in key economic variables over time. (7)

touch point All possible areas of a business where customers communicate with that business. (18)

trade allowance A price reduction offered by manufacturers to

intermediaries, such as wholesalers and retailers. (15)

trade sales promotion Sales promotion activities targeting a channel member, such as a wholesaler or retailer. (15)

trademark The exclusive right to use a brand or part of a brand. (8)

trend analysis forecasting Estimating future sales based on past sales. (7)

trust The condition that exists when one party has confidence in an exchange partner's reliability and integrity. (5)

tweens Pre-and early adolescents, ages 9 to 14. (3)

two-part pricing A price tactic that charges two separate amounts to consume a single good or service. (17)

U

unbundling Reducing the bundle of services that comes with the basic product. (17)

undifferentiated targeting strategy Marketing approach that views the market as one big market with no individual segments and thus requires a single marketing mix. (6)

uniform delivered pricing A price tactic in which the seller pays the actual freight charges and bills every purchaser an identical, flat freight charge. (17)

unique selling proposition A desirable, exclusive, and believable advertising appeal selected as the theme for a campaign. (14)

unitary elasticity A situation in which total revenue remains the same when prices change. (16)

universal product codes (UPCs, bar code) Series of thick and thin vertical lines, readable by computerized optical scanners, that represent numbers used to track products. (8)

universe The population from which a sample will be drawn. (7)

unsought product A product unknown to the potential buyer or a known product that the buyer does not actively seek. (8)

untargeted e-mail marketing (spam) A mass e-mailing sent to unqualified e-mail addresses. (web 19)

UPCs *See* universal product codes.

usage-rate segmentation Dividing a market by the amount of product bought or consumed. (6)

V

value The enduring belief that a specific mode of conduct is personally or socially preferable to another mode of conduct. (4)

value-based pricing Setting the price at a level that seems to the customer to be a good price compared to the prices of other options. (17)

variable cost A cost that varies with changes in the level of output. (16)

vertical conflict A channel conflict that occurs between different levels in a marketing channel, most typically between the manufacturer and wholesaler or between the manufacturer and retailer. (11)

viral marketing Marketers encourage their customers to send personal messages to their friends as the Internet's version of word-of-mouth referrals. (web 19)

visible minority Persons, other than Aboriginal peoples, who are non-Caucasian in race and non-white in colour. (3)

W

want Recognition of an unfulfilled need and a product that will satisfy it. (4)

warehouse membership club A limited-service merchant wholesaler that sells a limited selection of brand-name appliances, household items, and groceries on a cash-and-carry basis to members, usually small businesses and groups. (12)

warranty A confirmation of the quality or performance of a good or service. (8)

Web community A carefully selected group of consumers who agree to participate in an ongoing dialogue with a particular corporation. (7)

Web-based interactions Communications between customers and organizations using Web vehicles. (18)

Y

yield management systems (YMS) A technique for adjusting prices that uses complex mathematical software to profitably fill unused capacity by discounting early purchases, limiting early sales at these discounted prices, and overbooking capacity. (16)

Z

zone pricing A modification of uniform delivered pricing that divides the country (or the total market) into segments or zones and charges a flat freight rate to all customers in a given zone. (17)

CHAPTER 1

1. Hollie Shaw, "Tim Hortons Looks to Go Global," *The Windsor Star*, May 15, 2010, A16; Hollie Shaw, "Staying Fresh with Smart Marketing," *Financial Post*, March 1, 2006, FP3; "Breakfast Sandwich Heats Up Tims Quarterly Sales," *Globe and Mail*, January 6, 2007, B6; www.timhortons.com.

2. "Glossary of Definitions," www.marketingpower.com/index, July 2006.

3. Philip Kotler and Kevin Keller, *Marketing Management*, 13th ed. (Upper Saddle River, NJ: Prentice-Hall, 2009), 12.

4. Geoff Kirbyson, "City Candy Firm Signs National Retail Deals: Clodhoppers to Appear in Video Outlets," *Winnipeg Free Press*, March 21, 2003, B1; www.kraves.com.

5. Woody Driggs, "Serving up Customer Delight," *Customer Relationship Management*, April 2008, 14.

6. Rekha Balu, "Listen Up," *Fast Company*, May 2000, 312.

7. Marc Gunther, "Coca-Cola's Green Crusader," *Fortune*, April 28, 2008, 150.

8. "Molson Coors Enters Russia with Coors Light," "Molson Coors-Si'Hai Beer Company Launches in China," and "Molson Coors Acquires Majority Stake in New Joint Venture with Si'Hai Beer Company of China," www.molsoncoors.com, accessed October 1, 2010.

9. Robert Bibb and Eric Gehm, "The 360-Degree View," *Customer Relationship Management*, June 2001, 23–24.

10. "Ask Yourself, What the Hell Really Works Here?" *Fast Company*, May 2001, 82.

11. "Many Companies Not Working to Earn Loyalty," *Quirk's Marketing Research Review*, October 2008, 80.

12. Jeffrey M. O-Brien, "A Perfect Season," *Fortune*, February 4, 2008, 61–66.

13. Robert Levering and Milton Moskowitz, "The 100 Best Companies to Work For," *Fortune*, January 20, 2006, 127–52.

14. A. G. Lafley and Rom Charan, "The Consumer Is Boss," *Fortune*, March 17, 2008, 122.

15. Don Steinberg, "Just Play," *Inc. Magazine*, October 2008, 124–34; Ethan Smith, Yutari Iwatani Kane, and Sam Schechner, "Beatles Tunes Join Rock Band Game," *Wall Street Journal*, October 30, 2008, B3; Dan Gallagher, "Is 'Guitar Hero' Hitting Its Peak?" *Market Watch*, December 12, 2008, 12; and http://www.harmonixmusic.com.

16. CBC, *Venture*, "Wormboy," broadcast February 6, 2005; Cindy Rovins, "Getting into the Big Box: By Thinking Outside the Box," *In Business*, January/February 2007, 14–16; Jessica Damiano, "Product Review: Worm Poop," Newsday.com, April 3, 2007; Daphne Gordon, "Recycled Bottles Are Perfect Packaging for Organic Fertilizer," *Toronto Star*, February 4, 2006, A17; "Worm Your Way to Healthy Products," *Good Times*, April 2007, 20; "Worm Poop: The Fertilizer of Choice," *Barrie Life and Times*, August 9, 2006, 25; www.terracycle.net.

CHAPTER 2

1. Scott Anderson, "Rona Aims for 10–15% EPS Growth," *Financial Post* (www.financialpost.com/markets/news-releases/story.html?id=2482458), January 25, 2010; Eric Lam, "Rona Improves Q1 Sales and Profits," *Financial Post*, May 12, 2010, 23; Hollie Shaw, "Rona Targets 'Do-It-for-Me' Consumers," *Financial Post*, February 21, 2006, FP1, FP3; Marina Strauss, "Rona Could Ask: Do You Want Gas with Those Nails?" *Globe and Mail*, August 10, 2006, B3; www.rona.ca; www.homedepot.ca.

2. Kate Maddox, "Marketer of the Year: Dan Henson, VP-CMO, General Electric, Co.," *BtoB's Best*, October 22, 2007.

3. Joseph Pereira, "Toys 'R' Us Unwraps Plans for Expansion," *Wall Street Journal*, May 22, 2008, B1.

4. Bertrand Marotte, "Coutu's Deal for Eckerd Stores Vaults Chain into the Top Ranks," *Globe and Mail*, April 6, 2004, B1, B16.

5. Marina Strauss, "Low Frills, High Stakes," *Globe and Mail*, May 12, 2010, B1, B5.

6. www.norco.com/profile/index.htm.

7. www.nike.com, May 14, 2010.

8. Store review, Bass Pro Shops, flyfishingabout.com, December 1, 2008.

9. Khanh T. L. Tran, "Nike Puts Its Swoosh on MP3 Players, Walkie-Talkies, Heart Monitors," *Wall Street Journal*, May 10, 2008, B1, B4.

10. Niraj Sherth, "India Liquor, Tobacco Firms Shift Tack," *Wall Street Journal*, May 6, 2008, B8; Kounteya Sinha, "Surrogate Ads Luring Kids to Smoking: Study," epaper.timesofindia.com, December 1, 2008; "Surrogate Ads Will Be Stopped, Assures I&B," timesofindia.indiatimes.com, December 1, 2008.

11. Richard Siklos, "Bob Iger Rocks Disney," *Fortune*, January 19, 2009, 80–86; Peter Sanders, "Disney Focuses on Boys," *Wall Street Journal*, January 8, 2009, A3; http://disney.go.com (accessed on May 15, 2010).

12. CBC, *Venture*, "Town Doctor: Welcome to Tofino," broadcast February 20, 2005; CBC, *Venture*, "PEI Meets Doug Hall," broadcast March 13, 2001; www.island.net/~whales/; www.tofinobusiness.com; www.cavendishfigurines.com; www.eurekaranch.com; www.gov.pe.ca/business/; www.islandwindcraft.com.

CHAPTER 3

1. Marina Strauss, "Low Frills, High Stakes," *Globe and Mail*, May 12, 2010, B1, B5: Marina Strauss, "Grocers Developing Appetite for Ethnic Market," *Globe and Mail*, April 5, 2004, B1, B6; Aparita Bhandari, "Ethnic Marketing—It's More Than Skin Deep," *Globe and Mail*, September 7, 2005, B3; Andy Mukherjee, "Halal Finally Spotted on the Radar Screen," *Globe and Mail*, August 11, 2006, B6.

2. Marc Gunther, "Tree Huggers, Soy Lovers, and Profits," *Fortune*, June 23, 2003, 98–104.

3. John Carey, "Big Strides to Become the Jolly Green Giant," *Business Week*, January 29, 2009, 57.

4. "Globally, Companies Are Giving Back," *HR Magazine*, June 1, 2007, 30.

5. This section is adapted from Archie B. Carroll, "The Pyramid of Corporate Social Responsibility: Toward the Moral Management of Organizational Stakeholders," *Business Horizons*, July–August 1991, 39–48; see also Kirk Davidson, "Marketers Must Accept Greater Responsibilities," *Marketing News*, February 2, 1998, 6.

6. www.wm.com (accessed May 18, 2010).

7. Gunther, 104.

8. Konrad Yakabuski, "Bombardier's New Image Problem," *Globe and Mail*, June 29, 2005, B4; Bertrand Marotte, "Bombardier Lands Big Order in China," *Globe and Mail*, November 7, 2006; www.studentsforafreetibet.org;

www.actionnetwork.org; www.savetibet.org; www.bombardieroutoftibet.org.

9. "Actions Contributing Most to Ethical Behavior and Compliance Identified," *Workspan*, February 1, 2007, 1; Anusorn Singhapakdi, Skott Vitell, and Kenneth Kraft, "Moral Intensity and Ethical Decisionmaking of Marketing Professionals," *Journal of Business Research*, March 1996, 245–55; Thomas Dunfee, Craig Smith, and William T. Ross, Jr., "Social Contracts and Marketing Ethics," *Journal of Marketing*, July 1999, 14–32; Jay Handleman and Stephen Arnold, "The Role of Marketing Actions with a Social Dimension: Appeals to the Institutional Environment," *Journal of Marketing*, July 1999, 33–48; and David Turnipseed, "Are Good Soldiers Good? Exploring the Link between Organizational Citizenship Behavior and Personal Ethics," *Journal of Business Research*, January 2002, 1–16.

10. O. C. Ferrell, Debbie Thorne, and Linda Ferrell, "Legal Pressure for Ethical Compliance in Marketing," *Proceedings of the American Marketing Association*, Summer 2005, 412–13.

11. Kerry Capell, "Thinking Simple at Philips," *Business Week*, December 11, 2006, 50.

12. "Tech Companies Try Wooing Women with Girlie Marketing," *Wall Street Journal*, August 26, 2003, B1, B4.

13. Norma Ramage, "Mark's Keeps an Eye on the Ladies," *Marketing Magazine*, February 10, 2003, 2.

14. Elisabeth A. Sullivan, "HOG-Harley-Davidson Shows Brand Strength As It Navigates Down New Roads—and Picks Up More Female Riders Along the Way," *Marketing News*, November 1, 2008, 8.

15. "Targeting Tweens," *Chain Store Age*, July 1, 2007; Statistics Canada, *Population by Sex and Age Group*, CANSIM, table 051-0001, December 30, 2009.

16. "Literal Fitness for Kids," *Brandweek*, September 24, 2007, 16; "Spas for Pre-Tween Set: More Businesses Are Offering Pampered-Treatment Packages for Kids," *Vancouver Sun*, October 30, 2006, C3.

17. "Understanding Tweens and Teens," *Youth Market Alert*, August 1, 2007, 7; "EPM Offers Advice for Marketing to Tweens and Teens," *Research Alert*, June 1, 2007, 5; Statistics Canada, *Population by Sex and Age Group*, CANSIM, table 051-0001, December 30, 2009.

18. "Teens Prefer Real Friends to Online Ones," *Quirk's Marketing Research Review*, August 2008, 6.

19. Linda Morten, "Targeting Generation Y," *Public Relations Quarterly*, Summer 2002, 46–49.

20. Hollie Shaw, "Serving Generation Y," *National Post*, April 1, 2006, FP9.

21. "'Gen Y' Fave," *Brandweek*, July 28, 2008, 13.

22. "Gen Xers and Their Concerns Are Reshaping the Retail Landscape,"

Montreal Gazette, June 13, 2007, B1; "Gen X Slackers Get Serious," *Brandweek*, June 30, 2008, 8.

23. "The Changing Face of Boomers," *Advertising Age*, July 7, 2008, 1, 10; www.vespa-canada.ca; www.piaggio-canada.ca.

24. Dick Chay, "New Segments of Boomers Reveal New Marketing Implications," *Marketing News*, March 14, 2005, 24.

25. Howard Willens and Leslie Harris, "The Mature Market . . . Is It for Real?" *Quirk's Marketing Research Review*, May 2001, 40–43.

26. Statistics Canada, *Population Projections of Visible Minority Groups, Canada, Provinces and Regions*, Catalogue no. 91-541-XIE, www.statcan.gc.ca/, July 2006.

27. Dalson Chen and Chris Thompson, "City's Visible Minorities to Rise Rapidly," *Windsor Star*, March 10, 2010, A1, A4; "The Numbers Behind Multicultural Marketing in Canada," *Marketing*, Cultural Diversity in Canada Supplement, May 2006, 9.

28. "Bringing Harmony to Multicultural Marketing," *Marketing*, Cultural Diversity in Canada Supplement, May 2006, 8.

29. Bob Meyer, "Local Supermarket Caters to the World," *Windsor Star*, April 19, 2004, C9.

30. Andre Mayer, "New Magazine Will Focus on Asian Women," *Globe and Mail*, August 6, 2003, B9.

31. "Making Multicultural Work," *Marketing*, Cultural Diversity in Canada Supplement, May 2006, 5; "The Web Goes Multicultural," *Advertising Age*, November 29, 1999, 51, 54.

32. "Creating the Digital Dividend," *Business2.com*, March 6, 2001, 60.

33. Canadian Statistics, *Economic Indicators— Canada*, www.statcan.gc.ca/.

34. Statistics Canada, CANSIM, table 111-0009, *Median Total Income, by Family Type, by Provinces and Territory*, May 2010, www.statcan.gc.ca/.

35. Canadian Statistics, *Economic Indicators–Canada*, www.statcan.gc.ca/.

36. Ibid.

37. RE$EARCH Infosource Inc., *Canada's Top 100 R&D Spenders 2009*, www.researchinfosource.com.

38. "Masters of Innovation," *Business Week 50*, Spring 2001, 162.

39. Stacy Perman, "Automate or Die," www.ecompany.com, July 2007, 60–67.

40. "Yes, Innovations Do Pay Off, Study Finds," *International Herald Tribune*, August 30–31, 2008, 15.

41. Brent Jang, "CanJet Blames Rivals for Its Demise," *Globe and Mail*, September 7, 2006, B8.

42. "KC, P&G's Lotion Tissue War Is Nothing to Sneeze At," *Brandweek*, September 18, 2008, 12–13.

43. Katrina Brooker, "A Game of Inches," *Fortune*, February 5, 2001, 98–100; www.pg.com; Procter & Gamble 2009 Annual Report.

44. "Starbucks Targets Growing China Market," *AsiaPulse News*, June 13, 2006;

Jeffrey S. Harrison, "Exporting a North American Concept to Asia," *Cornell Hotel & Restaurant Quarterly*, May 2007; Dexter Roberts, "Starbucks, Caffeinates Its China Growth Plan," *Business Week Online*, October 26, 2006.

45. Erica Johnson, "Bringing up Brainy: A Look at the Educational Toy Market," *CBC Marketplace*, broadcast January 16, 2005; www.commercialfreechildhood.org; www.babyeinstein.com; www.brainybaby.com; www.geniusproducts.com; Wendy Melillo, "Advocacy Group Targets Baby Einstein," *Adweek.Com*, May 1, 2006; Timothy Noah, "Baby Einstein Replies," *Slate.com*, January 31, 2007; Barbara Meltz, "Baby Videos Denounced over Ads," *International Herald Tribune Business*, May 2, 2006 (www.iht.com).

END OF PART 1 CASES

1. "Beneath the Skin," *Brand Strategy*, May 2008, 20–23; Jack Neff, "Retouching Ruckus Leaves Dove Flailing," *Advertising Age*, May 12, 2008, 1, 53; "Dove (D)evolution," *Business Week*, November 12, 2007; www.unilever.ca; Keith McArthur, "Advertising to Women Gains Super Yardage," *Globe and Mail*, February 7, 2006, B3, www.statcan.gc.ca/.

2. Shireen Dean "Don't Be Fooled," www.greenwashing.net, March 12, 2009; "Going Green," www.thrall.org/special/goinggreen.html, March 12, 2009; www.cutco.com.

CHAPTER 4

1. Rebecca Harris, "Bagging a Winner," *Marketing Magazine*, March 23, 2009, 34–35.

2. Maria Zain, "Ikea Ignites Desire through Ideas," January 30, 2008, http://corporate-marketing-branding .suite101.com/article.cfm/ikea_ignites_ desire_through_ideas, accessed February 3, 2010.

3. "iPhone," www.apple.ca, accessed February 3, 2010.

4. Suzanne Bidlake, "P&G to Roll Laundry Tablet in Europe," *Advertising Age*, March 1, 1999, 18.

5. Kristin Laird, "Marketers Plan to Get Social in 2009," *Marketing Magazine*, December 13, 2008.

6. Charles Zamaria and Fred Fletcher, "Canada Online: Year 2 Report 2007," *Canadian Internet Project*, www.ciponline.ca, accessed February 3, 2010; and Miniwatts Marketing Group, *Internet World Stats*, www .internetworldstats.com, accessed February 3, 2010.

7. Allen Weiss, Nicholas Lurie, and Deborah MacInnis, "Listening to Strangers: Whose Responses Are Valuable, How Valuable Are They, and Why?" *Journal of Marketing Research*, August 2008, 450–61.

8. Jean-Marc Leger and Dave Scholz, "Advertising Avalanche," *Marketing Magazine*, November 11, 2002, 25–26.

9. Associated Press and Marketing Staff, "Toyota Launches Ad Blitz to Reassure Customers ," *Marketing Magazine*, February 1, 2010; Chris Vander Doelen, "Toyota's Recall Nightmare," *Windsor Star*, February 2, 2010, A3.

10. Ernest Beck, "Boosting Diageo's Spirits," *Wall Street Journal*, February 23, 2001, B1.

11. *Canadian Driver*, "2010 Buyers Guide," www.canadiandriver.com/newcarbuyersguide?modelyear=2010, accessed February 4, 2010; and "2003 Buyers' Guide," *Carguide*, February 2003.

12. Jonah Berger and Grainne Fitzsimons, "Dogs on the Street, Pumas on Your Feet: How Cues in the Environment Influence Product Evaluation and Choice," *Journal of Marketing Research*, August 2008, 450–61.

13. Virgin corporate websitewww.virgin.com, accessed February 4, 2010.

14. Jeffrey Inman and Russell Winer, "Impulse Buys," *Wall Street Journal*, April 15, 1999, A1; David Silvera, Anne Lavack, and Fredric Kropp, "Impulse Buying: The Role of Affect, Social Influence, and Subjective Well-Being," *Journal of Consumer Research*, 25(1) (2008), 23–33.

15. Associated Press, "Customer satisfaction scores improve for Detroit Three," *Marketing Magazine*, August 18, 2009. Online: http://www.marketingmag.ca/english/news/marketer/article.jsp?content=20090818_140053_5480. Used with permission of The Associated Press. Copyright © 2010. All rights reserved.

16. Princeton Research Survey Associates, "Consumer Behavior, Experiences, and Attitudes: A Comparison by Age Groups," *AARP*, March 1999.

17. Amy Goldwasser, "What Is the Good Life? An A–Z Guide to Living Large," *Inc.*, October 2003, 71.

18. Zappos.com website, www.zappos.com, accessed March 18, 2010.

19. Paula Andruss, "Delivering Wow Through Service," *Marketing News*, October 15, 2008, 10.

20. Hyundai Canada website, http://hyundaicanada.com/Pages/About/Awards.aspx, accessed February 4, 2010.

21. www.heinz.com/health-wellness/focus-foods/dietary-preferences.aspx#diet, accessed February 4, 2010; Stephanie Thompson, "Marketers Embrace Latest Health Claims," *Advertising Age*, February 28, 2000, 20–22.

22. Soya World Inc. website, www.soyaworld.com, accessed February 4, 2010.

23. Statistics Canada, "Canada's Ethnocultural Mosaic, 2006 Census: National Picture," www.statcan.gc.ca, accessed February 4, 2010.

24. Chris Daniels, "The Slumdog Effect," *Marketing Magazine*, March 23, 2009, 39–40.

25. Graham Watt, "History and the Canadian Way," *Marketing Magazine*, May 1, 1995, 8.

26. Innovative Research Group, the Dominion Institute, and the *National Post*, "Canadians' Values Similar to Other Advanced Democracies," The Canadian Values Study, September 28, 2005, www.innovativeresearch.ca/Canadian%20Values%20Study_Factum%20280905.pdf, accessed February 4, 2010.

27. Citizenship and Immigration Canada, "Welcome to Canada: What You Should Know," Citizenship and Immigration Canada website, www.cic.gc.ca/english/resources/publications/welcome/wel-17e.aspwww.cic.gc.ca, accessed February 5, 2010.

28. Elliott Ettenberg, "Les Blokes Canadiens," *Marketing Magazine*, March 13, 1995, 8; "A Common Border Does Not Mean Shared Values," *Marketing Magazine*, January 25, 1993, 3.

29. Jack Bensimon, "Big Differences in Small Towns," *Marketing Magazine*, January 12, 2009, 35.

30. Statistics Canada, "Languages," Statistics Canada website, www41.statcan.gc.ca/2008/50000/ceb50000_000-eng.htm, accessed February 6, 2010; Eric Blais as quoted in Matt Semansky, "Plus Ca Change," *Marketing Magazine*, October 27, 2008, 24.

31. Statistics Canada, "Aboriginal Peoples," Statistics Canada website, www41.statcan.gc.ca/2008/10000/ceb10000_000-eng.htm, accessed Feb 6, 2010; TD Economics, "Aboriginal Peoples in Canada," www.td.com/economics/special/db0609_aboriginal.pdf, accessed February 6, 2010.

32. Statistics Canada, "Ethnic Diversity and Immigration," Statistics Canada website, www41.statcan.gc.ca/2008/30000/ceb30000_000-eng.htm, accessed, February 6, 2010.

33. Ibid.

34. Canadian Media Directors' Council, "*Media Digest*, 09/10," *Marketing Magazine*, 15.

35. Ibid., p. 25; Matt Semansky, "Pink Triangle Makes Fabulous Purchase," *Marketing Magazine*, February 8, 2008; Rogers Magazine Service, www.rogersmagazineservice.com, accessed February 6, 2010.

36. Rebecca Piirto Heath, "Life on Easy Street," *American Demographics*, April 1997.

37. Most Expensive Cars in the World: Top 10 List 2009–2010, www.thesupercars.org/top-cars/most-expensive-cars-in-the-world-top-10-list-2007-2008/ accessed February 7, 2010; Top Ten Most Expensive Pens in the World, 2009, www.moleskinerie.com/2009/09/top-10-most-expensive-pens-in-the-world.html, accessed February 7, 2010.

38. Elia Kacapyr, "Are You Middle Class?" *American Demographics*, October 1996.

39. Rebecca Piirto Heath, "The New Working Class," *American Demographics*, January 1998, 51–55.

40. Suein L. Hwang, "Dot-Coms Head Down-Market for Dollars," *Wall Street Journal*, July 16, 2001, B1.

41. Eve Lazarus, "Tourism BC Wants Mexicans To Go Downhill," *Marketing Magazine*, February 5, 2008.

42. Mike Farrell, "Statsthought 7.1," *Strategy*, June 2009, p. 22; *Ping*, Youthography website, www.youthography.com, accessed February 8, 2010.

43. Ronald Clark, James Zboja, and Ronald Goldsmith, "Status Consumption and Role Relaxed Consumption: A Tale of Two Retail Consumers," *Journal of Retailing and Consumer Services*, January 2007, 45–59.

44. Matt Haig, "Teenage Clicks," *The Guardian*, October 25, 2001, 46.

45. Neil E. Boudette and Gina Ghon, "Brawny BMW Seeks 'the Idea Class'," *Wall Street Journal*, August 2, 2006, B1.

46. Katie Delahaye Paine, "How Do Blogs Measure Up? Forget Reach and Frequency. Success in Today's Marketplace Is Measured Not By How Broad Your Reach Is But By How Deep Your Network Is," *Communication World*, Sept.–Oct. 2007, 24, 5, 30; Technorati website, technorati.com, accessed February 8, 2010.

47. Michelle Warren, "Blogger Knows Best," *Marketing Magazine*, April 6, 2009.

48. Chenting See, Kevin Zheng Zhou, Nan Zhou, and Julie Juan Li, "Harmonizing Conflict in Husband-Wife Purchase Decision Making: Perceived Fairness and Spousal Influence Dynamics," *Journal of the Academy of Marketing Science* (Fall 2008), 378–94; Michel Laroche, Zhiyong Yang, Kim Chankon, and Marie-Odile Richard, "How Culture Matters in Children's Purchase Influence: A Multi-level Investigation," *Journal of the Academy of Marketing Science* (Spring, 2007), 113–16.

49. Ibid.

50. Derek Gale, "Who's the Boss?" *Restaurants & Institutions*, February 1, 2007, 117, 2, 50.

51. Karin Ekstrom, "Parental Consumer Learning or 'Keeping up With Their Children'," *Journal of Consumer Behavior* (July/August 2007), 203–17.

52. Canadian Media Directors' Council, "*Media Digest*, 09/10," *Marketing Magazine*, 17–25.

53. Matthew Klein, "He Shops, She Shops," *American Demographics*, March 1998, 34–35.

54. FindGift.com website, www.findgift.com, accessed February 10, 2010.

55. Jennifer Wells, "What Women Want," *Report on Business Magazine*, December 2008, 20.

56. Jeff Beer, "Dove Begins 'Real Men' Push," *Marketing Magazine*, February 4, 2010.

57. www.owlkids.com, accessed February 11, 2010; Janice Rosenberg, "Tweens Mesh Latest Fads, Moms and Dads," *Advertising Age*, February 14, 2000, 40.

58. Statistics Canada, "Census Families by Number of Children at Home," *2006 Census*, www.statcan.gc.ca/, accessed February 11, 2010; Laura Pratt, "Not Like the Other," *Marketing Magazine*, December 9, 2002, 25.

59. Anil Mathur, George Moschis, and Euehun Lee, "A Longitudinal Study of the Effects of Life Style Status Changes on Changes in Consumer Preferences," *Journal of the Academy of Marketing Sciences*, Summer 2008, 234–46.

60. Welcome Wagon website, www .welcomewagon.ca, accessed February 11, 2010.

61. Mitsubishi Motors Canada, www .mitsubishimotors.ca, accessed February 11, 2010.

62. Nora J. Rifon and Molly Catherine Ziske, "Using Weight Loss Products: The Roles of Involvement, Self-Efficacy, and Body Image," in *1995 AMA Educators' Proceedings*, ed. Barbara B. Stern and George M. Zinkhan (Chicago: American Marketing Association, 1995), 90–98.

63. Lisa Vickery, Kelly Greene, Shelly Branch, and Emily Nelson, "Marketers Tweak Strategies as Age Groups Realign," *Wall Street Journal*, May 15, 2001, B1.

64. Lawrence Papoff, "Ford of Canada: The Blue Oval Takes Aim at Women Car Buyers," www.canadianautoworld.ca/ focus.php.

65. Loretta Chao and Betsy McKay, "Pepsi Steps into Coke Realm," *Wall Street Journal*, September 12, 2007.

66. Fashion Trendsetter, www .fashiontrendsetter.com, accessed February 11, 2010.

67. Laura Petrecca, "Axe Ads Turn up the Promise of Sex Appeal," *USA Today*, April 17, 2007.

68. David Menzies, "Cheque Mates," *Marketing*, August 27, 2007, 30; Feedback, "Universal Energy 'Set Up' By Menzies," *Marketing*, October 29, 2007, 4; Ellen Roseman, "Energy Marketing Needs Curbs," *Toronto Star*, October 18, 2008, B-2; Scott Simpson, "Gas Marketer Fighting BCUC ruling," *Vancouver Sun*, February 10, 2009, C.3; Gordon Jaremko, "We'll Fire Wrongdoers, Chairman Says," *Edmonton Journal*, May 23, 2004, D-5; Tony Cote, "Safeguard Enbridge Account Number, Man Warns," *Ottawa Citizen*, June 17, 2002, B-8.

69. Joshua Rosenbaum, "Guitar Maker Looks for a New Key," *Wall Street Journal*, February 11, 1998, B1, B5.

70. Elizabeth J. Wilson, "Using the Dollarmetric Scale to Establish the Just Meaningful Difference in Price," in *1987 AMA Educators' Proceedings*, ed. Susan Douglas et al. (Chicago: American Marketing Association, 1987), 107.

71. Sunil Gupta and Lee G. Cooper, "The Discounting of Discounts and Promotion Thresholds," *Journal of Consumer Research*, December 1992, 401–11.

72. Mark Stiving and Russell S. Winer, "An Empirical Analysis of Price Endings with Scanner Data," *Journal of Consumer Research*, June 1997, 57–67. See also Robert M. Schindler and Patrick N. Kirby, "Patterns of Rightmost Digits Used in Advertised Price: Implications for Nine-Ending Effects," *Journal of Consumer Research*, September 1997, 192–201.

73. "Listerine Mouthwash and PocketPaks," Cassie Awards, *Marketing Magazine*, November 18, 2002, Cassies 9 ; and Listerine website, www.listerine.ca, accessed March 18, 2010.

74. Mike Sundell, "Snow Job," *Marketing Magazine*, December 9, 2002, 13.

75. "Toyota Recalls Vehicles over Accelerator Problems," CanWest News, January 21, 2010; Matthew Philips, "Toyota's 'Tylenol Moment,'" *Newsweek*, February 15, 2010.

76. Kenneth Hein, "Teens Schizophrenic About Their Brands: Millennials Have Complex Feelings About Brands Unless, Of Course, It's Apple," *Brandweek*, June 18, 2007.

77. Dove Canada website, www.dove.ca/en/#/cfrb/mission_ statement.aspx, accessed March 18, 2010.

78. Deborah Ball, "Despite Downturn, Japanese Are Still Having Fits for Luxury Goods," *Wall Street Journal*, April 24, 2001, B1.

79. American Express Canada website home.americanexpress.com/home/ca, accessed March 18, 2010.

80. "Woolly Bully," *Canadian Business*, February 1996, 22.

81. International Chamber of Commerce's new initiative: BASCAP—Business Action to Stop Counterfeiting and Piracy www.icc-ccs.co.uk/bascap/ digest/Cases.htm, accessed September 11, 2007; Global Brand Protection Directory, www.iccwbo.org/bascap/id12418/index. html, accessed September 11, 2007.

82. Steven Lipin, Brian Coleman, and Jeremy Mark, "Pick a Card: Visa, American Express, and MasterCard Vie in Overseas Strategies," *Wall Street Journal*, February 15, 1994, A1, A5.

83. Eva Friede, "Love and Lingerie: Dos and Don'ts," CanWest News, February 10, 2009.

84. Westjet website, www.westjet.com, accessed March 18, 2010; Norma Ramage, "WestJet on the Fly," *Marketing Magazine*, June 20, 2005; Norma Ramage, "Go East, Young Airline," *Marketing Magazine*, December 12, 2005.

85. General Motors of Canada website, www.gm.ca/gm/english/may-the-best-car-win/chevrolet/equinox, accessed March 18, 2010.

86. All Bran Canada website, www.allbran.ca, accessed March 18, 2010; Sarah Dobson, "Kellogg Running Tasty Campaign for All-Bran," *Marketing Daily*, www. marketingmagazine.ca, August 1, 2006;

Rob Gerlsbeck, "Food Follies," *Marketing Magazine*, May 22, 2006.

87. Miriam Jordan, "Debut of Rival Diet Colas in India Leaves a Bitter Taste," *Wall Street Journal*, July 21, 1999, B1, B4.

88. This application exercise is based on the contribution of P. J. Forrest (Mississippi College) to "Great Ideas in Teaching Marketing," a teaching supplement that accompanies Lamb, Hair, and McDaniel's *Marketing*. Professor Forrest's entry, titled "Print Ad Projects for Consumer Behavior," was a winner in the "Best of the Great Ideas in Teaching Marketing" contest held in conjunction with the publication of the eighth edition of *Marketing*.

89. Based on Susan Mohammad, "What Armani Can Learn from Hooters," *Canadian Business*, October 12, 2009, 79.

90. Based on Business News Networks: "The Psychology of Spending Behaviour " September 11, 2009, 12:40 p.m., http://watch.bnn.ca/#clip212293.

CHAPTER 5

1. Anchor Lamina corporate website, www.anchorlamina.com, accessed April 8, 2010, www.answers.com/topic/ anchor-lamina-inc, accessed April 8, 2010; http://investing.businessweek .com/research/stocks/private/ snapshot.asp?privcapId=96885, accessed April 8, 2010.

2. Michael D. Hutt and Thomas W. Speth, *Business Marketing Management: B2B*, 9th ed. (Cincinnati: Thomson, 2007), 4.

3. "VIA Receives First Environmentally Enhanced F-40 Locomotive from CAD Railway Industries," Canada NewsWire, July 16, 2009; "Canadian Army Buying New Combat Vehicles," CanWest News, July 8, 2009; "Energy for 50,000 Manitoba Homes Blowin' in the Wind," Canadian Press, March 22, 2010.

4. Statistics Canada, "Electronic Commerce and Technology," *The Daily*, April 24, 2008, www.statcan.gc.ca/.

5. Statistics Canada, "Enterprises That Use the Internet," www40.statcan.gc.ca/ l01/cst01/econ146b-eng.htm, accessed April 8, 2010.

6. Statistics Canada, "Electronic Commerce and Technology," *The Daily*, April 20, 2006, www.statcan.gc.ca/.

7. Hutt and Speth, *Business Marketing Management*, 4.

8. NetGenesis, *E-Metrics: Business Metrics for the New Economy*, www.spss.com.

9. Mary E. Morrison, "Industrial Buyers Shopping Online," *BtoB Magazine*, October 13, 2008, 19.

10. "RSS," Wikipedia, accessed at http://en.wikipedia.org/wiki/.

11. "B2B Marketers Missing Out on Influencing Buyers Online," *Marketing Matters Newsletter*, Chicago: American Marketing Association, on-line, October 28, 2008.

12. "Grainger Introduces SupplyLink Site," *BtoB Magazine*, on-line, July 24, 2008.

13. "Disintermediation," Wikipedia, accessed at http://en.wikipedia.org/wiki/.

14. Ibid.

15. Bridor corporate website, "What Sets Us Apart" and "Our Tailor-Made Solutions," www.bridor.com, accessed April 9, 2010.

16. Kate Maddox, "Marketers Look to Boost Customer Retention," *BtoB Magazine*, on-line, May 5, 2008. Reprinted with permission of Crane Communications.

17. "Para Paints and Lowe's Announce Partnership," Canada NewsWire, March 15, 2010.

18. "ProMetic Forms Strategic Alliance with Denmark's Novozymes," Canadian Press, February 2, 2010.

19. Steven Reinberg, "The Issue: DHL Turns to Rival UPS," *Business Week*, June 11, 2008, on-line.

20. Erin White, "A Cheaper Alternative to Outsourcing: Choice Hotels and 1-800-Flowers Swap Call-Center Employees," *Wall Street Journal*, April 10, 2006, B3.

21. Robert M. Morgan and Shelby D. Hunt, "The Commitment-Trust Theory of Relationship Marketing," *Journal of Marketing*, 58(3) (1994): 23.

22. Ibid.

23. Steve Bodow, "The Care and Feeding of a Killer App," *Business 2.0*, August 2002, 76–78.

24. Geoffrey York, "BlackBerry's Arrival in China up to Partner, RIM Says," *Globe and Mail*, January 11, 2008, B.7; Aileen McCabe, "BlackBerrys Slow to Crack Lucrative Chinese Market," CanWest News, September 24, 2007, 1; Bloomberg News, Reuters, "BlackBerry Imminent for China, Says Research In Motion," *International Herald Tribune Tech/Media*, www.iht.com/articles/2006/12/07/business/rim.php.

25. "Bombardier to Supply 23 FLEXITY Outlook Trams to Linz, Austria; The 2009 European Capital of Culture selects Bombardier once again," *Marketwire*, July 3, 2009.

26. Statistics Canada, "Gross Domestic Product by Industry," January, 2010, www.statcan.gc.ca/; *Fortune*, "The Global 500," http://money.cnn.com/magazines/fortune/global500/2009/maps/index.html, accessed April 10, 2010.

27. Statistics Canada, "Retail Trade January 2010," www.statcan.gc.ca/pub/63-005-x/63-005-x2010001-eng.pdf, accessed April 10, 2010; Retail Council of Canada, "News-Media," www.retailcouncil.org/news/media/profile/www.retailcouncil.org/media centre/facts.asp.

28. Statistics Canada, "Wholesale Trade, Operating Statistics, by Province and Territory (Canada)," www40.statcan.gc.ca/l01/cst01/trad35a-eng.htm, accessed April 10, 2010.

29. Industry Canada, "Establishments Wholesale Trade (NAICS 41)," Canadian Industry Statistics, www.ic.gc.ca/cis-sic/cis-sic.nsf/IDE/cis-sic41etbe.html#est1, accessed April 10,

2010; Statistics Canada; and Alex Hays (2005), "Wholesalers: A Key Link in Canada's Economy," Analytical Report, Statistics Canada.

30. Statistics Canada, "Government Finance: Revenue, Expenditure and Surplus," *The Daily*, Tuesday, June 16, 2009, www.statcan.gc.ca/.

31. Paul Emanuelli, "Understanding Government Procurement Policy in the Era of Globalization," *Purchasing B2B*, December 2002, 36.

32. Ibid.; Laura Eggertson and Marja Hughes, "Unlocking Procurement Barriers," *Summit*, March 2003, 12; Internal Trade Secretariat, "Agreement on Internal Trade," Consolidated Version, Chapter 5 (Procurement), January 2006, www.ait-aci.ca, p. 5; Backgrounder-Agreement on Internal Trade, Office of the Prime Minister of Canada website, http://pm.gc.ca/eng/media.asp?id=2385, accessed April 10, 2010.

33. Statistics Canada, "Federal General Government Revenue and Expenditures (Expenditures and Surplus or Deficit)," www40.statcan.gc.ca/l01/cst01/govt02b-eng.htm, accessed April 10, 2010; Statistics Canada, "Consolidated Provincial and Territorial Government Revenue and Expenditures," www40.statcan.gc.ca/l01/cst01/govt55a-eng.htm, accessed April 10, 2010.

34. Statistics Canada, "Tables by Subject: Government Financial Statistics," www40.statcan.gc.ca/l01/ind01/l3_3764_3766-eng.htm?hili_govt48, accessed April 10, 2010.

35. Statistics Canada, "Satellite Account of Non-profit Institutions and Volunteering," *The Daily*, December 21, 2009, www.statcan.gc.ca/, accessed April 11, 2010.

36. Charity.com website, "Canadian Registered Charities," www.charity.com/canadiancharities.shtml, accessed, April 11, 2010; and Statistics Canada, "Charitable Donors," www40.statcan.gc.ca/l01/cst01/famil90-eng.htm, accessed April 11, 2010.

37. Statistics Canada, "North American Industry Classification System (NAICS) 2007—Canada," www.statcan.gc.ca/, accessed April 11, 2010.

38. Ibid.

39. CAE Corporate website, News Room, "CAE USA Expands C-130 Tampa Training Center," www.cae.com, accessed April 11, 2010; Nicolas Van Praet, "Investors Dump Shares After CAE Loses Contract," CanWest News, September 26, 2003, 1; Shot Kortje, "Aviation-support Shares Ascend with Airline Stocks," *Globe and Mail*, March 30, 2010, www.theglobeandmail.com/globe-investor/investment-ideas/features/stock-trends/aviation-support-shares-ascend-with-airline-stocks/article1516720/, accessed April 11, 2010.

40. SAQ website, www.saq.com, "B2B-About Us," www.saq-b2b.com/wx/en/MEMBERSZONE.PRESENTATION.STATIC_PAGES_DISPLAY_PREP/ABOUT_US, accessed April 11, 2010.

41. Purchasing Management Association of Canada corporate website, www.pmac.ca, "Certified Professional Purchaser," www.pmac.ca/education/cpp_accreditation.asp, accessed April 11, 2010.

42. Marshall Lager, "Listen Up," *Customer Relationship Management*, March 2007, 24–27.

43. "Amex Canada Sees Travel Turnaround: Buying Pros Help Control Costs," *Purchasing B2B*, April 2002.

44. Kate Maddox, "Relevant Content Connects with C-suite," *BtoB Magazine*, October 13, 2008.

45. Ibid.

46. "Right Channeling: Making Sure Your Best Customers Get Your Best Service," Right Now Technologies, online at www.rightnow.com, June 3, 2008.

47. Purchasing Management Association of Canada corporate website, "PMAC Code of Ethics," www.pmac.ca/about/ethics.asp, accessed April 11, 2010.

48. This application exercise is based on the contribution of Gregory B. Turner (College of Charleston) to "Great Ideas in Teaching Marketing," a teaching supplement that accompanies Lamb, Hair, and McDaniel's *Marketing*. Professor Turner's entry, "Student Ethics versus Practitioner Ethics," received an Honourable Mention in the "Best of the Great Ideas in Teaching Marketing" contest held in conjunction with the publication of the eighth edition of *Marketing*.

49. Jonathan Karp, "How Bikers' Water Backpack Became Soldiers' Essential," *Wall Street Journal*, July 19, 2005, B1, B2; "CamelBak Introduces New Line of Strength/Stealth Technology Responding to Law Enforcement and Military Needs; R&D Innovations Protect Against Infrared Detection, Provide Strongest Hydration Reservoir Available," *PR Newswire*, January 27, 2005; Mark Riedy, "The Birth of CamelBak," *Mountain Bike*, Summer 2004, 104; "CamelBak Announces Chem-Bio Hydration Reservoir for Military," *Law Enforcement and First Responders*; "New Reservoir Is World's Only Hands-Free Hydration System That Withstands Exposure to Chemical and Biological Agents to Provide Safe Drinking Water in All Combat Environments 24/7/365," *PR Newswire*, August 26, 2004; Sipsey Street Irregulars, "Praxis: Tactical Water, Part Two—The CamelBak," December 23, 2009, http://sipseystreetirregulars.blogspot.com/2009/12/praxis-tactical-water-part-two-camelbak.html, accessed April 11, 2010.

50. Based on SMED corporate website, http://www.smed.ca/company/falkridge.asp; CBC, *Venture*, "Turning Smed Around," January 19, 1999; International Interior Design Association, Northern Pacific Chapter, www.iida-wa.org/nl_sp03_board_retreat.html.

CHAPTER 6

1. Julie Harrison, "Women Only," *Windsor Star*, April 3, 2010, F1-2; and Georgian Court Hotel Vancouver website, www.georgiancourthotelvancouver.com/hotels-bc-canada-downtown-boutique-ladies-only-orchid-floor.html, accessed April 13, 2010.
2. Jeromy Lloyd, "Seneca College Targets Key Demographic," *Marketing Magazine*, July 23, 2008; Seneca College website, www.senecac.on.ca, accessed April 14, 2010.
3. Kokanee Beer website, www.kokaneebeer.ca, accessed April 14, 2010.
4. All population numbers in this section sourced from Statistics Canada, www.statcan.gc.ca/; "Canada's Population Estimate," *The Daily*, March 25, 2010; "Population by Sex and Age Group," *Summary Tables*, www40.statcan.gc.ca/l01/cst01/DEMO10A-eng.htm, accessed Thursday, March 25, 2010.
5. Anna R. McAlister and T. Bettina Cornwell, "Preschool Children's Persuasion Knowledge: The Contribution of Theory of Mind," *Journal of Public Policy & Marketing*, Fall 2009, 175–85; Anna R. McAlister and T. Bettina Cornwell, "Children's Brand Symbolism Understanding: Links to Theory of Mind and Executive Functioning," *Psychology & Marketing*, March 2010, 203; "Brand Recognition as Early as Three Years Old: All Types of Marketing Offensives Should Be Regulated!," Canada NewsWire, March 3, 2010.
6. Misty Harris, "Advertisers Have New Target: Your Baby," CanWest News, October 25, 2009.
7. "Spin Master Launches Liv(TM), a Bold New Fashion Doll Line That Celebrates What's Cool About Being a Real Teen Girl," Canada NewsWire, July 31, 2009.
8. Canadian Media Directors' Council, *Media Digest 09/10*, 18–25.
9. Statistics Canada, "Population by Sex and Age Group," Summary Tables, www.statcan.gc.ca/, accessed April 14, 2010; 2007 YTV Tween Report, www.corusmedia.com/ytv/docs/2008/YTV_Kidfluence_2007.pdf, accessed April 14, 2010.
10. Nichole L. Torres, "It's Child's Play," *Entrepreneur*, December 2001, 24–26.
11. Youth Culture Group Corporate website, www.youthculture.com, accessed April 14, 2010; and Canadian Media Directors' Council, *Media Digest 09/10*, 51.

12. Kate Calder, "Disney XD Unveils Results of Pan-EuroTween Study," *KidScreen*, February, 2010, 22.
13. Bacardi website, www.bacardi.com, accessed April 14, 2010.
14. Calvin Leung, "On Target," *Canadian Business*, August 18, 2008, 45; Lavalife Prime website, http://prime.lavalife.com/mature/welcome.act, accessed April 15, 2010.
15. Patricia Pearson, "The Golden Oldies," *Toronto Life*, October 2009, 82.
16. Canada Newswire, "Announcing Canada's 10 Most Admired Corporate Cultures(TM), 2008," November 19, 2008, www.newswire.ca/en/releases/archive/November2008/19/c2116.html, accessed October 22, 2010; Westjet corporate website, "The Experience," www.westjet.com, accessed May 6, 2010.
17. Statistics Canada Population Estimates and Projections, "Population by Sex and Age Group-2009," www.statcan.gc.ca/, accessed April 14, 2010.
18. Kristin Laird, "Hitting the Mark," *Marketing Magazine*, April 19, 2010, 18–22.
19. Ross Kenneth Urken, "EA Sports' Ads Feature New Stars: John (and Jane) Q. Public," *Wall Street Journal*, July 25, 2008, on-line.
20. Laird, "Hitting the Mark."
21. Ibid.
22. James Matheson, "Lancome's Men Skin Care," Ask Men website, http://ca.askmen.com/fashion/product_guide_150/191_fashion_product.html, accessed April 17, 2010.
23. "Average Total Income by Economic Family Types," *Families, Households, and Housing*, www.statcan.gc.ca/; Statistics Canada, "Expenditures Per Household Canada," *Spending Patterns in Canada 2008*, www.statcan.gc.ca/pub/62-202-x/2007000/t001-eng.pdf, accessed April 17, 2010.
24. Associated Press, "P&G Says Sales Are on the Rise," *Marketing Magazine*, January 28, 2010.
25. Statistics Canada, "Population by Home Language, by Province and Territory (2006 Census)," *Summary Tables*, www40.statcan.gc.ca/l01/cst01/demo61a-eng.htm, accessed April 17, 2010; Statistics Canada, "Detailed Language Spoken Most Often at Home," 2006 Census, released April 8, 2008, http://cansim2.statcan.gc.ca/cgi-win/cnsmcgi.pgm?Lang=E&SP_Action=Result&SP_ID=50006&SP_Par=50000&SP_TYP=60&SP_Sort=-2&SP_Portal=2, accessed April 17, 2010.
26. Toronto Symphony Orchestra website, "Chinese Brochure," http://files.tso.ca/PDF/Chinese/1011_brochure_chinese.pdf, accessed April 20, 2010; Statistics Canada, "Projections of the Diversity of the Canadian Population: 2006 to 2031," www.statcan.gc.ca/pub/91-551-x/91-551-x2010001-eng.pdf, accessed April 20, 2010; Loretta Lam,

"Music to Ethnic Ears," *Marketing Magazine*, May 19, 2003, 10–11.
27. Statistics Canada, "Census Families by Number of Children at Home," *2001 Census*, www.statcan.gc.ca/; Statistics Canada, "Type of Dwelling and Population by Type of Dwelling," *Canadian Statistics: Families, Households, and Housing*, www.statcan.gc.ca/; Statistics Canada, "Families, Households and Housing," *Canada Yearbook Overview 2008*, www41.statcan.gc.ca/2008/40000/ceb40000_000-eng.htm, accessed April 10, 2010; Statistics Canada, "Household Size, by Province and Territory (2006 Census)," www40.statcan.gc.ca/l01/cst01/famil53a-eng.htm, accessed April 21, 2010.
28. Dove For Men website, Dove For Men Super Bowl Commercial, http://content.dove.us/mencare, accessed April 21, 2010.
29. Melissa Burdon, "The Power of Personas," *Marketing Magazine*, August 28, 2006.
30. Canadian Press, "Alcohol Sales Free Flowing Through Quebec," *Marketing Magazine*, August 24, 2009.
31. Ken Mison, "Cutting Back on Wasted Mail," *Marketing Magazine*, February 11, 2002, 18.
32. Ken Jones and Michael Pearce, "The Geography of Markets: Spatial Analysis for Retailers," *Ivey Business Journal*, March–April 1999, 66–70.
33. Tetrad Computer Solutions website, "Environics Canadian Demographics: PrizmC2" www.tetrad.com/demographics/canada/environics/prizmce.html, accessed April 21, 2010; "Analytics and Geodemographics," www.geomedia.ca/about_us/partners.
34. Rebecca Harris, "Turning Green," *Marketing Magazine*, June 11, 2007.
35. President's Choice website, "PC Green," www.presidentschoice.ca/LCLOnline/liveArticles.jsp?articleId=lcloa34025&type=details, accessed April 22, 2010.
36. Joanna Pachner, "Faster Hotter Sooner," *Financial Post Business*, March 6, 2007, www.canada.com/nationalpost/financialpost/story.html; Statistics Canada, "Food Services and Drinking Places (Canada)," www40.statcan.gc.ca/l01/cst01/serv42a-eng.htm, accessed April 22, 2010; Canadian Restaurant and Food Service Association, "Statistics-Units," www.crfa.ca/research/statistics/default.asp#units, accessed April 22, 2010.
37. Greg White, "Boycotting Boomers," *Marketing Magazine*, October 3, 2005; CBC News Online, "Quebec Wal-Mart Closes Earlier Than Planned," April 29, 2005, www.cbc.ca.
38. Ellen Byron, "Aiming to Clean Up, P&G Courts Business Customers," *Wall Street Journal*, January 26, 2007, B1, B2.
39. Eve Lazarus, "Tea's Time," *Marketing Magazine*, September 25, 2006.
40. Canadian Association of Retired People website, www.carp.ca; *Zoomer Magazine*

website, "Zoomer Magazine Media Kit," http://zoomermedia.ca/ratecards/ ZOOMERMAG_MEDIAKIT.pdf, accessed April 26, 2010.

41. Fatburger website, "Locations by State," www.fatburger.com/Location/ LocationsByState.aspx?c=ca, accessed April 27, 2010; Eve Lazarus, "Fat Chances," *Marketing Magazine*, April 3, 2006.

42. Lululemon corporate website, www .lululemon.com, accessed April 27, 2010.

43. Tara Perkins, "Money-Losing Lewiscraft Says It Could Close 10 of 90 Stores This Month," Canadian Press NewsWire, January 10, 2006; David Paddon, "Spinrite in Nasty Spin Cycle as Slow Demand Sparks Flood of Low-Priced Yarn," Canadian Press NewsWire, March 30, 2006.

44. Ryan Bigge, "One Beer, Two Solitudes," *Marketing Magazine*, May 5, 2003, 12–13.

45. www.futureshop.ca.

46. Dell Canada corporate website, www.dell.ca; Blinds-To-Go corporate website, www.blindstogo.com, accessed April 27, 2010.

47. www.photogiftcard.com; Sarah Dobson, "Restaurants Offer Personalized Gift Cards," *Marketing Daily*, December 20, 2005.

48. Chuck Stogel, "Callaway Gets 'Personal' With $30M Campaign," *Brandweek*, February 12, 2007, 14.

49. Rogers website, www.rogers.com, accessed April 27, 2010.

50. "New Vehicle Warranty: 2011 Coverage at a Glance," www.toyota.ca.

51. Kleenex Products, Kleenex website, www.kleenex.com, accessed April 27, 2010.

52. Danny Kucharsky, "Mega Bloks Target Kids at Retail," *Marketing Magazine*, November 12, 2001, 4.

53. D'Arcy Jenish, "Up in the Air," *Maclean's*, April 2, 2001.

54. Tim Horton website, www.timhorton.com, accessed April 28, 2011.

55. C. Simms and P. Trott, "An Analysis of the Repositioning of the 'BMW Mini' Brand," *Journal of Product & Brand Management*, 2007, 297–309.

56. Geoff Colvin, "Selling P&G," *Fortune*, September 17, 2007, 163–69.

57. "Cottonelle Turns into Cashmere in New Campaign," *Marketing Daily*, June 15, 2005.

58. Michael Adams, "Blink Again," *Marketing Magazine*, April 4, 2005, 20.

59. This application exercise is based on the contribution of Kim McKeage (University of Maine) to "Great Ideas in Teaching Marketing," a teaching supplement that accompanies Lamb, Hair, and McDaniel's *Marketing*. Professor McKeage's entry, "Students Practice Making Market/ Product Grids on Themselves," received an Honourable Mention in the "Best of the Great Ideas in Teaching Marketing" contest held in conjunction with the publication of the eighth edition of *Marketing*.

60. Case Study: Jerry Adler, "Attack of the Diet Cokes," *Newsweek*, May 14, 2007; "Coke's New 'Coke Zero' Faces Tough Going" *UPI NewsTrack*, June 13, 2005; Duane D. Stanford, "0: That's Zero. As in No Calories," *Atlanta Journal-Constitution*, March 20, 2007; "Coca-Cola Co.," MMR, October 30, 2006; www.cocacolazero.com.

61. Business News Network (BNN), "Midday Markets: Marketing to Boomers—Part 1," March 17, 2010, http://watch.bnn.ca/ #clip277446; CBC, "Boom, Bust, and Echo," *National Magazine*, March 7, 1996; Robert Deangelo, "Dara Torres Biography—The Complete Olympic Dara Torres Bio," http://ezinearticles.com/?Dara-Torres-Biography—The-Complete-Olympic-Dara-Torres-Bio&id=1436097, accessed May 11, 2010.

CHAPTER 7

1. Government of Canada website, http://canada.gc.ca, accessed April 30, 2010.

2. Angus Reid, "Market Research Liberated," *Marketing Magazine*, September 25, 2007.

3. Cruise Line Industry Association, "2010 Cruise Industry Media Update," www.cruising.org/pressroom-research/ 2010-cruise-industry-media-update, accessed May 2, 2010.

4. "Cruise Ship Trips Sail to New Heights," *Calgary Herald*, March 14, 2007, F10.

5. Cruise Line Industry Association, "2010 Cruise Industry Media Update."

6. Royal Caribbean Cruise Lines press release, October 28, 2009, "Royal Caribbean International Takes Delivery of Much Anticipated Oasis of the Seas," www.oasisoftheseas.com/ press-room.php, accessed May 2, 2010.

7. Emily Gravelle, "Good for You," *Canadian Grocer*, November 2009, 43.

8. Ibid.

9. Ibid.

10. "Why Some Customers Are More Equal Than Others," *Fortune*, September 19, 1994, 215–24.

11. Sunil Gupta, Donald Lehmann, and Jennifer Ames Stuart, "Valuing Customers," *Journal of Marketing Research*, February 2004, 7–18.

12. Carey Toane, "Burger King Gets Mad, Even," *Strategy*, April 1, 2010, 19.

13. Robyn Lee, "Burger King Releases the Angry Whopper," January 6, 2009, http://aht.seriouseats.com/archives/ 2009/01/burger-king-releases-the-angry-whopper.html.

14. "Burger King Pours Bourbon Whopper into Canada," *BurgerBusiness*, www.burgerbusiness.com/?p=2991, accessed May 6, 2010.

15. WestJet corporate website, "The Experience," www.westjet.com, accessed May 6, 2010.

16. Toane, "Burger King Gets Mad, Even."

17. Michelle Halpern, "Youthful Ambitions," *Marketing Magazine*, June 20, 2005.

18. Ibid.

19. Canadian Press, "History Magazine Rebranding Without Sexual Connotation," *Marketing Magazine*, January 13, 2010.

20. Michael Fielding, "A Clean Slate," *Marketing News*, May 1, 2007, 9–10; X-14 Brand website, www.x14brand.com, accessed May 7, 2010.

21. Ibid.

22. Statistics Canada, "Census Release Dates and Topics," www.statcan.gc.ca/.

23. "Respondents Lie and Good Ideas Die," *Quirk's Marketing Research Review*, May 2007, 48–54.

24. D. Randall Brandt, "Improve the Customer Service," *Quirk's Marketing Research Review*, January 2006, 68.

25. "The APA Reports on Used Car Retailing," Canada NewsWire, March 5, 2010; Automobile Protection Association website, "Report on the APA Used Car Retailing Investigation with CTV's W-FIVE," www.apa.ca, March 6, 2010.

26. "Watch and Learn," *Marketing News*, February 1, 2006, 60.

27. Carey Toane, "Evolutionary Rise," *Strategy*, November 1, 2007.

28. Raymond R. Burke, "Virtual Shopping: Breakthrough in Marketing Research," *Harvard Business Review*, March/April 1996, 120–31.

29. Ellen Byron, "A Virtual View of the Store Aisle," *Wall Street Journal*, October 3, 2007, B1, B12.

30. Ibid.

31. Ibid.

32. Karl Feld, "Do You Know Where Your Data Came From?" *Quirk's Marketing Research Review*, November 2007, 24–31.

33. Internet World Stats website, "Internet Usage Statistics: The Internet Big Picture World Internet Users and Population Stats," www.internetworldstats.com.

34. Andrea Zoe Aster, "Consumer Research Goes Online," *Marketing Magazine*, June 7, 2004; Gary Bennewies, "Amused and Angry about Angus," Letters to the Editor, *Marketing Magazine*, November 20, 2006.

35. Conversation with Craig Stevens, Senior VP E-Rewards, based on company research (November 2, 2007); also see "Market Research," *Marketing News*, September 15, 2007, 16.

36. Tim Macer and Sheila Wilson, "Online Makes More Inroads," *Quirk's Marketing Research Review*, February 2007, 50–58.

37. Lee Smith, "Online Research's Time Has Come as a Proven Methodology," *CASRO Journal*, 2002, 45–50.

38. Bill MacElroy, "International Growth of Web Survey Activity," *Quirk's Marketing Research Review*, November 2000, 48–51.

39. Based on a conversation with Jerry Thomas, CEO Decision Analyst, Inc. This firm has one of the largest Internet panels in the world.

40. Gregory S. Heist, "Beyond Brand Building," *Quirk's Marketing Research Review*, July/August 2007, 62–67.

41. Ibid.

42. Ibid.

43. "CGM Overview," www.nielsenbuzzmetrics .com, August 27, 2007.

44. Pete Blackshaw, "The Pocket Guide to Consumer Generated Media," www.clickz.com, August 28, 2005; Paul Verna, "User-Generated Content: More Popular than Profitable," www.emarketer.com, January 2009, accessed February 13, 2009.

45. "BrandPulse Insights," www.nielsenbuzzmetrics.com, August 28, 2007.

46. "Behavioral Issues," *Brandweek*, October 20, 2008, 21–25.

47. Ibid.

48. Ibid.

49. Carl McDaniel and Roger Gates, *Marketing Research*, 7th ed. (Hoboken: John Wiley & Sons, 2007).

50. Phone conversation between Kevin Bender, Information Resources, Inc., and Carl McDaniel, April 17, 2000.

51. David Menzies, "Four First Class Flops," *Marketing Magazine*, April 23, 2001.

52. Sheena Sharp, "New Techniques for Corporate Foresight," *Research Conference Report*, May 1998, 7–8.

53. Toane, "Burger King Gets Mad, Even," 19.

54. www.redlobster.ca.

55. BNN, *After Hours*, "New Paradigm for the Used Vehicle Sector," broadcast September 24, 2009; Dennis DesRosiers, presentation to University of Windsor Automarketing Class attended by authors A. J. Faria and William J. Wellington at the University of Windsor, October 2009; DesRosiers Automotive Consultants Inc., corporate website, www.desrosiers.ca/ accessed May 14, 2010.

END OF PART 2 CASES

1. "Axl Rose Demands Apology, Payment from Dr. Pepper," November 27, 2008, www.nzherald.co.nz/music/news/article .cfm?c_id=264&objectid=10545353, accessed March 19, 2009; *Billboard*, "Dr. Pepper Issues Challenge to Guns N' Roses," MSNBC.com, March 27, 2008, www.msnbc.msn.com/id/23830713/, accessed March 19, 2009; "Guns N' Roses Dr Pepper Promo Misfires," CNNMoney.com, money.cnn.com/2008/ 12/02/news/companies/guns_drpepper/ index.htm, accessed December 10, 2008; Chris Harris, "Guns N' Roses Chinese Democracy Release Means Free Dr. Pepper for All," MTV, October 16, 2008, www.mtv.com/news/articles/ 1597200/20081016/guns_n_roses.html, accessed March 19, 2009; Andre Paine, "Guns N' Roses Lawyer Blasts Dr. Pepper," Reuters, November 26, 2008, www.reuters.com/article/ idUSTRE4AP9NM20081126, accessed

March 19, 2009; Karen Robinson, "Dr Pepper 'Disappointed' by Guns N' Roses' Lawsuit Threat over Free Soft Drinks," *The Dallas Morning News*, www.dallasnews.com/sharedcontent/ dws/dn/latestnews/stories/ 120308dnmetdrpeppersuit.27890a50 .html, accessed March 19, 2009.

2. Randy Carroll, "One Size Does Not Fit All," *Canadian Underwriter*, October 2009, 16; Insurance Brokers Association of Ontario corporate website, www.ibao.org, accessed May 14, 2010; Navicom corporate website, www.navicominc.com, accessed May 14, 2010.

CHAPTER 8

1. Andy Hoffman, "More Kit Kats Is Good. Too Many Is Not," *Globe and Mail*, September 9, 2006, B3; "Eggo Lesson: Expand Your Product Category," *Fortune*, October 31, 2005, 166–68; www.Nestle.ca; www.leggomyeggo.com.

2. Shawna Richer, "Guitars for Stars," *Globe and Mail*, October 1, 2003, R1, R2.

3. "Oral-B Unveils Age-Pegged Toothbrushes for Kids," BusinessWeek Online, October 4, 2001, www .businessweek.com/reuters_market/8/ REUT-8KW.HTM.

4. Todd Wasserman, "P&G Seeks Right Ingredient to Wash Out Laundry Woes," *Brandweek*, August 8, 2005, 5.

5. "Kool-Aid Announces New Products and Better-For-You Brand Direction," *Yahoo! Finance*, May 27, 2008.

6. Vanessa L. Facenda, "Procter Dishes Out 3-Tiered Dawn Attack," *Brandweek*, September 24, 2007, 4.

7. Sonia Reyes, "Minute Maid Juices Up Calcium Fortified Line," *Brandweek*, March 13, 2000, 323.

8. Mike Beirne, "Hershey Chews on Gum, Mint Plans; Jolly Rancher Eyes Preemptive Strike," *Brandweek*, February 26, 2001, 9.

9. Vanessa L. Facenda, "In Search of More Growth, P&G's Febreze Hits the Road," *Brandweek*, August 6, 2007, 6.

10. Julie Jargon, "Campbell's Chief Looks for Splash of Innovation," *Wall Street Journal*, May 30, 2008, B8.

11. Peter Gumbel, "Big Mac's Local Flavor," *Fortune*, May 5, 2008, 115–21.

12. "The 100 Best Global Brands 2009," www.businessweek.com; accessed June 7, 2010.

13. Brian O'Keefe, "Global Brands," *Fortune*, November 26, 2001, 102–10.

14. Nirmalya Kumar and Jan-Benedict Steenkamp, "Premium Store Brands: The Hottest Trend in Retailing," www.marketingprofs.com, March 20, 2009.

15. Michael Fielding, "No Longer Plain, Simple," *Marketing News*, May 15, 2006, 11–13; Matthew Boyle, "Brand Killers," *Fortune*, August 11, 2003, 88–100; Lauren Gold and Michael Gold, "Change the Rules of Private-Label Packaging," *Marketing News*, November 22,

1999, 20–21; Susan Bourette, "Private Label Share," *Globe and Mail*, November 30, 1998, B1, B3.

16. Marina Strauss, "Zellers Takes Page from Target," *Globe and Mail*, April 19, 2003, B3.

17. Frederic M. Biddle, "American Express, Lexus in Co-Brand Pact," *Wall Street Journal*, February 9, 2000, B12.

18. Michelle Wirth Fellman, "Ti-Gear: Owning Up to a Name," *Marketing News*, October 26, 1998, 2; www.golfgearin.com; www.iwantgolf.com.

19. Jim Edwards, "Brand Defense," *Brandweek*, August 25–September 1, 2008, S1, S2.

20. Cristin Schmitz, "Courtroom Barbie," *Financial Post*, May 26, 2005, FP3; Supreme Court of Canada, Citation: *Mattel, Inc. v. 3894207 Canada, Inc.*, 2006 SCC, Docket: 30839, June 2, 2006, scc.lexum.umontreal.ca/en/2006/2006 scc22/2006scc22.html.

21. Jonathan Eig, "Food Companies Grab Kids' Attention by Packaging Products as Toys, Games," WSJ.com, October 26, 2001, www.interactive.wsj.com.

22. Kenneth Hein, "Miracle-Gro Seeds TV, Radio, Print; $20M Push Targets Spring Planters," *Brandweek*, February 12, 2001, 4.

23. Paul Brent, "Guinness Pours It On," *Financial Post*, October 28, 2005, FP8.

24. "Environmentally Responsible Packaging: Convenience vs. Conscience," www.retailwire.com, April 30, 2008.

25. Alissa Walker, "Spin the Bottle," *Fast Company*, June 2008, 54.

26. George Anderson, "Consumers Want More/Different Info on Labels," www.retailwire.com, July 17, 2008.

27. Peter Wonacott, "Buick Maintains Its Shine in China," *Globe and Mail*, July 22, 2004, B6; www.autonews.com; "2009 China Sales Report," *JATO Dynamics*, www.autonewschina.com, June 2010.

28. Bo Svensson, "Protecting the Finished Product," *Automotive Industries*, February 2006, 14.

29. Jack Neff, "When the Worm Poop Hits the Fan, Market It," *Advertising Age*, April 23, 2007; Adam Aston, "Now That's Really a Turf War," *Business Week*, April 23, 2007; Angus Loten, "After a Good Fight, David Forced to Settle with Goliath," www.Inc.com, September 24, 2007.

30. CBC, *Marketplace*, "Faking It," broadcast April 9, 2006; CBC, *Venture*, "Counterfeit Crusader," broadcast December 21, 2003; "Largest Counterfeit Tobacco Seizure in BC History: CBSA and RCMP Seize over 50,000 Cartons of Illegal Tobacco," *Canada Border Services Agency*, May 5, 2010; Denise Ryan, "Canada Flooded with Counterfeit Products," *Calgary Herald*, June 24, 2007, 5; "Counterfeit Toothpaste Falsely Labelled as Colgate Found to Contain Harmful Bacteria," *Health Canada*, www.hc-sc.gc.ca, accessed June 11, 2010;

Criminal Intelligence Service Canada, "Counterfeit Pharmaceuticals in Canada," Central Bureau Report, Strategic Analytical Services, August 2006; "RCMP Seize an Estimated $1 Million of Counterfeit Merchandise," Canada NewsWire, March 12, 2004; "Six Plead Guilty to Sale of Counterfeit Merchandise," *Saskatoon Star-Phoenix*, June 10, 2004, A12. The following news stories can be viewed on your computer through *CBC News Archives* at www.cbc.ca: "RCMP Sweep Nets Huge Seizure of Knock-off Clothing," November 17, 2006; "Police, Merchants Battle Counterfeit Goods," September 25, 2006; "Synthetic DNA Separates the Prada from the Prado," September 1, 2006; "Counterfeit DVDs, Video Games Worth $50,000 Found in Calgary Home," August 8, 2006; "Counterfeit Luxury Items Snapped up in Raids," May 19, 2005. The following news stories can be viewed on your computer through *CTVglobalmedia Archives* at www.ctv.ca: "Beijing Market Selling Knockoff Canadian Coats," December 26, 2005; "Police Raids Seize 150,000 Illegal DVDs in T.O.," November 27, 2005.

CHAPTER 9

1. Joanna Pachner, "Retro Cool: Entrepreneur Revives the Pop Shoppe," *Globe and Mail*, June 3, 2010, 16; Joanna Pachner, "Other Brands That Have Been Resurrected," *Your Business*, June 3, 2010, 5.
2. Jana McGregor, "In Focus," *Business Week*, April 28, 2008, 61–72; Reena Jana, "In Data," *Business Week*, September 22, 2008, 48.
3. "The Value of New Product Time to Market," www.retailwire.com, November 21, 2008.
4. Gary Strauss, "Squeezing New from Old," *Globe and Mail*, January 4, 2002, B1, B2.
5. Gerry Khermouch, "Beefeater Gin Sets New Bottle, First Radio Ads on Renewal Drive," *Brandweek*, December 4, 2000, 17.
6. Melanie Warner, "P&G's Chemistry Test," *Fast Company*, July/August 2008, 71.
7. Renee Hopkins Callahan, Gwen Ishmael, and Leyla Nomiranian, "The Case for In-the-Box Innovation," *Innovation Brochure*, Decision Analysts, 2010.
8. Jeff Jarvis, "The Buzz From Starbucks Customers," *Business Week*, April 28, 2008, 42, 44.
9. Ibid.
10. Ian Wylie, "Calling for a Renewable Future," *Fast Company*, May 2003, 46–48.
11. Suzanne Vranica, "Mensa Members Find Their Way into Focus Groups for Marketing," WSJ.com, February 26, 2002.
12. Chuck Salter, "The Faces and Voices of the World's Most Innovative Company," *Fast Company*, March 2008, 74–96.
13. Philip Brasher, "Teens Sample Milk from Vending Machines," *Fort Worth Star-Telegram*, April 5, 2001, 10A.
14. John Gaffney, "How Do You Feel about a $44 Tooth-Bleaching Kit?" *Business 2.0*, October 2001, 125–27.
15. George Anderson, "New Products Fail to Make Impression," *RetailWire*, November 20, 2009 (online).
16. "Roadtrek: The Motorhome That Drives Like a Van," *Home and Park Motorhomes*, 100 Shirley Avenue, Kitchener, Ontario, N2B 2E1.
17. Michael Fielding, "Driving Into the Global Market," *Marketing News*, November 1, 2008, 14–17.
18. Zena Olijnyk, "Beat China on Quality," *Canadian Business*, November 7–20, 2005, 61–65.
19. Jenny Mero, "John Deere's Farm Team," *Fortune*, April 14, 2008, 121, 126.
20. Daniel B. Honigman, "Who's on First?" *Marketing News*, November 1, 2008, 16.
21. "When Will It Fly?", *The Economist*, August 9, 2003, 332.
22. James Daly, "Restart, Redo, Recharge," *Business 2.0*, May 1, 2001, 11.
23. Chris Pereira, "Wii Play Is the Best Selling Game," 1Up.com, January 15, 2009; Chris Pereira, "December NPDs; Wii and DS Combine for OVER 5 Million," 1Up.com, January 15, 2009; Kathy Shwiff, "New Sony Game Nears Breaking Even," *Wall Street Journal*, December 30, 2008; Daisuke Wakabayashi, "Hope Fades for PS3 as a Comeback Player," *Wall Street Journal*, December 29, 2009; Jonathan V. Last, "Playing the Fool," *Wall Street Journal*, December 30, 2009.
24. CBC *Venture*, "IdeaFetch," broadcast November 29, 2006; Brian Calamese, "Guardian by PetSafe Launches National Invention Contest," Guardian press release, May 22, 2006; "PetSafe Fetches Next Big Pet Idea," PR Newswire, www.prnewswire.com; "PetSafe's 'IdeaFetch' Contest," DoggieNews.com; www.doggienews.com; www.petsafe.net; www.ideafetch.ca.

CHAPTER 10

1. Max Chafkin, "And the Money Comes Rolling In," *Inc.com*, January 1, 2009, www.inc.com/magazine; "Making Money Making Dates," *National Post*, Canada.com, July 20, 2007, www.canada.com; Lee Gomes, "PlentyOfFish Owner Has the Perfect Bait for a Hugh Success," *Wall Street Journal*, May 23, 2007, B1; "Plentyoffish.com Dating Site Review," *Strategy*, July 15, 2009, 22; http://www.plentyoffish.com.
2. Statistics Canada, www.statcan.gc.ca/, Employment by Industry and Sex, CANSIM table 282-0008, January 29, 2010; Statistics Canada, Environments, Accounts, and Statistics Division, Total and Environmental Revenues by Industry, Catalogue no. 16F0008XIE, February 1, 2010.
3. Statistics Canada, www.statcan.gc.ca/, Employment by Industry, Catalogue no. 71F0004XCB, January 29, 2010.
4. Statistics Canada, www.statcan.gc.ca/, Gross Domestic Product, Expenditure-Based, Catalogue no. 13-001-XIB, May 31, 2010.
5. Ibid.
6. www.basspro.com.
7. Valarie A. Zeithaml, Mary Jo Bitner, and Dwayne Gremler, *Services Marketing* (New York: McGraw-Hill, 2009).
8. Paula Andruss, "Delivering WOW Through Service," *Marketing News*, October 15, 2008, 7.
9. Zeithaml, Bitner, and Gremler, *Services Marketing*.
10. Michael Applebaum, "One Tough Customer," *Brandweek*, March 19, 2007, 19–22.
11. Chris Daniels, "A Room for All Seasons," *Marketing*, February 4, 2002, 6, 7; www.fourseasons.com.
12. Much of the material in this section is based on Christopher H. Lovelock and Jochen Wirtz, *Services Marketing*, 6th ed. (Upper Saddle River: Prentice-Hall, 2007).
13. Wendy Perrin, "Bells and Whistles," Special business supplement to *Condé Nast Traveler*, 21–22.
14. Lovelock and Wirtz, *Services Marketing*.
15. Windsor-Essex County Development Commission, *Auto and MTDM Sector Strategic Plan*, March 2009.
16. Christina Binkley, "Soon, the Desk Clerk Will Know All About You," *Wall Street Journal*, May 8, 2003, D4.
17. Sue Shellenberger, "To Win the Loyalty of Your Employees, Try a Softer Touch," *Wall Street Journal*, January 26, 2000, B1.
18. Carmine Gallo, "Bringing Passion to Starbucks, Travelocity," *Business Week*, January 2, 2008, on-line.
19. Robert Passikoff, "Why Starbucks Has Ground to a Halt," *Brandweek*, November 10, 2008, 16.
20. Richard Bloom, "Canadian CEOs View Their Companies as World Class: Poll," *Globe and Mail*, January 21, 2004, B1, B5.
21. Statistics Canada, www.statcan.gc.ca/, Consolidated Federal, Provincial, Territorial, and Local Government Revenue and Expenditures, CANSIM table 385-0001, February 24, 2010; Statistics Canada, www.statcan.gc.ca/, Public Sector Employment, Wages, and Salaries, CANSIM table 183-0002, February 24, 2010.
22. Canada NewsWire, "Midnight Movie Marathon at Rainbow Cinemas to Benefit Two Charities," January 21, 2004, 1; www.gateway.proquest.com.
23. *Tribute*, www.tribute.ca.
24. CBC, *MarketPlace*, "Left a Loan," broadcast February 28, 2007; www.iaplife.com; www.carhelpcanada.com; The Canadian Life and Health Insurance OmbudService, www.clhio.ca.

CHAPTER 11

1. Lisa Kadane, "The New Party Animals; Direct Sellers Deliver Cocktails and Crostini With a Side of Shopping," *Edmonton Journal*, January 2, 2010, F7; Mary Teresa Bitti, "Laid Off? Why not Throw a Party? Direct Selling Firms Doing Well in Economic Downturn," *National Post*, May 25, 2009, FP4; "Company's Plan for Warehouse at Airport Nixed," *Times-Colonist*, January 31, 2008, B3.

2. Nicole Harris, "'Private Exchanges' May Allow B-to-B Commerce to Thrive After All," *Wall Street Journal*, March 16, 2001, B1; Michael Totty, "The Next Phase," *Wall Street Journal*, May 21, 2001, R8.

3. www.avoncompany.com/about/gettingavon.

4. Wade Lambert, "Publisher Puts Story Machines in London Tube," *Wall Street Journal*, February 22, 2001, B1.

5. Starbucks Annual Report, 2008.

6. Matthew Schifrin, "Partner or Perish," *Forbes Best of the Web*, May 21, 2001, 26; Jonathan Eig, "H.J. Heinz, Japan's Kagome Agree to Investments as Part of Alliance," *Wall Street Journal*, July 26, 2001, B11.

7. Jonathan Welsh, "Auto Makers Now 'Slam' Cars Right in the Factory," *Wall Street Journal*, October 30, 2001, B1.

8. Kyle Cattani and Vincent Mabert, "Supply Chain Design: Past, Present and Future," *Production and Inventory Management Journal*, Vol. 45, No. 2, April 2009, 47–57.

9. Andrew Reese, "Finding the Strategic Price," *Supply & Demand Chain Executive*, October/November 2009, 28; www.dod.mil; www.cmcusa.org.

10. Rob Wherry, "Ice Cream Wars: Dreyer's Conquered Supermarket Freezers. Now It's Going After the Corner Store," *Forbes*, May 28, 2001, 160.

11. David Hannon, "Leverage RFID for Streamlined Logistics," *Purchasing Magazine*, April 2008, 20; Bill Vlasic, "Global SUV Fuels GM's 'Revolution,'" *Detroit News*, August 1, 2004, 1A, 8A.

12. Tamara Audi, "Ailing Sheraton Shoots for a Room Upgrade," *Wall Street Journal*, March 25, 2008, A1.

13. Ellen Neuborne, "Big Brands (Small Companies)," *Business Week*, August 13, 2001, 12.

14. Marina Strauss, "In Small-Town Ontario, Store Wars Fought with Lawyers and Lobbyists, Not Coupons," *Globe and Mail*, August 28, 2006, B1, B11.

15. Evan West, "These Robots Play Fetch," *Fast Company*, July/August 2007, 49–50.

16. Stacy Perman, "Automate or Die," *Business 2.0 Online*, July 2003.

17. www.balancedscorecard.org, accessed July 9, 2010.

18. Monica Isbell and Chris Norek, "How Global Trade and Transportation Trends Impact North America's Transportation Infrastructure," *CSCMP Explores*, Spring 2008, 3.

19. Greg Keenan, "Border Study Calls for New Crossing," *Globe and Mail*, November 5, 2003, B1, B6.

20. George Anderson, "Best Buy Focusing RFID Efforts at Front of Store," www.retailwire.com, accessed June 6, 2010.

21. www.roadway.com; www.inboundlogistics.com.

22. Caitlin Kelly, "Rolling Onward," *Supply Chain Management* on-line, September 30, 2001.

23. Renee Boucher Ferguson, "Outsourcing Supply Chains," *eWeek*, April 2, 2001, 17.

24. www.ford.com; "Ford Hands Off Vehicle Delivery to Third Party," *Logistics Management and Distribution Report*, March 2000.

25. www.appleinsider.com, accessed July 9, 2010.

26. www.iphonetoolbox.com, accessed July 9, 2010.

27. Ken Bensinger, "Can You Spot the Fake?" *Wall Street Journal*, February 16, 2001, W1; Todd Zaun and Karby Leggett, "Motorcycle Makers from Japan Discover Piracy Made in China," *Wall Street Journal*, July 25, 2001, A1.

28. "Air Canada Extends Simplified Internet Fares to U.S. Flights," *Globe and Mail*, January 27, 2004, B2.

28. William Hoffman, "Dell Chief Targets Supply-Chain Gaps," *Shipping Digest*, March 12, 2007; Clay Risen, "Dell Takes on India," *World Trade Magazine*, September 2006; David Hannon, "Dell Flies in the Right Direction," *Purchasing*, November 17, 2005.

30. Chris Sorensen, "Big Profits Seen at Air Canada Cargo Unit," *Financial Post*, May 26, 2005, FP1, FP3. See also CBC, *Venture*, "Cargojet," broadcast February 15, 2004; www.cargojet.com; Kathlyn Horibe, "Canada's Maindeck Additions," *Air Cargo World Online*, www.aircargoworld.com, August 2006; Chris Sorensen, "Big Profits Seen at Air Canada Cargo Unit," *Financial Post*, May 26, 2005, FP1, FP3.

CHAPTER 12

1. Sunny Freeman, "Lululemon Targeting 45 Markets for Showroom Openings to Create Brand Buzz," Canadian Press, March 25, 2010; Lululemon corporate website, www.lululemon.com, accessed May 16, 2010; Canadian Press, "Lululemon Goes from Minority to Majority Shareholder in Aussie Yoga Brand," Canadian Press, May 12, 2010.

2. Retail Council of Canada, "2006/2007 Profile of the Canadian Retail Industry," www.retailcouncil.org/mediacentre/profile.asp, accessed May 17, 2010; Paul M. Jacobson, "The Structure of Retail in Canada," Retail 2004, Industry Canada, www.strategis.ic.gc.ca.

3. Statistics Canada, "Retail Trade January 2010," www.statcan.gc.ca/pub/63-005-x/63-005-x2010001-eng.pdf, accessed April 10, 2010; Statistics Canada, "Table 3 Canadian Economic Accounts Key Indicators," *The Daily*, Monday, March 1, 2010.

4. Statistics Canada, "Retail Trade, Operating Statistics, by Province and Territory (Canada)," www.statcan.gc.ca/, April 1, 2010.

5. Statistics Canada, "Table 1: Summary Statistics for Retail Trade, 2008," *Retail Trade 2008*, www.statcan.gc.ca/, accessed June 4, 2010; Statistics Canada, "Table 3: Summary Statistics for Non-Store Retail Trade, 2008," *Retail Trade 2008*, www.statcan.gc.ca/, accessed June 4, 2010.

6. http://honesteds.sites.toronto.com; www.truserv.ca; www.northwest.ca; www.hartstores.com; www.sr-store.com accessed May 18, 2010.

7. David Schultz, "The Definitive Ranking of the Nation's Biggest Specialty Chains," *Stores* on-line, August 2001.

8. www.mooresclothing.com, accessed May 10, 2010.

9. Statistics Canada, "Table 4-1: Average expenditure per household, Canada, provinces and territories, recent years—Canada," Spending Patterns in Canada 2008, www.statcan.gc.ca/, accessed June 4, 2010; Statistics Canada, "Retail Store Sales by Selected Commodity," Retail Sales by Type of Product, www.statcan.gc.ca/, accessed June 4, 2010.

10. Statistics Canada, "Food Expenditure in Canada 2001," 11, www.statcan.gc.ca/; Don Little and Leslie Bennett, "Food Services Competition in the 1990s," *Analytical Paper Series: Services Indicators*, Statistics Canada, July 2000.

11. Loblaws website, www.loblaws.ca/LCLOnline/home.jsp?_requestid=416717A, accessed June 4, 2010.

12. Citizenship and Immigration Canada, "Facts and Figures 2008—Immigration Overview: Permanent and Temporary Residents," www.cic.gc.ca, accessed June 4, 2010.

13. Couche Tard website, "Our Company," www.couche-tard.com/corporatif/the-network.html, accessed June 4, 2010.

14. Walmart 2010 Annual Report, www.walmart.com; "Fiscal 2010 End-of-Year Store Count." Walmart 2010 Annual Report, www.walmart.com; www.walmart.ca.

15. Press Release, "The Creativity Collection by Paris Hilton Is Now Available at Zellers Across Canada!," Canada NewsWire, December 17, 2009; Hollie Shaw, "Bay Kicks Off Line of Clothes: New Lines Aim to Draw Customers to Exclusive Brands," *National Post*, March 9, 2007, FP3; www.zellers.ca.

16. Walmart 2010 Annual Report, www.walmart.com; Calvin Leung, "Joseph Mimran Stages a Comeback: Meet Joe Fresh," *Canadian Business*, November 6–19, 2006, 49.

17. www.tescopoly.org, accessed June 19, 2008.

18. www.dollarstore.ca; Nancy Kwon, "Know Thy Enemy," *Canadian Grocer*, February 2007, 26.

19. CBC News, "Wal-Mart Canada to close Sam's Club stores," www.cbc.ca/money/story/2009/02/27/walmart-samsclub .html, accessed June 6, 2010.

20. "Research: Canada's Foodservice Industry," www.crfa.ca, accessed June 6, 2010.

21. Statistics Canada, "Retail Non-store Industries, Operating Statistics, by Province and Territory (Canada)," www40.statcan.gc.ca/l01/cst01/trad40a-eng.htm, accessed June 6, 2010.

22. Dana Flavelle, "New Fit for Vending Machines: Mark's Work Wearhouse Tries New Technique to Sell Its Clothes at Two GTA Locations," January 15, 2010, www.thestar.com/news/gta/article/7510 19, accessed June 6, 2010.

23. Gene Marcial, "Vending Machines Are Learning to Love Plastic," *Business Week*, August 13, 2007.

24. David Hayes, "Postcard from Tokyo: Rise of the (Vending) Machines," this.org/magazine/2009/06/02, accessed June 6, 2010.

25. Ibid.

26. www.usatech.com, accessed June 19, 2008.

27. Statistics Canada, "Retail Non-store Industries, Operating Statistics, by Province and Territory (Canada)."

28. Amy Lo, "Selling Dreams the Mary Kay Way," *AsiaWeek*, June 29, 2001.

29. Statistics Canada, "Retail Non-store Industries, Operating Statistics, by Province and Territory (Canada)."

30. www.justwhiteshirts.com, accessed June 6, 2010.

31. Canadian Media Directors' Council, *Media Digest 09–10*, 13.

32. Michelle Warren, "Counting on Catalogues," *Marketing Magazine*, March 6, 2006.

33. Ibid.

34. Jamie Tarrant, "Unlisted Numbers: Are the Hidden Costs of the CRTC's Do-Not-Call Registry Worth the Consumer Convenience?" *Western Standard*, April 24, 2006, 18.

35. CRTC website, "Telecom Decision CRTC 2007-48," July 3, 2007, www.crtc.gc.ca/eng/archive/2007/dt2007-48.htm, accessed June 6, 2010.

36. www.theshoppingchannel.com, accessed June 6, 2010.

37. Canadian Media Directors' Council, *Media Digest, 09–10*, 71-72; Internet World Stats, "Top 20 Countries With the Highest Number of Internet Users," updated, September 20, 2009, www.internetworldstats.com/top20.htm, accessed June 6, 2010.

38. Statistics Canada, "E-Commerce: Shopping on the Internet," *The Daily*, November 17, 2008.

39. Amazon.Com Annual Report 2009; www.amazon.com, accessed June 7, 2010.

40. www.outfitters.ca, accessed June 7, 2010.

41. Michelle Warren, "Plugged In," *Marketing Magazine*, November 19, 2001;

Chris Daniels, "Keeping Control of Explosive Growth," *Marketing Magazine*, November 17, 2003.

42. www.ebay.com.

43. Canadian Franchise Association, "Canadian Franchise Association Members," www.cfa.ca.

44. Ibid.; www.franchisedirectory.ca; "Canadian Franchise Market," www.royalbank.com/franchise/market_ca.html; www.franchise.org.

45. www.dominos.com.

46. Canadian Franchise Association, "Canadian Franchise Association Members-KFC," www.cfa.ca; International Franchise Association, www.franchise.org; KFC, "About Us," www.kfc.com; all accessed June 8, 2010.

47. www.franchise.org, accessed June 8, 2010.

48. Matthew McLearn, "The Ode: Dack's Shoes," *Canadian Business*, February 15, 2010, www.canadianbusiness.com; press release, "Quality Footwear Retailer Dack's Slips in to Bankruptcy; Closing Last 6 Stores," *Canadian Press*, December 16, 2009.

49. Robert Beaudoin And Daniel Charron, "Dressing Up Croteau," *Marketing Magazine*, September 16, 2002.

50. Susan Catto, "The People in your Neighbourhood," *Marketing Magazine*, March 23, 2009.

51. Scott Gardiner, "A Truly Awesome Database," *Marketing Magazine*, April 29, 2002.

52. www.amazon.ca; www.tigerdirect.ca; www.rugman.com; www.fridgedoor.com.

53. www.canadiantire.ca; www.presidentschoice.ca.

54. Press release, "Canadian Tire Celebrates the Grand Opening of Q in Mississauga," Canada NewsWire, September 6, 2006.

55. canada.frenchconnection.com; Street Talk, "FCUK's 'front end,'" *Marketing Magazine*, July 14, 2003; David Menzies, "Complain, Complain, Complain," *Marketing Magazine*, November 20, 2000; Jennifer Campbell, "FCUK's Risque Ads Get the Boot," CanWest News, October 20, 2003, 1.

56. Mike Moriarty et al., "Growth Opportunities for Global Retailers," The A.T. Kearney 2007 Global Retail Development Index, at www.atkearney .com, accessed January 2, 2008; Pamela N. Danziger, "The Global Luxury Market: Exploring the Mindset of Luxury Consumers in Seven Countries," Consumer Research Center Special Report, June 2007; Eoin Gleeson, "How China Fell in Love with Louis Vuitton," www.moneyweek.com, August 6, 2007; Shaun Rein, "Chinese Seek Quality from Multinationals," www.forbes.com, October 3, 2007; "Corporate FDI Plans Constant Despite Credit Market Turmoil," A.T. Kearney, December 10, 2007, www.atkearney.com, accessed January 2, 2008; "A World of Retail: The Top Emerging Countries for Global

Retail Expansion," WWD, December 11, 2007, 38; Aaron Dalton, "Amazing Asian Mega-Malls," www.forbestraveler.com, April 27, 2007; "Global Luxury Goods Market Growing at 9% Per Year Despite Uncertain Signals," Bain & Company, www.bain.com, November 14, 2007; Jessica Pallay, "Home Coming; Mohan Murjani Brings His Expertise to India's Booming Retail Scene," WWD, November 14, 2007, 22; "Asia 2015: Promoting Growth, Ending Poverty," The World Bank, http://go .worldbank.org/70UUD3QSY0, accessed January 7, 2008.

57. www.westedmontonmall.com, accessed June 8, 2010.

58. http://www.heartlandtown.com, accessed June 8, 2010.

59. "Highland Village: A Supercenter with a View," *Retailing Today*, December 10, 2007.

60. Nick Wingfield, "How Apple's Store Strategy Beat the Odds," *Wall Street Journal*, May 17, 2006, B1.

61. Kate Murphy, "A Sales Pitch Right Under Your Nose," *New York Times*, September 13, 1998, 8.

62. Sara Silver, "Motorola's New Devices Target Retailers," *Wall Street Journal*, January 14, 2008, B4.

63. www.homer.ca/shopping, accessed June 8, 2010.

64. Laura Severs, "Stores Turn to Technology to Improve Customer Satisfaction," *Business Edge*, June 1, 2007, www.businessedge.ca, accessed June 8, 2010.

65. "USA Technologies Expands into $4B Office Coffee Industry," www.usatech.com, February 18, 2009; www.verisign.com/verisign-inc/news-and-events/news-archive/us-news-2006/page_039937.html, accessed October 30, 2007.

66. Industry Canada Office of Consumer Affairs, "Mobile Commerce: New Experiences, Emerging Consumer Issues," *Consumer Trends Update*, Winter 2010, www.ic.gc.ca, accessed June 8, 2010; Samantha Murphy, "Getting iReady: M-Commerce to Pick-Up Steam in United States," *Chain Store Age*, August 2007.

67. "Contemporary Pop Up Shop," *Toronto Life Magazine*, June 8, 2010, www.torontolife.com; "New Pop-Up Stores: Wired, illy, Mishka, Toys 'R' Us," www.newyorkology.com, November 14, 2007.

68. Ibid.

69. Norml website, "Umbro Champions Collection Pop-Up Shop," Tuesday, May 25, 2010, www.normlclothing.com/blog/umbropopupishere; Peter Sayer, "Apple Opens Largest European Store-in-Store in Paris," *PC World*, June 29, 2007, http://pcworld .about.com/od/companynews/Apple-openslargest-European-s.htm; "Kolo Opens First Manhattan Store-Within-a-Store at Kate's Paperie

in Soho," *PRNewswire*, May 30, 2007; Paul Nunes and Brian Johnson, *Mass Affluence: Seven New Rules of Marketing to Today's Consumer* (Cambridge: Harvard Business School Press, 2004) 182.

70. This application exercise is based on the contribution of Amy Hubbert (University of Nebraska at Omaha) to "Great Ideas in Teaching Marketing," a teaching supplement that accompanies Lamb, Hair, and McDaniel's *Marketing*. Professor Hubbert's entry, "Discovery of Strategic Retailing Factors," was a winner in the "Best of the Great Ideas in Teaching Marketing" contest conducted in conjunction with the publication of the eighth edition of *Marketing*.

71. Ryerson Research News, "Top Green Retailers Find Sustainability Makes Good Business Sense," February 18, 2010, www.ryerson.ca/news/news/Research_News/20100218_green.html

72. Ibid.

73. "When Buying Green, Consumers Want to Shell Out Less Green," June 9, 2010, www.greeningretail.ca/news/.

74. Mountain Equipment Co-op corporate website, www.mec.ca.

75. Ibid.

76. Greeningretail, "Mountain Equipment Co-op," www.greeningretail.ca/featured/archive.dot#mec.

77. "Canadian Tire Outlines Strategy for Growth Focused on 'Core' Business," Canada NewsWire, April 7, 2010.

78. "Canadian Tire Strategy," Business News Network, April 7, 2010, [04-07-10 7:35 AM], http://watch.bnn.ca/#clip285839.

79. "Canadian Tire Outlines Strategy for Growth Focused on 'Core' Business,."

80. Ibid.

81. "Canadian Tire Strategy."

END OF PART 4 CASES

1. Associated Press, "The Boss Is Owning up to a Mistake," January 31, 2009, http://music.yahoo.com/read/news/12176684, accessed February 1, 2009; "Bruce Springsteen Plans Wal-Mart Only 'Greatest Hits'," *Rock & Roll Daily*, December 22, 2008, www.rollingstone.com/rockdaily/index.php/2008/12/22/brucespringsteen-plans-wal-mart-only-greatest-hits/, accessed February 1, 2009; Andrew Clark, "Springsteen Says Wal-Mart Album Deal was Mistake," February 1, 2009, www.guardian.co.uk/music/2009/feb/01/bruce-spring-steenwal-mart, accessed February 1, 2009; Jonathan Cohen, "Wal-Mart Snags Exclusive Springsteen Hits Set," Billboard, December 23, 2008, www.billboard.com/bbcom/news/wal-mart-snagsexclusive-springsteen-hits-1003924662.story, accessed February 1, 2009; "The Boss Says the Band Made a Bad Call," NME News, www.nme.com/news/bruce-springsteen/42451, accessed February 1, 2009; Peter Rakobowchuk, "Union Sees Partial Win After Top Court Rules in Favour of Wal-Mart," Canadian Press, November 27, 2009.

2. "Loblaw's New President Charts a Course to Return the Grocer to Its 'Glory Days' of Being Canada's 'Best' as Well as Biggest Food Retailer," *Natural~Specialty Foods Memo*, May 3, 2008, www.naturalspecialtyfoodsmemo.blogspot.com/2008/05/retail-memo-loblaws-new-president.html.

3. Joanna Pachner, "This Little Yogurt Went to Market," *Report on Business Magazine*, October 2008, 92.

4. "Loblaw, Targeting Wal-Mart Like Efficiency, Still Battling Supply Chain Re-Design Woes," *Supply Chain Digest*, January 26, 2006, hwww.scdigest.com/assets/NewsViews/06-01-26-1.cfm?cid=129&ctype=content.

5. Pachner, "This Little Yogurt Went to Market."

6. "Loblaw, Targeting Wal-Mart Like Efficiency, Still Battling Supply Chain Re-Design Woes."

CHAPTER 13

1. Jeromy Lloyd, "James Ready Lending a Helping Hand," *Marketing Magazine*, May 7, 2009; "Share Our Billboard Campaign," *Marketing Magazine*, June 15, 2009; Russ Martin, "James Ready to Party Near Campus," *Marketing Magazine*, October 15, 2009; www.jamesready.com.

2. Stuart Elliot, "Subway's New Campaign," *New York Times*, September 22, 2003.

3. Ian Austen, "In a Quebecer's Heart, Pepsi Occupies a Special Place," *New York Times*, July 30, 2009, www.nytimes.com/2009/07/31/business/media/31adco.html.

4. Austen, "In a Quebecer's Heart, Pepsi Occupies a Special Place"; Danny Kucharsky, "Relaxed Meunier Featured in Diet Pepsi Spots," *Marketing Daily*, June 26, 2003; Lara Mills, "Campaigns With Legs," *Marketing Magazine*, May 15, 2000.

5. Andrew McMains, "'Absolut World' Debuts," *ADWEEK*, April 27, 2007, www.adweek.com; Jeremy Mullman, "Breaking With Bottle Fires up Absolut Sales," *Advertising Age*, February 18, 2008.

6. Ibid.

7. www.absolut.com/iaaw/, accessed June 23, 2008.

8. Mullman, "Breaking with Bottle Fires up Absolut Sales."

9. Stuart Elliott, "In an 'Absolut World,' a Vodka Could Use the Same Ads for More Than 25 Years," *New York Times*, April 27, 2007.

10. Canadian Press, "Montreal Sells Itself as Global 'Lab' for New Advertising Strategies," *Marketing Magazine*, August 25, 2009.

11. State of the Blogosphere 2008, technorati.com; accessed February 2009; Royal Pingdom, "Internet Numbers 2009- Social Media," royal.pingdom.com/2010/01/22/internet-2009-in-numbers/, accessed June 14, 2010.

12. Jason Fry, "Blog Epitaphs? Get Me Rewrite!" *Wall Street Journal*, February 27, 2006, www.technorati.com/weblog/2006/02/81.html.

13. Tania Ralli, "Brand Blogs Capture the Attention of Some Companies," *New York Times*, October 24, 2005, C6; www.thebarqsman.com, accessed June 14, 2010.

14. "Blogs Can Offer a Big Advantage to Brands—If They're Honest," *New Age Media*, March 23, 2006.

15. Peter Sanders, "Starwood's Web Log Caters to Loyalty," *Wall Street Journal*, April 12, 2006, B3.

16. www.philips.com.

17. Ibid.

18. Michelle Warren, "Allstream Speaks With Its Customers," *Marketing Magazine*, October 27, 2003, 3.

19. Kim Hart, "A Flashy Facebook Page at a Cost to Privacy," *Washington Post*, June 12, 2008, www.washingtonpost.com, accessed February 2008; www.allfacebook.com/2009/facebook-privacy, accessed February 2009; Ralph Gross and Alessandro Acquisti, "Information Revelation and Privacy in Online Social Networks (The Facebook Case)," ACM Workshop on Privacy in the Electronic Society, November 7, 2007; Jeromy Lloyd, "Talks With Facebook 'Very Positive,' Says Privacy Commissioner," *Marketing Magazine*, August 18, 2009; Jordan Adler, "Chatter: Facebook Privacy Updates," *Marketing Magazine*, May 27, 2010.

20. The AIDA concept is based on the classic research of E. K. Strong, Jr., as theorized in *The Psychology of Selling and Advertising* (New York: McGraw-Hill, 1925) and "Theories of Selling," *Journal of Applied Psychology* 9 (1925), 75–86.

21. Apple Quarterly Sales, www.apple.com; Bob Keefe, "During the Holiday Quarter, Apple Sold 14 Million iPods, Which Equates to More Than 100 a Minute," *Atlanta Journal Constitution*, January 11, 2006, C-1; www.appleinsider.com, accessed January 2006;" iTunes Store Tops 10 Billion Songs Sold," www.apple.com/pr/library/2010/02/25itunes.html, accessed June 15, 2010.

22. Thomas E. Barry and Daniel J. Howard, "A Review and Critique of the Hierarchy of Effects in Advertising," *International Journal of Advertising*, 9 (1990), 121–35.

23. Canadian Media Directors' Council, "Ethnic Media," *Media Digest*, 09/10, 15.

24. Louise Kramer, "In a Battle of Toothpastes, It's Information vs. Emotion," *New York Times*, January 17, 2007, C6.

25. This application exercise is based on the contribution of Lyn R. Godwin (University of St. Thomas) to "Great

Ideas in Teaching Marketing," a teaching supplement that accompanies Lamb, Hair, and McDaniel's *Marketing.* Professor Godwin's entry, "Taboo or Not Taboo: That Is the Question," was a runner-up in the "Best of the Great Ideas in Teaching Marketing" contest held in conjunction with the publication of the eighth edition of *Marketing.*

26. This application exercise is based on the contribution of David M. Blanchette (Rhode Island College) to "Great Ideas in Teaching Marketing," a teaching supplement that accompanies Lamb, Hair, and McDaniel's *Marketing.* Professor Blanchette's entry, titled "Applying Semiotics in Promotion," was a runner-up in the "Best of the Great Ideas in Teaching Marketing" contest held in conjunction with the publication of the eighth edition of *Marketing.*

27. Sam Schechner, "Winfrey Firm to Produce HBO Shows," *Wall Street Journal,* December 17, 2008; Guy Brighton, "Campfire's True Blood Campaign," *New York Times,* accessed February 19, 2009; Lynette Rice, "Ad Campaign for HBO's True Blood' Confuses Thirsty Consumers," *Entertainment Weekly,* July 22, 2008, online at www.ew.com, accessed February 23, 2009; www.bloodcopy.com; www.hbo.com/ events/trueblood/; Douglas Quenqua, "The Vampires Are Coming, but Only After Months of Warnings," *New York Times,* July 15, 2008; Jeff Beer, "Campfire Sinks Its Creative Teeth into True Blood," http://creativity-online.com/ ?action=news:article&newsId= 130134&sectionName=behind_ the_work, accessed February 19, 2009.

28. "AD WEEK: Advertising in a Digital Age," *Business News Network,* January 27, 2010, [01-27-10 4:45 PM].

CHAPTER 14

1. www.mastercard.ca, "Sponsorships," accessed June 13, 2010; Chris Daniels, "Priceless Promotions," *Marketing Magazine,* December 12, 2005.

2. Canadian Media Directors' Council, "Net Advertising Volume by Medium (Canada—Millions of Dollars)," *Media Digest,* 10–11, 12.

3. Statistics Canada, "Canada, Total Number of Jobs, Advertising and Related Services," Labour statistics consistent with the System of National Accounts, by North American Industry Classification System (NAICS), annual (2007), CANSIM, www.statcan.gc.ca, accessed June 18, 2010.

4. Bradley Johnson, "Global Marketers," Ad Industry Jobs: Advertising Age Data Center, www.adage.com, accessed February 2009.

5. Canadian Media Directors' Council, "Television," *Media Digest,* 10–11, 16.

6. Natalie Zmuda, "What Went into the Updated Pepsi Logo" *Advertising Age,*

October 27, 2008, www.adage.com, accessed February 2009; Natalie Zmuda, "Pepsi, Coke Try to Outdo Each Other with Rays of Sunshine," *Advertising Age,* January 19, 2009, www. adage.com, accessed February 2009; Jim Edwards, "Pepsi's New $1 Million Logo Looks Like Old Diet Pepsi Logo," *BNET Industries,* October 27, 2008, http://industry.bnet.com/ advertising/1000270.

7. Amitava Chattaopadhyay and Kunal Basu, "Humor in Advertising: The Moderating Role of Prior Brand Evaluation," *Journal of Marketing Research,* November 1990, 466–76.

8. www.buckleys.com, accessed June 18, 2010.

9. Rajiv Grover and V. Srinivasan, "Evaluating the Multiple Effects of Retail Promotions on Brand Loyalty and Brand Switching Segments," *Journal of Marketing Research,* February 1992, 76–89; see also S.P. Raj, "The Effects of Advertising on High and Low Loyalty Consumer Segments," *Journal of Consumer Research,* June 1982, 77–89.

10. Chevrolet, www.gm.ca/gm/english/ vehicles/chevrolet/real-reactions/ overview, accessed June 18, 2010.

11. www.shell.ca, accessed June 18, 2010.

12. www.madd.ca, accessed June 18, 2010; and #Taxi website, www.poundtaxi.com, accessed June 18, 2010.

13. "What Is Windows 7.0?," www.microsoft .com; Mary Jo Foley, "Microsoft Earmarks Another $200 million for Windows Advertising," *ZDNet,* June 20, 2008, http://www.zdnet.com/blog/ microsoft/microsoft-earmarks-another- 200-million-for-windows-advertising/ 1453, accessed June 18, 2010.

14. www.gm.ca, accessed June 18, 2010.

15. Iain Marlow, "Bell Aliant sues Rogers Over Internet Ads," *Globe and Mail,* February 15, 2010, http://www .theglobeandmail.com/report-on- business/industry-news/marketing/ bell-aliant-sues-rogers-over-internet-ads/ article1468899/, accessed June 15, 2010.

16. "Absolut Vodka Must Pull Campaign in Italy," February 2, 2001, www .adageglobal.com.

17. Fahad S. Al-Olyan and Kiran Karade, *Journal of Advertising,* Fall 2000, 69.

18. Tim Hortons website, www .timhortons.com, accessed June 19, 2010; www.youtube.com, "Tim Hortons Coffee Commercial—Welcome Home," www.youtube.com/watch?v= BzmHwF2G4Vk, accessed June 19, 2010; www.youtube.com, "Tim Hortons Sidney Crosby Commercial," www.youtube .com/watch?v=CSlMIuOEenE, accessed June 19, 2010.

19. www.timhortons.com, accessed June 19, 2010.

20. Virgin Mobile Canada website, www.virgin.ca, accessed June 19, 2010.

21. Ibid.; Paul-Mark Rendon, "Virgin Mobile Out to Crush Wireless Rivals," *Marketing Daily,* March 2, 2005; www.telusmobility.com.

22. www.telusmobility.com, accessed June 24, 2010.

23. Laura Q. Hughes and Wendy Davis, "Revival of the Fittest," *Advertising Age,* March 12, 2001, 18–19; www.hersheys .com/chocolateworld/, accessed January 2006.

24. Dalson Chen, "Racy Billboards Called 'Disgusting'" *Windsor Star,* March 6, 2010, www.windsor.com, accessed June 20, 2010; Dalson Chen, "Windsor Billboards Removed for Being Too Racy," *Windsor Star,* March 11, 2010, www.windsor.com, accessed June 20, 2010.

25. "'FT' Creates World's Biggest Newspaper," *Advertising Age,* October 20, 2003.

26. Press release, Clio Awards, www.clioawards.com/winners/image_ pop.cfm? medium_id=4&media_ directory=billboard&website_entry_ id=200729270&is_c=0&image_no=1.

27. Russell Abratt and Deanna Cowan, "Client Agency Perspectives of Information Needs for Media Planning," *Journal of Advertising Research,* November 1999, 37.

28. Canadian Media Directors' Council, "Net Advertising Revenue by Medium (Canada—Millions of Dollars)."

29. Canadian Media Directors' Council, "Consumer Magazines," *Media Digest,* 10–11, 43.

30. Ibid. 44–49.

31. Canadian Media Directors' Council, "Radio," *Media Digest,* 10/11, 24.

32. Canadian Media Directors' Council, "Television," 16–23.

33. Rogers Media, "TV Guide Channel," Canadian Advertising Rates and Data Service, February 2007.

34. "Super Bowl 2010: Ratings Set Record, Beat M*A*S*H Finale," *Wall Street Journal,* February 8, 2010, http://blogs.wsj.com/speakeasy/2010/ 02/08/super-bowl-2010-ratings-a-smash, accessed June 22, 2010; Chris Zelkovich, "Grey Cup a Ratings Champion," *The Star* (Toronto), December 1, 2009, www.thestar.com/sports/football/cfl/ greycup/article/732817–zelkovich-grey- cup-a-ratings-champion, accessed June 22, 2010; Chris Zelkovich, "Super Ratings Show Strength of Grey Cup and World Juniors, Too" *The Star* (Toronto), February 9, 2010, http://thestar.blogs .com/sportsmedia/2010/02/here-are- the-top-weekend-sports-ratings-on- english-canadian-television-as-complied- by-bbm-canada–1-nfl-super-bowl- sunda.html, accessed June 22, 2010; William Houston, "Cup Ad Rates Good, but Long Way From Super," *Globe and Mail,* November 19, 2008, http://v1. theglobeandmail.com/servlet/story/ RTGAM.20081119.wspt_truth19/ BNStory/ALLAN+MAKI/, accessed June 22, 2010.

35. Jim Edwards, "The Art of the Infomercial," *Brandweek*, September 3, 2001, 14; Ian French, "A Primer on DRTV," *Marketing Magazine*, August 25, 2003; Lynda Rinkenbach, "Ford Meets Fear Factor," *Marketing Magazine*, June 21, 2004.

36. Gergana Koleva, "Don't Buy It," *MarketWatch*, January 24, 2008, on-line.

37. Matt Semansky, "West 49, Glassbox Partner on TV Skateboard Show," *Marketing Magazine*, October 26, 2009.

38. Matt Semansky, "Citytv Takes Rona Renovation Show West," *Marketing Magazine*, May 29, 2009; "CRTC 'Keeping an Eye' on Product Placement Trend," *Marketing Magazine*, November 21, 2005.

39. Hollie Shaw, "FP Marketing: The Distracted Mind of a PVR Owner," *Financial Post*, January 26, 2010, http://network.nationalpost.com/np/blogs/fpposted/archive/2010/01/26/fp-marketing-the-distracted-mind-of-a-pvr-owner.aspx#ixzz0rcZ7BE2k.

40. Suzanne Vranica, "TV-Ad Test to Show If Less Is More; NBC Universal's Trial Run Will Measure Effectiveness of Fewer Commercials," *Wall Street Journal*, April 5, 2006, B3

41. Charles Rex Arbogast, "Pregnant Cause," *Globe and Mail*, February 1, 2007, S1; Barbara Martinez, "City Sight: Giant Ads Spring from Holes in the Ground," *Wall Street Journal*, August 18, 1999, B1, B10.

42. Canadian Media Directors' Council, "Out-of-Home & Transit," *Media Digest*, 09/10, 58–70.

43. Matt Semansky, "New and Unusual," *Marketing Magazine*, June 25, 2007, S3.

44. Mike Esterl, "Going Outside, Beyond the Billboard," *Wall Street Journal*, July 21, 2005, B3.

45. Ryan Woo, "Adidas Wows Japan with Vertical Soccer Field," *Wall Street Journal*, September 22, 2003, B1.

46. Virgin Atlantic Airways, www.theloerieawards.co.za/winners/search/?show=1, accessed January 2006.

47. Canadian Media Directors' Council, "Internet and Mobile Media," *Media Digest*, 09/10, 71–80; Internet World Stats, "Internet Usage and Population in North America," www.internetworldstats.com/stats14.htm, accessed June 22, 2010.

48. Canadian Media Directors' Council, "Internet and Mobile Media," *Media Digest*, 09/10, 71–73.

49. Todd Wasserman, "Search Marketers Finding New Homes on Client Side," *Brandweek*, February 5, 2007, 6.

50. www.bmwfilms.com.

51. Jack Neff, "Floors in Stores Start Moving," *Advertising Age*, August 20, 2001, 15.

52. Suzanne Vranica, "Think Graffiti Is All That's Hanging in Subway Tunnels? Look Again," *Wall Street Journal*, April 4, 2001, B1, B4.

53. Christopher Lawton, "Videogame Ads Attempt Next Level," *Wall Street Journal*, July 25, 2005, B6; "Video Game Advertising Gets a Boost," *USA Today*, December 16, 2004, B-1; Derek Sooman, "World's First Video Game Advertising Network," October 20, 2004, www.techspot.com; www.massiveincorporated.com, accessed January 2006; www.microsoft.com/presspass/press/2006/may06/05-04-MassiveIncPR.mspx, accessed May 20, 2006.

54. Canadian Media Directors' Council, "Internet and Mobile Media," *Media Digest*, 09/10, 74.

55. Eve Lazarus, "Sympatico Reaching out to Media Buyers to Encourage Wireless Move," *Marketing Magazine*, March 23, 2010.

56. Paul Korzeniowski, "Cell Phones Emerge as New Advertising Medium," *TechNewsWorld*, November 16, 2005, www.technewsworld.com/story/46630.html, accessed June 23, 2008; Philip John, "Going Mobile: Cell Phone Advertising Leaps Forward by Moving Sideways," *Mediaweek*, September 17, 2007, www.mediaweek.com, accessed June 23, 2008.

57. Jeremy Curthoys and Christopher W. Kendall, "Ambush Marketing and the *Sydney 2000 Games (Indicia and Images) Protection Act*: A Retrospective," in Nancy A. Miller, "Ambush Marketing and the 2010 Vancouver-Whistler Olympic Games: A Prospective View," *Intellectual Property Law Journal*, 22 (1), 2009, 75–86.

58. Miller, "Ambush Marketing and the 2010 Vancouver-Whistler Olympic Games: A Prospective View," 82.

59. Nancy Armour, "2 Dutch Women in Court for WCup Ambush Marketing," *Associated Press*, http://g.sports.yahoo.com/soccer/world-cup/news/world-cup-officials-women-were-dressed-to-shill–fbintl_ap-wcup-orangedress.html, June 15, 2010, accessed June 15, 2010.

60. Damian Inwood, "Lululemon Irks Olympic Officials with 'Rogue' Clothing Line," *CanWest News*, December 16, 2009.

61. Nancy Armour, "World Cup Officials: Women Were Dressed to Shill," *Associated Press*, http://g.sports.yahoo.com/soccer/world-cup/news/world-cup-officials-women-were-dressed-to-shill–fbintl_ap-wcup-orangedress.html, June 15, 2010, accessed June 15, 2010.

62. Juan Sanchez, "The Water Horse: Legend of the Deep" *CultureBuzz*, www.culturebuzz.com/a_live_advertising_monster_japan_article_1566.html, accessed February 12, 2008.

63. Canadian Media Directors' Council, *Media Digest*, 10/11.

64. Annette Bourdeau, "Brilliant: Zig Scares Up Viral for Scream," *Strategy*, December 2006, 9.

65. "No Virgins Here," *Marketing Magazine*, March 7, 2005, 1.

66. James Cowan, "Mad Men and the Art of Stealth Branding," *Canadian Business*, December 7, 2009, 71; Adam Bluestein, "Prime-Time Exposure: How Companies Can Make a Splash in the Big-Money World of TV Product Placement—Without Spending a Dime," *Inc.*, March 2008, 66, accessed June 23, 2008; www.sourcewatch.org/index.php?title=Product_placement; Kris Oser, "How a Product Placement Strategy Worked for Yahoo," AdAge.com, January 31, 2005, http://adage.com/latestnews; http://money.howstuffworks.com/product-placement.htm; "Product Placement Spending in Media 2005," www.pqmedia.com, accessed January 2006.

67. Philip J. Hart, "Product Placement For Dummies," *Marketing Magazine*, May 5, 2003.

68. Ibid.

69. Bluestein, "Prime-Time Exposure: How Companies Can Make a Splash in the Big-Money World of TV Product Placement—Without Spending a Dime"; www.sourcewatch.org/index.php?title=Product_placement.

70. www.bmw.ca, accessed June 24, 2010.

71. Meetings Canada.Com, "Canadian Sponsorship Spending Survived the Recession: Study," April 27, 2010, www.meetingscanada.com/public/content.jsf?id=/canadian-sponsorship-spending-survived-the-recession-study-20711, accessed June 23, 2010; "Sponsorship Spending," IEG sponsorship, www.sponsorship.com accessed February 2009.

72. Beverley Smith, "CN Stays on Board Women's Open," *Globe and Mail*, April 13, 2010, S.4; Sarah Dobson, "Kane Tees It Up for CN," *Marketing Magazine*, July 21, 2006; Canadian Women's Open website, www.cncanadianwomensopen.com, accessed June 23, 2010.

73. Red Bull website, www.redbull.com, accessed June 23, 2010; Red Bull Air Race website, www.redbullairrace.com, accessed June 23, 2010;

74. Kristin Laird, "CauseForce Get Physical to Fight Cancer," *Marketing Magazine*, January 22, 2010.

75. www.bitc.org.uk/resources/research/research_publications/corp_survey_3.html, accessed January 2006.

76. Kristin Laird, "Canadian Tire Jumpstarts Fundraiser," *Marketing Magazine*, May 26, 2009.

77. www.stjude.org/corporate/0,2516,410_2034_16782,00.html, www.thinkbeforeyoupink.org/Pages/InfoMktgCampaigns.html, and www.bitc.org.uk/752resources/research/research_publications/corp_survey_3.html, accessed January 2006.

78. www.playstation.ca, accessed June 23, 2010.

79. Ann Zimmerman, "Wal-Mart Enlists Bloggers to Combat Negative News," *Wall Street Journal*, March 7, 2006, D7.

80. Ibid.

81. "Blogs Can Offer a Big Advantage to Brands—If They're Honest," *New Age Media*, March 23, 2006, 15.

82. George Anders, "eBay to Refund Millions After Outrage," *Wall Street Journal*, June 14, 1999, B8; George Anders, "eBay Scrambles to Repair Image After Big Crash," *Wall Street Journal*, June 14, 1999, B1, B4.

83. Eric Reguly, "No Accents Please: BP's PR Woes Start at the Top," *Globe and Mail*, June 17, 2010, B.2.

84. Adapted from David Dunne, "Crisis? What Crisis?," *Marketing Magazine*, January 10, 2005.

85. Gail Schiller, "iTVX Unveils Evaluation Tool To Gauge Product Placement," *Brandweek*, February 4, 2008, 8.

86. Susanne Courtney, "Measuring PR," *Marketing Magazine*, October 30, 2000.

87. This application exercise is based on the contribution of S. J. Garner (Eastern Kentucky University) to "Great Ideas in Teaching Marketing," a teaching supplement that accompanies Lamb, Hair, and McDaniel's *Marketing*. Professor Garner's entry, "Creating Advertising for Illegal Products/Services," was a runner-up in the "Best of the Great Ideas in Teaching Marketing" contest conducted in conjunction with the publication of the eighth edition of *Marketing*.

88. This application exercise is taken from Chuck Williams, *Management*, 3rd ed. (Cincinnati: South-Western, 2005). The idea to include a crisis management exercise in this chapter came from a contribution by Jack K. Mandel (Nassau Community College) to "Great Ideas in Teaching Marketing," a teaching supplement that accompanies Lamb, Hair, and McDaniel's *Marketing*. Professor Mandel's entry, "Putting Students in the Line of Fire to Learn Crisis Management Techniques," received an honourable mention in the "Best of the Great Ideas in Teaching Marketing" contest held in conjunction with the publication of the eighth edition of *Marketing*.

89. Associated Press, "PlayStation Graffiti Ads Spark Controversy," *Marketing Daily*, January 5, 2006.

90. Joe Kovacs, "Fowl-Mouthed Slogans Too Hot for Burger King," *WorldNetDaily*, July 28, 2005, www.worldnetdaily.com, accessed January 20, 2009; Elaine Walker, "Crispin + Bogusky Revs up BK's Image," *Miami Herald*, August 1, 2005; Andrew LaVallee, "Burger King Cancels Facebook Ad Campaign," *Wall Street Journal*, January 15, 2009, http://blogs.wsj.com/digits/2009/01/15/burger-king-cancels-facebookad-campaign/, accessed January 20, 2009; Brian Grow, "Burger King: Raunch With Those Fries?" *BusinessWeek*, August 15, 2005, i3947, 9; Todd Wasserman, "Burger King Doesn't Have It Your Way," *BrandWeek*, January 19, 2009, www.brandweek.com/bw/content_display/current-issue/e3i4edf08b57868094d4c25f75cbb9-bab13, accessed January 20, 2009; Suzanne Vranica, "Fresh Palates for Burger King," *Wall Street Journal*, December 4, 2008, http://online.wsj.com/article/SB122834728675077461.html, accessed January 20, 2009.

91. Business News Network, *The Street with Michael Kane and Patricia Lovett-Reid*, "Olympic Advertising Bonanza?," February 12, 2010 : [02-12-10 8:15 AM].

CHAPTER 15

1. "No Forecasts—Just Lessons Learned in a Tough Year," *Automotive News*, January 4, 2010, 12; www.gm.ca, accessed June 25, 2010.

2. www.gm.com, accessed June 25, 2010.

3. Mark Rechtin, "Mendel: Honda on Track Despite Lost Share," *Automotive News*, May 24, 2010, 4.

4. Jeannine Fallon and Chintan Talati, "Cash for Clunkers Results Finally In: Taxpayers Paid $24,000 per Vehicle Sold, Reports Edmunds.com," Press Release, October 28, 2009, http://www.edmunds.com/help/about/press/159446/article.html; Tony Van Alphen, "GM Has Cash for Customers' Old Cars," *Toronto Star*, September 17, 2009, B2; Good Car Bad Car, "Canada Auto Sales By Brand May 2010," www.goodcarbadcar.net/2010/06/canada-auto-sales-may-2010.html, accessed June 26, 2010.

5. Van Alphen, "GM Has Cash for Customers' Old Cars"; Good Car Bad Car, "Canada Auto Sales By Brand May 2010."

6. "Annual Report: Industry Report, October 2008," *PROMO Magazine*, promomagazine.com, accessed February 2009.

7. Ibid.

8. Bob Duff, "Fine Dining for Spits," *Windsor Star*, April 28, 2010; "Windsor Spitfires versus Barrie Colts," Cogeco Cable Windsor, Local Station Cable 11, April 27, 2010; "Its the 35th Anniversary of the Worst Promotion Idea in Sports History," www.fark.com/cgi/comments.pl?IDLink=4428597&hl=Its-35th-anniversary-of-worst-promotion-idea-in-sports-history, accessed June 24, 2010; "14 Regrettable Professional Sports Promotions," www.sloshspot.com/blog/07-13-2009/14-Regrettable-Professional-Sports-Promotions-187, accessed June 24, 2010.

9. Coupon Industry Association of Canada, "Coupon Fact Sheet for the Year 2006—Coupon Use in Canada," www.couponscanada.org, accessed June 26, 2010.

10. "Drawing a Crowd by Cutting Up Designer T-Shirts," Canada NewsWire, September 23, 2009; www.jeanmachine.com, accessed June 26, 2010; "Jean Machine Canada Discounts: Capture 10% Off Every New Arrival With Your Cell or Digital Camera," http://dealcetera.com/jean-machine-canada-discounts-capture-10-off-every-new-arrival-with-your-cell-or-digi/, accessed June 26, 2010.

11. David Menzies, "Mail-In Rebates RIP," *Marketing Magazine*, September 12, 2005.

12. www.businessweek.com/bwdaily/dnflash/nov2005/nf20051123_4158_db016.htm, accessed February 2008.

13. Sarah Schmidt, "McDonald's Recall Puts Spotlight on Cadmium Dangers," CanWest News, June 4, 2010; "McDonald's Signs Promo Deal with DreamWorks," *Marketing Daily*, July 29, 2005; "Right Up Their Alley; McDonald's, Toys 'R' Us Share a Holiday Happy Meal," *PROMO Magazine*, December 1, 2001, 11.

14. www.tequilaaficionado.com/article.php?sid=336, accessed February 2008.

15. "Canadian Tire Introduces New Reward in Celebration of Canada's Iconic Loyalty Program," Canada NewsWire, November 30, 2009; "Canadian Tire Money," corp.canadiantire.ca/EN/AboutUs/Pages/CanTireMoney.aspx, accessed June 26, 2010; Eymbert Vaandering, "Hey, Big Spender," *Marketing Magazine*, January 14, 2002. See also "Working Knowledge," *Building Loyalty 2006*, 10 (An Advertising Supplement to *Marketing Magazine*), www.marketingmag.ca.

16. "Working Knowledge," *Building Loyalty 2006*, 5.

17. Working Knowledge," *Building Loyalty 2006*, 6; CBC News, "Loyalty Programs' Popularity Surges: Study," August 20, 2009, http://www.cbc.ca/consumer/story/2009/08/20/loyalty-survey.html, accessed June 26, 2010; Rob Lewis, "Air Miles and Aeroplan Top Loyalty Programs in Canada," April 15, 2009, http://www.techvibes.com/blog/air-miles-and-aeroplan-top-loyalty-programs-in-canada, accessed June 26, 2010; Rick Ferguson and Kelly Hlavlinka, *The Big Sort: The 2009 COLLOQUY Loyalty Marketing Census*, Loyalty One Colloquy, April 2009.

18. "Working Knowledge," *Building Loyalty 2006*, 5; Danny Kucharsky, "Consumers Drawn to Loyalty Rewards," *Marketing Magazine*, May 6, 2002.

19. Jacqueline Nunes, "Program Is Good Medicine: Shoppers Drug Mart Optimum Card One of the Most Successful," *Toronto Star*, April 1, 2010, 4.

20. TD website, "The GM Card," http://www.tdcanadatrust.com/tdvisa/gm.jsp#1, accessed June 26, 2010; Credit Cards Canada, http://www.creditcardsco.ca/co-branded-credit-cards.html, accessed June 26, 2010.

21. Vincent Alonzo, "Money Isn't Everything," *Sales and Marketing Management*, April 2000, 47–48.

22. www.caramilk.com, accessed June 27, 2010.

23. www.harveys.ca/eng/index.php, accessed June 27, 2010; http://www.facebook.com/HarveysCanada?ref=ts.

24. Tim Hortons Roll Up the Rim t Win website, www.rolluptherimtowin.com/

en/fun.php?winnercalendar, accessed June 27, 2010.

25. Paula Kozbial, "Show Off," *Canadian Grocer*, October 2008, 42.

26. Patricia Odell, "Steady Growth," *PROMO Magazine*, December 1, 2009; Stephanie Fagnani, "A Taste of Success: The Practice of Product Sampling Combines Favorable Location, Product Innovation, Thorough Promotion, and Timely Execution," *Supermarket News*, August 27, 2001, 33.

27. Eve Lazarus, "Touch, Feel, and Taste," *Marketing Magazine*, August 1, 2005.

28. Kristin Laird, "Riceworks' Sampling Program Goes Outside This Summer," *Marketing Magazine*, June 24, 2010.

29. Geoffrey A. Fowler, "When Free Samples Become Saviors," *Wall Street Journal*, August 14, 2001, B1, B4.

30. Kristin Laird, "Banana Boat Heads to Camp," *Marketing Magazine*, June 28, 2008.

31. Ibid.

32. Kristin Laird, "John Frieda Highlights Blonde Haircare at Special Event," *Marketing Magazine*, June 21, 2010.

33. Andrea Aster, "Signage of the Times," *Marketing Magazine*, March 21, 2005.

34. "Point-of-Purchase: $17 Billion," *PROMO Magazine*, October 29, 2001, 3; "In Praise of Promotion," PROMO Xtra, www.promomagazine.com, accessed January 2009.

35. Aster, "Signage of the Times."

36. Paul Brent, "Chip Power," *Marketing Magazine*, August 14, 2006.

37. Kristin Laird, "Everyone's a Winner at East Side Mario's," *Marketing Magazine*, January19, 2010.

38. www.marketingsherpa.com/article.html?ident=29788, accessed February 2009.

39. www.couponinfonow.com/Couponing/2007trendsoverview.cfm, accessed February 2009.

40. Kristin Laird, "Promo-Post Launching New Click-And-Save Service," *Marketing Magazine*, June 4, 2009.

41. Scene website, www.scene.ca/programbenefits.aspx, accessed June 27, 2010.

42. Libby Estell, "Economic Incentives," *Sales and Marketing Management*, October 2001, S2, S4.

43. www.trade-show-advisor.com/trade-showsurvey.html, accessed February 2008.

44. Elana Harris, "Standing Tall," *Sales and Marketing Management*, December 2000, 84.

45. Michael Beverland, "Contextual Influences and the Adoption and Practice of Relationship Selling in a Business-to-Business Setting: An Exploratory Study," *Journal of Personal Selling and Sales Management*, Summer 2001, 207.

46. Richard Morrison, "The Business Process of Customer Retention and Loyalty," *Customer Interaction Solutions*, October 2001, 4.

47. "The Right Questions and Attitudes Can Beef Up Your Sales, Improve Customer Retention," *Selling*, June 2001, 3.

48. Larry Rigs, "Hit 'Em Where They Work," *Direct*, October 15, 2003; www.directmag.com.

49. Maura Schreier-Fleming, "7 Habits of Less Successful Salespeople," MLM Knowhow, www.mlmknowhow.com/articles/marketing/7habitsless.htm, accessed November 5, 2010.

50. Jean Halliday, "Chrysler Web Offerings Draw Sales Leads," *Automotive News*, December 5, 2005, 22.

51. Alf Nucifora, "Need Leads? Try a Networking Group," *Business News New Jersey*, November 14, 2000, 22; Catherine Seda, "The Meet Market," *Entrepreneur*, August 2004, 68; Jim Dickie, "Is Social Networking an Overhyped Fad or a Useful Tool?" *Destination CRM*, January 21, 2005; Kristina Dell, "What Are Friends For?" Time, September 21, 2004.

52. Mike Grebb, "The Customer Connection: Living Up to Your Sales Pitch," www.sammag.com, March 1, 2001.

53. B. Weitz, S. Castleberry, and J. Tanner, *Selling* (Burr Ridge, IL: McGraw-Hill/Irwin, 2007), 196–97.

54. www.bicworld.com; www.BIClink.com.

55. Scott Cressman, "Eight Tips for Highly Effective Presentations," *Sales*, www.sammag.com, May 1, 2001.

56. Sherri Telenko, "Smoke Signals," *Canadian Jeweller*, September/October 2006, 127:5, 42.

57. www.chanimal.com; "chatrooms" link at the "Overcoming Objections" Web page, link to www.chanimal.com/html/objections.html.

58. www.expedia.ca, accessed June 28, 2010.

59. Media Newsroom, "RBC Insurance Opens Its First Retail Insurance Office," Royal Bank of Canada, July 11, 2005, www.rbc.com.

60. Weitz, Castleberry, and Tanner, *Selling*, 17–22.

61. www.ge.com.

62. Laura Fowlie, "Many Employers Catnapping Over Potential of Learning by Mouse," *Edmonton Journal*, March 17, 2004, F7.

63. www.oracle.com/index.html.

64. Libby Estelle, "Rewarding and Improving Performance Motivate Employees and Customers to Grab the Brass Ring," *Sales and Marketing Management*, October 2001, S1, S4.

65. Geoffrey Brewer, "The 7 Traits of Great Sales Leaders," *Sales and Marketing Management*, July 1997, 38–46.

66. This application exercise is based on the contribution of John Ronchetto (University of San Diego) to "Great Ideas in Teaching Marketing," a teaching supplement that accompanies Lamb, Hair, and McDaniel's *Marketing*. Professor Ronchetto's entry, "Sales and Customer Service Experiential Journal and Paper," was a winner in the "Best of the Great Ideas in Teaching Marketing" contest held in conjunction with the publication of the eighth edition of *Marketing*.

67. Statistics Canada, "Food Highlights," http://www.statcan.gc.ca/pub/21-020-x/2009001/aftertoc-aprestdm1-eng.htm, accessed June 29, 2010.

68. Kristin Laird, "McDonald's Serves up Fresh, Free Coffee for All," *Marketing Magazine*, April 20, 2009.

69. Ibid.

70. Jonathan Paul, "McDonald's Big Bean Blitz," *Strategy*, June 2009, 21.

71. "Tim Hortons Says Profits up but Pondering Price Hikes," *Marketing Magazine*, August 7, 2009.

72. North American International Auto Show website, "History," http://www.naias.com/about-naias/show-history.aspx, accessed June 29, 2010.

73. Ibid.

74. Business News Network, "Trading Day: Inside Toyota," broadcast January 12, 2010, [01-12-10 2:40 PM].

END OF PART 5 CASES

1. Lisa Belkin, "Moms and Motrin," *New York Times*, November 17, 2008, accessed March 21, 2009; Matthew Herper, "Twitter Moms Sink Motrin Ad," Forbes.com, November 2008, blogs.forbes.com/sciencebizblog/2008/11/twitter-moms-si.html, accessed March 21, 2009; Linda A. Johnson, "Slings and Arrows: Online Backlash Ends Motrin Ad," *USA Today*, November 17, 2008, www.usatoday.com/money/economy/2008-11-17-4080031906_x.htm, accessed March 21, 2009; Peter Kafka, "Twitterers, Bloggers Praise Motrin for Giving Them Something to Do Last Weekend," *MediaMemo*, November 17, 2008, mediamemo.allthingsd.com/20081117/twitters-bloggerspraise-motrin-for-giving-them-something-to-dolast-weekend/, accessed March 21, 2009; Scott Lackey, "Motrin Attacks Moms and Child Carriers: Twitter Users Fight Back," *The New Advertising*, thenewadvertising.blogspot.com/2008/11/ motrin-attacks-moms-and-child-carriers.html, accessed March 21, 2009; "MotrinGate: Twitter Moms Abuzz over Motrin Video," November 16, 2008, blog.guruofnew.com/new-stuff/motringate-twitter-moms-abuzz-over-motrinvideo, accessed March 21, 2009; Laura Petrecca, "Offended Moms Get Tweet Revenge over Motrin Ads," *USA Today*, November 18, 2008, www.usatoday.com/tech/products/2008-11-18-motrin-ads-twitter-N.htm?POE=click-refer, accessed December 10, 2008; Joyce Schwarz, "Motrin Twitter Flurry Update," *Hollywood2020*, November 16, 2008, hollywood2020.blogs.com/hollywood2020/2008/11/motrin-twitter.html, accessed March 21, 2009.

2. Interbrand website, "Best Global Brands 2009," http://www.interbrand.com/best_global_brands.aspx, accessed June 29, 2010.

3. Coca-Cola Company, "Annual Report," www.cocacola.com, accessed June 29, 2010.

4. Coca-Cola Slogans, http://www.angelfire.com/oh/cocacolaantiques/slogans.html, accessed June 29, 2010; Coca-Cola Slogans in America 1886–, http://en.wikipedia.org/wiki/Coca-Cola_slogans#Slogans.2C_1886_-_2010_in_America, accessed June 29, 2010.

5. Kristin Laird, "Coke Opens Happiness in Canada," *Marketing Magazine*, July 30, 2009.

6. Ibid.

7. "Coca-Cola Canada Opens Happiness at the Vancouver 2010 Olympic Winter Games," Canada NewsWire, February 9, 2010.

8. Ibid.

CHAPTER 16

1. James Cowan, "Retail: The Genius of Dollarama," *Canadian Business*, February 15, 2010, 38; Marina Strauss, "The Best Bet for Your Bottom Dollar," *Globe and Mail*, August 2, 2003, B1, B3.

2. Franziska Volckner, "The Dual Role of Price: Decomposing Consumers' Reactions to Price," *Journal of the Academy of Marketing Science*, Fall 2008, 359–77.

3. Ibid.

4. Tom Krazit, "Intel Gained Back Some Chip Market Share on the Heels of Advanced Micro Devices' Abysmal First Quarter," *ZDNet News*, accessed July 15, 2010.

5. Tammo Bijmolt, Harold Van-Heerde, and Rik Pieters, "New Empirical Generalizations on the Determinants of Price Elasticity," *Journal of Marketing Research*, May 2005, 141–56.

6. "India's Mobile Users Hit 4.5 Million," CNN.com, September 19, 2001.

7. "Financing Deals for New Cars Shake Up Market for Used Cars," *Wall Street Journal*, November 16, 2001, B1, B4.

8. "What the Traffic Will Bear," *Forbes*, July 3, 2008, 69.

9. Michael Mendano, "Priced to Perfection," *Business2.com*, March 6, 2001, 40–41.

10. Anne Kadet, "Buyer Beware," *Smart Money*, May 2006, 90–95.

11. "Behave," *Marketing News*, September 15, 2008, 13–15.

12. Simona Rabinovitch, "Pay-What-You-Can Hits Canada," *Canada Travel Guide*, AOL Travel Canada (travel.aol.ca), July 16, 2010.

13. David Henderson, "What Are Price Wars Good For? Absolutely Nothing," *Fortune*, May 12, 1997, 156.

14. Christina Passariello, "Beauty Fix: Behind L'Oreal's Makeover in India: Going Upscale . . . When Cheap Shampoo Didn't Sell, Company Tapped the Rising Class," *Wall Street Journal*, July 13, 2007, A1, A8.

15. "Price Buster," *Wall Street Journal*, July 17, 2000, R12.

16. Press release at FreeMarkets.com, accessed July 2010.

17. Jason Kirby, "West Jet's Plan to Crust Air Canada," *Maclean's*, May 4, 2009, 38–41.

18. "Wal-Mart Puts the Squeeze on Costs," *Fortune*, June 9, 2008, 16.

19. Praveen Kopalle and Donald Lehmann, "The Effects of Advertised and Observed Quality on Expectations About New Product Quality," *Journal of Marketing Research*, August 1995, 280–90; Akshay Rao and Kent Monroe, "The Effect of Price, Brand Name, and Store Name on Buyers' Perceptions of Product Quality: An Integrative Review," *Journal of Marketing Research*, August 1989, 351–57; Gerard Tellis and Gary Gaeth, "Best Value, Price-Seeking, and Price Aversion: The Impact of Information and Learning on Consumer Choices," *Journal of Marketing*, April 1990, 34–45; Dawar Niraj and Phillip Parker, "Marketing Universals: Consumers' Use of Brand Name, Price, Physical Appearance, and Retailer Reputation as Signals of Product Quality," *Journal of Marketing*, April 1994, 81–95; R. Chandrashekaran, "The Implications of Individual Differences in Reference to Price Utilization for Designing Effective Price Communications," *Journal of Business Research*, August 2001, 85–92.

20. Margaret Campbell, "Says Who? How the Source of Price Information and Affect Influence Perceived Price (UN)fairness," *Journal of Marketing Research*, May 2007, 261–271.

21. Steven Levy, "How Apple's iPhone Ate the New iPods," *Newsweek*, September 17, 2007; Chris Nuttall, "Apple Apologizes to Early Buyers of iPhone After New Discounts," *Financial Times*, September 7, 2007; Lev Grossman, "Apple's New Calling: the iPhone," *Time*, January 9, 2007.

22. Marketplace, *Busted: easyhome*, broadcast April 2, 2010, episode #37-09; http://www.easyhome.ca; Industry Canada, Office of Consumer Affairs, *Consumer Handbook: Tips for Consumers Considering Rent to Own*, http://www.ic.gc.ca/eic/site/oca-bc.nsf/eng/ca02381.html; Industry Canada, Office of Consumer Affairs, *Rent-to-Own: Portrait of an Industry and Its Clientele*, Option Consommateurs.

CHAPTER 17

1. Stewart Thornhill, "Go Big or Go Boutique?" *Financial Post Magazine*, October 2009, 55.

2. Thomas Nagle and George Cressman, "Don't Just Set Prices, Manage Them," *Marketing Management*, November/December 2002, 29–33; Jay Klompmaker, William Rogers, and Anthony Nygren, "Value, Not Volume," *Marketing Management*, June 2003, 45–48; Kent Monroe and Jennifer Cox, "Pricing Practices That Endanger Profits," *Marketing Management*, September/October 2001, 42–46.

3. Allison Wellner, "Boost Your Bottom Line by Taking the Guesswork Out of Pricing," *Inc.*, June 2005, 72–82.

4. "Why P&G's Smile Is So Bright," *Business Week*, August 12, 2002, 58–60.

5. Patrick Brethour and Janet McFarland, "Forzani Agrees to Pay Record Fine," *Globe and Mail*, July 7, 2004, B1, B22.

6. Andy Hoffman, "Labatt Convicted in Quebec Discount Beer Case," *Globe and Mail*, November 24, 2005, B10.

7. Bertrand Marotte and Simon Tuck, "Paper Firms Hit with Record Price-Fixing Fines," *Globe and Mail*, January 10, 2006, B2.

8. Nicolas Van Praet, "Profitable WestJet Accuses Air Canada of Using Court-Protection to Reduce Fares Below Cost," CanWest News, October 20, 2003, 1; "Small B.C. Airline Accuses Insolvent Air Canada of Predatory Pricing," Canadian Press NewsWire, April 16, 2003.

9. Miriam Jordan, "A Retailer in Brazil Has Become Rich by Courting the Poor," *Wall Street Journal*, June 11, 2002, A1, A8.

10. James Areddy, "Chinese Customers Overwhelm Retailers with Team Tactics," *Wall Street Journal*, February 28, 2006.

11. Marina Strauss, "Bargain Hunters Are Reaping the Spoils of Grocers' Price Wars," *Globe and Mail*, March 15, 2004, B11.

12. "Value Pricing," *Marketing News*, January 15, 2008, 8.

13. Joel Urbany, "Are Your Prices Too Low?" *Harvard Business Review*, October 2001, 26–27.

14. Rui Zhu, Xinlei Chen, and Srabana Dasgupta, "Can Trade-Ins Hurt You? Exploring the Effect of a Trade-In On Consumers' Willingness to Pay for a Product," *Journal of Marketing Research*, April 2008, 159–170.

15. Ibid.

16. Charles Quigley and Elaine Notarantonio, "An Exploratory Investigation of Perceptions of Odd and Even Pricing," in *Developments in Marketing Science*, ed. Victoria Crittenden (Miami: Academy of Marketing Science, 1992), 306–9; "Nine Cents of Separation," *American Demographics*, May 1998, 41.

17. Dilip Soman and John Gourville, "Transaction Decoupling: How Price Bundling Affects the Decision to Consume," *Journal of Marketing Research*, February 2001, 30–44.

18. www.aircanada.com; CBC, *Venture*, "Air Wars," broadcast January 27, 2002; Richard Blackwell, "Dogfight Ends, War Continues," *Globe and Mail*, May 30, 2006, B1, B3; Keith McArthur, "Rivals Grab Bigger Piece of Air Canada's

Market Share," *Globe and Mail*, April 21, 2004, B1, B6; Keith McArthur and Jacquie McNish, "Air Canada: A Knight, a Cash Grab," *Globe and Mail*, April 3, 2003, B1, B9; "Small B.C. Airline Accuses Air Canada of Predatory Pricing," Canadian Press NewsWire, April 16, 2003; Nicolas Van Praet, "Profitable WestJet Accuses Air Canada of Using Court-Protection to Reduce Air Fares Below Cost," CanWest News, October 20, 2003, 1.

END OF PART 6 CASES

1. www.ryanair.com; Arlene Fleming, "The World's Biggest Airlines," airtravel.about .com/od/airlines/a/bigair.htm, March 22, 2009; Steve Keenan, "Ryanair Finds Another Charge," Times Online, May 20, 2008; Ginny McGrath, "Outrage over Ryanair's Toilet Charge Plan," Times Online, February 27, 2009; "Ryanair to Abolish Check-In Desks," BBC News, February 21, 2009.
2. Rachel Metz, "Amazon's New Kindle E-book Reader Gets Slimmer," AP News, February 9, 2009; Richard Quest, "Sony Reader vs. Amazon Kindle," CNN.com, December 18, 2008.

CHAPTER 18

1. www.westjetvacations.com, accessed June 30, 2010.
2. Garin Tcholakian and Emily Wexler, "WestJet Vacations Get Personal," *Strategy*, June 2009, 7.
3. Ibid.
4. Joseph Hair, Robert Bush, and David Ortinau, *Marketing Research: Within a Changing Information Environment*, 4th ed. (Burr Ridge, IL: McGraw-Hill/ Irwin, 2009).
5. www.mitchell1.com and www.ondemand5.com, accessed February 2009.
6. Brian Clifton, "Advanced Web Metrics with Google Analytics," 2008; www.google.com/ analytics/ features.htm; www.google.com/ analytics/benefits.htm; ww.google.com/ analytics/ case_study.
7. Michael Burns, "CRM Survey 2010," *CA Magazine*, April 2010, 11.
8. www.netsuite.com/portal/products/ neterp/main.shtml and www.oracle.com, accessed February 2009.
9. "Bridgestone/Firestone Minds the Gap," directmag.com/mag/marketing_ bridgestonefirestone_minds_gap/, accessed February 2008.
10. Lorne Hill, "As Nimble as the Little Guys," *Marketing Magazine*, February 12, 2001.
11. http://us.playstation.com/psn/ community/index.htm, accessed July 3, 2010.
12. SAP Customer Success Story, "Playstation.com Chooses mySAP CRM," www.hp.com.
13. Ibid.
14. "SPC Card Announces Canada's Largest Youth Shopping Loyalty Program," Canada NewsWire, July 27, 2005; www.5thbusiness.com/ page.aspx?_id=success_stories _spc.htm, accessed July 3, 2010; www.spccard.ca/ about.aspx, accessed July 3, 2010.
15. www.bestbuy.ca, accessed July 3, 2010.
16. www.mypedigree.ca, accessed July 3, 2010.
17. www.chaptersindigo.ca, "iRewards," accessed July 3, 2010.
18. www.sony.com.
19. "Online Quotes Key Demand From Insurance Shoppers," *Digital Marketing Report*, April 21, 2003.
20. Ben Gose, "Give and Take: Direct Giving Websites Rely on Fees to Help Cover Costs," *Chronicle of Philanthropy*, August 7, 2008, www.philanthropy.com, accessed February 2009; Sue Hoye and Elizabeth Schwinn, "Competition for Donations Is Going Global, Fund Raiser Predicts," *Chronicle of Philanthropy*, August 7, 2008, www.philanthropy.com, accessed February 2009; Rachel Emma Silverman "A New Generation Reinvents Philanthropy," *Wall Street Journal*, August 21, 2007, www.online.wsj.com, accessed February 2009; www.kiva.org.
21. www.canadahelps.org/Info/3/16/41/ss; accessed July 3, 2010.
22. www.modestneeds.org.
23. *Webster's Dictionary*, (New York: Random House, 2008).
24. "Realtors Continue to Educate Themselves," *Toronto Star*, March 26, 2010, 11.
25. "The Key to Effective CRM: Building an Interactive Dialog," www.marketing3.nl, presentation in Utrecht, The Netherlands, December 4, 2003.
26. www.shoppersdrugmart.ca; Chris Daniels, "Vendor Bender," *Marketing Magazine*, April 5, 2004.
27. www.unilever.com.
28. Bank of Montreal, www2.bmo.com, accessed July 4, 2010; Lesley Young, "Cutting Through All the Hype About CRM," *Marketing Magazine*, February 12, 2001.
29. "The Key to Effective CRM: Building an Interactive Dialog."
30. "Brandes Investment Partners Taps Angoss for On-Demand Sales Analytics," Canada NewsWire, January 12, 2010.
31. Young, "Cutting Through All the Hype About CRM."
32. Jennifer Myers, "Can't Live Without You," *Profit*, November, 2009, 52.
33. "Case Studies—Retailing/ Merchandising: Best Customer and Loyalty Programs," www.mooresponse.com.
34. Stephen Baker, "Math Will Rock Your World," *BusinessWeek*, January 23, 2006, 54–62.
35. Jaimie Seaton, "Stave Solves the Relationship Puzzle," *1to1 Magazine*, August 4, 2003, www.1to1.com.
36. B. Weitz, S. Castleberry, and J. Tanner, *Selling* (Burr Ridge, IL: McGraw-Hill/ Irwin, 2007), 196–197.
37. "Visa Gold Passport," www.laurentianbank .com, accessed July 4, 2010; "Tailored Rewards for Laurentian Bank VISA Gold Credit Card Holders Through a New 'Passport' Program," Canada NewsWire, December 17, 2003, 1.
38. Lesley Young, "When Three Heads Are Better Than One," *Marketing Magazine*, December 8, 2003; Scott Gardiner, "A Truly Awesome Database," *Marketing Magazine*, April 29, 2002.
39. Jane Zarem, "Nike's 'Smart' Loyalty Program," *1to1 Magazine*, March 2002.
40. www.fairmont.com, accessed July 4, 2010; Catherine Allen, "Getting the Most Out of Loyalty," *Marketing Magazine*, December 1, 1997; George S. Day, "No Two Customers Are Alike," *National Post*, June 16, 2003, FE5.
41. Whiskas website, whiskas.ca, accessed April 4, 2010.
42. Kit Davis, "Track Star, RFID Is Racing to Market," *Consumer Goods Magazine*, June 2003, www.consumergoods.com.
43. www.rogers.com, accessed July 4, 2010.
44. Ibid.; David Carr, "The Renaissance Rep," *Marketing Magazine*, April 16, 2001.
45. Paul Delean and Roberto Rocha, "Odds Slim of Missing Data Being Used for Fraud, Experts Said," CanWest News, January 20, 2007.
46. Carrie Harrison, "E-Mail Marketing in a Private World," *Marketing Magazine*, March 8, 2004.
47. CRTC website, "Telecom Decision CRTC 2007-48," July 3, 2007, www.crtc.gc.ca/eng/archive/2007/ dt2007-48.htm, accessed June 6, 2010.
48. The idea for this application exercise came from the contribution of Kenneth J. Radig (Medaille College) to "Great Ideas in Teaching Marketing," a teaching supplement that accompanies Lamb, Hair, and McDaniel's *Marketing*. Professor Radig's submission, "Direct Mail Assignment," was a runner-up in the "Best of the Great Ideas in Teaching Marketing" contest held in conjunction with the publication of the eighth Edition of *Marketing*
49. Joan Voight, "Getting a Handle on Customer Reviews," *Adweek*, June 25, 2007; "Online Shoppers Give Thumbs Up to Customer Product Reviews," *Business Wire*, January 9, 2007; Ken Magill, "Petco Tests Product Reviews," *Direct*, March 1, 2006; www.petco.com, accessed July 4, 2010.
50. CBC, "Gift Card Gotcha," *Marketplace*, January 31, 2007.

END OF PART 7 CASES

1. Erik Larsen, "Google Probed in London; Privacy Group Asks for Investigation," *The Gazette*, June 23, 2010, B8.
2. "10 Bizarre Sights in Google Street View," *Times Online*, June 1, 2007, technology.timesonline.co.uk/tol/news/ tech_and_web/article1870949.ece, accessed March 22, 2009; Jo Adetunji, "Google's Spy in the Streets Triggers a

Wave of Protests," *The Guardian*, www.guardian.co.uk/technology/ 2009/mar/21/google-streetview- privacy-images, accessed March 21, 2009; Warwick Ashford, "Google Street View Raises Privacy Concerns," *Computer Weekly*, March 21, 2009, www.computerweekly.com/Articles/ 2009/03/20/235346/google-streetview- raises-privacy-concerns.htm, accessed March 21, 2009; Brian Cooper, "Google Street View Continues to Raise Privacy Concerns," *Search Engine Guide Blog*,

February 2, 2009, www.searchengineguide .com/brian-cooper/googlestreet-view- continues-to-raise-pr.php, accessed March 21, 2009; Miriam Ellis, "Google Street View—Not Illegal, Maybe Antisocial," *Search Engine Guide Blog*, July 31, 2008, www.searchengineguide .com/miriam-ellis/google-streetview- not-illegal-maybe-ant.php, accessed March 21, 2009; Richard Wray, "Google Launches Street View in UK," *Guardian News and Media Limited*, March 19, 2009, www.guardian.co.uk/business/2009/

mar/19/google-street-view-uk/print, accessed March 21, 2009.
3. Melita Kuburas, "Kraft Whips up What's Cooking for the Masses," *Marketing Magazine*, January 22, 2010.
4. Katie Bailey, "Kraft Stuffs Dinner into Convenient Mobile App," *Marketing Magazine*, December 3, 2009.
5. Kraft Canada website, www.kraftcanada .com; Lesley Young, "One Bite at a Time," *Marketing Magazine*, November 5, 2001.

Index

N.B. All page numbers beginning with "19-" refer to material that can be found in Chapter 19, on the book's website.

Philips Electronics, 58
Philips Magnavox, 414
PhoneBusters, 19-26
Photo Gift Cards, 183
physical flow process, 335
Pillsbury, 115
Ping, 108
Pink Panther, 258
pioneer advertising, 439–440
PIPEDA. *See* Personal Information Protection and Electronic Document Act
Pixar, 42
Pizza Hut, 253, 300, 585
Pizza Pizza, 380
place (distribution) strategy, 528, 530. *See also* marketing channels; retailing; supply chain pricing
    nonprofit organizations, 313–314
    services marketing and, 305
    web marketing and, 19-14–19-15
place of business, 366
Planet Hollywood, 389
planned obsolescence, 250
planning, 22
PlantBottle, 507
PlayStation 3, 294, 461, 468, 576
Please Mum, 424
PlentyOfFish, 297
point-of-purchase (PO) display, 482
point-of-sale interactions, 579
Polaroid Colorpack camera, 279
political factors affecting consumer behaviour, 73–75
Polo Ralph Lauren, 330
Pop Shoppe, 271, 330
pop-up-shops, 393
POP.com, 19-21–19-22
population, 62
Porsche, 8, 409–410
Porter, Michael, 19-5
portfolio matrix, 31–33
    defined, 32
position, 184
positioning, 184
    bases for, 185–186
    perceptual mapping, 185
    repositioning, 186
possession processing, 303
Post-it Notes, 276
Postal Walk, 173
Powerade, 108
PowerBar, 174
Prada, 120, 268, 353
preapproach, 491
predatory pricing, 547–548
predictive modelling, 586
premiums, 478–479
President's Choice, 8, 102, 118, 254, 371, 384–385, 436, 456
President's Choice Financial, 385
President's Choice Green Products, 174
prestige pricing, 533
Prevish, Leslie, 61
price, 512. *See also* price strategy
    business buying, 151
    competition and, 528
    cost determinant of, 523–527
    defined, 512–513
    demand determinant of, 516–521
    demands of large customers, 532
    distribution strategy and, 528–530
    importance of, 512–513
    Internet and, 530–532
    pricing objectives, 513–516
    promotion strategy, 532
    quality and, 532–533
    sales-oriented pricing objectives, 515–516
    stages in the product life cycle, 527–528
    status quo pricing objectives, 516
    targeting technology, 521–522
    yield management systems and, 521–522
price bundling, 554
Price Chopper, 22, 51
price discrimination, 547
price equilibrium, 518
price fixing, 547
price lining, 511, 553–554
price shading, 559
price skimming, 543–544
price strategy
    choosing, 543
    cost-oriented tactics, 559

defined, 543
    demand-oriented tactics, 559
    ethical issues in, 548
    fine-tuning base price, 549–556
    geographic pricing, 551–552
    inflation and, 558
    legality and ethics of, 546–548
    nonprofit organizations, 314–315
    positioning base, as, 185
    product line pricing, 557
    realistic, 8–9
    recession, during, 560–561
    services marketing and, 306
    setting price, process of, 542–546
    too low prices, 551
    web marketing and, 19-19–19-20
priceGrabber.ca, 19-14
pricegrabber.com, 531
Priceless.com, 410
Priceline, 9
PriceSCAN.com, 531
primary membership groups, 107–108
Print Measurement Bureau (PMB), 167, 318
printed magazines, 448
privacy, 19-27
    and regulation, 19-27–19-28
    EU and, 19-28
    guidelines for e-mail marketers, 19-28
    web and, 19-25–19-28
privacy legislation, 590, 592–593
private brand, 254–255
private exchange, 332
private label brand, 384–385
Private Manufacturers' Association, 254
PRIZM, 173
Pro Plan, 340
problem child, 32
process, service as a, 303
processed materials, 148
Procter & Gamble, 8, 24, 33, 65, 71, 76, 77, 92, 115, 149, 169, 177, 180, 186, 250, 251, 254, 255, 280, 281, 283, 338, 340, 342, 425, 438, 515, 544–546
procurement, 344
producer factors, 338–339
product, 246
    selecting to buy on-line, 530–532
product advertising, 439–441
    common appeals, 443
    developing and evaluating advertising appeals, 443–444
    executing the message, 444–446
    executional styles for, 444–446
    identifying, 442–443
    post-campaign evaluation, 446
product (service) strategy
    services marketing and, 303–305
product and trade name franchising, 380
product assortment, 384
product category, 177, 287
product characteristics, 328–329
product class, 185
product decisions
    nonprofit organizations, 313
product design, 27
product development, 277
    defined, 31
    global issues, 283
    importance of new products, 272–274
    new product failure, 282
    process of, 275–282
    R&D, 77
    spread of new products, 284–287
    Web 2.0 tools, using, 275
product differentiation, 184–185
product experience, 94
product factors, 338
product items, 248
product launch
    MobileMe, 320
product life cycle (PLC), 287–291
    diffusion process and, 291
    four stages of, 288
    marketing management implications, 290–291
    price determinants, 527–528
    promotional mix and, 422–423
    styles, fashions, fads, 288
product line, 248
product line contraction, 251, 253
product line depth, 249
product line extensions, 251

product lines, 272–273
product mix, 248–253, 249
product mix width, 249
product modification, 250
product offering, 384–385
product placement, 459
product trial, 589
product use, 185
product/service differentiation competitive advantage, 28–29
production innovations, 28
production orientation, 5
products
    branding, 254–257
    defined, 246
    global issues, 262
    labelling and, 260–261
    packaging, 258–262
    product items/lines/mixes, 248–253
    promotional mix and, 421–422
    relationships among, 557
    warranties, 263–264
    web and, 19-13–19-14
professional services pricing, 553
professional volunteers, 314
profit maximization, 513–514, 525–526
profits, 512–513
    price strategy and 542–543
    profit-oriented pricing objectives, 513–514
ProMetric Life Sciences inc., 136–137
promotion, 314
    defined, 406
    goals and AIDA concept, 418–419
    goals and tasks of, 413–414
    web marketing and, 19-15–19-19
promotion strategy
    retailing and, 385
    services marketing and, 305–306
promotional discount (trade allowance), 550
    characteristics, 417
    defined, 414
    factors affecting, 421–426
    factors affecting, diagram, 426
promotional mix, 414–417. *See also* integrated marketing communications; personal selling; public relations; sales promotion
promotional selling
    sales management, 495–499
promotional strategy
    defined, 406
    price decisions and, 532
proper location, 386
provincial legislation, 74
Prudential, 256
psychographic segmentation, 171–173
psychographics, 115
psychological pricing, 554
public relations, 457–465. *See also* advertising; integrated marketing communications (IMC)
    Coca-Cola, 508
    defined, 416, 417, 457
    functions of, 458
    major tools, 458–461, 463
    managing unfavourable publicity, 463–464
    measuring impact, 464
    web, 19-19
Public Relations Society of America (PRSA), 458
public service advertisement (PSA), 314
Public Works and Government Services, 140
publicity, 457
Puck, Wolfgang, 65
Puffs Plus, 76
pull strategy
    defined, 425–426
    vs. push strategy, 425–426
pulsing media schedule, 456
pumpbiz.com, 332
purchaser (family), 110
purchasing contract, 152
Purchasing Management Association of Canada, 145, 153,
    Code of Ethics, 154
purchasing power, 70
Puretracks.com, 588, 634
PURL, 571
push marketing strategy, 473
    vs. pull strategy, 425–426
    defined, 424–425
push money, 484
Puzzles, Stave, 587
pyramid of corporate social responsibility, 52